The First Woman in the Republic

New Americanists
A Series Edited by Donald E. Pease

The First Woman in the Republic

A Cultural Biography of

Lydia Maria Child

CAROLYN L. KARCHER

DUKE UNIVERSITY PRESS   *Durham and London 1994*

© 1994 Duke University Press   All rights reserved
Printed in the United States of America on acid-free paper ∞
Typeset in Janson Text by Keystone Typesetting, Inc.
Library of Congress Cataloging-in-Publication Data appear
on the last printed page of this book.

Quotations from letters in the Anti-Slavery Collection, Boston Public Library by courtesy of the Trustees of the Boston Public Library; quotations from Child manuscripts at Cornell courtesy of the Division of Rare and Manuscript Collections, Cornell University Library; quotations from Child's uncollected letters to Charles Sumner, bMS Am 1, by permission of the Houghton Library, Harvard University; quotations from David Child family letters courtesy of Milton Emerson Ross; quotations from letters about spiritualism to Charles Follen, Martha Griffith Browne, and Lucy Ann Brooks in Child's *Collected Correspondence* courtesy of the Arthur Conan Doyle Collection, Humanities Research Center, University of Texas, Austin; quotations from letters in the Washburn, French, Stearns, Horace Mann, and Horace Mann II Papers courtesy of the Massachusetts Historical Society.

An earlier version of Chapter 1 appears as the introduction to *HOBOMOK and Other Writings on Indians*, Carolyn L. Karcher, ed. New Brunswick, NJ: Rutgers the State University, © 1986. Reprinted by permission Rutgers UP; a small portion of Chapter 13 appeared in "Censorship, American Style," *Studies in the American Renaissance* 1986: 283–303, ed. Joel Meyerson (Charlottesville: UP Virginia, 1986); part of the "Hilda Silfverling" section of Chapter 14 was published in different form as "Patriarchal Society and Matriarchal Family in Irving's 'Rip Van Winkle' and Child's 'Hilda Silfverling,'" *Legacy* 2 (Fall 1985): 31–44; the antislavery fiction section of Chapter 14 appeared in substantially the same form in Shirley Samuels, ed., *The Culture of Sentiment: Race, Gender, and Sentimentality in Nineteenth-Century America* (New York: Oxford UP, 1992) 58–72 and in an earlier version in *Women's Studies International Forum* 9 (1986): 323–32; a portion of Chapter 16 appeared in "From Pacifism to Armed Struggle: Lydia Maria Child's 'The Kansas Emigrants' and Antislavery Ideology in the 1850's," *ESQ: A Journal of the American Renaissance* 34 (3rd Qt. 1988): 141–58; the first section of Chapter 17 appeared in substantially the same form in *Race Traitor* 1 (Winter 1993): 21–44; a significant portion of Chapter 19 appeared in preliminary form as "Lydia Maria Child's *A Romance of the Republic*: An Abolitionist Vision of America's Racial Destiny," in Deborah E. McDowell and Arnold Rampersad, eds., *Slavery and the Literary Imagination* (Baltimore: Johns Hopkins UP, 1989) 81–103. Permission to reprint is gratefully acknowledged.

To H. Bruce Franklin and Jane Morgan Franklin
Beloved Mentors

Contents

Illustrations

(following page 486)

Lydia Maria Francis, age 24, engraving after the portrait painted by Francis Alexander in 1826; courtesy Library of Congress

David Lee Child in his early thirties, portrait said to be by Francis Alexander, ca. 1828

Engraving of Convers Francis and his parsonage at Watertown, where Child wrote *Hobomok*; by permission of the Boston Athenaeum

Child's sketch of the view from her home at Cottage Place (1832–35), from the manuscript "Autobiography" she compiled in 1875; by permission of Cornell University Library

Ellis Gray Loring and Louisa Gilman Loring; by permission of the Massachusetts Historical Society

Daguerreotype of Child at age 54, made in 1856, while she was writing "The Kansas Emigrants"; by permission of the Schlesinger Library, Radcliffe College

Photograph of John Brown by James Wallace Black, 1859; by permission of the Boston Athenaeum

Cabinet Photograph of Harriet Jacobs by Gilbert Studios, Washington, D.C.; by permission of the owners, courtesy of Jean Fagan Yellin

Carte de visite photograph of Child at age 63 by John Adams Whipple, 1865; by permission of the Boston Athenaeum

Engraving of Child at age 63, by F. T. Stuart, Boston, after the photograph by John Adams Whipple, 1865; by permission of the Schlesinger Library, Radcliffe College

Photograph of David Lee Child at age 75, taken in 1870; courtesy Library of Congress

Photograph of the Child cottage in Wayland, Massachusetts; by permission of the Wayland Historical Society

Preface and Acknowledgments

For half a century Lydia Maria Child (1802–80) was a household name in America. The famous antislavery agitator William Lloyd Garrison hailed her as "the first woman in the republic." The Radical Republican Senator Charles Sumner credited her with inspiring his career as an advocate of racial equality and sought her advice on Reconstruction policy. Samuel Jackson, an African American correspondent of Garrison's newspaper, *The Liberator*, proposed enshrining her alongside John Brown in the pantheon of his people's white benefactors. The suffragist leader Elizabeth Cady Stanton cited Child's encyclopaedic *History of the Condition of Women* (1835) as an invaluable resource for feminists in their battle against patriarchal ideology. The Transcendentalist theologian Theodore Parker pronounced her monumental *Progress of Religious Ideas* (1855) "*the* book of the age; and written by a *woman!*" A newspaperman ranked her popular weekly column of the 1840s, "Letters from New-York," "almost at the head of journalism in America. . . ." Edgar Allan Poe praised her novel *Philothea* (1836) as "an honor to our country, and a signal triumph for our countrywomen." The *National Anti-Slavery Standard* proclaimed her *Romance of the Republic* (1867) "one of the most thrilling books . . . ever written, involving the rights of the colored people — not excepting Uncle Tom's Cabin." And Child's earliest biographer, the abolitionist Thomas Wentworth Higginson, converted by her 1833 *Appeal in Favor of That Class of Americans Called Africans*, paid tribute to it as the "ablest" and most comprehensive antislavery book "ever printed in America." Tracing her "formative influence" on the activists of his generation back to the "intellectual provision" she had furnished them in their youth, he reminisced: "In those days she seemed to supply a sufficient literature for any family through her own unaided pen. Thence came novels for the parlor, cookery books for the kitchen, and the 'Juvenile Miscellany' for the nursery."[1]

Secure though her reputation seemed in the wake of the Civil War, Child was erased from history when the backlash against Reconstruction that began even before her death destroyed almost everything she had fought for. She survived in public memory only through a children's Thanksgiving song whose authorship none but specialists could identify: "Over the river and through the wood, / To grandfather's house we go."[2] Ironically, it projects a cozy image of New England family life belied by the poverty, hardship, and isolation Child endured over a long career of self-sacrificing political advocacy. No less ironically, she is most often reintroduced to the public these days not as an author in her own right, but as the editor of a slave narrative which had originally required her endorsement and authentication before a publisher would print it: Harriet A. Jacobs's *Incidents in the Life of a Slave Girl* (1861). Child herself might have relished this status reversal as the consummation of her life's work. When the African American minister Hiram R. Revels won a U.S. Senate seat in 1870, she exulted: "His election is an epoch in our history. It marks the first great step in the emancipation of the white race from the enslavement of an unjust and absurd prejudice."[3] But contrary to her hopes, the overturn of Reconstruction in her last years marked a giant step backward, relegating the prospect of the white race's emancipation from prejudice to an indefinite future and sweeping the antislavery movement into near oblivion.

Child would languish in obscurity for nearly a century. Not until the Civil Rights movement created a more favorable climate for reassessing the abolitionist legacy would reprints of her works begin to appear, and then only in facsimile editions for libraries. The first biography to bring Child back before the public in the mid-1960s, Helene G. Baer's *The Heart Is Like Heaven* (1964), reflected the fashionable distaste for radical reformers, sentimentalizing Child as an adoring wife who took up antislavery politics solely to please her husband. The second, Milton Meltzer's *Tongue of Flame* (1965), honored her courage as a reformer and held her up as a role model; written primarily for the audience Child herself had addressed in the *Juvenile Miscellany*, however, it necessarily smoothed out complexities beyond the grasp of youthful minds.[4] Although a trickle of scholarly articles and book chapters followed in the 1970s,[5] no doubt stimulated by second-wave feminism and the birth of Women's Studies, the real breakthrough came with Milton Meltzer and Patricia G. Holland's expert editing of Child's complete correspondence, issued both in microfiche and in a beautifully annotated one-volume compendium (1980, 1982). Arranged in chronological order, some 2,600 letters, hitherto scattered in more than sixty libraries and private collections, laid the basis for a solid biographical study. With Deborah Clifford's *Crusader for Freedom* (1992), Child's multifaceted life finally received the full-length scholarly treatment it had so long cried out for.[6] Meanwhile, feminist literary critics were starting to anthologize Child's fiction and journalism.[7] Encouraged by this development Rutgers University Press launched its American Women Writers Series with Child's *HOBOMOK and Other Writings on Indians* (1986), an editing project I undertook while conceptualizing *The First Woman in the Republic.*

Child attracted me because she boldly tackled problems of racial, sexual, and economic justice that our society has yet to resolve — problems she never allowed cynics to dismiss as insoluble. Fittingly, I first encountered her through "Prejudices against People of Color, and Our Duties in Relation to This Subject," the most controversial chapter of the antislavery *Appeal* whose publication in 1833 had cost her the patronage of the literary establishment and subjected her to boycott and ostracism. In it she charged: "[N]o other people on earth indulge so strong a prejudice with regard to color, as we do." And she urged an end to all forms of racial discrimination, from employment bans to antimiscegenation laws.[8] Reading this powerful call for redress at a historical moment that paralleled Child's — the early 1970s, when the Vietnam war was still raging and the Black Panthers, the American Indian Movement, and antiwar activists were under siege — I could not help recognizing its continuing relevance.

Besides playing a major role in the crusade against slavery and racism, Child campaigned for justice toward Native Americans. From 1829, when she took up the cause of the Cherokee, to the 1870s, when she championed the beleaguered Plains Indians, she dissented from the widely held theory that the Indians were "*destined* to disappear before the white man." The term "savages," she maintained, applied better to whites than to Indians.[9]

Child also participated in the movement for women's rights. Though she preferred at first to defy patriarchal ideology implicitly, by transgressing the bounds of woman's sphere to speak on behalf of the slave, rather than explicitly by denouncing the restrictions imposed on her sex, she took an increasingly militant stand as she resolved the personal conflicts that inhibited her at the outset. In one of her many public testimonials on the issue, she wrote: "[S]ociety can never be established on a true and solid foundation so long as any distinction whatsoever is made between men and women with regard to the full and free exercise of their faculties on all subjects, whether of art, science, literature, business or politics."[10]

As a writer, Child showed an uncanny ability to pinpoint and respond to new cultural needs. She pioneered almost *every* department of nineteenth-century American letters: the historical novel, the short story, children's literature, the domestic advice book, women's history, antislavery fiction, and journalism. Not least among her accomplishments, she anticipated an acute need of our own time by publishing an anthology for the elderly, designed to promote positive images of old age (*Looking toward Sunset*, 1865). Her corpus amounts to forty-seven books and tracts (including four novels and three collections of short stories), with enough uncollected journalism and fiction to fill one or two more, not to mention a correspondence rivaling Garrison's in extent.

Despite their nineteenth-century resonances, many of her writings strike familiar notes today. The homeless derelicts she described so movingly in *Letters from New York* roam our streets in greater numbers than ever. The diagnosis and remedy Child offered as she contemplated the slums and prisons of 1843 — "If we can abolish *poverty*, we shall have taken the greatest step towards the abolition of *crime*" — remain timely in 1994.[11] Even her advice on infant care, sex education of adolescents, and psychological health for the aging often has a startlingly modern ring.

Child's life, too, has much to teach. She acted on her principles, no matter what the cost; when her conscience prompted her to fight for the liberation of African Americans, she sacrificed the fame she had dreamed of and the livelihood she depended on. Poverty did not discourage her, nor did she ever yield to the temptation to recapture her lost popularity by renouncing the abolitionist cause. Chronic depression induced her not to retreat into her own misery, but to seek comfort in working for others. Through decades of setbacks, she faced ugly realities unflinchingly and never deluded herself with shams. Yet she died confident in the ultimate triumph of justice.

Though consistent in living out the ethic she preached, Child suffered from deep emotional splits that produced endless contradictions for her. Born a baker's daughter, she proudly identified herself with the "middle class" of "farmers and mechanics, who work with their *hands*." "Aristocracy is *always* my aversion, whether in the form of English noble, Southern planter, or Boston respectable," she liked to say.[12] Still, her tastes drew her to the milieu she professed to scorn, and with few exceptions, her closest friends belonged to the upper classes. Elevated by her domestic manual, *The Frugal Housewife* (1829), to the status of a national authority on homemaking, Child yearned in vain for a home of her own as she and her husband moved from one cheap boarding house to another, driven by the poverty to which his debts and the couple's abolitionist politics consigned them; even when she inherited her father's cottage at age fifty-four, she vacillated between her love of rural tranquillity and her hankering for metropolitan stimulation. A children's writer and purveyor of advice to mothers, she grew up motherless and remained childless. A professional author who supported her husband on her earnings, she celebrated the old-fashioned virtues of "good wives." An extraordinarily passionate woman who violated all sorts of sexual taboos in her fiction, hotly defended the sexual instinct as natural to both women and men, and privately justified divorce, she resigned herself to a sexually unsatisfying marriage. And for the sake of protecting that marriage, strained by her husband's financial irresponsibility, Child held back from involvement in women's rights agitation that her own example had helped spark. An artist rather than a reformer by temperament (or at least so she claimed), she craved beauty and abhorred strife and controversy, yet her emotional identification with the oppressed and her fierce sense of justice propelled her into the "rough work of reform."[13] Simultaneously visionary and practical, she could soar into the realm of the imagination while shrewdly managing her everyday business. Mystic and skeptic rolled into one, Child longed for religious faith, but her wide-ranging research in religious history only fortified her doubts.

The First Woman in the Republic covers all these facets of Child's career, focusing on the central problems in nineteenth-century American culture that she worked out in her life and writings: the creation of a national literature reflecting the experiences and aspirations of both sexes and all races; the redefinition of womanhood and the struggle to reconcile the conflicting demands of domestic responsibilities, sexual desires, professional ambitions, and political commitments; the extension of the country's egalitarian creed to disfranchised groups; and the quest for a faith free of sectarian dogmatism and enriched by the most commendable teachings of the world's diverse religions.

By vocation Child was a woman of letters. She made her greatest contributions as a reformer through her writings, and it is her writings that best distill the lessons her life continues to offer on the social problems with which she wrestled. Thus, I have centered this biography on Child's works and structured it to spiral around and flow from the key texts in her corpus. Her writings and her life are, of course, inextricably twined. She regularly translated personal concerns into political and literary insights, and repeatedly meshed her own deepest needs with those of her culture. I have tried to explore the biographical ramifications of her works as fully as possible, but without submerging Child the cultural critic in Child the individual. I have also tried to preserve the vitality of Child's own voice, to quote directly rather than to dilute her language through paraphrase and summary, and to adapt my analysis to the tone of her prose, unobtrusively interweaving text and commentary.

The extensive quotation and detailed literary analysis distinguishing this biography from most others serve several purposes. First, I wish to stimulate interest among literary scholars, historians, and publishers in recovering Child's writings, so that they can be studied, assigned in courses, and enjoyed by the wide audience they deserve. Second, I have sought to provide the close reading necessary to establish the significance of Child's fiction and cultural criticism. Third, I have aimed to furnish a potential model for analyzing the works of other neglected literary figures.

Accordingly, I have contextualized Child's writings by reconstructing the historical and cultural matrix out of which they grew, by restaging the debates surrounding the specific issues she was addressing, and by comparing Child's achievements with those of her contemporaries in all the genres she practiced. Such contextualization is indispensable to restoring authors like Child to their rightful place in our literary canons and historical textbooks. We can neither grasp their nuances nor attune ourselves to their idioms without immersing ourselves in the cultural production of the period.

The process of close reading and contextualization I have adopted is new only in the sense that I have applied it to an author hitherto deemed unworthy of serious study. I have merely treated Child with the same respect that "major" authors like Melville and Hawthorne generally receive. Just as critics have shown that even the "minor" works of Melville and Hawthorne repay careful analysis, I have assumed — and I hope demonstrated — that this is no less true of Child's works, from her domestic manual *The Frugal Housewife* (1829) to the novel she considered the capstone of her career, *A Romance of the Republic* (1867). When studied attentively, Child's fiction exhibits a structural complexity and symbolic richness akin to her more famous literary peers'. Similarly, her *Letters from New York* (1843), which exemplifies Transcendentalist literary style at its most innovative, challenges comparison with the essays of Emerson and Thoreau.

Child was much more than a literary woman, however, and my project is consequently larger than that of the traditional literary biography. Instead, as the subtitle "A Cultural Biography" is meant to suggest, I have attempted to view nineteenth-century America through the window of Child's mind. Child presents an exceptionally revealing perspective on that tumultuous era. Engaged in the leading intellectual and social movements of her time, she devoted her life and writings to transforming the United States into a multiracial egalitarian republic. In the process, she articulated penetrating critiques of nineteenth-century America's dominant ideology and formulated alternative cultural possibilities, particularly in the domains of race and gender relations. Through her eyes, we can recapture both the America she struggled to change and the America she envisioned in its place.[14]

The dedication of this book to H. Bruce Franklin and Jane Morgan Franklin represents more than the acknowledgment of a personal debt. It pays tribute to the courage, self-sacrifice, and principle with which Bruce and Jane have been carrying on the unfinished revolution of Lydia Maria Child and her abolitionist comrades. Like Child's, their example inspires continued struggle for freedom, justice, equality, and human dignity. Bruce and Jane have also contributed to this book in countless ways, direct and indirect. It is not too much to say that I owe my career as a scholar to Bruce, whom I had the good fortune to have as my freshman English teacher at Stanford. He and Jane encouraged me to undertake this biography, helped me reconceptualize key chapters, and rigorously critiqued the manuscript, Bruce in its entirety and Jane several sections of it.

The debt I owe to my husband, Martin, is equally immeasurable and longstanding. Without his unstinting support — intellectual, moral, financial, and domestic — none of my books would have been possible. By inviting me to read drafts to him while chapters were in progress, he helped catch stylistic infelicities and problems of focus at early stages. He also read every chapter, providing many helpful suggestions.

The book has further benefited from the criticisms of numerous friends and professional colleagues, who saved me from embarrassing errors and forced me to refine my ideas. Milton Meltzer, Deborah Clifford, Joan Hedrick, Andrea Kerr, and Joyce Sparer Adler read the whole manuscript (Andrea and Joyce twice). Jane Tompkins, Celia Morris (Eckhardt), Dorothy Sterling, Jean Fagan Yellin, Lucy Freibert, Lisa Johnson Ponder, Ira Berlin, Gordon Kelly, Patricia G. Holland, and Rodney Olsen read significant portions of it, as did Amy Kaplan, Donald Pease, Robert McGrath, Nancy Bentley, Shalom Goldman, Keith Walker, and other members of the Dartmouth Institute on "The U.S. and Its Others." I would also like to acknowledge the invaluable critiques of Richard Slotkin and Milton Sernet, who read the manuscript for Duke University Press, and two anonymous scholars who read it for another press.

Fellow scholars working on Child have shown extraordinary generosity toward me. Milton Meltzer and Patricia Holland sent me all the files they had compiled while editing Child's letters, as well as one containing letters discovered since the publication of their microfiche edition. Deborah Clifford shared with me her notes on the *Massachusetts Journal* and her list of the books Child borrowed from the Boston Athenaeum, even lending me her apartment in Cambridge for two weeks while I was doing research in Boston area libraries. And as this book was going to the press, she put me in touch with Megan Marshall, who supplied me with transcripts of Peabody family letters that discuss Child and the reception of *Hobomok* and *The Rebels*. Lisa Ponder sent me her M.A. thesis and course papers on Child, photocopied several of Child's rare works for me, and pooled ideas. Stimulating discussions with Margaret Kellow, Bruce Mills, and Susan Koppelman have also enriched this book. In addition, all of us are greatly indebted to Milton Emerson Ross, grandson of Child's niece, Lydia Maria

Child Haskins, who has kindly made his treasure trove of family letters available to visiting scholars. Besides putting up with the invasion of his privacy by a stranger and giving me an oral history of the Child and Haskins families, he allowed me to borrow and mail back to him the letters I could not finish perusing during my brief stay.

Librarians at many institutions have greatly facilitated my research. Elizabeth Miller of the Norridgewock Library wrote a long and detailed reply to my inquiries about the Preston family and Child's years in Maine. Jo Goeselt, Curator of the Wayland Historical Society, took Deborah Clifford and me to see Child's cottage and the family tombstones and sent me photocopies of many documents in her collection, as well as a photograph of the Child home. At the Boston Public Library, Dr. Laura V. Monti, Keeper of Rare Books and Manuscripts, translated a letter David Child had written in Spanish, and Giuseppe Bisaccia, Curator of Manuscripts, helped decipher several illegible letters, while Eugene Zepp furnished a desk lamp and expedited the delivery of manuscripts. At the Boston Athenaeum, Catharina Slautterback and Sallie Pierce, Curator of Prints, located the photographs of John Brown, Convers Francis, and Child in old age that appear in this book. At the Houghton Library, Harvard University, Jennie Rathbun and other reference librarians searched the Sumner Papers and sent me photocopies of Child's uncollected 1872 letters. I am also grateful for the courtesy of Eva Mosely, Curator of Manuscripts, and Marie-Helene Gold, Head of Prints and Photographs at the Schlesinger Library, Radcliffe College; Peter Drummey, Head Librarian of the Massachusetts Historical Society; librarians at the New York Public Library, who sent me the manuscript of "The Kansas Emigrants"; and the American Antiquarian Society. Diane Arecco, Research Associate at Prints and Photographs of the New York Historical Society, and Barbara Hatcher of Words & Pictures Research turned up an unpublished story by Child while unavailingly trying to find a youthful portrait of David Child. I owe most, however, to the Library of Congress, where I carried out the bulk of the research for this book (and its predecessors). I particularly wish to thank Bruce Martin, Head of Stack and Reader Services, Barbara Natanson of Prints and Photographs, and the staff in the Rare Book Room: Robert Shields, Anthony Edwards, Charles Kelly, Peter Van Wingen, and above all Clark Evans, for their patient assistance.

Several historians gave me especially valuable guidance. Dorothy Ross, Rodney Olsen, and Ira Berlin not only pointed me toward many primary and secondary sources, but challenged me to reconceptualize important issues, while Ira's superb courses at the University of Maryland on the comparative history of slavery laid the foundation for my research. I am further indebted for a number of insights to the students in my course on nineteenth-century American women radicals, particularly Donald Dingledine, Carolyn Sorisio, and Esther Schwartz-McKinzie.

The task of verifying the quotations and footnotes in this book required a large team of researchers in several cities. I am grateful for the conscientious work of Amie Martin and Anne-Marie Kent at the University of Massachusetts, Boston, who checked citations to manuscripts in Boston area collections and to the *Massachusetts Journal*, which Anne-Marie also searched for additional stories or articles by Child; Noreen Groover

Lape and Donald Dingledine of Temple University, who checked all the other quotations and notes; Mark Taylor; and Andrea Kerr, who took time out from her own research to check sources Noreen and Don were unable to obtain in Philadelphia. I also wish to thank Lydia Maningas for retyping ten chapters in WordPerfect.

At Duke University Press Reynolds Smith and Bob Mirandon have both earned my undying gratitude. Bob's meticulous and sensitive copyediting strengthened the manuscript without disputing stylistic preferences. Reynolds committed the Press to publishing this book unabridged, worked hard to procure the subventions needed to do so, helped me to improve the afterword, and put his personal imprint on the references to Child's Thanksgiving song, "Over the River and through the Woods."

Finally, I wish to thank the institutions whose financial support made this book possible and the individuals whose recommendations proved crucial to winning that support: the American Council of Learned Societies for fellowships in 1982 and 1986–87; Temple University for a funded Study Leave in 1989–90; the Dartmouth Institute on "The U.S. and Its Others" for a fellowship in spring 1993; Jane Tompkins, Annette Kolodny, Sacvan Bercovitch, Dorothy Ross, William W. Freehling, Richard Slotkin, Sterling Stuckey, and Deirdre David; and the Mary Duke Biddle Foundation and the National Endowment for the Humanities, whose subsidies kept this book affordable.

Chronology of Lydia Maria Child

1802   *February 11*: Lydia Francis born to Convers Francis and Susannah Rand Francis in Medford, Massachusetts, the youngest of five surviving children.

1811   Convers Francis, Jr., matriculates at Harvard University.
Susannah Francis (sister) marries and moves to Charlestown, Massachusetts.
Susannah Rand Francis (mother) bedridden with tuberculosis.

1814   *May*: Susannah Rand Francis (mother) dies of tuberculosis.
August: Susannah Rand (grandmother) dies.
September: Mary Francis (sister) marries Warren Preston and moves to Norridgewock, Maine (still a province of Massachusetts).
Lydia Francis enrolls in Miss Swan's Academy, Medford.

1815   *March*: Susannah Francis (sister) dies.
Summer: Lydia Francis sent to Norridgewock to live with Mary Francis Preston.
Father Rale's church bell disinterred in former Indian village of Norridgewock.

1817   *June*: Reads *Paradise Lost*; writes first surviving letter to Convers.

1819   Reads Scott, Gibbon, Addison, Shakespeare, Samuel Johnson.
Maine inhabitants vote for independent statehood.

1820   Moves to Gardiner, Maine, to teach school; reads Scott's *Ivanhoe*, Byron's *Don Juan*, Thomas Moore's *Lalla Rookh*; introduced to Swedenborgianism.
Maine statehood made contingent on admission of Missouri as slave state.

1821   *Late summer*: Moves in with Convers Francis, Jr., now pastor of First Church (Unitarian) of Watertown, Massachusetts; is baptized in her father's church in Medford (Congregational) and takes the name Lydia Maria.

1822   *February 17*: Joins the Swedenborgian Society of the New Jerusalem in Boston.

1824   *Summer*: Writes *Hobomok* in six weeks; first review appears in July.
December: Publishes *Evenings in New England*, meets David Lee Child (DLC).

1825   *June*: Attends public reception in Boston for General Lafayette.
December: Publishes *The Rebels*.

1826   *January 3*: DLC reviews *The Rebels* in inaugural issue of *Massachusetts Journal*, which he edits until 1832.

Spends winter of 1825–26 boarding at Madame Canda's academy in Boston; meets Emily Marshall and the artist Francis Alexander, who paints her portrait. *Fall*: opens school in Watertown; starts publication of *Juvenile Miscellany* (1826–34); publishes her first short story, "The Rival Brothers," in *The Token* for 1827.

1827   *October*: Engaged to DLC.

Gives up her school, boards at Madame Canda's academy; publishes *Emily Parker*, *The Juvenile Souvenir*, and six stories for the annuals, including "The Lone Indian" (*The Token* for 1828).

1828   *October 19*: Marries DLC.

Publishes "The Indian Wife," "The Church in the Wilderness" (*The Legendary*), *Moral Lessons in Verse*, and *Biographical Sketches of Great and Good Men*, writes *The First Settlers of New England*, begins editing literary columns of the *Massachusetts Journal*.

November: Andrew Jackson elected, resulting in a falloff of subscriptions to *Massachusetts Journal*.

1829   *Early January (or late December 1828)*: *The First Settlers* privately printed.

January 15 and 19: DLC convicted of libel in two lawsuits.

August: Reviews a lecture by Frances Wright for the *Massachusetts Journal*, writes "Chocorua's Curse."

October–November: William Lloyd Garrison reprints Child's "Comparative Strength of Male and Female Intellect" in the *Genius of Universal Emancipation* and hails her as "the first woman in the republic."

November 12: Publishes *The Frugal Housewife*.

1830   *February*: DLC loses his appeal of his libel conviction and is jailed for about six months.

Teaches school in Dorchester, Massachusetts, for several months.

June or July: Meets Garrison.

September: Publishes her first antislavery story in *The Juvenile Miscellany*, "The St. Domingo Orphans."

1831   *January*: Publishes *The Little Girl's Own Book* and a second antislavery story in the *Miscellany*, "Jumbo and Zairee"; Garrison founds the *Liberator*.

June 15: Publishes *The Mother's Book*.

August: Editorializes against racial prejudice in the *Massachusetts Journal*; Garrison praises Child's "Noble Commentary"; DLC responds to the Nat Turner revolt by defending the right of the oppressed to rebel.

1832   *January*: DLC attends founding meeting of New England Anti-Slavery Society.

February: *Massachusetts Journal* fails.

The Childs move to Cottage Place.

Publishes *The Biographies of Madame de Staël, and Madame Roland* and *The Biographies of Lady Russell, and Madame Guyon*.

1833 *April*: Publishes *Good Wives*.

August 5: Publishes *An Appeal in Favor of That Class of Americans Called Africans*

December: American Anti-Slavery Society founded in Philadelphia.

1834 *January*: Joins Boston Female Anti-Slavery Society (BFASS).

May: Mass cancellation of subscriptions forces LMC to give up editorship of *Juvenile Miscellany*.

October: Publishes *The Oasis*; DLC undertakes defense of the *Panda* crew, charged with piracy.

December: Organizes first Anti-Slavery Fair with Louisa Loring.

1835 *February*: LMC goes to Washington to plead for clemency to the *Panda* crew; appeal fails and case closes in May.

May: Boston Athenaeum cancels Child's free library privileges; Maria Weston Chapman's attempt to purchase her a paying membership apparently fails.

August 1: Helps save George Thompson from an antiabolitionist mob.

August 8–14: The Childs accompany George Thompson to New York, en route to England, where they are to serve as agents for British antislavery societies; instead, DLC is arrested for debt on the quay; they spend the next six months boarding with Quaker farmers, Joseph and Margaret Carpenter, in New Rochelle; there LMC helps desegregate a village school.

Fall: The Childs attend a meeting of the Philadelphia Female Anti-Slavery Society, where they encounter Angelina Grimké; in Philadelphia, Benjamin Lundy persuades DLC to join his projected free labor colony in Mexico; LMC publishes *History of the Condition of Women* and *Authentic Anecdotes of American Slavery*; Boston mob attacks BFASS and nearly lynches Garrison.

1836 *January*: Publishes *The Evils of Slavery, and the Cure of Slavery* and *Anti-Slavery Catechism*; writes *Philothea* (finished by spring and published in late summer).

May: Conquest of northern Mexico by proslavery Texans forces Lundy to abandon plans for colony; the Childs stay with DLC's parents in West Boylston, Massachusetts; LMC later moves in with her father in South Natick, Massachusetts.

August: LMC collects evidence that helps Ellis Loring win the case of the slave child Med, an important precedent for abolitionists.

October: DLC goes to Europe to study beet sugar production.

1837 Spends winter with father in South Natick, publishes *The Family Nurse*.

May 9–12: Represents BFASS at first Anti-Slavery Convention of American Women (New York).

Fall: DLC returns from Europe; the Childs board with the Lorings.

1838 *May*: New England Anti-Slavery Convention overrules protests by orthodox members and votes to allow official participation of women in its proceedings and committees; the Childs move to Northampton to start beet farming; they circulate antislavery petitions.

1839 *May*: LMC participates in New England Anti-Slavery Convention, serves on the business committee; opponents of women's full membership found rival Massachusetts Abolition Society.

Spends winter of 1839–40 in Boston, where DLC later joins her; participates in BFASS schism and serves as president pro tem; attends Margaret Fuller's Conversations and Emerson's lectures; publishes four pieces, including "Charity Bowery," in inaugural issue of *Liberty Bell*.

1840   *May*: LMC returns to Northampton; DLC attends American Anti-Slavery Society Meeting in New York, which splits over appointment of women as officers and committee members.

Convers Francis, Sr., buys the Childs a farm and lives with them until March.

December: LMC publishes "The Black Saxons" in *Liberty Bell* for 1841.

1841   *May*: LMC moves to New York to edit *National Anti-Slavery Standard*; boards with Quaker Isaac T. Hopper and begins visiting New York with his son, John Hopper.

June: Vacations in Brookline, Massachusetts, with the Lorings; visits Brook Farm.

August 19: Inaugurates "Letters from New-York" ("LNY") column in *Standard*.

October: Visits DLC in Northampton.

December: Publishes "The Quadroons" in *Liberty Bell* for 1842.

1842   *February–May*: Editorializes in favor of disunion; fracas with Garrisonians.

December: DLC files for bankruptcy in Northampton and goes to Washington as correspondent for *Liberator* and *Standard*; LMC publishes "Slavery's Pleasant Homes" in *Liberty Bell* for 1843.

1843   *February*: Separates financial affairs from DLC's and decides to remain in New York regardless of his plans; writes first "LNY" in favor of women's rights; begins editing "LNY" for publication as book.

May: Resigns from editorship of *Standard* after months of dissension; DLC replaces her as editor in August, but he spends winter in Washington again.

Late August: Publishes *Letters from New-York*; first edition sold out by December.

December: Inaugurates new "LNY" column in *Boston Courier*.

1844   *February*: In uncollected "LNY" defends Amelia Norman for having attempted to murder her seducer; helps to rehabilitate her.

May: DLC resigns editorship of *Standard*, returns to Northampton.

October: Meets Ole Bull.

December: Margaret Fuller arrives in New York as correspondent for Greeley's *Tribune*; Child and Fuller renew intimacy; LMC publishes two volumes of *Flowers for Children*.

Begins circulating in a milieu of literati, musicians, and artists that includes Poe, James Russell Lowell, Parke Godwin, Ole Bull, and William Page.

1845   *January*: With "Thot and Freia," begins publishing short stories in *Columbian Lady's and Gentleman's Magazine* and occasional pieces in Poe's *Broadway Journal*.

February: Publishes *Letters from New York. Second Series*; reviews Fuller's *Woman in the Nineteenth Century* for *Broadway Journal*.

December: Ole Bull leaves for Europe.

1846   *July*: Visits father in Wayland, Massachusetts.

August: Fuller leaves for Europe.

December: Publishes *Fact and Fiction* and third volume of *Flowers for Children*.

1847   *March*: John Hopper elopes with Rosa De Wolf.

May: Publishes "The Man That Killed His Neighbors," her last story for the *Columbian Lady's and Gentleman's Magazine*; moves to New Rochelle farmhouse of Joseph and Margaret Carpenter.

July: Begins publishing stories in *Union Magazine of Literature and Art*.

September: Mary Francis Preston (sister) dies.

December: Visits family and friends in Massachusetts.

1848   *April*: Begins research for *The Progress of Religious Ideas*; meets Dolores.

Late fall: DLC hired by his brother John Childe to supervise railway construction in Tennessee.

1849   *March*: Thinking she is about to die, burns 339 letters; renews contact with the Lorings; returns to the Hoppers', where she rents attic room.

September: DLC returns from Tennessee and is not rehired by John Childe; the Childs enjoy second honeymoon.

1850   *June*: The Childs move with Dolores to West Newton, Massachusetts, where they rent a farm from Ellis Loring.

1852   *May* 7: LMC summoned to deathbed of Isaac T. Hopper, promises to write his biography.

1853   *August*: Publishes *Isaac T. Hopper: A True Life*, vows proceeds to Hopper's family; Dolores returns to New York.

December: The Childs move into her father's home in Wayland, where she nurses her father for the next three years; LMC attends Anti-Slavery Fair for first time in many years.

1855   *November–December*: Publishes *The Progress of Religious Ideas*; *A New Flower for Children*; and "Jan and Zaida" in *Liberty Bell* for 1856.

1856   *Early spring*: Writes four stories for her collection *Autumnal Leaves*.

May 22: Charles Sumner caned in the U.S. Senate by Preston Brooks; civil war rages in Kansas between anti- and proslavery settlers.

October–November: Serializes "The Kansas Emigrants" in *New York Tribune* during last week of 1856 electoral campaign; writes "Song for the Free Soil Men"; organizes sewing circle in Wayland for antislavery settlers in Kansas; DLC campaigns for Frémont; Frémont loses to James Buchanan; LMC publishes *Autumnal Leaves*.

Thanksgiving Day: father, Convers Francis, dies.

1857   *Summer*: Meets Mattie Griffith.

December: Publishes "The Stars and Stripes. A Melo-Drama" in *Liberty Bell* for 1858.

1858   *May*: Publishes "Loo Loo" in *Atlantic Monthly*; Ellis Loring dies on May 24.

1859   *May*: The Childs attend New England Anti-Slavery Convention; John Brown walks out of it.

October 16–18: John Brown and his men raid Harpers Ferry, Virginia.

October 26: LMC writes to John Brown and Governor Henry Wise, asking permission to nurse Brown in prison.

November–December: Publishes exchanges with Brown, Governor Henry Wise, and Mrs. Margaretta Mason in *Tribune* and answers dozens of letters a day; raises funds for the families of Brown and his men; helps Garrison organize Tremont Temple ceremony to honor Brown; attends all-day prayer meeting for Brown at a black church.

1860 *January*: Publishes *Correspondence between Lydia Maria Child and Gov. Wise and Mrs. Mason*.

February: Completes *The Right Way the Safe Way*, personally addresses and mails more than a thousand copies over the next year.

Late summer: Edits Harriet Jacobs's *Incidents in the Life of a Slave Girl*.

October: Publishes *The Patriarchal Institution* and mails out hundreds of copies; publishes *The Duty of Disobedience to the Fugitive Slave Law*, sending copies to newly elected Massachusetts legislators; raises funds to free Thomas Sims.

November: Lincoln elected; the Childs board for the winter with Lucy Osgood in Medford.

December: Attends two antislavery meetings mobbed by conservatives; South Carolina secedes.

1861 *January 24*: Attends another antislavery meeting mobbed by conservatives.

February: Possibly attends Convention for the Indians, writes "Willie and Wikanee" and submits to *Knickerbocker* (not published).

April: The Childs return to Wayland; the Civil War breaks out with the capture of Fort Sumter by the Confederacy.

July: Attends party for Harriet Beecher Stowe; Union defeat at Battle of Bull Run.

Writes anonymous pro-emancipation articles for newspapers, sends relief supplies to "contrabands," knits for abolitionist-led regiments.

1862 *August–September*: Publishes "Emancipation and Amalgamation" and "L. Maria Child to the President of the United States."

Winter: Starts and puts aside *A Romance of the Republic*, begins work on *Looking Toward Sunset*.

1863 *March*: Publishes "Willie Wharton" in *Atlantic Monthly*.

April 7: Convers Francis (brother) dies.

June: Ell-wing of Wayland cottage burns down.

July: New York draft riots; Massachusetts 54th decimated in attack on Fort Wagner, Robert Shaw killed.

1864 *January*: Meets Edmonia Lewis at Anti-Slavery Reception.

Lobbies for education and training programs for freedpeople, redistribution of confiscated plantations to freedpeople and poor whites, reelection of Lincoln.

Begins work on *Freedmen's Book*.

November: Publishes *Looking Toward Sunset*.

1865   *January 31*: House of Representatives passes Thirteenth Amendment, abolishing slavery.

April: Frances E. W. Harper lectures in Wayland; Lee surrenders to Grant at Appomatox, ending Civil War; Lincoln assassinated.

May: Begins writing articles for *Independent*.

November: Publishes *The Freedmen's Book*, begins outlining *A Romance of the Republic*.

1866   *March*: Publishes "Poor Chloe" in *Atlantic Monthly*.

Publishes articles in *Independent* criticizing Andrew Johnson's Reconstruction policies.

1867   *July*: Publishes *A Romance of the Republic*.

1868   *April 11 and 18*: Publishes "A Plea for the Indian" in *Standard*; reissued as *An Appeal for the Indians*.

May: Louisa Loring dies.

Writes many articles over the next few years for *Standard*, *Independent*, *Woman's Advocate*, and *Woman's Journal* advocating black suffrage, land redistribution, protection for the freedpeople, woman suffrage, Indian rights.

1870   *January 27*: Attends closing meeting of Massachusetts Anti-Slavery Society and last Anti-Slavery Festival.

April 16: *National Anti-Slavery Standard* ceases publication after ratification of Fifteenth Amendment, enfranchising black men; replaced by monthly *Standard*, then weekly *National Standard*, again monthly through December 1872.

December: Publishes "Resemblances between the Buddhist and Catholic Religions" in *Atlantic Monthly*.

1871   *October*: Publishes "The Intermingling of Religions" in *Atlantic Monthly*.

1872   Tries to dissuade Sumner from supporting Greeley in 1872 election, publishes articles urging voters to support Grant.

1874   *March*: Charles Sumner dies.

September 17: DLC dies in Wayland.

November: Democrats recapture Congress, ushering in end of Reconstruction; LMC visits with the Sewalls and goes to spend winter with the Shaws on Staten Island, returning to Wayland in the spring.

1876   *May*: Attends Free Religious Association meeting, visits the Alcott family.

Winter: Begins spending winters in Boston, where she regularly attends Free Religious Association meetings.

1878   *May*: Publishes *Aspirations of the World*.

1879   *May*: Shortly after a visit with LMC, Garrison dies.

August: Publishes tribute to Garrison in *Atlantic* (her last article).

1880   *October 20*: Dies in Wayland.

Abbreviations

BPL Boston Public Library, Anti-Slavery Collections

CC *The Collected Correspondence of Lydia Maria Child, 1817–1880*, ed. Patricia G. Holland, Milton Meltzer, and Francine Krasno (Millwood, N.Y.: Kraus Microform, 1980)

CWL *The Collected Works of Abraham Lincoln*, ed. Roy P. Basler, 8 vols. (New Brunswick, N.J.: Rutgers UP, 1953)

DAB *Dictionary of American Biography*

GL *The Letters of William Lloyd Garrison*, ed. Walter M. Merrill and Louis Ruchames, 6 vols. (Cambridge, Mass.: Belknap P of Harvard UP, 1971–81)

JM *Juvenile Miscellany*

LIFE *William Lloyd Garrison, 1850–1879: The Story of His Life Told by His Children*, 4 vols. (1885–1889; New York: Arno P, 1969)

MHS Massachusetts Historical Society

NAR *North American Review*

SL *Lydia Maria Child: Selected Letters, 1817–1880*, ed. Milton Meltzer, Patricia G. Holland, and Francine Krasno (Amherst: U of Massachusetts P, 1982)

Prologue
A Passion for Books

My Dear Brother, — I have been busily engaged in reading "Paradise Lost." . . . I could not but admire such astonishing grandeur of description, such heavenly sublimity of style. I never read a poem that displayed a more prolific fancy, or a more vigorous genius. But don't you think that Milton asserts the superiority of his own sex in rather too lordly a manner? Thus, when Eve is conversing with Adam, she is made to say, —

> *"My author and disposer, what thou bid'st*
> *Unargu'd I obey; so God ordained.*
> *God is thy law, thou mine: to know no more*
> *Is woman's happiest knowledge, and her praise."[1]*

This precocious letter, written at age fifteen, aptly introduces one of nineteenth-century America's most original writers and reformers, Lydia Maria Francis Child.[2] When it was first published in a selected edition of Child's correspondence, two years after her death in 1880, reviewers familiar with her controversial career as an advocate of racial, sexual, and religious equality immediately recognized it as casting her "mental horoscope."[3] Addressed to her elder brother, Convers Francis, then finishing his studies at Harvard Divinity School, Child's comments on *Paradise Lost* reflect the mind of a young woman sensitive to literary genius but unawed by patriarchal authority, impatient of the restraints placed on her sex, and already prone to reject orthodoxy and think for herself. Her letter to Convers also gives a foretaste of the rhetorical strategies that would enable Child to exert such a powerful influence on her contemporaries during her half century as a cultural spokesperson. Not only does this largely self-educated fifteen-year-old bolster her interpretation by citing chapter and verse, as she would in the many polemical works she would go on to write, but under the guise of tactfully deferring to her university-educated brother, she firmly reasserts her independence. "Perhaps you will smile at the freedom with which I express my opinion concerning the books which I have been reading," she writes ingenuously, hastening to assure Convers that she "willingly acknowledges the superiority of [his] talents and advantages, and . . .

fully appreciates" the "condescension and kindness" he has shown toward her. Nevertheless, she remains undaunted by his insistence that her criticism of Milton is unfounded. "I perceive that I never shall convert you to my opinions concerning Milton's treatment to [sic] our sex," she replies jauntily, confident that truth lies on her side, whatever Convers's claims to greater erudition.[4] The same reliance on her own inner convictions would again and again lead her to challenge time-honored institutions — in the 1820s by exploring the tabooed subject of interracial marriage and championing the cause of the Indians,[5] in the 1830s by calling for the immediate abolition of slavery and denouncing all forms of racial discrimination, in the 1840s by taking up the defense of "fallen women" and demanding the extension to women of sexual as well as civil and political rights, in the 1850s by denying the historical truth of Christianity and urging respect for the world's other religions, and in the 1860s and 1870s by crusading for a genuine Reconstruction of American society on the basis of universal equality.

The intellectual boldness and self-assurance Child reveals in her earliest surviving letters are all the more remarkable in the light of her background. As she informed her brother's biographer, her parents had been "hard-working people, who had had small opportunity for culture," and during her childhood, there had been "nothing like literary influences in the family, or its surroundings."[6] An autobiographical fragment Convers left among his papers likewise conveys the impression of "intensely industrious and rigidly economical" folk, whose arduous struggle against the poverty they had known in their youth had forced them to dispense with education and to limit their reading to didactic works.[7] The "little book-case" that graced the Francis home offered only the plainest fare: "an odd volume of Cowley, Orton's 'Expositions of the Old Testament,' Forbes's 'Family Book,' some histories of England and of the Revolution, and Watts's 'Improvement of the Mind.' "[8]

Yet ever since Child could remember, she and Convers, six years her senior, had shared "a passion for books" that had differentiated them from their parents and three older siblings, James, Susannah, and Mary. Long after Child had made a name for herself as the author of more than thirty works, many of them best-sellers, she went so far as to ascribe her own "literary tendencies entirely to [Convers's] early influence." "When I came from school," she reminisced, "I always hurried to his bed-room, and threw myself down among his piles of books. As I devoured everything that came in my way, I, of course, read much that was beyond my childish comprehension. I was constantly calling upon him to explain: 'Convers, what does Shakespeare mean by this? What does Milton mean by that?' " The picture she conjured up of her brother no doubt applied to them both: "Whatever work he was set about, he always had a book in his pocket; and he was poring over it, at every moment of leisure."[9]

Moments of leisure were few, however. By trade a baker, whose famous "Medford crackers" were sold widely in the region and even exported to England, their father, Convers Francis, Senior, did not encourage the intellectual aspirations that his two youngest children had somehow developed. Although he had built his bakery into a "flourishing" business by the time his youngest daughter was born on February 11,

1802, he remained a "great believer in manual labor" and "a somewhat severe exactor of labor from his children." Musing on his father's death at age ninety, Convers still marveled at the old man's tenacious industry: "He devoted himself to his work with an eagerness and an unsparing exertion of strength which used to seem to me prodigious," he noted in his diary.[10] Mr. Francis also set an "unsparing" pace for the rest of the family. No matter how deeply "buried" in their books, young Convers and Lydia had perpetually to be "unearthed" for the performance of the innumerable tasks involved in running a thriving household enterprise and family farm: "[T]he farm-work and bake-house-work followed [them] up sharply; . . . [they] had to make hay, weed the garden, set the hens, tend the shop, turn the 'dumb-betty,' and hang out the clothes."[11]

Despite such obstacles, Child recollected, Convers had "early manifested an earnest desire to go to college." Initially, their father had not been "inclined to favor his wishes; for he . . . considered a college-education something out of the line of himself or his family." He yielded to the persuasion of two eminent figures in their native Medford, Massachusetts: the Reverend David Osgood, pastor of the Congregationalist Church the Francis family attended; and Dr. John Brooks, the family physician and future governor of Massachusetts. According to Child, Brooks had insisted: " 'Mr. Francis, you will do very wrong to thwart the inclinations of that boy. He has remarkable powers of mind; and his passion for books is so strong, that he will be sure to distinguish himself in learning; whereas, if you try to make anything else of him, he will prove a total failure.' "[12] Thanks to this intercession, Convers entered the sacred precincts of Dr. Hosmer's college preparatory academy, reserved for the elite of Medford's 1,400 inhabitants: "There was an air of aristocracy about it," he recalled in his autobiography; "sons of rich men from other towns came to it as boarding-scholars; and only 'the better sort,' in the town, sent their children to it. . . . so that when I, the baker's boy, was transferred from the town school to it, it was a promotion which made me tremble."[13]

In an era preceding the establishment of colleges for women, there was no one to intercede for Convers's equally promising sister, who was obliged to fend for herself once her brother matriculated at Harvard in 1811. After outgrowing the "dame school" where she and Convers had learned their letters, Child had to content herself first with the meager offerings of the "common town school, where Tom, Dick, and Harry, everybody's boys, and everybody's girls, went as a matter of course," then with the hardly more stimulating regime of Miss Swan's Female Academy, which she attended for a year at age twelve.[14] The divergence of the siblings' paths had far-reaching consequences. Convers, whose "promotion" enabled him to marry a woman of "the better sort," would continually shy away from embracing causes likely to offend his new associates. No such inhibitions would trouble his sister, who would take pride in her identity as a baker's daughter and retain her fierce hatred of "aristocracy" to the end of her life. Indeed, the experience of being denied the education lavished on her brother sowed the seeds of a feminist consciousness in Child, as it did in two women's rights leaders of the 1830s and 1840s who acknowledged her as a forerunner—Sarah Grimké and Elizabeth Cady Stanton.[15] Equally formative, the experience of being cast on her own intellectual resources liberated Child from dependency on the authority of the conservative professors who dominated the universities and vocally opposed the radical reforms she would later champion.

Of course, as a nine year old, Child could not have foreseen that she would learn more from making her own education, in defiance of a father "alarmed at her increasing fondness for books," than Convers would from his courses at Harvard.[16] The loss of her cherished brother and mentor must simply have felt overwhelming. Scenes of brothers and sisters torn apart in early youth recur obsessively in Child's fiction.[17]

Exacerbating the young girl's misery was her mother's slow decline. Susannah Rand Francis had borne seven children in twelve years, of whom five had survived and the sixth had been stillborn. By age thirty-six, when her last baby arrived, the strain of repeated childbearing, prolonged hard times, and incessant domestic drudgery had fatally sapped her health. Perhaps already laboring under the first symptoms of the tuberculosis to which she would succumb at forty-eight, Susannah seems to have greeted her baby daughter with scant enthusiasm. Unlike Convers, Child would never write fondly of "the devoted, anxious care with which [my mother] watched over my welfare," or of the "blessed power for good" that the bond between them exerted over her life. Apparently, Susannah had "heaped the full measure of her love" on Convers and her older children and had "little left for her youngest daughter."[18] All her life Child would suffer from an unfulfilled craving for love, intensified by a passionate temperament for which New England decorum allowed no outlet. Until Convers's departure for Harvard, Child had relied on him and on her favorite sister Susannah for the affection she so desperately needed. But the very year Convers left home, Susannah married and moved away, and their mother withdrew into her final illness. For the better part of three years, just when the lonely preadolescent girl required most mothering, Susannah Rand Francis lay bedridden with tuberculosis. "[S]o much accustomed" did Child grow to her dying mother's "pale face, and weak voice" that she could hardly remember a prior state.[19]

Guilt and ill-concealed resentment haunt the only direct account Child left of her mother — an autobiographical story entitled "My Mother's Grave" (1828), published in her children's magazine, *The Juvenile Miscellany*. What that story reveals is the inner turmoil of a girl who cannot forgive her mother for not having had the strength to nurture her during the most critical period of her youth. "At first, it is true, I had sobbed violently — for they told me she would die," Child confides, "but when, day after day, I returned from school, and found her the same, I began to believe she would always be spared to me" (311). Was she also unconsciously denying that her mother's illness had reversed their proper roles — that it was now her responsibility to care for the mother who could not care for her? The wrenching incident Child proceeds to relate would suggest so.

She had come home one afternoon "discouraged and fretful," having done her work "wrong-side-outward" and consequently forfeited her place at the head of the class. Although she had found her mother "paler than usual," she was in no mood to supply an invalid's wants. That day she needed more than the "affectionate smile, that always welcomed [her] return." Thus, when her mother requested her to "go down stairs, and bring her a glass of water," Child reacted "pettishly" by demanding "why she did not call the domestic to do it" (312). Nor was she melted by the "look of mild reproach" her mother gave her as she asked, "And will not my daughter bring a glass of water for her poor sick mother?" She performed the task grudgingly: "Instead of smiling, and kissing her, as I was wont to do, I sat the glass down very quick, and left the room." She did not even return to bid her mother goodnight. Alone in the "darkness and silence" of her room, however, Child could not sleep. Her mother's pale face and trembling voice pricked her conscience, as those never-to-be-forgotten words of reproach echoed in her ears. She determined to ask forgiveness, but it was too late — her mother had "just sunk into an uneasy slumber," from which she would not awaken.[20]

Child would spend a lifetime coping with the psychic wounds left by her mother's illness and death: unresolved anger toward her parents, the guilt and chronic depression that typically result from anger deflected inward, and an insatiable yearning for love. Consciously and unconsciously, she would keep trying to compensate for having failed her mother at the hour of her death. Forty years later, for example, she would all but drop her writing to nurse her irascible father through his protracted last illness. She would make similar sacrifices for her husband, not only by nursing him in his old age, but by subordinating her professional and emotional needs to his for most of their married life and repressing the anger this generated in her, with disastrous psychological consequences.

Though Child seems never to have recovered from the trauma she commemorated in "My Mother's Grave," she did succeed in turning her compulsive quest for atonement and her thwarted desire for nurture to productive uses. In assuming the vocation of a writer for mothers and children, she would step symbolically into her mother's role and offer a generation of young readers the mothering she herself had not received. She would even devote one of her domestic advice books, *The Family Nurse* (1837), to the household care of the sick — the very service she had rebelled against rendering. Ultimately, Child would extend her nurturing far beyond the domestic sphere to embrace nearly all the wronged and oppressed of her society: Indians threatened with dispossession; enslaved, fugitive, and free but ostracized African Americans; martyred abolitionists;[21] "fallen women"; prisoners; the urban poor; Irish and Chinese immigrants; the elderly.

The need for atonement that helped prompt a career of self-sacrificing advocacy for others is undisguised in "My Mother's Grave," written explicitly so "that those children who have parents to love them, may learn to value them as they ought" (311). Significantly, that story remained Child's sole tribute to her mother. The painful memory of her unfilial conduct — and the poignant, if unreasonable, anger she acted out toward her mother for abandoning her by dying — overclouded her girlhood. As an adult, Child rarely spoke of her years in Medford, except to say that they were "cold, shaded, and uncongenial." "Whenever reminiscences of them rise up before me, I turn my back on them as quick as possible," she told her friend Lucy Osgood, daughter of the pastor who had helped send Convers to Harvard.[22]

Twelve years older than Child, Lucy Osgood took the place of a mother after Susannah Rand Francis retreated into invalidism. Perhaps as important in the long run, Lucy and her elder sister Mary furnished Child with the only positive role models of intellectual women she encountered in her youth. Educated at home by their father, they had learned Latin, Greek, and Hebrew and ranged widely in his well stocked library. "Their extensive reading," their erudition, and "their depth and independence of thought" had made them "objects of [her] childish veneration," teaching her that women, too, could master the subjects she longed to study. At the same time, the Osgood sisters' "old-fashioned skill and diligence" in the womanly arts of "sewing, knitting, netting, and crocheting," which they took "especial satisfaction" in consecrating to the production of "comfortable articles for those who were in need," counteracted the stereotype of the unfeminine pedant, held up to deter girls from intellectual pursuits.[23] The Osgoods' example must have gone far to immunize Child against the anxieties generated by the most notorious local embodiment of the female intellectual — an "aged" spinster named Hannah Adams, who had authored a history of the Jews and supposedly "unsexed herself by her learning." Looking back on the obstacles literary women had once faced, Child remarked wryly of Hannah Adams: "She was said not only to be unconscious of a hole in her stocking, but to be absolutely unable to recognize her own face in the glass; and if *that* was not being unfeminine, pray tell me what *could* be."[24] When she followed Hannah Adams into authorship, she avoided such strictures by modeling her deportment on the Osgood sisters'.

If her own parents did not manage to satisfy Child's hunger for love and thirst for education, they did nonetheless bequeath to her many of the principles she would defend so eloquently. The habits of tireless industry and rigid economy they inculcated in her would stand her in good stead during a struggle against poverty as taxing as any her parents had known, and she would transmit their lessons to a wide audience in *The Frugal Housewife* and *The Juvenile Miscellany*. Child's parents also showed her that thrift and self-denial must go hand in hand with generosity toward poorer neighbors. Every week they sent a Sunday dinner to their children's first teacher, the old, tobacco-chewing spinster Ma'am Betty, who held a "dame school" in her untidy bedroom. And every Thanksgiving eve they invited "all the humble friends of the household — 'Ma'am Betty,' the washerwoman, the berry-woman, the wood-sawyer, the journeymen-bakers" — for a festive meal. In the ample, old-fashioned kitchen, the gathering of twenty or thirty working folk "partook of an immense chicken-pie, pumpkin-pies (made in milk-pans), and heaps of doughnuts. . . . and went away loaded with crackers and bread by the father, and with pies by the mother, not forgetting 'turnovers' for their children."[25] The one memory of her youth that she liked to recall, Child would immortalize this picture of a traditional New England Thanksgiving in her poem, "Over the river and through the wood, / To grandfather's house we go," which generations of American children have sung without knowing the name of the author.[26]

Commenting on the Francis family's Thanksgiving bounty, the abolitionist Thomas Wentworth Higginson surmised in his 1868 biographical sketch of his old friend: "Such homely applications of the doctrine 'It is more blessed to give than to receive' may have done more to mould the Lydia Maria Child of maturer years than all the faithful labors of good Dr. Osgood, to whom she and her brother used to repeat the Westminster Assembly's Catechism once a month."[27] Child would in fact rebel aggressively against the dour Calvinist creed Dr. Osgood preached, to which her father clung till his dying day, despite Osgood's own capitulation to Unitarianism. But her parents' Christian ethic would inspire her deep commitment to relieving the suffering of the poor.

Child's parents also taught her political principles that went beyond Christian charity. The elder Convers Francis prided himself on being the son of a "liberty man, . . . reported to have killed five" redcoats at the battle of Concord: "The sound of the old Revolution . . . was still in his ears, and he detested slavery, with all its apologists and in all its forms."[28] He kindled the same ardent love of "right and freedom" in his daughter. From an early age, stories about slavery in Massachusetts — and about local heroes who had fought against it — shaped Child's consciousness. One incident her parents must often have related to her had occurred when she was three years old: the rescue of the escaped slave Caesar in 1805, which had earned Medford the honor of being the first American town to shield a fugitive against recapture. Like the Francises, Caesar, a tailor, and Nathan Wait, the blacksmith who took primary credit for the rescue, were "mechanics," or artisans, the class Child identified as the backbone of the antislavery movement in Massachusetts; hence, it is quite possible that her parents were among the Medford "friends" who informed Caesar of his right to "be a free man if he chose."[29] Child may also have learned from her mother of another incident she recounted in both her *Authentic Anecdotes of American Slavery* (1835) and her *Atlantic Monthly* sketch "Poor Chloe" (1866). Illustrating the callousness slavery produced, it involved a workingwoman in Gloucester, Massachusetts, who had received a black infant as a present from a wealthy slaveholder and had nourished it with her own milk, only to sell it into Virginia at age five in order to buy herself a brocade gown for Sabbath wear.[30] The hatred of slavery such stories aroused in Child no doubt predisposed her to embrace the abolitionist cause.[31] Yet of the five Francis siblings, Child alone seems to have inherited her parents' Revolutionary creed. Her eldest brother, James, a farmer, would espouse the racist politics of the Democratic party, and her beloved Convers would take almost a decade to follow her timidly into the abolitionist camp.[32] If her sister Mary sympathized any earlier with her antislavery views, she left no record of it, though Mary's daughters, Sarah Preston Parsons and Mary Preston Stearns, would be committed abolitionists by the 1850s. Ultimately, perhaps as decisive a factor as her parents' teachings in transforming Child into an antislavery activist was the marginal position she occupied in both her family and her society. Denied the rewards of parental approbation and professional recognition, she learned to seek instead the reward of her own conscience.

Unfortunately, the senior Convers Francis's exemplary qualities did not include the ability to comfort a desolate twelve-year-old girl grieving for her dead mother. Gloomy and withdrawn by temperament, he seemed to turn his back on her. And when she sought consolation in her books, he fretted. "He was a good man, and meant to be kind, — but he was not used to showing tenderness," Child would write of her father in her thinly disguised autobiographical novella, *Emily Parker* (1827):

> When he came in from work, he would always inquire what she had done during the day. If she had accomplished a great deal, he would praise her industry; but he did not talk with her, during the long winter's evenings, — and it was only by the subdued tone of his naturally stern voice, and the prolonged kiss he sometimes gave her, when she bade him good night, that Emily knew he blessed her in his heart, both for her own, and her mother's sake.[33]

Under his grim exterior, of course, her father was wrestling with his own sorrow. As a devout Calvinist, he may have been undergoing the crisis of faith common to so many New Englanders, who struggled in vain to reconcile themselves to the possibility that God might choose to damn their loved ones. Child would later attribute the "especial grudge" she developed against her parents' "fierce theology" to her father's incurable terror of "going to hell" — and to his insistence that she, too, would "have to burn hereafter" for her apostasy.[34] Adding to the disconsolate widower's cares was the severe economic depression that the War of 1812 had triggered throughout New England as a result of the embargo on trade with Britain. What finally enabled him to decide how to solve his domestic problems was the marriage of his daughter Mary, who had been running the Francis household and serving as a surrogate mother to her younger sister for the past three years.

Devastated at the prospect of losing her last mainstay, Child had refused to attend Mary's wedding and secluded herself with her kitten "until all was over."[35] Mary's departure for Norridgewock, Maine (then a province of Massachusetts), had left her widowed father to cope by himself with a straitened business, a large house and farm, and a wayward, bookish adolescent daughter. The solution he settled on was to sell the bakery, move in with his son James, and dispatch Lydia to her newly married sister in Norridgewock, who could cure her of her notions and initiate her into the domestic avocations befitting a woman. Meanwhile, as if to complete the disintegration of the family, both Child's favorite sister, Susannah, and her grandmother, Susannah Rand, died.[36]

Bereft of intellectual companionship and maternal tenderness; barred from the portals of knowledge through which the baker's son, but not his daughter, might enter the realm of refinement and culture depicted in the books both of them cherished; and banished like an unwanted burden from the only home she had known — Child must have felt abandoned by the entire world. Ten years later, she poured her unassuaged grief over her mother's death and her "desperate resentment" toward her father into her first novel: *Hobomok, A Tale of Early Times* (1824). Her heroine, Mary Conant, too, endures the pain of being deprived one by one of a friend's "cheering influence," a role model's "firm support," and a mother's "mild, soothing spirit." Unlike Child, however, Mary plays the part of a dutiful daughter, choosing to nurse her dying mother rather than return with her lover to England. Through her heroine's sacrifice, culminating in an emotionally resonant deathbed farewell of mother and daughter, Child granted herself absolution from shame and guilt. But she vented her anger against her surviving parent, whom she blamed for having rejected her. Refusing to remain isolated in an atmosphere of "unreciprocated intellect" with a morose, austere father, Mary spites him by fleeing into the wilderness with an Indian — a parody of the exile from civilization that Convers Francis, Senior, like his fictional representative, Roger Conant, had chosen for his daughter.[37]

Actually, as Child seems to have realized by the time she wrote *Hobomok*, the move from Medford to Norridgewock turned out to be as liberating as her heroine's sojourn in the wilderness. True, Norridgewock lacked the advantages that Medford's proximity to the cultural centers of Boston and Cambridge afforded. Yet it also lacked the rigid class structure of the older town, which reserved those advantages for an elite the Francis family did not belong to. In Norridgewock, Child drew her social identity not from her father the baker, but from her brother-in-law, Warren Preston, a respected lawyer and future county probate judge. Thus, she could mingle freely with the cultured Massachusetts families, university graduates, and professional men comprising the village's one thousand inhabitants.[38]

Moreover, as the shire town of Somerset County, Norridgewock became a hub of activity when court was in session. During those three busy months, lawyers and judges from all over the region converged on the little town. Many gathered in the Prestons' parlor, where Child could eavesdrop on legal and political debates. Chief among the issues raging in that turbulent period following the War of 1812 was whether the District of Maine should seek independent statehood, or secede from the U.S. government as well as from Massachusetts. The question of statehood was intimately connected with the dispute over slavery that erupted into the open in the Missouri crisis of 1819–20; for Maine's admission to the Union as a free state became contingent on granting Missouri admission as a slave state, contrary to the provisions of the 1787 ordinance banning slavery from the Northwest Territory. These discussions must have played a key role in initiating Child into the legal and political complexities of the slavery controversy. She would devote an entire chapter of her 1833 *Appeal in Favor of That Class of Americans Called Africans* to the "Influence of Slavery on the Politics of the United States," citing the case of Maine and Missouri as a prime illustration of how the South's ruling oligarchy held the entire country hostage to proslavery interests.[39]

Besides intellectual stimulation and political education, the Preston household provided emotional sustenance. The close bond Child formed with her sister Mary is evident in the affectionate letters through which she attempted to maintain their intimacy after leaving Maine in 1821. "I have a million things, which I wish to say to you, every day — but I cannot put them in a letter," she writes in one, begging for a long, newsy reply. "Do not feel that your letters are uninteresting to me," she pleads. "I assure you that you would not, if you could read my heart when I receive them."[40] "I do wish you could find it in your heart to write oftener," she complains in another letter, reporting a conversation with a recent visitor from Maine, whose gossip about "a pretty-black-eyed sister of mine" had overwhelmed her with nostalgia.[41]

From Mary, Child learned the domestic skills she would impart to thousands of readers in *The Frugal Housewife* (1829). Like the heroine of her novella *Emily Parker*, "Before she was fifteen . . . she could spin more yarn, and weave more cloth in a day, than any girl on the Kenebec" [*sic*]. Nor was this all: she could make the best "butter and cheese . . . in the country" and display her "ingenuity" by stitching quilts and braiding carpets "which a Bostonian might have mistaken for Marseilles" manufacture.[42] (A specimen of Child's handiwork preserved in the Medford museum — a christening dress she sewed for one of her nieces — makes good her boast.) The experience of helping to bring up the Preston children also taught her much of the wisdom she distilled into *The Mother's Book* (1831) and the *Juvenile Miscellany* (1826–34), which together made this motherless child and childless woman a national authority on childrearing. The *Miscellany*, for example, regularly featured dialogues between Aunt Maria and her charges and even referred to the young Prestons by their own names in one story ("The Little Traveller").[43]

Child's years in Norridgewock had their greatest impact, however, in awakening her sympathy for the Indians, who would inspire some of her best early fiction and draw her into her first political cause. Despite the amenities on which it prided itself, Norridgewock was still unmistakably a frontier town in the second decade of the nineteenth century. Bears, wolves, and foxes made occasional forays into the surrounding farms, and remnants of the Abenaki and Penobscot Indian tribes lived or camped close by, in the towering hemlock forests that skirted the shores of the Kennebec River.[44] The Abenaki hamlet of Norridgewock, seven miles upriver from the present town, had been the site of a massacre in 1724. English troops had wiped out the inhabitants and razed the village with its Catholic church, also killing the French Jesuit resident priest, Sebastien Rale. English settlers had then usurped the land once farmed by the Abenaki. Norridgewock's buried past was literally disinterred by a storm in 1815, the very year Child arrived. Heavy winds overturned an ancient oak tree, exposing Father Rale's cracked, corroded church bell, which had lain entangled in its roots for almost a century. Child would ponder the lessons of this tempestuous return of the repressed in two provocative stories: "Adventures of a Bell" (1827) and "The Church in the Wilderness" (1828).

The Maine wilderness opened up vistas more exotic than any that Convers discerned from Harvard. It unleashed Child's literary imagination, inviting her to explore recesses into which few American writers of her day dared to venture. And it exposed her at an impressionable age to a culture that seemed to foster physical strength, independence, and survival skills in women, instead of celebrating an ideal of feminine delicacy and stultifying domesticity.

One winter, while Child was staying with friends in Winslow, a Penobscot woman from an encampment in the vicinity showed up at the door. "She had waded four miles through very deep and almost unbroken snow, to beg for salt fish," being unable to obtain her usual food because of the heavy snowfall. The following day, to the astonishment of Child's hosts, the woman returned "with a new-born babe strapped to her back." She had given birth the preceding evening, she told her white interlocutors, and in accordance with her tribe's custom, had washed the baby in the river, after "first cut[ting] a hole in the ice with her hatchet." This time she requested a sack of potatoes, which she "slung . . . over her shoulders, with her baby," retracing her four-mile hike through the snow "with vigorous strides."[45] Child never forgot the encounter. Almost twenty years afterward, in her *History of the Condition of Women*, she generalized about the "hardy constitutions" Indian women shared with the "female peasantry of Europe" and described how "[w]hen an infant is a few hours old, they carry it to some neighboring stream and plunge it in the water, even if they have to break the ice for that purpose."[46] As late as 1873 she cited the incident in an article on the "Physical Strength of Women," in which she argued that "whole classes of women develop into robustness, and perform with ease and safety what are generally considered masculine labors," thus proving the alleged weakness of women to be the result not of "Nature" but of "false education and enfeebling habits."[47] Thanks to her youthful acquaintance with Indian women, Child began making such cross-cultural comparisons long before other feminist theorists, and unlike most of her contemporaries, she did not fall into the error of holding up the women of her own race and class as the norm for her sex.

On another occasion Child visited the Penobscot chief, Captain Neptune, and "ate supper with [his] tribe in a hemlock forest, on the shores of the Kennebec." Although Child probably did not know it, Neptune occupied an eminent niche in Maine annals. Not only did he adroitly defend his people's hunting and fishing rights during his fifty-year tenure as lieutenant governor of the Penobscot, but he exercised considerable spiritual power as a shaman and reputedly enjoyed flaunting his sexual prowess. Neptune himself interested Child much less, however, than his "handsome nephew [Etalexis], a tall, athletic youth, of most graceful proportions." The "majestic young Indian" cast such a spell over her that when she ran across a group of Penobscot in Hoboken, New Jersey, after a lapse of a quarter-century, his image sprang to life again before her mind's eye: "Long forgotten scenes were restored to memory, and . . . I seemed to see him as I saw him last — the very dandy of his tribe — with a broad band of shining brass about his hat, a circle of silver on his breast, tied with scarlet ribbons, and a long belt of curiously-wrought wampum hanging to his feet." Gazing at this Indian "Apollo Belvidere" with "girlish curiosity," Child had "raised the heavy tassels of [his] wampum belt" and "playfully" asked old Captain Neptune, why *he* didn't wear such finery. The chief, who had been "quietly . . . puffing his pipe, undisturbed by the consciousness of wearing a crushed hat and a dirty blanket," had replied disdainfully, " 'What for *me* wear ribbons and beads? . . . Me no want to catch 'em *squaw*.' " "He spoke in the slow, imperturbable tone of his race," Child noted; "but there was a satirical twinkle in his small black eye, as if he had sufficiently learned the tricks of civilization to enjoy mightily any jokes upon women."[48]

By her own account, Child's contacts with Indians in Maine were not limited to such infrequent encounters. "I used to go to the woods, and visit the dozen wigwams that stood there, very often," she reports in one of her *Juvenile Miscellany* sketches, "The Indian Boy."[49] She never went empty-handed, for the effects of their brutal dispossession lingered on among the impoverished Abenaki and Penobscot. But the cultural enrichment Child derived from these contacts made them more than visits of charity. As she watched the Indians weave and dye baskets, listened to the stories they told, and daydreamed about the freedom their mode of life seemed to offer, she was imperceptibly developing into the "author of *Hobomok*."

Like her heroine Mary Conant, Child may have indulged in romantic fantasies of eloping with an Indian. In dwelling on Hobomok's "tall, athletic form," "manly beauty," and "elastic, vigorous elegance of proportion" (16, 36), was she expressing the attraction she had felt toward Etalexis?[50] Did the rebellious impulses she shared with her heroine sometimes take the form of wondering whether marrying an Indian "whose nature was unwarped by the artifices of civilized life" might be more desirable than submitting to the restrictions "civilized life" imposed on women (121)?

One restriction to which Child refused to submit was the curtailment of her education. Unlike Medford, Norridgewock boasted neither a female seminary nor a male college preparatory academy, but once again it did allow Child access to the same opportunities for education open to the town's best families. There, the baker's daughter could attend summer classes given by students from Bowdoin College. Better still, she could range through the shelves of the town library, where Warren Preston, one of its founders, officiated as librarian.[51]

Encouraged from a distance by Convers, Child tackled Samuel Johnson, Addison, Gibbon, Scott, Milton, and Shakespeare, recording her opinions, ambitions, and assessments of herself in lively letters. At times, she audaciously declared her independence. "Whether the ideas I have formed . . . be erroneous or not," she responded tartly when Convers accused her of misreading *Paradise Lost*, "they are entirely my own." At others, she humbly admitted to a need for greater intellectual self-discipline and maturity: "I am aware that I have been too indolent in examining the systems of great writers; that I have not enough cultivated habits of thought and reflection upon any subject. The consequence is, my imagination has ripened before my judgment; I have quickness of perception, without profoundness of thought; I can at one glance take in a subject as displayed by another, but I am incapable of investigation."[52] The self-criticism was astute, and she obviously fulfilled her intention of remedying the shortcoming she noted, for "investigation" was to prove her forte in the many historical works she went on to publish.

Most suggestive are her comments on Scott's women characters, prefiguring as they do the rebellious heroines Child would before long create in her own fiction:

> I always preferred the impetuous grandeur of the cataract to the gentle meanderings of the rill, and spite of all that is said about gentleness, modesty, and timidity in the heroine of a novel or poem, give *me* the mixture of pathos and grandeur exhibited in the character of Meg Merrilies; or the wild dignity of Diana Vernon, with all the freedom of a Highland maiden in her step and in her eye; . . . or even the lofty contempt of life and danger which, though not unmixed with ferocity, throws such a peculiar interest around Helen MacGregor.

In *life* I am aware that gentleness and modesty form the distinguished ornaments of our sex. But in *description* they cannot captivate the imagination, nor rivet
the attention.[53]

Identifying with these "wild" and daring Highland lassies, so much akin to the Indian
women she admired, allowed Child to escape vicariously from a feminine ideal she
found as boring in life as in literature.

While unconsciously preparing for a career of authorship, consciously Child was
studying to be a schoolteacher. In March 1820, a month after her nineteenth birthday,
she wrote Convers to announce "the good news": "I leave Norridgewock, and take a
school in Gardiner." What delighted her most about the prospect was that she would
be earning her own living. "Not that I have formed any high-flown expectations," she
quickly interjected. "All I expect is, that, if I am industrious and prudent I shall be
independent."[54] She did not yet realize, apparently, how radical an aspiration independence was for a nineteenth-century woman.

Like the heroine of her autobiographical novella, *Emily Parker*, Child now found
herself "established at the head of a pleasant school" and boarding with a family whose
genteel standard of living outclassed the Prestons' (36). Did she also, like Emily, feel
torn between rival suitors: a rakish wit who sought to woo her with lessons in drawing
and music, and a serious-minded philosophy student whose humble class background
resembled hers? If so, she did not confide her secrets to Convers or Mary. In a "Letter
from New-York" of the 1840s, however, Child reminisces about a former flame who, in
her "youthful days," had been "the very Magnus Apollo of [her] imagination":

I listened to him in reverence, and took truth (or fancied I took it) upon his
authority; for it seemed to me that he knew all, and that I could never hope to be
half as wise as he. We met ten years after, and I knew not what to say to him! We
walked in the summer woods, and it reminded him of Thompson's *Seasons*, which
he recited, as of old. But I, in the meantime, had become intimate with Wordsworth, and dwelt in friendly companionship with Herder, Schiller, and Jean Paul.
Strangely, like some meagre, foreign tongue, his words fell upon my ear.[55]

This reminiscence suggests that the kind of lover Child may already have been seeking
was an intellectual mentor who would allow her to explore ideas and feelings her
society deemed dangerous, especially for women. The intermingled titillation and
terror with which she was reacting at the time to her latest literary samplings — Byron's
Don Juan and Thomas Moore's *Lalla Rookh* — reinforce such an impression. "I can give
you no idea of the anguish I felt when I read this shocking specimen of fearless and
hardened depravity. I felt as if a friend had betrayed me," she wrote to Convers after
advancing far enough in *Don Juan* to decide that she wanted to read no further.[56]

Simultaneously, Child was undergoing a crisis of faith, mirrored in her persona
Emily Parker's wild swings from "fearless" speculation on religious subjects to "mor-
bid" repudiation of "human learning as a sin" and back again to cynical mockery of
religion (18–20, 42–44). She had left her father's Calvinism behind in Medford, but the

prosaic Unitarian creed the Prestons and Convers professed did not satisfy the "glow-ing and poetic" imagination Child shared with her heroine (19). Whether through a Gardiner beau or through independent investigation, Child discovered the works of the Swedish visionary Emanuel Swedenborg during this period. The seer's doctrine of "correspondences," which postulated that every aspect of the physical universe sym-bolized a spiritual truth, exerted an instant appeal. It "seemed a golden key to unlock the massive gate between the external and spiritual worlds," and when "applied to *Scripture*," it promised access to "a store-house of jewels," Child later recalled.[57] Swe-denborg's philosophy of "conjugial love," with its emphasis on the complementarity of the sexes, must also have attracted her. Not only did it grant women a more significant place in his religious scheme than either Calvinism or Unitarianism conceded to them, but it sanctioned and transfigured the kinds of sexual fantasies Child would express in *Hobomok*. Indeed, one historian has compared the "symbolic significance of sex" in Swedenborg's "marriage mysticism" to the place it occupies in Tantric Buddhism.[58]

Worried at the prospect that Child might convert to this heterodoxical religion, Convers admonished her against yielding to an unexamined impulse. "I am in more danger of wrecking on the rocks of skepticism than of stranding on the shoals of fanaticism," she retorted, claiming that the "beautiful theory" of Swedenborgianism "plays round the imagination, but fails to reach the heart." She added wistfully: "I wish I could find some religion in which my heart and understanding could unite."[59] She would echo that wish with more and more poignancy over the years. Belying the assurances she gave Convers, however, she joined Boston's Swedenborgian New Church in February 1822, after deciding that neither the "ordinances" of her father's church nor the preach-ing of her brother's provided the spiritual sustenance she needed.[60]

By then, Convers himself had been ordained as a Unitarian minister and occupied the pulpit of the First Church in Watertown, Massachusetts. Though Child had spent little more than one school year in Gardiner, she leaped at the invitation to move into his parsonage, where she took up residence late in the summer of 1821. As if to signal her intention of assuming an identity she had chosen for herself, instead of one given to her by her parents, she had herself rebaptized Lydia Maria and asked her friends to call her Maria rather than Lydia, which "some associations of childhood" made "unpleas-ant" to her.[61] Reuniting with her family after an eight-year separation gave Child a new perspective on her class origins. For the first time she noticed how uncouth her father and her eldest brother, James, seemed, compared to the Prestons and the family with whom she had been boarding in Gardiner. The prospects of seeing James's children "growing up so ignorant and awkward as they will at home" distressed her, prompting her to inquire confidentially whether Mary would consider sending for James's eldest daughter to fill the place she herself had vacated.[62]

Convers, on the other hand, represented the social respectability and refinement toward which Child now aspired. He was marrying the daughter of a well-established minister, Abby Bradford Allyn, and taking charge of a prosperous congregation, which had furnished him with a fine house and excellent salary. Watertown, located a few miles away from Cambridge, offered opportunities for cultural enrichment far beyond any Child had ever known, and Convers held the key to them. As a graduate of Harvard Divinity School, he enjoyed access to the leading intellectual circles of the Boston area. He introduced his sister to luminaries who played an important role in her intellectual development — chief among them Ralph Waldo Emerson, then finishing his studies at Harvard; John Gorham Palfrey, a Unitarian clergyman and historian who wrote for the influential *North American Review*; and George Ticknor, professor of German literature at Harvard and arbiter of Boston's literary world.[63]

Even more vital to Child's education was the impressive library Convers had already begun to build — a library featuring many rare manuscripts and numbering 7,000 or 8,000 volumes by the time he died in 1863.[64] There, Child could at last satisfy to the full her "passion for books." And there, fittingly, she would launch the literary career for which she had so long been schooling herself.

I

The Author of *Hobomok*

"I did not mean . . . that my wildest hopes, hardly my wildest wishes, had placed me even within sight of the proud summit which has been gained either by Sir Walter Scott, or Mr. Cooper. . . . Still, barren and uninteresting as New England history is, I feel there is enough connected with it, to rouse the dormant energies of my soul; and I would fain deserve some other epitaph than that 'he lived and died.' "[1]

Hobomok, A Tale of Early Times (1824) opens with an autobiographical vignette depicting its author's dramatic entry onto the American literary scene. Bursting into the study of a friend we can easily recognize as Convers Francis, the young artist-to-be brashly announces "his" intention to write "a new England novel" — an intention prompted, as Child's was, by a Mr. "P[alfrey]'s remarks concerning our early history." Through her male persona, Child articulates her unwomanly aspiration to express the "dormant energies of my soul" and to win an epitaph in the male sphere of public action instead of in the female sphere of domestic life. Like Convers, her fictional persona's friend agrees to further the enterprise by procuring "as many old, historical pamphlets as possible." And like Child, her persona self-consciously surveys a literary landscape dominated by Sir Walter Scott and James Fenimore Cooper, and proceeds to stake out the ground that remains unexplored.

This vignette, which constitutes the preface to the novel, suggests how Child met the challenge of defining herself as an author in an era when authorship was still almost entirely the prerogative of an educated male elite. She began by identifying herself so thoroughly with her elder brother that she all but assumed his gender. Just as she had taken refuge in his bedroom and "devoured" his books while he was fitting himself for college, so she now ensconced herself in his study and enlisted his aid in fulfilling her literary ambition. At age seven or eight, it had not occurred to her that the books of a schoolboy six years her senior were beyond her "childish comprehension."[2] No more did it occur to her at age twenty-two that she could not claim the right to a public career her brother took for granted. Child seems never to have suffered from either the fear of unsexing herself or the paralyzing sense of inadequacy that inhibited so many other nineteenth-century women writers.[3] In keeping with her male identification, she looked for literary precursors among male writers, showing no discernible awareness of being disqualified by gender from inheriting (or appropriating) their mantle. Simultaneously, she treated their texts with the same iconoclasm she had displayed as a fifteen year old when she had questioned Milton's "lordly" assertion of maculine superiority.[4] Intuitively recognizing the problems posed by patriarchal literary conventions, she boldly revised them to accord women greater freedom and dignity.

The anxiety Child acknowledges in the preface to *Hobomok* is not that of a woman entering a domain reserved for men. It is the anxiety of an American seeking to demonstrate that *New* England's history offers as much scope as *Old* England's (and Scotland's) for the homegrown novelist hoping to emulate Scott.

Aspiring American writers indeed faced a daunting prospect in 1824, as they groped for direction. Irving had just published *The Sketch Book* in 1819–20, Cooper *The Spy* in 1821 and *The Pioneers* in 1823. As for predecessors like Susanna Rowson, Hugh Henry Breckinridge, and Charles Brockden Brown, none had succeeded in solving the problem that confronted the writers of Child's generation — the creation of a distinctive national literature rooted in American soil.

Rowson and Brown, however, had identified key elements of such a solution. In *Reuben and Rachel* (1798) Rowson had provided an epic that not only commemorated the discovery, conquest, and settlement of the New World, but probed the complex relations between its European and Indian peoples. And in *Edgar Huntly* (1799) Brown had transferred the Gothic novel from a European to an American setting, where "[t]he incidents of Indian hostility, and the perils of the western wilderness" replaced sadistic priests and haunted castles as mainsprings of terror.[5] Of the two, Rowson came closer to furnishing Child with a congenial model; for unlike most of her successors, she perceived that the interactions between Spanish and English settlers and Indians had taken a range of forms besides wars of extermination — forms that included the assimilation of Indian converts into early colonial Spanish and English society, the assimilation of European captives into Indian tribes, and a degree of cross-fertilization among the various cultures. Even more significantly, Rowson, who self-consciously announced in her preface that she presumed to write "[f]or my own sex only," had revised the historical record to give women a leading role.[6]

It is intriguing to speculate about the influence Rowson might have had on Child, whose historical fiction would exhibit the same protofeminist thrust and revisionist daring. By a curious coincidence, Rowson was running a school for girls in Medford during Child's infancy, and she died in Boston the year *Hobomok* appeared on the local market.[7] But no evidence suggests that the two women's paths ever crossed, or that Child ever read *Reuben and Rachel*, though she did express an unflattering opinion of Rowson's best-selling novel of seduction, *Charlotte Temple* (1794): "[It] has a nice good moral at the end, and I dare say was written with the best intention, yet I believe few works do so much harm to girls of fourteen or fifteen."[8]

Writing when the historical novel was still fluid, Rowson never managed to shape it into a paradigm that an emergent national literature could adopt. Not until Scott brought the historical novel to maturity in the second decade of the nineteenth century — the decade when Child was sharing her impressions of his novels with Convers — did American writers find a genre suited to their purposes.

Designed specifically to forge a nationalist consciousness and cultural identity in the newly independent United States, the American historical novel inevitably exhibited the same central contradiction as American history itself — the contradiction between an ideology based on the premise that all men are created equal and a political structure based on the assumption that people of color and white women do not fall under the rubric "men." Like its British prototype, the American version of the genre developed by Scott celebrated the triumph of a technologically advanced civilization over a tribal society. Unlike Scott, however — identified by birth with one of the defeated ethnic groups whose heroic struggle against Norman and British invaders he memorialized — American writers belonged to the conquering race, which constituted their sole audience. Their mission was not to reconcile the victor with the vanquished, nor to offer a healing vision of the two groups' eventual amalgamation under the victors' hegemony. Rather, it was to justify the complete obliteration of the vanquished race and at the same time to assert the victors' own cultural independence vis-à-vis the British they had just overthrown.[9]

Ironically, as American writers were to find, the key to establishing a distinctive cultural identity lay in exploiting the culture of the very race their compatriots were so brutally extirpating. An early nineteenth-century critic writing for the *North American Review*, the journal that was to formulate the first major theory of American literature, put the case bluntly. The United States was "deficient in literature" because its "colonial existence," inherently "opposed to literary originality," had deprived it of the basis for a true national literature. "The remotest germs of literature are the native peculiarities of the country in which it is to spring," he pointed out, and a "National literature seems to be . . . the legitimate product, of a national language." Yet colonialism had saddled Americans with a literary tradition rooted in another continent and with a language suited perhaps to describing the serenity of the Thames, but far too "tame" to convey the "majesty of the Mississippi" or the grandeur of Niagara. These handicaps notwithstanding, the critic contended, America did in fact have an indigenous literature that displayed "genuine originality," "haughty independence" of foreign influences, and poetic vigor equal to soaring with the eagle and thundering with the cataract: "the oral literature of its aborigines." Critics in later numbers of the *North American Review* were quick to draw the inference: if American writers could mine the linguistic and mythological riches of this literature, they would develop the means of escaping their humiliating cultural subservience to England.[10]

The reliance, for their prime claim to originality, on borrowings from a culture the nation was currently destroying — a culture whose destruction, indeed, the nascent "American" literature had the task of rationalizing — was not the only contradiction to beset the historical novels that appeared in response to such promptings. The mission of declaring the nation's cultural independence involved the further problem of defining its relationship to the colonial past. On the one hand, Americans had rebelled against patriarchal authority both by casting off the yoke of the king and by rejecting the worldview of their Puritan Founding Fathers as superstitious and bigoted. On the other hand, they needed to legitimate the political system they had erected in the place of the old aristocratic and theocratic orders they repudiated.

The novelists who took up the challenge of creating an authentic national literature in the 1820s envisioned diverse solutions to the problems of racial conflict and patriarchal authority.[11] They ranged from the symbolic marriage of cultures to the elimination of Indians.

In *Logan, A Family History* (1822) John Neal conjures up what is potentially the most radical solution — a white man who goes Indian, marries into an Indian tribe, and fights on the side of his adopted people, putting his technological skills at their service in order to lead them " 'forth, from barbarianism and ignorance, to liberty and light!' " Yet Neal proves unable to follow through on this conception, which often seems to repel him. Throughout the novel, the hero is more attracted to a married white woman than to his Indian wife, and after he leads her tribe in a bloodthirsty reprisal raid, he wallows in self-loathing. Not surprisingly, Neal ends up killing off all his principal characters.[12]

In *Koningsmarke* (1823) James Kirke Paulding briefly flirts with the possibility that whites might wish to permanently embrace Indian ways — a possibility discussed nervously by several eighteenth-century writers who noted that although "thousands of Europeans" were living as Indians, "we have no examples of even one of those Aborigines having from choice become Europeans!"[13] Paulding's purpose is merely satiric, however; his true view, expressed in a long disquisition preceding his hero and heroine's captivity among Indians, is that destiny has slated the primitive red man for "extinction" and the " 'wise white man' " for "final ascendency." Foreshadowing his future role as an apologist for slavery and white supremacy, Paulding also hints at the threat of an impending alliance between Indians and blacks; he then symbolically forestalls such a consummation by bringing his grotesque black characters to ignominious ends.[14]

We are all familiar with the formula for resolving racial conflict that prevailed historically and found consummate expression in the only novels of this period to survive in our literary canon — those of James Fenimore Cooper.[15] Cooper's scenario presupposes that on a national level the encounter between "savage" and "civilized" races can take but one form — war — and can lead to but one outcome — the total defeat and extinction of the "savage" race. Though drenched in violence and replete with scenes of Indian tomahawking, scalping, and torture, Cooper's novels do not glorify the extermination of the Indians, as do those of Paulding and his later competitor, Robert Montgomery Bird. Instead, they mourn the "vanishing" of the red man as tragic but inevitable, and they pay tribute to the noble qualities of those Indians who ally themselves with whites. Through Cooper's great mythic creation, the Indianized frontiersman Hawk-eye, and through the friendship between Hawk-eye and the noble Indians Uncas and Chingachgook, the *Leatherstocking Novels* also seek to mediate the conflict between "savage" and "civilized" ways of life. Yet Cooper's scenario allows no role in America's future, either for Uncas and Chingachgook or for Hawk-eye — all three are doomed to die without issue. In lieu of a reconciliation between Indians and whites, Cooper's *The Pioneers* (1823) provides a reconciliation between Tory and Revolutionary. Obviously serving to reestablish patriarchal authority in the new order emerging from the routing of Indian savages and British tyrants, this solution leaves Anglo-American women on the sidelines — precisely the position they occupy in the political system.

Excluded as they were from the benefits that American democracy conferred on their male peers, middle- and upper-class white women often identified consciously or unconsciously with other excluded groups. In the 1830s an awareness of being "bound with" black slaves would propel a significant number of American women into the abolitionist movement.[16] In the 1820s it led some of the women writers who helped shape the American historical novel to imagine alternatives to race war, genocide, and white male supremacy as modes of resolving the contradictions that riddled their society.[17] Child's career — which as we shall see followed a trajectory from portraying Indians sympathetically in her fiction, to agitating against Andrew Jackson's Cherokee removal policy, to assuming a leading role in the struggle against slavery, to campaigning for black suffrage, woman suffrage, and a more humane Indian policy after the Civil War — illustrates how closely these phenomena are connected.

When Child sat down to write *Hobomok* in 1824, she took her cue directly from one of the critics who had been calling on American writers to exploit the matchless resources that America's panoramic landscapes, heroic Puritan settlers, and exotic Indian folklore afforded the romancer. Leafing through an old volume of the *North American Review* in her brother's study as she was whiling away the hours between morning and afternoon Sunday services, she had come across a long review of a narrative poem entitled *Yamoyden, A Tale of the Wars of King Philip, in Six Cantos*, by James Wallis Eastburn and Robert Sands (1820). *Yamoyden* represented a landmark in American literature, proclaimed the reviewer, John Gorham Palfrey, whom Child had met through Convers. "We are glad that somebody has at last found out the unequalled fitness of our early history for the purposes of a work of fiction," he pontificated. That history, Palfrey went on, contained all the elements Scott had put to such effective use in his novels of border warfare — indeed, the "stern, romantic enthusiasm" of America's Puritans; the "fierce," "primitive" character of her Indians, "with all the bold rough lines of nature yet uneffaced upon them"; and the vast scale of her picturesque scenery surpassed anything Scotland could boast. "Whoever in this country first attains the rank of a first rate writer of fiction," predicted Palfrey, "will lay his scene here. The wide field is ripe for the harvest, and scarce a sickle yet has touched it."[18]

The prediction kindled Child's imagination. Had she not encountered Indians in the forests of Maine? And had she not read her Scott, as well as her annals of Puritan history? "I know not what impelled me," she later recalled; "I had never dreamed of such a thing as turning author; but I siezed [*sic*] a pen, and before the bell rang for afternoon meeting I had written the first chapter, exactly as it now stands. When I showed it to my brother, my young ambition was flattered by the exclamation, 'But Maria did you *really* write this? Do you *mean* what you say, that it is entirely your own?' "[19]

Whether in fact *Hobomok* was entirely the fruit of Child's imagination, or owed more than she admitted to the epic poem that had occasioned Palfrey's momentous review, is an open question. The parallels between *Hobomok* and *Yamoyden* extend far beyond the titles that announce the two works' self-conscious use of native themes. Both describe their Indian title characters as "cast in nature's noblest mould." Both feature Anglo-American heroines who elope with Indian lovers in defiance of paternal wishes. And both model themselves after Shakespeare's *Othello* in having their dark-skinned heroes win the love of a white woman through eloquent recitals of their exploits and adventures.[20] True, Palfrey's detailed summary of *Yamoyden* could have sufficed to provide Child with the germ of her plot, and the idea of drawing for inspiration on English literature's most memorable account of an interracial wooing was obvious enough to have occurred to her independently. In any case, if she did literally write the first chapter of *Hobomok*, "exactly as it now stands," the very day she read Palfrey's review, she had already conceived the embryo of a plot that differed substantially from *Yamoyden*'s, whatever hints she subsequently derived from directly consulting the poem cited so frequently in her epigraphs.

The differences illuminate the enormous gap that divided even the most pro-Indian male writers of this period from their female counterparts, where their perceptions of the relationship between white supremacy and patriarchy were concerned. For Eastburn and Sands were unmistakably pro-Indian. To the great annoyance of Palfrey, who chastised them for "sentimentality," they presented the bloody uprising of 1675–76, led by the Wampanoag sachem Metacom ("King Philip"), from the Indians' point of view. Portraying the Puritans as "remorseless oppressors" and the Indians as "cruelly wronged,"[21] they showed that the Indians were merely reacting against a long series of encroachments on their lands and rights, climaxing with the incident directly responsible for the uprising—the Puritans' execution of three Wampanoag warriors. Still, Eastburn and Sands, like Cooper, centered their epic on race war and ended it with a reassertion of patriarchal authority. The love affair between the Nipnet Yamoyden and the Puritan Nora, which initially points toward an alternative future for the two warring races, and a larger role in determining her own destiny for the Anglo-American woman, culminates in tragedy. Nora is captured and delivered over to her father, who generously forgives her disobedience; Yamoyden sacrifices his life to save his hitherto estranged father-in-law from an Indian's tomahawk; and Nora dies in her husband's arms as her father promises to raise the couple's baby.[22] What becomes of this baby the poem's epilogue does not specify, but the concluding lament over the tragic outcome of the marriage and of the Indian uprising intertwined with it does not portend a hopeful resolution for the child of the racial conflicts that have doomed the parents. No doubt this reassuring negation of a threat to white supremacy and patriarchal authority saved Eastburn and Sands from the censure Child would reap when she followed their lead in violating the taboo against interracial marriage.

At the time she wrote *Hobomok*, Child evidently had a much lower level of political consciousness on the Indian question than Eastburn and Sands did. She had not yet begun to contest the Puritan chroniclers' version of the wars that decimated the Indians, as she would five years later in a book aimed at arousing opposition to the U.S. government's "crooked and narrow-minded policy" toward Indians: *The First Settlers of New-England* (1829).[23] Nor had she come to see the Indians who defended their people's sovereign existence and territorial rights, rather than those who sided with the whites, as the true heroes of an American national epic. Unlike Yamoyden, who joins King Philip's uprising despite the pleadings of his English wife, Child's Hobomok betrays an Indian conspiracy to save his white beloved and her family from massacre. Child also stereotypes Hobomok's adversary, Corbitant, a militant foe of the English "usurpers," as a villainous "bad Indian" (30).[24]

What dictates the plot of *Hobomok* is not its author's awareness of racial issues, but her rebellion against patriarchy. Nevertheless, the result is a revolutionary insight into the connection between male dominance and white supremacy. This insight suggested to Child the central theme of *Hobomok* and indeed of her entire life as a reformer and writer: interracial marriage, symbolizing both the natural alliance between white women and people of color, and the natural resolution of America's racial and sexual contradictions. Thus, if we are to understand *Hobomok* and the alternative vision of race and gender relations it introduces into American literature, we must take as our starting point the defiance of patriarchy that governs its fictional strategies.

Even the most seemingly conventional strategies Child uses turn out to be subversive. The book's main formal device, for example, the pretense of relying on "an old, worn-out manuscript" (6), allows Child to appropriate the narrative authority of the Puritan chroniclers while rewriting the hagiography they had bequeathed to posterity. It also allows her to evade the sanctions against female authorship by speaking through a series of male narrators. (Signed "By an American," *Hobomok* was published anonymously, for Child had been "gravely warned . . . that no woman could expect to be regarded as a *lady* after she had written a book.")[25]

Under the cover of her principal male narrator, the purported editor of the "old, worn-out manuscript" allegedly written by an ancestor who debarked at Naumkeak in 1629 (6), Child announces at the outset that her source demands considerable revision. Its style is "antiquated and almost unintelligible," its content too familiar to readers brought up on John Winthrop's *Journal*, William Hubbard's *General History of New England*, and Nathaniel Morton's *New England's Memorial* to bear repetition: "Every one acquainted with our early history remembers the wretched state in which [newcomers] found the scanty remnant of their brethren" at Naumkeak, she asserts. Hence, Child plans to substitute her own language and to "pass over" her source's "dreary account of sickness and distress" (7). The effect of these revisions, of course, is to undermine the authority of the original text and to deflate the myth that such "dreary" accounts served to consecrate — the myth of heroic martyrs battling God's enemies in the wilderness. The deflation is quite explicit in Child's description of the colony as it appeared to her ancestor, with " 'six miserable hovels' " constituting " 'the whole settlement of Naumkeak' " and a few " 'sickly and half starved' " inhabitants presenting " 'a pitiful contrast to the vigorous and wondering savages who stood among them' " (7–8).

A glance at Child's sources, which cite "half a score of houses" in lieu of "six miserable hovels,"[26] reveals how consciously she went about writing an alternative history of the Puritan experiment — one that highlighted its underside and shifted the focus from the saints to the sinners, from the orthodox to the heterodox, from the white settlers to the Indians, from the venerated patriarchs to their unsung wives. To begin with, the historical prototypes of her principal male characters all occupied either marginal or deviant status in the Puritan community.

Roger Conant and John Oldham were disaffected members of the Plymouth colony. Oldham, in fact, had been expelled from Plymouth for fomenting dissension, along with the Reverend John Lyford, to whose lechery Child alludes (19). Later, Oldham's murder by Indians, which Child's *The First Settlers of New-England* would blame on his hot temper, helped touch off the Pequot War.[27] Ironically, in *Hobomok* Child transforms this humorless bigot into a "jocular" gadfly who blasphemes "the mysteries of godliness" and laughs at "his own disgraces with the most shameless effrontery" (11–12). As for Conant, credited by Hubbard "with courage and resolution to abide fixed in his purpose, notwithstanding all opposition and persuasion he met,"[28] Child brings him to his knees by forcing him to accept his daughter's successive marriages to two men his religion brands as outcasts: the Indian Hobomok and the Episcopalian Charles Brown.

Even more historically marginal than Oldham and Conant, the Episcopalians Samuel and John Brown are mentioned only briefly in the chronicles. They never reappeared in Naumkeak after their banishment by John Endicott for "speeches and practices tending to mutiny and faction."[29] Fusing them into her hero Charles Brown, however, whom she pointedly names after the king the Puritans had fled, Child awards him the hand of her heroine and an honorable place in the colony that has previously exiled him.

As an Indian, the historical Hobomok was by definition a marginal figure in Puritan eyes, albeit a valued ally. Sometimes confused by the chroniclers with the god whose name he bore — a deity that a Puritan woman was hanged for allegedly taking as her husband in 1653[30] — Hobomok did earn this accolade for furthering the colonists' "peace . . . with the natives":

> Hobamak, who came to live amongst the English, he being a proper lusty young man, and one that was in account amongst the Indians in those parts for his valour, continued faithful and constant to the English until his death. He, with the said Squanto, being sent amongst the Indians about business for the English, were surprised by an Indian Sachem named Corbitant, who was no friend to the English . . . and offered to stab Hobamak, who being a strong man, soon cleared himself of him; and with speed came and gave intelligence to the Governour of Plimouth. . . .[31]

Though retaining these details, Child goes her sources one better by elevating Hobomok to the rank of title character, marrying him to her Puritan heroine, and integrating the couple's son into white society—a daring inversion of her Puritan ancestors' "errand into the wilderness."[32]

Repeatedly, Child revises patriarchal script by turning the peripheral into the central, the central into the peripheral. Nowhere is this more obvious than in the leading roles she accords the wives and daughters of the patriarchs, literally invisible in the chronicles. On the one hand, Child emphasizes the heroism of women like Mrs. Oldham, careworn but uncomplaining despite the vicissitudes her quarrelsome husband has brought on her, or Mrs. Conant and Lady Arabella Johnson, fated to wither and die under the blast of New England's harsh climate, "victims to what has always been the source of woman's greatest misery—love—deep and unwearied love" (25, 111). On the other hand, Child holds up as role models the younger women who refuse to submit to patriarchy—the lively Sally Oldham, so adept at exposing the cant of the Puritan elders, and the heretical Mary Conant, whom Child will empower to transmute the errand of conquering or converting the Indian into an errand of embracing his ways.

Mirroring Child's disparate selves—Sally the down-to-earth, fun-loving young woman who prides herself on her domestic skills and humble class origins; Mary the poetic dreamer who yearns for escape to an upper-class world where she can satisfy her taste for refinement and beauty—*Hobomok*'s paired heroines function very differently from their counterparts in male-authored novels. The temperamental and physical contrast between them proves deceptive. Sally's "roguish blue eyes" reflect the same impatience with her society's strictures as Mary's "large, dark eyes, with their deep, melancholy fringe" (59). It is just that Sally's nonconformity takes humorous forms: sending her "sanctified looking" wooer packing after landing him in the mud; precipitating a minor crisis in the Plymouth church by proposing to the messenger who has brought her a marriage offer from another elder; and reacting to her minister's "fatherly advice" at her wedding by "wish[ing] in mercy" that he would hurry through it (18–19, 22, 61). Instead of serving as Mary's decorous foil or rival (in the mode of Cooper's Alice and Cora and Scott's Rowena and Rebecca), Sally enacts a comic version of her friend's departures from patriarchal script and provides Mary with unstinting support in the teeth of the Puritan community's ostracism. She thus sets up a variant standard by which to judge Mary.

For her part, Mary quickly wrests control of the plot from those twin personifications of patriarchal authority, the tyrannical father intent on determining her fate and the male narrator intent on recording it. From the very first chapter—the chapter Child dashed off in response to Palfrey's review while her brother was preparing to deliver his Sunday sermon—it is apparent that Mary's rebellion against her father involves a rejection of his religious, racial, and sexual ideology, as well as an affirmation of her right to follow the inclinations of her heart. Neither Mary nor her mother shares Conant's religious convictions. Yet in the name of those convictions, Conant has uprooted them from their home in England, subjected them to the hardships of the bleak Puritan outpost he would have them regard as "a second Canaan," and forbidden Mary to wed the lover of her choice, the Episcopalian Charles Brown (7, 9–10). With unexpected psychological acumen for a twenty-two-year-old woman living in a pre-Freudian age, Child hints that Conant has mistaken a grudge against his father-in-law for religious inspiration, and that he is unconsciously inflicting on his wife and daughter the psychic wounds he himself once received as a victim of patriarchal tyranny, repudiated and consigned to poverty by his wife's highborn family (8, 119). Conant's case illustrates how patriarchal tyranny perpetuates itself by transforming scarred sons into obdurate fathers.

Conversely, the rebellion of his wife and daughter illustrates how the cycle of patriarchal tyranny can be arrested. Having learned a different lesson than her husband has from "[t]he remembrance of her own thwarted inclinations," Mrs. Conant adjures him on her deathbed to consent to Mary's and Charles's marriage (47, 108).

Mrs. Conant also dissents privately from her husband's narrow creed. In its stead, she articulates a religion of the heart that transcends the theological controversies of Puritan and Episcopalian. To her, such "[m]atters of dispute" as doctrines, forms, and ceremonies represent the shadow of religion, not its substance. Even the Bible often strikes her as "a flaming cherubim, turning every way, and guarding the tree of life from the touch of man." The alternative to which she turns for religious inspiration is the book of nature: "[I]n creation, one may read to their fill. It is God's library — the first Bible he ever wrote" (76).

Here, in embryo, a dozen-odd years before Emerson proclaimed it, is the Transcendentalist gospel.[33] But more to the point, through Mrs. Conant, Child is asserting her own right to the role of preacher-theologian that society had granted her brother Convers. It was a right she would exercise more openly in her future career, first as an abolitionist, then as the author of *The Progress of Religious Ideas, through Successive Ages* (1855), which scandalized nineteenth-century readers by putting Hinduism, Muhammadanism, and Buddhism on an equal footing with Christianity.

Child projected most of her iconoclasm not onto Mrs. Conant, but onto Mary. Noting that the evening star sheds the same light on the "cross-crowned turrets of the Catholic," the "proud spires of the Episcopalian," the "distant mosques and temples" of the East, "the sacrifice heap of the Indian, and the rude dwellings of the Calvinist," Mary discerns an analogy with the light of faith. "It cannot be," she concludes, that "as my father says, . . . of all the multitude of people who view" these "cheering rays, so small a remnant only are pleasing in the sight of God" (47–48). So Child would conclude in *The Progress of Religious Ideas*, where she would write in the preface: "While my mind was yet in its youth, I was offended by the manner in which Christian writers usually describe other religions. . . . I recollect wishing, long ago, that I could become acquainted with some good, intelligent Bramin, or Mohammedan, that I might learn, in some degree, how their religions appeared to *them*."[34]

The plot of *Hobomok* symbolically fulfills this fantasy, expressed recurrently in Child's writings, and sometimes specifically formulated as the desire to be turned into an Indian for a while, "that I might experience the fashion of their thoughts and feelings."[35] Through Mary Conant, Child vicariously marries an Indian and lives the invigorating life of the Penobscot and Abenaki women she had observed at first hand in Maine. Mary's odyssey also spells out the fantasy's underlying implication — that questioning the dogmas of a culture which relegates nonwhite, non-Christian peoples to inferior status entails joining with those peoples in throwing off the yoke of the Great White Father.

The scene that climaxes the novel's opening chapter dramatically reveals where Mary's repudiation of her father's bigotry will lead her. After an evening of "much holy and edifying discourse" (12), punctuated by her father's harangues against Episcopalians, Mary steals out of the house by full moon and plunges into the woods. There, in a setting the Puritan fathers identified with the pre-Christian matriarchal world of nature and its tabooed sexuality — a world they peopled with witches, demons, and Indians cavorting in blasphemous orgiastic rites[36] — Mary performs what can only be called a ritual of witchcraft. Its purpose is to ascertain whether Brown will become her husband despite her father's interdiction — that is, whether matriarchal nature will prevail over patriarchal culture, primitive sexuality over civilized repression, and female witchcraft over male Puritan ideology. Drawing a "large circle" on the ground, walking around it "three times," and retracing her steps backward, Mary chants:

> Whoever's to claim a husband's power,
> Come to me in the moonlight hour.
>
> .   .   .   .   .
>
> Whoe'er my bridegroom is to be,
> Step in the circle after me. (13)

Although Mary's witchcraft does not produce the result she expects, it foreshadows the course her rebellion against her father will take; for it succeeds in conjuring up, one on the heels of the other, the two men who will serve as her vehicles for defying her father's authority and challenging the values he represents. Hardly has she completed her incantation than, to her horror, the Indian Hobomok leaps into the circle in place of the lover she is awaiting. At first, she takes him for a ghost (oddly in keeping with the historical Hobomok's role as a *pniese*, or shaman).[37] But he explains that he has come to perform a ritual of his own, which consists of throwing a bough on a heap of rocks, to "make the Manitto Asseinah green as the oak tree," and pronouncing "a short incantation" (14). The coincidence symbolizes the historic affinity between ancient European and Indian fertility cults,[38] as well as the unconscious bond between the female victims of male dominance and the nonwhite victims of European racism.

Hobomok's ritual, too, produces a result he does not expect, but one that foreshadows the course his relationship with Mary will take: just as he and Mary are leaving the woods, the Episcopalian Charles Brown suddenly appears. Described by Mr. Conant earlier in the evening as a "sprig from [the] tree of corruption" and a strange graft on the Puritan settlement's "pleasant plants" (9–10), Brown indeed seems almost to have emerged from the Indian's boughs. He accounts for his arrival, however, by saying that he had dreamed Mary was in danger. As Brown and Mary walk off together, Hobomok brings his ritual to a close by invoking his tutelary deity Abbamocho (a variant name for Hobomok): "Three times much winnit Abbamocho said; three times me do" (14). Once again, the parallel emphasis on threefold repetition establishes Hobomok's ritual as an extension of Mary's.

What is the significance of the two lovers Mary's witchcraft has conjured up, and what is the relationship between them? It is initially tempting to speculate that the Episcopalian and the Indian embody opposite alternatives to the bigotry and asceticism of Roger Conant's Puritan world, from which Mary is so desperately seeking escape. If so, the Episcopalian would seem to personify the rich cultural heritage Mary has been forced to leave behind in England, and the Indian the tantalizing wilderness she has been forbidden to explore. Reduced to its simplest terms, this formulation would equate the Episcopalian with culture, the Indian with nature, and the combined appeal of the two men with the hunger Mary feels for the aesthetic and sensuous pleasures Puritan society bans. Child herself suffered intensely from the hunger she projected onto her heroine, and it similarly drew her in opposite directions — on the one hand, toward the upper-class milieu of her brother's associates, with their tastefully decorated residences; on the other, toward identification with Indians, whom she imagined as free from the emotional and sexual restrictions under which she chafed. In life as in fiction, these different sides of Child's temperament would repeatedly attract her to men who fulfilled very different needs for her.

Child provides a good deal of textual warrant for such an interpretation of Mary's Episcopalian and Indian lovers. As if to equate Brown with aristocratic culture, she traces Mary's acquaintance with him back to the ancestral mansion of Mary's maternal grandfather, where painting, sculpture, and poetry had left a deep impress "upon her young heart," and where she herself had been "the little idol of the brilliant circle" (46–47, 78). In this setting, Mary had greeted Charles as the very incarnation of the arts she had come to worship, the epitome of all her aspirations. There, Mary had "mingled with [Charles] in the graceful evolutions of the dance, while her young heart in vain strove to be proof against the intoxicating witchery of light and motion. And there, as she gazed on his lofty forehead, stamped with the proud, deep impress of intellect, and watched the changeful lustre of his dark, eloquent eyes, that alternately beamed with high or tender thoughts, she too became covetous of mental riches, and worshipped at the shrine of genius" (78). Child's evocation of the scene fuses the aesthetic, the sensual, and the spiritual.

Summing up everything Charles represents for Mary are the gifts he and her grandfather send her after the Puritan elders have exiled Charles from Naumkeak for the crime of trying to reintroduce a religion they associate with the Whore of Babylon. A miniature of himself in a "glittering enclosure; and a splendid [Episcopal] prayer-book printed for the royal family," and bearing the arms of England and the portraits of King Charles and his "handsome . . . French queen" (103–5), the twin gifts graphically highlight the magnificence of the aristocratic culture Charles personifies and the barrenness of the Puritan world that has banished him. Their message is clear: all Mary needs to do to regain her rightful station in life is to take up this prayer book and follow her lover back to England, where she can partake with him in the "mental riches" she covets.

On the face of it, the Indian lover whom Mary's witchcraft has conjured up ahead of Charles, and with whom she will elope after hearing that Charles has perished at sea, would seem to exert an entirely different appeal. "[U]nwarped by the artifices of civilized life," Hobomok displays a "tall, athletic form," a "healthy cheek," and "manly beauty": "This Indian was indeed cast in nature's noblest mould. He was one of the finest specimens of elastic, vigorous elegance of proportion, to be found among his tribe" (16, 36, 121). Though "rich . . . in native imagination," Hobomok's "uncultivated mind" is no match for Charles's, Child implies (135). Conversely, she shows, Charles is no match for Hobomok in the Indian's native element, the world of nature into which he melts at the end of the book (142).

If the dichotomy of nature versus culture differentiates the Indian from the Episcopalian, it also associates the Indian with women, traditionally consigned to the outskirts of culture.[39] That may be why Child describes Hobomok's creed in almost the same terms as she does Mrs. Conant's and Mary's. Accordingly, Mary finds in Hobomok a kindred spirit sharing her "native fervor of imagination" (35). The affinity between them lies deeper than Mary realizes. Just as Hobomok has looked upon Mary "with reverence, which almost amounted to adoration," ever since she nursed his sick mother back to life, so Mary will offer herself in marriage to Hobomok on her own mother's grave (33, 120–21). Once again, Child's symbolism hints at the factors that create a natural alliance between white women and people of color: roots in similar matriarchal traditions and a common victimization under European patriarchy.

Ultimately, to schematize the relationship between Mary's Indian and Episcopalian lovers as a dichotomy between nature and culture proves misleading, however, for the novel consistently links the two men to each other, as well as to its female rebels against patriarchy and Puritanism. Brown's very surname associates him with the "tawny" Indian—an association reinforced by his "dark, eloquent eyes" (78, 84). To the Puritans, in any case, both Episcopalians and Indians are minions of the devil, "the Black Man." Thus, Roger Conant calls the Episcopalian a worshiper of Baal. Mary may think she loves Brown for his "intellect" (78), but her Puritan father knows better—he scents in the Episcopalian's allure "the flesh-pots of Egypt" (9).

Just as Brown, the standard-bearer of culture, discloses affinities with nature, so Hobomok, that prince of nature, discloses affinities with culture. Like Othello, who wins Desdemona's love through spellbinding accounts of his adventures and of the exotic peoples he has encountered, Hobomok wins Mary's through "long stories, abounding . . . with metaphors" and fabulous "descriptions of the Indian nations," couched in "the brief, figurative language of nature" (84–87, 133). Breathing a natural poetry, his narratives are closer to the elegant literature Mary learned to value so highly in England than anything Puritan Naumkeak can boast. Among them is a story of intertribal marriage that culminates in the exchange of the tomahawk for the peace pipe (86–87)—an echo of the novel's interracial marriage plot through which Child aligns her own narrative with Hobomok's. In analogous fashion, the native artistry

Hobomok displays when he tells Mary how to arrange the shells of the wampum belt she is making for him reveals his kinship with the artists who produced the paintings in her grandfather's mansion (86). Such aesthetic impulses, Child underscores, have no place in Naumkeak, whose Puritan inhabitants are preoccupied by "the fierce contests of opinion" and blind to "the latent treasures of mind or the rich sympathies of taste" or the spectacular pageantry of nature (91). It is because Hobomok feeds her craving for poetry and beauty that Mary prefers him to her fellow settlers, with whom she has nothing in common.

Like Brown, Hobomok also feeds Mary's craving for idolatry—the reverse of the continual diminishment she receives from her father and the Puritan elders who regard women as foolish and sinful temptresses. In both cases, the idolatry is at once quasi-religious and erotic, promoting Mary from the status of a "frail carcase" to that of a goddess, and offering her a spiritual role Puritanism denies her. For Brown, Mary is the "little fairy" who has inspired him to plant the "Episcopal mitre in the forests of America"; for Hobomok, she is a "bright . . . emanation from the Good Spirit" (9, 46, 84).

Like Brown's, Hobomok's "idolatry" excites Mary sexually. As Child puts it, "female penetration knew the plant, though thriving in so wild a soil; and female vanity sinfully indulged its growth." Even before Brown's reported death, Mary accompanies Hobomok on a hunt by torchlight that arouses in her the same mixture of aesthetic, sensual, and spiritual feelings she had experienced while dancing with Brown (78, 84–85, 88–89, 121).

In short, the attraction Mary feels for her Episcopalian and Indian lovers is at bottom the same. Both represent a fusion of nature and culture. Both foster the aesthetic impulses Puritan society contemns. Both fulfill the spiritual aspirations thwarted in Mary by a religion that has ruled out the feminine principle (spiritual aspirations that had led Child to Swedenborgianism). Both embody the sexuality Puritanism seeks to repress. And both provide a means of defying patriarchal authority, as vested not only in Mary's father, but in the society for which he stands.

So closely does the plot intertwine the two lovers, whom Mary's incantation summons to "Come to me in the moonlight hour" and "Step in the circle after me," that it irresistibly identifies them as doubles. Again and again, the identities of Mary's Episcopalian and Indian lovers merge as her quest for the one leads her to the other. Again and again, the object of that quest turns out to be what Charles and Hobomok alike offer Mary: the right to define her own "fate," choose her own religion, reclaim her own sexuality, assert her own worth.

A few examples must suffice to illustrate this insistent pattern of doubling. The most striking of them occur in chapter 17, which opens and closes with scenes reenacting the episode in the forest. At the outset, Hobomok materializes out of Mary's thoughts while she is mourning Charles's death, the news of which the Indian has carried to Naumkeak. Like a projection of Mary's own unconscious desires, he arrives as if in answer to the question barely formed in her mind: "What now had life to offer?" (121). Recognizing the parallel with the earlier episode, Mary immediately concludes that fate has decreed her marriage to Hobomok. Then she had defied her father's proscription of Charles by using witchcraft to ascertain her fate for herself. Now she spites him by invoking a parody of his Calvinist creed — "the utter fruitlessness of all human endeavour" to resist heaven's mandates — as a rationale for violating every principle he holds dear (122). Appropriately, Mr. Conant himself telescopes the two scenes when he attempts to throw the Episcopal prayer book that Mary associates with Charles into the fire, thereby precipitating her elopement with Hobomok.

Crowning the pattern of doubling in chapter 17 is the marriage ceremony with which the chapter ends. Not only does the ceremony correspond detail for detail with the rituals Mary and Hobomok have performed in the forest, complete with wand, circle, incantation, repetition in patterns of three, and retracing of steps "backward"; it climaxes with the intrusion of Brown's ghostly presence. The pipe Hobomok produces for his guests to smoke, eliciting from Mary a "piercing shriek," turns out to be the one Brown had sent him from England as a token of friendship, in the very package containing the miniature and the Episcopal prayer book destined for Mary (104–5, 125). A phallic symbol, as well as a traditional Indian artifact used in rituals of bonding, and later adopted by Europeans, the pipe cements the unity of Mary's Indian and Episcopalian lovers. In effect, she has married them both. Therein, perhaps, lies the significance of the fantasies she has acted out in chapters 1 and 17.

Once we realize that in Child's plot Hobomok and Brown actually function as doubles, rather than rivals, we can discern more than one meaning in the transformation Hobomok undergoes after three years of marriage: "he seems almost like an Englishman," notes Mary's friend Sally Oldham (137). We can also understand why Charles himself undergoes a reverse transformation in the interim — shipwrecked on an "East India" vessel, cast on the coast of Africa, and held prisoner for three years, he experiences the lot of the peoples the English have been colonizing (145). Much in the way dreams work, Child's plot repeatedly turns Charles into Hobomok, Hobomok into Charles.

The ending of the novel can best be read as the consummation of Mary's secret desire to enjoy both of the lovers her witchcraft has conjured up in defiance of her father's prohibitions. Charles materializes in the forest exactly as he did in the opening chapter, surprising Hobomok as the Indian is hunting game for Mary and their infant son. In the first scene Hobomok had appeared to be a ghost summoned by Mary's witchcraft. Now Charles, paralleling his mysterious arrival on that former occasion, when a dream that Mary was in danger had aroused him from sleep, appears to Hobomok to be a ghost. Previously, Mary had yielded to "fate" in marrying Hobomok. Now, Hobomok yields to "fate" by nobly ceding Mary to her first lover. Again acting as the agent of Mary's unconscious wishes, he recognizes that Mary loves Charles better than himself, "for even now she prays for him in her sleep" (139). Hence, his decision to go away without consulting her — a decision that manipulates Charles into taking Mary back despite "[d]isappointed love, a sense of degradation, perhaps something of resentment" (139). The "chaos of agony" Charles undergoes before determining to marry a woman his society would deem "fallen" echoes the "chaos in Mary's mind" as she contemplates marrying an Indian (121, 139). The linkage emphasizes that both marriages represent breaches of Anglo-America's sexual codes.[40]

In the very act of reclaiming his bride from her Indian husband, Brown once again merges with his ostensible rival. The interview at which Brown asks Mary to be his wife, a few hours after the Indian has ceremonially divorced her, takes place in Hobomok's wigwam, and the words with which Charles greets Mary's son by Hobomok — "He is a brave boy" — are "the last words his father said to him" before leaving for the hunt that morning. Indeed, the name Mary has given the child — Charles Hobomok Conant — identifies him metaphorically as her son by both lovers (it is "Indian custom," Mary explains, for a child to take the surname of its mother).[41] Accordingly, Charles promises, "He shall be my own boy" (148–49). Confirming the symbolic significance of this pledge, the denouement supplies Charles and Mary with no other offspring; instead, it follows "the little Hobomok" into maturity, as a university education converts him into an Englishman.

Child's radical revision of patriarchal script thus culminates not in the reassertion of patriarchal authority, but in its overthrow; not in the death of a heroine who has dared to challenge the religious, racial, and sexual ideology on which patriarchy rests, but in her achievement of happiness, enabling the triumph of the alternative values she has embraced. Mary returns to the Puritan community on her own terms, unscathed by her violation of its taboos against miscegenation and divorce. Far from paying any price for her transgressions, she finds herself rewarded by the unprecedented opportunity to remarry. And this time the Puritan elders who earlier banished her chosen lover for heresy fully countenance her marriage and the couple's reintegration into the community as religious dissidents. Even that personification of patriarchal authority, Mr. Conant, capitulates. Softened by the suffering he has undergone since Mary's elopement and blaming himself for having driven her to it, he joyfully agrees to hold the wedding under his roof. In return, Mary and Charles reserve a place for him at their fireside and tolerate his religious views — a bold reversal of roles.

The final element in the resolution of religious, racial, sexual, and generational conflicts with which the novel ends is the assimilation into Anglo-American society of the child embodying the marriage of America's white colonists and Indian aborigines — the alternative Child offers to white supremacy and race war. At the request of Mr. Conant, half of the family's legacy goes toward educating Charles Hobomok Conant, who distinguishes himself at Harvard and finishes his studies in England, eventually losing all traces of his Indian identity and melting into his mother's people. Child hints that he will reenact his mother's interracial marriage by taking as his wife "the laughing little Mary Collier," whose name betokens Sally Oldham Collier's solidarity with her friend Mary Conant.

This resolution, however, conspicuously excludes Hobomok himself. In the last analysis, his function as Charles's double does not counteract the telltale signs of authorial ambivalence that mar the intermarriage plot: the suggestion that Mary elopes with Hobomok in a fit of mental aberration (120–21); the Indians' furtive performance of the wedding ceremony "for fear of exciting the suspicion of their white neighbours," as if Child were projecting onto the participants her own sense of engaging in a forbidden rite (124–25); the lurking shadow of a "hawk" threatening to despoil the "nest" of the interracial family (137, 140) — Hobomok's archenemy Corbitant, the "bad Indian" whose specter typically haunts the "good Indian" in frontier novels;[42] Mary's damaging acceptance of her culture's verdict that her marriage with an Indian has "degraded" and "disgrace[d]" her (135, 148); and above all Child's awkward and abortive handling of the marriage. Nor does interpreting Hobomok and Charles as dual aspects of the same character negate the sinister implications of the Indian's convenient decision to forgo his rights and leave his English rival in possession of his patrimony. As several critics have pointed out, Child ultimately succumbs to the familiar white fantasy that the Indian will somehow disappear.[43]

Moreover, the happy ending she has provided represents a betrayal of the alliance with people of color that had allowed Mary to liberate herself from patriarchal oppression. It also belies the ideal of a mutually enriching cultural intermarriage, which Mary's attraction to Hobomok and the symbolic fusion of her two lovers' identities might suggest. Granted, Child does envisage assimilation in lieu of Indian genocide — and she is alone among early nineteenth-century novelists in doing so (though writers like William Byrd and Robert Beverley had advanced the idea in the eighteenth century). This said, her conception of assimilation amounts to cultural genocide. Only if Indians cease to be Indians, it implies, can they earn a place in the society that is dispossessing them. That is why Hobomok must "go far off among some of the red men in the west" (139), leaving to his half-English son the questionable honor of joining white society.

In short, despite its insights into the connections between male dominance and white supremacy, and despite its daring revisions of patriarchal script, Child's response to the call for an authentic national literature does not succeed in resolving the central contradictions of the American historical novel, nor those of American history itself: that white Americans win their political freedom at the expense of the Indians they exterminate and the Africans they enslave, and that they achieve their cultural independence by expropriating the cultures of the peoples they have systematically debased, devalorized, and deprived of an independent identity.

Nevertheless, *Hobomok* does offer a more progressive vision of race and gender relations than the one ultimately encoded in the American literary canon. Child breaks out of the mold in which American writers had hitherto found themselves imprisoned by the sources they drew on as they sought to create a distinctive national literature — the Puritan narratives of captivity and Indian war that served to justify white conquest. In *Hobomok* the threat of Indian hostilities occupies little more than two out of twenty chapters and is quickly dissipated. Moreover, that staple from the captivity narrative which garnishes virtually every historical novel set in the early colonial period — the scene of Indians swooping down on a helpless community, barbarously murdering most of the inhabitants, and carrying the remnant into captivity — is absent. Contrary

to tradition, Mary's departure into the wilderness with Hobomok is completely voluntary (albeit riddled with ambivalence), and its context is not warfare between Indians
and whites, but conflict between the Puritan patriarchy and the rebels against it. In
these respects *Hobomok* is more revolutionary than its best-selling nonfictional competitor, James Everett Seaver's *Narrative of the Life of Mrs. Mary Jemison* (1824), the
story of an actual white woman's assimilation and marriage into an Indian tribe that has
taken her captive.[44]

The subversive possibilities Child's innovations portended did not escape contemporary reviewers, who hastened to spell out the guidelines American writers would have
to follow. While commending the anonymous author for "well conceived" characters,
skill at rendering the "strange mixture of good sense, piety, fanaticism, and intolerance,
which distinguished our puritan ancestors," and success at capturing the "Indian character . . . and language," reviewers united in pronouncing the novel's plot "in very bad
taste, to say the least."[45] Their summaries were telling: "A high born and delicate
female, on the supposed death of her lover, has, in a fit of insane despondency, offered
herself as the wife of an Indian chief, and has become such, according to the customs of
his nation. . . . At the end of that time, her white lover returns; her copper one with
great magnanimity relinquishes her and departs, and she is married to the former."[46] As
this summary suggests, what reviewers found so "unnatural" and "revolting . . . to every
feeling of delicacy in man or woman" was the sexual freedom Child had allowed a
woman of their own social class — freedom to choose her mate without regard to race
or class; freedom to take the initiative in proposing marriage; freedom to divorce,
remarry, and retain custody of her child — freedom, in sum, to flout every law of
patriarchy without suffering the consequences. Hence the contrast between their reactions to the interracial love plots of Child's *Hobomok* and of Eastburn and Sands's
Yamoyden, which had avoided censure by punishing its erring heroine with death.
   Still, the men who ruled the early nineteenth-century literary establishment saw
enough potential in *Hobomok*, as a historical novel serving nationalist aims, to encourage its author to persevere. Charitably imputing the faults they had criticized to "inexperience in this kind of writing," they expressed the hope "that the author may amend
them and at the same time retain all the other qualifications for a good writer, which are
here exhibited." The amendment they had in mind is chillingly obvious from one of the
passages singled out for praise and quotation: the deathbed scene of Mrs. Conant and
Lady Arabella Johnson, both exemplary Puritan wives who have dutifully endured the
hardships of exile for their husbands' sake.[47] The message, of course, was that American
writers had the responsibility of inculcating the values the white male governing elite
deemed appropriate; and foremost among the values prescribed for women, as the
martyrdom of Mrs. Conant and Arabella Johnson testified, were a submissiveness and
self-sacrifice that could literally prove deadly.
   Curiously, *Hobomok* found more favor with reviewers than the safer novels produced
the same year by two rival women writers who, like Child, veiled their gender in

anonymity: Harriet Vaughan Cheney's *A Peep at the Pilgrims in Sixteen Hundred Thirty-Six. A Tale of Olden Times* and Eliza L. Cushing's *Saratoga: A Tale of the Revolution*. Of the three, Child's was the only one that the *North American Review* predicted would "stand the test of repeated readings," thanks to its author's talent for "genuine pathos," "graphic descriptions of scenery," and "forcible delineations of character."[48] The judgment may not have been wholly objective, since the *North American*'s editor, Jared Sparks, was a personal friend of Convers Francis. Given the objections reviewers had raised to the plot of *Hobomok*, however, they might have been expected to point out the ideological merits of novels that better conformed to their canons.

A comparison of *Hobomok* with its analogues reveals the extent of Child's radicalism. Covering almost identical ground, Cheney's *A Peep at the Pilgrims* features a love affair between a Puritan maiden (more docile than Mary) and an Episcopalian suitor (who obliges her father by converting to Puritanism). It even includes Hobomok among its historical characters, though relegating him to a walk-on part utterly devoid of dignity. Cheney also offers a glimpse of alternative relations between whites and Indians — the friendship that unfolds between her heroine, Miriam Gray, and the women of the Pequot sachem Mononotto's household, after Miriam is captured in an Indian attack. Repeatedly saved from death by their intervention, and treated with great kindness and delicacy, Miriam begins to accommodate to Indian life, learning how to weave baskets and embroider moccasins with porcupine quills. In its depiction of such details and its portrayal of Indian women (all but absent from *Hobomok*), *A Peep at the Pilgrims* sets new directions. But Cheney does not attempt to envisage the prospect of a long-term or permanent accommodation, let alone intermarriage between Indians and whites. Instead, she lets the historical outcome of the Pequot War — the massacre of the Pequots and the enslavement of the tribe's few survivors — limit her imagination and determine her plot.

Likewise throwing Child's daring into relief is Eliza L. Cushing's portrayal of Indian-white relations in *Saratoga*. True, Cushing does plead for bringing the Indians "within the pale of civilized life" so that the "mild light of christianity" can "shed on them its softening influence." She also allows friendships between her Indian and white characters to develop further than Cheney does, hinting that white women might benefit from emulating the courage and hardihood of their Indian sisters. Yet Cushing squelches the possibility of a love relationship between the white hero and the Indian woman who helps him to escape from captivity. Indeed, her Indian protagonists decline marriage with each other, opting for the status of mere appendages to the whites they have chosen to serve.[49]

Against the backdrop of these contemporary novels, and of such immediate predecessors as John Neal's *Logan* and James Kirke Paulding's *Koningsmarke*, *Hobomok* stands out for having reoriented the American historical novel toward exploring a radical alternative to race war and white male supremacy — a marriage of the races that would allow people of color and white women a more equal role in defining the nation's destiny. The significance of this achievement becomes especially apparent in the light of the three novels that Child's example inspired to venture into the forbidden domain of miscegenation.

Two years after the publication of *Hobomok*, James Fenimore Cooper issued what may well have been his answer to its challenge: *The Last of the Mohicans* (1826). Shifting the focus back to race war as the correct prototype of relations between whites and Indians, Cooper raises the specter of a love affair between a white woman and an Indian only to dispel it. Lusted after by the evil Magua and devotedly worshiped by the noble Uncas, Cooper's voluptuous heroine Cora, it turns out, is not white after all — her mother was "descended, remotely, from that unfortunate class who are so basely enslaved to administer to the wants of a luxurious people." This not only accounts for Cora's raven tresses and "complexion . . . charged with the color of the rich blood, that seemed ready to burst its bounds." It also accounts for a contemporary reviewer's perception of her, contrary to Cooper's manifest intention, as "quite a bold young woman, [who] . . . makes rather free, we think, with the savages." "We mean no offence whatever to the colored population of the United States; . . . and we acknowledge it to be a vile and abominable prejudice," commented the reviewer; "but still we have (and we cannot help it) a particular dislike to the richness of the negro blood in a heroine."[50] As if to forestall just such an objection, Cooper in fact takes care to block every possibility of interracial marriage in *The Last of the Mohicans*. Killing off Cora and Uncas, along with Magua, he buries the would-be lovers in separate graves, so that even in death their blood will not mingle. And when the Indian maidens hymn the "future prospects of Cora and Uncas" in the " 'blessed hunting grounds of the Lenape,' " the scout Hawkeye shakes his head, "like one who knew the error of their simple creed."[51]

But the ghost of *Hobomok* was not so easily laid. Before another year was out, a woman writer sought to amplify, rather than foreclose, the possibilities Child had opened up. Catharine Maria Sedgwick's *Hope Leslie; or, Early Times in the Massachusetts* (1827) is in many ways a more progressive as well as a more accomplished novel than *Hobomok*. Shattering American literary precedent, it embodies the noble Indian not in a warrior, but in a woman. A truly impressive literary creation, Sedgwick's Magawisca is more than a match for Cooper's Uncas and Chingachgook. And unlike both Cooper's and Child's noble Indians, Magawisca remains loyal to her people. Granted, Sedgwick does not allow Magawisca the marriage with the white hero, Everell Fletcher, which the novel fleetingly appears to promise. Instead, modeling her work on Scott's *Ivanhoe*, she casts Magawisca in the role of Rebecca and reserves the role of Rowena for her heroine, Hope Leslie. Even so, she does go further than Child in two other respects. First, she elaborates on the idea of an alliance between white women and Indians, turning it into a political — and feminist — gesture of solidarity, when Hope Leslie helps Magawisca escape from prison. Second, she arranges the only lasting Indian-white marriage in the nineteenth-century frontier novel — the marriage between Hope's sister Faith, captured and adopted by Indians in her early childhood, and Magawisca's brother Oneco.[52]

Despite these advances, Sedgwick avoids following Child's lead in presenting inter-marriage and assimilation as viable alternatives to Indian genocide. Magawisca, like Cooper's Indians and their friend, Hawk-eye, sees no possibility of reconciliation or integration with whites: "[T]he Indian and the white man can no more mingle, and become one, than day and night," she tells Everell and Hope when they urge her to remain with them. As if to prove her point, Faith and Oneco remain childless. In contrast to Mary Conant, Faith Leslie can never be reintegrated into white society. By marrying an Indian and adopting his people's ways, she has irrevocably regressed to savagery.[53]

The qualifications with which Sedgwick hedged herself when she hazarded enter-taining the tabooed idea of racial intermarriage did not suffice to grant *Hope Leslie* a role any more significant than that of *Hobomok* in altering the form of the American histor-ical novel—or the shape of the American literary canon. Notwithstanding the real merits of Sedgwick's novel, and the enormous popularity it enjoyed in its day, *Hope Leslie*, like *Hobomok*, would lie forgotten for well over a century.[54] The last word on the subject of Indian-white relations, be they sexual or military, would be Cooper's. Once again, it seems to have come in response to a woman novelist's challenge.

In *The Wept of Wish-ton-Wish* (1829) Cooper authoritatively revised Sedgwick's plot, forcing it into the less subversive mold of Eastburn and Sands's *Yamoyden*. Ruth Heath-cote, like Faith Leslie (and like the historical Eunice Williams on whose story both Sedgwick and Cooper drew), is captured by Indians as a child, adopted by the tribe, and eventually married to an Indian chief. She, too, regresses to savagery, forgetting her mother tongue and the religion of her fathers and embracing Indian ways. And unlike Faith, but like Mary Conant, she actually bears her Indian husband a child. The end of the novel rights all wrongs and restores order, however. Paralleling the denouement of *Yamoyden*, Ruth's husband, Conanchet, is killed by an Indian enemy (though at the behest of the Puritans), and she dies by his side, overcome with grief and shock. Lest the abortive end of their marriage not suffice to counter the threat Sedgwick had introduced by permitting her Anglo-Indian couple to survive unharmed, Cooper puts into the mouth of Conanchet the moral that it is futile for people of different races to violate the ban of nature and the Great Spirit. In a final twist, he symbolically purges Ruth of her distasteful liaison, restores her virginity, and brings her back into the Anglo-American fold. Just before her death, she suddenly loses all memory of her long sojourn among the Indians and mentally reverts to her state at the time of her cap-ture—the state of a five-year-old girl. As for the infant lying in her lap—an infant whose mixed blood, according to her husband, makes it unfit to live among Indians—Cooper literally expunges it from the novel. Neither in his summary of the surviving characters' fates nor in his descriptions of the gravestones commemorating the dead does he account for the mixed-blood baby. The dismissal of intermarriage from the history and literature of white America could hardly have been more definitive.[55]

Child refused to acquiesce in that dismissal. The young woman who had stood by her insight into *Paradise Lost* at age fifteen, regardless of her older brother, would like-wise stand by her insight into America's racial and sexual contradictions at age twenty-two, regardless of her literary elders. She had instinctively recognized the taboo-ridden issue of interracial marriage as both the crux of those contradictions and the key to resolving them, and she would persist in exploring its ramifications, whatever the cost.

Setting what would become a pattern in Child's works, *Hobomok* uncannily predicts her future career; the novel imagines in fiction the political issues Child would address polemically and act on as a reformer a few years hence.[56] Not only does the intermarriage plot foreshadow Child's literal espousal of the Indian cause during the Cherokee removal controversy later in the decade, but it also prefigures the campaign against antimiscegenation laws with which she would inaugurate her career as an antislavery agitator in 1833, and it adumbrates her lifelong conviction, developed with progressively greater political awareness in subsequent writings, that the destiny of the American nation lies in the fusion of its races and cultures. *Hobomok* forecasts Child's commitment to the struggle for women's rights as well—a struggle she would define in the 1840s to include sexual freedom. No less centrally, the novel's condemnation of Calvinist bigotry and its recognition that Protestants, Catholics, Muslims, Hindus, and aboriginal animists must all be "pleasing in the sight of God" points ahead toward the crusade for religious toleration that would culminate in the "eclectic Bible" Child published two years before her death—a Bible featuring a higher proportion of non-Christian than of Christian sacred texts. Finally, *Hobomok* reveals Child's conflicting aspirations toward respectability and marginality, acceptance by her society and rebellion against it, signaling how she would seek to resolve those conflicts—by refashioning her society to conform with her ideals.

Although Child's novelistic imagination prophesied the radical course she would soon take, she did not yet choose to translate fiction into reality. In the wake of *Hobomok*, she was savoring her first taste of fame. She was not ready to forfeit the patronage of a literary establishment that had clearly indicated its willingness to smile on her if she followed its dictates. The wine of success was too heady.

2

Rebels and "Rivals":
Self Portraits of a Conflicted Young Artist

Praises and invitations have poured in upon me, beyond my utmost hopes. . . . "I should think more highly of the talent of the woman who could write 'Hobomok,' " Mr. H. says, "than of any other American woman who has ever written, though to be sure it has its faults." — "Say nothing of its faults," urges the editor of the "North American"; "they are the faults of genius, and the beauties weigh them down." The Misses Osgood hold up their hands, and exclaim, "prodigious, prodigious!"[1]

Reveling in her new celebrity as the author of a novel that had achieved a succès de scandale in Boston's staid literary world, Child reported her triumphs to her sister Mary in Norridgewock with girlish zest. What she did not tell Mary, however, was that she herself had engineered her rise to fame through a shrewd, but most unladylike, act of self-promotion. Nor did she acknowledge the unanticipated discomfort she was feeling in the glamorous social milieu she had so longed to enter — a discomfort she would project onto the heroine of her second novel, *The Rebels, or Boston Before the Revolution* (1825). As a female writer in an age when the term was almost an oxymoron, as a self-educated social interloper in circles dominated by Harvard-trained intellectuals and Boston Brahmins, as an inveterate iconoclast with a yen for respectability, and as a young woman who aspired to independence rather than marriage, but who was also struggling to contain the powerful sexual impulses she had expressed in *Hobomok*, Child faced a major challenge. She would have to carve out a new identity for herself and learn how to reconcile her conflicting needs and ambitions while negotiating the limits of early nineteenth-century gender roles.

Publishing a novel in the 1820s meant incurring a great financial risk. The American book trade was still in its infancy, and most authors had to help subsidize and promote their own works.[2] Hence, Child had invested $495, no doubt borrowed from her father or Convers, in the publication of *Hobomok*. She had had a thousand copies printed, to be retailed at seventy-five cents each. But sales had been disappointingly slow in the wake of the *North American Review*'s initial verdict that the plot was "revolting." By March 1825, almost "half the edition" remained unsold, and Child stood $98 in debt.[3]

Determined to recoup the loss, she had set about producing her first potboiler, a children's book titled *Evenings in New England* (1824), which appeared just in time for the profitable New Year's market.[4] Yet she still dreamed of winning literary laurels. The plot of another historical novel was simmering in her mind, and she wanted to prove her mettle. She could not chance it unless *Hobomok* gained a wider audience. The solution occurred to Child when she learned that one of Convers's associates, the eminent Harvard professor George Ticknor, had spoken flatteringly of her maiden work.

The personification of the Boston aristocracy and the Harvard intelligentsia, Ticknor played the role of a literary kingmaker. His patronage all but assured a young author a brilliant future, and his vote of censure could end a promising career (as Child would later discover). "[N]o man could consider himself of any account in the world if he was not admitted to Mr. Ticknor's study," recalled one prominent victim of the kingmaker's ostracism, the controversial Transcendentalist clergyman Theodore Parker.[5] No wonder Child felt that "[t]o have been praised by such a man was sufficient to urge me on to mightier efforts."[6]

Her reaction to Ticknor's eulogy of her talents was nevertheless brash. Showing anything but the "trembling diffidence" she professed, let alone a proper regard for feminine decorum, she sat down to write to this literary magnate behind Convers's back. "There is nothing in life like the beatings of pure, youthful ambition, — of a soul excited by praise and expanding over its own glorious visions," Child confided. Inspired by Ticknor's tribute to *Hobomok*, she had "already commenced a new work," but her "energy and enthusiasm" had been sapped by the statement of accounts she had received from her publisher. She was appealing to Ticknor because she believed that unlike most men, he would sympathize with "a heart chilled and a mind prostrated by discouragement" over the poor reception of her "unfortunate book." "You may ask, what do you wish, or expect me to do?" she went on ingenuously: "I answer, your influence in the literary and fashionable world is very great, and a few words timely spoken by you would effect more than my utmost exertions. Your judgment would have much weight with those whose taste is law, and your notice would induce many to purchase, who would otherwise regard the subject with a very natural indifference."[7] She would never have presumed to make such a request, Child added, had Ticknor not "voluntarily praised [her] trifling production." With unerring instinct, she had struck all the right notes.

Ticknor immediately obliged. To Child's embarrassment, he even indicated his willingness to help cover the $98 dollar debt she found so onerous. More importantly, he persuaded his friend the historian Jared Sparks, editor of the *North American*, to include a second notice of *Hobomok*, enhanced with extracts from the most praiseworthy scenes, in an omnibus review of ten "Recent American Novels."[8] And he began inviting Child to literary soirees at his exclusive Boston salon.

As Ticknor's latest protégée, "the brilliant Miss Francis" suddenly found herself the toast of the patrician world over which he presided. Witty, vivacious, and exuberant, she enchanted these jaded sophisticates with her natural manner, which seemed to blow the fresh air of the Maine wilderness into their overheated drawing rooms. Physically, this petite, dark-haired, dark-eyed young woman did not cut an arresting figure. Her complexion was too "florid," her features too strongly marked for the tastes of her contemporaries. But as soon as a subject aroused her enthusiasm, her face would light up, transfusing her with an irresistible vitality. An interlocutor could not help sensing the passionate convictions that generated Child's displays of eloquence.[9]

If Ticknor himself left no description of her during this period, a worshipful adolescent did. Sixteen-year-old Margaret Fuller, who met Child in the summer of 1825 and began reading Locke and Madame de Staël with her a year and a half later, summed up the attraction her friend exerted: "She is a natural person, — a most rare thing in this age of cant and pretension. Her conversation is charming, — she brings all her powers to bear upon it; her style is varied, and she has a very pleasant and spirited way of thinking. I should judge, too, that she possesses peculiar purity of mind."[10] Fuller herself would eventually become famous for her Conversations, but she would cultivate a style very different from her untutored friend's.

By June 1825 the visibility Child had gained through Ticknor procured her an invitation from the governor of Massachusetts, Levi Lincoln, to attend the event of her life — a public reception for General Lafayette. The French war hero had been feting the fiftieth anniversary of the American Revolution by touring the country he had helped liberate, and he was returning to Boston to join in memorializing the Battle of Bunker Hill. Child had described his triumphal entry into Boston the previous summer in her *Evenings in New England* (which had perhaps earned her the honor of greeting the general now). This time she enjoyed the thrill of having Lafayette kiss her hand — a kiss that she vowed "should 'never be washed off.' "[11]

Amid the flurry of anniversary celebrations, Child completed her own commemoration of "Boston before the Revolution," *The Rebels*. She dedicated it to her new benefactor, George Ticknor. As Child seems to have dimly realized, he was a problematic choice. Fiercely conservative, he was at heart a Tory rather than a Revolutionary. His total lack of sympathy for the oppressed peoples with whom she impulsively identified may not have become obvious to Child until she espoused the antislavery cause in the 1830s, but she must have already perceived that he embodied convention itself. Before inscribing the dedication, she made a point of ascertaining whether he had any "fears that the character of the book" might prove "disgraceful to him."[12]

It is hardly surprising, then, that the novel Child credited to Ticknor's inspiration marked an ideological retreat. By shifting her setting from the wild frontier to civilized Boston, she was moving from the margins to the center of her culture. And by replacing Puritan and Indian characters with Tories and Revolutionaries, she was choosing a topic that enabled her to channel her rebellious energies in a socially approved direction. She could now link her personal revolt against the tyranny of the Fathers with the nation's.

Unlike the Puritan settlers, the heroes of the Revolution had not built their struggle for freedom on the suppression of their religious and racial adversaries. *The Rebels* thus presents a far less revisionist interpretation of American history than *Hobomok* had. Whereas Child had parodied the Puritan chronicles on which she had based *Hobomok*, she adheres faithfully to her main source for *The Rebels*—William Tudor's 1823 biography of James Otis.[13] Accordingly, her principal historical characters are no longer cranks or exotics, but major figures: the Revolutionaries James Otis and Samuel Adams; the Tory Thomas Hutchinson, lieutenant governor of Massachusetts; and the evangelist George Whitefield. The sole exception, significantly, is the Calvinist minister Mather Byles, a Tory sympathizer, who serves as an excuse for Child to deliver another blistering attack on the creed of her youth.

Child's rendering of the political and religious rhetoric of the day is in fact the most successful feature of *The Rebels*. The discourse she re-created had such an authentic ring that a speech she put into the mouth of Otis and a revival sermon she invented for Whitefield found their way into nineteenth-century schoolbooks, to be memorized by generations of pupils as bona fide transcriptions. Among those who learned these "high-sounding periods" by heart without realizing they had originated in "a young lady's romance" was the abolitionist Thomas Wentworth Higginson.[14]

Despite the novel's patriotic treatment of the Revolution, timed to coincide with the national jubilee, elements of the subversiveness that animates *Hobomok* persist in *The Rebels*. Once again, hostility toward Calvinism and patriarchy pervades the book, and a feminist impetus governs both characterization and plot. In *Hobomok*, Child had depicted the religious and social order founded by New England's Puritan Fathers as one peculiarly oppressive to women. The question she explores in *The Rebels* is whether the new order ushered in by the Revolution would be any better for women—whether it would confer liberty on *them*, as well as on their menfolk. Through a spectrum of female characters representing different classes and political viewpoints—chief among them the strong-minded spinster, Miss Sandford, and the heroine, Lucretia Fitzherbert—Child attempts to show that the Revolution indeed elevated women from the status of inferiors and pawns to that of respected if not fully equal partners in the society to which they had helped give birth.

Miss Sandford, the sister-in-law of Governor Hutchinson, with whom she shares the guardianship of Lucretia, represents the position women occupied under the old order.[15] A doughty mouthpiece of protofeminist ideas, she goes off like a "bullet" at the sound of the words "female inferiority."[16] These words are most frequently uttered by the Reverend Mather Byles, who pontificates that "[w]omen should only speak when it is necessary" (25). Child uses Miss Sandford's exchanges with Byles to discredit the patriarchal ideology she associates with Calvinist doctrine and Tory politics. Far from being innately superior, she shows, men like the Reverend Mr. Byles maintain their power simply by disparaging women and denying them the right to participate in intellectual discourse. When he is unable to best Miss Sandford in argument, for example, Byles resorts to that unfailing masculine weapon, aspersions on her femininity. "I never knew a woman that could not have been married if she wished it; and I certainly never knew one but that wished it, if she could," he sneers (96). By allowing Miss Sandford to hold her own in debate with a historical clergyman famous for his caustic wit, Child demonstrates that if women are willing to brave ridicule, they can reclaim the realm of ideas from the men who guard it.

Nevertheless, Byles typifies the formidable obstacle that Calvinist clergymen will pose to women's advancement. Child's exposé of their bigotry would not go unnoticed — Calvinists "took umbrage" at her caricature of Byles. Shrugging off their imprecations with magisterial disdain, Child wrote to her sister Mary: "I do not think it worth while to battle with them or their doctrines. As mankind advance in the steady march of free and rational principles their absurd tenets will die away, together with image worship, pilgrimages to Mecca, and holy alliances. Indeed, their present extraordinary zeal is but the convulsive spasm of approaching dissolution."[17] Although Child *would* set out to battle with Calvinist doctrine four years later in *The First Settlers of New-England* (1829), her main target in the satire she directs against the Reverend Mr. Byles is the misogyny to which Calvinism lent religious sanction.

Despised as an old maid and thwarted in her intellectual aspirations, Miss Sandford all too painfully illustrates women's oppression under the old theocratic and political order. Because she remains committed to the Tory regime her brother-in-law, Governor Hutchinson, champions, however, she cannot provide a model for a feminist challenge to patriarchal authority. When forced to choose between feminist and Tory principles, Miss Sandford chooses the latter. Hence, notwithstanding her own decision to remain single, she tries to pressure her ward, Lucretia Fitzherbert, into a marriage of convenience with Governor Hutchinson's nephew, Frederic Somerville, who proves to be a scoundrel.

It is Lucretia, rather than Miss Sandford, who rebels against the patriarchal authority vested in Governor Hutchinson and the British king he serves. In the process, she fuses her own struggle for independence with her country's and exemplifies the role women will play in the new republican order.

Lucretia resembles her creator in so many ways that it is impossible not to take her for a self-portrait.[18] Like Child, who frequently described herself as "very ugly," Lucretia is "very plain" (unusual for a heroine of the 1820s).[19] Recalling contemporary accounts of Child with "her face all aglow,"[20] Lucretia's face is "transiently lighted up with expression that almost atoned for the want of beauty" (10). She, too, impresses observers with her "vivacity and good sense" (205) — traits that friends repeatedly attributed to Child.[21] Above all, she shares the intellectual daring and the rich fantasy life of the young woman who had taken refuge from her loneliness in romantic novels and woodland rambles: "[Lucretia's] mind, vigorous as an eagle's wing, and rapid as the streams of Chili, had been early left to her own guidance. Under such circumstances, imagination had become her favourite region; but the glowing climate that brought the weeds to rank luxuriance, did not scorch the beauty of the flowers. She was wont to examine every thing in the illusive kaleidoscope of fancy . . ." (87). The echoes of Child's youthful comments on Scott's "wild" heroines are hard to miss ("I always preferred the impetuous grandeur of the cataract to the gentle meanderings of the rill," she had written).[22]

Through her heroine, Child explores tendencies she fears in herself. Lucretia "possessed a large share of that freedom of thought, that boldness of investigation, which renders exalted talents a peculiarly dangerous gift," she notes. "Such minds, while they proudly avoid the shoals of superstition, are too apt to be wrecked on the rocks of scepticism" (84). Unconsciously, she again echoes her confession to Convers: "I am in more danger of wrecking on the rocks of skepticism than of stranding on the shoals of fanaticism."[23] She also criticizes her heroine for having failed to learn "the important lesson of self-control" — a failure that threatens to undermine Lucretia's "great purity and rectitude of purpose" (147–48). Revealingly, Child goes on to warn against the very propensities she herself had shown in *Hobomok*: "[t]he fearless reasoning, the contempt of quiet virtues, the restlessness under the salutary shackles of society, against which a vigorous understanding and a glowing imagination ought to be peculiarly guarded" (148). Was she discovering that to get along with her new associates, she would have to curb her own "fearless reasoning"? Was she, too, feeling restless under the "shackles" imposed by the patricians she had so eagerly courted? And had she begun to doubt whether those shackles were in fact "salutary"?

Lucretia's reaction to the world of the British aristocracy, into which her Tory fiancé, Frederic Somerville, initiates her, would suggest so: "Wealth is a glittering and much coveted bauble; but the heart cannot nestle in it, and cling to it, in its hour of loneliness," she repines. "What do I care for Turkey carpets, Parisian mirrors, and Chinese vases, when every being around me is as chilling as the tessellated marble of our grand saloon?" (194). Even the excitement of meeting the leading intellectual and cultural figures of the day — the statesman Edmund Burke, the actor David Garrick, the painter Joshua Reynolds, and the writers Samuel Johnson and Oliver Goldsmith — does not overcome Lucretia's sense of alienation. Was Child finding the celebrities she was meeting in Ticknor's salon equally unsatisfying?

The course Lucretia ultimately elects presages Child's future career as uncannily as *Hobomok* does. This time, however, the authority figure against whom her heroine rebels — the Tory Governor Hutchinson, who has taken her under his wing and adopted her into his aristocratic milieu — is no longer a projection of Child's Calvinist father; rather, he resembles her patron George Ticknor. In following the dictates of her conscience, Lucretia casts her lot with the Revolutionaries at the cost of forfeiting her guardian's patronage — just as Child would forfeit Ticknor's on joining the antislavery movement in 1833.

The eeriest autobiographical parallels occur in a scene peripheral to the plot — the storming of Governor Hutchinson's mansion and the ransacking of his famous library by a Revolutionary mob. In that scene Lucretia snatches up two rolls of manuscripts she sees lying on Hutchinson's desk as he is desperately trying to save his most precious records. One is his unfinished *History of the Colony and Province of Massachusetts-Bay*, the other "the original manuscript of Hubbard's History" (38) — both key documents in colonial New England archives.[24] Thus, symbolically usurping Hutchinson's role as the custodian of New England's history, Lucretia reenacts Child's revision of Puritan history in *Hobomok* and heralds the contributions she would make to rewriting the history of Indians, African Americans, women, and non-Christian peoples in subsequent works. Child could not know it at the time, of course, but a library would also be the site of her future rupture with Ticknor, who, like Hutchinson, was already helping to assemble some of New England's most important collections of rare books and manuscripts. To facilitate Child's historical research, Ticknor would grant her library privileges at the Boston Athenaeum, only to withdraw them after she published her *Appeal in Favor of That Class of Americans Called Africans*.[25]

Lucretia's break with Hutchinson takes a different form — public denunciation of his nephew Somerville as a perfidious fortune hunter — but Child does project onto her heroine her own sense of being a social impostor. At the climax of the novel, Lucretia learns that she is not in fact an aristocrat, as she had supposed, but the granddaughter of a pariah, the witch Molly Bradford, who had exchanged her in the cradle with the legitimate Fitzherbert heiress for the sake of assuring her a more prosperous life. Although Molly's surname ironically conjures up the governor and historian of the Plymouth colony, William Bradford, she herself represents the heretics and troublemakers he had excluded from his community of saints; her practice of witchcraft, moreover, invites us to view her as another Mary Conant. Molly also represents the "rabble" that surged to the forefront of the Revolution's earliest phase — the Boston Massacre of March 5, 1770. She raises the loudest taunts against the British troops who brandish fixed bayonets and loaded muskets against a crowd of angry citizens, and in the opening salvo of the Massacre, she becomes one of the Revolution's first martyrs. Molly's revelation of her granddaughter's parentage consequently redefines both Lucretia's class and her national identity. Henceforward, Lucretia, too, must take her place among the "rabble," where she will be free to forge a new identity for herself, based no longer on birth, privilege, and marital alliances, but on the moral worth earned by her own actions.

Moralizing on Lucretia's odyssey, Child comments prophetically: "Wealth, with all its imposing pageantry, and rank with its embroidered baldrick and blazing star, had been idols before which her imagination had bowed with scarcely inferior homage; and she had proved their utter insufficiency to satisfy the soul in its hour of trial. . . . She now began to estimate men and things according to their real value, — to appreciate qualities according to their usefulness, not according to their lustre" (300). For Child, life would imitate art less than a decade later, when her embrace of African Americans would brand her in patrician eyes as a pariah. Like Lucretia, she would regard her expulsion from her patron's mansion as liberating and spend the rest of her life proclaiming her detestation of aristocracy.

Throughout *The Rebels*, Child pointedly links her heroine's evolution with the American colonists'. As agitation against the Stamp Act develops into revolt against British rule, Lucretia begins to question the Tory values she has been taught and to exchange

Tory for Republican associates. Her staunchly patriotic friend Grace Osborne, whose family has championed the Revolutionary cause from the outset, replaces her patroness Miss Sandford in her affections, and Grace's brother Henry wins Lucretia's hand after she rejects Somerville. In parallel fashion, the book's narrative point of view shifts gradually away from the Tory Hutchinsons and toward the Revolutionaries with whom Lucretia comes to align herself.

Though manifestly an inadequate vehicle, the romance plot involving Lucretia, her Tory fiancé Frederic Somerville, her friends the Osbornes, and the witch Molly Bradford functions as a political allegory, illuminating the connections between the public and private spheres. Lucretia reenacts the ordeal of the American colonies as they sever their ties with the mother country and construct an independent, democratic identity for themselves. The Tory Somerville, who initially woos Grace Osborne, but abandons her for Lucretia on the latter's sudden accession to wealth, personifies the treachery and rapacity of British overlords bent on draining the colonies of their riches. Grace, who dies of grief after Somerville's betrayal gives "additional fervour" to the patriotic sentiments "ever deeply imbedded" in her heart (210), embodies the wrongs the American people have endured at the hands of the British — wrongs her brother Henry will avenge. And Molly Bradford incarnates both the spirit of the Revolution and its plebeian origins.

The marriage between Lucretia and Henry Osborne in which the romance plot culminates also serves to consummate the political allegory. Through Henry, Lucretia marries the Revolution, which her wronged friend, Grace, and her heroic grandmother, Molly, have both died to bring into being, and which her husband, Henry, will carry to completion. She thus assumes the role of an auxiliary partner in the nation's destiny. The final sentence of the novel characterizes Lucretia as the domestic exemplar of the civic virtue her husband has displayed "in the senate and the field" (304). In short, it invokes the post-Revolutionary ideology that the historian Linda Kerber has dubbed "Republican motherhood."[26] This ideology dignified women's role in the new order by endowing their domestic responsibilities with political significance, but it reserved the sphere of politics for men. Child's endorsement of it marks the limits of the feminist consciousness she had attained by 1825. The Founding Fathers of the American Republic had won her allegiance because unlike their Puritan predecessors, they did not denigrate women. She did not yet recognize how far short of granting women equal status their creed of "Republican motherhood" fell.

Child's political allegory evidently escaped reviewers of *The Rebels*. They pronounced the narrative "greatly deficient in simplicity and unity" and criticized it for failing to connect "the historical events . . . with those of a domestic nature."[27] In truth, they could hardly be blamed. Melodramatic and weakened by a profusion of implausible complications, her plot simply could not support the symbolism with which she had freighted it.

The objections that J. C. Gray of the *North American Review* voiced to the ending are nevertheless indicative of the opposition Child faced in challenging patriarchal ideals.

While praising the characterization of Lucretia as a successful attempt to "render a heroine interesting without beauty," Gray judged that after her repudiation of Somerville, she should have been "consigned, like her friend Grace, to an early grave, or to a hopeless celibacy." Seeing her emerge "comfortably married" from the ordeal of breaking her engagement and exposing her lover's duplicity, he complained, was as disappointing as having a "long expected duel . . . prevented by an amicable arrangement, in which case, as we have heard it aptly said, '*the generous public* will be satisfied with nothing but bloodshed.'" The metaphor suggests that a woman who flouts patriarchal convention, however justifiably, must be punished. Otherwise, it is hard to account for Gray's almost willful misinterpretation of "the marriage between the high spirited Lucretia" and the patriotic Osborne as a "prudent calculation." Like the reviewers of *Hobomok*, Gray reenforced his prescriptions by selecting for extensive quotation a deathbed scene illustrating both the fate of an exemplary heroine (Grace Osborne) and the "pathetic" style an exemplary author ought to cultivate.[28]

Although Child failed to achieve her aims in *The Rebels*, she had undertaken some ambitious tasks: to inject serious political discourse into the American historical novel; to reorient the subgenre of novels about the Revolution—hitherto concerned mainly with celebrating the colonists' heroism in battle—toward exploring the issues that had generated their struggle for independence; and to extend the political revolution against patriarchal authority into the domestic realm of gender relations. The endeavor already foreshadows her tracts and newspaper articles advocating equal rights for Indians, African Americans, and women, in which she would draw extensively on the ideology of the Revolution. It also sets her apart from her contemporaries.

Comparisons with works that might have served Child as models are instructive. Both in Cooper's two novels of the Revolution—*The Spy. A Tale of the Neutral Ground* (1821) and *Lionel Lincoln: or, The Leaguer of Boston* (1825)—and in Eliza L. Cushing's *Saratoga; A Tale of the Revolution* (1824), the military aspect of the war overshadows the political, and debates between Tory and Revolutionary characters center almost wholly on such questions as whether the British or the Americans are braver soldiers and which side is destined to win. In contrast, Child's characters argue over whether the mob violence that has rocked Massachusetts has been instigated by the "arts of demagogues" or the "tyranny of rulers." Her characters attempt to resolve the dispute by examining the merits of the colonists' grievances—local governments appointed by the king rather than elected by the people, a spoils system that enriches "parasites and plunderers" at the people's expense, the "enslaving principle of taxation without representation" (55–60). Child's penchant for political discourse becomes especially apparent when one juxtaposes *The Rebels* with *Lionel Lincoln*, which picks up the thread of pre-Revolutionary history only four years after the Boston Massacre, but once again reduces political discussion to a minimum and concentrates instead on the battles of Concord, Lexington, and Bunker Hill.

It is the relationship established between revolution and patriarchy, however, that provides the best touchstone for differentiating Child from her competitors. Symptomatically, the patriarchal Washington presides over Cooper's *The Spy*, eliciting silent devotion from the novel's most memorable character, the Yankee pedlar Harvey Birch, and taking a fatherly interest in the heroine, Frances Wharton. True, Cooper allows Frances the extraordinary feat of scrambling up a mountaintop alone at night to help her Loyalist brother, Henry, escape recapture by her Revolutionary lover. Nevertheless, Cooper carefully circumscribes Frances's role in a military contest directed by men. Both she and her sister Sarah take their political opinions straight from the men they love, and Frances triumphs over a rival for her lover's hand specifically because she is "mild, gentle, and dependent."[29]

Going further than Cooper, Eliza Cushing in her novel *Saratoga* does link her heroine's Revolutionary sympathies with rebellion against patriarchy.[30] "[F]irm in her principles and attachments," Catherine Courtland has sided with the Revolutionaries out of the conviction that their cause is just, and she even tries to dissuade her Tory father from taking up arms against them. She also rejects the wealthy Tory aristocrat her father would have her marry, insisting on her right to choose her husband for herself. Her choice of a Revolutionary lover thus represents an assertion of her political allegiance as well as a protest against patriarchal authority. Yet Cushing ends *Saratoga* with the reconciliation of Tory father and Revolutionary daughter. Child on the contrary ends *The Rebels* with the rupture between Lucretia and her Tory guardian, Governor Hutchinson, devoting the novel's next-to-last page to moralizing on Hutchinson's downfall. Unlike her literary peers, the twenty-three-year-old author of *The Rebels* shows unmistakable signs of becoming a rebel herself.

At least one of Child's new acquaintances recognized her intellectual boldness, not with concern, but with a thrill of sympathy. On January 3, 1826, the inaugural issue of the *Massachusetts Journal* carried a front-page review of *The Rebels* that extravagantly praised *Hobomok* as well. "The author is so extensively and so favorably known as the writer of a previous and very powerful production founded on the earliest history of New England," proclaimed the reviewer, "that the present work in our opinion needs nothing more than its own title page to bring it fairly, and even advantageously before the public." He went on to pay homage in the same breath to the woman and the work: "It has been said that personal beauty is a good letter of recommendation. We will add that a work, whose title page discloses the fact that the author has previously written a tale so beautiful as 'Hobomok,' needs no letter of recommendation from any one." The extract the reviewer chose to reprint from *The Rebels* was not a "pathetic" deathbed scene, but a stirring political oration—the fictitious speech by James Otis that would soon reappear in nineteenth-century schoolbooks. He left no doubt as to whose eloquence he ranked higher—Otis's or the young novelist's. "If *James Otis* spoke in this fashion, the wonder is that the Revolution did not begin sooner," he trumpeted. The reviewer was David Lee Child, who had just assumed the editorship of the *Massachusetts Journal*, a triweekly newspaper sponsored by Daniel Webster and John Quincy Adams.[31]

By January 1826 David Lee Child and Lydia Maria Francis had known each other for a little over a year. They had met on December 2, 1824, when Convers and his wife,

Abba, had invited David to dinner, shortly after his arrival in Watertown to study law with his uncle, Tyler Bigelow. The author of *Hobomok* had been sufficiently impressed to note in her diary: "Mr. Child . . . possesses the rich fund of an intelligent traveller, without the slightest twinge of a traveller's vanity."[32]

David Lee Child was more than well-traveled. Steeped in the Greek and Latin classics; fluent in French, German, Spanish, and Portuguese; full of piquant insights into history and current politics — he was a one-man university. In addition, he had the dashing mien of a Byronic hero, with his high forehead, patrician nose and mouth, dark hair, and dreamy eyes. David had just returned from a two-year sojourn in Portugal and Spain, where he had originally gone to serve as secretary of legation in Lisbon under minister plenipotentiary Henry Dearborn, Jefferson's former secretary of war, as well as a Revolutionary hero and veteran of Bunker Hill. He had attracted Dearborn's attention in 1819 by publishing a pamphlet debunking another alleged hero of Bunker Hill, Israel Putnam. David was teaching classics at the prestigious Boston Latin School — the position he had taken on graduating from Harvard in 1817 — but he had leaped at the chance to exchange the staid job of a pedagogue for the glamorous political and diplomatic career Dearborn offered him. After a trip to Washington and Virginia in 1821, during which David had met the most famous politicians of the day — among them Daniel Webster, John C. Calhoun, and John Randolph — he had embarked for Lisbon in July 1822.[33]

Europe was then in the throes of a struggle between liberal and reactionary forces. In April 1823, nine months after David landed in Portugal, the French government under Louis XVIII invaded Spain to put down the liberals who had come to power there and were forcing the Spanish king to install a constitutional system.[34] At such a crisis, when the cause of liberty throughout the world seemed at stake, David could not bear to remain on the sidelines, even if throwing himself into the fray meant abandoning an "honorable and lucrative destiny" and renouncing "ease for hardship, gain for loss, & safety for danger." The French and their backers in the Holy Alliance had committed an act of "infernal piracy." Their "damnable project" had to be defeated. Armed with a letter of introduction from his friend John James Appleton, he headed for Spain in May 1823 to join the army of General Lopez Baros.[35] To David's disgust, the war for liberty turned into a rout. Refighting the campaign in a letter to an unnamed correspondent, he explained how, had he been in charge, he would have kept track of the enemy's movements through spies, forced the opposing army into action on his "chosen ground," "animated" his troops with his own "enthusiasm," and "made in Spain another Thermopylae."[36]

This fiery, articulate champion of freedom struck the author of *Hobomok* as the very incarnation of her romantic fantasies. "He is the most gallant man that has lived since the sixteenth century; and needs nothing but helmet, shield, and chain armour to make him a complete knight of chivalry," Child confided to her diary six weeks later, on meeting David again at the home of a Watertown friend (the widow Lois Curtis, sister-in-law of George Ticknor).[37] If she sensed that her "knight" bore a dismaying resemblance to Don Quixote, she did not admit it to herself.

The two continued to spend "many delightful evenings" together, during which David dazzled Child with his brilliance and drew her into political discussions of the kind she was re-creating in *The Rebels*. "I do not know which to admire most[,] the vigour of his understanding, or the ready sparkle of his wit," she mused after one such discussion. David's ideas interested her so much that she jotted them down in a diary entry of May 3, 1825: "Talked of the political position of England — said war was necessary to her existence. Spoke of the tendency to decline which marks all institutions, particularly republican. Laughed as he mentioned the tremendous *squirearchy* of America."[38] Equally smitten, David rhapsodized the same month in his own diary:

> [T]he etherial, high-souled, high-reaching Maria! the elegant, pure, powerful-minded Maria! . . . I know of no mind with which it seems to me, my soul could hold such sweet converse as with the eloquent, susceptible, correct, & brilliant spirit which animates the pleasing beautiful form of Maria. I would love her dearly if the fates were not adverse to it. She is the only lady in Watertown, who has made any impression upon me of a serious & enduring kind, i e to say of *a tender kind*.[39]

Nevertheless, as David's cryptic allusion to "adverse" circumstances indicates, no proposal followed. Instead, he moved to Boston to set himself up as a lawyer and edit the *Massachusetts Journal*.

A major factor in delaying any commitment between the lovers must have been the state of David's finances. At age thirty-one, he still had not begun to earn a steady living. The erratic career path he had followed to date betrayed a disturbing tendency to flit from one enthusiasm to another and to sacrifice prospects of stable employment for the sake of pursuing dreams of glory, albeit with idealistic motives. David's stint in the Spanish army had cost him his diplomatic appointment, which had not been re-newed on his return to Portugal. To the great disappointment of his aging parents, who had counted on his contributing to their support, he had arrived home without a penny to show for his years abroad. Indeed, he had already accumulated a mountain of debts — another ill-omened pattern in his life.[40] At a stage when he should have been firmly established in a profession, he was making his third vocational debut and relying on his parents to bail him out of his financial morass. "At present I know not where I shall get money to pay my quarterly board wh[ich] will become due in about a month," he complained in a letter written two weeks before he met Child. Ironically, David was responding to a request for help from his father, who was also struggling to get out of debt. Suggesting that his father sell a horse and recover a small sum lent to someone else, David added pointedly: "I . . . wish that after providing for the comfort of Mother yourself Lydia & sisters my wants may rank next & be attended to *for all my old debts*."[41]

If David was not in a position to marry by 1825, neither was Child in any hurry to forfeit the independence she valued so highly. A new world had just opened up to her since the publication of *Hobomok*, and she was eager to explore it. Yet unlike David, Child was also determined to find a means of fulfilling her ambitions without depending on anyone for financial assistance. So far her literary endeavors had not paid her keep, whatever social rewards they had brought her. If she wanted to support herself, she would have to resort again to schoolteaching, reserving the interstices of her schedule for writing. "[W]ith the view of fitting [herself] for a large and genteel, and perman[en]t school," Child decided to perfect her French and drawing skills by enrolling in Madame Angeline Canda's famous academy for young ladies. Conveniently, the plan allowed her to follow David to Boston in the winter of 1825–26.[42]

David was far from being the only admirer to court the "brilliant Miss Francis," however. The flamboyant young author Nathaniel Parker Willis, a notorious dandy who would win a name for himself by editing several well-regarded literary periodicals and churning out gossipy sketches of European high society, "struck up quite an intimacy" with her. "[H]e was a man of undoubted genius, and of very fascinating manners," Child judged in retrospect, though his adulation of moneyed aristocrats led him to make poor use of his talents. She commented wryly on their brief flirtation from the vantage point of old age: "How well I remember our walks on the Common, he looking down from his slender height upon my slender shortness; for I was slender then. I seem to see him as he was then, young, and fair of aspect, in tall white hat, buff vest, and new light-colored French gloves; all in the pink of the mode, of course. He was full of worldly ambition *then*, talking much of the high position he meant to conquer for himself."[43] Despite his "fascinating manners," Child must have found Willis unbearably snobbish, as well as superficial. A social climber who prided himself on his solidly respectable antecedents and traded on his father's reputation as the editor of a leading Congregationalist weekly, he would never have dreamed of marrying a baker's daughter, let alone a woman with the iconoclastic bent the author of *Hobomok* had revealed.[44]

A more serious contender for Child's heart was the painter Francis Alexander, whom she described to her sister as "young, unmarried, —and my *especial* friend" ("Do not smile!" she exhorted Mary).[45] The artistic side of Child's nature had always yearned for gratification, and she delighted in visiting Alexander's studio. His portraits even inspired her to compose some verses. She also enjoyed bantering with him. While pretending to puzzle over what his first initial F. stood for—"it cannot be for funny, nor foolish, nor finical, nor fanatic,—but it may be fanciful, and I am sure it is Famous Alexander"—she assured him playfully of her own straightforwardness: "there are more *naturals* than either *flats* or *sharps* in my scale of notes; now, if with all this information, we cannot *chord* whenever we meet, you must be 'fit for treason, sacrilege, and crimes.'"[46]

Notwithstanding her coquettish badinage, the role Child assumed toward Alexander was less that of a marriageable young lady exhibiting her charms to a prospective suitor than of a motherly art patron furnishing moral and material support to a protégé—a role she would extend to a large circle of artists and musicians in later years. When Alexander succumbed to discouragement, for example, she chided him: "[T]hrow off that sickly sensibility that leads you to distrust yourself and suspect others! It will be the ruin of you, if you indulge it." An artist should emulate, not envy or despise his rivals, Child admonished Alexander, urging him to cultivate self-confidence: "You have genius—why do you care whether Mr. —— or Miss —— acknowledge it or not? Above all why do you care that another is more appreciated, while you are undervalued?" One of Alexander's rivals had benefited greatly by going to Europe to study, and Child suggested that he should do likewise — advice he took in 1831.[47]

Not content with praising and counseling Alexander, Child sought to increase his clientele. She brought her French teacher, Madame Canda, and her classmate, the renowned beauty Emily Marshall, to his studio, apparently procuring him a commission from the latter. She even sat for a portrait herself in the spring of 1826. A three-quarter view of a lively young woman whose fashionably dressed black hair and demure, semidécolleté gown with puffed, lace-edged sleeves belie the trace of defiance in her expression, it hangs today in the Medford Historical Society. Child would always insist that it flattered her too much to be a good likeness. "There is a glow and enthusiasm about it which belongs to the author of 'Hobomok,' rather than to L. M. Francis," she wrote to her sister Mary, for whom she had ordered the portrait as a gift. "If it has any fault, it is because the artist has *too much* genius — He wanted to make a Sappho of me, and to pour over my very ugly face the full tide of inspiration." But she begged Mary not to risk hurting Alexander's feelings by criticizing the portrait in public. "[H]e has all the susceptibility of genius," she warned.[48]

In the same letter Child announced that she would be taking charge of a school in Watertown almost as soon as she left Boston that summer. After her winter of basking in the favor of the Brahmin elite, she was not looking forward to the comedown. Nor was she looking forward to moving back in with her sister-in-law Abba. "She is jealous of every compliment paid to my talents, of every attention I receive, even from my brother," she complained to Mary. Those attentions had included "[b]ooks, rings, pictures, trinkets, and an elegant India comb, 11$," besides a steady stream of invitations. It was hardly surprising that Abba was finding the contrast between the duties of a minister's wife and the glories of a literary lion hard to digest. But Child also admitted that her social prominence had brought her "vexations and afflictions" and that she had made some well-deserved enemies among her new associates. "Oh, how often I have wanted you to fly to, for advice and assistance. If people knew half the extent of my vehement, and impetuous temperament, they would give me credit for governing myself as well as I do," she confided to her sister. Nostalgic for her family and friends in Maine, she wished she could exchange her school in Watertown for a "*first rate one*" in her old haunts. Child did not divulge the cause of her outburst, but her assertion that she had settled on schoolteaching as a profession because she would "probably never marry" is suggestive. Had David thrown himself into politics and editorial work and drifted out of her life? Was she discovering that the other men who paid tribute to her brilliance shied away from marrying such an independent-minded woman?[49] Or was she frightened by the sexual desires being aroused in her by men's admiration? The fiction she began writing that fall provides no clear answers, but it does reflect a mind "torn and convulsed by contending passions."[50]

Fortuitously, at a juncture in Child's career when she could no longer spare the time for novel-writing, a new literary outlet appeared on the scene: the gift book, or annual. An attractive volume that made an ideal New Year's present, "with its sentimental title and its gold and vellum bindings and its elaborate and expensive embellishments," the gift book featured sketches, poems, essays, and short stories representing the latest products of American talent.[51] From the outset, editors and publishers recognized the importance of using the medium to boost the development of a national literature, both by relying exclusively on American contributors, and by calling for "original pieces . . . illustrative of American history, scenery, and manners."[52]

In important respects the gift book fitted the needs of American writers better than the historical novel. The "*Waverley*-model," despite its adaptability, yoked Scott's American heirs to a borrowed vehicle and cast them in the role of imitators — the very role they so desperately wished to escape. For women, moreover, that model was doubly problematic. Scott and his chief American disciple Cooper had fashioned the historical novel into a solidly patriarchal genre, and Child's efforts to subvert the conventions they had established had met with strong resistance from some reviewers, as we have seen.[53]

By comparison, the gift book offered several advantages: the fluidity of an emerging medium; the premium it put on brevity and variety; and the profitability of a genre that sold well and required no financial investment by authors. As an astute critic in the April 1829 *North American Review* pointed out, the short selections favored by the annuals were "especially suited to the instant genius of our land," giving literary apprentices the exposure they needed while allowing them to "practise those niceties and beauties of expression, hereafter to be worked in upon more enduring materials. . . ." The short story bore the same relationship to the novel that the "cartoons of the Indian artists" did to "the more matured and nobler fresco" of European artists, he suggested. The metaphor endowed the new genre with greater signficance than this critic perhaps intended, for it implied that American writers had at last discovered a literary form as native to their shores as the Indian. So indeed it proved, according to the first serious student of the American short story, Fred Lewis Pattee. "Cooper was 'the American Scott,' Irving was 'the American Addison,' and Bryant was 'the American Wordsworth,' but the native writers of short fiction for the annuals and the periodicals were producing something that had no prototype" in England, asserts Pattee — a genre that "first won its way . . . as literature distinctively and uniquely American."[54]

If we exclude selections with no discernible "American" content, gift book fiction fell into four overlapping categories: sketches of domestic manners; regional or local color fiction; historical fiction; and Indian tales. Child contributed a few pieces to the first category — notably, "The Sagacious Papa," "The Recluse of the Lake," and "Harriet Bruce" — but they do not match the achievements of Catharine Maria Sedgwick and Eliza Leslie, who reigned supreme in this domain.[55] As for the second category, best represented by James Kirke Paulding's Irvingesque pictures of the Dutch in old New York,[56] Child eschewed it altogether. Her forte lay in historical fiction and Indian tales, where she left a valuable legacy. Unlike her contemporaries, Child did not use these subgenres to commemorate ancestral triumphs over British tyrants and Indian savages.

Instead, she adapted them to more subversive ends. Her best short stories illuminate the hidden recesses of the American psyche, probe the relationship between sexual and political repression, expose the ills threatening the nation's future, and rewrite American history from the viewpoint of its victims.[57]

Only a year after the gift book made its debut in 1825 with *The Atlantic Souvenir*, Child published her first story, "The Rival Brothers. A Tale of the Revolution."[58] Signed "By the Author of новомок," it shares the revisionist thrust of the novel that had propelled Child to fame. Not only does "The Rival Brothers" present a woman's perspective on the Revolution—a perspective radically different from that of America's Founding Fathers—it also returns to the exploration of women's sexual fantasies. The dark figure onto whom Child projects those fantasies in the story, however, is no longer an Indian, but a Tory.

Picking up ideologically where *The Rebels* leaves off, "The Rival Brothers" focuses on the experiences of humble folk like Child's own parents and grandparents, rather than aristocrats like the Hutchinsons. Child had often heard her father, Convers, tell of the hardships his family had undergone during the five years his father, Benjamin, was away fighting in the Revolutionary army. With no breadwinner and eleven mouths to feed, the senior Convers's mother, Lydia, had been reduced to sending the children out begging. One day Convers himself had trudged barefoot through the snow to the gristmill in hopes that the miller could spare a little cornmeal—only to be told that another needy supplicant had just been given the last spoonful. The family would have starved if a neighbor had not come to the rescue with some potatoes.[59]

Child highlights this aspect of the war—so often neglected by male writers—in a vignette of the heroic sacrifices women had performed behind the scenes while men were acting in "the public theatre of a sympathising world": "To fasten the knapsack round a father's neck, to fill the cartridges of a beloved husband, and see him go forth to battle, when his little ones are crying for bread, and his desolate home is left at the mercy of the ravager; to have none left to dig the grave of an only son, and to consign him to the cold, damp earth, wept over only by the aged and the helpless, require no ordinary effort of human strength" (49–50). "The Rival Brothers" reminds readers that "the fortitude of our mothers" deserves to be commemorated along with "the courage of our fathers" (49).

Yet the most striking feature of the story—and the most revealing of its author's inner turmoil—is its recurrent motif of psychosexual conflict. This motif surfaces at three different points: in the narrative frame, in the characterization of the eponymous rival brothers, and in the heroine's vacillation between her two suitors.

The narrative frame introduces a couple enjoying a stimulating conversation during a ride through the woods. "[D]eriving new charms from the scene around"—a scene of twittering birds and "butterflies, like gay coquettes, weary of conquest, closing and spreading their gorgeous wings in languid indifference"—the couple's intercourse is charged with sexual overtones. As the two converse, "thoughts spring spontaneously from the tongue, attended with all the contagious exhilaration of wit and talent," and the narrator responds "every instant with increasing pleasure" to her companion's words. But suddenly a nightmare figure that seems to erupt from the Puritan conscience arrests the conversation at its height. "[F]rightful and loathsome-looking," the apparition embodies the consequences of abusing intellectual gifts and violating sexual bans:

> The lofty and projecting forehead, and the bold, rigid contour of the head, all indicated the possession of prodigious power; and "the spark of hell burning in his eye," proved that power had been exerted for the prince of darkness. He was clothed in the squalid and tattered drapery of exceeding poverty; and deeply had age graven upon his iron visage the lines of guilt and passion. The painter and the sculptor could not have found a more fitting personification of pestilence or crime. (34)

It is as if the narrator has conjured up a nemesis to punish her for indulging in forbidden thoughts — or as if the criminal represents the shadow self of the companion to whom she has been listening with such excitement.

Child sets up a direct relationship between the criminal and the couple whose intimacy he shatters, when she identifies him as a man well known to the narrator's companion. The story of this "depraved wretch," transmitted to the narrator by her companion, redefines the fratricidal strife between Tory and Revolutionary in psychosexual terms. Joseph and William Warner, the one a "furious Tory," the other a "firm and decided Whig," vie for the love of the heroine, Frances Leslie. Frances, in turn, projects onto her rival lovers the war raging within her between "imagination" (her sexual impulses) and "reason" (her values, as reflected in the qualities she seeks in a prospective spouse). Though "reason" tells Frances that the gentle and industrious William is "a thousand times more fitted to make her happy," "imagination" draws her to Joseph, in whom she sees "a character torn and convulsed by contending passions" — her own mirror image.

Child unmistakably indicates the sexual essence of the attraction: "[Frances's] gentle nature shrunk from his ferocity, and she dreaded an influence which she always found tumultuous and exciting; but, like the bird charmed by a rattlesnake, the greater her fear the more powerful the attraction" (39). Still, the fascination that men like Joseph exert for women is more than sexual, she stresses. At its basis lies "that worship of power, which exists in every human mind" (38). If women all too often tend to fall under the spell of "unprincipled," domineering men, mistaking "boldness . . . for strength and moral insanity for intellectual vigour" (39), it is because they are blindly seeking access to power through men — the only route patriarchy allows them.

Frances's fate illustrates the danger of yielding to such unconscious drives. It also suggests that the demonic Joseph may be the alter ego of the virtuous William — that the terrors of unbridled sexuality lurk beneath the illusions of love. After the two brothers join opposing armies — Joseph malignantly cursing his patriot brother and father as he leaves for the British camp — Frances believes she has resolved her inner conflict in William's favor:

Left to the quiet communion of her own spirit, Frances found that her affection for [William] had taken deep and vigorous root. . . . for it is one of the strangest perversities of love, that absence strengthens it far more than constant presence. The memory of his devotedness to her and her widowed parent was associated with every thing around her; and each day, some deficiency in their household comfort reminded them of the industry and kindness which had so promptly supplied their wants. (51–52)

Does Frances's love for William grow in his absence because he does not really interest her in the flesh? Are her sexual desires more potent — and more deadly — than she realizes? Such would appear to be the implications of her behavior when she receives a reply to her declaration of love, ostensibly from William, but written in a style more characteristic of Joseph, with "violent protestations of unalterable attachment" (52). This letter summons her to a secret twilight rendezvous in the woods, at which Joseph greets her instead of William. Brandishing William's sword, which he has obtained by trickery, he reproaches Frances for "broken promises and disappointed hopes," and murders her when she "refuse[s] to pollute her soul with false vows" (56). Her body is found with "her long, fair hair . . . tangled in the shrubbery" and the sword lying "all bloody at her side" (54) — a depiction highly evocative of rape. The eery psychodrama ends with William dying in battle and his Tory brother Joseph surviving to haunt the narrator and her companion long after the Revolution.

Unlike *Hobomok* and *The Rebels*, "The Rival Brothers" offers no escape from patriarchal tyranny, no prospect of sexual liberation. On the contrary, it warns against the kinds of sexual fantasies that *Hobomok* licenses. Whereas Mary Conant violates taboo with impunity and wins both of the dark lovers she desires, Frances Leslie is raped and murdered when she allows her sexual desires to betray her. "The Rival Brothers" also reverses the optimistic political outcome of *The Rebels*. Instead of celebrating the downfall of a Tory patriarch, it suggests that the forces of Toryism have persisted in the American body politic; and instead of signalizing the complementary ways in which the two sexes reap the benefits of the Revolution in the domestic and political spheres, it hints that women will find the men who dominate the new order indistinguishable from those who "ravage[d]" their homes under the old.

Despite these differences, "The Rival Brothers" exhibits the same iconoclastic spirit that *Hobomok* does. Not surprisingly, it would elicit the same charge of bad taste from at least one reviewer. Confessing "a special dislike" for "The Rival Brothers," he would pontificate: "Unmingled and incredible atrocity is a bad subject for any pen."[60]

If precisely these features give "The Rival Brothers" its fascination for modern readers, Child's grim tale nevertheless prompts biographical questions. What are we to make of the political and psychosexual interpretations the story invites, and how can we account for its pessimism? No external evidence would seem to point yet toward any development in Child's political consciousness. The story may express her awareness of narrowing options, however, as she confronted the barriers to winning the freedom and literary laurels of which she had dreamed two years earlier. Clues to the psychosexual anxieties the story betrays are sparse. None of the men in Child's life resembles Joseph, but intriguing parallels do link William with the hero of a much later story, also named William, and clearly modeled on David.[61] Did Child dimly sense the lack of sexual ardor in David that would frustrate her so deeply in their marriage? Or did she simply fear that her own passion might lure her into a marriage she would find stifling? Child's letters do not say. Rather, the picture they reveal of her is buoyantly self-confident.

Shortly after "The Rival Brothers" greeted readers on their New Year's gift tables, Child sat down in her unheated schoolroom to write her sister a retrospective of the past season. Fortune had kept "smiling beyond [her] utmost hopes," she reported to Mary. "The rich and fashionable" patrons she had expected would "consign [her] to oblivion" once she left their parlors for a suburban schoolhouse had remained "as attentive as if [she] were their equal." "I sometimes ask myself can I be the same individual I was . . . two years ago? Can it be that I am on terms of intimacy — nay that I even regard with contempt some of these great people, who used to frighten me at a distance?" she marveled.[62]

The secret of Child's continuing popularity lay in a new turn her literary career had taken the previous September. The Boston publishing firm of Putnam and Hunt had invited her to edit a children's magazine, the first of its kind in the United States. And *The Juvenile Miscellany* had produced a sensation.

3

The Juvenile Miscellany:
The Creation of an American Children's
Literature

"I know what that shout means among the children," said Miss Amy; "the Miscellany has come."

So I ran down stairs and saw Papa with the book in his hand, stooping down to Mary, who was stretching up her neck, and Emily, who was standing tip-toe to get a look at it; while little black Dinah showed her white teeth for joy. Fortunately, there were two numbers, and as soon as they had been ex-am-in-ed by the elder members of the family, Mary took one copy, and Emily the other. I soon heard dear little Emily spelling Ju-ve-line. Then I begged Mary to find Emily an easy place to read; and Mary was good-na-tur-ed enough to stop in the midst of a pretty story, and show her the "Sailor's Dog." Then little Emily looked very earnest, and spelt almost a page, until the bell rang for eight o'clock.[1]

This lively description of "A Family Scene" in Charleston, South Carolina, re-creates the excitement with which the entire household greeted each bimonthly number of Child's *Juvenile Miscellany*. Written by one of the *Miscellany's* chief contributors, the transplanted Bostonian Caroline Howard Gilman, the vignette also captures the spirit of a magazine that served as primer, storybook, "library of entertaining knowledge," and purveyor of moral values. The relations it pictures between parents and children, older and younger siblings, master and servant, suggest the social mission of nineteenth-century children's literature: to promote domestic harmony, provide behavioral models for parents and children to emulate, foster a desire for education, and bridge the gap between the privileged classes and their subordinates.[2]

The presence of the slave child, "little black Dinah," and even more tellingly, the silence as to her actual status (Gilman would soon become an apologist for her adopted region's "peculiar institution"), indicates the conservative nature of this mission.[3] The cultural establishment that sponsored the *Juvenile Miscellany* conceived of children's literature as a buttress for the dominant society's hierarchies of race, class, and gender — not as a site for challenging them.[4]

When Child founded the *Juvenile Miscellany* in 1826, however, she did not perceive the contradiction between promulgating the moral, social, and political ideology of America's white middle class and furthering a vision of racial equality that threatened white hegemony. For most of its eight-year existence, the magazine successfully combined aims whose incompatibility would not become apparent to either its editor or its audience until controversy over slavery polarized the country in the 1830s.

The reminiscences of readers brought up on the *Miscellany* testify to how skillfully Child packaged her dual message and how imaginatively she fused didacticism with entertainment. "No child who read the *Juvenile Miscellany* . . . will ever forget the excitement that the appearance of each number caused," wrote the abolitionist and woman's rights advocate Caroline Healey Dall in 1883, three years after Child's death.[5] The tableau Dall sketched of the neighborhood hubbub on delivery day confirms that Caroline Howard Gilman was not simply puffing the magazine in "A Family Scene."

"The children sat on the stone steps of their house doors all the way up and down Chestnut Street in Boston, waiting for the carrier," recalled Dall. "He used to cross the street, going from door to door in a zigzag fashion; and the fortunate possessor of the first copy found a crowd of little ones hanging over her shoulder from the steps above. . . . How forlorn we were if the carrier was late!" Half a century later, Dall fondly remembered her favorite stories; their mere titles — "Garafelia," "Ferdinand and Zoe," "The Easter Eggs" — still conjured up "vivid pictures of past delight."

Though the *Miscellany* had long been eclipsed by vastly more sophisticated children's magazines, Dall pronounced it superior to its successors "in simplicity, directness, and moral influence." She went on to pay Child the tribute of ranking her above all the children's writers who had inherited her mantle, including Louisa May Alcott, whose popularity has endured into our own day. "Never did any one cater so wisely and so well for the unfolding mind," she asserted.

Alcott herself indirectly acknowledged Child's influence by borrowing a famous episode in *Little Women* — Jo March's decision to help raise money for the family by selling her hair — from a *Juvenile Miscellany* story.[6] Her contemporary Lucy Larcom, an editor of the post–Civil War children's magazine *Our Young Folks*, credited the *Juvenile Miscellany* with inspiring the founding of the millworkers' periodical in which she made her literary debut: *The Lowell Offering*.[7]

Yet another New England writer molded by "that delightful pioneer among children's magazines in America" was the abolitionist Thomas Wentworth Higginson. His 1868 biography of the woman to whom he attributed his conversion to antislavery opened with his "earliest recollections" of the persona she assumed in so many of the *Miscellany*'s dialogues and sketches: "she came before us . . . as some kindly and omnipresent aunt, beloved forever by the heart of childhood, — some one gifted with all lore, and furnished with unfathomable resources, — some one discoursing equal delight to all members of the household."[8]

What accounts for the "delight" Child's juvenile readers took in the magazine, and why did it leave such a lasting impression on them? A prime factor was the novelty of the entertainment and instruction the *Miscellany* offered. Dall, Alcott, Larcom, and Higginson belonged to the first generation of American children to enjoy a magazine and a body of literature produced especially for them. The centuries-old fairy tales and fables we now think of as children's literature did not acquire that function until well into the nineteenth century; in fact, the eighteenth-century British writers who invented the genre of children's literature strongly disapproved of frivolous stories about fairies and witches, which tended, in their view, to warp youthful minds.[9]

A genre self-consciously aimed at socializing children was born at a historical moment when several related developments were interacting to create a need for such a medium.[10] First, the industrial revolution had transformed family relations by taking economic production out of the home and relocating it in factories. Formerly, all but the wealthiest men and women had shared responsibility for earning the family's livelihood and had relegated childrearing to the interstices of household production; as soon as children were old enough to work, they either participated in the family enterprise or were bound out as apprentices. In the industrial era, however, the productive occupations women had once controlled, such as spinning, were taken over by machines. The factory system no longer allowed for combining remunerative work with child care; instead, it demanded a full-time labor force. Reduced to economic dependency, married women of the middle class found themselves redefined purely as homemakers and childrearers.[11]

Second, an unprecedented idealization of childhood accompanied the separation of the domestic and economic spheres. Previously, Europeans had regarded children as miniature adults. Around the age of seven the child began wearing the same clothes and joining in the same household tasks and pastimes as adults. The concept of childhood as a distinctive state of consciousness requiring careful nurture and protection against adult realities did not exist. No one considered it necessary to shield children from exposure to sexuality, for example, since the assumption of the child's pristine innocence had not yet taken hold.[12] Significantly, a new concern for the moral edification of children arose earliest in the middle class, whose economic activity was laying the groundwork for the industrial revolution.

Third, the moral values the middle class stressed — hard work, productivity, usefulness, frugality, self-denial, sobriety, orderliness, punctuality — though originating in the desire to lead a pious life, proved crucial to the development of capitalism. These values, constituting what Max Weber called the "Protestant ethic," sharply distinguished the middle class from both the aristocracy it sought to displace and the working class it sought to regiment.[13]

From the perspective of the middle class, its twin adversaries were mirror images of each other. The idle and profligate aristocracy monopolized power and privileges it had not earned, unjustly barring the advancement of the hard-working, talented entrepreneurs who were revitalizing the British economy. The lower class, equally averse to honest labor and prone to lewd and disorderly conduct, perpetually threatened to disrupt production. Both aristocracy and lower class wasted the society's resources, impeded economic development, and set a bad example to middle-class youth. Against the feudal order of fixed social classes determined by birth, the middle class formulated a new ideology based on the premise that "[m]erit, talent, and hard work should dictate social, economic, and political rewards." According to this ideology, the individual should rely neither on inherited privileges nor on charity but on his or her own unaided efforts: "[T]he individual alone in the market place of merit and talent . . . determined for himself his success or failure."[14]

The future of the middle class hung on the successful transmission of its ideology; middle-class youth must continue to practice the virtues responsible for their fore-bears' prosperity, and other classes must come to accept the bourgeois worldview. Hence, it was no coincidence that some of the very political theorists who formulated bourgeois ideology—John Locke, Joseph Priestley, William Godwin, Mary Woll-stonecraft—also played a role in the creation of children's literature, and that the most influential practitioners of the new genre—Maria Edgeworth and Anna Letitia Bar-bauld—came from the same political circles.[15]

Edgeworth and Barbauld profoundly influenced American writers of Child's genera-tion. Child's first foray into children's literature—*Evenings in New England* (1824)—explicitly invokes these precursors. "To write books for children, after Miss Edgeworth and Mrs. Barbauld have written, is indeed presumptuous," Child concedes, realizing that her readers will compare her book with its famous prototype, Barbauld's *Evenings at Home; or, The Juvenile Budget Opened* (1792). The justification she offers for daring to invade the province of her illustrious predecessors is that their works, "[e]xcellent" though they might be, "are emphatically *English*." By substituting "American scenes and American characters," she has attempted to adapt an English model to the needs of her compatriots.[16] In short, a common nationalist impulse lies behind *Evenings in New England* and *Hobomok*, published six months earlier: American children, like American adults, require a literature of their own—a literature that reflects their circumstances, addresses the problems their society poses, and inculcates values suited to a democratic republic.

Of course, the values Child had infiltrated into *Hobomok* were anathema to the parents who eagerly seized on *Evenings in New England*. Ironically, she had followed up a book denounced as "revolting . . . to every feeling of delicacy in man or woman" with one hailed for "nourishing the plant of virtue in its tenderest age, and protecting the blossom of innocence at a time, when it may so easily be withered and destroyed by the rude assaults to which it is exposed."[17] The paradox is symptomatic of tensions at the heart of Child's career, which repeatedly found her poised between articulating her culture's deepest convictions and pushing those convictions to their most radical limits. In no phase of her career would the tensions surface more dramatically than in her heyday as a children's writer.

When Child assumed the vocation of an American Mrs. Barbauld, she undertook a complex task. In the 1790s Barbauld had represented the vanguard of the bourgeois revolt against aristocratic privilege. A modern historian has described her as "per-haps the most important woman radical" of her day, after Mary Wollstonecraft.[18] Transposed to the United States of the 1820s, however, Barbauld's *Evenings at Home* would have sounded strangely conservative in some ways and uncomfortably radical in others.

The book's setting—a "mansion-house . . . inhabited by the family of FAIRBORNE"— betrays the aristocratic character of eighteenth-century British society. As spelled out in "A Dialogue on Different Stations in Life," class distinctions are strongly marked, and mobility between classes is minimal. For example, on coming home from a visit with the daughter of Sir Thomas Pemberton, Sally Meanwell asks why the Meanwells do not have a richly furnished mansion or ride in a coach like the Pembertons. Her mother answers: "Sir Thomas had a large estate left him by his father; but your papa has little but what he gains by his own industry." She reminds Sally that the Meanwells are better off than "Mr. White the baker, and Mr. Shape the taylor," whose children are happy to receive Sally's cast-off dolls, and that they, in turn, are better off than "Plow-man the labourer," whose children are "dirty and ragged" and suffer from hunger and cold. Never does Mrs. Meanwell suggest that even by hard work, a farm laborer can rise into the artisanal class, or a capitalist into the landed aristocracy.[19]

Accordingly, education serves not to level but to reinforce class distinctions—and the gender distinctions deriving from them. "[I]t is the purpose of all education to fit persons for the station in which they are hereafter to live," Mamma explains to Kitty in "Dialogue, on Things to be Learned." She adds pointedly: "you know there are very great differences in that respect, both among men and women." Kitty's education must train her to perform a middle-class woman's household tasks: marketing, making and mending clothes for the family, and bringing up the children. Thus she must master sewing, handwriting, and enough accounting "to prevent our being overcharged in any thing, and to know exactly how much we spend, and whether or no we are exceeding our income, and in what articles we ought to be more saving." In addition, she should study "the nature of plants, and animals, and minerals, because we are always using some or other of them," and acquaint herself with geography and history (*English* history, as Barbauld's sketches of King Alfred and King Canute indicate). Unlike Miss Rich, Kitty cannot afford to waste time on drawing and music unless circumstances permit.[20] And unlike George and Harry in another dialogue, she will acquire her education primarily from her mother rather than from a tutor. Moreover, her mother's circumscribed role in her education will drive home the inferior position women occupy in a middle-class English household of the 1790s—for it will be the father, not the mother, who reads aloud to the children and teaches them about the world.[21]

If by the 1820s republican America had advanced far beyond the society to which Barbauld had applied her lessons on class and gender, it had never caught up with her radicalism on an issue Americans preferred not to discuss: the assault on "savage" peoples carried out in the name of "civilization." In Barbauld's England, agitation against the slave trade and colonialism had formed part of the bourgeois vanguard's revolt against the old order. Hence, the socialization of bourgeois children could include fostering their sympathy for the victims of colonialism—a component of early bourgeois ideology that would become a liability under a bourgeois regime as dependent on slavery and colonial conquest as the aristocracy it had overthrown.

Listening to his father read about how the Danes used to kidnap Greenlanders on the pretext of instructing them in Christianity and using the converts "to civilize their countrymen," little Edward asks whether "civilized nations [have] any *right* to behave so to savages" and whether "savages [can] think about right and wrong as we do?" "Why not!" answers Father; "are they not *men*?" He proceeds to teach his son that there are "no important difference[s] between ourselves and those people we are pleased to call savage, but in the degree of knowledge and virtue possessed by each."[22]

Barbauld's thinly veiled attack on the colonial ideology used to justify the African slave trade was all too relevant to the United States in the decade that began with a major concession to slaveholders—the Missouri Compromise of 1820—and ended with a congressional vote authorizing Indian removal in 1830. Yet this very fact made Barbauld a doubly problematic model for Child, who inherited both her radicalism and her role in shaping bourgeois ideology to the needs of her generation.

Child's modifications of her prototype in *Evenings in New England*—and later in the *Juvenile Miscellany*—provide fascinating insight into the formation of nineteenth-century American culture and ideology. Her first priority is to substitute American for English history lessons. Accounts of Indian tribes, Plymouth Rock, and Revolutionary generals replace anecdotes about English kings. Even when one of the children protests against this patriotic diet and begs for an old-fashioned story about foreign "kings and nobles," their aunt responds with a description of Lafayette's 1824 visit to Boston.

Signaling major changes in the status of women that further differentiate republican America from aristocratic England, the aunt (and in the *Juvenile Miscellany*, the mother) has now taken over the leading role in the children's education, which Barbauld had accorded to the father and the tutor. In dialogues obviously modeled on Child's own experience of helping to bring up her Norridgewock nieces and nephews, Aunt imparts lessons in history, natural science, trade, and manufactures, as well as moral principles and social values. Nor does she distinguish between her nephew's and niece's educational programs. The dialogues Aunt conducts with Robert on "Personification," "The Rainbow," and "Aurora Borealis" are interchangeable with those she conducts with Lucy on "Oracles," "Trees," "Botanical Hints," and "Gobelins Tapestry." Although Lucy appears less interested than Robert in history, Aunt does not humor her complaint that she is "tired to death of reading" about "battles and revolutions"; instead, Aunt proposes a systematic plan of study, using historical plays and novels to supplement factual texts (9–10).

The issue of class, which had bulked so large in Barbauld's *Evenings at Home*, has metamorphosed into a concern for preserving republican simplicity and virtue in a society offering the possibility of upward mobility. For example, Aunt tells Lucy that "our happiness depends very little upon wealth," but a great deal upon doing "what we know and feel to be right" (59)—advice that poignantly foreshadows the sacrifices Child would make for her principles less than a decade later.

Similarly, a fable about an overly ambitious oak tree illustrates the moral: "Never be anxious to change a humble situation, which you have long proved to be quiet and happy, for the uncertain comforts of wealth, parade, or fame" (28). When the oak's ambition to leave her obscure village for glamorous Boston is realized, she encounters "quite as many chimney-sweepers and beggars, as she [does] fine ladies and gentlemen" in the city. Languishing in the "smoky and unwholesome" air, she is ultimately cut down to make way for a new street (26–28). Urbanization and industrialization, the fable seems to warn, threaten to introduce disparities of wealth into a relatively egalitarian, rural society. Yet these socioeconomic transformations also provide greater opportunities for advancement than in Barbauld's England.

The task of educating children for the station they would occupy in life would prove much more complicated in a society where distinctions among Mr. Meanwell the capitalist, Mr. Shape the tailor, and Plowman the laborer were no longer so clear-cut and permanent, but where the promise of upward mobility could not always be fulfilled. Class conflicts lurk beneath the surface of *Juvenile Miscellany* stories, in which destitute widows and orphans typically succeed through persevering hard work in earning the respect and charity of the rich and thereby climbing up to the plateau of middle-class prosperity.

American bourgeois ideology could neither mask nor resolve conflicts involving race, however, which displaced class discrimination onto targeted Others. To extend the promise of upward mobility to Indians and African Americans, whose extorted land and labor furnished the nation's wealth, would mean overturning the economic foundations of the American republic. Thus, American children's literature could not follow Barbauld's lead in denying the existence of "important differences between ourselves and those people we are pleased to call savage."[23]

Child began struggling with this dilemma in *Evenings in New England*, where the issues of Indian dispossession, the African slave trade, and slavery itself crop up repeatedly in dialogues between Aunt and Robert. Though Aunt consistently transmits the approved ideological message, she never quite manages to allay Robert's humanitarian concerns. It is as if the adult representing the ideology of the dominant society and the youth representing the instinctive sympathies of the heart are vying for Child's allegiance.

The very first selection in *Evenings in New England* betrays Child's discomfort with the subjugation of Indians and Africans in republican America. Intended simply to illustrate the concept of "Personification," it gratuitously cites examples that draw children's attention to the violence of white conquest. Personifying Africa is a "dark looking, naked figure, grappling with a lion, and casting a terrified look upon the vessel which he sees off the coast" (1–2) — an allusion Aunt must explain to Robert, who does not understand why the man should be "alarmed at a ship," when "our merchants send a great many pretty things to Africa." Personifying South America is an "Indian digging up whole shovelfulls of pure gold, and exchanging it with a dark looking man for a rod of iron" (2–3). Aunt cannot personify North America as honestly — the Republic wrapped in her stars and stripes merely looks back from a distance at an Indian holding a bow and arrow. The relationship between the two figures, Aunt tells Robert, symbolizes the "savage state" from which the nation has progressed (3); but by noting that Europeans have replaced the Indians who formerly inhabited North America she also hints at a more sinister meaning of the symbol.

In the dialogue "Indian Tribes," Robert raises the question implicit in Aunt's evasive emblem: "if [Indians] were so very thick when Maine was first settled, where can they all have fled?" (73). The answer that "war and various diseases" have decimated them does not satisfy Robert. "But what right had we to take away their lands?" he persists (74). While assuring Robert that in most cases "the Indians sold their land willingly, and were paid honourably," Aunt admits: "they are too often cruelly imposed upon" by "artful, dishonest men" (74). "How I do wish something could be done to make all the Indians as happy and prosperous as we are," exclaims Robert (78). Pessimistic about whether this "desirable" end can be achieved, Aunt predicts that the Indians will ultimately "cease to exist as a distinct people." Yet Child gives the last word to an Indian spokesman: "You have driven us to the sea-shore, and still you ask us to move on" (78). Soon her white adult mouthpieces would adopt the Indian viewpoint themselves.

The conflict between the white adult's ideology and the white child's emotional impulses is particularly striking in "The Little Master and His Little Slave." A dialogue between Aunt and Robert, it frames a narrative told by a slave to his master's children, and repeated by them to their mother, whose interruptions construct an inner dialogue. On each level a child voices instinctive revulsion against slavery, which an adult tries to contain within a framework of prescriptive commentary.

At the outset, Robert blurts out: "the people at the southward must be very cruel, or they would not keep slaves as they do" (138). Rebuking him for his injustice toward "our southern brethren," Aunt articulates the position shared by well-meaning northern and southern whites in the 1820s, before the founding of a radical abolitionist movement. Slavery is indeed an "indelible stain" on the country's honor, she grants, and "every one that has a single particle of human kindness could not but rejoice to see the Africans released from a state of servitude and oppression." Southerners, however, are not to blame for an institution fastened on the American colonies by the British. "Many of their best men would gladly be rid of it," and Aunt does not doubt that "some time or other," their desire will be fulfilled (138). The process must be gradual, she cautions:

> The negroes are very numerous, and they have been so unused to liberty, that they would become licentious and abandoned if left to themselves. Therefore, all that a good man can do, at present, is to make all the slaves in his power as comfortable as possible, to instruct their children, to give freedom to those who deserve it, to use all his personal influence to remove the evil, and to wait patiently till the curse of slavery can be entirely and safely removed from the land. (139)

In short, Aunt believes emancipation can best be hastened by promoting a spirit of goodwill toward white southerners and by acknowledging the efforts of those who are conscientiously preparing their slaves for freedom.[24]

To convince Robert that "kind masters and grateful slaves are very numerous at the

South," Aunt proceeds to read him the story of "The Little Master and His Little Slave." Yet the story reveals that contrary to Aunt's claims, whippings, forced sales, and the separation of families are essential means of disciplining a refractory labor force, even in "kind" households.

The unmanageable slave child, Ned, causes so much trouble on the plantation and sets such a bad example to his fellow slaves that his master and overseer agree he must be sold. Only the intercession of the master's son, little Edward, saves Ned. (Their identical names — Ned is later referred to as "Eddy" — betoken the white child's identification with the slave). Shielding Ned against the overseer's whip with his own back, Edward promises to "make him good" if his father will give Ned to him (142). The slave expresses his gratitude in a double entendre that ironically equates the kind slaveholder with his brutal overseer: "Now, young master," he says, "this rope ties me to you, as fast as it tied me to the whipping-post" (145). As Ned's metaphor suggests, he will remain a slave. At the end of the story, which Edward's daughters have learned from another slave and recounted to their mother, Ned continues to face the same alternatives of submission or punishment after reaching adulthood. Now it is his mistress, the children's mother, who wants to send this "heedless and inattentive" house slave back to the plantation for field work (146).

Like the dialogue that frames it, the story of "The Little Master and His Little Slave" illustrates the process by which adults socialize children into shifting their sympathies from the slave to the master. Guided by their mother, who strongly disapproves of their fraternizing with slaves, Edward's daughters will follow in his footsteps and grow up to be kind slaveholders. Similarly, Robert arrives at the prevailing antislavery position toward which his aunt has been leading him. Although he still "cannot bear the idea of keeping slaves" — once again Child projects her own humanitarian fervor onto the young boy being socialized — he readily concedes the point his aunt reiterates: "that our Southern brethren have an abundance of kind and generous feeling" (146). Putting himself in their place, he imagines what he would do if he had "a little slave": "I would teach him to read, and write, and cypher, and then I would send him to the island of Hayti, where he might be as free and happy as I am" (147). With one significant difference, his antislavery sentiments have been channeled into a solution formulated by slaveholders like Jefferson and Madison and embraced by the vast majority of the American public: gradual, voluntary emancipation and the expatriation of the freed slaves, so that they would no longer menace either a union built on slavery or a republic unwilling to admit people of color as equal citizens. That difference, however — the substitution of Haiti (a republic founded by slave revolutionaries and not recognized by the U.S. government until the Civil War) for Liberia (the puppet state for emancipated slaves established by the slaveholder-dominated American Colonization Society) — signals Child's predisposition toward the radical abolitionist doctrine she would adopt seven years later.[25]

Not surprisingly, *Evenings in New England* met with "much more unqualified approbation than 'Hobomok,'" as Child reported in a letter to her sister Mary.[26] She had redirected her radical impulses toward a socially sanctioned end—appropriating for her compatriots the legacy of a major bourgeois preceptor. Child's audience immediately recognized that *Evenings in New England* furnished the blueprint for an American children's literature. Praising its "miscellaneous" combination of "fable, dialogue, historical incidents, . . . precept, . . . [and] . . . lessons on the works of nature and art," the *North American Review* asserted: "The book cannot fail to amuse children, it cannot fail to instruct and make them better [by] . . . laying the foundation of a character, which in after life will secure to them the respect of the wise, and the benedictions of the good."[27]

The following year the publisher John Putnam invited Child to edit a magazine for juveniles modeled on *Evenings in New England*. Perhaps because she feared that such a commitment would deflect her from the literary work on which she hoped to build her reputation, Child undertook the project reluctantly. "[S]ome Boston ladies finally persuaded me into it," she confided to Mary.[28] Their role in initiating Child into her new vocation reveals how closely the emergence of children's literature is connected to the economic changes that invested women with the primary responsibility for rearing children, and to the political ideology that apotheosized them as republican mothers. Awarded the sacred task of "instructing their sons in the principles of liberty and government," middle-class American women were naturally among the first to feel the need for an American children's literature.[29]

Financial pressures also spurred Child to accept Putnam's invitation. The profession of letters was highly precarious for American writers of the early nineteenth century, and nearly all of them supplemented the scanty income derived from novels and short stories by resorting periodically to more lucrative genres—histories, biographies, travelogues, political hack writings, religious works, domestic advice books, children's literature—or to ancillary occupations like schoolteaching, which Child was already pursuing.[30]

If she at first regarded the launching of a children's magazine as a deviation from her true vocation, Child soon changed her mind. Writing to Mary four months after issuing the first number of the *Juvenile Miscellany* in September 1826, she sent a pointed message to an old friend from Norridgewock days, the aspiring writer Nathaniel Deering. "Tell N. Deering that children's books are more profitable than any others, and that I am American enough to prefer money to fame." By then she could boast that the *Miscellany*'s subscription list stood at "850 names" and was "every day increasing." "It seems as if the public was resolved to give me a flourish of trumpets, let me write what I will," she remarked naively (little dreaming of the abuse she would receive when she started writing indictments of slavery). "Valuable gifts, jewels, beautiful dresses pour in upon me, invitations beyond acceptance, admiring letters from all parts of the country."[31] As these enthusiastic tributes indicate, the *Miscellany* had filled a vital cultural need at just the right moment.

With the inventiveness she showed so often in her career, Child quickly turned the magazine into a sophisticated professional enterprise. She enlisted a network of contributors that included most of the leading women writers of the day: Lydia Huntley

Sigourney, Catharine Maria Sedgwick, Eliza Leslie, Sarah Josepha Hale, Caroline Howard Gilman, Hannah Flagg Gould, Anna Maria Wells, and a host of others who can no longer be identified. (Contributors typically published under pseudonyms or initials, while Child left her pieces unsigned.) Each of them produced works commissioned especially for the *Miscellany* and tailored to fit the various regular series it featured. Sigourney, Gilman, Gould, Hale, and Wells supplied poems and occasional sketches. Sedgwick, Leslie, "F." of Stockbridge, "Mater," and Child herself provided domestic fiction. "A.B.F." authored moral dialogues between "Mother and Eliza" and "Botanical" dialogues between Mother and Harry. "D**" detailed the habits of insects, and "X.Y.Z." the wonders of "Conchology." "F." (possibly Convers Francis) devoted the column "Scripture Illustrations" to explicating obscure biblical references by drawing on travelers' accounts of Middle Eastern customs. Child, who wrote from one-fourth to one-third of every 108-page number and practiced all these genres, specialized in biographical sketches of American heroes, dialogues on "American History," translations of European fairy tales, and stories of Indians, blacks, and ethnic groups from other continents.[32]

The wide range of selections, enhanced with illustrations and supplemented with riddles, ensured that the *Miscellany* would appeal to children of both sexes and many ages. Every issue opened with an engraved frontispiece accompanying the lead story and closed with verses, puzzles, and the answers to the preceding issue's "conundrums." Fusing "amusement" with "instruction," as the magazine's subtitle proclaimed, fiction served to inculcate moral principles, and whimsical sketches ("Letter from Summer to Winter," "Complaint of the Letter H to his Brother K") conveyed lessons in geography and spelling.

Any modern reader would find the magazine oppressively didactic. Nevertheless, its nonsectarian approach toward forming youthful minds was both liberal and innovative for its day. To appreciate the *Miscellany*'s pioneering character, one need only glance at its chief competitor, *The Youth's Companion*, which began publication seven months later, in April 1827 — under the editorship of Nathaniel Willis, the father of Child's dandified beau.[33] Willis's "Prospectus" clearly distinguished his aim from Child's. Unlike extant "Literary Magazines for youth, which exclude[d] religious topics" or emphasized "mere amusement," the *Youth's Companion* would give priority to "articles of a religious character." Accordingly, Willis's four-page weekly consisted almost entirely of brief anecdotes centering on children's conversion experiences or exemplary deaths. The titles speak for themselves: "Death Bed Scene of a Child Six Years Old," "A Child's Prayer for His Minister," "Force of Conscience." Moreover, despite Willis's claim that the *Companion* would be broader in scope than "Tract and Sabbath School Magazines," he borrowed the preponderance of his selections from those sources.

Willis's narrow religious focus left no room for educational articles, like the natural history essays and dialogues that occupied such a prominent place in the *Miscellany*. Even when Willis introduced a natural history department in the *Companion* (perhaps in response to the popularity of the *Miscellany*'s), he gave it a biblical stamp. A brief

article on "The Elephant," for example, assembled biblical references to the animal and speculated about whether to identify it with Job's Behemoth. In contrast, Child and her contributors were using natural history in the spirit of the Deist Thomas Paine and the Unitarian scientist Joseph Priestley — to exemplify the workings of an "All-Wise Providence" that had fashioned all creatures for the "necessities of their situation."[34]

Further, because the *Companion* eschewed anything that smacked of levity, riddles and conundrums were out of the question. Willis did eventually bow to the public taste for illustrations, but the tiny engravings he squeezed sideways into the upper left-hand corner of the *Companion* betrayed the reluctance with which he must have followed Child's lead.

Indeed, nothing could testify more eloquently to the *Miscellany*'s role as a trendsetter in the field it inaugurated than its gradual infiltration of its conservative rival. Within a few months of its founding, the *Youth's Companion* was already reprinting poems, didactic dialogues, and moral sketches from the *Miscellany*. At first, Willis confined himself to borrowings compatible with the *Companion*'s religious orientation, such as the poem "Mother, What is Death?" by Gilman and the pious account of "The Deaf, Dumb, and Blind Girl" by Sigourney. Yet before long he began reprinting Child's biographical sketches of William Penn, Tadeusz Kościuszko, and Baron de Kalb (Lafayette's Polish and German analogues). By September 1828 he was even reprinting Child's celebrated stories, "The Cottage Girl" and "Garafelia" — material he had formerly stigmatized as "frivolous."[35]

Revealingly, the only items Willis never borrowed from the *Miscellany* were Child's stories about Indians and blacks. Constituting the magazine's most original feature, they also mark the limits of the influence Child exerted on the development of the fledgling genre. Willis realized what the young woman from whom he learned his craft refused to admit — that children's literature could not fulfill its socializing mission if it defied the prejudices of the dominant society. Hence, he contented himself with accounts of converted Indians and pious slaves.[36]

Although the *Youth's Companion* and the *Juvenile Miscellany* represented opposite poles in the spectrum of early nineteenth-century American children's literature, which ranged from Calvinist orthodoxy to Unitarian liberalism, they shared a commitment to inculcating the middle-class value system. American children's literature of the 1820s, like its British prototype of the 1790s, had a critical role to perform while the nation was shifting to an industrial capitalist economy. Along with schools, churches, and the myriad societies for the Promotion of Industry, Frugality, and Temperance that sprang up in the mid-1820s, children's literature served to disseminate the bourgeois work ethic so essential to capitalist production. As one historian has explained, the objective of all these cultural agencies was to create "an orderly society" in which "[c]itizens would be self-reliant, hard-working, and sober; obedient to their superiors; attentive to their labors; and self-disciplined in all their pursuits.[37]

Indoctrination in the bourgeois virtues is ubiquitous in the *Miscellany*. "Industry conquers every thing" reads the motto on the opening volume's frontispiece, which pictures a man tilling the fields, against a symbolic backdrop of paired beehives. Through sermons, dialogues, biographical sketches of bourgeois heroes, and stories of children whose industry, frugality, and perseverance overcome all obstacles, Child and her contributors drive home the message that sound work habits and austere living earn their rightful reward.

Symptomatically, Benjamin Franklin appears often in early issues of the *Miscellany*. A recurrent figure even in British classics of children's literature, Franklin personified the conjunction of the Protestant ethic and the spirit of capitalism.[38] In fact, Max Weber illustrates the hallmarks of the capitalist ethos — obsessive concern with making and saving money as ends in themselves, and "strict avoidance of all spontaneous enjoyment of life" — by quoting copiously from the famous passage in Franklin's *Advice to a Young Tradesman* beginning: "Remember, that *time* is money."[39] Franklin had urged his compatriots to emulate the diligence responsible for his fabled rise from "Poverty and Obscurity . . . to a State of Affluence and some Degree of Reputation in the World"; and lest they miss the point, he catalogued the thirteen virtues he deemed paramount — temperance, silence, order, resolution, frugality, industry, sincerity, justice, moderation, cleanliness, tranquillity, chastity, humility — and scrupulously charted his method of acquiring them.[40]

Child's own parents had proved the validity of both the principles Franklin articulated and the democratic promise of upward mobility that his career exemplified. Convers and Susannah Rand Francis, too, had struggled out of poverty into comparative affluence, thanks to their unwearied industry and rigid economy, and two of their children had advanced from the ranks of artisan-shopkeepers into the intelligentsia, by applying themselves equally industriously to their studies. The Francis family had likewise known the sense of community responsibility that tempered the harsher aspects of Franklin's philosophy. Just as Franklin had founded institutions for the public good and sponsored charities for the relief of the poor, Convers and Susannah had looked after less fortunate neighbors like Ma'am Betty, and, in turn, notables like Governor John Brooks and the Reverend David Osgood had helped further their son Convers's education. No wonder, then, that Child devoted the *Miscellany* to transmitting the bourgeois ideology Franklin had so compellingly propounded.

Child's first New Year's message to *Miscellany* readers, "Value of Time," invokes Franklin's authority. "It is your duty, — a solemn, and serious duty, — to make good use of the time God has given you," she exhorts. Assuring children that it is vital to their happiness to be "always employed," she advises: "Make a regular arrangement of your time. Devote some hours to study, some to walking, some to work, and some to play." Significantly, however, when Child quotes Franklin's dictum "Time is money," she amends it to reflect what she values most highly: "time is learning too. That is, a diligent use of it, will procure both wealth and knowledge."[41]

Child similarly adapts Franklin's message to her own ends in her biographical sketch of him, which singles out three causes for his "rise in the world": the "spirit of enterprise" he manifested, the "habits of close observation" he cultivated, and the "economy" he developed into a fine art. Franklin was "frugal in his own expenses; frugal in his system of politics; and frugal even in his words," comments Child pithily, foreshadowing her appropriation of his role in *The Frugal Housewife* two years later (1829). The qualification she immediately adds — "Yet his economy seems to have had no touch of meanness" — is characteristic of a woman repeatedly portrayed by her contemporaries as "denying herself every luxury and many common comforts, in order to compass the power to relieve or to prevent suffering."[42] Child proceeds to credit Franklin with a style of generosity she herself would practice to the end of her life: "He was always willing to lend money to those who were entering life destitute; and when these people were able and willing to pay him, he would often say, 'Lend it to the first poor tradesman you find, who is industrious and honest; and tell him to lend it to another, as soon as he is able to spare it. In this way, with a small sum of money, I shall do good to the end of time.' "[43] Summarizing the lessons of Franklin's career, Child holds it up as a model of middle-class virtue that the idle rich would do well to imitate — a pervasive theme in children's literature.[44] "[I]f the laugh of the gay and fashionable, should ever make industry and economy appear like contemptible virtues," she admonishes her readers, "let them remember that Benjamin Franklin, a poor, hard-working mechanic, became by means of these very virtues, a philosopher, whose discoveries were useful and celebrated throughout Europe" (2: 22–23). Once again, Child's version of Franklin's success story subtly modifies it to stress his acquisition of knowledge, rather than wealth, and to define usefulness to humanity as his ultimate achievement.

Franklin is only the best-known of the exemplars Child enlists to school her juvenile readers in the values they must internalize, if they are to become the hard-working, enterprising citizens the American republic needs. Like Franklin, two of the other paragons she cites — the traveler John Ledyard and the painter Benjamin West — demonstrate that by resolutely adhering to these values, Americans can win recognition for their country, as well as for themselves.[45] Ledyard teaches "the important lesson of *perseverance*" by braving the snows of Lapland and Siberia and the "[b]urning sands" of the African desert, and by pursuing his voyages of discovery, even when reduced to "utter poverty." And West shows how much "industry, ingenuity, and perseverance" can accomplish, when he becomes "an artist of first rate eminence — admired and respected by the nobility of London, Paris, and Rome — " after fabricating a paintbrush with a black cat's tail and learning from the Indians how to make red and yellow paint.[46]

Although all of the bourgeois heroes the *Miscellany* celebrates in its biographical sketches are men, Child preaches the same values to girls in her didactic dialogues and stories. A particularly interesting instance is "Mother and Eliza" in the first number of the *Miscellany*. Markedly different from the mother-daughter dialogues later contributed by "A.B.F.," it seems to reflect Child's feminist and antiracist concerns.[47]

In response to Eliza's complaint that the composition her teacher has assigned is beyond her capacity, Mother tells a story contrasting a little girl who gives up too easily with her brother who perseveres. The little girl, Mother suggests, has never learned to persevere, because her thoughts have been occupied by dress and other "trifling amusements," and "trifles always tend to weaken the character, and excuse exertion." Her brother, meanwhile, has "thought more of the necessity of studying and improving himself," because he has been "fitting for college" and preparing "to become a man." Implying that girls ought to be given the same training and opportunities as boys, Mother reiterates "the necessity of being interested in something important, solid and useful."[48] Mother realizes, however, that sermons on perseverance are not enough, and that little girls must be given confidence in their abilities. Thus, she suggests a composition based on an account Eliza heard of a sea captain's visit to China. Once Eliza has recalled the details of that account, she sees that she has more than enough material for a composition. At the same time, the captain's description of the Chinese serves to amplify Mother's lesson on perseverance, by compelling respect for a foreign people who exhibit the prime bourgeois virtues. The Chinese are so "industrious" and "ingenious," Eliza remembers, that they contrive to perform several tasks simultaneously. The women, for example, iron clothes by sitting on them, which leaves their hands and feet free for other work! Such a people, comments Mother, would not say "because a thing was difficult, that *they could not do it*" (1: 42).

If Child preaches perseverance and industry to girls and boys alike, her fiction nevertheless reveals inadvertently that the rewards of practicing those virtues are far greater for boys. The story "The Industrious Family" (1831) illustrates the constraints of gender even as it seeks to transcend them. Its competent, responsible heroine, Ellen Temple, may well be Child's answer to Charlotte Temple, the fallen woman who gave her name to Susanna Rowson's best-selling novel of seduction ("few works do so much harm to girls of fourteen or fifteen," Child warns in *The Mother's Book*, published the same year as "The Industrious Family"). The eldest in a family of orphans, Ellen dutifully raises her brothers and sisters:

> She was a good Latin, Italian, and French scholar, painted beautifully, and played with great taste on the harp and guitar. But for all she was so accomplished, she thought it no shame to work with her own hands for the support of her orphan brothers and sisters. For several years after her father's death, she was too poor to pay a domestic; and the noble-minded girl, without a murmur, made the butter, cooked the food, and kept the little swarm of children as neat and busy as so many bees.[49]

Ellen's industry, frugality, and self-denial shield the family against starvation and inspire her brothers and sisters to emulate her.

Child's point is that they *must* emulate her for the family to survive. This is not a story of female self-sacrifice, but of socialization into the bourgeois virtues that ensure individual and collective prosperity — among them respect for manual labor. Hence, it is as important for Ellen's brother John to exercise self-denial as it is for Ellen to "work with her own hands." Like Child's brother Convers, John has a passion for books, and "if he had cared only about pleasing himself, he would have read from morning till night; but he knew this would be selfish; and he cheerfully worked in the garden and about the house, without allowing himself an hour a day for his favorite occupation."[50]

Ultimately, a fairy godfather shows up in the person of a sea captain uncle who rewards the children for their assiduity. The moral that God helps those who help themselves is explicit: "God always provides a way for such industrious, kind-hearted little ones" (221). Child's insistence on male self-denial is equally explicit—because John has shown himself to be "a good, hard-working boy, willing to deny [himself] for the sake of others" (225), his uncle enables him to fulfill his dream of attending college.

The disparity between the rewards the male and female siblings earn, however, drastically undercuts Child's efforts to establish a single standard of virtue for both sexes. While John becomes "a lawyer of great reputation" and his brother, William, also helped by their uncle to pursue his studies, makes "a large fortune by his success in machines" (228), what of Ellen and her sisters? The best to which they can aspire is to marry men like their brothers—a clergyman in Ellen's case, and wealthy manufacturers in the case of her sisters.

This gender inequality is all the more conspicuous in a magazine that marks such an advance beyond the strict sexual stereotyping of early British children's literature, with its unrelieved subordination of women to men.[51] Yet it is also symptomatic of the contradictions that pervade nineteenth-century children's literature—and the bourgeois ideology it promulgates. Again and again, the egalitarian claims of bourgeois ideology conflict with the patently inferior position it accords women, the poor, and people of color.

"The Industrious Family," like most stories in the *Miscellany*, presents poverty as a temporary reverse, which hard work and frugality can always overcome. As "F. of Stockbridge" puts it in a similar story, "In this favored land, no one, who is blessed with health, and willing to be industrious and economical, need be destitute of the comforts of life."[52] Child specifically attributes her young protagonists' good fortune to their industry and self-denial. "I am sure you need not ask if they prospered in the world," she writes in an aside to readers (221). "The prudent and industrious generally contrive to accomplish their purposes, in one way or another," agrees "F. of Stockbridge." The children's status as orphans underscores the message that they have had nothing to rely on but themselves. Commenting on the ubiquity of orphans in children's literature, the historian Isaac Kramnick explains: "Orphans allow a personalization of the basic bourgeois assumption that the individual is on his or her own, free from the weight of the past, from tradition, from family." By definition, orphans are responsible "for their own fate," forced back on "their own hard work, self-reliance, merit, and talent."[53]

How ironic, then, that Child must resort to a deus ex machina—the proverbial rich uncle—to rescue the children from poverty. This device, so frequent in *Miscellany* stories, implicitly acknowledges that hard work and frugality do *not* suffice, that the poor cannot be left to rely on themselves, but must instead be helped out of poverty and given financial support if they are to acquire the education needed for upward mobility. As a vehicle for solving the problem of poverty, the deus ex machina also masks the reality of class conflict. Usually, this figure is not a relative, but a rich person who expects some deference in return for charity. Needless to say, neither giver nor recipient ever questions the social structure or suggests that charity may be a right, not a privilege to be earned by good behavior. The traditional happy ending of such stories — a marriage between the poor person and the rich patron's son or daughter — neatly averts class conflict by promising selective upward mobility.

The story "Louisa Preston" (1828) is typical.[54] Its heroine, a poor washerwoman's daughter, is almost thwarted in her attempts to educate herself for a career as a primary schoolteacher: "[I]t took so much of her time to assist her mother in washing, to mend her brother's clothes, and to tend the baby, that it seemed to be almost impossible for her to get her lessons" (58). In addition to the heavy workload she must carry in a household too poor to allow her the leisure for studying, Louisa faces the obstacle of class snobbery, as her rich schoolmates taunt her for her patched clothes. Predictably, Child moralizes: "But to the industrious and persevering, nothing is impossible; and Louisa Preston, with all her discouragements, was always the best scholar in school" (58).

The opportunity for Louisa to achieve her goal arises when it is announced that the student who demonstrates the most thorough command of ancient and modern geography will earn "a handsome copy of Miss Edgeworth's 'Moral Tales,' and one year's education at the best school in the city" (64). Twice, however, Louisa is forced to drop out of school for weeks at a time to nurse her mother and sister through serious illnesses. Thus, her rich classmate Hannah White ends up winning the prize.

Realistically, the story recognizes that poor students cannot compete on equal terms with their rich classmates and that the odds against them are overwhelming. What finally allows Louisa to fulfill her ambition is the charity she earns through her virtuous behavior. First, the mothers of her classmates, hearing of Louisa's "good character," present her with "plain, neat suits of clothes" and give her mother "constant employment" (69). Then, her rival Hannah, who had formerly made fun of her, publicly admits that Louisa would have earned the prize had she not been obliged to nurse her mother and sister. As a result, the school examiners give prizes to both girls. In the end, Louisa not only succeeds in becoming a teacher, but she manages to send her brother to college. Consummating her advancement to middle-class status, she marries Hannah White's brother.

The threat of class conflict is very much on the surface of this story, which honestly acknowledges the enormous gulf between rich and poor. Yet Child defuses that threat by showing how the barriers of class can be transcended. Louisa's virtuous behavior literally reconciles class conflicts: it elicits the charity of the rich, sets a standard of morality they come to emulate, and culminates in a marriage of classes (paralleling the recurrent interracial marriages in Child's fiction for adults). The fact Child overlooks is that such a solution puts the burden of reconciliation on the poor and obfuscates the causes of poverty.

If adopting bourgeois habits of industry, perseverance, and self-denial opens the door to upward mobility, by implication the reverse is also true — the poverty of those who fail to achieve upward mobility can be blamed on their stubborn persistence in lower-class habits of sloth, improvidence, and drunkenness (the epitome of self-indulgence). "The Brothers, or . . . The Influence of Example" (1827) takes precisely this line. The story contrasts two pairs of poor brothers who respond differently to upper-class programs for the socialization and uplift of the working class. The first pair, Charles and George, work during the week to help their widowed mother support the family, and they attend the Sunday school provided for the village poor. The second pair, Lying Harry and Skulking Dick, waste their time playing truant in the woods and getting drunk. Worse, they exert a pernicious influence over all the poor boys of the village by denouncing the Sunday school as a sop for poor folk, about which "the Squire and the Parson feel mighty grand." George temporarily falls under their sway and nearly forfeits the respect of the other villagers, but thanks to his brother Charles's virtuous example, he repents in time.[55]

Here, as in "Louisa Preston" and "The Industrious Family," hard work and sobriety earn Charles and George the charity they need to further their education; and education, in turn, allows them to rise in the world. Charles obtains a post in "one of the best schools in the state — the income of which made him much richer than he ever expected to be," and George invents a machine and becomes a wealthy manufacturer. In "The Brothers," however, Child meets the threat of class conflict head-on, explicitly drawing a social rather than an individual moral: "New England is a blessed land. In every corner of it there are people willing and able to assist those who are anxious to gain knowledge" (2: 219). That is, Charles and George owe their good fortune not merely to their own efforts, but to a society that deals justly with the poor and rewards the well-deserving. Such a society obviously needs no redistribution of wealth to eliminate poverty.

Because they reject this ideological premise, Lying Harry and Skulking Dick come to bad ends — if they accepted it, they would realize that it is in their interests to conform to their superiors' ethic of hard work and sobriety. Growing so dissolute that no one will employ them, they sink deeper into poverty, until they are finally imprisoned for robbery. Although he learns his lesson too late, Skulking Dick endorses the story's moral with his dying breath. His fate, he admits, is the result of Harry's bad example; had he followed Charles' path, he, too, might have become a prosperous middle-class citizen.

Interestingly, recent historical studies tend to support the contention that workers who adopted their employers' bourgeois ethic did actually enjoy greater upward mobility than the "traditionalists" who "clung to customs and habits inherited from the loose . . . morality" of the preindustrial era. Often, however, these "model workers" were "bound by ties of kinship, religion, or neighborhood" to their employers, and thus they were more prone to embrace an ideology that blamed poverty on "idleness and self-indulgence rather than [on] exploitation."[56]

Stories like "The Brothers" naturally minimize such factors. Even more significantly, they omit an alternative represented by a third group of workers, whom Paul Faler calls "rebel mechanics" — the alternative of adopting the bourgeois moral code while rejecting bourgeois ideology. The rebels articulated what the Lying Harrys and Skulking Dicks inchoately felt — that their employers' wealth was the product not just of "hard work, self-reliance, and shrewdness," but also of "petty fraud and heartless extortion." "The most vigorous opponents of capitalist exploitation," they used bourgeois work discipline "in their own class interest" to struggle for higher wages, and they refused to be bought off by the promise of selective upward mobility.[57] In short, they embodied the specter of class conflict that nineteenth-century children's literature sought to exorcise.

Paradoxically, children's literature harked back to the past even while it looked ahead to the future. As an instrument for creating the disciplined labor force required by the developing industrial capitalist economy, children's literature helped propel nineteenth-century America into a new era. Yet when confronting the terrible urban poverty produced by industrial capitalism, the genre offered a solution rooted in the communal ethic of the preindustrial village.

None of Child's *Miscellany* stories dramatizes the contradiction more poignantly than "The Cottage Girl" (1828). What makes this tale of urban poverty particularly revealing is that Child rewrote it in 1856, after three decades of mushrooming urbanization and accelerating immigration had completely transformed the America of her youth. Titling the new version "Rosy O'Ryan," she registered the changes: the replacement of the native-born American poor by still poorer Irish immigrants; the widening gap between them and the rich in cities that intensified the anonymity of the destitute; the diminishing opportunities for upward mobility. She also noted the elements of a future solution — solidarity among the poor themselves. Nevertheless, she ended the story as she had in 1828, by symbolically restoring the rural community of the past.[58]

The two versions of "The Cottage Girl" are revealing in another respect. Issues of class and gender intersect in both, but "Rosy O'Ryan" expresses the heightened feminist consciousness fostered by the women's rights movement of the 1830s and 1840s. In addition, it exhibits increased familiarity with the lives of urban working-class women, thanks to the nine years Child had spent in New York from 1841 to 1850, during which she had frequently visited slums, asylums, and prisons.

Set in Boston (though its oddly incongruous title foreshadows the rural haven the story offers its heroine), "The Cottage Girl" can no longer assume a village community like that of "Louisa Preston," in which the plight of a deserving poor family comes naturally to the attention of prosperous neighbors, whose charity can be relied on. Instead, the wealthy seem unaware of the misery around them and unconcerned about the welfare of the washerwomen and scullions they hire to do their menial labor. "The rich people, for whom [Mrs. Wood] worked with patient drudgery, paid her wages, and thought nothing more about her," writes Child ("Rosy" 159). To dispel this callous indifference, she brings home to her readers what poverty means. "[I]t is harder work than many rich little girls imagine, to earn enough to eat, and coarse clothes to wear," she points out, explaining why Mrs. Wood, "a poor woman, whose husband had left her with two little children, to support herself as she could," ends up dying of overwork ("CG" n.s. 1: 3).

In the 1856 version, which fleshes out the hardships such a woman faces, Child turns the deserted Mrs. Wood of "The Cottage Girl" into a battered wife, whom she renames Mrs. O'Ryan: "Mary O'Ryan was a poor Irish woman, whose husband spent all his wages for strong drink. She went out to do washing and scouring, and left her little ones at home for some kind neighbour to look after; as many a poor woman is obliged to do. When she returned after a day of hard work, she often found her husband intoxicated, and he would beat her cruelly, to make her give him the money she had earned" ("Rosy" 158).

Of course, the portrayal of the Irish husband as a drunkard and wife-beater falls into ethnic stereotyping. Now, however, Child recognizes that lower-class women must work—and leave their children in the care of neighbors—regardless of whether or not they have husbands. In fact, the death of her husband at least gives Mrs. O'Ryan "control of her own wages" ("Rosy" 160). The problem is the inadequacy of those wages and the severance of the bonds that had once prompted rich people to relieve the distress of their poor neighbors.

In both "The Cottage Girl" and "Rosy O'Ryan," the only person who comes to the help of the distressed mother is a "poor washer-woman" (named Mrs. Kinsey in the former, Mrs. Wood in the latter). "A great many people in Boston would have helped . . . if they had known" of the family's need, Child concedes in "The Cottage Girl," yet she implies that their ignorance is almost willful. Those who see the hearse go by know that it is "some poor person['s], because no carriages and very few people" follow it. Still, they do not think to inquire about the circumstances. Child contrasts their heedlessness with the washerwoman's kindness: "Every night, after she had finished her hard day's work, she used to go in and ask how neighbor Wood did, and give the children a portion of her own supper" ("CG" n.s. 1: 5, 7). In "Rosy O'Ryan" Child sharpens her social criticism, pointedly commenting: "Benevolence is commendable in the rich, who can give away ten dollars without depriving themselves of any thing they need; but in the sight of God and angels it is less beautiful and holy than the generosity of the poor. No one knew how often Mrs. Wood was obliged to deny herself a cup of tea, or a morsel of meat, because she had used up her small funds to feed Mary O'Ryan's famishing children" ("Rosy" 159).

Child develops the bonding of the two women into a major theme of "Rosy O'Ryan," where the washerwoman Mrs. Wood shelters Mary O'Ryan and her children during Mr. O'Ryan's drunken sprees, and the two enjoy a "rivalry of mutual kindness" for a year before Mrs. O'Ryan takes ill ("Rosy" 160–61). Another new element Child adds to "Rosy O'Ryan" is the transformation of the friendship into a cross-ethnic alliance. By making Mrs. Wood English and Mrs. O'Ryan Irish, Child suggests that feminist sisterhood and class solidarity can transcend ethnic divisions.

Yet Child never perceives the sisterhood and solidarity of the poor as alternatives to the charity of the rich. If the poor can alleviate each other's suffering, they cannot help each other to achieve upward mobility. And upward mobility remains the only solution Child can envision to the problem of poverty. Thus, despite having shown that the urban rich are utterly oblivious of poverty, Child must find a way of eliciting their charity in order to save the washerwomen and her adopted children from the fate of the dead mother. Suddenly, employers and landlords who have hitherto failed to manifest the slightest curiosity about the struggling family learn of the washerwoman's generosity and resolve to assist her.

That assistance inevitably takes the form of transplanting the family to a rural environment and providing the children with opportunities for advancement. Adopted by
a wealthy family, the son becomes a "prosperous" manufacturer in the 1828 text, and a
"civil engineer . . . profitably employed in the construction of railroads" in the 1856
text, where his adopted family suffers financial reverses obliging him to make "his own
way in the world" ("Rosy" 188). His sister can only improve her status through marriage. She grows up with the washerwoman, refusing to abandon her even when invited
to join her brother's family some years later, but ultimately "marrie[s] a sensible,
industrious man, who own[s] a good farm" ("CG" n.s. 1: 18–19; "Rosy" 188).

The divergence of the children's paths raises several issues the story attempts to
address but fails to resolve satisfactorily. First, it calls attention to a major disadvantage
of upward mobility—the gulf created between a successful individual and the family
and class he or she leaves behind. Second, it suggests the unnaturalness of class distinctions, which literally subvert the principle of human brotherhood by dividing brother
from sister. Third, it reflects the limitations that gender places on upward mobility.

Child's response to all three issues is to bridge differences. Although the sister
initially finds it "strange" that "*her own brother—her twin brother*, too . . . should be
dressed so much better" than she is, she tells herself she is glad he is "so well off" and
philosophizes: "after all, I don't believe he is a bit happier than I am" ("CG" n.s. 1: 15–
16). For his part, her brother has an impulse to "put on a frock, and come to work in
[his sister's] garden." (In "Rosy O'Ryan" he has the opposite impulse of wanting to
support his sister and her adopted mother, "so that they need not work so hard," but
the washerwoman, speaking for Child, admonishes him: "work is a good thing; and
nobody can be happy without it" ["Rosy" 183]). The irony Child confronts here is basic
to bourgeois ideology: once attained, the bourgeois goal of acquiring wealth and bet-
tering one's condition threatens the ethic of hard work and frugality that distinguishes
the virtuous middle class from the idle rich.[59] Hence, the upwardly mobile individual
must relearn the necessity of hard work from the poor.

Also serving to bridge the class differences between brother and sister in "The
Cottage Girl" is charity. The brother's wealthy adopted parents send his sister "to a
good school" and make her frequent "presents of neat, suitable clothing" ("CG" n.s. 1:
18). Not only has Child reconstituted the village environment of "Louisa Preston,"
with its communal ethic binding rich and poor; she has actually converted the two
classes into one big family in which all have their proper places. Significantly, she
cements the union of rich and poor through the ritual that had epitomized the communal ethic in the Medford of her childhood. Every Thanksgiving, brother and sister sit
down together at her "plain, but plentiful table," which symbolizes their reciprocal
relations ("CG" n.s. 1: 18–19).

The difference the story does not succeed in bridging is that of gender. As in "The
Industrious Family," Child cannot realistically provide male and female siblings with
the same opportunities for advancement. No amount of schooling can permit a girl to
become an engineer or manufacturer. By taking her urban orphan out of the city and
marrying her off to a farmer, Child implies what a number of feminist historians have

argued — that most women were better off under the domestic economy of the past, in which they controlled many remunerative activities, than they were under industrial capitalism.[60] Child's solution to the problem of urban workingwomen's immiseration is thus to restore them to their previous status as productive members of self-sufficient rural households. This solution becomes especially obvious in "Rosy O'Ryan," which ends with a catalog of the productive occupations in which Mrs. Wood and her adopted daughter engage on the farm: Mrs. Wood "made many hundred pounds of butter for the market; and when she was too old to do that, she sat in her rocking-chair, sewing woolen mats, or knitting stockings for all the family. . . . Rosy was too busy to attend much to a flower garden; but she *would* find time to put a few seed in the ground" so as to enjoy the sight of flowers "while she was skimming milk in her pantry" ("Rosy" 188–89).

In their very celebration of bourgeois ideology, stories like "The Cottage Girl," "Rosy O'Ryan," "Louisa Preston," "The Brothers," and "The Industrious Family" repeatedly betray that ideology's contradictions. Promising all citizens equal opportunity to enjoy the benefits of American democracy, the stories distribute opportunities and benefits unequally among men and women, rich and poor. Serving to socialize children into an industrial capitalist society, they repudiate the consequences of capitalist development and resurrect the rural past. Extolling individualism and self-reliance, they re-create class relations of mutual dependency. Blaming poverty on idleness and hymning the rewards of hard work and self-denial, they depict a world in which the poor die of overwork and the rich pay others a pittance to do their cleaning, washing, and sewing. Yet these stories also convey the power and persuasiveness of the ideology they promulgate. It is easy to understand why Child's juvenile readers and their parents found the magazine so compelling.

The organs of the cultural establishment provide ample evidence of how highly Child's contemporaries valued the ideological work the *Juvenile Miscellany* performed. The prestigious *North American Review*, while admitting that children's literature lay "beyond our jurisdiction," made a special point of recommending the *Miscellany* and expressing "respect for an accomplished lady, to whom we have been indebted for entertainment in former times." Sarah Hale's *Ladies' Magazine* reviewed several numbers and urged "every family where there are children" to subscribe. Indeed, wrote Hale, "grown people would not find their time misspent while perusing its pages, which is more than we would be willing to say in favor of, at least, one half of the new publications that are thronging us. . . ." Perhaps the most telling index of the *Miscellany*'s cultural significance is the amount of exposure it received in the *American Traveller*, a gossipy, widely circulated Boston newspaper with an attractive literary page. The *Traveller* greeted each issue of the *Miscellany* as it appeared, occasionally reprinted selections from it, and singled out "The Cottage Girl" for special praise as a story set in "this city" and "calculated to rivet the attention, please the fancy and improve the mind." This newspaper's many enthusiastic reviews best sum up the achievement of the magazine it hailed as the " 'Children's North American' ":

The fair editor . . . has a peculiar tact for extracting the pith from subjects, dry and obscure in themselves, though important and useful, and presenting it to her youthful readers in the most pleasing and attractive forms.

Miss Francis, with the aid of several lady contributors of high literary attainments, succeeds, beyond the anticipations of her friends, in sustaining the popular character of the Juvenile Miscellany; and each successive number . . . presents us with something new, something palatable, and something to gratify and instruct the tender juvenile mind.

[T]he whole [is] adapted to the juvenile capacity, and eminently calculated to give a proper direction to the expanding passions and sympathies of the heart. . . . [T]he useful lessons and valuable principles of *"Aunt Maria,"* will hereafter, we are confident, in many instances, be remembered as the first incentives to distinction and usefulness.[61]

Within a year of founding the *Miscellany*, Child had achieved her goal of professional independence. The magazine was not only winning universal acclaim, but clearing $300 a year in profits for its editor—more than enough to support her. Child was leading an extraordinarily busy, productive life—teaching school for six hours a day; carrying on an extensive correspondence with contributors, printers, and subscribers; writing her share of each bimonthly number; continuing to submit fiction to the gift books through which she sought to maintain her literary reputation; and enjoying the attention being lavished on her by a large circle of admirers.[62] But whether or not she suspected it, her freedom as a single woman was drawing to a close.

4

A Marriage of True Minds: Espousing the Indian Cause

I blush that I should have been absolutely engaged more than a week without having found a moment to tell you of the important news. Mr. Child's extreme devotion, and my own excess of happiness, must form my excuse for this negligence. Indeed, dear sister, I am happy, — happy, beyond my own imagination, — and that is saying much. . . . Since an explanation has taken place, I find that mutual interest has long existed between us and that we have both been playing hide and go seek, for various idle reasons; but it is all ended, now, — and I am happier than ever any woman was in reciprocated affection.[1]

Child's ecstatic letter to her sister Mary, announcing her engagement to "D. L. Child Esq" on October 18, 1827, intimates that despite their instant attraction to each other almost three years ago, she and David had been carrying on an elaborate masquerade to avoid getting drawn into marriage. "Their intercourse was mostly banter and mutual criticism, amounting sometimes to what might be taken as evidence of mutual repugnance," confirms an adolescent observer of their peculiar courtship, George Ticknor Curtis, at whose mother Lois's home in Cambridge the couple frequently met. The proposal scene, on which young Curtis had eavesdropped, had followed the same odd pattern. David had arrived on horseback at nine o'clock in the evening, and the "*dé-nouement*" had taken all of four hours. "Mr. Child pressed his suit most earnestly," the unseen fifteen-year-old witness later recalled. "The lady was a long time in making up her mind. Ten o'clock came, then eleven, then twelve." In the interval, "grown impatient and no doubt very cold and hungry," the horse David had left tied to a post at the Curtis's front door kept pawing the wooden steps of the porch and stomping away, repeatedly forcing the no less impatient lover to interrupt his wooing and run outside to pacify his mount. At last, just as the clock struck one, horse and rider departed. Once the clatter of hoofs had receded, the author of *Hobomok* burst into her friend's room to tell her that she was engaged to David Lee Child.[2]

Meanwhile, her fiancé hastened to communicate the thrilling news to his mother: "I am the luckiest dog that ever lived. I am E-N. en, G-A-G. engag, E-D. ed — ENGAGED, for to be married; & to one of the brightest & best of beings; to one, the latchet of whose shoes I am not worthy to unloose; one who possesses the intellect of Johnson & the goodness & learning of Lady Jane Gray; & the gentleness & attraction of Aspasia." In his excitement over having negotiated this rite of passage so successfully by winning the hand of a paragon, David "almost forgot to mention the name of the Lady." He added in a postscript: "It is *Lydia*, a very excellent name & in right good odour in our family," being the name of his mother and sister (though his bride to be cordially detested it).[3]

Why the protracted game of "hide and go seek," belying the diary entries in which Child had recorded her admiration for David's gallantry, wit, and intellectual "vigor," and David had sung the praises of the "high-souled, high-reaching . . . powerful-minded Maria"?[4] Each had different reasons for fending off marriage.

David may have been hoping to put both the *Massachusetts Journal* and his fledgling legal practice on a firmer footing before asking the "brilliant Miss Francis" to share his life. Whereas she had already made a name for herself as a writer, he had hardly begun to fulfill his ambitions for a distinguished career in journalism, law, and politics. What did he have to offer this literary lion, so courted by the Boston aristocracy? Not until the autumn of 1827 had his prospects improved sufficiently for him to take the plunge. By then, the *Massachusetts Journal* had achieved recognition as an articulate exponent of John Quincy Adams and Daniel Webster's Whiggish National Republican ideology, and David had acquired visibility as an orator at local political rallies, even managing to get himself elected to the Massachusetts state legislature.[5]

For her part, Child must have felt loath to sacrifice her cherished laurels on the altar of domesticity. The family role models to whom she might have looked as she contemplated marriage were not encouraging. She had watched her mother die at a young age, worn out with domestic drudgery and frequent childbearing; she had helped her sister Mary run a busy household and care for five small children, born in quick succession; and she was taking note of the perpetual nagging and invalidism through which her sister-in-law Abba vented frustration with her wifely duties.[6] Marriage would leave little time or energy for writing — especially on the tight budget that might be expected of a newspaper editor.

On the other hand, Child had always hungered for love, and David seemed in many respects to be a perfect match for her. Their backgrounds were strikingly similar. Like the senior Convers Francis, David's father, Zachariah Child, belonged to the middle class of small "farmers and mechanics, who work with their *hands*."[7] The seventh of twelve siblings, David had grown up doing chores on a farm in West Boylston, north of Worcester. He also shared with his future brother-in-law Convers the distinction of having earned admission to Harvard purely on the strength of his intellectual gifts and contrary to family tradition (of David's four brothers, only John, the youngest, would pursue a higher education — in his case at West Point). David, in fact, had known real poverty in his youth; much as his prospective father-in-law had been reduced to begging for food during the Revolution, David had had to lug water from neighboring farms whenever his father's well ran dry. The difference was that his father remained in poverty all his life (due, as Child would learn the hard way, to habits of procrastination and carelessness with money that he had passed on to David).[8]

Like Child, David was seeking a route out of his parents' drab existence and into the charmed circle of the Boston elite, but for David the route was politics. His mentors — politicians like Massachusetts Senator Daniel Webster, current Governor Levi Lincoln, Congressman and future Governor Edward Everett, and former Secretary of War and Minister to Portugal Henry Dearborn — frequented the same milieu as Child's patron George Ticknor. If David's erratic career is any indication, however, he may well have been feeling the same discomfort with their exclusiveness and conservatism as Child was, except that instead of projecting his conflicts of identity and class loyalty onto fictional characters, he acted them out by recurrently sabotaging his own professional goals in the name of some higher ideal.

David's affinities with Child lay even deeper than their marginal social status and the psychological tug of war it generated in both of them. Their commonalities extended to an ambiguous gender identity as well. All her life, Child would feel torn between the "feminine" and "masculine" sides of herself — a condition she described as "the heart of a man imprisoned within a woman's destiny."[9] The male persona she had assumed in the preface to *Hobomok* had served not merely to mask her unfeminine accession to authorship, but to express her ambition for the glory toward which a man could aspire. David's behavior, on the contrary, suggests that he may have suffered from something like the heart of a woman imprisoned within a man's destiny. Again and again, following a pattern that bears a suspicious resemblance to the syndrome psychologists have dubbed the "fear of success" — a syndrome most prevalent among women, though also found among men of marginal status — David would defeat his own ostensible aims by scattering his energies, failing to be "prompt and punctual," disregarding details requiring meticulous attention, ignoring warning signals, and abandoning projects uncompleted.[10] In short, he seems to have resisted internalizing the bourgeois virtues Child hymned in her *Juvenile Miscellany* stories — virtues our culture has coded as "masculine."[11] From this perspective, the opposite side of David's character — the bullheaded combativeness he so often displayed, beginning with his Spanish military adventure — can be seen as both an overcompensation for the "feminine" tendencies he felt in himself and an inverted expression of them, taking the form of an unconscious quest for martyrdom; such a reading would explain why his campaigns against wrongdoers invariably ended up costing him far more dearly than they did his opponents.

The two lovers' ambiguous gender identity may well have drawn them to each other. In David, Child recognized a man much like William in "The Rival Brothers" — gentle, kind, and tender, noble and idealistic (though fatally haunted by a demonic double, as she may also have intuited). In Child, David recognized a woman who combined the masculine intellect of the redoubtable Samuel Johnson with the feminine attractions of two women who had likewise crossed gender boundaries by mastering knowledge reserved for men — Lady Jane Grey and the courtesan Aspasia, consort of Pericles.[12]

Forming yet another bond between the lovers was their exposure at an impressionable age to cultures outside the Anglo-American orbit — that of the Abenaki and Penobscot Indians in Child's case, that of the Iberian peninsula's intermingled Catholic and Moorish populations in David's. The cross-cultural vantage point that both of them derived from this exposure predisposed them to question their society's racial hierarchies, as well as the class and gender systems in which they occupied such marginal positions. The author of *Hobomok* could scarcely have happened on a man more likely to sympathize with her vision of interracial marriage as an alternative to white supremacy than the "intelligent traveller" who had fought against tyranny and injustice in Spain.[13]

Nevertheless, profound differences in character, temperament, and taste — differences that may partially account for the lovers' delay in cementing an engagement — would dog the Childs' marriage. Schooled by her parents in frugality, orderliness, punctuality, perseverance, and above all a horror of indebtedness — the epitome of everything the middle-class despised in the idle rich and slothful poor — the editor of the *Juvenile Miscellany* would find herself tied to a man who had already proved constitutionally incapable of keeping track of money, meeting commitments, or carrying tasks to completion — a man who had been resorting since early youth to borrowing recklessly from everyone he could dazzle with his eloquence and brilliance. Extraordinarily passionate for a nineteenth-century New England woman, and driven like her heroines Mary Conant and Frances Leslie by powerful sexual urges, the author of *Hobomok* would be doomed to disappointment in a husband she would describe as "kind" rather than ardent.[14] Multifaceted in her talents and tastes, Child would discover that although David admired her intellect and applauded the gift for political discourse she had revealed in *The Rebels* — a gift he would help her to develop — he did not share the aesthetic and mystical impulses that attracted her to artists like Francis Alexander and the musicians she would later frequent, and to the philosophy of Emanuel Swedenborg.

If Child was too deeply in love to pay much attention to her lover's flaws, her father was not so easily misled. The retired baker had never had much use for learning and saw little to recommend in a thirty-three-year-old intellectual who, ten years after graduating from Harvard, was only now settling into a profession and still not earning a secure income. Whatever David's attainments, warned the old man, he threatened to be a poor provider. Mr. Francis may also have heard rumors that David owed money to a great many people and that instead of taking on legal cases from which he could extract enough to repay his debts, he was defending penniless clients without charge. David had the business acumen of the proverbial fool who had gone about "cutting stones with a razor," he judged.[15]

Her father's croaking did not deter Child. She felt sure she could bring in enough income from her writing to help David support the household — in fact, she may have looked forward to marrying a man whose financial dependence on her would make him unlikely to ask his wife to give up her literary career. For the time being, their engagement would even allow her to drop schoolteaching and move back to Boston, where she could board with Madame Canda, up the street from David's rooms, and devote full time to her writing.[16]

The year that intervened before the wedding was Child's most productive so far. Besides editing the *Miscellany*, she published the nation's first gift book for children, the *Juvenile Souvenir* (1827), modeled on the *Atlantic Souvenir*; a didactic novella titled *Emily Parker, or Impulse, not Principle* (1827); a collection of *Moral Lessons in Verse* (1828); a volume excerpted from the *Miscellany* — *Biographical Sketches of Great and Good Men* (1828); and six stories for the annuals: "The Young West-Indian" in the *Atlantic Souvenir* for 1828; "The Lone Indian," "The Recluse of the Lake," and "Adventures of a Rain-Drop" in the *Token* for 1828; and "The Indian Wife" and "The Church in the Wilderness" for Nathaniel P. Willis's gift book, *The Legendary* (1828).[17]

From a biographical point of view, the most intriguing of these works is *Emily Parker*. While ostensibly aimed at an audience of adolescent girls, it not only retraces the milestones of Child's own life — the death of her mother, her girlhood and apprenticeship as a schoolteacher in Maine, her adoption by the Boston aristocracy; it also once again portrays a heroine torn between two lovers representing different sides of herself. And once again, it pits a man much like David — an idealistic but sexless young college student of humble background, named George Wilson — against a Byronic upper-class rake, Dr. Fox, who exhibits the same "tyrannical" proclivities as Joseph in "The Rival Brothers." This time the heroine marries the rake, who soon neglects her for other women and gambles away his fortune. Meanwhile, at age thirty her rejected lover is "appointed Professor of metaphysics in a highly respectable college" and wins the praises of all for "his talents, his learning, and his domestic virtues." Had Child ever hesitated between David and the "fascinating" Nathaniel P. Willis (or the "Magnus Apollo" she had met in Maine)? Was she trying to convince herself that she had made the right choice, that her fiancé would defy her father's predictions?[18]

Unfortunately, David's affairs in 1828 did not bear out Child's faith. Writing in July to David's sister Lydia, whom she had met on a visit to his family home the previous Thanksgiving, Child admitted to feeling "low spirited." David had been "exceedingly occupied with politics and business" and "working like a very cart-horse." As a result, she had "seen him less than usual" that summer.[19] The truth was, he had become embroiled in libel suits that were going to cost him hundreds of dollars in legal defense fees. First, David had charged a superintendant of construction at Massachusetts State Prison, the stonecutter Samuel R. Johnson (apparently a Jacksonian), with siphoning off large sums of money by stinting the prisoners and accepting kickbacks on supplies of rough stone. Then he had accused State Senator John Keyes, chairman of the committee of accounts and currently running for reelection, of favoritism in granting a state printing contract to a "reprobated Jackson press" without opening the sealed bids of other printers. However well-founded, such allegations took on a highly partisan character when publicized in the editorial columns of a major party newspaper during a bitter political campaign between incumbent National Republican President John Quincy Adams and his Democratic opponent, Andrew Jackson. In addition, David had opened himself up to libel actions by his equally partisan foes, because he had relied on the word of informants he considered trustworthy, without bothering to cross-check their testimony for accuracy.[20]

Meanwhile, though the *Massachusetts Journal*'s political supporters commended David's "upright and undeviating course" as editor, the paper was in serious financial trouble. The precise cause of the problem is impossible to ascertain in the absence of surviving records, but it seems fair to speculate that subscriptions had not kept pace with expenses and that David had responded, as was his wont, not by scaling down operations and trying to balance income with outgo, but by borrowing more to keep the *Journal* afloat. Like a compulsive gambler with the mirage of a big win dangling in front of his eyes, he tended to double the stakes when he was losing, as if to manipulate the fates into siding with him. Still, the *Massachusetts Journal* had acquired a good reputation among National Republicans, and David could be very persuasive. He managed to procure $15,000 worth of loans — on top of those he already owed — from wealthy patrons, among them the textile magnate Abbott Lawrence; "the richest man in Massachusetts, Peter Brooks"; his former benefactor, Dearborn; and Webster.[21]

After David had "candidly" revealed the state of his finances to Child, she had suggested it might be "prudent" to defer their marriage until the following spring. For the first time, she was beginning to get a glimmering of the trials that awaited her, and she was finding the prospect sobering. "Your brother has been so anxious to relieve all the distress in the world, that he has done himself wrong," she confided to Lydia. "I love him the better for it — " she added bravely, "but it makes me look forward to the expenses of housekeeping with anxiety and fear." Apparently David succeeded in convincing his practical fiancée that they could live more cheaply together than by continuing to board out separately. Foreshadowing the role she would soon assume as the household's sole breadwinner, she calculated that the $300 a year she earned from the *Miscellany*, added to David's meager income, would suffice to support them if they were "economical" — especially since she had already purchased most of the furniture.[22]

The wedding was thus set for the evening of Sunday, October 19, 1828. If any doubts persisted, they were quickly swallowed up in the whirl of activity that propelled the couple toward the great event. The dressmaker had been working for a whole week on her trousseau, Child reported to Mary, who could not make the long journey from Norridgewock: "I have a claret-colored silk pelisse, lined with straw-colored silk, made in the extent of the mode, enough to make anybody stare; one black figured levantine silk, and one swiss muslin." It was a wardrobe better suited to the "brilliant Miss Francis" of George Ticknor's salon than to the Frugal Housewife of the years to come. For the ceremony, over which Convers officiated, with David's cousin Clarissa Bigelow acting as bridesmaid, Child wore a wedding gown of India muslin trimmed with white satin. The large gathering of family and friends regaled themselves in the parsonage with thirty-five pounds of cake.[23]

The next day the Childs took up housekeeping in the "proper little martin box, furnished with very plain gentility," which they had rented on Harvard Street in Boston. For several weeks they were inundated with "company, — company, — company" — long visits from David's mother and brother John, and constant calls from wellwishers — amid which Child complained of "domestics changed three times!" "Oh, dear! the miseries of housekeeping!" she groaned to her mother-in-law, hoping that her latest helper would stay.[24] Lois and George Ticknor Curtis were among the first guests Child entertained in what George remembered as a "very humble home" with "no servant" (or at least none of the type who staffed the establishments of wealthy Bostonians). Providing a rare glimpse of the couple's married life in those early weeks, he described the frugal meal Child had prepared and served with her own hands: "a savory dish, consisting of a meat-pie, perhaps mutton, baked in a small oven," with "roasted or baked potatoes," and Indian pudding. "There was no dessert, and no wine, no beverage of any kind but water, not even a cup of tea or coffee," he noted disconcertedly, but the new bride had not given any sign of minding her privations, and her husband had appeared "breezy, cheerful, and energetic as ever."[25]

With all the excitement, Child was finding "little time to write, and less to read," though she hastened to add: "I don't care — I am as willing to be useful in one way as in another." The form of usefulness toward which she was gravitating was to throw herself wholeheartedly into David's enthusiasms. Adopting his overly optimistic view, Child informed her mother-in-law that "[n]obody, whether friendly to him or not," had any doubt David would win his libel defense against Keyes, and that despite the probability of an electoral victory by "that political scavenger, Jackson," the *Massachusetts Journal* and its editor had "never stood so high, or so advantageously with the respectable part of the community as they do now."[26]

From the start, the Childs defined their marriage as a political partnership. It was a partnership in which each would influence the other and the two would reconsecrate their talents to combating injustice and espousing the cause of America's oppressed peoples of color. David would encourage his wife to engage openly in political discourse, rather than content herself with exploring political ideas through the medium of fiction. Child, in turn, would direct David's attention to the wrongs of the Indians, which had captured her imagination since her youth in Norridgewock and inspired her best fiction to date.

Soon after entering on her new life as a married woman, Child shouldered responsibility for the literary columns of the *Massachusetts Journal*. While continuing to edit the *Miscellany* and contribute to the annuals, she increasingly channeled her literary energies into David's newspaper. She also undertook a work that marks her debut as a political writer: *The First Settlers of New England: or, Conquest of the Pequods, Narragansets and Pokanokets: As Related by a Mother to Her Children, and Designed for the Instruction of Youth.*[27] A revisionist history of America's colonization, stressing the atrocities committed against the Indians by English Puritans and their Spanish Catholic predecessors, the book resembles the educational dialogues conducted by Mother and Aunt Maria in the *Miscellany* and *Evenings in New England*. Yet unlike these earlier works, *The First Settlers* no longer attempts to portray European colonists in a patriotic light or to gloss over their depredations; on the contrary, it launches both a searing indictment of European bigotry and rapacity and a passionate defense of Indian rights. Even more sharply differentiating it from Child's previous writings is the overt political stand *The First Settlers* takes on the latest phase of the perennial Indian question—the controversy over whether or not to uproot the Cherokee from their hereditary lands in Georgia so as to transport them beyond the Mississippi, along with other Eastern Indian tribes.

The idea of transferring the Indian population en masse had originated with Jefferson, but it had lain dormant until revived by Monroe in 1817. Jefferson, Monroe, and Monroe's successor, John Quincy Adams, had all made the tribes' removal contingent on their agreement to sell their lands. The trouble was that none of the tribes wanted to sell. The Cherokee, in particular, had formally resolved not to part with another foot of territory. Instead, as Child reminds readers of *The First Settlers*, the Cherokee had opted to follow the advice Washington had given them in 1796, after defeating them in battle: "to quit the chase, and practise the arts of agriculture, and become herdsmen and artisans; with the assurance that, should they accede to the proposal, the United States would take them under . . . protection, and guarantee to them their land within specific limits" (v). Tribal leaders had welcomed the agents Washington had sent to instruct the Cherokee in the cultivation of cotton and flax, the raising of sheep, and the use of government-furnished spinning wheels and looms. And the results had far outstripped the prophecies of their sympathizers.

By the mid-1820s the Cherokee had shown dramatic evidence of progress toward "civilization." According to a New England-educated Cherokee named David Brown, whose testimony Child cites in *The First Settlers*, his people now boasted prosperous farms with a wide variety of crops, extensive peach and apple orchards, and large flocks of sheep and other domestic animals. They also exported cotton downriver to New Orleans and manufactured woolen and cotton cloth for domestic consumption (*FS* 260–61). Nor was their progress confined to the material sphere. A Cherokee named Sequoyah had devised an alphabet, literacy was spreading, schools were multiplying, and churches were flourishing. Indeed, Brown went so far as to claim that Christianity had become "the religion of the [Cherokee] nation" (*FS* 260). In July 1827 the Cherokee had even held a convention to ratify their own constitution. It affirmed their status as "one of the sovereign and independent nations of the earth, having complete jurisdiction over its territory, to the exclusion of the authority of any other State, and it provided for a representative system of government, modeled upon that of the United States." The following February they had begun issuing their first newspaper, the *Cherokee Phoenix*. Printed in Cherokee and English and edited by the articulate Elias Boudinot, it broadcast their successes to the American public. Among the newspapers that regularly exchanged copies with the *Phoenix* was David's *Massachusetts Journal*.[28]

Despite the Cherokee successes, pressure for removal had continued to build, especially from the state of Georgia. In 1802 Georgia had ceded its claim on what became Alabama and Mississippi, with the proviso that the federal government would "extinguish existing Indian land title in the state"—land title that the United States had already bound itself to respect with "solemn guarantees" to the tribes. The Cherokee occupied 15 million acres of fertile land, which Georgian planters were determined to seize. Because the production of slave-grown staples quickly exhausted the soil, the slave system depended for its survival on perpetual expansion. The availability of cheap virgin land into which to expand served two vital purposes. First, it allowed the large planters to relocate, once their holdings became unprofitable. Second, it offered poor whites and small farmers a chance to acquire plantations themselves; in turn, the hope of upward mobility kept the small fry loyal to the planter aristocracy. The Cherokee stood in the way of both these objectives, even though they had adopted their white neighbors' slave economy (a fact Child apparently had not learned).[29]

Reacting with outrage to the Cherokee constitution, the Georgia state legislature passed a resolution declaring "[t]hat all the lands, appropriated and unappropriated, which lie within the conventional limits of Georgia belong to her absolutely; that the title is in her; that the Indians are tenants at her will, . . . and that Georgia has the right to extend her authority and laws over her whole territory and to coerce obedience to them from all descriptions of people, be they white, red, or black, who may reside within her limits." A year later, in December 1828, the legislature explicitly pronounced "all laws made by the Cherokee Nation . . . null and void" as of June 1, 1830.[30]

The accession of Andrew Jackson, who had plainly indicated his sympathy with Georgia's position and his commitment to Indian removal, brought the dispute to a head.[31] Jackson's victory at the polls in November 1828 may also have been the stimulus that prompted Child's first foray into contemporary politics. Throughout the electoral campaign David had been printing fierce denunciations of Jackson in the *Massachusetts Journal*, highlighting Old Hickory's brutal record as an Indian fighter — and as a slaveowner. One article, for example, had recalled Jackson's "wanton cruelty" and flagrant violations of international law and the U.S. Constitution in 1818. Invading Spanish-held Florida without a congressional declaration of war, Jackson had led four thousand mounted volunteers in pursuit of "defeated and fugitive Indians and runaway negroes," and during that expedition he had summarily executed two English traders living among the Indians and two Seminole chiefs captured by stratagem. In an editorial note introducing the article, David had pointed out that its author had chaired the Senate committee charged with investigating Jackson's conduct, which had narrowly escaped an official vote of censure.[32] Another article had quoted a military dispatch Jackson had sent from the battlefield of the Horseshoe in 1814, in which he had announced his intention to "EXTERMINATE" his Indian foes, of whom "[f]ive hundred and fifty-seven were left dead" and "no more than TEN had escaped."[33] Several articles had also accused Jackson of "negro trading" and cruelty toward the slaves on his plantation, one of whom had been murdered by an overseer in a case Jackson had hushed up.[34] The intermingling of the Indian removal question with the slavery issue in these articles hints at the significance the Cherokee cause would assume as a dress rehearsal for many of the crusaders who, like the Childs, would soon join the abolitionist movement.[35]

While David excoriated Jackson for his past record, he did not yet challenge the ideological assumption shared by all too many opponents, as well as advocates of Cherokee removal — that the Indians were slated for extinction. Thus, when a Georgia newspaper editorialized that the Cherokee must be forced to leave, and "the sooner the better," because "[t]he safety of the many must supersede the convenience of the few," David commented: "It makes the heart sink to read such desolating sentiments, and to note such sanguinary purposes. It is melancholy enough to think, that by a law of nature these native proprietors must disappear from the scenes of human action, but it is doubly so, when Christian agency is employed to hasten their exit."[36]

In *The First Settlers* Child sets out specifically to counter this self-defeating belief in the Indians' inevitable demise, which so drastically undercuts the effectiveness of their would-be champions. Basing her book on the premise that what has decreed the Indians' extinction is not a "law of nature," but the "crooked and narrow-minded policy" Anglo-Americans have adopted toward the native inhabitants of the continent ever since Puritan times, she calls for radical change. Unless the United States brings its treatment of the Indians into conformity with the "religious and civil . . . principles which form the basis of our government," she argues, the American republic will undergo "the calamitous reverses which have fallen on other nations, whose path to empire has been marked by the blood and ruin of their fellow-men" (iv).

The disjuncture between the issue of Cherokee removal — addressed primarily in the preface and the last twenty-five pages of the book — and the subject announced in the subtitle *Conquest of the Pequods, Narragansets and Pokanokets*, suggests nevertheless that Child may have written *The First Settlers* at two different stages. Originally, she seems to have conceived it simply as a lesson in Puritan history, modeled on those she was offering in the *Miscellany*, though far more revisionist in orientation. She may in fact have completed the 200-page section on the colonization of America, constituting the bulk of the work, during the summer of 1828 when David was tied up with his own affairs. The idea of extending her history of past injustices toward Indians into the present and of applying the conclusions she had drawn from her research on New England Indians to the Cherokee controversy seems to have occurred to her as an afterthought. At least that is the impression conveyed by the organization of the text, which moves backward in time from the Puritans to Columbus, and then abruptly shifts to the 1820s in a section demarcated from the preceding by a line drawn across the page.

Child had ended her analysis of the English and Spanish colonial ventures by moralizing:

> In surveying the disastrous events of this history, we find that nations and individuals are alike punished for their crimes, by a perpetual reaction, which subjects them to the like sufferings and privations which they caused to fall on others. . . .
>
> The causes which have produced . . . [the cyclical rise and fall of empires] will forever continue to operate until mankind are sufficiently enlightened, virtuous, and magnanimous to allow their fellow beings to enjoy in peace the bounteous provisions of nature which have been so graciously bestowed on them. (216, 219)

Tacked on after this passage is a section headed "Illustrations, Anecdotes, &c." It opens by paying tribute to the Osage and Winnebago chiefs recently defeated in Wisconsin, and it proceeds to cite a number of authorities who have either spoken out against Indian removal or recognized the Indians' virtues and rights. Child's inclusion of congressional speeches among these citations — a new addition to her repertoire — and her references to several works published in the fall of 1828 provide further evidence that she may have enlarged the scope of the book and updated her research while finishing the manuscript in the weeks following her wedding. The new familiarity she was acquiring with current political debates through the *Massachusetts Journal*, and the involvement she had come to feel in an election that had brought an avowed partisan of Indian removal to power, seem to have given her the courage to develop the political implications of the book she had started out to write.

Even without the preface and the concluding section, however, Child's revisionist history of the Puritans' Indian wars already lends itself to undermining the ideological grounds for Indian removal by demolishing the religious sanction the Puritans had invoked for their genocidal mission. Like *Hobomok*, though much more deliberately, *The First Settlers* seeks to redefine the past in order to lay the basis for altering the future course of American history.

Child's evolution toward an increasingly radical political stance can also be detected in the protofeminist cast she gives to the dialogue between "Mother" and her daughters Caroline and Elizabeth in *The First Settlers*. Superficially, the format of a mother educating her daughters in American history appears conformable with the ideology of Republican motherhood. The Republican Mother, "an educated woman who . . . placed her learning at her family's service," was supposed to " 'inspire her brothers, her husband, or her sons, with such a love of virtue, such just ideas of the true value of civil liberty . . . that future heroes and statesmen, when arrived at the summit of military or political fame, [would] exaltingly declare, it is to my mother I owe this elevation.' "[37] Yet Child's Republican Mother is inspiring daughters, not sons; and her manner of preparing her daughters for "the performance of the high duties, which devolve on your sex in all the relations of life" (252), is to teach them to question the authority of the Puritan patriarchs who have transmitted a falsified version of history to posterity. Moreover, by enlisting her daughters' sympathies for the Indians — in the present as well as in the past — this Republican Mother is implying that women's "high duties" extend beyond the home, that they entail applying the ethic governing the home to society at large. Women who inform themselves of their country's history and raise their voices against violations of the national creed, she is suggesting, are not overstepping the bounds of their sphere, but fulfilling their sacred responsibilities as mothers — a bold expansion of the Republican Mother's role.

Accordingly, the models "Mother" holds up to Caroline and Elizabeth for emulation are all women who have either challenged patriarchal authority or exercised political power themselves. The first is a Puritan woman named Mrs. Oliver, reviled by John Winthrop for having publicly contradicted the Puritan magistrates and exhibited " 'a masculine spirit' " (93).[38] Taking issue with Winthrop, "Mother" hails Mrs. Oliver as "the only person who, in that season of gloom and superstition, ventured to profess a rational belief," entitling her to "the respect and esteem of enlightened christians of the present day" (91). The other exemplars "Mother" cites for her daughters are Queen Isabella of Spain and her Carib Indian contemporary, Queen Anacaona of Santo Domingo. Both rulers obviously demonstrate that women can do more than wield indirect influence over husbands, brothers, and sons — that they can govern kingdoms directly and acquit themselves creditably. The lesson is not lost on Caroline and Elizabeth, who find it "extraordinary, that two female sovereigns, so celebrated as Isabella and Anacaona, should have lived at the same period of time" (240). "Mother" immediately drives the point home: "The common notion, that women are incapable of occupying high and responsible stations in society, is not sustained by history or experience. The few females, who have attained sovereign power, have, in most instances, discharged the important duties which devolved on them, with dignity, and an attention to humanity and the rights of their subjects, which is not commonly found in kings" (241).

Besides redefining the ideology of Republican Motherhood in protofeminist terms, Child uses the format of the mother-daughter dialogue to privilege the viewpoint of women and children and to exploit the nineteenth-century belief in the child's intuitive perception of truth. The subversive potential of this rhetorical strategy becomes evident as Caroline and Elizabeth respond to the Puritan texts their mother reads to them — among them John Winthrop's *Journal*, William Hubbard's *Narrative of the Troubles with the Indians in New England*, and Thomas Prince's *Chronological History of New England*. Again and again, the children express "natural emotions of compassion" that pernicious social influences stifle in adults. Again and again, they display an understanding of religion unwarped by "fanaticism and bigotry" (213).

For example, as Caroline listens to Hubbard's account of how the Puritans pursued the remnants of the Pequots through the swamps and sold the survivors into West Indian slavery, she identifies with the Pequot mothers and children. "What can exceed the distress of those mothers," she exclaims, "who, after witnessing the destruction of their fathers and husbands and brothers, saw their young sons forced from them, and sent to a foreign land, there to be sold for slaves. I picture to myself my little brother among these captives, in vain calling for help, and stretching his eager arms towards his unhappy mother, who is herself a slave, and unable to give him any relief" (29–30). Elizabeth is even more shocked by the details of the war against the Narragansetts, who had succored Roger Williams and his dissident faction in Rhode Island and sided with the English during the Pequot War. The colonists should have felt "bound by the ties of gratitude and honour" (87) to refrain from turning against their former allies, she observes. And Caroline comments, "How very wicked and odious it seems to speak of God as guiding and assisting to destroy a people so worthy of respect and esteem, and to whom [the settlers] were so much indebted!" (89).

The children identify with Indians not merely as victims of white treachery and cruelty, but as warriors in a patriotic struggle for national liberation. Indignant at the Puritan chroniclers' vilification of Indian leaders like the Pokanoket chief Philip, who had led a bloody uprising against the Puritans in 1675–76, Caroline remarks: "It would seem that the colonists thought that the Indians had no right to defend themselves, or [to] prevent them from taking possession of their country" (139). She then proceeds to put herself in Philip's place, conjecturing that after "all the sacrifices and concessions he had made had failed to procure him any permanent peace . . . [he] was determined to submit no longer to the insults and impositions of the English" (145).

The children's reactions make it seem natural to sympathize with Indian resistance to white encroachments. What appears *unnatural* is the Puritans' ferocious persecution of Native peoples. The strategy is so effective that the reader is scarcely aware of Child's radicalism in turning two hundred years of national ideology upside down.

While Caroline and Elizabeth instinctively recognize Native peoples' right to defend their land, it is "Mother" who supplies the facts and arguments legitimizing the children's sentiments. "Mother" continually challenges the Puritan chroniclers' authority and disputes their allegations against the Indians. The pretexts for both the Pequot War and the reprisal expedition against the Block Island Narragansetts, for instance, were the isolated murders of English adventurers by Indians. "Mother" notes, however, that the victims were all men of bad character, whom the Puritans themselves had previously indicted for "atrocious offences" (7–8, 64).[39] Thus, she contends, the murdered men were very likely the "aggressors" in incidents for which the Indians made amends, and for which the Puritans nevertheless retaliated by massacring entire tribes (9–12). Similarly, she discredits Hubbard's efforts to "excuse and extenuate" the colonists' harsh treatment of Philip's brother Alexander, and she discounts the charge that Philip was already plotting rebellion when he appealed to the English for justice five years before taking up arms against them (131–32). Instead, "Mother" affirms, "The natural discernment of Philip unquestionably led him to conclude that the English had determined on his ruin; and he therefore preferred to risk all, and die bravely, defending his country, than become their slave" (145). However violent the tactics Philip and his warriors used against the English, she emphasizes, it must be remembered that they were fighting "to preserve themselves and their country from subjugation to usurpers, whose ingratitude and perfidy they held in abhorrence" (161). The children draw the lesson she leaves unstated: "How many heroes, among civilized nations, have had statues and monuments erected to their memories for the same patriotism which was deemed criminal in Philip" (169)!

The pro-Indian point of view Child adopts in *The First Settlers* reveals her maturation of political consciousness since publishing *Hobomok*. No longer does she reserve her sympathy for Indians like Hobomok, who side with the English against their own people. On the contrary, she now portrays such figures as enemy collaborators "induced by artifice or rewards to betray their country" (77). Especially pitiful, in her eyes, are the Christian Indians — deluded wretches taught to deem it "their duty to betray their unbelieving countrymen, who were already doomed to never-ending wo for their unbelief" (77). Sausaman, the Christian Indian who betrayed the conspiracy organized against the English by the Pokanoket chief Philip, deserved to be executed for treason, Child contends. "Philip no doubt considered him as a traitor and renegade, who had justly forfeited his life," she has "Mother" explain to the girls. And when Elizabeth infers that "Philip only exercised a legal act of justice, in putting to death a traitorous subject," "Mother" agrees (143).

The most radical aspect of *The First Settlers*, however, is its dismantling of Puritan religious ideology. Repeatedly, Caroline and Elizabeth raise the question of how the Puritans could have claimed religious sanction for their butchery of Indians. "Mother" answers by analyzing the psychosocial consequences of Calvinist doctrine:

> [A] sect, — who ascribe to God passions highly vindictive and unjust, — who represent this universal Parent as having formed rational creatures for the express purpose of inflicting on them torments the most excruciating and endless, without allowing them any chance or power to escape, — and who also believe, that the small number, whom he has ordained to be happy, have been redeemed by the sufferings and blood of a benevolent and perfect being, who has given himself a willing victim to satisfy divine vengeance, — may have believed themselves authorized to inflict all the evil in their power on wretches who are born to suffer. (31)

In short, anticipating the insights of twentieth-century historians like Richard Slotkin and Richard Drinnon, Child argues that the Calvinist God is the product of a sadistic imagination and that the men who conceived such a God inevitably acted out the sadistic impulses they projected onto him. Because they viewed human nature as hideously vile and depraved, human life could have no value in their eyes. When the Puritans put Indian villages to the torch, they were merely imitating the God who had consigned these loathsome creatures to the eternal fires of hell before their birth. One need have no compunctions about inflicting suffering on "wretches who are born to suffer."

At the same time, Child suggests, the Puritans themselves suffered from the intense anxiety that sadism begets. She portrays them as trapped in a vicious cycle in which anxiety induces efforts to allay it through self-punishment and punishment of others — tactics that only intensify the original anxiety, leading to renewed inflictions:

> However strong were their convictions of the justice of their cause, however plausible were their arguments in defence of their usurpations, they were unable to silence the voice of conscience; and they vainly attempted to escape from the remorse, which, with all its terrors, seizes on the hearts of the guilty, by redoubling their superstitious observances. They fasted and prayed, and the austerities, they imposed on themselves and others, destroyed in a great degree all social enjoyment; and, whilst they were systematically planning the destruction of the Indians, they were sharply engaged in discussing with each other points of faith altogether unimportant or incomprehensible. (13–14).

The consequence of Puritan psychology that principally concerns Child is the legacy it has left of attitudes and policies toward Indians. "People seldom forgive those whom they have wronged," she points out, "and the first settlers appear to have fostered a mortal aversion to the Indians, whom they had barbarously destroyed" (13). Their rationales for dispossessing and exterminating Native peoples were still being invoked by their descendants, as the case of the Georgians testified (23). Hence the importance of exposing the Puritans' crimes and of repudiating the religious tenets that sanctioned them.

Among these tenets, Child particularly stresses the myth of the chosen people, which the Puritans had inherited from the Jews. "[L]ike the Israelites," she notes, the Puritans believed themselves "authorized by God to destroy or drive out the heathen, as they styled the Indians" (32). And like the Israelites, they believed God had promised another people's land to them. The Puritans had defined Christianity as a religion of war, pitting the armies of the Saints against the armies of Satan, the New Israel against the Canaanites of a new promised land.[40] Child calls for redefining Christianity as a religion of peace, mercy, and brotherly love, dedicated to bringing about a world in which all peoples can dwell together in harmony.

Throughout *The First Settlers*, Child counters the belief that the systematic extermination of Indians has been divinely ordained to make way for a superior people. From the Puritans on, she shows, this belief has allowed Anglo-Americans to evade responsibility for obliterating entire nations. It has paralyzed opposition to each new injustice against the Indians and deadened the moral sensibilities of the perpetrators. That is why Child ends the book by applying the lesson of her revisionist history to the current debates over Cherokee removal. The progress the Cherokee have made disproves the often reiterated dictum that "the Indians are incapable of becoming a civilized people, or of assimilating" with whites, Child asserts. It also disproves the comforting notion that Indians "voluntarily retire at the approach of the whites" (259). On the contrary, Child insists, the Cherokee have "adopt[ed] our arts, our religion, and husbandry; in the hope of being permitted to retain what is left of their native inheritance." "It is, in my opinion, decidedly wrong, to speak of the removal, or extinction of the Indians as inevitable," she concludes; "it surely implies that the people of these states have not sufficient virtue or magnanimity to redeem their past offences, by affording the sad remnant, which still exist, succour and protection" (281).

The ultimate solution Child offers to racial conflict simultaneously harks back to *Hobomok* and foreshadows her long career as an abolitionist. "Our heavenly Father . . . has made of one blood all the nations of men, that they may dwell together," she premises, quoting what would become a favorite abolitionist text; thus, the best means of showing "our obedience to [his] will" is for "people of different colours to unite" in marriage (66). Child even goes on to meet objections against amalgamation with "inferior" races by citing evidence that Europeans had derived their arts and sciences from the dark-complexioned peoples of Asia and Africa (67–69)—evidence on which she would base key chapters of her groundbreaking *Appeal in Favor of That Class of Americans Called Africans* four years later. Europeans had benefited in the past and would benefit in the future from the mingling of races, she implies.

Speculating about how large-scale intermarriage between English colonists and Indians might have altered the course of history, "Mother" suggests to Caroline and Elizabeth:

> The primitive simplicity, hospitality, and generosity of the Indians would gradually have improved and softened the stern and morose feelings resulting from the false views of religion, and the superstitious reverence in which the settlers viewed

the characters of the Israelites, whose example they believed themselves authorized to follow. Our arts and sciences would have imparted to the Indians new light
and vigour. The pure religion of Jesus would have strengthened and confirmed
their innate convictions of the character and attributes of the Almighty, and the
example of our divine master and instructer would have taught them to subdue
their wayward passions, and evil propensities. (65)

Here, as in *Hobomok*, Child describes the religion the Indians have imbibed from
nature as closer to the "pure religion of Jesus" than the "superstitious" dogma the
Puritan settlers have allegedly imbibed from the Old Testament. The concept of assimilation she formulates in *The First Settlers* marks a significant advance, however. Rather
than the mere Anglicization of the Indian, she now visualizes a genuine interchange
between Indians and whites, with influences traveling in both directions. The Indians'
superior ethic of "simplicity, hospitality, and generosity" would convert the settlers
from Calvinist bigots into true Christians. Once the settlers themselves actually lived
by the "pure religion of Jesus," they would be able to transmit it to the Indians. In turn,
that religion would raise the Indians to a higher ethical level, refining the reverential
impulses manifested in their innate belief in a Great Spirit and restraining such "wayward passions" as their proverbial vengefulness. It is nonetheless symptomatic that in
the domain of "arts and sciences," the interchange between the two peoples remains
one-sided. Child can appreciate the Indians' ethos, but not their culture.

Even more symptomatic is the argument Child uses to clinch her analysis of what
American society could have gained from an Indian policy of assimilation rather than
extermination. By "intermixing" with the Indians, she claims, the descendants of the
Puritans might have saved the nation "from the hordes of vagrants, who have been
allured to our shores, like vultures by the scent of prey, that they might seize on the
spoils of the natives whom we have destroyed" (65–66).

Those "vagrants," of course, were the immigrants who gravitated toward Andrew
Jackson's Democratic party. Rootless, penniless, and unruly, they represented the specter of class war that threatened to reproduce European conditions in America. The
Jacksonians' answer to this threat was to extend the process of electoral democratization begun in the wake of the Revolution, when property restrictions on white male
suffrage were gradually eliminated. The enfranchisement and glorification of the
workingman offered the new class of unskilled immigrant laborers the illusion of
equality. In exchange, they were to support the interests of the southern planters who
dominated the Democratic party — interests starkly dramatized by the dispossession of
the Cherokee to make way for white slaveowners.[41]

Repudiating the ideal of a democracy built on white supremacy, Child envisions in its
place a multiracial republic in which Indians would provide a bulwark against a foreign
proletariat: "[T]hough we might not be able to boast, 'the glorious result of ten millions of white inhabitants,' the red men who would have formed a part of our population, would have been to us a wall of defence; neither would the innocent blood we have
so profusely shed, which cries aloud for vengeance, subject us to the fearful retribution

which has fallen on the guilty nations who have established themselves on the ruins of their fellow men" (66).

However progressive racially, Child's Whig alternative to the Jacksonians' white supremacism perpetuates the same polarization of white proletariat and nonwhite subject races. By playing into the hands of the racist demagogues who have perennially succeeded in deflecting white workers' hostilities away from their class enemies and toward racial Others, it inadvertently guarantees the persistence of the very antagonisms Child wishes to eliminate. This monumental failure of vision would haunt the reformers of Child's generation and stymie their efforts to reconstruct the nation on the basis of racial equality after the Civil War.

In its advocacy of intermarriage as a solution to America's race problem; in its arguments against white supremacy; in its championship of an oppressed people's right to fight for freedom; in its thoroughgoing critique of the religious ideology used to justify colonial conquest (a critique that already questions the privileging of Christianity as revealed truth) and in its assertion of women's equal capacity to occupy "high and responsible stations" (241) as well as to participate in political debates involving the nation's future — The First Settlers adumbrates ideas that would be central to Child's thinking for the rest of her life. It is undoubtedly one of the most radical works she would ever write.

The question thus arises: why did The First Settlers escape the censure that overwhelmed Child in 1833, when she advanced many of the same ideas in her Appeal for African Americans? The search for clues in contemporary reviews merely uncovers another mystery: The First Settlers apparently left no trace of its reception. Of the organs that regularly reviewed Child's novels, gift book fiction, writings for children, and domestic advice books — the North American Review, Sarah Hale's Ladies' Magazine, N. P. Willis's American Monthly Magazine, and the American Traveller — none commented on The First Settlers. Even more puzzling is the Cherokee Phoenix's failure to notice the book, although it regularly reprinted speeches and articles by white supporters and occasionally featured articles from the Massachusetts Journal, culling Child's "Hints to People of Moderate Fortune," for example.[42] The silence that might seem most inexplicable — that of the Massachusetts Journal itself — points toward the only possible solution of the mystery: contrary to the practice she had followed since enlisting Ticknor's help in publicizing Hobomok, Child did not promote The First Settlers. Indeed, she may actually have decided not to put it on the market.[43]

Why would Child have gone through the expense of having the book privately printed (not to mention the labor of writing it), only to consign it to oblivion? The likeliest explanation is that by the time The First Settlers came off the press, the Childs were caught in an acute financial crisis. After Jackson's election, subscriptions to the Massachusetts Journal had fallen off by the hundreds, as former Adams supporters, including many newspaper editors, had jumped on the Jackson bandwagon. Characteristically David had responded by choosing this inopportune moment to launch a new daily edition of the paper, on top of its weekly and triweekly editions — a move that of course exacerbated his financial difficulties.[44]

Meanwhile, in mid-January the two libel cases pending against him came up for trial. The judge in the Keyes case, Marcus Morton, a Jacksonian, openly tilted toward his fellow party member, urging the jury to consider all the extenuating circumstances in Keyes's favor and all the indications of malicious motives and inconsistent testimony on the part of David and his supporting witnesses. "If [the defendant] has failed in your opinion to establish the truth of the [corruption] charge [against Keyes]," Morton instructed the jury, "then the law implies malice in the publication." On January 15, after a trial of three days and an evening of deliberation, the jury returned a verdict of guilty. David now owed several hundred dollars' worth of legal fees and found himself facing a prison sentence, which he appealed to the Massachusetts Supreme Court. The guilty verdict and damages of $15 in the Johnson libel case four days later seemed almost anticlimactic.[45]

Undaunted, David returned to the charge. When a witness sent him further evidence of Johnson's corruption after the trial, David rehashed the details of the stone-cutter's alleged misdeeds in two long articles. "Let the facts and evidence be examined, and we have no fear of the judgment which may follow," he trumpeted (though the court had just rendered judgment). He went on to bait his foes by predicting: "When a certain class called the 'exclusives' shall have discovered that the mere *name* and *proclamation* of libel *actions* and *indictments* will not *put down this press*, they will let it alone."[46] In addition, David published a belligerent letter to Keyes, ending with an exhortation to the "electors of Middlesex" to remember the facts against their representative — precisely the gesture that had provoked Keyes's libel suit in the first place. No wonder people began calling him "David *Libel* Child, because he was always libelling somebody."[47]

If David's truculence in the wake of his libel convictions appears almost foolhardy, the letters of support he received from other newspapers provide a different perspective. His fellow editors saw him as a martyr to freedom of the press. Noting that David had "received his information from a more credible channel" than the norm for journalists, the editor of the *New York Commercial Advertiser* warned: "If we poor editors are to be punished for every free word spoken of a candidate for public office, in the heat of an electioneering contest . . . it will be worse than the old gag law." The *Wicasset Citizen* of Maine agreed: "If the publication of Mr. Child was a libel, scarcely a publisher of a newspaper in the country could escape the charge of one." "Mr. Child was influenced by no other motives than the desire to discharge his duties faithfully to the public, by making known what he considered material to forming a correct judgment of the conduct of public affairs," concluded the *Boston Daily Advertiser*.[48]

While Child must have found these tributes to her husband's courage and public spiritedness highly gratifying, she felt "sick with anxiety" as she contemplated the prospect of bankruptcy. "[I]n a state little short of insanity," she appealed desperately to her erstwhile benefactor George Ticknor. The contrast between this letter and the one she had written to him four years earlier could hardly be more poignant. "Owing to the temporary pressure of circumstances, my husband is very much involved, and must speedily be ruined, unless five thousand dollars can be raised to assist him," Child explained. Four wealthy backers had agreed to help, "but they wait—and wait—and want to see how much each is willing to do; and the misery is, my husband cannot stand it a fortnight longer." Could Ticknor possibly advance a thousand dollars, against Child's furniture and books as collateral? She would not make this request were she not convinced, "[a]fter a careful and cool investigation of the state of affairs," that David was right in thinking his paper would be "valuable property by and bye," if they could just "weather this stormy cape." She was writing without David's knowledge, Child added. In front of him, she tried to appear "cheerful," but the effort was costing her so much that she could "neither eat, nor sleep." Helplessly watching her literary fortunes get entangled with David's, she was perhaps revealing more than she meant to when she confided: "There is no mental suffering equal to the hourly dread of losing all the little, one has earned by years of hard exertion."[49]

Whether or not Ticknor came through with the loan (which seems improbable), the ordeal established a pattern in the Childs' marriage. David continued to accumulate debts as he recklessly defied political enemies and the rules of sound business practice, and Child increasingly took over the burden of supporting the household. From now on, she realized, she would have to orient her literary talents primarily toward genres that made money.

The First Settlers clearly did not fall into the money-making category. In fact Child could not have found a combination more likely to alienate the audience she had so skillfully built up through the *Miscellany* than the book's diatribe against Calvinism, its advocacy of interracial marriage, and its violation of the taboo against "female interference or usurpation of authority, in directing the affairs of state."[50] Had she attempted to promote *The First Settlers* (which she had prudently issued anonymously), she would have risked literary boycott just when she could least afford it. Under the circumstances, it is hard to avoid suspecting that she simply chose—whether deliberately or by default—to let the book die stillborn.

The decision may have marked a political retreat, but it was wise on more than one count. Rhetorically, *The First Settlers* could never have achieved its ostensible aim of arousing sympathy for the Cherokee, since its religious iconoclasm would have offended the sensibilities of the principal readers it was addressing—mothers and children. Child's rejection of Calvinist doctrine and the authority of the Old Testament would also have needlessly antagonized the Calvinist missionaries who were leading the white opposition to Cherokee removal.[51] Instead of being welcomed as an instrument of the cause, the book would have drawn sectarian fire and diverted the energies of the missionaries away from their main task. Nor could a book couched in the language of Republican Motherhood and designed for the nursery have served to mobilize the politicians and opinion-makers capable of acting on the Cherokee question. A peculiar hybrid, counterproductive on every score, *The First Settlers* is essentially an apprentice work. Child had not yet found her voice as a propagandist.

Nevertheless, she had identified her vocation as a reformer. And with the same prescience she would show in the abolitionist movement, she had enrolled in the antiremoval crusade at a very early stage — months before the main white spokesman of the Cherokee cause, Jeremiah Evarts, began publishing his widely read "William Penn" letters in August 1829, and well over a year before Congress debated the Indian Removal Bill in May 1830.[52]

Furthermore, *The First Settlers* does seem to have influenced David, at least. He stopped lamenting the threat of Cherokee removal and began agitating against it. "The Indians have a right, a natural right to the soil which they cultivate," and the U.S. government must respect its treaty obligations, he proclaimed in June 1829. In August he hailed reports that the Cherokee were holding mass meetings at which they vowed a "war of extermination" to defend their land: "We applaud the determination of these remnants of a noble race, to perish on their fathers graves, rather than be driven from their heritage." And in September, reacting to news of a group formed to support the president's removal policy, he editorialized in accents that evoke John Brown:

> We call upon all men in this land, white, black and red; bond and free, christian and heathen to resist, as we will in our sphere, the murders and rapine, which are here meditated. We hope the Cherokee Phoenix will make known to the nation the sympathy which is felt for their wrongs, and will cheer them on to resist unto death.
>
> . . . We have heard several respectable men say that they should deem it a duty *to take arms* to protect the Indians and to preserve public treaties inviolate. If the administration does not respect the treaties of the United States and the rights of the Indians, but yield them up to the caprice and cupidity of the Georgians, then do we feel confident that a CIVIL CONTEST between sister states is not distant, and the sooner it comes the better.[53]

As late as 1831, David's militant championship of the Cherokee cause earned him a personal letter of thanks from Chief John Ross, head of the majority die-hard faction of the tribe, which resisted removal till the bitter end. Child pasted it into a scrapbook and treasured it for the rest of her life.[54]

Yet the solidarity movement of "white, black and red; bond and free, christian and heathen" that David envisioned did not materialize under the pro-Cherokee banner. Although white missionaries and the Cherokee formed a strong alliance, they kept their campaign narrowly focused on averting removal. The mainstream Whig politicians who delivered eloquent speeches in Congress against removal had even more limited goals.[55] Without a long-range agenda that challenged the government's entire Indian policy, the crusade to save the Cherokee was bound to peter out, once the forces of white expansionism won their inevitable victory in Georgia.[56]

By the time U.S. troops dispatched the Cherokee on their Trail of Tears in 1838, those advocates of Indian rights who understood the need to attack America's white supremacist system at its roots had begun fighting for the abolition of slavery. Besides the Childs, they included the former slaveholder James G. Birney, who had served as a

lawyer for the Cherokee Nation from 1826 to 1832; the New York City merchant
Arthur Tappan, a financial mainstay of evangelical causes ranging from missionary
societies to abolition; the Quaker poet John Greenleaf Whittier; and William Lloyd
Garrison. They would necessarily bring to the abolitionist movement both the lessons
they had learned from the campaign against Cherokee removal and the unresolved
contradictions that had stymied it.[57]

The ideological and rhetorical flaws in *The First Settlers* herald several of the principal contradictions abolitionists would face — suspicion of immigrant workers (especially Irish Catholics), whom abolitionists would often inadvertently antagonize while
championing people of color; and sectarian disputes over religious orthodoxy and
women's rights, which would split abolitionists into warring camps in 1839. Child
would never entirely free herself of her biases against Catholic immigrants (whose
plight she publicized in the 1840s), but she would try to mediate and transcend sectarian disputes, once she embraced her new vocation and mastered the art of propaganda. In her later pleas for justice toward African Americans and Indians, she would
steer clear of introducing extraneous issues that could only divide the audience she was
trying to reach and deflect attention from the causes she was trying to further.[58] At the
same time, by addressing these works to the public at large, she would doff the veil of
Republican Motherhood and step boldly into the political sphere.

In 1829, however, Child was not yet prepared to shift from literature to politics. The
author of *Hobomok* still succeeded best at creating sympathy for the Indians through her
fiction.

5

Blighted Prospects: Indian Fiction and Domestic Reality

One remembers writing his first book as distinctly as he recollects the first time he saw the ocean. Like the unquiet sea, all the elements of our nature are then heaving and tumultuous. Restless, insatiable ambition, is on us like a fiery charm. Every thing partakes of the brightness and boundlessness of our own hopes. . . . It then seems strange how mortals can avoid being intellectually great. . . .

. . . We then write because we cannot help it — the mind is a full fountain that will overflow — and if the waters sparkle as they fall, it is from their own impetuous abundance. . . .

The last book, like the first, may indeed be written because we cannot help it: not that the full mind overflows — but the printer's boy stands at our elbow. We then look to bookseller's accounts for inspiration, hunt for pearls because we have promised to furnish them, and string glass beads because they will sell better than diamonds.[1]

Titled "The First and Last Book," this poignant retrospective of Child's career, which rounds out her first collection of fiction and verse, *The Coronal* (1832), sums up the psychological transformation she had undergone since gate-crashing the literary world with her daring interracial romance seven years earlier. As her use of masculine pronouns betrays, Child had started on her race for glory with so little consciousness of the limits imposed on women writers that she had essentially thought of herself as a man. The "[r]estless, insatiable ambition" she describes; the confidence she expresses in her ability to achieve not mere popular success, but intellectual greatness; the phallic metaphor of the "impetuous," overflowing fountain, which conveys her youthful sense of her creative powers — all align her not with the typical female scribbler, who shrank from publicity and professed to write only when induced by divine fiat or desperate financial need, but with the male genius who, like Whitman, proclaimed himself a "kosmos," or like Melville, thundered "Give me a condor's quill! Give me Vesuvius' crater for an inkstand!"[2]

By the time Child published *The Coronal*, she had suffered a rude awakening. After the critical failure of *The Rebels* (1825), and concomitantly, the enthusiastic reception of *Evenings in New England* and the *Juvenile Miscellany*, she had learned to redefine herself primarily as a woman writer, seeking moral influence and economic independence rather than intellectual greatness, though continuing to maintain a foothold in the sphere of belles lettres through her gift book fiction. Within three months of her marriage in October 1828, Child no longer enjoyed even the satisfaction of controlling her income and balancing her literary and financial goals. Instead, she found herself at the mercy of David's spiraling debts. As a nineteenth-century wife, she now fell under the coverture law, which meant that all her earnings and the copyrights to her books belonged to her husband. Once David lost the Keyes libel suit in January 1829, financial exigency became the driving force behind Child's literary career, dictating how she would use her talents. She had metamorphosed from a literary prophet deciphering the "open volume of poetry and truth" for her acolytes into a jaded professional author churning out copy for the market and looking only to "bookseller's accounts for inspiration" (282–84).

The Coronal marks the transition between these two phases of Child's career. Twelve out of thirty-one selections, including several poems, first appeared in the *Atlantic Souvenir*, *The Token*, or Nathaniel P. Willis's short-lived gift book, *The Legendary*. One poem originated in the *Juvenile Miscellany*. Seven stories and sketches had been written specifically for the *Massachusetts Journal*. The remainder apparently served as fillers for *The Coronal*.[3]

The most impressive stories in the volume, however (besides "The Rival Brothers," discussed in chapter 2), are "The Lone Indian," "The Indian Wife," and "Chocorua's Curse," which span the same period as *The First Settlers of New England* and reflect the same passionate concern for the Indians' plight. To these must be added the most complex and original of Child's Indian tales, "The Church in the Wilderness," which she had contributed to *The Legendary* along with "The Indian Wife," but inexplicably omitted from *The Coronal*.[4] All four stories display the spirit of "[r]estless, insatiable ambition" and "tumultuous" energy that had animated *Hobomok*. But they also translate the humanitarian agenda of *The First Settlers* into a new kind of protest fiction, which Child would soon hone into a fine art. In this respect, too, as well as in their darkened mood and uncharacteristically muted criticism of patriarchy (especially noticeable in "Chocorua's Curse," written on the heels of David's libel conviction), Child's Indian stories signal a turning point in her career. For the better part of the next fifteen years, domestic usefulness and social reform would replace literary ambition as the fulcrum of her creativity.

The historical moment at which Child produced the bulk of her Indian stories saw the convergence of two phenomena — an unprecedented Indian vogue in the literary marketplace and the physical elimination of Indians from the eastern United States, as one tribe after another was forcibly transported beyond the Mississippi. The irony spoke volumes. Culturally as well as politically, American nationalism fed off the Indian's stolen birthright. The creation of a "native" American literature required the appropriation of the Indian heritage — indeed, of Indians themselves — as surely as the building of a powerful modern state required the appropriation of Indian land. Both appropriations reduced the Indian to the white man's subject. Inevitably, the stories that filled the literary annuals echoed the controversy over the Indian's destiny then reverberating through the halls of Congress.[5]

The dominant modes served to justify the ruthless slaughter of America's Native population, by portraying Indians as bloodthirsty savages. A flagrant but not atypical example is William Leete Stone's "A Romance of the Border," whose climactic scene of a warrior tomahawking a helpless woman announces its debt to Puritan narratives of captivity and Indian fighting: "his eyes flashing fire, and his distended nostrils breathing vengeance and fury, . . . his uplifted hatchet twinkled for a moment in the air, and was in the same instant planted deep in the lovely temples of the beautiful Alice Johnson!" Chronicling a massacre perpetrated during the Revolution by the famous Mohawk chief Joseph Brant, who had sided with the English, the story's every detail drives home the message that no accommodation is possible with such perfidious enemies — that if allowed to survive, Indians will threaten the nation's very existence.[6]

Less obviously, but no less effectively, stories purporting to lament the degeneration of the noble savage into a sot promoted the myth of a race doomed to "fade away" at the approach of white "civilization." William J. Snelling's "Te Zahpahtah. A Sketch from Indian History," for instance, depicts the drunkenness and brawling that destroy the Dacotahs from within, despite their chief's efforts to save them. The Indians' primitive ethos cannot withstand exposure to white society, Snelling implies, and civilization offers no remedies — all too receptive to its vices, Indians remain stubbornly impervious to its virtues.[7]

Only a half-dozen stories in the gift books of the Indian removal era attempt to articulate the Indian's viewpoint, hold whites accountable for the state of war between the two peoples, or envision alternatives to genocide. Four of them are Child's. The other two — John Neal's "Otter-Bag, the Oneida Chief" and the anonymous "Narantsauk" — follow in her wake. This fact defines Child's contribution to the genre of Indian fiction and illuminates the political perspective distinguishing her from most of her literary peers.

Once again, as in *Hobomok*, Child severs Indian fiction from its roots in the Puritan captivity narrative and adapts it to a diametrically opposite purpose. Yet Child's four Indian tales of 1827–29 go further than *Hobomok*. Now her aim is not simply to repudiate the bigotry of her Puritan forebears, but to do justice to the Indian. This entails highlighting America's sorry history of racial conflict and squarely confronting the white rapacity and bad faith responsible for it. Unlike *Hobomok*, "The Lone Indian," "The Indian Wife," "The Church in the Wilderness," and "Chocorua's Curse" offer no happy endings, because Child has come to realize that her novel's ending is not happy for the Indian. On the contrary, these stories dramatize the tragic miscarriage of the very alternatives *Hobomok* and *The First Settlers* entertain — brotherhood, intermarriage, assimilation, cultural syncretism, and symbiosis. Pervaded by images of ravaged forests and blighted lives, they also warn of the price the nation will pay for its dispossession of the Indian.

The political thrust of Child's Indian fiction is immediately evident in "The Lone Indian" (1827).[8] The lead story in *The Coronal*, coming right after the poem "Caius Marius," which opens the collection, its placement indicates how much importance Child attached to mobilizing support for the Indian cause. The juxtaposition of the story and the poem implicitly link the evicted Mohawk chief, brooding over his devastated land, with the exiled Roman general, brooding among the ruins of Carthage, the Tunisian city Rome had destroyed. At the same time, by identifying her protagonist Powontonamo as a Mohawk and his bride Soonseetah as an Oneida — two of the Six Nations constituting the Iroquois Confederacy — Child pointedly takes issue with Cooper, who had vilified the Iroquois the previous year in *The Last of the Mohicans* (1826). Not only does she create sympathy for the very Indians Cooper had stigmatized as "ravenous varments" and "greedy and lying . . . varlets";[9] she portrays them in the familiar language of domesticity. Powontonamo loves Soonseetah "as fondly, deeply, and passionately, as ever a white man loved," Child tells her readers.[10] And to encourage their emotional identification with her Indian protagonists, she conveys the breakdown of cultural values and tribal structures through the metaphors of home and family dear to nineteenth-century audiences, rather than through descriptions of the rampant alcoholism that so horrifyingly epitomized the white assault on Indian culture.

Child's most revolutionary gesture, however, is to present Powontonamo's story entirely from his point of view, allowing him to articulate his outrage at white arrogance and ingratitude without the mediation of a competing white voice. Even her third-person narrator speaks from within an Indian language zone and describes English practices through Indian eyes.[11]

As Child argues in *The First Settlers*, so she shows in "The Lone Indian" that "the natives would gladly have allowed the English to dwell with them" in harmony — a possibility whites rejected.[12] "[F]rank, chivalrous, and kind," Powontonamo treats whites generously when they come to buy land: "he met them with an open palm, and spread his buffalo for the traveller" (154). Although Mohawk prophets warn that the English will soon grow so numerous as to drive off the game on which the Indians depend for food, Powontonamo does not heed them. The traditional ethic by which he has always lived prescribes sharing his surplus with needy strangers, and he cannot believe that a territory as vast as the American continent will be overrun by a single race.

He soon learns otherwise, as the baleful "strokes of the axe levelling the old trees of his forests" (156) announce that the English live by a very different ethic. "[T]he ravages of the civilized destroyer" systematically lay waste to the environment the Indians have treated as sacred: "Where were the trees, under which he had frolicked in infancy, sported in boyhood, and rested after the fatigues of battle? They formed the English boat, or lined the English dwelling. Where were the holy sacrifice-heaps of his people? The stones were taken to fence in the land, which the intruder dared to call his own. Where was his father's grave? The stranger's road passed over it, and his cattle trampled on the ground where the mighty Mohawk slumbered" (156–57). The accents in which Child condemns this despoliation are not merely Powontonamo's, but those of the great Shawnee chief Tecumseh. "Where today are the Pequot? Where are the Narraganset, the Mohican, the Pocanoket and many other once powerful tribes of our people?" Tecumseh had demanded less than two decades ago: "They have vanished before the avarice and oppression of the white man. . . . Look abroad over their once beautiful country, and what see you now? Nought but the *ravages of the paleface destroyers*" (italics added).[13]

Compounding desecration with barefaced effrontery, the white man who has seized the Indian's domains, after being welcomed into them as a guest, now accuses the Indian of trespassing. "[Y]our squaw has been stripping a dozen of my trees, and I don't like it over much," a white farmer tells Powontonamo at a moment when the irate chief can "ill brook a white man's insolence." With the fury of a "raging panther" and an "ambushed rattlesnake," Powontonamo reminds "the unconscious offender" that he is "chief of the Mohawks" and that "[t]hese broad lands are all his own" (157–58). But by then it is too late to restore his rights.

As game disappears and Powontonamo's tribe dwindles, "the English [swarm], like vultures around the dying," and the Mohawk prophets' warnings are fulfilled (157). The crowning blow comes when Powontonamo's wife and son die of a fever they have caught from the English. At the end of the story no trace of Powontonamo or his family remains. Even the tree he has planted over the grave of his wife and son has been cut down by "the white man's axe," and "[n]one ever knew where Powontonamo laid his dying head" (159–60).

Child reverses the significance of the "vanishing" Indian convention to which Powontonamo's story initially appears to conform. Though she dispatches Powontonamo across the "distant Mississippi, . . . where no man called him brother; and [where] the wolves of the desert . . . howled the death-song of the Mohawk Eagle," the last glimpse she provides of the country he has left behind flatly contradicts the myth that a higher civilization has taken the Indian's place. Whereas *Hobomok* culminates in a vision of the Anglo-American nation as a "mighty tree" whose branches shelter the peoples of the earth — the fertile outgrowth of a plantation that had begun as a "tender slip" needing the Indian's protection to survive (150) — "The Lone Indian" reveals only the denuded landscape Powontonamo sees when he decides to quit his native land:

The Englishman's road wound like a serpent around the banks of the Mohawk; and iron hoofs had so beaten down the war-path, that a hawk's eye could not discover an Indian track. The last wigwam was destroyed; and the sun looked boldly down upon spots he had visited only by stealth, during thousands and thousands of moons. The few remaining trees, clothed in the fantastic mourning of autumn; the long line of heavy clouds, melting away before the coming sun; and the distant mountain, seen through the blue mist of departing twilight, alone remained as he had seen them in his boyhood. (159–60)

In short, "The Lone Indian" gives the lie to the ideological justifications for Indian removal invoked by nearly all Child's contemporaries. It contrasts starkly, for example, with such apologias as I. M'Lellan's "Hymn of the Cherokee Indian," whose Cherokee speaker conveniently endorses the belief that Providence has reserved the American continent for a race capable of taking full advantage of its resources, and exhorts his people:

> Let us yield our pleasant land
> To the stranger's stronger hand;
> Red men, and their realms must sever,
> They forsake them, and for ever![14]

Child does not let her readers take refuge in this comfortable evasion. Instead, she forces them to confront the human and environmental cost of the nation's unbridled expansionism. The expulsion of the Indian results in continental blight, not "improvement," she implies.

One could hardly find a better indicator of the place "The Lone Indian" occupies in literary history than the enthusiasm with which Child greeted John Neal's "Otter-Bag, the Oneida Chief" when it appeared in *The Token* for 1829, just as she was completing *The First Settlers*. Rejoicing that "men of high intellectual endowments, have been touched with the wrongs and unmerited sufferings of our Indians, and have come forward to vindicate their rights," Child hailed Neal for so ably exposing "the futility and injustice of the arguments used in defence of our wresting from the Indians their land" (*First Settlers* 254–55). In his authorial preface to the story, Neal indeed articulates a powerful protest against the ideology of Indian removal through the mouth of an imaginary Indian spokesman, but he abandons this device in the story proper. Otter-Bag himself is a stereotypical "good Indian" ally on the model of Hobomok, not a proud chief like Powontonamo, who meets whites as their equal, and Neal presents him through two white observers. Doubly distanced, the Indian is also silenced by the very question the narrative sets out to answer — whether or not Otter-Bag was guilty of the treachery with which he was charged by the white fellow soldiers who "butchered" him. It is as if white interests must dictate the Indian's story, even in a narrative that asks us to do him justice. Rare is the identification Child achieves with her Indian protagonist by allowing him to speak for himself.

Rarer still is the greatest achievement of Child's Indian fiction — its persistence in exploring alternatives to the displacement of America's native inhabitants by white settlers. What gives her stories their power is their convincing reconstruction of a past that might have led to a better future for the two races — and for the American continent the white race has been plundering. The might-have-been that they conjure up so vividly makes it impossible to accept the necessity of reenacting the sordid past — impossible to accept the scenario already prescribed for Georgia's Cherokee and Florida's Seminole.

While "The Lone Indian" suggests that Powontonamo's tragedy might have been averted had whites chosen to respect his tribal ethic and share the land accordingly, "The Church in the Wilderness" and "The Indian Wife" examine the alternatives of cultural syncretism and intermarriage mapped out in *The First Settlers*. French Catholic missionaries and fur traders had elected precisely these options, foreclosed by English Puritans.[15] Child thus probes the French colonial experience. The question she raises is whether the French came any closer than the English to developing relations with the Indians that allowed for mutual enrichment, in lieu of European enrichment at Indian expense. "The Church in the Wilderness" and "The Indian Wife" offer different answers to this question.

The lead story in Nathaniel P. Willis's new gift book, *The Legendary*, "The Church in the Wilderness" focuses on a historical incident of 1724 that counterpoints the French and English modes of colonization: the English massacre of an Abenaki Indian hamlet served by the French Jesuit priest, Sebastian Rale, a master of the cultural syncretism through which his order sought to win the Indians to Catholicism and to advance French colonial aims. Because it took place in Norridgewock, the massacre resonated with special significance for Child. Remnants of the Abenaki tribe still frequented the site of their forebears' mass grave, and memorials of the carnage perpetually turned up to haunt the white settlers who had usurped the land. In Child's words: "The soil is fertilized by the blood of a murdered tribe. Even now the spade strikes against wampum belts, which once covered hearts as bold and true, as ever beat beneath a crusader's shield, and gaudy beads are found, which once ornamented bosoms throbbing with as deep and fervent tenderness, as woman ever displayed in the mild courtesies of civilized life."[16]

The accidental disinterment of Father Rale's long-lost church bell in 1815, the year Child arrived in Norridgewock, no doubt aroused her interest in the massacre, especially since the find reanimated the controversy that had swirled around the Jesuit in his lifetime. During her stay, Child seems to have sought information about Rale from many sources: the British annalists who excoriated him as a warmonger and blamed him for provoking the massacre in which he and his congregation perished; the French chroniclers who hailed him as a saint; "the old inhabitants of Norridgewock"; and Abenaki oral tradition, from which Child seems to have learned that Rale had lost his influence over the tribe by the time the British attack occurred — a fact confirmed by twentieth-century ethnologists. Shortly before Child left Norridgewock, a new "Biographical Memoir of Father Rasles," which attempted to strike a balance between French and British accounts, again drew her attention to this fascinating chapter of colonial history. She probably continued her research in Convers's fine collection of documents and in Harvard University archives to which he gave her access. Discussions with her brother, who would later publish his own "Life of Sebastian Rale" in his friend Jared Sparks's *Library of American Biography* (1845), may well have stimulated the two stories Child based on the Norridgewock massacre: "Adventures of a Bell," written for the *Juvenile Miscellany* (March 1827), and "The Church in the Wilderness" (1828).[17]

Even the version addressed to a juvenile audience unsparingly depicts the savagery the English displayed in an assault that had leveled the Abenaki settlement and left almost no survivors. The aspect of Rale's mission and of the French colonial model that seems to have appealed most strongly to Child's imagination, however, is the alternative of cultural intermingling they posed to wars of extermination—an alternative whose import many of her contemporaries likewise understood, as the revival of interest in Rale during the Indian removal era attests.[18] Child also pursues hints her sources furnished of racial amalgamation at Norridgewock—the means of Indian-white reconciliation she had envisioned in *Hobomok*. When British soldiers had found the body of a mixed-blood chief among their slain victims, they had jumped to the conclusion that the Jesuit priest had fathered a natural son by his Abenaki servant—an error French historians had corrected by identifying the chief as the son of Rale's friend, the Baron de Castine, who had married an Abenaki woman and left their children in the care of her people.

Extrapolating from these kernels of fact, Child centers "The Church in the Wilderness" around the "mixture of nations" (6). All of her protagonists act out different variations on this theme. Through characters who cross cultural, racial, or sexual boundaries, Child explores the viability of solving the "Indian problem" by breaking down the barriers between Indians and whites.

The historical Rale had combined cultural syncretism with strict maintenance of sexual boundaries. Child assesses the limitations of this approach. Probing the contradictions generated by Rale's priestly vow of celibacy, she suggests that his denial of his own sexuality may have played a role in undermining the model of Euro-Indian relations he personified. The religious mission to which he had consecrated his life required that he assimilate into his converts' society, in accordance with Jesuit custom. Thus, in Child's story he has lived in the wilderness for thirty years, "sharing the dangers and privations incident to savage life" (4). Not only has he mastered Indian languages so thoroughly that "his utterance could not have been distinguished from that of a native, had it not been for a peculiarly softened cadence, and rapid enunciation" (4); he has also acquired an Indian "quickness of eye and ear" (12). Nevertheless, Rale's religious mission has forbidden him to consummate his relationship with his adoptive tribe by marrying an Abenaki woman. As a result, he has firmly repressed his sexual and emotional cravings: "A restless light in his small, hazel eye, and the close compression of his lips, betokened one, who had, with a strong hand, thrown up dykes against the overflowing torrent of his own mad passions" (4). Anticipating Freud, Child theorizes that Rale may have experienced a return of the repressed: "let man do his worst, there are moments when nature will rebound from all the restraints imposed on her by pride, prejudice, or superstition" (4). In short, Child portrays the priest as riven by deep conflicts between his spiritual calling and his sexual impulses—conflicts he tries to resolve by pouring the "love he could not wholly stifle within him" into two adopted children (4).

Products of intermarriages, Rale's adopted children symbolize a sexual as well as cultural "mixture of nations" (6). The first, Otoolpha, "The Son of the Stranger," is the orphaned offspring of the Baron de Castine "by a beautiful young Abnakis." Less than a year after Rale invites Otoolpha's Abenaki nurse to "take up her abode in his own wigwam" (4), a second mixed-blooded infant turns up abandoned in the woods (almost as if growing out of this domestic arrangement), and Rale adopts and raises the girl along with Otoolpha. The Indians name her Saupoolah, "The Scattered Leaf," signifying that "her parentage and tribe were unknown," and that she is to be "engrafted . . . on the tree of Abnakis" (5).

On one level, Child's reference to the priest's cohabitation with his adoptees' Abenaki nurse hints at the sexual liaison her English sources alleged. On another level, as the fruit of Rale's "marriage" with Indian culture, Saupoolah and Otoolpha represent the sublimation of his sexual impulses. The priest indeed seems to recognize this by inflicting "long and painful . . . penances . . . upon himself, for an all-absorbing love, which his erring conscience deemed a sin" (9). Yet Child's characterization of Otoolpha and Saupoolah serves larger purposes. The Jesuit's mixed-blood adoptees become her vehicles for imagining solutions more promising than his to the problem of reconciling European and Indian value systems, and thus avoiding race war. They embody the dissolution of racial boundaries and the fusion of cultural types that might have produced a far more vigorous and vibrant America, had it occurred on a wider scale:

> [T]hese extraordinary young people grew up with a strange mixture of European and aboriginal character. Both had the rapid, elastic tread of Indians; but the outlines of their tall, erect figures possessed something of the pliant gracefulness of France. When indignant, the expression of their eyes was like light from a burning-glass; but in softer moments, they had a melting glance, which belongs only to a civilized and voluptuous land. Saupoolah's hair, though remarkably soft and fine, had the jet black hue of the savage; Otoolpha's was brown, and when moistened by exercise, it sometimes curled slightly around his high, prominent forehead. (6)

Superior in physique and broader in emotional compass than their parent stocks, Rale's Euro-Indian adoptees illustrate the advantages Child sees in intermarriage.

Child also presents these mixed-bloods as agents for the dissolution of political boundaries that could have followed from the amalgamation of races and cultures. When Otoolpha and Saupoolah visit a nearby English settlement to trade their handmade baskets for beads, they make friends with an Englishwoman, Mrs. Allan. On one occasion Mrs. Allan saves Saupoolah from drowning, at the risk of her own life. After they grow up, Otoolpha and Saupoolah "protect Mrs. Allan from a thousand petty wrongs and insults, with which her white brethren were not unfrequently visited" (6). Such neighborly reciprocity between Indians and whites, Child implies, could have offered another alternative to race war.

The dissolution of boundaries Child imagines through her mixed-blood characters even extends to gender. Refusing to conform to the manners and roles prescribed for girls, Saupoolah enjoys a freedom many a European girl would envy: "From the first dawn of reason she gave indications of an impetuous, fearless, and romantic spirit. The squaw who nursed her, together with the little Otoolpha, tried in vain to curb her roving propensities. At four and five years old, she would frequently be absent several days, accompanied by her foster brother. . . . [T]hey could cross streams, leap ditches, and thread their way through the labyrinths of the wilderness, with the boldness and sagacity of young hunters . . ." (5). Such freedom, Child concedes, is not typical for Indian women. If European civilization idealizes women as fragile decorative objects to be confined to the parlor, Indian culture assigns them toils that "weigh down the springs of the soul, till the body refuses to rebound at its feeble impulses" (8). Still, Child seems aware that Indian culture, unlike European, provides room for those who deviate from gender norms. As the twentieth-century Indian scholar Paula Gunn Allen explains, many tribes had traditions of "gender designation based on dreams," innate preference, or familial need, permitting individuals to live "for all practical purposes" as members of the opposite sex. Far from being looked down on, such transsexual "men" and "women" were often accorded special respect as shamans. Fittingly, Child endows Saupoolah with shamanistic powers that have earned her the title "Daughter of a Prophet" (13). Although Saupoolah is not transsexual, since she marries her foster brother rather than a lesbian partner, she does correspond closely to the " 'warrior woman' or 'manly hearted woman' who acted as a man in both hunting and warfare" among certain tribes. Even after her marriage, she continues to hunt with Otoolpha, never adopting female avocations.[19]

By challenging boundaries of race, culture, and gender through her mixed-blood characters, Child shows that contrary to American ideology, these boundaries do not grow out of nature, but violate it. The products of a biracial heritage and an Indian upbringing, Otoolpha and Saupoolah exemplify the harmony with nature that intermarriage might have made as available to Europeans as to Indians: "Many were the bold and beautiful thoughts which rushed upon their untutored imaginations, as they roamed over a picturesque country, sleeping in clefts where panthers hid themselves, and scaling precipices from which they scared the screaming eagles. Perhaps cultivated intellect never received brighter thoughts from the holy rays of the evening star, or a stormier sense of grandeur from the cataract, than did these children of the wilderness" (8). Free from artificial restraints, the thoughts of Otoolpha and Saupoolah partake of the wildness and power of nature itself.

In sum, Child uses her two mixed-blood protagonists to suggest the many benefits Europeans could have derived from intermingling racially and culturally with the Indians — benefits that range from the peaceful exchange of goods and services to the reeducation of peoples who have systematically warred against nature and sought to root natural impulses out of themselves.

Historically, however, neither the cultural syncretism practiced by Rale nor the sexual amalgamation of Indian and European embodied by Child's imaginary mixed-bloods survived in Norridgewock. Instead, the British razed the settlement and imposed their own colonial model of white supremacy and Indian extermination. Thus, Child devotes the second half of "The Church in the Wilderness" to examining the factors responsible for the Franco-Indian defeat.

Chief among these factors, she surmises, is the breakdown of Rale's relationship with the Abenaki. She depicts the unraveling of his life's work as a return of the repressed that leads the priest to transfer his allegiance from his Indian family to his European fellow colonials. Again extrapolating from a kernel of fact—the discovery among the victims of the Norridgewock massacre of a gravely wounded English boy named William Mitchell, captured by the Abenaki in a raid six months earlier—Child now introduces this boy into the story, renaming him William Posonby and giving him a French mother, whom she identifies as Rale's long-lost beloved. The priest, she reveals, has taken orders because the woman he sought to marry succumbed to pressure to make a wealthy match (16). French society has induced Rale and his beloved to act against nature—unlike the Indians he proposes to "civilize." As the son who should have been his—the fruit of a loveless marriage of convenience that has "driven [Rale] to a life of solitude and self-denial" (16)—William Posonby incarnates the priest's repressed sexuality, which Child conjures up out of his past to haunt him.

It is on a night when he has been dreaming of France and of "a bright, laughing girl, who had won his heart in early youth" (10) that Rale finds William in the forest beside the body of his dead mother. Like an externalization of the forces Rale fears in himself, apocalyptic portents flash through the skies as the priest approaches the refugees. William and his mother, Rale learns, had fled from Indian captors, who had subjected the boy's English father to a "horrid and lingering death" (16). The two had intended to appeal to Rale for protection, but William's mother had collapsed on the outskirts of Norridgewock.

This resurgence of Rale's past marks a turning point in his mission among the Abenaki. William replaces Otoolpha and Saupoolah in his affections, and the priest even begins to display "occasional harshness" toward the half-Indian children he once loved so dearly. Realizing that the actual object of his passion is William's dead mother, he resorts to ever more strenuous self-repression. "The gloom with which he had long looked upon the world" deepens, reinforcing his motives for "giving up his whole soul to the stern dictates of Jesuitical maxims" (15–16). The syndrome recalls Child's psychoanalysis of the Puritans, whose own brand of religious fanaticism justified their extermination of the Indians: "they vainly attempted to escape from the remorse, which, with all its terrors, seizes on the hearts of the guilty, by redoubling their superstitious observances" (*First Settlers* 14). Rale, she suggests, has turned into the very counterpart of his Puritan foes, with whom he has far more in common than with the Indians, despite the differences between the French and English colonial models; the same projected self-hatred that fuels the Puritans' genocidal Indian wars dooms the Jesuit's alternative strategy of cultural syncretism.

Child dramatizes this insight by reversing the pattern the first half of the story has set up. The priest's substitution of the Anglo-French William Posonby for the Franco-Indian Otoolpha and Saupoolah precipitates a series of loyalty conflicts that destroy cross-cultural alliances and culminate in all-out war. As the Abenaki sense that their priest has reverted to his European identity, they cease to trust him, and their former prophet Wautoconomese regains his ascendancy. Meanwhile, hostilities between the Abenaki and the encroaching English colonists daily increase. To appease the "Evil Spirit [that] had governed them ever since William Posonby came among them,"

Wautoconomese and the Abenaki tribal council decree the sacrifice of the boy (18–19). Rale pleads in vain and finally agrees to a counterproposal of Otoolpha's—a "war against every white man, woman, and child" in the region, which, if successful, need not require the immolation of William (19). But this plan compels Saupoolah, in turn, to choose between friendship with Mrs. Allan and loyalty to her people. When Saupoolah warns Mrs. Allan of the coming attack, in defiance of Rale's and Otoolpha's prohibition, she confronts her friend with the same terrible dilemma, which the Englishwoman resolves in the opposite way by alerting her countrymen and thereby ensuring the annihilation of the Abenaki.

Child presents the ensuing massacre as the climax of a chain reaction that has spread suspicion and antagonism throughout the community, dividing priest from parishioners, European from Indian, adoptive father from children, and most tragically in the case of Otoolpha and Saupoolah, husband from wife and the "Indian" from the "European" self of the mixed-blood. Following oral tradition, Child describes the British invaders as bursting into Norridgewock while Rale is celebrating mass, and she portrays the priest as stabbing himself with the sword buried in William Posonby's breast.[20] Though historically inaccurate, these details convey symbolic truths. The Norridgewock massacre certainly represented a travesty of the Puritans' boasted Christianity. "Not one escaped; not one," Child writes of the Abenaki men, women, and children the British mowed down as they fled (22). Moreover, whether or not Rale suffered from the repressed sexual desires she attributes to him, he did, in a sense, commit suicide by refusing to surrender and provoking his enemies into dispatching him. As a modern historian has argued:

> [D]eath swift and sure would be preferred to anything life could offer him. If he surrendered or was taken, he must spend the rest of his life in a Boston jail. . . . But even life and freedom would be worse than captivity. His work among his Indians was ended. The village he had spent his lifetime in serving was . . . destroyed; his converts were dead or scattered; . . . his whole life-work was to vanish like a dream. He saw that his children, as he called them, would never again receive him, even if he lived.[21]

In keeping with the tragic significance Child discerns in the English victory at Norridgewock, "The Church in the Wilderness" ends with all traces of alternative cultural models obliterated: "Before the setting of the sun, the pretty hamlet was reduced to ashes; and the Indians slept their last sleep beneath their own possessions. . . . For many years two white crosses marked the place where the Jesuit and his English boy were buried; but they have long since been removed. The white man's corn is nourished by the bones of the Abnakis; and the name of their tribe is well nigh forgotten" (23). Child leaves her readers with the chilling image of a civilization that has founded its prosperity on genocide.

Because of the comparisons the Norridgewock massacre inevitably evoked between French Jesuit and English Puritan relations with Indians—especially at a moment when the nation was debating whether Indians and whites could coexist—the 1724 episode inspired several other literary renditions. Seven months after "The Church in the Wilderness" came off the press, the actor Edwin Forrest sponsored a contest for plays featuring Indian heroes. In response, an ambitious young author with whom Child had flirted in Maine, Nathaniel Deering, produced *Carabasset*, named after an Abenaki chief slain at Norridgewock. Almost simultaneously, an anonymous story titled "Narantsauk," the Abenaki pronunciation of Norridgewock, appeared in the *Atlantic Souvenir* for 1829. Eight years later, Child's friend John Greenleaf Whittier published what became the most famous version of the Norridgewock saga, the narrative poem "Mogg Megone" (1836), named for another slain Abenaki chief. The different perspectives these works offer on the same events and characters shed new light on Child's political agenda.[22]

Both *Carabasset* and "Mogg Megone" are filled with unrelenting depictions of Indian savagery. Sharing the belief that nature has destined the Indians for extinction and made them impervious to "civilizing" influences, neither Deering nor Whittier ascribes any efficacy to Rale's missionary work. Of the two, Whittier, a Quaker pacifist who by 1836 was strongly committed to abolitionism, surprisingly betrays the more virulent anti-Indian and anti-Catholic prejudices. Stereotypical in every respect, his Mogg Megone thirsts for blood, lusts after a white woman, and drinks himself into a beastlike stupor; and his Rale proves to be a murderous fanatic who actively incites the Abenaki against the British. Significantly, when Whittier creates a character personifying the crossing of cultural boundaries, it is a white man who has regressed to savagery: the "swarthy" outlaw Johnny Boniton.[23]

Only the anonymous author of "Narantsauk" attempts, like Child, to imagine alternative relations between whites and Indians.[24] Reviewing the story in the *Ladies' Magazine*, Sarah Hale noted its striking similarity to "The Church in the Wilderness." "Father Ralle seems in a fair way of obtaining that fame for piety and disinterested benevolence, which he undoubtedly deserved," she commented, adding: "and we are glad to see American writers doing justice to the Indian character, though at the expense of our own ancestors."[25]

In one major respect the author of "Narantsauk" actually goes further than Child, envisioning an interracial alliance she never considers—an Indianized white man who takes up arms to defend the Indians against the British. This hero, a British aristocrat named Arundel, also embraces Child's favorite solution to the race problem—intermarriage—by wedding the half-Abenaki daughter of the Baron de Castine. Reflecting an authorial ambivalence absent from "The Church in the Wilderness," however, "Narantsauk" perpetually seeks to erase its mixed-blood heroine's Indian identity. Unlike Saupoolah, her counterpart in "Narantsauk," Clara, is given a white education in a convent, as her name suggests, and "Narantsauk"'s Rale even tries to persuade her to "take the veil." Arundel is "alarmed" by the very traits in Clara that give Child's Saupoolah her charm: "an independence, a fearlessness of consequences, a sportive gaiety that he was aware would create much surprise among the primitive dames of New England, and ill comported with the titled dignity of the elder branches of his

family in Britain." Contemplating "with some repugnance . . . the blot upon his es-
cutcheon" of a half-Indian wife, he conceals Clara's ancestry when he introduces her to
his aristocratic relatives. Perhaps most tellingly, the couple settles not in America, but
in England. Ultimately, the anonymous author of "Narantsauk" cannot endorse the
prospect of a racially mixed America, which Child had espoused as early as *Hobomok*
and translated into much bolder cultural terms in "The Church in the Wilderness."[26]

What emerges most plainly from these comparisons is the daring of Child's efforts to
imagine her way out of her culture's dead ends. More committed than ever to breaking
down the racial, cultural, and sexual barriers she sees as the root of America's violent
history, Child reveals an insight into the psychosexual dynamics of racism that none of
her literary rivals seems to have achieved. She also reveals a distinctive understanding
of how barriers erected against outsiders imprison and impoverish insiders. The ideal
that "The Church in the Wilderness" holds up in lieu of race war — a society enriched
by racial and cultural intermingling and freed from the compulsion to stifle human
nature — is still radical today.

If Child's opening story in *The Legendary* presents the marriage of races and cultures
fostered by the French colonial system as a tragically aborted alternative to the genocide practiced by the English, its companion piece, "The Indian Wife," takes a darker
view. It exposes French colonialism as no less destructive to the Indians, notwithstanding its veneer of tolerance for cultural syncretism. In this story Child uses intermarriage as a metaphor for a more insidious mode of victimization, which reduces a people
to the status of dependents — submissive wives who have been seduced into matrimony
only to be abandoned when they have lost their birthright.

The Sioux heroine Tahmiroo, who incarnates the plight of her people, falls prey to
the wiles of the greedy and treacherous French fur trader Florimond de Rance precisely because he is able to bridge the cultural gap between them. On the one hand, he
appears willing to accommodate to Indian ways: "the facility with which his pliant
nation conform to the usages of savage life, made him a universal favourite; and, at his
request, he was formally adopted as one of the tribe."[27] On the other hand, he appeals
to the affinity Tahmiroo feels for European ways; "a creature all formed for love," she
has the temperament and demeanor "appropriate to protected and dependant women
in refined countries" and thus proves all the more susceptible to European "deference
and courtesy" toward women (163–64).

Under different circumstances this adaptability to each other's cultures might herald a
truly reciprocal relationship between Indian and European. But in a colonial context,
where the Sioux' "extensive lands on the Missouri [are] daily becoming of more consequence to [the Frenchman's] ambitious nation," the relationship will necessarily involve dominance and exploitation. Accordingly, Tahmiroo's attempts to master French,
which she studies "with a patience and perseverance to which the savage has seldom
been known to submit" (169), her embrace of Catholicism, her "close observance of . . .
European customs," and her imitation of European dress merely speed her degeneration into a "slave" (164, 169). As for de Rance, his marriage with a Sioux chief's daughter

and his assimilation into his wife's tribe are nothing but means of acquiring a fortune that he can repatriate to France.

Even the children embodying the union of the two peoples become pawns in a struggle between colonizer and colonized. Symbolizing his theft of his Indian wife's birthright, de Rance seeks to estrange his aptly named daughter Victoire "from her mother, and her mother's people" and eventually takes her to Quebec to "gratify his ambitious views" for her future (171–72). Tahmiroo, in turn, transformed by this perfidy from a gentle, devoted wife into "as bitter and implacable [a foe] as the most blood-thirsty of her tribe," "instil[s] a deadly hatred of white men" in her son and brings him up as "the veriest little savage that ever let fly an arrow" (175). Rather than give the child up when her husband returns from Quebec to reclaim him, Tahmiroo ultimately chooses to commit suicide in a manner that ritually dissolves her European marriage and reunites her and her son with their Indian ancestors. Decking the boy in her most prized wampum belts and attiring herself in her wedding finery, so that "when her father meets her in the spirit-land, he will know the beads he gave her" (178), she paddles their canoe over the falls of St. Anthony.

In short, "The Indian Wife" turns *Hobomok* on its head and unmasks the betrayal its happy ending represents. By reversing the Indian and European partners' genders, Child highlights the colonial power relations that the marriage of Mary and Hobomok obscures. De Rance's abandonment of Tahmiroo and his decision to reintegrate their children into white society clarify the significance of Mary's departure with little Hobomok. As long as Indians remain subordinate partners to be discarded at will, the story suggests, intermarriage hardly constitutes an alternative to race war.

This assessment corresponds with modern historians'. Describing the exploitation of Indian women involved in the fur trade, for example, Sara Evans writes:

> As guides or as wives, they lived in a social and economic structure organized around the needs of male European traders. When they decided to return to Europe, traders were notorious for abandoning wives of many years, sometimes simply passing them on to their successors. Such practices contributed to the increased reluctance of Indian women to have any relations with white men. . . . [U]nlike their traditional sisters who had virtual control over their offspring, traders' wives experienced the assertion of patriarchal authority most painfully when their children — especially their sons — were sent away to receive a "civilized education."[28]

Detail for detail, Child had formulated the same critique in "The Indian Wife" more than a century and a half earlier.

Despite its insights into the dynamics of interracial marriages that occur in colonial situations, "The Indian Wife" suffers from weaknesses inherent in tales of victimization. Besides being excessively sentimental, it misrepresents the Indian as a helpless, "infantile" creature all too easily duped by whites (162–63). The tragic ending also lends itself to being interpreted as condemning intermarriage.

Child corrected many of these weaknesses when she rewrote the story almost two decades later, titling the new version "Legend of the Falls of St. Anthony" (1846). By then, long experience as an antislavery propagandist and intensive research on the status of women in Western and non-Western societies had sharpened her political consciousness. She gave her Indian heroine, renamed Zah-gah-see-ga-quay, greater maturity and dignity; developed the Sioux chief Wee-chush-ta-doo-ta into a character whose national pride and distrust of whites counterbalance his daughter's pathetic "idolatry" of her undeserving French husband; and ended the story with the marriage of Zah-gah-see-ga-quay's daughter, now renamed Felicie, to a "wealthy Frenchman" — a symbolic endorsement of race-mixing as a long-term solution.[29]

Child's most interesting revisions are the comments she interpolates on the favorable contrast that Indian marriage and child custody mores present to those of white civilization. When the Frenchman Jerome de Rance asks the chief for his daughter's hand, for example, Wee-chush-ta-doo-ta reveals an awareness of the double standard governing white men's relations with women of color. "If a paleface marries an Indian woman," objects the chief, "he calls her his wife while he likes to look upon her, but when he desires another, he walks away and says she is not his wife. Such are not the customs of the red men" (205). Indeed, white captives who married into Indian tribes were treated equally in all respects, as Child could expect her readers to know. Mary Jemison's best-selling 1824 narrative of her life among the Seneca was only one of many popular works attesting to this.[30] Lest readers miss the point, Child takes pains to inform them that "[a]ccording to Indian custom, the mother's right to her offspring amounts to unquestioned law. If her husband chooses to leave the tribe, the children must remain with her" (208). No nineteenth-century woman would have needed reminding that the laws of "civilized" societies, on the contrary, licensed the cruelty of men like Jerome de Rance by giving fathers "unquestioned" custody of the children.

While Child's revisions of "The Indian Wife" reflect her intellectual growth, they also confirm that she had intended the story as a political protest against the continuing violation of Indian rights guaranteed by solemn treaties. No doubt that was a reason why she chose to publish it in the *Massachusetts Journal*, as well as in *The Legendary*. At least one review indicates that "The Indian Wife" did succeed in capturing readers' sympathies. When Sarah Hale held it up for emulation in the *Ladies' Magazine* as a story displaying "the skill of true genius," she stressed the identification Child elicited with the Indian heroine: "The interest, awakened at the opening of the legend, never for a moment flags till we weep over the fate of the 'Startled Fawn' and her beloved boy, when 'they went to the Spirit Land together.' It is stories told like this, with power and pathos, without circumlocution or intricacy, . . . which appear best calculated for a work like the Legendary."[31]

The political sentiments generating this "power and pathos" become especially obvious when one compares "The Indian Wife" with "The Indian Bride," an anonymous story published in the *Atlantic Souvenir* for 1832. The differences are telling. The French hero of "The Indian Bride," significantly named St. Pierre, devotes himself sincerely to civilizing and Christianizing the Natchez, but falls victim to the tribe's vengeance against his people in a war the French provoke. When he elopes with the chief's daughter, the Natchez pursue the lovers and burn them at the stake. Completely negating any sympathy for the wrongs the Natchez have suffered at the hands of the French (wrongs the author acknowledges), the story climaxes with stereotypical scenes of Indian savagery: flames licking the bodies of a well-meaning white man and his Indian beloved, and "the ghastly spectacle of mangled and consuming carcasses" in a French encampment the Natchez have left a "smouldering heap of ruins."[32]

Unlike the author of "The Indian Bride," Child does not idealize the French adventurers who settled among Indians. Nor does she pander to the dread of Indian violence that the captivity narrative had planted in the American psyche. As she would write forty years later in her *Appeal for the Indians*, "so much has been said of [the Indians'] horrid cruelties, and they have taken such deep hold of the popular mind, that it would be like throwing petroleum on a flaming village for me to repeat them."[33] Above all, she places the blame for racial conflict squarely on the shoulders of white colonists. Not Indian savagery, she emphasizes, but white duplicity, has poisoned the relationship between the two peoples.

With "The Indian Wife" and "The Church in the Wilderness," Child's literary productivity reached the peak of six stories for the annuals in one year. Not until the 1840s would she match the output of fiction she achieved during the twelve months before her marriage, when she wrote the bulk of the stories collected in *The Coronal*. Instead, Child began diverting her creativity into other channels. Initially, as *The First Settlers* suggests, she seems to have turned away from fiction out of an impulse to register her political protest against Indian removal more directly. By the time her abortive tract was ready, however, financial rather than political imperatives dictated Child's priorities.

The disastrous falling off of subscriptions to the *Massachusetts Journal*, just after David had borrowed so heavily to keep the paper afloat, and concurrently, the expenses of his libel suits, meant that Child now saw rebuilding the *Journal*'s subscription list as one of her most urgent tasks. She must have calculated that she could earn more from her stories in the long run by using them to attract subscribers to David's newspaper than by selling them to the annuals. Although this move would cost Child her visibility in the literary sphere, since her stories were much likelier to be reviewed when published in the annuals, it would win her a visibility in the political sphere that only one other woman in America then enjoyed—the notorious Frances Wright, coeditor of the radical *Free Enquirer* and pioneer female lecturer. All in all, the trade-off was not necessarily a sacrifice, except for the harassing worry about how to make ends meet.

Child could not know it, of course, but when she accepted the challenge of adapting the *Massachusetts Journal* to a broader audience and turning it into a family newspaper that would appeal to female as well as male household members, she was gaining invaluable long-range experience, She was in fact serving her apprenticeship as the future editor of the *National Anti-Slavery Standard*. That paper would benefit from many of the lessons she learned as she sought to enhance the *Journal*'s literary columns and thus increase subscriptions.

In addition to political news and editorials, the *Journal* now started featuring a series of anecdotal "Light Readings" extracted from various sources; regular reviews of annuals, periodicals, and new novels; cultural criticism, including evaluations of art exhibitions; and sketches and stories "For the *Massachusetts Journal*." Her new responsibilities gave Child the opportunity to step into the shoes of the men who had reviewed *Hobomok* and *The Rebels*, and she clearly took pleasure in delivering rather than merely receiving critical judgments. Assessing Cooper's latest novel, *The Wept of Wish-ton-Wish* (1829), for example, she pronounced it "far short" of his previous fiction. She went on to pay the patriarch back in his own coin: "In his Indians and his Puritans, Mr. Cooper has succeeded very well; but his women are just such as he has always painted—One is gentle, fair-haired and insipid; another, whom he would have spirited and energetic, is as *brusque* as a mastiff."[34]

Child also instructed the public on such topics as "Philosophy and Consistency," "Politeness," "Comparative Strength of Male and Female Intellect," and "Hints to People of Moderate Fortune." It would be through these articles, many of which were reprinted in other newspapers, that she would attract the attention of William Lloyd Garrison.[35] As a cultural critic, Child staked out an ambiguous position. Her "Hints" on domestic economy, though squarely within woman's sphere, articulated political values that applied to larger public issues, as Garrison recognized. At the same time, Child took an increasingly conservative stand on questions of gender.

In "Comparative Strength of Male and Female Intellect," for example, she argued forcefully against the doctrines of sexual equality that Frances Wright was currently preaching. (Ironically, this was the article Garrison chose to reprint, though he would go on to become an ardent champion of women's rights). If "women are now apt to be dissatisfied with praise for mere elegance of mind, quickness of perception, and promptness in the application of their knowledge," Child charged; if they were aspiring "to the more solid reputation of . . . profundity and vigour," it was because "usurpers are easily made giddy with power." Child urged women to content themselves with the status that novelists like Catharine Maria Sedgwick had attained, instead of "contesting for the honors" of politicians like Daniel Webster. Speculating about whether "a different course of education, moral, intellectual, and physical," might change women's "natures" and transform them into "gladiators on the arena of science," Child reached conclusions diametrically opposed to those she would later propound in her essays on women's rights. "[T]here can never be a state of society in which the experiment can be fairly tried," she asserted: "The very circumstance that women do not *need* as much acuteness and vigour of intellect as men, is to me a powerful argument that they do not *possess* it; for it is the wonderful adaptation of every thing to the place it is intended to fill, which constitutes the delightful order of the universe, and makes the vast system of mind and matter a perfect mansion of glories."[36] The phrase "mansion of glories" indicates that Child was parroting Emanuel Swedenborg, whose religion solaced her greatly as she struggled to cope with her new adversities in the months following David's libel conviction.[37] But more to the point, she was also publicly acknowledging her husband's superiority and pledging to refrain from "contesting for [his] honors"— even while helping him improve his newspaper.

Child again locked horns with her feminist adversary—the troubling voice of the younger self she was trying so hard to bury as she embraced wifehood—in the summer of 1829, this time in a "Letter from a Lady, concerning Miss Wright," whom she had just heard lecture in Boston. Frances Wright's attacks on religion, the family, and the cult of True Womanhood, which she viewed as obstacles to the creation of a truly democratic, egalitarian society, had earned her the epithet of a "Sampson in petticoats who is trying to pull down the pillars of the social edifice about our ears"—an epithet Child quoted. Child agreed with Wright's detractors that "[t]empted by self-conceit and a love of notoriety, she goes about preaching doctrines, which, if they have any effect at all, must be ruinous to the peace and good order of society." Yet she forbore from joining the hue and cry or casting aspersions on Wright's character. Like Mary Wollstonecraft before her, Wright was "an erring woman, not an abandoned one," Child contended. And like Wollstonecraft, Wright "argued against the established usages of civil society, not because her own depravity sought an excuse for lawless indulgence, but because she idly deemed she had discovered the pure elements of freedom and philosophy." For her part, Child affected a jaded indifference to ideas that were causing more clamor than they deserved. "The older and more reflecting part of [Wright's] audience," among whom she classed herself, "had read all her arguments, over and over again, in the infidel writers of the French Revolution" and knew "how utterly fallacious" the premises of "her specious system" were. Impressionable young listeners would soon learn the same wisdom from experience. "As for those who plead this woman's authority for giving a loose rein to impulse, they probably would have been vicious if they had never heard her. . . ." Child's parting shot betrayed that she took Wright more personally than she let on, however. "Miss Wright should go to Spain—there is *real* ignorance and superstition; here she fights with windmill giants,—amuses for a moment,—and is forgotten." That is, Child was rejecting Wright in favor of the "intelligent traveller" she herself had married, who had been to Don Quixote's country and knew how much better off women were in America.[38]

Had she been willing to listen to Wright, Child might have spared herself serious psychological damage as well as fourteen years of what she would come to call "pump[ing] water into a sieve."[39] Yet in truth, Wright proved no more able to apply her own philosophy of women's rights than those who closed their ears to it. Barely a year after lecturing in Boston, she ended up jettisoning her feminism when an unwanted pregancy forced her to marry a man much less progressive than David.[40] There were simply no models of emancipated womanhood or authentically egalitarian marriages for that generation. Even if there had been, Child was too deeply in love to question the course on which David had embarked. It seemed more rewarding to put aside her own career goals and to throw herself into supporting his. The feminist insights she had expressed in *Hobomok*, "The Church in the Wilderness," and *The First Settlers* were the first casualty of her effort to live up to her culture's ideal of wifely duty. They would not be the last. Meanwhile, she was at least mastering a new craft.

Although Child's output of fiction slackened once she redirected her energies toward sustaining the *Massachusetts Journal*, its quality remained high. Many of the uncollected sketches she produced for the *Journal*'s column of "Original Miscellany" deserve to be reprinted. They are particularly notable for experimentation with new forms. In her "Annals of a Village," for example, Child tried her hand at adapting the "narrative of community" that the English writer Mary Russell Mitford had popularized. In satiric pieces like "The Miseries of Knowledge," "The Winds," and "Leaf from a Reviewer's Journal," she poked fun at humorless psuedointellectuals, "theological pugilists" of the blue-lipped Calvinist variety, and the politics of literary criticism. And in sketches like "The Stage Coach," she described a parade of human types, capturing their idiosyncracies in pithy phrases.[41]

After assuming her role as unofficial literary editor of the *Massachusetts Journal*, Child published only one more story in a prestigious gift book: "Chocorua's Curse" in *The Token* for 1830. Haunted like her other Indian tales of the late 1820s by images of poisoned relationships, obliterated communities, plundered nature, and blasted promise, it is by far the bleakest. Its dark mood reflects more than Child's pessimism about staving off another crime against the Indians under Andrew Jackson's presidency. Beneath a text about the spiraling violence that had blighted the nation's prospects lurks a subtext about the uncontrollable self-destructiveness of a husband whose failures would blight Child's literary career and the couple's marriage.

Returning to the theme of "The Lone Indian," "Chocorua's Curse" dramatizes the clash between incompatible cultures—one viewing nature as a source of life to be venerated or propitiated, the other treating it as an enemy to be subjugated. In "The Lone Indian," Child had hinted that whites, too, would suffer the consequences of despoiling the land they have seized from the Indians. In "Chocorua's Curse," she shows how this despoliation leads to the destruction of an entire white community, even where whites and Indians have lived side by side in harmony.

Child probably derived the idea for the story from Thomas Cole's 1829 painting, "The Death of Chocorua," based on a legend of the Mount Chocorua region in New Hampshire. According to this legend, an Indian chief killed by local whites had cursed the land with a bane making its waters deadly. Child had surely seen Cole's painting exhibited in Boston that winter, and the dramatic scene it pictured—a prostrate Indian on the edge of a cliff, with a white man's rifle pointed at him and a second white man beckoning others to follow—must have appealed to her imagination. An engraving of the painting, retitled "Chocorua's Curse," illustrated her story in *The Token*. One historian has speculated that the volume's editor, Samuel Griswold Goodrich, may have commissioned Child to provide a narrative accompaniment for Cole's artwork.[42] If so, Child elaborated considerably on the legend Cole had recorded. Her embellishments reflect her characteristic preoccupations: exploring the bases for peaceful coexistence of whites and Indians, probing the responsibility whites bear for precipitating mutual hostilities, and prophesying disaster for both races if whites persist in their irresponsible course.

The prehistory Child supplies for the Chocorua legend stresses that "[n]o cause of quarrel had ever arisen" between the region's white colonists and Indians until whites set the cycle of catastrophe in motion through their war on nature. Symbolically, the poison they have prepared for a "mischievous fox, which had long troubled the little settlement," ends up killing the nine-year-old son of the Indian prophet Chocorua, when he accidentally drinks it on one of his frequent visits to the home of the white settlers Cornelius and Caroline Campbell. The tragedy dooms the friendly relations that have hitherto prevailed between the colonists and their Indian neighbors. Chocorua revenges himself by murdering Caroline Campbell and her children. Retaliating in the same "wild, demoniac spirit of revenge" (165), Cornelius leads a vigilante expedition against the prophet. In his death agony Chocorua invokes a curse on the community, conjuring the Great Spirit to breathe death and destruction on it. As he prophesies, the combined forces of nature indeed wreak their fury against the Indian's foes: "The tomahawk and scalping knife were busy among them, the winds tore up trees and hurled them at their dwellings, their crops were blasted, their cattle died, and sickness came upon their strongest men." The Indian prophet's curse continues to haunt the region "[t]o this day," Child warns (referring to the legend behind her story and Cole's painting). Such, she hints, might be the fate of a nation that has forgotten the ancient lesson of human survival so central to Indian culture — respect for nature and its creatures.[43]

Child's vision of a white community blighted by its arrogant disposal of the Indian's birthright invites comparison with the more typical vision of America's history and destiny articulated in Timothy Flint's "The Indian Fighter," published in the same issue of *The Token* as "Chocorua's Curse." Its white hero, like Cornelius Campbell, devotes his life to vengeance after his fiancée is captured and eventually slain in an Indian raid. In contrast to Child, however, Flint presents Indian violence as totally unprovoked and describes it in gruesome detail. His story culminates in the white hero's absolution and the Indians' annihilation. Having "long since become a Christian," the Indian Fighter revisits the scene of his vengeance and finds his enemies' bones "bleaching" on the ground and their skulls housing rattlesnakes. It is the white man's God, and not the Indian's, whose curse prevails, as the Indian Fighter prophesies that He "who operateth by the silent and irresistible hand of time . . . will soon subdue all our enemies under our feet."[44]

"Chocorua's Curse" rejects this ideological justification of Indian genocide not only by exposing its consequences, but by exploring the cruel irony that underlies a history of violence ultimately devastating to both peoples. The two men who poison each other's existence, the story suggests, are actually mirror images of each other. Both Cornelius Campbell and Chocorua tower above their fellows, but neither has succeeded in living up to his potential because of his society's limitations. As a result, both smolder with pent-up frustration.

Verbal echoes emphasize the kinship between the white settler and the Indian prophet. Child even describes Cornelius in Indianlike terms:

His stature was gigantic, and he had the bold, quick tread of one who had wandered frequently and fearlessly among the terrible hiding-places of nature. His voice was harsh, but his whole countenance possessed singular capabilities for tenderness of expression; and sometimes, under the gentle influence of domestic excitement, his hard features would be rapidly lighted up, seeming like the sunshine flying over the shaded fields in an April day. (163)

In his small New Hampshire colony, Cornelius is a "master spirit." He throws "the spell of intellect" over his companions, who cannot help sensing his superiority. Under favorable conditions, his "intellectual energies" and talents "would unquestionably have worked out a path to emolument and fame," but both in England and in America, his political views have proved "too liberal and philosophical for the state of the people" (163–64). The thwarting of his ambitions has produced "a haughty spirit, strongly curbed by circumstances he could not control, and at which he scorned to murmur" — a spirit stamped on his face (163).

Chocorua mirrors almost all these traits. Likewise "an object of peculiar respect" in his community, which acknowledges him as a prophet, he, too, has great intellectual endowments that circumstances have not permitted him to develop: "He had a mind which education and motive would have nerved with giant strength; but growing up in savage freedom, it wasted itself in dark, fierce, ungovernable passions" (164). His face, too, reveals his frustration: "There was something fearful in the quiet haughtiness of his lip — it seemed so like slumbering power, too proud to be lightly roused, and too implacable to sleep again. In his small, black, fiery eye, expression lay coiled up like a beautiful snake" (164).

Of course, Child's stereotyped portrayal of Chocorua reflects her ethnocentric misconceptions about a culture she sees as "savage," anarchic, and intellectually primitive. Still, through the elaborate parallels she creates between Chocorua and Cornelius, Child implies that could they but recognize their brotherhood, these two men who have so much in common hold the key to each other's fulfillment. The peaceful symbiosis in which their communities initially live and the friendship that grows up between Chocorua's son and the Campbell family herald the possibility of mutually beneficial exchanges. What blasts this promising relationship is the failure of each to accommodate to the other's way of life.

Once again, as with the theme of interracial marriage in "The Indian Wife," Child has revised a central motif of *Hobomok* and given it a pessimistic twist. The identification of Cornelius and Chocorua as doubles culminates in murder, not in marriage. The peace pipe that fused Mary Conant's Indian and Episcopalian husbands has metamorphosed into the fox poison that incites a war to the death between Indian and white. "Little Hobomok," whose brilliant future as a university graduate symbolized the Indian's assimilation into white society, has become an Indian child blighted by his contact with whites and destined never to reach manhood.

"Chocorua's Curse" likewise revises the theme Child associates so closely with the double motif in *Hobomok* — rebellion against patriarchy. Here, however, Child's revision marks a retreat rather than an advance from her earlier insights. The very experiences that have sharpened her understanding of national politics — her first foray into polemical writing, her increasing share in editing the *Massachusetts Journal*, and the impact of Andrew Jackson's election on David's financial situation—have also committed her to submerging her own identity in her husband's and unconditionally supporting his course. Thus, it is precisely at the point where the story's radical political message intersects with the conservative domestic ideology it preaches that its repressed subtext surfaces.

"[S]trongly curbed by circumstances he could not control," cheated by unfavorable political contingencies out of the "emolument and fame" his "talents and ambition" deserve to win him, and "too liberal and philosophical" to cater to the prevailing religious and political ideology, Cornelius Campbull irresistibly evokes David Lee Child, as his wife sees him through the idealizing medium of her devotion. Correspondingly, Child's portrait of Caroline Campbell reveals that the author of *Hobomok* no longer identifies with the rebellious heroines of her youthful novel, but with its loyal Puritan wives.

Like Mrs. Conant (and like Child herself), Caroline Campbell has "incurred her father's displeasure" by marrying a man of whom he disapproves (163). And like Mrs. Conant, Caroline has followed her husband into the wilderness on an errand he has unilaterally imposed on her. Child had once described Mrs. Conant and Arabella Johnson as "victims to what has always been the source of woman's greatest misery—love—deep and unwearied love" (111). Now, however, she denies that Caroline's marriage has involved any sacrifice, notwithstanding the poverty and isolation to which it has consigned her: "It seemed a hard fate for one who had from childhood been accustomed to indulgence and admiration, yet Mrs. Campbell enjoyed more than she had done in her days of splendour; so much deeper are the sources of happiness than those of gaiety" (163–64).

Repudiating Frances Wright's critique of marriage and domestic ideology for the third time in six months, Child asks: "To such a woman as Caroline Campbell, of what use would have been some modern doctrines of equality and independence?" She answers that those doctrines are based not on experience but on theoretical abstractions contrary to the instincts of nature:

> With a mind sufficiently cultivated to appreciate and enjoy her husband's intellectual energies, she had a heart that could not have found another home. The bird will drop into its nest though the treasures of earth and sky are open. To have proved marriage a tyranny, and the cares of domestic life a thraldom, would have affected Caroline Campbell as little, as to be told that the pure, sweet atmosphere she breathed, was pressing upon her so many pounds to every square inch! (164)

A note of defensiveness nevertheless creeps into the assertion in which Child's paean to domesticity culminates: "Over such a heart, and such a soul, external circumstances have little power; all worldly interest was concentrated in her husband and babes, and her spirit was satisfied with that inexhaustible fountain of joy which nature gives, and God has blessed" (164).

Protest though she may that "external circumstances" have not shaken her faith in the marital creed she upholds, Child's plot belies her. Caroline pays with her life — and those of her children — for sacrificing her own needs to her husband's. Caroline's fate suggests that at the deepest level of her consciousness, Child may have sensed how dangerous her wholehearted espousal of her culture's domestic ideal would prove. But her obsession with refuting Frances Wright also shows that she was determinedly repressing that awareness.

Child's depiction of her heroine as happier in adversity than "in her days of splendour" echoes a letter she herself had written to her sister-in-law on the eve of David's conviction for libel: "I have tried to be as saving as possible — I certainly have denied myself every superfluity. I have dropped *all* my acquaintance. I neither visit, nor receive visits. We never ride — never go to the threatre, or any place of public amusement. It seems queer to me, — I used to go about so much; but after all, I am happier than I ever was."[45] Again protesting too much, Child had gone on to assure Lydia that she and David had not "rushed thoughtlessly into matrimony and ruin" and that their rigid economy was merely a temporary expedient, "lest the pressure of too many untoward circumstances meeting together should destroy prospects otherwise flattering." Child was doing her best to hang on to her illusions. But the "brilliant Miss Francis" was no more, and the author of *Hobomok* was about to give way to the author of *The Frugal Housewife*.

The very week that Child attended Frances Wright's lecture in late July 1829, she made a desperate attempt to save her literary career by turning her gift book fiction to financial account. Writing to the publishers of the *Atlantic Souvenir*, Carey & Lea of Philadelphia, Child asked them to tell her "candidly" whether a collection of her stories for the annuals would be profitable and if so, what terms they would offer her. "Do not advise me to it unless you think I can make *something*," she underscored.[46] Apparently Carey & Lea did not so advise. Not until two years later did Child find a publisher willing to undertake the project on terms favorable enough to justify the venture: the firm of Carter and Hendee, which had recently issued her domestic advice books *The Frugal Housewife* (1829) and *The Mother's Book* (1831), then going through their sixth and second printings, respectively.[47] By that time Child had resigned herself to the fact that fiction simply would not pay her husband's bills.

Issued no longer with the hope of winning her the laurels of which she had once dreamed, but rather with the aim of making money, *The Coronal* (1832) represents the author of *Hobomok*'s valedictory to the literary world. Child dedicated it wistfully to "the Author of Hope Leslie," Catharine Maria Sedgwick, to whom she was now surrendering the field of Indian fiction they had worked in sisterly rivalry. Four years would elapse before she would yield to the longing to write another novel and almost fifteen years before she would resume publishing stories in major periodicals.

Nowhere does Child more poignantly express her conflicted responses to the price her marriage was exacting of her literary career than in the two short pieces with which she ends *The Coronal*: the poem "To a Husband, Who presented, as a New-Year's Offering, a *Heart* and a *Laurel wreath*, the leaves of which were not very abundant," and the sketch "The First and Last Book." Wryly commenting on the vanity of the literary ambitions she is renouncing, while reaffirming the higher valuation she places on conjugal love, Child announces in the poem, "I care not for the wreath of laurel." The moral she draws from "Its *scanty* leaves" is that "fame's fairest amplest dower" would not compensate her for the loss of her husband's love (281). Yet coming from the husband responsible for arresting her pursuit of artistic distinction, and timed for New Year's when the annual gift books in which Child had published her best stories traditionally made their appearance, the "offering" of a stunted laurel wreath surely resonates with ironic significance, whatever Child may have intended. "The First and Last Book" registers the same ambivalence. The novelty of authorship having worn off, Child admits, the "cares of the world press heavily on the spirit," and the "smiles of the public no longer have power to kindle us into enthusiastic energy" (283). To seek fame is to roll the "stone of Sisyphus," the erstwhile aspirant for glory has come to realize. Experience has taught her that she must produce not for the muse but for the market. Publishers' ledgers now supply her "inspiration," and if she hunts for pearls, it is only because she has "promised to furnish them." Most often, she "string[s] glass beads because they . . . sell better than diamonds" (284). Though the game has proved to be "a battle, hardly worth the winning," she hastens to reiterate, she has found happiness in a higher sphere "over which the world has no power": "Religious hope, and deep domestic love, can meet no change. . ." (285).

The juxtaposition of these closing pieces with "Chocorua's Curse," placed directly before "To a Husband," betrays the anxieties underlying Child's zealous promulgation of domestic ideology. She could not afford to question the power of "deep domestic love" to withstand the worldly trials that threatened to overwhelm her. Almost as soon as she sent her last story off to *The Token*, she gave herself up to the task of stringing "glass beads." With the publication of *The Coronal*, Child bade a long farewell to pearls and diamonds.

6

The Frugal Housewife: Financial
Worries and Domestic Advice

*I have kept thinking the darkest time had come, and that the clouds must break away; but still a
darker one would come. . . . I have had serious thoughts of taking a school; and perhaps I shall do
so. But it is uncertain whether I could get one large enough to be profitable . . . and if my poor
brain will but hold out to meet the demands of booksellers from various parts of the Union, I can
do better than I can with a common-sized school. . . .*

    *I have had two boarders all winter; and I now have one, who is likewise a scholar. This has
taken up my time very much.*[1]

Apologizing to her sister-in-law for the long interval since her last letter, Child lifted
the curtain that hid her domestic life from public view. To put food on the table and pay
the rent after deducting monthly expenses and the reimbursements due on David's
debts and legal fees, Child was resorting to a combination of the many expedients
by which middle-class women traditionally contributed to the support of their families when poverty or widowhood necessitated: writing whatever would sell, taking in
boarders, and even contemplating a return to schoolteaching — everything except sewing. Neither her frenetic attempts to earn more income nor the severe privations she
had accepted for the sake of economy — privations that included cutting herself off
from friends whose invitations she could not afford to reciprocate — seemed to have
alleviated David's financial situation. The *Massachusetts Journal* still teetered on the
brink of bankruptcy. And another devastating blow had just fallen: in February 1830
David had lost his appeal of the Keyes libel conviction. He was now preparing to go to
prison for an incarceration of some six months. (Ironically, the Massachusetts Supreme
Court would end up reversing the original libel conviction, but only after David had
served his sentence.)[2]

    That was what Child meant when she told her sister-in-law that her horizons had
kept growing darker, long after the darkest day seemed to have dawned. The exigencies
she described to Lydia had driven her to write *The Frugal Housewife* — her latest effort at
stringing "glass beads." Deposited for copyright in mid-November 1829, the book was

already going into its second edition three months later. It had sold so quickly that no copies were available to send to David's family by the time Child forced herself to renew communication with her in-laws. Over the next two years, it would net at least $2,000—more than three times the sum Child was earning from *The Juvenile Miscellany*.[3]

Although Child had turned to writing domestic advice books out of desperation, she succeeded in tapping into a cultural need born of changing economic conditions. In late eighteenth-century England and early nineteenth-century America, the industrial revolution had shifted the locus of economic production from the home to the factory. As a result, the role of women was undergoing a major transformation. Home production had allowed married women to supervise children while engaging in artisanal activities that helped generate income for the family. The factory system no longer permitted such arrangements. Not only did it involve long hours of uninterrupted work outside the home, but it required a full-time labor force. Both conditions tended to exclude married women, though large numbers of single women and children did get drafted into factory labor.[4]

For women of the class to which Child belonged—"respectable mechanics" who "work with their *hands*, own a house, with or without some acres of land" and earn modest incomes "from their own labor"—the new economic order dramatically reduced their occupations. It is thus no coincidence that an ideology glorifying homemaking and childrearing arose to confine women to the home at a historical moment when increased leisure might have freed them to take advantage of career opportunities currently opening up for middle-class men. By holding out to women a "sphere" of their own and assigning it the vital function of preserving the nation's moral purity, the ideology of domesticity served to keep them from claiming for themselves democratic rights that the bourgeois creed of individual freedom tacitly reserved for men.[5]

While domesticity was being redefined as an art that demanded concerted study, increasing geographical mobility was carrying young wives away from the mothers and grandmothers on whom they had traditionally relied for guidance in running a household and bringing up children. To fill the breach, a new genre emerged: the domestic advice book. Typically, such books lectured wives on their "domestic duties" and provided information on every aspect of women's household role, from marketing and cookery to health care and "the Instruction of Children." By the time Child published *The Frugal Housewife* in 1829, the genre was well established in England and the United States.

Indeed, recalled Child, so great was the "variety of cookery books already in the market" that the first booksellers she approached "declined publishing" *The Frugal Housewife* for fear it would not prove competitive. What convinced her publishers to risk launching yet another such volume on a seemingly overstocked market was Child's insistence that among all those available, not one was "suited to the wants of the middling class in our own country"—the readership to which she had addressed *The Frugal Housewife*. "Books of this kind have usually been written for the wealthy: I have written for the poor," she explained (6). "[T]he sale of more than six thousand copies in one year," she concluded with justifiable pride, had shown her to be right in believing that an advice book on domestic economy for the poor and "middling" sort was badly needed.[6]

A glance at the most popular domestic advice manuals of the late 1820s confirms Child's assessment of the difference between *The Frugal Housewife* and its rivals. Leading the field was a British work Child had reviewed for the *Massachusetts Journal* in December 1828: Frances Parkes's *Domestic Duties; or, Instructions to Young Married Ladies on the Management of Their Households and the Regulation of Their Conduct in the Various Relations and Duties of Married Life* (1825). Despite its many reprintings in the United States as well as in England, Parkes's book was clearly suitable only for upperclass ladies. As Child pointed out in her review, the "whole tone" of the work was adapted to"wealthy, aristocratic England": "the economy, the benevolence, all the duties inculcated, presuppose great wealth, high station, and fashionable habits. We should indeed tremble for the twenty four *Disunited States* of this Republic, if we thought such books would become necessary here."[7]

Parkes's subject headings unmistakably indicate her intended audience: "Morning Calls," "Dinner Parties," "Collections of Works of Art," "Servants. — Number. — Choice of. — Food of. — Management of. — Conduct to. — Indulgence to." The bulk of her advice concerns the adjustment of the young bride to her new role as wife and household supervisor; hence, one of the first topics Parkes takes up is whether a bride must renounce her former friends on cleaving to her husband. Her main object is inculcating the proper attitude toward "domestic duties" rather than providing practical tips on housekeeping. When the issue of "economy" — so vital to Child and her "middling" audience — engages Parkes's attention at all, it is merely to discuss the problem of guarding against dishonesty in the servants to whom marketing is entrusted and to recommend that housewives check prices and closely oversee household expenditures.[8]

The idea of producing an American substitute for Parkes's *Domestic Duties*, aimed at women of her own social class, may well have occurred to Child in the process of reviewing the book. If so, she would quickly have encountered an American predecessor: Eliza Leslie's *Seventy-Five Receipts for Pastry, Cakes and Sweetmeats*. Issued by the firm that had printed Child's *First Settlers*, Munroe & Francis, it had run into twenty editions by 1827. Leslie, too, was a respected literary woman and even a contributor to the *Juvenile Miscellany* — an added incentive for benefiting from her example. Though more properly a "cookery book," Leslie's *Seventy-Five Receipts* would have struck Child as liable to the same sort of criticism she had directed at Parkes's volume. Most of Leslie's recipes are much too elaborate for housewives on small incomes. Besides such luxuries as ice cream and almond custard, her book includes seventeen recipes for jams and preserves — an item *The Frugal Housewife* advises the "economical" to forgo (81). Child in fact refers readers "who can afford to be epicures" to Leslie's "Seventy-five Receipts," explaining that since she herself has "written for the poor," she has "said nothing about *rich* cooking" (6). As with Parkes, Leslie's concept of "economy" reflects little understanding of what it means to live in straitened circumstances. Her sole concessions to readers who must count pennies are to suggest that they reduce the amount of "spice, wine, brandy, rose-water, essence of lemon" and other "seasoning" recommended, and to assure them that "if done at home, and by a person that can be trusted," any of her pastries can be produced "in the best and most liberal manner at ONE HALF of the cost of the same articles supplied by a confectioner."[9]

Belying its title, even the English *Frugal Housewife* — whose existence Child discovered only after arranging to have her own book published in England — offered no advice on economy. Like Leslie's, its recipes were devised to gratify the tastes of readers who could afford such luxuries as lobster sauce, artichoke pie, and venison pastry.[10]

Child's *The Frugal Housewife* furnishes a striking contrast. Unlike all other domestic advice books of the period, it does not take for granted that its readers rely on servants to do their housework. Nor does it lament the dearth of qualified servants and suggest solutions to this problem (as Catharine Beecher does in her 1841 *Treatise on Domestic Economy*). Nor does it moralize on the virtues of women's doing their own housework (as William Alcott does in his 1837 manual, *The Young House-keeper*).[11] Instead, Child addresses her advice specifically to readers who cannot afford hired help, except perhaps occasionally.

"Dedicated to those who are not ashamed of economy," *The Frugal Housewife* shares with other women struggling to make ends meet on scant budgets the helpful hints Child had gleaned from her own painful experience. It also provides an unintendedly revealing perspective on her private ordeal. "People who have little to spend, should partake sparingly of useless amusements; those who are in debt should deny themselves entirely," Child admonishes her readers (103). As she had confided to Lydia, she was following that precept to a tee: "I neither visit, nor receive visits. We never ride — never go to the theatre, or any place of public amusement."[12] Child had likewise learned the hard way that "the prudent, the industrious, and the well-informed" may fall victim to poverty along with the improvident and the ignorant; she is obviously speaking for herself when she assures readers that in such cases a "*useful*" and "judicious education is all-powerful in enabling [people] to *endure* the evils it cannot always *prevent*" (111).

Reflecting the spirit of her dedication, from the very first sentence of her "Introductory Chapter," Child's emphasis is on the art of "economy" rather than the art of housewifery. "The true economy of housekeeping is simply the art of gathering up all the fragments, so that nothing be lost," she begins, adding: "I mean fragments of *time*, as well as *materials*. Nothing should be thrown away so long as it is possible to make any use of it, however trifling that use may be; and whatever be the size of a family, every member should be employed either in earning or saving money" (3). Her purpose, she underscores, is "to teach how money can be *saved*, not how it can be *enjoyed*" (6).

As these remarks indicate, the ideology governing *The Frugal Housewife* is not the cult of domesticity, but the ethic of industry, frugality, and plain living. Homilies on the dignity of housekeeping and the prestige the housewife enjoyed as "the sovereign of an empire" — in which the works of Beecher and Alcott, for example, abound — are conspicuously absent from *The Frugal Housewife*.[13] Only in the chapter "Education of Daughters," included among the "Hints to Persons of Moderate Fortune" Child appended to subsequent editions, does she come close to enunciating the tenets of domestic ideology. There, citing the case of a mother who has failed to train her daughter in domestic skills on the plea that she should be allowed to "*enjoy herself all she can, while she is single*," Child comments: "Instead of representing domestic life as the gathering place of the deepest and purest affections; as the sphere of woman's *enjoyments* as well as of her *duties*; as, indeed, the whole world to her," this mother's "pernicious" philosophy denigrates marriage as a "necessary sacrifice of . . . freedom and . . . gayety"; that is, it "teaches a girl to consider matrimony desirable because 'a good match' is a triumph of vanity, and it is deemed respectable to be 'well settled in the world' " (95). Even while advocating that mothers prepare daughters for the "important duties of domestic life," however, Child inveighs against the "universal error" of encouraging girls to "exaggerate the importance of getting married" (91–92) — a theme rarely sounded in advice books.

Far more typical of the ideological concerns central to *The Frugal Housewife* are the subjects covered in other chapters of "Hints to Persons of Moderate Fortune": the avoidance of luxury and needless expenditure ("Furniture," "Travelling and Public Amusements"); the wisdom of recognizing "the advantages of a situation in which we *are* placed, instead of imagining the enjoyments of one in which we are *not* placed" ("Philosophy and Consistency"); the cultivation of inner resources as a means of surviving misfortune ("How to Endure Poverty"); and the critique of the "extravagance . . . sapping the strength of our happy country" ("Reasons for Hard Times"). Like Child's stories in *The Juvenile Miscellany*, these essays in *The Frugal Housewife* seek on the one hand to combat a growing disdain for "all manual employment" as "degrading" and on the other hand to inculcate the values needed by a burgeoning capitalist state and democratic republic. "If young men and young women are brought up to consider frugality contemptible, and industry degrading," Child points out, "it is vain to expect they will at once become prudent and useful, when the cares of life press heavily upon them" (94, 97). Spelling out the political implications for her readers, she warns: "[L]et any reflecting mind inquire how decay has begun in all republics, and then let them calmly ask themselves whether we are in no danger, in departing thus rapidly from the simplicity and industry of our forefathers" (99).

At bottom, however, the impetus that generated *The Frugal Housewife* was practical rather than ideological. Only as an afterthought had Child incorporated into the book the "Hints to People of Moderate Fortune" she had begun publishing in the *Massachusetts Journal* six months earlier.[14] In its original form she had geared *The Frugal Housewife* simply toward offering pointers on how to cope with the day-to-day tasks a low-income housewife must perform.

Child had conceived the book primarily for women who still lived in rural villages like the Medford and the Norridgewock of her youth and the Wayland of her old age, the last home she would know. Thus, her instructions frequently refer to the conditions of rural life. For example, she reminds readers to "set the handle of your pump as high as possible, before you go to bed" in the winter, and to cover the pump with a "rug or horse-blanket" when the temperature reaches extreme lows — a trick she must have learned in Norridgewock.[15] "[A] frozen pump is a comfortless preparation for a winter's breakfast," she cautions, no doubt speaking from sad experience (16). Similarly, she urges country dwellers to teach their children how to make fans from the feathers of turkeys and geese and how to "prepare and braid straw for their own bonnets, and their brothers' hats" (3). "The sooner children are taught to turn their faculties to some account, the better for them and for their parents," she stresses (3).

At the same time, Child realized that many of her readers already lived in cities, and she sought to adapt her advice accordingly. In some cases these attempts betray the persistence of Child's rural habits of thought, as when she rather lamely suggests that city dwellers ask friends in the country to procure them "lard, butter, and eggs" in bulk for winter use (14–15). In other cases she distinguishes between what is economical for country and city dwellers, recommending that city dwellers cut down recipes to use smaller quantities of eggs, butter, and lard, substitute cheaper ingredients, or simply eschew such dishes altogether (61, 75). In still others she proposes genuine alternatives to city dwellers, such as exchanging "ashes and grease for soap," in lieu of either manufacturing their own or purchasing it at costly rates (22).

At the height of *The Frugal Housewife*'s popularity in the 1830s, the readers Child addressed probably constituted a majority of the nation's adult female population. Not until well into the next decade would the diffusion of household technology and the advance of urbanization give significant numbers of middle-class women access to running water and other conveniences described by Catharine Beecher in her more modern *Treatise on Domestic Economy* (1841). Correspondingly, it was a year after the publication of Beecher's volume that reprintings of *The Frugal Housewife* began to slack off with the twenty-eighth edition of 1842. Hitherto reprinted almost every year, and as many as twelve times between 1829 and 1832, Child's manual was reissued only twice in the mid-1840s, once in 1855, and once each in 1860 and 1870.[16] By then, the class most in need of advice on "How to Endure Poverty" lived in crowded city tenements where Child's strategies for economizing no longer applied.

As late as 1883, however, Caroline Healey Dall wished "we could see a new edition" of a book she judged unique for its orientation toward people of modest means. "Modern cooking schools and modern cookery books invariably cater to the taste of those who live in luxury," she complained. Child's book, on the contrary, "showed people how to make broth instead of *bouillon*, brown bread instead of 'angel's food,'" and "simple, inexpensive desserts" instead of "*méringues* or *soufflés*."[17]

In accordance with Child's emphasis on frugality — rather than on domesticity as a fine art, applied "science," or cultural ideal — the opening section of *The Frugal Housewife* is devoted to "Odd Scraps for the Economical." The title is apt; the chapter is literally a scrap bag of tips on how to "avoid waste in your family" by preventing spoilage, removing stains, and restoring "rusty" silks, "faded" cottons and carpets, "soiled" bonnets, "bunchy" mattresses, and smelly feather beds to a state "as good as new" (8, 9, 12–13, 15, 19). In later chapters Child extends the principle of salvaging everything possible even to "injured" meat, "tainted" butter, soured dough, and moldy cake (57, 70, 73, 114).

Advice on economy constitutes almost half the book in the first edition and a still larger proportion in subsequent editions. It also informs the book's other sections. The list of "Simple Remedies," for example, which includes some eight cures for dysentery and four preventives for lockjaw, must have served in part to obviate doctors' fees for prevalent illnesses. Financial considerations likewise govern the choice of recipes in the section comprising the actual cookbook. The headings are indicative: "Cheap Common Cooking," "Cheap Cakes," "Cheap Custards," "Common Pies."[18] Recipes typically appeal less to the palate than the pocketbook. Thus, Child recommends liver as "the cheapest of all animal food" and pig's head as "a profitable thing to buy," commenting of the latter: "It is despised, because it is cheap; but when well cooked it is delicious. . . . It tastes like roast pork, and yields abundance of sweet fat, for shortening" (43, 46).

Although the recipes Child offers are much plainer than those of rival cookbooks, the need for economy dictated a far greater expenditure of time manufacturing articles that wealthier people purchased in shops, such as soap, candles, stockings, yeast, and bread. As Child points out, "those who are under the necessity of being economical, should make convenience a secondary object" (9). *The Frugal Housewife* conveys a vivid picture of how arduous domestic chores in low-income homes could be. The need for economy entailed buying food products in bulk when they were cheapest (contrary to recommendations in cookbooks designed for the wealthy),[19] checking them constantly for signs of spoilage, and periodically taking measures to restore them to a semblance of freshness (8–9). It entailed making feather beds with feathers plucked from the fowls used for cooking, and when they grew old, ripping them apart, washing and drying the feathers, and sewing them up again (12)—a process that also applied to mattresses. It entailed cutting up old clothes "no longer capable of being converted into garments" and "braiding them for door-mats" (13). And it entailed saving the grease from cooking to boil into soap, an operation that consumed many hours and involved "great difficulty in making soap '*come*' " (23).

Such chores may not have been part of Child's daily routine in her Boston home, but she surely remembered many of them from her youth in Medford and Norridgewock and would perform them again when she returned to rural life, briefly in Northampton, Massachusetts, in 1838–39 and 1840–41, permanently in West Newton and Wayland, Massachusetts, in 1850. Whether or not Child resorted to making her own soap, candles, and feather beds to save money, she was reduced to at least some of the measures for salvaging damaged goods that she recommended to her readers. Even in old age, she would complain of spending an inordinate amount of energy battling mold, fermentation, and spoilage.[20]

In its form as well as in its content, *The Frugal Housewife* reflects Child's desperate financial straits and harried frame of mind during the period of its composition. The conflicting demands on her time—editing the *Juvenile Miscellany*, helping to run the *Massachusetts Journal*, paying bills and calculating expenses, cooking and cleaning for boarders—must have forced her to write in the interstices of an already overcharged schedule.

The Frugal Housewife reads as if Child had flown between her kitchen and her desk, jotting down whatever ideas came to mind while she was performing her household tasks. Particularly in "Odd Scraps for the Economical," Child seems to have made no effort to organize material in a logical manner. Advice on removing spots is jumbled together with directions on storing Indian meal, brushing teeth, and protecting woollens against moths; and scattered instructions on cleaning the same items — carpets, gloves, and tortoise shell combs among others — occur in several different places (9, 10, 11, 13, 20). In the first edition, even the section on "Cheap Common Cooking" is a hodge podge, with no attempt to group like items together and no subtitles setting off recipes from one another — a surprising omission in view of other contemporary cookbooks' sophisticated formats. As Sarah Hale delicately phrased it in reviewing *The Frugal Housewife* for the *Ladies' Magazine*, "There is not sufficient system in the arrangement of items."[21]

What most disturbed reviewers of *The Frugal Housewife*, however, was not the book's defects of organization, but its violations of the genteel code prescribing the demeanor of upper-class ladies. Sarah Hale, for example, objected strenuously to a lady's showing such an unseemly preoccupation with money. Quoting the opening sentences of *The Frugal Housewife*, in which Child asserts that every member of the family should be "employed either in earning or saving money," Hale demurred: "Now we do not think that either in earning or saving money consists the chief importance of life. . . . Our men are sufficiently money-making. Let us keep our women and children from the contagion as long as possible." In short, Hale was countering advice suited to the poor with a cultural ideal of "true womanhood" applicable only to the prosperous.

To establish her superior authority as a spokesperson for her sex, Hale cited her experience as a mother — an experience she knew Child could not claim. "[H]ad she ever watched, with a mother's anxiety over the developement of mind and character in those she wished to train to usefulness and virtue," Hale protested, Child would have been more careful "to distinguish between the spirit of that economy which is seeking to be rich, and that which is seeking to enrich or assist others." Whether deliberately or not, the barb must have wounded Child deeply, for she made no secret of her desire for children. But more to the point, Hale tellingly misconstrued the purpose of *The Frugal Housewife*, confusing a strategy for survival with a program for getting rich — an error symptomatic of her class blinders. Hale's strictures extended to the book's very language. She reproached Child for such "vulgarisms" as the use of the word "emptings," which she alleged, was "not found in any dictionary" and heard only "among the most ignorant." Despite her reservations, Hale recognized that Child had intended to benefit women. Moreover, as a widow who had entered on her own literary career in order to support her five children, she could not but have felt a certain kinship with a sister writer likewise dependent for her livelihood on her pen. Thus, Hale took care to temper her criticism of *The Frugal Housewife* with a tribute to the "proof" Child's example had furnished "that learning, imagination, genius, do not unfit a lady for domestic usefulness."[22]

No such compunctions restrained Child's former beau, Nathaniel P. Willis, now editor of the *American Monthly Magazine*. His vindictive attacks gave the distinct impression that he felt a sense of personal as well as class betrayal at seeing a woman he had once courted stoop to publishing a book like *The Frugal Housewife*. Willis explicitly framed his objections to the language and spirit of the book in terms that emphasized the class barriers Child had transgressed. Noting that *The Frugal Housewife* was "written for the lower classes," he sarcastically hailed its "thorough-going, unhesitating, cordial freedom from taste":

> No word is used where there was a plainer or ruder one to be had. No misplaced attempt is made to . . . qualify expressions to which a delicate ear is unused. . . . We read the book under some apprehension that we should detect traces of breeding in it — that, as it was written by . . . a celebrated lady, there would occur glimpses of refinement, and distaste to the task. We feared that the rude creatures for whose benefit it was designed, . . . would feel that it was not written by one who entered with a pleased sympathy into even the coarsest of their wants, and took a genial satisfaction in what others might call the repugnant details of such matters. It was a most unnecessary apprehension.[23]

As if to repair the breach in the walls guarding the sanctuary of upper-class culture against uncouth intrusions, Willis went on to allude pointedly to the humble origins that branded Child as an interloper in polite society. "There is a lingering succulence about some of the descriptions of dishes which could only have been engendered from recollection," he sneered. He proceeded to list a half-page of extracts illustrating the book's unforgivable crudeness. Heading the list were the recommendations with which Child had opened her "Odd Scraps for the Economical": "Look frequently into the pails to see that nothing is thrown to the pigs, which should be in the grease-pot." "Look to the grease-pot and see if nothing is there which might serve to nourish your own family." Willis also cited examples of Child's colloquial diction, indelicate references to animal body parts, mention of details "at which a palate of tolerable nicety would revolt," and apparent fondness for foods rightly despised by genteel readers:

> "Hard gingerbread is *nice* to have in the family."

> "The heart, liver, &c., of a pig is *nice* fried."

> "The navel end of the brisket is the best for salting and corning."

> "Calf's head should be cleansed with very great care; particularly the lights. . . . It is better to leave the wind-pipe on, *for if it hangs out of the pot while the head is cooking, all the froth will escape through it.*"[24]

Stung by the criticisms of her erstwhile peers in Boston's elite literary circles, Child hastened to purge the second edition of the "vulgarisms" for which she had been excoriated. She diligently substituted "yeast" for "emptings" and "good" for "nice" wherever she caught the offending words. She also followed Hale's suggestions for more substantive revisions, significantly improving the organization and introducing "a few receipts on a more liberal scale" (among them instructions on cleaning gold jewelry) for the benefit of people disdaining to be thought "*obliged* to practice such rigid economy."[25]

No doubt to her relief, Hale responded with immediate commendation in the April number of the *Ladies' Magazine*. "If the fact that a book sells, is any proof of its popularity," she acknowledged, "Mrs. Child has the honor of having written the most approved work of these 'hard times.' The second edition is nearly sold. We are glad of this, because we believe the book was written to do good — and that it will do good. 'The Hints [to Persons of Moderate Fortune]' &c. are excellent — and the arrangement of the whole is now correct and judicious."[26]

Meanwhile, Willis continued to lampoon *The Frugal Housewife* in the *American Monthly Magazine*. He ended a sketch titled "A Morning in the Library" with a young man's threat to punish his cousin for being such a "horrid creature" by lending her "the Frugal Housewife."[27] And in his "Editor's Table" of the same month, while cataloguing the many recent disruptions of class and gender relations that seemed to have turned the world upside down, he commented, "It is odd that General Jackson [a frontiersman and self-styled spokesman for the common man] should be President — odd that Fanny Wright should be a man, and Mr. Owen [also an ardent champion of women's rights and coeditor with Wright of the *Free Enquirer*] a woman, . . . and very odd that any body can think 'hard gingerbread is nice.' " In other words, Willis was associating Child with the radical feminist from whom she had sought so obsessively to distance herself; and he was associating the book she had "written for the lower classes" with three figures whose championship of the working classes made them anathema to elite Bostonians: Andrew Jackson, who had opened the Democratic party and the electoral process up to the urban masses; and Frances Wright and her colleague, Robert Dale Owen, who affiliated themselves with the more radical Workingman's party and with the English socialist movement led by Owen's father, Robert Owen. Willis may also have been insinuating that like Wright and Owen, the Childs had unsexed themselves by deviating from normal gender roles. He could hardly have chosen a more cutting way of disavowing and discrediting the woman he had squired around Boston only three years earlier.[28]

By this time, Willis's cavils had become a standing joke between the Childs. Writing to David in August 1830 from a pension at the beach where she had gone to take a week's respite, Child remarked of the food: "every thing is '*nice*,' hard gingerbread and all."[29]

Besides Willis and Hale, one other literary acquaintance greeted *The Frugal Housewife* with a response that must have given Child a pang, though it was intended kindly. Catharine Maria Sedgwick, who had taken Child under her wing after the publication of *Hobomok*, followed in her footsteps with *Hope Leslie* (1827), and lent her reputation to the contributors' list of the *Juvenile Miscellany*, wrote to express surprise at meeting her "in a new department of writing." Child's "condescension" in undertaking a work that benefited the human species by multiplying "the common comforts of life" was truly admirable, Sedgwick ventured; but she added, "I trust you have not forsaken the department for which the rich gifts of nature so eminently qualify you." Perhaps to spur her into returning to the fold, she also sent Child her latest novel, of which she was awaiting the reviews with "drooping" courage. Sedgwick could not know, of course, how hard it had been for Child to abandon fiction for domestic advice books and how small a part "condescension" had played in directing her toward this "new department," but her well meant admonition must have hurt.[30]

Ironically, in the very months that *The Frugal Housewife* was instating Child as an authority on homemaking, her dream of securing a domestic haven in a "snug little cottage" with "just income enough to meet very moderate wants" was being thwarted. Faced with David's impending prison term, Child had concluded that she could no longer afford to maintain a household, even by taking in boarders. If she could break the lease on their house, she told Lydia, she had calculated that it would be cheaper to "dispose of part of my furniture, and board out." The decision cost her dearly. "I do hate to give up *home*," she mourned.[31]

The months of David's imprisonment were surely the "darkest time" Child had yet seen. At first, she moved in with the family of her friend Emily Marshall, the famous beauty she had met at Madame Canda's school in the winter of 1825–26. The Marshalls provided emotional support, but the contrast between their elegant establishment and the "proper little martin box" in which Child had been living so frugally since her wedding could scarcely have failed to prompt unwelcome thoughts. While Child was enduring a cruel separation from her husband, Emily was blissfully engaged; and unlike David, Emily's fiancé, William Foster Otis, a descendant of the James Otis whom Child had celebrated in *The Rebels*, and the son of Boston's mayor Harrison Gray Otis, would be able to offer her a life of refinement and luxury. Over the past year Child had dropped her acquaintance with the aristocratic Bostonians who had patronized her as the "brilliant Miss Francis." Now she was back among them, but in the humiliating role of a dependent, rather than a petted literary lion. Accentuating the humiliation, the Marshalls' wealthy neighbors could gawk at "seeing Lydia Maria Child go by, with long curls hanging over her shoulders, and a tin pail in her hand," carrying meals three times a day to the prison where her husband languished behind bars. In between trips to the jail, moreover, Child had to run the *Massachusetts Journal* in David's absence and somehow still find time to edit the *Miscellany*. Small wonder if she published nothing else that year.[32]

Child took on yet another burden when a teaching position opened up in Dorchester Heights, where her father was now living. But the strain of trying to continue her editorial work after spending all day in a schoolroom proved more than she could handle, especially combined with the oppressive atmosphere of her father's home. By July, Child had to admit defeat. Though David had finally been released, her friends the Marshalls insisted on taking her to the beach with them to recover from her exhaustion. "How I do wish you were here!" she wrote David, with no trace of cooling love despite the ordeal they had been through. "It is nonsense for me to go a 'pleasuring' without you. My sleep don't do me any good; and every pleasant sight makes my heart yearn, because you are not with me." That morning Child had gone down to a "little cove between two lines of rocks," taken off her stockings, and "let the saucy waves come dashing and sparkling into my lap." Sadly she had recalled "the beautiful time we had, when we washed our feet together in the mountain waterfall." During their courtship, she had not dreamed of the trials that awaited her and David. But she did not confess to any regrets. "My dear husband, I *cannot* stay away a week," she ended her letter. "We lost a great deal of life by not being married sooner, and I am determined to waste no more precious hours of happiness. Don't forget. . . ."[33]

David reciprocated with similar sentiments when it was his turn to leave that October for a trip to New Hampshire, where he went to gather material for some articles on Daniel Webster and to pick up additional subscribers for the *Massachusetts Journal*: "I have passed thro many grand & beautiful natural scenes, but without you I lacked sense and enthusiasm to enjoy them. I live upon the hope that the time will come when I shall have leisure and other means to indulge my strong desire to carry you to such places and to select such a residence as will gratify our taste." He went on to tell his wife how much he missed her and appreciated her loyal support: "You cannot imagine how often I have thought of your bright and affectionate face looking up so kindly and confidingly in mine. It makes my heart melt & the tears come to think how sweetly you have borne yourself to me in the severe trials which I have brought upon you — " Yet David's letter also struck a note that would recur more frequently as the chances of improving his financial situation became increasingly remote. The humiliation of his position was clearly taking its toll, and he was not finding it easy to apologize perpetually for the trials he had inflicted on his wife or to keep showing the gratitude he knew he owed her. "I had need to be absent to learn how necessary you are to me," he admitted — a strange comment after the long separation they had just undergone during his stint in jail. And no sooner had he paid tribute to his wife's heroism than he began describing the "unearthly beauty" of his landlady's daughter, whose sad story took up more space in his letter than his loving words. There followed a two-page account of his talks with New Hampshire farmers about Daniel Webster, written for the *Massachusetts Journal*. Betraying a sense of inadequacy in comparison with the gifted literary woman he had married, David tried to anticipate her evaluation of his style: "I do not know, my dear Maria, that the above will not appear flat and uninteresting. I have written it in a dull fashion. I wish you would judge impartially whether it or any part of it is fit for the paper."[34] The conflicting feelings he was displaying — emotional dependency on his wife and the unconscious resentment such dependency inevitably breeds; a discomfiting awareness of having failed as a husband and provider; and a tendency to measure himself morally and professionally against his wife, with predictable consequences for his ego — boded ill for the Childs' marriage.

Though reunited, the couple could not afford to resume housekeeping. It would be almost three years before they would enjoy another brief moment of conventional home life — appropriately on a street named "Cottage Place" — and decades before they would actually inherit a home of their own: the Wayland, Massachusetts, farmhouse into which the senior Convers Francis finally settled. Instead, the years to come would find the Childs moving from one boardinghouse to another and staying "here and there, dependent upon the hospitality" of friends and family members. "This makes the *fifth* time my furniture has been removed, since we began to board out," Child complained to her sister-in-law the following August.[35] And she admitted to her mother-in-law: "Sometimes I get a little fidgetty, because I want to go to housekeeping so much,—and it is such a long, long way out of the woods yet. But when I fidget my husband only looks sad, and says, 'It *is* a shame such a good creature as you can't have every thing you want;' and then, you know, it is *impossible* to withstand such kindness—and I brighten up, and am as cheerful as the day is long."[36] The effort to repress her discontent and maintain her idealized image of David is almost palpable.

Intensifying Child's impatience with this unsettled mode of life was the yearning for a baby that she confided to her mother-in-law in the same letter. Although claiming to desire it "even more for my husband's sake, than for my own," she acknowledged that on the way home from a visit to David's family, the sight of a toddler "shaking all its little curls" had made her "heart ache." She must have been acutely conscious of the irony behind the occasion for her letter: the June 15 publication of her latest domestic manual, *The Mother's Book* (1831).[37]

As with *The Frugal Housewife*, Child defended *The Mother's Book* against the charge of "adding another to the numerous books on education" and affirmed: "I do not know of one adapted to popular use in this country."[38] Once again, investigation bears her out. The chief works on "education" available to the American public in 1831—and the term "education" accurately characterizes their subject matter—were either British or European; none duplicated the ambitious scope of *The Mother's Book*, which covered every aspect of childrearing, from "developing the Bodily Senses in earliest Infancy" to "Management during the Teens."[39] Predating and probably influencing such rivals as John Abbott's companion volumes *The Mother at Home* and *The Child at Home* (1833) and Lydia Huntley Sigourney's *Letters to Mothers* (1838), *The Mother's Book* clearly establishes Child as a pioneer in the field.[40]

"It has been jestingly said, that 'they who have no children, always know how to manage them well,'" Child would write apologetically on issuing a new edition of *The Mother's Book* in 1844.[41] "Childless myself, I can only plead my strong love for children, and my habitual observation of all that concerns them." These qualities pervade both *The Mother's Book* and its immediate predecessor, *The Little Girl's Own Book*, published in January 1831.[42] Like *The Frugal Housewife*, Child's books for mothers and daughters differ significantly from those of her contemporaries in their practical, unsentimental, undoctrinaire approach and in their orientation toward the needs of women from less privileged sectors of the "middling" class. Essentially, they elaborate on principles she had dramatized in *The Juvenile Miscellany* and adumbrated in the chapter of "Hints to Persons of Moderate Fortune" subtitled "Education of Daughters."

Chief among those principles, as she reiterated in her preface to *The Little Girl's Own Book*, was that "[i]n this land of precarious fortunes, every girl should know how to be *useful*," and all parents should educate their daughters in a manner enabling them "to fulfil the duties of a humble station" as well as "to dignify and adorn the highest." Child's own experience had certainly taught her the necessity of preparing girls for every possible contingency. Within a few dizzy years, she had risen from baker's daughter to darling of Boston's salons, only to fall into the role of frugal housewife, beset by a poverty worse than any that her brothers and sisters had known in their straitened youth. Thus, Child designed *The Little Girl's Own Book* to encompass not only a large variety of games, sports, riddles, intellectual exercises, educational dialogues, stories, and poems, but also crafts and housewifely skills that could be turned into means of earning or saving money, such as basket weaving, lacemaking, patchwork, beadwork, knitting, sewing, and mending.

In contrast, Eliza Leslie's *The Girl's Book of Diversions; or, Occupation for Play Hours* (1831), published in the wake of Child's manual, assumes an audience of families who can afford to bring up their daughters as marriageable young ladies of leisure. Lacking both the "useful" activities and the games designed to teach history, geography, natural history, arithmetic, and French, which Child had interspersed with lighter amusements in *The Little Girl's Own Book*, Leslie's compendium of "diversions" revealingly includes a game called "Speculation, or Matrimony." Also reflecting the more ample means of Leslie's audience is an entire section devoted to "Plays with Toys" — a category Child's book omits.[43]

Given the differences between the two works, Child was justifiably annoyed when the *American Traveller* reported, on the authority of Leslie's publishers, Munroe & Francis, "that the plan of Miss Leslie's American Girl's Book was projected and copy sent to the publishers in the summer of 1830, *before Mrs Child conceived of such a book; but hearing of this one probably was the cause of her hastily making up a volume*, which does contain poetry and an original story, where The American Girl's Book is filled with details of methods to make articles of amusing and useful work." Indignantly denying the charge, Child explained that her book had been inspired by the "popularity of an English volume, called The Boy's Own Book," and that she had learned of Leslie's parallel enterprise only when Munroe & Francis had contacted her own publishers, Carter and Hendee, in response to the latter's advertisement of Child's forthcoming book, then already in press. She had great respect for Leslie's talents, Child stressed, and would never have sought to preempt a sister writer's project. She went on to spell out the ethic she believed writers and publishers alike ought to follow: "The field of competition is open to all; and warmly and cheerfully do I wish success to those who deserve it. Miss Leslie had an unquestioned right to make a Girl's Book; and if she made a better one, it ought to rival mine. I merely complain that the size, shape, title, and arrangement, and materials are so similar to mine, that purchasers bringing orders from a distance might easily take one for the other."[44]

The process of putting together *The Little Girl's Own Book* must have fired Child's ambition to try her hand at a comprehensive advice book on childrearing. Her research for the earlier volume would naturally have led her to realize the need for such a manual and to notice the total absence of any on the market. She may also have derived the idea for *The Mother's Book* from encountering the works of the Swiss educator Johann

Heinrich Pestalozzi, either during her stints as a schoolteacher or while preparing educational materials for *The Juvenile Miscellany*. Pestalozzi's theories on early childhood education, which highlighted the role mothers could play in stimulating sensory development and intellectual curiosity, as well as in forming moral attitudes, were exerting widespread influence around 1830. One of the periodicals that regularly reviewed Child's own writings for juveniles—the *American Journal of Education*—published frequent articles on Pestalozzi's teachings; and Child's publishers, Carter and Hendee, brought out an abridged American edition of his *Letters . . . on the Education of Infancy. Addressed to Mothers* in 1830. This may have been the work referred to as *The Mother's Book* in an 1829 article summarizing "Pestalozzi's Principles and Methods of Instruction" for the *American Journal of Education*.[45] If so, it resembled Child's mainly in its title, being too abstract and limited in scope to serve as a handbook for mothers.

The task Child set herself was to translate the Pestalozzian precepts she found useful into concrete terms, rooted in the day-to-day realities of the nursery, and to incorporate the subject of infant education into a larger survey, extending into the teen years and devoting special attention to the upbringing of girls (all but ignored by Pestalozzi). It was a bold enterprise for a childless woman. Still, Child had spent her girlhood helping to raise her nieces and nephews in Norridgewock, and recently her friend Louisa Gilman Loring had had a baby, in whom Child had been taking a keen interest that would eventually ripen into a lifelong bond. Louisa is one of several possible candidates for the "intelligent and judicious mother" Child acknowledged in the preface as the source of many suggestions in *The Mother's Book*. Yet whatever Child owed to conversations with the mothers among her friends or to treatises by European authorities, *The Mother's Book* bears the unmistakable stamp of personal observation by a shrewd and sympathetic analyst of children's behavior.

The "plain practical good-sense" toward which Child aspired is evident from the first chapter. Eschewing the homilies on the "Responsibility" and "Privileges of the Mother" with which her American successors, John Abbott and Lydia Sigourney, open their manuals, Child begins with the need to develop the infant's sensory awareness by arousing his or her attention with objects of "bright and beautiful colors" and "sounds pleasant and soft to the ear" (3)—an idea borrowed from Pestalozzi.[46] Every time an infant handles, drops, or picks up an object, she explains, "he adds something to the little stock of his scanty experience" (3). In a subsequent discussion of habit formation, Child warns against waiting for an infant to cry before taking care of his needs and showing him affection. "Who can blame a child for fretting and screaming," she asks, "if experience has taught him that he cannot get his wants attended to in any other manner?" (23).

Although she underscores the importance of surrounding the infant with an "atmosphere of love," Child refrains from the gushing effusions that typify Sigourney's treatment of this subject.[47] And unlike Sigourney, she recognizes that "people of moderate fortune cannot attend exclusively to an infant" (4), let alone solve the problem of competing household duties in the manner Sigourney recommends—by engaging "an efficient person in the nurse's department" and "competent assistance, in the sphere of manual labour," so that a mother can "become the constant directress of her children, and have leisure to be happy in their companionship."[48] Instead, Child describes a scenario in which a busy mother must rely on "sisters, or domestics" for babysitting (as Child's sister Mary had relied on her) while performing other chores. In such cases, she advises, a mother should remember to give her infant an occasional smile when occupied in the same room, or "endearing appellations" when in an adjoining room, since a feeling of "safety and protection" will be "alike conducive to his happiness and beneficial to his temper" (4–5).

Her ensuing chapters on cultivating the "affections" and the "intellect" and perfecting the art of child "management" are similarly filled with helpful pointers. For example, Child suggests dealing with ill humor not by scolding — "This, in all probability, will make matters worse" — but by distracting the child's attention to "pleasant thoughts" or soothing him or her with "little kind offices," such as gently "washing the face and combing the hair" (24–25). In the same spirit, she stresses that while it is important to use games as means of introducing concepts and encouraging "habits of thought," if a child is impatient to play and resists being fed information, "it is unwise to cross his inclinations," because "forced instruction is apt to injure the temper, and give an early aversion to knowledge" (11–12).[49]

Even where Child concurs with other authorities, her emphasis is often different. To take a prime instance, all nineteenth-century authorities agreed that inculcating obedience as early as possible was crucial and that parents should be consistent in enforcing compliance with any rules they laid down. Abbott and Sigourney introduce the principle of obedience at the outset and present it as the "first step towards religion."[50] Child, however, subordinates her discussion of obedience to the goal of convincing mothers that a "silent influence" and moral example inspiring "right *feelings*" is more efficacious than "direct rules and commands" (22, 25–26). She treats obedience largely as a practical matter. "[T]here are cases where rules must be made; and children must be taught to obey implicitly," she notes. "For instance, a child must be expressly forbidden to play with fire, to climb upon the tables, &c." (26). Advocating that punishment for disobedience be "as mild as it can be and produce the desired effect," she warns against "[p]unishments which make a child ashamed," since "a sense of degradation is not healthy for the character" (30, 37–38).

By late twentieth-century standards, of course, the style of childrearing promoted in *The Mother's Book* may seem repressive rather than liberal. Child fully shared her contemporaries' belief that a mother must "drive evil passions" like anger and resentment out of her own heart and try to prevent them from taking root in her children's (3–5, 9). Many of her techniques for fostering approved moral attitudes — reacting with "sorrow" to a child's misdeeds, for example (28) — would strike a post-Freudian reader as guilt-inducing and manipulative. Yet situated in historical context, *The Mother's Book* emerges as a pioneering contribution to the literature of childrearing.[51]

The differences between *The Mother's Book* and its rivals furnish a key to understanding a major rift in nineteenth-century American culture. While most of the authors who formulated and promulgated the ideology of domesticity sought to keep women within their sphere, a small cadre of reformers began challenging the doctrine of "woman's sphere" and developing much more flexible concepts of gender, class, and race, though they did not necessarily reject domestic ideology wholesale. *The Mother's Book* belongs at the head of this alternative lineage. Unlike such texts as Abbott's *The Mother at Home*, Sigourney's *Letters to Mothers*, Alcott's *The Young House-keeper*, and Catharine Beecher's *Treatise on Domestic Economy*, *The Mother's Book* does not glorify homemaking and childrearing as women's highest vocation. It simply offers advice on how best to fulfill the responsibilities women most commonly assumed in nineteenth-century households, particularly in those of moderate income.

The ideology discernible between the lines of *The Mother's Book* is not the cult of domesticity, but the democratic humanitarianism that lies at the heart of the movements for social justice to which Child would shortly dedicate her life. The resemblance is no coincidence, for Child had met William Lloyd Garrison the previous year and was already avidly reading his newspaper *The Liberator* and gathering material for her 1833 *Appeal in Favor of That Class of Americans Called Africans*. Along with her latest stories in the *Juvenile Miscellany*, *The Mother's Book* reflects her evolution toward Garrisonian abolitionism.[52] The style of childrearing she advocates in the book — one in which "ill-humor and discontent are driven away by the influence of kindness and cheerfulness" and " 'evil is overcome with good' " (25) — foreshadows her espousal of the pacifist ethic Garrisonian abolitionists would call "nonresistance." In parallel fashion, her emphasis on developing "right *feelings*" and motivating children to do good not for the sake of winning rewards or avoiding punishments, but for the sake of satisfying their own consciences, fosters a character trait indispensable for future social reformers, but undesirable for members of an entrenched elite: the inner strength needed to brave public opinion in defense of unpopular causes. "It is not true that we always meet a return for kindness and generosity" or that we necessarily win the "good opinion of others" by doing what we think right, Child writes, almost as if anticipating the abuse she would receive two years later for her courageous stand against slavery and racial prejudice. Thus she urges parents not to "pollute" good actions with wrong motives by promising children that they will gain by good conduct. Those who expect rewards for their good conduct are bound to be disappointed, she warns, "and not being accustomed to act from any better motive, they will cease to be benevolent" except when it pays. Ultimately "[n]othing is a safe guide but the honest convictions of our own hearts" (38–44). She would sound that theme throughout her career as an abolitionist.

Even more prophetic of Child's participation in the struggles for racial equality and women's rights are the democratic values *The Mother's Book* upholds. The chapter on "Politeness" is typical. Differentiating between genteel manners and the consideration for others' well being that is "the very life and soul of politeness," Child maintains: "a truly benevolent, kindhearted person will always be distinguished for what is called native politeness, though entirely ignorant of the conventional forms of society" (109–10). She adds: "True politeness may be cherished in the hovel as well as in the palace" (114). Her ensuing criticism of a "very prevalent fault among children" — "want of politeness to domestics" — reenforces the message that politeness is not a function of gentility (116). Attitudes of superiority are "peculiarly preposterous" in a republic, she underscores; moreover, given the financial vicissitudes to which the American economy is subject, "those who are servants now may be mistresses next year; and those who *keep* domestics now may *be* domestics hereafter" (117).

The egalitarian thrust of Child's exhortations becomes especially evident in the light of Catharine Beecher's chapter "On Domestic Manners." Contrary to Child (whose abolitionist philosophy she would vociferously reject), Beecher argues that "certain grades of superiority and subordination are needful, both for individual and public benefit." Furthermore, she attributes the "defect in American manners" to the refusal to observe the "proprieties" defining what "style of deportment and address" is appropriate for each grade: "thus we see, to an increasing extent, disrespectful treatment of parents, from children; of teachers, from pupils; of employers, from domestics; of the aged, from the young," she complains. Beecher applies this hierarchical view of society to the relations between men and women. The "privileges" of the "female sex," she contends, rest on women's acceptance of a "subordinate station." Hence, she orients her *Treatise on Domestic Economy* toward preparing women for their roles as wives and mothers, even going so far as to recommend that until girls reach the age of fifteen, their "intellectual culture . . . ought to be made altogether secondary in importance" to their "domestic education."[53]

Child envisages a much greater degree of mobility and variability in the social positions girls are destined to occupy. Her views on how they should be educated differ accordingly. While agreeing that a "knowledge of domestic duties is beyond all price to a woman," she sees "no necessity that the gaining of such information should interfere with intellectual acquirement" (146). In fact, she uses almost the same phrase — "above all price" — to refer to "the power of finding enjoyment in reading" (20). A love of reading is even more important for girls to cultivate than for boys, Child affirms, not only because it enables them to be better wives and mothers, but because it offers a means of expanding the restrictive bounds of woman's sphere: "It cheers so many hours of illness and seclusion; it gives the mind something to interest itself about, instead of the concerns of one's neighbors, and the changes of fashion; it enlarges the heart, by giving extensive views of the world . . ." (86). Girls should maintain a balance between domestic and intellectual education, Child asserts, for both are vital: "If a girl feels interested in nothing but books, she will in all probability be useless, or nearly so, in all the relations dearest to a good woman's heart; if, on the other hand, she gives all her attention to household matters, she will become a mere drudge, and will lose many valuable sources of enjoyment and usefulness" (21).

Indicating the significance Child attaches to instilling a love of reading, she devotes a whole chapter to "Advice concerning Books." She particularly recommends "History, Voyages, Travels, Biography." Novels, she suggests, "should form the *recreation* rather than the *employment* of the mind" (87), but should not be prohibited, as long as they are "pure in spirit and in language." The same is true of fairy tales for younger children, which most nineteenth-century educators decried as frivolous. Replying to the common objection that fairy tales prevented children from learning to distinguish between reality and fiction, Child defends them on surprisingly modern grounds: "I do not believe chidren ever think they are true. During my own childhood, I am very sure I regarded them as just what they were, — as efforts of the imagination — dreams that had a meaning to them" (92). She would carry this insight further in the 1844 edition of *The Mother's Book*, where she would argue in an interpolated passage: "The love of fiction is . . . founded in an universal instinct; and all universal instincts of human nature should be wisely employed, rather than forcibly repressed" (94). Few nineteenth-century educators shared Child's understanding of the vital function the imagination performed for the human psyche.[54]

The same regard for the "universal instincts of human nature" impels Child to risk public censure by alluding to a topic avoided by her peers — one on which she feels "very anxious to say a great deal; but on which, for obvious reasons," she knows she can "say very little" (151). "[T]he want of confidence between mothers and daughters on delicate subjects" is "the greatest evil now existing in education," she specifies. She proceeds to reason that curiosity about such matters is "perfectly natural and innocent" and should be "frankly met by a mother," instead of being greeted with "mystery and embarrassment" or turned aside with "lies." "Mothers are the only proper persons to convey such knowledge to a child's mind . . . and it is an imperious duty that they should do it," Child insists (151–52). To speak so openly about a tabooed subject in a domestic manual written to earn badly needed income demanded the kind of courage Child was about to show in her antislavery *Appeal*. This aspect of *The Mother's Book* also recalls the "author of *Hobomok*" and prefigures the increasingly bold treatment of sexuality in Child's fiction of the 1840s.

Child's discussion of sex education in "Management during the Teens" leads naturally into the chapter with which she ends *The Mother's Book*: "Views of Matrimony." Unlike Catharine Beecher, Child does not predicate the upbringing of girls on the expectation that they will marry and be supported by their husbands throughout their lives. Taking a stand that anticipates the feminist argument of Margaret Fuller's *Woman in the Nineteenth Century* (1845), Child urges women to remain single rather than sell themselves for the sake of economic security. Marrying for money is "absolutely unprincipled," and "marrying for a home is a most tiresome way of getting a living," she avers (164). She also recognizes that even when women marry, they cannot be sure their husbands will be stable breadwinners (as she herself had learned from bitter experience), and that widowhood often throws women back on their own resources. Thus, she advises them to learn bookkeeping and acquire "a general knowledge of the *laws* connected with the settlement of estates" (136). While hastening to disclaim any "wish to see American women taking business out of the hands of men," Child reiterates: "I wish they were all *capable* of doing business, or settling an estate, when it is *necessary*" (136).

Girls as well as boys, Child stresses, should be "brought up with a dread of being dependent on the bounty of others" and educated in a way that will enable them to "support themselves respectably" if they have to. For that purpose they should develop all their faculties to the utmost and place no limits on the pursuit of knowledge. "I do not believe that *any* kind of knowledge ever unfitted a person for the discharge of duty," Child declares categorically, in response to those who fear the danger of "unfitting girls for the duties of their station." On the contrary, knowledge "multiplies our resources in case of poverty" and empowers us to be "useful to others" (136–38). "I believe a variety of knowledge . . . would make a man a better servant, as well as a better president; and make a woman a better wife, as well as a better teacher" (139–40).

True, the grammar of Child's sentence equates wifehood with servitude and registers the greater scope for advancement open to men; nonetheless, implicit in her views on the education of girls are the same egalitarian convictions she would articulate in her antislavery tracts and articles on women's rights. Like *The Mother's Book*, those later works would reject the concept of a hierarchical society in which some occupied a "superior" and others a "subordinate station." They, too, would plead eloquently against arbitrary barriers to self-development, serving to keep the "subordinate" in their "station." They, too, would assume the basic equality of all human beings and insist on the need to equip all alike with the means to exercise their rights and improve their status.

The potentially dangerous liberalism of *The Mother's Book* did not escape the notice of reviewers. Both the *American Annals of Education* and the *American Monthly Review* pointedly announced that they could not "subscribe to all its sentiments," though they praised the book for its "sensible" and "uncommonly . . . instructive" advice, particularly on the handling of infants and young children.[55] Only Sarah Hale endorsed it without qualification, perhaps because she found confirmation for her ideology of "woman's sphere" in the fact that a woman writer who "could so soar and shine in the regions of imagination" had shown herself "content to . . . do good."[56]

Notwithstanding the reservations of reviewers, *The Mother's Book* won Child a tremendous ovation from the public, probably because it fulfilled a need that no other work on the market yet addressed. "[T]he Mother's Book . . . sells with astonishing rapidity," Child wrote to her sister-in-law in August. After only six weeks, the first edition was exhausted and the publisher could not "get another edition ready soon enough" to meet popular demand. It would go through five printings by 1833. "I have never received so many congratulatory letters on the publication of any book," Child reported.[57]

Despite the "remarkable degree of success" she had achieved, Child confessed to being in a "discouraged mood." "Every thing we [meaning "I"] can earn goes to pay debts," she complained to Lydia, " — and yet it seems as if we should never get out of difficulty."[58]

That October, wistfully recalling what she and David had "said, and thought, and felt, three years ago," on the eve of their wedding, she assured David he need not fear the "decay" of her love, for she was "miserable" when apart from him. "In all that relates to external circumstances, our married life has been a stormy journey," Child acknowledged. "But in all other respects, my dear husband, have we not realized all, and *more* than we then hoped? *I* at least have; and by the blessing of God, I will try to be a more 'perfect wife' than I have been." The note of self-blame in that vow — as if Child were redirecting responsibility for her "stormy" married life from David's failures toward her own inability to bear them without complaint—would grow more strident as her husband's prospects worsened.[59]

Written while Child was supervising the printing of *The Coronal* from her publishers' headquarters in Lancaster, a town near Worcester, her letter registers a triple irony. She had sacrificed her financial independence for marriage and her vocation as a writer of fiction for the task of producing remunerative domestic advice books, yet she still did not enjoy the benefits that domestic ideology promised to women. Torn between her professional responsibilities and her wifely impulses, she wished she could follow the promptings of her "heart," "leave the printing here to take care of itself, jump into the stage, and come right back home"; but even if she did so, she realized bleakly, she would not find the domestic haven she craved: "[A]las, I *have* no home to come to—no corner in which to fix up my things for the winter. Oh, how I do long to be settled!"[60]

The tension between Child's allegiance to domestic ideology and her marked deviations from it, both in her advice books and in her life, resurfaced in the project she undertook on the heels of *The Mother's Book*—the creation of the *Ladies' Family Library*, another of her historical innovations. Launched in 1832, this five-volume series supplied women with precisely the literary fare Child had recommended in *The Mother's Book*—biographies, histories, and if not travelogues, at least travelers' accounts of women in distant lands. It comprised three volumes of biographical sketches, celebrating women notable for both intellectual achievement and feminine virtues (1832, 1833), and a two-volume *History of the Condition of Women, in Various Ages and Nations* (1835).[61] As with the reasons Child had given in *The Mother's Book* for encouraging women to cultivate a love of reading, the *Ladies' Family Library* extended the parameters of the domestic sphere even while idealizing women's roles as companionate wives and Republican mothers. Child clearly conceived the series with a dual aim: promoting women's education through informal channels at a historical moment when most women did not have access to institutions of higher learning; and offering a variety of role models to emulate in a period of social ferment that heralded new opportunities for some women. Once again, she was recognizing and responding to a cultural need almost as soon as it had arisen.

If the wide spectrum of women Child holds up for imitation represents the gamut of available social choices, it also mirrors the conflicts among her different selves—feminist rebel, aspiring literary genius, incipient political activist, and "perfect wife." She opens the series in volume 1 with two women of formidable intellectual powers who had boldly challenged the political tyranny of male authorities: Madame Anne-Louise-Germaine Necker de Staël and Madame Jeanne-Marie Phlipon Roland.[62] A brilliant and versatile writer whose command of German and English philosophy had inspired Child and her young friend Margaret Fuller to study her *De l'Allemagne* (1813) together in the winter of 1826–27, Madame de Staël had dared to stand up to Napoleon. Persecution and banishment had failed to silence her, as economic boycott and ostracism would fail to silence Child after she pledged herself to the antislavery cause. De Staël's romantic novel *Corinne, ou l'Italie* (1807), akin in spirit to *Hobomok*, had also conjured into being the persona of the female artist-intellectual—a persona many would come to associate with Margaret Fuller, the "Yankee Corinna."[63] De Staël's contemporary Madame Roland likewise had striking affinities with Child and Fuller and uncannily foreshadowed their future careers. A committed republican, she had participated in the French Revolution alongside her Girondist husband, evoking both the Childs' partnership in the antislavery movement and Fuller's partnership with her lover, Angelo Ossoli, in the Italian Revolution of 1848. At the same time, Madame Roland embodied the female author-revolutionary in a more conventional guise than Child would choose to assume. Perceiving that "a woman who acquires the title [of author] . . . forfeits the affection of the male sex, and provokes the criticism of her own," Madame Roland had opted for writing her political tracts under her husband's name and allowing him to take credit for them (143, 208–10). Indeed, she had gone to the guillotine in his place. Child's portrayal of Madame Roland suggests the contradictory feelings with which she was struggling as she reshaped her career after her marriage: on the one hand, guilt at failing to live up to the standard of the "perfect wife" set by a woman who had renounced literary ambition; on the other hand, a dim recognition of how deadly it could be for a wife to submerge her own identity in her husband's.

The second and third volumes of the series, *The Biographies of Lady Russell, and Madame Guyon* (1832) and *Good Wives* (1833), continue the trend toward more conventional images of women discernible in the shift from Madame de Staël to Madame Roland. Child probably felt she had to counterbalance intellectuals and revolutionaries with pious Christians and exemplary helpmeets if she wanted to maximize sales. The high proportion of quoted material, especially in volume 3, gives one a sense of hackwork rather than of genuine engagement with the subject (a reminder that Child was simultaneously researching and writing her ambitious antislavery *Appeal* and editing the *Juvenile Miscellany*). Nevertheless, the biographical sketches in these volumes betray wrenching personal anxieties. Child's account of Lady Russell's suffering when her husband is unjustly beheaded, for example, resonates with the sentiment she acknowledged in a letter to David about his seemingly unmerited adversity: "Nothing disturbs my faith in Providence so much as your good actions and bad fortune."[64] Equally symptomatic is the tone of self-abnegation that pervades the dedication of *Good Wives* (and echoes Child's poem "To a Husband, Who presented, as a New-Year's Offering, a *Heart* and a *Laurel wreath*, the leaves of which were not very abundant"): "To my husband this book is affectionately inscribed, by one who, through every vicissitude, has found in his kindness and worth, her purest happiness, and most constant incentives to duty." In keeping with this dedication, an inordinate number of the biographies in *Good Wives* credit the virtues of wives entirely to their husbands and praise women for being "zealous in the only politics which belong to woman—viz. loyalty to her husband"—an astonishing stand for Child to take at a time when she was about to invade the tabooed sphere of antislavery politics.[65] It is impossible to avoid concluding that Child was desperately striving to be a "good wife" by attributing her achievements to David and by suppressing any resentment she felt at having to orient her literary talents toward the goal of earning enough money to pay his debts.

However unsuccessfully Child worked through the role conflicts she projected into the biographies of the *Ladies' Family Library*, she managed to turn them into a vehicle for helping her readers to resolve similar problems, as she had in *The Frugal Housewife* and *The Mother's Book*. The biographies of Madame de Staël and Madame Roland would prove great favorites with women's rights advocates, among them Margaret Fuller and Elizabeth Cady Stanton.[66] All three volumes received glowing reviews. "We know of no works better fitted for the perusal of ladies in all conditions of life, than the Ladies' Family Library; and we know of no person who could have better fulfilled the task of editing these volumes than Mrs. Child," wrote "U.U." in the *Ladies' Magazine*, greeting the series as "an *oasis* in the dreary desert" of contemporary literature. Predictably, reviewers united in pronouncing *Good Wives* "decidedly the best of [Child's] works." "Every wife, mother and daughter in the land should read this book," pontificated the *Southern Quarterly Review*: "Mrs. Child disclaims the character of a philosopher, but she knows how to teach the art of living well, which is certainly the highest wisdom, and there are few living writers in the English language, of either sex, who employ a style more pure, unaffected, nervous and elegant." Explaining its preference for *Good Wives* over the other volumes in the series, the *Ladies' Magazine* pointed out that though Child's characterizations of Madame de Staël and Madame Roland were "spirited and interesting," these two women's "brilliant beauties" were "not *examples* for the daughters of republican America." "The time for the display of such heroism and daring fortitude has gone by, and women are now called upon to exercise the more quiet, yet more important virtues of domestic life," claimed Sarah Hale's oracle. Whatever Child's feelings about having her least creative work universally hailed as her best, she had tried so hard to practice the wifely virtues she preached that she must have been gratified when her "eloquent, yet simple, dedication 'TO MY HUSBAND,'" was cited as "sufficient to recommend the volume to all *good wives*."[67]

Good Wives was the last work Child wrote before the publication of her antislavery *Appeal* abruptly ended her popularity and cost her the patronage of Boston's aristocrats. She would not make another foray into the domestic advice market until 1837, with *The Family Nurse; or, Companion of the Frugal Housewife*.[68] Once again, she resorted to the genre out of desperation. "If any other than very practical works would sell extensively," she admitted in the preface with surprising candor, "I fear I should still be lingering in more poetic regions" (4). The Childs' financial situation had reached a nadir, however. Now, added to the problem of David's debts, both the *Massachusetts Journal* and David's legal practice (or what there was of it) had collapsed, and Child had lost her own sources of income. *The Mother's Book* had dropped out of favor as soon as Child's antislavery manifesto had appeared; suddenly going out of print, it was not reissued until 1844.[69] *The Juvenile Miscellany* had succumbed to parental boycott in 1834. Although *The Frugal Housewife* and *The Little Girl's Own Book* did not suffer the same fate, perhaps because they did not seem to be indoctrinating the young with subversive values, their sales had noticeably slowed. And previously the four works combined had not sufficed to meet the Childs' expenses.

True, Child had slight grounds for hoping that another domestic advice manual would counter the public hostility that had killed her earlier best-sellers. Nevertheless, writing was her only real means of support. She could not afford to give up, but neither could she help betraying her despondent mood in the preface to her new work. "For many reasons," she confessed, the compilation of *The Family Nurse* had been "an arduous and disagreeable task" (4). One reason was the dilemma she faced in trying to describe the symptoms and treatment of bodily disorders in "language plain enough to be understood" without being "indelicate, in the world's estimation." Willis's sarcasms regarding the crude language of *The Frugal Housewife* still rankled, yet Child saw no way of refining a work "very obviously not intended for the drawing-room." As a result, the book had lain "unfinished" for a long interval until she had determined to repudiate "false modesty."

Child's resistance to the task of writing *The Family Nurse* may also have had deeper roots. Temporarily staying with her father again while David was away in Europe, she may have found herself reliving the pain of her mother's three-year illness and the guilt of her own failure to be the model daughter and tender nurse she felt she should have been. In a sense, she had been using her domestic manuals as means of atoning for her childhood sin of behaving badly toward her dying mother. *The Frugal Housewife* had paid tribute to the style of plain living and hard work she had learned from her mother. *The Mother's Book* had enabled her to step into her mother's role and symbolically re-create her childhood as she would have liked to remember it. And *The Family Nurse* allowed her to act out a revised version of the deathbed scene that continued to haunt her more than twenty years later — this time by offering the world the nursing she had been unwilling to give her mother.

Like her other domestic manuals, *The Family Nurse* contained a wealth of practical advice. In preparing it, Child had consulted the best medical texts of the period, as well as "aged relatives and judicious nurses." She had also submitted it to a practicing physician and member of the Massachusetts Medical Society for review, with the aim of ensuring that the book would be perfectly "*safe*" (3).

The book's careful organization reflected the thought and labor Child had put into it. It opened with several pages of "Hints for the Preservation of Health" and "Hints to Nurses and the Sick." Then followed a section on "Food and Drink for Invalids," which included recipes and instructions on the stage of illness or convalescence for which each was appropriate. "Children" occupied a quarter of the book, beginning with advice on prenatal care and diet during nursing and proceeding to detail the diseases prevalent in each age group and their remedies. The last half of the book particularized the uses of medicines and herbs every household should keep in stock and described standard methods of treatment. A glossary and index facilitated consultation of the book in emergencies. Child had learned a great deal since throwing together *The Frugal Housewife*.

The glimpse that *The Family Nurse* provides of health care in an era when most diseases, from croup to dysentery, were treated by inducing vomiting and purging, reveals a side of nineteenth-century women's lives veiled by paeans to the "angel in the house." Relegated to women, nursing involved a multitude of unpleasant and burdensome tasks that indeed defied genteel language and belied the public image of the lady. Child's reluctance to finish the book surely reflects her awareness of the contradictions between domestic ideology and the realities of "woman's sphere."

Sadly, *The Family Nurse* did not repay the time and effort Child had expended on it, let alone help alleviate her financial difficulties. It was the only one of her advice books that was never reprinted. Perhaps it fell victim to the Panic of 1837. Alternatively, it may have overlapped too much with the medical texts from which Child had drawn her information. It is also probable that by embracing the abolitionist cause, Child had simply forfeited the moral authority she had once enjoyed. Henceforth, the domestic advice market would be closed to her.[70]

The final irony of Child's career as a purveyor of domestic advice was that *The Family Nurse* would prove to be the book most relevant to her life. Although a stable home would elude her for decades and her yearning for children would remain permanently unsatisfied, she would end up nursing her father and David through the incontinence of old age.

7
Children's Literature and Antislavery: Conservative Medium, Radical Message

After conducting the Miscellany for eight years, I am now compelled to bid a reluctant and most affectionate farewell to my little readers. May God bless you, my young friends, and impress deeply upon your hearts the conviction that all true excellence and happiness consist in living for others, not for yourselves. In whatsoever situation Divine Providence may place you, be governed by this spirit, in all things, both great and small, and you will find peace within your own hearts, while you prove a blessing to those around you. I intend hereafter to write other books for your amusement and instruction; and I part from you with less pain, because I hope that God will enable me to be a medium of use to you, in some other form than the Miscellany.[1]

Child's poignant valedictory to the juvenile readers she had been nurturing since 1826 encapsulates the contradictions of her role as a children's writer. She had helped shape children's literature into a powerful medium for socializing the young into the value systems adults wanted them to internalize. From the beginning, Child had used the genre to inculcate the principles she held most vital to a democratic republic — principles that included a commitment to equal rights for all and the courage to stand by one's inner convictions, as well as the practice of the middle-class virtues — industry, frugality, temperance, self-denial, and perseverance. By building the *Juvenile Miscellany* into the most popular children's magazine of its day, she had succeeded in exerting enormous influence over a generation of New England youth. Yet the extent of that influence and of the financial remuneration that had directed Child toward the genre in the first place — indeed, the very survival of the *Juvenile Miscellany* — depended on strict adherence to one condition: remaining safely within the stockade of the national ideology. Child could not comply. As she had ever since her girlhood in Maine, she irresistibly strayed toward the outlying wilderness inhabited by racial Others. Twice during her eight-year tenure as editor, she risked her reputation by espousing the cause of those Others. On the first occasion — the 1829 publication of *The First Settlers of New England*, with its double-barreled attack on the U.S. government's "crooked and narrow-minded [Indian] policy" and on the Calvinist theology that had historically sanctioned Indian genocide — she wrote under the cover of anonymity and ultimately chose not to promote or distribute the book, averting a probable debacle.[2] On the second occasion — her decision to dedicate her literary talents to the crusade against slavery, prompted by her meeting with William Lloyd Garrison in June 1830 — she did not flinch from the sacrifice when an irate public cast her off and consigned her beloved *Miscellany* to bankruptcy.[3]

Spanning the years when Child was preparing to join the abolitionist movement, the *Miscellany* offers precious clues to the evolution of her political consciousness at that critical juncture — an evolution of which she left no private record. The magazine also offers illuminating insights into the difficulties that reformers of Child's generation would confront when they tried to address the issues of Indian dispossession, slavery, and racism as they had addressed the issue of white poverty. Interspersing bourgeois success stories that affirmed the nation's utopian claims with protests against racial prejudice, which patently gave the lie to those claims, the *Miscellany* endeavored to harmonize conflicting views of American society and conflicting prescriptions for its ills. The conservative social philosophy the magazine upheld defined the plight of destitute whites in individual terms and suggested individual remedies — hard work, education, charity toward the deserving, and selective upward mobility. The plight of the peoples a white nation had debased and enslaved was manifestly collective, however, and the redress of racial injustice demanded collective remedies — an overall change in the nation's policies, the repeal of discriminatory laws, and an accompanying transformation of white attitudes. Juxtaposed with each other, the *Miscellany*'s stories about whites and racial Others starkly reveal the limitations of bourgeois ideology as an instrument for revolutionizing a racist society.

Happy endings are far less frequent for Child's Indian and black protagonists, and they seldom take the forms of upward mobility or restoration to a rural haven. After all, what made the dream of returning to the country and purchasing their own farms a continuing possibility for many poor whites was the theft of Indian land. And what furnished the cheap raw materials on which northern manufacturers, as well as southern planters, depended for their profits was black slave labor. How, then, could Child extend to her Indian and black protagonists the solutions she held out to her white orphans?[4]

The contradictions with which Child wrestled in the *Miscellany* dated back to the very origins of American democratic ideology. No one illustrated those contradictions more tellingly than Thomas Jefferson, who had fathered both a political creed proclaiming the equality of all mankind and a body of theory postulating the innate inferiority of Africans.[5] As the sociologist Donald L. Noel has explained, the simultaneous development of egalitarian and racist ideas was not accidental, but logical: "In the absence of notions of equality, brotherhood, and justice, members of one group can exploit members of other groups with few qualms and no compulsion to construct a unique justifying rationale." Such rationales, Noel argues, are peculiar to societies in which the "blatant clash" between egalitarian values and exploitative institutions necessitates an ideology that reconciles the two by denying the humanity of the exploited groups.[6]

Thus, the challenge Child faced in her stories about Indians and blacks lay in countering the white supremacist assumptions that excluded racial Others from the American creed of equality and denied them the benefits of democracy. To accomplish this task, she could not resort to fictional formulas drawing their power of conviction from the dominant cultural mythology, as she could for the white poor. Instead, she had to combat deeply held stereotypes of Indians and blacks as savages and subhuman creatures; redefine the meaning of equality and humanity to encompass all the country's inhabitants; and reenvision the United States as a multiracial republic. In the case of Indians this effort entailed exploring the historical basis for peaceful relations with whites, disputing the inevitability of the Indians' extinction, and demonstrating the feasibility of bringing them within the fold of white "civilization." In the case of blacks, the problem was more daunting, since arousing white readers' sympathies for them required exposing the horrors of the slave system that undergirded the American republic. Such an enterprise threatened to unleash a controversy of mammoth proportions, one that many feared would eventuate in tearing the nation asunder.

Child tackled the "Indian problem" much earlier than the issue of slavery, both because her contact with the Abenaki and Penobscot in Maine had brought it closer to her and because it seemed less freighted with dangerous consequences. Occupying the same position *Hobomok* does at the outset of Child's literary career, and revising Puritan history along similar lines, a story that deliberately reverses the captivity narrative opens the very first number of the *Juvenile Miscellany*.

Like *Hobomok*, "Adventure in the Woods" (1826) dramatizes an alternative to race war and genocide: it shows how a community prospers when Puritan colonists overcome their dread of savages and treat their Indian neighbors with Christian charity.[7] The story begins by dismissing the colonists' fears of Indians as the product, literally, of a childish imagination. Although the two peoples are at peace with each other when the Wilson family lands in New England, Child specifies, young Benjamin and Rachel are "very much afraid" of Indians: "[T]hey had heard frightful stories about their wickedness and cruelty—and their dark skins, and long black hair, their strange dresses and language made them appear very frightful creatures to children who had never seen any thing like them before" (1: 7).

As in *Hobomok*, it is the female members of the community who initiate relations of reciprocity and trust between Indians and whites, which prove crucial to the survival of both. One day a "poor sick Indian woman, unable to follow her tribe who were wandering to the north," comes to the Puritan village begging for food. Mrs. Wilson sees her sitting under a tree, invites her into the house, and gives her bread. "In exchange," the woman leaves "two bright blue feathers," which Rachel shows her father and brother on their return home from the fields. Mrs. Wilson's charity reaps its reward the following year. On an "excursion in search of wild fruits," Rachel and Benjamin get lost in the woods, where the Indian woman finds them. Child pointedly deflates the expectations the scene arouses in readers brought up on captivity narratives. When Benjamin throws "his arm round his sister as if to protect her" from the old woman, Child comments: "but of that there was no need" (1: 8, 11). Recognizing Rachel and remembering her mother's kindness, the woman takes the two children home to their parents, carrying the "weary little girl in her arms" the whole way.

Significantly, the male sibling is the one who continues to view the Indian as a savage foe in this scene, while the female sibling now personalizes her as "the squaw who once came to the village for food" (1: 11). Not the male sphere of war, but the female sphere of domestic nurture, Child implies, furnishes the proper model for Indian-white relations. Through her charity toward a needy sister, Mrs. Wilson has saved her family and set an example for her husband and son to follow. Accordingly, Mr. Wilson presents the Indian woman with a pocket knife—his equivalent for the two feathers she gave his wife the previous year—to thank her for her kindness. The roles of benefactor and beneficiary have been reversed and a permanent bond established between Indian and white. The Indian woman revisits the family every year, "bringing some token of remembrance, and returning loaded with presents." A new image of the Indian has replaced the bugaboo that frightened the children at the outset: "the children loved her . . . and never saw an Indian without thinking of their Adventure in the Wood" (1: 13).

Child's efforts to counteract negative stereotypes of the Indian and to refute fatalistic predictions of the race's demise take a variety of forms in the *Miscellany*. Biographical sketches of figures like William Penn and the Puritan missionary John Eliot emphasize that some whites did succeed in maintaining friendly relations with the Indians by dealing justly with them.[8] Historical accounts of the Pequot War, King Philip's War, and the Norridgewock massacre portray Indians as victims rather than instigators of brutal extermination campaigns.[9] Reminiscences of Indians whom Child had known in her Norridgewock days provide examples of native virtues paralleling the industry, ingenuity, and self-denial valued by bourgeois society.

These personal reminiscences furnish valuable insight into the relations Child formed with Indians, showing how she learned to extend her sympathies to racial Others. At the same time, their often condescending tone betrays an ethnocentrism Child would never fully overcome.[10]

"The Indian Boy" (1827) describes a Penobscot youth named Alexis, whom Child had befriended in Maine.[11] After his grandmother sends him twice in one week to ask for flour, and the boy explains that the old woman is ill, Child replies: "I will give you some meal, to-day, because I think you are a very good boy, and would not tell a wrong story." The next day she sets out to visit his grandmother's wigwam, where she finds Alexis "weaving baskets, as fast as he could make his fingers fly." He makes "brooms and baskets all the time," his grandmother reports, and always turns his earnings over to her. That very morning, he has finished "a beautiful, open-work basket" promised to Child. Later, as Alexis grows older, he accompanies his father on hunting expeditions and becomes "the swiftest runner, and the best hunter in his tribe." But he still gives his grandmother the money he earns from selling his furs. The sketch ends by admonishing white children not to "laugh at people, because they do not know every thing that has been taught us." Even though Alexis has "never been to any school," Child points out, "he knows the names and uses of every tree, far and wide," and can "tell little white boys a great many things they never heard of" (2: 31).

"The Indian Boy" epitomizes the awkward results of trying to adapt the conventions of children's literature to bridging the gap between white and Indian children. True, Alexis exemplifies many of the virtues preached in the *Miscellany*: he works industriously at Indian crafts, keeps his promises, devotes himself to his grandmother's welfare, saves his earnings for the family, and strives to perfect himself in the skills prized by his people. Nevertheless, Child cannot honestly portray him as winning the same rewards for these virtues as his white peers would. Relegated to an ever more precarious existence on the periphery of a white society that has deprived Indians of their livelihood, his people must rely on the patronizing charity of white benefactors who, like Child, feel compelled to verify whether or not an Indian reduced to begging for food is telling a "wrong story." Exhortations against sentiments of racial superiority are of little avail against these realities.

Only in one of her *Miscellany* sketches, "Pol Sosef. The Indian Artist," does Child hold out the hope — very tentatively formulated — that an Indian boy might follow the path of advancement marked out for the magazine's white protagonists. Dated January 1831, this sketch reflects the political awareness Child had developed since participating in the debates over Cherokee removal and beginning her research on slavery. Accordingly, it uses a more sophisticated two-pronged approach toward counteracting prejudice against Indians, first by explaining the principles on which their traditional mode of life is based, then by citing evidence of their progress in mission-run schools.[12]

Child dramatizes the clash between Indian and white value systems through an anecdote pitting Penobscot women against a prosperous Maine landowner. The women have built temporary wigwams on the white proprietor's "fine timber-lot" and have proceeded to cut down "his best trees, to make baskets and brooms" — their usual occupation during the winter, while their menfolk are absent on hunting expeditions. "[T]hey cannot be made to believe that the woods belong to one man more than another," Child observes. Not only does she allow the women to confront the irate proprietor with their own philosophy of land use, but she gives them the last word: "You have wood enough to burn — what for you want more wood? When you die, you no carry wood with you" (n.s. 5: 278–79). The Indian view of natural resources as the collective inheritance of all human beings, to be used only as needed and left for future generations, may make more sense than the bourgeois concept of private property that permits one man to monopolize resources merely for the sake of enriching himself, Child hints.[13]

Though improvident by middle-class American standards, she goes on to argue, Indians have revealed "talents nowise inferior to our own," and experiments in educating them have produced encouraging results: "I have seen let[t]ers from a young Cherokee, written in the fairest Italian hand I ever looked upon, and expressed in terms well chosen and elegant" (n.s. 5: 280–81).[14] Child's main example of Indian educational achievement, of course, is the artist who gives the sketch its title: Pol Sosef, the son of a Penobscot chief and the brightest student at an Indian school founded by a French priest in 1828. Inspired to begin painting after a visit to Bangor, when he saw his first works of Western art, Pol Sosef distinguished himself sufficiently to be sent to study with a Bangor artist. "It is yet uncertain how far the experiment will succeed," Child grants; "but should he prove to have real genius, how the world will stare at the INDIAN ARTIST! He will be a greater wonder than West was to the Europeans" (n.s. 5: 284). The artist Benjamin West, whose biography Child had sketched in an earlier *Miscellany* selection, had confounded European notions of American inferiority; so might Pol Sosef confound theories about the impossibility of civilizing the Indian, Child intimates.

In her account of West, Child had noted that a party of visiting Indians had taught him "how to prepare the red and yellow colors, with which they painted their ornaments."[15] Her comparison of Pol Sosef with West does not spell out the lesson behind the origins of West's art, however — that cultural influences have traveled in both directions, with white Americans often turning to the Indians for inspiration in their effort to create an "indigenous" art. On the contrary, Child's language inescapably suggests that she conceives of art in European terms and regards an Indian artist as an anomaly. To rise to the level of whites, she assumes, Indians would have to master the arts of white "civilization." Pol Sosef and the "young Cherokee" writer with whom Child associates him prove the Indian's ability to do so. Yet in *The First Settlers*, Child had recognized that even when Indian nations did sacrifice their cultural integrity and accept "civilization," as the Cherokee had, white guarantees of equal rights did not materialize.

The contradictions typified by sketches like "Pol Sosef" and "The Indian Boy" are prophetic. Child would broaden her concept of assimilation over the years, but she would never abandon it. Nor would she abandon her belief that the problem of Indian-white conflict, like the problem of class conflict, could be solved by inculcating the proper social virtues in both the dominant and the subordinate group and providing opportunities for individual advancement.

On the other hand, these sketches attest to the formative influence of Child's early contacts with Indians in fostering her deep commitment to racial egalitarianism. Unlike most of her contemporaries, she cherished a multiracial, if not a multicultural, vision of American society. The values she sought to instill in American children consistently included respect for members of other races.

The *Miscellany* featured a striking number of selections about people of color — Chinese, Turks, New Zealanders, South Sea Islanders, Eskimos, and Africans, as well as Indians and African Americans — which sharply distinguished it from rival magazines. *Miscellany* readers learned that the pursuit of knowledge and the practice of industry and frugality were not confined to Anglo-Saxons; that non-Christian nations could exhibit "habits and manners . . . which in many respects may well make us blush for our own"; that untaught "savages" could show great intelligence; that cannibals could be "kind-hearted"; and that American customs could appear as strange and benighted to the natives of Tongataboo as those natives' customs appeared to Americans.[16] Closer in spirit to the travelers' accounts from which they were drawn than to the reports of missionary endeavors that constituted the standard juvenile fare of the period, Child's entertaining articles about alien cultures do not seem to have antagonized her readership. In fact they probably contributed to the *Miscellany's* popularity.

The public did not react negatively to Child's message of racial equality until she applied it to African Americans. Only then did the threat this ideal posed to the American social order become apparent. In the 1820s the United States had not yet entered on the phase of imperialist conquest that would redefine the distant peoples of Asia and the Pacific as enemies. At home the Indian question no longer touched the economic interests of Child's New England subscribers. The dispossession and extermination of New England's Indian tribes had long since occurred, and the few remnants could safely be regarded as objects of humanitarian sympathy. The theater of Indian-white conflict had shifted to the South, where the Cherokee and Seminole were being hounded out of their tribal lands. And that theater was far enough away to permit championship of the victims (though Child kept the Cherokee removal controversy out of the *Miscellany*).[17]

In contrast, the issue of slavery involved interests vital to the entire nation. With the 1793 invention of the cotton gin, an institution that had appeared moribund at the turn of the nineteenth century was by the 1820s generating enormous profits both on the cotton plantations of the South and in the burgeoning textile factories of the North. Moreover, southern states had indicated from the outset that their adherence to the Union depended on the North's willingness to leave slavery unchallenged. For some three decades controversy over slavery had been staved off by maintaining the fiction that a process of gradual, voluntary emancipation was already under way and that the South, if left to regulate its own affairs, would eventually follow the example of the North by legislating slavery out of existence in one state after another. Meanwhile, humanitarian reformers channeled their energies into what seemed the most practical scheme for effecting emancipation: "Colonization," or the repatriation of free blacks to Africa.[18]

When Child published the book that furnished the model for the *Juvenile Miscellany—Evenings in New England* (1824)—she fully concurred in the prevailing view of the slavery question, which no white writer had yet disputed. By the time she wrote *The First Settlers of New England* five years later, however, she was entertaining ideas that would ineluctably propel her toward a more radical position. Pronouncing the notion of African inferiority "as untrue, as it is wicked and base," and dismissing it as a "shallow pretext" for depriving blacks of "all the rights of men," she implied that blacks, like Indians, could be assimilated into American society through intermarriage (*FS* 65–69). In short, she had come to repudiate the belief that slavery could not be abolished unless blacks were expatriated en masse—a pillar of Colonizationist doctrine.

Still, it took Child almost two more years to overcome her qualms about espousing a politically divisive cause.[19] While pleading for the Indian in early volumes of the

Miscellany, she remained conspicuously silent on slavery. Indeed, the magazine's sole mention of the subject before 1830 is a description of slaves in Baltimore by a traveler signing himself "F." (probably Convers Francis), who concludes: "It cannot be too much regretted that such a thing as slavery exists; but so far as concerns the actual situation of slaves at the South, I think New England prejudices have been violent and unreasonable."[20]

Not until after her catalytic meeting with Garrison in June 1830 did Child begin introducing antislavery material into the *Miscellany*. But once she committed herself to investigating the slavery question and promoting emancipation, the magazine immediately registered the change in her orientation. From September 1830 on, nearly every issue of the *Miscellany* carried some reference to slavery, be it a story, an article, an anecdote, or a bit of information tucked away in an unlikely context. Many of the facts and arguments Child amassed for her juvenile readers would reappear in her 1833 *Appeal in Favor of That Class of Americans Called Africans*, often repeated verbatim.[21]

Having digested the lesson of her previous attempt to combine children's literature with political advocacy, Child did her best to avoid the errors of rhetorical strategy that had made *The First Settlers* unmarketable. She took care not to offend her audience's political and religious sensibilities through direct attacks on the South's peculiar institution and the hypocrisy the clergy displayed in sanctioning it. Instead, she undermined the assumptions that permitted well-meaning people to continue tolerating slavery.

It was in the *Miscellany* that Child first developed her preferred rhetorical strategy for winning a hearing from an unsympathetic audience. As she later described it to her fellow abolitionist Caroline Weston: "I often attack bigotry with 'a troop of horse shod with felt'; that is, I try to *enter* the wedge of general principles, letting inferences unfold themselves very gradually."[22] She would use this approach in nearly all her commercially published works, deploying it as advantageously to further the causes of women's rights, sexual freedom, and religious liberalism as to advocate racial justice.

The strategy of the "troop of horse shod with felt" takes many forms in the *Miscellany*. Frequently, Child slips her antislavery message into articles of the type the *Miscellany* regularly featured. Reviewing an arithmetic primer under the column "New Books," for example, Child cites the British abolitionist Thomas Clarkson on the "mental dexterity" Africans show by performing "long and complicated" mathematical calculations "*in their heads*" with a "despatch and accuracy, surpassing . . . the European method" of ciphering on paper. Such evidence, she suggests, would seem to refute those who claim Africans to be "a baser race than the whites, approaching . . . the brute creation." At the very least, it illustrates the "efficacy of the early and assiduous exercise of the mind" — a principle applicable to children of every race. "[W]e must not permit this occasion to pass," she adds, "without telling all good little readers that it is very rash, and must be very offensive in the sight of God, whose children we all are, for any portion of the human family to arrogate to themselves a superiority over others. There is no real superiority but pureness of heart and goodness of conduct."[23]

Similarly infiltrating the *Miscellany*'s geography department, articles innocuously titled "Some Talk about Cuba" and "All about Brazil" describe tropical paradises flawed by slavery — "the greatest evil that can exist in any country" and one that "is sure to bring misery upon those who encourage it, as well as upon those who suffer by it." Child does not spell out the implications for her own country. She merely comments on the conditions slavery produces in other countries and allows readers to draw the logical conclusions:

> It would make my heart ache to tell you how the poor negroes in Brazil are abused; how they are starved to death, and whipped to death; and how often despair and rage leads them to murder their masters and kill themselves. Poor creatures! They are treated like wild beasts, and what wonder is it that they become so? Their masters say they are lazy and careless. Everybody would be lazy and careless, if they had nothing to hope for. The negro fares none the better for being industrious. He cannot have his earnings to buy a meal for himself, a ribbon for his wife, or a whistle for his little boy. He works while the whip is held over him, and he knows that his children, if they live, must do the same. Are not such things as these enough to make anybody lazy and revengeful? The Africans are naturally kind and obliging; it is ill treatment that renders them otherwise.[24]

Child again resorts to "a troop of horse shod with felt" when she manipulates the conventions of the moral tale — a staple of juvenile literature — to plead against racial prejudice. Neither the title nor the format of "William Peterson, the Brave and Good Boy" hints at any departure from the typical eulogy of an exemplary youth. As the "industrious" son of a washwoman and a wood sawyer who have "placed their chief dependence upon him," William resembles many other *Miscellany* heroes. Not until after relating how he has given his life to save a group of skaters who have fallen into a hole in the ice does Child reveal that "William Peterson was a colored boy" and the skaters he rescued "all white boys." By that point she can risk articulating the moral of her "*true* anecdote": "I believe no generous-minded white children, will be tempted to speak unkindly, or uncivilly, to people whom God has made of a color different from their own."[25]

Child's antislavery writings in the *Miscellany* illuminate not only the content of her research and the maturation of her style as a propagandist, but the route of her progression toward the abolitionist ideology she would propound in the *Appeal*. Dating from September 1830, her earliest antislavery story, "The St. Domingo Orphans," clearly reflects Child's need to surmount a deep-seated fear of race war before she could embrace Garrison's doctrine of immediate emancipation.[26] Once again, it was Thomas Jefferson who had given that fear its classic formulation in explaining why Colonization was a prerequisite for ending slavery: "Deep-rooted prejudices entertained by the whites; ten thousand recollections, by the blacks, of the injuries they have sustained; new provocations; the real distinctions which nature has made; and many other circumstances, will divide us into parties, and produce convulsions, which will probably never end but in the extermination of the one or the other race."[27]

Occurring six years after Jefferson's prophecy, the massive Santo Domingo slave uprising of 1791–1804 had seemed to give credence to the widespread belief that "insurrections would be the inevitable result of any attempt to remove [slavery]" (*Appeal* 86). As Child would confess in the *Appeal*, she, too, had originally attributed "the horrible massacres of St Domingo" to the effects of "sudden freedom" (86). Hence, her first step toward ascertaining whether emancipation could be safely undertaken had been to delve into the history of the Santo Domingo revolution. Her research would ultimately convince her that the rebellion had preceded and induced, rather than followed, the abolition of slavery in Santo Domingo, and that emancipation had not produced any disturbances until Bonaparte "made his atrocious attempt *to restore slavery* in the island" (*Appeal* 86).

An early offshoot of this research, "The St. Domingo Orphans" betrays the racial fantasies Child had to dispel in order to refute Jefferson's fallacious logic. The specter of the bloodthirsty black savage bent on exterminating whites haunts the story, which also reverberates with echoes of Indian captivity narratives. Speaking in the accents of Mary Rowlandson, Child describes how whites are "butchered by these unfeeling wretches" and how a "ferocious soldier" "cut the head [of a white woman] from her body so suddenly, that her blood flew all over her unfortunate daughters" (n.s. 5: 82, 86). To exorcise the phantasm of the savage avenger, Child conjures up the counterimage of the "good" black, reminiscent of Hobomok and his role in saving the Conant family from massacre. Yet the fears she seeks to repress continually resurface. Linking "good" and "bad" blacks, for example, are family ties and identical names: the "affectionate" Maria who hides Mrs. Jameson and her daughters from vengeful slaves is the daughter of the "savage creature" who boasts of having killed his master; and the "bad negress" who betrays the fugitives is "likewise named Maria" (n.s. 5: 81–84). The plot, too, blurs distinctions between "good" and "bad" blacks. Thus, when the widow of "the bloodthirsty tyrant Dessalines" — herself "very tender-hearted" — tries to atone for his cruelty by befriending Mrs. Jameson's orphaned daughters, she unwittingly delivers them into treacherous hands.

If the story does not succeed either in exorcising racist fantasies or in questioning the proslavery interpretation of the Santo Domingo revolution, it does grope toward insights central to the abolitionist analysis Child would develop in the *Appeal*. Albeit tentatively and inchoately, "The St. Domingo Orphans" suggests that the perpetuation of slavery might pose a greater threat than immediate abolition; that the true savages might be the whites whose greed leads them to enslave their fellow human beings, rather than the blacks who revolt against their oppressors; and that the racial distinctions on which New World slavery is based are dangerously misleading.

Saved from death by Dessaline's widow and entrusted to another white survivor on her way to the United States, the orphans fall victim to the very slave system their parents upheld. Their friendless, orphaned status puts them in a position much like that of blacks in a slave society. Since no one can testify to their identity, they find themselves without recourse when their perfidious guardian forces them "to call themselves mulattoes, and sign a paper in the presence of witnesses, which declared that their parents had sold them to her as slaves." "[E]xposure to a West-Indian sun had made them so dark, that they were easily mistaken for mulattoes," explains Child (n.s. 5: 91).

In short, contrary to the ideology justifying black slavery, the orphans learn that so long as any class of people can be enslaved, no one is immune to enslavement. As slaveholders' daughters, they have relied on the evidence of skin color and on the bonds of race and class to protect them. Yet all the signs differentiating black from white, slave from free, have failed them, and a human sympathy transcending racial and class barriers has proved their best protection. As Child puts it (in a formulation whose attempted reversal of racist stereotypes continues to equate whiteness with virtue and blackness with evil), the widow of Dessalines, "though her face was black," has shown her heart to be white, while the orphans' "wicked" guardian, a racial peer, has turned out to have "a white face and a black heart" (n.s. 5: 91). Moreover, in the orphans' case black and white have dissolved into shades of ambiguous brown. The fiction that skin color determines legal status has broken down in the face of racial intermixture and climatic conditions, both of which produce a range of colors making it impossible to differentiate those entitled to dominance from those subject to enslavement.

The outcome of the story illustrates the difficulties Child faced in trying to adapt the conventions of children's literature to antislavery protest. Because her Santo Domingo orphans are slaves, she cannot resort to the formulas she invokes in her stories of white orphans. Industry, frugality, and sobriety cannot earn slaves the reward of upward mobility. Nor will neighbors who perceive them as black extend a helping hand to rescue them from slavery. To create a happy ending, Child literally has to summon foreign intervention: a hitherto unmentioned French grandmother traces and rescues the orphans through the French consul, and the girls hasten to take refuge in France from the slavery of Republican America.

The finale once again reveals a deeply ambivalent attitude toward the Santo Domingo rebels. For the rest of their lives, Child writes, the orphans recall their black benefactors with "tears of gratitude," and they "never [allow] a ship to sail to St. Domingo without carrying some token of affectionate remembrance to the good widow of the blood-thirsty Dessalines" (n.s. 5: 94). On the one hand, Child invites the inference that the orphans have received better treatment from blacks — even in the throes of history's most violent slave insurrection — than from members of their own race. On the other, the last words of the story are "the blood-thirsty Dessalines."

However unsatisfactory as an antislavery story, "The St. Domingo Orphans" apparently enabled Child to work through the psychological and ideological obstacles that had stood in the way of her conversion to abolitionism. Much of Child's subsequent antislavery fiction, including the two principal stories she went on to publish in the *Miscellany*, would develop the themes she adumbrated in "The St. Domingo Orphans." Significantly, the one theme that would never reappear in her corpus would be the fear of black savagery.

Child's next antislavery story for the *Miscellany*, dated January 1831, marks a significant advance in her thinking over a four-month period. Already she has clearly moved beyond her initial concern lest "sudden freedom" provoke "horrible massacres" by vengeful slaves. From histories of slave uprisings, she has turned to investigating the slave trade; and from the plantations of the New World, her research into the innate racial character of blacks — a question repeatedly raised in debates over the feasibility of immediate emancipation — has led her to the villages of Africa. The shift of focus indicates a corresponding shift of political allegiance. Not the white, but the black victims of the slave system now command her sympathies; not the savagery of blacks, but that of whites now arouses her revulsion.

Based on an actual case publicized in both the Colonization Society's *African Repository* and Nathaniel Willis's *Youth's Companion*, Child's "Jumbo and Zairee" registers her increasing disagreement, though not yet her outright break, with Colonizationist doctrine.[28] A comparison of the three accounts inspired by the case shows why Child concluded in the *Appeal*: "the Colonization Society . . . tends to put public opinion asleep, on a subject where it needs to be wide awake" (133).

A perfect candidate for the Colonization Society's benevolence, the historical "Abduhl Rahahman, the Unfortunate Moor," had been a prince of Footah Jallo (Futa Jallon), a Muslim state in the interior of Guinea, before falling into the hands of an enemy tribe and being sold into slavery in distant Mississippi. While in Footah Jallo, he and his family had sheltered an American doctor and nursed him through a "long and painful illness." Years after the prince's enslavement, this doctor miraculously turned up in Mississippi, recognized his former host, and unavailingly sought to purchase and emancipate the prince. Finally relinquished at the end of his life by his owner, the prince was now seeking the Colonization Society's help in sending him back to Africa along with his wife and as many of his children as subscribers could raise money to redeem.[29] The Colonization Society carefully presented the prince's claims to sympathy in terms that did not challenge the slave system. It capitalized on the romantic appeal of Abduhl Rahahman's royal blood, stressed the alleged racial superiority of the Moor to the Negro, cast responsibility for the prince's enslavement on his fellow Africans rather than on whites, highlighted the becoming gratitude of the white doctor, glossed over the mean-spiritedness of the prince's owner in refusing to part with him until old age had diminished his usefulness, smugly celebrated the benevolence of the Colonization Society's white patrons, touted the commercial advantages the United States might derive from using the prince to open up trade relations with Timbuctu and other cities of the interior, and perorated in a burst of sanctimonious enthusiasm: "We see in these events [of the prince's life] that God's ways are not as our ways, nor His thoughts as our thoughts. We see why Prince was not permitted to return with his Moorish disposition and his Moorish sword; that Providence continued him here so long until grace had softened his heart. He will now return a messenger of peace."[30]

Though himself a Colonizationist, Nathaniel Willis of the *Youth's Companion* took exception to the coverage singling out the prince for special consideration. "Abduhl Rahahman is not the only African, who has claims upon our sympathies," he objected in an editorial on "Slavery": "There are at this moment many hundreds of thousands of Africans in our country who are slaves to white men, and have no prospect of becoming free. There may not be any among them who were *princes* in Africa; but they are all *human beings*, who were torn from their country, from their homes, from their parents and neighbors and friends and sold into cruel bondage."[31] Despite his championship of all African slaves as fellow human beings and his acknowledgment of the slave system's cruelty, Willis hewed to the standard Colonizationist line. "Strange as it must seem," he lamented, "mercy to the colored people themselves requires, that they should *for the present* continue as they are," since most of them are "unfit to take care of themselves and their families," and "many of them are very wicked. . . ." He did nevertheless stipulate that both slaveholders and "the governments of the states, are certainly under every obligation" to educate the slaves and "to take every possible measure to give them liberty in a gradual way."[32]

Of course, Child had expressed similar views in her 1824 *Evenings in New England*.[33] By 1831, however, she was no longer willing to take refuge in the plea that most slaves were unfit for freedom, nor was she advocating the piecemeal approach of emancipating slaves individually, once they had shown that they "deserved" freedom. Instead, she was envisaging the emancipation of entire plantations as the owners came to realize that slavery was "wrong in the sight of God" (n.s. 5: 299).

Cited by historians of children's literature as an unusually "outspoken indictment of slavery" for a mainstream juvenile audience,[34] Child's "Jumbo and Zairee" radically revises the story of Abduhl Rahahman. To begin with, Child transforms the prince from a Moor of Footah Jallo into a "negro" of the Guinea Coast, the capital of the slave trade. She thus eliminates the spurious distinction between "superior" and "inferior" African races and relocates the action to an area where whites did not rely on African intermediaries to procure slaves for them, but personally engaged in the business of kidnapping. The first paragraph of the story pointedly underscores the direct involvement of white Americans in the slave trade: "I am very sorry to say the Americans have sometimes stolen the negroes, and sold them for slaves," Child tells her young readers, immediately after introducing them to the "two pretty negro children," Jumbo and Zairee (n.s. 5: 285).

As suggested by the device of centering the narrative on these fictional children and relegating the prince himself to a minor role, Child's second major departure is to orient her version of the Abduhl Rahahman saga specifically toward enlisting young people's sympathies for the victims of slavery. From the outset, she portrays Jumbo and Zairee in terms with which the children reading about them in the *Miscellany* can identify. Like their white peers, they "listen to . . . stories by the hour together," love each other tenderly, become "very much attached" to adults who treat them affectionately, share whatever they have with needy strangers, and get into trouble when they fail to obey their mother. Hence, their experiences bring home to sheltered white children the inhumanity of a system under which Africans are kidnapped, "put in a dark hole with a great many other wretched negroes," transported across the ocean in loathsome conditions, "thrown overboard" if they die, or, if they survive, "driven to the market-place to be sold" in a strange land, separated from their remaining loved ones, and subjected to brutal beatings by their overseers (n.s. 5: 289–93).

Child's graphic descriptions of white cruelty to Africans and her wholesale indictment of slavery as an institution represent a third major departure from Colonizationist
sources. Child minces no words exposing and denouncing the outrages practiced by
her country while it "boasts of being the only true republic in the world! the asylum
of the distressed! the only land of perfect freedom and equality!" Scornfully dismissing such boasts, she exclaims, " 'Shame on my country — everlasting shame.' History
blushes as she writes the page of American slavery, and Europe points her finger at it in
derision" (n.s. 5: 294–95).

Even more significant, however, is Child's fourth major departure — the sympathetic
depiction of African culture with which she counters the Colonizationist argument that
slavery served the providential purpose of Christianizing the African. Drawing on
Mungo Park's *Travels in the Interior Districts of Africa* (1799) and Olaudah Equiano's *Interesting Narrative* of his own kidnapping and enslavement (1789) — works she would
cite at length in the *Appeal* — Child sketches a society very different from the stereotypes of African savagery disseminated by apologists of slavery.[35] Its keynote is hospitality toward strangers. When the Englishman Mr. Harris is shipwrecked on the
shores of the land belonging to Jumbo and Zairee's father Prince Yoloo, the African
sovereign takes the unfortunate white man into his family and clothes and feeds him "as
if he had been his own son." "[T]he English king could not have treated a guest with
more kindness and generosity," Child comments (n.s. 5: 285). She also shows that
unlike Abduhl Rahahman's master in Mississippi, Prince Yoloo does not try to retain a
stranger who longs for his own people, homeland, and native tongue.

Far from softening savage hearts and converting warriors into messengers of peace,
as the Colonization Society had claimed of Abduhl Rahahman's enslavement, moreover, Child proceeds to demonstrate that the kidnapping of Prince Yoloo's children by
white slavers "turn[s] the kindness of a savage heart into gall and bitterness" (n.s. 5:
291) and poisons the prince and his wife against all whites. The prince now swears
revenge against the entire white race and vows never again to save a white man from
death. His wife "hate[s] the sound of a white man's name," bans any mention of their
departed guest, and heaps imprecations on a people she views as worse than the crocodiles she wishes had swallowed her children instead. Although the couple's suspicions
of their guest's involvement in the kidnapping are groundless, since it occurs after his
ship has sailed out of sight, Child subtly establishes the collective responsibility whites
share for slavery. Symbolically, at least, it is no coincidence that the children are
kidnapped when they insist on seeing Mr. Harris off, contrary to their parents' orders,
and that they innocently mistake a party of white slavers for friends who will convey
them to him. After all, Mr. Harris does eventually settle on an American plantation and
stock it with slaves. In this sense, Child implies, Prince Yoloo and his wife are right to
feel that the white man has requited their hospitality with base ingratitude.

Child's final and most prophetic departure from her Colonizationist sources consists
in bringing Mr. Harris to a true understanding of the debt he owes his African benefactors. Several years after the abduction of his children, Prince Yoloo himself, like his
prototype Abduhl Rahahman, is captured in a war against an enemy tribe, sold to

American slave traders, and miraculously thrown together again with the white man he once befriended. The recognition restores the former relations between the two as Mr. Harris, "forgetting black and white, master and slave, . . . [falls] into Yoloo's arms, and clasp[s] him warmly to his bosom" (297–98). Unlike the doctor who tried to purchase and repatriate Abduhl Rahahman, however, Mr. Harris realizes through this providential encounter that his responsibility extends further — that he must emancipate not only the prince and his children (who belong to other owners), but the slaves on his own plantation. "I have tried to show my gratitude to the negroes by being a kind master," he explains; "but I am satisfied this is not all I ought to do. They ought to be free. What is wrong in the sight of God, cannot be made right by the laws of man" (n.s. 5: 298–99). Thus, he buys a ship and sends all the slaves in his possession back to "their native country," except for "[t]wo old negroes [who] preferred remaining with him."

The narrative ends with the family of Jumbo and Zairee at last reunited "under the pleasant shade of their native cocoas," where they "repeat to their neighbors, the story of the good white man" (n.s. 5: 299). Though appropriate for slaves recently uprooted from Africa, the denouement of course obfuscates the problem embodied by the "two old negroes" who elect to stay in America. What of those — constituting the vast majority of the slave population — whose "native country" was America, not Africa? How could Colonization offer a viable solution to *them*? In January 1831 Child evidently was not ready to answer such questions, which free black leaders were insistently raising. Whatever her impatience with the Colonization Society's timidity, she continued to regard its program of repatriation as a practical means of ending slavery. But she was not lagging behind other progressive whites. Even her mentor Garrison had barely begun to reassess the merits of Colonization.[36]

Child would later recall having reached complete agreement with Garrison by the end of 1831.[37] Yet precisely when and how she made the transition to the radical abolitionist stand she took two years later in the *Appeal*, where she definitively rejected Colonization and called for immediate emancipation and the integration of blacks as equal citizens, is impossible to infer from her subsequent contributions to the *Miscellany*. None addresses the issue of slavery as forthrightly as "Jumbo and Zairee," and Child's next important antislavery story, "Mary French and Susan Easton," did not appear until May 1834, nine months after the *Appeal*.[38]

If it offers no further clue to the timetable of Child's political evolution, "Mary French and Susan Easton" does reflect the analysis of slavery she formulated in the *Appeal*. The subtitle of the *Appeal*'s opening chapter — "Inevitable Effect [of Negro Slavery] Upon All Concerned in It" — might well serve as the epigraph for this somber story about two little girls, one white, the other black, who find themselves kidnapped together into slavery. The key significance Child assigned to the issue of racial prejudice, which occupies four chapters of the *Appeal* and links the abolition of slavery to the goal of granting "free people of color . . . equal civil and political rights and privileges with the whites" (*Appeal* 146), also defines her aims in this story. Exploiting the full potential of insights embryonic in "The St. Domingo Orphans," "Mary French and Susan Easton" dramatizes the dangers of reserving democratic rights for those perceived as white. Slavery has no boundaries in the story, located in free territory on the western bank of the Mississippi, and it is literally no respecter of persons.

The situation Child sets up in her parable of a rural Eden blighted by slavery and racism is rooted in a widespread social problem. Kidnappers prowled throughout the country, seeking slaves for the insatiable southern market, and free blacks were almost as vulnerable to them as fugitive slaves, due to Black Laws that hardly distinguished between the two groups, often barring both from testifying in court.[39] One such kidnapping, thwarted by a Quaker family in Pennsylvania, had recently inspired a story Child brought to the attention of *Miscellany* readers in her "New Books" column for March 1832: Eliza Leslie's "The Travelling Tin-Man."[40] The case on which Child based her heroine Mary French's experience, however, involved a stolen white girl "afterwards discovered to have been stained black, and sold for a SLAVE," as a headnote informed readers in a revised version of the tale, reprinted in the abolitionist children's magazine *The Slave's Friend*.[41] Child combines elements of both cases in "Mary French and Susan Easton."

The device of pairing a white and a black victim of slave kidnapping allows Child to explore the problem of race relations from different angles. She begins with the only perspective offering any hope for the future — the children's. Innocent of racial distinctions, Mary and Susan grow up playing together as equals, though Mary is the daughter of white homesteaders and Susan of an "honest, industrious" former slave, emancipated for having "saved his master from the bite of a rattlesnake" (3rd. ser. 6: 186). Emblematic of the biracial egalitarian society their friendship heralds is the black-and-white-spotted rabbit the girls cherish and tearfully recall after their abduction.[42] The emblem governing the present and determining the plot, however, is the rattlesnake — an obvious allusion to the evil that makes a mockery out of freedom in a would-be Eden, most cruelly for free blacks like Susan's parents, but ultimately for the nation at large, as Child shows.

The French and Easton families' contrasting reactions to their children's disappearance indicate how dangerously oblivious whites are to the threat slavery represents to their own liberties. The meaning of the biblical injunction to "love thy neighbor as thyself" totally eludes the Frenches, though the Eastons are their only neighbors "within several miles," and though the two children have disappeared together (3rd ser. 6: 186). When Paul Easton raises the possibility of slave kidnappers, naturally the "first thought" to occur to a black father, "his neighbor French" immediately discounts it, "because he thought the kidnappers could have no motive for stealing a white child, which the laws allowed no man to sell or buy" (3rd ser. 6: 199–200). In short, Mr. French views the problem of slave kidnapping, so vital to blacks, as of no concern to himself. Similarly, when Mr. French sets out in search of Mary, he makes no effort to rescue Susan; it never occurs to him that his neighbor Easton cannot "go in search of *his* child, because a free colored man travelling was liable to be taken up and sold, or shot through the head for a runaway slave" (3rd ser. 6: 201). Mr. French's inaction is all the more chilling given his legal power to save Susan by testifying in court to her free parentage — a recourse denied to blacks in many states.

The children's own reactions parallel their parents', presaging how little chance their friendship has of surviving the forces pitted against them. Susan quickly recognizes the peddler who has decoyed them for a "wicked kidnapper" and tries to prevent him from hurting her friend (3rd ser. 6: 190–91). Yet when the peddler takes a horsewhip to Susan, Mary stands passively "crying and sobbing, on the spot where he had left her." It is as if she already senses that the easiest means of saving herself lies not in identifying with Susan, but in differentiating herself from her black friend. Revealingly, after the peddler blackens her skin, cuts and frizzes her hair, and sells her into slavery, the plea Mary will use to procure her freedom is that she is white. Her ability to prove her claim by washing the black coloring off her skin forces her purchaser to free her, for "he knew that the laws would not allow him to keep a white child in slavery" (3rd ser. 6: 198).

True, Mary does speak up for her friend once she has obtained her own freedom. "[I]n a timid voice," she begs her purchaser to locate Susan and restore her to her family, pointing out that the Eastons' status as free blacks entitles their daughter to freedom, too. But when the master's son, who has so far proved very sympathetic to Mary, retorts that "*niggers* are used to being slaves," Mary does not have the "courage to say any more," even though she cannot "understand what right they had to take honest Paul Easton's daughter, and make her a slave, any more than they had to make a slave of *her* father's daughter" (3rd ser. 6: 198–99). She pursues the matter no further and returns home with her father, weeping for her lost playmate, but unable to brave the disapproval she would face if she insisted on siding with "niggers."

Throughout the story, Child emphasizes the delusiveness of an ideology that grounds democratic rights for whites on the oppression of blacks. Again and again, she drives home the message that those who form the habit of degrading one class of human beings easily extend the same contempt to others.

"Hardened" by trading in slaves and licensed by society to treat all blacks as "niggers" subject to reenslavement at will, the peddler, for example, has ceased to make the distinction between "niggers" and whites. "There! Now you are almost as good-looking a *nigger* as t'other one," he tells Mary after darkening her skin. What he has come to realize is that he can turn anyone he chooses into a "nigger" to be sold for profit. Significantly, he gets away with his ploy and is never apprehended.

Child provides a still more telling example in a passerby to whom the children call out for help as the peddler is transporting them south. Ready to intervene for white children, he changes his tune when the peddler identifies them as nothing but "refractory" slaves. "Give 'em a touch of the whip; that will quiet their tongues," he says with a shrug, driving off "without taking further notice" (3rd ser. 6: 193). Only later does the full irony of the encounter emerge (though it is lost on both the passerby and the French family). Responding to the advertisement Mr. French has put in the newspaper, the passerby recalls the incident, but he can give the Frenches no information, having failed to take an interest in children he had perceived to be black slaves. As Child spells out in the version she published in *The Slave's Friend*: "If his heart had not been hardened by the wicked system of slavery, he would have stopped and spoken to the children, and they might both have been saved."[43]

In the end, only Mary is "saved," and a story that opens with a white and a black child playing together as naturally as the black and white markings intermingle on their iconic spotted rabbit closes with contrasting tableaux of two families tragically separated by slavery and racism:

> Mr. French's house was a house of joy. But poor Mr. Easton and his wife . . . never could gain any tidings of their lost child. She is no doubt a slave, compelled to labor without receiving any wages for her hard work, and whipped whenever she dares to say that she has a right to be free. Yet the only difference between Mary French and Susan Easton is, that the black color could be rubbed off from Mary's skin, while from Susan's it could not. (3rd ser. 6: 202).

The divergent endings of Mary's and Susan's stories sum up the contradictions Child struggled unsuccessfully to resolve in her role as a purveyor of values to the young. For eight years she had preached the dominant creed promising the reward of upward mobility to all who practiced the middle-class virtues of industry, honesty, frugality, and self-denial. In her fiction she had consistently represented her white protagonists as triumphing over the odds against them through the exercise of these virtues. And she had repeatedly confirmed that the disparities between rich and poor in America existed not because of the social system, but because of individual circumstances, surmountable by the determined efforts of the poor and by the discriminating charity of the rich.

Over the years, however, Child's increasing involvement in the cause of the Indians, and especially in the abolitionist movement, had compelled her to recognize disparities that could not be attributed to individual circumstances or remedied by individual efforts. In addressing the issue of slavery she had had to confront a social and political problem that imperatively demanded a social and political solution. The case of Susan Easton defied the logic of American bourgeois ideology. Paul Easton had been honest, industrious, and self-sacrificing enough to risk his life for his master. But he had been unable to protect his daughter from *downward* mobility, much less secure for her the benefits of his hard work. Nor had his virtues and respectability earned him the assistance of his more fortunate neighbors, as in *Miscellany* stories about the white working class. Meanwhile, his daughter's playmate had obtained her freedom merely by proving herself to be white — a result of birth, not merit.

"Mary French and Susan Easton" offers no comforting solutions to the wrenching problems it dramatizes. Unlike the stories responsible for the *Miscellany*'s popularity, it does not celebrate the harmonious workings of a just society, but exposes a structural defect so fundamental that it threatens to destroy the entire edifice. And it implies that if whites hope to avert such a catastrophe, they must give up privileges they enjoy at the expense of blacks.

How did the *Miscellany*'s readership respond to this disturbing story? Records are disappointingly sparse. None of the men and women who later paid tribute to the magazine's formative influence on them mentioned any antislavery stories among those they recalled with special fondness. The only reference I have found to the reception of

"Mary French and Susan Easton" is an 1837 advertisement in Garrison's *Liberator* for the abolitionist-funded children's magazine, *The Slave's Friend*: "This volume . . . contains the story of Mary French and Susan Easton, which children always read with intense interest, and which they will find it hard ever to drive from their minds."[44]

By then, of course, the *Miscellany* had ceased to exist. Even before "Mary French and Susan Easton" appeared in the May 1834 number, outraged parents had already canceled their subscriptions to the magazine en masse. That very month Child announced that the *Miscellany* was "about to be discontinued, for want of sufficient patronage." She bade her "reluctant" farewell to her "little readers" in the following number.[45] Turned over to the editorship of Sarah Hale, who would later achieve record-breaking subscriptions for *Godey's Lady's Book*, the *Miscellany* sputtered for another two years before finally expiring.

The abrupt collapse of a periodical so beloved by the public raises a host of intriguing questions. Were Child's subscribers reacting solely to the publication of her antislavery *Appeal*, as all of her biographers, beginning with her contemporaries, have maintained?[46] Did they fear that a woman who overstepped her sphere by tackling the controversial issue of slavery in the male arena of politics would exert a dangerous moral influence over their children? Or had parents noticed the sudden rash of antislavery commentary in a periodical that had preserved an all but total silence on the topic for the first four years of its existence? Had the magazine's insistent criticism of racial prejudice irritated them? In particular, were they concerned about the subversive impact that stories like "Jumbo and Zairee" and "Mary French and Susan Easton" might be having on children whose parents, teachers, and ministers were attempting to assure them that most blacks, unlike whites, were better off for the time being under the paternal guardianship of kind masters?[47]

Historical evidence is too scanty to permit any firm conclusions, but there are indications that even before the *Appeal* came off the press in August 1833, public enthusiasm for the *Miscellany* may have waned and parental subscribers may have grown restive. The *American Traveller*, which had been reviewing almost every issue, skipped two in 1831 (including the one containing "Jumbo and Zairee"); after May 1831, when the *Traveller* complimented Child for the last time on "improvements" in the magazine's format that "enhance its favor with a discerning and merit-rewarding public," it took no further notice of the *Miscellany*. Meanwhile, the paper's coverage of the September 1831 Nat Turner insurrection and of "incendiary" activities by abolitionists registered growing hostility to agitation against slavery.[48] Paralleling the *Miscellany*'s apparent loss of favor with an establishment organ, by January 1833 persistent rumors had begun to circulate that "Mrs. Child . . . is about to give up the editorship" of the magazine. Forced to issue a denial, Child informed subscribers that "she never has had the slightest intention of leaving them until they leave her."[49] Since Child had not yet assumed a public role in the abolitionist movement, it seems fair to speculate that the rumors reflected dwindling subscriptions caused by mounting dissatisfaction with the new direction the magazine was taking.

Whether or not parental support for the *Miscellany* was indeed flagging before 1833,

Child would have confronted a changed climate of opinion by 1834, even if she had not published the *Appeal*. The mid-1830s saw an upsurge of mob attacks against abolitionists and African Americans, amid which calls for censorship of antislavery publications became so vociferous that Child would have found it almost impossible to slip stories like "Jumbo and Zairee" and "Mary French and Susan Easton" past vigilant parents. The *Appeal* surely hastened Child's fall from grace and extended the ban to her other works, but it could not have deprived her of many subscribers who would have accepted her antislavery message had she confined it to the medium of children's literature.

On the contrary, her broad influence as a children's writer depended on using the genre to promulgate rather than question the dominant creed. Antislavery children's literature stood no chance of winning a mass audience.[50] Child herself eventually bowed to the limitations of the genre. When she returned to children's literature as a source of income in the 1840s, she collected many of her *Miscellany* stories along with new items in a series of volumes titled *Flowers for Children*. Of the fifty-five selections she included, none addresses the issue of slavery and only two are aimed at counteracting racial prejudice: "The Little White Lamb and the Little Black Lamb" and "Lariboo. Sketches of Life in the Desert."[51] The first, written for toddlers, is the least interesting and most innocuous of her *Miscellany* sketches, merely affirming that God has created both white lambs and black, white children and black, and loves them equally. The second, an adventure story about an African woman saved by a panther that guides her across the desert, presents an exotic and attractive picture of Africa and compels an identification with the heroine that transcends race consciousness; yet its promotion of sympathy for Africans is too subtle to have made it an effective weapon against racism. Not until the crisis of the late 1850s renewed Child's commitment to mobilizing every possible instrument in the struggle against slavery would she again attempt to use children's literature for that purpose. Even then, she would set the long antislavery story with which she led off *A New Flower for Children* (1856) — "Jamie and Jeannie" — not in America, but in South Africa.[52]

Although the conservative socializing mission of children's literature clashed with the radical message Child sought to propound in her antislavery stories for the *Miscellany*, to conclude that the magazine failed to transform its juvenile readers' racial attitudes would nevertheless fly in the face of historical testimony. Of the children who had pored over stories describing how little girls and boys like themselves were torn from their parents, kidnapped into slavery, and subjected to brutal tortures throughout their lives, a sizable cadre grew up to share the revulsion against slavery, the passionate identification with its victims, and the determination to fight for a multiracial egalitarian America that inspired the editor of their favorite magazine. The parents who canceled their subscriptions and railed against abolitionist agitators could not efface the impression the *Miscellany* had made on their children or stifle the humanitarian sentiments it had awakened in them. The ranks of Child's young fans included some who went on in their turn to become antislavery writers, activists, and moral preceptors of the young — Thomas Wentworth Higginson, Caroline Healey Dall, Lucy Larcom, Louisa May Alcott, and the orientalist and radical theologian Samuel Johnson — as well as scores of unknown activists in local antislavery circles. Wherever Child's abolitionist work took her over her long career, wrote Dall, "[s]he never went into any neighborhood so obscure that, within a radius of three or four miles, it did not hold many who had sat upon doorsteps waiting for the *Juvenile Miscellany*, or who, as young men and women, had not . . . recognized it as a leading influence in their lives."[53]

Like Child herself, these readers viewed their commitment to liberating African Americans from slavery and racial prejudice not as a contradiction, but as an extension of the ethic the *Juvenile Miscellany* preached in such stories as "Louisa Preston" and "The Cottage Girl," where charitable neighbors help smooth the path of industrious poor folk. They, too, merely wished to eliminate the obstacles that prevented people of color from competing on equal terms with their white compatriots for the chance to better their fortunes. For them, as for Child, the source of the moral fervor that inspired their lifelong dedication to a despised cause lay in the very political and religious traditions the *Juvenile Miscellany* upheld — the democratic creed of equal rights for all and the Christian ethic of brotherly love and self-sacrifice. While recognizing the limitations entailed on the abolitionist movement by its ideological heritage, we should not minimize the strength its adherents drew from their conviction that the dream of upward mobility could be guaranteed to everyone.

The final word on whether or not Child achieved her dual aims as an agent of socialization and as a voice of radical reform rightly belongs to the children whose consciousness she molded. Decades after the demise of the *Juvenile Miscellany*, several of these former children felt moved to write to the woman they credited with propelling them into the abolitionist movement.

Driven out of his Unitarian pulpit for his radical political and religious opinions, the orientalist Samuel Johnson responded with such a thrill to Child's 1860 tract in defense of John Brown that he dashed off a letter to thank her for having launched him on his own quest for freedom. "I don't know whether I ever told you with what delight I fed on your little Juvenile Miscellany long ago — " he confided:

> You little knew how many young spirits you were quickening by that wonderful gift to children (as I still regard it); nor yet how many opening minds you brought to clearness & freedom of thought as to Gods Presence with all races & ages, by your "Progress of Religious Ideas." And just as little can you conceive how many men & women all over the half-awakened land you have *now* been teaching the grand possibilities that come of fearlessly following the best conviction & the best impulse.[54]

Johnson clearly equated the moral lessons he had learned from the *Miscellany* with the liberating mission of religious tolerance he ascribed to Child's *Progress of Religious Ideas* and the call for the overthrow of slavery he extrapolated from her eloquent tract on Brown. What linked the three in his mind was the cardinal principle Child had emphasized in *The Mother's Book* — the importance of "fearlessly following" the "honest convictions of our own hearts."[55]

The occasion that prompted Sarah Van Vechten Brown to write to Child was the receipt of her 1868 *Appeal for the Indians*, sent to Brown at the behest of the New York abolitionist Gerrit Smith. Recalling the "widely extended & powerful influence" Child had exerted thirty-four years before through her *Appeal in Favor of That Class of Americans Called Africans*, Brown affirmed: "I well remember . . . the delight with which it was read, & the zeal with which it was circulated, by a little group of schoolgirl abolitionists, of which I had the honor to be one." "[A]lthough I am altogether unknown — to you," she went on, "you have been my friend from an early day, ever so long ago as when the Juvenile Miscellany was the delight of my childish heart." Like Johnson, Brown left no doubt about the connection she saw between the *Miscellany* and Child's other writings: "Your influence over me has always been ennobling, & purifying, & elevating, & stimulating to benevolence & charity."[56]

Nothing could more eloquently sum up the significance Child's young readers discerned in her stories of struggling orphans, and the way in which they transferred to their adult commitments the moral imperatives they deduced from their childhood reading, than the tribute of Melissa E. Dawes, an abolitionist correspondent who had adopted a Civil War orphan (of unspecified race). Describing herself as "an obscure humble woman," Dawes, like Sarah Van Vechten Brown, associated her embrace of the antislavery cause with her reading of her idol's stories for children. "I have known you by your writings and loved you, from my childhood," she explained. "It was then I saw upon the fronticepiece of some [of] the first numbers of the Liberator Slavery depicted in all its horrors and at that time I knelt down and called God to witness that one soul should be consecrated to the divine work of Emancipation. . . . I want to thank you in the name of the blessed Jesus for what *you* have done for His poor." The stimulus that elicited her letter — the sight of her ward crying over a well-thumbed volume of Child's *Flowers for Children* — encapsulated the legacy of stories cherished and passed on from one generation to another and attested to their continuing power to change young readers' lives by arousing their sympathy for human suffering: "[A]s the tears trickled down her cheek and her voice choked I longed to tell you that you might have the reward, And when I thought that half a Century had rolled its rounds since those words were penned I envied the soul that could thus stir the fountains of the human heart."[57]

8

"The First Woman in the Republic"
An Antislavery Baptism

Let me say, then, that — taking her for all in all — she is the first woman in the republic.

The encomium at the head of this chapter appeared in an article of November 20, 1829, headlined "MRS. CHILD" in bold capitals and featured prominently in the editorial column of the *Genius of Universal Emancipation*, an antislavery newspaper issued from Baltimore by the Quaker Benjamin Lundy. Its author was William Lloyd Garrison, who at age twenty-four had recently joined Lundy as coeditor of the *Genius*, having previously edited several ephemeral newspapers and worked briefly as a journeyman printer at the offices of David Lee Child's *Massachusetts Journal*.[1]

The commendation, prefacing an extract from Child's "Hints to People of Moderate Fortune," was in fact Garrison's second tribute in three weeks to the wife of his quondam employer. On October 30 he had reprinted an article from the *Massachusetts Journal* on the "Comparative Strength of Male and Female Intellect," which he had ascribed to "Mrs. Child, (formerly Miss Francis,) a writer who is not surpassed, if equalled, by any other female in this country, and whose genius is as versatile as it is brilliant." Indeed, Garrison had asserted, Child's anonymous contributions to the *Massachusetts Journal* were "worthy of the strongest intellect of the most sagacious politician."[2] Now he pronounced even his earlier "panegyric" inadequate. Not only did Child excel such rivals as Lydia Huntley Sigourney, Sarah Josepha Hale, and Catharine Maria Sedgwick in "depth and expansion of mind," Garrison judged, but she had shown that she could "impart useful hints to the government as well as to the family circle." Through her "Hints to People of Moderate Fortune," published in the *Massachusetts Journal* and currently receiving "extensive circulation" in other newspapers, she was "doing more to reform the manners of the age" and to "restore the simplicity of the good old days of our fathers" than any other writer, "male or female," since Benjamin Franklin. The author of *Poor Richard's Almanac* would be proud to claim Child's "Hints," Garrison added, "for they embody his wisdom, his sagacity, and his wonderful knowledge of human nature." Exhorting Child to reissue these essays in book form, he went on to comment that her magazine, the *Juvenile Miscellany*, likewise deserved a nationwide circulation commensurate with the "admirable" influence it was exerting on the "rising generation." He ended by expressing an intense desire to meet the literary woman who had excited in him a "curiosity . . . greater than toward any other 'north of the Potomac.' "

Clearly, Garrison was already dreaming of enlisting this eloquent and discerning critic of American society in the antislavery cause.[3] Many months would go by before he would find an opportunity to do so, however. At the very moment he was eulogizing Child's talents as a political writer, he was engaged in his first major antislavery battle — the exposé of a Newburyport, Massachusetts, merchant named Francis Todd, who had transported a shipload of slaves from Baltimore to New Orleans. The slave-trading allegation publicly leveled against a wealthy New Englander (though true) would land Garrison in a Baltimore jail for seven weeks on a libel conviction. Not until the New York philanthropist and future abolitionist leader Arthur Tappan paid Garrison's fine would the crusading editor be free to visit Boston in early June 1830.[4]

Meanwhile, the Childs were probably receiving the *Genius of Universal Emancipation* in exchange for the *Massachusetts Journal*, a common practice among editors during a period when local newspapers could not afford to hire correspondents to cover news from distant cities. They were also following the Garrison libel case through other newspapers and hotly debating the advisability of agitating the question of slavery, particularly in the confrontational manner Garrison had adopted. "[I]t was the theme of many of our conversations while Garrison was in prison," Child later recalled, crediting David with being "wide awake before I was."[5] By November 1830, when Garrison was back in Boston for good, David was defending him in the columns of the *Massachusetts Journal*. Rather than censure, he proclaimed, Garrison "deserved praise for 'covering with infamy' as 'thick' as he could any slave-dealer, slave-owner, . . . or slave-agent or driver in the world."[6] David was one of the first to whom Garrison confided his intention of founding the *Liberator*, which would begin publication on January 1, 1831. Yet while David applauded, Child herself pronounced Garrison "too ultra, too rash" for her taste.[7]

David's prior receptivity to Garrison may reflect the similarity of their pugnacious editorial styles. Or it may date back to their earlier acquaintance. In April 1827 both men had participated in an abortive campaign to reelect John Quincy Adams, in the course of which David had spoken at a Faneuil Hall rally that Garrison had covered for the *Newburyport Herald*. During his stint on the *Massachusetts Journal*, the youthful journeyman printer had greatly admired the "vigor and dash" of his employer's writing, as well as the "candor, good sense, and sterling independence" David had shown as editor. Garrison may well have tried to proselytize his employer when he began collecting signatures for antislavery petitions in August 1828, after being spurred into antislavery activism by Benjamin Lundy. He would pay tribute to David half a century later as one of "the very earliest of my anti-slavery friends and co-laborers," though by then he could no longer recollect how much contact he and David had had with each other at the *Journal* office.[8]

It was Maria Child, rather than David, however, whom Garrison most wished to proselytize as he set about building an antislavery movement in June 1830. His extravagant tribute to her as *"the first woman in the republic"* indicates that he considered a meeting with her important enough to attempt arranging it amid a flying visit to Boston on his emergence from prison. Through his former employer and fellow editor, he had a natural entrée to her as well as a strategic ally in the effort to involve her in the crusade against slavery. Thus, on both sides the stage was set for a catalytic encounter.

Child would remember the event vividly almost fifty years afterward. "I little thought then that the whole pattern of my life-web would be changed by that introduction," she wrote on hearing the news of Garrison's death in May 1879.

> I was then all absorbed in poetry and painting, — soaring aloft, on Psyche-wings, into the etherial regions of mysticism. He got hold of the strings of my conscience, and pulled me into Reforms. It is of no use to imagine what might have been, if I had never met him. Old dreams vanished, old associates departed, and all things became new. . . . A new stimulus siezed [sic] my whole being, and carried me whithersoever it would. "I could not otherwise, so help me God."[9]

The language inescapably suggests a religious conversion. Like the Old Testament prophets on whom the word of the Lord descended, commanding them to preach to a recalcitrant people; like the early Christians filled with the spirit of God at Pentecost and empowered to see visions and speak in foreign tongues, Child felt herself possessed and transformed. Inspired by Garrison's ardent fellow feeling for the slaves,[10] impelled by his sense of urgency, and deeply moved by his appeal to her conscience, Child reconsecrated her art to the service of her sisters and brothers in bonds.

Nevertheless, she did not espouse on the spot the doctrines that would come to characterize Garrisonian abolitionism. For one thing, in June 1830 Garrison had scarcely begun to formulate them.[11] More to the point, Child was far too independent-minded to embrace a creed she had not thoroughly investigated. Garrison had aroused her sympathy for the slaves and induced her to devote her life to working for their emancipation, but before she could publicly advocate abolition, she had to wrestle with a host of troublesome questions.

For example: Granted that slavery was a gigantic moral evil, was the condition of southern slaves really so intolerable? Wasn't it in the masters' interests to treat their slaves kindly, and didn't simple expediency result in making cruelty the exception rather than the rule? Besides, wasn't it the constitutional prerogative of the slaveholding states to regulate their own internal affairs, and, if so, what right did the North have to meddle with slavery? Wouldn't agitation of the issue anger the South and thereby threaten the Union? Didn't the Colonization Society, founded in 1816, provide a vehicle for gradual emancipation through its program of resettling free blacks in Africa? Was any other means of emancipation safe or feasible? If the slaves were "turned loose," would they go on a rampage against whites? Would emancipation bring economic ruin? What lessons should be drawn from the contrasting precedents offered by the Santo Domingo uprising of the 1790s and the process of gradual abolition by legislative fiat in the northern states? In the event that Colonization should prove unworkable, could blacks and whites coexist in harmony once slavery was abolished? To what extent did racial prejudice on one side and racial hatred or biological inferiority on the other pose insurmountable obstacles to the integration of blacks into the American body politic? Was there evidence that racial prejudice was not universal and that blacks were not inferior?

These questions, and the unresolved issues lurking behind them, had stymied antislavery activism for several decades, ever since the ratification of the Constitution with its fatal compromises tacitly recognizing slavery. In 1830 Child did not have access to a body of antislavery literature to which she could turn for answers. True, protest against slavery had started in the late seventeenth century, and earlier generations of abolitionists had argued persuasively that slavery violated Christian principles and secular doctrines of natural rights.[12] Yet American abolitionists of the pre-Revolutionary period had not had to face constitutional barriers to legislative action. Nor did British and French antislavery theory always apply to the United States, where slavery was practiced not in distant colonies, but in states that formed an indissoluble part of the nation and benefited from disproportionate political representation in Congress.

In short, to refute the objections that conservative opponents raised to antislavery agitation, Child had to collect facts from a wide variety of sources and synthesize them into a coherent argument addressing all aspects of the slavery controversy — moral, legal, economic, political, and racial. This amounted to nothing less than writing her own textbook on the subject — the first of its kind. The project would consume three years before reaching fruition in her ambitious *Appeal in Favor of That Class of Americans Called Africans* (1833). During that interval Child would immerse herself in the debates over slavery covered in Garrison's weekly newspaper, *The Liberator*; read a staggering array of scholarly and polemical works; join David in exchanging opinions with Garrison through the editorial columns of the *Massachusetts Journal*; further hone her ideas in discussions with friends who, like David and herself, were gravitating toward Garrison's brand of antislavery activism; and participate vicariously through David in the founding of the New England Anti-Slavery Society. In the process Child would evolve toward the fully developed abolitionist ideology she would articulate in the *Appeal*.

As Child was researching and conceptualizing the *Appeal*, she found Garrison's *Liberator* an invaluable mine of information. The paper not only supplied her with innumerable facts she would use, but directed her toward works to consult for more extensive research. It recorded shocking cases of slave abuse; quoted fugitive slave advertisements from southern newspapers; cited draconian laws against slaves and free blacks, North as well as South; publicized cases of kidnapping involving northern free blacks illicitly sold into southern slavery; and reprinted voluminous extracts from books, tracts, speeches, sermons, congressional debates, and newspaper articles, representing all schools of thought, pro- and antislavery.

The *Liberator* can even be said to have influenced the way in which Child defined the parameters of her subject. Nearly all the issues Child tackled in the *Appeal* can be traced back to articles in Garrison's paper. Probably most important for contextualizing the unparalleled emphasis Child would give to counteracting racial prejudice — a theme that would dominate four of the *Appeal*'s eight chapters — were the *Liberator*'s repudiation of Colonization as a fraudulent, racist substitute for genuine antislavery action; its concerted campaign against all forms of anti-black discrimination in the North, ranging from color bars in schools, jobs, and transportation facilities to laws prohibiting interracial marriage; and its receptiveness to contributions by African American writers, which served both to demonstrate their intellectual capabilities and to expose white sympathizers to the viewpoint of the class they hoped to benefit.

Through the *Liberator*'s African American correspondents, for example, Child learned that blacks categorically opposed repatriation to Africa and cogently defended their right to enjoy the same privileges as other American citizens.[13] Their eloquent protests surely helped sensitize her to the day-to-day indignities and impediments African Americans faced as a result of racial discrimination. The *Liberator* may also have prompted her to read (or reread) the most trenchant analysis an African American writer had thus far produced of his people's oppression — David Walker's 1829 *Appeal to the Coloured Citizens of the World*, which a correspondent signed "V" extensively quoted and reviewed in May 1831. Along with the militant summons to resistance for which it is famous, it presented a searing denunciation of the Colonization scheme that may well have influenced both Garrison and Child. Some have suggested that Child titled her own *Appeal* with Walker's in mind.[14]

While Child was gathering information and forming her opinions, she and David engaged in a journalistic dialogue with Garrison. They felt their way toward new perspectives on the slavery question in their *Massachusetts Journal* editorials, and he responded in the *Liberator* by prodding them toward more radical positions. These exchanges offer fascinating glimpses of Child's evolution toward the *Appeal*.

On January 15, 1831, Garrison reprinted an article from the *Massachusetts Journal*, which sought to defend Colonization without adopting the Colonization Society's postulate that racial antipathies could not be overcome because they were rooted in human nature.[15] Bemusedly, the author of the article (possibly Maria Child, since it appeared underneath one of her own contributions) noted the "very violent prejudices against Colonization to Africa" expressed by blacks. "The Boston negroes have the impression, that the whites care little whether the poor Africans live or die, provided they can get rid of them with safety to themselves," she (or David) reported: "The negroes therefore say, 'the whites brought us here, in a cruel manner and from sordid motives, for their service and pleasure, and now that we . . . are increasing so as to be inconvenient, they would ship us off. We won't go from this continent. If we go anywhere, it shall be to Canada, . . . where we can become respectable, wealthy, and hold offices, as we may under the laws of England.'" Though admitting that she had not been "able to reply" to such strictures, Child could not agree with the view that the Colonization scheme veiled a sinister design to annihilate America's free black population through exile to an insalubrious climate. Nor could she relinquish the belief that emigration to Liberia offered blacks an opportunity to escape racial proscriptions and found a "powerful and glorious nation." She did, nevertheless, concede that the "exclusion of negroes of good character and competent qualifications from offices of honor and emolument" in their native land was "wholly indefensible on principles of natural law, religion, or the constitution of the United States." It was an acknowledgment marking a fundamental departure from the Colonizationist ideology of racial separatism and indicating how close the Childs had come, as early as January 1831, to accepting Garrison's premise that blacks could be safely integrated into American society as equal citizens.

Garrison's comments in the footnotes he appended to the article measured the precise distance the couple still needed to travel from Colonizationist to abolitionist ideology. Pointing out that prejudices against Colonization were not confined to Boston blacks, but "pervade[d] the breasts of our free colored population throughout the country," he suggested that blacks could hardly be blamed for distrusting the motives of those who were "anxious to send them to Africa," but "refuse[d] to meliorate their condition here." No people, he insisted, should have to emigrate to improve their status. As for the bright future Child conjured up for the exiles in Liberia, Garrison dismissed it as a "delightful hallucination."

Eight months later, the Childs' dialogue with Garrison had progressed to a point of almost complete accord on the most radical feature of his ideology — his call for an end to racial discrimination. Under the headline "A Noble Commentary," Garrison prefaced another reprint from the *Massachusetts Journal* with the words: "Since we commenced the publication of the Liberator, we have seen nothing in the newspapers which has given us more unfeigned pleasure." An incisive condemnation of American racial prejudice, the article, he predicted, would "find a response in the bosom of every true patriot, and add another rose to the wreath of independence which crowns the head of its author."[16] Despite its placement on the editorial page of the *Massachusetts Journal*, the style almost surely identified the author as Maria Child. Indeed, she would incorporate much of it virtually unchanged into *An Appeal in Favor of That Class of Americans Called Africans*.[17]

This is not to say that by August 1831 Child was ready to advocate immediate abolition, as she would in the *Appeal*. On the contrary, in a passage of her *Massachusetts Journal* editorial tactfully overlooked by Garrison, she explicitly disclaimed the intention of entering the controversy over slavery. She even pronounced it "ungenerous to raise an outcry against the southern states for an evil which their best men regret as deeply as we do — an evil which it is far more easy to *condemn* than it is to *remedy*." Her aim, she specified, was rather to foster a spirit of self-criticism in the North. "[A]re *we* governed by right feelings in our deportment towards the negroes?" she asked, urging northerners to examine their own hearts.

Child proceeded to argue that racial prejudice was not only "contrary to the spirit of the Bible, and contrary to the spirit of the Declaration of Independence," but indefensible on rational grounds and politically embarrassing in a republic. "It is a singular fact that we *republicans* are abundantly more exclusive" in racial matters "than our monarchical neighbors," she remarked, playing on American national pride: "In England, it is common to see respectable and genteel people open their pews when a black stranger enters the church; and at hotels, nobody thinks it a degradation to have a colored traveller sit at the same table." A "well authenticated anecdote" about a black expatriate in London named Prince Saunders served to illustrate Child's point. Calling on an American family at the breakfast hour, the gentleman was not invited to join them at the table but was kept standing while they ate. Only when they had risen did the hostess, "with an air of sudden recollection," ask if he had had breakfast and offer him a cup of coffee. His "dignified" reply that he was "engaged to breakfast with the Prince Regent this morning" drove home the irony that British aristocrats could treat a black man as an equal while American republicans made a mockery of their egalitarian creed by refusing to apply it to their dark-skinned compatriots.

"We are well aware that this is not the popular side of the question — that we shall be called vulgar, and radical," Child went on. Undaunted, she confronted the inevitable challenge: "Would you have us invite negroes to our parties, and give them our daughters in marriage?" The onus, she retorted, was on the prejudiced to supply "a *good* reason why a virtuous, well-educated black should not be invited!" Yet her stand on "mixed marriages" fell short of the one she would take in the *Appeal*. "[T]hey are in bad taste, and are unnatural," she averred, oddly echoing the very words reviewers had used to disparage the plot of *Hobomok*, and simultaneously contradicting the defense of interracial marriage she had formulated in *The First Settlers of New England*.[18] It was the sole statement in the article to which Garrison took exception. "We agree with the editor of the Journal & Tribune, that, at the present time, mixed marriages would be in bad taste, but not that 'they are unnatural,'" he demurred, adding that only in the case of different species could amalgamation be termed "unnatural."

Embedded in Child's unfortunate concession to popular prejudice against interracial marriage was a covert critique of antimiscegenation laws, however. They were unnecessary, she intimated, because such marriages "would never take place except in very rare instances." Instead, "we would leave men free to choose their wives, as they are to choose their religion," she concluded. She would expand on this argument in the *Appeal*, where she would openly call for rescinding the Massachusetts antimiscegenation law, couching her plea in nearly identical language, but no longer stigmatizing interracial marriage as "unnatural" or "in bad taste."[19]

Child even anticipated the *Appeal* in the witty peroration of her *Massachusetts Journal* editorial. Pointing out that the Turks, whose "narrow bigotry" had become a byword, had recently passed a law "imposing a fine upon whoever shall call a Christian a dog," she exhorted her readers: "Let us try to keep pace with the Turks in candor and benevolence." In the later work she would suggest that a "residence in Turkey might be profitable to those Christians" who characterized prejudice as eternal and irremediable, for "it would afford an opportunity of testing the goodness of the rule, by showing how it works both ways" (231). Garrison would reprint a long extract from this article in his 1832 *Thoughts on African Colonization*.[20]

The editorial pages of the *Liberator* and the *Massachusetts Journal* once again revealed the increasing ideological convergence between the Childs and Garrison when the Nat

Turner revolt burst upon the nation on August 21, 1831. That night a small, powerfully built, thirty-year-old African American from Southampton County, Virginia, who believed he had been commissioned by God to free his people, led a party of his fellow slaves from plantation to plantation, killing every white person they encountered — a total of fifty-five before they were routed by white troops forty-eight hours later. Garrison interpreted the uprising as the fulfillment of his prophecy that death and destruction would rain down on the country until it repented of its sins and freed the slaves. Though "horror-struck" at the bloodbath (which ultimately claimed the lives of some 120 blacks in the gruesome reprisals), he insisted that no one who justified the patriots of the American revolution for resorting to arms had the right to condemn the slaves. David Child agreed. "[W]e will never swerve from the principle that the oppressed and enslaved of every country, Hayti and Virginia as well as France and Poland, have a right to assert their 'natural and unalienable rights' whenever and wherever they can do it, and that they also have a right to judge of the fitness of the occasion," he maintained, in a statement Garrison reprinted in the *Liberator*.[21]

The only difference between the two men's reactions was that Garrison subscribed to the "pacific precepts of Jesus Christ," which enjoined all believers without exception to return good for evil,[22] whereas David, who had fought in Spain's war against French domination, feared simply that the odds against the slaves were too heavy for such a revolt to succeed. Under current circumstances, he thought, an attempt like Turner's could accomplish nothing but "to inflict useless misery" on both slaves and masters. "God grant that it may come to good," he apostrophized.

In the midst of these editorial exchanges, the increasing frequency of the *Liberator*'s references to Maria Child suggests that she may already have joined the circle of antislavery friends Garrison was gathering around him. In May 1831 an advertisement in the *Liberator* announced that *The Mother's Book* was "in the press." A brief extract from *The Mother's Book* appeared in December. Evidently Child did not object to letting Garrison publicize her work in his reputedly "incendiary" newspaper. More tellingly, two sketches with low-key antislavery messages followed in January 1832: "The Moral of an Alarm Watch" and "Stand from Under!"[23]

The first sketch, reprinted anonymously from the *Massachusetts Journal*, drew a lesson from the common experience of sleeping through the ringing of an alarm clock because "the drowsy ear" has become "accustomed to the sound." Child specifically applied the lesson to slavery, citing the case of a "New-England lady," who, after "residing at the South a few years" no longer found herself " 'shocked at the idea of keeping slaves.' " "They who disregard" the alarm clock's warning "soon cease to hear its voice," Child moralized.

The second sketch was a ghost story set on board a slave-trading ship and narrated by a sailor with "misgivings about the business." It symbolically pictured slavery as an evil spirit haunting the ship and warning the crew to "Stand from Under!" Boldly signed "By Mrs. Child," in the format not of a borrowed reprint, but of a voluntary contribution, it represented yet another step toward Child's public identification with Garrison and the antislavery movement.

It is surely no coincidence that Child took this step in January 1832, for during that very month David played a prominent part in the founding of the New England Anti-Slavery Society. Over the previous year he had frequently visited the "dingy," third-story office, with its ink-spattered windows, where Garrison printed the *Liberator* with his own hands, ate at the long editorial table piled high with mail and newspapers, and slept on the floor.[24] The men who congregated there all shared the Childs' growing conviction that "[t]he hour of national expiation had come, and men and women must needs obey the summons."[25] These comrades in struggle included the gentle Unitarian clergyman Samuel J. May, to whom Child would dedicate her *Appeal* "as a mark of gratitude, for his earnest and disinterested efforts in an unpopular but most righteous cause"; May's cousin, the lawyer Samuel E. Sewall, whom David had known since their days at Harvard, where all three had graduated in the class of 1817;[26] May's brother-in-law Bronson Alcott, whose wife Abba May had attracted Child "by her prompt decisions concerning the right and wrong of things" when both were still unattached;[27] the Quaker poet and future laureate of the abolitionist movement, John Greenleaf Whittier, like Child a prize literary recruit; the Congregationalist minister Amos A. Phelps, whose 1834 *Lectures on Slavery and Its Remedy* would draw heavily on Child's *Appeal*; the printer and editor Oliver Johnson, later Garrison's first biographer; and the lawyer Ellis Gray Loring, who had studied under David at the Boston Latin School, and whose wife Louisa Gilman Loring was intimate with Child before either married.[28]

As they prepared to brave social censure, the Childs must have engaged in many soul-searching discussions with their associates, and especially with their closest friends, the Lorings. Sensitive and refined, tenderly attached to each other and to their baby daughter "Nony," naturally inclined toward domestic privacy, and "reluctant to believe in the existence of evil," Ellis and Louisa, like Child, found the "rough work of reform . . . unavoidably distasteful." "The thousand nameless sacrifices to conscience made by such characters are by no means among the smallest offerings laid on the altar of humanity," Child wrote long afterward, speaking as much for herself as for the Lorings.[29] For her part, Child would have much preferred to indulge her propensity toward mysticism and her taste for art and poetry, or at least to devote herself to securing the permanent home she yearned for. Of the four, David was the only one who could claim to relish disputation and combat. But he also aspired to a career in politics that abolitionist advocacy would doom. Soberly, the two couples and their young comrades faced the prospects of revilement, isolation, professional boycott, thwarted ambition, and financial hardship. But none turned back.

By late 1831, no doubt spurred by the Nat Turner revolt, the men in Garrison's circle began laying plans to form an antislavery society and spiritedly debating whether or not to base it explicitly on the principle of immediate emancipation. According to Oliver Johnson, all of the fifteen men who met in Samuel Sewall's law office on November 13 "admitted the duty and safety of setting the slaves free at once; but six of the number doubted the wisdom of incorporating that principle into the constitution of the society, believing that it would excite popular prejudice, and thus tend to defeat the object in view."[30] Though David and his fellow lawyers Sewall and Loring headed the list of doubters, they joined Garrison and Johnson in drafting the constitution of the New England Anti-Slavery Society. David even presided over the historic meeting of January 6, 1832, at which the constitution was adopted. (Child did not attend, since the society had not yet opened its meetings to women, as it soon would.)[31]

Symbolically heralding the obstacles that abolitionists would face, a "fierce northeast storm, combining snow, rain and hail," pelted the crusaders who struggled through the slush on this "dismal night" to seal their commitment to the antislavery cause. The meeting place was equally symbolic. A schoolroom in the basement of the African Baptist Church, located in the black neighborhood known as "Nigger Hill," it betokened the solidarity these early abolitionists felt with African Americans, the ostracism they risked by associating with a pariah class, and the racial uplift they hoped to promote by furnishing blacks with opportunities for higher education. Yet indicative of a paternalism abolitionists would never quite overcome, no African Americans participated in founding the New England Anti-Slavery Society, despite a well-established tradition of black antislavery activism; instead, blacks were invited to join after whites had set the society's initial agenda.[32]

That agenda was spelled out in the second article of the society's constitution: "The objects of the Society shall be, to endeavor, by all means sanctioned by law, humanity and religion, to effect the abolition of slavery in the United States; to improve the character and condition of the free people of color, to inform and correct public opinion in relation to their situation and rights, and obtain for them equal civil and political rights and privileges with the whites."[33] The point of contention between radicals and moderates lay not in this clause, but in the preamble enunciating the "right to immediate freedom from personal bondage." Still unconvinced that it was expedient to alienate potential supporters by making "immediate emancipation" a cardinal doctrine of the new society, David, Sewall, and Loring withheld their signatures from the "apostolic" roster of twelve names making up the original membership. All three quickly changed their minds, however, and by the following year Sewall had accepted a position on the board of managers and David and Loring were serving as counselors.[34]

Concurrently, Child took her final step toward assuming the role of the despised antislavery agitator. In August 1833, when, as Samuel May recalled, "the number, the variety, and the malignity of our opponents had become manifest," she startled friends and foes alike by publishing *An Appeal in Favor of That Class of Americans Called Africans*. "We had seen her often at our meetings," May reminisced. "We knew that she sympathized with her brave husband in his abhorrence of our American system of slavery; but we did not know that she had so carefully studied and thoroughly mastered the subject."[35]

Compounding the "exultation" in antislavery ranks that "such an author — ay, such an *authority* — should espouse our cause just at that crisis" was the stature Child had by now attained. In 1833, some four years after Garrison had hailed her as "*the first woman in the republic,*" she stood at the apex of her literary fame. Only a month earlier, the most prestigious journal of American letters, the *North American Review*, had crowned her with its laurels in a twenty-five-page appraisal of her entire oeuvre. Uncannily echoing Garrison's very words (though attributing the phrase "the first woman in the republic" to a comment Napoleon made to Madame de Staël), the editors of the *North American* reiterated his prophetic judgment: "[W]e are not sure that any woman in our country would outrank Mrs. Child." Like Garrison—but for diametrically opposite reasons— they, too, recognized in Child "just the woman we want for the mothers and daughters of the present generation."[36] It was as if rival camps—one representing social dominance, the other radical egalitarianism and the contumely that went with its advocacy—vied for the privilege of offering her leadership.

Serenely true to the inner convictions she had always exhorted her readers to heed, Child turned her back on the prize laid at her feet by the arbiters of the literary world— a prize she had long coveted—and cast her lot with America's oppressed people of color. "Hardly ever was there a costlier sacrifice," wrote her friend Wendell Phillips. "Narrow means just changing to ease; after a weary struggle, fame and social position in her grasp; every door opening before her; the sweetness of having her genius recognized."[37] Still, Child did not flinch. "I am fully aware of the unpopularity of the task I have undertaken," she avowed in her preface to the *Appeal*; "but though I *expect* ridicule and censure, I cannot *fear* them."

An Appeal in Favor of That Class of Americans Called Africans provided the abolitionist movement with its first full-scale analysis of the slavery question. Indeed, so comprehensive was its scope that no other antislavery writer ever attempted to duplicate Child's achievement; all subsequent works would focus on individual aspects of the subject that Child covered in eight thoroughly researched and extensively documented chapters.[38] Even today, the book's wide-ranging scholarship, consummate rhetoric, and signal prescience command attention.

Child's very title is "pregnant with the gist" of her entire argument (as May aptly notes);[39] every word inspires reflection and challenges prejudice. Child simultaneously "appeals" to her readers' human sympathies, subverts their intellectual categories, and redefines the national identity of her subjects and her readers alike. African Americans, she quietly asserts, are Americans, not Africans; compatriots, not foreigners. They can no more be "called" Africans than Americans can be called Britons. They are an assimilable "class," not a biologically separate race.

In her preface Child subtly negotiates the transition from *The Mother's Book* and the *Juvenile Miscellany* to the *Appeal*. Addressing the audience that had hitherto revered her as a model for women and children, and speaking in the familiar tones of nineteenth-century womanhood, she implores it in the name of her past services to grant her a hearing on an admittedly unfeminine topic:

> Reader, I beseech you not to throw down this volume as soon as you have glanced at the title. Read it, if your prejudices will allow, for the very truth's sake:—If I

have the most trifling claims upon your good will, for an hour's amusement to yourself, or benefit to your children, read it for *my* sake: — Read it, if it be merely to find fresh occasion to sneer at the vulgarity of the cause: — Read it, from sheer curiosity to see what a woman (who had much better attend to her household concerns) will say upon such a subject: — Read it, on *any* terms, and my purpose will be gained.

With her confident allusion to her purpose, however, Child shifts into the "masculine" discourse of political critique that she will use throughout the major portion of the book. "The subject I have chosen admits of no encomiums on my country," she remarks drily; "but as I generally make it an object to supply what is most needed, this circumstance is unimportant; the market is so glutted with flattery, that a little truth may be acceptable, were it only for its rarity." Earlier, she had stormed a market glutted with cookbooks and childhood "education" treatises for wealthy Europeans. Now she proposes to defy a market glutted with chauvinistic self-congratulation. In her previous ventures she had shrewdly calculated on reaping financial dividends while fulfilling a social need. This time she faces the prospect of financial ruin and public vilification, secure in the knowledge that she is advancing "the inevitable progress of truth and justice." "I would not exchange the consciousness" of performing such a mission "for all Rothchild's wealth, or Sir Walter's fame," she concludes in her valedictory admonition to readers who balk at following her into her new realm.

What is initially most striking about the 230-page treatise this preface so disarmingly introduces is its solid historical grounding. Organized with flawless logic, the book moves from past to present, from history to political economy, from fact to argument, from problem to solution. It opens with a "Brief History of Negro Slavery. — [and] Its Inevitable Effect upon All Concerned in It" (chapter 1), succeeded by a "Comparative View of Slavery, in Different Ages and Nations" (chapter 2). Occupying almost a third of the book, these chapters situate American slavery in a worldwide context that includes ancient Israel, Greece, and Rome, as well as Africa, the Caribbean, and Latin America. Through a detailed analysis of the laws regulating slavery in these various societies, Child shows that "Modern slavery . . . in all its particulars, is more odious than the ancient; and . . . that the condition of slaves has always been worse just in proportion to the freedom enjoyed by their masters" (35). As the most democratic society in history, the United States has the most stringent slave codes, she points out. "Slavery is so inconsistent with free institutions, and the spirit of liberty is so contagious under such institutions," Child explains, "that the system must either be given up, or sustained by laws outrageously severe; hence we find that our slave laws have each year been growing more harsh than those of any other nation" (75–76). In both her comparative approach and her astute insights, Child anticipates twentieth-century scholars who have revolutionized the study of slavery.[40]

After this geohistorical survey, Child proceeds to explore the economics and politics of the slavery controversy. Chapter 3, "Free and Slave Labor. — Possibility of Safe Emancipation," counters fears that emancipation would entail economic disaster and insurrectionary violence. The introduction of a free labor system would improve the economy of the South, she asserts, since slave labor has such serious disadvantages: "*where* slaves are employed, manual industry is a degradation to white people, and indolence becomes the prevailing characteristic" (78). As for the risk of unleashing another Santo Domingo, an "impartial and careful examination" has convinced her that "slavery causes insurrections, while emancipation prevents them" (86). In chapter 4, "Influence of Slavery on the Politics of the United States," Child turns the tables on defenders of the status quo by arguing that the real threat to the Union lies not in agitation of the slavery question, but in the South's political dominance and commitment to furthering its own interests at all costs. Because of the constitutional clause allowing the slaveholding states to count three-fifths of their slave population in determining their allotment of congressional seats, the South has acquired " 'entire control of the national policy' " and has used that control "to protect and extend slave power" (114–15). The accession of new slave states has already secured "a renewed and apparently interminable lease to the duration of slavery," and the insatiable thirst for more slave territory portends future wars of conquest, warns Child, referring to the looming annexation of Texas (127–28).

In her pivotal chapter, "Colonization Society, and Anti-Slavery Society," placed at the center of the book, Child examines the two parties' opposing solutions to the problem of slavery: gradual emancipation accompanied by repatriation to Africa versus immediate emancipation followed by the bestowal of "equal civil and political rights and privileges with the whites" (146). Since the principal point at issue between Colonizationists and abolitionists is whether prejudice against blacks can and should be overcome, she devotes the rest of the book to answering that question. Chapters 6 and 7, "Intellect of Negroes" and "Moral Character of Negroes," demolish the rationale for prejudice — the myth of the Negro's biological inferiority and savage past — by resurrecting accounts of Africa's ancient civilizations and recalling numerous modern instances of blacks who have distinguished themselves by their talents. The final chapter, "Prejudices against People of Color, and Our Duties in Relation to This Subject," condemns racial discrimination and urges Americans to repudiate attitudes and practices inconsistent with their republican creed.

Although the *Appeal* violates the prevailing norms of feminine discourse by its very engagement in political controversy, as well as by its authoritative display of erudition and its preoccupation with such matters as law, economics, and congressional apportionment, it simultaneously presents a woman's perspective on slavery. Repeatedly, Child focuses on the special ways in which slavery victimizes women and makes a mockery of the domestic ideology glorifying "true womanhood." In the process, she pointedly reveals the limitations on her own freedom as a woman that link her to her sisters in bonds.

"There is another view of this system, which I cannot unveil so completely as it ought to be," she writes. "I shall be called bold for saying so much; but the facts are so important, that it is a matter of conscience not to be fastidious" (19). Her ensuing comments on the sexual exploitation of slave women are muffled in circumlocutions:

> The negro woman is unprotected either by law or public opinion. She is the
> property of her master, and her daughters are his property. They are allowed to
> have no conscientious scruples, no sense of shame, no regard for the feelings of
> husband, or parent; they must be entirely subservient to the will of their owner, on
> pain of being whipped as near unto death as will comport with his interest, or quite
> to death, if it suit his pleasure.
>
> Those who know human nature would be able to conjecture the unavoidable
> result, even if it were not betrayed by the amount of mixed population. (19)

On the one hand, Child acknowledges, she herself cannot speak as plainly as she ought
to because to do so would be to compromise her womanhood by the standards of
nineteenth-century ideology. On the other hand, she shows, the slave woman has no
right to the "protection" this ideology imposes on the white woman, no right to
preserve the sexual purity deemed essential to true womanhood.

Child takes her analysis to a deeper level when she turns to the effects of slavery on
the white mistress. "[A]uthentic records of female cruelty" indicate that the slave
system perverts the womanhood of the mistress as hideously as it does that of the slave,
Child suggests. Significantly, the case she chooses to cite involves a New England
woman, thus inculcating the lesson that the system operates on everyone who comes
under it. Originally "amiable" and "affectionate," this woman has metamorphosed into
a "fiend" since moving South and acquiring slaves: "One faithful negro woman nursed
the twins of her mistress, and did all the washing, ironing, and scouring. If, after a
sleepless night with the restless babes (driven from the bosom of their own mother,) she
performed her toilsome avocations with diminished activity, her mistress, with her own
lady-like hands, applied the cow-skin, and the neighborhood resounded with the cries
of her victim" (24–25). Having shunted onto the black woman the responsibilities of
motherhood and domesticity that supposedly constitute a true woman's glory, the slave
mistress has become the mere caricature of a "lady." She has, in fact, become a mas-
culinized brute, Child implies.

The woman's perspective Child brings to bear on slavery determines her choice of
supporting illustrations in many other sections of the *Appeal*, as we shall see. Yet she did
not originate the female antislavery discourse she so brilliantly manipulates. Rather,
she perfected and carried to a new plane of sophistication a discourse initiated by
women in the British antislavery movement of the early nineteenth century, and pursued by such American pioneers as the Quaker Elizabeth Margaret Chandler, who
edited the female department of the *Genius of Universal Emancipation* and helped launch
its analogue in the *Liberator*. Child also took many cues from African American women
writers she encountered through the *Liberator* — notably Maria Stewart, Sarah Douglass, and Sarah Forten — who developed a parallel discourse.[41]

The distinctiveness of the *Appeal* lies not in the particular arguments it advances, but
in its all-encompassing synthesis of facts and arguments from an unprecedented array
of sources. Among Child's precursors, the British abolitionist Thomas Clarkson had
detailed the horrors of the slave trade. The American legal scholar George Stroud had

exhaustively studied southern slave laws and demonstrated their harshness. David Walker and Garrison had dissected Colonizationist ideology and exposed its racism and illogicality. The Abbé Grégoire of the French Amis des Noirs had vindicated blacks against charges of inferiority by amassing examples of their achievements in science, art, and literature. And the American historian Alexander Everett, though a conservative on the slavery question, had promulgated the theory that Africa was the cradle of the civilization Europe had derived from the ancients.[42]

Child not only drew on these prior writers, but she evidently developed her analysis in conjunction with David. At the January 1833 annual meeting of the New England Anti-Slavery Society, he had delivered a marathon speech in support of the proposition that "the free People of Color and Slaves in this land of Liberty and Law, have less liberty, and are less protected by law, than in any other part of the world." Garrison and Whittier would later remember it as "a masterly and exhaustive analysis and exposure of the 'peculiar institution'" and "the best and fullest exposition of our principles and objects" to date.[43] Subsequently expanded for publication, David's speech, *The Despotism of Freedom*, overlaps with the *Appeal* in comparing the southern slave system to its biblical, classical, Caribbean, and Latin American analogues. Shared anecdotes, witticisms, and literary borrowings suggest that the Childs researched their projects simultaneously and pooled their ideas. Yet the *Appeal* is far broader in scope than *The Despotism of Freedom*.[44]

Neither David nor any of Child's predecessors had sought to weave the diverse strands of antislavery thought into a single panoramic tapestry. Nor had anyone sought to combine them with the economic and political analysis she offered in her third and fourth chapters, which constitute an early formulation of the "free labor" ideology the Republican party preached in the 1850s.[45] One recent historian has even credited Child with having articulated the first major statement of the "slave power" thesis.[46] The most original feature of the *Appeal*, however, distinguishing it from all other antislavery tracts by white Americans, is its concerted refutation of racist ideology.[47] This motif governs four out of eight chapters and recurs elsewhere as a subtheme. It is not too much to say that it motivates Child's rhetorical strategy, which aims at overturning ethnocentric stereotypes and inducing readers to think in unaccustomed ways.

Thus, in her history of slavery and the slave trade, Child draws frequent analogies between European Christians and the peoples they denigrate. To illustrate the "bigotry" fostered by the slave trade, she describes how Moors and Arabs base their right to enslave "heathen tribes" on the idolatry of their victims, yet refuse to proselytize them for fear of forfeiting the pretext for the lucrative traffic in human flesh. Having decoyed her readers, Child springs her trap: "This is precisely like our own conduct," she notes. "We say the negroes are so ignorant that they must be slaves; and we insist upon keeping them ignorant, lest we spoil them for slaves" (5).

Later, Child uses the same technique to puncture the hackneyed claim that the slave trade rescued Africans from "the despotism and wars, which desolate their own continent" (15). Pointing out that "the white man is himself the cause of these wars," and that we have no right to judge for other peoples where they will be best off, she reverses the argument: "If the Turks, or the Algerines saw fit to exercise this right, they might carry away captive all the occupants of our prisons and penitentiaries" (15).

In yet another twist, Child shows that instead of bringing Africans out of savagery and into civilization, the slave trade has actually brought the savagery of African coastal raids to the United States. In American cities, as in African villages, "[a] free man of color is in constant danger of being seized and carried off by . . . slave dealers. . . . Wherever these notorious slave jockeys appear in our Southern States, the free people of color hide themselves, as they are obliged to do on the coast of Africa" (31). David Child would elaborate on this analogy between the African and the American interstate slave trades in a report on the domestic slave trade presented at the New England Anti-Slavery Convention of 1834.[48]

While arguing that the slave trade prevented the economic development of Africa—a thesis upheld by recent scholars[49]—Child takes pains to counteract the stereotype of Africa as the "dark continent." In her chapters on the "Intellect" and "Moral Character of Negroes," she provides a wealth of information about African history and culture, relying on such sources as the travel accounts of Mungo Park and Major Denham, the narrative of the African-born slave Olaudah Equiano, the treatise of the Abbé Grégoire, the *Biographie Universelle*, and the *English Family Library*. She cites the "mechanical skill" displayed by African leather workers, jewelers, and weavers; the eloquence exhibited by minstrels and orators; and the existence of cities presenting " 'a prospect of civilization and magnificence' " (160–61). Most memorable is Child's long account of the Angolan queen Zhinga, who "could neither be subdued by force of arms, nor appeased by presents" (161–65).[50]

Zhinga obviously attracted Child's attention both as a woman and as an African who exemplified outstanding "bravery, intelligence, and perseverance" (161). But Child's admiring portrait also serves another purpose. It is one of many passages in the *Appeal* that defend the resort to armed resistance. A few pages later, Child pays tribute to Toussaint L'Ouverture, describing the Santo Domingo revolution not as an outbreak of barbarism, but as a heroic struggle for freedom (175–78). Just as she had earlier vindicated the right of the Wampanoag chief Philip to lead an uprising against the Puritan settlers who had taken over his people's land,[51] so she now extends the same sympathy to slave rebels like Toussaint and perhaps Nat Turner: "By thousands and thousands, these poor people have died for freedom. They have stabbed themselves for freedom—jumped into the waves for freedom—starved for freedom—fought like very tigers for freedom! But they have been hung, and burned, and shot—and their tyrants have been their historians!" (180)

Recognizing that oppressors monopolize the power to write history, Child predicts that the oppressed will seize it once they liberate themselves: "When the Africans have writers of their own, we shall hear their efforts for liberty called by the true title of heroism in a glorious cause" (180).

Child's sweeping refutation of racism culminates in her chapter "Prejudices against People of Color, and Our Duties in Relation to This Subject." Asserting that northern racial prejudice is "even more inveterate" than its southern counterpart, she charges:

"[O]ur cold-hearted, ignoble prejudice admits of no exception — no intermission. . . .
Those who are kind and liberal on all other subjects, unite with the selfish and the
proud in their unrelenting efforts to keep the colored population in the lowest state of
degradation" (208–9). Unsparingly, Child catalogs the forms of discrimination practiced against blacks in schools, churches, jobs, and travel facilities, and she describes the
violence with which whites have enforced them. To dispel at the outset the bugbear
traditionally invoked to justify such discrimination, she begins with the "unjust law"
prohibiting "marriages between persons of different color." In her 1831 *Massachusetts
Journal* editorial, she had attacked antimiscegenation laws under the cover of anonymity, allowing readers to attribute her views to David. It took much greater courage
to advance in her own name, as a woman, views that men like Garrison had been
anathemized for expressing. "I am perfectly aware of the gross ridicule to which I may
subject myself . . . ," she writes; "but I have lived too long, and observed too much, to be
disturbed by the world's mockery" (209).

Child's argument boldly equates freedom of marriage with freedom of religion — the
principle that had led New England's Puritan founders to emigrate to America: "A man
has at least as good a right to choose his wife, as he has to choose his religion. His taste
may not suit his neighbors; but so long as his deportment is correct, they have no right
to interfere with his concerns" (209). The equation redefines as sacred an exercise of
individual "taste" that society stigmatizes as indecent. Revealingly, however, Child
here speaks in male accents. She does not dare couch her defense of interracial marriage in terms of a woman's sacred right to choose her husband regardless of race. Still,
the examples she cites are white women who have chosen to live in common-law
marriages with black men, and she refers to them in a manner that implies personal
acquaintance: "I know two or three instances where women of the laboring class have
been united to reputable, industrious colored men. These husbands regularly bring
home their wages, and are kind to their families" (210). Moreover, as in her analysis of
the slave system, Child focuses on the ways in which antimiscegenation laws victimize
women:

> If by some of the odd chances, which not unfrequently occur in the world, their
> wives should become heirs to any property, the children may be wronged out of it,
> because the law pronounces them illegitimate. And while this injustice exists with
> regard to *honest*, industrious individuals, who are merely guilty of differing from us
> in a matter of taste, neither the legislation nor customs of slaveholding States exert
> their influence against *immoral* connexions. (210)

True, Child distances herself from these women by intimating that she does not share
their tastes.[52] She does, nevertheless, challenge the sexual and racial double standard,
once again focusing on how it oppresses women.

This time Child cites the case of New Orleans' famous quadroon concubines, a class
of women as refined as their upper-class white sisters, yet forced by the slave system and
the color bar into illicit relations with white men: "White gentlemen of the first
rank . . . often become seriously in love with these fascinating but unfortunate beings.

Prejudice forbids matrimony, but universal custom sanctions temporary connexions, to which a certain degree of respectability is allowed, on account of the peculiar situation of the parties. These attachments often continue for years — sometimes for life — and instances are not unfrequent of exemplary constancy and great propriety of deportment" (210).

Having anticipated and disposed of the plea that racial discrimination is necessary to prevent intermarriage, Child devotes the rest of the chapter to showing how discrimination functions to prevent blacks from improving their status. Her most telling examples involve the virulent opposition to higher education for African Americans. Not only are blacks systematically excluded from white schools, Child points out, but mobs have repeatedly prevented the founding even of segregated academies and colleges for African Americans.

Among the instances Child cites, one must have resonated with special significance for her, since it dramatized the obloquy a white woman must face if she allied herself with women of color. During the very months when Child was writing the *Appeal*, a Quaker teacher named Prudence Crandall had attempted to open a school for "young ladies and little misses of color" in Canterbury, Connecticut. The irate citizens of Canterbury had smeared her door with filth; poisoned her well with excrement; organized a boycott against her and her students among the town's merchants; served a warrant on one of her students under an obsolete vagrancy law, threatening the young woman with a public whipping on her "*naked body*"; and actually imprisoned Crandall herself for one night in a cell previously occupied by a murderer. The case was going through the courts as the *Appeal* came off the press, and it would climax the following year in the mob destruction of the school.[53] Child acknowledged its role in steeling her own resolve to defy racial prejudice when she dedicated the *Appeal* to Samuel May, who had been leading Crandall's defense.

The explanation that a self-styled "Friend of the Colonization Cause" gave for the vendetta against Crandall's school — an explanation Child paraphrases and rebuts in the *Appeal* (213) — illuminates her reasons for according so much importance to the issue of interracial marriage. What purpose, asks this writer, can an institution like Crandall's serve?

> Why, to break down the barriers which God has placed between blacks and whites — to manufacture "*Young Ladies of color*," and to foist upon community a new species of gentility, in the shape of sable belles. They [Crandall and her abolitionist supporters] propose, by softening down the rough features of the African mind, in these wenches, to cook up a palatable morsel for our white bachelors. After this precious concoction is completed, they are then to be taken by the hand, introduced into the best society, and made to aspire to the first matrimonial connections in the country. In a word, they hope to force the two races to amalgamate![54]

Child must have recognized in this scurrilous broadside a foretaste of the public reaction to the *Appeal*. Yet she perceived — and had the courage to maintain publicly — that it was vital to carry the defense of racial integration to its logical conclusion by affirming the right to intermarriage. Since Colonizationists were leading the campaign against efforts to promote African American uplift and integration, Child formulated her most radical statement on interracial marriage in her chapter on Colonization and antislavery:

> Perhaps, a hundred years hence, some negro Rothschild may come from Hayti, with his seventy *millions* of pounds, and persuade some white woman to *sacrifice* herself to him. . . . Shall we keep this class of people in everlasting degradation, for fear one of their descendants *may* marry our great-great-great-great-grandchild?
>
> While the prejudice exists, such unions cannot take place; and when the prejudice is melted away, they will cease to be a degradation, and of course cease to be an evil. (140)

Thirty-four years later (well short of the "hundred" envisioned here) Child would translate this prediction into a novel advocating interracial marriage as the ultimate solution to racial prejudice: *A Romance of the Republic* (1867).

As Child had somberly expected, the *Appeal* outraged a public that had just canonized her as a paragon of feminine virtue. No portion of it touched a rawer nerve than her indictment of northern racial prejudice. In a vitriolic ten-page rejoinder a prominent Colonizationist clergyman, Leonard Bacon, indignantly contested the charge that prejudice was more rampant in the North than in the South. Characterizing the Prudence Crandall case as exceptional and blaming abolitionists for having fomented the excitement, he personally denied ever having sought to "discourage or embarrass the people of color, in their struggles after knowledge and respectability." "If Mrs. Child has any confessions [of her own] to make, very well," he sneered; "only . . . let her not attempt to impute the same guilt to the public sentiment of New England."[55]

Negative reviews were the least of the trials Child had to face. Her beloved Convers, to whom she had looked up all her life, dismayed her by counseling prudence and charity toward southerners and exhibiting the constitutional timidity of a minister dependent on a wealthy congregation for support. Her elder brother, James, who had named his daughters Lydia Maria and Mary Conant, turned hostile; a Jacksonian Democrat, he could not stomach either "niggers" or "nigger-lovers." Her father, though he sympathized warmly with her abolitionist principles, did not extend the same sympathy toward David, but instead blamed his son-in-law for the heavy financial price of the couple's antislavery activism. Only David's family backed the couple wholeheartedly (David's sister Lucretia would express her ardent identification with the abolitionist cause by naming her three children George Thompson, William Lloyd Garrison, and Lydia Maria Child).[56]

Friendships, as well as family ties, gave way under the pressure of social disapproval. Lois Curtis, under whose roof David had proposed to Child, now snubbed the couple. Relations grew strained with morally earnest but conservative Lucy Osgood, who had mothered Child in her lonely youth and applauded her triumphs of authorship. Child herself felt compelled to stop seeing Emily Marshall, despite the kindness the Marshalls had always shown her; their paths in life had diverged after Emily's 1831 marriage into one of Boston's most aristocratic families, and Child had feared both that she would no longer find in her friend's "spirit an echo to the voice of mine" and that Emily's father-in-law, Boston mayor Harrison Gray Otis, would consider it politically embarrassing if she received an abolitionist in her home. When Emily died giving birth in 1836, Child's remorse knew no bounds.[57]

Abolition also came between Child and Catharine Maria Sedgwick, to whom she had dedicated *The Coronal*. Sedgwick noticeably "cooled" after Child sent her a copy of the *Appeal* and invited her to contribute to her projected antislavery gift book, *The Oasis*. In her tardy and temporizing reply, Sedgwick accepted only on condition that she not be viewed as "an advocate of the principles of the abolitionists." Slavery was "a dark & fearful subject," she ventured, and some abolitionist leaders were "foolish & doubtful zealots," besides which she could not see why abolitionists and Colonizationists were attacking each other when they had the "same aim." As Child judged bitterly in retrospect, Sedgwick "sincerely wished well to the negroes, but she could not bear to *contend* for them, or for anything else. . . . She was very deficient in moral *courage*" and "*afraid* of reformers," as well as of the slavery question.[58]

In addition to the pain of broken friendships, Child bore the cost of professional blacklisting as her erstwhile patrons among the Boston aristocracy mobilized against her. Former admirers like Harvard professor George Ticknor slammed their doors in her face, cut her dead in the street, and enforced a policy of ostracism toward anyone who violated the ban against her. The future attorney general of Massachusetts, James T. Austin, a political enemy of David's who several years later would defend the mob killing of an abolitionist editor as a patriotic act, hurled the *Appeal* out the window with a pair of tongs. The Boston Athenaeum withdrew the free library privileges Ticknor had induced the trustees to confer on Child in a token of esteem only one other woman, Hannah Adams, had been accorded (library privileges Child desperately needed for her research in progress on *The History of the Condition of Women*). Most damagingly, readers boycotted her writings, and parents canceled their subscriptions to the *Juvenile Miscellany. The Mother's Book* promptly went out of print, the *Miscellany* folded, and even sales of *The Frugal Housewife* plummeted, reducing Child's already meager income to a pittance.[59]

Although the *Appeal* destroyed Child's literary popularity and evicted her from Boston's salons, it propelled her to the forefront of the abolitionist movement, elevating her to a position of unparalled political influence for a woman. Abolitionists immediately hailed the *Appeal* as a "powerful auxiliary to the Anti-Slavery cause." "We were particularly struck with the appearance of extensive research which characterizes the work," commented the reviewer for the *Unionist*, a newspaper founded to support Prudence Crandall: "Written in a style, easy, simple and elegant; enlivened with occasional flashes of wit, rich in important facts, happy illustrations and forcible, conclusive reasoning—its satire delicate but keen; its appeals touching and powerful; its reproofs grave, just and severe, yet couched in a language courteous and dignified—it is altogether one of the most valuable publications which have for a long time fallen under our eye." Asserting that it was "impossible for any candid mind and unprejudiced person to read this book . . . without becoming a decided Abolitionist," the reviewer urged that copies be distributed to "every friend and every enemy of our cause." "[A]n armory well stored with weapons of approved temper," it would arm friends for combat and not only disarm enemies, but "enlist [them] under the banner of justice," he predicted.[60]

Abolitionist reviewers universally echoed his judgment. "[T]hat heart must be harder than the nether mill-stone, which can remain unaffected by the solemn truths" the *Appeal* so ably propounded, Oliver Johnson averred. "[I]t cannot fail to afford incalculable aid to the cause of universal emancipation," agreed a correspondent who praised the "noble independence" Child had shown by "hazard[ing] her glorious reputation" in defense of an "injured people."[61]

Soon, anecdotes bearing these reviewers out began appearing in the *Liberator*. A prominent Colonizationist and manager of the American Bible Society complained that his wife and daughter had gone over to the enemy since reading the *Appeal*. "I will not read the book," he swore, because "I do not mean to be an abolitionist." The heiress of a large slave estate, induced by friends to read the *Appeal* while on a visit to the North, had "thrown [it] down in anger," only to find herself impelled to take it up again and yield at last to its persuasion. Promising to free her slaves, she had determined to learn how to do her own housework. (One can imagine her being handed *The Frugal Housewife* to help her on her way.)[62]

As these anecdotes indicate, Child played an instrumental role in bringing women into the movement at an early stage. Indeed, reviewers again and again expressed the hope that women would be "provoked to emulation, by the example of Miss Crandall and Mrs. Child." "[W]e need the aid of our virtuous and principled females," they proclaimed. "[N]othing great and good can be accomplished in our country without their assistance. . . . Should *they*, one and all, lend their aid to the cause of emancipation, we might safely predict, that at no distant period, this horrible stain, this humiliating reproach, would be wiped away from our nation forever!"[63]

Child's influence was by no means confined to women. With her calm, rational tone; her method of allowing facts to speak for themselves; and her technique of framing conclusions as rhetorical questions that engaged the reader in a dialogue—she succeeded in converting readers repelled by Garrison's scathing denunciations and alien to the world of religious revivalism out of which Garrison had emerged. Men trained in the discourses of legal argumentation, scholarly induction, and Unitarian-style preaching responded to the *Appeal* in a way that they could not respond to the thunderous accents of the evangelical exhorter summoning sinners to repentance—the rhetoric that was Garrison's forte.

The *Appeal* recruited into abolitionist ranks a new cadre of leaders who would extend the antislavery movement in many directions. A roll call of those who would credit the *Appeal* with exercising a "formative influence" on their thinking—and often with changing their lives—furnishes a gauge of the political authority Child achieved. It includes the Unitarian minister William Ellery Channing, idol of the Boston aristocracy and a vital mediator between abolitionists and their conservative opponents; his fellow Unitarian, John Gorham Palfrey, Massachusetts state legislator and quondam editor of the *North American Review* (in which he had published the review of *Yamoyden* that had sparked Child's literary career); the brilliant, Harvard-trained lawyer Wendell Phillips, star orator of the antislavery movement and second only to Garrison in its councils; the Transcendentalist militant Thomas Wentworth Higginson, who went on to lead the first black regiment in the Civil War, publish the first collection of African American spirituals, write the first biography of Margaret Fuller, and introduce the world to the poetry of Emily Dickinson; the Massachusetts senator and future vice president under Ulysses S. Grant, Henry Wilson; and, above all, the towering leader of the Radical Republicans, Charles Sumner, largely responsible for the legislative victories of Reconstruction. Over a forty-year period these men would read Child's publications, heed the advice she offered in adroit letters on public policy, and seek her endorsement of the aims and strategies they pursued. Higginson's 1868 testimonial best sums up their considered judgment of the *Appeal*: "As it was the first anti-slavery work ever printed in America in book form, so I have always thought it the ablest; that is, it covered the whole ground better than any other."[64]

The decades following the publication of the *Appeal* would find Child's name blazoned on an editorial masthead and her articles featured prominently in the major newspapers that shaped antislavery and later Radical Republican ideology; her books and pamphlets distributed to members of Congress, as well as to antislavery lecturers, for whom the *Appeal* constituted required reading; and her utterances targeted for rebuttal by opinion-makers of the dominant camp. Baptized in the fires of abolitionism and reconsecrated as a proselytizer for the cause of black liberation, she would indeed become what Garrison titled her at the dawn of her career: *"the first woman in the republic."*

9

An Antislavery Marriage: Careers
at Cross-Purposes

Why, sir, whilst the thunders of a Garrison were rocking this land, . . . almost all its population were as hard as the rocks. . . . But when the melting notes of a Mrs. Child began to move upon the minds of the people, like the voice of mercy from Calvary, all the population that heard it seemed to melt as if by the magic touch of the finger of an angel of mercy.[1]

This tribute by the Reverend Henry Ludlow encapsulates the new identity Child had assumed in the wake of the *Appeal*. Canonized as a saint for her sacrifice of fame and livelihood to plead on behalf of an oppressed people, credited with the divine power to create light out of darkness and to bring a sinful nation to repentance, she occupied a position rivaling Garrison's in the abolitionist pantheon; indeed, the Reverend Mr. Ludlow cast her in the role of Christ and associated Garrison with the Old Testament prophets. "One Mrs. Child has done more to wake up the people to effort in this cause of God and humanity, than all the men that went before her in this country," he contended.

Similar panegyrics abound in the abolitionist press. An admirer who encountered Child on a boat to New York in February 1835 wrote enthusiastically to the *Liberator*:

> This lady is truly an ornament to her sex, to our metropolis, to our country. Possessing not only talents of the highest order, but elevated and noble senti- ments, pure and philanthropic principles, a fearless and undaunted spirit, she is admirably qualified to act a distinguished part in that great work of benevolence in which she has enlisted; the redemption from bondage and degradation of "that class of Americans, called Africans."[2]

In a more rationalistic vein, a speaker replying to the "sneers" of men who pronounced women incapable of understanding politics cited "the works of Mrs. Child, a woman, upon this subject." Compared with her antislavery writings, he asserted, "all that the greatest *statesmen* in the country (who, of course, do understand the subject) have ever written and spoken, upon the other side, is straw and stubble."[3] Such eulogies testify to

Child's stature as an antislavery propagandist, second only to Garrison in her output and influence, and ranked above him by those who preferred her low-key, modulated style.

For the third time in her life Child had dramatically redirected her career and come before the public in a vastly different guise. Just as the baker's daughter had metamorphosed into the author of *Hobomok* and the aspiring literary genius had donned the garb of the Frugal Housewife, so the oracle of domestic advice now stepped forth as the angel of the abolitionist cause, whose talismanic *Appeal* magically converted lifelong bigots into devoted friends of the slave. While embracing her new vocation, Child nevertheless continued to suffer from agonizing conflicts as she sought to reconcile incompatible private needs and public roles. She still longed to win literary distinction in the realm of the imagination where she had always been most at home, felt more driven than ever to live up to the ideal of the "perfect wife," and craved her husband's love above all else, even as she mastered the male discourse of antislavery polemic and boldly defied the taboos barring women from the political sphere. These conflicts are discernible in every aspect of her life and work over the next half-decade. They find expression in the range of her corpus, which includes four more antislavery classics: *The Oasis* (1834), *Authentic Anecdotes of American Slavery* (1835, 1838), an *Anti-Slavery Catechism* (1836), and *The Evils of Slavery, and the Cure of Slavery* (1836); a two-volume *History of the Condition of Women, in Various Ages and Nations* (1835); a novel reflecting her penchant for Transcendentalist mysticism, *Philothea* (1836); and her last domestic advice book, *The Family Nurse* (1837). Within the works themselves, Child's ambivalences surface not only in prefaces frankly avowing her preference for romantic fantasies over practical realities, but in conceptualizations that straddle opposing allegiances, like the literary and artistic cast of *The Oasis* and the curious avoidance of feminist theory in the *History of Women*. Child's self-divisions also permeate her letters; and they simultaneously shape and restrict the forms of activism she chooses. Ultimately, the civil war raging inside her would block her literary productivity altogether.

Paralleling and interacting with Child's battle of selves, David was undergoing his own destructive role conflicts. The political partnership the couple had cemented after their marriage had at first corresponded to Child's idealized description of the Rolands'. Like her idol, Madame Roland, who had lent her literary skills to her husband's political work but allowed him to take credit for her writings, Child had helped run the *Massachusetts Journal* and, under the cover of anonymity, contributed increasingly to its editorial as well as its literary columns. But with her husband's blessing, she had broken out of that mold to address the issue of slavery.

Besides initiating Child into political journalism, David had blazed the path that led her to write her *Appeal*. As editor of the *Massachusetts Journal and Tribune* (the last avatar of his newspaper, by 1830 reduced to a weekly), he had devoted unusually extensive coverage to abolition.[4] In addition to occasional reprints from the *Liberator*, he had published articles attacking antimiscegenation laws and defending the establishment of colleges for African Americans (then being furiously opposed by local elites). He had given further proof of his courage in editorials praising Garrison and championing Nat Turner amid the hysterical reaction of a press that blamed the revolt on abolitionist incendiaries. But in February 1832 the *Journal and Tribune* had folded, leaving David bereft of his main mouthpiece and source of professional identity, just when his wife was reaching the peak of her popularity.

Despite the *Journal's* collapse, David had gone on to publish one of the movement's earliest and most militant antislavery tracts, *The Despotism of Freedom*. In the process of researching and writing it, David had shared many of his ideas with his wife and encouraged her to publish a tract of her own. Yet no sooner had she done so than her performance had eclipsed his. While reviewers had lavished praise on the style of the *Appeal*, they had complained of *The Despotism of Freedom*, "The style of Mr. Child, is not what would be called easy, flowing and elegant."[5] It was Mrs. Child, not Mr. Child or the Childs as a couple, whom the abolitionist public elevated to celebrity. In the political partnership the Childs had established, husband and wife had all but reversed roles.

Such a reversal would still be very difficult for most husbands to accept today, but in an era when the ideology of domesticity and separate spheres reigned supreme, it must have been excruciatingly painful for both Childs to adjust to. After David's death, Child would confess to one of his college classmates: "It has always been a source of regret to me that my dear husband lacked facility in imparting his great store of knowledge to others. It was always a laborious task to him to write, or to speak to an audience; so that few knew how to appreciate him at his real value."[6] As the two were pioneering a new model of conjugal relations and struggling to repress feelings of competitiveness toward each other that contradicted their ideals, neither of them could yet admit that talents and accomplishments had been unevenly divided between them. Nor could they find a satisfactory solution to the problem. Both Childs had shown themselves to be intensely ambitious, yet ambition inevitably triggered competitiveness and guilt. Both were thus trying desperately to quell or deny their ambitions at greater and greater psychological cost.

David's role conflicts probably did not originate in rivalry with his wife, but lay much deeper. Long before his marriage, he had formed a pattern of sabotaging the career he thought he wanted — most obviously when he left his post at the American legation in Portugal to fight in Spain's war for self-determination. Whether because he felt secretly inadequate or out of place in the world of letters he had compelled to open its doors to him by dint of his intellectual powers, or whether because he could not decide between his aspirations for upward mobility and his class identity as a farmer's son, David repeatedly veered away from the intellectual occupations for which his Harvard education had equipped him. He would bring to his new career as an antislavery activist the same clashing impulses and unresolved problems of identity that had dogged all his previous ventures. And once again, they would have a disastrous impact on his wife's career.

Child had already weathered one experience of letting her husband's needs dictate her professional priorities. As a new bride, however, she had found it relatively easy to talk herself into sharing David's optimism about his prospects. She had not yet observed his work habits and financial irresponsibility at close hand, nor had she come crashing up against his poor judgment. Now that David had lost two libel suits he had confidently expected to win, and contracted debts totaling more than $15,000 without managing to set the *Massachusetts Journal* on a sound financial footing, Child could no longer maintain her faith in her husband's ability to succeed professionally. She had to willfully shut her eyes to the mounting evidence that he was causing much of his own ill luck (as she would confess ten years later).[7] Moreover, this time David would have nothing to offer her in return for again deflecting her career. Instead of initiating her into a new vocation, he would be depriving her of all her literary resources.

The record of the couple's careers after the *Appeal* drew Child into the political limelight reveals a brief period of successful partnership in antislavery activism; then, on Child's part an explosion of creativity followed by sudden silence; and on David's several years of flailing around, during which he drifted to the margins of the abolitionist movement, carrying his wife with him, as he sought to translate his antislavery ideals into a financially rewarding enterprise. It is a record full of paradoxes. Interestingly, one of Garrison's sons would put his finger on the central paradox after Child's death, when a selected edition of her letters first became available to the public. "[T]his work fails to throw light on the problem why so exceptionally gifted a couple as David Lee and Lydia Maria Child did not make more of themselves," he noted, drawing attention to "the reader's sense of an anti-climax in their public careers." The two questions that most puzzled him were why "the author of 'Hobomok,' 'The Rebels,' and 'Philothea' was not led to produce an anti-slavery romance anticipating 'Uncle Tom's Cabin'"; and why David—"a scholar, a classical teacher, a journalist, an able lawyer, at one time a member of the Massachusetts Legislature, an indefatigable writer, who rendered infinite service in unmasking the pro slavery conspiracy which fomented the . . . annexation of Texas," ended up withdrawing almost completely "from an agitation in whose beginning he bore so conspicuous a part."[8] The answers to those questions seem to reside in the difficulties the Childs wrestled with in the 1830s— David's professional failures and their effect on both his ego and the couple's marriage; the unacknowledged rivalry between husband and wife and the unconscious resentment it generated in both of them—resentment that could be repressed only by total self-censorship; and, finally, the mutually destructive interaction between David's tendency to cast himself in the role of a Child requiring perpetual mothering and Child's compulsion to sacrifice everything to her insatiable hunger for love.

However darkly the decade ended for the Childs, their new life as abolitionists began happily. Child would always look back with special fondness on that early phase of consecration to the cause, when the hearts of Garrison's apostles were knit together as one. The year before her public espousal of abolition, Child's earnings from *The Frugal Housewife* and *The Mother's Book* had at last enabled her to exchange the discomforts of cheap boardinghouses for the "humble little home" of which she had so long dreamed: "a very small cottage, with a *very* small garden *filled* with flowers." She and David called it "Le Paradis des Pauvres." Located at Cottage Place on the Neck in Roxbury, it overlooked the harbor. "The sea dashed under the windows, and was often sparkling with moon-beams when we went to bed," Child reminisced in a manuscript "Auto-biography" of 1875.[9]

Enhancing the charms of this home was its proximity to the Lorings. Their little daughter, "Nony," would toddle over regularly to play with the Childs' gray cat—and to receive the extra mothering Child wished she could bestow on a daughter of her own. In turn, the Childs would often drop in on the Lorings for a chat over the breakfast table, at which Ellis and Louisa liked to loiter until late in the morning. Frequently, other abolitionist visitors could be found there. Ostracized by their former associates, the young reformers kept up each other's spirits by banding together and reconstituting a tight circle of friends, bound no longer by class but by political commitment. Their numbers were so few in those days that they hailed each new convert with excitement. Child particularly liked to recall one occasion when she arrived at the Lorings' as they were rejoicing over their latest recruit. " 'Oh Maria, how we wanted you here last evening!' " Ellis had exclaimed: "We had a charming visitor. A young gentleman beautiful in person and full of talent. He told us a friend had lately induced him to read several things on the subject of slavery; among the rest your Appeal. . . . When he left us he said, 'Perhaps I shall be compelled to declare myself an Abolitionist; for I confess I don't see how any man can honestly evade this great question.' " The "beautiful young man," it turned out, was Wendell Phillips, soon to emerge as one of the abolitionist movement's most spellbinding orators.[10]

Another intimate, whose home on Poplar Street provided a haven for abolitionists during that early phase, was Henrietta Sargent. She and her elder sister, Catherine, served "cozy dinners" and "nice cups of tea" to the friends who gathered to strategize or exchange experiences of rebuffs.[11] Before long, Maria Weston Chapman and her husband, Henry, a merchant who had forsworn dealing in cotton, joined the group, providing it with what became its social headquarters—the parlor of their Chauncy Place mansion. "[V]ivacious, witty," and regal, Chapman cut a splendid figure, with her "dazzling complexion," "golden hair," and "swift eyes of clear steel-blue." Child delighted in quoting her aphorisms, among which her favorite was "*God* often makes use of instruments, that *I* would n't touch with a pair of tongs." Equally committed to abolitionism, Chapman's sisters Deborah, Caroline, Lucia, and Anne Warren Weston managed an integrated primary school on Boylston Street. The clan also included Henry's sister Ann Greene Chapman and Chapman's cousin Ann Terry Greene, who lived with the Chapmans and would shortly marry Wendell Phillips. It was she who had given him Child's *Appeal* to read.[12]

Abolitionists needed all the strength they derived from their support networks for outside their close-knit social circle they confronted a cruelly hostile world. Lawyers like Loring and Sewall lost wealthy clients (though they could afford these losses better than David, thanks to family inheritances). Ministers like Samuel J. May and Amos Phelps lost their pulpits. Men and women who had held secure positions in society found themselves the targets of snubs, sneers, and malicious gossip. Attending church became an ordeal rather than a comfort, as fellow parishioners turned their backs, and disapproving ministers sermonized against un-Christian attacks on slave-holders. To her dismay, Child discovered that her Swedenborgian congregation was no exception. "[B]itterly pro-slavery, and . . . intensely bigotted," her pastor, Thomas Worcester, would not support abolition until 1864, when Child's tract *The Right Way the Safe Way* (1860) convinced him that "it was *safe* and *profitable* for the sinner to repent," as she commented acidly.[13]

Opponents of abolitionism did not confine themselves to ridicule, social ostracism, economic boycott, and religious excommunication. Determined to quash a movement they viewed as a threat to the nation's economic prosperity and political unity, the elites who benefited from ties to the South used every means of repression at their disposal. They barred antislavery speakers from churches and public meeting halls. Finding that this did not suffice, they unleashed a campaign of mob violence against abolitionists. Across the country, beginning in October 1833 and rising to a peak in the "mob year" 1835, crowds of thugs led by "gentlemen of property and standing" stormed aboli-tionist meetings, pelting the speakers and participants with brickbats and rotten eggs. Mobs also threatened prominent leaders with lynching, vandalized abolitionist offices, destroyed antislavery printing presses, and precipitated orgies of arson that leveled homes, assembly halls, and entire African American neighborhoods. In the South they broke into post offices, ransacked the mails for antislavery publications, and burned the "offensive documents" in bonfires set under effigies of abolitionist leaders, whom they hung in mock lynchings.[14]

But the movement continued to grow in dialectical relation with the onslaught against it. Indeed, one historian has argued that what prompted the ferocity of the antiabolitionist campaign was the rapid proliferation of abolition societies after 1832 rather than the launching of Garrison's *Liberator* in 1831 or the fears generated by the Nat Turner revolt later that year.[15] By December 1833, less than two years after Garrison's band of twelve apostles had founded the New England Anti-Slavery Soci-ety—the first to pledge itself to the goal of "immediate abolition"—forty-seven such associations had sprung up in ten states, and abolitionists were ready to form a cen-tralized national organization, the American Anti-Slavery Society, with headquarters in New York.[16] Symbolizing their intention of completing the work of the Founding Fathers by fulfilling the promise of liberty and equality set forth in the Declaration of Independence, abolitionists chose Philadelphia as the site of their national convention and issued a Declaration of Sentiments that spelled out the relationship they saw between their enterprise and their Revolutionary forebears':

> Their principles led them to wage war against their oppressors, and to spill human blood like water, in order to be free. Ours forbid the doing of evil that good may come, and lead us to reject, and to entreat the oppressed to reject, the use of all carnal weapons for deliverance from bondage; relying solely upon those which are spiritual. . . .
>
> Their measures were physical resistance. . . . Ours shall be such only as the opposition of moral purity to moral corruption—the destruction of error by the

potency of truth—the overthrow of prejudice by the power of love—and the abolition of slavery by the spirit of repentance.

Besides committing the American Anti-Slavery Society to pacifist means, the Declaration of Sentiments vowed to work within the legal limits prescribed by the U.S. Constitution. The signers ended by echoing and redefining the Declaration of Independence's rousing conclusion as they pledged to deliver their country from the curse of slavery and "to secure to the colored population of the United States, all the rights and privileges which belong to them as men, and as Americans—come what may to our persons, our interests, or our reputation—whether we live to witness the triumph of Liberty, Justice and Humanity, or perish untimely as martyrs in this great, benevolent, and holy cause."[17]

The Childs did not participate in the historic occasion because they could not afford the expense of traveling to Philadelphia, but David played an active role in the New England Anti-Slavery Society, which remained the primary forum of abolitionists in the Boston area. Through 1834 the couple's political partnership functioned well, with neither partner predominating. David collaborated with Child on her project of editing an antislavery gift book, *The Oasis*, to which he contributed three articles. They attended antislavery meetings together, at which Child took a backseat, as was customary for women, while David delivered speeches and proposed resolutions.

At the August 1 celebration of the British Parliament's abolition of slavery in its West Indian colonies, David gave the key oration.[18] He also maintained a high profile at the New England Anti-Slavery Convention that May. As part of the group's effort to combat racial discrimination, he volunteered to compile a list of "taverns, stages, and steam-boats" that accommodated blacks on equal terms, so that abolitionists could confine their patronage to facilities compatible with their principles. In addition, David presented a detailed report on the domestic slave trade, which he showed to be as cruel as the banned African slave trade. The legal argument he formulated in the report was especially significant. By demonstrating that the Constitution's interstate commerce clause gave the federal government the authority to abolish the domestic slave trade, David furnished abolitionists with a concrete means of legislating against slavery within the limits of the Constitution, which barred any federal interference with the states' internal affairs.[19] Strategically, moreover, abolition of the interstate trade would have dealt the slave system a mortal blow, since the profitability of slavery in the upper South depended on exporting surplus slaves from its declining plantations, while the economic viability of slavery in the deep South states carved out of the Louisiana Purchase depended on a perpetual replenishment of the labor supply. Thus, David was here engaged in a central abolitionist endeavor.

The same was true of David's work in two related areas that offered scope for interracial cooperation: the protection of free blacks against kidnapping and the founding of academies to train them for middle-class professions. The kidnapping of free blacks occurred on such a large scale that blacks had organized vigilance committees in their communities to identify suspected kidnappers, mobilize witnesses to testify in favor of friends and neighbors claimed as fugitive slaves, and mount rescue operations where legal avenues failed.[20] White abolitionists proved to be invaluable allies in kidnapping cases, both by bringing them to public attention and by supplying legal advice and testimony in court. In 1833, while serving as a justice of the peace, David recorded and appended to *The Despotism of Freedom* the sworn affidavits of three Boston blacks who attested to the kidnapping of numerous relatives and friends. He was immediately accused of libel by one of the alleged kidnappers — an indication of how much harassment abolitionists risked in such solidarity efforts.[21]

David's last significant contribution of 1834 was to participate in the founding of a college pledged to admit "colored youth of good character on equal terms with whites of like character" — the Noyes Academy in Canaan, New Hampshire. Along with his friend Samuel Sewall, David served as a trustee of the institution. He even signed up to join its faculty as "Paramount Instructor," though he never fulfilled this intention. When the Noyes Academy opened its doors in the winter of 1835, David was preoccupied with what would prove to be the last legal case of his career. And within six months the college would meet the same fate as Prudence Crandall's school two years earlier. Once again, opponents fomented hysterical fears that the "village was to be overrun with negroes from the South" and that "paupers and vagabonds" would "inundate the industrious town." This time they did not bother to pass retroactive laws or to file suit against the school's managers. Instead, three hundred self-styled patriots, who professed to be acting in "the spirit of '75," tore the offending building down and dragged it into a swamp with the help of a hundred yoke of oxen.[22]

If David did not have the opportunity to teach at the short-lived interracial college he had helped found, he did have the satisfaction of receiving two major votes of confidence from his fellow abolitionists. In January 1835 — the height of his prominence in Garrisonian ranks — he was elected vice president of the Massachusetts Anti-Slavery Society and nominated for the U.S. Senate in a bid to put up a "thorough abolitionist" candidate. Endorsed separately by Garrison, the letter of nomination in the *Liberator* must have deeply gratified David: "If we look for a man well skilled in national politics, manly and independent in his opinions, fearless and eloquent in avowing and supporting them, one who has clear, correct and honest purposes, and sound and settled principles of action on such subjects as will come before the Senate — where shall we find a better Senator, than David Lee Child?"[23] David's dreams of combining his political ambitions with his abolitionist ideals would never materialize, however. No "thorough abolitionist" stood a chance of being elected to national office in 1835 (indeed not until 1848 would Salmon P. Chase become the first antislavery politician to win a Senate seat); and by the time a handful of politicians representing antislavery congressional districts had succeeded in penetrating the House of Representatives in the 1840s, David had lost all professional credibility.

While David was formulating abolitionist strategy, campaigning against racial discrimination, and attempting to establish institutions for African American uplift and black-white solidarity, Child was busy extending the outreach of the antislavery movement, both through personal contacts and through her writings. No allies then seemed more vital to recruit than the clergy, and no clergyman in Boston wielded a greater influence than the dean of Unitarian ministers, William Ellery Channing. Notwithstanding his reputation for liberalism, Channing was firmly opposed to abolitionist agitation and had tried to prevent his parishioners from joining antislavery societies.[24] Many of Child's abolitionist friends — among them the Lorings, Chapmans, Sewalls, and Sargents — attended his church, and though they defied his proscription, they recognized him as a crucial adversary to convert. Child acted as their emissary.

Soon after writing the *Appeal*, Child sent Channing a copy. The book made such a strong impression on him that he walked all the way from his fashionable neighborhood on Mt. Vernon Street to her "Paradis des Pauvres" at Cottage Place to thank her for having aroused his conscience to the duty of breaking his silence on slavery. The conversation lasted three hours. Channing "expressed great joy at the publication of the 'Appeal'" and urged Child "never to desert the cause through evil report or good report"; inveterately ambivalent, however, he worried that she "went too far." It was the first of numerous exchanges, which gradually overcame the genteel minister's qualms about identifying himself with a group of reformers he and his wealthy patrons viewed as noisy fanatics.[25]

Two years later, Channing produced his own book, *Slavery* (1835), in which he condemned the institution "in language [as] strong, bold, and displeasing to oppressors" as any abolitionist's — but simultaneously criticized abolitionists for advocating immediate emancipation, fomenting "excitement" among their foes, admitting blacks into their societies, and seeking a mass base for their movement instead of relying on the sober and judicious. Published in the throes of the "mob year," Channing's lukewarm endorsement of their cause bitterly disappointed abolitionists, who had hoped he would act to stem the tide of hostility against them. In a long review Child tactfully but plainly exposed the fallacies in Channing's strictures, while praising him for speaking out against slavery.[26]

At Loring's behest, she also visited Channing repeatedly in the mid-1830s to continue the dialogue in person. Child liked to depict herself as a "busy *mouse* . . . gnawing away the net-work, which aristocratic family and friends are all the time weaving around the *lion*,"[27] but she often grew impatient with Channing's shilly-shallying. "What a pity that a mind like his should be bound round with Lilliputian cords," she raged after one such visit. "My soul has suffered many a shivering ague-fit in attempting to melt, or batter away, the glaciers of his prejudice, false refinement, and beautiful *theories*, into which the breath of life was never infused by being boldly brought into *action*."[28] Though she vowed never to "approach him, or his tribe" again, Loring prevailed on her to return to the charge. On the next occasion she admitted that Channing "had progressed (as we Yankees say) considerably since I last conversed with him." True, he "still betrayed his characteristic timidity" — "Almost every sentence began with, 'I am doubtful,' or 'I am afraid'" — but he had abandoned his objections to the tactic of petitioning Congress and had even agreed to let his signature head the 1836 "Boston Petition for the abolition of slavery in [the] District of Columbia."[29] He would take increasingly bolder public stands in support of abolitionist initiatives over the next few years, joining in the campaign against the annexation of Texas as well as in protests against mob violence and the infringement of civil liberties.[30]

Shortly before his death in 1842, Channing would pay Child a moving tribute. In a pair of letters thanking her for her labors on behalf of the oppressed and acknowledging the "profit" he had derived from her writings, he would confess that he had found her courageous example both inspiring and chastening: "I had heard so often of your brave endurance of adversity, and was conscious of having suffered so little myself for truth and humanity, that I almost questioned my right to send you encouraging words," the famous minister would admit to the woman who characterized herself as a "mouse." Frankly owning to his innate "shrinking from the work of reform" that Child had shouldered without repining and impelled him to undertake in spite of himself, he would humbly affirm: "But on this very account the work is good for me. I need it . . . to save me from a refined selfishness, to give me force, disinterestedness, true dignity and elevation, to link me by a new faith to God, by a deeper love to my race, and to make me a blessing to the world."[31]

Channing was only one of the many key opinion-makers Child brought into anti-slavery ranks. She did not enjoy allaying the scruples of nervous clergymen, however, and preferred to concentrate on her true vocation — influencing the general public through her writings.

Once the *Appeal* was off her hands, Child set about repackaging its antislavery message for a broader audience. Always a shrewd literary entrepreneur, she realized that the Christmas and New Year's gift book offered an ideal medium for winning new converts to the abolitionist cause. A tasteful volume timed for the holiday season, modeled on the *Token* and *Atlantic Souvenir*, and featuring poems, fictional and nonfictional narra-tives, witty anecdotes, and biographical sketches, along with a judicious sprinkling of ideological statements, might win admittance into drawing rooms firmly barred against the *Appeal* or the *Liberator*. And a feminine genre read in a domestic setting could enlist essential allies for the cause within the confines of "woman's sphere," where domestic ideology accorded wives and mothers moral influence over husbands and sons.

Child designed every detail of *The Oasis* to attract as wide a spectrum of readers as possible — and to educate them in undiluted abolitionist principles by appealing to their aesthetic senses. The volume's patterned green cloth binding with the title stamped in gold on the spine between two vignettes presents the inviting appearance typical of the gift book. The title, *The Oasis*, likewise conforms to genre, recalling such analogues as The *Amaranth, The Amulet,* and *The Talisman*.[32] Yet it simultaneously prompts reflection. Taken literally, it suggests the topography of Saharan Africa and conveys a subtle reminder that Western civilization originated in Egypt (as the poem and engraving "Ruins of Egyptian Thebes" reiterate in the text). Taken symbolically, it refers to the moral desert of slavery, in which the abolitionist movement stands as an oasis.

The title page conveys its message iconographically. Framed by the mottoes "Strike, but hear!" and "The *Truth* shall make us free" is an engraving of an open Bible, resting on a rock that rises, like Mount Sinai, out of storm clouds. Beneath the Bible lies a pile of chains, which the Bible partially conceals, and enveloped in the clouds is a serpent shooting its forked tongue at the sacred text—twin allusions to the clergy's use of Scripture to justify slavery. But the sun is rising behind the mountain, illuminating the open page and portending the ultimate triumph of light over darkness, truth over falsehood, freedom over slavery. The iconography continues throughout the volume, which is lavishly illustrated in the classic gift book tradition—except that the subjects are preponderantly African.[33]

To enhance the literary quality of *The Oasis*, Child sought works by the best poets in antislavery ranks: John Greenleaf Whittier and his sister, Elizabeth; Hannah Flagg Gould, a former contributor to the *Juvenile Miscellany*; and Eliza Lee Cabot Follen, also a popular children's writer. In addition, Child made a point of including a black voice among the authors. Thus, she solicited a narrative by the former slave James Bradley, who had bought his own freedom and gone on to study at Lane Seminary in Ohio. Complementing Bradley's autobiographical sketch is Child's article "Voices from the South," which re-creates the eighteen-day debate over slavery and abolitionism at Lane, culminating in the mass conversion of James Bradley's white classmates, many of them southern slaveholders. That event—one of the most dramatic in antislavery annals—had dominated the *Liberator*'s headlines in the spring of 1834 and brought a new influx of recruits into the abolitionist movement, some of whom would assume major roles in years to come.

Child also involved David in the project—a strategy that served both to maintain the couple's political partnership and to incorporate the theme of slave resistance into *The Oasis* without violating gender conventions. David provided a biographical sketch of Henry Diaz, slave hero of Brazil's war against the Dutch; an account of "The Three Colored Republics of Guiana" founded by slave maroons, exemplifying blacks' bravery and capacity for self-government; and a legal analysis of "Judicial Decisions in Slave States" and their implications.

Yet Child herself wrote the bulk of *The Oasis*. Her opening statement "To the Public" strikes the keynote. "Even if you would *allow* me to exert the power of persuasion against the perfect freedom of your own conclusions," Child assures her readers, "I should have no wish to avail myself of that power." Instead, she "beseech[es]" them "not to trust the gross misrepresentations of interested or thoughtless persons" but to "examine candidly, and judge in freedom," what the truth is. "I have great confidence in the good sense and good feelings of the American people," she affirms.

Her preface articulates the purpose implicit in so many of the engravings and selections: "to familiarize the public mind with the idea that colored people are *human beings*—elevated or degraded by the same circumstances that elevate or degrade other men" (vii). The same purpose, of course, had animated the *Appeal*, yet *The Oasis* presents pictorially and dramatically the themes Child had developed analytically in its predecessor. Using narrative and visual representation rather than argument, selections like "Malem-Boo," "Henry Diaz," "Joanna," "Scipio Africanus," and "History of

Thomas Jenkins" challenge racial prejudice by creating positive images of African culture; promoting sympathy and respect for blacks; celebrating their intellectual achievements, military prowess, and moral virtues; championing their right to fight for freedom; defending intermarriage; and showing that other white nations have rewarded deserving blacks with honorable positions.

The most innovative of these selections is undoubtedly Child's story "Malem-Boo. The Brazilian Slave." The only piece in *The Oasis* to be illustrated by two full-page engravings and two vignettes, it showcases the cause of the slave and arouses readers' sympathies through art as well as fiction. Child was one of the first writers to realize the potency of fiction as a medium for overcoming readers' prejudices and converting them to abolitionism. Having pioneered the genre of antislavery fiction in *The Juvenile Miscellany*, she now oriented it toward adult readers. "Malem-Boo" is in fact an adult version of her children's story "Jumbo and Zairee," likewise centered on a family kidnapped from Africa.[34] Here, however, she shifts the focus to the father and develops the African setting in richer detail.

Combating the stereotypes of African savagery that served to justify slavery and the slave trade, the story draws an idyllic picture of life in the village where Malem-Boo and his wife, Yarrima, live with Yazoo, her infant son by an earlier marriage: "It is difficult to imagine human happiness more perfect than that enjoyed by these untaught children of nature," Child writes, applying to Africans the language of Romantic primitivism generally reserved for Indians and Polynesians: "Their hut, plastered with clay, and thatched with Palms, might have seemed rude to one accustomed to European luxury; but Yarrima knew nothing of this. Her husband was doatingly fond of her; and little Yazoo, her infant son, grew every day more intelligent and interesting. Then nature herself was so beautiful in that sunny clime!" (23). As in her Indian fiction, Child specifically translates harmony with nature into sexual freedom, and racial Others into vehicles for protesting against the sexual repressiveness of "civilized" society—a recurrent theme in her writings. "Among those primitive people, courtship is not a tedious process. The rules of civilized life have not as yet taught them to divorce their words and actions from the true affections of the heart," Child explains in describing how swiftly love leads to marriage for Malem-boo and Yarrima (23).

The evil that mars the family's bliss comes not from within their own society, but from Europe, in the person of "the cruel slave-trader" (24). To underscore the extensiveness of the slave trade, Child makes Yarrima doubly a victim of it—first when she and Yazoo are kidnapped from among her people, the Caffres, and carried overland in a coffle from which she escapes; next when Yazoo is kidnapped from the village near the Zambese in which she has settled with Malem-boo. Child pointedly contrasts African generosity and love with "Christian avarice, and civilized cruelty" (29). On learning of Yazoo's abduction, Malem-boo offers the whites all his gold in exchange for his stepson, only to be seized himself along with his gold.

In her ensuing account of the Middle Passage, Child spares few of its gruesome horrors: the dense packing of the captives into noisome holds; the daily weeding out of the diseased and dead slated to be thrown overboard; the whippings administered to make the captives "dance"; the suicides. Yet she also shows the victims' resistance and emphasizes the strength of African family ties. To save his stepson's life, Malem-boo gives the boy his own portion of water, for which act he is separated from the child and "lashed till his blood flowed freely on the deck" (33). Malem-boo eventually wins the battle of wills by going on a hunger strike until Yazoo is restored to him. Later in Brazil, after being sold apart from Yazoo, he refuses to work despite whippings, torture, starvation, and repeated resales. Only when his fourth master, an American, purchases the boy and promises the two their freedom "as soon as they had earned money enough to pay the price of their own bones and sinews" does Malem-boo cooperate; for now "exertion" has become "a matter of life and death" (39–40). Of his new master, Child comments drily: "Mr B——— . . . lavished thousands in matters of taste, or pleasure; but it never occurred to him that he could well afford to send Malem-boo and his child to Africa, without receiving any ransom" (40). By 1834 Child had acquired a keener understanding of the "kind" slaveholder's limitations than she had had while writing "Jumbo and Zairee" almost four years earlier.

In contrast to the happy ending she had offered the juvenile readers of "Jumbo and Zairee" by reuniting the entire family in Africa, Child leaves the ending of "Malem-boo" unresolved—a striking formal innovation for the time. "[S]hould Malem-boo regain his freedom, there is great danger that the avarice of white men will again enslave him, before he can reach his native shore," Child points out with uncompromising realism. As for Yarrima, Child suggests that the only reunion she can hope for is in "that better Africa, beyond the sky." In keeping with the iconographic character of *The Oasis*, the closure Child provides for the story is visual rather than verbal: a vignette of a bird hovering over an empty nest.

Technically and thematically, "Malem-boo" represents a rare achievement in antislavery fiction. The genre would ultimately develop in a different direction, toward a critique of American slavery rather than a vindication of African culture. Yet Child's first antislavery story for adults remains a hauntingly original contribution, at once lyrical and brutally honest in rendering a society superior in many ways to those of Europe and America, but ravaged by the slave trade.

Like the *Appeal*, *The Oasis* received universal praise in abolitionist circles. Garrison, who judged it "beautifully executed and powerfully written," predicted that it would "produce quite a sensation." "[T]his is a work of a high literary character, and worth double its price," agreed Nathaniel Southard, noting the attractive blend of "valuable information, thrilling incident, and interesting description," all conveyed in "a very agreeable style."[35]

Surprisingly, the most favorable and substantive review appeared not in the abolitionist press, but in the *Boston Daily Advocate*. The author, evidently an admirer who did not share Child's abolitionist convictions but continued to enjoy her writings, "especially commend[ed]" *The Oasis* to "those who have imbibed ungenerous prejudices against the most talented female in America, because she has espoused the hopeless and unpopular cause of the slave." If the book did not "change their feelings on the subject of slavery," he asserted, it would at least "compel" such readers to "respect the motives, and admire the disinterestedness of a female, who ventures so fearlessly and yet so unassumingly, in the profitless cause of philanthropy." He himself found in *The Oasis* the same qualities he had always esteemed in Child's works: "excellent sense and practical utility," combined with "what would seem to be their opposites, a fine imagination and a high-wrought enthusiasm of feeling and purpose." "[N]o sickly sensibility" marred the book, he assured readers hostile to abolition. Rather, they would be struck by its "elevated spirit of humanity, free from the fanaticism that weeps over imaginary and incurable evils, or the folly that seeks to establish equalities in conditions that are fundamentally irreconcilable."[36]

His forecast proved overly optimistic. Nevertheless, a scathing personal attack by an antiabolitionist reviewer did furnish telling evidence of the book's effectiveness as propaganda. "Mrs. Child has prepared . . . poison in the shape of an Annual. . . . She has insidiously endeavored to steal upon the early impressions of the mind, to tingle [tinge?] it with error under the treacherous form of amusement," he fumed. Though intended as a dismissal, the cutting jibe with which he ended his review constituted an inadvertent tribute: "[W]e would suggest to the authoress a return to her usual species of composition, fiction, as this volume bears evident marks of the vigor of that talent."[37]

Reviews alone do not provide a sufficient gauge of the book's readership and currency. References to the *Oasis* repeatedly crop up in the *Liberator*. For instance, a letter Garrison published "[t]o show how deep an interest is felt in the anti-slavery cause by some individuals at the south" also indicates how devoted a following Child commanded there in progressive circles. Its author, a correspondent from Maryland, had seen *The Oasis* advertised in the *Liberator* and requested three copies of the book and one of the *Appeal*. "I want to get the people, in my own section of country, to thinking on the subject of slavery, if possible," he explained.[38] Child's works seemed to him to be particularly well-adapted to that purpose. He was in fact incurring a tremendous risk by ordering "incendiary" publications outlawed in the South. Only four months later, a student from Lane Seminary, Amos Dresser, would be publicly whipped on his naked back in Nashville, Tennessee, for being found with three antislavery works in his possession, among them *The Oasis*.[39]

Garrison himself offers the best example of the influence *The Oasis* exerted. While editorializing on the upcoming election of 1834, he advised abolitionists to interrogate candidates about their stand on slavery and withhold their votes from those who would not commit themselves to emancipation — the practice of British Quakers, as described in an "instructive and pithy anecdote" by "Mrs. CHILD, in her beautiful anti-slavery annual, called 'THE OASIS.' "[40]

The Oasis even inspired a poem. When J. H. Le Roy presented a copy of the book to a friend whom he hoped it would convert to abolitionism, he inscribed on the flyleaf a long, versified plea that echoed Child's preface to the *Appeal* and summed up what she had sought to accomplish through an antislavery gift book:

> Read, read it! for the sake of him
> Whose hand has traced this line;
> Read, read it! though you ne'er again
> Look on a gift of mine.[41]

Despite the high repute *The Oasis* enjoyed, its sales disappointed Child. In the hopes of reaching a broader audience than an antislavery press could have commanded, she had had the book published commercially at her own expense by the prestigious firm of Allen and Ticknor, which had taken over her previous firm, Carter and Hendee.[42] The engravings and binding represented a considerable investment, and Child borrowed $100 each from Samuel Sewall and Ellis Loring to finance the venture. Five years later, she was still struggling to repay the debt. Too proud to let her more prosperous friends take over the burden, she even tried to make them accept interest on the loan. Of course, they indignantly refused. Remonstrating with her, Loring claimed not to remember how much he had advanced her. Speaking for Sewall as well, he added: "The Oasis was no private affair of yours. It was an offering to the cause — a most costly one — and one which [Sewall] exceedingly urged your making. He was very sanguine of its pecuniary success."[43]

There was actually good reason to be "sanguine" about the "pecuniary success" of an antislavery gift book, as Maria Chapman would demonstrate the very year this exchange of correspondence took place (1839). Modeled on *The Oasis*, but executed on a more modest scale, financed through outright donations, and sold at the yearly Anti-Slavery Fair, Chapman's *The Liberty Bell* would become the fund-raising abolitionist literary annual Child had hoped to launch. "[I]t always doubles the money invested in it," the organizers of the Fair would claim.[44] Child had simply made the mistake of trying to publish and market *The Oasis* through commercial channels.

As *The Oasis* came off the press in October 1834, David was embarking on a legal case that would result in derailing the Childs' lives, threatening their antislavery partnership, marginalizing them in the abolitionist movement, and disrupting his wife's career. Despite the precarious state of his finances and the near extinction of his law practice, he undertook — gratis — the defense of a Spanish crew charged with piracy. The Spaniards' schooner, the *Panda*, had allegedly pirated an American brig, the *Mexican*, in 1832. Captured in 1834, the *Panda*'s crew of twelve sailors included several "men of color (Peruvians) and one negro," whose chances of obtaining a fair trial were very slim, especially during a period of uproar over abolitionist agitation. No doubt that was one reason why David volunteered to serve as their counsel, though his fluency in Spanish must also have been a major factor. The trial took place in mid-November 1834 and lasted two weeks. Joined by the fledgling lawyer George Hillard (who would go on to become Charles Sumner's law partner), David "made a masterly plea in [the crew's] defence," but the jury rendered a split verdict, acquitting five and judging the other seven guilty. After a motion for a new trial failed, Hillard prudently withdrew from the case. David, on the contrary, insisted on exhausting every possible resource. Convinced of his clients' innocence, he sent Child to Washington in February 1835 to appeal personally to Attorney General Benjamin Butler and President Andrew Jackson for a stay of execution.[45]

It was almost unheard-of for a woman to make such a long journey virtually alone, and the couple could ill afford the cost of the trip. "[D]esolate and discouraged" though she felt as she traveled across the wintry landscape, Child seems to have espoused David's latest enthusiasm almost as uncritically as she had earlier accepted his assurances that he would win his libel suits and turn the *Massachusetts Journal* into a profitable concern. She told Attorney General Butler that when she thought of "seven men, six of whom are husbands and fathers, being hung first, and proved innocent afterward," she was ready to "go to the ends of the earth to prevent it." In the same breath, however, she asserted that "if sure they were pirates," she would "never shed a tear for them." Did the qualification betray any secret misgivings? If so, she did not admit to them. According to legend, she "cast herself on her knees" before President Jackson, begging for the men's lives, but "[h]is only reply was, 'By the Eternal, let them hang!'" (Jackson later yielded to the pleas of the chief mate's beautiful wife, granting first a reprieve and then a pardon to her husband, Bernardo de Soto). Nevertheless, as David pursued the appeal to the bitter end on another expedition to Washington that May, Child seemed to be having second thoughts. Passing on to David word that the Spanish consul did not believe relatives of the defendants would "*ever* send a single cent to defray expenses," she admonished him: "You must *think* of this; though you know me well enough, to know that I would not allow it to weigh much in the balance with human life."[46] Fortunately, she never learned the unsavory truth — that de Soto not only confessed many years later to having participated in the crime for which he had been pardoned, but exonerated himself by claiming that he had shipped on the *Panda* believing her to be a slaver rather than a pirate vessel.[47]

The *Panda* episode, so reminiscent of David's military adventure in Spain, typified his self-destructive quixoticism. Albeit with noble motives, he had staked his reputation on a case that promised no monetary recompense and tested no significant legal principle — a venture that sidelined him from the important antislavery work he had been doing, subjected him to the odium of having championed yet another unpopular cause, and left him fighting for his financial survival. A decade earlier, when he had abandoned his diplomatic post in Portugal to fight in an ill-starred war, he had merely damaged his own prospects (and disappointed his parents' hopes). Now besides completing the ruin of his law practice, he was wreaking havoc on his wife's career just as she was reaching the peak of her productivity and achieving preeminence in her new field.

By May 1835, while Child was in the midst of her latest project, the two-volume *History of the Condition of Women* that would round out her *Ladies' Family Library*, David was coming to the conclusion that some drastic move would be necessary to restore him to solvency. As Child contemplated leaving her beloved Cottage Place, she tried to comfort herself with the thought that their troubles had brought her and David closer to each other. "How much we have suffered and enjoyed together since you first called me wife! and how has all the suffering and the enjoyment knit together the fibres of our hearts!" she wrote to David (then on his way to Washington). Her word order implied that the suffering had exceeded the enjoyment. Revealing the psychological toll that her unconditional support of David was taking, she went on to deflect blame for their adversities from David to herself, and even to embrace the chastisement she believed her unwomanly ambition had brought upon her: "I wish I had been as uniformly good and kind as you have been; but my ambitious and impatient temperament needed a world of trouble to tame it." Although the thought of uprooting herself was "exceedingly painful," she continued, anything would be preferable to living without David. "The truth is, I have formed the habit of depending on you for all my sunshine," she acknowledged abjectly. She ended with a plaintive postscript: " 'I want to go home'; but my home is gone away."[48]

What Child was apparently steeling herself to endure was not simply a resumption of boardinghouse life, but emigration to the frontier, where she had heard that "devastating sickness" was "sweeping off whole colonies." Ever since his return from Spain, David had periodically toyed with the idea of starting afresh in the West, and he would revive the plan several times in the next few years.[49] To Child's relief, a more attractive option turned up — an antislavery mission to England, initiated by the British abolitionist George Thompson.

In the fall of 1834 Garrison had arranged to bring Thompson to the United States on a lecture tour.[50] An electrifying orator credited with having mobilized the British masses to support emancipation in the West Indies, Thompson set out to "abolitionize" the American masses too. The American press immediately vilified him as a foreign subversive bent on breaking up the Union and provoking civil war. Angry mobs gathered wherever he spoke, and on several occasions, he barely escaped lynching. During his stay in Boston, Thompson developed a close relationship with the Childs. They squired him around to lectures and helped protect him from the thugs who dogged him. In turn, he accompanied Child on the New York-Philadelphia leg of her journey to Washington.[51] Sympathetic to the Childs' plight and appreciative of their talents, Thompson procured positions for them in England as agents for British antislavery societies. Caroline Weston, an indefatigable organizer, immediately set about raising part of the money to pay the Childs' salaries. Explaining the many "collateral advantages" of having the Childs represent American abolitionists in England, she inadvertently spoke only of "Mrs. Child": " — she will be in communion — with the good & gifted there — & information from such a source through such a channel must have great weight — & do great good — she will observe & report for our advantage — she will write for foreign periodicals — and books of hers which will reflect honour upon us all — . . . can be produced more advantageously there than here — "[52]

The couple's departure from Boston was set for August 8, barely allowing Child the time to finish her *History of the Condition of Women* before embarking. On August 6 the Childs held an auction at Cottage Place to dispose of their belongings. The following night they gathered with their friends at the Lorings' for an emotional farewell. "It seemed like one of the church meetings of old," wrote Caroline Weston to her sisters Ann and Deborah in Weymouth:

> "Ellis dear" in his sweet & quiet way said "it has been proposed, that before we separate we should unite in prayer — . . ." Thompson fell on his knees — & almost all the others — & there went up such earnest & fervent supplications as one does not hear in these times — you can imagine the scene better than I can describe it — there was much weeping — & feeling — then . . . one by one with the most solemn leave taking the company departed —[53]

Adding to the emotional intensity of the occasion was the threat of mob violence. Thompson had just eluded a Boston lynch mob on August 1, and the Childs had volunteered to spirit him away with them to New York (where they were supposed to catch their ship), dodging the mobs on his track and secreting him in the home of friends in Brooklyn. Dangers beset them at every stage of the trip. "Had I committed some monstrous crime, I could not have performed this journey with more uncomfortable sensations," Child wrote to Louisa Loring from New York. Passing through Newport, Rhode Island (where they stopped to say goodbye to David's younger brother John and his "aristocratic" wife, as well as to pay a last visit to Channing), they found the "steam-boat . . . full of Southerners," who hounded Thompson with "malignant looks and scornful jests." New York, virtually under siege, reminded Child of Paris during the 1789 French Revolution (as described by Thomas Carlyle), "when no man dared trust his neighbor." Child graphically relayed to Louisa the tense atmosphere of the city and the frayed state of her nerves:

> Private assassins from N. Orleans are lurking at the corners of the streets, to stab Arthur Tappan [president of the American Anti-Slavery Society]; and very large sums are offered for any one who will convey Mr. Thompson into the slave states. I tremble for him, and love him in proportion to my fears. He is almost a close prisoner in his chamber — his friend deeming him in imminent peril the moment it is ascertained where he is. . . . My faith has at times been so weak, that I have started, and trembled, and wept, like a very child; and personal respect and affection for him has so far gained the mastery over my trust in Providence, that I have exclaimed in anguish of heart, "Would to God, I could die for thee!"[54]

More than fear of a mob attack seemed to lie behind Child's outburst. She had clearly come to love the charismatic Thompson (who would inspire crushes in many abolitionist women). At this difficult crisis of her marriage, was she fighting a tendency to compare David to men who seemed to embody all the qualities he lacked (including a dynamism that aroused her sexually)?[55] Or was she displacing onto Thompson concerns she felt for her own psychological safety as her marriage deteriorated and her career risked shipwreck? Did she identify with Thompson as a "close prisoner in his chamber" because she felt similarly trapped in her wifely role, yet terrified of the lawless world that would tear her to pieces if she dared to venture out?

In the long letter Child wrote to Louisa about the journey, she buried its traumatic anticlimax in three parenthetical sentences. Just as she and David had been boarding the ship bound for England, David had been arrested on the quay in New York. David's partner on the *Massachusetts Journal and Tribune*, George Snelling, "not content with leaving the whole burden" of the newspaper's debts to his associate, had filed suit against him and procured an injunction against letting David leave the country. Overcome with humiliation and disappointment, Child had sat down and wept on the quay.[56] She was still hoping that David could somehow arrange matters in time for them to sail the following morning, but no such miracle occurred. Instead the lawsuit with Snelling and the upheavals and uncertainties of the Childs' domestic lives would drag on interminably. For the next six years David's desperate pursuit of one chimera after another would keep the couple in limbo and soon make it impossible for Child to write. Their promising partnership as antislavery activists had foundered on the careless business practices and unresolved career conflicts that had finally caught up with David, and Child would not succeed in reestablishing it until she redefined the terms of their marriage.

IO

The Condition of Women:
Double Binds, Unresolved Conflicts

To their friend MRS. CHILD, the true, the noble, the irreproachable, who made the first 'APPEAL' in behalf of the AMERICAN slave.[1]

This inscription graced a gold watch presented to Child by the "anti-slavery Ladies" of Lynn and Salem, Massachusetts, to bid her farewell before she embarked on the aborted voyage to England. Both the gift and the occasion betoken the complexities of Child's career as a female antislavery activist. The gift attests to the veneration in which other antislavery women held Child and the inspiration they derived from her example. Presenting themselves as "endeavoring to do a little in support of the cause of abolition, for which you have done so much," the women of Lynn and Salem made clear that they saw themselves as following in Child's footsteps.[2] The occasion — a trip to England undertaken because it offered a means of employment to David Child and canceled because he was arrested for debt — signals the perpetual disruption that his financial predicament effected in his wife's social relations. It also epitomizes the sacrifices Child's marriage exacted of her — sacrifices of personal ties, stable living and working conditions, and professional aspirations as a writer and reformer. The need to preserve her marriage at all costs complicated Child's responses to what came to be called "the woman question" — the explosive debate over woman's proper place that polarized the antislavery movement in the late 1830s. Bent on repressing her resentment toward her husband for continually thwarting her career goals, she could not take the leadership role that her radical sisters expected of her in championing their right to equal partnership with men. Instead, she imposed uncharacteristic restrictions on herself, first as an antislavery activist and later as an analyst of the female condition.

At the outset, the acclaim that had greeted the *Appeal* had promoted Child overnight to the status of an honorary man in a male-dominated movement. Hitherto a silent observer at meetings of the New England Anti-Slavery Society, which she had been attending since early 1832, she emerged in the wake of the *Appeal*, testifies Samuel May, as one of the "presiding geniuses in all our councils and more public meetings, often proposing the wisest measures, and suggesting . . . weighty thoughts, pertinent facts, [and] apt illustrations."[3] Her example also emboldened other women who, like herself, had been accompanying their husbands to meetings, to play a more active role in them. Among them May cites the formidable Maria Weston Chapman, who would later dominate Garrison's circle, assuming the editorship of the *Liberator* during his absences,[4] and the writer Eliza Lee Cabot Follen, wife of the German émigré clergyman Charles Follen. Eulogizing these pioneers for their contributions to the antislavery cause during a period when taboos against women's speaking in public remained unchallenged except by Quakers, May describes how they enlisted male allies to transmit their views: "Repeatedly . . . did I spring to the platform, crying, 'Hear me as the mouthpiece of Mrs. Child, or Mrs. Chapman, or Mrs. Follen,' and convulsed the audience with a stroke of wit, or electrified them with a flash of eloquence, caught from the lips of one or the other of our antislavery prophetesses."[5]

Child's submission to the rules governing women's participation in mixed public assemblies — a course in which she persisted long after women lecturers had ceased to be a novelty — contrasts strikingly with her fearless defiance of such conventions in her writing. It points to a deep ambivalence about whether to accept or reject the restraints her culture placed on women's freedom, whether to consider herself a circumscribed woman or an honorary man, whether to elect a female or a male forum for her antislavery work. She would manifest this ambivalence again and again as women began to join the movement in greater numbers and as different models of female antislavery activism arose.

Even in the initial stages of the antislavery movement, Child could have found models among Quaker women for full participation in meetings with men. Several Quaker women attended the December 1833 founding convention of the American Anti-Slavery Society, and one of them, the future women's rights leader Lucretia Mott, took the floor repeatedly to propose ideas the convention ended up adopting.[6]

True, Child could not claim the long Quaker tradition of women preachers that helped Mott gain acceptance, not only by members of her own sect, but by Evangelicals whose religious principles enjoined women to "keep silence in the churches" (1 Cor. 14:34). Yet on one occasion the Evangelical Lewis Tappan (soon to become a staunch opponent of women's rights) actually implored Child to take the podium in order to reignite a sputtering antislavery meeting in New York. "You will doubtless recover from your embarrassment in a few moments," he assured her when she declined. Annoyed by her refusal, he proceeded to lecture her: "[Y]ou really ought to make an effort to overcome your reluctance, when you reflect how much good you can do, and how much the audience will be interested, if you allow me to announce that Mrs. Child of Boston is about to address them."[7] As Tappan's plea indicates, Child's talents had won so much respect that strictures against female speakers did not apply to her. She had proved herself too valuable a commodity to be confined to woman's sphere when she was needed in a wider field.

Nevertheless, Child did not avail herself of the chance to enjoy the full benefits of her status as an honorary man. Her reluctance to violate the taboo against women's public speaking cannot be ascribed to diffidence. Her friends have memorialized her as a scintillating conversationalist with a gift for witty repartee.[8] Confirming their accounts, Child herself described how she once buttonholed a fellow passenger in the stagecoach, a conservative opponent of abolition, and demolished his sophisms in front of his associates. "I burnt him up like a stroke of the sun, and swept his ashes up after him," she boasted to Louisa Loring, adding ingenuously: "[N]ever in all my life was I half so brilliant and witty. It seems to have produced the effect of an electric shock upon the members in the stage. Every day or two some new echo comes back to me from the neighboring towns." In view of her refusal to lecture when given the opportunity (several months before this incident), it is astonishing to find her lamenting to Louisa in the same breath: "Oh, if I was a man, how I *would* lecture! But I am a woman, and so I sit in the corner and knit socks."[9]

Why did Child repress the ambition she confided to her most intimate friend? Her criticisms of Frances Wright in her 1829 articles for the *Massachusetts Journal* suggest one reason: she did not want to be associated with the pioneer female lecturer who had been denounced as a "Sampson in petticoats . . . trying to pull down the pillars of the social edifice."[10] Another reason might be her unwillingness to compete with David in yet another arena. From the beginning, she had established herself as a more competent breadwinner and a more successful editor than he, and reviewers tacitly recognized her as the better writer of the two.[11] Child clearly found it painful to know that her husband's talents were less valued than her own and that he was increasingly regarded as a professional failure.[12] Particularly in an era when women were supposed to be subordinate to their husbands, neither she nor David could have adjusted without difficulty to their reversal of roles. By refraining from lecturing, Child was leaving David at least one domain of preeminence. Had she chosen to compete with him on the lecture platform, she probably would have excelled him there, too. Commenting on David's defects as a public speaker, Garrison had written: "Mr. Child's delivery is most unhappy—his matter is always better than his manner. His voice is harsh and stubborn, and when exerted, grates painfully upon the ear."[13] David himself did not discourage his wife from lecturing, however. "I should feel ashamed now and forever after if I . . . suffered any consideration connected with myself, to oppose any obstacle to this, more than to any form of service, to which her judgment and the full feelings of her generous heart may impel her," he affirmed. All the same, his unenthusiastic tone and convoluted syntax suggest that he, too, may have been trying to repress feelings of rivalry of which he was "ashamed."[14]

Child could of course have elected an alternative model of antislavery activism that would not have involved competition with David. Evangelical women had acquired considerable experience in organizing female auxiliary societies for such benevolent causes as temperance and moral reform. Building on that experience and on the example of women in the British antislavery movement, they began forming female antislavery societies as early as 1832. At its inaugural convention in December 1833 the Evangelical-dominated American Anti-Slavery Society (AASS) specifically called on women to intensify their efforts. "The influence of women, under God, is omnipotent," proclaimed one of the resolutions unanimously approved at the convention:

> [W]oman can exert her soothing and gentle influence amidst the wildest of the storm. She was created to hush the awry passions of political and personal strife; and to point man away from sordid and selfish pursuits, to the high and holy object of doing good to his species. . . . The baser tendencies of ambitious feeling cannot lure her from the single aim before her eye — that of aiding in the disenthrallment and redemption of her sisters and brethren in bondage. Let the females of this nation organize themselves into Anti-Slavery Societies, on principles kindred with those promulgated by this convention. . . .[15]

Yet Child resisted appeals framed in the language of true womanhood and patterned on conventional forms of women's activism as stubbornly as she rejected invitations to transgress the code that prohibited women from addressing mixed audiences. Despite the urging of the women who founded the Boston Female Anti-Slavery Society (BFASS) in October 1833, she refused to lend her prestige to the enterprise because she objected to the idea of a "distinct female society." Rethinking the question in January 1834, she conceded to Charlotte Phelps, the group's first president: "I may be in the wrong, and others in the right. In this, and all other matters, each one must act in freedom, according to his own perceptions of right and wrong, advisable or unadvisable." She consequently agreed to keep her reservations to herself and to pay dues, though not to assume any office in the society. "The plain truth is, my sympathies do not, and never have, moved freely in this project," she admitted.[16]

Still, Child ended up playing a much more active role in the BFASS than she had set out to. The circle of women friends she formed in the process also became an important source of emotional support during a period when the instability of her home life and the uncertainty of David's prospects were subjecting her to great stress. In addition to Louisa Loring and Charlotte Phelps, the group included Henrietta Sargent, one of four women Child would count among her dearest lifelong friends; the members of the Chapman-Weston clan; Mary S. Parker, who ran an abolitionist boardinghouse at which the Garrisons frequently stayed; and Susan Paul, daughter of the well-known minister of the African Baptist Church, Thomas Paul, and herself a teacher and choir director at a black primary school.

The most enterprising of them was undoubtedly Maria Weston Chapman, described by Garrison's sons as "the soul of the Boston Female A.S Society."[17] Beginning in 1835, Chapman wrote the society's annual reports, issued under the title *Right and Wrong in Boston*, maintained a regular correspondence with antislavery sympathizers abroad, and spearheaded fund-raising drives. Child judged her "one of the most remarkable women of the age." "Her heart is as large and magnanimous as her intellect is clear, vigorous, and brilliant," Child told Lucretia Mott.[18]

Child developed a warm relationship with Susan Paul, too. Mindful of the need to break down racial barriers, she always went out of her way to sit beside African American women at antislavery gatherings and to ensure that they felt welcome.[19] Her own precarious position on the edge of the middle class probably made her seem more approachable to blacks than did abolitionists from the Boston elite. Thus, when Paul found herself faced with a financial crisis, Child was the one she turned to for help. Child immediately wrote to a wealthy philanthropist, describing Paul's circumstances with the sympathy of a woman who understood from experience how scrupulously Paul had hitherto "avoided incurring the slightest debt" and how much she had suffered before pocketing her pride and requesting a loan.[20]

Child also used the opportunity to sensitize Paul's benefactor (who was not an abolitionist) to the impact of racial prejudice on African Americans. Paul's plight, she explained, had arisen because discrimination produced a severe dearth of affordable housing for blacks. The psychological effects of prejudice were worse: "The few individuals among them, who have any considerable degree of intelligence or refinement, are, like Tantalus, continually tormented with the sight of fruit they may not eat, and fountains at which their thirsty souls are not allowed to drink." She went on to write movingly of how abolitionism had transformed her consciousness: "[I]n former years . . . the colored population came and went before my eyes, like shadows. I never paused to reflect that they were, like myself, immortals pent up in the prison-house of time. I never asked whether the windows of *their* prison were more darkened than my own — whether their limbs were not cramped by the narrow walls of the dungeon assigned to them by the will of the strongest." Contrary to the popular stereotype of abolitionists, she had not become a woman of " 'one idea' " in espousing the cause of blacks, Child added pointedly. Rather, her conversion to abolition had made "*every* form of human suffering . . . doubly interesting" to her: "*Every* shackle on *every* human soul not only arrests my attention, but excites the earnest inquiry 'What can *I* do to break the chain' "?[21] Through her tactful appeal, Child showed that she practiced the society's ideals.

Although Child had joined the BFASS with strong reservations about the merits of separate female organizations, by the fall of 1834 she had thrown herself into the typically female activity of organizing a Christmas fund-raising fair for the benefit of the New England Anti-Slavery Society. This project, which she initiated and took charge of together with Louisa Loring, netted $300.[22] Among those who attended was thirteen-year-old Sarah Southwick, who had grown up on the *Juvenile Miscellany* and was eagerly looking forward to meeting its celebrated editor. Like other abolitionist children, Sarah and her sister had been encouraged by their mother to produce some articles for the fair. Catching sight of the needle-book she had made on the table over which Child was presiding, she asked its price as a way of opening a conversation. To her mortification, Child "looked at it, and replied, 'It is marked fifty cents, but it is not well made, and you may have it for two shillings.' " Sarah nevertheless recovered sufficiently from her hurt pride to purchase a copy of *The Oasis*. She and her mother, Thankful, remained active in the Boston Female Anti-Slavery Society throughout its existence.[23]

The success of this first fair sparked emulation by female antislavery societies throughout the North. Maria Weston Chapman and her sisters, in particular, would develop the annual "bazaar" of the BFASS into a grand social event that would help sustain the *Liberator* and the AASS with several thousand dollars each year.

Despite her preference for advancing abolitionist aims through masculine forums, no one understood better than the creator of the *Juvenile Miscellany*, *The Frugal House-wife*, and *The Mother's Book* how to translate a female medium into a vehicle for radical ideas. As Child put it in her account of the 1836 fair organized by Chapman: "The ladies have ever regarded the pecuniary benefit derived from these sales as but *one* of several reasons in their favor. The main object is to keep the subject before the public eye, and by every innocent expedient to promote perpetual discussion."[24]

Child also realized that antislavery fairs offered women who felt uneasy about over-stepping the bounds of their "sphere" a traditional mode of contributing to the cause and displaying their creativity. Women who never would have dreamed of publishing tracts or newspaper articles, much less speaking out publicly against slavery, expressed their political sentiments through the mottoes they inscribed on articles they sewed and baked for the fair. Among the items sold at the 1836 fair, for example, were boxes of wax wafers (used to seal documents), bearing the motto, "The doom of Slavery is *sealed*"; needle-books marked with "May the use of our needles prick the consciences of slaveholders"; "[s]mall silken bags of perfume, for bureau drawers," embroidered with the biblical verse, "The kingdom of heaven is like unto leaven, which a *woman* hid in three measures of meal, until the whole was leavened"; and ornamental match stands adorned with the maxim, "LIGHT, whether material or moral, is the best of all Re-formers." Child herself had sewn a patchwork cradle quilt made up of small stars; on the central star she had transcribed a poem by Eliza Lee Cabot Follen, exhorting the mother who clasped her child in her arms to "Think of the *negro*-mother, / When *her* child is torn away." In short, antislavery fairs generated an elaborate female discourse, fusing political activism with housewifely arts and reworking domestic emblems into a trenchant abolitionist iconography.[25]

If Child successfully manipulated this female discourse and invented new forms of antislavery activism for women, she never overcame her discomfort with separate female organizations. As late as 1839 she would tell Lucretia Mott: "They always seemed to me like half a pair of scissors."[26] Ultimately, Child could not embrace either of the alternatives available to her as an activist: full partnership with men, including the free exercise of her talents as a speaker; or a leadership role in female auxiliary societies, where she could use her political as well as her domestic skills, but remain within a woman's sphere. Instead, she opted for an awkward compromise between the two. She continued to assign priority to participating in male organizations through male mouthpieces, and she grudgingly put her creativity and managerial aptitude at the service of female antislavery groups, though only until 1840.

The roots of Child's ambivalence probably lie in her youth. The dynamics of her parents' relationship — her father domineering, her mother self-effacing until she took to her bed and died of consumption — must have convinced Child at an early age that identification with the parent who possessed authority and power offered the surest means of acquiring those attributes herself. Her special bond with Convers could only have reinforced the pattern. He effectually helped make her an honorary man by initiating her into the world of the intellect. Yet she soon outclassed him in that world, as she eventually outclassed David. Indeed, the *Appeal* simultaneously confirmed her superiority to both of her beloved male mentors—to Convers because he still held himself aloof from abolitionism, to David because her book had surpassed his in intellectual breadth and stylistic grace.

Thus, Child found herself in a double bind. Identifying with men, she refused to be relegated to the lesser sphere of a female organization. At the same time, male identification entailed loyalty to the men who had promoted her to her honorary status. Indebted to Convers and David for treating her as an equal and giving her access to the male domains of scholarship and politics, she did not want to eclipse them on all fronts. Hence, Child compensated for her success in the field of polemical writing by stifling her likely gifts in the even more masculine field of oratory, which her two mentors had staked out, Convers as a clergyman, David as a political speaker.

Child's ambivalent gender identity and the excruciating conflicts to which it gave rise — between her "masculine" ambition for success and her "feminine" craving for love, between her impulse to rebel against her culture's restrictions on her freedom and her effort to live up to its crippling ideal of the "good wife"—inform her *History of the Condition of Women, in Various Ages and Nations* (1835), filling it with pregnant silences. It was precisely while she was struggling to bring this work to fruition that David was contemplating going West to recoup his ruined fortunes. Clinging with all her strength to her belief in her husband, Child was in no mood to pursue the implications of her research on "the condition of women." If she wanted to preserve her marriage, she could not afford to think too deeply about women's subjection to male dominance, which would have fueled the anger she was trying so hard to repress. Accordingly, she confined herself to description and eschewed theory and polemic.

The circumstances of the book's composition and publication reproduced the tensions of her career. The culmination of her *Ladies' Family Library*, directly preceded by *Good Wives* (1833), the *Appeal* (1833), and *The Oasis* (1834), *The History of the Condition of Women* stands at the crossroads of Child's vocations as a purveyor of domestic advice and as a subversive political agitator. Reorienting her five-volume series toward questioning rather than endorsing the traditional female roles that earlier volumes had seemed to celebrate, it also met the need that abolitionist women were feeling for a broader definition of womanhood compatible with their new activities. Symbolically, just as Child was reaching the most critical stage of her writing, the Boston Athenaeum canceled her free library privileges, and her friends in the BFASS took George Ticknor's place as her patrons. No sooner did Maria Chapman learn of Child's predicament than she set about raising funds to purchase her a paying membership at the Athenaeum, which required $100. With her wonted energy, Chapman managed to procure almost the full sum in one day by explaining the circumstances to those she contacted: "Mrs. Child is writing a book & she can't go on with it, because the directors of the Athaeneum library have revoked the permission which they gave her some years ago to take out what books she chose. . . . [T]hese books she *must* have, or give up her book."[27] Child was "moved even to tears" by the gesture of solidarity. "I have never in my whole life, met with anything that gratified me more, or affected me so deeply," she wrote in her letter of thanks. Ultimately, the directors of the Athenaeum refused to allow her a paying membership either, but the $100 gift did buy Child respite from the financial worries that were also interfering with her writing.[28] Completed on the eve of her supposed departure for England, the book appeared on the market in September.[29]

A landmark text anticipating some of the most recent trends in feminist scholarship, Child's two-volume *History* explores the commonalities and differences in the status of women across the globe, from ancient times to the mid-nineteenth century, from the remotest tribes of Siberia, Africa, and the Pacific islands to the nations of Europe and the Americas.[30] Among the indicators Child examines are marriage customs reflecting each society's valuation of women as drudges, sexual objects, reproducers, childrearers, or simply property; laws regulating virginity, adultery, concubinage, polygamy, prostitution, and divorce — and the differential application of such laws to men and women; patrilineal versus matrilineal reckoning of descent, paternal versus maternal custody of children, and the extent of discrimination between males and females when disposing of surplus children through infanticide or sale; women's occupations in relation to men's; their access to education, moneymaking activities, political power, the priesthood, and other avenues to prestige; and the degree of personal freedom or confinement they experience. In addition, Child notes variations within a society created by class, and she describes changes over time produced by economic development and social stratification.

As in the *Appeal*, Child takes a comparative approach to her subject, setting the institution of male dominance, like the system of slavery, in transhistorical and cross-cultural contexts. Once again, the project involved consulting and synthesizing an enormous range of sources. The records of Child's borrowings from the Athenaeum include Greek and Roman classics; works of biblical and classical scholarship; church histories; encyclopedias and compilations by French philosophes; travel accounts of North and South America, the Caribbean, Africa, the Near East, Asia, the Arctic Circle, and the islands of Southeast Asia and the Pacific; and early histories of women that served her as models.[31] Far more complicated than her research for the *Appeal*, however, the task Child faced in collecting these data necessitated sifting through sources that often mentioned women only in passing.[32]

The ambitiousness of Child's enterprise and the self-conscious inclusiveness of her vision become especially obvious when one compares her history with the work from which she took her cue: William Alexander's *The History of Women, from the Earliest Antiquity, to the Present Time; Giving an Account of Almost Every Interesting Particular Concerning that Sex, among All Nations, Ancient and Modern* (1779).[33] Although Child derived her main categories of analysis and much of her information about the ancient world and post-Roman Europe from this source, she vastly expanded its coverage by turning to travel literature for material on non-Western societies. She also reorganized the facts Alexander had presented under topical chapter headings ("Female Education," "Employments and Amusements," "Matrimony") by substituting a geographical framework ("Asia," "Asiatic Islands," "Africa," "Europe," "America," "South Sea Islands"). The result is to shift the focus from disparate customs to whole cultures, making it possible to reconstruct the place of women within specific cultures and to draw connections between women's treatment and other aspects of the culture. Only in one instance does Child depart from her geographical framework: she intercalates a chapter on "Women in Slave-holding Countries" between the sections on Europe and the Americas. Here, the result is to shift the focus from diverse cultures to a single institution. "[B]ecause slavery everywhere produces nearly the same effects on character," she explains, it can most usefully be analyzed under a heading that subsumes national particularities (2: 212).

Essentially recapitulating the *Appeal*, this chapter testifies to how closely *The History of Women* resembles the earlier work, not only in its comparative methodology and encyclopaedic scholarship, but in its political perspective and rhetorical strategy. Indeed, the two books can be read as complementary halves of one monumental opus aimed at eradicating all forms of oppression. The interconnections between *The History of Women* and the *Appeal* neatly illustrate the parallels that a growing number of women would soon discern between their own status and that of the slaves for whose liberation they were fighting.

Just as Child weaves a special interest in women into the antislavery argument of the *Appeal*, so she weaves protest against slavery into the feminist inquiry of *The History of Women*. Implicit and explicit analogies between women and slaves punctuate the book: the Babylonian practice of auctioning marriageable girls, pricing them according to their beauty, like the quadroon slaves on the auction blocks of New Orleans (1: 24); the raffling of imported European wives to British colonists in India (1: 129); the New Holland natives' kidnapping of wives from enemy tribes in a manner reminiscent of the slave trade (1: 207); the flourishing "trade in female slaves . . . for the harems of Turkey and Persia" (1: 47); the Circassian recourse to punishing premarital sex and adultery by selling women offenders as slaves (1: 45); the almost universal diffusion of bride price and dowry systems defining marriage as an economic transaction in which wives are purchased and daughters are sold; the widespread view of wives as "slaves," commodities, and creatures of "an inferior race," shared by Bedouins (1: 37), Cochin Chinese (1: 137), Tartars (1: 163), Sumatran Battas (1: 194), Moors (1: 237–38), and Greenlanders, among others (2: 243).

While presenting a bleak picture of women's enslavement in these non-Western societies, Child reiterates a central thesis of the *Appeal* — that the forms of slavery found in other cultures have still been much less inhumane than the "peculiar institution" of the antebellum South. Athenian slave women, she points out, could seek refuge in the temple from the sexual advances of masters and could "demand a change of owners" (2: 29–30). The Turks, despite their reputation for cruelty, do not keep slaves for life or perpetuate inferior status through antimiscegenation laws: "Female slaves are free by law at the end of six years, and allowed to form the most advantageous marriages they can" (1: 70). Spelling out the comparison, Child adds: "It is a singular fact, that the

Mohammedan nations treat slaves better than the Christian; and that, among Christians, the Catholic nations treat them better than the Protestant" (1: 71). Similarly, Child emphasizes that "the domestic slavery of the Africans is altogether of a milder character, and more resembles Hebrew servitude, than the slavery existing among white men" (1: 266).

Reinforcing the continuity between the *Appeal* and the *History of Women* is the detailed and sympathetic account Child furnishes of Africa, drawing on the same sources she had cited in her chapters on the "Intellect" and "Moral Character of Negroes." Once again, a comparison of Child's and Alexander's histories of women illuminates the commitment to revising racist stereotypes that informs Child's approach to her subject. By beginning her eighty-page chapter on Africa with Egypt and Carthage, which Alexander had situated in the ancient Near East and consistently placed after Israel in his chapters, Child radically redefines the prevailing concept of Africa as a region of perpetual savagery that had contributed nothing to world civilization. She asserts that the Egyptians originally migrated from Ethiopia, that the site of their ancient civilization lay in the south, and that "their complexion was black" (1: 217–18, 230) — facts since confirmed by twentieth-century scholars.[34] The redefinition of Egypt as African adds another dimension to her exploration of the status of women in Africa, since women enjoyed more freedom and greater prestige in Pharaonic Egypt than in any other culture of the ancient world.

Child also pointedly takes issue with Alexander's portrayal of Africans in the few pages he allots to sub-Saharan peoples. Where he finds "a general sameness and uniformity," she stresses diversity: "The various African tribes differ as much in personal appearance as the inhabitants of the numerous Asiatic kingdoms" (1: 246). Where he finds ugliness, she cites many examples of beauty:[35]

[Fulah] women are slender and graceful, with languishing eyes, and soft voices. The Wolofs are tall and well-shaped, with prominent and rather aquiline noses, lips not very thick, black complexions, uncommonly sweet voices, and a very frank, mild expression of countenance. . . .

The color of the Mandingoes is black intermixed with yellow. They have regular features, with a frank, intelligent expression. The women are almost universally well-shaped and handsome. . . . The Kaffers, or Caffres, have . . . the European conformation of head and features; their complexion is glossy black, their eyes large and sparkling, their teeth are beautifully white and regular, and the expression of their countenances bright and good-humored. Travellers all agree in describing the men as uncommonly noble and majestic figures. The women are of lower stature, rather muscular than graceful; but many of them have very handsome faces. (1: 246–47)

Having contended that Africans are attractive even by European standards, she proceeds to challenge ethnocentric notions of beauty: "The Africans consider our color quite as great a deformity as we regard theirs. . . . Many of them suppose that the pale color of Europeans is owing to a leprous disease" (1: 262).

Child's antiracist agenda merges with her feminist agenda when she describes the roles African women play in their societies. Unlike the majority of their Asian and European counterparts, Child shows, African women often engage in prestigious activities typically reserved for men: "In time of battle the African women encourage the troops, supply them with fresh arrows, and hurl stones at their enemies. In some tribes it is common for them to unite with the men in hunting the lion and the leopard" (1: 254). Most relevant to Child's sisters in the antislavery movement is the participation of African women in political "palavers." Quoting a traveler who had "attended a palaver, or council, in Southern Africa," Child reports that the women " 'took an eager interest in the debate — cheering those whose sentiments they approved, or bursting into loud laughter at any thing they considered ridiculous' " (1: 254).

Child's dual agendas likewise shape her chapter on the Americas. It, too, begins by redefining the very concept of "America" as a land discovered and settled by Europeans. Instead, Child opens the chapter with "American Indians," followed by "Women of the Arctic Regions," "South American Women," and last of all "Women of the United States" — an organization that decenters the United States. Although Child concurs with most European observers in her erroneous view of Indian women as quasi-enslaved drudges, she underscores that male tyranny never takes the form of sexual abuse among Indians: "In this respect, their deportment towards women is abundantly more praiseworthy than that of civilized nations" (2: 231). Child also mentions a fact suggesting more equality between men and women than Europeans generally acknowledged: "Both girls and boys are early taught to endure without a murmur the utmost rigors of climate, excess of labor, and the extremity of pain" (2: 235). Along the same lines Child notes evidence indicating that Indian women exercise significant power and influence. "[I]n time of battle, they often encourage and assist the warriors," she points out, echoing her description of African women (2: 237). They additionally serve as "the physicians of their tribes" and "claim the gift of prophecy" interchangeably with men (2: 239). Huron and Iroquois women even participate in tribal councils. "Huron women might appoint a member of the council, and one of their own sex if they chose. They could prevail upon the warriors to go to battle, or to desist from it, according to their wishes" (2: 241).

Throughout *The History of Women*, Child's antiracist agenda is far more explicit than her feminist agenda, however. Nothing more tellingly betrays Child's ambivalent attitude toward feminist advocacy than her deliberate refusal to draw conclusions or deduce theories from the wealth of facts she amasses. Even Sarah Hale noticed Child's uncharacteristic reticence. "[F]rom her we did anticipate somewhat more of the philosophy of history. There are but very few attempts to trace causes from the effects described," she complained. While commending the "honesty of purpose in all that Mrs. Child prepares, which gains the confidence of the reader," Hale expressed disappointment over the restrictions Child had imposed on herself: "In the few general remarks she has ventured, there is so much good sense, that we only regret in these volumes she should have transcribed so much, and written so little."[36]

Her criticism was on target. *The History of Women* totally lacks the analytical framework Child had supplied in its antislavery companion volume. The first editions lacked even a preface. When Child added one to the 1845 edition, it only highlighted the book's omissions:

> This volume is not an essay upon woman's rights, or a philosophical investigation of what is or ought to be the relation of the sexes. If any theories on this subject are contained in it, they are merely incidentally implied by the manner of stating historical facts. I have simply endeavored to give an accurate history of the condition of women, in language sufficiently concise for popular use. Those who reflect on this highly interesting and important subject will find in the facts thus patiently collected much that will excite thought, and many materials for argument.

As Jean Fagan Yellin remarks, Child's "preface to the *Condition of Women* reads very differently from that of *An Appeal*"; it does not affirm her fearlessness in the face of "ridicule and censure," but bristles with "denials and disclaimers."[37]

Despite Child's reluctance to formulate them, theories and arguments in favor of women's rights *are* unmistakably "implied" in the book's "manner of stating historical facts." First, the overwhelming diversity Child shows in the kinds of labor women have performed and in the functions they have fulfilled militates against any monolithic concept of womanhood, let alone the concept of "true womanhood" that served to confine nineteenth-century American women to the domestic sphere. Second, the widespread treatment of women as beasts of burden, created especially to discharge the heaviest and most disagreeable tasks, undermines a major rationale for women's subordinate status — their physical weakness compared to men. Third, the existence of societies that have accorded women more equal status, and the many instances of women's having exercised political power even in societies defining them as subordinates, prove that male dominance and female subjection are neither natural nor inevitable. Fourth, the extreme variation in sexual mores — and the sexual freedom some societies have allowed women — similarly confirm that no sexual arrangements are inherently natural, and thus point toward the possibility of challenging nineteenth-century America's repressive and hypocritical ideology of the double standard.

Within less than a decade two major works of feminist theory published by Child's friends — Sarah Grimké's *Letters on the Equality of the Sexes, and the Condition of Woman* (1838) and Margaret Fuller's *Woman in the Nineteenth Century* (1845) — would explicitly advance the ideas she had "incidentally implied." Both would support their contentions by referring repeatedly to the "many materials for argument" her *History* had furnished.

Grimké's work would charge men with having "made slaves of the creatures whom God designed to be their companions and coadjutors in every moral and intellectual improvement." Citing many examples from Child's *History*, and quoting her at length, Grimké would maintain that "women are capable of acquiring as great physical power as men"; that they are equally capable of directing the affairs of state; and that the shibboleths about "the sphere of man and the sphere of woman, are mere arbitrary opinions, differing in different ages and countries." She would issue a militant challenge to men: "All I ask of our brethren is, that they will take their feet from off our necks, and permit us to stand upright on that ground which God designed us to occupy."[38]

In *Woman in the Nineteenth Century* Margaret Fuller would pick up where Grimké left off. Exhorting women to cultivate "independence of Man" and learn to "stand alone," she would prophesy the advent of a female messiah who would "vindicate their birthright for all women."[39] More daringly, Fuller would tackle an aspect of Child's research overlooked by Grimké — its invitation to reevaluate contemporary sexual mores in the light of information about other cultures. Child's analysis of the ways in which women had been exchanged as commodities and bought and sold as sexual objects throughout history would serve Fuller as the basis for a concerted attack on the double standard and the marriage of convenience, which she would characterize as legalized prostitution. "It is idle to speak with contempt of the nations where polygamy is an institution, or seraglios a custom, when practices far more debasing haunt, well-nigh fill, every city and every town," she would stress, echoing Child's assertion that "Licentiousness abounds in all cities" and that "it is not confined to a class of women avowedly depraved, but sometimes lurks beneath the garb of decency, and even of elegance" (2: 205).[40] Fuller would proceed to detail practices Child had only hinted at. Men who shamelessly frequented prostitutes and seduced unprotected girls, she would point out, were freely received in society and if they were wealthy, pursued as desirable matches for daughters sheltered from any sexual knowledge. When women protested, they were told they "should know nothing about such things." At the same time, they were brought up to exhibit their persons and to court attention with the aim of attracting rich husbands, just as prostitutes ogled rich clients. Fuller would urge women to reject the double standard, both by refusing to tolerate licentiousness in men and by acknowledging prostitutes as their sisters and giving them "tender sympathy, counsel, employment."[41] "It is a *bold* book, I assure you," Child would comment of *Woman in the Nineteenth Century*, admitting ruefully to Louisa Loring: "I should not have dared to have written some things in it, though it would have been safer for me, being married."[42]

While Grimké and Fuller formulated the theories for which Child had contented herself with laying the groundwork, their books by no means superseded hers. *The History of the Condition of Women* went through a total of six printings, of which four coincided with the period when Child's reputation among the general public was at its nadir — a fact that surely testifies to how important a need it filled on the market. Fuller confirmed as much in her review of the 1845 edition for the *New York Tribune*. Drawing attention to the significance of "[t]he words *Fifth Edition* on the title page," she predicted: "As long as there are copies of this popular book to be procured . . . readers will hasten to seek for it."[43] Once again, Child had displayed her ability to anticipate a new demand at a pivotal moment and thus to direct the course of cultural change.

Whatever her own ambivalence about openly advocating women's rights, Child's exhaustive study of the cultural and historical variations in women's status prompted some of her sisters in the antislavery movement to reexamine the grounds for circumscribing their proper sphere of action. Indeed, the leaders of the women's rights movement specifically paid tribute to its influence on them in their *History of Woman Suffrage*. Child's book was "the first American storehouse of information" on women's history and "undoubtedly increased the agitation" for equal rights, they recalled.[44] The reasons for its impact and timeliness can best be understood through a review of the developments that eventually led to a schism in abolitionist ranks over the "woman question."

Child's *History* appeared just as abolitionist women were beginning to claim a larger role for themselves. Until 1835 many had wrestled with self-doubts about whether they were overstepping woman's sphere by taking a public stand on a controversial political subject. The statements they had issued in response to the taunting question raised by antiabolitionists — "What Have Ladies to Do with the Subject of Anti-Slavery?" — had been based on a traditional concept of woman's moral influence. "It is not hers to arouse and astonish a nation by the thunders of the Senate, the lightning flashes of the bar, or the more lofty eloquence of the pulpit," they had humbly agreed, "but hers it is to fashion and to mould those characters, who afterward go forth to proclaim to the world the principles, and thoughts, and feelings, which she has given them." Hence, they had invoked their responsibility as mothers and their capacity to "feel for our enslaved sisters" as justifications for collectively protesting against a system that itself violated woman's natural delicacy.[45]

In the very months when Child was researching her *History* and organizing the Boston Female Anti-Slavery Society's first annual fair, however, events were propelling women toward more radical forms of activism than most had originally envisaged. Besieged by escalating violence against abolitionists, women attending antislavery meetings sometimes found themselves in the unprecedented position of defending male abolitionists from mobs that did not dare to assault white "ladies." As a female correspondent to the *Liberator* put it, the women had learned that instead of relying on men to protect them, "they must defend themselves, and *soldier-like*, protect their male friends from rude assailants, and *bear them off* amidst the *hisses*, &c. of the mob."[46]

Child herself underwent such an experience during a meeting held on August 1, 1835, to commemorate the first anniversary of emancipation in the British West Indies. Although David was one of the speakers, the chief target of the mob was George Thompson. Child immediately recognized the troublemakers in the audience: "a line of men in fine broadcloth," exchanging frequent "nods and glances" with a group of red-faced "truckmen, in shirt sleeves," whose courage had been fortified by rum. "When the meeting closed, the heart of every abolitionist beat with a quickened pulse, for Thompson's safety. . . . [T]he stairway and entry were lined with desperate-looking fellows, brandishing clubs and cart-whips." Thompson's supporters had planned to help him escape through a secret back exit, at which they had stationed a "carriage with swift horses" to rush him away, but women's collaboration was crucial to the success of the ploy. The women's task was "to keep Mr. Thompson apparently engaged in lively conversation, and to follow him as he moved along gradually, till he came to the place where he could slip behind the curtain" concealing the secret exit. They were then to remain there as if waiting for him, in order to give him time to get a head start before the mob discovered his whereabouts and set out in pursuit. "[H]uddled" around the curtain with her sisters from the Boston Female Anti-Slavery Society, Child recalled, "[m]y heart, meanwhile, throbbed so violently, that I felt as if I should sink upon the floor. But we did not sink, any of us." Soon Samuel May returned with the news that Thompson had managed to effect his escape.[47]

When Boston's most famous outbreak of antiabolitionist violence occurred in October 1835, the Childs were staying in New Rochelle, New York, where David was trying to sort out his future plans while awaiting the results of the lawsuit against him by his ex-partner, George Snelling. This time the members of the BFASS confronted a mob that vented its fury directly against them. Inflamed by rumors that Thompson (whom the Childs had actually spirited out of town) was going to address the women at their annual meeting, several thousand rioters, once again headed by the "wealthy and respectable," gathered outside the Anti-Slavery Office to "*snake Thompson out.*" The women continued with their proceedings while the "mob hurled missiles at the lady presiding" and shouts drowned out the secretary as she tried to read her report. When the mayor of Boston finally arrived, he merely urged the women to go home, on the plea that he could not guarantee their safety. Reminding the mayor that his "personal friends" were "the instigators of this mob," Chapman asked, "have you ever used your personal influence with them?" "If this is the last bulwark of freedom, we may as well die here, as any where," she proclaimed. The women did ultimately cut short their meeting, whites and blacks reportedly walking arm in arm through the hostile crowd that included many men "we had, till now, thought friends." (Only later did they learn that upon their departure, the mob turned against Garrison, who had been doing editorial work in an adjoining room, and came near killing him before he was rescued by a group of sympathizers and housed in the city jail for the night—the sole protection the mayor could offer him.[48])

Having faced down Boston's ruling elite, the women emerged from their ordeal with strengthened confidence in their ability to determine their duty for themselves, without deferring to male authority. By the time Child wrote to them several weeks afterward, her sisters in the BFASS no longer needed to be reassured about their right to speak out against an evil that was threatening to destroy the nation. They had already digested the lesson of the anecdote Child quoted from her biography of Madame de Staël: "When Bonaparte told a French lady that he did not like to hear a woman talk politics, she replied, — 'Sire, in a country where women are beheaded, it is very natural they should like to know the reason.'" And they had gone beyond Child's own application of that lesson: "where women are brutalized, scourged, and sold, shall we not inquire the reason?"[49] Instead, they were prepared to ask by what right men who had flaunted their contempt for female delicacy, Christian charity, and constitutional liberties could prevent women from acting in accordance with their consciences. Further still, they were prepared to reconsider the validity of any distinctions between the moral duties of men and women.

Reflecting how highly Child's sisters valued her support, however, when the BFASS finally reconvened its disrupted annual meeting on November 19, the secretary read Child's letter aloud to the group, which included "over a hundred and thirty" women, among them the visiting British feminist Harriet Martineau and the wife of George Thompson. The society's secretary also mentioned the letter in her report of the meeting for the *Liberator*, and Maria Chapman reprinted it in *Right and Wrong in Boston*.[50] It seems logical, then, to suppose that Child's friends, who had just contributed to financing the research for her newly published *History of Women*, would have greeted it as a godsend and eagerly exploited the evidence it provided for challenging the ideology of woman's sphere. Certainly Sarah Grimké did so, and it is suggestive that she wrote her *Letters on the Equality of the Sexes, and the Condition of Woman* at the behest of Mary S. Parker, president of the BFASS, which sponsored the Grimké sisters' lecture tour of New England in 1837.[51]

If Child helped inspire the feminist militancy of friends like the Grimkés, Maria Chapman, the Westons, and Abby Kelley, they soon outstripped her in their radicalism. Before long, they were pressuring her to "come out concerning the Rights of Women" as "a legitimate branch of the anti-slavery enterprise."[52] Meanwhile, however, Child was retreating precipitately from the feminist insights that her *History of Women* had suggested to her friends, for she and David were weathering the most prolonged crisis they had yet endured.

During the trying months that followed his arrest for debt at Snelling's instigation, David considered and rejected one career option after another. At first he talked of leaving for England in October.[53] Then after meeting the Quaker Benjamin Lundy (Garrison's former coeditor on the *Genius of Universal Emancipation*) in the course of a week's visit to Philadelphia, David seized on a new idea. Lundy was currently seeking recruits for a racially integrated settlement he was planning to establish in the state of Tamaulipas, Mexico, which he intended as a pilot project to demonstrate the feasibility of emancipation and the superior profitability of free labor. It was the kind of project that might have attracted support in the 1820s, when antislavery advocates still thought in terms of gradual, piecemeal emancipation schemes, coupled with some form of colonization; by 1835, however, radical abolitionists had moved beyond such utopian approaches, and Lundy was finding few takers among them.[54] Garrison had pointed out the ideological and practical shortcomings of the project almost as soon as Lundy had publicized it in the summer of 1835. Not only was a "colonization scheme" inherently objectionable, he had contended, but "[t]he experiment proposed [was] too limited, and . . . slow in its results, to aid essentially the anti-slavery cause." Besides, Garrison had warned, the political situation of the region was highly unstable, and a free labor colony there would consequently involve "unavoidable perils, real privations," and possible "loss of life."[55] By the time David met Lundy in fact, war was raging between proslavery settlers in Texas and the government of Mexico, which had recently abolished slavery.

Far from deterring David, the danger apparently attracted him. Once again, as in Spain, he thrilled at the prospect of actually fighting for freedom, rather than merely writing or speechifying about it. "Anxious to give the most decisive proof of the genuineness and ardor" of his sentiments, he even went so far as to write to Señor Castillo, the Mexican chargé d'affaires, proposing to raise a military corps consisting "either wholly or principally of colored persons" to aid the Mexicans. The real purpose of the Texans' "corrupt rebellion" — and of their American abettors' championship of it — he noted, was "the extension and perpetuation of the most cruel and detestable system of slavery" ever seen "on the face of the earth."[56]

It is impossible to doubt the sincerity of David's commitment to solidarity with people of color in the struggle against slavery and white supremacy. And he certainly showed an accurate understanding of the proslavery expansionism that incited the campaign to annex Texas and northern Mexico. Perhaps under different historical circumstances David might have turned into a John Brown, instead of remaining an inveterate Don Quixote. Yet coming on the heels of the *Panda* case and recalling his Spanish adventure, his enthusiasm for emigrating to a war zone and enlisting in the defense of Mexico suggests a desperate flight from his past failures. That is, it suggests an adolescent fantasy of proving his manhood by winning glory or martyrdom on the battlefield — a fantasy with suicidal overtones.

Lundy himself, though he willingly transmitted David's letter to Castillo, envisioned his free labor colony rather as a practical and profitable philanthropic undertaking than as an intervention in the war between Texas slaveholders and Mexico. But the financial aspect of Lundy's scheme also appealed to David, since it seemed to offer him a chance to redeem his reputation as a failure in business by earning a quick fortune. He proposed joining Lundy as a partner, with a commitment to "furnish half the colonists, *and share half the lands*." Lundy replied that he already had a partner, but he promised David at least "*half a league* of land" and "ample means to realize something handsome, in a comparatively short period." Feeding David's hopes, Lundy assured him: "A wide door is open, there, for a man of enterprise; and my project will present him with a large field for its exercise." David's participation in his free labor colony represented a major "coup" for Lundy, who had been deeply hurt by Garrison's dismissal of the project. He was even more overjoyed to be able to announce that Mrs. Child would be accompanying the group.[57]

Child herself tried to sound equally enthusiastic in informing the Lorings of David's decision to renounce the mission to England in favor of pioneering a free labor settlement on the Mexican frontier. Confessedly, she had hoped to "make some profitable literary arrangements" in England, "by which we could have been enabled to pay the debts we so much desire to pay," but she could write books anywhere, she claimed. She inadvertently revealed the obstacles contradicting that claim when she went on to allay the Lorings' fears about proslavery hostilities in the region. "[F]our or five hundred miles from the scene of disturbance," Lundy's grant lay in "unsettled" country, "far up from the sea, and not in the way of direct communication between any great towns." In short, Child would be subjected to the drudgery of a pioneer farm wife and cut off from libraries, booksellers, and publishers.[58]

Was the desire to reassert himself as the main breadwinner in the family also an unconscious element in David's preference for Mexico over England? Or was he yielding to his persistent impulse to escape from intellectual pursuits, and simply ignoring the damage that his western odyssey would do to his wife's literary career? Whatever the mixture of genuine idealism, quixotic self-destructiveness, unconscious rivalry with his wife, and selfish disregard of her needs that motivated David, Child refused to exercise the latitude she might have had in determining their future. Her own inner compulsions drove her to self-sacrifice — be it for the cause of freedom or for the husband whose love she craved above all else. And what she felt most driven to sacrifice was the intense ambition that conflicted with her ideal of the "good wife."

The agonizing conflicts with which Child had been wrestling since her marriage — between professional ambition and self-sacrificing love, feminist assertiveness and womanly self-effacement, sexual passion and commitment to a sexually unfulfilling marriage, political activism and religious mysticism, literary and "useful" vocations — surface with grim clarity in a novel she completed as she and David were preparing to leave for Texas in March: *Philothea: A Romance* (1836). The world of the imagination had always provided a refuge for Child, and the writing of *Philothea* seems to have served as a therapeutic outlet during the months of uncertainty following the aborted trip to England. It allowed her to express the poetic, mystical side of her nature that she had had to bury after assuming the roles of Frugal Housewife and antislavery agitator. But *Philothea* also reveals the terrifying psychological price Child was paying by subordinating all her other needs to the goal of saving a marriage that was becoming increasingly unsatisfying.

Paradoxically, what gave Child the leisure to write her first novel in almost a decade was the loss of her cherished home and many professional occupations. Since September 1835 she and David had been boarding with the Quaker abolitionists Joseph and Margaret Carpenter at their isolated farmhouse in New Rochelle. Spared the tasks of cooking and cleaning, the work of political organizing, and the editorship of the defunct *Miscellany*, Child had more time to herself than she had had in years.

Initially, she and David had agreed to write antislavery articles for the commercial press in exchange for financial support from the American Anti-Slavery Society, pending a rescheduled departure for England. Child had soon given up trying to place articles in New York newspapers, however. Half of those she submitted had been rejected, she complained to Loring, and another portion had been "lost." Instead, she produced three more abolitionist tracts: *Authentic Anecdotes of American Slavery* (1835), *The Evils of Slavery, and the Cure of Slavery* (1836), and an *Anti-Slavery Catechism* (1836).[59] Displaying the range, versatility, and sense of audience that earned her such renown as a propagandist, each tract cast the antislavery argument in a new format. *Authentic Anecdotes* recorded and verified atrocities committed against slaves. *The Evils of Slavery* cited slaveholders themselves on the cruelty and economic inefficiency of their institution and proffered the "cure" of emancipation, as demonstrated by the encouraging results of abolition in the West Indies. Most original was the *Anti-Slavery Catechism*, which deserves a closer look.

Disarmingly appropriating a religious genre associated with conventional piety, it implicitly affirms the religious nature of the antislavery enterprise. Because nineteenth-century Protestantism assigned the mission of catechizing children to mothers, the catechism format also domesticates and feminizes the task of antislavery proselytism, which opponents pronounced beyond the bounds of woman's sphere. The familiar question-answer structure sets readers at ease and helps allay their suspicions of the radical doctrines propounded by abolitionists. Engaging readers in a dialogue that allows them to voice the concerns and objections typically raised by antiabolitionists, Child answers them in detail one by one.

Among the questions she puts in the mouth of her imaginary interlocutor: "Ought not the slaves to be fitted for freedom, before they are emancipated?" "[D]on't you think it would be dangerous to turn the slaves at once loose upon the community?" "[T]hey say your measures are unconstitutional." "[W]ould you at once give so many ignorant creatures political power, by making them voters?" And most explosive of all: "Is there any truth to the charge that you wish to break down all distinctions of society, . . . introduce the negroes into our parlors," and "promote the amalgamation of colored and white people?"[60]

In response, Child explains how abolitionists hope to bring about emancipation and how they envisage the transition from slavery to freedom, from inequality to equality. Abolitionists have never advocated "any legislative interference with the Southern States," she contends: "They merely wish to *induce the Southerners to legislate for themselves*; and they hope to do this by the universal dissemination of facts and arguments, calculated to promote a *correct public sentiment* on the subject of slavery . . ." (35).

Regarding the future of the emancipated slaves, Child denies that abolitionists have ever planned to turn them loose or to endow them instantly with voting rights and social equality. Rather, she describes what amounts to an extended apprenticeship as wage laborers and wards of the state: "[Abolitionists] merely wish to have the power of punishment transferred from individuals to magistrates; to have the sale of human beings cease; and to have the stimulus of *wages* applied, instead of the stimulus of the *whip*. The relation of master and laborer might still continue; but under circumstances less irksome and degrading to both parties" (18). Abolitionists recognize that "[a]n educated person will not naturally like to associate with one who is grossly ignorant," Child concedes. All they ask is that the children of the ignorant be granted "as fair a chance . . . to obtain an education, and rise in the world" as the children of the privileged (32–33). In sum, Child redefines the slaves' future integration as a problem of class, not race. And she holds out the same solution to them as to the working-class heroes of her *Juvenile Miscellany* stories: the gradual elimination of inequality through education and upward mobility.[61]

Besides continuing to write for the antislavery cause, Child was practicing her abolitionist principles in a new way at the Carpenters' — by sharing in an interracial household. Joseph and Margaret had accepted as boarders three black orphans (the children of an emancipated slave), and at their table black and white members of the household (including several black domestics) took their meals together — an unheard-of arrangement for the period. "The pleasure this gives me shows how my democracy increases with my years," Child commented to her mother-in-law.[62] She had also taken it upon herself to integrate the village school by accompanying the children there and ensuring their welcome.[63]

The peaceful atmosphere of the Carpenter home, the sense of living out her abolitionism despite the separation from her Boston comrades, and the publication of her three latest abolitionist tracts freed Child to indulge her longing for respite from "extended usefulness." She had in fact been chafing under her confinement to remunerative or practical works, she admitted in the preface to *Philothea*. She had started the novel four or five years ago, but the "spirit of the times" had perpetually forced her to abandon the "ideal" for the "actual": "[T]here have been seasons when my soul felt restless in this bondage, — like the Pegasus of German fable, chained to a plodding ox, and offered in the market; and as that rash steed, when he caught a glimpse of the far blue sky, snapped the chain that bound him, spread his wings, and left the earth beneath him — so I, for awhile, bid adieu to the substantial fields of utility, to float on the clouds of romance."[64] The metaphor conveys the feeling of enslavement Child had not permitted herself to acknowledge in her *History of the Condition of Women*. It also hints at a reason for her identification with the slave, of which she may not have been fully conscious. Like a woman on the auction block, sold as a physical commodity without regard for her immortal soul, she, too, may have felt as if her most sacred attribute — her literary talent — were being "offered in the market." A dream she proceeds to relate points toward yet another implication of the metaphor — that the "plodding ox" to which her Pegasus has been yoked is the husband who has cut short her flight in the sphere of romance (both literary and literal) by saddling her with his debts. In the dream, Child awakens to find that spring has suddenly transfigured her garden at Cottage Place, and the "radiance of morning" has transmuted the harbor in the distance into "'fairy land.'" Rapturously, she and David gaze on "a multitude of boats, with sails like the wings of butterflies," and among them, "a multitude of statues, that seemed to be endowed with life; some large and majestic, some of beautiful feminine proportions, and an almost infinite variety of lovely little cherubs." But as the two stand "absorbed in the intensity of delight," "an old woman with a checked apron" shatters their idyll with the words: "'Ma'am, I can't afford to let you have that brisket for eight pence a pound'" (vii–viii). Child offers her readers the interpretation David had ventured: "'The first part of it was dreamed by Philothea; the last, by the Frugal Housewife.'" Yet the haggling old woman seems to personify something more sinister — the financial worries that were sapping Child's creativity and destroying her marriage.

As Child's preface, with its invocation of her Paradis des Pauvres at Cottage Place, glosses over the deterioration of her marriage, her dedication repairs the breach with her other male mentor by announcing her debt "To my brother, the Reverend Convers Francis, of Watertown, Mass., to whose early influence I owe my love of literature. . . ." The gesture reasserts the bond she and Convers still shared — a love of Trancendentalist philosophy — at a time when abolitionism had come between them. Published a few weeks before Emerson's *Nature* and the first meeting of the Transcendental Club, over which Convers presided, *Philothea* expresses the same belief in the reality of visionary experience and the illusoriness of the material world. Child's heroine, Philothea (recognized by all her friends as an idealized self-portrait), thrills to Plato's disquisitions on the "everlasting harmony between the soul of man and the visible forms of creation," "associate[s] all earthly objects with things divine," hears the "music of the stars," and sees "the shining of god-like wings" everywhere in nature (40, 52, 72).[65]

The novel fuses Child's penchant for mysticism with her current political concerns. Set in Pericles' Athens, it counteracts racial prejudice by subtly reminding readers of Greek philosophy's Afro-Asiatic roots.[66] At Pericles' court, Plato engages in "earnest conversation with [the] learned Ethiopian" Tithonus and the Persian Artaphernes (35). The "sable" Tithonus cuts a "magnificent" figure with his "vigorous and finely-proportioned limbs." Testifying to the high level of civilization his people have achieved (and to the close relations between Ethiopia and Greece), he presents Pericles' consort Aspasia with "a beautiful box of ivory, inlaid with gold" and "wrought with exquisite skill," which "excite[s] universal admiration" (36).

While showing the ancient Athenians to be innocent of prejudice against Africans, Child uses her Greek setting as the medium for an allegorical critique of Andrew Jackson's America.[67] "[B]eneath the mask of democracy," political demagoguery and mob tyranny rule a society that has driven its most principled citizens into exile — a society that strives "to drown the din of domestic discord in boasts of foreign conquest" (109). Like the Childs, the philosopher Anaxagoras and his granddaughter Philothea prefer to live in poverty and obscurity rather than betray their ideals. And like Child, Philothea finds consolation in mysticism.

Belying the novel's affirmation of a religious faith and spiritual love that transcend all worldly sorrow, however, is its chilling embrace of death, to which its heroine repeatedly consecrates herself. First, Philothea gives up her lover, Paralus, to follow her grandfather into exile and to remain with him until he dies. Then, after Paralus has degenerated into the state of "one that dies while he lives," she marries him, deliberately accepting a relationship in which she will be her husband's "nurse" in lieu of his sexual partner (191, 204). "Pure and blameless . . . — with a mind richly endowed by the gods," yet stricken with a mysterious disease and lost in a dreamworld, Paralus uncannily resembles David. The ailment Child ascribes to Paralus suggests that David may have been suffering from a sexual dysfunction. At the very least, it suggests that at some level of her consciousness, Child may have come to fear her husband's "deficienc[i]es in business matters" (and perhaps in sexual matters as well) were "*incurable*," as she would later conclude.[68] Nevertheless, Child's idealization of Paralus indicates her unwillingness to reevaluate either her husband or her marriage at this stage. Paralleling Child's subordination of herself to David, Philothea perceives Paralus as a spiritual mentor who enjoys closer contact with transcendental realities than she does, even though it is she who sustains him. When Paralus finally dies, Philothea, too, wastes away. It is as though Child were anticipating the death of her marriage.[69]

If Philothea personifies the self-denying feminine ideal Child was aspiring to fulfill, her foil Aspasia embodies the assertive, ambitious, sexual self she was evidently trying to repress. David had once compared his prospective bride to Aspasia, but Child portrays this Greek celebrity in terms that evoke her own 1829 description of Frances Wright: "Tempted by self-conceit and a love of notoriety, she goes about preaching doctrines, which, if they have any effect at all, must be ruinous to the peace and good order of society."[70] "There is no immortality but fame," insists Aspasia, boasting: "Is there in all Greece a poet who has not sung my praises? Is there an artist who has not paid me tribute? . . . To the remotest period of time, the world . . . will hear of Aspasia the beautiful and the gifted!" (28). Philothea retorts: "When men talk of Aspasia the beautiful and the gifted, will they add, Aspasia the good — the happy — the innocent?" (29). Child herself could have echoed Aspasia's boast without adopting Philothea's qualification; she had reaped fame for both her intellectual gifts and her moral virtues. Yet in her depiction of Aspasia, she identifies the desire for fame with self-prostitution.

Aspasia recalls Child's caricature of Wright not only in her "self-conceit and . . . love of notoriety," but in the feminist and atheistical doctrines she preaches. Just as Wright's detractors had accused her of promulgating and practicing "free love," Aspasia, a courtesan, has prevailed on Pericles to divorce his wife and marry her. She has gone on to challenge the subordination of women in Greek society by inviting women to soirees previously open only to men, urging them to renounce the "tyrannical custom" of wearing veils, and encouraging them to perform in public (24). Philothea's friend Eudora welcomes such innovations. "What is the use of a beautiful face, if one must be shut up in her own apartment forever? And what avails skill in music, if there is no chance to display it?" she demands. But Philothea counters: "Why should a true-hearted woman wish to display her beautiful face, or her skill in music, to any but those on whom her affections are bestowed" (16)? Like those who vilified Wright as a "Sampson in petticoats," Child figures Aspasia as simultaneously attacking the edifices of society and of religion. Hence, Aspasia derides the stories of the gods as "fables" and greets Philothea's belief in a "future existence" with "an incredulous smile" (26–27).

Child categorically rejects the model of liberated womanhood Aspasia/Wright incarnates. Instead, she espouses the self-effacing model Philothea offers. Though Philothea, like Aspasia, has "great intellectual gifts," which have won her "a degree of respect not usually bestowed upon women of that period," she chooses to exercise them in a purely domestic setting: "the restraint of public opinion was unnecessary to keep her within the privacy of domestic life; for it was her own chosen home." Eschewing authorship in her own right, she copies the manuscripts of her grandfather and plays the humble role of "auditor to the philosophers, poets, and artists, who were ever fond of gathering round the good old man." That is, she acts as an auxiliary rather than a rival of men. She also practices the virtues of "industry and frugality" that Child had celebrated as a purveyor of domestic advice. "Living in almost complete seclusion," as Child had after her marriage, she devotes herself to such domestic duties as preparing "frugal repast[s]," and she reserves the pursuit of artistic and intellectual pleasures for her "leisure hours" (76).

Against the model of Philothea, Child holds up Eudora as an example of what happens to women when they succumb to the baneful influence of an Aspasia or a Frances Wright. "[T]ransformed into a vain, restless, ambitious woman, wild for distinction, and impatient of restraint" (77), Eudora falls prey to the blandishments of the seducer Alcibiades and alienates her true love, the noble Philaemon. Eudora thus learns from experience how dangerous ambition can be for a woman. Forced to flee to Persia, where Philaemon ultimately forgives and marries her, she adjusts to a far more repressive confinement of women than she had chafed against in Greece.

Philothea, Eudora, and Aspasia all represent projections of the selves Child wished or feared to be. Through Philothea, she embraces a stifling domestic ideal and belittles her formidable literary talents, reducing herself to the lowly "copyist" of her male mentors. Through Eudora and Aspasia, she punishes herself for the ambitions and sexual desires she equates with exhibitionism and promiscuity. The three women also represent perversely distorted images of the public and private identities Child was struggling to reconcile in her life: the domestic expert and loving spouse, the literary lion and darling of Boston's salons, the political advocate and heroine of the antislavery movement. Publicly, Child had succeeded in negotiating the transition from each persona to the next with consummate grace. Privately, as *Philothea* shows, the conflicts among her different selves were tearing her apart.

In sum, *Philothea* seems to repudiate the theories and arguments "incidentally implied" in Child's *History of the Condition of Women*. Far from exposing the arbitrary tyranny of the practices that restrict women to a narrow sphere in male-dominated societies, the novel discredits feminist rebellion, idealizes traditional feminine roles, and apotheosizes a deadly self-sacrifice as the highest virtue. Yet it also registers the awareness Child was trying so hard to repress—that she was killing the most vibrant part of herself by abnegating her independent identity and allowing an "incurable" husband to direct the course of her life.

Ironically, the novel that so stridently proclaimed its author's renunciation of ambition restored her to a measure of the literary fame she had forfeited. Just as the reviewers of *Hobomok* had indicated their willingness to reward Child if she would use her talents to uphold rather than to subvert their values, so the reviewers of *Philothea* welcomed her back into the literary fold and intimated that they would gladly regard the *Appeal* as an aberration, provided she would put abolitionism behind her. Sarah Hale assured readers of the *Ladies' Magazine* that *Philothea* had "nothing in common with the 'Frugal Housewife,' or the 'Appeal, &c.'—except the directness of expression and energy of purpose, which always mark the writings of the authoress." *Philothea* did "credit to Mrs. Child, and to her sex," she judged. Cornelius Felton of the *North American Review*, recalling that the "early writings of Mrs. Child" had given "brilliant promise of future eminence in the path of imaginative literature," expressed "pleasure at meeting [her] again in the calm and gladsome light of literature" after a hiatus he had viewed "with some surprise and more regret." He found her heroine "a beautiful creation," "a lovely dream of Mrs. Child's imagination." The novel would "take a permanent place in our elegant literature," he predicted: "Every page of it breathes the inspiration of genius." Most surprising was the praise of Poe in the *Southern Literary Messenger* — a mouthpiece of proslavery ideology. Poe pronounced *Philothea* a work of "no common order" that placed the "well known" author of *Hobomok*, *The Frugal Housewife*, and *The Mother's Book* "in a new and most favorable light": "we turn to these pure and quiet pages with that species of gasping satisfaction with which a drowning man clutches the shore." Poe especially liked the passages describing the "dreamy, distraught, yet unembittered existence of the husband, revelling in the visions of the Platonic philosophy" — which must have reminded him of his own obsessed heroes. The novel was "an honor to our country, and a signal triumph for our country-women," he concluded, adding that its "purity of language" and "lofty morality" recommended it for use in "our female academies." Once again, Child had won her way back into respectability.[71]

Besides earning the acclaim of the critics, *Philothea* would enjoy considerable popularity in Transcendentalist circles. Young Henry David Thoreau, a senior at Harvard, copied two pages of extracts from the novel into his notebook. And Thomas Wentworth Higginson remembered it as "one of those delights of boyhood which the criticism of maturity cannot disturb." The novel also appealed to Child's friends in the Boston Female Anti-Slavery Society. On her return to Boston in April 1836, they gathered at Louisa Loring's to hear Child read the manuscript, and Anne Warren Weston reported that her sister Maria thought it "very fine." Perhaps Child's comrades shared some of her ambivalence about redefining their roles as women.[72]

Shortly after Child finished *Philothea*, proslavery Texans conquered the region that included Lundy's Tamaulipas land grant, forcing him to abandon his plans for a free labor colony. He and David now shifted their energy toward a far more effective use of their talents than the original scheme would have been — lobbying against the threatened annexation of Texas. In a series of articles they unmasked annexation as a plot to expand the southern slave empire and increase the slave states' representation in Congress. These articles furnished John Quincy Adams and other free-soil advocates with vital facts and arguments in the ensuing congressional debates over annexation, which eventuated in delaying it for almost a decade.[73]

Meanwhile, however, the Childs were again in limbo. In May 1836 George Thompson renewed the invitation for them to take up residence in England, now to edit a periodical that British abolitionists were planning to found. The organizers already had "subscribed fifty pounds sterling" to meet the Childs' initial expenses, he informed them. Additionally, he assured Child that Britain's two premier literary journals, the *Westminster Review* and the *Edinburgh Review*, badly wanted "an able American writer." Child was well-esteemed in England, where all her commercial works since *The Frugal Housewife* had been reissued by British firms, some in numerous printings. A stint in

English literary circles would have given a tremendous boost to her career, while the intellectual stimulation she would have derived from interacting with some of the best minds in a European metropolis would have broadened her horizons and perhaps directed her onto new paths. "With a settled prospect of doing *something somewhere*," Child reported to Louisa, "I find hope again springing up in my heart. I do not wake up, as I have for months past with a load on my heart."[74]

Her rejoicing was premature. This time David, who had hitherto shown no caution where his own financial gambles were concerned, insisted on watertight guarantees. First, he consulted an American diplomat familiar with living conditions in England, his old friend from the legation in Portugal, John James Appleton. Appleton, whom Child characterized as "a very calculating, prudent man, with great experience of the ways of the world," balanced the Childs' "expenses" against their "prospects" and concluded that they would "do well in England." Not satisfied with this, David then wrote to Thompson in Child's name, claiming, as she told Louisa, "that *I* am not willing to try my chance in a foreign country, without some degree of *certainty* concerning support—such as a specified number of subscribers already gained."[75] Of course, Thompson could provide no such certainty. Nor had Child herself ever required that kind of security in the past. On the contrary, she had always relied on her own shrewd assessment of the market, sometimes even going against the advice of publishers, as in the case of *The Frugal Housewife* and *The Mother's Book*. Moreover, she had succeeded in all her purely commercial ventures, and during her editorship of the *Juvenile Miscellany*, she had proved herself capable of multiplying subscriptions overnight.[76] It is hard to avoid suspecting that the real problem was not the alleged lack of financial backing in England, but David's unacknowledged reluctance to find himself once again eclipsed by his brilliant wife in a literary milieu where she would have many more opportunities than he for earning income.

During the spring and summer of 1836 the Childs hit a psychological nadir. After a brief visit to Boston alone in April, where Child felt "like a troubled spirit" without David, the couple moved in with David's parents in West Boylston. There, David "digged and ploughed, and built fences, and laid stone wall, until his hands [were] as hard as horn," and Child kept "very busy ironing, sweeping, washing dishes, sewing &c for [David's] aged mother." Awaiting word from Thompson, Child tried to take comfort in the apple blossoms and nesting birds. Thanks to the beauties of the countryside, the consciousness of being useful again, and especially her reading of the late-medieval mystic Thomas à Kempis, she announced to Louisa, she was happier than she had been for many months. Thomas à Kempis's counsel to renounce all earthly desire had been "a *real* source of consolation," she confided. Quoting a passage in which Thomas represented God as telling a sinner that "thy salvation depends upon thy being sometimes left in the full perception of thine own impotence and wretchedness," she applied the lesson to herself: "My long cloudy state of religious darkness is clearing away. I see more clearly what is required of me, and am more willing to *give up*."[77] Child was doing her best to achieve the deadly self-abnegation she had idealized in her heroine Philothea.

As the hope of going to England receded and David talked of migrating to Illinois, Child's religious resignation turned to weary despair. "Unless God sees that it is necessary for your spiritual progress, I hope you never *may* be able to realize that state of mind when *rest* is the first, the last, the *only* good desired," she wrote Louisa. Further complicating the Childs' situation and delaying its resolution, David's former partner George Snelling changed his mind about settling out of court. In July Child finally decided to leave David in West Boylston and go stay with her father in South Natick (about forty miles away), where she would have the leisure to write something remunerative.[78]

Overwhelmed with loneliness and weighed down by her father's congenital gloom, however, Child spent more time writing to David than she did on her current project — compiling *The Family Nurse* (1837). "I feel as if I would travel ten miles, if I could only sit and knit behind the wood-pile, speaking to you now and then while you were at work," she repined after finding no letters from David at the post office. Seeking to cheer David as well as herself, she went on to invoke the lessons she had learned from Thomas à Kempis:

> I *hope* the various and continuing trials through which we have passed will not prove in vain — that they will serve to widen and deepen our sympathies for all the suffering of the human family — that they will strengthen and elevate our affection for each other, that they will enable us to place our trust in God rather than man. I *believe* that they *are* working this effect. From no other point of view, but our present lowly one, could either of us see so distinctly the numerous errors of our past lives. I believe we shall both come out of this fog purified and strenthened; and that you will *yet* be placed in a situation where the energies of your mind and the good feelings of your heart will have a fair field of action.

Child's letter nevertheless reveals that far from bringing them closer, the stress she and David were undergoing was destroying their marriage. Blaming herself for their deteriorating relationship, as she had so often before, Child tried to wring a word of endearment from David: "If we can but live *together*, and you still love me, notwithstanding my many faults, and my frequent failures in duty, I will not ask for more of *this* world's goods. *Do* you love me? God only knows how deeply and tenderly I love you; and how often the tears start to my eyes because I cannot relieve your troubles."[79]

David apparently replied only by pouring out his discouragement in a "sad letter" that has not survived. Despondent about his future prospects, flagellating himself for his past "errors of judgment," and smarting over his loss of status, he seems to have withdrawn emotionally. Child's letters convey the impression that her husband was too immersed in his own misery to show much affection. She reacted by attempting to bolster his ego — and by disparaging herself in the process. "Few men have done more good in the world than you have done. Few are more *truly* respected, though thousands are more popular," she assured David. She proceeded to credit him with the role of preceptor in their marriage and to bewail her failure to live up to the same standard of conjugal devotion:

I weep when I think how selfish and unreasonable I have often been. . . . God knows that I consider my union with you his richest blessing. It has made me a better and a happier woman than I ever was before. . . . [Y]ou have been to me a most kind, considerate, and forgiving husband; and I have ever loved and respected you with my whole heart. How many times have you guided me when I was wrong! How many times have you strengthened me, when I have been weak! How often restored me to my balance, when I have been perverse and unreasonable![80]

Obviously hurt by David's unresponsiveness, when she wrote again several days later, Child put on a jaunty front and indulged in humor at her own expense. "What if I *do* write three or four letters to your writing one?" she asked. Adopting the pose of a lovesick girl languishing after an indifferent suitor, she told David:

If *you* are inclined to laugh about the little heart at South Natick, which morning, noon, and night is filled with yearning to see you, and with tender recollections of many passages that have occurred since we journeyed through life together, — why you *may* laugh. . . . This makes the fifth letter I have written to you since I have been here; but what of that? It has been a great comfort to me to write them, and perhaps it has been *some* comfort to you to receive them.[81]

Painful to read, these letters present the spectacle of a successful, independent-minded woman reduced to pleading abjectly for love and abasing herself to the husband responsible for sabotaging her career.

Yet Child did not utterly renounce control of her fate. She suggested to David a practical way out of his impasse — to apply for the editorship of the American Anti-Slavery Society's newspaper, *The Emancipator*, which Amos Phelps was about to vacate. The job would allow David to earn much-needed income while the Snelling lawsuit was pending, and unlike the western frontier, New York City, where the paper was based, would be a good place for Child to research and write the history of slavery she was meditating. David could take the editorship for three to six months and decide later "whether to proceed to Illinois," Child urged. David pursued the suggestion, and Garrison strongly promoted his candidacy. *The Emancipator* needed an editor competent to "unravel" the intricacies of political subjects like the annexation issue, he pointed out. "I cherish a profound regard for your extensive acquirements, your solid talents, your vigor and originality of mind, and your disinterestedness, generosity and magnanimity of soul," Garrison told David, adding that he had "dwelt . . . upon the importance of securing your assistance at this time because I believe you would do justice to that branch of our cause."[82] But ignoring Garrison's recommendation, the New York Evangelicals in charge of the AASS ultimately replaced Phelps with another Evangelical, Joshua Leavitt.[83] Although religious parochialism probably influenced the choice, the New Yorkers were also shrewd businessmen. They knew David owed his predicament largely to the debts he had mounted up during his editorship of the *Massachusetts Journal* — a fact that did not bode well for his ability to keep the *Emancipator* on a sound financial footing.

Nothing could more clearly have indicated the collapse of the Childs' antislavery partnership than the gap that opened between them in the summer of 1836, as David remained immobilized in West Boylston and Child continued to write and work for the cause in South Natick and Boston. David could hardly have helped feeling sidelined when a critical slave case arose that August, which his wife was instrumental in taking to court and his friends Loring and Sewall were instrumental in winning. Abolitionists had been looking for an opportunity to test whether Massachusetts law automatically freed any slave voluntarily brought into the state by visiting slaveholders. The occasion arrived when Child learned at a meeting of the Boston Female Anti-Slavery Society that a New Orleans slaveholder vacationing in Boston had brought a young black girl with her. Along with a delegation of her friends, she called on the family "to ascertain beyond doubt whether the child was a slave, [and] whether there was intention to carry her back to New Orleans." The women then turned the evidence over to Loring and Sewall, whom they chose to litigate the case of the "slave child, Med." In an argument widely acclaimed for its impressive command of legal precedent and brilliant exposition of the consequences that would ensue from applying slave law in a free state, Loring convinced Chief Justice Lemuel Shaw to rule that Massachusetts law did not recognize an institution "contrary to the principles of justice, and of nature, and repugnant to the provisions of the Declaration of Rights." Though Shaw pointedly restricted the scope of the verdict to avoid undermining the 1793 Fugitive Slave Law (auguring how he would enforce the buttressed version of that law in the 1850s), abolitionists rejoiced in a major victory. Freed and adopted by Garrison's partner, Isaac Knapp, "little Med" was renamed "Maria Somersett" in honor of Maria Child and the main legal precedent on which Loring had relied, the famous Somerset case argued by the eighteenth-century British abolitionist Granville Sharpe.[84]

Loring's triumph in the Med case must have brought home to David how thoroughly he had marginalized himself since wrecking his legal practice in the ill-fated *Panda* case the previous year. Despite his fund of legal knowledge, he no longer had the credibility to represent abolitionists in court, unlike Loring and Sewall, with whom he had stood shoulder to shoulder at the outset. The public acknowledgment of his wife's role in a case from which he had been excluded could only have reinforced his sense of having lost his prominent place in antislavery ranks. Small wonder if he was exploring alternative avenues to distinction, which would take him far from the scene of his past failures and remove him from competition with his literary wife and lawyer friends.

As the Med case was winding up, the Childs left for New York, apparently to inquire personally about taking over the editorship of the *Emancipator*.[85] "Five minutes" after they had landed in the city, however, an opportunity far more appealing to David turned up. David's friend George Kimball, a co-founder of the Noyes Academy who had planned to accompany Lundy to Tamaulipas but had since moved to Illinois, met David in New York with the news that several "wealthy gentlemen" in Alton, Illinois, were proposing to form a company to manufacture beet sugar, which they hoped to market as a substitute for slave-grown cane sugar. They were looking for someone willing to learn the process, still a closely guarded secret in the United States, though widely diffused in France and Belgium. If David would volunteer, they would fund the trip to Europe. Naturally, he leaped at it.[86]

From David's perspective, the attractions of the scheme were manifold. First, he had long supported the "free produce" movement and its goal of boycotting the products of slave labor. The discovery of beet sugar seemed providential. As Child explained to another "free produce" sympathizer, the millionaire philanthropist Gerrit Smith, "[t]his simple vegetable, having the *color* of blood but not its *stain*," furnished the stone that could down the Goliath of slavery.[87] Second, the manufacture of beet sugar offered a field of antislavey activism that David could pioneer unrivaled. Fluent in French and well-versed in farming, he was ideally suited for the mission of studying beet growing and sugar production in France and Belgium. And that mission would enable him to travel through Europe as an abolitionist celebrity with an original agenda, not as an appendage of his famous wife. Third, launching a new industry promised David a means of earning a fortune and thus restoring his sense of manhood. The financial motive, which had also drawn him to Lundy's free labor colony, became stronger than ever when David learned that he had lost the Snelling lawsuit and now owed his former partner a staggering $9,750, on top of all his previous debts.[88]

As she had done so often before, Child repressed her misgivings and frustration and tried to support David's decision, though she keenly felt the injustice of being forced to renounce her own dream of going to England. "My poverty, but not my will, consented to remaining behind, while one I loved so much was going where I so much wished to go," she confessed to her mother-in-law.[89] Child's persistent denial of her own needs would cost her dearly. Her literary productivity, so extraordinary until then, would come to an abrupt halt. The depression and emotional withdrawal she had betrayed in *Philothea* would deepen. Above all, the unresolved conflicts she had projected onto her three female protagonists would continue to hold her back, even as other women in the antislavery movement were questioning the ideology that kept them subordinate to men.

Among those radical women, none more forcefully embodied the challenge to the doctrine of separate spheres than the South Carolina slaveholders' daughter-turned-Quaker Angelina Grimké, whom Child had met during the same visit to Philadelphia that had introduced David to Benjamin Lundy. The intersecting trajectories of Child's and Grimké's antislavery careers, the shifting positions they occupied in the controversy over the "woman question," and the reciprocal influence they exerted on each other illustrate the common problems that bound Child to her abolitionist sisters as they struggled to define new roles for themselves. It was no small irony that what brought the two women together at a juncture when Child was allowing herself to be swallowed up in her husband's chimeras was the Philadelphia Female Anti-Slavery Society's invitation to David to address the group.

Child was deeply impressed by this young woman, "born and educated at the south," who felt such a passionate sense of solidarity with the slaves. "A lady told [Angelina] that she suffered her heart to be too much engrossed with the subject of slavery — that the suitable time had not yet come, for action," Child reported. "She replied, very mildly, 'If thou wert a slave, toiling in the fields of Carolina, I apprehend thou wouldst think the time had *fully* come."[90] Angelina was equally impressed with the famous New England writer whose masterful indictment of slavery and racism had proved a woman's ability to match or surpass a man's intellectual power. She had read the *Appeal* some months earlier and been "much pleased" with it, as she had confided in a letter to the *Liberator* describing how she had been "brought into deep and solemn exercise of mind" on the subject of slavery.[91] At the moment of their encounter, Child's ideas on the equality of the sexes were far in advance of Angelina's. "I verily believed in *female subordination until* very recently," Angelina later acknowledged to a friend.[92]

By the time the two women renewed their acquaintance at the Anti-Slavery Convention of American Women in May 1837, however, they had reversed roles. In the interim, Angelina had been playing an increasingly prominent part in both Philadelphia and New York antislavery circles, where she had been giving women's groups an inside view of the slave system. Child, in contrast, had been participating less and less in Boston antislavery activities, for she had withdrawn into a deep depression.

Returning to South Natick after David's departure for Europe, Child spent the winter of 1836 and the spring of 1837 holed up with her chronically doleful father. "Father . . . *wants* to make me happy; but he so habitually looks on the dark side, that I believe he would keep the very larks from singing," she complained to her sister-in-law. "To contend with his gloom and my own too, has sometimes seemed a hopeless task."[93]

Though recognizing that she may have inherited her tendency to depression from her father, Child had a special reason for being "gloomy almost to madness." As she spelled out to both Lydia and Louisa Loring, she had received only three "rather business like" letters from David in six months. The first, brief and uncommunicative, had not contained a single word of affection. Written three months later, the second, albeit somewhat "more loving," had been mostly taken up with a communication to David's friend George Kimball "about machinery &c." Child could barely repress her anger at her husband's selfishness and irresponsibility. With surprising candor, she told her sister-in-law that she had all but ceased to care when she and David would be "reunited" and where they would go once he came back: "I have so much lost my interest in all things connected with this life, that I care but little about anything." Speculating about whether it would pay to manufacture beet sugar as an alternative to slave-grown cane sugar, she avowed: "I have a sort of superstition that his customary bad luck will follow him in every thing. The fact is, I no longer have any hope concerning these matters." But she hastened to add, "it seems to me I can be content to have him with me in the poorest and dreariest corner of the world."[94]

Child unburdened herself even more frankly to Louisa. She had recurrently felt "out of sorts with matrimony" in past months, she divulged, after receiving David's second letter. She also noted David's vagueness about both "his '*pecunary*' affairs" (mimicking her father's pronunciation) and his probable date of return, which he had set for some time in May or June (actually he would not come home until late fall). "[H]ow he is to stay abroad so long is more than I can imagine, without he 'adds in the Year of our Lord into the sum of his profits,' " she commented drily.[95] But several weeks later, apparently after receiving a third letter, she was already reproaching herself for her lack of faith in David and deflecting her anger against him toward herself. "Does n't my husband write dear good letters?" she gushed to Louisa: "They have almost wrought a miracle in my feelings. To tell the truth, when I was in Boston, waiting so long for a line from him, I had a foolish *jealousy* that he was pleasuring away in Europe, forgetful of his poor old wife. With all my experience of his true and affectionate heart, this was exceedingly absurd and unreasonable." Attributing her querulousness to "repeated disappointments and discouragements," she assured Louisa that David's "dear letters" had "dissipated all my envy of 'old maids,' like mist before the sun."[96]

Only two of David's letters from Europe have survived, dated February 12 and June 7. Neither seems to be the one Child found so comforting. Characteristically, their closely written pages are filled with impersonal cultural and political commentary, no doubt intended for publication in the *Liberator*. As in the letter David had written to Child from New Hampshire six years earlier, he implies that he appreciates her more when he is away from her: "It is a strange inconsistency and caprice of human nature not to appreciate happiness until it is gone." What makes him miss his wife is neither the desire to share the experience of Europe with her nor a yearning for physical intimacy, but a reminder of her domestic nurturing: "A few days ago I happened for the first time to resort to ball of white yarn, and when I found a pin [?] that you had put in the end to keep it from unwinding, this little incident brought you before me and made my heart rise to my mouth." Anticipating Child's reaction to a letter so lacking in affection despite its length, he writes: "Now my love I calculate that your [illegible] heart is quite grieved, and your lips ready to give me a good [crossed out] scolding because I write about that [crossed out] what you do not care a button for." As if to blame his wife for his coldness toward her, he explains: "I have not yet got over the electric shock, which the only letter I have recd since any of mine were received, gave me." His sole effort to express love rings false: "I do feel fairly homesick, and compare my present existence with the delightful years I have passed in your sweet & enchanting society, to some black dream, or to one of falling from the high beams."[97]

If the degeneration of the Childs' marriage is painfully obvious in these letters, so is Child's inability to face it. Doing without David seemed more unbearable than "the poorest and dreariest" existence with him.[98] Hence the paralyzing depression she was experiencing—the result of anger turned inward. So unyielding was its grip that Child could no longer function. For the first time in her life, she was suffering from writer's block. She could not finish the antislavery novel she had started that winter and would eventually destroy. And she had all but given up abolitionist work.

When women antislavery activists decided to hold a "Female Convention" in New York the following spring, Child opted out, even though the BFASS had voted to pay all her expenses. She did not want to take money away from the two other delegates, Susan Paul and Mary Parker, she claimed. But her confession to Henrietta Sargent, one of her most intimate friends in the group, lay closer to the truth: "I am in a vacillating and discouraged state of mind. I feel as if I had no more to do in the world — or at least no *power* to do any more."[99] Fortunately, Sargent and Chapman, to whom Child appealed for help in deciding where her duty lay, convinced her that it lay in accepting the mandate to represent her sisters at the convention. Her participation in that event, where she would share the limelight with Angelina Grimké, would reenergize Child and take her out of herself, at least temporarily. But it would not overcome her ambivalence about whether to espouse a female model of antislavery activism or to elect complete equality with men on a gender-integrated platform — the course Angelina and her sister Sarah had come to favor.

A historic milestone, the four-day Anti-Slavery Convention of American Women that opened on May 9, 1837, was not only "the first public political meeting of U.S. women," but "the first interracial gathering of any consequence."[100] Some two hundred women attended, including many members of black female organizations. No men were admitted. Rejecting an offer by the abolitionist Theodore Weld to help run the meeting, the women tartly rejoined that "they had *minds* of their own and could transact their business *without* his direction" (4).[101] The antiabolitionist press viciously lampooned the convention as an "Amazonian farce" staged by "a monstrous *regiment* of women": "The spinster has thrown aside her distaff — . . . the matron her darning-needle — the sweet novelist her crow-quill," the young mother her infant, and "the kitchen maid her pots and frying-pans — to discuss the weighty matters of state." Reporters also targeted "Mrs. Child" and the "sisters Grimké" for special mention.[102] An index of their notoriety, the publicity Child and the Grimkés attracted accords with the dominant roles they played at the convention. Child and Angelina presented the largest number of resolutions and consistently took the most radical stands, with Sarah running a distant third.[103]

Three controversial issues arose at the convention: racial prejudice, "the province of woman," and religious sectarianism. The latter two in particular sparked dissension that presaged the schisms about to erupt in the abolitionist movement at large. More subtle in its effects, prejudice divided abolitionists along racial rather than ideological lines, segregating blacks from all but the most progressive white sympathizers.

Deeply committed to fighting against prejudice, Child and Angelina joined in bringing the issue to the forefront. After a resolution against the Colonization Society and the racism it fostered had elicited "touching appeals from the colored members of the Convention," Angelina denounced the "unnatural prejudice against our colored population" as "one of the chief pillars of American slavery" (19). She went on to bring the lesson home to abolitionists, whose prejudices she had noticed with dismay in Philadelphia and New York. Her resolution exhorted women "to pray to be delivered from such an unholy feeling, and to act out the principles of Christian equality by associating with [blacks] as though the color of the skin was of no more consequence than that of the hair, or the eyes" (19). Child proposed two resolutions that translated Angelina's into concrete terms by addressing the problems of job discrimination, economic opportunity, and segregation. It was "the duty of abolitionists to encourage our oppressed brethren and sisters in their different trades and dealings by employing them," she asserted. She also urged abolitionists to "use all our influence in having our colored friends seated promiscuously in all our congregations" and to "take our seats with them" in churches "disgraced with side-seats and corners set apart for them" (24).

Indicating the two women's reversal of roles since their meeting in Philadelphia, however, Angelina and not Child was the one to propose the most hotly debated resolution of the convention:

> That as certain rights and duties are common to all moral beings, the time has come for woman to move in that sphere which Providence has assigned her, and no longer remain satisfied in the circumscribed limits with which corrupt custom and a perverted application of Scripture have encircled her; therefore that it is the duty of woman, and the province of woman, to plead the cause of the oppressed in our land, and to do all that she can by her voice, and her pen, and her purse, and the influence of her example, to overthrow the horrible system of American slavery. (13)

What made this statement so controversial was the implicit challenge it posed to the orthodox interpretation of the Bible—a challenge Sarah Grimké would spell out a few months later in her first letter on the equality of the sexes. Like her seventeenth-century precursor Anne Hutchinson, Angelina was here claiming the right to reinterpret Scripture for herself, without the aid of an erring clergy. She was also claiming, as Sarah would in more detail, that Providence had assigned woman a status equal, and not subordinate, to man's, contrary to clerical dogma. Evangelical women could not assent to such a proposition without denying their creed. Twelve women who voted against it insisted on having their names recorded when the resolution passed over their objections. All but two belonged to the New York-based group of abolitionists whose male kin would quit the American Anti-Slavery Society in 1840 when women were named to its business committee and governing board.

Interestingly, Child, who had of course supported the resolution, moved the following day that it be reconsidered, in deference to the feelings of the Evangelicals. Perhaps she already sensed and was trying to head off the rumblings of the bitter schism that the clergy would soon succeed in fomenting. Yet the very same morning, she herself introduced resolutions opposed by three of the same orthodox women. Directed against the most powerful benevolent organizations of the Evangelical establishment, her resolutions criticized the Bible and missionary societies for taking donations from slaveholders and recommended that "followers of Christ . . . ascertain with fervent prayer, what God will have them to do in this matter" (14–15). If Child was choosing the ground on which to wage a struggle, she was apparently signifying that she felt more comfortable taking her stand against sectarian bigotry generally than against orthodox notions of "woman's sphere" specifically.

Their first opportunity to run their own antislavery convention gave women invaluable political experience. In the long run, it prepared some for the radical step of demanding woman suffrage eleven years later, at the groundbreaking Seneca Falls

Women's Rights Convention, organized by Lucretia Mott and Elizabeth Cady Stanton. In the short run, the most significant political initiative to emerge from the four-day meeting was a campaign to collect a million signatures on petitions to Congress for the abolition of slavery and the slave trade in the District of Columbia — a campaign that would also further women's political education and whet their appetite for a larger share in determining the nation's destiny. It was Child who explained the benefits of circulating petitions and suggested how to coordinate the campaign (21).[104]

The 1837 Convention marked the peak of Child's involvement in female antislavery activism. Although she had moved that "a Convention of Anti-Slavery Women be held annually . . . until slavery is abolished" (23), she never attended another. When Caroline Weston and Lucretia Mott tried to enlist her in the conventions of 1838 and 1839, she replied that she had "never . . . entered very earnestly into the plan of female conventions and societies." They had probably contributed to "the freedom of women," she conceded, "but in every other point of view . . . their influence [had] been very slight." It was a revealing formulation, once again suggesting the low priority Child assigned to advancing the "freedom of women" at a time when feminists like Mott, Weston, Chapman, and the Grimkés had already recognized the need for women to emancipate themselves if they were to aid effectively in the emancipation of the slaves.[105]

Consummating the reversal of roles between Child and the Grimkés, Angelina and Sarah went on to blaze the path Child had balked at reconnoitering. Engaged by the American Anti-Slavery Society as lecturers, they shortly began speaking not only to women's groups, but to mixed audiences at which they drew huge crowds. Meanwhile, Child turned a deaf ear to pleas by Theodore Weld and others urging her to follow the Grimkés' lead.[106]

As the Grimkés' lecture tour provoked increasing opposition from the clergy and mounting consternation among abolitionists of orthodox persuasion, Child strongly supported the sisters in a course she rejected for herself. Yet she remained uneasy with direct advocacy of women's rights. In long conversations with Angelina and Sarah, she advised them "not to *talk* about our right, but simply [to] go forward and *do* whatsoever we deem a duty," as she reported in an 1839 letter to the *Liberator*. It was a strategy that served a double purpose: to sidestep a controversy threatening to deflect attention from the struggle against slavery, and to defuse the anger against the oppressor that protest against oppression inevitably arouses in the oppressed. The Grimkés answered that they found such a strategy crippling and ultimately self-defeating. "[T]hey considered the establishment of woman's freedom of vital importance to the anti-slavery cause. 'Little can be done for the slave,' said they, 'while this prejudice blocks up the way.'" Dismayed by Child's timidity on the issue, "[T]hey urged me to say and do more about woman's rights, nay, at times they gently rebuked me for my want of zeal," she recalled. But she stuck to her position: "In toiling for the freedom of others, we shall find our own." That is, Child envisaged women's emancipation as a byproduct of their unselfish labors, rather than as a goal in its own right.[107]

Still, the Grimkés' arguments for a more militant stand were not lost on Child, and the years to come would bring yet another reversal of roles between them. Angelina, who married Theodore Weld in May 1838, would suddenly confront the difficulties Child had been contending with for ten years. Overwhelmed by the all-consuming tasks of housekeeping and childrearing on a poverty-level income — tasks for which the Grimkés' upbringing as southern ladies had ill-prepared them — the sisters would withdraw from antislavery activism for decades.[108]

On receiving her first letter from Angelina six months after the wedding, Child joked: "I began to think it was with you as with a girl, who being met by a person with whom she had formerly lived at service, was asked, 'Where do you live now, Nancy'? 'Please, ma'am, I dont live anywhere now; I'm married.' "[109] Child might have been speaking of herself, for she had given up her writing to help David grow sugar beets on a farm in Northampton, Massachusetts. In her case, however, the domestic drudgery and professional extinction that David's latest ill-fated venture brought on her finally precipitated the long delayed crisis in the couple's marriage. That crisis would liberate Child at last from her thralldom to the ideal of the "good wife," which had cost her so much suffering, and enable her to explore alternative identities for herself and her sisters.

I I

Schisms, Personal and Political

"I have never been so discouraged about abolition, as since we came into this iron-bound Valley of the Connecticut," wrote Child to Henrietta Sargent, about six months after settling in Northampton, Massachusetts.[1] Her discouragement stemmed from many sources, some personal, some political; for the new phase of her life beginning with the move to Northampton in May 1838, encompassing her stint as editor of the New York-based *National Anti-Slavery Standard* from 1841 to 1843, and ending with her decision to resume her literary career in May 1843, witnessed the simultaneous disintegration of her marriage and of the antislavery movement.

David's attempt to launch the production of beet sugar in Massachusetts as a means of undercutting one of the slave South's most lucrative staple crops—cane sugar—represented his last serious gesture toward establishing himself in a financially re-munerative enterprise. From the start, it was dogged with ill omens. The Illinois Beet Sugar Company, which had sent him to Europe with the promise "to pay all his expenses and give him a liberal salary beside[s] . . . dissolved in air" during his absence, and "he never received a cent."[2] Months of uncertainty had followed, during which the Childs had lived with the Lorings—an arrangement Child had found so "galling" to her "pride of personal independence," despite the two families' long-standing inti-macy, that she had insisted on reimbursing them for "board" as soon as she received her next royalty payment.[3] Finally, David had landed a prospect of employment with a company willing to set up a beet sugar factory in Northampton—only to have that company, too, die stillborn when the entrepreneurs who were to have financed it lost money speculating in silks.[4] Meanwhile, David had ordered several hundred dollars' worth of machinery in Europe, which Child ended up having to pay for out of her earnings from *The Frugal Housewife*. "It is a dreadful hard time that you have, but I expect you will rest on a bed of roses by & by," he assured his wife with undaunted optimism.[5]

Still struggling against the growing conviction that David's misfortunes were largely of his own making, Child kept his precarious financial situation to herself until much later, meeting the inquiries of concerned Boston friends with studied silence.[6] Instead, she wrote jauntily about her "Herculean labors" in the beet field David had planted on an acre of rented land (which turned out to have lost much of its fertility). "I often go and help him weed three or four hours night and morning," rising "sometimes at 3 o'clock, sometimes at 4; when all the world, except the birds, are asleep. Think of that Mrs. Remarkable Lazy-bones!" Child boasted to Louisa. To spur each other on, she and David conjured up pictures of the "loitering breakfasts . . . running almost into midday" in the Loring household, and "jibed and jeered about" whether anything "short of saving Ellis' life" — or that of little Med, the young girl they had all participated in rescuing from slavery — would "tempt Louisa to bestir herself at this hour."[7]

The lowly status the Childs had assumed as farmers had not prevented them from being "treated with a good deal of politeness" by the local aristocracy, much to their surprise. Clearly, the author of *Hobomok* and former editor of the *Juvenile Miscellany* had retained the aura of a celebrity even after her fall from grace. "Once more I have it in my power to be the favorite of the class denominated first," she noted, predicting ruefully that as soon as she confronted the "grandees" with "Anti Slavery Petitions" to sign, she would become "like the man who had spent a night . . . revelling in fairy palaces, and awoke in the morning to find himself alone on a cold and barren heath."[8] Though Child hastened to disown the metaphor as "exaggerated," it conveyed more truth than she liked to admit. Fame and patronage had indeed made the baker's daughter feel like a Cinderella "revelling in fairy palaces," and she was finding the life of a social pariah unbearably dreary, especially now that she could no longer draw strength from a circle of antislavery friends within easy reach.

An incident that occurred on a visit to David's brother John in nearby Springfield brought this realization home to her. A little girl presented her with a "beautiful bunch of flowers, saying she 'had gathered them for the lady who told her such pleasant stories in the Miscellany.' " "Renovated" by the gesture, Child confessed to Louisa, "I think the absence of sympathy and popularity, to which I had been accustomed has stifled my spirit with a sort of night-mare oppression. . . ."[9]

Nevertheless, Child did not yield to the temptation of basking in the favor of Northampton's elite. Rather, she took advantage of the opportunity to "place the anti-slavery lever" through earnest conversations and tracts.[10] She and David also busied themselves with "that most odious of all tasks," circulating antislavery petitions. "We are resolved that the business shall be done in this town more thoroughly than it has been heretofore. But 'Oh Lord, sir!' " she wrote Henrietta.[11]

While the Childs were gathering signatures on petitions against the annexation of Texas and in favor of ending slavery and the slave trade in the District of Columbia, abolitionist women in Lynn, Dorchester, Plymouth, Brookfield, and Boston were braving scurrilous innuendoes to address a still more explosive issue — the racial discrimination codified in Massachusetts's "Marriage Law." Echoing the arguments Child had formulated in her *Appeal*, they were petitioning the state legislature for the "repeal of all laws making a distinction between people of color and white citizens," their prime target being the law against interracial marriage.[12] It would have been impossible to garner support for such a petition in Northampton, but Child did not remain on the sidelines. When the legislators sneered that there was not "A VIRTUOUS WOMAN AMONG" the signers and deplored the poor judgment or lack of chivalry shown by male kin in allowing women to air matters "which cannot be investigated without raising a blush," she fired off an indignant letter to the legislature demanding that "her name may be publicly recorded with the honorable women of Lynn, as protesting against said law." Contrary to the legislators' insinuations about her sisters, she added pointedly: "That [your petitioner] is not made the ignorant tool of evil-designing persons, during the recent excitement, is evident from the fact that she six years ago published a book, in which she mentioned this very law, as a violation of the principles of justice and freedom."[13]

Child's expectation of being sent to "Coventry" by Northampton's "upper circles" for her antislavery activities proved unwarranted in the case of Judge Joseph Lyman and his wife, foremost among the town's "River Gods."[14] Their library featured a full set of the *Juvenile Miscellany*, and Anne Jean Lyman had read *Philothea* "with much emotion."[15] "Mrs. Lyman seems determined that she *will* get acquainted with me, though she is the very embodiment of aristocracy," Child confided to the Lorings. Her new friend could hardly have differed more strikingly from the radical comrades-in-arms Child had left behind in Boston: "[She] Hates republics, hates democracy in every form, of course hates reforms of all sorts, and loves to have woman a graceful vine that droops and dies, unless it can find some stately oak around which to twine itself." All the same, Child admitted to liking her. Whatever the notions she professed, Mrs. Lyman herself was "anything but a drooping and twining vine" and possessed "noble impulses, and a brave, imprudent frankness." Thus, Child concluded: "If she can manage to like me, anti-slavery, rights-of-woman, and all, it must be because she respects the daring freedom of speech which she practices."[16] Long afterward, Child would reminisce to Mrs. Lyman's daughter Susan, with whom she maintained a correspondence that lasted into old age: "Both of us were as direct and energetic as a loco-motive under high pressure of steam; and, coming full tilt from opposite directions, we sometimes ran against each other with a clash. But no bones were ever broken."[17]

Another friend who helped sustain Child through a period she would forever recall as the bleakest in her life was the Unitarian minister John Sullivan Dwight. A kindred spirit, he shared her penchant for Transcendentalism, as well as her passion for music and her commitment to social justice. In fact he would soon join the utopian community of Brook Farm, a haven for Transcendentalist reformers, and ultimately he would make a name for himself as a music critic. Calling on Child shortly after her arrival in Northampton, he found her in the midst of her domestic chores, "with a dirty gown and hands somewhat grimmed," but "in fifteen minutes," they had taken flight into the spheres of mysticism and were "high up in the blue."[18]

Apart from these rare intimates, Child found Northampton thoroughly uncongenial. The town's charming old houses and scenic views of the Berkshires did not compensate for the bigotry of its 3,700 inhabitants, who uncannily resembled the dour Puritans portrayed in *Hobomok*. Northampton prided itself on a heritage of religious orthodoxy dating back to Jonathan Edwards and the Great Awakening of the mid-eighteenth century. Child judged the result acerbically: "Calvinism sits here enthroned, with high ears, blue nose, thin lips, and griping fist."[19] "Orthodoxy has clothed most of the community in her straight-laced garments. There is organing, and psalm-singing, and praying, and preaching, and reverence for 'the divine ambassadors of Christ,' and saving of souls, &c more than enough; but of genuine love to the neighbor, as a child of one common Father, the manifestations seem to be of the smallest."[20] Boarding at the home of a local farmer exposed her to the full brunt of this "intellectual desert." "We live in a North room, without a gleam of sunshine" or a single tasteful object to beautify it, Child complained to the Lorings, asking them to imagine having to stare morning and night at grim portraits of Calvinist ministers and "ancient wood engravings" of gloomy biblical scenes, all in "black wooden frames," lined up over the mantelpiece "like 'four and twenty little dogs all of a row.' " As if the surroundings were not depressing enough, the family was "so narrow, so uninformed, so bigotted" that Child felt she would "gladly walk a hundred miles and back again" for a single "hour's talk" with Louisa and Ellis.[21]

Northampton's political conservatism matched its religious orthodoxy. The town was a favorite summer resort for southerners, and dense networks of kinship and business bound its citizens to proslavery interests. In a letter to Theodore Dwight Weld, then collecting material for his famous tract, *American Slavery As It Is*, Child listed scores of Northamptoners in all walks of life — schoolteachers, ministers, storekeepers, merchants, doctors, dentists, judges — who had resided in the South, held or traded in slaves, disseminated proslavery propaganda, or connected themselves to the institution through close kin.[22]

A "rich slave-auctioneer" named Thomas Napier lived "within call" of the Childs, and his loud prayers grated on their ears. "Hear the pious old thief, trying to come paddy over the Lord!" David used to exclaim, striking up his accordion "to drown sounds so discordant to [their] feelings." A leading member of the local Congregational church, Napier contributed $250 a year to the minister's salary, served as a deacon, and taught Sunday school classes, in which he promulgated the doctrine that "Africans are the descendants of Ham, and God has especially ordained them to perpetual slavery." Not surprisingly, the minister, in turn, preached against reforms and barred his pulpit to antislavery lecturers.[23]

Southerners frequently brought pampered slaves with them when they visited relatives in Northampton, parading them through the town as "samples of the general condition of their bondsmen" and loudly trumpeting that no abolitionist could entice them away. Well-aware that such slaves usually "left children, or other near ties, behind them," Child wrote a strong letter to Napier's niece, who had arrived in Northampton with her slave Rosa in tow. Rosa sought Child out, indignant at learning that this notorious abolitionist had allegedly "called her a well-fatted pig, and her children puppies," but Child read her a copy of the letter and "easily convinced her, . . . that I had said nothing about her, but compared the happiness of slaves to that of well fed pigs; and spoke of them as liable to be sold" to different purchasers, "like dogs, and their . . . puppies." Within half an hour they were "the best friends imaginable." Rosa's story turned out to be all too familiar — her old mistress had provided in her will that Rosa and her children were to be free after the death of the mistress's granddaughter, but the heirs had conveniently lost the document and seemed disinclined to respect it. At Rosa's request, Child wrote to Angelina Grimké, who had known the family in Charleston, asking her to appeal to their honor. Before Angelina could respond, Rosa faced the agonizing choice between abandoning her children if she claimed her freedom under Massachusetts law, or returning to a probable lifetime of slavery in Charleston, with the risk of being sold apart from her children in any case. "The struggle in her mind . . . was evidently severe & painful," but she accompanied her mistress back to the South, still hoping that Angelina could somehow help her. Meanwhile, the Napiers announced triumphantly that Child had failed to "coax [Rosa] away from her beloved mistress."[24]

"Never in my life have I witnessed so much of the lofty slave-holding spirit," Child fumed to Abby Kelley. "Will moral influence ever reach these haughty sinners? Never. Much as I deprecate it, I am convinced that emancipation must come through violence."[25] The Welds and Garrison had arrived at the same verdict in the wake of the antiabolitionist riots that had raged for half a decade.[26] But Child's sojourn in the hinterland, where abolitionism exerted little influence, had taught her a more chilling lesson about the prospects of overcoming racial prejudice. "I have ceased to believe that public opinion will ever be sincerely reformed on the question, till long after emancipation has taken place," she reported to Henrietta. "I mean that, for generations to come, there will be a very large minority hostile to the claims of colored people; and the majority will be largely composed of individuals, who are found on that side from any and every motive, rather than hearty sympathy with the down-trodden race."[27] The proof, to Child, lay in the tepidness of Northampton's self-styled abolitionists, who "evidently consider[ed] abolition as secondary to the advance of sectarian doctrines."[28] Those belonging to the Congregational church, for example, did not object to having their minister draw his salary from the proceeds of slave auctions. "They never open their lips — so highly do they value 'the peace of the church,'" Child wrote in disgust to Abby Kelley, lamenting, "oh, how I have hungered and thirsted after the good, warm abolition-sympathy" of Boston.[29]

Even as Child wrote, however, bitter conflicts were rending the abolitionist community. Trouble had first erupted during the Grimké sisters' speaking tour in the summer of 1837. Conservative clergymen, opposed to antislavery agitation because it tended to split their churches and undermine their authority, had pounced on the spectacle of women's lectures to "promiscuous" audiences as a bugbear with which to frighten the orthodox away from abolitionism and back into the fold.[30] In a pastoral letter authored by a minister who would later publish an overt defense of slavery, the General Association of Massachusetts Congregational clergy pontificated: "*Deference and subordination are essential to the happiness of society, and peculiarly so in the relation of a people to their pastor.*" Parishioners had no right to force "perplexed and agitating subjects" upon a church "*at the hazard of alienation and division*"; nor should they invite lecturers to address them on issues their ministers had judged wisest to leave in abeyance. Especially fraught with peril, warned the pastoral letter, were practices that "*threaten the* FEMALE CHARACTER with wide-spread and permanent injury" by violating the New Testament's injunctions as to the "appropriate duties" of woman: "[W]hen [woman] assumes the place and tone of man as a public reformer, . . . she yields the power which God has given her for protection, and her character becomes unnatural. If the vine, whose strength and beauty is to lean upon the trellis work and half conceal its clusters, thinks to assume the independence and the overshading nature of the elm, it will not only cease to bear fruit, but fall in shame and dishonor into the dust."[31] A New Hampshire abolitionist shrewdly sized up the clergy's real concern: "some ministers . . . seem to think, that if women are permitted to speak in behalf of the suffering, the clerical vocation is in danger."[32]

Despite its patently antiabolitionist agenda, the pastoral letter achieved its aim of provoking a schism in antislavery ranks that pitted orthodox Christians against religious liberals and freethinkers. Almost immediately, "clerical" abolitionists began defecting from the camp of William Lloyd Garrison and dissociating themselves from his harsh "abuse of gospel ministers and excellent Christians not ready to unite with anti-slavery societies."[33] In a series of "Clerical Appeals," ministers and seminarians who identified themselves (sometimes spuriously) as abolitionists condemned the introduction of "heresies" into the antislavery cause, singling out "public lectures of females" for special opprobrium. Garrison and his supporters responded with outraged denunciations of the "schismatics," and by the fall of 1837 the *Liberator* was publishing little but the "criminations and recriminations" the two sides were trading.[34] At first the clerical disaffection siphoned off only a small minority of abolitionists, mostly latecomers to the movement. By the time the Childs left for Northampton in May 1838, however, one of their oldest compeers, the Reverend Amos Phelps, had joined the schismatics in protest over the New England Anti-Slavery Convention's vote to allow the official participation of women in its proceedings and committees. Soon he was leading a conspiracy to secure control of the antislavery movement for the orthodox faction or, failing that, to start a rival antislavery society. Within months, the counterrevolution had engulfed orthodox abolitionists of sterling credentials, among them the men who headed the American or "parent" society based in New York.

Why had men and women who had been able to transcend their denominational differences and work harmoniously together for half a decade suddenly begun quarreling so ferociously over ancillary issues?[35] The most plausible explanation lies in the contradictory results that their campaign of "moral suasion" had produced. Abolitionists had hoped to "promote a *correct public sentiment* on the subject of slavery" through the "universal dissemination of facts and arguments," as Child had explained in her *Anti-Slavery Catechism*.[36] Or to adopt the language of Evangelical abolitionists, they had hoped to bring a sinful nation to repentance. This process was to have culminated in a collective decision to legislate slavery out of existence. Instead, every strategy that abolitionists had devised had seemingly gone down to defeat. Antislavery lecturers had never succeeded in penetrating the South, where local laws and vigilante groups threatened them with death; and throughout the North, mobs had hounded them and churches had barred their doors. Abolitionist editors saw their presses destroyed and their lives endangered time and again; the most notorious case had occurred in November 1837, when Elijah Lovejoy, editor of the *Alton Observer*, had been killed defending his fourth press against a mob. The tracts that the American Anti-Slavery Society had spent thousands of dollars printing and mailing to southern opinionmakers had reached no farther than the post office. After southern mobs had burned the first shipments in 1836, many postmasters had simply refused to deliver abolitionist literature, supported by a ruling of U.S. Postmaster General Amos Kendall. The latest antislavery initiative — the plan to inundate Congress with petitions — had provoked the passage of a "gag-rule" stipulating that "all petitions, memorials, resolutions, propositions, or papers relating in any way or to any extent whatever to the subject of slavery or the abolition of slavery shall, without being printed or referred, be laid upon the table and that no further action whatever be taken thereon." The rule remained in effect from 1836 to 1844.[37]

Faced with such intransigence, thoughtful abolitionists were compelled to question whether "moral suasion" would suffice to end slavery. Child was not alone in fearing that emancipation "must come through violence."[38] Yet neither she nor anyone who shared her fears was ready to advocate an armed onslaught against slavery — a course that would have been suicidal in the 1830s, even if not forbidden by pacifist scruples.

At the same time, the very extremes to which opponents had gone to suppress antislavery agitation won new adherents to the cause. Often, the recent recruits did not share the deep identification with the slaves and the commitment to racial egalitarianism that had inspired pioneers like Garrison, the Childs, the Grimké sisters, and Theodore Weld. As Child put it, these "*nominal* abolitionists" had " 'their dander up' " about "their own rights of petition" and civil liberties (and about the South's political domination of the North), "but few really sympathize[d] with the slave."[39] Already they were lowering the tone of the antislavery movement. The African American abolitionist Theodore S. Wright summed up the problem lucidly:

> Three years ago, when a man professed to be an abolitionist, we knew where he was. He was an individual who recognized the identity of the human family. Now a man may call himself an abolitionist, and we not know where to find him.... Free discussion, petition, anti-Texas, and political favor converts are multiplying.... It is an easy thing to talk about the vileness of slavery at the south, but ... to treat the man of color in all circumstances as a man and brother, that is the test.[40]

The miscarriage of their original strategy threw abolitionists into disarray and reignited religious and political differences they had hitherto managed to subordinate to their immediate goal. The prospect of a much longer battle than they had anticipated also sapped the will of many who had been prepared for martyrdom, but not for indefinite banishment from their churches and social circles. Religious faith had always fortified abolitionists against persecution. As they turned back to it for strength to meet the challenge of a protracted siege, it led them in opposite directions. Orthodox abolitionists wanted to renew their ties to the churches. Garrisonian radicals, on the other hand, wanted to find substitutes for the dogmas and outward forms that no longer satisfied their religious yearnings. Child had increasingly given herself up to the mysticism that inspired *Philothea*. Garrison had come to espouse a creed he called "nonresistance," which held that all human government was evil and that the true Christian should recognize only the "dominion of God, the control of an inward spirit."[41]

These divergent religious tendencies implied divergent strategies for the antislavery movement. In the hope of conciliating the clergy and attracting more support from conservative churchgoers, the orthodox faction sought to improve the movement's "public image" by insisting that it repudiate women's rights, nonresistance, and other "heresies." Anxious to preserve the character of a vanguard movement, the Garrisonians objected to trammeling their most ardent activists and consequently favored a platform that would maximize adherents' freedom of opinion. Each party accused the other of saddling the cause with "extraneous" issues and sacrificing the slave to sectarian interests. Both shamelessly jockeyed to secure the undivided loyalty of the African American community, whose true interests, instead, lay in maintaining its neutrality and defining its own agenda.[42]

"Oh! how my heart is grieved by these dissensions! I wish our dear and much respected friend Garrison would record them more sparingly in his paper," wrote Child to Lucretia Mott, as she noticed the degree to which abolitionists were wasting their energies attacking each other while proslavery forces gained ground in Congress.[43] The publicity given by her comrades to their internecine feuding and the vituperativeness of their mutual accusations made her "sick at heart, discouraged, and ashamed," she confessed to Loring. While more inclined to blame the orthodox party after a year of observing the "sectarian zeal, and cunning, and obstinate perseverance, with which Calvinism seeks to build itself up and shut others out," she could not help seeing that "the spirit is manifestly wrong on both sides."[44] Her sojourn in Northampton, where the vast majority of abolitionists identified with the orthodox faction, gave her a special perspective on the schism. In a letter marked "Not to be published in any part," Child tried to share that perspective with Caroline Weston, one of her most politically minded friends in the Boston Female Anti-Slavery Society. "It is too evident now, that with real enemies of the cause, and half-and-half abolitionists, are mixed up a *large* class of sincere friends of emancipation, according to their honest but limited views thereof," she asserted. None of these sincere but limited orthodox abolitionists would believe that men like Amos Phelps and Henry B. Stanton, who had sacrificed so much for the antislavery cause, were actually plotting against it, and nothing was gained by proving their "narrow sectarianism," since Northamptoners considered that a "virtue." Hence, Child had become "convinced that every move Garrison can make against" the rival party "re-acts against the Liberator." Far from serving the interests of truth and free speech, as Garrison believed, his policy of reprinting and refuting his adversaries' charges merely fanned the flames. Child would take the lesson to heart on assuming the editorship of the *National Anti-Slavery Standard* two years later.[45]

Publicly, however, Child defended Garrison. In a letter she and David sent to the Massachusetts Anti-Slavery Society in time to have it read at the January annual meeting, they pleaded for unity and toleration: "Shall we stop to settle creeds, while our brother lies wounded and bleeding by the way-side? . . . If [Mr. Garrison's] religious views differ from most of us, candor must compel us to admit that he devotes a very small portion of his paper to the expression of them." Garrison had a claim on "every true-hearted abolitionist," the Childs pointed out, for his "clear, strong voice of warning and rebuke . . . woke us all from our slumbers."[46]

The pressure of circumstances soon drew Child deeper into the controversy. Although she had told Caroline that her "yearnings to be in Boston" had been somewhat curbed by "relief at being distant from the scene of contention," she returned to the city in late May 1839, ostensibly to look for work.[47]

The Childs' first year in Northampton had left them in worse financial straits than ever. David had "toiled like a very slave," but so far his beet sugar enterprise had not generated a dollar of income. The expenses of setting it up had been "paid entirely from the slender proceeds" of Child's "literary exertions." Moreover, the creditors he had accumulated over the years were clamoring for reimbursement. His former partner on the *Massachusetts Journal* had "re-commenced his persecutions," and recently, to Child's mortification, Chief Justice Lemuel Shaw—whose respect abolitionists could ill afford to jeopardize—had called to collect money David had long ago borrowed from the late Major Thomas Melvill.[48]

"I must *earn* something this summer. I am willing to do *anything*. . . . *What* to do I know not," Child wrote in desperation to Louisa. At first, she toyed with the idea of making beet sugar candy. Nothing came of the scheme, perhaps because the 1,200 pounds of sugar David produced would not have sufficed to make it profitable.[49] She also considered resorting to her old standby in times of distress—schoolteaching—but hesitated to commit herself because of uncertainty about David's future plans. She had given up on literature, she told Louisa, since her "'false position' toward the 'spirit of the age'" had apparently "cut off profit as an author." Swallowing her pride, she had even written to Samuel Goodrich, editor of *The Token*, in which she had published so many stories, "to see if I cannot get some sort of editing, or compiling, or writing, or coloring maps." This, too, failed to materialize.[50] "Dearest and best of friends, shall we *ever* again, 'in the wide sterility of this world lay out a garden of household love, and fill it with flowers. . .'?" Child wrote mournfully to David from Boston. She had just learned that David's arrival in the city was going to be further delayed, and it was beginning to seem "as if in everything connected with *you* I was to be forever disappointed." "Dearest *do* you love your forlorn little wife? or do you feel just about as happy without her as with her? I dont know what I *shall* do if you dont love me," she repined with some of her former abjectness. But she also sounded a new note of teasing defiance as she announced that she had rented a shared room: "Tired of waiting for *your* movements, . . . I have taken up with a new companion, and gone to house-keeping without your lordship." Still, she conceded that it made sense for David to finish manufacturing his beets into sugar before joining her in Boston. The fame of his experiment had preceded him, she added, reporting wryly that when she had gone to buy West Indian free-labor sugar, the grocer had told her that a domestic variety would shortly be available, for "they 'were making beet sugar on a *great scale* in the western part of the state.' "[51]

A ray of good fortune heartened Child a few months later when David won a silver "medal and a Diploma from the Mechanics' Institute, for the first Beet Sugar made in America," as well as a $100 premium from the agricultural society.[52] For a brief moment it looked as though the fame and success he had dreamed of earning were within his grasp. The *Boston Courier* saluted his achievement and glowingly reviewed his treatise on *The Culture of the Beet, and Manufacture of Beet Sugar.*[53] The *Journal of Commerce* proclaimed: "[H]andsomer or better flavored brown sugar we never met with. . . . If such sugar can be produced at the same price as cane or maple, it will have a great run. We conceive that Mr. Child . . . is rendering an important service to the American public, and we hope to himself also."[54] The Adelphic Union invited David to lecture on the "History of the Beet Sugar Enterprise." And Garrison devoted an editorial to hailing David's "invaluable work" and commenting on how favorably it had been received by the commercial press. Evidently David had managed to convince him that beet sugar would quickly supplant cane sugar in the free states and increase their "general productiveness and prosperity . . . at least fifty per cent."[55] No wonder Child harbored "a comfortable pre-sentiment that the tide is soon going to turn."[56]

Her spirits had in fact risen well before David's prospects had improved. As she confided to her sister-in-law in a letter describing her activities in Boston, "I now feel happier than I have for several years, though our pecuniary fortunes are at the lowest ebb."[57] The truth was that she was once again in her element after a year of intellectual and emotional starvation. Accompanied by the Lorings, Caroline Sturgis, and other afficionados of Transcendentalism, she was attending Emerson's lectures in Cambridge, "merry-making" along the way.[58] She was also participating in the Conversations that Margaret Fuller, whom she had known twelve years ago as a precocious adolescent, was holding with women to help them acquire the "precision in which our sex are so deficient" and to ascertain collectively "how we may make best use of our means for building up the life of thought upon the life of action." The group included several of Child's friends from the BFASS, and they were challenging Fuller to extend her feminism to her enslaved sisters.[59] Above all, Child was savoring the exhilaration of resuming her place in a sophisticated, highly politicized circle of antislavery women. No longer a frustrated bystander, she was actively fighting to save the antislavery movement.

Child had arrived in Boston just in time to throw her support to the Garrisonians in the critical New England Anti-Slavery Convention of May 28, 1839. The showdown took place over Amos Phelps's resolution that "gentlemen only" be enrolled as members of the convention. Overwhelmingly defeated, Phelps and his allies withdrew to form a new state organization that would "exclude women and non-resistants." The victorious party then named Child and Maria Weston Chapman to the business committee charged with drafting the resolutions to be voted on at the convention—a breakthrough for women. The following day Child again joined Chapman on a business committee when they attended a special meeting of "Friends to the Liberator," called to reaffirm the value of the paper against its detractors and to devise new means of financing it. Clearly the two women impressed their male colleagues with their talents in this capacity because, two weeks later, Samuel J. May wrote to request that Garrison enlist them to frame resolutions for a county antislavery meeting he was organizing. "I like to preach from their texts," he said. They continued to serve together throughout Child's stay in Boston, appearing on business committees at the annual meetings of the New-England Non-Resistance Society in October (where they shared the honors with Lucretia Mott and Thankful Southwick) and of the Massachusetts Anti-Slavery Society in January (where David now took his place among the male members).[60]

Meanwhile, Child played a prominent role in the bitter feud that was tearing apart the BFASS. The party lines replicated those of the Massachusetts and American societies. President Mary S. Parker and her corps of officers remained loyal to the orthodox "new organization" led by Phelps, whose deceased wife had founded the BFASS. At the January quarterly meeting Parker had procured a majority vote to donate the proceeds of the traditional December fair to the American Society in New York, then in the hands of orthodox sympathizers. Maria Chapman's minority faction had strenuously objected, accusing Parker of having concealed her sectarian partisanship. After failing to obtain a reconsideration of the vote in the light of subsequent developments, Chapman had launched a counter-fair in October, to raise funds for the Garrisonian-dominated Massachusetts society, or "old organization."[61]

Child had come into the imbroglio "cool and unbiassed." As she divulged to her sister-in-law, she had secretly feared that Chapman had been "unjust" toward the Parker clique and "somewhat blinded by her zeal." But once on the spot, she had quickly changed her mind. "The scenes in our Female Anti Slavery meetings are painful and disgusting," she informed Lydia.[62] The Parker clique used parliamentary maneuvering to control the proceedings, challenging the membership status of women in the opposing faction, refusing to call on them in the debates, and falsifying the vote count in the election for new officers. Child herself was subjected to a personal attack when she urged the need for a president capable of conducting meetings more impartially. The current secretary, Lucy Ball (whom one historian has identified as a woman of color light enough to pass), recalled that Child had opposed the formation of the female society at its inception and claimed that she had also been unwilling to open its membership to women of color "because it would make the anti-slavery cause unpopular." Ball added pointedly that "[s]he hoped the colored friends would notice this."[63] When Child's friend Anne Warren Weston rose to "defend her abolition character," Child cut her off, saying: "If it could not stand without defence, it might fall. She [Child] should content herself with a simple denial of the statement as to the admittance of colored people. That she had considered the formation of a distinct female society inexpedient, was correct." The group's infighting was aired for months in the

Liberator, while the commercial press chortled over the "jangling and discord" of women who had hitherto "spared neither lungs nor shoe-leather" against "that 'abominable abomination,' the system of slavery." The "petticoat agitators" now seemed "only to agitate themselves," jeered the *Boston Transcript*.[64]

As another quarterly meeting approached in April 1840 with the group's conflicts still unresolved, Child appealed to her sisters through the columns of the *Liberator*: "Is there no way of avoiding a recurrence of such disagreeable, mortifying, and discreditable collisions?" She had chosen this "mode of communicating," she explained, because it had proved almost impossible to get a hearing at meetings: "the moment the minority touch the real grounds of the difficulty, the cries 'out of order,' 'out of order,' resemble the din of Congress." She then spelled out the underlying issue: "we want to know whether two thirds of our Society really do wish, by the reappointment of our old Board, to give us the appearance of sustaining the new organization."[65]

Her appeal failed, and the Parker faction peremptorily dissolved the society. Now acting as president pro tem, Child called a special meeting, which 120 members attended. Choosing new officers, the BFASS rededicated itself to its original principles, condemned the "new organization" as "much more detrimental to the cause of the slave than Colonization," and pledged its support to Garrison and the *Liberator*.[66] Throughout the fracas, Child had "struggled against" her innate aversion to "*disagreeable scenes*" and strongly upheld Chapman's faction. Yet she could not suppress nagging doubts about whether either side was really in the right. As she would admit to Ellis Loring three years later, a dim awareness that abolitionists were merely "fighting in the spirit of *sect*" had been "growing" on her "ever since the split in the Female Anti slavery society."[67]

During the year Child spent in Boston, however, she perceived sectarianism mainly among the orthodox intriguers who were trying to "get Garrison formally disowned by the abolitionists of Massachusetts." Convinced that they were raising a hue and cry against "Non-Resistance, Woman's Rights, &c.," as a pretext for winning adherents to an abolitionist program sufficiently diluted to be acceptable to the clergy, she published two long analyses of the controversy, both couched as letters to Garrison. In the first, she addressed herself to the orthodox claim that nonresistants and women's rights advocates had taken over the Massachusetts Anti-Slavery Society and were deflecting it from its original purpose. She began by pointing out that nonresistants constituted only a tiny minority of the society. Although their belief that all governments were evil prevented them from voting, they had never sought to impose this belief on others; all they asked was to be left free to choose forms of antislavery action that they could conscientiously practice. The vast majority of the Massachusetts society's membership strongly advocated political action, and the society as a whole had endorsed it in resolutions that "solemnly conjured" all who "voted on *any* occasion . . . to carry their *abolition principles* to the polls, triumphant over every consideration of interest or party." Thus, argued Child, partisans of the orthodox faction had no grounds for demanding that "the Society should declare it the imperious duty of every abolitionist to go to the polls, and advise any man to withdraw from the Association, who failed to do this." Surely, they rather than the nonresistants were the ones guilty of forcing a "foreign topic" onto the antislavery agenda.[68]

"With regard to the Woman Question, . . . the case is much the same," Child continued. Antislavery women had "sedulously avoided" the subject of women's rights — they had simply worked for the cause in any way their consciences prescribed. Their opponents were the ones who were agitating the issue by insisting that the society officially limit women's means of action. "For my individual self," Child added,

> I now, as ever, would avoid any discussion of the woman question in anti-slavery meetings, or [news]papers. But when a man advises me to withdraw from a society or convention, or not to act there according to the dictates of my own judgment, I am constrained to reply, "Thou canst not touch the freedom of my soul. I deem that I have duties to perform here. I make no onset upon your opinions and prejudices; but my moral responsibility lies between God and my own conscience."[69]

Child's letter elicited an enthusiastic response from one male reader. "What a woman! what an intellect is hers! And now shall we speak about the *equality* of the sexes? with whom shall we compare her?" he exclaimed, characterizing Child as "the Aurora of the cause." He had been particularly impressed by the reticence toward women's rights that the Grimkés had criticized in Child: "She has said very little about her own rights, but she has done and suffered much for the rights of the slave."[70]

Unfortunately, no one from the orthodox faction seems to have joined in the praise. The conflict raged unabated, and by the spring of 1840 both sides were furiously mobilizing for the May Anniversary Meeting, at which each aimed to take control of the parent society in New York. Child's second letter to the *Liberator*, published on March 6, served to undermine the orthodox faction's credibility by showing that "those, who are now loudest in their opposition to what is called the Woman Question, are . . . warmed by a zeal of somewhat recent date." James G. Birney, Lewis Tappan, and Alanson St. Clair (Sinclair), for example, had declared themselves in favor of withdrawing from the American Anti-Slavery Society unless it rescinded its 1839 "vote to allow women a participation in its meetings." (At least so Child had heard.) Yet she recalled encounters with all three men that contradicted their present stand. Birney had once told her he found it " 'natural and proper' " that women should serve as delegates to antislavery conventions — an innovation his colleagues in Ohio had adopted well in advance of New Englanders. Tappan had importuned her to address a mixed audience in New York, though he now allegedly based his objections to women's rights on Saint Paul. And Sinclair had vociferously advocated admitting women as delegates to a convention held only a year and a half earlier, at which he had "rebuked" Child "in language . . . bordering on rudeness" for her perceived lukewarmness.[71]

Child had never come so close to delivering a personal attack, and she never would again. She may well have judged the results counterproductive. Both Birney and Tappan wrote immediate replies. They specifically disavowed any intention of founding a new national antislavery society if their faction did not prevail at the upcoming anniversary (though they were to do just that). Birney's rejoinder, which Child shared with her friend Caroline Weston, but decided not to publish or refute, indignantly denied having stigmatized the American society's enfranchisement of women as a violation of its constitution. "You never saw, such a piece of malicious twaddle as his letter was," fumed Caroline to her sister Anne.[72] Tappan's reply, addressed to Garrison and published in the *Liberator*, was more temperate. Regretting the necessity of taking issue with an "excellent woman and faithful friend of the anti-slavery cause," he explained that his disapproval of women's lecturing to "promiscuous assemblies, or mixing with men in meetings for business," was not "founded on St. Paul," but on the conviction that "the public mind is diverted from the anti-slavery cause by this novel course."[73]

Clearly, Child's letter had backfired; far from discomfiting the leaders of the opposing camp, it had given them a chance to reiterate their opinions, to the possible detriment of her own credibility. The experience perhaps played a role in her subsequent decision to keep such personal attacks out of the *National Anti-Slavery Standard* during her tenure as editor.

Child had looked forward to attending the fateful anniversary in New York, which she considered "one of the most important antislavery meetings ever held."[74] A restaging of the "old struggle for Freedom . . . in a new form," its outcome would determine the destiny of both the national society and the movement at large, she believed. The BFASS had elected her a delegate, and the Massachusetts society, which had chartered a boat for its supporters to ensure maximum attendance, had volunteered to pay the Childs' expenses. As so often before, however, David's priorities intervened, and she found herself heading back to Northampton instead. Only David would enjoy the privilege of participating in the climactic event that resulted in the triumph of Garrison's party — and a permanent schism in antislavery ranks.[75]

David had no doubt cherished the hope that the favorable publicity his sugar beet experiment had received would attract investors. He had demonstrated the feasibility of manufacturing beet sugar in New England, but he had yet to demonstrate that the enterprise could be profitable. So far he had been operating on "Slater's straps" (suspenders), as Maria Chapman pointed out. Child bristled at the term. "My husband is very remarkable for mastering difficulties, and doing whatever he tries," she retorted loyally. "His soul has been almost worried out of him by want of funds, and by delay after delay occasioned by cheap machinery; but he has made perfect sugar; and finds his skill in no way deficient to the task he has undertaken."[76] Still, the fact remained that Chapman was right. The venture could not succeed financially without a major outlay of capital. Beet sugar production required much expensive machinery (evidently the amount David had purchased in Europe did not suffice, because he borrowed money from his brother John to purchase more in 1840). Production also required a substantial labor force since sugar did not grain well unless the manufacturing process was carried out very rapidly.[77] Like any new product, finally, beet sugar had to be manufactured in large enough quantities to be sold at a competitive price.

The key to meeting these conditions was capital, but David could hardly have chosen a less propitious moment for obtaining it. The nation was still reeling from the disastrous Panic of 1837, the worst economic depression in its history. Hundreds of firms had fallen victim to the spiral of bank failures, customer defaults, and curtailed demand—among them the two companies that had originally agreed to underwrite David's enterprise.[78]

Yet David could not bear to abandon his dream after having invested so much labor and money in it and come so close to fulfilling it. At this critical juncture, his father-in-law held out a solution. The senior Convers Francis had long wished to live with his daughter. Restless and constitutionally morose, he had moved thirteen times over the past twenty years. Having exhausted his welcome with his eldest son, James, he had somehow become possessed of the idea that if only his daughter would take him in, "he should be perfectly contented." Thus, he proposed to advance the Childs $3,000—the sum he expected to bequeath to his daughter—for the purpose of setting them up on a farm in Northampton, where he would reside with them. Child frankly "dreaded the experiment," and her brother James warned her that she would "never be able to stand it."[79] Besides, David already owed the old man several thousand dollars, borrowed during previous emergencies—a debt on which Child had been faithfully paying interest for many years. But this time filial duty converged with what appeared to be mutual convenience.

Mr. Francis spent $1,000 on a hundred acres of "remarkably fine" but direfully "neglected" farmland: "There were scarcely any fences, a barn in ruins, and an old shantee with two little rooms and a low garret." He had earmarked the remaining $2,000 for buildings, fences, and equipment. Almost immediately, however, the agreement began to unravel.[80]

Arriving in Northampton early in May 1840, summoned by an urgent letter from David, Child found her father laid up with a leg "severely bruised by a fall from a wagon" and with his temper already fraying under this unaccustomed confinement. For three weeks Child had to dress her father's leg several times a day in addition to her other tasks: arranging furniture "tumbled in heaps on the floor" and doing all the cooking and washing for him, David, and "a stout Irish laborer, who works and eats as much as two other men." Never in her life had she felt so bone-weary, she complained to her mother-in-law: "At night my feet ached so that I could not sleep, and I almost cried with the pain." She added ruefully: "I do not think continued adversity does good to *my* character. . . . I know prosperity is considered a dangerous trial; but I should like to have it; and I say, as the old woman did, 'I dont care how fiery the trial may be.'" The physical labor was far from being the worst of her tribulations. "Uneasy and gloomy," her father was proving even more burdensome than Child had feared: "Sometimes it seems to me as if I *should* die. We do everything we can to please him, and he is very kind and obliging; but everything, both great and small, goes wrong in his eyes."[81]

Six weeks later, Child announced to Louisa that she and David had severed their "pecuniary connection" to her father. The old man had begun complaining to the "domestics and neighbors" that he had "done so much for his daughter as to deprive himself of a home." He had been especially unpleasant to David, who had "borne all manner of provocations with wonderful calmness and patience—never giving a hasty word, though continually fretted at, even when he was trying most to please." The only way out was to "decline the expenditure of another dollar by father." This left the Childs with "a barn unpaid for, no house to live in, no fences to our fields," and no money with which to pay the carpenter, let alone buy the necessary machinery for sugar manufacture. To bail them out, David ended up mortgaging the improvements on the farm to his brother John.[82]

Moreover, canceling their financial obligation did not relieve the Childs of the old man's company. He remained with them for many months, casting an intolerable damper on their spirits, interdicting the little pleasures they liked to offer themselves, and further straining their relationship. "He is unacquainted with sentiment, and has a violent prejudice against literature, taste, and even the common forms of modern civilized life," Child explained to Louisa. When she could snatch a few minutes for reading in the course of her unending housework, she had to do so surreptitiously, "father having a strange determination to believe that literature always leads to beggary." David could not read to her in the evenings, as had been their custom, "because father cannot abide reading aloud." And whenever David displayed any of the "sentiment and romance that characterized our early love," the old man sneered at it as " 'childish folly.' " Through it all, Child was tortured with "the fretting, conscience-stricken feeling that I should fail in filial duty unless I continued to renew my efforts," as she admitted to her brother Convers. Referring again to the domestic toil she habitually described as the least of her inflictions, she exhorted him: "Thank God that you are not a woman! *Great* labors do but strengthen the intellect of a well-balanced character; but these million Lilliputian cords tie down the stoutest Gulliver that ever wrestled in their miserable entanglement"[83]

Indeed, during this terrible year in Northampton, Child experienced to the full what she had called "the condition of women." Trapped between the demands of an authoritarian father and an ineffectual husband, reduced from a literary celebrity to a household drudge, she had never before felt so oppressed by the weight of patriarchy. "If there were no other escape from such a position, I am afraid I should eventually seek it in drunkenness, or suicide," she wrote darkly to Louisa.[84]

The "escape" that presented itself was providential, though Child characterized it as a "*driving*" rather than a "*leading*" of Providence." She had just resolved to leave Northampton for the second time in search of work to pay expenses on the farm, when urgent "intreaties" came from Garrisonian headquarters in Boston. The *National Anti-Slavery Standard*, founded in 1840 as the organ of the regenerated AASS in New York, desperately needed a "judicious editor, warmly interested in the cause." Could the Childs jointly take on the job? The salary would be $1,000 a year. They gratefully accepted, with the understanding that David would remain in Northampton, supplying occasional editorials, while Child would actually manage and write for the paper.[85]

The farewell was wrenching (Child compared it to "being hanged"), perhaps because the couple had had "glimpses of real sunshine" after the departure of Mr. Francis in March, perhaps because both sensed that a phase of their marriage was ending forever. Child crowded so much work into one day preparing the "shantee" for David that the neighboring farmers' wives assured her she would "break down." She cleaned out cobwebs, scoured, "scraped lint, and made finger cots, and labelled medicines, and cut, made, and mended a good supply of summer clothing"; she set out "household utensils" for David to use and "packed the rest carefully"; and she delayed leaving until she could engage a housekeeper who would bake David's bread and scrub his floors.[86]

On the long journey to New York and in the months that followed, Child gradually gathered the strength to face the painful questions she had been evading for so many years. Could all of David's failures really be blamed on ill luck and other people's broken promises? Hadn't he always had a tendency to overlook obstacles, ignore danger signals, and incur major expenditures without proper guarantees? Why had he decided to launch a new enterprise during a disastrous economic crisis? Why had he bought costly machinery in Europe without the authorization of his financial sponsors? And why hadn't he dropped the project once his sponsors had abandoned him? If hardheaded capitalists had chosen not to risk investing in an untried industry under unfavorable conditions, had it been anything less than foolhardy for someone in David's circumstances to hazard the venture on the tiny sum his father-in-law had agreed to advance?[87]

Then there was the troubling matter of David's debts, some $9,000 claimed by his former partner on the *Massachusetts Journal* and countless thousands borrowed from other creditors. Shouldn't David have felt morally obliged to reimburse these loans before borrowing more? Such carelessness must have been deeply disturbing to a woman who had long prided herself on her scrupulousness about money matters and who had insisted on paying "board" when she stayed with friends, to avoid the least taint of dependency. "My own views of doing business are always to choose *safe* ground, however narrow," she would later specify, defending the prudent financial policy she adopted as editor of the *Standard*.[88]

In retrospect, Child would attribute David's "want of success" to two irremediable character defects inherited from his father: a propensity for getting into financial "entanglements" and an inability to be "prompt, and punctual to his engagements."[89] During the "fourteen years of uninterrupted adverse fortune" she had endured since her marriage, Child would admit to Louisa, she had felt a "constantly increasing conviction that the cause [was] incurable." Had she heeded that conviction and pursued her own career, instead of following David to Northampton, "it would have been better for us both, and saved a great deal of wasted time and energy," she concluded.[90] Child would be even more explicit in a letter to Francis Shaw: "I have turned aside from my true mission [literature] to help Mr. Child in various emergencies; or rather to *try* to help what did not admit of help. I have allowed my thoughts to be frittered away on pecuniary calculations how to meet current expenses, when there were always elements at work, which upset my calculations."[91] Over the years, as David persisted in involving himself in unprofitable schemes, Child would come to speak of him with humorous detachment. A letter she wrote to Louisa in 1847 wryly summed up her husband's self-defeating career. Appropriately, Child used as a metaphor a sleigh ride that Susan Lyman had described taking with David in Northampton.

> It was *so* characteristic of him. . . . [T]hey struck off into unknown paths, through the depths of a wood, and went tumbling over stumps and rocks, and tearing down perpendicular hills, till [Susan] began to think it would be a miracle if they ever reached home with unbroken bones. At last they met two surveyors, and Mr. Child asked, "Can you tell us where we are?" "Where do you wish to go?" inquired one of the men. "Nowhere in particular," replied Mr. Child. "Very well," rejoined the man, "you are on the straight road there."
>
> Susan adds, "So we kept on, and arrived there, and found no one at home."

Explicating the metaphor, in case Louisa had missed its point, Child commented: "Poor David! He drives on at much the same result in *all* the affairs of life. He constantly reminds me of Emerson's remark that 'Some men expend infinite effort to arrive nowhere.' "[92]

If her illusions about David had ended, she was at least psychologically free to make a new life for herself.

12

The National Anti-Slavery
Standard: Family Newspaper
or Factional Organ?

Were you an abolitionist in the good old days of persecution from without, and of cordial, heart-filling sympathy from our little world within? Oh, the brave old days! — When sects were fused together by the heat of a holy zeal! It was worth living for, to have been thus raised above worldly considerations, selfish aims, and the circumscribed vision of creeds, into the open sunlight of universal love, the bracing atmosphere of free opinion![1]

With this evocation of the spirit that had animated the abolitionist movement at its outset, Child inaugurated her editorship of the *National Anti-Slavery Standard* and set the tone she would maintain throughout her two-year tenure. Her aim would be to recapture the self-sacrificing idealism of pristine abolitionism and to rechannel the energy that had been dissipated in sectarian infighting toward the goal of winning new recruits to the cause.

When Child took over the paper on May 20, 1841, it had been embroiled in strife for almost a year. Indeed, the *Standard* owed its birth to the 1840 schism, for it was founded to replace the American Anti-Slavery Society's previous organ, the *Emancipator*, which the orthodox faction had taken with it on withdrawing to form the rival American and Foreign Anti-Slavery Society.[2] The *Standard*'s opening editorial, written by James C. Jackson, who would manage the paper until the return from Europe of its first official editor, Nathaniel P. Rogers, reflected the contradictory purposes the new organ was supposed to fulfill. On the one hand, Jackson proclaimed, "the will of the Society" dictated that the *Standard* "should be conducted on the broad principle of the universal fraternity of the human race, irrespective of sect, party, sex[,] color or country." Hence, the paper would welcome as "co-laborers" all who embraced the movement's fundamental principles: love of freedom, abhorrence of slavery, and commitment to immediate emancipation. With "corresponding liberality," it would "admit the discussion of both sides" in debates concerning strategy. On the other hand, Jackson warned, the *Standard* would condemn the "spirit of new organization . . . as inimical to the broad and noble platform from which the Anti-Slavery enterprize first started." In particular, it would condemn the "American Church" as the bulwark of slavery.[3] Neither the paper's sponsors nor its editors could seem to agree on whether its mission was to reunify abolitionists around their original ideals or to attack deviations from what Garrisonian radicals considered the correct line. The unresolved contradiction would dog the *Standard* during Child's editorship and would ultimately drive her from her post.

Until Child's accession, attacks predominated. Between them, Jackson and Rogers published more than twenty editorials and communications rehashing the causes of the schism.[4] In a typical editorial Rogers pronounced "New organization" to be a more formidable "*enemy* of the anti-slavery cause" than "slave-driving" itself. "We must unmask new organization. That is the great business of anti-slavery," he contended.[5] The unmasking often took the form of personal attacks on the opposing faction's leaders. For example, Rogers wrote of the Southerner James G. Birney, who had joined the abolitionist movement in 1835 after emancipating his slaves: "Friend Birney's anti-slavery is more of the Old England type than the New. It spent itself nearly, when he freed his own slaves. The sooner he retires from the northern service for the southern, the better for him and the cause."[6]

Even more destructive than the vendetta against "new organization" was the prolonged sparring into which Jackson entered with African American leaders over their decision to hold a "Colored Convention." "We oppose all exclusive action on the part of the colored people," Jackson editorialized, arguing that separatism only increased racial prejudice.[7] When the editor and correspondents of the *Colored American* objected to the "dictatorial" spirit and "superior" attitude Jackson had shown, he charged them with "aristocracy of the skin," or what we would today call "reverse racism." "It matters not how long they have been in this '*school of Democracy*,' they are bad scholars," he pontificated, advising them to go back to the "rudiments" and, "like 'good dutiful children,' learn their A, B, C."[8]

Although dissatisfaction with the course of the *Standard* had prompted Child's appointment, her Garrisonian colleagues held widely different views as to the policy they wanted her to follow. Rogers naturally hoped she would vindicate him by adopting the same hard-hitting editorial style he had chosen. On welcoming her to the editorial chair, he urged her to ignore her "womanhood" in the "warfare before her" and to emulate "the maid of Orleans . . . when she led France to the rout and expulsion of England from her native shores."[9] Ellis Loring, who had heartily disapproved of Rogers's belligerence and played an instrumental role (along with Abby Kelley) in engineering his replacement by Child, "long[ed] for a dignified and temperate discipline of principles," as manifested in "dispassionate statements of facts." "If the Anti Slavery organizations cannot find better business in future than they have been engrossed by, for a year or two back, they will assuredly die," he predicted.[10] Conversely, Chapman, her sisters, and their confidant Edmund Quincy worried whether Child would "fail at her duty to New Orgn.," as Quincy put it in a letter to Chapman. "I should hardly dare to trust her with the Standard," wrote Anne Warren Weston to her sister Deborah, after learning of Child's belief that Garrison should disregard his critics and "*go strait on*." Reporting to Chapman that Loring felt more confidence in the paper's survival under Child's editorship, Anne commented: "You know his temperament."[11]

For her part, Child assumed the editorship determined to rely on her own moral judgment in righting the paper's course. Like Loring, she was convinced that it was time to lay the schism to rest and recall abolitionists to their actual task — the emancipation of the slaves. In her "Prospectus" for the year to come, she pointedly announced that the reasons for the "divisions in the anti-slavery ranks" were now "sufficiently understood," thanks to their "full expositions by the late able and true-hearted editor," and that she would consequently allot "very small space . . . to such discussions." Whenever "[f]idelity to historical Truth" necessitated any reference to past disputes, she promised, "facts" would be "disentangled from personal controversy, as much as possible."[12]

Child's address "To Abolitionists" offered a healing philosophical overview of the schism.[13] Drawing on her reading of the mystic Emanuel Swedenborg, she theorized that "the everlasting duality in man's soul always had, and always must, split men into two parties, on every new application of old principles to existing institutions, or modes of thought." She called the first the "'conservative'" or "'stop there'" party, the second the "'reform'" or "'go ahead'" party. She then set the schism in a comparative historical context, using the same analytical method she had exploited so successfully in the *Appeal* and the *Condition of Women*. The primitive Christians and later their heirs of the Reformation era had likewise split into "stop there" and "go ahead" parties, she noted. In each case, one group had sought to limit the application of a newly perceived truth, while the other had pursued all the "collateral bearings" such a truth suggested.

In the case of the antislavery movement, the central insight that no human being could claim another as property had prompted victims of oppression all over the world to ask "How does this principle apply to *my* condition? Do laws and customs leave *me* the free exercise of all my powers?" "The debased Hindoo, and the fiery Chartist," as well as the American woman, had begun asking, "Am *I* too not a chattel? Be true to your principle, and cut the cords that fetter *me*, body and soul." Defusing the issue of women's rights by recontextualizing it, she contrasted the reactions of "stop there" and "go ahead" minds to the Grimké sisters' path-breaking lectures. The first "looked back anxiously to St. Paul to arrest the progress of this innovation." The second "boldly asked, 'What if I do differ from St. Paul? So he differed from Peter on some points.'"

Child similarly recast the debate over nonresistance, tracing it to its origins in the question of what attitude to take toward slave insurrections. Initially, she recalled, abolitionists had not only denied charges that they sought to "excite insurrection," but they had implored slaves to "wait quietly for their emancipation to be effected by the exertion of moral power" because murder was "contrary to the gospel of Christ." "Conservative" minds had drawn the line here. "Reforming" minds had gone on to ask: "Then what right had *we* to fight at Bunker Hill? What right had we to promote insurrection among the *Poles* . . . ?" They had quickly realized that abolitionists must either repudiate "all war [as] a violation of the gospel" or prepare themselves for the day when it would become "a *duty* to send swords and standards to *black* Poles."

The antislavery movement had room for both "stop there" and "go ahead" partisans, Child insisted: "Let Peter and Paul fulfill their respective missions" and cease to quarrel with each other. "All conservative minds are not necessarily narrow and base, nor all reforming minds honest and true," she added. Each could be motivated either by conscientious scruples or self-seeking impulses. She concluded by reminding abolitionists that their duty remained the same in spite of their divisions: "The slave still stands in chains, counting the time of his redemption by minutes, while we count it by years."

"*Well done!*, faithful, dear Maria," wrote Loring commending her debut in the *Standard* as "brilliant" and "heavenly-spirited." She had shown the "[c]andour & true toleration" so vitally needed among antislavery leaders, and she had proved herself "capable of looking at the dividing questions from the opposite . . . point of view" as well as her own. "I am most thankful that there is, at last, an Anti Slavery paper that I can open with satisfaction," he rejoiced.[14]

Child needed all the moral support her friends could give her, for she found her path beset with unanticipated obstacles. "I have been crying, like a fool, today," she wrote Loring right after her first meeting with the American Anti-Slavery Society's executive committee in New York. Its two "colored members," Thomas Van Rensalaer and William P. Powell, had urged the necessity of "cutting down" her salary of a thousand dollars a year, "saying they earned their money too hard to spend it so lavishly." They could not know that because of her "sensitiveness about taking money at all in the Anti Slavery business," Child had voluntarily reduced her own salary from the $1,200 originally proposed; nor could they know that she had been contending with a degree of poverty and hard physical labor comparable to any they themselves had experienced (Van Rensalaer owned a restaurant and Powell ran a temperance "Sailor's Home").[15] Rather, they were projecting onto Child the growing resentment of African Americans over white abolitionists' failure to treat them as equal partners in the antislavery movement. As they saw it, the *Standard* was absorbing resources that might have gone to the support of an African American newspaper like the *Colored American* or the *Mirror of Liberty*, both of which were languishing for want of adequate funds, and Child was occupying a position that might have been filled by a black editor — a possibility that evidently had never occurred to the white directors of the American Anti-Slavery Society (AASS).

Child also faced the hostility of two white men who felt they had been unjustly passed over — the *Standard*'s former temporary editor, James C. Jackson, and its local managing editor during Rogers's tenure, Oliver Johnson. Both men thought "*they* ought to have been editors, and that there was no call for the Society to throw away its money in paying me," Child reported to Loring.[16] Jackson eventually switched his allegiance and assumed the editorship of a new organization paper in upstate New

York, but Johnson continued undermining Child from within Garrisonian ranks in his role as AASS agent and member of the executive committee.

Added to these demoralizing "jealousies and heart-burnings" where she had hoped to encounter friendly collaboration, the challenge of editing a political newspaper — a milestone for a woman — was proving far greater than Child had expected. She was keenly aware of the twin precedents she was setting as a female editor and as a wife elevated to a rank above her husband's. In her greeting "To the Readers of the Standard,"[17] she frankly acknowledged that "Mr. Child's . . . experience in editing" the *Massachusetts Journal*, "his close observation of public affairs," and his professional inclinations would have made him a more logical choice as editor in chief, and that had he been free to move to New York, she would have served as assistant editor. "But in any other point of view, it is quite unimportant that the arrangement is reversed," she affirmed, undercutting her seeming concession to the gender prescriptions she was nullifying. The masthead she designed for the *Standard* translated her statement into visual terms: it displayed the couple's names in bold capitals at the top of the page, right under the paper's title, hers in the left corner — LYDIA MARIA CHILD, EDITOR — David's in the right corner — DAVID LEE CHILD, ASSISTANT EDITOR. The antiabolitionist press did not miss the opportunity for crude witticisms. "The male child . . . has not *grown* into puberty enough to be worthy of being promoted to at least a joint labor with his wife," gibed the *New-York Courier and Enquirer*.[18] The Childs adopted the practice of signing their editorials with their initials, LMC and DLC. This allowed each to assume responsibility for her or his own opinions, but it also increased Child's visibility.[19] In general, David supplied editorials on political subjects — the threatened annexation of Texas; the latest statements of such Whig politicians as Henry Clay, Daniel Webster, John Quincy Adams, and Joshua Giddings; and the campaign to restore the right of petition in Congress — and Child covered the range of antislavery ideology and social and cultural criticism, though she, too, occasionally commented on political developments.

Gender role reversal was not the only handicap Child labored under as a pioneering woman editor. "In addition to what men editors have to perform, I am obliged to do my own washing and ironing, mending and making, besides manifold stitches for my husband's comfort," she reminded her colleagues of the *Pennsylvania Freeman*.[20] Fortunately, she did not have to do her own cooking and housekeeping since she was boarding with the family of the Quaker Isaac T. Hopper.

She did have to master an "irksome" new craft, however, and except for helping David with the *Massachusetts Journal*, she had little prior experience to fall back on. Newspapers of the mid-nineteenth century typically consisted of articles reprinted from each other. In lieu of sending out reporters to cover events in other cities, editors read through endless piles of "exchange papers" from which they selected extracts. Child had always found politics distasteful, and now she had to immerse herself in the medium and "take more pains than a man would do, in order to avoid any inaccuracy or oversight in *state affairs*."[21] "This reading of papers and pamphlets, and poring over Congressional documents, is perfectly intolerable, unless sustained by the conviction that I am doing some good to the anti slavery cause," she complained to Loring.

Moreover, filling the *Standard*'s four pages of six long columns each — equal in dimensions to today's newspapers, but with much smaller print — was no easy task: "The type is fine, and that large sheet swallows an incredible amount of matter."[22]

Initially, Child regarded her work primarily as an onerous sacrifice imposed on her by David's financial circumstances and the needs of the abolitionist movement. "How I do long to get out of this infernal treadmill! How I do long to be re-united to my dear husband, and have some quiet, domestic days again!," she lamented after four months in the editorial chair, assuring Loring that "[n]othing *but* Mr. Child's pecuniary distress would keep me here another month."[23]

Her attitude changed abruptly after a visit to David in Northampton, timed to coincide with their thirteenth wedding anniversary. From a distance, she discovered to her surprise that the *Standard* had become a "favorite child," as she admitted in a "Letter from the Editor."[24] The inadvertent pun revealed more than she consciously recognized; in effect, she was imperceptibly transferring her allegiance from the Child she had married to the one she had begun to fashion out of her intellect. The brief reunion with David was "one of almost unmixed pain," Child confided to Loring. "David looked so thin and over-worked, that I should hardly have known him." The woman she had engaged to cook and clean for him had "proved most negligent and unfaithful," and Child spent her entire visit setting the household back into "comfortable train." Once again the couple laid plans for the future, and once again Child convinced herself that she saw a light at the end of the road. But as if she already sensed that she had to disengage herself emotionally from David and carve out an independent vocation for herself, she announced in the very next paragraph: "The ruling idea of my life, at this present showing, is to make the Standard a first-rate paper." No longer counting the months till the expiration of her first year's contract, Child now expressed a "wish to retain the charge of the Standard" indefinitely, if she could arrange a means for David to live with her while she took "entire care" of the paper. "The fact is, I am getting attached to the plaguy thing, and feel a keen interest in its success," she told Loring.[25]

Child gave an unmistakable indication of how possessive she was becoming toward her "plaguy" ward when Philadelphia abolitionists invited her to merge the *Standard* with their organ, the *Pennsylvania Freeman*. They proposed to "insert 3 columns per week" on any topics they chose and pay half price for a thousand copies of the *Standard*, which they would distribute in Pennsylvania. Child promptly rejected an arrangement that would have entailed relinquishing her editorial control over the paper and changing its character. "The Freeman is filled with twaddling articles, without intellectual life and spirit, generally; and moreover, it is always betwixt & between on points of principle," she wrote privately to Loring. Besides, she did not see why she should let Philadelphia abolitionists make a profit on her newspaper and use it to pay their office expenses. If they wanted a merger, she stipulated, it must be on her terms. Let them suspend publication, send her communications which she would publish subject to the same conditions as any others she received, and allow their subscribers to choose between the *Standard* and the *Emancipator* (since the *Freeman* tried to cater to both old and new organizationists). She could not "conscientiously edit" a paper that advocated policies she considered detrimental to the cause, nor could she publish any sectarian material or personal attacks whatsoever, she specified. They accepted.[26]

By the following spring, Child was speaking of her editorship as a mission Providence had conferred on her. "When I reflect on the peculiar and trying situation of the Anti-Slavery cause, and see how few in our ranks combine earnest love for the cause, with clear vision and cautious discrimination, I feel as if I were raised up for this crisis," she wrote to Louisa. Admittedly, she continued to feel "heart-sick for husband and home, and rural life," but what assuaged the pain of separation was "the consciousness of presenting weekly portions of truth to 16,000 readers; for at the lowest estimate, as many as that read the Standard."[27]

The circulation figure Child cited was extraordinary for an antislavery newspaper. It represented a subscription list of 4,000 — up from 2,500 at the time she took over the *Standard* from Rogers — multiplied by the number of readers in an average household. The tally would climb to 5,000 subscriptions by the end of Child's second year. During the same period the *Liberator* steadily lost subscribers.[28] How did Child achieve such a feat? The answer lies in the innovations she introduced into antislavery journalism and the meticulous attention she devoted to her craft.

In format, the *Standard* resembled the *Liberator* and other antislavery newspapers. The front page featured news articles, congressional speeches, major antislavery addresses, and other documents of the kind. Editorials, communications from readers or antislavery agents, and scattered small news items and advertisements occupied the second and third pages. The back page was reserved for miscellany, which usually included a column of poetry and sometimes other literary matter (though Garrison used the space for nonresistance articles).

Within this basic framework, Child set about transforming a dry, partisan organ with a limited audience into a "family newspaper" whose varied content would appeal to a wide range of readers. As she later explained, abolitionists already had a plethora of newspapers oriented toward the ideological needs of specific factions. What the cause lacked was "a medium of communication with the *people*." In order to win subscribers who "would not take an exclusively anti-slavery periodical," she deliberately enlarged the scope of the *Standard* by increasing the "proportion of literary and miscellaneous matter" in its columns. Her goal was to create an antislavery newspaper that people of many political tendencies would read for its feature items, and to use it as a vehicle for educating such readers in abolition principles. By "drawing them with the garland of imagination and taste," she would induce them to "look candidly" at the controversial issues of slavery and racial prejudice.[29]

Accordingly, as with the *Massachusetts Journal*, Child developed the literary department of the *Standard* into a major attraction. She serialized Frances Trolloppe's neglected novel of western travel, *Jonathan Jefferson Whitlaw*, valuable for its "true representation of society in the slave-holding South West,"[30] and Caroline Kirkland's "Forest Life," a series of sketches depicting living conditions on the frontier with unaccustomed realism. She reprinted copious extracts from Charles Dickens's *Ameri-*

can Notes, passages from de Tocqueville's *Democracy in America* and Emerson's essays, and a large selection of short stories, among them Nathaniel Hawthorne's temperance tale, "A Rill from the Town Pump." And she reviewed Harriet Martineau's historical novel about Toussaint L'Ouverture and the Santo Domingo uprising, *The Hour and the Man*. Eventually Child opened a column on the miscellany page for nonliterary folk as well: "Housekeepers and Farmers." It offered advice taken from domestic and agricultural manuals, one of which was Catharine Beecher's newly published *Treatise on Domestic Economy*.[31]

On the editorial page, Child herself furnished what became the *Standard*'s most popular literary item, a column she titled "Letters from New-York." These freewheeling sketches described the sights, institutions, and denizens of the nation's largest metropolis, sliding from the material into the moral and spiritual realms, from pictorial representation into social criticism and philosophical speculation. They integrated abolitionism into a comprehensive philanthropy that encompassed the issues of urban poverty, prison reform, women's rights, capital punishment, religious toleration, and justice toward all ethnic minorities — African Americans, Indians, Jews, Irish immigrants. The accompanying editorials commented not only on slavery, but on such topics of current interest as Mormonism, Puseyism, Transcendentalism, utopian socialism, homeopathy, and the Second Advent movement led by William Miller. Indeed, they often overlapped with the "Letters from New-York."

The "garland of imagination and taste" also enhanced Child's presentation of antislavery doctrine. Many of her editorials took the form of narratives or allegories — factual in content, but akin to fiction in style. "Annette Gray," "They have not wit enough to take care of themselves," "Follow the North Star," "The Slaveholder Seeking Light," and "Lewis Clark," retold the stories of the fugitive slaves Child had encountered, detailing their sufferings, emphasizing their resourceful strategies for survival and escape, transmitting their hard-won insights into their oppression, illuminating hidden corners of the slave system, and exposing the pitiful sophistry of the proslavery argument.[32]

Two of Child's most original editorials — "The Deserted Church" and "The Iron Shroud" — dramatized the economic and political self-destructiveness of the "peculiar institution" through evocative metaphors. In "The Deserted Church," Child conjured up a desolate landscape of abandoned plantations and rotting villas, overgrown with a "choking wilderness of weeds." Her central trope — a "mouldering" church occupied only by birds and bats, its ornate pulpit buried in dust, its "gilded Bible, still open, probably at the place where religious services had last been read" — symbolized the fate of a Christianity prostituted to uphold slavery. Recalling the biblical prophecies about the fall of Babylon and the destruction of Jerusalem, this godforsaken scene, explained Child, epitomized the blight produced by slave agriculture, which quickly exhausted the soil and therefore required constant expansion into new territories: "The whole range of the country between the Atlantic and the Pacific seems needed to keep alive a system, which, like the locusts of Egypt, devours every green thing it passes over."[33]

Similarly, in "The Iron Shroud" Child borrowed a trope from a story she had read in an English periodical and applied it to the political evolution of the past decade. Just as, in the story, a dungeoned prisoner of state found the "walls of his prison . . . every day closing in upon him" until they finally "crush[ed] him in their iron embrace," so Child discerned multiplying signs that "the walls *are* closing in upon the foul system [of slavery], and that it must inevitably be crushed." Ever since the launching of the abolitionist crusade, she noted, "Slaveholders and their abettors have been our most powerful agents . . . and they will be so unto the end. They cannot help it, let them resolve as much discretion as they may." All the measures they had taken to stamp out opposition to slavery — "[t]he outrage on the United States mail, the murder of Lovejoy, the Boston and New-York mobs, the burning of Pennsylvania Hall," and most recently, the "war upon the right of petition" — had instead "conspired to do our work" by awakening the public to the threat slavery posed to civil liberties. Yet the defenders of slavery could not solve their difficulties by tolerating abolitionist agitation either. "Would it have been safe for their system to have Congress receive petitions for its abolition, and allow free discussion thereon?" Child asked rhetorically. "Most manifestly not." She proceeded to sum up the other forces arrayed against the South: the shift in northern public opinion revealed in the mainstream press's unexpected sympathy for insurgent slaves in two recent uprisings on board the Spanish ship *Amistad* and the Virginian brig *Creole* — incidents that had marked serious defeats for southern diplomacy; the economic competition offered by cotton grown in India; the growth of antislavery sentiment in Kentucky and western Virginia; the South's increasing political isolation and vulnerability to slave revolt, Indian attacks, and possibly invasion from Mexico and the Caribbean in case of war. "Surely the walls *are* closing around slavery," she concluded.[34]

In yet another instance of how inventively Child adapted the *Standard* to the purpose of reaching "the *people*," her editorial "Great Race between the North and the South" even used a cartoon as a vehicle for illustrating the superiority of free labor. It depicted free labor as a man riding a galloping donkey and dangling beets on a pole in front of its nose to make his mount go faster. The juxtaposed vignette of slave labor showed "two idle men" (the master and the overseer) trying to flog a balking donkey — a visual pun on the comparative effectiveness of beets and beatings as stimuli (and perhaps a covert plug for beet sugar versus cane sugar). Not only had the creature "planted his fore-feet out, with the most indomitable obstinacy," Child pointed out, but he had his "hindfoot . . . lifted for a kick at his tormentors." The paired vignettes also contrasted the ignorance and debasement slavery enforced (symbolized by the blinders and downcast head of the "slave" donkey) with the enterprising spirit free labor fostered, symbolized by the "free" donkey's unencumbered and upheld head. Child followed up the pictorial lesson with a long extract from her chapter on free versus slave labor in the *Appeal*.[35]

Clearly, Child intended such editorials for readers with little or no prior exposure to abolitionist ideology. Likewise for their benefit, she introduced the column "A, B, C, of

Abolition," in which she reprinted her *Anti-Slavery Catechism*. And with the double purpose of inspiring new recruits and rekindling the "holy zeal" of veteran abolitionists, she commissioned from Samuel J. May a series of "Anti-Slavery Reminiscences" about the "brave old days" when the movement's pioneers had stood united against persecution.[36]

Child did not confine herself to the "A, B, C, of Abolition," however. Instead, she sought to increase her readers' political sophistication by teaching them to analyze the organs of public opinion more critically and by enabling them to detect the censorship and misrepresentation through which proslavery interests maintained their hegemony. Contrary to popular belief, she argued in one of several incisive editorials on "The Press," newspapers only functioned as the "mouthpieces" of the people when the people were already well-informed on a subject. Otherwise, "an unprincipled minority" could simply take advantage of the people's "ignorance and indifference" to fill "honest minds with prejudices, by presenting false statements, and making up false issues." Such had been the case with the subject of slavery, she asserted: "Facts have been so uniformly suppressed, and falsehoods so industriously circulated [by the "organs of political parties and religious sects"], that now, after ten years of laborious effort to gain the ears of the people, a large proportion of intelligent citizens honestly believe that our principles and measures are totally opposite to what they really are."[37] Mainstream periodicals had consistently refused to publish the "undoubted facts and plain statistics" abolitionists had collected to prove the cruelty and unprofitability of slavery and the success of emancipation in the West Indies, she charged. Among the telling examples of censorship Child cited was a short passage the *North American Review* had deleted from an article of David's on beet sugar; it had contained statistics on the mortality rate among slaves on Louisiana sugar plantations — drawn from official documents of the U.S. government and unaccompanied "by any anti-slavery remarks" — which David had adduced to establish the greater "*humanity*" of beet sugar manufacture, since it did not involve "such waste of life." Remarked Child drily: "The editor, Professor Palfrey, had, the last we knew, a slaveholding brother in New Orleans." For the further edification of readers, she republished the censored statistics in an adjacent column.[38]

If she hoped to counteract the negative influence of the mainstream press and to develop the *Standard* into a truly effective "medium of communication with the *people*," Child realized, she could not inculcate antislavery principles through editorials alone. She had to make the paper a leading source of current news about the slavery controversy generally and abolitionist activity in particular. Thus, she gave extensive coverage to the congressional debates over the gag rule abrogating the right of petition; the attempts by antiabolitionist congressmen to censure and even expel Representatives John Quincy Adams and Joshua Giddings for their antislavery speeches; the military expeditions indicating plans to annex Texas and foment a war with Mexico; the long-drawn and bloody Seminole War in Florida, aimed simultaneously at seizing Indian land, closing off a haven for fugitive slaves, and recapturing the fugitives who had intermarried with the Seminoles; the agitation against the 1793 Fugitive Slave Act sparked by the arrest in Boston of a slave named George Latimer; and the campaign that Massachusetts abolitionists were waging against Jim Crow transportation and antimiscegenation laws.

Rather than simply reprint news articles as she found them, Child compared and synthesized different versions of the same events and tightened the prose to condense information and maximize space for other items. She exercised even more editorial control over the communications sent to her by abolitionists, "disentangling roots, and throwing rocks out of the path" to improve their readability, and eliminating redundancy, sectarian bias, and personal attacks. In addition to striving for literary quality in her news coverage, Child made a special point of soliciting independent accounts of abolitionist gatherings and protest meetings, so as to avoid having to lift "stale" news from the *Liberator* weeks after the fact. Thanks to this policy, the *Standard* provided a far more dramatic account than the *Liberator* of at least one major episode in abolitionist annals: Frederick Douglass's speaking debut at an antislavery meeting in Nantucket, described for Child by Henrietta Sargent.[39]

In sum, every department of the *Standard*—from the news on the front page to the literature and miscellany on the back page, from Child's own editorials to her subscribers' letters to the editor—bore her impress and served to attract as broad a readership as possible. The literary distinction Child injected into antislavery journalism and the tone of principled impartiality she succeeded in maintaining amid the crossfire of warring sects won the *Standard* unprecedented popularity and earned her encomiums from many quarters.

"I rejoice . . . that L. M. Child is doing so much for the cause & for woman by acquitting herself so nobly in the Editorial Chair," wrote Lucretia Mott from Philadelphia. Mott went on to quote the opinion of Philadelphia's influential Unitarian minister William H. Furness that the *Standard* was "becoming one of the best papers in the country." William Ellery Channing, whom Child had worked so hard at converting to abolitionism, broke a long silence to tell her that he had been subscribing to the *Standard* ever since learning that "it had passed into your hands" and that he had been particularly "delighted" with her "Letters from New-York." Several key members of the "new organization" joined in the acclaim. The wealthy landowner Gerrit Smith, a founder of its political arm, the Liberty party, sent Child twenty dollars toward her salary, "saying he had read every paper thoroughly since [she] began to edit it—that he was delighted with the ability that sustained it, and the kind spirit that breathed through it." Lewis Tappan, leader of the American and Foreign Anti-Slavery Society, called at the *Standard* office to order a subscription and "expressed his admiration of Mrs. C." And Joshua Leavitt, editor of the *Emancipator*, contrasted Child flatteringly with Rogers and Garrison (a tribute she interpreted as a "dagger-thrust" aimed at "those tried and true friends of universal freedom"). The chorus of praise culminated in a testimonial by the Garrisonian radical Wendell Phillips, who assured Child that "all classes here [in Boston], the *ultra*, the moderate, the half converted, the zealous, the indifferent, the active, all welcome the *Standard*, and that it is fast changing them all into its own likeness of sound, liberal, generous, active, devoted men and women, without partiality and without hypocrisy. . . ."[40]

From the start, however, dissenting voices in the Garrisonian camp belied Phillips's enthusiastic assessment. Not surprisingly, the disgruntled Oliver Johnson was among the first to articulate the reservations of "ultra" Garrisonians, who numbered among them Chapman, the Weston sisters, Edmund Quincy, Abby Kelley, and, of course, N. P. Rogers. In a private letter to Chapman, which he claimed he would not have written "to one less friendly to Mrs. C. than yourself," Johnson complained that the *Standard* was too "*agreeable* . . . under Mrs. Child's administration." It lacked the "fire" of the *Liberator* and did not "sufficiently expose the corruptions of the Church." Moreover, he warned, "[i]ts agreeableness is attracting the support of some half-and-half-, milk-and-water sort of abolitionists, who will always new organize in an emergency." Pointing out that the *Standard* was "often complimented at the Liberator's expense," Johnson carped: "I don't want our papers to become too popular, lest it should require too much time and sacrifice hereafter to take care of their reputation."[41]

What the "ultras" refused to recognize was that "attracting the support of . . . half-and-half-, milk-and-water . . . abolitionists" was vital to the progress of the antislavery cause, for in the long run this group would tip the political scale in favor of ending slavery at any cost—if necessary through war. Child, on the contrary, had formulated her editorial policy precisely with the aim of recruiting subscribers from this pivotal group and then cultivating a true abolitionist consciousness in them. Although she adapted the content and rhetorical style of the *Standard* to the tastes of a varied public, she never diluted the essence of the antislavery message: uncompromising insistence on the duty and feasibility of abolishing slavery immediately, rooting out all forms of racial discrimination, and opening the doors of equal opportunity to free blacks. Nor did her aversion to controversy prevent her from speaking out strongly in defense of Garrisonian principles when abolitionists of the opposing camp took stands she considered deleterious to the cause.

Child's denunciation of prosouthern apologists and advocates of Colonization could be as harsh as Garrison's. She scornfully dismissed the often repeated allegation that the abusiveness of abolitionists had driven the South into hard-line championship of a system it had once deplored as a curse. Calling the South's previous posture a "convenient arrangement" of "[p]lunder in the hand, and philanthropy on the lips," Child contended: "At no time would the south have admitted slavery to be an evil, if called upon to remove that evil. Truth, however kindly spoken, if spoken in earnest, would have unmasked their hypocrisy." Child similarly answered a correspondent who thought that an unsigned editorial on Colonization "could not have been written by the 'amiable editor,' because its language was so harsh." No one's "detestation of that scheme could surpass my own," she responded tartly, asserting that the omission of her initials had been accidental.[42]

As in all her earlier publications, Child also assigned high priority in the *Standard* to combating racial prejudice. Her editorial "Unwritten Wrongs" pointed out that to African Americans, "our boasted free institutions are a bitter jest." To bolster the ongoing campaigns against Jim Crow transportation and segregated schooling, she cited cases of blacks who had died of exposure as a result of being denied seating inside stagecoaches or ship cabins, and she noted the triple injustice of taxing blacks to support public schools they were barred from attending, yet blaming them for lacking the intellectual culture they were not allowed to acquire.[43] Another editorial, "Our Anglo-Saxon Ancestry," exploded the white supremacist boast that "tyranny could never bow the proud spirit of the Anglo Saxon into tame submission," as it had the spirit of the Negro. "The plain, unvarnished truth is, our Anglo Saxon ancestry were slaves," Child reminded her readers. Drawing on the French historian Augustin Thierry's *Norman Conquest of England*, she elaborated on the many parallels between Anglo-Saxon and African American slaves: neither had succeeded in overthrowing their rulers "under circumstances of such overwhelming tyranny"; among both groups, "love of liberty" had prompted many to take refuge in forests, mountains, and swamps and to form "bands of partisans" or "brigands"; among both, the masses of slaves had secretly venerated these brigands as heroes, for "the smothered love of liberty shows itself in the manner of hating those whom they have the will to conquer, without the power; of loving those who contend with their oppressors; and of sympathizing with those who elude their vigilance"; among both groups, finally, women had been "compelled, willing or unwilling, to submit entirely to their master's orders."[44]

More important than her own editorializing against prejudice was the receptiveness Child showed to African American writers' views. She reprinted not only the speeches of Frederick Douglass and William C. Nell, but a long article from the *Northern Star and Freeman's Advocate*, "a paper edited with much intelligence by our colored brethren in Albany." It castigated white abolitionists for their failure to live up to their promises of "opening every avenue, and destroying every barrier in their power that was closed against us, or that retarded our progression." Blacks did not expect to intermarry with whites, or "mix in their parties of pleasure," but they did hope that abolitionists would set the example of patronizing black businesses and of training black youth for remunerative trades, wrote this black critic. "Until abolitionists *eradicate prejudice from their own hearts*," he concluded, "they never *can* receive the unwavering confidence of the people of color." "The rebuke is too well deserved," commented Child, urging abolitionists to "profit by the hints" of their "colored brethren."[45]

The themes Child emphasized in the *Standard* had always been central to antislavery doctrine; veteran abolitionists of all factions could still unite around the call for immediate emancipation, the dismissal of Colonization, and the denunciation of racial prejudice. The controversies that divided abolitionists focused instead on determining how best to achieve their aims. Child's editorship of the *Standard* coincided with a period when abolitionists of all factions were experimenting with new strategies of agitation as their old strategies of moral suasion were proving inadequate. The "new organization" was relying more and more heavily on electoral politics and trying to build an antislavery "third party." Perhaps under the influence of African Americans, some new organizationists were also moving tentatively toward an endorsement of slave insurrection. Meanwhile, Garrisonians were recommending individual and collective withdrawal from the Union as a formula for ending the North's complicity in slavery and hastening the fall of the system in the South. It was in her handling of these issues that Child faced the ultimate test of her editorial policy.

Like other Garrisonians, Child considered it crucial for abolitionism to retain the character of a moral rather than a political movement. She quickly attained the status of a leading spokesperson for this ideological position. The high value Garrison attached to her eloquent editorials on the subject is obvious from the number he reprinted in the *Liberator*; indeed, even Rogers reprinted a few in his newspaper, the *Herald of Freedom*.[46] While Child went out of her way to credit the men who embraced the Liberty party with "patriotic and unselfish" intentions, she strongly criticized the mode of activism they had chosen. "No reformer can make use of political machinery, as a means to effect his ends, without moral injury to himself, and serious detriment to the cause he advocates," she contended. When abolitionists entered the political arena, she explained, the short-range goal of winning votes inevitably replaced the long-range objective of inculcating correct principles. As a result, their moral fervor lessened and they gradually lost sight of their original ideals: "They who once leaned on principles as the sheet-anchor of the soul, by degrees come to spend their strength in vain efforts to keep a sure footing on the revolving platform of temporary expediency; until at last, by trusting in man, they forget to trust in God."[47]

At the same time, Child recognized the absolute necessity of political action and the indispensable role it would play in bringing about abolition. She simply disagreed with the Liberty party's narrow concept of political action, especially decrying the tactic of creating a separate antislavery party. In a dialogue titled "Talk about Political Party," she outlined the alternative approach that she and her fellow Garrisonians favored. Abolitionists should "work *through*" political parties, "but not *with* them," she argued. By exerting their moral influence on voters and politicians, and by acting as a united pressure group that both parties would have to court, abolitionists could promote a change in public opinion that would automatically express itself through political channels. Parties and politicians "do *our* work; we do not *their's*," Child specified. She cited a number of practical objections to the third-party scheme. First, she maintained, by dividing and siphoning off a significant proportion of the antislavery constituency, it prevented abolitionists from holding the balance of power between the two major parties and thus obtaining concessions from both, as abolitionists had successfully done in Massachusetts and Vermont before the founding of the Liberty party. Second, a party built on a single issue could not hold together; either it would split over the political differences that aligned some abolitionists with the Whigs and others with the Democrats, or its members would bolt whenever other political interests vied with their commitment to abolition. Third, an abolitionist minority party would never be able to elect more than a token handful of representatives to state legislatures and Congress. "Two or three radical abolitionists," even if they were "anti-slavery to the back-bone," could not achieve as much as "*twenty*" or "fifty" men like the antislavery Whig Joshua R. Giddings, "who have a strong motive for obliging the abolitionists," Child asserted. She ended with an urgent plea against dissipating the movement's moral power by "sustaining a fallacious and mischievous scheme."[48]

Garrison found Child's "Talk about Political Party" so "replete with the good sense, clear discrimination, and catholic spirit, which usually characterize the writings of this estimable woman" that he reprinted it in full and defended it warmly against an attack by a prominent Liberty party advocate, the former AASS president Beriah Green. Accusing Green of exhibiting a "contemptuousness of spirit" and "inclination to caricature" totally unwarranted by the rational, fair-minded tone of Child's article, Garrison conjectured that a double animus lay behind his attack. Not only was Green incapable of "estimat[ing] at its true value, any thing that may be said or written by a woman," but he was perturbed by the impact Child's arguments were having on Liberty party men and anxious to keep the "moral contagion from spreading"; in fact, Green's letter was addressed not to Child herself but to a Liberty party correspondent who had confessed to being " 'greatly interested' in her 'talk,' and constrained to adopt her views."[49]

Child again felt compelled to speak out in protest when radical members of the Liberty party issued statements that in her view imperiled the antislavery movement by contributing to the general "misconception, and misrepresentation of our objects." In January 1842 Liberty party conventions at Williamsburg, New York, and Peterboro, New York, passed a series of resolutions applauding the slave rebels of the *Creole* for having "acted in accordance with the principles of our Declaration of Independence"; urging other slaves to follow their example; pledging that "should the slaves at the South endeavor to gain their natural rights and liberty, 'peaceably if they can, *forcibly if they must*,' " Liberty party abolitionists would not intervene against them but would pray for their victory; and arguing that the South's slave laws could "be repealed only by concentrated political action . . . at the North." At the Peterboro convention, Gerrit Smith also read an "Address to the Slaves of the United States," in which he advised them to feel no compunction about appropriating whatever they needed to make their escape — "the horse, the boat, the food, the clothing" — anywhere along their route.[50]

Child herself had frequently expressed sympathy for slave rebels, including those of the *Creole* and *Amistad*, and she had praised such heroes as Toussaint L'Ouverture and Zhinga in the *Appeal*. Though a pacifist, she agreed that "[i]f any people on earth have a right to fight in self-defense, the captured and enslaved negro has most peculiarly that right," as she had explicitly stated in her New York letter on the *Amistad* captives, published only a few weeks earlier.[51] Her objections to the Liberty party's Williamsburg and Peterboro resolutions lay primarily in the adverse impact that such official statements, emanating from abolitionists as a group, would have on the public; after all, northern opinion-makers had only recently justified suppressing antislavery agitation through mob violence and censorship, on the pretext that abolitionists were seeking to foment slave insurrections.

Thus, Child issued a disclaimer in the name of the American Anti-Slavery Society, repudiating the Williamsburg resolutions "without reserve, as being broadly at variance with the principles" abolitionists had originally professed. Reprinting the second and third articles of the 1833 AASS constitution, she reminded abolitionists that the society had vowed " 'never, in any way, [to] countenance the oppressed in vindicating their rights by a resort to physical force.' " Her reaction to the Peterboro resolutions was more muted. To avoid "misconstruction of our motives," she suggested an alternative wording for the most controversial resolution: "It should be stated that while we think it wrong to *excite* insurrection, we consider it equally wrong to take part against the oppressed in case of insurrection." She also took issue with the theory that the North could force the South to repeal its slave laws. The U.S. Constitution gave the states jurisdiction over their own internal affairs, she pointed out. The only recourse abolitionists had was to "convince slaveholders that emancipation is a sacred duty, and therefore the highest expediency"; if slaveholders could not be "saved by moral influence, they must go to destruction in the way of their own choosing." To impose abolition on the South against its will, she added, would only be counterproductive: "the disease would still exist, ready to break out again in aggravated forms."[52]

Child expended special tact on Gerrit Smith's address to the slaves, which she acknowledged "comes from one of the kindest of human hearts; (God's blessing rest upon it!) — and . . . finds a response in *every* feeling heart." The "novelty" of addressing the slaves directly in this bold manner might have "one good effect," Child conceded — to "arrest popular attention, by startling prejudice and timidity." Yet it would produce many more ill effects. To begin with, neither the slaves nor the "free-colored people of the South" had much chance of receiving a message from northern abolitionists, at least without its being "intercepted by the masters." Smith's address would not only inflame the South and "diminish what little confidence" the northern public had in "the discretion and practical wisdom of abolitionists"; worse, it would "throw new and powerful obstacles in the way of escape" for most slaves. Masters would "redouble the vigilance and precautions of tyranny," and fugitive slaves, if they followed Smith's advice to steal what they needed, would meet with far less sympathy, have more difficulty finding people to shelter them, and "be constantly liable to be taken on a *writ of theft*." Child's prediction was fulfilled sooner than either she or Smith expected; that summer a Kentucky slave named Nelson Hackett, who rode his master's racehorse to safety in Canada and took along a gold watch to sell if he needed cash, was remanded by the Canadian authorities as a thief, in a portentous reversal of Canada's usual policy.[53]

Militant declarations by African Americans elicited similarly nuanced reactions from Child. In the wake of the Supreme Court's 1842 *Prigg* v. *Pennsylvania* decision, which reinforced the federal government's jurisdiction over fugitive slave cases (and correspondingly nullified more liberal laws in the free states), kidnappings of former fugitives and freeborn blacks were dramatically increasing. The African American *People's Press* responded by calling on blacks to prepare themselves for violent resistance: "Let it be known to the kidnappers and their myrmidons, that we think our lives of less worth than our liberties; and *their* lives of infinitely less value than either — and they will let us alone." Child politely dissented. "We hope the colored population will rely upon the laws, and not trust themselves to carry dangerous weapons," she editorialized: "Leaving principle entirely out of the question, it is the very worst *policy* they can pursue. If they can but be manly, firm, and uncompromising, without being violent, they will infallibly gain the strong voice of popular opinion and popular prejudice on their side." She went on to cite the example of Boston's "colored citizens," who had also resolved not to "permit ourselves nor brethren to be transferred to the southern prison-house," but who had opted for petitioning the state legislature and Congress to nullify or repeal the 1793 Fugitive Slave Law.[54] Essentially, Child was asking African Americans to place their dependence not on their own resources and capacity for self-defense, but on the goodwill of the white majority. Nevertheless, she was at least eschewing the dictatorial style J. C. Jackson had assumed when he had condemned the separatism of colored conventions.

In using her editorial position to define what she considered to be the wisest and most principled policy for abolitionists to follow at this crucial juncture, Child did not exempt her own faction from criticism. When she felt that leaders of the "old organization," including Garrison himself, endangered the cause through rash actions or ill-advised statements, she exercised the same prerogative of tactful demurral toward them as toward those outside their camp. Such an occasion arose as Garrisonians began formulating a radical new strategy that paralleled the endorsements of violence emerging from sectors of the Liberty party and the African American community. Frustrated, like their rivals, by the seeming impasse at which the antislavery movement had arrived after a decade of agitation, Garrisonians, too, found themselves reevaluating the pledges they had made at the outset of their crusade. Not yet ready to abandon their commitment to nonviolence, they focused instead on reevaluating their original pledge to uphold the Constitution, respect the compact binding the free North to the slave South, and preserve the Union.

Child herself was actually one of the first to conclude that "there was no other way for the free States to clear themselves of being accomplices in tremendous guilt" than to "take measures for a peaceable separation" from the South. In an unsigned editorial of February 1842, titled "The Union," which appeared on the same page of the *Standard* as her comments on Gerrit Smith's "Address," she acknowledged that she had reached that verdict more than two years earlier.[55] The stimulus that prompted her editorial was a letter from a Boston friend (possibly Maria Chapman or Abby Kelley), announcing that Garrisonians had just launched a campaign to repeal the Union.[56] While supporting the initiative, Child cautioned that "petitions of this kind" should be "most carefully worded; not for the sake of policy, or disguise; but [so] that our real views and wishes may be distinctly understood." She proceeded to articulate the rationale for repealing the Union. The Constitution obliged northern citizens to surrender fugitive slaves when the master could prove his claim to them, and it used northerners' tax dollars to put down insurrections. "What, then, can we do, but insist upon such changes in the Constitution, as will relieve us of all *partnership* in this nefarious business? And if this is refused, what remedy is there but a peaceable separation, for conscience' sake?"

In the ensuing weeks Child reprinted many letters and editorials on the disunion question, both pro and con, from other newspapers (as did Garrison in the *Liberator*).[57] She spelled out her own position most fully in a long editorial of March 31, 1842.[58] It began by listing the grounds on which she objected to the Union. First, she pointed out: "It is a sham, and not a reality. It professes to be union, and *is* coercion. We are *called* the United States, and we *are* the Disunited States." Using an analogy that reverberated with personal significance, she compared the Union, as currently constituted, to a "marriage" in which " 'the disparity seemed to be all on one side.' " In such an unequal partnership, based on coercion, "We are tied, not united; soldered, not fused," Child contended. Second, "To keep up the appearance of union, the American people are fast becoming accustomed to the relinquishment of those real principles, on which free institutions *must* rest, if they exist at all." Third, the collaboration of the free states played a vital role in perpetuating slavery. "We are the standing army of the South, ranged in dense platoons, with bayonets pointed toward the trembling slaves. Without our help, southerners would not even *try* to sustain their peculiar institutions," Child stressed. Those who thought they could individually withdraw from partnership in guilt by severing their connection with the government were deluding themselves, she added, for their property was still taxed and they were still counted in the census. Fourth, by resorting to mob violence, censorship, and war to maintain the slave system at all costs, Americans were "aiding and abetting to harm the cause of freedom throughout the world."

Having summed up her reasons for favoring a repeal of the Union, Child suggested possible compromises. For example, the North might seek to modify the Constitution for the purpose of establishing a "partial union . . . absolving us from *direct* partnership in slavery." This would weaken the slave system sufficiently to bring about abolition and thus lay the basis for a true union. Child reminded her fellow northerners, however, that in attempting to end their partnership in crime, they should not forget their responsibility to the South. Since northerners had contributed to the growth of slavery, they should not leave the South to grapple unaided with "bankruptcy and insurrections." As long as there remained any hope of persuading the South to save herself from disaster, Child urged, duty to both master and slave required that the North "strive . . . to bring her *out* of the condition *into* which we have helped to bring her."

Child ended by reiterating the need for the "utmost circumspection, and forbearance" in approaching the question of renegotiating the Union. "No measure should be taken because it is startling, or new," she warned. Instead, northerners should aim to extricate themselves from participation in slavery "with the least injury to [their] fellow-creatures, and the least danger to the welfare of [their] country."

Child saw it as her mission to lay down principles but leave readers free to decide for themselves how best to translate those principles into action. To prescribe any particular course of action, she believed, would be to violate the spirit of the broad platform, based on respect for each individual's freedom of conscience, which distinguished the old organization from the new. And to prescribe a "startling . . . new" course that conscientious people might justly be unable to support would be ruinous, she felt.

Thus, she reacted with consternation to the fiery editorial Garrison issued on April 22, right before the May 1842 annual meeting, in which he proclaimed:

> The milk that has hitherto been used must now give place to meat. . . . New ground must be occupied, and skirmishing must give way to a general engagement. . . .
>
>   The first [question to be settled at the annual meeting] . . . is the duty of making the REPEAL OF THE UNION between the North and the South, the grand rallying point until it be accomplished, or slavery cease to pollute our soil. We are for throwing all the means, energies, actions, purposes, and appliances of the genuine friends of liberty and republicanism into this one channel, and for measuring the humanity, patriotism and piety of every man by this one standard.[59]

Child considered it "imprudent" of Garrison to have unilaterally announced that "the chief business of our anniversary was to dissolve the union; . . . *before* the Society had at all deliberated what was best on a subject so very important" and even more "rash to throw out such an enunciation, without any explanation of the *means to be used*"; she also took exception to the idea that "a set in Massachusetts were going to measure every man's 'humanity patriotism and piety,' by their willingness to dissolve the union."[60]

Her consternation turned to alarm when New York's leading antiabolitionist newspapers pounced on Garrison's editorial and blazoned it as the proof that they had always been right in denouncing abolitionism as "treason to the Union of the States." James Watson Webb of the *New-York Courier and Enquirer* editorialized that his patriotic warnings had been disregarded for fifteen years, while abolitionists had grown in numbers and boldness; now these "incendiaries" had dropped their "mask" and openly admitted their "infamous purpose." "The avowed object . . . of this Convention, is treasonable, revolutionary, and dangerous. If held, it will rouse a feeling in the public mind, such as has never yet been witnessed," he threatened in a barely disguised incitement to mob violence. While Webb called on the mayor and the police to prevent abolitionists from engaging in sedition, Judge Mordecai Manasseh Noah of the New York court of sessions convened a grand jury and charged it to indict the "agitators" if their advocacy of disunion provoked a "disastrous breach of the public peace."[61]

Child responded swiftly to avert the danger of another outbreak like the notorious New York riots of 1834, which had also targeted an antislavery meeting. She and James S. Gibbons, chairman of the AASS executive committee, sent a circular to all the New York newspapers, disclaiming responsibility for Garrison's announcement that the dissolution of the Union would be the main item on the agenda at the annual meeting and denying that the AASS had committed itself to promoting "an object . . . entirely foreign to the purpose for which it was organized." At the same time, she and Gibbons emphasized that the society would exercise the right to discuss any subjects it deemed proper at its annual meeting and would not be "deterred from the fearless discharge of duty by threats of violence."[62]

Garrison greeted the circular with "unfeigned surprise, deep mortification, and extreme regret," construing it as a personal rebuke from a valued coadjutor.[63] His own instincts, moreover, ran diametrically counter to Child's. Never one to back down in the face of threats, Garrison intensified his rhetoric. "Slavery is a combination of DEATH and HELL, and with it the North have made a covenant," he trumpeted. Summoning his troops to "Demand the repeal of the Union, or the abolition of slavery," he perorated: "People of the North! if the South be wholly dependent upon you for protection in prosecuting her bloody enormities, who are the real slaveholders, the real slave-traders, the real slave-drivers, the real slave-plunderers, but YOURSELVES? You cannot extricate yourselves from this position without a repeal of the Union."[64]

In substance, Garrison's analysis added nothing to Child's. "There is probably very slight, if any, difference between my views about the Union" and those of Garrison and his most radical supporters, she underscored in letters to Chapman and Wendell Phillips. As for Garrison's inflammatory editorial, "[i]f precisely the same ideas had been *worded* a little differently, they could not have been made such effectual use of by our enemies." The divergence lay in the rhetoric and political strategy each of them espoused. A born agitator, Garrison sought to galvanize the masses into action; an intellectual whose mainsprings were reason and conscience, Child sought to promote the formulation of a better policy through a "calm, rational appeal" to "intelligent and judicious" minds.[65]

Neither Garrison nor his followers understood Child's stand, however. Responding to her friends' "vehement" protests against what they perceived as disloyalty to Garrison and opposition to airing a controversial subject, Child insisted that they were "fight[ing] with a man of straw." "I have no *disposition* to 'wash my hands of Garrison,'" she assured Chapman, "for the simple reason that I have the highest respect for his ability, the most perfect confidence in his integrity of purpose, and a general unity with his principles." Similarly, she was perfectly willing to have the question of disunion "fully and freely discussed" both in the *Standard* and at the annual meeting, "provided it is done in a rational and manly style" and not in a style of "cat-hauling."[66]

In the end, both Child and Garrison felt vindicated by the results of the annual meeting. Child thought she had succeeded in averting mob violence and creating the conditions for a thoughtful debate in which widely varying opinions were "uttered with perfect harmony and brotherly kindness." "The tone of our meetings implied an unanimous conviction that the North could not continue her present connection with the South, without being a direct partner in the guilt of slaveholding; and that our duty as individuals, and as a society, required us to use all moral means to deepen and strengthen this conviction," she reported in the *Standard*. Garrison, who had absented himself to avoid influencing the debate, interpreted this consensus as an endorsement of the stand he had taken in his editorial. Swayed by "circumstances of great peril," he concluded, Child had committed an "error of judgment" but not a "compromise of principle" in issuing her circular. He was sure that she must "heartily regret its publication"; Child was sure that she "should do just the same thing next week, under similar circumstances."[67]

The disagreement over tactics, though irresoluble, did not lessen the two editors' mutual respect for each other's contributions. A month after recovering from his "deep mortification" at Child's disclaimer, Garrison paid another extravagant tribute to the writer he had hailed thirteen years earlier as *the first woman in the republic*." In an editorial marking the second anniversary of the *Standard*'s founding, he pronounced the paper "an honor to the literature and philanthropy of the land" and praised the "rare dignity, excellent judgment, and perfect fidelity" with which Child had sustained it.[68] Despite having begun "without a single subscriber," he noted, the *Standard* now stood "on a more solid basis than any other anti-slavery periodical." He went on to recapitulate Child's distinguished career. "It would not be easy to name another person in the crowded ranks of anti-slavery, who has made greater sacrifices, or exhibited superior moral courage or devotedness, in the cause of emancipation," he asserted. "The acquisition of so gifted an intellect and so large a heart to the anti-slavery cause, in its infancy, . . . filled my breast with joy, and served greatly to refresh my spirit." Crediting Child's *Appeal* with having helped produce the "surprising change, in public sentiment," which was becoming increasingly apparent, Garrison turned to assessing the talents and character traits she displayed as editor of the *Standard*. "Mrs. Child has very few superiors as a writer," he observed. "Her style is clear as crystal, and elegantly simple; combining that rare quality, practical good sense, with great poetic beauty. . . . She utters her opinions calmly and frankly, and studiously avoids an oracular or dogmatical air." Garrison not only showed himself able to appreciate a style that differed entirely from his own; he also revealed keen insight into Child's temperament and surprising sympathy even with what he regarded as her limitations. "The field of controversy is not so much to her taste, as the grove of contemplation, or the arbor of poesy," he conceded,

> but her clear perception of wrong, and her large benevolence of soul, impel her to go into the moral arena, not so much to achieve a triumph over others as to discharge a sacred duty. She addresses herself more to the understanding than to the conscience, and is therefore better adapted to be an auxiliary than a leader in the work of reform. Between her fondness for literary pursuits and her sympathy for the oppressed, there is a visible struggle; and each in turn receives its due share of attention, to the relief of her heart, and the gratification of her intellect.

Besides proclaiming his high esteem for Child, Garrison was implicitly affirming that a "diversity of tastes and temperaments — of gifts and attainments — " was "essential to the advancement" of the antislavery cause. He proceeded to register his concern about the growing tendency of abolitionists to be "impatient or censorious toward each other" in matters that pertained to temperament rather than creed. Addressing himself to those who objected to the *Standard* because they found it "too literary, too quiet in its tone, too nice in its phraseology," he reminded them that many readers conversely objected to the *Liberator* and the *Herald of Freedom* (edited by Rogers) because they considered these papers to be "conducted in bad taste, almost in a bad spirit." "I cannot find it in my heart to complain, . . . that my friend Mrs. Child is not disposed to make either of us her editorial pattern," Garrison avowed. What counted ultimately was "our union of hearts as the friends of the perishing slave." He closed with a generous acknowledgment of David Child's input into the *Standard* as well.

Characteristically, Child reprinted in the *Standard* solely the portion of Garrison's editorial that advocated a "Diversity of Gifts with Unity of Purpose." Indeed, she all but ignored "Garrison's glorification article," referring to it only once in a letter dismissing the idea of reproducing four hundred copies of it for the English market as a means of advertising the *Standard*.[69] She could not so easily ignore the complaints to which Garrison had tried to respond.

Though the fracas over Child's circular had blown over, it had brought to a head the mounting dissatisfaction of Garrisonian fire-eaters with a newspaper they found "too tame" to serve as the organ of the American Anti-Slavery Society. Led by Maria Weston Chapman, the malcontents included the Weston sisters, Edmund Quincy, N. P. Rogers, and the *Standard*'s traveling agents Abby Kelley, John A. Collins, and Stephen S. Foster, Kelley's future husband. Significantly, Wendell Phillips, the greatest intellect among Garrison's radical followers, held himself aloof from the campaign against Child's editorial policy. Like Garrison, Phillips recognized the key role Child played in bridging differences among factions, attracting more moderate supporters, and lending respectability to the movement. "Let Rogers madden" and "Abby Kelley tread a pirate deck," he urged, but let Child pursue her own course unimpeded. "Because New Hampshire [Rogers's native state and a hotbed of radicalism] is crazy shall there be no more letters from N.Y., no more articles 'rightly dividing the word of truth,' on the whole reasons of division in our ranks?"[70]

The fire-eaters did not agree. Chapman privately accused Child of substituting "flapdoodle" for the "roast Beef" the *Standard* needed. In fact, Chapman went so far as to claim that the paper owed its unrivaled circulation to her own salesmanship rather than to Child's editing. "No body know[s] better than I what it *took* to make the Standard the popular paper it was during Mrs. Child's reign," she told her sister Caroline a year after Child's resignation, when subscriptions had plunged from 5,000 to 1,300.[71] Collins blamed "the tone of the Standard" for the failure of his fund-raising drive as AASS general agent (a failure others attributed to the hostility Collins was arousing by using antislavery meetings as vehicles for winning converts to utopian socialism).[72] Kelley, Foster, and Rogers were currently denouncing the churches as a "brotherhood of thieves" and exhorting abolitionists to "come out" of Babylon by cutting their ties with any religious sects and political parties that did not unequivocally condemn slavery. They wanted the *Standard* to endorse "come-outism" and abandon "the half-souled and the hypocrite" to "their ephemeral existences." "We must have a Standard around which *all true hearts* can rally," insisted Abby Kelley (laying the accent on "true" rather than "all").[73] Chapman, too, was "*determined* that the popularity of the Standard should be *forced* to sustain the come-outisms of church and state," as Child informed Loring. But Chapman and Quincy also had a covert agenda — to discredit "new organization" once and for all and to ensure a crushing defeat for the Liberty party in the 1842 and 1844 elections. This agenda, which they were busily implementing as editors pro tem of the *Liberator*, required that the *Standard* open its columns to partisan attacks against their opponents, beginning with Joshua Leavitt, editor of the *Emancipator* and the most able exponent of political abolitionism.[74]

Child balked. "Taste, principle, and philosophy would alike forbid me to prepare such hyena soup with brimstone seasoning, as suits many of our friends," she wrote Phillips.[75] Firmly refusing to go along with Chapman's strategy, Child admonished her friend and former ally in the Boston Female Anti-Slavery Society schism: "You know we always differed on certain points. I never could enter into your partisan spirit; never could see that we were bound to conceal all the faults of our own side, while we blazoned all those of our opponents." She proceeded to spell out the alternatives: the *Standard* could either remain "a good family anti-slavery newspaper . . . intended . . . to gain the ear of the people at large," or it could become a "controversial and agitating paper" adapted to the tastes of "veteran abolitionists." The two policies could not be "mixed, any more than fire and water." If the *Standard* began printing articles "for and against Liberty Party, for and against New organization, for and against" individual figures in the movement, it would turn into "only another edition of the Liberator," in which case it ought to be merged with the *Liberator* and printed in Boston, "to save expense." Child hoped the society would decide which it wanted, but if it opted for an organ of agitation, she would step down from the editorship, for she could not conscientiously promulgate come-outism, let alone engage in sectarian feuding. Come-outism was "as narrow and coercive" in its insistence that abolitionists leave their churches as the new organization had been in its insistence that "all men must vote, or all must belong to the Liberty Party," Child pointed out. The imposition of such a requirement would end up driving the "*best* spirits" out of the old organization, she predicted, since "Anti slavery does not, and cannot, supply the *religious* wants of our nature."[76]

Further embittering the dispute over editorial policy was a financial crisis caused by the Massachusetts board's decision to back Collins's scheme for enlarging the society's "sphere of operations" through an ambitious program of local conventions. As Child explained in a letter to the board, on taking over the *Standard* she had "arranged everything on a safe and economical scale" and thereby succeeded in meeting "all present expenses" and in reducing the paper's debt to a mere $800 of the "old load" incurred on its founding. But her colleagues had scorned her system of management as overly "*cautious*"; they had forced Collins's "scheme of large adventure" on her, with the result that the *Standard* was now $2,000 in debt: "[We are] scarcely able to pay our printers a weekly allowance to save their children from hunger; buying paper of one man, till we are so deeply in debt that he will let us have no more, and then getting more of another man, with the same result; dunned by our landlord for rent; sniffed at . . . because we cannot pay . . . what we owe."[77] Sharp-toned as Child's letter was, it did not mention that because of the arrears in her salary and her unwillingness to accept any money before the printers had been paid, she had had "only 37½ cts in [her] purse for three months past," and "not a single decent seasonable dress in which to cross the threshold of the street door."[78]

After the many years Child had spent repressing her misgivings about David's financial gambles and struggling to pay off the debts he accumulated, she must have felt a dreary sense of déjà vu in confronting her situation at the *Standard*. Driving home the coincidence, even while she was writing to the board, David was taking advantage of a new law allowing debtors to file for bankruptcy and thus cancel their pecuniary obligations. Symbolically, among the personal possessions sold at auction to pay off David's creditors, to whom he now owed almost $30,000, was the gold watch presented to Child by the ladies of Lynn and Salem. "When poverty comes in at the door, love goes out the window," Caroline Weston commented acerbically on Child's letter to the board. The gibe was doubly apropos.[79]

It was one of the cruelest ironies of Child's life that at the very moment when she was reluctantly facing David's financial irresponsibility and beginning to extricate herself from his "entanglements," she should have found herself reenacting the same painful conflicts over money with her colleagues of the antislavery movement. Her two great loves — the man and the movement embodying her ideals — seemed fated to disappoint her simultaneously. As her twin marriages disintegrated, she adopted the same formula for divorce in both cases, avoiding a public rupture, but distancing herself emotionally, ending her financial and professional involvement, and redefining her personal priorities.

Child began preparing to resign from the *Standard* in January 1843. The catalyst that prompted her decision, as she confided to Loring, was an editorial by Edmund Quincy in the *Liberator*, written on seeing the news of Arthur Tappan's bankruptcy announced in the *Standard*. In her own editorial on the subject, Child had expressed regret for Tappan's misfortune, recalling that Tappan had paid Garrison's fine during his 1830 imprisonment in Baltimore and spent much of his wealth financing antislavery projects. Quincy, however, had sanctimoniously asserted that "misfortune, no more than death, exempts any man from the just memory of his deeds," and he had gone on to berate Tappan for his role in transferring the *Emancipator* to the new organization during the 1840 schism — a dereliction that ought to have "consigned [Tappan] . . . to the Penitentiary," he claimed.[80] This editorial, wrote Child, "took the last scales from my eyes" and forced her to recognize that abolitionists were "fighting in the spirit of *sect*; a spirit which I abhor, in all its manifestations." "The feeling that will not allow us to express a word of sympathy for the misfortunes of a man, who has done and sacrificed so much for anti-slavery as Arthur Tappan has, merely because his bigotry led him into *one* mistake, *cannot* be a right feeling," she expostulated. Rejecting the plea that such attacks were necessary to keep new recruits to abolitionism from joining the enemy camp, Child answered: "*all* sectarian attacks and wrangling are justified in the same way. It *always* seems necessary to be narrow and one-sided."[81]

She articulated that insight publicly in her editorial "Sects and Sectarianism," her boldest repudiation of the line Garrisonian fire-eaters were laying down for the movement. Reverting to the analogy she had drawn in her opening address to *Standard* readers almost two years earlier, Child contended that sectarianism was now impeding the progress of abolitionism just as it had hindered the progress of the Reformation.

"In every subdivision of opinion, the hateful old spirit of sect continues to show itself," she warned. Those who sought to "limit the free exercise of opinion" and those who branded "timidity as treachery, . . . bigotry as malicious falsehood," and honest disagreement as "time-serving" compromise were equally guilty. "The only way to cast out the demon of sectarianism, is by the calm but earnest promulgation of Truth" for its own sake, and not for the sake of "building up any party, or attacking any party," Child insisted.[82] Greeted with outrage by Chapman, the Westons, and Abby Kelley, Child's editorial elicited more "liberal expressions of unity" from subscribers than any she had written for weeks, acknowledged James Gibbons.[83]

By this time Child was beyond caring. "My feelings are completely and forever alienated from the anti-slavery *organization*. I cannot go with them, without fighting with my own best instincts," she told Loring. Ever since the schisms had begun five years ago, she had found it harder and harder to work with her antislavery colleagues: "Things deemed necessary for the support of the cause seem to me to be *wrong*." From now on, she would abide by her convictions. It would be many, many years before Child would attend another antislavery meeting or participate in another fund-raising fair. She would even leave town every May at anniversary season, to avoid abrasive encounters with the erstwhile comrades-in-arms whose censoriousness had wounded her so deeply. As she later divulged to Loring, she had come very close to a nervous breakdown during her last months at the *Standard*: "Such a night-mare was on me, that I *could* not write, either one thing or another. I have not yet recovered from the effects of it. It will yet take great quantities of music, and blossoms, and serene engravings, to restore me to my former self." Nevertheless, Child assured Loring, he need not fear her "turning *against* the anti-slavery organization," since she was not driven by "personal or selfish feelings," but was acting in accordance with the "honest dictates of conscience."[84]

Child kept her promise. Her "Farewell" to *Standard* readers made no mention of her disagreements with Garrisonian fire-eaters. It merely reiterated the editorial principles she had followed and hinted that she felt temperamentally unsuited to the work she was relinquishing: "[T]he freedom of my own spirit makes it absolutely necessary for me to retire. I am too distinctly and decidedly an individual, to edit the organ of any association." In turn, the AASS voted her a resolution of thanks, and Garrison affirmed that her resignation would be "deeply regretted by a large portion" of the *Standard*'s readers and "by a wide circle of admiring friends." He also ventured to hope that Child would continue to write for the paper—a hope she quickly squelched through Loring. Neither Child nor Garrison could entirely gloss over the conflict, however. Lest readers draw an "unjust inference" from Child's valedictory statement, Garrison felt compelled to deny that any "official attempt was made to interfere with the freedom of her spirit." And he went on to argue that though a " 'family newspaper' " might be more popular, the AASS needed a newspaper "signalized for its daring and hardihood in carrying on the war against whatever arrays itself in opposition to our cause."[85]

Ironically, while Child was becoming estranged from her old antislavery associates, David was enjoying a rapprochement with them. Having finally conceded the failure of his sugar beet experiment in October 1842, he had accepted an assignment to cover the debates in Congress for the *Liberator* and the *Standard* that winter — an arrangement prompted by the Garrisonians' desire to outrival Joshua Leavitt's dispatches from Washington in the *Emancipator*.[86] Although the Whig bias and narrow political focus of David's articles disappointed many Garrisonians — Lucretia Mott pronounced them "dull miserable affairs" far inferior to Leavitt's — he still emerged as the leading contender in the search for a successor to Child.[87] Some people no doubt hoped that the paper would continue to benefit from Child's prestige if David replaced her at the helm. Others valued his editorial experience and "vast fund of general and political knowledge." Chapman, who adamantly refused to take on the editorship of the *Standard* herself, despite the fervent pleas of Abby Kelley and Garrison, seems to have had her own reasons for favoring David. She knew that his political enemies had dubbed him David Libel Child, in honor of the combativeness that had landed him with three libel suits during his editorship of the *Massachusetts Journal*, and she thought he could be relied on to undertake the personal attacks Child had stigmatized as "*dirty* work." "He will be a king" compared to Child, she judged. Abby Kelley vehemently disagreed: "I consider L. Maria far better qualified, notwithstanding her 'hatred of the work of Reform'" (and notwithstanding Kelley's charge two months earlier that Child had "disgraced and degraded the Standard to the level of new organization"). Observing that "D.L.C. has some-how a killing influence on every thing he touches," Kelley prophesied darkly, "we shall all go over the dam if he takes [the *Standard*]": "Heaven avert such a catastrophy."[88]

Child herself had reacted unenthusiastically to the idea of David's exchanging one precarious means of livelihood for another, but she did not stand in his way. "He leaves me to be a very free individual, and I wish to do the same by him," she told friends; and whenever asked about whether she concurred with his political opinions or editorial positions, she answered: "I make no effort to influence David's mind. I never inquire what his editorials are to be, and never read them till the paper is issued."[89] Given her visceral abhorrence of personal controversy and sectarian infighting, however, she must have watched with dismay as David yielded to the pressures she had so steadfastly resisted.

Within less than six weeks of his accession, David reprinted a long article by Edmund Quincy, rehashing the Garrisonians' grievances over the transfer of the *Emancipator*, adduced as proof that the leaders of the Liberty party could not be trusted to be "true to the slave." The following week David issued his first editorial on "The Embezzlement of the Emancipator," in which he accused Joshua Leavitt of having stolen the paper from the AASS because he "saw no *future for him*" in Garrisonian ranks and wanted to "create . . . an anti-slavery future" for himself as editor of the *Emancipator*.[90] (Was David still rankling over the Tappans' appointment of Leavitt to the editorship he himself had applied for in 1836?)[91] David also published the article as a *Standard* extra. Members of the opposing faction retaliated with libel threats, which he welcomed "[w]ithout bravado," and the battle was on. For almost two months, the Leavitt affair dominated the *Standard*'s editorial columns to the exclusion of much more significant developments in the movement.[92]

Exactly what Child had predicted had come to pass: "if you put in a little [attacking], the other side claims to put in a little in reply, and so on, like a shuttle-cock." Again and again Child had emphasized that if Garrisonians tried to use the *Standard* to "fight with abolitionists of all stamps but their own," they would forfeit the large audience she had built up and find themselves left with a paper like the *Liberator*, which would "repel all but a limited number."[93] David's experience not only bore her out, but it confirmed the wisdom of her decision to let her course be guided solely by her own principles, rather than by the contradictory demands of hostile factions. David's attacks on Leavitt alienated everyone outside the Chapman clique, yet they failed to reconcile fire-eaters angered by his refusal to endorse come-outism; at the same time, his increasingly obvious tilting toward the Whig party and its candidate Henry Clay, a moderate Kentucky slaveholder, irritated Democrats in abolitionist ranks and disgusted those who, like Child, firmly opposed compromises with "temporary expediency" and stood pledged never to support a proslavery candidate under any circumstances.[94] By the time David resigned from the *Standard* in May 1844, its subscriptions had fallen below the *Liberator*'s.

Typically, when David headed back to Northampton for an indefinite stint of hardscrabble farming and odd jobbing, he left a trail of debts in his wake. Having again spent several months in Washington reporting on congressional affairs, he had not paid his board in New York and owed money to an Irish worker. As so often before, it would be up to Child to pay his debts.[95]

The couple's relationship no longer stood on the same footing, however. In the spring of 1843 Child had taken a momentous step. "I have resolved to separate my pecuniary affairs entirely from David's, and to stay fixed here [in New York], let him experiment where he will," she informed the Lorings. "I *do* hope he won't get into any more entanglements, but I feel no security about that. I mean to keep my earnings out of the way."[96] She had spent fourteen years "pump[ing] water into a sieve," Child noted bitterly, but she had finally recognized that she "must put a stop to it, or die." Determined to take control of her destiny again, she vowed: "I *can* put a stop to it; and I will put a stop to it." Under New York equity law a wife could keep her property from her husband's creditors by transferring it to another male custodian. Child named Ellis Loring as her legal surrogate. She was not acting in a "selfish or monopolizing spirit," she explained; rather, by protecting her earnings from David, she was ensuring that they would be of use "to *him* as well as myself." Nor did she seek an actual divorce—she had simply given up relying on David to make a home for her. Instead, she would build a "nest" for herself in a "city of strangers," with "no old associations to give me pain." She would keep "a warm corner" ready for David whenever he chose to settle down, but she would no longer allow him to derail her life.[97]

Child had always considered literature to be her true vocation. Accordingly, she now proposed to devote herself to the "attainment of literary excellence."[98] As she contemplated the future, renewed hope, energy, and confidence surged through her. "Such powers as I have, are in their maturity now; and I feel a resolution I never felt before — to cast from me all the fetters of sand which have so miserably bound me down to unprofitable drudgery," she wrote Loring. The road to eminence was crowded, she realized, and "a great deal of dust [was] flying." Nevertheless, she expected to hear the call, "Make room there! Let Mrs. Child's carriage pass."[99]

13
Letters from New York:
The Invention of a New Literary Genre

She is capable of much intellectual exertion. . . . Her mind does not run in channels with other persons; her thoughts are not others' thoughts. . . . Her tastes are decidedly social and domestic; and she has strong connubial love and affection. . . . [T]his head indicates a combination of qualities peculiarly calculated to confer and enjoy domestic happiness. She likes the society of [intelligent and cultivated] men better than that of women, and feels more interest in the subjects on which they converse. . . . She enjoys herself with a book and pen more than in household arrangements, or general society. . . . She has great resolution, spirit, and force . . . more than an ordinary degree of moral courage; is never afraid to defend what she thinks right. . . . [F]rom a child, [she] was always ambitious to excel in some department. . . . Her imagination is strong and vivid. . . . She has a great versatility of talent. . . .[1]

This shrewd analysis of Child's character by the phrenologist L. N. Fowler, allegedly based only on an examination of her head with no knowledge of her name or writings and no conversation between consultant and client, appeared in the *American Phrenological Journal* of September 1841. "The *hit*, it seems to us, is very remarkable," commented Garrison on reprinting it in the *Liberator*.[2] Child agreed. "You may be as sceptical as you like," she protested when Ellis Loring scoffed at such claims for "the truth of phrenology as an accurate and valuable science"; even if Fowler "had read *all* my books," Child insisted, "I do not see how he could tell all he *did* tell, without the 'devil helped him.'"[3] Fowler's report clearly indicated that he *had* read Child's works, perhaps after the initial interview, for he mentioned details he could hardly have gleaned from the bumps on her head: her "deep interest in the welfare of children," her liking for "method in household affairs," her "prudent" attitude toward money, her "radical . . . notions," her commitment to "moral, social, and intellectual reforms," her penchant for "analogical" reasoning, her religious iconoclasm and "quick perception of the ridiculous and the incongruous." Yet Child was right to feel that the famous phrenologist had exhibited uncanny insight into her personality. Not only had he noted the male identification and preference for the companionship of "intelligent and cultivated men" that had so complicated her attitude toward the "woman question," but he had put his finger on one of the deepest and most painful conflicts in Child's life — the conflict between the "strong connubial love and affection" that had driven her to cling to David for twelve years at such great sacrifice and the sense of intellectual and moral vocation that had finally impelled her to rebuild a professional career alone in New York.

Child would never succeed in reconciling her craving for love with her need for self-fulfillment. Marriage remained the only acceptable channel through which a respectable woman of her era and culture could satisfy her yearning for heterosexual love. And ever since the move to Northampton, marriage to David had meant burial in a rural backwater with no prospect of escape from drudging poverty and perpetual financial "entanglements." If Child had left Northampton unwillingly in 1841, without any intention of renouncing her marriage, she made a conscious choice three years later when she elected to pursue her literary ambitions in New York rather than return with David to Northampton after his abortive editorship of the *Standard*. The choice did not require forgoing love altogether, although it did entail sublimating her sexuality. During the nine years Child spent in New York, from 1841 until 1850, she sought emotional outlets for her desires in highly charged platonic relationships with other men and in an intoxicating new world of music and art.

On launching the New York phase of her career, Child began to express the unfolding sides of herself in the richest and most innovative body of writings she had yet produced. Besides editorials in the *Standard* and three volumes of children's stories, her output comprised the series of journalistic sketches titled "Letters from New-York," which she had inaugurated in the *Standard* and continued in the *Boston Courier*. It additionally included the short stories she published in the abolitionist annual the *Liberty Bell*, the *Columbian Lady's and Gentleman's Magazine*, and the *Union Magazine of Literature and Art*.[4]

In reclaiming the literary vocation she had sacrificed soon after her marriage, Child did not abandon her commitment to social reform. She simply reversed the relationship between her artistic imagination and her political consciousness. She had begun her career by dramatizing political issues in fiction before analyzing them in polemical tracts and acting on them in the public sphere. She now redirected her political energies toward creating literary forms suited to promoting the changes she advocated in racial, sexual, and class attitudes.[5]

Three men nourished the creativity that flowered in Child's newspaper sketches and magazine fiction: Ellis Loring, who came to replace David as her intellectual adviser and critic; John Hopper, the twenty-six-year-old son of her Quaker host, Isaac T. Hopper, and her chief escort in the rambles through the city retraced in "Letters from New-York"; and later Ole Bull, the Norwegian violinist whose music Child described as having "stirred the depths of my soul, and kindled my whole being."[6] Child started transferring her affection from David to Ellis and John soon after moving to New York in May 1841. "I cannot live without being beloved," she admitted to her friend Francis

Shaw that very month; and though she was referring to David, she was simultaneously acknowledging the emotional need that drew her to men better able to make her feel "beloved" at a stage of her life when David had failed her.[7] Intriguingly, it was in a letter to David of July 1841 that Child first signaled the shift — almost as if she were warning him not to take her for granted any more. She had just come back from a brief vacation with the Lorings at their summer home in Brookline, to which she had traveled with Ellis. Sitting on the deck of the steamer late into the night, as Ellis sheltered her from the rain "under his cloak," they had "passed for lovers," she announced. Their conversation had been "anything but lover-like; being on the most abstruse philosophical subjects," she hastened to assure David. Yet she went on to needle him with an account of her recent excursion to Greenwood cemetery with John Hopper. "How do you think *I* spent the 5th" of July, Child teased. "In the most romantic way imaginable. John wanted to get me away from the noise and heat of the city." They had passed a delightful afternoon picnicking on "oranges and cake" in a verdant setting. "While John slept under the trees," she had written an editorial, and, on awakening, he had read aloud to her while she "wove oak garlands."[8]

If David responded to the nudging, he left no record of it. The paucity of letters between the couple during their long separation — and the frequency of Child's complaints, in the surviving correspondence, about receiving so few letters from David — suggests that he ignored his wife's playful disclosures. More acute and less self-absorbed than her husband, Loring reacted almost immediately to Child's developing intimacy with John by admonishing her against the perils she was courting. She replied with a frankness so disarming as to leave no room for censure. Loring's "caution" had made her "smile," she claimed:

> My charms were *never* very formidable, and at this period I think can hardly endanger a young man of 26, passionately fond of the beautiful. If there is danger in being absolutely necessary to each other's happiness, for the time being, we are both in great peril. You who want me to sustain the Standard may as well be thankful that it is so; for I absolutely *could* not stay in N.Y., away from my husband, if I had not [John] to walk with me, read to me, bring me pictures, and always greet me with a welcoming smile. . . . That I can disturb *his* peace of mind seems to me scarcely possible; and he will not *mine*, except the pain of parting from a friend sometimes makes us regret that we ever formed the acquaintance.[9]

Exploiting the thirteen-year age difference between them, Child presented John to the world as her "adopted son." The maternal guise allowed her to entertain an unconventional relationship in full view of all her friends, and to speak of it with breathtaking openness. Thus, as she prepared for David's arrival in New York two years later, she could write unabashedly to Loring: "I hardly care what happens to me, if I can only manage not to be separated from John. I have come to be *afraid* to lean upon David in all matters connected with a *home* and *support*; I am weary of moving about; and John is such a good hand to lean upon, and manages all my affairs so well." As long as she took care to specify that John supplied the "place of a real son," she could boldly confess, "my affections have got so entwined around him, that it would almost kill me to have to leave him." And wrapped in the mantle of motherhood, she could contemplate without impropriety the idea of a ménage à trois in which "David and he and I can live together, and bless each other."[10]

With all the freedom it permitted her, the pretext of a mother-son relationship ultimately frustrated the passion for a younger man that Child might have expressed sexually had she lived in a less repressive culture. Too honest and discerning to lie to herself, however she may have veiled the nature of her attachment to John from her friends, Child could not always maintain the subterfuge. "It is as well to be dead outright, as not to have somebody to love, and somebody that you've a right to love," she wrote to Loring early in her intimacy with John.[11] Instead of filling the gap left by a broken marriage, the "ingenious kindness, and perpetual vicinity" of a platonic lover sometimes increased her loneliness. "His thousand little delicate attentions remind me so much of Mr. Child, and yet are so insufficient for the cravings of a heart so fond of domestic life as mine," she confided to Loring.[12] And to her friends Maria White Lowell and Francis Shaw, she hinted of "fierce spiritual conflicts," "dark wanderings," "withered hopes," and uncontrollable sadness at the sight of young lovers.[13]

Child may at first have perceived John as a reincarnation of the David she remembered from their courtship—the Byronic hero, newly home from the war in Spain, who had struck her romantic imagination as "the most gallant man that has lived since the sixteenth century."[14] David had proved deficient in the passion his chivalric pose had led Child to expect of him, but John unmistakably exuded it. "[I]mpulsive and ardent," he chafed under the restraints of Quaker decorum as much as Child did under the shackles of New England propriety and the cult of True Womanhood. Reminiscing about John's "irrepressible" liveliness and love of "healthy, good-humored fun," an acquaintance commented that he seemed "to have been intended by Nature as a protest against broad-brimmed hats and solemn faces" (the badges of Quakerism). John was "born to make the world *laugh at itself*, to cure dyspepsia, physical and moral," he added. John and Child immediately recognized each other as kindred spirits. At thirty-nine, an age proverbially attractive to young men of the type awakened sexually by an older woman, Child could still be aroused into the vitality that had charmed the aristocratic patrons of the "brilliant Miss Francis." Her obvious need for companionship must have appealed to John's protective instincts. Besides, the attentions of an abolitionist heroine and literary celebrity, would have been flattering to any young man. Witty and "electric," "little Zippy Damn," as John nicknamed Child, brought out the side of him that his staid parents had tried in vain to curb. John adored the theater and "might have made his fortune as a comedian," but until Child's arrival in the household, he had had to indulge this taste surreptitiously. Now he could legitimately exercise the prerogative of squiring Child to plays and concerts she could not have attended without a male escort.[15]

Professionally, as well as temperamentally, John may have represented the man Child had thought she was marrying in choosing David. John, too, was a lawyer, but one who had a faculty for business. Committed like David to abolitionism and the relief of human suffering, John expressed his philanthropy without plunging into quixotic adventures.

For two years Child and John were inseparable. They promenaded Broadway and the Battery in the evenings, sometimes staying out until midnight; took weekend expeditions into the country; went to church together, John accompanying Child to her Swedenborgian services because his "curiosity [was] a good deal excited about the doctrines"; visited prisons and slums; and frequented art galleries, theaters, concert halls, and the opera house. John also read through Child's works, "buying a collection of all I ever wrote," as she proudly informed Loring.[16]

Then David came from Northampton to take over the editorship of the *Standard*. His sojourn in New York, which lasted approximately from August 1843 to January 1844, did not fulfill Child's fantasy of a ménage à trois. While claiming that David was "getting strongly attached" to John, she acknowledged that her evenings had suddenly become "quite solitary": "David is always on the editorial tread-mill in his own room; John has a great increase of anxieties and cares."[17] Evidently the Childs' estrangement grew, perhaps widened by disagreement over editorial policy and by the declining subscriptions that testified to David's inability to match his wife's success. His departure for Washington after only five months likewise points to a rift between them. At the same time, John's romantic pleasure in Child's company seems to have been dampened by the intrusion of her husband. The "anxieties and cares" Child noticed may have marked the beginning of his gradual disengagement, which would culminate in 1847 with his marriage. Child's anticipation of the "regret" she would feel at having made herself vulnerable to so much pain, once the inevitable moment of parting arrived, would prove all too prophetic.

In dedicating *Letters from New York* (1843) to John, Child publicly asserted that her volume of city sketches had grown out of jaunts like the one she had described to David. "[M]ost of the scenes mentioned in these Letters we have visited together," she wrote. Moreover, her companion had shared the "love for nature and poetry" and the "genial sympathy for the whole family of man" that imbued the book. Thus, contrary to appearances, "pages . . . so deeply tinged with romance and mysticism" were not an "unfit offering to one who has the crowning merit of the nineteenth century—that of being a cautious and energetic 'business man.' " Whether consciously or not, Child was implicitly crediting John with qualities David lacked: good business sense and an appreciation for the poetic side of herself. She was also deliberately using *Letters from New York* as she had once used her contributions to the *Massachusetts Journal*, to lend her prestige to the man she loved; for her "adopted son" had let it be known that a public tribute by a well-known author would "help him some in his [law] business."[18]

Until John induced her to change her mind, Child had intended to dedicate *Letters from New York* to Loring, who had played an even greater role in fathering the book. As the opening paragraph of Letter I indicates, her column in the *Standard* had originated in an imaginary conversation with Loring about how her view of New York had changed after a few months of living there:

You ask what is now my opinion of this great Babylon; and playfully remind me of former philippics, and a long string of vituperative alliterations, such as magnificence and mud, finery and filth, diamonds and dirt, bullion and brass-tape, &c. &c. Nor do you forget my first impression of the city, when we arrived at early dawn, amid fog and drizzling rain, the expiring lamps adding their smoke to the impure air, and close beside us a boat called the "Fairy Queen," laden with dead hogs.[19]

The conversation had continued in subsequent letters, with Child defending New York and Loring urging the superiority of Boston: "you deem me heretical in preferring the Battery to the Common, consecrated by so many pleasant associations of my youth"; "[y]ou think my praises of the Battery exaggerated" (15, 17). Writing to Loring in January 1842, six months after launching the column, Child acknowledged, "I *thought* I addressed [the letters] to an abstraction; but I find you are *always* in my mind as the person addressed."[20]

Whomever Child imagined as her audience, what charmed her readers was their sense that she was speaking personally to each of them. As her friend of Medford days, Lucy Osgood, put it in renewing contact with Child after a lapse of more than a decade, "I could fancy many of your letters from New York addressed to myself, so strong was the impulse on reading them to carry on the discussions as if you were present — to assent with acclamation to some of your opinions & query others."[21] Even reviewers echoed this sentiment. For example, Charles F. Briggs, coeditor with Poe of the *Broadway Journal*, ascribed the popularity of *Letters from New York* to Child's ability to make every reader "feel as though they had been addressed to himself personally."[22]

Indeed, the "you" in *Letters from New York* constantly expands outward. Sometimes "you" metamorphoses from an intimate friend, with privileged access to Child's innermost thoughts, into a fan who has learned to know her almost as intimately through her writings: "You know that religion has always come to me in stillness; and that the machinery of theological excitement has ever been as powerless over my soul, as would be the exorcisms of a wizard. You are likewise aware of my tendency to *generalize*; to look at truth as *universal*, not merely in its particular relations; to observe human nature as a *whole*, and not in fragments" (79). At other times, Child gives her readers the illusion of eavesdropping on whispered revelations to a chosen confidante and thereby gleaning precious lessons for themselves: "I feel that these are thoughts that should be spoken into your private ear, not published to the world. To some few they may, perchance, awaken a series of aspiring thoughts, till the highest touch the golden harps of heaven, and fill the world with celestial echoes" (182). Occasionally, Child assumes the stance of a celebrity being interviewed by the press for the benefit of an audience anxious to be guided by her opinions: "You ask what are my opinions about 'Women's Rights'" (245). Even on such occasions, she personalizes her audience and opens herself up to it: "You seem very curious to learn what I think of recent phenomena in animal magnetism, or mesmerism, which you have described to me. They have probably impressed your mind more than my own; because I was ten years ago convinced

that animal magnetism was destined to produce great changes in the science of medicine, and in the whole philosophy of spirit and matter" (130). Turning the tables, she
also invites her readers to participate in a dialogue and share their private thoughts and
experiences with her: "Is your memory a daguerreotype machine, taking instantaneous
likenesses of whatsoever the light of imagination happens to rest upon? I wish mine
were not; especially in a city like this. . ." (88).

Clearly, Child achieved these effects at least in part because she did mentally address
the letters not to "an abstraction," but to a real reader, with whom she could have the
"intellectual or spiritual communion" she sorely missed in New York. "You can't
conceive how lonely I am," she complained to Loring, reproaching him for not having
written. She who loved to "look upward" found herself continually obliged to "descend
to a lower plane" among her associates, none of whom boasted Loring's sophistication
and erudition.[23]

Not only had Child conceived "Letters from New-York" with Loring in mind; she
had enlisted his help in turning her sketches for the *Standard* into a book adapted to a
wider audience — her first step toward reestablishing her literary reputation. Requests
to collect and reissue these popular pieces in a form that would earn them the "general
perusal and appreciation which their merits deserve" had come from quarters as diverse
as the *New York Tribune*, *Graham's Magazine*, and the publishers of the *Democratic
Review*.[24] Hence, as Child told Loring, punning on her title, she intended to make the
work her "letter of introduction to the literary world, where I have so long been a
stranger."[25] While preparing the manuscript for the press, Child asked Loring to
"[a]lter, amend, strike out, or add" anything necessary to improve the style, and she
accepted most of his editorial suggestions.[26] She also consulted him on which letters to
retain and which to delete from the book. Although she disregarded his advice to
reprint the entire series, and instead dropped three of the most radical antislavery
letters without involving him in the decision, she did let him persuade her to include
the letters championing women's rights and condemning capital punishment, which
she had initially planned to omit.[27]

The self-censorship Child exercised as she reoriented *Letters from New York* toward
readers who would never have subscribed to the *Standard* provides fascinating insight
into her ability to measure the distance between an antislavery audience and the general public. Despite the bitterness of her breach with Garrisonian fire-eaters, Child had
not renounced her abolitionist ideals. Nor did her reconsecration to the pursuit of
"literary excellence" imply that she had embraced an aesthetic of art for art's sake. On
the contrary, she assured Francis Shaw: "Formed as my character now is, I cannot do
otherwise than make literature the honest agent of my conscience and my heart." If she
no longer worked *with* "organized reformers," she did "work to the same *end*" through
her writings: "I belong to the group of *sappers* and *miners*, instead of laying rails on the
open direct road."[28]

Yet the strategies Child adopted as an antislavery propagandist and as a literary artist
differ more in degree than in kind. Even in the *Standard* she had sought to entice
unconverted readers into "look[ing] candidly at anti-slavery principles" by "drawing

them with the garland of imagination and taste."[29] In repackaging *Letters from New York* as a book for the commercial market, Child simply increased the size of the garland and enveloped her antislavery message more ingeniously. Besides reducing the proportion of antislavery material, Child eliminated the letters most likely to offend readers who considered abolitionists meddlesome fanatics (a prime instance being her vivid description of the antiabolitionist mob from which she had helped rescue George Thompson). She also excised passages addressed to an in-group of comrades-in-arms, substituting the word "reformers" for "abolitionists" and deleting the names of prominent figures in the movement. Still, at least nine of the forty letters she reprinted from the fifty-eight that had constituted the original series in the *Standard* offered some antislavery commentary, direct or indirect, central or peripheral.[30] The most memorable of these is her moving portrayal of "The Eloquent Coloured Preacher," Julia Pell, which captures the power and richness of African American religious rhetoric and shows the sermon of an unlettered black woman to be "not unworthy of Milton" in "poetic conception" (77).

The enduring significance of *Letters from New York* does not lie in its subtle testimony against slavery and racism, however. It lies rather in Child's pioneering depiction of the modern city—pioneering both as social criticism and as literary genre. Child arrived in New York—the nation's largest metropolis—just as massive immigration and industrialization were transforming the urban landscape, producing extremes of luxury and misery on a scale never seen before in America's white population. Unlike her Transcendentalist contemporaries, Child did not shrink from the sordid scenes that confronted her in the streets of a noisy, crowded city, but set about chronicling the epic of capitalist development and proletarian destitution.

Her opening letter sets the tone and announces the leading theme of the book:

> Wealth dozes on French couches, thrice piled, and canopied with damask, while Poverty camps on the dirty pavement, or sleeps off its wretchedness in the watch-house. There, amid the splendour of Broadway, sits the blind negro beggar, with horny hand and tattered garments, while opposite to him stands the stately mansion of the slave trader, still plying his bloody trade, and laughing to scorn the cobweb laws, through which the strong can break so easily.
>
> In Wall-street, and elsewhere, Mammon, as usual, coolly calculates his chance of extracting a penny from war, pestilence, and famine; and Commerce, with her loaded drays, and jaded skeletons of horses, is busy as ever fulfilling the "World's contract with the Devil." (13–14)

Child's irony accentuates the contrasts between opulence and "wretchedness," "splendour" and filth, while her strong verbs and graphic details force readers to realize that the nabob who "dozes" in his "stately mansion" has extorted his surfeit by starving—and often literally selling—the worker who "camps" on his pavement after a lifetime of drudgery. The prosperity generated by "Commerce," she pointedly observes, rests on the "jaded skeletons" of those condemned to serve as beasts of burden.

In the letters that follow, Child presents haunting vignettes that encapsulate the daily lives of the poor: a "ragged urchin" staggering under a load of newspapers, his face "blue, cold, and disconsolate," his childish voice "prematurely cracked into shrillness, by screaming street cries, at the top of his lungs" (95); "two young boys fighting furiously for some coppers, that had been given them and had fallen on the pavement" (96); "a ragged, emaciated woman" sitting in front of a store window displaying "large vases of gold and silver, curiously wrought" (96–97); another woman "with garments all draggled in New-York gutters," lying in the street where she had "fallen in intoxication" (98); infantile match sellers, wearily trudging from door to door with their "dirty little basket[s]," and grabbing the money offered to them "with a hungry avarice, that made my very heart ache" (193–94); two small girls with "scanty garments fluttering in the wind" and "blue hands . . . locked in each other" as they struggled through snow drifts and stopped every now and then to exchange the single "pair of broken shoes," bound with rags, that they shared (278–79).

While seeking to awaken sympathy for a class of people commonly viewed with disgust and fear, if seen at all, Child also takes her genteel readers on a tour of the institutions designed to segregate the poor from the rich and to punish any transgression of boundaries: prisons, insane asylums, almshouses, and orphanages. In the process she questions the moral distinctions between the inmates of these institutions and the respectable men and women who look down on them from their comfortable social sanctums. The "shrewd business man" who has gained his wealth through " 'good bargains' " and shady transactions is as much a thief as the clerk who "borrows some money from his employer's drawer" in an emergency, perhaps with the intention of restoring it, Child contends. Both have derived their false values from "the maxims of trade, the customs of society," and the gospel of moneymaking. The only difference is that one has succeeded and the other has failed. The businessman has been "honoured" for his wealth and awarded a magistracy; the clerk has been caught and sent to prison (203). Child applies the same analysis to the " 'street-walkers' " who form such a large proportion of the penitentiary inmates on Blackwell's Island. Challenging her readers to reject the double standard of gender and class, she charges:

> The men who made [prostitutes] such, who, perchance, caused the love of a human heart to be its ruin, and changed tenderness into sensuality and crime — these men live in the "ceiled houses" of Broadway, and sit in council in the City Hall, and pass "regulations" to clear the streets they have filled with sin. And do you suppose their poor victims do not *feel* the injustice of society thus regulated? Think you they respect the *laws*? . . . Their whole being cries out that it is a mockery. . . . (202)

The real criminal, Child insists, is the society that "make[s] its own criminals." Anticipating a debate still raging today, she argues that the cure is not to build more "penitentiaries and prisons," but to "change . . . the structure of society" so as to redistribute its benefits more equitably: "If we can abolish *poverty*, we shall have taken the greatest step towards the abolition of *crime*." Meanwhile, she asserts, the prison system actually tends to "*increase* crime," because "coercion . . . rouse[s] all the bad passions in man's nature, and if long continued, harden[s] the whole character" (204).[31]

Child would pursue the topic of prison reform in her "Letters from New-York" for the *Boston Courier*, several of which describe the efforts of philanthropists like her Quaker host, Isaac T. Hopper, and her friend Eliza Farnham to rehabilitate prisoners by treating them kindly, furnishing them with well-stocked libraries and recreational opportunities, and finding employment for them after their release.[32] In her letter about the institutions she visits on Blackwell's Island and neighboring Long Island Farms, however, she explains why "[b]enevolent institutions and reformatory societies perform but a limited and temporary use" and "do not reach the ground-work of evil" — the repression and perversion of natural human instincts (205). The model orphanage of Long Island Farms illustrates her point. Though "clean and comfortable," it fails to provide "the aliment which the spirit craves": love. Instead, it regiments the children and turns them into robots:

> Everything moves by machinery, as it always must with masses of children, never subdivided into families. In one place, I saw a stack of small wooden guns, and was informed that the boys were daily drilled to military exercises, as a useful means of forming habits of order, as well as fitting them for the future service of the state. Their infant school evolutions partook of the same drill character; and as for their religion, I was informed that it was "beautiful to see them pray; for at the first tip of the whistle, they all dropped on their knees." Alas, poor childhood, thus doth "church and state" provide for thee! The state arms thee with wooden guns, to play the future murderer, and the church teaches thee to pray in platoons, "at the first tip of the whistle." (209)[33]

The alternative, Child repeatedly affirms, is for the "natural spontaneous influences of society" to "supply men with healthy motives, and give full, free play to the affections, and the faculties" (205–6).

Written simultaneously with her antislavery editorials, and published alongside them, Child's "Letters from New-York" reflect the broadening of her horizons and the deepening of her political consciousness that resulted from her exposure to a more cosmopolitan city than her native Boston. Not only does Child now reveal a far more sophisticated understanding of poverty and class relations than she had shown in her *Juvenile Miscellany* stories of the late 1820s; she also reveals greater sensitivity to the plight of the white working class than many of her fellow abolitionists. During precisely the same period, Garrison, N. P. Rogers, and Wendell Phillips would undergo a parallel awakening sparked by their encounters with working-class poverty in England. Concurrently, at the Transcendentalist community of Brook Farm, Child's friends John Sullivan Dwight and Francis Shaw were exploring utopian socialism as a solution to poverty — an experiment Child followed with keen interest.[34] Yet by wrestling with the problem of urban poverty in New York, where it was taking the form it would assume in the United States, Child came closer to discerning the challenges of the future.

The critique she formulated of capitalist society in letters like the one about Blackwell's Island was as radical as the militant antislavery protest she edited out of the book. Well-aware that her readers might find her championship of the poor no less threatening than her indictment of slavery and racial prejudice, Child once again seduced them with the "garland of imagination and taste." Although social criticism is ubiquitous in the book, only in a few cases does it occupy entire letters. Child's ostensible subject is New York's tourist attractions. She invites her readers to admire the view of the Battery at dawn; strolls with them down Broadway, through Union Park and Castle Garden, "along the Bowery to Bloomingdale, on the north" (16); introduces them to that New York fixture, P. T. Barnum's American Museum, and to wandering street musicians, apple sellers, vendors of "Hot corn! . . . Lily white corn!" (14); leads them to Rosh Hashanah services at a Jewish synagogue, mass at the Catholic cathedral, Sunday worship at a black Methodist church; and takes them on excursions to Hoboken, Weehawken, Greenwood Cemetery, Ravenswood, Staten Island, Rockland Lake, Orangetown, Croton Reservoir, and the Navy Yard at Brooklyn. Celebrating the ethnic diversity and multicultural vitality of New York, she transforms the city from an unfamiliar and frightening world into a stimulating metropolis, where her readers can learn to feel at home as they rub shoulders with Americans of all backgrounds.[35] Again and again, Child demonstrates that the soul in need of "Nature's healing power" can find it in "blossoms by the dusty wayside," even "amid the rattle and glare of the city" (163).

If Child defends the city against romantic detractors, she unforgettably evokes the alienation its denizens can experience under a capitalist economy that commodifies all aspects of human life. Where anonymity fosters the "wild license which prevails in times of pestilence," she suggests, nothing is sacred, and everything is for sale:

> Life is a reckless game, and death is a business transaction. Warehouses of ready-made coffins, stand beside warehouses of ready-made clothing, and the shroud is sold with spangled opera-dresses. Nay, you may chance to see exposed at sheriffs' sales, in public squares, piles of coffins, like nests of boxes, one within another, with a hole bored in the topmost lid to sustain the red flag of the auctioneer, who stands by, describing their conveniences and merits, with all the exaggerating eloquence of his tricky trade. (68–69)

Mourning and revelry furnish interchangeable occasions for profit, Child notes wryly, and integuments for dead and living bodies are marketed with the same avidity. The spectacle of an auctioneer crying up the "conveniences and merits" of coffins may well have reminded her of the slave auctions at which buyers inspected the teeth, muscles, and skin of their human merchandise and traders advertised the selling points of the fellow beings they dispatched into living death.

Meditating on "this dense crowding of human existence, this mercantile familiarity with death" in the teeming financial capital of modern America, Child acknowledges: "It has sometimes forced upon me, for a few moments, an appalling night-mare sensation of vanishing identity; as if I were but an unknown, unnoticed, and unseparated drop in the great ocean of human existence; as if the uncomfortable old theory were true, and we were but portions of a Great Mundane Soul, to which we ultimately return, to be swallowed up in its infinity" (69). In such moods, she divulges with surprising frankness, alienation can lead to suicide. Were she to indulge her penchant for metaphysical speculation and her "curious search into the invisible," she might end up wandering into extinction. Thus, she resolutely "expel[s]" ideas so dangerous to follow to their ultimate conclusion: "I find it wiser to forbear inflating this balloon of thought, lest it roll me away through unlimited space, until I become like the absent man, who put his clothes in bed, and hung himself over the chair; or like his twin-brother, who laid his candle on the pillow, and blew himself out" (69). Child eerily renders the shadowy line between sanity and insanity, self-preservation and self-destruction. Yet she banishes horror with humor, maintaining an ironic detachment that defuses the revelations she seems to offer.

Along with the new vision they conjured up of urban America, Child's journalistic sketches launched what her contemporaries recognized as a new literary genre — a genre Margaret Fuller, Fanny Fern, Grace Greenwood, and Gail Hamilton would all help shape. In the words of Thomas Wentworth Higginson: " 'Letters from New-York' . . . were the precursors of that modern school of newspaper correspondence in which women have so large a share, and which has something of the charm of women's private letters, — a style of writing where description preponderates over argument and statistics make way for fancy and enthusiasm."[36] Child gave her readers "a new sensation," he recalled. Interestingly, he went on to link the style of her letters with their substance by crediting their "tone" with prompting "a fresh inquiry into the foundations of social science." Though Child "did not call herself an Associationist," unlike her friends at Brook Farm, her social criticism paralleled theirs, "and her highest rhapsodies about poetry and music were apt to end in some fervent appeal for some increase of harmony in daily life," Higginson observed. This interweaving of personal sentiment, social protest, poetic depiction, and mystical speculation is in fact the most original feature of *Letters from New York* and no doubt contributed significantly to the book's popularity.

The style of free association Child invented verges on stream of consciousness. Describing it, she wrote: "I never can pen a letter without making myself liable to the Vagrant Act. . . . My pen . . . paces or whirls, bounds or waltzes, steps in the slow minuet, or capers in the fantastic fandango, according to the music within."[37] "Flibber-tigibbet himself never moved with more unexpected and incoherent variety" (69). Perhaps because the letters initially served her as "a safety valve for an expanding spirit, pent up like steam in a boiler" (270), Child let herself go in them, allowing her unconscious mind to take over. As a result, metaphors and symbols seem to unfurl in an endless procession, often billowing out of everyday sights and experiences. A typical example is the series of associations that springs from the sense of being hemmed in by brick walls during the "damp, sultry days" of a New York August, so "oppressive . . . to mind and body." As Child grimly contemplates the source of her discomfort, her physical suffocation reminds her of the spiritual suffocation she endured during her two years in Northampton, and that in turn sets her to philosophizing about religion:

> The sun staring at you from bright red walls, like the shining face of a heated cook. Strange to say, they are *painted* red, blocked off with white compartments, as numerous as Protestant sects, and as unlovely in their narrowness. What an expenditure for ugliness and discomfort to the eye! To paint bricks their own colour, resembles the great outlay of time and money in theological schools, to enable dismal, arbitrary souls to give an approved image of themselves in their ideas of Deity.
>
> After all, the God *within* us is the God we really believe in, whatever we may have learned in catechisms or creeds.
>
> Hence to some, the divine image presents itself habitually as a dark, solemn shadow, saddening the gladsomeness of earth, like thunder-clouds reflected on the fair mirror of the sea. To others, the religious sentiment is to the soul what Spring is in the seasons, flowers to the eye, and music to the ear. In the greatest proportion of minds these sentiments are mixed, and therefore two images are reflected, one to be worshipped with love, the other with fear. (23–24)

After ending her philosophizing with a plea for religious tolerance, Child reins herself in and comments self-consciously on her own mental processes: "Whence came all this digression? It has as little to do with New-York, as a seraph has to do with Banks and Markets. Yet in good truth, it all came from a painted brick wall staring in at my chamber window. What a strange thing is the mind! How marvellously is the infinite embodied in the smallest fragment of the finite!" (25). She then turns to the scenes beneath her window that relieve the harshness of the "sectarian brick wall" opposite her: "a little, little, patch of garden, trimly kept, and neatly white-washed," belonging to a black woman named Jane Plato, and a pair of interlaced trees, an ailanthus and a catalpa, which Child imagines as "two lovely nymphs, suddenly transformed to trees, in the midst of a graceful, twining dance" (25, 111). With another self-conscious flourish, she anticipates her readers' reactions to her fantasies and bids them to watch her bring them back to reality:

> But I must quit this strain; or you will say the fair, floating Grecian shadow casts itself too obviously over *my* Christianity. Perchance, you will even call me "transcendental" . . . .
>
> Have patience with me, and I will come straight back from the Ilissus to New-York — thus.
>
> You too would worship two little trees and a sunflower, if you had gone with me to the neighbourhood of the Five Points the other day. (26)

The rest of her letter catalogs the varieties of "human misery" and "human degradation" infesting this notorious slum, and draws a moral from the neighbourhood's origins:

It is said a spacious pond of sweet, soft water, once occupied the place where Five Points stands. It might have furnished half the city with the purifying element; but it was filled up at incredible expense — a million loads of earth being thrown in, before perceivable progress was made. Now, they have to supply the city with water from a distance, by the prodigious expense of the Croton Water Works.

This is a good illustration of the policy of society towards crime. Thus does it choke up nature, and then seek to protect itself from the result, by the incalculable expense of bolts, bars, the gallows, watch-houses, police courts, constables, and "Egyptian tombs". . . . (27)

Imperceptibly, Child has coaxed her readers to extend their sympathies from the author with whom she has given them an illusion of such intimate rapport to the thousands of slum dwellers around her. By inviting them into the private recesses of her mind as it floats from one association to the next, she has also enabled her readers to discern the connections uniting the individual, social, physical, and spiritual planes. Despite an appearance of having wandered far from her point of departure, she has actually returned to it; for the "incredible expense" of filling in a pond, only to breed a hideous slum, resembles the useless "expenditure for ugliness and discomfort to the eye" of painting bricks "their own colour"; correspondingly, "the great outlay of time and money" for "theological schools" that inculcate sectarian narrowness and religious gloom, resembles the "incalculable expense" of maintaining police forces, prisons, and courts to punish the crimes that society itself generates. In each case an artificial force has "choke[d] up nature," and the result has been individual and collective suffering.

As engagingly as Child presented her radical message — and as skillfully as she adapted it to the tastes of a nonabolitionist audience — she did not succeed in allaying the fears that generally kept commercial publishers from handling abolitionist books. The Langley brothers, publishers of the *Democratic Review*, had been sufficiently taken with Child's "Letters from New-York" to solicit the manuscript, but after completing their negotiations with her they insisted on further cuts. They "informed me that they did not want to trammel me, but it would injure their business very much if any expression in a book they published should prove offensive to the South," Child wrote in disgust to Louisa Loring.[38] Closely associated with the Democratic party, which combined unconditional support of slavery and white supremacy with advocacy on behalf of white wage laborers and Irish immigrants, the Langleys no doubt hoped to capitalize on the appeal that Child's sketches of urban poverty would exert for the Democrats' northern constituents, yet to purge the book of antislavery passages incompatible with the party's platform.[39] Child had been willing to delete her strongest antislavery letters for the sake of winning a hearing from readers who would not have tolerated a frontal attack on their prejudices, but she could not conscientiously agree to eliminate all references to slavery, merely for the sake of pandering to the racist sensibilities of Democratic voters.

The alternative of letting an abolitionist press issue the book was equally unacceptable, since it would have consigned Child anew to the very ghetto she was trying to escape. Hence, she politely declined her former colleague Oliver Johnson's offer to print *Letters from New York*. "I am exceedingly anxious to get well-established in business connexions here, and make publishers and printers *desirous* to be in connection with me," she explained to Loring, whom she asked to relay the message.[40] Child's overtures to other commercial publishers failed, however, and she finally decided to borrow enough money to print the book at her own expense. Significantly, the firm that took the risk of putting its imprimatur on an abolitionist book, even under those conditions, belonged to distant cousins on her father's side: Charles S. Francis in New York and J. H. Francis and his partner, James Munroe, in Boston.[41]

To their mutual astonishment, *Letters from New York* sold out its first print run of 1,500 copies within four months and went through ten more printings in seven years.[42] Sharing the good news with Francis Shaw, who had helped her finance the venture, Child admitted: "The great popularity of that volume surprises me; for it is full of ultraisms." With her usual insight, she suspected that one secret of the *Letters'* success might be the "fascination" always aroused by "whatever gives out *itself* freely."[43] The reviews confirm her hypothesis. Writing for William Henry Channing's short-lived progressive journal *The Present*, for example, Thomas Wentworth Higginson (then making his literary debut) quoted the dictum that "the inward experience, the real life, of any one person" constituted "the most interesting and profitable" of all literary subjects. He went on to apply it to *Letters from New York*: "[W]e have before us a real living person, whom we may know and love as such. . . . [I]n all the thoughts that crowd up from the clear well-spring within her, we take a share; and when we close the book, we feel we have found a new friend, whose character we know thoroughly and trust entirely . . . one who looks keenly, thinks deeply, feels earnestly, and speaks fearlessly."[44]

Higginson also indicated another major attraction the *Letters* held, particularly for a public undergoing the throes of rapid urbanization — Child's ability to find the Beautiful not only in conventional romantic settings, but "equally in the dark gray city, where beats the sorrowing, striving heart of man." Nearly every reviewer echoed him in praising the book's honest yet sympathetic depiction of city life. The *Democratic Review* credited Child with having captured "the infinite novelty which an open eye and soul will find in and about a great city." The more conservative *Knickerbocker* exclaimed with uncharacteristic enthusiasm: "Here is a woman who knows 'how to observe.'" Child need not have apologized for the book's "'romance and mysticism,'" the *Knickerbocker* opined: "to our conception, its pages exhibit a far greater amount of *truth*, undeniable, and of deep import to society at large, and to our own metropolitan community especially." Summing up the themes previous reviewers had sounded, Margaret Fuller paid *Letters from New York* the ultimate compliment in the *Dial*: "It is, really, a contribution to *American* literature, recording in a generous spirit, and with lively truth, the pulsations in one great center of the national existence. . . . The writer never loses sight of the hopes and needs of all men, while she faithfully winnows grain for herself from the chaff of every day, and grows in love and trust, in proportion with her growth in knowledge."[45]

Revealingly, the one dissenting voice in the chorus of acclaim excoriated Child for fostering a "sympathy with the oppressed which warps reason." In an effort to counteract the influence *Letters from New York* seemed to be exerting as it entered its third printing, the ultraconservative *American Whig Review* devoted fifteen pages to ridiculing the book's social philosophy, which it dismissed as "the fungal growth of an oversensitive heart." The ragged paupers Child sketched with such pathos were figments of a sentimental imagination, declared the reviewer, Donald G. Mitchell, himself a writer of sentimental sketches. The actual slum dwellers and vagabonds of New York were too degraded to inspire the compassion she sought to arouse in readers. What Mitchell found most pernicious, however, was Child's premise that "society makes its own criminals." Reminding his readers that "society" meant "you and I, and the million," he retorted that the real cause of crime was "the known and accredited tendency of humanity to evil doing, unless restrained." In her zeal to do justice to the criminal, he added, Child evidently deemed it "a matter of very little importance whether justice is done to those who are not criminal" (an argument familiar to late twentieth-century readers). "[W]e like her writings," Mitchell admitted grudgingly, and "others like her writings as well as ourselves." Thus, he ended by imploring Child to redirect her "considerable" influence away from "satirizing civil justice" and toward denouncing "the crying evils of social life." Foremost among the evils he targeted, perhaps alluding to Child's separation from her husband, was woman's failure to fulfill "her right vocation" in the home.[46]

Letters from New York achieved Child's aims. It revived her literary career, gained her a broader audience for the progressive ideas she advocated, and secured her readmittance into the commercial publishing world that had closed its doors to her a decade ago. It also furnished her with a "letter of introduction" to the New York literati. Soon Child began circulating in a milieu that included the poet William Cullen Bryant, editor of the New York *Evening Post*; his son-in-law, Parke Godwin, a reformer with ties to the Associationist movement, who shared Child's interest in Fourierism and leaned toward antislavery politics; the poet James Russell Lowell, who had married Child's friend from the Boston Female Anti-Slavery Society, Maria White, a poet in her own right; and Charles F. Briggs and Edgar Allan Poe, coeditors of the *Broadway Journal*.

Poe and Lowell left memorable sketches of Child that capture the transfiguration this nondescript, middle-aged little woman underwent whenever an idea, a political issue, or a person in need awakened her dormant passion. "Mrs. Child, casually observed, has nothing particularly striking in her personal appearance," wrote Poe. "Her dress is usually plain, not even neat — anything but fashionable." But he noted that her expression became "highly intellectual" as soon as she entered into an "animated" conversation: "Her bearing needs excitement to impress it with life and dignity. She is of that order of beings who are themselves only on 'great occasions.'" Poe also paid tribute to both her "energetic and active philanthropy" and the "high merit" of her writings.[47]

Lowell, though he portrayed Child condescendingly, conveyed the magnetism of
her personality and the depth of her sympathy for human suffering:

> There comes Philothea, her face all aglow,
> She has just been dividing some poor creature's woe,
>
> .   .   .   .
>
> The pole, science tells us, the magnet controls,
> But she is a magnet to emigrant Poles,
> And folks with a mission that nobody knows,
> Throng thickly about her as bees round a rose;
>
> .   .   .   .
>
> Yes, a great heart is hers, one that dares to go in
> To the prison, the slave-hut, the alleys of sin,
> And to bring into each, or to find there, some line
> Of the never completely out-trampled divine. . . .[48]

Child's contacts with these prominent men of letters, all of whom edited important
periodicals, would help her to find outlets for the journalism and fiction she produced
in the wake of *Letters from New York*.

By December 1843 the book's Boston and New York publishers were already vying
for the privilege of issuing a second edition—this time on terms favorable to the
author—and Joseph T. Buckingham, editor of the *Boston Courier*, had invited Child to
contribute a second series of "Letters from New-York" to his newspaper, as she informed Loring.[49] The transfer of her column from the *Standard* to a mainstream organ
exponentially increased her readership and all but restored Child to her former popularity. *Courier* subscribers greeted the "Letters" with the same excitement that had once
prompted children to sit on their doorsteps waiting for the *Juvenile Miscellany*. "The
counting-room of the *Courier* was filled by an eager crowd, half an hour before the
proper time, on the days when [the Letters] were expected," recalled Caroline Healey
Dall: "The paper came damp from the press, and many a delicate glove bore traces of
the fervor with which the owner had grasped the sheet. Men read it as they walked
slowly up School Street. Young women ran into Munro and Francis' bookstore for
their first glimpse. These letters were read aloud at the tea-table, and the next day
everybody passed their bright sayings along."[50]

Child's column in the *Courier* differed markedly from its predecessor in the *Standard*,
however, for her perpetually evolving career had entered yet another phase. Freed from
the editorial grind, the demands of activism in a social movement, and the burden of
David's debts, Child had thrown herself into the arts with the fervor of a proselyte and
the hunger of a New England mechanic's daughter who had never been allowed aesthetic pleasures. She could hardly have chosen a more propitious moment. New York
was just attaining cultural predominance. Aspiring painters, sculptors, musicians, sing-
ers, and actors were flocking to the city. Professional critics had not yet emerged, which
left room for a talented amateur to carve out a place for herself as a reviewer of concerts
and exhibitions. Child proceeded to do exactly that in her *Courier* letters.

Though the gratification of her taste for music and art represented an unaccustomed luxury, it did not spell an abandonment of the ideals that had inspired her throughout her life. Rather, she extended her philanthropy in a new direction. With the same ready sympathy she had always shown, she took a personal interest in forwarding the careers of the artists she admired. She obtained patronage from wealthy friends for the silhouettist Auguste Edouart, the painter William Page, and the sculptor Horace Kneeland; secured theater engagements for the actress Jeannie Barrett, whom she rescued from alcoholism; and promoted the concerts of the Norwegian violinist Ole Bull, the destitute Bohemian composer Antony Philip Heinrich, the singer Julia Northall (an orphan struggling to support herself and her many siblings), and the pianists Edward Walker and Henry Christian Timm. By collecting $400 each from ten contributors, she enabled Kneeland to cast his equestrian statue of George Washington in Berlin. She wrote to William Wetmore Story and Charles Sumner giving them advance notice of Julia Northall's Boston concert and asking them to "speak a friendly word" for her protégée, whom she also praised in a well-timed "Letter from New-York." When the importunate Heinrich complained of having been turned away from her door with the message that she was "too much engaged to see strangers," and insinuated that his poverty-stricken appearance may have occasioned the slight, she replied: "I never in my life asked any questions concerning a man's coat; but should I accidentally learn that his coat was thread-bare, it would be an *inducement* for me to set aside engagements to see him." The exchange initiated a long correspondence in which Child good-humoredly put up with Heinrich's jealous disparagement of Ole Bull and graciously apologized for having hurt his feelings by referring to him as "the mad musician" in a "Letter from New-York" that she had written especially to advertise his forthcoming Boston concert.[51]

By 1845 Child had gathered around her a large circle of devotees for whom she played the role of a muse. Having invested in a piano (a rare extravagance for her) and plunged into the study of musical theory, she impressed musicians with her genuine appreciation of their artistry. "Old Father Heinrich insists upon calling me 'Queen of Song.' Heaven help my subjects, if they are as ignorant as their queen," she wrote amusedly to Anna Loring, Louisa and Ellis's teenaged daughter. "I seize every opportunity of hearing good music, and the time and expense is rewarded by slow gradual improvement of ear and taste; and that is the most that the 'Queen of Song' can say for herself." Yet musicians evidently recognized in her a kindred spirit and refused to take her humble professions of ignorance seriously. As she reported with childlike wonder to Anna:

> Timm, our best pianist, ... whose exquisitely delicate and graceful style of playing rejuvenates my blood every time I hear him ... has ... [s]ent to ask it as a *favor* that I will *allow* him to come and play to me, on my piano! Walker, the inventor of the Harmonic Attachment, has done the same. It is really *too* funny. What will happen next, I know not. Perhaps Franz Liszt will beg of me to *condescend* to listen to him, while he extemporizes fantasias of his own, or transposes some of Beethoven

sonatas, for my edification. Really, it is the oddest thing, how such a little dot of a magnet draws the big musicians![52]

By far the most eminent of the musicians Child's "magnet" attracted was Ole Bull, whom she credited with having "awakened . . . a new sense" in her.[53] An international celebrity said to be the model for Ibsen's *Peer Gynt*, Bull drew enthusiastic crowds everywhere he performed and won the adulation of women on two continents.[54] Child first heard him play in December 1843 and reviewed the concert in her inaugural "Letter from New-York" for the *Courier*. She renders the experience in the language typically used to describe a religious conversion. Initially, she avows, she had refused to "join the throng who are following this Star of the North," because "I never like lions"; but the power of Ole Bull's music "overcame like a miracle":

> I felt that my soul was, for the first time, baptised in music; that my spiritual relations were somehow changed by it, and that I should henceforth be otherwise than I had been. I was so oppressed with "the exceeding weight of glory," that I drew my breath with difficulty. . . . [I]t seemed to me as if such music should bring all the world into the harmonious beauty of divine order. I passed by my earthly home, and knew it not; for my spirit seemed to be floating through infinite space. Afterward, I felt like a person who had been in a trance, seen heaven opened, and then returned to earth again.[55]

In a classic illustration of the link between religious and sexual ecstasy, Child shifts at this point into the language of romance. Comparing herself to a "romantic girl of sixteen," she confesses an impulse to wear a "broken string of [Ole Bull's] violin . . . as a relic." She proceeds to descant on how Bull's physical appearance "increases the charm" of his music: "[H]e looks pure and natural, vigorous yet gentle, like Adam in Paradise. His inspired soul dwells in a healthy body, and looks out with wondrous intensity from the depths of his plaintive, earnest eyes. The religious sentiment must be strong in his nature; for Teutonic reverence, mingled with impassioned aspiration, shines through his honest Northern face, and runs like electricity through all his music." Child's fusion of sexual and religious imagery culminates in her invocation of the Swedenborgian theory that music is to the universe "what woman is to man" — that it represents "the feminine principle, the *heart* of the universe."

Child would be even more explicit about her adolescent "hero-worship" in a letter to Ellis Loring, written while Bull was performing in Boston five months later. Eagerly anticipating the Lorings' reaction to the concert, she relived the thrill of her first exposure to his music. "I would have compassed sea and land to get one of his violin strings for a bracelet. I was wild," she admitted unabashedly. Bull had sent her an engraving of his portrait, she added, "with the nicest of letters in elaborate English" (perhaps a token of thanks for her extravagant review in the *Courier*): "The divine man! How I love to look upon him!" He had also promised to call on her when he returned to New York — a prospect that frightened Child because he seemed "so like a god." Expecting that Loring would give a party for Bull, as he often did for visiting "lions," Child asked him to speak of her and convey the "joy" she took in her idol's portrait.[56]

Long afterward, Child would explain the impact Ole Bull had had on her by recalling that she had been "laboring under discouragement and severe depression" at the time. She did not specify the reasons for her despondency, but they can be conjectured from her circumstances in December 1843. David was about to leave for Washington, barely five months after settling in New York, and John may already have been turning to "*young* lady friends," for he would enter on an abortive engagement in 1844. Faced with the breakdown of her marriage and the looming end of her compensatory relationship with John, Child may have been feeling as if the dream of love had eluded her forever. Ole Bull had dispelled her bleak mood with his rejuvenating music that December evening: "He gave a fresh impulse to my soul, kindled in me a new life, made a bright Indian Summer in the dreary autumn of my existence."[57]

As with her love for her "adopted son," Child did not try to conceal from herself the nature of the "intense devotion to music" that Ole Bull had aroused in her. "I fly to [music], as other weary and wounded spirits fly to fanaticism in religion," she wrote with characteristic candor to Louisa. "Such a cloud all the time hangs over my life, from David's incurable tendencies, and the changes in me produced thereby, that I have no choice between a listless and moping melancholy, or a *desperate* effort to keep young, and bright, and cheerful. In this state, music came to me like an angel. I should have gone mad without it."[58]

Child at last met the man who had turned her "dreary autumn" into "Indian summer" when he came back to New York for a second series of concerts in October 1844. The day after his opening performance, which had left her with "nerves . . . so excited, that I came home and wept that the time must come . . . when I could hear Ole Bul no more," the famous violinist visited her at the Hopper home, just as she was in the midst of a letter about him to Anna Loring. The two struck up an immediate friendship. "[F]ree, gushing, spontaneous," Bull appealed to the side of Child that rebelled so fiercely against genteel conventions. He did not conform to society's demand that men and women "conceal their individuality, and repress their inward life," she wrote to Anna, and consequently might seem gauche to staid Bostonians like her father, Ellis (who had been disappointingly unresponsive to the "Star of the North"): "But alone in my humble little parlor, where he can laugh, shout, clap his hands, or tell his sorrows, as the mood may be, — he is a most delightful person — gentle as the flute, various as the violin, lively and *naive* as the oboe. I never admired any human being so much."[59] Whether because Loring had shown himself unable to sympathize with her enthusiasm for Ole Bull, or because Child found it easier to share her feelings with "romantic girl[s] of sixteen" who loved music as passionately as she did, she increasingly preferred to confide in Anna Loring and Susan Lyman, the daughter of her old friend in Northampton. Anna would in fact end up marrying a German concert pianist, and Susan, who accompanied Child to a concert by Ole Bull while on a visit to New York, agreed that she, too, "dated the birth of a new sense" from his music.[60]

Bull paid court to Child throughout the remainder of his stay in the United States, which lasted until December 1845. "[H]e has done being afraid of me, as a literary lady," Child reported to Anna not long after his first visit. The two saw each other often. "He invites me to rehearsals, . . . because he knows I am trying to understand the construction of musical compositions, and to accustom my ear to the harmony of different parts." In exchange, Child gave him copies of the literary works he inspired in her, among them a fable about creativity titled "Thot and Freia," to which he took a "particular fancy." During a rehearsal of his new composition "The Solitude of the Prairie," he leaped from the stage and went "bounding up to the dark corner of the opera" house where Child was sitting to ask her with a boyish smile, "Is *that* from Freia's harp?"[61] Utterly captivated by Bull's exuberance, Child pronounced the Norwegian musician "the most genuine child of nature and genius, that it was ever my good fortune to know."[62]

Bull also called on Child frequently in her little parlor at the Hoppers', where he played his violin for her private enjoyment and composed music on her piano. On one of these occasions she finally obtained the violin string she had been coveting as a "relic." Wreathing it in "Immortelles," she decorated his bust with it on his birthday, which she was still celebrating with Susan Lyman more than a year after his departure. As she confessed to another admirer of Ole Bull, the Salem socialite Marianne Silsbee, the celebration included "the highly improper proceeding" of climbing on the piano to kiss her idol's portrait. "Dont you *tell*!" she exhorted Silsbee.[63]

Ole Bull clearly reciprocated the attachment in his own way. Despite a multitude of younger feminine votaries, he chose to spend his last nights in New York with Child (and John Hopper, who kept them company). A raging northeast storm that delayed the sailing of his ship obliged him to remain "a fixture" in her parlor for three days. The prolonged farewell was an appropriate finale for an episode of Child's life filled with sturm und drang. "[O]n my sweet-toned piano he circumnavigated the globe of music — playing Norwegian, Russian, Polish, Hungarian, Spanish, Italian, French, Irish, and all sorts of airs; patiently instructing me the while in the different effects produced by changes of key and rhythm." Re-creating the scene for Anna, Child wrote its closure with mixed emotions: "Well, I thank God for what he *has* been to me. I shall never look upon his like again — the strongest, the gentlest, the freshest of human beings."[64]

Sadly, her idol was destined to disappoint her. He never returned "one syllable of answer" to the many letters she wrote to him. "He has so pained me by his uniform indifference and total neglect, that I often wish I had never heard of him," Child complained to Marianne Silsbee. Yet she kept up the birthday ritual all the same. Musing on why she cherished his memory so "tenderly," when he did not deserve her love as much as "other friends, who treat me with lavish kindness, whose characters are more in unison with my own, and whose qualities are more worthy of my entire approbation," she could only conclude: "He claims ever the privileges of 'a little child,' in whom one must forgive much, on account of winning ways, and not *meaning* any harm."[65] Ironically, she had once again fallen for a man with the charms and failings of the Child she had married.

Whatever the personal dynamics of this "Indian summer" relationship, it undoubtedly directed Child's creativity into new channels. The spirit of Ole Bull presides over the second series of *Letters from New York*, published in February 1845,[66] as unmistakably as the presence of John Hopper and the voice of Ellis Loring hover behind the strolls and dialogues Child conducted with her readers in the first series. Three of the book's thirty-one letters hail Ole Bull by name. Reviews of his concerts — "Ole Bul heard for the first time" and "Ole Bul's Niagara and Solitude of the Prairie" — occupy strategic framing positions as the second and penultimate letters. "The Romance of Thot and Freia," avowedly inspired by Ole Bull, comprises a fourth letter. In addition, two letters describe the varieties of music to be heard in New York — ranging from the elitist institutions of the Philharmonic and the Italian Opera to the popular bands in outdoor parks and aboard steamboats; three use examples from music to illustrate Swedenborg's doctrine of correspondences and Fourier's socialist theory; and music crops up incidentally in other letters.[67]

Instead of dedicating the book to "the Norwegian minstrel" (177), however, Child conferred that honor on a mutual friend and fellow enthusiast of his music — the young German businessman Edmund Benzon, who escorted her to many of the concerts she reviewed, bought her tickets to the opera, and shared her bent for mysticism. Child may have been referring specifically to Benzon when she compared Bull to friends whose "lavish kindness" earned her gratitude but failed to evoke the same tenderness in her.[68]

As a whole, the second series of *Letters from New York* reflects the shift in Child's interests from social reform to mysticism and the arts. True, she devotes three letters to antislavery and one to prison reform; yet if her interview with the former slave Charity Bowery and her detailed account of successful rehabilitation efforts at Sing Sing and other prisons rank among the most historically significant pieces in the volume, they do not sound its leitmotif. Indeed, the antislavery selections date from an earlier period, being reprints from the *Liberty Bell* and the *Standard*.[69]

Child's deep identification with "the people at large" nevertheless informs her perspective on the arts. She pointedly dissociates herself from the "fashionables" who scorn the places of entertainment frequented by the working classes, such as Vauxhall, in the Bowery. "They who think exclusive gentility worth the fetters it imposes, are welcome to wear them. I find quite enough of conventional shackles, that cannot be slipped off, without assuming any unnecessary ones," she comments (171). Similarly, Child takes special pleasure in the Arts Union because it exhibits the works of bank tellers, clerks, shopkeepers, and farmers alongside those of professional artists, and because it aims to "scatter abroad works of native art among the masses of people, who are not able to pay such high prices as the rich can afford" (218). Such institutions, she hopes, will counteract the "grovelling tendencies" deriving from the nation's "too eager . . . pursuit of gain" (215–16, 218).

Child's refocusing of her energies on aesthetic and spiritual concerns is also discernible in the lesser prominence the second series accords to New York itself. As her friend John Sullivan Dwight put it in reviewing the book for *The Harbinger*, published by Brook Farm's Fourierist supporters: "They might be called Letters from Fairy Land, or from the Spirit World. Yet they are true to their title, and do give veritable impressions of New York. Professing only to introduce us into the heart of the great city, the writer introduces us also into another great world, which is her own inward life; and lets the two worlds illustrate one the other."[70] Margaret Fuller likewise noted the dual focus of the second series, characterizing it as a "New-York Spectator" interfused with passages in which "fancy takes flight above experience, or the mind, rooted in reality, raises its eyes with assurance to the region of spiritual laws."[71] While the vivid depiction of city life remains the *Letters'* chief attraction, essays on other subjects — Mammoth Cave in Kentucky, Transcendentalism, speculations about states of existence prior to and following life on earth — take up a good third of the book. The title *Letters from New York* is no longer "altogether appropriate," Child acknowledges in her preface, though she coyly denies having chosen it "on account of the unexpected popularity of the first volume." Appropriately titled or not, the second volume sold as well as the first and garnered even higher praise from the critics.[72]

The selections of the second series often have the feel of essays or narratives rather than letters, as if Child preferred to move on to another literary form, rather than duplicate her previous success. Stylistically, they tend far less toward free association. Child's column in the *Standard* had been an outlet for the side of herself that she could not express in her regular work as an abolitionist editor. Now one senses her chafing against the constraints of the genre she herself had invented. Where Child is at her most creative, she is clearly breaking out of the journalistic mold altogether and stretching her wings in the sphere of fiction.

"The Romance of Thot and Freia" best exemplifies Child's evolution toward a new mode. It also illustrates the role Ole Bull played in that evolution. Beginning on the model of the first series of *Letters from New York*, as a dialogue with an unnamed intimate (clearly Ellis Loring), it quickly metamorphoses into a "fairy legend," which Child uses to articulate her view of the difference between "genius and talent, inspiration and skill," a conventional Romantic theme (176). The choice of figures from Norse mythology to represent these concepts obviously links the definition of genius to Ole Bull, whose merits Child is defending against charges that her favorite lacks a sound mastery of technical skill.[73]

At the same time, by identifying genius/inspiration with the goddess Freia, and talent/skill with the inferior masculine deity Thot, Child is translating the debate over the relative merits of the two principles into a feminist fable that overturns the patriarchal view of the woman artist as an inferior and unnatural creature. Thot, an Aasgaardsreja, or spirit "not good enough for heaven, or bad enough for hell," embodies "Art, Science, or Skill" (177–78). Quintessentially masculine, he resembles "a man of iron, with an eye that looked as if he thought creation was his anvil, on which he could fashion all things" (179). Freia, goddess of Love, or Feeling, has stirred the depths of his soul with the music of her harp, in which Thot has recognized "the tones to which the trees grow, and the blossoms unfold" (179). But rather than give himself up to Freia's magic, Thot wants to make her his "slave," so that he can acquire her creative power and use it to dethrone the gods (180). In describing his "intense desire to press farther into the inmost heart of all being" and to "penetrate" the "secret" of life, Child resorts to the imagery of rape: Thot devises a spell to "bring Freia into his power," then "seize[s] her, and mounting the fiery steed" he has requisitioned from the Aasgaardsreja, gallops away with her (179, 182). Simultaneously, Child exposes male violence as impotent to capture the secret of life. The Freia conjured into being by Thot turns out to be only a specter, and the worlds he creates with his stolen power prove lifeless and "petrified" (186–87). After a final desperate attempt to "extort from [Freia] the primeval word of her being" or "chain [her] forever," Thot finds "the corpse of a mortal woman" at his feet (182, 190) — a denouement recalling that of Nathaniel Hawthorne's "The Birthmark," in which the mad scientist Aylmer's effort to transcend the limitations of nature ends up killing his beautiful wife, Georgiana.[74]

Child's feminist fable does not allow the masculine principle of Art/ Science/Skill its deadly triumph over the feminine principle of Love/Feeling, however. Unlike Hawthorne's Georgiana, a helpless victim of the masculine drive for dominance, Freia represents the female power to create life, which cannot be extinguished without destroying all life in the universe. Thus Freia reveals to Thot in a dream that he has all along been under an illusion: "Thou hast never enslaved *me*. . . . If thou *couldst* fetter me with thy triangles and squares, the universe would stop its motions" (191). Child proceeds to substitute an androgynous vision of creativity for the masculine vision Thot has vainly tried to fulfill. "Thou and I, dear Thot, are one from all eternity. Thou hast made this mournful separation, by reversing the divine laws of our being," Freia explains (191). In seeking to take possession of Freia's creative power, he has lost touch with the side of himself that she embodies. Hence, he has produced nothing but sterility and death. Only if he humbly resigns himself to the influence Freia will exert on him in dreams can he achieve reunion with her and thereby recover his creative potential. The embodiment of their union will be a child whose soul will be "filled with [Thot's] struggling aspirations to reproduce all Nature," but who will receive that gift entirely "from Freia's harp" (193). His mission will be "To be strong in manhood, and yet remain a child in spirit. To let Nature breathe through his soul, as the wind through a tree. To believe all she tells him, and reveal it in immortal music" (192–93).

The child is of course the "minstrel of the North," Ole Bull, but Child's feminist fable has redefined the artist as the union of the feminine and masculine principles — a union in which the feminine predominates. To become an artist, she implies, a man must learn to become like a woman and accept the tutelage of the creature he has always deemed inferior. Underscoring her feminist message, Child portrays Thot as continually tempted to reassert his masculine primacy. "Why should I receive from her? She understands not the laws of her own being," he rages. "No, . . . but she obeys them," Freia's "tuneful" voice replies, and Thot ultimately submits to it (193). Child has also redefined the muse as a far more active figure than in classical tradition, for

Freia is a creator in her own right, not merely an instrument to be "invoked" at will by the male artist.

Through her fable, Child was reclaiming the right to assume the role of artist as well as muse, to give free play to her own creative powers as well as celebrate those of other artists. If she modeled her "child of nature" on Ole Bull, she projected herself into Freia. With "Thot and Freia," Child made her transition from journalism back to fiction. Though she would continue to publish "Letters from New-York" in the *Boston Courier*, she would channel her genius for innovation primarily into a group of short stories comprising her finest achievement to date in the genre. "The periodicals, which have so long ignored my existence, begin to send in requests for contributions, in quite respectful style," Child wrote to her friend Sarah Shaw in November 1844.[75] One such request had come from the *Columbian Lady's and Gentleman's Magazine*, and Child had sent "Thot and Freia" in response. "It is a matter of indifference to me whether you take it or not," she professed, with a self-protectiveness born of the innumerable affronts she had endured since falling out of public favor. The *Columbian* took it, and her feminist fable led off its January 1845 issue.[76] After a lapse of fifteen years, Child was at last back in circulation as a writer of commercial magazine fiction.

14

Sexuality and Marriage in
Fact and Fiction

I do not wonder that so many men are libertines; I had almost said, I do not blame them. Nature is so outrageously dammed up, her strongest instincts are so repressed, her plainest laws are so violated, in the present structure of society, that nature will revenge herself, in spite of all we can do. . . . You cannot make men and women have a horror of each other; the impulses of nature are too strong. But this is a subject on which I dare not speak, though I have thought more busily upon it, than upon any other, for the last ten years. I am, in fact, unqualified to speak, because here lies the weak side of my own nature. "The strong necessity of loving" has been the great temptation and conflict of my life; yet I sincerely believe that few women are more pure-minded than myself.[1]

When Child wrote this astonishingly candid letter to Francis Shaw in August 1846, she was struggling to come to terms with the thwarted needs that had impelled her to reevaluate her culture's repressive sexual mores. Shaw had evidently expressed concern about her "more than usual tendency to low-spirits." Their friendship dated back to the 1820s, when both had joined the Swedenborgian Church of the New Jerusalem, and they shared a fascination with George Sand, whose sexually daring novels Shaw had been translating.[2] Shaw had indicated that he, too, was questioning the sexual double standard, and he had asked Child whether she approved of concealing "the *real* situation of the world" from young women — one of the hypocritical practices their mutual friend Margaret Fuller had recently denounced in *Woman in the Nineteenth Century* (1845).[3] Perhaps emboldened by his letter (which has not survived), Child unburdened herself more freely than she ever had to anyone else.

Her depression, she explained, stemmed from the failure of her marriage, which had left her "isolated" and loveless, though she was "naturally very affectionate and domestic." Since her decision three years ago to separate her financial affairs from David's "in self-defence" and to pursue her "own avocations without any reference to his whereabout or whatabout," the two had followed "more and more divergent" paths. David had been "living in the woods, with animals and coarse men"; in the meantime, she herself had been "growing more refined and poetic every day, under the influences of music, pictures, and mystical contemplation." Much as they loved each other, they had become increasingly estranged. "[T]his above all things makes me sad," she confided.

Yet when Child went on to say that she had "thought more busily" about the problem of "dammed up" instinctual drives than about any other subject "for the last ten years," she hinted that her marriage had ceased to fulfill her long before David's "*incurable*" propensity for ill-advised financial ventures had led to an open break. Ten years earlier, in fact, while trying to cope with David's emotional (and perhaps sexual) withdrawal after the collapse of his legal practice, Child had explored the self-divisions generated by a failing marriage in her novel *Philothea* (1836). Still committed then to saving her marriage at all costs, she had opted for a culturally sanctioned solution to what she called "the great temptation and conflict" of her life — her craving for love. She had embraced the traditional feminine ideal typified by her heroine Philothea's asexual purity and self-sacrificing devotion to an invalid husband, and she had rejected the alternative the feminist Frances Wright had offered in the late 1820s — championing women's right to sexual freedom. Now, as a result of her disengagement from David, Child was free to reconsider issues she had previously foreclosed. The language of her letter to Shaw, with its emphasis on the "laws" and "instincts" of "nature" and its metaphor of sexuality as a river that should not be "dammed up" suggests that she may have been reading the works of utopian radicals like Wright's mentor, Robert Owen, whose sexual philosophy and "infidel" attacks on religion had once repelled her. She was certainly reading analogous works by the French socialist Charles Fourier, cited repeatedly in *Letters from New York*.[4]

Marking the distance Child had traveled since *Philothea* and reflecting the new influences on her thinking, her writings of the 1840s reveal a pronounced evolution toward feminist militancy and sexual liberalism. They likewise attest to her passionate sympathy for all who found themselves unable to conform to nineteenth-century bourgeois society's rigid sexual code. In life, Child expressed that sympathy not only by speaking up for rebels in her own circle, like Margaret Fuller, whose unconventional marriage to a younger man after the birth of their son scandalized acquaintances, but by befriending a host of "fallen women," from the alcoholic actress Jeannie Barrett to the seduced working girl and would-be murderer Amelia Norman. In her fiction Child dramatizes the theme of forbidden sexuality and "dammed up" nature under many guises, projecting herself into slave women denied the right to choose their own lovers and coerced into unwanted sex with their masters, unwed mothers punished for the crime of yielding to the " 'strong necessity of loving,' " and thwarted lovers of both sexes who must learn to sublimate the passions they cannot act out. At her most daring, she also expands the limits of the possible through stories that conjure up utopian worlds in which sexual desires can enjoy free play.

Fittingly, Child issued her first unequivocal endorsement of the women's rights cause the very month that she decided to set her priorities and choose her place of residence independently of David—in February 1843.⁵ She had hitherto tempered her support of the cause by aligning herself with those "women who most gladly would have avoided discussion on the subject of their own rights," had they not been "reluctantly drawn into controversy" by the need to defend the Grimké sisters against clerical detractors. "To me this 'vexed question' has ever been distasteful," Child had confessed in an editorial of July 1841, titled "Speaking in the Church." "[I]f I must, at the bidding of conscience, enter the arena and struggle for human rights, I prefer they should be the rights of others, rather than my own."⁶ Accordingly, Child had taken a stand in solidarity with the Grimkés rather than in vindication of women's rights per se. And she had assumed an attitude of ironic detachment toward the orthodox clerics who had "urged women to become missionaries, and form tract societies," but who had reacted with such consternation to the spectacle of female antislavery lecturers. Like the sorcerer's apprentice in the German legend, Child had commented dryly: "They have changed the household utensil to a living, energetic being; and they have no spell to turn it into a broom again."⁷ Until the final months of her tenure as editor, however, Child had stubbornly resisted importunities to "come out concerning the Rights of Women." Then in two of her last "Letters from New-York," she broke her self-imposed silence and defined her position on the "vexed question."⁸

In tone and content, these letters unmistakably represent a new departure. Not that Child had entirely surmounted her "strong distaste to the subject, as it has been generally treated" by advocates and opponents alike; indeed, she had considered omitting her letters on women's rights from the book, and when she revised them for the volume, she reiterated her old complaint that "much of the talk about Women's Rights offends both my reason and my taste" (245, 250).⁹ What so sharply distinguishes her "coming out" on women's rights from her earlier statements is instead the anger against men that Child articulates for the first time since the youthful novels written before her marriage.

Anger boils over again and again in Child's exposé of the interlocking methods men have used to keep women in subjection—methods ranging from "physical force" and verbal ridicule to "gallantry" and intellectual condescension. "[P]hysical force" is the prime engine of the social system built on women's oppression, Child contends: "[W]hosoever doubts it, let her reflect why she is afraid to go out in the evening without the protection of a man" (247). Men's vaunted "gallantry" toward women, so often cited as a privilege women would forfeit if they obtained the equality they demanded, actually serves to blind women to their true situation, explains Child:

> [I]t is merely the flimsy veil which foppery throws over sensuality, to conceal its grossness. So far is it from indicating sincere esteem and affection for women, that the profligacy of a nation may, in general, be fairly measured by its gallantry. This taking away *rights*, and *condescending* to grant *privileges*, is an old trick of the physical-force principle; and with the immense majority, who only look on the surface of things, this mask effectually disguises an ugliness, which would otherwise be abhorred. (247)

Bristling with terms of opprobrium—"foppery," "grossness," "trick," "ugliness," "abhorred"—Child's language no longer strives to distance emotion. Gone is the magisterial objectivity she had maintained in her 1835 *History of the Condition of Women*. Gone, too, is the posture of wry aloofness and chivalric solidarity she had adopted in "Speaking in the Church." Child is now speaking for herself, not for "others," and drawing on personal experience, not just on her fund of historical knowledge.

The examples Child uses to illustrate men's intellectual condescension toward women are particularly telling. "There are few books which I can read through, without feeling insulted as a woman; but this insult is almost universally conveyed through that which was intended for praise," she writes. "Just imagine, for a moment, what impression it would make on men, if women authors should write about *their* 'rosy lips,' and 'melting eyes,' and 'voluptuous forms,' as they write about *us!*" (248). Child's bitterness about the stereotyping of women as vacuous sex objects wells up out of her long battle against a male-dominated literary establishment whose severe restrictions on the freedom of "women authors" have fettered her throughout her career.

The anger Child expresses against the ideologues who teach women to depend on men for their self-esteem dates back even further. The two she names—Emerson and Milton—are both closely associated with the intellectual tutelage of her brother Convers. Child had met Emerson through Convers in the 1820s and had attended his lecture series in Boston and New York. Unlike Convers, however, she had become increasingly critical of Emerson's abstractions and evasions. Apparently she had also become increasingly resentful of the sage's inability to recognize women as intellectual peers, for she attacks Emerson's differing advice to women and to men in his lecture "Being and Seeming." "*Men* were exhorted to *be*, rather than to *seem*, that they might ... in God's freedom, grow up into the full stature of spiritual manhood; but *women* were urged" to "*be*, rather than *seem*" in order to "*gain hearts*" and make themselves "more *pleasing*" to men, Child notes. Still rankling over the affront, she recalls that it had "brought a flush of indignation over my face." In the next breath, she quotes the passage from *Paradise Lost* that had troubled her at age fifteen, when she had first challenged Convers's intellectual authority: "'*God* is thy law, *thou* mine,' said Eve to Adam. May Milton be forgiven for sending that thought 'out into everlasting time' in such a jewelled setting. What weakness, vanity, frivolity, infirmity of moral purpose, sinful flexibility of principle—in a word, what soul-stifling, has been the result of thus putting man in the place of God!" (249–50).

It is as if she has recaptured the feminist rebelliousness of her youth in the act of freeing herself from her marriage. No longer bound by her loyalty to male mentors, she has shed her identity as an honorary man and let herself feel the anger she has repressed for so many years at the "soul-stifling" she has endured as a woman.

The process of redefining her relationship to the women's rights movement was more than an intellectual endeavor for Child. It also involved the renewal of her bonds with women. Although Child's rupture with Maria Chapman, the Weston sisters, and Abby Kelley had cut her off from one feminist sisterhood, she constructed another in its place. The women friends Child cultivated after leaving the *Standard* enabled her to recover or develop sides of herself that the Frugal Housewife and antislavery activist had had to renounce. These friends included Lucy Osgood, with whom Child conducted a lively correspondence on theological and literary matters; Marianne Devereux Silsbee (wife of the mayor of Salem, Massachusetts) who shared Child's passion for music and her taste for bold-spirited women writers, though the two disagreed sharply over slavery; and above all, Margaret Fuller, whose stint as literary editor and book reviewer for Horace Greeley's *New-York Daily Tribune* in 1845–46 rekindled an intimacy that had ended with Child's marriage. In addition, Child extended the bonds of sisterhood to a group of sexual outcasts she recognized as alter egos—"fallen women" victimized because they, too, had suffered from a thirst for love and unjustly ostracized because they had yielded to the desires she herself was restraining at such great cost.

One of the many friends Child had sacrificed on the altar of abolitionism, Lucy Osgood had begun subscribing to the *Standard* in the changed climate of 1843. "Letters from New-York" had "revived" her "old feeling of familiarity with the mind of the editor," and she had greeted those on women's rights with particular enthusiasm. On rereading the letters Child had written to her in the 1820s, she had found to her delight that "however the Apostle of Freedom might have lost sight . . . of the scenes & associates of other days, she had never lost herself—that the L. M. Francis of 1826 . . . is the identical L. M. Child of 1843 . . . with the same aspirations after good, the same impatience of wrong, the same independence, originality & honesty."[10] Osgood represented a link with Child's past and with an older generation of strong-minded women who never openly challenged patriarchal authority, yet preserved a certain intellectual independence. Curiously, it was this spinster daughter of a clergyman who would perceive Child's deep affinities with George Sand. "You are perfectly right," Child would marvel at her friend's acumen.

> I have always known that George Sand was my twin sister. . . . I never read a book of hers without continually stumbling on things that seem to have been written by myself. . . . She *is* my double; and if the external influences of our lives had been the same, I should doubtless have been like her, faults and all. . . . The affections in her nature are too strong for her intellect, and they have befooled her. Don't I know how to sympathize with *that*?[11]

Like Osgood, Marianne Silsbee apparently felt impelled to write to Child after reading her "Letters from New-York." In her case, the letters that inspired her sense of rapport with the author were probably Child's enthusiastic tributes to Ole Bull. The letters on women's rights may also have struck a sympathetic chord in her, for she sent Child a "very beautiful edition" of the British feminist Anna Jameson's *Characteristics of Shakespeare's Women*, signing the gift "from a woman who had benefited much from Mrs. Child's characteristics."[12] Despite Child's intense hatred of aristocrats and the Silsbees' equally violent aversion to abolitionists, the kinship these two passionate women felt with each other was strong enough to induce Child to visit the Silsbees in Salem—a rare departure from her reclusiveness. The letter Child wrote to Silsbee about Charlotte Brontë's *Jane Eyre* suggests that each fulfilled the other's need for a confidante to whom she could pour out her romantic fantasies and heterodox thoughts. Referring to Brontë's hero, Rochester, stigmatized as "unloveable" by many critics, Child exclaims to Silsbee: "*I* could have loved him with my whole heart." She proceeds to air her "*private* opinion . . . that a real living Jane Eyre, placed in similar circumstances," would not have left Rochester on learning that he was already married, but "would have obeyed an *inward* law, higher and better than outward conventional scruples." "The tyrannical law, which bound him to a mad and wicked wife, seems such a mere figment!" Child protests.[13]

If she herself could not act on the view that the "tyrannical law" binding her to an estranged husband and preventing her from taking her sexual freedom was "a mere figment," she did nonetheless defend the breaking of marital ties in life as well as in fiction. Writing to Louisa Loring about the separation of Louisa's cousin John King and his wife, Jane Tuckerman, Child boldly affirms: "[W]hen people *are* incongruous and mutually *feel* that they are, it is the wisest and best thing to separate, let society say what it may. Nay *I* go so far as to consider it positively *wrong*, under such circumstances, to live together in the married relation." A loveless marriage maintained for appearances' sake is nothing but "legalized prostitution," she asserts, adding pointedly: "I know it is a dangerous subject to speculate upon; but experience and observation have *forced* upon me a close attention to it. . . ."[14]

Child's ensuing arguments imply even more strongly that she is covertly justifying her own decision to part ways with David. Using an analogy she had elsewhere applied to David's "deficienc[i]es in business matters," she says of the Kings: "They can neither of them help their temperaments, any more than they can help the color of their eyes, or the height of their persons."[15] Child then cites the example of another separated couple, the Jamesons. Her description of their incompatible temperaments corresponds at least partially to her own and David's, for she, like Anna Jameson, was "impulsive, warm, and poetic," and David seems to have become "cold, sluggish, and legal" as a result of his failures and defeats.[16] Obviously projecting, Child divines that Mrs. Jameson had left her husband because "[s]he *could* not feel herself freezing to death by inches." At the end of her letter she finally speaks directly of herself, inviting Louisa to make the connection: "Oh, my God what fierce conflicts I have had under my sober exterior of practical common sense! How I *have* suffered! how I *have* wept!"

Of the women toward whom Child gravitated in the mid-1840s, none would better have understood her "fierce conflicts" than Margaret Fuller. Since the days when they had set about studying Madame de Staël together almost two decades before, both had developed into extraordinarily complex, multifaceted women who towered intellectually above their peers. Both had passed through a Transcendentalist phase before moving on to an engagement with social reform. Both had formed an early feminist consciousness that would flower in a pioneering work on the condition of women. Both traveled in social circles that encompassed the Lorings, the Shaws, the Alcotts, the Kings, the Storys, Caroline Sturgis, Emerson, and William Henry Channing, to name only the most important of their common friends. And both were struggling with unfulfilled sexual desires. Although their careers had repeatedly intersected, the older woman and the younger woman had followed the same paths in different directions. The daughter of a congressman from a well-connected family, Fuller had enjoyed social and educational privileges denied to Child. Yet her father's sudden death, plunging the family into genteel poverty, had forced some of the same sacrifices on Fuller that David's debts had imposed on Child. She, too, had laid aside ambitious intellectual projects in order to earn money to support her family (by teaching school, rather than by writing domestic advice books), and she, too, had given up a longed-for trip to Europe because her family's needs took precedence. While Fuller was floating in a Transcendental realm, however, Child was writing antislavery tracts and collecting signatures on petitions. Conversely, while Fuller was assuming the role of a trailblazer for other women in her Conversations, and formulating the feminist theories she would bring to fruition in "The Great Lawsuit" (1843) and *Woman in the Nineteenth Century* (1845), Child was retreating from her own feminist insights and withdrawing into the self-abnegating mysticism of *Philothea* (1836). Symbolizing their reversed roles, in 1839, four years after publishing her *History of the Condition of Women*, Child was attending the Conversations over which Fuller presided. Still, Fuller drew heavily on Child's research and continued to look up to her as an embodiment of the ideals that eventually led the younger woman to emulate the elder's social activism. "In former days, you used to tell me much which I have stored in memory as I have in my heart the picture of your affectionate, generous, and resolute life," she wrote Child in March 1844.[17] That December she arrived in New York to enter on the journalistic career Child herself had just relinquished and to school herself in the work of reform that Child had temporarily forsaken for literature and the arts.

During Fuller's two-year stay in New York the two friends saw each other frequently, read and reviewed each other's work, attended plays and concerts together, visited and reported on the same penal and reformatory institutions, and concerned themselves in different ways with the rehabilitation of "fallen women."[18] Because Fuller's residence at the Greeleys' was so far uptown, she occasionally spent the night with Child after evenings at the theater. "[T]hey are, indeed, pleasant hours we pass together," Fuller wrote to Anna Loring. "Mrs. Child . . . is so entertaining, and her generous heart glows through all she says, and makes a friendly home around her." For her part, Child admitted to Anna that she had at first been put off by Fuller, "having the idea that she was coldly critical and intellectual," but that Fuller had dispelled such notions with her ardent reaction to Ole Bull's "Niagara." When Fuller, too, had recognized that "Ole Bul is a *poet*-musician, that his conceptions are *romantic* and full of *genius*," Child had thrown her arms around her, and they had become "sworn friends." "I like her extremely," Child confirmed to Louisa. "She is a great woman, and no mistake."[19]

Anxious to "help the sale" of Fuller's *Woman in the Nineteenth Century*, Child took the trouble to procure it in proof and give it advance reviews in the *Boston Courier*, the *New-York Daily Tribune*, and the *Broadway Journal*—an astute move by which she stole a march on the male reviewers who would rake Fuller over the coals.[20] Her comments on the book show how much sustenance she drew from the relationship with Fuller—the only woman she had ever met who challenged her intellectually and questioned society's sexual codes more boldly and openly than she herself dared to.

Praising the "vigorous" style and "free energetic spirit" of the book, Child asserts that the occasional opaqueness of Fuller's language "does not arise from affectation, or pedantic elaboration"; rather, "it is the defect of a mind that has too many thoughts for its words; an excess by no means common, either in men or women." Having transformed a "defect" into a virtue, Child tackles what she fears may prove the chief obstacle to the book's success: "It contains a few passages that will offend the fastidiousness of some readers; for they allude to subjects which men do not wish to have discussed, and which women dare not approach." She then turns the tables on Fuller's prospective critics and forces them on the defensive: "the clean-minded will not sneer; for they will see that the motive is pure, and the object is to ennoble human nature." In summing up the message of *Woman in the Nineteenth Century*, Child articulates the concerns she herself has been wrestling with for ten years. Though phrased impersonally, her purported restatement of Fuller's inquiries reverberates with personal overtones and irresistibly recalls her confessional letter to Francis Shaw: "There is a great deal of unuttered thought and suppressed feeling, concerning the terrible discords of society, as it now exists. The passion of love, divorced from the pure and elevating sentiment, is felt to be unsatisfactory, as well as degrading. More and more earnestly rise the questions, '*Is* love a mockery, and marriage a sham? What is woman's true mission? What is the harmonious relation of the sexes?' "

If Child was asking these questions as she fought the temptation to satisfy her need for love outside of marriage, Fuller was confronting them as a single woman of thirty-five, buffeted for the second time in her life by an unrequited passion. Apparently the two women guessed each other's secrets, but volunteered no confidences. Child knew that Fuller was seeing the German Jewish businessman James Nathan, a friend and compatriot of Edmund Benzon, to whom she had dedicated the second series of *Letters from New York*. The couple sometimes rendezvoused at the Hopper home and probably accompanied Child and Benzon to concerts.[21] When Nathan left for Europe in June 1845 and did not write for months, Child must have noticed Fuller's dejection. She testified to her solicitude by making the long trip across town to Fuller's residence — an "extraordinary civility" as she put it — on hearing that her friend was unwell, and by leaving a note offering her services "either as nurse, or as a sympathizing listener to the outpourings of a sad heart."[22] Child's own painful position seems to have been equally obvious to Fuller and Nathan. In a letter to her lover referring to earlier conversations the two had had about Child, Fuller speculated that her friend had "married very young, before she knew much of herself" and that she did not always have "the surest instincts as to selecting" appropriate objects for her self-sacrificing love. Intriguingly, the worldly Nathan, who had shocked and wounded Fuller with a sexual proposition, observed that Child was a woman of " 'deep passion.' "[23]

Perhaps as a result of struggling to contain sexual impulses in themselves that they felt to be illicit, both Child and Fuller came to identify strongly with "fallen women." Child's forays into this sphere preceded Fuller's, and her example may well have inspired the passage in *Woman in the Nineteenth Century* that calls on the more fortunate to "[s]eek out these degraded women, give them tender sympathy, counsel, employment."[24] Both Child and Fuller also owed a debt to the Evangelical women of the Moral Reform movement, who had campaigned against prostitution in the 1830s, and to Quaker prison reformers like Child's host, Isaac T. Hopper, and his daughter Abby Hopper Gibbons, who were currently pioneering methods of rehabilitating incarcerated women as well as men.[25] The two friends deviated from their Evangelical and Quaker precursors, however, by claiming greater sexual freedom for women, Child in her fiction of the 1840s, Fuller in her defense of George Sand and Mary Wollstonecraft, and later in her liaison with Angelo Ossoli.[26]

Child first publicly espoused the cause of fallen women in January 1844, when she risked scurrilous attacks on her character to champion Amelia Norman, a young workingwoman indicted for having tried to murder the gentleman rake who had seduced and abandoned her. She visited Norman in prison, enlisted the aid of John Hopper in finding her a lawyer and raising funds for her defense, and covered the trial in "Letters from New-York."[27] According to Fuller, who paid tribute in *Woman in the Nineteenth Century* to her friend's "nobleness . . . toward an injured sister," Child helped turn the tide of public opinion in Norman's favor and suggested some of the arguments Norman's lawyer used to win over the jury, which ultimately acquitted her.[28]

The burning attack Child launches against the double standard in her "Letter from New-York" on the Norman case goes well beyond the feminist militancy of her 1843 "coming out" on women's rights. Once again, her language explodes with anger against men. Child scornfully details the tactics used by the seducer's lawyer to smear Norman as a prostitute and then insist that "no evidence concerning her character or [his client's] should be admitted" — a position the judge sustained. Quoting the address to the jury in which this lawyer had asked "whether it would be worse to have the virtue of their daughters ruined, or their young and generous sons brought home stabbed by the hands of prostitutes," Child replies:

> I had no doubt that if all deeply injured women were to undertake to redress their wrongs in this bad way, there would be a huge pile of dead citizens. (I even thought it not impossible that some of the honorable court themselves might be among the missing.) . . . It unquestionably was an argument that came home to men's business and bosoms. Yet I felt no very active pity for their terror. I indignantly asked what had been done to the twelve thousand men, who made these poor creatures prostitutes?

Ridiculing the lawyer's "lively picture of poor innocent men tempted, betrayed, and persecuted by women," Child contends that even if men are at times "led astray" by prostitutes, as well as the reverse, they do not suffer the same emotional consequences that women do. The temptation to which men succumb is "merely animal," she argues, whereas the "seductive influence of the affections . . . often leads woman to ruin, through the agency of her best impulses."

Child did not content herself with publicizing Norman's case and helping to obtain her acquittal. She took the young girl home with her after the trial, nursed her through illness and depression, gave her the strength to begin life anew, and found a job for her with a sympathetic family in New England. Almost two years later, she was still exerting herself for Norman, this time by trying to arrange for her to "go to Europe as a waiting-maid, for one or two years, preparatory to learning a trade."[29] Child saw her private rehabilitation work as an extension of her public campaign against the prison system. "When I look at this poor misguided girl, now so useful, and improving daily in her views of things, and think what she *would* have been, had they sent her to Sing Sing, my feelings with regard to society's treatment of criminals grow stronger and stronger," she wrote to a friend.[30]

Norman was only one of the women Child rescued "from the gutter" and attended "as a sister till she learnt to love her as one," to quote Fuller's account of her friend's efforts for the "once beautiful and celebrated" actress Jeannie Barrett.[31] Barrett's embarrassing relapse into alcoholism on the opening night of a theater engagement Child had secured for her led Fuller to conjecture that the woman she admired so much did not always show good judgment in choosing whom to befriend. Yet the truth was that Child had the generosity to take chances with unpromising cases and the patience to persist despite setbacks.[32] In Barrett's case her persistence paid off, for the actress did eventually control her drinking enough to make a successful comeback. The private appeals Child made for other protégées also indicate that she approached her charity work without illusions. In trying to obtain training in a millinery establishment for the purported widow of the murderer John C. Colt, for example, Child wrote: "Ought we not to assist her, even at the risk of being disappointed in our hopes?"[33] And when she sought a position for a reformed drunkard named Amelia Wilson, Child warned: "This girl *may* possibly give you trouble by an intemperate fit . . . but I do not *think* she will." The advice she gave Wilson's prospective employer encapsulates the spirit of her labors for erring sisters: "Never let *her* know, or perceive, that she is considered a subject of benevolence. It is by that fatal mistake, that so many promising cases are ruined. Human souls yearn for sympathy, and that degree of equality which is the rightful basis of all our separate and diverse gifts and missions. Instead of this, people in general give *condescension*, and thus undo the work they really wish to do."[34]

In reaching out to women like Jeannie Barrett and Amelia Norman, Child was acknowledging that she had shared their temptations and avoided their fate not through any innate superiority but through what she called "the external influences of our lives."[35] She was also acknowledging the "bonds of womanhood" that restricted her freedom and linked her to her sisters — a psychological gesture she had been unable to make in the days when she had defined herself as an honorary man and resisted being relegated to the lesser sphere of "female societies."[36]

Child's shift from male to female identification and from speaking for "others" to speaking at least symbolically for herself is discernible not only in her public and private affirmations of feminist sisterhood, but in her fiction. Child's three earliest stories of the 1840s — "The Black Saxons" (1841), "The Quadroons" (1842), and "Slavery's

Pleasant Homes" (1843), published in Maria Weston Chapman's abolitionist annual *The Liberty Bell*— speak for "others."[37] In keeping with the mission of fighting for "human rights" that Child had undertaken "at the bidding of conscience," her antislavery fiction strives to arouse the sympathies of her genteel white readers for a despised and downtrodden race.[38] Even within this fictional subgenre, however, Child shows evidence of realigning herself with women and reorienting herself toward the sexual concerns that will dominate her fiction for the rest of the decade. "The Black Saxons," written in November 1840 while Child was still in Northampton, adopts the viewpoint of a male slaveholder as he eavesdrops on a debate among male slaves over whether or not to murder their masters.[39] "The Quadroons" and "Slavery's Pleasant Homes" focus on the sexual exploitation of slave women and reflect Child's growing awareness of being personally oppressed by a code of marital and sexual relations that victimizes all women.

An overview of the stories Child wrote between 1840 and 1849, the dates of her first and last periodical contributions of the decade, confirms the pattern. Fifteen out of twenty-seven explore the subject about which Child admitted to Francis Shaw that she dared not speak openly, though she had "thought more busily upon it, than upon any other, for the last ten years."[40] The proportion is higher still—ten out of fifteen—in the collection of stories she titled *Fact and Fiction* (1846). Failed marriages, thwarted or forbidden sexuality, and erotic fantasies haunt this striking body of work, which includes six tales of marital betrayal or dissension ("The Quadroons," "Slavery's Pleasant Homes," "The Beloved Tune," "The Children of Mount Ida," "Home and Politics," and "The Prophet of Ionia"); five dramatizations of cross-group sexuality (between blacks and whites in the two antislavery tales, between Indians and whites in "A Legend of the Falls of St. Anthony," between Jew and Greek in "A Legend of the Apostle John," between upper and lower caste in "The Hindoo Anchorite"); three narratives of fallen women ("Elizabeth Wilson," "Rosenglory," and "Hilda Silfverling"); two stories of rival lovers ("The Brothers" and "The Rival Mechanicians"); and two visions of sexual liberation ("Hilda Silfverling" and "She Waits in the Spirit Land").[41]

With their daring protest against the repression of nature's "strongest instincts," these stories represent a woman writer's effort to challenge prevailing notions of female sexuality and to break the silence Anglo-American literary convention had imposed on the topic of sexual desire. Their frequent autobiographical resonances also suggest that the medium of fiction allowed Child the distance and imaginative freedom to examine aspects of her life too painful to confront directly—in particular the disintegration of her marriage and the emotional deprivation of her childhood.

To read Child's fiction primarily for the autobiographical revelations it offers would do violence to its serious social purpose and considerable literary merit, but neither can one ignore vital clues to the private sources of her remarkable psychosexual insights. Stories like "The Quadroons" (1842), "The Children of Mount Ida" (1845), "The Beloved Tune" (1845), and "Home and Politics" (1848)—all of which portray husbands who desert their wives in order to pursue selfish aims—shed a far harsher light on the Childs' marriage than the couple's surviving correspondence does. "The Beloved Tune," a story about an intemperate husband, registers Child's awareness that in his *"incurable"* urge to gamble on dubious schemes promising quick enrichment, David suffered from an addictive drive. The recurrence in the other three stories of a husband's political ambition as the cause of the couple's estrangement would seem to indicate that David's attraction to politics was also a significant factor in the Childs' estrangement.[42] Just as Corythus in "The Children of Mount Ida" abandons Oenone to fulfill his dreams of glory at the court of Ilium, David had twice left Child for prolonged sojourns in Washington in 1843 and 1844—sojourns that seem to have rekindled the zest for party politics he had displayed in the 1820s. Just as George Franklin in "Home and Politics" bankrupts his family by staking everything he owns on Henry Clay's victory in the 1844 election, David had incurred thousands of dollars in debts during the election of 1828, filed for bankruptcy in 1843, and thrown himself into Clay's campaign of 1844—a move that had shocked many abolitionists. Explaining David's position to Francis Shaw, who shared her abhorrence of Clay (a moderate Kentucky slaveholder), Child had written: "Mr. Child, who is the most honest and unselfish man I ever knew, is carried away with the idea that Texas is *the* question on which the extension of American slavery depends, and that Henry Clay is the only man that can save the country from annexation. I smile; for ever since I can remember men have been expending their energies in *saving the country*; and what comes of it?"[43] She may well have feared that like Edward in "The Quadroons," whose "honest fervour" and "sincere patriotism" imperceptibly turn into political ambition, David had become "involved in movements which his frank nature would have once abhorred" and was "watching the doubtful game of mutual cunning with all the fierce excitement of a gambler" (64–65). The imagery of addiction and "mental intoxication" that she uses to convey both Edward's and George Franklin's obsession with politics is certainly suggestive. And her assessment of George (like David a lawyer by training) needs little modification to apply to David: "By the study and industry of years, he had laid a solid foundation in his profession, and every year brought some increase of income and influence. But he had the American impatience of slow growth. Distinguished in some way he had always wished to be; and no avenue to the desired object seemed so short as the political race-course."[44] Selfish, unprincipled, irresponsible, and driven, the husbands in these stories give the impression that at some level of her consciousness Child may have recognized facets of David's character belying her description of him in letters as "honest and unselfish," "noble" and "kind," though a bumbler through no fault of his own.[45]

At the same time, Child seems to have modeled her victimized women on the self who could not "live without being beloved"—the self who had written to David: "Dearest *do* you love your forlorn little wife? . . . I dont know what I *shall* do if you dont love me."[46] When Oenone senses the emotional withdrawal of Corythus, manifested in his tendency to "forget that she was in existence," she asks plaintively, "you *do* love me; do you not?" (27). Abandoned by Corythus, she wastes away. The quadroon Rosalie and her daughter, Xarifa, similarly cannot "live without an atmosphere of love" (72). Alice Franklin of "Home and Politics," who, like Child, had idealized domesticity and "longed inexpressibly for a home," goes mad when her husband's bankruptcy wrecks her "little bower of beauty."[47] Looking back from the perspective of her failed marriage on the role of the "good wife" that she had once celebrated in her domestic advice books and tried to emulate in her life, Child seems to have judged this ideal deadly to women. In "The Children of Mount Ida," where Oenone inadvertently stimulates the political ambition of Corythus by revealing his royal identity and glorifying the court of Ilium in her clairvoyant trances, Child indicates that the wife who allows herself to be totally absorbed in her husband's identity contributes to destroying herself and her marriage.[48] (This lesson escaped Charles F. Briggs of the *Broadway Journal*, who ironically praised Child for having "unconsciously we suspect, drawn the portrait of a perfect woman, a wife and mother, in Oenone, a very different being from the Glumdalclitches who form the ideal of Miss Fuller's women.")[49] Together, these stories present a devastating critique of marriage, evidently distilled from the adversities and "withered hopes" that made Child confess to Francis Shaw: "In spite of myself, the sight of youthful love always throws a melancholy shadow over my soul."[50]

The most startlingly autobiographical of the stories in which Child reevaluates her marriage is "The Brothers." Its protagonists, two Quaker siblings named David and Jonathan, fall in love with the same woman. Jonathan declares his love before David has an opportunity to do so (thus sparing the bride the need to choose between them). All spend their lives together in a ménage à trois like the one Child had imagined for herself, but David must stifle his passion, channeling it into unselfish acts of charity. It is hard to miss the implications of a story that rewrites Child's life to give her John instead of David and to cast David rather than herself in the role of the disappointed lover forced to sublimate sexuality in self-sacrifice. It is also telling that "The Brothers" is one of the two stories in *Fact and Fiction* to depict a happy marriage (the other being "The Youthful Emigrant," in which the woman takes the initiative to propose marriage).

Tantalizing though such glimpses of Child's inner life may be to the biographer, they should not obscure the real significance of her fiction — its courageous and innovative treatment of subjects her culture sought to veil in mystification. Nor should they obscure her achievements as an artist. If Child used her fiction as an instrument for working out her marital and sexual conflicts, she also perfected it as an art form. As her friend John Sullivan Dwight put it in reviewing *Fact and Fiction* for Brook Farm's journal, *The Harbinger*, "Mrs. Child's . . . is a remarkably *progressive* genius. Each successive yield from her mind's store-house is of a deeper, finer, and more solid quality. . . . Nothing is more remarkable than the variety of the flowers woven into this wreath of 'Fact and Fiction.' They are of all climes and of all spheres of passion."[51] Child's stories of the 1840s differ markedly from the historical fiction she was writing in the 1820s. Their range, diversity, and experimentation with such genres as science fiction and the "documentary" tale[52] reflect the intellectual maturation and mastery of her craft that she had now attained. The best of these stories devise new literary strategies for promoting the two causes Child found most pressing — the abolition of slavery and the liberalization of sexual mores.

Child had begun developing the short story into a vehicle for converting readers to abolitionism as early as the 1830s, first in the *Juvenile Miscellany* (1830–34), then in her antislavery gift book, *The Oasis* (1834).[53] None of her *Miscellany* and *Oasis* stories attempted to probe the sordid recesses of master-slave relations, however, or to depict the institution as it was practiced in the United States. The first writer to do so was a young lawyer named Richard Hildreth. When his anonymously published novel *The Slave; or, Memoirs of Archy Moore* had appeared in 1836, Child had greeted it as a major contribution to the "progress of the cause." "People of the dullest minds and the coldest sympathies are thrilled by it, as if their benumbed fingers had touched an electric chain," she had reported in a letter to the *Liberator*. Praising its unsparing delineation of slavery and its accuracy of detail, she had ended her panegyric with the wistful avowal: "If I were a man, I would rather be the author of that work, than of anything ever published in America."[54] The qualification "if I were a man" poignantly testifies to Child's awareness of the limitations imposed on nineteenth-century women writers. No woman could assume the viewpoint of a rebellious male fugitive and narrate his story in the accents of "fiery indignation" he would naturally use — the device she had most admired in *Archy Moore*.[55] Hildreth's success nevertheless fired Child's ambition to write an antislavery novel aimed at women readers. She would have to formulate a different approach, she realized, for any work that "took the *same* ground as Archy Moore would seem utterly tame in comparison."[56]

The novel she started some time between fall 1836 and spring 1837 apparently centered on the activities of abolitionist women, featuring her friend Maria Weston Chapman as a "prominent character," according to Caroline Weston.[57] Prevented by writer's block from completing it during David's absence in Europe, Child seems to have destroyed the manuscript. Not until November 1840 would she find it possible to take up the task she had laid aside in 1837. At that point the demands of the occasion — Chapman's request for contributions to her fund-raising gift book, *The Liberty Bell* — and the burdens of housework in Northampton and then of editorial work in New York combined to direct her toward the short story rather than the novel.

As Child's comments on *Archy Moore* indicate, she recognized that fiction had the potential to arouse the "benumbed" sympathies of hostile or indifferent readers by impelling them to imagine themselves in the place of slaves. She also recognized that fiction would lose its attraction for such readers if it strayed too close to the disturbing contents of the antislavery tract. The challenge she faced was to exploit the emotional appeal of fiction without sacrificing the veracity of factual documentation. Her three stories for *The Liberty Bell* — "The Black Saxons" (1841), "The Quadroons" (1842), and "Slavery's Pleasant Homes" (1843) — address this problem in different ways.

"The Black Saxons," which focuses on the theme of slave revolt and refutes the myth of the loyal contented menial, offers a variant of the male model established by Hildreth. In lieu of impersonating a slave rebel, Child enters the consciousness of a kindhearted, scholarly slaveholder named Mr. Duncan, caught between the conflicting influences of the " 'system entailed upon him by his ancestors' " and of "republican sympathies" and "democratic theories deeply imbibed in childhood" (190, 193). Through Mr. Duncan, she induces readers brought up on the ideals of the American Revolution to apply those ideals to African American slaves. Anticipating the insights of twentieth-century scholars like E. J. Hobsbawm, she also propounds a philosophy of history developed further in her 1842 editorial, "Our Anglo-Saxon Ancestry."[58]

By coincidence, Mr. Duncan finds himself reading Thierry's *History of the Norman Conquest* on an evening during the War of 1812, when all of his slaves have asked for permission to attend a prayer meeting in the woods. As he ponders the fate of his Saxon ancestors, who "sank to the condition of slaves" after their defeat by Norman invaders, he wonders how many unknown heroes continued to resist Norman rule. "[C]onquerors write their own History," he notes (190–91), echoing Child's assertion in the *Appeal* that the slaves' "tyrants have been their historians!"[59] But he speculates that oppressed peoples have "minstrels of their own; unknown in princely halls, untrumpeted by fame, yet singing of their exploits in spirit-stirring tones, to hearts burning with a sense of wrong." Thus, reading between the lines of the conquerors' history, Mr. Duncan interprets the legends of outlaws like "Robin Hood and his bold followers," who took refuge in the forests and harried their oppressors in periodic raids, as evidence of a prolonged struggle for freedom. "Troubled must be the sleep of those who rule a conquered nation!" he moralizes (191).

Ironically, Mr. Duncan does not see any connection between his Saxon ancestors and his slaves until he rings the bell for a glass of water and remembers that he is alone in the house and that prayer meetings in the woods have become unusually frequent of late. Suddenly he recalls hearing that British troops are about to invade the state and that an escaped slave named Big-boned Dick has been "holding a rendezvous for runaways, in the swampy depths of some dark forest" — a thought that comes "unbidden and unwelcome, into incongruous association with his spontaneous sympathy for Saxon serfs, . . . and his admiration of the bold outlaws, who lived by plunder in the wild freedom of Saxon forests" (192–93).

Child does not bring Mr. Duncan to free his slaves — a denouement she views as unrealistic, given "the prejudices of [his] education, and the habits of his whole life" (193). Rejecting a pat moral ending, she opts for a strategy that allows her simultaneously to articulate and to distance herself from the militant spirit of rebellion Hildreth's hero had voiced. Mr. Duncan decides to accompany his slaves in disguise to their next prayer meeting, which turns out, as he had guessed, to be a secret convocation to determine the best means of obtaining their freedom. There, he listens as they debate how to secure their liberty — whether by bloodlessly deserting to the British, or by first murdering their masters. All agree that they do not want to "work . . . for nothing any longer" and that they should take advantage of "a good chance" to end their bondage (197, 199). They disagree only on whether or not to revenge themselves on their masters in the process. Child endorses the romantic racialist notion that the African temperament is innately docile, predisposing blacks against violence except under "excessive provocation."[60] Hence, she divides the debate along racial lines: those who most vociferously advocate murder are mulattoes, while those who carry the day by invoking the example of Jesus are full-blooded blacks. She does not foreclose the possibility of violent reprisals, however, for "not a few" leave the meeting "in wrathful mood, muttering curses deep" (203). The slave to whom Child gives the last word — an "uncouth" black who speaks in dialect — argues (as Frederick Douglass would in his 1845 *Narrative*) that "knowledge" is the key to freedom.[61] Urging his fellow slaves to master literacy, whether or not the British troops land, he promises: "and den, by'm bye, you be de British *yourselves!*" (200, 202).

Child ends the story by shifting from fiction to fact — a technique that not only emphasizes her purpose in telling it, but reinforces the warning it conveys to those who, like Mr. Duncan, confine their "republican sympathies" and "democratic theories" to white men. Several years after his adventure in the woods, she writes, Mr. Duncan visited Boston "and told the story to a gentleman, who often repeated it in the circle of his friends" (204). Child claims to have "told it truly," as she heard it, "with some filling up by imagination." Neither in the "real" nor in the "fictitious" story does the threatened slave revolt materialize — Mr. Duncan "contented himself with advising the magistrates to forbid all meetings whatsoever among the coloured people until the war was ended" (204). But Child leaves both Mr. Duncan and the reader with the knowledge that black Robin Hoods and Wat Tylers are lurking in the forests, ready to lead a strike for liberty.

In her next antislavery story, "The Quadroons" (1842), Child turned away from the male mode of "The Black Saxons" and set about adapting the conventions of women's fiction to expose an aspect of the slave system that she had first broached in the *Appeal* — the sexual exploitation of slave women and its "degrading effect . . . on the morals of both blacks and whites."[62] This "delicate" subject had dominated women's antislavery discourse for a decade, yet it remained out of bounds for polite literature, and the custodians of social respectability continued to stigmatize the radicals who dared to speak of it as unwomanly. Testifying to the stranglehold such taboos still exerted as late as 1840, an angry note in the *Liberator* berated the "fashionable, exclusive, and delicate-nerved, ladies of the north, who cannot condescend to append their 'honorable' names to an anti-slavery petition, and who manifest a most refined and exquisite indignation at the idea of a woman employed in procuring signatures to such a paper. . . ." Such self-styled "ladies," not the brave activists they accused of transgressing woman's " 'appropriate sphere,' " had actually " 'unsexed' themselves of all the sympathies and emotions which belong to woman's nature as God made it," charged the writer.[63]

In "The Quadroons" Child sought to create a literary form capable of appealing to the very sensibilities that prevented "fashionable, exclusive, and delicate-nerved ladies" from inquiring into the condition of their enslaved sisters. The problem she wrestled with was how to transmute the unsavory facts she had collected in the *Appeal* into fiction palatable enough to attract unsympathetic consumers. It was an enterprise fraught with contradictions: the conventions of romance must serve to dispel readers' romantic illusions about slavery; a language shorn of ugly details must convey the violence of the institution to an audience convinced that abolitionists exaggerated its cruelty; a code of gentility that did not protect slave women against rape or white women against their husbands' philandering must govern fictional treatment of sexuality; above all, a heroine representing a concession to racial prejudice must somehow serve to counteract prejudice.

The fictional strategy Child devised in "The Quadroons" was to personify the evils of slavery in a figure that has come to be known as the "tragic mulatto."[64] Light-skinned and genteel, the "tragic mulatto," with her mixed racial origin, embodies the hypocrisy of the South's sexual code, which dogs her throughout her life. Her tragedy consists in sharing the sensibilities, tastes, and moral standards of the white readers she resembles, yet being subject to the sexual exploitation and abuse endured by the black slave woman whom most readers refuse to acknowledge as their sister. Rosalie and her daughter, Xarifa, exemplify different versions of the tragic mulatto's plight. Both love white men barred by law and custom from marrying them. Rosalie's conscience, as strict as any white woman's, requires that her mother's church, at least, sanction her union with Edward, even if "the ceremony gave her no legal hold on Edward's constancy" (62); when he takes a white wife ten years later, she refuses to carry on an illicit relationship and soon dies of grief. Xarifa's lot is more sordid. Several years after her mother's death, she finds herself claimed as property by the creditors of her white grandfather's estate. Auctioned off to a profligate, who kills her white lover, she dies a "raving maniac" (76). Meanwhile, Edward has drunk himself to death, having sacrificed the woman he sincerely loved to his society's perverted racial and sexual code; and his white wife, whom he married solely to advance his political fortunes, has learned that she, too, has been nothing but a pawn in the hands of the men who rule her world. The story's twin plots inspired a long line of variations on the tragic mulatto theme, beginning with Stowe's *Uncle Tom's Cabin* (1852) and William Wells Brown's *Clotel* (1853).[65]

Melodramatic and sentimental, "The Quadroons" is dangerously flawed from a modern perspective: its heroines' preference for white lovers suggests a repudiation of their African roots, and their clinging dependency and utter lack of inner resources grossly misrepresent slave women. Yet these very defects may explain why the story struck such a responsive chord in nineteenth-century white readers.

Child herself found found "The Quadroons" embarrassingly cloying, as she admitted in her cover letter to Chapman. "You and Caroline [Weston] will laugh at it heartily," she ruefully anticipated, "but the young and romantic will like it. It sounds, in sooth, more like a girl of sixteen, than a woman of forty; and I can give no rational account how I happened to fall into such a strain. The fact is, I was plagued to death for a subject, and happened to hit upon one that involved much love-making."[66] Child's letter indicates her awareness of the conflicting demands her fiction had to meet from sophisticated antislavery activists and unconverted general readers. But it also conveys the impression that the story had welled up out of her unconscious. She clearly projected onto Rosalie and Xarifa the side of herself that had uncritically embraced her culture's pernicious ideal of womanhood. Her readers may well have shared her covert sense of identification with these pathetic victims of a sexual code under which all women suffered.

Although "The Quadroons" achieved Child's aim of formulating a literary strategy that could enlist genteel readers in the antislavery cause, it does not seem to have satisfied her aspiration to harness the imaginative power of fiction without softening the indictment of slavery she had presented in her tracts and editorials. She attained that goal in one of her greatest stories — "Slavery's Pleasant Homes. A Faithful Sketch" (1843) — which still ranks among the masterpieces of antislavery fiction. This story portrays a darker-hued slave heroine who, unlike Rosalie and Xarifa, rejects the dubious honor of a white gentleman's attentions, chooses a lover from among her fellow slaves, and dies resisting her master rather than mourning the loss of her white lover.[67] It also fuses the narratives of female sexual exploitation and male rebellion by dramatizing a slave's murder of his master in retaliation for the rape and murder of his wife.

Child evidently based "Slavery's Pleasant Homes" both on newspaper articles she had read over the years and on interviews with fugitive slaves. Her skillful use of these sources gives the story an unmistakable ring of authenticity. Two of the articles that inspired her plot date back to the early 1830s. Indeed, Child had cited them in the chapter of the *Appeal* titled "Moral Character of Negroes." The first, derived from "a Georgia paper," had reported the murder of an overseer by a slave "goaded to frenzy" at seeing his wife whipped. "The Georgia editor viewed the subject only on one side," Child had noted dryly, "viz. — the monstrous outrage against the white man — the negro's wrongs passed for nothing!" (201). She similarly ends "Slavery's Pleasant Homes" by quoting from "Georgian papers" and pointing out their one-sidedness. The second article, which had appeared in the *Liberator* in 1832, explained the circumstances behind the murder of an overseer on a plantation in Santa Cruz belonging to a prominent Bostonian. The murder had been touted by antiabolitionists as evidence of "what diabolical passions these negroes have!," and the newspapers had called the perpetrators "negro devils" and "incarnate fiends"[68] — slurs Child cites in her purported extracts from the southern and northern press in "Slavery's Pleasant Homes." As Garrison had reported in the *Liberator*, however, further investigation of the case revealed that the overseer had taken "a fancy to two of the negroes' wives," "chained [them] to [his] bed-post, and flogged [them] unmercifully, to compel them to submit to his orders."[69] The outraged husbands had taken "justice into their own hands" and stabbed the overseer to death. In "Slavery's Pleasant Homes" Child focuses on the tragedy of one young slave couple and shifts the blame for the wife's rape from the overseer to the gentleman slaveholder — an alteration that makes her story a more damning indictment of the slave system than the *Liberator* article on which she founds it.

The aspect of the Santa Cruz incident that had most strongly engaged Child's imagination, leading her to incorporate it into her defense of the Negro's "Moral Character," had been the murderers' loyalty to their fellow slaves. Although they themselves had escaped detection, they had voluntarily confessed their guilt to save those who had been wrongly charged with the crime from execution (206). Despite an act of moral heroism surpassing that of Damon and Pythias, Garrison had editorialized, "Not a voice was raised in their favor, and they were shot like dogs" — a comment Child echoes in the final sentences of "Slavery's Pleasant Homes."

What apparently revived Child's memory of the incident and suggested the idea of turning it into a story for the *Liberty Bell* was a new outbreak of "Horrible Events" publicized by the southern press in 1842. Reprinting the *Natchez Free Trader*'s grisly account of a lynching conducted to punish a gang of slaves for their "unheard-of cruelty" toward two white women, Child had speculated that as in the Santa Cruz incident, whose particulars she recalled for *Standard* readers, an inquest would prove that the slaves' "demoniac" fury had been "incited by brutal outrages on *their* wives or daughters. . . ."[70] Whenever she read of barbarities committed by either blacks or Indians, Child moralized, she always asked herself: "What was *their* side of the story? What long-continued, insupportable wrongs drove human nature to such frightful atrocity, such reckless desperation?" She sought to provide an answer in "Slavery's Pleasant Homes."

Child set her scene not among field slaves — a class about whom she knew little and who were too uncouth to attract the sympathies of her genteel readers — but among the house slaves and wealthy owners of an elegant mansion. For details illustrating the intercourse between slaves and masters and setting forth the household arrangements that lent themselves to sexual intrigues, she relied on the reminiscences of the fugitives she had encountered. Two in particular, "Annette Gray" and "Robert Lee," whose narratives she had published in the *Standard*, supplied her with many of the specifics responsible for the story's unusual realism.[71]

Child had probably worked out the main outlines of her plot when an article about the sequestration that southern "chivalry" imposed on the upper-class white woman caught her eye. Appearing in the *Portsmouth Journal*, and reprinted by Child in the *Standard*, it portrayed southern ladies as products of a social system that reduced them to denatured harem slaves:

> A seclusion, almost Mahommedan, is demanded of [woman] by the exactions of southern fashion. . . .
>
> . . . The Odalisque of the harem is delicate as the half-opened petals of the rose of the East, and this is all her boast, for when this fragile attractiveness is faded, her whole mission in life is over. . . .
>
> . . . [T]here is apparent, upon a close observation of southern life, a species of lurking and secret jealousy of women — an oriental desire of confining her to a state of restriction and surveillance — an overweening anxiety in man to engross all her social as well as domestic relations to himself alone. . . .

Shifting to another analogy, the author then compared the "boasted, yet bastard chivalry of the South" to its medieval prototype. Under both systems of chivalry, he (or she) asserted, woman is "regarded, in external form, as a goddess, to be worshipped, but at the same time and in reality, as a child and plaything, to be allowed no will of her own."[72]

The metaphors of the harem slave and the plaything must have struck Child as peculiarly appropriate, for she developed them into central conceits of a story aimed at exposing slavery's desecration of the home. In her *History of the Condition of Women* she had long ago noted the many cultural practices setting women "in the light of property," equating them with slaves, subjecting them to male tyranny, and defining them as sexual objects.[73] There, however, she had shrunk from exploring the connections between the interlocking systems of slavery and patriarchy, with the different types of oppression they entailed for women of color and their privileged white sisters. Now the timely publication of the *Portsmouth Journal* article at the right juncture in her psychological development seemingly prompted her to devote her most trenchant story for the *Liberty Bell* to this theme.

Grounded in Child's twin studies of slavery and the status of women, based on actual incidents reported in the press or recounted by slaves, elaborating on metaphors popularized by Romantic literature, and addressed to the women readers of gift book fiction, "Slavery's Pleasant Homes" brilliantly counterpoints fact and fiction as it attempts to re-create the slave's "side of the story." Its technical virtuosity instantly strikes a modern reader. From the outset, the interplay between the title "Slavery's Pleasant Homes" and the subtitle "A Faithful Sketch" suggests a conflict between rival literary modes — romance and realism.[74] Readers who want romance, it hints with self-conscious irony, had better beware of looking for it in a plantation setting.

The deflation of romantic stereotype begins in the very first sentence: "When Frederic Dalcho brought his young bride from New-Orleans to her Georgian home, there were great demonstrations of joy among the slaves of the establishment, — dancing, shouting, clapping of hands, and eager invocations of blessing on the heads of 'massa and missis;' for well they knew that he who manifested most zeal was likely to get the largest coin, or the brightest handkerchief" (147). Immediately afterward, Child introduces the metaphor that defines the plantation not as a Christian home, but as an Islamic seraglio. "The bride," she observes, borrowing the language of the *Portsmouth Journal*, "had been nurtured in seclusion, almost as deep as that of the oriental harem" (148). Through this metaphor, Child establishes a parallel between Frederic Dalcho's bride Marion and her slave foster sister Rosa. Both occupy the position of harem slaves to whom Frederick will claim exclusive sexual access in the tradition of the Oriental despot.

Having intimated that slavery turns the home into a harem, Child proceeds to examine the resulting perversions of domestic relationships. Marion and Rosa have "grown up from infancy together," suckled by the same mother, yet Marion's consciousness of her superior rank warps the affection she feels for her foster sister: as "soon as the little white lady could speak, she learned to call Rosa *her* slave" (148). Raised to be nothing more than a "pretty little waxen plaything," Marion in turn treats Rosa as a plaything, decorating her with jewels like a doll. Both women suffer diminishment, but of the two, Rosa suffers more, for nature has endowed her with greater beauty and vitality. Recalling the Odalisque to whom the *Portsmouth Journal* had compared the southern lady, Marion is "as fragile and as delicate as the white Petunia blossom." In contrast, Rosa is "beautiful as a dark velvet carnation" — a longer lasting and hardier flower. "[L]ike a glittering star," capable of generating its own light and heat, she has been set "in attendance upon the pale and almost vanishing moonsickle," whose feeble rays merely reflect the light of the sun.[75]

The violation of nature is equally flagrant in the case of Frederic and his "handsome quadroon brother" and "favorite slave," George. As George remarks bitterly: "we grew up side by side, children of the same father; but I am his slave. Handsomer, stronger, and more intelligent than he; yet I am his *slave*" (149, 156).

Reflected in the distorted sibling relationships is the sexual license of the harem. Inevitably, the marriage of Marion and Frederic will follow the pattern long since set by Frederic's father, when he indulged in a liaison with a slave and reared her son alongside his wife's. As if to heighten the difference between natural and perverted sexual relations, Child makes the developing love between Rosa and George arouse Frederic's lust. The scene pulsates with dramatic intensity:

> [Rosa] wore about her neck a small heart and cross of gold, which her lover had given her the night before. [George] smiled archly, as he glanced at it, and the answer from her large, dark eyes was full of joyful tenderness. Unfortunately, the master looked up at that moment, and at once comprehended the significance of that beaming expression. He saw that it spoke whole volumes of mutual, happy love; and it kindled in him an unholy fire. He had never before realized that the girl was so very handsome. . . . [H]e glanced at his young wife. She, too, was certainly very lovely; but the rich, mantling beauty of the slave had the charm of novelty. (150–51)

Of course, few slaves could have afforded gold ornaments. Still, by drawing on romantic convention and depicting Rosa and George in an attitude familiar to genteel readers, Child is enabling those readers to identify with slaves. The gift itself, moreover — a heart and cross of gold — serves to foreshadow the outcome of the young slaves' love and to symbolize the brute reality beneath the gilded surface of their lives. Their hearts are indeed destined to be crucified in a manner that will shock readers out of their romantic fantasies.

For Rosa and George a natural expression of "mutual, happy love" finds an unnatural consummation, spelling out the meaning of slavery and patriarchy. Pursued by her master, Rosa cannot rely for protection on either her lover or her mistress. George is but a slave, and a revelation that would raise "a storm" in his "proud and fiery" heart would only endanger them both (151). As for Marion, her own helplessness soon becomes apparent. Noticing her husband's "singularly capricious and severe" treatment of George, she tries to "remonstrate with him" and to learn why he opposes the lovers' marriage, but the intercession merely subjects her to a sharp retort that leaves her in tears. At last, events reach their inescapable climax: "One night, Marion was awakened by the closing of the door, and found that Frederic was absent. She heard voices in Rosa's apartment, and the painful truth flashed upon her. Poor young wife, what a bitter hour was that!" (152).

Child's staging of the scene faithfully reproduces the details furnished to her by "Annette Gray" and "Robert Lee," both of whom had described the master's habitual midnight visits to the chambermaid as "distinctly audible" to his wife, as well as to the attendants who slept on the floor of her room.[76] She also patterns the ensuing confrontation between Rosa and Marion on Gray's narrative. Like Gray, who "could not look [her] mistress in the eye" after such visits and "could [not] help hanging [her] head for shame," Rosa avoids "looking in [Marion's] face, and [keeps] her eyes fixed on the ground." And like Gray's mistress, who was sometimes "violently cross, and scolded me for every thing," but would then try to "make up" for her outbursts, Marion "angrily" accuses Rosa of "awkwardness" and gives her a "blow," but soon melts into tears, and the two end up weeping in each other's arms (153). If Child follows Gray's narrative in muting the usual consequences of the slave mistress's impotence to control her husband's promiscuity — the redirection toward her slave of the jealous rage she cannot direct toward her husband — she allows no illusions about the southern mistress's ability or willingness to break the silence that legitimizes the slave system's sexual duplicity and violence. Neither woman, she comments pointedly, "sought any further to learn the other's secrets" (153). After this scene, Marion all but disappears from the story.

Meanwhile, her husband unleashes against Rosa the full fury of his own jealousy. "[E]xasperated . . . beyond endurance" by Rosa's manifest preference for George, whom she continues to meet secretly in defiance of their master's orders, Frederic swears to "overcome her obstinacy, or kill her": "[O]ne severe flogging succeeded another, till the tenderly-nurtured slave fainted under the cruel infliction, which was rendered doubly dangerous by the delicate state of her health. Maternal pains came on prematurely, and she died a few hours after" (155). With exquisite rhetorical tact, Child succeeds in evoking a scene whose every element is unmentionable in polite society: a husband's rape of his wife's foster sister; a gentleman's sadistic flogging of a "tenderly-nurtured" woman; a pregnancy resulting from illicit sex;[77] a miscarriage induced by violence.

Adding another dimension to the pattern of disrupted domestic relations that Child exposes in "Slavery's Pleasant Homes" is the connivance of a mulatto slave named Mars, who spies on Rosa and George and informs the master of their stolen interviews. Since he, too, lusts after Rosa and derives his power to injure her from the institution that governs their lives, Mars acts as an extension of his master. Yet he originally belonged to Marion, whom Child does not exonerate from responsibility for Rosa's death. The name Mars, of course, symbolizes the essence of slavery — war. The god of war, Child implies, always presides over slavery, whether practiced by a kind mistress or a brutal master. On another level, Mars represents the fate of human brotherhood under slavery. Just as slavery has falsified the actual sibling relationships between George and Frederic, Rosa and Marion, so it has eroded the potential solidarity of the slaves themselves.

The final phase of "Slavery's Pleasant Homes" — and the most daring for a woman writer — shifts the focus from Rosa's victimization to George's revenge. Here Child's devastating indictment of slavery and patriarchy culminates in the justification of slave revolt. The passage setting the scene for George's retaliation against his master reiterates the motif of violated nature that runs through the story: "But a few months ago, how beautiful and bright was Nature — and now, how inexpressibly gloomy" (156). From this survey of the landscape, George's train of thought, as he stands over Rosa's grave, moves into recollections of the graceful girl whose lacerated body now lies "cold and dead beneath his feet." Significantly, Child leaves unformulated the thought that climaxes this series of associations when George looks toward his master's house and groans, "He murdered my poor Rosa."

Instead, she presents George's ensuing murder of Frederic through Marion's sleeping consciousness: "On that night, Marion's sleep was disturbed and fitful. The memory of her foster-sister mingled darkly with all her dreams. Was that a shriek she heard? It was fearfully shrill in the night-silence! Half sleeping and half waking, she called wildly, 'Rosa! Rosa!' But a moment after, she remembered that Rosa's light step would never again come at her call" (157). A tour de force, the technique fuses George's murder of Frederic with Frederic's prior murder of Rosa. The effect is to emphasize that the true criminals are Rosa's master and mistress. Symbolically, the dagger found in Frederic's heart when Marion awakens from her troubled sleep turns out to be "the one he had himself been accustomed to wear" (158). The slaveholder's violence, Child shows, has come home to him.

Child does more than exculpate George, however. She portrays him as a hero. Like his prototypes in the Santa Cruz case, George nobly confesses to the murder rather than let another man pay for the crime he himself has committed — even though that man is his enemy, Mars. Going beyond her source, Child underscores the contrast between George's generosity and the slaveholder's vindictiveness, between George's innate sense of justice and the injustice of a legal system that convicts a slave "with slaveholders for judges and jurors" (158). Whereas George cannot look on unmoved as his enemy is brought forward to be hanged, "Planters rode miles to witness the execution, and stood glaring at their trembling victim, with the fierceness of tigers" (159). Whereas George has compassion for the man whose tale-bearing has led to Rosa's murder, slaveholders have none for the slave whose wife the master has raped and flogged to death. Echoing Garrison's editorial on the Santa Cruz case, Child comments: "No voice praised [George] for the generous confession. They kicked and cursed him; and hung up, like a dog or a wolf, a man of nobler soul than any of them all" (160).

Child's finest stroke is to end her story by juxtaposing fact and fiction — a technique Melville would later use in "Benito Cereno" and *Billy Budd*.[78] Representing what conventionally passes for fact are newspaper accounts of the story Child has just told. "*Fiend-like Murder*," announces the headline in the Georgian papers. The article reads: "Frederic Dalcho, one of our most wealthy and respected citizens, was robbed and murdered last week, by one of his slaves. The black demon was caught and hung; and hanging was too good for him" (160). With barbed irony, Child notes that "The Northern papers copied this version; merely adding, 'These are the black-hearted monsters, which abolition philanthropy would let loose upon our brethren of the

South.' The role of the northern press, as she knew too well, was not to provide a different perspective on slavery, based on independent investigation, but to subserve the interests of slaveholders and the merchants, bankers, and textile manufacturers constituting their northern allies.

Child lets her readers decide whether the term "fiend-like murder" applies better to Rosa's or to Frederic's murder. She simply reminds them of the crucial facts the newspapers have omitted: "Not one was found to tell how the slave's young wife had been torn from him by his own brother, and murdered with slow tortures. Not one recorded the heroism that would not purchase life by another's death, though the victim was his enemy. His very *name* was left unmentioned; he was only Mr. Dalcho's *slave!*" (160). Through such omissions, Child suggests, the proslavery press has turned a victim into a criminal, a hero into a monster, a man into a thing.

Thus, having begun by puncturing the illusions of romantic fiction, "Slavery's Pleasant Homes" ironically closes by laying bare the mendacity of factual reportage. In the hands of the master class, both prove equally unreliable as media for transcribing what Child had called the slave's "side of the story." It is doubly appropriate that the story should come back full circle to the question of fiction versus fact, for that was the central question Child faced as an antislavery propagandist. She had tested the limits of the two modes available to her for arousing public sentiment against slavery and had found neither adequate. Tracts, eyewitness testimony, slave narratives, and antislavery newspapers provided a far more accurate view of life under slavery than romantic fiction could pretend to, yet "delicate-nerved ladies" did not want their sensibilities harrowed by graphic accounts of "indecencies" and "villainies" that "woman dare not name."[79] Stories like "The Quadroons" could move such readers, but only at the cost of dangerous concessions to the very prejudices and misconceptions abolitionists sought to overcome. In "Slavery's Pleasant Homes" Child succeeded in buttressing fiction with the authenticity of fact and charging fact with the emotional power of fiction. She did not succeed, however, in producing a story that "delicate-nerved ladies" and censorious gentlemen would read, much less one that a commercial publisher would risk handling. As a result, Child excluded her most incisive antislavery story from a collection centrally concerned with the theme she had explored in "Slavery's Pleasant Homes": *Fact and Fiction*.

In espousing the antislavery cause "at the bidding of conscience," Child had "enter[ed] the arena" of public controversy to "struggle for . . . the rights of others."[80] Longer than most of her radical sisters in the movement, she had resisted acknowledging that she identified with the slave because she, too, felt oppressed. When her disillusionment with her marriage at last forced her to confront her repressed anger and thwarted sexuality, Child's attention began to shift from the plight of the slave woman coerced into unwanted sexual relations toward that of the white woman punished for yielding to her sexual desires. Her rupture with the American Anti-Slavery Society naturally furthered this reorientation. Although Child did not totally suspend work for the antislavery cause — reprinting many of her antislavery writings in her commercially published volumes, for example, and helping fugitive slaves to elude pursuit and find employment[81] — she devoted the bulk of her fiction after 1843 to probing the sexual ideology that had entrapped her and to adumbrating alternative cultural possibilities. Her most impressive achievements in this domain are her three stories of fallen women — "Elizabeth Wilson" (1845), "Hilda Silfverling" (1845), and "Rosenglory" (1846) — and her Indian tale, "She Waits in the Spirit Land" (1846).

Child's stories of fallen women are striking for the tolerant attitude they take toward sexual laxity, especially in an era of sexual repression governed by an ideology of female "passionlessness."[82] Unlike the Evangelical moral reformers who first took up the defense of the fallen woman in the 1830s, Child's sympathy for these victims of the double standard did not lead her to support a more repressive code of conduct for both sexes.[83] On the contrary, it prompted her to put herself in the place of men who rebelled against genteel norms by becoming "libertines"; "I had *almost* said, I do not *blame* them," we may recall Child admitting to Francis Shaw.[84] Again and again, Child insists that sexual desire is a natural instinct in women as well as in men and that it is an appropriate expression of two people's love for each other. What is unnatural, she suggests, are the social codes banning sexual relations outside marriage, tabooing marriages between people of different classes and races, and defining women who transgress these sexual boundaries as pariahs. Thus, in "Elizabeth Wilson," "Rosenglory," and "Hilda Silfverling," Child portrays her fallen heroines as adolescent girls who merely succumb to the " 'strong necessity of loving,' which so pervades the nature of woman" ("EW" 127) — the same necessity she recognized in herself, as she confessed to Shaw. Child refuses to condemn them for it. Challenging her readers to reexamine the moral distinctions they make between themselves and the women whose case histories she fictionalizes, Child argues in "Rosenglory": "If the gay, the prosperous, and the flattered find it pleasant to be loved, how much more so must it be to one whose life from infancy had been so darkened? Society reflects its own pollution on feelings which nature made beautiful, and does cruel injustice to youthful hearts by the grossness of its interpretations" ("R" 249).

The autobiographical parallels that link Child to her fallen heroines reveal how deeply she identifies with them. Elizabeth Wilson, Susan Gray of "Rosenglory," and Hilda Silfverling all lose their mothers at an early age, as Child had; indeed, Elizabeth's traumatic memory of seeing her mother's body "with large coins on the eye-lids" ("EW" 128) may well be Child's. Like Child, Elizabeth not only grows up avid for love, but suffers from the emotional deprivation of being cast on the hands of a father whose idea of "parental duty" consists of providing food, clothing, and education in the three R's: "Of clothing for the mind, or food for the heart, he knew nothing; for his own had never been clothed and fed" ("EW" 128). For both Elizabeth and Susan, as for Child, separation from a beloved older brother compounds the pain of bereavement. All three of Child's heroines undergo the banishment from home that scarred her so indelibly as a girl of twelve, though unlike herself, Elizabeth and Susan are bound out to service, and Hilda, whose poor relatives "could not well conceal that the destitute orphan was a burden," voluntarily leaves to seek work in the city ("HS" 205). In short, Child projects onto her heroines the innate need for love and the formative experiences of bereavement and exile that shaped her own psyche, tracing the consequences they might have had under different external circumstances.

Lonely, unprotected by family ties or social position, and callously treated by their employers, these orphaned servant girls are "naturally prone to listen to the first words of warm affection" they hear, as Child writes of Hilda ("HS" 206). What follows for Hilda — "the old story, which will continue to be told as long as there are human passions and human laws" ("HS" 206) — applies to Elizabeth and Susan as well. That is, all three become defined as fallen women when their lovers fail to marry them. Yet Child does not blame her heroines' "fall" on rampant male sexuality, nor does she characterize their lovers as heartless seducers. For example, she writes of Hilda's lover Magnus: "To do the young man justice, though selfish, . . . he did not mean to be treacherous to the friendless young creature who trusted him. He sailed from Sweden with the honest intention to return and make her his wife; but he was lost in a storm at sea. . ." ("HS" 206). Similarly, Robert Andrews, the son of fifteen-year-old Susan Gray's first employers in "Rosenglory," "had no deliberately bad intentions; but he was thoughtless by nature, and selfish by education" ("R" 248).

In each case Child attributes the heroine's predicament to a hypocritical social code rather than to either partner's sexual licentiousness. That code prevents genteel men from marrying the servant girls with whom it allows them to trifle; hence, Elizabeth Wilson's lover abandons her for a "good-looking widow, with a small fortune" ("EW" 137), and Robert's mother dismisses Susan after catching the young couple in each other's arms. The code also requires genteel women to cooperate in enforcing the double standard, as Susan's next employer does by discharging her without her wages and accusing her of being "impertinent" for having insinuated that the master of the house made advances to her ("R" 253–54). In its deadliest manifestation the code dooms the unwed mother to "disgrace," tempting her to resort to infanticide — the crime for which Elizabeth Wilson is executed and Hilda Silfverling is "condemned to die" ("HS" 207).

While directing her censure at the social system rather than at the men who lead her heroines astray, Child explicitly presents it as a system designed and controlled by men to serve their interests. In "Rosenglory," the very magistrate who sends Susan Gray to Blackwell's Island later propositions her — a fact Child explains by invoking the feminist theory she had pronounced "distasteful" to her only five years earlier.[85] Had Susan "read or heard anything about 'Woman's Rights,'" Child points out, she might have understood why men could freely commit the acts for which they sentenced women to imprisonment: "it was because men made all the laws, and elected all the magistrates" ("R" 255).

Based on the story of Amelia Norman, "Rosenglory" dramatizes the views Child had articulated polemically in her account of Norman's trial. Curiously, the plot does not follow its heroine toward the rehabilitation Child had helped Norman to attain. Instead, it serves as a vehicle for Child's crusade against "society's treatment of criminals" by illustrating what might have happened to Norman had she been convicted and incarcerated with hardened offenders.[86] No longer able to obtain respectable employment after emerging from prison, Susan now accepts Robert Andrews's offer to support her as his mistress. And when he tires of her and tells her to "get [her] living as others in [her] situation" do ("R" 259) (the same words Norman's seducer had used), Susan does not try to kill her betrayer, as Norman had, but turns to prostitution and ultimately dies of disease — the fate nineteenth-century fiction typically meted out to the fallen woman.

Child's adherence in "Rosenglory" (and "Elizabeth Wilson") to the pattern of the classic fallen woman story might seem surprising in the light of contemporary analogues that depict the rehabilitation of the erring protagonist. Two such stories, Martha Russell's "Melinda Dutton" and C. M. Sisson's "The Reclaimed," actually appeared in the *Columbian Lady's and Gentleman's Magazine* a few months after "Rosenglory."[87] And Hawthorne's *The Scarlet Letter* (1850) readily comes to mind as the most famous example. Yet invariably (and *The Scarlet Letter* is no exception), narratives that allowed a fallen woman to repent for her sin did so at the price of repressing her sexuality and consigning her to a life of nunlike devotion to others. Such a resolution could hardly have attracted Child, who was all too familiar with the role of the sister of mercy. What engaged her imagination was the possibility not of redemption from sin, but of liberation from sexual taboos. She explored this possibility in "Hilda Silfverling" and "She Waits in the Spirit Land." Significantly, Child had to abandon the mode of realism and travel beyond the boundaries of her culture before she could envision a sexual order in harmony with nature. It was no coincidence that she traveled to the Scandinavian dreamland she associated with Ole Bull and to the Indian wilderness she had found so enticing in her youth.

A science fiction tale subtitled "A Fantasy" and set in eighteenth-century Sweden and nineteenth-century Norway, "Hilda Silfverling" begins as a conventional fallen woman story on the model of "Elizabeth Wilson." When it reaches its heroine's trial and conviction for infanticide on circumstantial evidence — the end of Elizabeth Wilson's story — it swerves from that model, however. Elizabeth eventually becomes at least an accomplice in infanticide because she is cast off by her father and stepmother for having brought "disgrace" on them with her pregnancy: "no kind Christian heart strengthened her with the assurance that one false step in life might be forgiven and retrieved" ("EW" 139). Hilda, on the other hand, succeeds in safeguarding the future of her baby by finding a surrogate mother — a Norwegian peasant woman working in Stockholm as a laundress — who agrees to adopt it.

Although the utopian world of the future will provide a refuge for Hilda, the patriarchal world of the present subjects her to unremitting persecution. Every institution of patriarchy acts against her. The society that has failed to protect her as an orphaned adolescent, and that offers her no means of raising the illegitimate child whose birth it stigmatizes as a "disgrace," self-righteously accuses her of infanticide when a baby is found "strangled with a sash very like one Hilda had been accustomed to wear" (207). Despite the absence of conclusive proof, a male tribunal sentences Hilda to death. A male scientist who has "discovered a process of artificial cold, by which he could suspend animation in living creatures, and restore it at any prescribed time," petitions to consign Hilda to this experiment in lieu of beheading. A male metaphysician seconds the proposal, for the sake of the knowledge to be gained by "put[ting] a human being asleep thus, and watch[ing] the reunion of soul and body, after the lapse of a hundred years." Male government officials approve the request, "for no one suggested a doubt of [the] divine right to freeze human hearts, instead of chopping off human heads, or choking human lungs" (208).[88] A male chaplain lends his sanction to the proceeding and finds himself too "embarrassed" by uncertainty over the fate of her soul in the interval to tender Hilda the customary religious solace. Male "public functionaries" install her in the icy provisional tomb to which patriarchal justice has condemned her, and in which she is surrounded by frozen embodiments of masculine ferocity—a bear, a snake, a crocodile, and a wolf (209–11). Hilda's final journey "in a close carriage from the prison to the laboratory" (209) sums up the essence of patriarchal society and what it represents for women.

The laboratory itself is Child's central symbol of the perversions resulting from the system of male dominance and class privilege that she probes in her stories of fallen women. "[B]uilt entirely of stone, . . . rendered intensely cold by an artificial process," illuminated only by the "dim and spectral" light "admitted from above through a small circle of blue glass," and devoted to arresting the life functions of natural creatures, the laboratory parodies and inverts the creative powers that patriarchy punishes in women (209). It also parodies Christianity, which it enlists in support of the economic rapacity this life-denying establishment upholds. Describing the "huge bear" lying on one of the laboratory's stone shelves, "with paws crossed on his breast, as devoutly as some pious knight of the fourteenth century," Child comments: "There was in fact no inconsiderable resemblance in the proceedings by which both these characters gained their worldly possessions; they were equally based on the maxim that 'might makes right'" (209).

So intolerable is the atmosphere of the laboratory that even the men who have "attended the prisoner, to make sure that justice was not defrauded of its due," cannot remain in it for more than a few minutes. The public functionaries hastily retire, "complaining of the unearthly cold," and the chemist in charge of the experiment presses Hilda to drink her potion quickly, "for I am getting chilly myself" (209–10). His parting words and the action that belies them reverberate with ironies, prophetically evoking the horrors unleashed by science and rationalized by doublespeak in our own century—the gas chambers, the atomic bomb, chemical and biological weapons, and the lethal industries polluting the planet. "You will fall asleep as easily as a babe in his cradle," he promises, as he "cover[s] his face with a mask, let[s] some gasses escape from an apparatus in the centre of the room," and rushes out of the laboratory, "locking the door after him" (210–11).

The second half of the story—which opens a hundred years later, after Hilda has been ceremoniously "resuscitated" in the presence of "a select scientific few" so that her physical symptoms can be carefully studied (212)—takes its heroine into a utopian world where she can begin life anew. Intriguingly, Hilda's rebirth and release from the laboratory in which she has been "frozen for a century" occurs on February 10, 1840—one day before Child's thirty-eighth birthday. That year in Northampton, Child had felt herself to be "freezing to death by inches" as she reached the nadir of her married life; in February 1843 she had celebrated her birthday by deciding "not to follow David's movements any more."[89] The synchronism suggests that in this 1845 "Fantasy," Child is imagining the possibility of reliving her own life through a persona magically enabled to cancel her past and make a fresh start. Accordingly, she fulfills in fiction the desires she has had to renounce in reality. She who had never recovered from the trauma of losing her mother and being expelled from home by her father allows her orphaned heroine to find a new home with surrogate parents: on awakening from her "centennial slumber" (214), Hilda goes to Norway, where she is adopted by a peasant couple who have recently lost a daughter. Forty-three years old in 1845, and acutely conscious of her advancing age, Child confers the gift of perpetual youth on her heroine: Hilda does not age in her sleep, like Rip Van Winkle, but remains "in the bloom of sixteen" (213) like Sleeping Beauty.[90] Although she herself had had to accept the consequences of an ill-starred marriage in a society that discountenanced divorce and remarriage, Child departs radically from the conventions governing stories of fallen women by awarding her heroine a second chance for happiness. The new lover she conjures up for Hilda—a Norwegian named Alerik Thorild, who turns out to be the great-grandson of Hilda and Magnus—reproduces the mother-son bond of Child's relationship with John Hopper and strikingly recalls both surviving accounts of John and her own descriptions of Ole Bull.

Like John, whom an acquaintance memorialized as "a whole theatre in himself," a born "comedian" with the gift of "cur[ing] dyspepsia, physical and moral," by making "the world *laugh at itself*," Alerik is an inveterate play actor and practical joker who cures Hilda of melancholy and keeps everyone around him laughing.[91] Like Bull, whom Child had characterized as "vigorous yet gentle," "free, gushing, spontaneous," and "earnest," Alerik is "vigorous," "expressive," "tender and earnest" (222, 231). Contrasting Bull with those who "repress their inward life" to conform to society's dictates, Child had rhapsodized: "he is a most delightful person—gentle as the flute, various as the violin, lively and *naive* as the oboe." She uses almost exactly the same words to explain why Hilda is so "delighted" by Alerik: "[H]is 'smile most musical'" was always "in harmony with the inward feeling, whether of sadness, fun, or tenderness. Then his moods were so bewitchingly various. Now powerful as the organ, now bright as the flute, now *naive* as the oboe" (231). Alerik even shares Bull's musical "genius." He plays the violin and the flute, improvising according to his moods: "Sometimes all went madly," "[s]ometimes . . . the sounds came mournfully as the midnight wind through ruined towers," and "when his soul overflowed with love and happiness, oh, then how the music gushed and nestled!" (231). Intensely "alive," Alerik's music stirs Hilda as powerfully as Bull's music stirred Child.[92]

Whatever private fantasies Child wove into "Hilda Silfverling," she conceived the story not as a covert outlet for her buried desires, but as a vehicle for transcending the limits that nineteenth-century social convention placed on women's sexual freedom and for exploring alternatives barred by cultural taboos. Hence, she rescued her heroine from the confines of the realistic fallen woman narrative by resorting to science fiction — a genre that feminist writers have found exceptionally conducive to reenvisioning gender roles and sexual practice.[93] She also drew on folklore — another field that permitted great imaginative license — casting Hilda in the role of Sleeping Beauty and Alerik in the role of a folk character Carroll Smith-Rosenberg has called "the ideal feminist hero": the Trickster.[94]

Tricksters appear in narrative cycles the world over, but Child probably derived her concept of this folk figure from Norse mythology, where his best-known avatar is the god Loki. The reasons why such a figure so aptly serves the purposes of a story concerned with sexual liberation become obvious when we note that folklorists have seen in the Trickster the "life of the body" personified — "*the spirit of disorder, the enemy of boundaries,*" hierarchies, and taboos. Among his/her many attributes are "indeterminate sex and changeable gender." Bawdy, libidinous, and incestuous, the Trickster often opts in his male incarnation for a "mother or grandmother bond." He/she generally enjoys "privileged freedom from some of the demands of the social code," defies authority, and indulges in "amoral and asocial" behavior. But creative as well as destructive, the Trickster may simultaneously perform the function of the Culture Hero or Savior. In addition, he/she is "independen[t] . . . of temporal and spatial boundaries," "perpetually young or perpetually aged," "ambiguously situated between life and death," "between the social cosmos and . . . chaos," between the human and animal worlds. Finally, both in word and deed the Trickster dissolves the distinction between reality and fiction or representation.[95]

Detail for detail, this description applies to Alerik Thorild. Inasmuch as he is both Hilda's lover and her great-grandson (hence an extension of her), he is at once male and female, "perpetually young" and more than a century old. Their love is certainly an incestuous "mother or [great-]grandmother bond." Hilda's hundred-year sleep has situated her, at least, beyond "temporal and spatial boundaries," "between life and death," and even between the human and animal worlds, since she has slept alongside bears, wolves, and crocodiles. Alerik occupies the same liminal place.

Appropriately, Child introduces him through the tales told about him — a self-conscious allusion to his origins in folklore. "Ah, he was such a Berserker of a boy!" Hilda's foster mother Brenda begins her recital of his pranks. The Berserker, Child informs us in a note, is "[a] warrior famous in the Northern Sagas for his stormy and untamable character" (218). Her conflation of the Berserker with the Trickster reflects Child's awareness that the roles of these two folk figures are analogous. Indeed, scholars have defined the Berserker in nearly identical terms: "a member of a special class free from the laws which govern ordinary members of society," "representing the wild and fantastic in contrast with law and order."[96] Brenda proceeds to portray Alerik as a "rogue" perennially inventing "mischief," yet loved by everyone in the village, and as a hoaxer who can make people doubt the evidence of their senses (219). "There will be no telling which end of the world is uppermost, while he is here," agrees Hilda's foster father, Eystein Hansen, predicting "plenty of tricks" now that Alerik has returned to the village (221).

The practical jokes Alerik plays illustrate the antiauthoritarian, "amoral," and "asocial" nature of the Trickster. Their chief victim is *"Father* Hansen," as Child consistently calls him, pointedly underscoring his patriarchal status. Alerik disrupts a wedding and drowns out Father Hansen's singing in church while the latter, a clergyman's assistant, is trying to lead the hymn in accordance with "immemorial custom" (221); paints the old man's house brown so that he cannot recognize it in the dark; and plies Father Hansen with drink at the Wolf's Head tavern, with the aim of tricking the old man into shooting and apparently killing him. By turning Father Hansen's world upside down, Alerik is enabling the creation of a new world in which equality will replace hierarchy, divisions will give way to unity, proscriptions will vanish, and sexuality will enjoy free play. In this sense, Alerik typifies the Trickster's duality as a destroyer who acts as a creator, savior, or culture hero.

Alerik's creativity takes many forms. At the Wolf's Head tavern he stages a parody of ritual death and resurrection (situating him "between life and death"), tells stories, sings songs, and convulses the audience with laughter. A craftsman as well as a verbal showman, "[h]e can make anything he chooses," Father Hansen tells Hilda (220). Alerik has carved a wolf's head that looks alive enough to bite (231) (pointing to the Trickster's "human/animal dualism" and evoking Loki's fathering of the wolf Fenrir).[97] And he has built an organ that he plays "like a Northeast storm" (220). Alerik expresses his creativity most obviously in his music, which transmits the sounds of nature and links him to the Norse goddess of Love and Feeling, Freia, and to the Greek culture hero Orpheus.[98] Like Freia and Orpheus, he symbolizes the power of love and art over death, as his relationship with Hilda indicates. Although he does not literally deliver Hilda from the underworld, he does empower her to live down her shame and find happiness again; and since he looks exactly like his great-grandfather Magnus, he almost seems to have come back from the dead himself to marry her.

This brings us back to Child's motive for endowing Alerik with the attributes of the Trickster. As the product (albeit at several removes) of Hilda's womb, Alerik clearly incarnates the male part of her. He also embodies and defends her forbidden sexual impulses. Both functions are in keeping with the Trickster's mission — to celebrate the "life of the body" and to defy taboos.[99] That is why, when Hilda reveals to him that he is her great-grandson, he merely "burst[s] into immoderate peals of laughter" (233). The prohibition against incest represents the primal sexual taboo. The child's encounter with it marks the end of innocent pleasure in sexuality and the beginning of guilt and repression. Thus, Alerik mobilizes all his creative resources to make a mockery of the criteria defining incest; by freeing Hilda from the fear of committing the primal sin, he can free her from all the taboos that prevent sexual fulfillment.

The roguish arguments he uses to confound Hilda dazzlingly display the Trickster's ability to efface the distinction between fact and fiction — the sign of a consummate artist. Citing the Pythagorean theory of metempsychosis, Alerik suggests that all creatures, human and animal, belong to the same family. "If these things are so, how the deuce is a man ever to tell whether he marries his grandmother or not?" he asks, reducing the concept of incest to absurdity (233, 235). He then compares Hilda's account of her entombment in the laboratory to an array of myths and fairy tales involving metamorphoses, interchanged identities, and disrupted categories. Hilda's story is neither more nor less "true" than the others, he implies. If true, such stories leave no means of differentiating between animate and inanimate; human, animal, vegetable, and mineral — hence, no means of ensuring against incest. If fictive, they may safely be disregarded. When Hilda appeals to the authority of memory and sensory experience, Alerik retorts with jests full of sexual innuendoes about his irrepressible libido — the hallmark of the Trickster. The bear Hilda remembers seeing on the shelf opposite her in the laboratory "must have been a great bear to have staid there," he teases: "If I had been in his skin, may I be shot if all the drugs and gasses in the world would have kept *me* there, with my paws folded on my breast" (236). Similarly, when Hilda attempts to distinguish her "true story" from Alerik's "fairy" stories, and the Christian religion from the myths to which Alerik has referred, he intimates that the Christian religion has proved at best ineffectual in protecting women like Hilda and may well have contributed to their oppression: "But tell me, best Hilda . . . what the Christian religion has to do with penning up young maidens with bears and crocodiles? In its marriage ceremonies, I grant that it sometimes does things not very unlike that, only omitting the important part of freezing the maiden's heart" (237). Alerik's subversion of the incest taboo culminates in invoking a literal reading of the Bible to authorize his marrying his great-grandmother: "I have read in *my mother's* big Bible, that a man must not marry his grandmother [emphasis added]; but I do not remember that it said a single word against his marrying his *great*-grandmother" (237). In the guise of the Trickster, Child has succeeded in delivering patriarchal religion into the custody of the women it would imprison.

As Alerik's creator, of course, Child herself has played the role of the Trickster. By assuming a male persona, she, too, has transcended the boundaries of gender. And she, too, has challenged the incest taboo (a proscription painfully relevant to her relationship with John Hopper). In the process she has daringly reclaimed the right to sexual satisfaction for women as well as for men — and for the female author and reader as well as for their fictional projections.

An analysis of the story's ending nevertheless reveals the problematic character of the Trickster tale as an instrument for reenvisioning gender and sexuality. The genre exposes the arbitrariness of the social order it parodies, but as a leading folklorist has pointed out, "it produces no real alternative, only an exhilarated sense of freedom from form in general," which may or may not yield fruit in social change.[100] In Child's case the trickster tale allowed her to imagine escaping the consequences of a sexual misalliance (be it an illicit love affair or an unhappy marriage) and building a new life with another spouse, but it did not enable her to imagine an alternative to the patriarchal institution of marriage.

On the surface, "Hilda Silfverling" reaches an idyllic consummation. The lovers embrace in the sunset while twittering birds serenade them — a coded representation of intercourse. Flouting patriarchal convention, their union results not in punishment for breaking the incest taboo, but in "harmony with the peaceful beauty of Nature." Their ensuing marriage also divests Father Hansen once and for all of his patriarchal authority: "reluctantly" yet "good-naturedly," he "cease[s] to disturb modern ears with his clamorous vociferation of the hymns" (240).

Lurking beneath the final tableau of conjugal bliss, however, is the ghost of Child's disappointment in her own marriage — a ghost that always dogged her at the sight of young lovers, as she had confided to Francis Shaw.[101] When Hilda murmurs drowsily to Alerik, "Oh, it was well worth a hundred years with bears and crocodiles, to fall asleep thus on thy heart," she inadvertently suggests a disturbing parallel, rather than a reassuring contrast, with the scene in which she was put to sleep in the scientist's laboratory. The ambiguity registers Child's awareness that under the unequal conditions prevailing in her society (and reflected in Alerik's playful domineering of Hilda), marriage almost inevitably stifled a woman's growth. She might transcend those conditions in "Fantasy," but she had found them well-nigh insurmountable in real life.

Along with science fiction and the Trickster tale, anthropology and ethnographic fiction have frequently served as vehicles for feminist writers exploring alternatives to the repressive social and sexual relations of their own culture. Fascinated since her youth with the greater sexual freedom seemingly permitted by American Indian culture, Child had turned to these vehicles again and again. Five months after publishing "Hilda Silfverling," she confronted the staid readers of the *Columbian Lady's and Gentleman's Magazine* with a story that explicitly held up the "natural" sexual mores of Indians as a model to emulate: "She Waits in the Spirit Land" (March 1846).[102]

Neighbors from childhood, Wah-bu-nung-o and O-ge-bu-no-qua imperceptibly fall in love as they reach adolescence. Their unfolding sentiments for each other develop freely, unimpeded by censorious adults and unmarred by the guilt and shame that burden their "civilized" counterparts. "The simple philosophy of the Indians had never taught that nature was a sin, and therefore nature was troubled with no sinful consciousness," explains Child (194). "[N]ature, subjected to no false restraints, manifests her innate modesty, and even in her child-like abandonment to impulse, rebukes by her innocence the unclean self-consciousness of artificial society." In short, Child contends, the indecency and prurience her readers associate with sexuality are the product of repression; sexuality itself is not inherently "unclean" or shameful, but only becomes so when subjected to "false restraints"; and the civilized man or woman who condemns sexual indulgence as evil is far less pure-minded than the native who yields to the impulses of nature with "child-like abandonment" (194).

Accordingly, Child depicts her young lovers' relationship as evolving literally out of nature. After a long period of ripening into sexual awareness while performing their daily tasks side by side, Wah-bu-nung-o and O-ge-bu-no-qua linger past nightfall in a romantic setting on a beautiful spring evening. Among trees that have reached "noble proportions, because they had room enough to grow upward and outward, with a strong free grace" and birds whose singing betokens the "mating season," the Indian youth and maiden enact their own mating ritual (195). He plays "a rude kind of flute" reserved for "courting," and she "warble[s] a wild plaintive little air": "He spoke of love; of the new wigwam he would build for his bride, and the game he would bring down with his arrow. These home-pictures roused emotions too strong for words" (196). The erotic scene Child conjures up culminates in a metaphor of intoxication — the closest she dared come to evoking orgasm.

Driving home the contrast with "artificial society," Child comments pointedly: "When [Wah-bu-nung-o and O-ge-bu-no-qua] returned, no one questioned them. It was the most natural thing in the world that they should love each other; and natural politeness respected the freedom of their young hearts. No marriage settlements, no precautions of the law, were necessary. There was no person to object, whenever he chose to lead her into his wigwam, and by that simple circumstance she became his wife" (196).

As in "Hilda Silfverling," however, Child proved unable to sustain the vision of sexual liberation she transcribed in "She Waits in the Spirit Land." Even when it carried her beyond the bounds of civilization, her imagination remained haunted by the sense of guilt for forbidden sexual desires that made her identify with the fallen woman. She might decry the "sinful consciousness" her culture fostered, but she could not escape it. Symptomatically, her Indian lovers never enjoy another night together. The very next afternoon, war erupts with a neighboring tribe, and O-ge-bu-no-qua is captured and subsequently killed — almost as if Child were unconsciously punishing herself for her erotic fantasies. Indeed, from the very beginning, Wah-bu-nung-o has foreseen in a dream that his beloved will "go to the spirit-land" and leave him to "mourn alone" — a presentiment that overshadows the lovers' bliss (195). Once his fears materialize, he ritually renounces war and devotes the rest of his life to protecting the enemy chief who killed his beloved, lest her persecutor precede him into the spirit-land and continue to torment her there. The selfless course he elects irresistibly recalls Child's own self-sacrificing life. Similarly, the relegation of the lovers' reunion to the spirit-land suggests that she saw no possibility of happiness in the world of the flesh.

"I am struck with the saddened tone of so many of the tales," wrote Ellis Loring on receiving his copy of *Fact and Fiction*.[103] Though "charmed" with the book, which he pronounced "worthy" of Child, he admitted that it had depressed him. Most of the stories were better suited to "younger or gayer hearts" than his, he ventured. For reasons of her own, Child herself seems to have intended the book as a message to the younger generation. She dedicated it to Anna Loring, whom she called the "Child of my Heart" (a formulation John Hopper had hit upon).[104] But she worried that Ellis and Louisa might "find something in the book unfit for Anna" — an indication of how consciously she had pushed her critique of her society's sexual code to the outermost limits of acceptable feminine discourse. "Amused" at her apprehension, Loring assured her that all three of them were deeply touched.[105]

Unfortunately, no one besides Loring responded to the new book, except for Child's friend of Northampton days, John Sullivan Dwight, who gave *Fact and Fiction* "extravagant praise" in Brook Farm's *Harbinger*.[106] Of the journals that had reviewed *Letters from New York* so favorably, none noticed *Fact and Fiction*. The *Broadway Journal*, which had hailed "The Children of Mount Ida" on its publication in the *Columbian Lady's and Gentleman's Magazine*, had ceased to exist. Margaret Fuller, who had reviewed Child's works in *The Dial* and the *Tribune*, had left for Europe by the time *Fact and Fiction* appeared. Fuller's successor at the *Tribune* gave *Fact and Fiction* only a brief blurb as a Christmas gift book, mentioning it under the column for miscellaneous "City Items" rather than for "New Books," and the *Knickerbocker* and the *Democratic Review* entirely ignored it. Even the abolitionist press overlooked the book, despite the antislavery stories it included.

The silence that greeted Child's return to her vocation as a writer of fiction must have deeply shaken her, perhaps playing a role in turning her away from the genre and dampening the ambition to make a literary comeback that had originally energized her. By February 1847 Child was complaining to Francis Shaw of an increasing disinclination to write. She had received several letters from the prominent British author and reformer Mary Howitt, urging her to contribute to the *People's Journal*, she told Shaw. "But some how or other, I do not feel sufficient interest in anybody or anything, to take pen in hand very earnestly. None of the world's prizes seem to me worthy of the trouble it takes to gain them."[107] In July, rejecting the overtures of another English journal that had contacted her through Shaw, she reiterated that she never "felt *moved* to write anything . . . in these days." The reasons she gave Shaw suggest that a combination of personal and professional disappointments had undermined her sense of purpose in life. "I seem to have hopelessly lost my interest in the world and all it contains," Child confided:

> Of literary ambition, I am sorry to say I have not one particle. The honors of this world are so worthless, and so indiscriminately given, withal, that I regard them with utter contempt. As for money, it is of no use for me to make more than enough to feed and clothe myself decently. I cannot make a position for myself, as *men* can. As for good done to others, I cannot get up a faith that my writings are, or can be, worth much in that way. So you see the *motive*, the *propelling power* to exertion is every way wanting. I wish it were otherwise; but I cannot help it. I am indifferent to the game of life, and weary of the battle.[108]

The devastating crisis of confidence Child was undergoing had multiple causes. Notwithstanding her denial, she had had enough "literary ambition" to assert in another letter to Shaw, exactly three years earlier: "I mean to devote the remainder of my life to the attainment of literary excellence."[109] On reentering the literary arena in 1843, she had cast aside the feminine self-effacement she had imposed on herself since her marriage and had boldly determined to compete with men for the "world's prizes." She had also cast aside her self-protective posture of disinterest in women's rights and let herself feel her oppression and the anger against men that it fueled in her. She had even dared to cast aside her allegiance to the nineteenth-century feminine ideal of asexual purity and to let herself feel the sexual passion she had tried for so long to repress. The tremendous risks she had taken had left her extremely vulnerable, and they had apparently yielded nothing but defeat. She had built great expectations on the success of *Letters from New York*, only to have the literary establishment once again remind her that she could not aspire to the rewards reserved for men. She had "come out" on women's rights, while realizing that she would not enjoy the fruits of the struggle in her lifetime. She had ceased to believe that her writings could "do good" because she no longer upheld her culture's moral code. Most painful of all, she had left her husband and fallen in love with two other men, yet she was still alone and sexually unfulfilled, and she knew she could never resolve the dilemma without becoming a social outcast.

Several events had converged with her dashed literary hopes to precipitate this crisis in 1847. Margaret Fuller's departure for Europe the previous August, had accentuated Child's loneliness in New York and evoked options she herself could not elect. The Lorings, too, were planning a trip to Europe early in 1847. Ole Bull had drifted out of her life. And that January John Hopper had begun courting a beautiful and musically accomplished young woman, Rosa De Wolf. By March it had become obvious that the young couple was heading toward marriage, although the bitter opposition of Rosa's wealthy antiabolitionist father seemed likely to delay matters. Putting a cheerful face on the prospect, Child wrote to Susan Lyman: "It would be right pleasant to me to live in the same nest with Rosa, and have her have a little child, that I could adopt for my own. A *musical* child it would be, of course; and if it was *very* magnificent, I would name it Ole." At the very moment when Child was comforting herself with these fantasies, however, John was taking advantage of an ostensible business trip to elope with Rosa. "The news of their marriage came upon me like a thunder-clap," Child admitted to Susan. With her usual realism, she immediately began preparations to move out of the Hopper household. Sharing a home with a young couple never worked well, she told Susan, "even in the case of a mother and her own and only son." The wistful postscript she added nevertheless betrayed how much the relationship had meant to her and how difficult it was to relinquish: "John used to think he could *never* get accustomed to living without 'little Zippy Damn,' and I thought I could not possibly get along without *him*. But human nature is a strange thing. It now seems as if it were at least three years, since we were mutually accustomed to be so dependent on each other."[110]

The phase of her life that Child would later describe as her "brief Indian summer in New York"[111] had ended, and with it the burst of creativity it had generated.

15

The Progress of Religious Ideas: A "Pilgrimage of Penance"

I have never been so much depressed in spirits. . . . You talk of my being a saint of the 19th century. Alas, I am poorly calculated for it now. The experience of the last eight years has terribly shaken my faith in human nature. However, I will try to do the best I can with what remains of my once strong and electric nature. Resignation to life is all I now aim at, or hope for. My external relations are too much at war with my interior life. I give up the long contested battle, and surrender myself prisoner.[1]

Addressed to Ellis Loring as Child was preparing to relinquish her hard-won independence forever, this chilling admission of defeat sums up the mood that would govern her life and dictate her choices for almost a decade, beginning with John Hopper's marriage in March 1847 and ending with her father's death on Thanksgiving day, 1856. It would be a decade of expiation, renunciation, and reassessment. Coinciding with the disappointment of her literary ambitions, the shock of losing the love relationship that had sustained her since the disintegration of her marriage — and perhaps the distress of squarely facing its real nature — would drive Child to undertake what she later called "a real pilgrimage of penance, with peas in my shoes, walking over rubble-stones most of the way."[2] Intellectually, that pilgrimage would culminate in *The Progress of Religious Ideas, Through Successive Ages* (1855), a formidable three-volume comparative history of religion in which Child would liberate herself once and for all from orthodox strictures, not only by disputing Christianity's claim to divine inspiration, but by rejecting the sexual asceticism so pervasive in Christian tradition. Accommodation rather than liberation would mark the terminus of Child's pilgrimage in other spheres of her life, however. Socially, she would finally accept the constraints her culture placed on her freedom as a woman, reassuming the bonds she had broken when she had left her husband and parted ways with her father. Emotionally, she would satisfy her craving for love in the only way she could: by nurturing the two men who needed her most. Psychologically, she would atone for her illicit passion through a series of sacrificial acts: moving back to rural Massachusetts for David's sake and "conforming [her] own tastes and inclinations to his";[3] writing a biography of Isaac Hopper (who had also played the role of a father in her life, not least as the father of her beloved John) and devoting its proceeds to his family; and, above all, nursing her father through three years of incontinence and growing senility until his death at age ninety.

Child embarked on the first stage of her penance — self-inflicted exile on the isolated New Rochelle farm of the Quakers Joseph and Margaret Carpenter, where she and David had stayed in 1835–1836[4] — almost immediately after John returned to New York with his bride. "Never was such a lonely place!" she wrote, describing the hermitage into which she had withdrawn. The Carpenter home was "thirty miles up in the country," and four miles from the train depot. "In the stillness of twilight the whizz of the very far-off steam-cars sometimes reaches my ears; and that is all I hear of the turmoil of the world," she announced to her friends. She had "not even heard a dog bark" since arriving, and had "met no living thing" on the road "except one pig and four geese." Completing the picture of anchoritic retreat, her tiny room was so "low-walled" that the ceiling almost hit her head.[5]

The rationale Child gave for burying herself in a spot so removed from the metropolitan stimulation of concert halls, art galleries, lecture rooms, and libraries, which she had cherished in New York, was that the "country air" would be "better for David." "For six or eight months past, the state of David's 'pecunary' affairs, and his decreasing health, have made me anxious to curtail my expenses by going into the country," she explained to Louisa. Couching the move as a transfer of maternal care from a son who no longer needed her to one who now took precedence, she added that heretofore, despite her concern for David, "I could never see my way clear about leaving my impulsive and ardent friend John without some companion who would make a home for him."[6] David already enjoyed "country air" in Northampton, however, and he showed no inclination to put their marriage back together. He spent barely a month visiting his wife in New Rochelle before returning to his chosen home. Although Child found the brief reunion "a faint gleam of the good old times," David's behavior would indicate that their estrangement persisted. He did not answer Child's frantic letters inquiring about his health and imploring him to rejoin her instead of spending the "cold dreary months" of winter "shut up" in his Northampton farmhouse.[7] "I am so much accustomed to his never coming, that 'I never expect him till I see him,'" Child at length admitted.[8] The truth was, David had nothing to do with her decision to seclude herself in New Rochelle; rather, she was engaged in a religious quest for absolution and solace, seemingly prompted by the guilt she felt over her love for John.

A story she published in April 1848, "The Hindoo Anchorite," spells out the meaning of that quest with tragic clarity.[9] It describes the life-throttling penance a Hindu sage undertakes, to atone for having yielded to his passion for "a beautiful girl of inferior caste," of whom he has become "desperately enamored . . . according to that powerful law of human nature which impels man to desire most that which is forbidden" (2: 151). When his beloved dies after a four-year liaison, the anchorite Kanoua strives to purify himself by bringing up their son "perfectly safe from the temptation which had dragged him downward in his own saintly career" (2: 151). Together, father and son pursue the Hindu ideal of "absorption in the Divine Mind" by "complete annihilation of the body" — literally achieving their goal in death (2: 153). The story reflects Child's sense of having violated a taboo for which she could only atone by sacrificing her "adopted son" and withdrawing from the world. It also expresses her desire for release from suffering. Like her Hindu protagonist, she sought that release through religion.

Child had turned to religion several times before during difficult periods of transition, most notably during the marital crisis reflected in *Philothea*. Although Swedenborgian mysticism continued to furnish her with a refuge from worldly troubles, Child had felt increasingly estranged from the Swedenborgian church, because of its leaders' dogmatism and hostility to abolition. During her years in New York she had renewed her search for a religion that could fulfill the conflicting demands of her social conscience, her reason, and her heart. She had attended churches of every denomination, including a Jewish synagogue and a Catholic cathedral, but had found none congenial. "My soul is like a hungry raven, with its mouth wide open for the food which no man offers," she lamented to Lucy Osgood:

> The Unitarian meetings here chill me with their cold intellectual respectability. Mr. Barrett, the Swedenborgian, has only transferred the padlock of his chain from St. Paul to Swedenborg. He is so narrow and bigotted, that when I come within his spiritual sphere, I feel like a bird under an exhausted receiver. At the Calvinistic meeting in the next street, the preacher, in his prayer, says, "We thank thee, O Lord, that there is a hell of despair!" I quote his very words. At the Episcopal churches, the minister, with perfumed handkerchief, addresses ladies in silks and satins, with prayer-books richly gilded, and exhorts them to contribute something toward building a chapel for the poor; it being *very* important that the poor should be taught sufficient religion to keep them from burning the houses and breaking open the stores of the rich.
>
> Now what can a poor sinner, like me, with such an intense abhorrence of shams, do in such places? . . . I assure you that it is hard work to keep from rushing out of the nearest window, through the painted glass, at the risk of demolishing the image of St Paul, or breaking Peter's sword, in my exit.[10]

However alienated by the custodians of organized religion, Child still longed for a faith in which she could find peace. Understandably, her spiritual quest grew especially urgent after the dissolution of the substitute "marriage" she had created for herself in New York. Such appears to have been her motive for retiring into "*complete* solitude" and "reading much about God and the soul."[11]

During her two-year sequestration in New Rochelle, relieved only by occasional visits from friends and brief trips to New York and Boston, Child succumbed to the most paralyzing depression she had ever experienced. Far from healing her wounds, her flight from the "turmoil of the world" left her feeling "all alone on a rock in the middle of the ocean."[12] "[N]ow I am really growing old; growing so in my *feelings*, which

I never before have done," she brooded, with the grim prospect of a solitary middle age looming before her.[13] Exacerbating her sense of having been cheated out of love and sexual satisfaction, her body retained its youthful energy. "Every spring in my machinery is elastic, every wheel is oiled," she commented ruefully to Susan Lyman.[14] Susan, who had just announced her engagement to a Calvinist minister named Peter Lesley, suffered from delicate health, as did John's bride, Rosa, and Child wished she could "by some magnetic process, impart . . . a portion of [her] strength" to her two young friends. She must also have wished she could receive a portion of their happiness.

The "discouraged, reckless, unhealthy state of mind" with which Child was vainly wrestling expressed itself in a recurrent dream of death — a dream so real to her that in March 1849 she actually devoted a week to setting her affairs in order and burning letters she considered compromising (339 in all).[15] Apparently she was reliving the trauma of her mother's death, which had occurred at almost the same age (forty-eight in the case of Susannah Rand Francis, forty-seven in Child's case).[16] If so, the association was perhaps triggered by the guilt and self-blame that linked her memory of having failed in filial duty toward her dying mother with her fear of having failed in wifely duty toward an aging husband, whom she perceived as having lost his moorings. It may also have been triggered by her sister Mary's death in September 1847. Although Child had totally lost touch with Mary, the news would naturally have revived memories of the triple bereavement she had experienced when her mother had died, her sister had "married and left home," and her father had dispatched her to Mary's distant household in Norridgewock. The curiously insensitive letter of condolence Child sent to her niece Sarah conveyed the impression that she was now identifying no longer with the twelve-year-old self who had so desperately needed a mother, but with the weary mother who had welcomed death as a release from the burdens of housekeeping and childrearing. Admonishing Sarah that her mother's death was "[s]ad for *you*, but not for *her*," Child wrote:

> From my earliest youth I have always had a very strong desire not to live to be very old.
> But though to her it was a blessing to depart, it must be a deep sorrow to you, who have always lived with her, and been accustomed to her constant maternal care. Your father must feel the separation from his life-companion more acutely than any other one can feel her loss.[17]

So completely had she transferred her allegiance that she could only conjecture an orphaned daughter's sentiments, reserving her sympathies instead for the parents by whom she had once felt abandoned. She was also indicating how fervently she wished to die, as she would confirm by literally preparing to die eighteen months later.

Ultimately, Child managed to convert a suicidal gesture into a therapeutic process. As she reread the hundreds of letters the Lorings and other dear friends had written to her, she realized that the isolation in which she had been languishing had been self-willed. Having "foolishly" taken a notion that the Lorings had "laid [her] on the shelf," she had forgotten what "friendly heart-warmth" pervaded their letters, and how much love and camaraderie the large bundles marked "Ellis and Louisa" contained. Though she burned them anyway, the "tender recollections" they aroused prompted her to renew contact with the "angels of blessing" who had stood by her so loyally, and to make "strong resolutions to keep out of the shadows."[18]

As with her preparation for death, Child's immersion in religious literature had a positive outcome, whatever the impulse behind it. Her extensive reading seems to have convinced her that no church or creed could supply the wants of her soul, that indeed no "revelation written for one age or in one age can be adapted to all ages" — not excepting the revelations the Old and New Testaments purported to chronicle.[19] As early as April 1848, she evidently conceived the idea of turning her private quest to public account, for she confided to Marianne Silsbee that she was "very busy in making extracts, and reading innumerable books" with a "literary project" in mind.[20] It was a project requiring "so much study, that 'the serpent has a file to bite,' with a vengeance!" she volunteered a few months later to Susan Lyman, whom she asked to send her a sampling of the "terrible anathemas and iron doctrines of Calvinism."[21] By then the drift of her research could already be discerned. The "investigations" she was pursuing gave "a terrible shaking to old customs and traditions," she hinted to Parke Godwin.[22] And to Marianne Silsbee she sarcastically underscored the implications of Harriet Martineau's newly published *Eastern Lands, Past and Present*:

> She says very coolly that most of the laws and institutions of Moses "he obtained from the Egyptians, from what source he received the remainder is unknown.". . . Now if that be the fact, how *awful* it has been to reverence them so long! Of *course*, God never inspired an Egyptian! Oh no indeed! He confined himself to his "peculiar["] people, the Jews; and a very peculiar people they were, it must be confessed.[23]

Although Child could have indulged more safely in disseminating such heterodox opinions had she oriented herself toward an esoteric audience, she chose instead to design her "book of religions, for the *common* mind."[24] The mission she undertook was to liberate her contemporaries from the shackles of dogma and bigotry — an endeavor she knew would arouse the ire of the clergy. From the outset, Child strove against anxieties that stymied her work, as she girded herself for the storm of abuse she expected. "I am not sustained by the least hope that my mode of treating the subject will prove acceptable to any class of persons," she acknowledged to her brother Convers a year after starting her research.[25] The following year, with the manuscript hardly any nearer completion — a most uncharacteristic delay for her — Child was still complaining, "My learned book is a dreadful tedious job, and one at which I work without much heart; for I foresee that it will make me unpopular."[26] *The Progress of Religious Ideas* would in fact take Child eight years to write. The protracted agony of its composition, repeatedly interrupted for months on end by unsettled living conditions, domestic responsibilities, financial worries, bouts of depression, and the writer's block induced by all these impediments, mirrored her efforts to resolve the conflicts that had launched her on her "pilgrimage of penance."

Chief among the questions Child faced while laboring on her monumental study was whether or not to rebuild her marriage. The conditions that had led her to separate from David remained unchanged. Since the collapse of his beet sugar experiment in 1843, David had gone "from one failure to another with unbounded enthusiasm," as Child's old friend Mrs. Lyman (Susan's mother) noted dryly. One year he had contracted to cart stones for the railroad. "He verily believes that he shall realize [a profit of] $2000 . . . for stone that will cost an outlay of only $150. I might try to convince him that the contractors must be crazy to make such a bargain; but it is of no use to argufy," Child reported in exasperation to Louisa.[27] Predictably, he had lost ten cents on every load—to which Mrs. Lyman had responded, "if he has got hold of anything by which he loses only ten cents a load, do encourage him in it!"[28] Another year David had planted tobacco and neglected to superintend its curing, letting it stay in the barn "till it was too dry to be rolled properly." Unburdening herself to Susan, Child fumed: "Sometimes these things make me laugh, and sometimes they make me cry."[29] Recently, having got wind of a scheme to make a fortune on peat, David had been planning to have the peat on his Northampton farm analyzed by an agricultural expert. "I want you to avoid expending money upon it; and if I were you, I would not talk much about it with any one. . . . So much for my old habit of *advising*," Child remonstrated.[30] Given David's "love of *vast* plans," what frightened Child more than the peat speculation was her presentiment—shrewdly accurate as it turned out—that he would "catch the California fever" and want to join the 1849 Gold Rush. "[I]f he succeeded in making any money, he would lose it all before he got back, by investing it in some magnificent plan to make *more*. He is not the person to be among such a set of swindlers and sharpers as swarm in California," she judged with brutal realism.[31] Meanwhile, David was serving an apprenticeship with his brother John in Tennessee, who as chief engineer of the Mobile Railroad Company was supervising the building of a railroad line from Mobile to Cincinnati. The wages were a mere forty dollars a month, out of which his travel expenses were to be paid, but Child was pinning her "*last* hope" on John—the only member of their family who had ever succeeded in business—to convert the apprenticeship into a steady job, at least for the next few years.[32]

She had few illusions that David could overcome the habits of carelessness, unreliability, and "*procrastination*" to which she attributed his checkered career. "I do not think he *can* change, if he tries ever so hard," she wrote bluntly to her mother-in-law.[33] The latest indication of how futile it was to try to help this overgrown Child had been the fate of the "four new shirts" she had sewn for him when he stopped in New Rochelle on his way to Tennessee: "One of them he left at West Boylston, by accident; the other three were stolen from him before he reached Cincinnati. So he had no good from them during his hardships in the woods. It is curious how much of my life has been spent pumping into sieves."[34]

Poor though the prognosis for his reformation might be, David's very helplessness tugged at Child's conscience. He was now well over fifty. How long could he endure the toll of hard manual labor? During his stint in Tennessee, he had caught typhus fever and lain ill for weeks "in a miserable log-hut, with only an old slave to nurse him."[35] Even under normal circumstances, his protracted bachelorhood had not taught him to cook healthy meals for himself, let alone wash and mend his own clothes. On each of his few short visits Child had spent days getting "his garments into comfortable and respectable condition."[36] "I have ripped open your carpet bag, in want of the key, and hired a strong woman, and had all your blankets and old rags washed clean. What a mess they *are*, to be sure!" she chided David, who had gone to see his mother in West Boylston after his return from Tennessee.[37]

Aside from feeling responsible for a husband so obviously unfit to fend for himself, Child was suffering from loneliness. Although she moved back to the Hoppers' in March 1849 (because the Carpenters could no longer spare the room they had been renting to her), the proximity to a young couple blissfully in love only intensified her loneliness. David's last visit, moreover, had offered "a little glimpse of the good old times. Thank God even for that *little* glimpse!" Looking back on it with "grateful and affectionate thoughts," Child begged David to return before setting off again for Tennessee. "I will try to make everything as pleasant as I can, and not to recall any pictures of our bad luck," she promised. "Come to your little old partridge as soon as you can. She is not in a state to drum much with quills or otherwise now; but she is capable of making a warm nest yet."[38]

David did return in September, and they enjoyed "quite a second honey-moon; a little flowery oasis in the desert of our domestic life," as Child confided to Louisa. Intriguingly, in the very next sentence, she asked: "What think you of Margaret Fuller's marriage and motherhood?" It was as if she were reading lessons for herself in the romantic outcome of Fuller's odyssey — her secret wedding with the Italian nobleman Angelo Ossoli, seven years her junior, during their participation in the 1848 Roman revolution. Yet in the midst of this "second honey-moon," Child could not repress misgivings about what a permanent reunion with David might mean, for she prefaced her account of their reborn happiness with the anecdote about David's shirts.[39] The same ambivalence crept into a letter Child wrote to Marianne Silsbee: "It is *so* pleasant to have a sympathizing friend in my loneliness. Domestic love *is* the best of earth's blessings, and worth having even at the price of many heavy drawbacks."[40]

The "domestic love" of which Child spoke was undoubtedly genuine. Deeply rooted humanitarian ideals had always constituted a strong bond between the Childs, and she had never ceased to characterize David as truly great-souled, however "mal-adroit . . . in all practical matters."[41] "I see no one who seems to me to have such a large, noble, generous, kind heart," she reiterated through the years.[42] If David did not share her enthusiasm for music and art, he did share her sense of humor, her detestation of "shams," and her religious iconoclasm. As she recounted to Ellis Loring: "I was reading to [David] the other day a poetical account of Chrishna's flute-playing, from the sacred Pouranas of the Hindoos. He remarked, with the utmost gravity, 'I always thought

Jesus would have been much more interesting, if he had taken an interest in the fine arts.'" In contrast, Loring, with whom Child had enjoyed greater intellectual companionship than with almost anyone else, had bridled at David's irreverence and huffily reminded them both that "the character and precepts of Jesus loom up in heavenly beauty above the other religious teachers of the world."[43]

Despite their many affinities, profound temperamental differences remained a source of frustration, as did David's apparent sexual deficiency. "I sometimes wish that he was more mercurial, or I was less so," Child confessed to Marianne Silsbee.[44] Still, the needs David didn't satisfy in her had to be weighed against the devastating loneliness she had been experiencing.

Child also had to weigh the "price" she would have to pay for "domestic love." The "many heavy drawbacks" of life with David came to the fore all too soon. Months went by without the expected summons from his brother John, forcing Child to conclude that her husband had again proved remiss. "Perhaps David may not always have been as prompt as he ought to have been; though I have no reason to *think* so, except from my knowledge of his character," she conjectured to Ellis Loring. She also suspected that John considered "David's abolition likely to be injurious to his own interests," since the railroad line he was building traversed slave territory, and David had not concealed his antislavery views during his sojourn in Tennessee.[45]

As a result of John's defection, which occurred after David had rented out his Northampton farm, leaving him at loose ends, the decision about whether or not to risk resuming conjugal life was all but taken out of Child's hands. The further problem now arose of determining where to reside. Initially, Child had counted on finishing her book in New York, where she had easy access to the libraries she needed. She had "paid *in advance*" for library privileges and had "many borrowed books which [she] could not spare, and should not like to carry."[46] Besides, she had reached "the most perplexing part of [her] troublesome book" (probably the "Retrospective View" in volume 2, summing up the resemblances between Judaism and other religions of the ancient world) and did not want to be interrupted. "I have been so *dreadfully* hindered ever since I began the confounded job!" she complained. "Obliged to toat *up* to N. Rochelle with all my books and papers; to go back and forth 36 miles to libraries; then obliged to toat *down* from N. Rochelle with all my books and papers." The thought of putting up with another dislocation at this stage was intolerable. Boarding at the Hoppers' had also presented the advantage of freeing Child from most domestic chores. But John and Rosa were occupying the apartment she had previously rented, and the tiny attic room the Hoppers had given her was much too small for two, and unbearably hot in the summer. Moreover, the cost of living in New York, affordable as long as Child had had only herself to support, would be prohibitive with a husband earning no income and perpetually subject to financial temptations.

Everything pointed toward the solution of returning to rural Massachusetts and renting a "humble little place, with three or four acres of ground," where David could "raise fruit and vegetables in the summer, and write Latin, or translate, or copy law papers, in the winter."[47] "In resigning myself to this inevitable destiny, and conforming my own tastes and inclinations to his, I find peace of mind; but it takes all the electricity out of me," Child wrote sadly to Loring. Once again, her thoughts wandered suggestively from her own marriage to Margaret Fuller's. Immediately after the news about herself and David, she commented to Loring on the proof their mutual friend Emelyn Story had just provided that Fuller had indeed married Angelo Ossoli, contrary to malicious reports that she had merely indulged in a sexual liaison with him and borne their son out of wedlock: "I was very glad to see [Emelyn Story's letter]; not on my own account; for I was perfectly satisfied to allow [Margaret] to manage her own affairs in her own way . . . ; but I was rejoiced to find that she had not imprudently put herself in the power of small female minds, of both sexes. . . . The love and tenderness induced by these new relations I think will greatly soften and beautify Margaret's character."[48] Child knew that the Ossolis, too, were contending with the dire poverty she and David had endured for so many years (and would soon encounter again), but she must have envied the tangible evidence that Fuller's handsome young husband had not taken "all the electricity" out of her.

If Child had eased her conscience and resolved her gnawing uncertainties about the future, she had hardly found "peace of mind." The brief respite from depression brought by her "second honey-moon" ended almost as soon as David's job with the railroad evaporated. When Child wrote, "I have never been so *much* depressed in spirits as I have this winter" — the letter to Loring quoted at the beginning of the present chapter — she was referring to the very months following her joyous reunion with David.[49] She would echo those words again and again in the years to come.

The most ominous indication of how much it would cost her to "conform[ ] [her] own tastes and inclinations" to David's was a paralyzing writer's block that forced her to suspend work on *The Progress of Religious Ideas*. As she explained to Loring: "It has been almost impossible for me to get on at all with my book; because I have been constantly tormented with the idea that I *ought* to be doing trifles that would bring in money quicker; but I *could* not do trifles, because feeling and imagination were dead within me."[50] The "trifles" she could not produce were the short stories into which she had poured so much "feeling and imagination" during her "Indian summer" of the mid-1840s. She had turned from fiction to religious history because she could no longer draw on the psychosexual energy that had inspired stories like "Hilda Silfverling" and "She Waits in the Spirit-Land." But now her repressed anger against David for once more derailing her career was preventing her from writing at all.

Since separating her financial affairs from David's in 1843, Child had been free to follow her literary bent, wherever it might lead. She continued to rely on her pen for a livelihood, yet thanks to her frugal habits, she no longer had to let pressing financial necessities dictate her choice of genre and subject matter, as in the days when David's debts had obliged her to rechannel her talents from fiction into domestic advice books. She had enjoyed writing her remunerative newspaper sketches, magazine fiction, and *Flowers for Children* of the 1840s. When her imagination had flagged, however, she had had the option of living off her royalties and savings while undertaking a massive project that would not generate any appreciable income. David's complete dependence on her changed all that, no doubt reawakening angry memories of the past, in addition to arousing terrifying worries about the future.

Child intended to forestall a repetition of the disastrous investments that had culminated in David's bankruptcy. She would control the family's finances from then on, and she would hold David to his "promise of not expending one dollar, without consulting me."[51] She would also take legal measures to keep her income and possessions "safe from the fangs of Massachusetts laws, so much less liberal to women, than those of N. York," by "quietly transfer[ring]" title to Ellis Loring, as her trustee, so that her "little goods and chattels" could not be seized to pay David's debts.[52] Nevertheless, she was essentially committing herself to support David for the rest of his life — an onerous charge that entailed drastically reordering her priorities.

How little she could rely on David to contribute even marginally to the family income became clear almost at the outset. He had earned nothing during his eight months in New York and had incurred extra expenses for board and laundry, yet when he finally landed an assignment to "write some Latin" documents, Child "*could* not get him" to set a firm deadline for himself.[53] Not only did she have to sacrifice her own needs to David's; she also had to assume the entire burden of making practical arrangements for the future and carrying out plans to move. "[T]he packing of our things has all *but* killed me," she exploded to Loring, as she and David were preparing to leave New York for Massachusetts in June 1850.

> Of *my* chattels I transport only necessary articles, with the exception of a few pictures, and plaster images rendered sacred by some association. But dear me how I *have* battled with David to burn a few of his barrels of old political pamphlets and M.S. about Gen. Jackson [dating back to the 1828 election]! By hook or by crook (mostly by *crook*) I have succeeded in destroying some two or three hundred pamphlets and newspapers, which I feel quite sure he never will miss. But O Lord! what dictionaries and documents still remain. My energy has not held out as it used to do; partly because I am growing old, but chiefly because I am in a very discouraged state.

As Child herself dimly realized, her "energy" was being diverted from the intellectual and creative work she treasured into the Sisyphean task of suppressing her rage against a husband who refused to grow up. Hence her persistent low spirits and unaccustomed fatigue.

In heading for a small farm in Massachusetts, after bidding farewell to the city where she had made her literary comeback, Child must have had an eerie sense of déjà vu. True, West Newton, a suburb of Boston, was not as far as Northampton from metropolitan amenities and cherished friends. The farm the Childs would be renting in fact belonged to Ellis Loring, who had been overjoyed to welcome them back. "I tell you clearly that we don't mean to part with you any more in this world. Make up your mind that we three [he, Louisa, and Anna] mean to love you so much that it will be impossible for you to leave us again," he had announced when Child had first asked him to help locate a suitable homestead.[54] Child had also defined the conditions very differently, setting modest goals and avoiding major expenditures. Still, she was about to plunge back into the mind-deadening domestic drudgery that had driven her to the verge of a suicidal depression in Northampton. And she was about to submit again to the double yoke of patriarchy by taking responsibility for her "poor old father" as well as for her "*incurable*" husband. The senior Convers's claims had played a role in her decision to leave New York, she told the Lorings, for he was now eighty-four, and she feared he would soon become "thoroughly imbecile" and need her care. She added ruefully: "It is a stinging blister to *me* to be with him, (may God forgive me for it) but it is a great comfort to *him* to see me sometimes. He is a kind good old man, though not agreeable to a poetic nature."[55] Child was not yet ready to share a household with her father, however — a contingency to which she would be reduced three years later. Instead, the family she reconstituted in West Newton included an adopted daughter — a young Spanish woman named Dolores.

Child's intensely charged friendship with this mysterious orphan, so much like a heroine of romance, began in 1848 during one of her periodic visits to New York from New Rochelle. Dolores had just fled a "brutal husband" in Spain and was trying to make a living by teaching Spanish and doing ornamental sewing, though she had been "educated in the midst of wealth and indulgence."[56] Always charmed by "tropical exuberance," which drew out the "impetuous," "fiery" side of her nature she had to "rein in" with her fellow New Englanders, Child took to Dolores so passionately that within weeks of meeting her, she was already writing: "I never pitied anybody so much in my life, and very rarely have loved anybody so much."[57] She invited Dolores to New Rochelle for a few days, and the two "talked like magpies" in French, "sometimes calling in the aid of very expressive pantomime."[58]

The attraction was complex. Like Anna Loring and Susan Lyman, Dolores fulfilled Child's need for a daughter. But to Anna and Susan, Child merely stood in the relation of an honorary aunt, whereas Dolores, "friendless and alone in a strange land," clung to her "like a drowning man to a rope." Child had been "avaricious of love" since her earliest years, and the hunger aroused by her youthful deprivation had never abated.[59] "[H]ow often, and how keenly do I feel, '. . . by none am I *enough* beloved,'" Child confessed to Sarah Shaw, one of her dearest friends.[60] Dolores, who had "no husband and children" to come "*between* us" (unlike Sarah) and no doting parents to take precedence (unlike Anna and Susan), could give her the "*exclusive*" love she craved. Nor did New England decorum inhibit Dolores's expressions of love. "She has called me an *angel*, over and over again; but getting to consider *that* a cold, inadequate expression," she had addressed Child in one letter as "My dear Heavenly Diamond" and closed with "un million de baisers, avec l'amour chaud d'un coeur passioné pour vous" (a million kisses, with the warm love of a passionate heart for you).[61]

Dolores represented more to Child than the daughter she had always wanted. She represented the self Child felt within the deepest recesses of her being. Temperamentally ardent, Child had found the milieu into which she was born "uncongenial" for as long as she could remember. "When I was quite a little girl, I remember imagining that gipsies had changed me from some other cradle, and put me in a place where I did not belong," she told Lucy Osgood.[62] It was because she felt that she "*ought* to have been a foreigner" that she was so "partial to the excessive warmth of foreigners."[63] She even acted out that sentiment by adopting the name "Mariquita," which Dolores seems to have given her.

Child identified with Dolores in other ways as well. "[M]y little Spanish friend . . . is about as independent as I am in her spirit. . . . I never saw such a capable, tasteful, energetic little creature, as she is," she wrote to Marianne Silsbee, with the expectation that Silsbee would "understand why it is I feel a *peculiar* sympathy for her."[64] She was referring to Dolores's pride, which she was actually hurting in the same way that her wealthy friends had repeatedly hurt hers — by showering gifts on her that she could not reciprocate and by forcing Dolores to remain in the position of a debtor. Dolores had just given Child a "Marie Stuart head-dress of crimson velvet," which she had "embroidered with gold," but pronouncing it "not suited to my insignificant person and forlorn condition," Child had offered it to Silsbee for ten dollars. "The money I shall appropriate to clothing for my poor Spanish friend," she explained, anticipating a stormy reaction from Dolores.[65] The very words she used to describe Dolores's attitude — "She is . . . extremely averse to being under any obligation to others" — were words she had often reiterated in rebuffing the many friends who had tried to alleviate *her* financial distress.[66]

Perhaps unconsciously, Child identified not only with Dolores's independence, resourcefulness, and pluck in the face of adversity, but also with her status as an abused wife. "She would be a jewel of a wife, to a man that knew how to appreciate her," Child commented to Silsbee immediately after praising Dolores's "energetic" self-reliance. The comment applied all too well to herself — and Child was feeling particularly unappreciated at this time, not having seen or heard from David for many months.[67] There was even an analogy between Dolores's legal situation and her own, for Dolores, too, was in "danger of her husband-in-law siezing" any property bequeathed to her, and her uncle in Spain was trying to make "such arrangements with the courts, that her brutal husband will not be allowed to *live* with her. . . ."[68] Of course, David could hardly have been called "brutal" by his worst enemy, but he had become a "husband-in-law," and the law still gave him power over his estranged wife.

Child had been planning to share an apartment with Dolores in New York and "unite our industry and economy to keep our little boat afloat."[69] "I will not under *any* circumstances desert her," she told the Lorings. "I am not Quixotic about seeking for such occasions. . . . but when God lays a forlorn fellow creature in my arms, and says, 'There! take her and warm her!' I cannot otherwise than do it." Thus, when David's job prospects vanished, Child decided to bring Dolores with her to Massachusetts and to "provide a way for her to get her living by teaching Spanish in schools or private lessons, with embroidery, netting &c to fill up spare hours."[70]

Despite Child's manifold precautions and strenuous efforts, nothing worked out as she had hoped in hiring the farm at West Newton. Once the excitement of settling in and greeting old friends subsided, Child sank into a mire of never-ending household chores: "Rat-gnawed meal bags to mend, straw beds, and coarse out of door frocks to make, old carpets to patch & darn," bread to bake, butter to churn, vegetables to pick and prepare, constant supervision to ensure that "nothing moulds, ferments, or freezes." "The weeks revolve and find me tired every night, without seeing my way out of the whirl," she lamented to Louisa, declining an invitation to visit the Lorings' country home in Beverly.[71]

In addition, financial problems resurfaced almost immediately. Because the Childs had arrived too late in the summer to raise food for "cow, pig, and hens" or to gather sufficient firewood, they had had to buy these costly items. The soil was so "full of rocks, stones, and stumps" that Child had had to hire an Irishman to clear the quarter acre needed for the following year's vegetables, since the work was beyond David's strength. On top of these things, Child discovered that David had contracted yet another debt, which had to be deducted from the income she had counted on from the Northampton farm. She had hoped that the sale of their surplus produce would generate a hundred dollars a year, but it soon became evident that their goods would not fetch enough in the market to cover the cost of raising them. Child had also expected David to pick up $200 or $300 a year doing translations and paralegal odd jobs, and she had done her best to obtain scholars for Dolores, advertising in several newspapers and contacting notables she would otherwise have preferred to avoid, but no opportunites had materialized for either of them. Worst of all, her publisher had notified her that the sale of her books had tapered off, "because I neglect to keep up an acquaintance with the public," but she found herself totally unable to write. "Even if I had *time* to write, all power of thinking, and still more of imagining, is pressed out of me by this perpetual load of anxiety," she complained to Loring.[72] She analyzed the vicious syndrome with almost clinical precision: "The dull monotonous life of the country kills my mind . . . stone dead. . . . Anxiety about money matters, and a sense of dependence makes the matter still worse, so that all my faculties go from me. The tendency to sadness, which I inherit from my father, increases under such circumstances."[73]

By the end of their first year in West Newton, Child had reached a state of utter panic and despair. "I toil incessantly, but I toil without the least ray of hope. . . . I . . . practise a degree of economy which pinches my soul till I despise its smallness," she wrote Loring, humiliated at having to live on his bounty when she had meant to pay him an annual rent. Reevaluating her endeavor "to provide a home for David's old age," she could only say: "I was trying to do what I thought was my duty. Whether I made a mistake or not, God knows; I do not."[74]

The sole alternative Child could now envisage was to join the North American Phalanx, the longest-lived and most successful of the utopian socialist communities that had proliferated in the 1840s.[75] Child had taken a warm interest in these experiments at implementing the theories of the French socialist Charles Fourier, especially while her friends John Sullivan Dwight and Francis Shaw were participating in the Transcendentalist community of Brook Farm. She would remain convinced to the end of her life that the "troublesome knot of employers and employed can never be disentangled, except by some process of Association, which shall apportion some manual labor to all, and some culture and recreation to all."[76] Apart from the North American Phalanx, however, none of the Fourierist communities founded in the 1840s had survived for more than a few years, and by 1852, the utopian movement had already waned. Not idealism, but desperation, impelled Child to consider so risky a solution to her financial and marital problems.

Explaining her motives in a "*confidential*" letter to Loring, on whom she had come to rely more and more heavily in the the throes of readjusting to her "inevitable destiny" with David, she wrote: "I am more than ever convinced that David can never 'make buckle and strap meet' by working for *himself* in any way." On the other hand, Child had heard from men whose opinions she respected — among them Francis Shaw and *New York Tribune* editor Horace Greeley, vice president of the North American Phalanx — that the nine-year-old community was "on a much more *safe* business foundation" than any of its predecessors, being run not by "spiritual loafers, as was Brook Farm," but by "practical men, enterprising mechanics and farmers." The Phalanx reportedly needed teachers. "If David could teach a certain number of hours in the day, and agree to keep a certain number of acres weeded, or hens fed, and be *paid* for it, it would be the *safest* situation for a man of his peculiarities." The Phalanx's proximity to New York City would also make it possible for Child to resume her literary career without leaving David. "[S]uch talent as I have is more recognized [in New York] than it ever was, or ever will be in Boston," she argued, indicating how much she was missing the varied professional contacts she had established in her adopted home. In many respects, Child acknowledged with devastating frankness, life in the Phalanx "would not be agreeable" to her, "but I *cannot* be agreeably situated while I am involved in David's destiny." Quoting the refrain Dickens put in the mouth of another long-suffering wife saddled with a feckless husband, she added wryly: "He is good and kind, and I have made up my mind that 'I never *will* desert Mr. Macawber' " [*sic*].[77]

Child planned to go to New York to "make minute inquiries about the Phalanx, without intimating to any one that *we* have any interest in the inquiries." Meanwhile, David was once again hankering to prospect for gold in California, where one of his nephews, "a practical managing Yankee," was going to investigate the opportunities for him. "If [David] goes to California," Child wound up, "I shall go to New York, dive into the thickest of the fight, allow myself to be lionized, sell comfort, repose, taste, everything but conscience."[78] Her longing vision of contending for the laurels she had spurned in the past would never reach fulfillment. David would not go to California, and the North American Phalanx would begin to disintegrate before the year was out, folding in 1854.

As if to confirm that the New York chapter of her life had closed forever, a strangely metamorphosed Ole Bull suddenly returned to the United States in 1852, not to revive Child's Indian summer with his music, but to bury her dreams in a utopian venture uncannily reminiscent of David's Northampton beet farm. Purchasing 11,000 acres in Pennsylvania from a land speculator, he founded an ill-fated colony for Norwegian immigrants, grandly named Oleana, which soon collapsed under a mountain of debts.

For Child, the fiasco would entail a last cruel irony by setting Ole Bull against that other sun of her Indian summer, John Hopper. As Bull's legal advisor, John would hound him with lawsuits for unpaid services long after Oleana had faded from memory. Lacerated by the two men's sordid quarrel, Child would refuse to revisit New York for many years and ask never to be reminded of John.[79]

In 1852 the pathetic denouement of Child's relations with Ole Bull and John Hopper still lay in the future, however, and the problem that absorbed her was how to extricate herself from a mode of life that had proved untenable. The catalyst that finally enabled her to break out of her writer's block, if not to recover her lost freedom, was the death of her venerable Quaker host in New York, Isaac Hopper, to whose bedside she was summoned that May. Because Hopper had played such a vital role in the fugitive slave rescue network called the Underground Railroad, as well as in the Quaker-led prison reform movement, Child had promised that she would "write his biography for the benefit of his children" and of posterity.[80] The acceptance of a commitment that could not be put off indefinitely, unlike her long-stalled *Progress of Religious Ideas* — a commitment, moreover, that Child could define as purely altruistic, since she was forgoing any profit from the book and framing it as a tribute to someone else's philanthropy — helped her to take a step indispensable to making time to write. "I have resolved, at *last*, to try to procure a good domestic this Fall," Child announced to Louisa in August:

> I have resisted coming to this conclusion, because I have uniformly found that I *cannot* write when my mind is anxious and discouraged; and if I could not write, where was the money to come from to pay the girl's board and wages? . . . But I see that I gain nothing by going on in this way. It is two years last week since we came here, and with my utmost diligence I have not found as much time to read or write, as I should have had in one month at board. Six weeks often passes without my even looking into a book or touching a pen.[81]

The only sensible course was to "trust to [her] poor old brain" and accept her friends' offers to tide her over financially until she could get on her feet. Already "stronger and more cheerful" at the prospect of returning to her real vocation, Child invited Louisa for a long visit while Ellis and Anna were away in Europe and then set about her task with a surge of her old energy.

The biography of Hopper was an ideal project for Child to undertake at a stage when she needed above all to convince herself that she still had the capacity to write. She could "work upon it at odd hours, and interrupted moments," as she could not on a subject as intellectually demanding as her history of religion, and she did not have to tax her dormant powers of invention.[82] The bulk of the book would consist of anecdotes about the hundreds of fugitive slaves, prisoners, and derelicts Hopper had assisted over a philanthropic career dating back to the 1790s. Child had heard Hopper narrate these anecdotes innumerable times during her seven years in his household, and both he and she had previously recorded many of them, Hopper in a column for the *National Anti-Slavery Standard* titled "Tales of Oppression," Child in her "Letters from New-York."

Thus, she could simply remodel existing accounts, infusing Hopper's rather pedestrian writing with the drama of his oral style and tightening her own prose where necessary.

Though the biography inevitably bears the marks of its disjointed composition, Child did succeed in her endeavor to make it "lively."[83] The portrait that emerges from it reflects her considerable psychological acumen. Departing from the convention of tracing a saintly life to a formative conversion experience, she dwells on the mischievous love of practical jokes that Hopper exhibited in his youth and shows how he channeled the instincts of a born trickster into the virtuous enterprise of helping fugitive slaves to outwit their pursuers. Similarly, she comments shrewdly on Hopper's striking resemblance to Napoleon, both in person and in character, noting that he might have been "a skilful diplomatist, and a successful leader of armies" had he not directed his energies toward benevolent rather than aggressive ends: "He battled courageously, not from ambition, but from an inborn love of truth. He circumvented as adroitly as the most practised politician; but it was always to defeat the plans of those who oppressed God's poor; never to advance his own self-interest."[84]

Child's strong identification with Hopper also allowed her to overcome some of the psychological barriers to self-expression that were preventing her from writing. In her efforts to control or deny feelings she found unacceptable — anger against David; envy of her happily married friends (Louisa, Rosa Hopper, Susan Lyman, Sarah Shaw); regret at having given up her independence — she had cut off the very lifeblood of her creativity: her unconscious mind. The censorship she had imposed on her feelings had resulted in silencing her altogether. Conversely, she would circumvent this self-censorship by turning her biography of Isaac Hopper into a vehicle for articulating her sentiments by proxy.

Hopper had in fact embodied the ideals Child held dearest, and he had paid as dearly as she for living by them. He, too, had lost friends, forfeited opportunities for advancement, and suffered crushing poverty for the sake of his principles. And he, too, had "walked straight forward in what seemed to him the path of duty, and snapped all the lilliputian cords with which [sectarian dogmatists] tried to bind him" (392) (metaphors Child often used of herself).[85] While Child consistently made light of her own sacrifices, however, she could write sympathetically of Hopper's:

> Many were hostile to Friend Hopper, and some were bitter in their enmity. Of course, it could not be otherwise with a man who battled with oppression, selfishness, and bigotry. . . . Moreover, no person in this world is allowed to be peculiar and independent with impunity. There are always men who wish to compel such characters to submit, by the pressure of circumstances. This kind of spiritual thumb-screw was often . . . tried upon Friend Hopper; but though it sometimes occasioned temporary inconvenience, it never induced him to change his course. (468–69)

Child identified not only with Hopper's unswerving commitment to principle, but with his horror of "incurring obligations." His refusal to avail himself of Quaker charitable funds because he thought they should be "reserved for those whose necessities were greater than his own" (290) found countless echoes in her life.[86] The affinities between Hopper and Child even extended to their class origins and attitudes. Like Child, who would never "avoid mentioning that [her] father was a mechanic," despite hints that she would "stand a great deal better with the upper classes" if she passed herself off as one of them, Hopper introduced himself as a former tailor and pointed out the "marks of the shears" on his hands when a wealthy host disparaged a fellow church member as the son of a mechanic (304).[87] "[H]e was totally and entirely unconscious of any such thing as distinctions of rank," Child commented — an observation that also applied to her and that differentiated them both from friends who self-consciously "tried to be democratic" out of "kind feelings" (339).

Child revealed herself most where she sought to be most reticent — in casting a veil over Hopper's sorrows. "[W]ho does not know that all the sternest conflicts of life can never be recorded!" she asked, in words that reverberate through her letters to friends: "Every human soul must walk alone through the darkest and most dangerous paths of its spiritual pilgrimage. . . . Much, from which we suffer most acutely, could never be revealed to others; still more could never be understood. . . . Therefore, the frankest and fullest biography must necessarily be superficial" (467–68).[88]

Besides freeing her emotionally, the biography of Hopper gave Child an opportunity to adumbrate theories she would subsequently develop in *The Progress of Religious Ideas*. Hopper had played an active part in two controversies over slavery that had bitterly divided the Quaker community — the schism between Orthodox and Hicksite Friends in the 1820s and the expulsion of active abolitionists — among them himself and his son-in-law James S. Gibbons, Child's coadjutor on the *Standard* — from Quaker meetings in the 1840s. The Quakers' betrayal of their antislavery heritage, which Child attributed to their increasing prosperity, confirmed a pattern she had noted in every religious group she had studied, including the primitive Christians — a tendency to degenerate into formalism and hypocrisy as soon as its adherents acquired worldly power. Child's research had led her to conclude that the spirit of religion could never be preserved through institutions, theological doctrines, or sacred scriptures — that it had to be experienced directly by each individual. Attachment to the form rather than the spirit of religion was a prime cause of sectarian strife, she believed. Yet she had found it excruciatingly difficult to preach that message in *The Progress of Religious Ideas*. The biography of Hopper offered her an unthreatening forum in which to introduce her iconoclastic theories. Though Hopper himself mourned his excommunication and clung to "the hope that the primitive character of Quakerism would be restored," Child argued that "his character grew larger, and his views more liberal, after the bonds which bound him to a sect were cut asunder" (465) — a transformation she herself had undergone and hoped to induce in the readers of her religious opus.

Psychologically and intellectually, the writing of Hopper's biography prepared Child to complete the ambitious task she had mulled over for so many years. Politically, it enabled her to begin refocusing her attention on the struggle against slavery, through which she would ultimately transcend her own suffering. The 160-odd pages Child devoted to Hopper's rescue work with fugitive slaves constituted her first public protest against the Fugitive Slave Law of 1850. Although she would not resume an active role in the abolitionist movement until 1856, she had taken an initiative vital to combating the personal and political discouragement that had throttled her.

Child's sprightly portrait of a Quaker hero and her vivid accounts of real-life cases corroborating "the pictures of slavery drawn by Mrs. Stowe" (vi) would make her biography of Isaac Hopper her most popular antislavery work. Selling more than 12,000 copies before 1860, it would be reprinted as late as 1881. Characteristically, however, Child refused to touch a penny for the biography. "It is the old gentleman's *deeds*, not my *words*, which will give interest to the book. His whole life was a struggle with pecuniary difficulties; and if his doings can make any money for his widow and children *now*, why, in God's name, let it be done!" she wrote heatedly to Loring, who had just negotiated a very favorable contract for her with a new publisher, John P. Jewett. Anticipating the response that her life, too, "was a struggle with pecuniary difficulties" and that she needed the money at least as much as the Hopper family did, she countered: "If I can only have *time* I will work myself out of my present tangle, without owing money to *anybody*. But God forbid I should put Friend Hopper up for sale for that purpose."[89]

With the debt to her surrogate father discharged, there remained a more onerous filial obligation to assume before Child could bring her "long procrastinated book on religions" to fruition.[90] Ever since her return to Massachusetts, her father had been conveying an obvious desire to move in with her. He visited more and more frequently, stayed longer and longer, and grew "more and more helpless" with advancing age. "As usual, he growls about everything; but . . . I am willing to do *anything* for his happiness," Child wrote resignedly.[91] So far the old man's "insuperable objections" to the house in West Newton had staved off a permanent arrangement. But by the end of her second year there, Child had decided that she could not continue to live rent-free on Loring's property with no prospect of being able to repay him.[92] While she was casting about for a solution in the spring of 1853, her father came down with erysipelas (a severe, infectious skin disease), and she went to his home in Wayland to nurse him. The conclusion seemed inescapable — she and David would eventually have to move in with him. As she explained to Loring, her father's "physical infirmities, and mental loneliness" demanded the presence of a nurse who would make it "a conscientious *duty*" to minister to his needs, and whom he would "*allow* to take proper care of him." Only she could fill that role. "The performance of the duty involves great privations," Child admitted; "but, like all other things, it has its compensations." She added bravely: "I only hope that I shall be able to carry it through, to the end, without his suspecting that it requires any sacrifice on my part."[93]

In shifting from her spacious household in West Newton to the cramped, primitive cottage in Wayland that she and David would share with her father for the next three years and inherit after his death, Child had to give up more than her domestic privacy — she had to give up the adopted daughter whose love had sustained her through the ordeal of resettling in rural Massachusetts. Unable to find work in the Boston area and as averse to economic dependency as Child was, Dolores would probably have chosen to go back to New York even if the cottage in Wayland could have accommodated another resident. But that realization only intensified Child's grief. "I never felt the bitterness of poverty as I do in being compelled to part with her. She *so* needs a sympathizing friend and protector, and I *so* need a loving daughter," she mourned.[94]

Despite the dislocation of packing up her belongings again and squeezing into "one very small room for sleeping, eating, writing, and all," Child succeeded in knuckling down to *The Progress of Religious Ideas* soon after moving permanently to Wayland in December 1853.[95] "I am working away at it diligently now; and if my poor old father continues well, I hope to get it done in three or four months," she reported to Francis Shaw in January.[96] Her ability to write under such adverse conditions, worse in many respects than those that had thwarted her in New York and West Newton, suggests that she had largely resolved the conflicts underlying her prolonged writer's block. By consecrating herself to the service of the patriarchs in her life — David, Isaac Hopper, and her eighty-seven-year-old father — she apparently liberated herself to challenge the authority of the patriarchs who presided over the world of the spirit. Even when her old anxieties resurfaced, she handled them with a new self-confidence. "My courage fails me dreadfully at times. Yet I feel re-assured by the conviction that it *must* be salutary, in the long run, to speak the plain truth on *all* subjects," she wrote to Shaw, giving him a foretaste of the "startling" boldness with which she was rejecting the "delusions" her culture enshrined as revelation.[97] She disposed similarly of the guilt that had once troubled her for not "writing something . . . likely to bring in money." "Perhaps you think I am perverse," she apologized to Loring. "But . . . I cannot write except just what happens to be *in* me. . . . Now this plaguey subject of religions *is* in my head, and *will* not go out, till it has said its say."[98]

The "three or four months" Child had projected for finishing the book stretched into many more. Nevertheless, by October 1854 the bulk of the manuscript was in the hands of the publisher, her cousin Charles S. Francis, and the terms of the contract were set: 15 percent on the retail price of the first two thousand copies sold, and 12.5 percent thereafter. The last remaining "stumbling block" was Francis's insistence on a " 'catching' " and "Christian" title, such as "The Divine Light" or "Glimpses of Faith." Child refused to agree to "clap-trap," however, and they compromised on "The Progress of Religious Ideas, Through Successive Ages" (a title at variance with the contents, as several reviewers pointed out).[99] After another year's delay, Child's magnum opus, comprising three 450-page volumes in small print, finally appeared on the market in November 1855.[100]

Like so many of Child's contributions, *The Progress of Religious Ideas* is a pioneering work. Encompassing all the major religions of the ancient world — Hinduism, Buddhism, Jainism, Confucianism, Taoism, and Zoroastrianism; Egyptian, Chaldaic, Graeco-Roman, and Celtic myths and cults; Judaism, Christianity, and Muhammadanism — the book sought to exhibit each "in its own light; that is, as it appeared to those who sincerely believed it to be of divine origin"; to illustrate "the beauties and the blemishes" of every religion through quotations from its own sacred scriptures; and to preserve "complete impartiality," eschewing favoritism toward Christianity or condemnation of other faiths.[101] Even more daringly, the juxtaposition of all these creeds drew attention to the striking parallels between the Judaeo-Christian Bible and older religious texts, between the story of Christ and the myths of "Crishna," Osiris, and Mithra, inviting readers to explore the influences that surrounding cultures had exerted on Judaism and Christianity over the centuries. No analogous study existed in English, as all Child's reviewers conceded.[102] Hitherto, interest in Oriental scriptures, comparative mythology, and Higher Criticism (the historical examination of the Old and New Testaments led by German scholars) had been confined to esoteric circles.[103] Child was the first to digest this vast body of research for "the popular mind" (ix).

Her motive, as Child explained in a preface "candidly" warning "bigoted" readers "not to purchase this book," was to promote religious tolerance: "I wished to show that *theology* is not *religion*; with the hope that I might help to break down partition walls" (vii). That is, her latest work, like her early narratives of interracial marriage and appeals against racial prejudice, had originated in the impulse to unify humankind:

> While my mind was yet in its youth, I was offended by the manner in which Christian writers usually describe other religions; for I observed that they habitually covered apparent contradictions and absurdities, in Jewish or Christian writings, with a veil of allegories and mystical interpretation, while the records of all other religions were unscrupulously analyzed, or contemptuously described as "childish fables," or "filthy superstitions." . . . I recollect wishing, long ago, that I could become acquainted with some good, intelligent Bramin, or Mohammedan, that I might learn, in some degree, how their religions appeared to *them*. (vii)

Child had attempted to fulfill this wish by reading the sacred texts of foreign peoples from their point of view, as nearly as she could approximate it, and she had conceived her book with the aim of showing that all religions contained sublime truths along with "more or less of the alloy necessarily resulting from our imperfect nature and uncompleted growth" (2: 184).

From a modern perspective, what is most remarkable about Child's study is her grasp of history. Instead of trying to derive a transhistorical essence from each group of religious texts, she traces the evolution they reflect in a given culture over time. Thus, she notes the increasing complexity of Hindu theology as it develops from the Vedas to the Code of Manu to the Mahabharata to the Puranas; and of Judaism as it develops from the Mosaic law of the Hebrews' nomadic stage to the Temple-centered worship of the preexilic kingdom to the apocalyptic prophecies imported from Persia during the Babylonian captivity to the Gnostic mysticism and Talmudic commentary of later periods. She also illuminates the transformation of Christianity from a Jewish sect into a new religion oriented toward a Graeco-Roman constituency, showing how gradually the concepts of the Virgin Birth, the Logos, the divinity of Christ, and the Trinity took shape, how violently these doctrines were contested by rival Christian sects, and how much Christianity borrowed from other religions of the ancient world.

The effect of Child's comparative historical approach is to decenter the Judaeo-Christian tradition and to undermine its claims as revealed truth. Structurally, she denies the priority of the Judaeo-Christian Scriptures by placing them after her account of Hindu, Egyptian, and Chaldaic texts and myths, whose antiquity she pointedly emphasizes. In the same fashion, she redefines Christianity as an extension of late Judaism by situating John the Baptist and Jesus not at the beginning of a new chapter, but toward the end of the chapter on Judaism, where she sandwiches them between the Jewish sects of the Roman era and the Talmud and Mishnah of the post-Dispersion period.

Throughout the book Child pursues a cluster of recurrent themes. First, she distinguishes between the religious sentiment and its codification in theology. True religion, she argues "does not consist in *doctrines* of any kind, but in *sentiments* of reverence toward God, and of justice and benevolence toward our fellow men" (3: 451). Every religion has originated in direct experience of the "Divine Spirit" and has translated its vision of divinity into lofty ethical principles, but all faiths have subsequently degenerated into empty formalism. Every religion has likewise endeavored to "resuscitate decaying forms" by resorting to "far-fetched explanations and allegories" (3: 419).

Second, Child insists that sacred texts cannot preserve the spirit of religion — they can only record what previous generations understood to be the Word of God, as expressed in the languages of specific cultures at specific historical moments. "[T]he very nature of a Written Revelation involves the necessity of ceasing to be adequate to the wants of society sooner or later; for a Revelation must necessarily be adapted to the then present state of the public mind," Child contends (3: 419). Hence, she concludes: "Up to a certain point, written Revelations aid the progress of nations; but after the state of society for which they were written has entirely passed away, they become a positive hindrance; because the *habit* of reverence remains after the *life* has gone" (3: 442). Child applies this postulate openly to Hindu and Jewish sacred texts, but she hints that it may also apply to some of St. Paul's Epistles: "forced into perpetual arguments, often of a metaphysical character . . . Paul taught theology," whereas "Christ preached a religion" (3: 449). Privately, she went further, discounting even the authority of Christ. "I do not believe [the Spirit of God] was ever shut up within the covers of any *book*, or that it ever *can* be," she wrote to Lucy Osgood. "*[B]reathings* of it, are in *many* books. The words of Christ seem to me *full* of it, as no other words are. But if *we* want truth, we must listen to the voice of God in the silence of our *own* souls, as *he* did."[104]

Third, Child highlights the role played by a class of professional interpreters and priests in hastening the degeneration of religion into theology. "The priesthood of all nations" — Hindus, Egyptians, Hebrews, Persians, and Celts — "had always acted upon the system that it was necessary to deceive the mass of the people, for their own good," she charges. Brahmin philosophers and Egyptian priests had jealously guarded their abstract concepts of an invisible supreme being, on the grounds that "elevated ideas of God and the soul were . . . above the comprehension of the populace" and might lead unsophisticated minds to atheism (3: 167, 1: 181). "The same idea of managing the people, for their spiritual benefit, prevailed among the Christian Fathers," Child asserts (3: 167). They altered, interpolated, and "forged" scriptures "for the purpose of giving authority to particular opinions or principles" (3: 168). In every case, she stresses, the "fear of trusting truth to . . . rest simply on its own merits," has "produced lamentable results" (3: 167). Whenever "religious ideas, studiously hidden from the people, become a monopoly of power in the hands of a privileged class" corruption inevitably ensues. "[L]eft to obey laws without knowing why they were ordained, and to observe the ritual of religion without comprehending its import," the masses sink into ignorance, superstition, and bigotry (1: 181).

Child minces no words in summing up her judgment of theology, which she pronounces uniformly deleterious in its impact:

> What destruction of the beautiful monuments of past ages, what waste of life, what disturbance of domestic and social happiness, what perverted feelings, what blighted hearts, have always marked its baneful progress! . . .
>
> . . . How much intellect has been employed mousing after texts, to sustain preconceived doctrines! . . . [P]assages of ancient books are taken up hundreds of years after they were written, and are used in a sense altogether foreign from the original intention. . . . And the human mind is not left free to pursue even *this* distorting process; but colleges of supervisors are appointed to instruct the young in what light everything *ought* to be viewed. (3: 451–52)

Fourth, Child exposes sectarian strife as the worst consequence of allowing a priestly class to idolatrize sacred texts and to substitute theology for religion. Here, she directs her heaviest artillery at Christianity. Montanists, Donatists, Nestorians, Monophysites, Arians, and Athanasians warred fiercely against each other, turning cities into "scenes of massacre and licentious outrage," Child points out, yet "[i]t requires an intellectual microscope to discover" the differences among the doctrines for which they contended (3: 28, 50). Moreover, "[t]hese sectarian controversies were often intertwisted with personal quarrels, growing out of mutual jealousy, and competition for power"—an insight Child must have derived from her painful experience of sectarianism in abolitionist ranks (3: 212).

In combating sectarianism and intolerance toward non-Christian religions, Child repeatedly urges her readers to consider the point of view of the peoples whose faiths were being assailed by Christian proselytizers. Greek and Roman peasants must have reacted "not only with deep grief, but with absolute terror" to the desecration of their temples: believing that the gods they worshiped had "protected them and their forefathers for ages, they expected storm, pestilence, and famine, as the inevitable consequence" of destroying their altars (3: 84–85). Similarly, the bitter persecution to which the Jews were subjected could hardly have "induced [them] to embrace" the creed of those who "plundered and slaughtered them":

> If we looked at the subject candidly, I think we should acknowledge as heroic martyrs, those men and women, who resisted constant appeals to their fears and their selfishness, and at the cost of incredible sacrifices and sufferings, still set their

faces steadfastly toward Jerusalem, and replied: "After this manner worship we the God of our fathers." Ever since I have reflected on the subject, I have never been able to do otherwise than reverence their firmness and their faith. (3: 440–41)

In addition to these religious themes — the distinction between religion and theology; the demystification of sacred texts; the discrediting of theology and its professional custodians; and the denunciation of sectarianism — Child also focuses on three main secular issues. As one might expect, the issue of slavery occupies a significant place in Child's examination of Judaism and Christianity, since proslavery apologists and abolitionists had been engaged for decades in a heated debate over whether or not the Bible sanctioned the "peculiar institution." With the honesty she displays in evaluating the evidence against the Bible's divine inspiration, Child reluctantly acknowledges its ambiguous stand on slavery. The Old Testament prohibited Jews from permanently enslaving each other, but directed them to buy their slaves from "strangers," whom they could keep as "bondmen forever" and "inherit . . . for a possession" (1: 409). The New Testament merely exhorted Christians to treat each other as brethren regardless of their worldly rank, and the early Christians, like the Jews, generally limited their humanity to their coreligionists. The best Child can say is that Christians often revealed conscientious scruples against slavery by manumitting their bond servants in their wills (2: 197; 3: 282–84).

A second issue of major concern to Child is the status of women. She comments on the degree of freedom women enjoyed under the various religions of the ancient world, notes whether or not they were allowed to perform priestly functions, analyzes the attitudes religious leaders exhibited toward women, and contrary to her policy of objectivity on other matters, measures religions against each other by their treatment of women. For example, she observes that the "condition of women in Egypt was prodigiously in advance of their enslaved sisters in Hindostan" (1: 195), and she contrasts the contempt for women among Asiatic nations with the sexual egalitarianism that prevailed among the Celtic tribes: "Men were themselves in a rude and barbarous condition, but such as it was, women were on the same level. Both sexes held consultation together in councils of state, and fought in battle with equal bravery. Among the Teutones, women were the only physicians. In Asia, there were always ten prophets to one prophetess. But Celtic nations believed that women were endowed with supernatural powers in a pre-eminent degree" (1: 377).

As with the question of slavery, Child recognizes that the record of Christianity is mixed where women are concerned. "Women were among the most devoted friends of Christ, by whom they were always treated with respect and sympathy," she affirms, but Paul and other apostles betrayed "old Asiatic habits of thought" in inculcating the subordination of women (2: 197–98). Child also points out that women gradually lost status in the church, "as the clerical order increased in dignity" and began to contest such practices as the ordination of women (3: 197). Far more forthright than her 1835 *History of the Condition of Women*, Child's confident handling of gender discrimination in *The Progress of Religious Ideas* unmistakably indicates that she has not retreated from her strong feminist stance of the 1840s, whatever compromises she may have made in her personal life.

The most striking sign of how successfully Child has resolved the conflicts that induced her "pilgrimage of penance" is the prominence she accords the issue of sexuality in her study of religion. If feelings of guilt about her sexual desires had impelled her to turn to religion for absolution, her probing of religious teachings on sexuality ultimately led her to reconsider a fundamental tenet of Indo-European culture: "[t]he abstract idea that Matter was the origin of Evil" (3: 454). Child traces this idea to Hindu philosophy and theorizes that it spread from a common source, either in India or in Egypt, exerting a profound influence on the Greeks through Pythagoras, Plato, and the Gnostics, and thereby impregnating Christianity. The "Oriental" concept of matter as evil was originally foreign to Christianity, Child claims, because the Jews "do not appear to have held the body in such hatred and contempt, as did the devout of many other ancient nations." According to Child, Jesus shared his people's healthy acceptance of the body. "Nothing approaching to asceticism on this subject is discoverable" in his teachings, and his few allusions to marriage "imply approbation of that institution" (2: 188). Once again, Child differentiates Jesus from Paul, whose preference for celibacy she sees as evidence of a transition toward asceticism (2: 189).

Child takes every opportunity to condemn asceticism. The perverse belief in the vileness of matter has wreaked havoc in human history, she charges:

> At a very early period, it introduced civil war into the house of life, by teaching men to regard the body as an enemy to the soul. Passions and instincts given for usefulness, and for enjoyment, were considered spiritual snares. . . . [T]o feel sexual attraction was yielding to the instigation of the Devil. In order to become angels, men tormented their poor material forms. They reduced themselves to skeletons, by . . . prolonged fasts; they scourged themselves till the blood flowed; they tore their flesh with hooks, and burned it with fire . . . to atone for the sin of having any bodily wants. From this horror of natural instincts arose the traditions of various nations that their holy teachers were born of virgins . . . to disconnect them with the alleged impurity of human passions. (2: 171)

As Child interrogates each religion's attitude toward the body, she boldly challenges her culture's squeamishness about sexuality. In discussing Hindu and Egyptian iconography, for example, she defends the worship of male and female sexual emblems representing the "Fructifying Principle, the Generating Power that pervades the universe" (1: 16–17, 157–58). Ancient peoples regarded "the great mystery of human Birth" with awe and reverence, she explains. "Were *they* impure thus to regard it? Or are *we* impure that we do *not* so regard it?" (1: 16). Through such reassessments, Child seeks to rid sexuality of the shamefulness with which her culture has invested it and to restore it to its rightful place as a natural part of human life.

"I successively fall in love with *every* religion I describe; except the Jewish," Child confided to Louisa while she was writing volume 1.[105] Despite her sincere efforts to maintain "impartiality," her biases are easily discernible. Among non-Christian cultures, to which she shows a strong attraction, the Greeks emerge as her favorites. In Greece, she avers, "[t]heories of God and the soul escaped from the locks and keys of priests into the minds of philosophers, who lectured upon them openly, excited other minds to investigation, and led the way to general discussion" (1: 330). Child clearly idealizes Greek culture, with its "worship of freedom and beauty" (1: 284–85), as the antithesis of the Christian orthodoxy against which she had been rebelling since her youth. This impulse leads her to minimize its defects by giving short shrift to the Greeks' views on women and by attributing the antimaterialist tendencies in Greek philosophy to Oriental influences.[106]

The obverse is true of her glaring prejudice against Judaism — a prejudice rooted in Christian orthodoxy's historical reliance on literal readings of the Old Testament to justify wars of extermination, religious intolerance, capital punishment, the subordination of women, and many other practices Child reprobates. "Every abominable practice in Christendom has . . . been sustained by arguments drawn from the Old Testament," yet large portions of the Old Testament were "adapted . . . to savage tribes, and . . . to semi-barbarous ages," she objects (3: 442). Child accentuates the ugliest features of the Old Testament as conspicuously as she glosses over the shortcomings of the Greeks. Nevertheless, she distinguishes scrupulously between the Jewish religion and the Jewish people, pleading eloquently against anti-Semitism. It is absurd to reverence "savage tribes of the desert, who went about slaughtering women and children, in the name of Jehovah," and at the same time to persecute their "enlightened" descendants, she contends. She also notes the irony that "Moses Mendelssohn, the great and the good, would not have been allowed to purchase an acre of land in Christian countries, where Joshua is regarded as directly and constantly inspired by God, though he allured marauding tribes to conquer innocent people. . ." (3: 441). (In response, one reviewer predicted snidely that Child's "vigorous defence of the Jews" would "elicit general approval" from them, but would not abate the prejudice against them, since "after all . . . [t]hey *did* crucify the SON OF GOD.")[107]

The supreme test of Child's "impartiality" is her assessment of Christianity. While recognizing that Christianity inherited nearly all of its doctrines from other religions of the ancient world and that the ethical precepts taught by Jesus have analogues in the teachings of Buddha, Socrates, Confucius, and the Old Testament prophets, Child still concludes that "Christianity contains within itself a vital element of progress, superior to any other spiritual influence by which God has yet guided the world" (3: 433). No other religion has identified itself so closely with the poor and downtrodden, and none has made "such an earnest and extensive effort to inculcate the brotherhood of man, and to exemplify it by practice," she maintains (3: 427, 429). Accordingly, the quotations Child selects to represent the "beauties and blemishes" of Christianity give the erroneous impression that Jesus and Paul never spoke in the harsh, intolerant accents of their Old Testament forebears.

Of course, Child's very goal of preserving "complete impartiality" seems hopelessly naive in the light of postmodern theory. As she herself admits, "a modern mind, so foreign to ancient habits of thought, and separated from them by the lapse of ages," can never recapture the sentiments of alien peoples who lived thousands of years ago (viii–ix). By the standards of her own day, however, Child was far in advance of her contemporaries. A book published sixteen years after *The Progress of Religious Ideas* — the Unitarian clergyman and Transcendentalist scholar James Freeman Clarke's *Ten Great Religions: An Essay in Comparative Theology* (1871) — provides a telling gauge of Child's radicalism.

Harvard-trained and versed in Greek, Latin, Hebrew, and German, Clarke paid condescending tribute to Child as a precursor whom he had superseded. Thanks to the burgeoning "science of Comparative Theology" and the wealth of Oriental texts translated since Child had completed her study, it was now possible "to accomplish something which may have a lasting value," he announced.[108] Yet Clarke's one-volume work actually supplied much less information about the religions it covered than Child's three-volume compendium had. Nor did it adopt the same approach of quoting extensively from each religion's sacred texts and allowing readers to draw their own inferences. Instead, every chapter opened with a judgmental introduction spelling out the defects of the religion in question. As his method so patently indicated, Clarke's purpose was not to promote religious tolerance (though he proclaimed allegiance to this ideal), but to demonstrate that Christianity alone had the potential to be a "catholic" rather than an "ethnic" religion. Thus, he argued speciously that all other religions had been "limited to a single nation or race," with the exception of Islam, which had spread by military conquest rather than by proselytism, and that all other religions had been "arrested" in their development, while Christianity alone had shown "the power of keeping abreast with the advancing civilization of the world" (29–30).

Child had in fact attempted to counteract just such partisanship in *The Progress of Religious Ideas*. Long acquaintance with Harvard-trained theologians like Clarke and her brother Convers and eight years of immersion in their writings had led her to believe that her "want of learning" was more of an asset than a liability in prosecuting her study of religion. "Thoughts do not range so freely, when the store-room of the brain is overloaded with furniture. . . . [L]earned men can rarely have such freedom from any sectarian bias, as the circumstances of my life have produced in me," she had asserted in her preface (ix). Clarke's exercise in "comparative theology" proved her point.

Reviews of *The Progress of Religious Ideas* confirm that, in 1855, merely to advocate an "impartial" comparison of Christianity with other creeds was to incur charges of sacrilege. Child had nowhere acknowledged the "divine origin and authority" of Christianity, complained the *New-York Evangelist*, accusing her of leaving room for the "inference" that "the Incarnation and Trinity of the Hindoos stand upon about the same level . . . as the corresponding article of the Christian faith."[109] "The author . . . appears to regard [the Christian Scriptures] as little better than the writings of Confucius, or the Shasters of the Hindoos," agreed the *New-York Observer*.[110] The *New Englander* went so far as to allege that Child exhibited "too great partiality for Paganism, and too great prejudice against the sacred Books of Christians." "If Mrs. Child had taken half the pains to present what is hideous and ignoble and irrational and immoral in the vedas and shastras, that she has to show what she calls the blemishes of the sacred Scriptures, it would have been far more creditable to her character, though it might have been less agreeable to her taste," charged this orthodox journal.[111] Even the liberal *Christian Inquirer*, which gave Child one of her most sympathetic reviews, judged on the one hand that she had spoken with too much "freedom . . . of certain dogmas and usages which the great majority of Christians regard as indissolubly connected with the very substance of Christianity" and on the other hand that "[i]n her desire to show the favorable side" of pagan religions, she had not presented "in equally vivid colors the baneful effects of the bad which was mixed with the good."[112]

Child herself had been so well prepared for such criticisms that she found the reviews more generous than she had expected. "There have been more commendatory notices, than fault-finding ones; and those who dislike the book have, with two or three exceptions, expressed their disapprobation in a mild and courteous tone," she reported. As usual, she took a long-range historical view of the situation and concluded: "Certainly the world has made some progress since the learned and benevolent Dr. Priestly had his house and library burned by a mob, and was constrained to become an exile from his native country, because he published what he conscientiously regarded as the truth, in opposition to prevailing theological opinions."[113] The book's sales also gave Child cause for satisfaction. Within two months of its publication, the first edition of two thousand copies had "already paid for itself."[114]

If hostile reviews did not disturb Child, the lukewarm reactions of her loved ones did. Understandably, her brother Convers had bristled at her condemnation of theology, which he called "the science of God" and held up as "the highest and best of all sciences."[115] The Lorings and the Shaws had been "silent as the grave" about the book.[116] Curiously, the two friends who greeted *The Progress of Religious Ideas* most appreciatively were fellow rebels against a Calvinist upbringing: Lucy Osgood, whose father had taught Child her catechism, and Peter Lesley, who had given up his pulpit shortly after marrying Susan Lyman. Osgood and her sister had read "every word" of the book aloud to each other and "rejoice[d] that this great work is the performance of a woman." Child need not have apologized for her "want of learning," Osgood assured her, for "if learning consists in a familiarity with the various phases & highest aspirations of the human mind in the remotest ages & most distant countries; in the power of comprehending the ancient metaphysical subtleties, & of presenting them before the common mind in language so simple, clear & forcible, that he who runs may read — if this be learning . . . I ask, where is there a more learned scholarly work than the Progress of Religious Ideas?"[117] Lesley's letter has not been preserved, but he evidently shared Osgood's admiration for the unself-conscious authority with which Child had treated a subject hitherto assigned to male custodians. "[A] jury of critics could not decide whether [*The Progress of Religious Ideas*] was written by a man or a woman," he opined.[118] He also delighted Child by perceptively remarking that she seemed to "*believe* in the supernatural, and yet to *ridicule* it." As she confessed to both Lesley and Osgood, she was indeed divided between these dual impulses: "one side of my mind tends to the extremest rationality, and the other to a reverential faith, that sometimes borders on superstition."[119]

Perhaps most gratifying to Child were the accolades *The Progress of Religious Ideas* won from the two ministers in abolitionist ranks whom she held in highest esteem — Samuel J. May, to whom she had dedicated the *Appeal*, and Theodore Parker, whose 1841 "Discourse of the Transient and Permanent in Christianity" had created such a furor that no other Unitarian clergyman would exchange pulpits with him (including his old friend Convers Francis).[120] Both hailed Child's book from the pulpit and recommended it to their congregations. "[I]t is the most valuable contribution to an enlarged, charitable and true theology, that has been made by any one in our country," May wrote Child, confiding that he ranked her work above Parker's. Parker himself pronounced the book "magnificent" and saluted it in his Thanksgiving day sermon as "*the* book of the age; and written by a *woman*!"[121]

In reflecting back on her career, Child drew an analogy between *The Progress of Religious Ideas* and the *Appeal*. The earlier work had sought to liberate her contemporaries from the shackles of racial bigotry, the later from the shackles of religious bigotry. Child could now measure the impact of the *Appeal* by the leaders it had converted to the antislavery cause — Wendell Phillips, William Ellery Channing, Charles Sumner, and countless unknown organizers of local abolition societies across the country. "Who can tell how many young minds may be so influenced by the Progress of Ideas as to materially change their career?" she wondered.[122] Over the years, testimonials would accumulate in answer to her query. "A thoughtful lady who lives near us . . . has been deeply studying your Progress of Ideas. . . . 'A shoemaker, has just been reading it with thorough enthusiasm, & declares it is the greatest book ever written — so that he is now raising money to buy it, averring that he cannot live without it.' "[123] "I found my wife last night reading your History of the progress of religious ideas. No book in my library, except the dictionary, oftener attracts my attention."[124] Nor were these obscure folk alone. "To how many of us has [*The Progress of Religious Ideas*] been the pillar of light through the wilderness of doubt in the last twenty years," wrote the famous suffragist Elizabeth Cady Stanton in her 1880 obituary tribute to Child. Fifteen years later, she would follow in Child's footsteps by publishing her controversial *Woman's Bible* (1895). "[I]t still requires courage to question the divine inspiration of the Hebrew Writings as to the position of woman," Stanton would avow as she reiterated the question Child had raised: "Why should the myths, fables, and allegories of the Hebrews be held more sacred than those of the Assyrians and Egyptians, from whose literature most of them were derived?"[125]

Child's "pilgrimage of penance" liberated her forever from the religious dogmas that had haunted her as she had struggled to come to terms with her loss of faith, her sense of spiritual isolation, her disillusionment with the husband who had once embodied her ideals, her alienation from the antislavery comrades she had revered as heroes, and her conflicted gender identity and sexual frustration. With the completion of that pilgrimage's final phase — nursing her father through his last illness — Child would be free to resume her public life.

16

Autumnal Leaves: Reconsecrated Partnerships, Personal and Political

I have felt such burning indignation at the ever-increasing insults and outrages of the South, and the cold, selfish indifference of the North! I have so longed to sieze [sic] a signal-torch, and rush over all the mountains, and through all the vallies, summoning the friends of freedom to the rescue! If they only would forget all minor differences, and form a solid phalanx to resist this gigantic evil, how soon the blustering despots would cower before them! At times, my old heart swells almost to bursting in view of all these things; for it is the heart of a man imprisoned within a woman's destiny.[1]

The outrage that triggered Child's blast of "indignation" was the shocking assault on the Massachusetts senator Charles Sumner by the South Carolina congressman Preston Brooks. On May 20, 1856, Sumner had delivered a fiery Senate oration in which he likened the armed takeover of Kansas by proslavery "ruffians" to a rape and caricatured the thugs' chief defenders in the Senate, Andrew P. Butler of South Carolina and Stephen Douglas of Illinois, as Don Quixote and Sancho Panza. Two days later, Brooks avenged what he considered an insult to the honor of the South, of his home state, and of Butler (a distant cousin). Entering the Senate chamber after adjournment, where Sumner was "busily . . . addressing copies of his speech" for the next mail, Brooks waited until the room was nearly empty and then confronted his bête noire with the words: "[Y]our speech . . . is a libel on South Carolina and Mr. Butler, who is a relative of mine." Before Sumner could reply, Brooks attacked him with a heavy, gold-headed cane, landing more than thirty blows on his victim's skull and shoulders as the senator vainly tried to "extricate himself" from his desk, and finally wrenched it loose from the floor to which it was bolted, only to collapse, drenched in blood.[2]

Intensifying Child's revulsion was the special regard she cherished for Sumner, both as a model statesman of uncompromising integrity and as a political disciple. In 1853, gratified by Child's praise for his "*magnificent* speech in Congress against the Fugitive [Slave] Law," Sumner had written to acknowledge the influence of her antislavery writings in forming his principles and teaching him to transcend personal and sectarian controversy.[3] "The tone which you helped me adopt so early is most in unison with my present position," he had affirmed.[4] Child had preserved Sumner's letter among her "choicest treasures" as an antidote to desponding moods in which she felt that she "*had* done nothing, a[n]d *could* do nothing, to arrest the course of violence and wrong!"[5] Now the vision of her disciple bleeding on the Senate floor brought on "painful suffocation of the heart, alternating with painful throbbings of the brain" — symptoms that lasted for "two or three days," unlike any her "strong constitution" had ever exhibited.[6] "My first impulse was to rush directly to Washington, to ascertain whether I could not supply to you, in some small degree, the absence of a mother's or sister's care," Child wrote to Sumner. Only the obligations that "chained" her to the bedside of her eighty-nine-year-old father kept her from acting on her maternal impulse.

Although Child attributed her symptoms to frustration at being denied the "safety-valve of *action*, to let off the accumulating steam,"[7] she appears to have been identifying physically with Sumner and reliving by association the trauma of her mother's death. Her urge to nurse her hero suggests a deep compulsion to return symbolically to her mother's deathbed, this time in the role of dutiful daughter, which she had angrily rejected at age twelve. She was in fact already playing that role, having devoted herself for the past three years to nursing her senescent father. In her preoccupation with fulfilling her private duties, however, she had "fallen into such a torpid state" that she had all but lost sight of the crisis through which the nation was passing.[8] The assault on Sumner galvanized Child into shifting her attention from the feeble body in her care to the disintegrating body politic beyond her portals. By enabling her to exercise the powerful urge to heal through which she sought assuagement for her psychic wound, yet to extend her nursing from the domestic to the national sphere, the incident liberated her from the severe depression she suffered when she immolated herself on the domestic altar.

Called back into the public arena by the national emergency that "Bleeding Kansas" and "Bleeding Sumner" epitomized, Child summoned the "friends of freedom to the rescue" with a literary "signal-torch" — her powerful story, "The Kansas Emigrants," serialized in the *New York Tribune*. Concurrently, she showed by example how seriously she took the need for antislavery partisans to forget their differences and "form a solid phalanx to resist this gigantic evil." Putting the bitter schisms of the 1840s behind her, she began rebuilding her old antislavery friendships, which once again assumed a central place in her life.

In the process of reconsecrating herself to the struggle against slavery, Child forged a more satisfying relationship with the husband who had so woefully disappointed her. As in the 1830s, she and David turned their marriage into an antislavery partnership. Yet no longer marred by unconscious rivalry on his part and wifely self-abnegation on hers, it now became a partnership of equals, allowing both to make full use of their talents. While Child's writings and letters of the late 1850s reflect the improvement in her marriage, they also reflect her continuing frustration at being "imprisoned within a woman's destiny." She would never retreat from the militant stand on women's rights that she had taken in the 1840s. On the contrary, she protested restrictions on women's freedom more and more vigorously, encouraging her sisters to go further than she had, and hailing every individual achievement as an advance for all women.

Until the blows against Sumner roused her from her torpor, however, Child had endeavored to submit to her "imprisonment" rather than to break out of it. Chastened by the failure of her attempt to make a new start with David in a modest home of their own, she felt "less disposed to struggle with [her] destiny."[9] As she wrote bleakly to Francis Shaw a few months after moving into her father's Wayland, Massachusetts, cottage in December 1853, "I have done building castles in the air. I do not now construct even the smallest paper ones. . . . All my dreams have settled into a stoical resignation to life, as it comes. I try to perform the present duty cheerfully, and do not look beyond it."[10] The "present duty" involved constant drudgery and almost unrelieved loneliness. "One day is *exactly* like another; each day has its laborious task," as well as its endless round of "sweeping, making beds, filling lamps, preparing meals, and washing dishes," not to mention sewing and mending.[11] The routine never varied, except when her father had "one of his poor turns," at which times he "required such *frequent* attention" that Child could not count on "two uninterrupted hours, day or evening."[12] Receiving friends under those conditions was out of the question, and visits to the Lorings and other intimates in Boston, sixteen miles away, had to be carefully rationed and limited to a few hours at a stretch. Her father did not take kindly to her brief absences. He would sit at the window waiting for her return and moaning, "Why *don't* my *darter* come? I'm afraid she is going to stay all night."[13]

Few women could lead the "fettered" existence to which habit had inured her, Child noted grimly.[14] Indeed, she herself would have pronounced it "unendurable" if she had had any inkling of what lay in store for her. "But the human mind can get acclimated to *any*thing," she philosophized, and the thought of "cheering [her] poor old father, in his descent into the grave" usually kept her "in a state of serene contentment."[15] Her loneliness and drudgery had one "pleasant compensation." As she explained to Marianne Silsbee, "The strong affections, which have made me expend all my resources so unreservedly for those I love, find solace in being an object of supreme importance to the two beings who depend upon me for their daily happiness. This tendency is ingrained in my nature, and has been the source of my greatest virtues, and my worst mistakes."[16]

The attack on Sumner shattered Child's mood of "stoical resignation" and made her chafe against her "fetters" with renewed impatience. The word "fetters," which recurs again and again in Child's letters, points to the psychological significance the issue of slavery now took on for her. When she had joined the antislavery movement in the 1830s, she had sacrificed literary, financial, and social standing to fight for the freedom of "others." When she reentered the fray in 1856, she was throwing off her own "fetters" as well as those that bound southern chattels and the northern public to the dictates of the Slave Power. Describing to Sarah Shaw the acute depression that overwhelmed her in the wake of Sumner's beating, Child metaphorically connected its personal and political causes:

The narrowing and fettering influences of my condition here [in Wayland] have something the same effect on me that the atmosphere of the Marshalsea prison had on Little Dorrit; and I *feel* my fetters more than I did when father was so ill as to require unremitting care. Now that I can safely dismiss him from my mind for hours, my wings begin to flutter, and I want to fly; but I *can*not leave him, because nobody else can do anything with him; and when *I* am away, he trains in an extraordinary fashion. The recent public events have also greatly discouraged me. To have labored so *long* against slavery, and yet to see it always triumphant! The outrage upon Charles Sumner made me literally ill. . . .[17]

As her sense of personal imprisonment converged with her fury at the nation's subjection to a perpetually "triumphant" Slave Power, Child experienced the paralyzing self-hatred that results from anger turned inward. "[T]his summer it has been all *night* within my soul," she lamented to Sarah:

I have never been so powerless to struggle against mental depression. All the time, I am weighed down with the miserable consciousness of having lived in vain. All my efforts seem to me so poor, that in glancing back upon them, I feel a profound contempt for them, and for myself. This state of mind of course kills any power there might be to do better; and for *that* also I reproach myself. It is a diseased state; but how to get well?

The answer to her question, Child found, lay in action. She could not strike off the domestic fetters she had assumed as a filial duty, but she could at least arouse her northern compatriots to strike off the political fetters they had allowed the South to impose on them.

Those fetters had multiplied dramatically over the thirteen years since Child had left the *Standard*. In 1845 abolitionists had finally lost their decade-long struggle to prevent the annexation of Texas — a struggle in which David had played a major role, culminating in his tract *The Taking of Naboth's Vineyard* (1845).[18] War with Mexico had swiftly followed, and by 1848 the United States had conquered a vast territory that threatened to expand the South's slave empire as far as the Pacific coast, and thus to tip the precarious balance of power between slave and free states in the South's favor. The ensuing confrontation between proslavery forces determined to enjoy the fruits of the war and antislavery forces determined to contain the "peculiar institution" within its current boundaries had resulted in the Compromise of 1850. In exchange for admitting one of the conquered territories, California, as a free state, and ending the slave trade (but not slavery itself) in the District of Columbia, the notorious agreement brokered by Henry Clay and Daniel Webster organized the remaining territories without "any restriction or condition on the subject of slavery." The worst provision was a draconian Fugitive Slave Law that effectually nullified the legal system of the free states, replacing it with the slave code of the South.[19] Four years later, proslavery forces made a mockery out of "compromise" when they pushed through the Kansas-Nebraska Act, which repealed the 1820 Missouri Compromise (also engineered by Henry Clay) and lifted the restrictions it had established against slavery in territory north of the 36°30″ line. Henceforward, all new territories would have the right to decide by "popular sovereignty" whether or not to allow slavery within their borders. "Of all our servile senates, none have been so completely servile to the slave-interest, as the present one," Child commented in disgust to Francis Shaw, whom she was keeping abreast of political developments during his sojourn in Europe. "I feel habitually as if I should be willing to pour out my blood, like water, if I could do anything to arrest the downward course of things."[20]

Although Child had withdrawn from the American Anti-Slavery Society, she had continued to help fugitive slaves on their way to freedom. Both the Hopper home in New York City and the Carpenter farm in New Rochelle served as stations on the Underground Railroad, affording many opportunities for direct contacts with runaways. Describing one such encounter to Marianne Silsbee, in the hope of appealing to her antiabolitionist friend's human sympathies, Child wrote: "A poor slave came to me the other day. He looked sad and weather-beaten. They had sold his wife and baby to far Louisiana, where he would never see them again. . . . I helped him on to Victoria's dominions, with the feeling of shame, which I always have, when obliged to tell men they cannot be free in our own country."[21]

The Fugitive Slave Law not only penalized such rescue work with stiff fines and six-month imprisonment terms, but prohibited "any court, judge, magistrate," or private citizen from obstructing the recapture of fugitives. It also offered what amounted to a bribe for enforcement: a ten-dollar fee to commissioners for every slave remanded, as against a five-dollar fee for cases decided against the claimant. The sight of fugitives being hunted down and sent back into slavery by officials of her native Massachusetts enraged Child. Hearing that Salem mayor Nathaniel Silsbee, her friend Marianne's husband, had "assisted in restoring a fugitive slave," Child vowed to "bury every friendship on earth, rather than shake hands" with such a man. "The coals of my free nature are burning yet, though the ashes of many disappointments cover them. Touch a hair of a slave's head, and a tongue of flame shoots up from the suppressed volcano!" she warned, revealing her pent-up rebellion against her own "fettered" existence in her ardent identification with the hounded fugitive.[22]

Child was particularly "pained and humiliated" when the slave Anthony Burns was "given up by Boston magistrates, and triumphantly carried back to bondage" in June 1854, "guarded by a strong escort of U.S. troops." The scene she sketched for Francis Shaw unmistakably indicated that the citizens of Boston had been reduced to slavery in their homeland: "The court-house was nearly *filled* with troops and hired ruffians, armed with cutlasses and bowie knives. No *citizen* was allowed to enter without a *pass*, as is the custom with *slaves*. . . . Men were even arrested and imprisoned for merely making *observations* to each other, which the ruling powers considered dangerous." What most "humiliated" Child about the episode was the impotence abolitionists had displayed in a bungling attempt to rescue Burns, which had left one person dead. She blamed the fiasco on the militant rhetoric that protesters at a Faneuil Hall rally had substituted for well-planned action: "[T]hey *talked* boldly of a rescue the next *morning* and so did more harm than good, by forewarning the Southerners and giving them time to summon a great array of U.S. troops. If they had *only* struck when the iron was hot, and used very slight precautions, I think the poor slave might have been rescued without shedding blood."[23] Actually, the rescue attempt had failed because of faulty coordination between its ringleaders and their allies at the Faneuil Hall meeting, who were supposed to have adjourned early and joined in storming the courthouse that evening.[24] Child could not have known of the plan, however, for David does not seem to have belonged to Boston's Vigilance Committee — one of the many biracial (but all-male) organizations founded to provide armed defense of blacks claimed as fugitives after 1850.

Despite the "towering indignation" with which Child reacted to fugitive slave cases in Massachusetts and to the "servile submission of the North" in Congress,[25] she remained too paralyzed by depression and overwhelmed by housework to contribute more than in small ways to the campaign against the nefarious 1850 law. It would fall to Harriet Beecher Stowe to mobilize public opposition through a soul-stirring antislavery novel such as Child had once aspired to write. Hailing *Uncle Tom's Cabin* (1852) as a "truly great work" and crediting it with doing "much to command respect for faculties of woman," Child wryly predicted that the book's "moderate sprinkling of Calvinism" would "make it acceptable to a much larger class of readers, who are not in the habit of taking in much humanity, unless stirred up with a portion of theology; like brimstone and molasses."[26] She herself did not testify publicly against the Fugitive Slave Law until the following year, in her biography of Isaac Hopper (1853). Nor did she return to antislavery fiction until after the completion of *The Progress of Religious Ideas* (1855). Her first forays in the field were curiously distant from the American scene: "The Adventures of Jamie and Jeannie," set in South Africa, which led off *A New Flower for Children* (1856), and "Jan and Zaida," set in the Dutch East Indies, which Child published in the 1856 *Liberty Bell*.[27] Though far less effective than her antislavery stories of the 1840s, these two narratives marked Child's reconsecration of her art to the service of abolitionism. Not since the collapse of the *Juvenile Miscellany* in 1834 had Child sought to use children's fiction as a vehicle for antislavery principles, and not since her rupture with Maria Weston Chapman in 1843 had she contributed to the *Liberty Bell*.

Child's rapprochement with her former comrades in the Boston Female Anti-Slavery Society began in 1853. Attending their annual fund-raising fair for the first time in fourteen years, she found it "heart-warming" to discover "how much [she] was cared for." She would gradually resume her place in the circle of antislavery women, yet the fair would never provide a satisfying sphere of action for her. "I feel 'like a cat in a strange garret' there," she complained, perhaps referring to the elegant surroundings and aristocratic clientele that had come to characterize the event under Chapman's entrepreneurial management.[28]

Except for the fair, Child still recoiled from the "bigotry and harshness" of her old Garrisonian associates.[29] "Mrs. Chapman . . . calls both Mrs. Stowe and Charles Sumner 'ephemeras'; and says, 'they will be and *must* be ephemeras, unless they deepen and broaden,'" Child reported in exasperation to Anna Loring. "That is," she translated for Anna, "unless they subscribe to the creed of the American Anti Slavery Society. All I can say is, I should like to be performing as glorious a mission, as *either* of those 'ephemeras.' "[30] Once the vanguard of a mass movement, Garrisonians had dwindled into a sect rigidly intent on maintaining its ideological purity. Their "creed" now consisted in denouncing the Constitution as a proslavery compact and calling for dissolution of the Union — positions that cut them off from voters and politicians who shared their abhorrence of slavery but who wanted to act against it within the system. While Child agreed with the Garrisonians' political analysis, she deprecated their "inability to acknowledge any one as a helper who d[oe]s not work for the cause in their way."[31] Unlike Chapman, for example, she recognized that the battle against slavery had to be waged simultaneously on many fronts and that it could not be won without enlisting recruits of varying ideological persuasion and encouraging them to use the weapons of their choice. As she commented to Sarah Shaw:

> In the early days of the Anti Slavery enterprise, it was a common thing for our speakers to say that *eventually* the work must be completed by *politicians*. How we should have *then* rejoiced over any man that would have stood up on the floor of Congress, with even *half* the courage of Giddings, Sumner, and Wilson! But *we*, in the mean time, have been marching ahead; and the van of the long army has the folly to despise the rear. As if there could be a van *without* a rear! As if *all* the forces were not *needed*, to attack the enemy at *all* his weak points! *I* say, God speed the van, and God bless the rear! And for my own part, I am willing to ride about, here and there, "promiscuous like," as I see occasion.[32]

Child's reflections point up both the realignments that had taken place on the political scene by the mid-1850s and the evolution they had prompted in her thinking. With the founding of the Republican party in 1854, electoral politics had become a much more viable means of advancing the antislavery cause than had been the case during her editorship of the *Standard* in the 1840s, when she had so earnestly remonstrated against turning abolition from a moral into a political movement. A coalition of former Liberty party abolitionists, antislavery Whigs, and Free-Soil Democrats, the Republican party had committed itself to opposing the extension of slavery, though not to abolishing the institution where it already existed. If its goals fell far short of the Liberty party's, its constituency was much broader, and its ranks in Congress had swelled. Meanwhile, the old mainstream parties were in disarray. The Whigs had all but disintegrated, and the Democrats were fissuring along sectional lines. As a result, the Republicans had a realistic chance to shape congressional policy and perhaps even to capture the White House. They were fielding their first presidential candidate in the 1856 elections: John C. Frémont, who had vowed to stop the encroachments of the Slave Power.[33]

Thus, when the assault on Sumner drew Child back into the fray, the arena toward which she gravitated was not the sectarian conclave of the American Anti-Slavery Society but the national platform Sumner had occupied as a Republican politician. "I want to mount the rostrum myself," Child confided to Sarah Shaw. "I have such a fire burning in my soul, that it seems to me I could pour forth a stream of lava. . . ."[34] Sumner had poured forth a "stream of lava" when he had execrated "The Crime Against Kansas." Taking up his bloodstained mantle, Child sought to fulfill his mission. Instead of a congressional speech, she used the medium of a short story: "The Kansas Emigrants." But she serialized it in a leading Republican newspaper, the *New York Tribune*, and timed it to influence voters in the closing days of the hotly contested 1856 election.[35]

The "crime" Sumner had exposed in his speech had sprung directly from the "popular sovereignty" provision of the 1854 Kansas-Nebraska Act, which allowed the citizens of a territory applying for statehood to vote on whether to define their state as "free" or "slave." Immediately after passage of the Act, pro- and antislavery settlers had begun racing for electoral dominance in Kansas. Quickly outnumbered, proslavery settlers had then resorted to violence and fraud. At every election thousands of Missourians poured over the border to vote in Kansas and to scare free-state voters away from the polls. The Kansas legislature thus elected had promptly passed laws on slavery identical with those in Missouri. In response, antislavery settlers had met to formulate their own constitution. Civil war had finally erupted between the two parties in December 1855, and on May 21, 1856, the day before the beating of Sumner, proslavery forces had "wiped out" the town of Lawrence, Kansas, a hub of free-state activism, demolishing its printing press and burning its hotel and homes to the ground.[36]

To Child, the fate of the country seemed to hang in the balance. For more than thirty years, slavery had been spreading like a cancer. With every compromise, the Slave Power had increased its representation in Congress and tightened its stranglehold over the body politic. If it triumphed in Kansas, Child predicted in a letter to Sarah Shaw, nothing short of civil war could extirpate it. "[W]ith all my horror of bloodshed, I could be better resigned to that great calamity, than to endure the tyranny that has so long trampled on us," she added ominously. But Child was not yet resigned to civil war, for she still saw an alternative: "If the Slave-Power is checked *now*, it will *never* regain its strength."[37] By turning the tide in Kansas, abolitionists could keep open the possibility of ending slavery peacefully (a possibility at best remote and in retrospect illusory). At this critical juncture, Child believed, it was imperative for abolitionists to unite behind the two groups standing against the Slave Power: the free-state settlers in Kansas, who were resisting it with arms, and the Republican party, which was challenging it at the polls.

Child sought to forge the divided ranks of antislavery partisans into a "solid phalanx" through "The Kansas Emigrants," aiming the story simultaneously at the Republican readers of the *Tribune* and at her erstwhile Garrisonian comrades. Republicans held the Union sacred and quailed at risking its dissolution. Child tried to persuade them that the cause of freedom was more sacred than the Union, and that a Union ruled by the Slave Power was not worth preserving. Garrisonians clung to their ideal of Christlike nonresistance and balked at endorsing armed struggle. Child asked them to weigh their peace principles against their antislavery goals and choose between them.

Appearing in the *Tribune* alongside the latest bulletins from Kansas, and based on incidents publicized in antislavery newspapers and travelers' accounts, "The Kansas Emigrants" combines the authority of fact with the emotional appeal of fiction.[38] So skillfully does Child meld the two that a reader turning from one medium to the other in the *Tribune*'s columns feels no disjunction. Her plot weaves the strands of disparate news reports into a coherent narrative patterned on the culture's most cherished epics: the voyage of the pilgrims and the American Revolution. It also elevates the free-state settlers to epic status by casting them as heirs of the nation's seventeenth-and eighteenth-century founders. Obviously evoking the Puritan leaders William Bradford and John Winthrop, the Kansas emigrants John and Kate Bradford and William and Alice Bruce reenact and fulfill their predecessors' uncompleted errand. They, too, leave "comfortable homes" and close-knit communities to brave hardships in a dangerous frontier outpost, because they consider it "a glorious privilege to help in laying the foundation of states on a basis of justice and freedom."[39] Unlike their forebears', however, the emigrants' concept of a just society includes equal rights for Indians, African Americans, and women. Accordingly, the "savage" enemies they face in their new environment are not Indians, but Missouri Border Ruffians, and the government whose usurpations drive them to revolution is not a British king's, but an American president's — the Democratic administration of Franklin Pierce, which has been openly conniving with these proslavery thugs.

After arousing sympathy for the emigrants as embodiments of traditional American ideals, Child shows them patiently enduring an escalating series of provocations by their proslavery adversaries. Targeted at Republican readers, Child's depiction of the Border Ruffians as thieving bullies serves to illustrate the incompatibility of slavery with free institutions and hence the futility of Union with slavery. At the same time, her portrayal of the emigrants as pacifists who "stand pledged to avoid bloodshed" (344) serves to enlist Garrisonians in their favor. John Bradford and William Bruce honor this pledge in the teeth of attempts on their lives. One night, "twenty or thirty fierce-looking men, armed with bowie-knives and revolvers" break into the Bradford home to lynch John for publishing abolitionist articles in the *Herald of Freedom* (339–40). Kate succeeds in holding them at bay by throwing herself across John's body and clinging to him so desperately that the ruffians cannot pry her away, even by pounding her with their fists. As in the incident Child used as her source — the near-lynching of the Parkville *Luminary*'s editor in April 1855 — only the intervention of a proslavery settler moved by Kate's bravery and loyalty finally saves John.[40] "[I]t required more courage to refrain from seizing my rifle," admits her husband, crediting Kate with giving him that courage, "than it would have done to discharge its contents among those rascals" (344).

What leads John and William to decide that "the hour for self-defence has come" is not fear for their own lives, but concern for the future of antislavery in Kansas (348). The free-state settlers have exhausted all peaceful remedies, Child emphasizes. They have appealed again and again to President Pierce and Congress for "redress and protection." Yet the president has appointed a governor "in league with the Missourians" to rule over Kansas and has exhorted the free-state settlers to obey laws forced on them "at the point of the bayonet" (346–47). As for Congress, both the Whig and Democratic parties have invoked "law and order" against the settlers and "refused to read well-authenticated testimony" on the fraud and violence invalidating the elections. Now that the governor has actually called out troops against the emigrants, they must either fight or give Kansas over to proslavery rule.

In December 1855 when Border Ruffians reinforced by Federal troops began massing against the free-state settlement of Lawrence, the *Liberator*'s Kansas correspondent, Charles Stearns (a distant relation of Child's by marriage), reached the same conclusion. "My non-resistance has at length yielded," he wrote. "I am sorry to deny the principles of Jesus Christ, after contending for them so long, but it is not for myself that I am going to fight. It is *for God* and *the slaves. Down with American Slavery!* will be my watchword." Like Child in "The Kansas Emigrants," he went on to implore his fellow abolitionists to come to the rescue. "March straight through Missouri, and proclaim *Liberty to the slaves!*" Stearns exhorted them. "The war, if once commenced, *will* not, *must* not cease until every slave throughout the Union is liberated."[41]

His ringing appeal did not win Garrison's endorsement. Instead, Garrison compared Stearns's abandonment of his peace principles to Peter's cowardly denial of Christ and expressed the hope that Stearns, like Peter, would soon repent.[42] Garrison spelled out the full implications of his views in a long letter published in the *Standard* on the same day that the opening number of "The Kansas Emigrants" appeared in the *New York Weekly Tribune*. Contrary to the message of "The Kansas Emigrants," the purpose of Garrison's letter was to advise abolitionists not to vote in the upcoming election, lest they "compromise with sin." Reiterating his long-standing dictum that the Constitution binding the free North to the slave South was a "COVENANT WITH DEATH," Garrison insisted that it would be better to lose Kansas than to renounce the nonresistance principles that prohibited his followers from upholding the Constitution by their votes, or from sanctioning violence.[43]

Child herself had gone through an agonizing reappraisal of her commitment to nonviolence. The "cruel outrages against unoffending citizens in Kansas" and the "attempted assassination" of Sumner for having "defended their cause," she admitted to him, had "sorely tried" her "peace-principles": "nothing suits my mood so well, as Jeanne d'Arc's floating banner and consecrated sword."[44] She still believed Christians ought to try to live up to the "injunction *never* to return injury for injury," and she ranked those who would die for "justice, truth, or freedom" above those who would kill for them, but she dissociated herself from the American Anti-Slavery Society's "narrow and intolerant" condemnation of the free-state settlers' recourse to arms. "I can never call those men murderers, who forsake home and kindred, and all that renders life agreeable, and with noble self-sacrifice go forth to suffer and to die in the cause of freedom," she explained to Sumner.

To win Garrisonian readers over to her position and induce them to support the struggle for a free Kansas, Child characterizes her hero, William Bruce, precisely as a man willing to die for the antislavery cause. Throughout the story, she presents him as the emigrant community's most articulate and revered exponent of abolitionist principles. At the free-state settlers' constitutional convention in Topeka, he argues so strenuously against racial restrictions that opponents suspect him of favoring the extension of voting and officeholding rights to African Americans (a measure Child subtly advocates [332]). He also makes "firm friends" of the territory's Indians by "treating them with justice and kindness, and with that personal respect, which they so well know how to appreciate" and "so rarely meet in white men" (304, 350). Bruce's acquiescence in the collective decision that "the hour for self-defence has come" thus carries special weight. The circumstances of his murder — based on an actual incident — dignify him as a martyr, for he is shot in the back by a party of Border Ruffians while on his way home, unarmed, from patrol duty in Lawrence, his hands as yet unstained by blood. In short, Bruce personifies the cause abolitionists would be betraying if "stern adherence" to the doctrine of nonresistance led them to abandon Kansas to proslavery rule, as Garrison advised.[45]

Through Bruce, Child issues an election eve appeal to abolitionists that directly counters Garrison's. Appearing posthumously to his wife, Alice, in a "prophetic" vision, Bruce shows her the prospect of a "Free Kansas" that resembles "dear New England" — a land "covered with farm-houses and fields of corn," churches and schools, and, presiding over all, "a great University on the highest of the hills," now called "Free Mont" (362–63). The election of Frémont, Child reminds her readers, can make this dream of "Free Kansas" a reality.

Recalling the campaign slogan "Free Soil, Free Speech, Free Men, Frémont," the vision of "Free Kansas" that Child holds out here encapsulates Republican ideology with its premise that free labor generates economic and cultural development.[46] Child knew, however, that all too many of her Republican readers wanted to define "Free Kansas" as a white preserve. The *Tribune*'s Kansas correspondent William Phillips, for example, had given a virulently racist account of the territory's Indian tribes and had recommended their "extradition" to "wilds further west" on the grounds that they could never "successfully mix" with whites.[47] Similarly, Charles Stearns had reported in the *Liberator* that the vast majority of Kansas emigrants were "mongrel" abolitionists "like Aunt Ophelia, in Uncle Tom's Cabin." The main reason they so "desperately opposed" slavery, he had discovered to his horror, was that "they 'don't want the niggers about them.'"[48] Indeed the delegates to the Topeka convention had voted overwhelmingly for a "Black Law" barring African Americans from Kansas (the law against which Child has William Bruce plead). As Garrison pointed out, most free-state settlers were "contending for their own rights *as white men*, not for the rights of all, without distinction of caste or color"[49] — although their ranks certainly included thoroughgoing abolitionists, among them the men who would accompany John Brown to Harpers Ferry. By endowing Bruce with abolitionist ideals mandating justice toward Indians and equal rights for African Americans, Child is urging both the combatants at the front and their Republican sympathizers at home not to reproduce the flawed America of the past, but to make "Free Kansas" the prototype of a regenerated America, true to its creed of liberty and justice for all.

The climax of the story suggests that a second American Revolution will be needed to usher this ideal republic into being. Drilling to "the tunes of '76," the free-state settlers show the "old spirit of Lexington and Concord" as they defy President Pierce's orders to "obey the laws" of a government they have not elected (346, 351–52). Nevertheless, Lawrence succumbs to a proslavery mob that hoists a "blood-red pirate flag, fit emblem of the Border Ruffians," alongside the United States flag, now a "suitable companion for it." "What cared New England that *her* six stars were there, in shameful 'Union' with that blood-red flag?" Child demands of her readers (358–59). Whether on the battlefield or in another constitutional convention, she implies, Americans will have to dissolve their "Union" with slavery and reconstruct their Republic on a sounder basis.

Child accords women a major role in creating the new society she envisions — one that will embrace them as equal partners. Women were in fact playing a prominent part in the free-state settlers' defense of their communities. Contrasting so painfully with her domestic confinement in Wayland, the exploits of her sisters at the front fired Child's imagination more than any other aspect of the struggle. "Never, never have my sympathies been so powerfully excited. Never have I been so proud of women as I have been while reading of your patient endurance and your undaunted heroism," Child wrote "To the Women of Kansas."[50] Published in the *Herald of Freedom*, her letter accompanied a box of clothes she had dispatched to the settlers, in her anxiety to alleviate their sufferings before winter set in. Not only had she organized a sewing circle in Wayland that had produced "about $60 dollars worth of clothing" for the emigrants, but she herself had cut up and sewn "more than 60 yds of cloth into garments," sitting up until late at night and "stitching as fast as [her] fingers could go."[51] "While I was making them, I seemed to hear the alarm-drum beat, and the rifle-shots whizzing at dead of night; and my heart bled with yours," Child told her sisters in Kansas.

The women with whom Child identified so passionately were undergoing the ordeal she would have faced, had she and David gone to Texas as planned in 1836, to pioneer a free-labor colony with Benjamin Lundy. But Kansan women were also engaging in the active political combat for which she longed as she sat at home twenty years later, nursing her dying father. By fighting against slavery in Kansas, they were liberating themselves and others from woman's sphere. Child projected these dual perceptions of her sisters' travail onto heroines embodying different sides of herself as well as different ideals of womanhood. In the process, she reevaluated the choices she had made in the past and formulated more satisfying options for the women of the future.

Alice Bruce, who " 'idolizes' " her husband and "would have sacrificed life itself" for him (308, 327), personifies the ideal of True Womanhood to which Child had conformed in the early years of her marriage, with disastrous results. "[I]n such natures love takes possession of the whole being" (308), Child notes, echoing her astute analysis of herself.[52] Like her namesake, Alice Franklin, in "Home and Politics," another of Child's self-portraits, Alice Bruce has centered all her aspirations on the dream of "a neat little wedded home" (337).[53] It is a dream incompatible with life in a war-torn frontier settlement, and Alice suffers cruelly from the "rupture of old ties" that William's decision to emigrate to Kansas imposes on her (308), just as Child had suffered when she had uprooted herself from her circle of friends in Boston to accompany David to Northampton after the Texas scheme had fallen through. William's reasons for joining the settlers whom John Bradford is leading to Kansas sound much like David's reasons for joining Lundy's free-labor colony in Texas. "I feel that all there is of manhood within me, will be developed by the exigencies of such a career. . . . If I remain here, I never shall do half I am capable of doing for myself and for posterity," he tells Alice (305). Forced, like Child, to choose between parting with the man she loves or sacrificing her own needs to his, Alice, too, chooses self-sacrifice.

In Alice's case, the upshot is tragic, for she does not possess the literary talents that enabled Child to maintain an independent identity. Nor does she share her husband's political convictions, as Child did. She exemplifies the "patient endurance," but not the "undaunted heroism," that aroused Child's sympathies for the women of Kansas. Entirely immersed in woman's sphere, she understands none of the issues over which pro- and antislavery settlers are battling, and William must shelter her from the brutal realities of the strife. His murder shatters her mind, since she has merged her identity so totally in his that she cannot exist without him. Ultimately she regresses into infantilism—"utterly helpless," "fed and tended" like a baby, and pleading tearfully, "I want my *mother*! I want to go home to my *mother*!" (353–54, 361). Her fate warns against the deadly consequences of overvaluing domestic love. Having paid the price of trying to live by the feminine ideal Alice represents, Child now judges that it has no place in America's future.

That future, which Alice glimpses in a "prophetic" trance just before her death, will belong to women like her cousin Kate Bradford, whose "undaunted heroism" in Kansas is helping to construct it. If Alice embodies the domestic side of herself that Child had celebrated in *Good Wives*, Kate embodies the activist self she had expressed in her antislavery writings. Typifying a revolutionary ideal of womanhood, which Child actually links to "the women of '76," Kate participates alongside her husband, John, in the crusade to make Kansas a free-state, as Child would certainly have participated in David's and Lundy's crusade to launch a free-labor colony in Texas (349). John's plans for the future of Kansas include a free-state university where Kate can be a professor— a radical notion for an era when women did not attend universities, let alone teach at them. "I, for one, will give you my vote," he assures her, in a veiled reference to the campaign for woman suffrage (316).

The Bradfords' marriage reflects both the political partnership the Childs had established as antislavery activists in the 1830s and the one they were reestablishing in the 1850s. During the very weeks when Child was writing "The Kansas Emigrants," David was traveling around New England organizing relief efforts for the Massachusetts Kansas Aid Committee and stumping for Frémont and the Republican party.[54] Compared to her situation in the 1830s, Child had achieved a greater degree of autonomy in her marriage. David's political work no longer threatened to disrupt hers. By participating vicariously, rather than literally, in the struggle for a free Kansas, Child could best exercise the literary talents through which she had always made her most significant contributions to the antislavery cause. Yet she remained trapped in the roles of

Frugal Housewife and Family Nurse that she had resumed as much for David's sake as for her father's. Denied access to the wider platform she could have occupied had she been born a man, she felt more keenly than ever before the injustice of the gender system that "imprisoned" the "heart of a man . . . within a woman's destiny."[55] Hence the excitement with which she hailed the revolution her sisters in Kansas were enacting.

In Kate Bradford, Child imagines herself free to display "the heart of a man." Like the women described by the *Tribune*'s correspondent as "enrolled, under lady officers, ready to defend their houses, if necessary," Kate takes to practicing with "rifle and pistol" after hearing that Border Ruffians have raped one of her neighbors (355).[56] She also performs a feat attributed to two matrons whose husbands, like John Bradford and William Bruce, edited the *Herald of Freedom*.[57] When supplies of ammunition run low, Kate and another woman volunteer to run a wagonload of powder kegs and percussion caps through enemy lines, hiding their dangerous cargo under their "ample skirts" (348–49). "They will never suspect that women carry such luggage," argues Kate, in an ironic comment on the vulnerability of a patriarchal order that denies women's sexuality to keep them subordinate.[58] After the sack of Lawrence, it is Kate who salvages the elements necessary to reconstruct Free Kansas from its ashes. She conveys small children and helpless sufferers to safety, finds a "suitable place to conceal some firearms for future use," and runs back and forth "pistol in hand" rescuing valuables from the "wreck." Her parting words to the mob prophesy the ultimate triumph of freedom over slavery: "You *think* you have silenced the Herald of Freedom, because you have demolished the printing-press; but you are mistaken. That trumpet will sound across the prairies yet" (360–361). The task of rebuilding American society on a foundation of true liberty, Child suggests, requires a new woman, ready to take her place in the public arena.

Child herself reentered the public arena in a new guise with "The Kansas Emigrants." Like Jeanne d'Arc, whom she had invoked in her letter to Sumner, she had seized a "signal-torch," summoned the "friends of freedom to the rescue," and exhorted them to "form a solid phalanx" against their country's foe. And like Sumner, she had "mount[ed] a rostrum" and delivered a political address to the nation. Published on election eve in the North's leading Republican newspaper (where it interrupted the serialization of Dickens's *Little Dorrit*), "The Kansas Emigrants" reached the largest circulation Child ever achieved in a work of fiction and effectually propelled her to the forefront of another masculine realm — that of electoral politics.[59]

Twenty-three years after issuing her abolitionist *Appeal*, however, Child had long since rejected the status of an honorary man. She no longer contented herself with quietly exercising her own rights, as she had once advised the Grimké sisters to do, but emulated her feminist friends in demanding equal rights for all women. As a campaign pitch addressed to voters — by definition male — yet couched in a woman's voice and accentuating the crucial role women were playing in the struggle to determine the nation's fate, "The Kansas Emigrants" implicitly claimed that women, too, deserved the right to vote.

Eight years earlier, Elizabeth Cady Stanton and Lucretia Mott had advanced the same claim at the first Women's Rights Convention, held in 1848 at Seneca Falls, New York. Their initiative seems to have caught Child's imagination and contributed to directing her toward electoral politics—an avenue she had previously shunned. For Stanton, whose husband, Henry, had launched the Liberty party after breaking with Garrison over the issue of political action, the call for woman suffrage came naturally; why let men monopolize a vehicle they had found so useful?[60] For Child, who attributed a large portion of her marital woes to David's involvement in electoral politics, and who regarded politics as a "snare . . . drawing honest souls out of a straight-forward line into all manner of serpent-like sinuosities," the desire to enter the political arena represented a major shift.[61] "I never was bitten by politics before; but such mighty issues are depending on *this* election, that I cannot be indifferent," Child explained to Sarah Shaw.[62]

Sharing with Sarah the keen interest she took in the Frémont campaign, Child repeatedly linked it with the campaign for woman suffrage. "What a shame that *women* can't vote!" she exclaimed. "Wait a while! Women-stock's rising in the market. I shall not live to see women vote; but I'll come and *rap* at the ballot-box. Won't *you*?"[63] Child took a woman's pride in Frémont's talented wife, who appealed far more to her than the official Republican candidate did. Jessie Benton Frémont had coauthored the popular reports of her husband's exploring expeditions, and Republican campaign songs celebrated "Frémont and our Jessie" together. "Is n't it pleasant to have a *woman* spontaneously recognized as a moral influence in public affairs? There's *meaning* in that fact," Child rejoiced with Sarah. If women could vote, they would "carry 'our Jessie' into the White House on [their] shoulders," she added.[64] In contrast, Child admitted to distrust of Frémont. Recalling his filibustering expedition to California in 1846, she pointed out that he had done "much to stir up that most unjust war with Mexico." She was supporting Frémont mainly because he had "pledged himself to oppose the extension of slavery, and it is for his interest to *keep* the pledge."[65]

Whatever Child's reasons for being so uncharacteristically "infected with *political* excitement,"[66] her new enthusiasm was bringing her closer to David. "*We* also talk of little else but Kansas and Frémont," she wrote Sarah.[67] Unlike her letters of the early 1850s, which rarely mention David except in connection with the financial problems Child was trying to solve, her 1856 letters to the Shaws frequently quote him as a political pundit.

The letters that the couple exchanged during David's promotional trip for the Kansas Aid Committee reflect their growing camaraderie even more strikingly. David, who had written so seldom during their separations of the 1830s and 1840s, neglecting to answer his wife's letters despite poignant entreaties, is the first to write this time: "Darling Blessed Mariquita   How I do miss my mate!" he repines, complaining that he is not enjoying the beautiful scenery of Pittsfield without her and begging her to send him "a diamond letter."[68] "Darling David has n't begun to think Mariquita has forgotten him; *has* he?" Child responds apologetically, enumerating the causes of her silence: the pressure of meeting the *Tribune*'s deadline for "The Kansas Emigrants," the "heavy job" of sewing she had undertaken for the free-state settlers, and the burden of nursing her father through his latest spell of ill health. A tone of self-assured independence has replaced the abject pleas for love and forgiveness that resound through the letters of the 1830s. Yet one also hears a teasing affection: "My nest seems so dreary without my kind mate! I have nobody to plague, nobody to scold at, nobody to talk loving nonsense to. . . . Dear soul! How I do long to see you, and to have one of our old cozy chats, and say over the old prayer, before we go to sleep."[69] These letters conjure up the picture of an aging couple enjoying each other's company, recapturing the intimacy of their days as newlyweds, and preserving it in private rituals.

The contents of their "cozy chats" can be inferred from the subjects that dominate the couple's correspondence: anxiety about the fate of Kansas, worry about the election returns, concern over the tactics of political opponents, and recital of the activities through which wife and husband are both working for the Republicans. "It seemed as if my heart would burst, if I could n't *do* something to help on the election," writes Child of her most recent effort: a "Song for the Free Soil Men," which she has arranged to have distributed around the country after getting it set to music by her friend John Sullivan Dwight. Similarly, David reports from the Berkshires that "[p]eople thank me for coming to organize them, & take hold with alacrity & earnestness" of relief measures for the Kansas settlers. Looking forward to David's return in time for election day, Child jokes: "If you *dont* come, I shall put on your old hat and coat, and vote *for* you."[70] The fantasy of going to the polls disguised in David's clothes suggests that she has come to view the assumption of his identity as a route to political empowerment.

In rebuilding her marriage on the basis of political camaraderie, Child ultimately directed her residual anger over her aborted career away from David and toward the patriarchal system that subordinated all women to men. That is, she translated it from personal into political terms. The most telling indication occurs in a July 1856 letter to Loring, ostensibly requesting his legal opinion on the Childs' tax liability for their Northampton farm, which had just been sold. The town of Northampton had imposed an excessively high property tax as a means of recuperating its losses on precisely the kind of ill-advised expenditure in which David had repeatedly involved Child without consulting her — an investment in a superfluous building that the town could not afford, and a "foolish law-suit." "I was not permitted to *vote* about the extravagant building, or the needless law-suit; yet here am I called upon to *pay* for them, out of my small means," fumed Child, vowing to "petition the Legislature to exempt me from *taxes*, or grant me the privilege of *voting*." The tax burden had in fact originated in David's purchase of the Northampton farm, for which Child had been reimbursing her father the principal and the interest ever since, but she deflected the blame first onto the town of Northampton and then onto the male sex generally. "Oh *what* a sex you are!" she chided Loring, who enjoyed provoking her feminist outbursts with his twitting. "It's time you were turned out of office. *High* time. You've been captains long enough. It's *our* turn now."[71] On another occasion Child pointedly exempted David from the "towering indignation" kindled in her by the law that obliged her to have David sign her will, though she had been the family's sole income-earner almost from the start. "I was not indignant on my own account, for David respects the freedom of all women upon principle," she wrote Loring: "But I was indignant for womankind made chattels personal from the beginning of time, perpetually insulted by literature, law, and custom. The very phrases used with regard to us are abominable. 'Dead in the law,' 'Femme couverte.' How I detest such language! I must come out with a broadside on that subject before I die."[72] In the 1830s Child had tried to protect her marriage by avoiding analysis of the wrongs women suffered under patriarchy, lest it unleash her repressed anger against David. Now she was allowing herself to feel that anger, while giving it political rather than personal expression. If she had not succeeded in liberating herself from the prison of a "woman's destiny," she had arrived at a healthier resolution of her conflicting needs for love and self-fulfillment.

Besides their political rapprochement, several other factors cemented the Childs' reconciliation. The move to Wayland drastically curtailed their expenses and relieved David of the need to help " 'make buckle and strap meet.' " With neither investments to recover nor rent to pay, they could comfortably live off Child's literary earnings.[73] Since finishing *The Progress of Religious Ideas*, she had turned back to remunerative genres, publishing what she considered to be her best book for juveniles, *A New Flower for Children* (1856), and preparing another collection of short stories, *Autumnal Leaves* (1857). Meanwhile, David had abided by the decision to grant his wife exclusive control of their finances. In the past he had spent her hard-earned money on impulse, without giving a thought to her household budget. Now he acknowledged humbly, "[t]he industry, frugality, & generosity of my noble & loving Mariquita is my sole reliance for the goods of this world," and he conducted himself accordingly.[74] Having at last abandoned his hopeless pursuit of business success, he was channeling his ambitions into carving a modest niche for himself in Republican party politics — an endeavor far more in harmony with Child's abolitionist ideals than David's predilection for the Whigs and Henry Clay had been.

Child's seclusion in Wayland and her absorption in the care of her father may have eased David's adjustment to his dependent role. On the one hand, he no longer had reason to feel threatened by a wife who stole the limelight from him. On the other hand, the physical helplessness of his father-in-law, rather than his own financial incompetence, had prompted Child's latest sacrifice.

The filial duty Child had elected to perform seems to have brought the couple closer in other ways as well. The resentment that her father had harbored against David for so many years, because of the money he had borrowed and the poor use he had made of it, slowly gave way to grudging affection as he came to rely on David for small services around the house. The old man's deteriorating condition increased this reliance, since David was now helping to "lift him up and lay him down" and to cope with his incontinence. "Father is groaning to have you come back; not merely because he has divers things to be attended to; but because he 'misses David,' " Child noted with satisfaction.[75]

Shared political leanings tightened the bond between father-in-law and son-in-law.

A *Weekly Tribune* subscriber, the old man no doubt took pleasure in discussing the news with David, whose party ties gave him an inside view of Republican strategy. At age ninety, he was following the Frémont campaign with intense interest and had set his heart on going to the polls, though too "[f]eeble" to walk. Just before the election, an attack of palsy completely disabled him, and he grumpily renounced his "cherished idea." "I don't care who is President. It will make no difference to *me*," he snorted. When reminded that it would make a difference to posterity, he snapped, "Posterity acts like the Devil." But recovering his strength in time for the "eventful day," he "insisted upon going to vote. 'My *first* vote was given for Washington,' said he, 'and my *last* shall be given for Frémont.'" David and Maria "lifted him carefully into the carriage, and drove him very slowly to the polls." David was "obliged almost to *carry* him" to the ballot box, where he "deposited his vote with trembling hands."[76] "The poor old man wept when he heard the result of the election": 174 electoral votes for the Democratic candidate, James Buchanan, compared to 114 for Frémont.[77] Having lost his only remaining interest in life, he retreated ever deeper into senility.

Finding his father-in-law so close to death, David had postponed his next speaking engagements for the Kansas Aid Committee. After a week of hanging between life and death, however, the old man seemed to be stabilizing, and it looked as though he might "linger all winter." "[I]t seemed a pity to have *two* well persons give up all their avocations" indefinitely, Child decided, so she persuaded David to return to the Berkshires.[78] Grateful to her for minimizing his burdens during the prolonged agony of her father's decline, David responded in kind. "It almost made me cry to see how carefully you had arranged everything for my comfort before you went," Child wrote: "So much kindling stuff split up; and the bricks piled up to protect my flowers." David's departure at a time when Child was awaiting her father's death nevertheless seems to have aroused the feelings buried within her since her mother's death: anger at being abandoned, self-blame for her own anger, and a resulting sense of unworthiness. "How melancholy I felt, when you went off in the morning darkness! It seemed as if everything about me was tumbling down; as if I never was to have a nest and a mate any more," she lamented. Immediately afterward, as if to cancel the implied reproach and direct it against herself, she added: "Good, kind, generous, magnanimous soul! How I love you! . . . I don't deserve that you should be so kind to me."[79]

Child soon regretted having told David she could dispense with him, for her father's condition rapidly worsened. As he weakened, he grew more and more restless, and she needed assistance to "lift him, or change his posture." Her back had almost given out in the effort to do so alone. "He . . . has to be cared for, in all respects, like an infant. His physical infirmities are dreadful—dreadful—and increase with his increasing weakness," she hinted darkly to Louisa, who had offered to come help. Hurtfully reminding her friend, as she so often did, of the class difference between them, Child replied: "If I *could* smile, I should smile to think of your little satin hands performing the offices that I have to perform many times in the day and the night."[80] She did, however, request the aid of the widow who was renting part of the house from Mr. Francis and who was washing his bedding.

For the first fortnight Child watched constantly at her father's bedside, trying to anticipate his "infirmities," and restricting herself to "cat-naps." But after she began to hear "wild Aeolian harps" and loud bells ringing in her ears, she realized she had better get some sleep, and she simply "fold[ed] thick cloths under him" at night.[81] "I think this *must* be the narrowest passage in my narrow life," she wrote Louisa. "I have often thought so before; but *now*, the closing walls must either recede and widen my prospects, or they must crush me. I feel as if every vestige of poetry had been trampled out of me in these last six weary years."[82] Her father waited as impatiently as she did for their "prison-gate to open." "Oh, how long must I wait?" he kept repeating. The end finally came on Thanksgiving morning, at 2 A.M. Child had thought that she would greet her release by rushing "out into infinite space" and "chasing a comet though the universe." Instead, she found herself utterly "desolate." "The occupation of my life seems gone," she told her friends dazedly:

> The old man loved me; and you know how foolishly my nature craves love. Never again can I be so important to any human being as I was to him. Always, when I came back from Boston, there was a bright fire-light in his room for me, and his hand was eagerly stretched out, and the old face lighted up, as he said, "You're welcome back, Maria." *This* time, when I came home, it was all dark and silent. I almost cried myself blind. . . .[83]

By reversing their roles and mothering him in his second childhood, she had finally earned from her father the love for which she had thirsted so desperately in her youth. But she had paid a heavy price for it.

It took Child more than a year to recover from her grief. Her father's death rekindled the yearning for faith that she had put behind her with *The Progress of Religious Ideas*. Once again, she was writing to Lucy Osgood: "[I]f I could only *find* a church, I would nestle into it, as gladly as a bird ever nestled into her covert, in a storm. I have staid away from meeting, because one offered me petrifactions, and another offered gas, when I was hungry for bread."[84] Child had always liked the Unitarian minister in Wayland, Edmund H. Sears, despite their doctrinal differences, and she now began regularly attending his church. His preaching, "pervaded by an *atmosphere* of Swedenborgianism," comforted her greatly. "My first and only deep religious experience came to me through that medium," she explained. "While I listen to him, the Spirit of my religious *youth* seems beckoning to me." "Ah would to God, he could give me back the undoubting faith, the poetic rapture of spiritual insight, which I *then* enjoyed."[85] As fervently as she desired it, faith eluded her. Questions about life after death also tormented her. "Can we be deceived in thinking the soul is immortal?" she wondered, thinking of her father: "Where does he exist? How does he exist?"[86] Fortuitously, the Reverend Mr. Sears addressed the subject in a series of sermons, one of which touched Child deeply by describing the "long pathway of old age" leading into immortality.[87]

Even more than religious solace, Child craved direct contact with her father's spirit.

The spiritualist mania sparked by the "Rochester rappings" of 1848 was then at its height, and many of Child's associates—among them Garrison, Thomas Wentworth Higginson, Francis Jackson, and his daughter Eliza Frances Eddy—firmly believed in the authenticity of such "manifestations" from the spirit world as table rappings and communications through clairvoyant mediums.[88] Hoping for a message from her father, Child attended a séance with her friend Eliza Eddy about five weeks after his death. The medium never mentioned her father but did give an uncannily accurate description of Child's dead sister Mary Preston and her daughter, together with a message "strikingly appropriate to the state of things in their surviving family."[89] Intrigued, but unsatisfied, Child then wrote a confidential letter to Garrison, asking him to arrange a séance for her with a nonprofessional medium who had "no pecuniary interest at stake." "I waver between belief and scepticism," she confessed. By posing a "*mental* question, concerning a subject known only to [her]self and a departed friend," Child wished to test the genuineness of the alleged communications, so as to determine whether or not to pursue this frustrating quest.[90] The opportunity she sought did not present itself until two years later, and the result was again "tantalizing and unsatisfactory." The answer to her mental question "proved unintelligible," but she received messages purporting to be from loved ones ostensibly unknown to the medium. Unwilling to dismiss the phenomenon as wholly the product of "deliberate imposture, or unconscious self-delusion," she persisted in the notion that "some great truths, scientific and psychchological" [*sic*] lay at the bottom of the mystery. Yet she concluded: "It *cannot* be trusted, and it is *well* that it cannot. We should become mere passive machines, if spirits told us just what to do and what to believe."[91]

At his death, the senior Convers Francis left his daughter the dwelling he had been occupying, the quarter acre of land surrounding it, and a four-acre woodlot, in addition to a share amounting to $3,200 of his modest personal estate—a legacy of $4,000 in all. The bulk of his property—a farm valued at $4,000, an eleven-acre woodlot, and another $3,200 share—went to his eldest son, James, who had been cultivating the farm for more than thirty years without paying rent or interest. Although James lived only two miles down the road, the relationship between him and his sister appears to have been thorny because of his Jacksonian Democratic allegiance and anti-black, antiabolitionist prejudices.[92] Despite having "received a *great* deal more" than either Child or Convers from their father's estate, he had expected to inherit the entire fifteen-acre woodlot, and he bitterly resented the bequeathal of a portion to his sister. His insinuations that Child had extorted it from her father as payment for her services deeply wounded her. Her father had made his will before she had gone to nurse him, she assured Loring, who was handling the settlement of the estate, and she had "scrupulously guarded" him against changing it, "for the feeling was too sacred to be *sold*."[93]

The property Child inherited from her father gave her a measure of financial security that eased her worries about the future. It constituted her sole capital, the proceeds from her writings having "gone to liquidate debts, and pay interest" (much of it on loans from her father). "But the debts are *paid*, and the interest *stopped*, thank God!" she rejoiced.[94] With a roof over her head and a small income to fall back on, she could begin anew.

For a while Child dreamed of selling the house and moving to a more urban location, where she could be "within walking distance" of cherished friends who "sympathized with . . . [her] views and tastes."[95] She delighted in concerts, art galleries, and lectures and thrived in a community of like-minded intimates. "[B]y nature the most social of the social," she had not become reclusive by choice. "I should have gone forth to meet others much more freely than I have done had I not been continually entangled in pecuniary difficulties," she admitted to her niece Sarah Preston Parsons.[96] Child felt very isolated in Wayland, a conservative village of small farmers, off the main transportation line to Boston. The Reverend Mr. Sears was the only person there with whom she enjoyed any "intellectual communion," and he lived two miles away on a back road.[97]

Two major obstacles precluded resettling in Boston, however. Child could not afford the high rents there, and David needed the outdoor exercise of chopping wood and raising fruits and vegetables. Over the years he had gravitated back to the farm life of his youth, and the bustle of a large metropolis oppressed him. Their basic predilections still conflicted. But both may also have dimly sensed that resuming their past life in Boston would endanger their comradely relationship by setting them in competition with each other again for the recognition of the public and the attention of their friends.

"It is unfortunate, and also absurd, that as I grow older, and must necesssarily have less and less of love, I grow more and more craving for it," Child commented wryly to Sarah Shaw.[98] She had just lost one of "the two beings" whose love she had bought by becoming "an object of supreme importance" to him.[99] With her father gone, her "desire to be more important than *any* one else can be" to her loved ones focused on David. She could fulfill that desire only by accepting the isolation in Wayland that David found congenial. "I . . . belong to the class . . . to whom it is more necessary to love than to be loved; though both are essential to my happiness," she told Sarah. As usual, she analyzed her situation with disarming honesty. "Bad, is n't it? for a childless woman of sixty years. But then my good David serves me for husband and 'baby and all.'"[100] The couple thus worked out a compromise. Remaining in Wayland, Child devoted herself as completely to David as she had to her father, but alleviated her loneliness with visits to the friends who satisfied her need for cultural stimulation, as well as for "more and more" love. On his part, David showed his appreciation by encouraging her visits, writing frequently when the two were apart, and expressing a depth of tenderness and affection that had never appeared in his early letters. Several days after leaving on a trip with his sister Lydia, for example, he wrote that he already had an "inexpressible longing" for the sight of his wife's face and "the sound of her voice." "O how I miss the dear little causeries that we carry on unawares in our quiet home, for which God & your kind old Father be praised," he added.[101] Sharing his epistles with Marianne Silsbee, who was visiting her in David's absence, Child reported proudly, "Mrs. Silsbee . . . told me I was 'a happy woman to have a husband that wrote me such charming love letters.' I told her I thought so too."[102] On another occasion, when Child had gone to Salem to nurse her late sister Mary's daughter, Susan Clapp, who was dying of cancer, David wrote: "I miss you sadly, but I have not a word to say that may cut short a moment of the consolation & benediction, which none know quite so well as I, that your presence is." Thanking her profusely for writing "so often & so charmingly" despite her "anxieties & cares," he assured her: "Your kind & simple & touching letters are better than the presence of most other women."[103]

As Child settled into the permanent "nest" she had wanted for so many years to build with her "mate," she gradually lost her taste for the pleasures of social intercourse. In taking over her father's cottage, she had returned literally and symbolically to her class origins. Inevitably, the gap between her "social position" and that of her friends widened, creating "barriers impalpable as mist, but insuperable as granite."[104] The Lorings, the Shaws, and other soul mates inhabited a world of wealthy "respectable[s]" in which Child felt increasingly ill at ease. When she sought "intellectual communion" there, she could "find no *simplicity*, no spontaneousness." "Everything is elaborate, self-conscious, Margaret Fullerish," she complained (curiously reverting to the image she had had of her deceased friend before learning to know her more intimately in New York). "The world seems to me one great 'Circumlocution Office,' conventionally arranged to prevent people from doing anything real, or saying anything real, or feeling anything real."[105] Soon the letters she wrote to David from her friends' homes sounded the refrain: "I like to have no house-work to do, and so be able to wear clean clothes; but nevertheless I want to get home to 'my nest and my mate.'"[106] Plagued by rheumatism and stomach ailments that required constant nursing, David stepped into her father's place. Now it was he who greeted her eagerly on her return from visits to Boston. "David . . . was at the foot of the hill, waiting for the stage; so I was glad I did not allow myself to be persuaded to stay in Boston till Monday," Child wrote after one such excursion. "Constant affection is such a rare blessing in this world, that it is wise to make the most of what one has." Unconsciously, she was echoing the letters she had written about her father.[107]

Summing up the evolution Child had undergone over the past decade, her aptly titled *Autumnal Leaves: Tales and Sketches in Prose and Rhyme* — the last collection she would publish of her magazine fiction — came off the press in November 1856, just before her father's death. Its sixteen prose selections encompass the phases of Child's life preceding and following *The Progress of Religious Ideas* (1855). Ten pieces date from the years when Child was adjusting to John Hopper's marriage (1847–49). Two of the remaining six signal her rededication to the antislavery cause. The earliest and latest selections — "The Rival Mechanicians" (January 1847)[108] and "The Kansas Emigrants" (October 1856) — mark the artistic high points of each phase and register Child's movement away from science fiction, fantasy, and folklore as genres for exploring psychosexual topics toward a powerful journalistic realism, suited to the political issues that had come to dominate her consciousness. Thematically, the other selections span Child's wide-ranging concerns as a social reformer: the promotion of sympathy for European emigrants ("The Emigrant Boy"); protest against capital punishment ("The Juryman"); the Quaker ethic of nonviolence ("The Man That Killed His Neighbors"); the dismantling of religious "partition walls" and class barriers ("The Catholic and the Quaker" and "The Eglantine"); women's rights and the institution of marriage ("The Brother and Sister" and "Home and Politics"); and the persistent fascination that clairvoyant phenomena exerted for her ("The Ancient Clairvoyant").[109]

A comparison of *Autumnal Leaves* with Child's 1846 collection, *Fact and Fiction*, immediately reveals the changed mood and character of her art. The sole representative of her earlier mode, "The Rival Mechanicians," no longer celebrates sexual freedom, but mirrors the "disappointed love and ambition" (155) from which Child had smarted as she awaited John Hopper's impending marriage to Rosa de Wolf and digested the indifferent reception of *Fact and Fiction*. Reworking themes Child had addressed in "Thot and Freia" (January 1845) and "Hilda Silfverling" (October 1845), "The Rival Mechanicians" plumbs the interrelationships between sexuality and creativity, nature and art, but brings the quest for sexual and artistic fulfillment to a tragic consummation. When two gifted watchmaker's apprentices vie with each other to inherit their master's business and win the hand of his granddaughter Rosabella by inventing the "most perfect piece of mechanism" (143), their pursuit of an art that emulates nature degenerates into a soul-destroying psychosexual contest. Child projects herself into the loser, a Genevan named Pierre Berthoud, whose "powerful intellect" does not appeal to Rosabella as much as the youthful grace of his French rival Florien, and whose "grand conceptions," though remarkable for "durability and strength," similarly fail to match the "tastefulness and elegance" of his competitor's creations (143–44, 158). "Stung" by his defeat, Pierre stabs Florien in a burst of passion and flees to the mountains, returning a year later to discover that Rosabella has died of grief after the slaying of her lover. Henceforth, the "machine-mad" Pierre has "only one object in life" — "to re-produce Rosabella" in an image that he comes to "love . . . almost as much as he had loved the maiden herself" (159). Although he accomplishes "all that art *can* do," he finds that no artistic creation, however lifelike, can substitute for life itself, and he ultimately dies at the feet of Rosabella's image, thwarted in his yearning for love (162–63).

A female version of the Pygmalion myth, "The Rival Mechanicians" differs significantly from the stories of driven inventors being written by Child's male peers. In contrast to Owen Warland in Hawthorne's "The Artist of the Beautiful" (1844) and Bannadonna in Melville's "The Bell-Tower" (1855), both of whom resort to art as an escape from sexuality and marriage, Child's Pierre Berthoud transforms his art into an outlet for the sexual passion he has been barred from satisfying through marriage. While Hawthorne and Melville are exposing the womb envy and misogyny of the male artist who aspires to bypass procreation,[110] Child is assessing the limits of sublimation from her vantage point as a female artist whose sexuality has been blocked and whose creations have been devalued. She is also expressing her sense of herself as a sexual misfit, trapped between "masculine" aspirations and "feminine" conventions.

After "The Rival Mechanicians," Child appears to have backed away from the psychosexual mode of her earlier fiction. The stories of illicit sexuality that occupy such a large proportion of *Fact and Fiction* are conspicuously absent from *Autumnal Leaves*. Indeed, Child seems to have deliberately excluded the last story she wrote in that vein: "The Hindoo Anchorite" (April 1848).[111] Even her antislavery fiction no longer focuses on sexual themes. In the place of the slave woman threatened by rape and concubinage, "Jan and Zaida" presents a slave family threatened by separation at the auction block.

The lesser prominence in *Autumnal Leaves* of stories depicting unhappy marriages also reflects Child's evolution toward a reconciliation with David. "Home and Politics" (August 1848) and "The Kansas Emigrants" (October 1856) show her reevaluating her marriage first from the perspective of a wife whose domestic happiness is destroyed by her husband's obsession with politics, then from the perspective of a wife who finds her liberation in a political partnership with her husband. Two intervening stories — "The Ancient Clairvoyant" (February 1849) and "The Eglantine" (ca. 1856) — offer tantalizing glimpses of the inner conflicts Child had to resolve along the way.[112]

"The Ancient Clairvoyant" is especially revealing because Child revised it so extensively for *Autumnal Leaves*, muting the original emphasis on marital incompatibility and greatly expanding the treatment of clairvoyance. Previously published in *Sartain's Union Magazine of Literature and Art* under the title "The Prophet of Ionia," the story has obvious affinities with Child's other Greek fictions, *Philothea* (1836) and "The Children of Mount Ida" (April 1845).[113] In all three stories the ostensible theme of clairvoyance seems to have served her as a cover for pondering the factors to which she attributed the failure of her marriage. *Philothea* hints at a husband's psychosexual dysfunction, "The Children of Mount Ida" highlights political ambition as the cause of a husband's infidelity, and "The Prophet of Ionia" centers on the "mismating of temperaments" between a mercurial wife and an introverted husband (4: 95). The psychosexual roots of Child's disappointment in her marriage may have been so painful to probe that she could only do so in her fiction by triply distancing the subject — transposing it to a geographically and historically remote setting, and displacing her own mystical preoccupations onto male characters.

Like Paralus in *Philothea*, Hermotimus in "The Prophet of Ionia" has clairvoyant faculties that identify him with the mediums who were attracting so much attention in the mid-nineteenth century. Preternaturally sensitive and "visionary," he spends much of his life in "lonely wanderings and profound reverie" (4: 94). His mystical inclinations correspond to the side of Child's temperament that drew her to Swedenborgianism — a religious penchant David did not share. David's visionary impulses took the form of dreaming up magnificent schemes through which to turn his reformist ideals to financial profit. What apparently links him in Child's imagination to her protagonists Paralus and Hermotimus is a different form of withdrawal from the world — lack of interest in sexuality. In David's case this problem seems to have manifested itself after marriage. In the case of Hermotimus, it becomes obvious enough during his youth for his father to decide that the "best cure" is "matrimony, and the cares of a family" (4: 94).

To arouse Hermotimus from his apathy, his father arranges for him to marry the "buxom" Praxinoe, who exudes sexual vitality and cares for nothing but worldly pleasures. "[L]ively," thrifty, "energetic," "ambitious," skilled in the domestic arts, and a votary of "comfortable housekeeping," Praxinoe seems to embody the side of Child's many-faceted personality that was least attuned to David (4: 94–95).

The portrait Child sketches of the ill-assorted couple recalls her oft reiterated complaint: "To pump water into a sieve for fourteen years is enough to break down the most energetic spirit."[114] Like Child's, Praxinoe's "cheerful temper" becomes "overclouded with consciousness that the energy and industry, on which she prided herself, were unappreciated, and well nigh useless" (4: 95). Paralleling the emotional withdrawal with which David seems to have reacted to the ascendancy of his wife's career at a time when his own was at a standstill, Hermotimus is wearied by Praxinoe's "restless activity" and "bewildered" at being distracted from his "profound contemplation" by her "triumphant accounts" of the products she has "added to the market stock" (4: 94–95). As with the Childs in the 1840s, the distance between Praxinoe and Hermotimus grows "ever wider and wider" (4: 95). For the fictional couple, the process is hastened by Hermotimus's clairvoyant trances, which receive favorable notice from priests and philosophers, but leave Praxinoe remarking that it would be "pleasant to know whether one's husband were really dead or alive" (4: 95). Praxinoe's frustrations, like Child's in Northampton, are exacerbated by moving to a "lonely habitation" in the mountains for the sake of Hermotimus's health. Child does not blame either partner for the breakdown of the marriage: both had "meant . . . well," she judges, "and they could not help it that their natures would not harmonize" (4: 97) — a verdict that echoes her comments about the marital difficulties of her acquaintances.[115] Still, she expresses more sympathy for Praxinoe, describing her predicament in language she often uses of herself: "[I]t was a hard trial for Praxinoe. Her nature had such tropical exuberance, poor child! She was such a lover of sunshine, and her lot had been cast in such cold and shady places" (4: 96).[116]

The denouement of the story explores options that life had not opened to Child, but betrays the guilt she seems to have felt at contemplating them. After successfully resisting sexual temptation by a "handsome, vigorous" neighbor, who urges her to procure a divorce (4: 96), Praxinoe earns her reward. Hermotimus falls into a deathlike trance from which he does not awaken, and with the concurrence of the priests, Praxinoe consigns his body to the funeral pyre. Though enabled at last to realize her "ambitious dreams" by marrying an "energetic, enterprising husband," Praxinoe continues to suffer from pangs of conscience for having desired and perhaps effected her husband's death. At the end of the story, "It seem[s] as if Hermotimus [is] destined always to cast his shadow across her sunshine" (4: 97).

Although Child retained the main outlines of the plot when she revised "The Prophet of Ionia" for *Autumnal Leaves*, she suppressed nearly all the passages quoted above. The later version, retitled "The Ancient Clairvoyant," devotes twice as much space to Hermotimus's mediumistic trances as to the couple's relationship, considerably softens the description of mismatched temperaments, and eliminates the suggestion that Hermotimus's ghost will forever haunt Praxinoe. It is as if Child has now laid the issue of marital incompatibility to rest and no longer wishes to dwell on it.

The note of reconciliation is even more pronounced in "The Eglantine," probably written in the spring of 1856.[117] Child's principal aim in the story is to promote the eradication of class barriers through intermarriage and the equalization of work and privileges. The double love plot nevertheless reverberates with autobiographical overtones, evoking both the denouement of *Hobomok* and the trajectory of Child's marriage. The heroine, Sibella Flower, an English nursemaid, finds happiness with another man when forced by class-conscious family members to renounce the aristocrat who loves her, but she is ultimately reunited with her first love. Through her portrayals of Sibella's two husbands, Child suggests both the qualities she misses in David and those she prizes in him. The aristocrat Edward Vernon, who writes verses to Sibella and presents her with a copy of Moore's *Melodies*, personifies the "poetic" side of Child's temperament, which attracted her to artists, musicians, and mystics, and which she externalized in such romantic heroes as Alerik Thorild. The "torch-flower" Edward hands Sibella when they meet again several years later, telling her that its "flame-colour might answer for Hymen's torch" (41), intimates that he also embodies Child's sexual desires. Conversely, the Yankee man-of-all-trades, William Wood, whom Sibella marries on emigrating to America, represents the moral and social ideals that led Child to espouse reformist causes and a man who championed them. Strikingly reminiscent of David, William is "poetic in his deeds" rather than in his thoughts, "gentle, good, and wise," rather than romantic (34–35). He does not discourse "eloquently about the beauties of scenery," but employs his "busy intellect . . . chiefly with history, science, and ethics" (34). "A teacher from New England, a farmer's son, who had worked with his hands in the summer, and studied diligently in the winter, till he had become a scholar of more than common attainments" (33), William even emerges from the same class background and follows the same career path that had led David to Harvard and a teaching position at the Boston Latin School in his youth. Like Child in the mid-1850s, her heroine discovers "after her morning-dream had vanished utterly" that her second lover furnishes "pleasant companionship for heart and mind" (34).

The ending of the story invites alternative interpretations. William's death in a railroad accident after a very brief marriage may indicate that Child's own "morning-dream" has not "vanished utterly"—that the romantic imagination she unleashes in her fiction still seeks a more satisfying lover. On the other hand, the account of the psychological healing the widowed Sibella undergoes may apply to Child: "Sibella never expected to know happiness again, but she had attained to cheerful resignation" (37). If so, the renewed happiness her heroine attains in a second marriage with her first lover may reflect Child's sense of having entered on a new and happier phase of her own marriage.

While the stories in *Autumnal Leaves* retrace Child's movement toward reconciliation with David and hint at the burial of her sexual passion in exchange for intellectual and political camaraderie, they also point toward more liberating options for the women of the future than she herself had enjoyed—options typified by the militant

Kate Bradford of "The Kansas Emigrants." In turning away from the issue of the sexual double standard, Child did not abandon her advocacy of women's rights. Rather, she redirected it toward the demand for access to the routes of empowerment: the vote, the university, the pulpit, the legal profession, the magistracy.

The most explicitly feminist story in *Autumnal Leaves*, "The Brother and Sister" (October 1847), draws lessons for the future from the wrongs of the past. Looking back on her youth, Child contrasts the opportunities for advancement presented to Convers and David with the obstacles blocking her own escape from the prison of "a woman's destiny." Like the two Francis children, Esther Golding and her brother, John, share a passion for books and save the pennies they earn from picking berries, gathering chips, and selling eggs, in order to acquire a "little library" (182, 185). "Esther was as eager for information, as her more vivacious brother," comments Child, "though, as a woman, her pathway of life was more obstructed, and all its growth more stinted" (183). Accordingly, it is John, not Esther (as it had been Convers, not Child), whom the village minister advises the family to send to college. To emphasize the injustice, Child gives Esther both the role of mentor that Convers had actually played in the Francis children's youth, and the role of economic provider that she herself had played in her marriage. First by coaching John in his lessons, then by earning money to pay for her brother's education, Esther helps to lead John "into broader avenues than she herself was allowed to enter" (183). Child proceeds to show how a woman's vistas narrow as a man's widen. While John, like David, finishes college and goes on to join the American embassy in Spain, Esther, like Child, remains "penned up within the small routine of petty cares, and mere mechanical efforts" (191).

Through John, Child raises a series of questions that neither of the siblings has enough intellectual sophistication to pursue until it is too late for Esther: "Why don't *women* go to college?" Why don't women have "freer scope" for their faculties? Why can't they become "lawyers, and ministers, and judges" rather than domestic drudges, or at best schoolteachers? "Why cannot women go abroad, and earn their own way in the world, as well as men?" These questions, she predicts, "will revolutionize the world. For as surely as there is a God of harmony in the universe, so surely will woman one day become the acknowledged equal and co-worker of man, in *every* department of life; and yet be more truly gentle and affectionate than she now is" (188–89, 191–92, 195).

Esther's death of consumption—an apt symbol of the "soul-stifling" she has endured[118]—finally impels John to set about trying to improve the status of women. Together with his wife—a woman of the same background, character, and talents as Esther—he establishes a Normal School for Young Women, whose graduates "aid in the redemption" of their sex and the "slow harmonizing of our social discords" (199). Unlike the pathetic victims of Child's "fallen women" stories, Esther at least has not suffered and died in vain.

Through the fiction written in the wane of her Indian summer Child similarly converts her own thwarted aspirations into stepping-stones toward freedom for her younger sisters. If the stories in *Autumnal Leaves* have lost the tropical exuberance of

Fact and Fiction, they have gained the blazing tones and invigorating crispness of the harvest season.

Child's reviewers enthusiastically agreed that "[t]he freshness and versatility of her pen have lost nothing amid the toils of her more elaborate researches," as the *Tribune* put it: "Mrs. Child . . . never writes from mechanical impulses, never tamely follows in any beaten track, and always trust[s] less to memory than to present inspiration. Her literary productions are the growth of wide and deep experience, of earnest contemplation, of high integrity in the pursuit of truth, and of a fearless adherence to hard-won convictions." Referring to the mixture of previously published and recent stories in the volume, Garrison's review in the *Liberator* pronounced them all " 'as good as new,' " and Oliver Johnson's in the *Standard* judged the new selections to be "as good as the old." Typically, the antislavery press tended to emphasize the book's "world-embracing philanthropy" and strong "incitements to noble living." More literary in orientation, the *Knickerbocker* commended the stories' "great simplicity and vigor of language," "picturesqueness of description," and "touching pathos," singling out "The Rival Mechanicians," "The Emigrant Boy," and "The Man That Killed his Neighbors" for special praise.[119]

While gratified by the book's reception, Child had ceased to harbor the hopes with which she had set out to reconquer her lost eminence in the 1840s. "In a literary point of view, I know that I have only a local reputation, 'done in water-colors.' . . . I am not what I aspired to be in my days of young ambition," she wrote soberly to her brother Convers. "In every direction I see young giants rushing past me, at times pushing past me somewhat rudely in their speed, but I am glad to see such strong laborers to plough the land and sow the seed for coming years."[120]

In art as in life Child now looked to a new generation of women to attain the goals that had eluded her. She avidly followed the progress of women writers and artists, welcoming each success as a contribution to "the cause of womanhood."[121] Charmed by the novels of Stowe, Child opined that she had "a larger dash of *genius* in her talent than any of the Beechers." She especially relished Stowe's "capital hits on the woman question" in *The Minister's Wooing*. "*Intellectually*, I should think Mrs. Stowe might feel" as indignant as her protagonist Candace "at being considered, by law Apostolic, a 'weaker vessel,' than *her* legal lord and master," Child surmised.[122] When Stowe's husband, Calvin, defended President Franklin Pierce, who had been his classmate at Bowdoin, Child exploded, "If I were his wife, I'd sue for divorce, and *take* it, if I could'nt *get* it by petitioning."[123] It was as if Child saw in Stowe a younger self onto whom she could displace the feelings hidden in the deepest recesses of her heart—awareness of her intellectual superiority to the husband for whom she had sacrificed so much, and regret at not having divorced him.

Eclipsing all other women writers in Child's eyes was Elizabeth Barrett Browning, whom she pronounced "A Milton among women!" Not only did Child identify her paragon with the poet she had once cited as woman's nemesis, but she ranked Barrett Browning as a far greater poet than her husband, Robert Browning (another revealing instance of such displacement). "What a wonderfully *alive* book is that Aurora Leigh!" Child thrilled, exulting in its bold flouting of "all conventional distinctions." "How glad I am that genius is under the *necessity* of being ever on the free and progressive side! How I delight in having old fogies tormented, always and everywhere!" When the "old fogies" retaliated with reviews that condemned the book for "coarseness" and sneered at its " 'leaning toward woman's rights, and other *isms*,' " Child raged: "Because Hercules is disguised in *petticoats*, he must be kept eternally at the *distaff*, forsooth!" In her discouraged state of mind, however, her admiration of Barrett Browning's genius led her to denigrate her own formidable accomplishments. "Aurora Leigh . . . withered me all up with its scorching superiority," Child admitted to Marianne Silsbee. Dismissing everything she had ever written as "mere pap for babies" in comparison, she felt "no heart to touch pen to paper again."[124]

No such abasement marred Child's appreciation of the French novelist George Sand, whom she explicitly recognized as her "twin sister," and whom she similarly championed against the sexual double standard applied to women writers. Pointing out that the very critics who praised Byron and Burns "to audiences of delighted women" made sure that women "would not dare to express admiration of [Sand's] genius and *her* large, loving sympathy with the whole human race," Child fumed: "As a woman, my sense of *justice* is outraged. . . . It seems that 'what is sauce for goose is *not* sauce for gander.' "[125]

Of the many women artists with whom Child came to identify as she transferred her "young ambition" to her successors, none meant more to her than the sculptor Harriet Hosmer. Recognizing Hosmer's promise, Child had warmly supported her decision to pursue her studies in Rome with a view to "becoming a *sculptor by profession*" — a pioneering venture for a woman of that era. "[I]f you happen to meet her [in Rome] pray speak encouraging words," Child had urged Francis Shaw.[126] When Hosmer returned five years later with an impressive statue of Beatrice Cenci and plans for one of "Zenobia in chains" (a resonant feminist symbol), Child greeted her as the reincarnation of her own dead dreams. "[H]er strong fresh nature really put new life into my old veins," she wrote to Sarah Shaw. "I was powerfully attracted toward her. How I wish she was my daughter!"[127] Child spelled out the reasons for the attraction in a letter to Hosmer herself. "You 'stood beside me, like my youth,' " she reminisced of the visit with Hosmer that she had found so exhilarating: "Oh, how much I regret that in my youth I did not take my *freedom*, as you have done! I have been very unwise to allow my mind to be tied down by so many Lilliputian cords of petty cares: But it *seemed* to me to be a duty; and there is no help for it, now." After this astonishingly frank reassessment of the scruples that had led her to sacrifice a successful career to an ill-starred marriage, Child proceeded to give Hosmer the advice she would have given to a daughter: "Go thou, and do otherwise!"[128]

In her choice of adopted daughters, Child always expressed the passions that dominated the current phase of her life. She poured her thwarted ambitions as a woman artist into Harriet Hosmer, as she had earlier shared her enthusiasm for Ole Bull and his music with Anna Loring and Susan Lyman and projected her self-pity as an abused wife onto Dolores. Accordingly, Child also confirmed her rededication to the antislavery cause during this period by finding an adopted daughter who resembled the youthful author of *An Appeal in Favor of That Class of Americans Called Africans* — nineteen-year-old Mattie Griffith, whose *Autobiography of a Female Slave* had appeared within weeks of *Autumnal Leaves*. The orphaned daughter of a Kentucky slaveholder, Griffith, like Angelina Grimké, had grown up instinctively feeling that slavery was wrong, yet unable to ascertain where her duty lay. Not until the "murderous assault" on Sumner impelled her to "devour his Speeches" had Griffith broken the impasse — a coincidence that reinforced the bond Child felt with her. The abolitionist ideology Griffith imbibed from Sumner had prompted her to emancipate the six slaves comprising "her *entire* property." She had then set about earning her living with her pen, while simultaneously testifying against slavery. Though Child found the *Autobiography* "sentimental and inflated" in style, she recognized a kindred spirit in this heroic young woman who had braved public opprobrium and financial ruin for the sake of her principles (and who shared her aversion to incurring obligations, as she soon learned). Child had immediately written to Griffith and induced abolitionists to "rally round her," procuring invitations for her to the Lorings' summer residence in Beverly and the home of Child's niece and nephew-in-law in Medford, Mary and George Luther Stearns.[129] Child and Griffith struck up a warm friendship after spending ten days together in the summer of 1857 and kept in close touch with each other. "I have never met with *any* person, who so *completely* identifies herself with the slaves, as she does," Child noted — the highest accolade she could bestow on an abolitionist.[130] Judging from her own experience, she predicted: "[M]y heroic Mattie *will* experience disappointment, and some disgust, at the bigotry and harshness of some of the abolitionists. But she will learn to do, as I have learned to do; to pass by their sharp corners without hurting myself more than can't be helped; and if they jostle me rudely, to bid God bless them, because they are earnestly walking straight-forward."[131] The imperceptible transition she made from Mattie to herself betrayed the extent to which Child was reliving her antislavery career through her latest adopted daughter.

Energized by her exchanges with Mattie Griffith and Harriet Hosmer, Child emerged from her mourning and began writing again. By November, she had finished her contribution to the next *Liberty Bell* — a lively melodrama titled "The Stars and Stripes," based on the story of William and Ellen Craft's escape from slavery.[132] By the following May (1858) her resuscitated literary imagination had flowered in a long story of interracial marriage for the *Atlantic Monthly* — "Loo Loo: A Few Scenes from a True History," which she would subsequently develop into her Reconstruction era novel, *A Romance of the Republic*.[133]

Meanwhile, Child was busily engaged in whitewashing and repapering the cottage in Wayland so that she could finally invite the Lorings to a home that would not shock Ellis's "fastidious taste." Just as she was pasting the two last pieces of fireboard over her chimney on May 24, an express letter arrived with news that would "crush all life and hope" out of her. Ellis was dead. "Nothing but the death of my kind husband could have caused me such bitter grief," Child wrote to Lucy Osgood.

> For thirty years, he has been my chief reliance. In moral perplexities, I always went to him for counsel, and he never failed to clear away every cloud. In all worldly troubles, I went to him, and always found a judicious adviser, a sympathizing friend, a generous helper. . . . [A]ll my little property was in his hands; and if I had ever so small a sum, even ten dollars, . . . he put it on interest, though it were but for a single month.[134]

No wonder Child described this bereavement as "a loss greater to me, in *every* way, than any one but myself can understand."[135]

Her assertion that only "the death of [her] kind husband could have caused [her] such bitter grief" indeed indicated the role Loring had played in her life and suggested the comparisons she could hardly have helped making between this surrogate husband and the man she had married. Besides shouldering the legal and financial responsibilities for which David had proved himself unfit, Loring had come to replace David as a soul mate for the poetic side of Child, sharing her enthusiasm for Transcendentalism and Romantic literature in much the way she attributed to the fictional Edward in "The Eglantine." Although stuffier and more conventional in his sexual attitudes than David, Loring had proved a far more affectionate husband to Louisa than David ever had to Child. The intensity of the bonds between Ellis and Louisa, obvious from the letters they exchanged during their rare separations, had been apparent to all their friends, and Child must often have winced at the contrast as she faced her disintegrating marriage in the late 1830s, her loneliness in the 1840s, and her problematic reunion with David in the early 1850s. On occasion she had even voiced her feelings. "How like your good Ellis to come *sooner* than he said!" Child had written to Louisa on receiving her friend's joyful letter announcing Ellis's imminent return from Europe. "When David was in Europe, he sent me word at five different times that he should sail one month from the date of his writing; and he *finally* came three months after the date he *last* fixed!"[136] The contrast between David's disastrous career and Ellis's status as one of the abolitionist movement's most successful lawyers must also have struck Child painfully.

While Loring's death deprived Child of the surrogate husband on whom she had relied so heavily, it consummated the reconciliation she had gradually been effecting with David. Inevitably, David came to supply many of the emotional needs Loring had been fulfilling for her — just as Loring had earlier taken over the functions David had abdicated. The chastening spectacle of Louisa's widowhood may also have brought the Childs closer. Seeing her friend retreat into a state of impenetrable apathy, "indifferent to everybody and every thing," Child may well have resolved to value her husband more, whatever flaws persisted in their relationship.[137]

In parallel fashion, the loss of the abolitionist comrade who more than any other had represented a link to her best memories of the movement helped Child complete her slow rapprochement with the American Anti-Slavery Society. Her impatience with the "miserable intolerance" that Garrisonians so often exhibited now gave way to nostalgia for "the good old *early* times of Anti Slavery, when all our hearts moved with one pulsation."[138] Symbolically, it was on an errand to her deceased friend's office that Child underwent this psychological transformation. As she was nearing the familiar address and nerving herself for the sight of Loring's empty chair, she suddenly heard her name called. The poet laureate of the abolitionist movement, John Greenleaf Whittier, whom she had not seen for fifteen years, stood behind her. They talked for two hours, recalling Ellis and their "noble selfforgetting days" of "working shoulder to shoulder, in such a glow of faith" and parted with the mutual determination to "forget the disappointment of cherished hopes and expectations" and to embrace "all those who truly sympathized with the slave, whatever might be their opinions, theological or political." "It seemed like the old meetings, when we were all brothers and sisters, like Christians of the Apostolic Churches," Child reported to another "very dear old friend" of that era, Henrietta Sargent.[139] She had experienced a Pentecostal renewal of the spirit that had swept her into the crusade against slavery.

17

The Example of John Brown

The fact is, I want to shoot the accursed institution from all quarters of the globe. I think, from this time till I die, I shall stop firing only long enough to load my guns.[1]

Conveying the militant mood and incessant activism triggered in Child by John Brown's October 1859 raid on the federal arsenal at Harpers Ferry, this metaphorical declaration of war encapsulates her response to the meteoric event that so many Americans recognized as heralding the final onslaught against slavery. Its context—a warm letter to Maria Weston Chapman, with whom Child was once again working closely — also betokens her reintegration into an antislavery army that was at last confronting the Slave Power in a "solid phalanx," as she had advocated during the Kansas crisis.[2] "I have never done so much anti-slavery work in any year of my life," Child would write, looking back on the turbulent interval between the Harpers Ferry outbreak and the 1860 election.[3] Besides circulating petitions, fund-raising, attending antislavery meetings, and writing a record number of political letters, she produced four major tracts that year, which she personally mailed by the hundreds to key opinion-makers; and she edited and helped publish and distribute a slave narrative now ranked as an African American literary classic: Harriet A. Jacobs's *Incidents in the Life of a Slave Girl* (1861). Paradoxically, however, Child did not intend to set off a civil war with the barrage of ammunition she fired against the "accursed institution." Rather, she still hoped to avert war by convincing southerners as well as northerners that the best interests of all classes lay in abolishing slavery peacefully before it was too late. The tension between the militant stance she urged against slavery and the pacifist ideals she upheld would pervade her writings of the "John Brown Year" and indeed of the entire Civil War era.

"ATTEMPTED INSURRECTION IN HARPER'S FERRY." The headlines that flashed across the country on October 17, 1859, jolting abolitionists, proslavery advocates, and compromisers out of a three-year stasis, likewise roused Child from the grief into which her successive bereavements had plunged her following the 1856 election—the peak of her activism for a Free Kansas. A few months earlier, Child had participated in the annual New England Anti-Slavery Convention for the first time in many years. The speeches, which she had found "edifying," had left her feeling more in harmony with her former comrades than she had since the 1830s.[4]

Savoring the pleasure of belonging to an antislavery community again, Child did not notice the tall, gaunt man with a streaming, iron-gray beard—soon to grip the nation's attention at Harpers Ferry—who stalked out of the convention fuming, "Talk! talk! talk!—that will never set the slave free. What is needed is action—action."[5] Nor did she know that John Brown was then collecting money for his secret mission from her nephew-in-law, George Luther Stearns, and five other backers, including her friends Gerrit Smith, Thomas Wentworth Higginson, and Theodore Parker.[6] Only after the fateful eruption would Child recall that David had actually met this fierce old guerrilla fighter, fresh from combat in Kansas, while Brown was enlisting the sponsorship of the Massachusetts Kansas Committee in 1857.[7] "I honor those who conscientiously fight for justice, truth, or freedom; but I revere those who will *die* to advance great principles, though they will not *kill*," Child had written of the men Brown was leading in the struggle for a Free Kansas.[8] Brown would win her honor and reverence on the first two counts, but she would remain unable to embrace him wholeheartedly on the third.

The capture of Harpers Ferry took even Brown's backers by surprise, for he had never fully divulged the details of his plan. He had merely intimated that it would involve swooping down on a plantation community in Virginia, liberating a large number of slaves, and organizing them into guerrilla bands that would operate out of fastnesses in the mountains and make periodic forays into slave territory for recruits and supplies. He had settled on Harpers Ferry—a choice his men had vehemently opposed when he had revealed it to them at the eleventh hour—primarily because an attack on a federal stronghold would maximize the shock value of such a strike against slavery. "[I]f we lose our lives it will perhaps do more for the cause than our lives could be worth in any other way," Brown had argued, as if already anticipating the martyrdom through which he would transform failure into success.[9]

Brown and eighteen of his twenty-one followers stole into Harpers Ferry by night on October 16, easily overpowered the watchman guarding the arsenal, and took over the town. Brown then sent a few of his lieutenants to spread the word among the slaves and seize hostages from among the leading slaveholders. With an eye to historical symbolism and "moral effect," he chose a grandnephew of George Washington as his chief hostage and forced him to hand over Washington's prized sword to one of the five African Americans in the small liberation army, Osborne Anderson.[10] Aiming to trade the hostages for a safe conduct out of Harpers Ferry, and at the same time to drive home an antislavery lesson by treating them humanely, Brown lingered in the town until the next morning.[11] Meanwhile, to "allay the fears of those who believed" he had come "to burn and kill," he allowed a train he had stopped at the station to proceed to its destination (and of course raise the alarm)—another gesture of misplaced humanitarianism. "I could easily have saved myself . . . had I exercised my own better judgment rather than yielded to my feelings," he later admitted.[12] Apparently he had never quite decided between two irreconcilable conceptions of the raid: first, as a spectacular hit-and-run operation aimed at recruiting slaves into his guerrilla force; second, as a heroic suicide mission aimed at inspiring a national crusade to destroy slavery once and for all.[13] Whatever Brown's intent, the latter conception ultimately prevailed. The very qualms that doomed him as a revolutionary canonized him as a martyr. Therein lay the secret of the profound influence he would exert on Child.

By noon on October 17 Brown's fatal errors had caught up with him. Virginia and Maryland militia had surrounded his band, and several of his men had been killed or disabled. The following morning, Federal marines under Colonel Robert E. Lee battered down the door of the engine house into which Brown had retreated with his prisoners. The victors found Brown's son Oliver dead, another son Watson dying, and his lieutenant Aaron Stevens critically injured — both of the latter from wounds they had received when they had ventured out under a flag of truce. One of Lee's officers lunged at Brown with a sword after he was "down" and had agreed to surrender, stabbing him and attempting to split open his skull.[14] None of the prisoners had suffered any harm, though several townsmen and one marine had been killed in the siege. In all, ten of Brown's men fell at Harpers Ferry, four were captured, two who fled the scene were subsequently apprehended, and five succeeded in escaping — among them Osborne Anderson, who would publish the only eyewitness account of the raid by an African American participant; and Francis Jackson Merriam, whose grandfather and mother were good friends of Child's and prominent members of Garrison's circle.[15]

Albeit militarily defeated, Brown wrested the laurels from his captors in the widely publicized interview he gave the day after the debacle. Speaking from his bloodstained pallet on the floor of the armory, Brown turned the interrogation into one of the most potent antislavery sermons the nation had ever heard. "I respect the rights of the poorest and weakest of colored people, oppressed by the slave system, just as much as I do those of the most wealthy and powerful," he proclaimed. When asked how he justified his acts, he invoked the Golden Rule: "I pity the poor in bondage that have none to help them: that is why I am here; not to gratify any personal animosity, revenge, or vindictive spirit." He specifically denied that he had intended to incite "a general rising of the slaves" — a denial he reiterated at his trial. Instead, he had "expected to gather them up from time to time, and set them free." He went on to admonish the people of the South against the illusion that they could dispose of the "negro question" by disposing of him. "[T]his question . . . must come up for settlement sooner than you are prepared for it," he warned.[16]

While considering Brown "sadly mistaken in his mode of operation," Child greeted his foray as "the 'Concord *Fight*' of an impending revolution."[17] Hardly had she read the first reports from Harpers Ferry than she wrote to John Greenleaf Whittier, asking him to commemorate Brown's heroism in a poem akin to the famous "Concord Hymn" in which Emerson had immortalized the "embattled farmers" who had "fired the shot heard round the world."[18]

Child herself elected a different mode of showing her solidarity with Brown—offering to nurse him. "Dear Capt Brown," she wrote:

> Believing in peace principles, I cannot sympathize with the method you chose to advance the cause of freedom. But I honor your generous intentions, I admire your courage, moral and physical, I reverence you for the humanity which tempered your zeal, I sympathize with your cruel bereavements, your sufferings, and your wrongs. . . .
>
> . . . I think of you night and day, bleeding in prison, surrounded by hostile faces, sustained only by trust in God, and your own strong heart. I long to nurse you, to speak to you sisterly words of sympathy and consolation.[19]

Once again, as in her reaction to the caning of Sumner, Child was expressing an impulse with complex roots and multiple meanings. Brown's "bereavements" as a parent and the "sufferings" he was enduring as he awaited a probable death sentence may have linked him in Child's mind with both the mother she had refused to nurse and the father to whom she had just devoted three years of filial care. Brown also represented an alter ego for Child. He had shown himself willing to lay down his life for the slave, and his self-sacrifice both inspired and humbled her. "Conscience twinges me now and then, that I ever turned aside from . . . duty [to the slave], to dally in primrose paths," Child would later acknowledge.[20] Brown's example no doubt provoked one of those "twinges." On the anniversary of his execution, she would confide to his widow: "I have resolved henceforth to wear only black and brown; that when I am tempted to grow tired of reform-work, which I must confess is foreign to my natural *taste*, I may think of John Brown's example. . . ."[21] By volunteering to nurse him in prison, Child was similarly affiliating herself with Brown and doing penance for having failed to live up to the standard of dedication he had set.

Events would direct her toward a much more productive means of honoring Brown's "example," however. She had always served the antislavery cause best through her writings. By a fortunate twist of fate, her letter to Brown would turn into one of her most famous antislavery tracts and "constitute a permanent portion of the thrilling history of the Harper's Ferry tragedy," as the *Liberator* put it. The result aptly illustrated Child's observation that "by far the most efficient co-laborers we [abolitionists] have ever had have been the Slave States themselves,"[22] for it was Governor Henry Wise of Virginia who began this transmogrification.

Child had sent her letter to Brown along with one addressed to the governor—officially Brown's chief custodian—in which she formally requested permission to nurse the wounded martyr. To avoid any imputation of seeking favors on false pretences, she identified herself at the outset: "I have been for years an uncompromising abolitionist, and I should scorn to deny it or apologize for it as much as John Brown himself would do." She also took pains to spell out how she and her fellow abolitionists viewed Brown's action. None had expected or approved of it, she asserted (perhaps not yet privy to her friends' role in financing Brown), but all felt the same sympathy for the fallen hero. Lest Wise misconstrue her stand on slave rebellion, she added pointedly:

"[I]f I believed our religion justified men in fighting for freedom, I should consider the enslaved everywhere as best entitled to that right." She nevertheless promised not to air her abolitionist opinions in Virginia, should Wise grant her permission to come.[23]

Wise replied with all the affable courtesy of a southern gentleman. Noting that she had a constitutional right to visit Virginia for the "avowed purpose" of ministering to a "captive in prison," he assured her that he would fulfill his duty to uphold the Constitution by protecting her. "Virginia and her authorities would be weak indeed — weak in point of folly and weak in point of power — if her State faith and Constitutional obligations cant be redeemed in her own limits. . . . Every arm which guards Brown from rescue on the one hand and from Lynch-Law on the other, will be ready to guard your person in Virginia," he claimed. At the same time, Wise cautioned Child against the "imprudence of risking any experiment upon the peace of a society very much excited by the crimes, with whose chief author" she seemed to "sympathise so much." He ended by lecturing her on the "error" of sympathizing with Brown yet professing "surprise" at his action. She was as guilty as Brown of having "whetted knives of butchery for our 'Mothers, sisters,' daughters 'and babes,'" Wise charged: "His attempt was a natural consequence of your sympathy."[24]

Evidently, Wise thought he had scored a propaganda victory from which the northern public might benefit, for he sent copies of his exchange with Child to the press. He quickly learned that he had underestimated an adversary who had long ago pierced the mask of southern chivalry and mastered the art of propaganda. Child wasted no time regaining the advantage in the battle to win over northern public opinion. She promptly sent an "Explanatory Letter" to the *New York Tribune*, accompanied by the answer she had received from John Brown in the interim.[25] Together, the two letters presented Brown and his abolitionist supporters not as bloodthirsty fanatics, but as unassuming and level-headed Good Samaritans. "My proposal to go and nurse that brave and generous old man, who so willingly gives his life a sacrifice for God's oppressed poor, originated in a very simple and unmeritorious impulse of kindness," Child affirmed. Other admirers of Brown in her circle, including her niece,[26] had shared that impulse, but her "age and state of health" had made her the most suitable candidate. She had packed her trunk with bandage supplies and prepared to "slip away quietly, without having the affair made public." Yet Governor Wise's admonition against inflaming an already "excited" populace had made her fear that her arrival might jeopardize whatever chance Brown had of obtaining a fair trial. Taking counsel with her husband, she had decided to await "a reply from Captain Brown himself" before proceeding (13).

Brown's letter served to provide renewed proof of his courage and selflessness. "I should certainly be greatly pleased to become personally acquainted with one so gifted; & so kind," he responded (indicating his awareness of Child's reputation). He no longer needed nursing, however, and his jailer, "a most humane gentleman" (to whom all the prisoners paid tribute), was giving him "every possible attention." Could he suggest "another channel" for the sympathies of his friends — to "constitute a little fund" for the support of his bereaved family, consisting of his wife, several helpless children, and the widows of the sons and kin who had fallen with him at Harpers Ferry (15–16)?[27] Published under the title "JOHN BROWN'S LETTER TO LYDIA MARIA CHILD. THE TRUE AID AND COMFORT TO THE DOOMED OLD MAN," the letter launched a fund-raising campaign for the martyrs of Harpers Ferry. Child would extend that campaign well beyond Brown's family members, reminding contributors not to overlook "the *other* sufferers . . . ; especially the *colored* men," and inquiring whether any of the African Americans had "left wives, children, or mothers, destitute."[28]

Child did not content herself with indirectly countering the chivalric pose Wise had struck as a statesman committed to upholding the Constitution he charged northern abolitionists with violating. She fired off a long rejoinder, which appeared in the *Tribune* a week later.[29] "Your constitutional obligation, for which you profess so much respect, has never proved any protection to citizens of the Free States, who happened to have a black, brown, or yellow complexion; nor to any white citizen whom you even suspected of entertaining opinions opposite to your own" on the slavery question, Child pointed out, referring to the imprisonment and enslavement of "colored seamen" whose ships touched at southern ports, and to notorious cases of men hounded out of the South for their supposed antislavery views (6–7). How could Wise consistently arraign Brown for treason, she asked, when he and his fellow southerners had "threatened to trample on the Constitution, and break the Union, if a majority of the legal voters" in the United States "dared to elect a President unfavorable to the extension of Slavery" (7)? Contrary to Wise's allegations, Brown's scheme was the "natural result" not of abolitionist agitation, but of "the continual, and constantly-increasing aggressions of the Slave Power," Child argued (9). She proceeded to recapitulate these aggressions, from the gag laws through which proslavery politicians had tried to muzzle free speech in Congress to the lynch law through which their henchmen had tried to impose slavery in Kansas. "[B]ecause slaveholders so recklessly sowed the wind in Kansas, they reaped a whirlwind at Harper's Ferry," she contended. She wound up by predicting that a majority of northerners "would rejoice to have the Slave States fulfill their oft-repeated threat of withdrawal from the Union" (12).

Thanks to Wise, Child's offer to nurse Brown, which she had meant as a private, womanly gesture, ended up attracting as much notoriety as had Brown's interview, and serving the antislavery cause almost as effectively. The governor's ungentlemanly effort to expose Child to public censure had gained her a "Southern audience" she could never otherwise have reached, she noted wryly.[30] Her audience multiplied tenfold nationwide when Margaretta Mason, wife of Virginia's Senator James M. Mason, joined the fray. Mrs. Mason's vituperative letter, published in the Virginia press, opened with the rebuke: "Do you read your Bible, Mrs. Child? If you do, read there, 'Woe unto you, hypocrites'" (16). Accusing Child of ignoring the "objects of charity" on her doorstep—the northern white poor—and confining her "sympathy" to a man who had sought to unleash a "servile war" against the men, women, and children of her own race, Mrs. Mason exhorted her to take a lesson in true charity from the slaveholding matrons of the South: "[W]ould *you* stand by the bedside of an old negro, dying of a hopeless disease, to alleviate his sufferings as far as human aid could? . . . Do *you* soften the pangs of maternity in those around you by all the care and comfort you can give? . . . Did *you* ever sit up until the 'wee hours' to complete a dress for a motherless child, that she might appear on Christmas day in a new one. . . ?" (16–17). As Child's large northern readership would have known, Mrs. Mason could hardly have chosen a more inappropriate target for such reproaches than the author who had dedicated so many years of her life to alleviating the sufferings of everyone around her, regardless of race. Mrs. Mason's parting shot misfired even more clumsily. Unaware that Child had been virtually tabooed in the South ever since publishing her first abolitionist book twenty-seven years earlier, Mrs. Mason pontificated: "no Southerner ought, after your letter to Governor Wise and to Brown, to read a line of your composition. . ." (17).

Like Governor Wise, the Virginian senator's wife would emerge badly worsted from her self-initiated public exchange with the abolitionist movement's most skillful propagandist. Child answered her in an eleven-page letter, which she sent to the *New York Tribune* with a confidential note to editor Horace Greeley. Her aim, she told Greeley, was to provide "entering wedges" for antislavery arguments that might sway voters in favor of the Republican party.[31] Taking her cue from Mrs. Mason, Child began with an array of biblical texts — eighteen quotations sustaining an antislavery interpretation of Christianity, compared to the two Mrs. Mason had cited for proslavery purposes. She followed with a trenchant summary of her myriad antislavery tracts, using southern law codes, advertisements for fugitives, the testimony of converted slaveholders, and the avowals of southern politicians to establish the brutality of slavery. She then urged Mrs. Mason to examine dispassionately the benefits the South would derive from emancipation, and to weigh them against the costs of maintaining an institution that depended for its survival on "despotic measures . . . to silence investigation." "Your letter to me is published in Northern papers, as well as Southern; but my reply will not be allowed to appear in any Southern paper," Child underscored (26). Southerners were not only sacrificing their own liberties but courting their own destruction for the sake of preserving slavery, she warned: "In this enlightened age, all despotisms *ought* to come to an end by the agency of moral and rational means. But if they resist such agencies, it is in the order of Providence that they *must* come to an end by violence." Turning at last to the "personal questions" Mrs. Mason had raised about her practical philanthropy, Child answered them impersonally "in the name of all the women of New England":

> It would be extremely difficult to find any woman in our villages who does *not* sew for the poor, and watch with the sick, whenever occasion requires. We pay our domestics generous wages, with which they can purchase as many Christmas gowns as they please; a process far better for their characters, as well as our own, than to receive their clothing as a charity, after being deprived of just payment for their labor. I have never known an instance where the "pangs of maternity" did not meet with requisite assistance; and here at the North, after we have helped the mothers, *we do not sell the babies*. (26)

There could be little disagreement as to which party had won the debate. In Garrison's words, "Mrs. Child has 'pulverized' Governor Wise . . . and thoroughly 'used up' Mrs. Mason."[32]

Reprinted in newspapers across the country, Child's correspondence with Brown, Governor Wise, and Mrs. Mason elicited scores of responses. Southerners smeared her with "the most *inconceivable* scurrility and abuse," their "violent and filthy" language furnishing "a new revelation of the degrading effects of the slave system upon human nature."[33] They also slandered her in the press, with the help of their northern "dough-face" allies. A correspondent of the New Orleans *Picayune*, for example, planted a rumor zealously circulated by antiabolitionist newspapers throughout the nation. "[T]he would-be sympathizer and nurse of the old rascal Brown," reported the *Picayune*, had abandoned a crippled daughter who was being generously supported by a Mississippi slaveholder.[34] In the same vein, a northern Democratic newspaper took advantage of a recent local tragedy that had produced a hundred casualties to sneer: "*Why is it . . . that we do not hear of the presence of Lydia Maria Child at this scene of woe?* It is true that she would find no . . . cold-blooded murderers" or "frag[ra]nt, intellectual, ideal Negro" to "clasp in a chaste, sisterly embrace. . . ."[35]

Such slurs did not typify the reaction of northern readers, however. The vast majority "overwhelmed" Child with "letters of laudation," frequently enclosing contributions to the fund for Brown's family and manifesting a degree of esteem for the old man himself that indicated an astounding transformation of public consciousness.[36] "It is not often that I read anything on the extreme abolition side of the slavery question with such hearty unmixed satisfaction," wrote a conservative northerner, convinced that "[h]undreds of thousands" had greeted Child's "admirable Epistle" to Mrs. Mason with the same enthusiasm.[37] "I know of nothing . . . that has commanded such universal respect & gratitude as these words of yours," echoed a well-known specialist in Oriental languages.[38] "You were inspired to write that letter. I hear of it all around me," confirmed Child's old friend Eliza Lee Cabot Follen, wishing it could be "sent to every house in the land."[39] African Americans were especially moved by Child's letter to Brown. The poet Frances Ellen Watkins [Harper], whose verses Child pronounced "very clever," wrote to thank her for paying tribute to a man who had "reached out his brave and generous hand to the crushed and blighted of my race."[40] And a "colored man in Ohio" asked Child for her photograph, which he wanted to enshrine alongside Brown's. "We desire to hand down to our posterity, in connection with the tragic scene at Harper's Ferry, the pictures of two honest persons," he explained.[41]

Child's abolitionist comrades soon realized that her exchanges with John Brown, Governor Wise, and Mrs. Mason were revolutionizing public opinion. To capitalize on an instrumentality they hoped would "work the overthrow of the slave system by . . . moral power, without the aid of invasion or insurrection," the American Anti-Slavery Society reissued the entire set of letters as a tract. Sold for five cents apiece (and less in large quantities), the *Correspondence between Lydia Maria Child and Gov. Wise and Mrs. Mason, of Virginia* reached the almost unprecedented circulation of 300,000 copies.[42] At Child's behest, the tract was also sent to British newspapers and to foreign progressives whose support abolitionists hoped to enlist, among them the writers Harriet Martineau, Mary Howitt, and Victor Hugo, and the Hungarian and Italian revolutionaries Lajos Kossuth and Giuseppe Mazzini.[43] If Harpers Ferry represented the "Concord Fight" of a second American Revolution, Child's incisive letters articulated the "Common Sense" that mobilized her generation to wage that struggle.

True, Child did not literally call for a war against slavery. Yet she did draw the battle lines and instill a determination to resist further encroachments by the Slave Power, whatever the cost. The tone of her *Correspondence* with Governor Wise and Mrs. Mason differs strikingly from that of her 1833 *Appeal* and her 1836 *Anti-Slavery Catechism*. Gone are the conciliatory rhetoric and the beseeching posture that characterized the earlier tracts. No longer does Child plead and reason with her interlocutor. The rhetoric of the *Correspondence* is accusatory and openly sectional, pitting "you" of the South against "us" of the North. It fuels the anger of northern readers who have reached the limits of their endurance after thirty years of submitting to southern dictation, and it serves notice to southern readers that the time for concessions and compromises has passed. The solution Child holds out is disunion, rather than war. If the South secedes, slavery will crumble, she implies. Slaves will be able to escape to the free states without fear of being remanded to their owners by northern judges, and slaveholders will have to face insurrections without the aid of Federal troops to suppress them. Meanwhile, the North will finally be free to "give the world the example of a real republic" (12).

In the end, of course, this scenario would prove chimerical. The northern public would not accept the dismemberment of the Union, and the slaveholding oligarchy would launch a preemptive strike to neutralize the threat to its peculiar institution. Although Child hoped to the last that her compatriots would elect to bring about emancipation by peaceful means, she steeled herself to "go steadily forward to the slave's rescue," be the consequence insurrection or civil war. Explaining the militant stance she had taken against Governor Wise and Mrs. Mason, she wrote to Sarah Shaw:

> I *force* myself to remember that, terrible as an insurrection would be to *white* women and children, the *black* women and children have, for many generations, been living in subjection to things *as* horrid, with no *Union*, no *laws*, no *public sentiment* to help *them*. . . . It is plainly wrong to be silent in view of such outrages as the colored people suffer in this country; outrages in which we at the North are compelled to become more and more *accomplices*; yet God alone knows how many John Brown's we *may* wake up, when we "cry aloud and spare not". . . . I *must* stand by the poor slave, come what will. . . . Nay, shrinking and quivering at every nerve, I would *still* do it, if I *knew* their pathway to freedom must be "over their master's bodies". . . . If we don't stand up, like men, [the slave states] will bring us more and more under the yoke. They will ruin *us*, without helping *themselves*; for the string drawn too tightly will snap at last, and the end will come in blood.[44]

Thus, seeing no possibility that silent complicity in slavery would avert either insurrection or war, Child did not flinch from the risk that her rhetoric might trigger a bloodbath. Loyalty to the slaves took precedence over every other consideration; if revolution alone could liberate them, she must be ready to abet it. Such was the lesson she derived from John Brown.

Amid the flurry of exchanging broadsides with Governor Wise and Mrs. Mason, answering twenty or thirty letters a week from admiring or irate readers, and collecting funds for the families of Brown and his men, Child anxiously followed the trials at Harpers Ferry. Within less than two weeks of their capture, Brown and four of his followers — the African Americans John A. Copeland, Jr., and Shields Green and the whites Edwin Coppoc and John E. Cook — were indicted and found guilty of murder, treason against the State of Virginia, and conspiracy to foment slave insurrection.[45] Brown was sentenced to be executed on December 2, the others on December 16. The trials of two remaining members of the band, Aaron Dwight Stevens and Albert Hazlett, were postponed until February.

At his sentencing, Brown transformed the brief statement he was allowed by the court into what Child called "a most effective anti-slavery document,"[46] reprinted by newspapers all over the country. "Had I . . . interfered in behalf of the rich, the powerful, the intelligent, the so-called great, or in behalf of any of their friends . . . every man in this court would have deemed it an act worthy of reward rather than punishment," he contended. Drawing attention to the New Testament prominently displayed in the courtroom, and again quoting the Golden Rule, he added:

> I am yet too young to understand that God is any respecter of persons. I believe that to have interfered as I have done . . . in behalf of His despised poor, was not wrong, but right. Now, if it is deemed necessary that I should forfeit my life for the furtherance of the ends of justice, and mingle my blood further with the blood of my children and with the blood of millions in this slave country whose rights are disregarded by wicked, cruel, and unjust enactments, — I submit; so let it be done.[47]

"What a success [Brown] has made of failure, by the moral grandeur of his own character!" Child exulted.[48] His moving words, crowned by his martyrdom, would do more to arouse the nation against slavery than he could ever have achieved by carrying out his original scheme, she predicted: "No peace and quietness for Slavery after this!"[49]

The day of Brown's hanging was marked by solemn observances. Child helped Garrison organize the evening commemoration at Tremont Temple, at which that lifelong nonresistant proclaimed to "[e]nthusiastic applause": "as a peace man — an 'ultra' peace man — I am prepared to say, 'Success to every slave insurrection at the South, and in every slave country.'"[50] Seeking an atmosphere "congenial to [her] tender state of mind," she spent the intervening hours attending an all-day prayer meeting at a black church. "*There* was no doubt of [Brown's] sanity, no division of opinion concerning the reverence and gratitude due to his memory," she observed with satisfaction. Child took comfort from the African American community's clear-cut verdict: "He was the friend of their persecuted race, and he had proved it by dying for them." She was especially touched by the eloquent prayer of an "old black man who informed the Lord that he 'had been a slave, and knew how *bitter* it was,' [and who] ejaculated, with great fervor: 'And since it has pleased Thee to take away our Moses, Oh, Lord God! raise us up a Joshua.' "[51]

Although Child longed to share her black brothers' and sisters' unambivalent response to Brown, her pacifist convictions posed an insurmountable obstacle. In one of the speeches she heard that night at Tremont Temple, the African American minister J. Sella Martin summed up the differences between his community's interpretation of the Harpers Ferry tragedy and that of the white speakers, most of whom had stressed Brown's assertion that he had not intended to "shed blood." "In my opinion, speaking as a military critic," Martin retorted, "this was one of the faults of his plan. In not shedding blood, he left the slaves uncertain how to act."[52] Child could not adopt the "military" viewpoint of an oppressed people who knew their liberation could only be won by arms. Indeed, she never fully resolved her contradictory feelings about Brown's recourse to violence. If he had not seized the arsenal, but had simply conducted a bloodless slave rescue, she would be "more completely satisfied with his martyrdom," she admitted privately to her niece. "But he liked Old Testament heroes better than I do."[53] Publicly, Child, like Garrison, maintained that none but pacifists who were prepared to condemn war "under *any* circumstances" had the right to condemn Brown. Others must judge him by the standard of the American Revolution. "It is very inconsistent to eulogise Lafayette for volunteering to aid in *our* fight for freedom, while we blame John Brown for going to the rescue of those who are a thousand times more oppressed than we ever were, and who have none to help them," she argued in a letter to the *Liberator*. Even pacifists would do well to examine their consciences before criticizing a man who had dared to sacrifice his life for his principles, she continued: "Instead of blaming [Brown] for carrying out his own convictions by means we cannot sanction, it would be more profitable for us to inquire of ourselves whether we, who believe in a 'more excellent way,' have carried our convictions into practice, as faithfully as he did *his*." She concluded that abolitionists had not exerted their "*moral influence*" strenuously enough to effect the peaceful emancipation they favored. Thus the end was coming "by violence; because come it *must*."[54]

Ultimately, Child would judge Brown not by external standards, whether religious or political, but by his moral effect on her: "Others may spend their time in debating whether John Brown did wrong, or not; whether he was sane, or not; all I know, or care to know, is that his example has stirred me up to consecrate myself with renewed earnestness to the righteous cause for which he died so bravely."[55] The lesson she would draw from John Brown, she vowed to his widow, would be to "work for the oppressed, as diligently and fearlessly in *my* line, as he did in *his*."[56]

After Brown's execution, Child's first concern was to provide for "the other sufferers" of Harpers Ferry. Unlike Brown's "sublime martyrdom," the hangings of his followers filled her with anguish. "Those poor *young* victims were not so raised above their fate, as their leader was. They wanted to *live*; & my heart ached for them," she wrote.[57] She particularly felt for the African Americans, "hung for trying to serve their oppressed brethren, when Washington and Warren are eulogised!"[58] Child noted with disgust that the Virginians had carried their "savage contempt" for blacks "to the very borders of the grave" by giving "the *colored* men meaner *coffins* than those of the white men."[59]

At this time Child also began corresponding with Aaron Dwight Stevens, one of the two surviving captives, to inquire whether she could do anything for him or his family or for the families of his late comrades. "You are not left alone," she assured him. "God and his angels are with you; and thousands and thousands of hearts in the Free States are earnestly praying for you. . . ." To comfort him through his ordeal, she transcribed three pages of religious verses. She later learned that her friend Rebecca Spring had sent Stevens a copy of *Autumnal Leaves*, and that it had "made a few hours pass less drearily."[60] He must have especially liked "The Kansas Emigrants," since he proceeded to reminisce about the brave women he had encountered in that embattled territory, one of whom had "fought thirteen men and whipped them with one wrist broken and a thumb put out of joint. . . ."[61] Hoping that the Virginia court could be induced to grant clemency to Stevens and his comrade Hazlett, Child collected three hundred signatures on a petition from Wayland—one among many sent from the North—but to no avail.[62] The two young men went to their deaths on March 16, 1860.

Child had originally planned to write a biography of Brown as a means of doing justice to his character for posterity and simultaneously raising money for his family, but she abandoned the project on learning that James Redpath, a journalist who had known Brown in Kansas, had already undertaken such a work. Her admirers tried in vain to persuade her to reconsider. "No *man* will do it as you will," urged her friend Eliza Follen.[63] Brown's brother, too, disappointed in Redpath's hastily prepared volume, sought to interest Child in lending her literary talents to a more lasting monument to the martyr. She persisted in her refusal, however, convinced that a second biography issued so soon after the first would not sell.[64] Her tribute to Brown would instead take the form of sowing "seed" in the "public mind" he had so thoroughly "ploughed up."[65]

Even before the hangings of Stevens and Hazlett brought the tragedy of Harpers Ferry to a close, Child set about writing a pair of tracts designed to influence the electoral campaign of 1860, which all parties recognized as pivotal. If the Republicans honored their pledge to oppose any further extension of slavery, their victory would reverse the forty-year trend that had added three new slave states and opened vast territories to plantation crops since the Missouri Compromise of 1820. By blocking the mechanism that kept slavery profitable, a Republican administration might well set the country on the path toward emancipation; for only continual expansion into virgin land could offset the soil exhaustion produced by slave agriculture, and only the perpetual creation of new markets for slaves could stem the decline of the institution in the older cotton- and tobacco-growing states.[66] Precisely this prospect had led the slave states to threaten that they would secede from the Union should a Republican win the presidency.

To promote the Republican cause, Child devised a two-pronged strategy, oriented toward wooing crucial sectors of the electorate that normally supported the Democratic party: "*reflecting* people at the South" and white workers in the North. A small but increasing minority of southerners, Child believed, knew their system was economically vulnerable and dreaded the specter of future John Browns and Nat Turners, but saw no way out of their dilemma. She addressed their concerns in *The Right Way the Safe Way, Proved by Emancipation in the British West Indies, and Elsewhere* (1860). Even more vital to the Republicans were northern workers, who were particularly susceptible to the argument that the "wage slavery" of the North was worse than the chattel slavery of the South—an argument the Democratic press laced with racist demagoguery. Child exposed the dangers of an alliance between northern workers and southern slavocrats in *The Patriarchal Institution, as Described by Members of Its Own Family* (1860). The twin tracts had actually originated as one, which she had published in 1836 under the title *The Evils of Slavery, and the Cure of Slavery. The first proved by the opinions of Southerners themselves, the last shown by historical evidence*. In updating this work and adapting it to a different exigency almost a quarter of a century later, however, Child radically revised her earlier conception of her audience. Nothing could more tellingly indicate the sectional polarization that had occurred since the 1830s than the necessity she recognized of dividing it into two separate tracts, as distinct from each other in rhetorical approach and factual content as the two audiences she now sought to reach were distinct geographically.[67]

On sending the manuscript of *The Right Way the Safe Way* to the American Anti-Slavery Society's publishing agent, Samuel May, Jr., Child explained, "I wrote it especially for the *South*. . . . My plan is to attack them with a 'troop of horse shod with felt.'" Hence, she suggested that the title page omit any mention of the American Anti-Slavery Society, giving only an address but no publisher. She even considered issuing the tract anonymously but decided that her notoriety would probably help rather than hinder its circulation. Copies should be mailed to each member of the current Congress, to the "Governor of *every* state; and to the editors of all the Southern newspapers," as well as to "such *individuals* the Southern States as we happen to know, or whose residence we know," Child directed. No doubt recalling the post office riots that had defeated the ambitious tract-mailing campaign of 1836, she added: "[T]o be efficacious, it ought to be done *quietly*; no sounding of the trumpet *before* it, in any of the newspapers."[68]

Child elaborated further on her aim and method in a letter to John Curtis Underwood, a northern lawyer who had made his home in Virginia until driven out of the State for supporting Frémont in 1856: "My zeal is exceeding great to convince the South that immediate, unconditional emancipation would be conducive to their safety and their prosperity. I compiled the evidence expressly for the *South*. For that reason, I forbore to make any allusion to slavery in the United States. I thought the evidence might make more *impression* upon them, if nothing was said to irritate them, or excite their prejudices."[69]

The Right Way the Safe Way presents a mere "*business*-view" of the slavery question,

Child announces at the outset (6). It thus eschews moral pleas and descriptions of cruel treatment, focusing almost exclusively on the economic and social results of emancipation in the West Indies. Proslavery apologists had inundated the press with claims that emancipation had wrecked the economies of the Caribbean islands and catapulted the freed slaves back into African "barbarism." Child systematically refutes these claims. She begins by quoting official reports of the British Parliament, which show that complaints of "impending ruin" in the West Indies date as far back as 1792, long before the abolition of the slave trade, let alone of slavery itself. Pointing out the "apparent anomaly" of sugar planters' inability to survive financially when their crop enjoyed a monopoly on the British market, Child traces it to the "system of slavery" and its deleterious effects on laborers, landowners, and agriculture generally (5). She then examines the effects of emancipation on Antigua, the Windward Islands, and Jamaica, drawing on James A. Thome's and Horace Kimball's extensive 1837 study for the immediate aftermath of the 1834 Emancipation Act, and citing other authorities for the period up to 1859. To bolster the thesis that emancipation has uniformly proved "safe," she includes a brief survey of the French West Indies, Java, South Africa, the South American republics, Mexico, and the Swedish and Danish colonies, all of which had successfully abolished slavery.

In the sections on the British West Indies, Child establishes through the recorded testimony of former slaveholders, estate managers, magistrates, teachers, missionaries, and freed slaves that no major disturbances occurred after emancipation; that the ex-slaves did not sink into idleness, but continued to labor; that profits increased rather than decreased; that crime and licentiousness diminished, while church attendance and the rate of marriage rose; that the freedpeople eagerly sought education, made rapid progress in school, and did not become unruly and dissatisfied on acquiring literacy. By 1859 the islands were covered with neat villages "built by emancipated laborers," many of whom owned "cottages of their own, and small freeholds" (42). Child also contrasts the case of Antigua, where the planters had opted for immediate emancipation in 1834, with those of the Windward Islands and Jamaica, where they had instituted an apprenticeship system. Belying the myth that slaves needed to be gradually prepared for freedom, Antigua had experienced the smoothest transition to a free society.

Child relegates Jamaica to a separate chapter because that large island presented a much less rosy picture, seemingly confirming proslavery allegations. Again highlighting a prior trend of decline, she argues that emancipation "did not cause, it only precipitated" the steep fall of sugar production from which the island was still suffering (55). The apprenticeship system had prolonged the agony by allowing the planters to postpone adjusting to free labor conditions. The main explanation Child offers for Jamaica's woes, however, is that "the spirit of slavery was more violent and unyielding there than in the other Colonies," leading to "a more furious opposition to abolition, and a more stubborn determination to make it operate badly, if possible" (55). The systems of wage labor and tenant farming with which Jamaican planters had replaced slavery had proved so extortionate that whenever able, blacks had preferred to scrimp together the means to purchase their own land rather than remain on the estates.

Astonishingly, 100,000 of them had succeeded in doing so by 1850. Almost invariably, they had turned "their land to better account, than to enter into competition with sugar makers" (78), choosing to grow food instead. Hence, the collapse of the Jamaican sugar industry. In short, Child suggests that by refusing to accommodate to emancipation, Jamaican planters sealed their own doom. Nevertheless, emancipation had produced "the germ of that middling class, which is the best reliance in every community, and which can never co-exist with slavery" (81).[70]

As propaganda, *The Right Way the Safe Way* fulfills its purpose effectively. Seldom intervening with editorial comments, Child lets quotations from her sources speak for themselves. "I have not advanced opinions, or theories; I have simply stated facts," she emphasizes in her conclusion. "Leaving the obvious considerations of justice and humanity entirely out of the question," she asks "candid readers" to judge whether the evidence she has provided has not shown immediate emancipation to be "a measure of plain, practical good sense, and sound policy" (94). In her last few paragraphs she answers the questions most commonly raised by southerners who were leaning toward emancipation but feared its consequences: "What would you *do* with the slaves, if they were emancipated?" And how is emancipation to be accomplished? Her solutions are disarmingly simple. It is the task of "legislators" to work out the constitutional procedures for abolishing slavery. Once emancipated, the slaves' "labor is needed where they are," and their former masters have but to substitute the stimulus of wages for the coercion of the lash. "[E]ducation and religious teaching, and agricultural improvements will soon follow, as matters of course." "[T]he transition from slavery to freedom" will necessarily involve "inconveniences," Child acknowledges in a final caveat, but they will be *slight and temporary; while the difficulties and dangers involved in the continuance of slavery are permanent, and constantly increasing*" (95–96).

With her usual sense of timeliness, Child anticipated what one historian has described as "a steady stream of pamphlets, newspaper articles, and speeches" on West Indian emancipation, beginning with the outbreak of Civil War and continuing until Lincoln issued the Emancipation Proclamation.[71] Hers was by far the most ambitious and influential of these documents. In the months leading up to the election Child personally mailed more than a thousand copies to members of Congress, governors, judges, and southerners whose addresses she had obtained either through acquaintances or through her own research. John C. Underwood sent her several hundred names, for example, and Child happened on five hundred more in the list of subscribers to one of her friend Peter Lesley's publications.[72] Even after the election, she kept mailing tracts at the rate of twenty-five a day. "I am res[olved] that it shall not be *my* fault, if the path to freedom lies through the Red Sea," she wrote to Congressman Sidney Edgerton of Ohio, one of the many politicians who credited her with converting him to abolition.[73] Although the vast majority of southerners did, of course, choose the "path . . . through the Red Sea," Child's tract won numerous converts in what would become West Virginia. Based on reports from correspondents there, Underwood assured her optimistically: "[Y]our Tract exactly meets the wants of the time. Emancipation will take place in Virginia sooner than anybody *out* of the State supposes."[74] The breakaway state of West Virginia indeed provided for gradual emancipation as of July 1863. The second edition of *The Right Way the Safe Way*, which Child published in March 1862 with the aim of encouraging emancipation in the Border Slave States, may also have exerted a palpable influence. Child mailed copies to all Maryland and Delaware legislators, and the legislature of Maryland did abolish slavery in 1864.[75] Delaware, like the other Border States, clung to slavery till the bitter end, but Child's tract generated enough interest there for the Wilmington newspapers to reprint "copious extracts" of it.[76]

Presenting a startling contrast to the low-key approach Child formulated for thinking southerners, the tract she aimed at northern workers — *The Patriarchal Institution, as Described by Members of Its Own Family* — bristles with sectional antagonism.[77] The mere subject headings raise hackles as they frame an indictment of the South: "SOUTHERN PROOFS OF THE 'CHIVALROUS AND HIGH-MINDED CHARACTER' PRODUCED BY SLAVERY"; "SOUTHERN PROOFS THAT 'THE PHYSICAL CONDITION OF SLAVES IS BETTER THAN THAT OF NORTHERN LABORERS'"; "SOUTHERN PROSPECTS FOR NORTHERN LABORERS AND MECHANICS"; "SOUTHERN AND NORTHERN DEMOCRATS NOW LEAGUED FOR THE EXTENSION OF SLAVERY." No longer does Child carefully refrain from mentioning American slavery; instead, she attacks it head on. The subject she does skirt is race. Unlike her 1833 *Appeal*, *The Patriarchal Institution* does not castigate its readers' prejudices or demand equality for African Americans. It uses a more indirect strategy to inveigle white workers into putting themselves in the place of the slaves they have been told are better off than themselves.

As in *The Right Way the Safe Way*, Child advances her entire argument through quotations drawn from other authorities — in this case southerners themselves. "[S]o arranged as to be very sarcastic," extracts from southern law codes, fugitive slave advertisements, articles in southern newspapers, and the speeches and writings of proslavery apologists counter every claim southerners have made for their "patriarchal institution."[78] Thus, giving the lie to "Southern Proofs that Slaves are 'Happy and Contented'" are nine pages of fugitive slave advertisements and two laws that sum up the essence of slavery: one imposing a fine for the mutilation of slaves, except "'by whipping, or beating, with a horsewhip'" and the other outlawing the killing of slaves, except by "'moderate correction'" (9–18). With even more devastating irony, long lists of runaways characterized by their owners as able to pass for white serve as "Southern Proofs that Slavery is a 'Parental Relation'" (25–28).

The technique, of course, is hardly new. Both Child and Theodore Weld had exploited it to the hilt in their tracts of the 1830s. What differentiates *The Patriarchal Institution* from those earlier tracts is that it appeals not to the humanitarianism of white readers generally, but to the self-interest of white workers in particular. The Democratic party had managed to convince large numbers of white workers that Republicans wanted to degrade them to the level of black slaves. Child reverses the argument. The very party posing as the champion of the northern working class has expressed open contempt for working people in its southern organs, she shows. The quotations she marshals from southern Democratic newspapers need no comment. One stigmatizes

"*Free* society" as a sickening "conglomeration of *greasy mechanics, filthy operatives,* [and] *small-fisted farmers* . . . hardly fit for association with a gentleman's body servant" (6–7). Another complains that the North's "*servile class*" is "*unfit for self-government*" and lectures: "*Slavery is the natural and normal condition of the laboring man, white or black*" (6). Proslavery theorists and politicians like Governor Wise have been explicitly advocating the extension of slavery "*into the very heart of the North*," and northern Democrats have been dancing to their tune, Child indicates (47).[79]

In her "Concluding Remarks," Child mimics the accents of proslavery apologists as she hymns the blessings that northern workers will share with southern slaves if they heed the Democrats' siren song and ally themselves with the Slave Power. "*Slavery is nothing more than labor obeying unchecked, unregulated and irresponsible capital,*" a convention of southern businessmen had declared enthusiastically (4–5). Playing on this theme, Child purports to explain why such a system offers "inducements" to "*laborers*" as well as to "*capitalists*":

> It is true you would receive no wages for your valuable services; but . . . you would be relieved from all the cares and responsibilities entailed upon property. . . . "A peck of corn a week" . . . might seem rather monotonous provender; but then you would be almost sure not to die of repletion, or dyspepsia. . . . [Y]our wife . . . might happen to be sold into a State far distant from the place where your own lot was cast; but . . . [t]he proverb says, "Variety is the spice of life"; and you could both forthwith form new connections, without the formality or expense of weddings. (50–51)

Only in the final paragraph does Child address northern workers in her own voice. "Slavery and Freedom are antagonistic elements. . . . Which do you choose? Momentous issues are at stake on your decision," she admonishes them (53). Inviting attention to itself, the shift in rhetoric reinforces the message that this Republican pamphleteer, unlike her Democratic counterparts, is speaking to working-class voters as intelligent fellow beings, capable of making educated choices.

Child had planned *The Patriarchal Institution* as a "Political Campaign Document." Perhaps with an eye toward having it distributed at the May nominating convention, she had even asked Massachusetts Senator Henry Wilson to submit it to the Republican committee.[80] Apparently the party regulars found the tract too radical for their purposes, however. The Republicans were trying to distance themselves from abolitionists, and *The Patriarchal Institution* clearly manifested an abolitionist's sympathy with the slave. In any case, the committee decided to request David to supply an alternative campaign document: a series of pamphlets exposing southern "outrages" against free speech, civil liberties, the "Federal Compact," and international law — that is, against the rights and principles of white citizens, rather than of African Americans.[81] The substitution bore out Child's often reiterated charge that Republican politicians tended to "think only of the interests of *white* men: they ignore the monstrous and perpetual wrongs that we are *helping* the South to inflict upon the *colored* race." Publication of *The Patriarchal Institution*, delayed until October, once again fell to the

American Anti-Slavery Society. Still, Child insisted on having the tract circulated before the November election. "[W]e may as well make the Republicans of some *use*," she remarked acidly.[82]

As with *The Right Way the Safe Way*, Child did the lion's share of the distribution work, personally addressing and mailing several hundred copies to northern "Governors, Judges, Counsellers, &c" whose names she found listed in the *American Almanac*. Suggesting that the society might do well to employ a clerk to dispatch "3 or 4000 of the Tract in a week," given the short time remaining until the election, she specified: "I would confine the circulation . . . pretty much to the *Free* States. . . . Every editor of a Republican newspaper, throughout the Free States, ought to have a copy."[83]

"I *must* stand by the poor slave, come what will," Child had summed up the lesson she had learned from John Brown. Hidden behind the scenes in *The Right Way the Safe Way* and *The Patriarchal Institution*, the slave comes to the fore in Child's last major projects of the "John Brown Year," undertaken simultaneously in the late summer of 1860: her tract *The Duty of Disobedience to the Fugitive Slave Act: An Appeal to the Legislators of Massachusetts* and her editing of Harriet Jacobs's *Incidents in the Life of a Slave Girl*.[84] The two projects overlap in more ways than one. Both look beyond the November election and seek to forestall a danger that Child feared more than a Republican defeat: the danger that once elected, the Republicans would cave in to southern threats of secession, abandon their campaign promises, and agree to yet another shameful "compromise" with slavery. Both ask readers to adopt the slave's point of view and "imagine how *you* would feel, under similar circumstances" (12). Both situate themselves in what had become by 1860 a well-established tradition of female political discourse. "[I]n view of all that women have done, and are doing, intellectually and morally, for the advancement of the world," writes Child in *The Duty of Disobedience*, "I presume no enlightened legislator will be disposed to deny that the 'truth of Heaven' *is* often committed to them, and that they sometimes utter it with a degree of power that greatly influences the age in which they live" (3). "I want to add my testimony to that of abler pens to convince the people of the Free States what Slavery really is," writes Jacobs in *Incidents in the Life of a Slave Girl*.[85] Both refer to the spectacular success of Harriet Beecher Stowe's *Uncle Tom's Cabin* (1852) and self-consciously manipulate the language of women's fiction, which she had raised to new heights.

The Duty of Disobedience to the Fugitive Slave Act petitions the legislators of Massachusetts to reenforce the State Personal Liberty Law. The current law merely granted apprehended fugitives a jury trial, but it did not prevent their being remanded if proved to be the "property" of their claimants. Pronouncing this insufficient, Child urges Massachusetts to emulate Vermont, which had passed a state law overriding and effectively nullifying the hated federal statute. It declared that any slave who entered the state, whether with or without the consent of his or her "owner," automatically became free, and that all laws inconsistent with those of Vermont were "hereby repealed" (36). Nothing less can absolve Massachusetts citizens of complicity in slavery, Child argues.

"Legislators of Massachusetts, can it be that you really understand what Slavery *is*, and yet consent that a fugitive slave, who seeks protection here, shall be driven back to that dismal house of bondage?" she demands. To induce such an understanding, she places her readers in the situation of a mulatto slave man whose parentage encapsulates the contradictions and injustices of the South's racial chattel system: "Suppose your father was Governor of Carolina and your mother was a slave" (5). The imaginary narrative she proceeds to construct borrows many details from the accounts of Jacobs, Frederick Douglass, and other fugitives as it takes this hypothetical "you" through typical phases of a mulatto slave's life: the sale of "your" mother, due to the mistress's jealousy; abuse by "your whiter brother"; secret efforts to achieve the literacy forbidden to slaves; the master's betrayal of his promise to let "you" buy "yourself"; his appropriation of "your" wife as well as of the installments "you" have paid toward "your" freedom; "your" sale and "your" desperate decision to flee (6–10). Quoting directly from Jacobs's narrative, Child describes how "You hide in a neighboring swamp, where you are bitten by a venomous snake, and your swollen limb becomes almost incapable of motion" (LMC 10; J 98, 113). The fate she awards "you" after "your" safe arrival in the North is not the freedom Douglass's and Jacobs's friends had purchased for them, however; rather, it is the reenslavement to which Boston had condemned Thomas Sims in 1851 and Anthony Burns in 1854: "Suddenly, you find yourself arrested and chained. Soldiers escort you through the streets of Boston, and put you on board a Southern ship, to be sent back to your master" (11).

Having taught her readers to imagine themselves as slaves, Child now reminds them of real-life fugitive slave cases. Most horrifying is that of Margaret Garner (immortalized by novelist Toni Morrison in *Beloved*), who had cut her baby daughter's throat and attempted to kill her other children, too, when tracked down and cornered by slave catchers. "Do you think that mother had a murderer's heart? Nay, verily. Exceeding love for her children impelled her to do the dreadful deed," contends Child, laying the blame on "those human hounds, who drove [Garner] to . . . choose between Slavery or Death for her innocent offspring" (18).

In short, Child casts her appeal to Massachusetts Legislators in the rhetoric of *Uncle Tom's Cabin*. She even steps into the role of Stowe's Mrs. Bird as she pleads with lawmakers who, like the fictional Senator Bird, had defended the Fugitive Slave Law because they "had never thought that a fugitive might be a hapless mother, a defenceless child."[86] Not until she has forced her readers to abandon their customary legalistic mode and to envision fugitives as human beings like themselves does Child evaluate the legal merits of the Fugitive Slave Act:

> Law was established to maintain justice between man and man; and this Act clearly maintains injustice. Law was instituted to protect the weak from the strong; this Act delivers the weak completely into the arbitrary power of the strong. "Law is a rule of conduct, prescribed by the supreme power, commanding what is right, and forbidding what is wrong". . . . [T]he Fugitive Slave Act . . . reverses the maxim. It commands what is wrong, and forbids what is right. (21–22)

As if to accentuate the subordination of legal to moral arguments, Child relegates to an appendix the expert opinions she has assembled in support of her verdict that the Fugitive Slave Act (she conspicuously eschews the more common term "law") is illegal. She chooses instead to end her *Appeal to the Legislators of Massachusetts* by literally assuming the posture of a slave: "I am a humble member of the community. . . . I am growing old; and on this great question of equal rights I have toiled for years, sometimes with a heart sickened by 'hope deferred.' I beseech you to let me die on Free Soil!" (23). It is a posture not altogether alien to her, she intimates, for like her slave sister, she has "no vote to give," and as a result she knows that her "tears" are "of little consequence" to her rulers (23).

"This admirable tract . . . displays equally its author's well-known power to touch the heart and moisten the eyes. Mrs. Child pleads for those in bonds 'as bound with them,'" commented the *Liberator*.[87] While true to the tone of Child's tract, the eulogy hardly captured the thrust of her political strategy. Child gave the newly elected legislators no time to forget their campaign promises and begin trading concessions. She ensured that they would have leisure to read her appeal "in the quiet of their homes, undisturbed by the distractions of the city" (or the temptations of the public arena).[88] Immediately after the election, she procured the winners' personal addresses and mailed "*every one* of them" copies not only of *The Duty of Disobedience to the Fugitive Slave Act*, but of *The Patriarchal Institution* and *The Right Way the Safe Way*. The second and third tracts would buttress the first by showing "what sort of system it *is*, that slaves run away from . . . and . . . how easily that system might be changed," Child explained.[89] She intended to guard against a Republican retreat by subjecting the victorious troops to a steady bombardment of abolitionist propaganda.

"It seems as if Slavery would be the death of me. . . . My indignation rises higher than it used to in my younger days. . . . If the monster had one head, assuredly I should be Charlotte Corday," wrote Child to her old friend Samuel Sewall.[90] Her reading of Harriet Jacobs's *Incidents in the Life of a Slave Girl* doubtless fueled this indignation, for the lecherous master who hounded his young slave for sexual favors and the jealous mistress who "pitied herself" but "had no compassion for the poor victim of her husband's perfidy" (33) incarnated the "loathsome, hypocritical features" of the peculiar institution.[91]

Jacobs had approached Child in late July or early August 1860 to obtain her editorial "advise and assistance."[92] She had been trying for several years to secure a publisher for the narrative she had written of her experiences as a slave, and the firm of Thayer and Eldridge had finally accepted the manuscript, on condition that Child write a preface for it. Though fearing rebuff from a "Satellite of so great magnitude," Jacobs had found Child a warm, "whole souled Woman."[93] Child, in turn, had been impressed with Jacobs's "quickwitted" intelligence and "great refinement and propriety of manner."[94] The friendship that sprang up between them would last for many years.

Child spent more than a month editing the manuscript, primarily for the purposes of "bring[ing] the story into continuous *order*," transferring the antislavery "remarks"

Jacobs had interpolated at various points to more "*appropriate* places" in the text, and occasionally deleting "superfluous words."[95] "I have very little occasion to alter the language, which is wonderfully good, for one whose opportunities for education have been so limited," she assured Jacobs. In letters to friends, Child repeated her praise of Jacobs's "lively and dramatic" style and confirmed that she had not "*altered* fifty words in the whole volume."[96] She did, however, acknowledge having made one major change for the sake of increasing the book's potential readership (at the cost of marring its narrative coherence): "I put the savage cruelties into one chapter, entitled 'Neighboring Planters,' in order that those who shrink from 'supping upon horrors,' might omit them, without interrupting the thread of the story."[97] Child had displayed the same hardheaded editorial judgment in adapting her own *Letters from New York* for a broader audience. During her editorship of the *Standard*, she had also taken similar liberties with the texts of her contributors, when she felt the needs of the cause required greater tact.[98]

Although Child assumed the role of an experienced professional advising a literary novice, she offered her suggestions in a manner that showed considerable sensitivity toward Jacobs. For example, she carefully explained why "the last Chapter, about John Brown, had better be omitted." Since Jacobs had fled her native North Carolina in 1842, John Brown did not "naturally come into [her] story." Besides, the manuscript was "already too long. Nothing can be so appropriate to end with, as the death of your grandmother." In a reverse instance, Child diplomatically indicated that Jacobs had not sufficiently elaborated on the repercussions of the Nat Turner rebellion, which did come naturally into her story. Using leading questions, Child prodded Jacobs to support her generalizations with specific details: "You say the reader would not believe what you saw 'inflicted on men, women, and children, without the slightest ground of suspicion against them.' What *were* those inflictions? Were any tortured to make them confess? and how? Where [*sic*] any killed? Please write down some of the most striking particulars, and let me have them to insert." Most important, Child expected Jacobs to claim an author's time-honored privilege of going over and possibly contesting editorial changes. "I suppose you will want to see the M.S. after I have exercised my bump of mental order upon it; and I will send it wherever you direct, a fortnight hence," she promised.[99]

Child's consideration for Jacobs extended to maximizing her profits and assisting with distribution. Believing the book exceptionally "well calculated to do service in the Anti Slavery cause," she helped persuade an abolitionist charitable fund, the Hovey Committee, to purchase a thousand copies. This would enable the publishers to take the risk of stereotyping an edition of two thousand, and "they ought, therefore, to make a generous arrangement with the author," Child pointed out. "When you bargain with them, please have an eye to her interest," she instructed Wendell Phillips, who had taken over Ellis Loring's responsibilities as the attorney handling Child's business transactions.[100] After the firm of Thayer and Eldridge suddenly went bankrupt in December 1860, forcing Jacobs to buy the plates and have the book privately printed, Child asked abolitionist friends in other cities to contact their local booksellers and try to interest them in purchasing several dozen copies at a discount. "The Boston book-sellers are dreadfully afraid of soiling their hands with an Anti-Slavery book; so we have a good deal of trouble in getting the book into the market," she complained.[101]

Child's promotion of Jacobs's writing continued through the Civil War. Not only did she mail copies of *Incidents* to Union troops as a means of arousing their hatred of slavery, but she included Jacobs's sketch of her grandmother in her 1865 anthologies *Looking toward Sunset* and *The Freedmen's Book*. In the latter, published after the war, she substituted Jacobs's real name for the pseudonym used in the book to protect those who had harbored her against retaliation. Child also publicized Jacobs's labors among the freed slaves in Union Army camps by forwarding her friend's vivid letters about these refugees to the *Liberator* and the *Standard*.[102]

Suggesting the intimacy the two women developed, Jacobs became one of the few overnight guests Child accommodated in her tiny Wayland cottage — a distinction she shared with Sarah Shaw, Marianne Silsbee, and Dolores.[103] The frugal habits of a white woman who had contended with poverty for much of her life and was used to doing her own housework must have helped put Jacobs at ease. Child no doubt told Jacobs that her own father, like Jacobs's grandmother, had been famous for his "nice crackers" (*Incidents* 6), and that she and Convers, like Jacobs and her brother, John, had benefited from the large clientele of village notables attracted by the family bakery. A common love of gardening provided another bond between the two women, Child sending Jacobs "fifty four different kinds of seeds" for the freedpeople in Georgia to plant in what Jacobs called "Yankee gardens."[104] Jacobs trusted Child enough to confide her worries about her son, Joseph, who had gone to Australia to dig gold and had disap-peared without a trace, after asking her to send him money through a third party for his passage home. In response, suspecting "foul play," Child wrote to relatives of David's in Australia, requesting them to have local clergymen launch a search by reading descrip-tions of the missing son from their pulpits.[105] Because Child's and Jacobs's letters to each other in later years have been lost, we can only speculate about the quality of their relationship.[106] Nevertheless, it seems to have been the closest friendship Child formed with an African American woman.

In the midst of Child's work on *Incidents in the Life of a Slave Girl* and *The Duty of Disobedience to the Fugitive Slave Act*, an opportunity arose for her to stand by the slave not merely as an advocate, but as an emancipator. She had never forgiven herself for her long interval of inaction on slavery, during which her native state had disgraced itself by remanding Thomas Sims and Anthony Burns to their masters under the provisions of the Fugitive Slave Law. Sims had nearly died of the flogging he had received on his return; he had recovered only to be "sold farther South," as Child recalled in *The Duty of Disobedience* (21). Now she learned that he had just written to his sister in Boston, informing her that his new master would be willing to sell him for $1,800. Child immediately volunteered to solicit contributions from "wealthy gentlemen" and ar-ranged for the lawyer Samuel Sewall to keep the money until Sims arrived. "I swore 'by the Eternal' . . . that as Massachusetts had sent him into slavery, Massachusetts should bring him back. I resolved, also, that it should all be done with *pro-slavery* money," she wrote to Sarah Shaw. "They told me that I had undertaken to 'hoe a very hard row.' . . . But I got it! I got it! I got it!"[107] After dispatching eighteen of the hundred letters she had thought might be required, Child received word that Charles Devens, the very U.S. marshal who had remanded Sims, wished to atone by putting up the entire sum himself, provided his name would be kept secret. History foiled Child's triumph, however, for Civil War broke out before negotiations with Sims's master could be completed. Sims would have to wait until the Union army liberated him in 1863. When Sims finally arrived in Boston, Devens sent him a hundred dollars through Child "to assist him till he could get into business."[108]

Sims's fate proved paradigmatic. For the nation, too, the "path to freedom" would lie "through the Red Sea," despite Child's heroic efforts to map out an alternative route. "[T]he crimes of this *guilty land* will never be purged away but with *blood*," John Brown had prophesied in his famous valedictory. Like Brown, Child would conclude that she had "vainly flattered [her]self" in hoping otherwise.[109]

The inexorable drift toward war accelerated sharply as the 1860 electoral campaign exposed the sectional fragmentation of the party system. The Democrats split into northern and southern wings, each with its own set of candidates. The Republicans did not even appear on the ballot in ten out of fifteen southern states. The sole group to seek a national constituency on the old model allying southern planters with northern merchants and capitalists was the ghost of the defunct Whig party, which now called itself the "Constitutional Union" or "Bell-Everett" ticket, after its candidates John Bell of Tennessee and Edward Everett of Massachusetts. The Bell-Everetts polled less than 3 percent of the northern vote, though the party's adherents would whip up a ferocious backlash against the winners they stigmatized as "Black Republicans."[110]

Child greeted the nomination and election of Abraham Lincoln with cautious optimism, judging him an "honest, independent man, and sincerely a friend to freedom."[111] She did not share the disappointment of those abolitionists who had wished the Republicans would nominate William H. Seward, renowned for his speeches proclaiming that there was a "higher law than the Constitution" and that slavery and freedom were headed toward an "irrepressible conflict." Seward, she noticed, had dropped his antislavery rhetoric as soon as he had started "baiting for a nomination." "When the Presidency touches the hem of a man's garment, all virtue goes out of him," she commented acerbically.[112] Her distrust of Seward would give way to loathing during the tense interregnum between the November election and Lincoln's inauguration on March 4, 1861. As the president-elect's appointee for secretary of state, Seward began doing exactly what Child had most feared—trying to conciliate the South by urging the repeal of northern state laws that obstructed the Fugitive Slave Act and by recommending the passage of an inalterable amendment to the Constitution that would permanently deny Congress the "power to abolish or interfere with slavery in any State."[113]

The flurry of "compromise" proposals paradoxically following the impressive Republican victory at the polls was generated by a veritable southern counterrevolution.[114] On December 20, 1860, South Carolina made good on its threats to secede, triggering a "chain reaction" throughout the lower South. Conservative businessmen, appalled at the prospect of losing their southern markets and plunging into economic ruin, swiftly mobilized to avert this catastrophe. Their political spokesmen, nearly all prominent members of the Bell-Everett faction, assured southerners that if they would hold out against secession, they would find "there is now a conservative element throughout the North . . . large enough and powerful enough to see that the South shall be sustained in every right guaranteed by the Constitution."[115] Simultaneously, Bell-Everetts reminded their fellow northerners that secession was already having a "serious effect upon business operations" and creating "distress among mechanics, laborers, and clerks, who have families to support."[116] Such caveats served to bolster their campaign for repeal of the Personal Liberty Laws, which, as Massachusetts conservatives argued in a widely reprinted address, "violated our great national compact," conflicted with "the Constitution and laws of the United States," and fed the fires of secession.[117] Child noted with "deep sadness" that the "respected and influential name" of Lemuel Shaw, chief justice of the Massachusetts Supreme Court, headed the list of signers (a list comprising a roll call of the Brahmins who had acted as patrons to her and David in their days as the "brilliant Miss Francis" and the ambitious editor of the *Massachusetts Journal*).[118] She must have thought of the distance Shaw seemed to have traveled since she had praised him in 1836 for his decision freeing the slave child Med. And she could hardly have helped remembering his role in the 1851 Sims case as the first northern judge to implement the Fugitive Slave Law. But she sent him copies of *The Duty of Disobedience*, *The Patriarchal Institution*, and *The Right Way the Safe Way*, along with a cover letter "respectfully and earnestly" asking him to read them "with candid attention."[119]

The conservatives Shaw represented did not intend to rely on argument alone to reverse the results of the election. "We have got a most powerful organization here, that will be heard from in due time," they boasted. "[O]ur fanatics . . . have had their day. . . . A John Brown meeting cannot be held in Boston now, no more than it could in Atlanta."[120] It was no idle boast. While politicians in Washington dithered and dickered with compromise proposals, a tidal wave of antiabolitionist riots engulfed the North. The "gentlemen of property and standing" who led them indeed chose a "John Brown meeting," held at Tremont Temple on the anniversary of the martyr's hanging, for their first show of strength. With the connivance of Boston's lame duck Bell-Everett mayor and Democrat-dominated police force, a mob "composed chiefly of North street aristocrats and Beacon street roughs" shouted down the pro-Brown speakers, drove them from the platform, and took over the meeting.[121] Frederick Douglass was "thrown down the staircase," fighting "like a trained pugilist," Frank Sanborn was "dragged out by the neck," and many African Americans in the audience were "knocked down and trampled upon" by the mob as they left the hall. An even more murderous mob waylaid those who attended the evening commemoration at the Reverend J. Sella Martin's church. To escape his pursuers, Wendell Phillips went home by a back way, sandwiched between Child and Chapman, his female bodyguards, and further protected by male friends who formed a close circle around him "with locked hands." Some thought his life was "in imminent peril," but Child believed the conspirators were "too *cunning* to give the abolitionists such an advantage." The thugs were "evidently drilled and organized carefully, to do no *more* than is necessary to effectually break up the meetings; because anything *beyond* that might excite popular sympathy for abolitionists," she judged shrewdly.[122]

Two weeks later, another Bell-Everett mob "directed by the cotton interest" and made up largely of "merchants' clerks" tried to disrupt a Sunday service at the Music Hall featuring Phillips as the main speaker. This time outnumbered inside the hall, the rowdies reserved their attack for the streets, where "they raised the Bell-Everett cry, 'All up,' and rushed towards" Phillips and his friends. Caught in the melee, "Mrs. Child was . . . 'tumbled up & down' somewhat," reported an abolitionist onlooker. To his gratification, she "left the field a victor" after "illustrating her Bunker Hill by collaring a burly rioter, — & her Non-resistance by preaching a broad cloth-Plugugly into immediate repentance & a promise to 'flee from the wrath to come.' "[123]

For Child the most frightening outbreak of mob violence occurred at the annual meeting of the Massachusetts Anti-Slavery Society on January 24, where she and David were slated to serve on the business committee. "I would rather have given $50 than attend," she confided frankly to Sarah Shaw, "but conscience told me it was a duty."[124] Notwithstanding her conviction that the thugs were seeking to intimidate rather than to kill abolitionists, Child spent a sleepless night, tormented by nightmare visions of Phillips's "noble head assailed by murderous hands, and I obliged to stand by, without the power to save him." Rising very early, she slipped into Tremont Hall "by a private labyrinthine passage." Phillips's friends were already present, "calm, but resolute and stern." All were armed, as were hundreds of other participants, though they had pledged not to use their weapons unless Phillips or any other abolitionist speaker were "*personally in danger*."

Shortly after the meeting opened, the mob "came tumbling in by hundreds" and "began to yell from the galleries." The ensuing pandemonium was "a full realization of the old phrase 'all hell broke loose,' " Child remarked wryly: "Such yelling, schreeching, stamping, and bellowing, I never heard." The rowdies drowned out two speakers and taunted Phillips for a full hour, sometimes with threats — "Throw him out!" "Throw a brick-bat at him!" — sometimes with gibes aimed at all abolitionists, as when they chanted "Tell John Andrew, Tell John Andrew, John Brown's dead" (referring to the Republican governor of Massachusetts who had proclaimed, "*Whatever may be thought of John Brown's acts, John Brown himself is right!*")[125] Suddenly "they all rose up," and the confrontation Child had dreaded seemed upon her: "[M]any clattered down stairs, and there was a surging forward toward the platform. My heart beat so, that I could hear it; for I did not *then* know how Mr. Phillips's armed friends were posted at every door, and in the middle of every aisle. They formed a firm wall, which the mob could not pass." An announcement that the police were on their way brought a temporary lull. Meanwhile, Phillips adopted the ruse of addressing his speech sotto voce to the "reporters stationed immediately below him," which "tantalized the mob" into silence. From the audience, David Child hailed the triumph with "three cheers for the conqueror."[126] But after adjournment of the morning session, abolitionists still had to brave the hooligans who had gathered to mob them in the streets.

At the afternoon session, the "uproar" was even louder. "The mob cheered and hurraed for the Union, and for Edward Everett," as well as for Boston's newly elected Democratic mayor, Joseph M. Wightman, and for Republican Congressman Charles Francis Adams, who had sponsored a "compromise" proposal to "give up New Mexico to the chances of slavery."[127] Alarmed for the safety of their property, the Tremont Hall trustees finally summoned the mayor to quell the riot, but misrepresenting their request, he instead ordered the meeting dispersed — "precisely what [the rioters] *wanted* him to do."[128] Though abolitionists called the mayor's bluff and forced him to comply with the trustees' demand, he subsequently canceled their evening session.[129] "S. Carolina still governs us," Child commented glumly. "I have now very little doubt that her whip will effectually frighten our merchants, and by their influence, combined with the South, the Republican leaders will be subdued into one miserable mush of concession."[130]

Child's suspicions that "an extensive and powerful league at the *North*" was conspiring with the South to subvert the Republican victory, possibly even through a coup d'etat, changed to near certainty after an unpleasant reunion with her friends the Silsbees. Knowing that Nathaniel Silsbee was "a ferocious Bell-Everett" and that Marianne blamed antislavery agitation for thwarting her husband's ambitions for a congressional seat, Child had determined to steer clear of politics.[131] "But S. Carolina came in, with sound of trumpet, as she does everywhere, now a days. . . . Mr. Silsbee grew red in the face, and his lips were occasionally tightly compressed." His fulminations struck Child as sinister enough for her to relay them to Charles Sumner, along with other rumors she had heard. "He did not blame the South for forming a Confederacy to protect their rights, he said. He upheld them in it. &c He said the Bell-Everett party had become an organization under *another name*." It had received pledges of large financial contributions from the "friends of 'law and order' to put down the Republican agitation." Not long afterward, another acquaintance Child encountered, whose father had supported the southern Democrats' candidate John C. Breckinridge for the presidency, confirmed that Democrats and Bell-Everetts had united to form a new organization. "Some of the richest gentlemen in Boston and some eminent lawyers were in league with it. Fifty millions of dollars would be forthcoming, if needed, to accomplish their object." That object, Child speculated, might be "the taking of Washington, and the placing of Breckenridge in the chair."[132] Nothing of the sort came to pass, of course, but Child was witnessing the genesis of an authentic conspiracy, the Copperhead movement, which was to operate against the Lincoln government throughout the Civil War.

In letters to abolitionist friends, Child conjured up an alternative scenario, much closer to the one that actually unfolded. "[P]artly from cowardice, partly from a sincere attachment to the Union, and partly from lures of personal ambition, which will be artfully held out to them, and partly from the selfish appeals of merchants and office-holders," Republican leaders, she predicted, might well be cajoled into "hugger-mug-gering up compromises" to which the rank and file of the "*party* would never consent, if their votes could be taken." As evidence that such a sellout was afoot, Child noted that the peace convention which Seward had called in Washington on February 4 (timed to coincide with the Confederate constitutional convention held in Montgomery) was meeting ominously behind "closed doors." "It is only despotisms that need secresy. The people ought to *know* what their rulers are about, before the mischief is accomplished," she protested.[133] Her sixth sense that the schemers were engineering an irrevocable compromise proved not far off the mark. A "proposed Thirteenth Amendment to the Constitution guaranteeing slavery in the states against any future interference by the federal government" did actually pass both the House and Senate a week before Lincoln's inauguration, and 40 percent of the Republican membership joined Democrats in supporting it.[134] Ultimately, Child placed more faith in the "blind fury of the Secessionists" than in the principles of the Republicans.[135] "My hope is that the South will scorn to accept *any* compromise, that the North will get on her knees to offer," she owned.[136] She had no illusions about what the consequences would be if the two sides deadlocked.

Having worked for thirty years to promote emancipation by peaceful means, Child now braced herself for the sole recourse that remained. "[M]uch as I deprecate civil war, I deliberately say even *that* is better than compromises of principle, at this momentous crisis," she wrote in February to her old comrade from the Boston Female Anti-Slavery Society, Henrietta Sargent. "Such epochs come in the history of individuals and of nations, when we are solemnly called upon to decide whether we will serve God or the Devil; and if we choose the latter, ruin is inevitable."[137] Hitherto, Child had served God by trying to avert war. She was at last ready to redefine her mission. When Union troops marched off to battle singing "John Brown's body lies a-mouldering in the grave / His soul goes marching on," she would exhort them to live up to their hero's creed by welcoming their black brothers into their ranks and fighting shoulder to shoulder with them till they had purged the last vestiges of the "accursed institution" from their "*guilty land*."[138]

18

Child's Civil War

Regarding war as a barbarism which demoralizes and disgraces civilized society, I am unable to enter into the military enthusiasm of the day. . . .

I confess to great apparent inconsistency of feeling during the course of events in the last few years. I detested war, with all my heart and soul; yet I was mortally afraid our terrible struggle would end too soon. I have never wavered in my convictions that peace principles were the highest and truest, and that human society would never be truly civilized till they were adopted. Yet . . . I dreaded to have the war end before Slavery was completely overthrown, because I foresaw that, if it did, another bloody war must inevitably follow.[1]

Throughout the four-year Civil War that produced the greatest mass carnage the world had ever seen, Child wrestled with the excruciating ambivalence she describes in this retrospective letter to the New York *Independent*, written in August 1865. Her revulsion against bloodshed and her disgust with the racism that governed public policy toward African Americans—often to the detriment of the war effort—weighed heavily on her spirits. Child's letters registered the marked change in her mood as the exaltation of the John Brown Year gave way to the attrition of endless combat, unredeemed by an abolitionist purpose. While rallying her compatriots around Brown's standard, she had felt "strong as an eagle" and "charged [so] . . . full of electricity" that political opponents found her "a torpedo to the touch."[2] In contrast, as she heard northern politicians, generals, editors, and citizens insist that the Union was fighting "a war to put down *treason*, not to meddle with *slavery*,"[3] Child sank into despondency. Her despondency turned to impotent fury when the Lincoln administration began ordering military officers to remand slaves who fled to Union army camps.

Personal as well as political factors contributed to Child's bleak mood. The war intensified her sense of isolation in Wayland, where many of her neighbors were Copperheads or anti-black Unionists.[4] The outbreak of hostilities in April 1861 and the shameful anti-black riots triggered by the Conscription Act in July 1863 also coincided with her last thwarted attempts to "extricate" herself from the "uncongenial" living situation that was "killing [her] soul."[5] Adding to the burdens of loneliness and domestic drudgery, the restriction of her physical mobility as she entered her sixties and David his seventies confined her more and more closely to her "prison."[6]

The defeat of her own aspirations toward freedom reinforced Child's lifelong solidarity with the slaves. In turn, the projection of her desire for escape onto the escapees from southern plantations sharpened the apprehension with which she followed the course of the War. "The fact is, I identify myself so completely with the slaves, that I am kept in alternating states of anxiety and wrath," she wrote in the summer of 1861, when Union troops were still routinely sending fugitives back to their masters. "If I wake up in the middle of the night, it is the first thing I think of." "Every instance of sending back poor fugitive slaves has cut into my heart like the stab of a bowie-knife."[7]

Determined to ensure that the war would result in genuine liberation for African Americans, Child concentrated her energies on advocating emancipation and the recruitment of black troops, supporting assistance programs that prepared refugees from slavery for productive lives, helping to launch a literacy campaign for the freedpeople, and lobbying for the redistribution of plantation estates among former slaves, poor whites, and Union soldiers. After the war, American society would have to be set on a new basis of equal opportunity for "people of all nations, and all complexions," she realized, and abolitionists must lose no time in guiding policy toward that goal.[8] Much of Child's Civil War activism, however, took a less public form than had her enterprises of the John Brown Year. While she continued to write for the *Liberator* and the *Standard*, she published a significant proportion of her pro-emancipation articles anonymously or pseudonymously in mainstream newspapers, with the hope of exerting greater influence on Unionists hostile to antislavery agitators.[9] Few of the wartime letters she wrote to politicians appeared in print, and none achieved the circulation of her famous correspondence with Governor Wise and Mrs. Mason. At a time when some of her younger sisters—among them Elizabeth Cady Stanton and Anna Dickinson—were advancing the Union cause from the rostrum she herself had once yearned to mount,[10] Child gravitated toward conventionally female types of activism: sewing for the ex-slave refugees and the Sanitary Commission; knitting for soldiers in abolitionist-led regiments; rolling bandages for hospital use; and participating in the annual fund-raising receptions that had replaced the antislavery fairs. Asked to write a pro-war tract for the soldiers, she refused point blank. "I have such a horror of war, it seems to me such a shocking barbarism, that I have a reluctance to having anything to do with it, except to alleviate the suffering it occasions," she explained.[11] She would work for the political aims of the war, as she defined them—the abolition of slavery, the conferral of equal citizenship rights on African Americans, and the fulfillment of the nation's republican ideals—but not for the war itself.

Significantly, Child's two most ambitious and enduring publications of the Civil War era performed a mission of personal and political healing. *Looking toward Sunset* (1865), an anthology presenting positive views of old age, once again displayed Child's ability to turn her deepest private needs to social account. *The Freedmen's Book* (1865), a reader comprising biographical sketches, poems, speeches, and stories by and about blacks, served to inculcate racial pride along with literacy and thus help the victims of slavery overcome their past.

During the ominous winter of 1860–61, marked by antiabolitionist riots, frenzied compromise negotiations, and preparations for war, Child was enjoying a "peaceful and pleasant" visit with Lucy Osgood.[12] Osgood had recently lost her sister, Mary, with whom she had shared her life for seventy years, and wanted a companion to fill the void. Child, on the other hand, longed for "a larger sphere of being" than her rustic cottage in Wayland, with its deadening round of domestic chores.[13] Boarding with Osgood in Medford, she thought, at least during the winter months, might offer the perfect solution to the problem of reconciling her need for intellectual stimulation and social "sympathy" with David's need for outdoor exercise and rural tranquillity. By paying $12 a month for meals they could avoid incurring any obligation. They both liked Osgood and harmonized with her opinions on most subjects. The house was large enough to allow privacy for all. Boston and Cambridge were within easy reach, and many other friends lived nearby. They would no longer be cut off from the world by icy roads once winter set in, and they could still spend their summers in Wayland, where David could garden and chop wood.[14]

Initially, the experiment seemed successful. Osgood was "always equable, always friendly, always instructive and agreeable." The two women read a variety of fiction to each other, providing relief from the "gloomy clouds . . . hanging over the country" — and from the political fare that David preferred.[15] For his part, David lived up to his promise to "*try* to be a good boy."[16] Nevertheless, the strain of adapting to the habits of another household (and possibly of sharing his wife with a valued friend) seems to have told on his health. No sooner did the couple return to Wayland in mid-April than David succumbed to a severe recurrence of his old enemy, dyspepsia (indigestion) — a stress-related ailment he had first developed during his years of living alone in Northampton. "I am deeply convinced that it is not safe for Mr. C. to stay long away from home," Child concluded sadly.[17] "David's constitution is so shattered, that nothing but great quiet and regularity keeps his physical machinery in tolerable order," she would later specify. "It is for his sake that I live as I do. I should myself like much better to be more in the midst of things."[18]

The Childs arrived home just in time to witness Wayland's reaction to the opening salvos of the long-expected war. On April 12, 1861, Confederate batteries bombarded Fort Sumter in Charleston harbor, forcing the starving federal garrison that had been defending it since December to surrender. Lincoln had cast the onus of starting the war on the Confederacy, and Confederate President Jefferson Davis had seized the gauntlet. Both won their gambles. Compelled to choose between aligning themselves militarily with the free North or the slave South, five of the undecided states joined the Confederacy — among them Virginia, a major prize. Meanwhile, the Confederacy's rejection of all the conciliatory overtures that Unionists had made since the election abruptly ended talk of compromise in the hitherto dissension-ridden North.[19] Lincoln's April 15 proclamation calling for 75,000 militiamen to put down the "insurrection" elicited an outpouring of patriotic fervor. Overnight, the entire North rallied to the defense of the Union. "Fort Sumter is lost, but Freedom is saved," editorialized the *New York Tribune*. "There is no more thought of bribing or coaxing the traitors who have dared to aim their cannon balls at the flag of the Union. . . . Democrat as well as Republican, Conservative and Radical, instinctively feel that the guns fired at Sumter were aimed at the heart of the American Republic."[20] Prior to the attack on Sumter, the crowds attending the Union meetings organized by conservatives had denounced abolitionists and clamored for concessions to the South. Now the same constituencies stood side by side with abolitionists and Republicans at Union meetings of unprecedented magnitude, where they denounced southern "traitors" and clamored for vigorous suppression of the "rebellion."

Although thankful to have lived "to see the day when it is risky to talk in praise of the South," Child suspected that little "right principle" underlay the "unanimous Union sentiment." Rather, she wrote cynically to Osgood: "Our merchants are alarmed about dangers to commerce; our national vanity is piqued by insults to the U.S. flag, likely to render it contemptible in the eyes of the world; great numbers of the people think there is an imperious necessity of defending the government *now*, lest there should soon *be* no government to protect us from utter anarchy; and still greater numbers are ready to rush into whatever is the fashion."[21]

Proving Child's point, a Union meeting David attended in Wayland dramatically illustrated the limitations of the average northerner's support for the war — and the chasm that divided the Childs from their neighbors. When David suggested that the U.S. government had a duty to harbor fugitive slaves and ought to welcome their offers to fight for the Union, "he was very violently treated, and almost mobbed," Child reported to Osgood. "He was told the war had 'nothing to do with the damned niggers'; the war was to preserve the *Union*." Typifying the community's attitude, the Childs' neighbor William Baldwin was "quite zealous for the stars and stripes," but expected "the worst part of the fighting [to] be 'putting down the niggers.' " Small wonder that "Union-shouts, and hurras for the U.S. flag, sound[ed] like fiendish mockery" to Child.[22]

For twenty years Child, like Garrison, had believed that only by withdrawing from the Union could the North end its complicity in slavery. Thus, she could hardly embrace a crusade to restore the Union unless its goal was also to abolish slavery. As she watched her neighbors' sons go off to war in their trim new uniforms, she thought of how soon these uniforms might be "draggled in blood and dust," and she agonized lest the young soldiers sacrifice their lives in vain. If she "could only be *sure*" they would "die for *freedom*," she told Osgood, she would find the losses easier to bear.[23] Child raged at news that General Benjamin Butler, who had just led a contingent of Massachusetts troops through Maryland, had volunteered their aid in putting down a threatened slave insurrection there. And when she heard that thirty Florida slaves who had "escaped to Fort Pickens and offered their services in defence of the U.S. were sent back to their masters, in chains," she exploded, "God knows I *want* to love and honor the flag of my country; but how *can* I, when it is used for *such* purposes?"[24] "If the U.S.

flag does not represent justice and freedom, it is to me merely a striped rag, and I care not who tramples it under foot." Besides being immoral, she argued, it was "absurd *policy* . . . [t]o send back those who want to *serve* us" when they would be "employed by rebels to help them in *shooting* us."[25]

This argument soon occurred to military and political leaders as well. Ironically, General Butler was one of the first to recognize its validity. On May 24, barely a month after his genuflexion to slaveholders' rights, he declared that slaves seeking refuge in Union army camps should be regarded as "contraband of war"—"goods . . . directly auxiliary to military operations"—hence that they should be confiscated and put to work for the Union army rather than remanded to their masters. He proceeded to apply this policy at Fort Monroe, Virginia. Secretary of War Cameron cautiously endorsed it, and on August 6, Congress legalized it in the Confiscation Act, which provided for the seizure of "slaves used in aiding the Insurrection." By the end of July, nine hundred "contrabands" had gathered at Fort Monroe, and Butler was beginning to hint that the government ought to regularize their status by emancipating them outright.[26]

The Lincoln administration, however, remained committed to the circumscribed goal of restoring the Union. Three border slave states—Delaware, Maryland, and Kentucky, Lincoln's birthplace and his wife's native state—had elected to stay in the Union. Lincoln was anxious to retain their loyalties, as well as to woo moderates in the Confederate states by showing that the Union government was abiding by its constitutional obligation not to interfere with slavery. A majority of the northern public favored this approach and agreed with Lincoln in considering emancipation by the federal government to be as unconstitutional as secession by the states.

The wartime political situation presented abolitionists with a very different challenge from any they had faced before. To win the war, the Lincoln administration needed the support of the Bell-Everetts and Democrats, who together had garnered more than 46 percent of the northern popular vote in the recent election.[27] The riots of the preceding winter had indicated how dangerous their opposition could be. Tactics of agitation, such as abolitionists had used for thirty years, would only polarize the northern public and split Lincoln's fragile coalition without advancing the cause of emancipation. Instead, abolitionists decided to build grassroots support for emancipation through a low-profile press campaign. In September 1861, Garrisonians, Republicans, and John Brown partisans banded together to form the Boston Emancipation League. Working "under cover," they planned to educate the public on the role slavery played in causing the war, undergirding the Confederate war machine, and prolonging the conflict, and conversely, on the impact emancipation would have in shortening the war and settling the disputes that had provoked it.[28] The Childs attended the group's opening meetings and helped formulate its strategy for turning the tide of "popular opinion . . . in the right direction" with "no more *publicity* than is necessary," as Child detailed it in a letter to Whittier.[29] Child herself undertook to plant anonymous articles in the mainstream press (an enterprise she had initiated independently and recommended that others pursue). Always alive to the power of popular media and the need for multiple channels of influence, she urged Whittier to compose some "spirit-stirring" songs and ballads for soldiers, "proclaiming what they went to fight for . . . — home, country, and liberty; and indignantly announcing that they did *not* go to hunt slaves. . . ." "Nothing on earth has such effect on the popular heart as Songs," she stressed.[30] Meanwhile, David had already begun a full-scale study of the legal basis for abolishing slavery under the war power. Published in four installments in the *Liberator* and reissued by the American Anti-Slavery Society under the title *Rights and Duties of the United States Relative to Slavery under the Laws of War*, it argued that "[c]onquerors have the right" to "dissolve the system of society which they find [in conquered territory], and substitute any other which they deem more conducive to the improvement and happiness of the vanquished, and the peace and safety of the conquering nation."[31]

Though agreeing with David that the "War Power is the *only* power that *can* abolish" slavery legally, Child doubted whether a presidential emancipation proclamation would be "politic" at this early stage. "Events may ripen public opinion for such a measure, but it is not *yet* ripened," she acknowledged privately to Sarah Shaw.[32] In a letter to the *Tribune* signed "Straight Line," Child offered a simple interim solution that would accomplish the purpose of protecting fugitive slaves in U.S. Army camps "without violating any existing legal obligation, and without exciting any disunity of parties."[33] Rebel masters, she pointed out, had "forfeited" their constitutional rights "by treason." Consequently, their slaves need never be surrendered. Although the "constitutional obligation" to return fugitives remained binding toward masters loyal to the Union, military officers were "not invested with any legal power" to do so:

> When a slave is claimed, a *civil process* is requisite to prove his identity, and the fact of the claimant's legal ownership of him in the State he ran from. Judges and jurors are not on hand in forts and camps, and military men have no right to proceed in such cases without due process of law. So far from being bound to give up a fugitive slave to the man who claims him, they are positively bound by our laws *not* to do it.

In such cases, Child proposed, let officers merely instruct fugitives: "If your master comes here to claim you, we have no legal power to protect you; but, on the other hand, we have no legal power to stop you from going where you choose." Slaves would know enough to keep out of harm's way, soldiers would be spared the "unsoldierly" task of slave-catching, and "the Government would be under no necessity of issuing a proclamation on the subject"; all the same, the "uniform practice" of the army would "prove that no fugitive slave who seeks protection under its banner is sent back to bondage."[34]

Despite her shrewd grasp of the contradictory pressures the Lincoln administration faced and her pragmatic willingness to suggest measures that fell short of the emancipation policy she would have preferred, Child seethed with "fiery indignation" over the indifference her compatriots exhibited toward the slaves.[35] "No class, except the old abolitionists, seem to take justice and humanity to the slaves at all into the account," she complained. "*They* are *property*, to be disposed of in *any* way, according as the laws of war, or the patching up of the Union, may seem to render expedient."[36] What particularly worried her in the early months of the war was the prospect of a quick northern victory, leading to the reestablishment of the Union on its "old foundations." The military strategy of Union Commander in Chief Winfield Scott was predicated on just this scenario, she noted. For proof, she cited a statement he had made "at a private dinner in Washington": "that 'we were fighting with *brethren*, and as little blood as possible ought to be spilled; that in ninety days the rebels would be effectually hemmed in, and then we would treat with them about terms.'" General Scott, she commented acidly, was a Virginian, and she could not "trust *any* Southerner's professions of neutrality."[37] She placed no more reliance on "the manhood of the North" than on the loyalty of southern Unionists. "My only trust is in the blind madness of Jeff Davis, and his coadjutors," she told her abolitionist friends. "Our consciences cannot be awakened, or our hearts touched, but our selfish passions *may* perhaps be goaded up to the sticking point" by southern "arrogance."[38]

Nothing but cruel "defeats and reverses," Child believed, would make her compatriots "come up manfully to the work of freedom" by teaching them the lesson they were "so slow to learn": "that we were not dealing with 'Southern *brethren*'. . . but with fierce, malignant, savage *enemies*; men rendered utterly *barbarous* by long practice of a hellish system."[39] Accordingly, she found herself in a painful predicament. She, a pacifist, was praying that the war would drag on and intensify in brutality; she, a northern patriot, was wishing that her side would suffer a crushing defeat.

The answer to her prayers came on July 21, 1861, when Union forces were routed at the battle of Bull Run. Precipitated by northern editors' calls for a major offensive, fought by raw troops on both sides, and marked by the ineptitude of "amateurs," the battle had at first appeared to be shaping into a Union victory. Then a series of blunders and mix-ups invisible to the correspondents reporting from the front had allowed the Confederates to gain the advantage, prompting a seemingly inexplicable order to retreat, which had thrown Union soldiers into a panic. Whether caused by the noise of retreating ambulances and baggage wagons or by the unexpected counterattack of fresh southern reinforcements emitting the bone-chilling scream that came to be known as the "rebel yell," the "infection of terror" had spread through the Union army in seconds. Suddenly "there was no army, only a flying rabble. . . . The only thought of the soldiers was for their personal safety. . . . The wounded were deserted in the hospitals. . . . Guns were thrown aside, and blankets and knapsacks were lost and trampled upon."[40]

Northern humiliation was total. But more horrifying to many than the disgraceful rout was the "*savage and deliberate slaughter of our wounded and helpless men by the Rebel troops.*" Quoting eyewitnesses, *New York Tribune* reporters alleged that Union surgeons treating patients were "charged on . . . by the Rebel cavalry," that wounded and dying soldiers were "deliberately stabbed with bayonets . . . and trampled with savage glee and malice under the horses' hoofs," and that a hospital was purposely "set on fire and burned to the ground, *broiling alive our suffering and helpless wounded men. . . .*"[41]

Though Child's "*reason*" judged the defeat salutary, her heart was "lacerated" by the misery it had inflicted. "Those poor wounded soldiers, panting for water, falling down exhausted, shot and stabbed in that state by their relentless pursuers, haunt me like spectres, night and day," she mourned. "My heart bleeds for the mothers of those sons."[42] Neither the mothers nor the sons were abstractions to her. Sarah and Francis Shaw's son, Robert, whom she had known since babyhood, was serving as a lieutenant in the Second Massachusetts Volunteers, and Child "watch[ed] the papers nervously" for news of him, frequently praying "in an agony of supplication, that his young life may be spared."[43] The maternal, nurturing side of her kept exclaiming: "Would that this dreadful war were over!" Yet the side of her that cried out for justice toward the slave replied: "I would not have it over, till the Lord's will be accomplished."

Like her hero John Brown, Child spoke increasingly in the accents of the Old Testament prophets and Puritan patriarchs as she sought to decipher the divine plan inscribed in the ordeal through which the nation was passing. "I have never felt the presence of God, as I do at this crisis," she wrote. "*His* guiding hand is plain in the course of events; even in this defeat." Characteristically, Child read the battle as "a terrible retribution for our selfish indifference to the wrongs of the slaves" — a retribution that had exposed northern whites to the tortures slaves had endured for centuries: "*They* have been mangled, and hunted like dogs, generation after generation, and we erected a brazen statue to the man who helped their tyrants do it [Daniel Webster, architect of the 1850 Compromise and its Fugitive Slave Law]. And now *our own sons* are mangled and hunted by the same barbarous power."[44]

Child was too realistic to think that the experience of having their sons treated as slaves would teach many northerners to "remember those in bonds as bound with them." Still, she did see evidence that the alleged atrocities committed by southern troops at Bull Run were advancing the work of emancipation faster than the best-conceived propaganda could. Her brother Convers, for example, had observed a "remarkable change . . . in conservative Cambridge. Men who were for killing Wendell Phillips if he spoke against slavery, are now cursing the institution and saying it *must* be abolished, whatever it may cost."[45] Child discerned a similar change in conservative Wayland, where people who had once loudly defended the enforcement of the Fugitive Slave Law now objected to having soldiers employed in that "mean, unmanly business" because it diminished the "moral dignity" of the Union cause.[46] "More and more, the reckless, barbarous South puts it out of the power of politicians to patch up the Union on the old guilty basis," Child rejoiced. "More and more, do men *perceive* that it is the Lord's work they are called upon to do, and that *success* depends upon their coming to it with *clean hands*" by ending the North's complicity in slavery.[47]

The gradual evolution of public opinion did not make Child feel any more at home in Wayland. A week before the battle of Bull Run, however, she enjoyed welcome relief from her isolation when invited to a "stylish party" in nearby Weston, attended by Harriet Beecher Stowe and her husband. The two famous women "got into a corner" and "dived at once into public affairs," "ignoring the party." "Mrs. Stowe's habitual stiffness of manner vanished the moment we spoke together," Child reported. To her delight, she discovered that her "favorite author, *par excellence*" was also a political soul mate. "She has no more faith in politicians than I have; and most especially does she distrust that selfish diplomat, [Secretary of State] William H. Seward, who exerts so much ingenuity to say what he does *not* mean," Child confided gleefully to Sarah Shaw. "Mrs. Stowe agreed with me in thinking that the spirit of the people would render it *politic* for him to walk straight. God and the people we *can* rely upon; the people, because God is now moving them." Child also commented perceptively on the "continual indications" Stowe gave of her "*Puritan* education." Among them she cited Stowe's assertion that she had been "convinced . . . slavery would be overthrown, ever since our Chief Justice [Lemuel Shaw] passed *under the chain*, to enter the Court House" during the trial of Thomas Sims. "[I]t was one of those *signs*, such as God inspired the old *Prophets* to enact, to reveal to the people the depth of their degradation; and, from that time to the present, [Stowe] thought the hand of God had been very remarkably and peculiarly manifest in the ordering of events."[48] Child reiterated the same faith in the "guiding hand" of God again and again in her letters of the period. She herself had begun to sound so much like Stowe that an anecdote she took pleasure in relating to friends could almost have come from *Uncle Tom's Cabin*: "The nurse of a sick child repeatedly told the mother she saw evident signs of recovery. 'But,' said the anxious mother, 'the medicine don't seem to produce the effects we expected.' 'Trust in God,' was the reply. 'He's *tedious*, ma'am, but He's *sure*.' "[49] Notwithstanding her hatred of Calvinism, the Civil War was bringing out her own "Puritan education."

For a brief moment at the end of the summer Child had a "pre-sentiment that God had sent" the country the "*man* to rule the *hour*."[50] On August 30, 1861, former Republican presidential candidate John C. Frémont, recently appointed commander of the army's Western Department in Missouri, issued the first emancipation proclamation of the war. It announced the confiscation of all property belonging to Missourians "who . . . take up arms against the United States," and it pointedly specified that "their slaves, if slaves they have, are declared free."[51] "*Laus Deo! — 'the beginning of the end,'* " exulted the *Liberator*.[52] The news made Child's "heart leap up, for the *first* time since Lincoln was chosen," for she felt certain that the "contagion" of Frémont's example would "spread like fire on the prairies." Emancipation under the war power was the "*only* step" that could "save the country, and bring this horrid conflict to a speedy close," she believed, and she had longed for "some bold and able military commander" to make canny use of that instrument.[53] Unfortunately, Frémont was too bold to suit Lincoln, who swiftly countermanded the proclamation, fearing it would jeopardize his efforts to keep Kentucky in the Union.[54]

The revocation threw Child back into despondency. Nevertheless, she urged her fellow abolitionists to "rally round" Frémont.[55] With "[p]ublic opinion . . . forming rapidly" and the "fate of the nation" hanging in the balance, Child judged it to be "the duty of every patriot to use quickly, on the right side, whatever influence he possesses."[56] Her contribution took the form of a letter to "Our Jessie," which she sent to William Cullen Bryant's *New York Evening Post*. Hailing both Jessie Benton Frémont and her "noble husband" for their "able and prompt adaptation to the present momentous crisis," Child assured them that "[a]ll feel the need of strong men and energetic measures." She proceeded to interpret the signs of the times for the American public, once again speaking in the apocalyptic accents of a native Puritan: "If we rightly exert the power which God has put into our hands, this may prove the last great battle, in open field, between the forces of Despotism and the forces of Freedom." Throughout the North, consciousness of the war's true significance was stirring in the "earnest wish of the people . . . to have their beloved country really and entirely free," Child affirmed. "It would be downright atheism to think" that "this mighty pulsation of the popular heart" was going to "prove all for nought," when the "hand of God" had never before been "so signally manifested in the course of human affairs." Like a revival preacher exhorting his flock to flee from the yawning gulf of hell by seizing the chance for salvation that God was holding out, she warned of the "degeneracy" and "suffering" the nation would incur "if we blindly and recklessly throw away the glorious opportunity for atonement which the Divine Ruler has placed within our reach."

> Seldom, indeed, does it happen in a war that one of the contending parties can secure victory and speedy peace by a measure which will also prove a real and permanent benefit to the defeated party. Seldom is the chance offered to any people to obey the dictates of justice and the impulses of humanity towards millions of oppressed fellow creatures, and thereby save for themselves an immense amount of bloodshed and expense, while they secure incalculable advantages to posterity. . . .[57]

Child intended her tribute to the Frémonts partly as a subtle rebuke to Lincoln and his wife.[58] If only "Our Jessie" were "the presiding genius of the White House, instead of that tawdry, fussy, pro-slavery dame [Mrs. Lincoln], we should see a different state of things!" she fumed to Sarah Shaw.[59] Describing Mrs. Lincoln as " 'two thirds secessionist and the other third fool,' " Child blamed her for Lincoln's tenderness toward her " '*noble* native state' " of Kentucky. "I rather think 'old Abe' *means* to be honest; but he is a narrow man, with faculties better adapted to splitting rails, than for the embodying of great principles in wise energetic measures," she opined; hence, it was all too easy for "his pro-slavery wife, and that serpentine Seward" to "keep him in leading-strings," as in the "old story of Adam and Eve and the serpent."[60] Child "whisper[ed]" such views only in the "*private* ear" of her closest abolitionist friends, however. "[W]e ought to be very cautious about publicly censuring the government," she realized.[61]

Indeed, Child and other abolitionists soon found themselves in the unaccustomed position of defending the U.S. government against attacks by their former antislavery comrades in England. Britain had declared "neutrality" at the beginning of the war (a diplomatic move that amounted to recognizing the status of the Confederacy as a belligerent power rather than a rebellious province).[62] Driven by strong economic and political interests, the British press had been tilting toward the Confederacy ever since. The British textile industry depended heavily on cotton imported from the American South, and the northern blockade of southern ports had effectually cut off the supply of this vital raw material. Many industrialists were pressuring their government to lift the blockade by force and to grant official recognition to the Confederacy. A leading British aristocrat, Lord Shaftesbury, had openly avowed: "I, in common with almost every English statesman, sincerely desire the rupture of the American Union. We justly fear the commercial and political rivalry of the United States."[63] Normally, British abolitionists would have sided with the Union, but the Lincoln administration's reluctance to proclaim emancipation lent plausibility to claims that "the North and the South [were] 'partners in guilt'" and that the North was "simply fighting for empire"[64]—two of the main arguments in favor of sanctioning a "rupture" so advantageous to Britain. In letters to the *Liberator* and the *Standard*, a number of prominent British abolitionists expressed their sympathy for the South's war of independence, berated the North for its aggression, and vociferously condemned the blockade that was causing British industrialists and workers so much hardship. Their animadversions reached a peak during the winter of 1861–62, when tensions between Britain and the United States almost erupted into war over the "*Trent* Affair."

In November an American naval captain intercepted the British steamer *Trent* on a voyage from Havana to London and arrested two southern passengers—James Mason of Virginia and John Slidell of Louisiana, whom the Confederate government was sending to the courts of England and France as ministers plenipotentiary. The northern public cheered, the British public denounced the "impressment" and "clamored for war," and the British government issued an "ultimatum demanding an apology and release of the Confederate diplomats." To Child's great relief, Lincoln complied: "One war at a time," he reportedly said. Heartily agreeing, Child admitted that the prospects of "another war, super-added to the one we are *playing* at, at such terrible cost," had filled her with despair. But the high-handed tone the British had adopted, so like that of a "bad-tempered step-mother," infuriated her. She determined to reply to an "irate epistle" in the *Standard* by the British abolitionist Harriet Martineau, which she had found particularly "imperious, insolent, and self-conceited" in its manner of announcing: "'I am Sir Oracle; when *I* speak let no dog bark'!"[65]

Though tempted to retort in kind, Child used the occasion to educate the British public. The Confederacy, she reminded British abolitionists, was "professedly based on the doctrines that . . . Slavery was morally, socially, and politically, a good institution, and that the African Slave Trade ought to be reopened, as a humanizing and missionary enterprise." She rehearsed the "violent enormities of slaveholding rebels" both before and during the war and asked why the British press had "scolded us for committing wrongs, which we have in fact suffered." Granting that the Union government had been "justly" reproached with "want of moral courage in not resorting to emancipation," she pointed out that the British had similarly "refrained from pursuing" an emancipationist policy during the Revolution for fear of alienating Loyalist slaveholders. She then compared the American government's "pacific" handling of the *Trent* affair with the British government's belligerent persistence in impressing U.S. sailors until "ten years of unavailing remonstrance" had culminated in the War of 1812. As a tactful gesture toward mending the breach between the two countries, Child acknowledged America's cultural debt to England. But she ended by warning British readers not to believe predictions that "the experiment of self-government, instituted by that noble band of pilgrims in the Mayflower, will prove a failure."[66]

Child's initiative sparked a campaign to win over British antislavery opinion. A month later, Garrison followed suit with a series of letters in the *Liberator*, aimed at rectifying the "general obfuscation of mind among *our English anti-slavery co-laborers*, respecting the nature of the civil war now going on in America."[67] Extending the work of the Emancipation League, this dialogue with transatlantic abolitionists played a significant role in helping to prevent British diplomatic recognition of the Confederacy.[68]

While energetically building emancipationist sentiment at home and promoting the Union cause abroad, Child kept her eye on what she considered the principal long-term goal of the war — raising the status of African Americans. She seized every chance to orient relief efforts for the freedpeople toward empowering them to better their own lot. Thus, Child responded creatively to an appeal in the *American Missionary* for the "contrabands" at Fort Monroe. No longer supported by the masters from whom they had escaped and not yet employed for wages by the U.S. government, these destitute fugitives were in dire need of warm clothing and bedding. The box of supplies Child put together — the first to arrive at Fort Monroe in November 1861 — contained "thread, tape, buttons, needles & knitting-needles," cloth, blankets, secondhand garments that she repaired herself, and warm hoods for women and woolen caps for men, which she made up out of the odd scraps she could "muster." Most important, Child assembled a small library for the men and women she was already looking forward to training for a productive future. She collected "20 picture books, and Primary School books," "re-stitched" them, and "enclosed them in good strong covers." And she supplemented the textbooks with antislavery literature of the kind she would later anthologize in her reader *The Freedmen's Book*:

> I gathered up all the Biographies of . . . runaway slaves, that I could find. I bound them anew, and pasted on the covers the Liberator heading of horses and men sold at auction. I sent 6 of my West India Tract, and cut from duplicate Liberators the Christ coming to rescue the oppressed, and the happy Emancipation scene of the children with their lambs &c; these I pasted on the covers, as nicely as if I were doing it for Queen Victoria. These, and a copy of Uncle Tom's Cabin . . . I did up in separate parcels, directed to two of the most intelligent "contrabands". . . .[69]

Like the revolutionary twentieth-century educator Paulo Freire, Child understood that the development of political consciousness was essential to the acquisition of literacy.[70]

By late 1861 Child could note with satisfaction that "the business of giving up fugitive slaves is pretty much over," enabling her to set about working for the soldiers with enthusiasm.[71] She began with the Kansas regiment of Colonel James Montgomery, a disciple of John Brown well-known to her niece and nephew-in-law the Stearnses, who were collecting a box of goods for his men. "I have put my heart into every stitch," Child wrote to Montgomery, "for I know that the hands and feet I help to cover will never move one inch to help tyrants recover their slaves."[72] Knitting till her fingers ached, she finished twenty pairs of mittens for the troops; two pairs of socks, one of mittens, and one of suspenders for Montgomery himself; and one pair of mittens for John Brown, Junior. In addition, she sent "some songs . . . to enliven the tedium of the camp" and several copies each of David's *War Power* tract, her own *Patriarchal Institution*, and Jacobs's *Incidents in the Life of a Slave Girl*. "They are not needed for your conversion, or for that of your noble comrades, but perhaps you can put them to some good use," she hinted to Montgomery.[73] Whites as well as blacks needed to be reeducated for the model republic Child hoped to see erected on the grave of the slave system.

As the war ground on through the winter of 1861–62, Child compared the state of the country to that of a ship adrift in a stormy sea "without a captain." She tried to comfort herself with her friend Francis Shaw's conjecture that Lincoln might be "providentially sent at this time, to keep pro-slavery a little drowsy, till the tempest of *events* carries the ship of state too far out to sea for them to manage it."[74] She also kept up her spirits by quoting Harriet Tubman, whose "uncouth utterance" she found "wiser than the plans of politicians": "Dey may send de flower ob dair young men down South, to die ob de fever in de summer, and de agoo in de winter. . . . Dey may send dem one year, two year, tree year, till dey *tired* ob sendin, or till dey use up *all* de young men. All no use! God's ahead ob massa Linkum. God won't let massa Linkum beat de South till he do *de right ting*."[75] Often, however, Child could not help feeling "so tired of the whole dreadful business, and so afraid that it will all be for nothing, or worse than nothing," that she could not bear to read the newspapers. "I left them unopened for three days, when David was absent," she confided to Osgood.[76]

The main event of the winter, coinciding with the *Trent* affair, was the U.S. Navy's capture of Port Royal, South Carolina, in November 1861, which inaugurated the most ambitious educational program for the "contrabands" of the Civil War era — a veritable "rehearsal for reconstruction."[77] As their masters fled to the mainland in disarray, the victory brought thousands of slaves from the long-staple cotton plantations of the South Carolina sea islands under Union control. Rising to the challenge of preparing this vast contingent of field workers for freedom and of showing they could be educated and taught to adapt to free labor conditions, missionaries, schoolteachers, and labor superintendents converged on Port Royal. Among them was the young African American abolitionist Charlotte Forten, whom Child had known and admired since the 1850s. Forten would record her impressions of the Sea Island blacks and their rich culture in two "beautiful articles for the Atlantic Monthly," from which Child would reprint an extract in *The Freedmen's Book*.[78]

Child herself felt so "powerfully drawn to be a teacher among the 'contrabands'" that it sometimes seemed she "*must* go, happen what would"; but as she told Sarah Shaw, "my good David would get sick if he went with me, or if he staid at home alone. The *nearest* duty must not be neglected."[79] For his part, David, now sixty-eight years old, had been chafing to "go into battle, and command a troop of horse" ever since the outbreak of the war.[80] Instead, both resigned themselves to the constraints of their advancing age and joined the Boston-based Educational Commission for the "contrabands," founded in February 1862.[81]

Stimulated by the opportunities she saw opening up at Port Royal and Fort Monroe, and anxious to divert her mind from the carnage that was making her "writhe with anguish" day after day, Child increasingly focused her energies on revolving plans for the uplift of the freedpeople.[82] The failure of the government and the public alike to manifest a sense of responsibility toward African Americans had depressed her more than any other aspect of the war, she lamented to the abolitionist Gerrit Smith: "Even should [the slaves] be emancipated, merely as a 'war necessity,' everything *must* go wrong, if there is no heart or conscience on the subject." Since Smith had expended large sums for the antislavery cause and donated a portion of his enormous landholdings to black farmers before the war, Child shared with him some of the ideas that had occurred to her as she had "thought, for hours together, of some *efficient* mode of helping the poor creatures, or rather of enabling them to help themselves." One scheme was to collect "a large colony" of freedpeople together and have "a few white men, who were their *sure* friends, establish manufactories, and employ them at fair wages." The model Child had in mind was that of the wealthy abolitionist merchant Charles Hovey, who had "carried on his extensive business" by "giving *every* person he employed, even the porters and errand boys, a share of the *profits* in addition to their wages. The result was that every one was interested in the prosperity of the establishment, and did their utmost to extend the business." Child felt certain that "[i]f our poor colored brethren could be brought under some such stimulus," they would "work wonders." The role she would most like to fill, she confessed ingenuously, echoing her former heroine Madame Roland, was that of "a Divine providence to the colored race."[83]

Child also shared her ideas with Francis Shaw, who had helped organize the Freedmen's Relief Association in New York and was contributing generously to its fund for paying the salaries of superintendents and teachers. Reiterating the suggestion she had made to Smith, she named the man she considered best-qualified to implement it: Frederick Law Olmsted, author of three extensive economic studies that demonstrated the superiority of free labor to slavery, based on information Olmsted had gleaned from his travels in the South and his experiences as a farmer in New York.[84] Would Shaw sound Olmsted out on the possibility of applying his free labor theories by launching a pilot project that would "employ 2 or 3000 'contrabands' in the culture of cotton" in Illinois? "With his great agricultural knowledge, . . . his enlightened views about labor," and his genuine sympathy for blacks, Olmsted would surely make such an enterprise "profitable . . . for all parties," Child thought. "The 'contrabands' ought to be employed on such terms that the more they *do* the more *money* they get," she stressed. "I wish white people could get rid of the idea that they must manage *for* them." At Fort Monroe the missionary in charge had taken it upon himself to deduct a portion of the contrabands' wages in order to apply it to the succor of the sick and the aged. Child objected strenuously to such practices. "*White* laborers would not work with much heart under such circumstances. They ought to pay them *wages* in proportion to their *work*, and let *them* form Relief Societies among themselves, so that they might feel that *they* did the benevolent work themselves," she insisted.[85] On the same principle, Child warmly supported the work her friend Harriet Jacobs undertook among the "contrabands" of Alexandria, Virginia, later that year. "I think it is good for the colored people to feel that they are helping their own unfortunate race," she wrote, explaining why she had chosen to give $15 for the "contrabands" to Jacobs rather than to a white philanthropist.[86]

The principal task confronting abolitionists in 1862 was still to secure a presidential emancipation proclamation, however. Hence, Child kept on sending "paragraphs and collections of facts, to the newspapers, to help public opinion on in the right direction."[87] In March she finally saw a ray of hope when Lincoln asked Congress to pass a joint resolution offering financial aid to "any state which may adopt a gradual abolishment of slavery."[88] Congressional sponsorship of gradual, compensated emancipation, Lincoln argued, would shorten the war, save money, and provide for a comparatively painless transition to freedom. The money currently being spent on the war could easily purchase every slave in the border states; the longer the war lasted, the less slaves would be worth. Eventually, Lincoln warned, recourse to a drastic means of "ending the struggle" might "seem indispensable." He invited slaveholders to consider "whether the pecuniary consideration tendered would not be of more value to the States and private persons concerned, than are the institution, and property in it, in the present aspect of affairs."[89]

Child greeted Lincoln's proposal with jubilation. The newspapers did not "seem to appreciate its *full* import," she wrote to *Tribune* editor Greeley. She proceeded to translate Lincoln's deliberately ambiguous language into "plain English": "If the rebels continue to resist, the U.S. gov. must and will resort to emancipation; and, gentlemen of the Border States, I ask you to reflect how much *your* slaves will be worth under those circumstances. Had n't you better accept of compensation from the U.S. before their market value is gone?"[90]

Child attributed Lincoln's initiative to rumors in the English press that Confederate agents James Mason and John Slidell were "offering to abolish slavery" in exchange for British and French aid to the Confederacy. "Bitter as the pill of emancipation would be to the South, . . . they would swallow it, rather than acknowledge themselves conquered by the U.S.," she believed. If the South embraced emancipation before the North did,

We should be the scorn and laughing-stock of the world; while England, by serving her own interest, would be covered with laurels for her justice and humanity. How she would boast of doing for freedom what the republic of the U.S. *refused* to do! The *tories* would effect *their* object of splitting the Union; and a measure that abolished American slavery, at the same time that it opened the cotton ports, would be prodigiously popular with the English *people*. England and France would secure a monopoly of Southern commerce, and we should be shut out.[91]

The scenario struck Child as irresistibly comic. "It would be such a charming piece of poetical justice, that I thought Providence *could n't* let it slip," she chuckled to Sarah Shaw. And she speculated that this very nightmare had " 'skeered' " Lincoln into putting out his "feelers" on emancipation.[92]

Because border state Unionists categorically opposed it, nothing came of Lincoln's proposal, despite the unanimous support of the Republican majority in Congress. Nonetheless, the country inched toward emancipation. On March 10, Congress enacted an article of war forbidding army officers to return fugitive slaves, even to loyal masters, "under penalty of court-martial."[93] On April 16 Lincoln signed a bill abolishing slavery in the District of Columbia. "After thirty years of arguing, and remonstrating, and pleading, and petitioning, and hoping, and fearing, and well nigh despairing, Slavery is *at last* abolished in ten miles square," Child commented drily to Anna Loring.[94] In June, Congress barred slavery from all the territories of the United States. And in July came the Militia and Confiscation Acts, the first allowing for the enrollment of African Americans in "war service," and the second decreeing the confiscation of all rebel property and declaring that slaves seized under the law "shall be forever free" — precisely the measure Frémont had been forced to retract a year earlier.

Still, Lincoln himself seemed to lag. When in May another abolitionist general, David Hunter, issued a military decree proclaiming the emancipation of all slaves in South Carolina, Georgia, and Florida, Lincoln again countermanded the edict.[95] "I sometimes wish he were a man *strong* enough to *lead* popular opinion, instead of *following* it so conscientiously," Child complained to Sumner.[96] Yet she made a special point of hailing the accomplishments of the 37th Congress in an article for the *Standard*, "Faithful Champions of Freedom in Congress." Antislavery politicians had displayed great "moral courage" in their long struggle to achieve these gains, Child noted, and they deserved an enthusiastic tribute from all abolitionists.[97] She also wrote personal letters of thanks to several politicians, taking advantage of the opportunity, as always, to air her concerns about the future. Praising Congressman William P. Cutler of Ohio for a speech attacking slavery as the "Public Enemy," for example, Child asserted that the problem of what to do with the emancipated slaves had a simple solution: "Take them away from Mr. Lash and place them with Mr. Cash." The real problem was going to be what to "do with their *masters*." True, "free institutions" would ultimately "change the moral and intellectual condition of the whole Southern people," but the process would take several generations, and "in their transition state, what a troublesome and dangerous set they will be to deal with!" As if already foreseeing the postwar debates over whether or not to grant the suffrage to the former slaves and deny it to ex-Confederates, Child added: "They talk about *slaves* being unfit to be trusted with legislation; doubtless it is true; but it seems to me that slave*holders*" are "even *more* unfit to legislate for free men."[98]

Simultaneously, Child tackled another issue that was preoccupying the public more and more as emancipation loomed closer. The bugbear of "amalgamation" had served for decades to squelch talk of emancipation, and the Democrats were loudly invoking it in the 1862 congressional election campaign. Indeed, Lincoln's fear of inflaming the race issue was one of the factors holding him back. To defuse this potential threat, he revived the long-discredited chimera of Colonization. Summoning a delegation of African American leaders to the White House on August 14, Lincoln told them: "There is an unwillingness on the part of our people, harsh as it may be, for you free colored people to remain with us." "I cannot alter [this fact] if I would." He asked them to renounce their "selfish" opposition to Colonization and help him recruit volunteers for an experimental colony in Central America or the Caribbean, which he hoped to develop into a large-scale emigration project after the war. "Can any sensible, humane, upright man read [Lincoln's address to black leaders] without a blush, alike for its author, and for the country which he officially represents?" exploded Garrison in the *Liberator*. Two thirds of the Republicans in Congress went along with the president, however, and appropriated $600,000 to support his Colonization scheme.[99]

In contrast to the moderate Republican strategy of using the "humbug" of Colonization to evade the race issue,[100] Child met anxieties about amalgamation head-on. Both in her letter to Cutler and in an article for the *Tribune* on "Emancipation and Amalgamation," she attempted to stake out a position that would allay voters' fears not by catering to them, but by refuting the misconceptions behind them.[101] "The horror that many people have of future social equality, and intermarriage of the races, makes me smile," she wrote to Cutler:

> [T]he fear is so contradictory of itself! If there *is* an "instinctive antipathy" [between the races], as many assert, surely that antipathy may be trusted to prevent amalgamation. If there is *no* instinctive antipathy, what reason is there for the horror? If the colored people are *really* an "inferior race," what danger is there of their attaining to an "equality" with us? If they are *not* inferior, what reason is there for excluding them from equality? *My* belief is, that when generations of colored people have had a fair chance for education and the acquisition of wealth, the prejudice against them, originating in their degraded position, will pass away. . . .

Prejudice could not be innate, Child implied, since she had been "born without it." She went on to cite the example of "colored acquaintance[s]" who ranked "very high . . . for intelligence, culture, and fine manners"—among them Charlotte Forten (whom she described without naming her). "What they *are* I believe that multitudes of them *might be*, under favorable influences," she emphasized. The talents of educated African Americans indicated the "possibilities of improvement now dammed up in the souls of [their] oppressed people." How "immeasurable" must be the guilt of a nation that kept such talents "dammed up" in an entire race while vaunting itself as the guardian of freedom![102]

Child's article on "Emancipation and Amalgamation" took a somewhat different tack. Answering readers convinced by *The Right Way the Safe Way*, but still worried "that negroes and whites will amalgamate if the slaves are freed," Child denounced the "outcry about future amalgamation" as "merely one of the artful dodges by which slaveholders and their allies seek to evade the main question." The "main question," she underscored, was the future prosperity of a "great nation." Statistical comparison of imports, agricultural productivity, and land values in Virginia and New York amply proved that slavery sapped a state's prosperity, while free institutions enhanced it. Was the preservation of a disreputable and unprofitable institution worth the sacrifice of a republic's destiny, she asked. Having shown what risks voters would be incurring if they heeded the lies of racist demagogues, Child exposed the fallacies in the demagogues' arguments. Those who had once predicted that emancipation would result in race war now claimed that it would result in amalgamation, she pointed out: "What a laughable contradiction there is between the two propositions!" Slaveholders' own statistics, moreover, revealed "thirteen times more amalgamation at the South than in the North." The implication was clear: amalgamation tended to *decrease* when white men no longer owned black women's bodies. Statistics from the West Indies confirmed that emancipation ended illicit relations between white men and black women; now the few unions that took place were legal marriages, sometimes between "white and colored . . . persons of high position." Yet Americans need have no fear that such "[l]egalized amalgamation" would ever become common among themselves as long as a "prevailing prejudice against color" remained an obstacle. "[W]hen that 'phantom dynasty' passes away with the centuries," Child predicted, "its disappearance will harm no one, and posterity will wonder at the power it once exercised, as we now marvel at the terror our ancestors had of witchcraft."[103]

In sending "Emancipation and Amalgamation" to the *Tribune*, Child was offering Republicans a model of how to handle the race issue in a principled and dignified manner, without pandering to the prejudices of voters. She may also have been responding specifically to Lincoln's flirtation with Colonization, since her article clearly delineated an alternative approach to the problem of Democratic race-baiting. But neither the Republican party nor the general public was ready to follow her lead.

By the time "Emancipation and Amalgamation" went into print, Child had lost all patience with Lincoln. She expressed her disgust with his seeming paralysis in an extraordinary personal appeal for a presidential emancipation proclamation. Featured prominently in the *National Republican*, the *Liberator*, and the *Standard* under the title "Mrs. L. Maria Child to the President of the United States," it was her most widely circulated political letter of the war years.[104] Child took as her point of departure Lincoln's latest unsuccessful plea to border state congressmen in July. She "respectfully" demanded: "how much longer [is] the nation . . . to wait for the decision of the Border States [to acquiesce in emancipation], paying, meanwhile $2,000,000 a day, and sending thousands of its best and bravest to be stabbed, shot, and hung by the rebels, whose property they are employed to guard." The American people had shown "almost miraculous patience, forbearance, and confidence in their rulers," as well as willingness to "sacrifice their fortunes and their lives," Child affirmed, "but they very reasonably wish to know what they are sacrificing them for." If they were going to continue to wage a struggle that was costing them so dearly, they needed to be "lifted up and sustained by great ideas of Justice and Freedom," not strung along by games of "diplomacy and strategy." "President Lincoln, it is an awful responsibility before God to quench the moral enthusiasm of a generous people," Child warned. By countermanding General Hunter's emancipation edict, Lincoln had acted as a fire "extinguisher" when the nation needed a "Drummond Light [limelight] in our watchtower." "I trust you will not deem me wanting in respect for yourself or your high position, if I say frankly that you seem to trust too much to diplomatic and selfish politicians, and far too little to the heart of the people," she admonished the President with a self-assurance that seems breathtaking even today.

Acknowledging Lincoln's sincere "wish to save the republic," Child went on to question the grounds for his "scruples" against proclaiming emancipation and enlisting black soldiers in the war. Now that the rebels had themselves spat and "trampled" on the Contitution, surely no "constitutional obligation" existed toward them, she argued. As for loyal slaveholders, "their name is not legion, nor their loyalty always of a kind that will stand much wear and tear." Nor did allegations that it would be "inhuman" to arm blacks hold any validity. "I cannot perceive why there is more inhumanity in a black man fighting for his freedom than in a white man fighting for the same cause," Child protested. If Lincoln was concerned about averting a slave insurrection, the best preventive would be to liberate the slaves and to organize them "under the instruction and guidance" of "just" officers. Child countered the racist stereotype of the black savage with the romantic racialist stereotype popularized by Stowe in Uncle Tom.[105] "[B]y nature docile" and "trained to habits of obedience," she hypothesized, the slaves would make good soldiers, and they would be "stimulated" to "bravery . . . by the most powerful motives that can act on human nature; the prospect of freedom on the one hand, and the fear of falling into their masters' power on the other." In an emotional crescendo, Child implored Lincoln to remember the "foul and cruel wrongs" that slaves had endured for so long and to heed the prayers they were uttering "in the secrecy of their rude little cabins."

"I can imagine, in some degree, the embarrassments of your position, and I compassionate you for the heavy weight of responsibility that rests upon your shoulders," Child added. Alluding as openly as she dared to the influence of Seward, she urged Lincoln to cease listening to the counsels of "devils that have squeezed themselves into the disguise of toads" and to place his "reliance on *principles* rather than on men." She ended by explaining that if she had written more forcefully than might have seemed respectful, it was because "night and day the plaintive song of the bondmen resounds in my ears:

> 'Go down, Moses, go down to Egypt's land,
> And say to Pharaoh: 'Let my people go.' "[106]

In short, Child was casting Lincoln in the role of Pharaoh and representing herself as a latter-day Moses responding to the call of "her" oppressed people.

Unbeknown to Child, Lincoln had in fact decided as early as July 13 — the day border state representatives turned down his last gradual emancipation proposal — that "[w]e must free the slaves or be ourselves subdued."[107] The military necessity of emancipation had "occupied his mind and thoughts day and night" for several weeks, Lincoln had told Seward and navy secretary Gideon Welles in a private conversation that would not be publicly revealed until 1872. On July 22 he had actually presented a draft of his Emancipation Proclamation to his cabinet, but two key cabinet members had dissuaded him from issuing it then: Postmaster General Montgomery Blair, who had contended that it might "cost the Republicans control of Congress in the fall elections," and Seward, who had advised waiting for a military victory, so that the proclamation would not appear to be a gesture of desperation—a suggestion Lincoln had found very shrewd. In blaming Seward for Lincoln's delay, Child was thus closer to the truth than even she suspected.

The Union's military situation was indeed bleak enough in July 1862 to give the impression that the government had reached its last resort. Ever since May the Union Army had been floundering from one defeat to another. The losing streak had begun when Confederate troops under Stonewall Jackson had chased Union forces headed by General Nathaniel Banks out of the Shenandoah Valley. Young Robert Shaw was in Banks's Second Massachusetts Regiment, which Child "watched closely" for the sake of Sarah and Francis. She read the papers "all of a tremble" when the retreat was announced, relieved not to find Robert's name on the list of killed and wounded, but uncertain of his fate. "There are sorrows so appalling, that the mere thought of them takes away the breath of the soul," Child wrote to Sarah after receiving news that Robert was safe. His comrades had "fought their way, inch by inch," through the Shenandoah, with Jeb Stuart's cavalry and the Rebel infantry in pursuit and local sharpshooters firing on the Yankee invaders "from almost every house." "A rifle-ball hit [Robert's] watch, and dented it deeply, thereby saving his life," Sarah reported to Child.[108]

Union General George McClellan's Army of the Potomac fared no better. Forced to fall back from Richmond, McClellan's forces reaped a disastrous series of defeats at the hands of Confederate General Robert E. Lee, leaving a total of 30,000 men killed and wounded on both sides in what came to be known as the Seven Days battles. The Union's reverses in Virginia culminated in Second Bull Run, which inflicted another 16,000 casualties on the battered bluecoats. Meanwhile, the Union offensive in the Mississippi Valley "bogged down before Vicksburg."[109]

Taking stock of the mounting toll and ferocity of the struggle, Child repeatedly described herself as "heartsick . . . of the war." "It is not merely our own soldiers that excite my pity," she wrote Sarah. "I cannot help compassionating the 'poor whites' of the South, led into wickedness and danger by men who care no more for their souls or bodies, than they would for so many blind dogs." In May she had been momentarily cheered by news that several hundred poor whites had "deserted from Georgia to the U.S. giving as a reason that they were 'tired of fighting the *rich men*'s war.'" Such incidents suggested that the war might be educating them for the future society Child dreamed would emerge from "this terrible process": "*they* will come up to the light, as well as the negroes; and they have been scarcely less wronged," she believed.[110] But by August, with no emancipation proclamation in sight despite unparalleled slaughter, Child was thoroughly demoralized. "Oh, it is sad, sad, to go on shooting and stabbing slaveholders, while we are regardless of the slave and while we are afraid to destroy the institution which occasions all the mischief," she groaned: "The Lord sends prophet after prophet to Pharaoh, to admonish him to 'let the people go.' But Pharoah prefers that the first-born of the land should be destroyed; and so they go to be sacrificed, thousands upon thousands; and sacrificed *in vain*; for God will *not* bless us, till we obey his laws." Once again, Child found herself inconsistently recoiling from the carnage and welcoming the Union defeats as "absolutely *necessary* to cure our blindness and perversity."[111] This time, however, she was wrong, for Lincoln had been waiting anxiously since July for a victory that would enable him to issue his Emancipation Proclamation from a position of strength rather than weakness.

The occasion finally arrived on September 22, after the battle of Antietam, when Union forces under McClellan turned back Lee's attempted invasion of Maryland in an engagement that produced 6,000 deaths and 17,000 casualties.[112] The *Tribune's* correspondent found corpses strewn "[o]ver acres and acres," sometimes "piled up almost like cordwood."[113] With all the bloodshed, the southern defeat proved inconclusive because McClellan did not "destroy the rebel army," as Lincoln had ordered, but allowed Lee's troops to escape over the Potomac.[114]

"Why was that army *allowed* to go back into Virginia?" demanded Child. "Why were they not intercepted? I believe they would have been, if General Mc'Lellan had not been playing false, for political purposes, as he has been from the beginning." McClellan's "object," Child surmised to Sumner, who she hoped would press for his removal, "was to prolong the war till the next presidential election, and then sell the country to slaveholders."[115] Her suspicions were widely shared, not only because McClellan had a history of avoiding battles and muffing golden opportunities, but because his closest political ties were with the "copperhead" faction of the Democratic party. To Child's outrage, his own staff officer brazenly admitted a few weeks later: " 'It is not our *game* to conquer the rebels, but to *worry out* both sections of the country, so that a compromise with Slavery can be effected.' "[116]

Lincoln, too, distrusted McClellan and deplored the aborted Union victory. Nevertheless, he judged that the time had come to keep his "covenant with God."[117] His Emancipation Proclamation of September 22 left much to be desired from an abolitionist point of view. True, it promised that all slaves in rebel territory would be "forever free" as of January 1, 1863, and it gave presidential sanction to the Confiscation Act forbidding the surrender of fugitive slaves. In these respects, Child recognized, the proclamation was "a great move onward," which would undoubtedly be "productive of considerable good."[118] Yet Lincoln still linked emancipation with plans to "colonize persons of African descent," provided their consent and that of a host government could be obtained. He also exempted slaves of loyal masters from the Confiscation Act. Most worrisome to Child was the grace period Lincoln allowed the Confederacy before emancipation would go into effect. "It certainly is not much to wait three months longer, after waiting thirty years," Child conceded; "but I can not divest myself of misgivings concerning contingencies that *may* intervene. . . . It is giving time to rebels in the South and traitors in the North to mature their plans."[119] By delaying so long, she feared, Lincoln was forfeiting the strategic advantages the country might have gained by emancipation. "We are again sacrificed to the Border States" for the sake of giving Kentucky "time to secure compensation," Child grumbled to Sumner. "I wish the Border States had *all* seceded in the beginning. They have been a mill stone about our necks."[120] Child also felt saddened by the lack of any idealism in Lincoln's message. "The ugly fact cannot be concealed from history that [emancipation] was done reluctantly and stintedly . . . merely [as] a war-measure . . . and that no recognition of principles of justice or humanity surrounded the politic act with a halo of moral glory," she wrote bitterly to Sarah Shaw.[121]

Child's tone began to change as Lincoln gave evidence of having committed himself firmly to emancipation. She was particularly reassured by the stiffening resolve he showed after Republican losses in the November elections. The Democrats had picked up votes in six states of the lower North, including New York, by denouncing the Emancipation Proclamation as "a proposal for the butchery of women and children" that would unleash "scenes of lust . . . rapine . . . arson and murder." McClellan had made no secret of his agreement with this view.[122] Notwithstanding the political fallout, Lincoln removed McClellan from command on November 7. "O, joy! joy!" Child hailed the news. "At last, I really believe 'old Abe' has got his back up. Like the old man in the fable, he has 'pleased nobody'; but he is at least determined that he won't 'lose his Ass into the bargain.['] . . . [H]aving tried everything else without success, we shall at last rely upon principle."[123] The definitive Emancipation Proclamation of January 1, 1863, did represent a distinct advance over its precursor. It announced itself explicitly as "an act of justice, warranted by the Constitution," and it accordingly invoked the "considerate judgment of mankind, and the gracious favor of Almighty God" on the measure. It also declared unequivocally that emancipated slaves would be "received into the armed service of the United States."[124]

Lincoln's shift toward the war policy Child had been advocating marked a turning point in her attitude toward him. From then on, he would steadily grow in her estimation. The transformation of the war into a liberation struggle, signaled by both the Emancipation Proclamation and the recruitment of black troops, enabled Child to embrace it with less ambivalence. She expressed her new fervor in a letter of late December to her nephew, William Lloyd Garrison Haskins, who had recently enlisted along with his brother, George Thompson Haskins. The two young men, named for famous abolitionists like their sister, Lydia Maria Child Haskins, were the sons of David's late sister, Lucretia. George would die of dysentery after only a few months' service — a fate he shared with countless thousands of Civil War soldiers — but Child would correspond faithfully with "Willie."[125] Aware that he would probably read the letters of his famous aunt aloud to his comrades, Child made a point of using them to inculcate abolitionist values.

Had Lincoln proclaimed emancipation at the start, she wrote to Willie, the war would already be over (a view most historians would dispute). "But, after all, it would not be fair to blame the President for moving so slowly. The *people* were not prepared to sustain him in any such measure; they had become too generally demoralized by long subservience to the Slave Power." Fortunately, the war had given the people an opportunity to redeem their country from the thralldom that had so dangerously undermined its free institutions. "If the white working-men of the North want to be secure of their *own* freedom, they must see to it that the black working-men of the South have *theirs*," Child stressed. Events of the past months had convinced her more than ever that "the wise Providence of God" was directing the war so as "to push us continually forward in the right direction, against the most stubborn resistance of our will." Whatever reverses and defeats lay ahead, she prophesied, "the *great* Battle of *Freedom* will surely be won." Speaking not only to Willie but to every soldier in the ranks, Child affirmed solemnly: "It is worth living for, worth dying for, my dear young friend."[126] This was what she had meant when she had reminded Lincoln that soldiers needed to be "lifted up and sustained by great ideas of Justice and Freedom." Realizing that the animation of a nation's moral purpose was a two-way process in which the troops, too, had an important role to play, Child asked her nephew to write to her about incidents that might "do good, by helping along public opinion." She would pass them on to Boston newspapers, she explained, to be published either under his name, or anonymously, as he preferred.[127]

Just as the plight of fugitive slaves and "contrabands" had most deeply engaged Child's sympathies during the first year of the war, so the heroic sacrifices of African American soldiers and their abolitionist officers now kindled her patriotic ardor in the wake of the Emancipation Proclamation. In November, as she reported to Willie, her friend Thomas Wentworth Higginson had gone to Port Royal to assume command of the First South Carolina Volunteers — the first regiment of slaves officially mustered into the Union army. He soon began sending personal dispatches from the front praising their performance. Not long afterward, Governor John Andrew of Massachusetts received the War Department's authorization to raise two regiments of free African Americans, the Fifty-fourth and Fifty-fifth Massachusetts. Andrew promptly appointed Robert Shaw colonel of the Fifty-fourth, and he asked Child's nephew-in-law George Stearns to head the recruitment committee.[128] (The first to sign up were the sons of Frederick Douglass, also a leading recruiter for the Fifty-fourth.) Over the next few months descriptions of these pioneer regiments filled the antislavery press, as reporters visited their training camps.

Again preaching to the troops through a letter to Willie, Child portrayed Robert Shaw as a role model for them: "a noble-hearted young gentlem[a]n, who left wealth and luxury, and a most happy home, to serve his country in her hour of need." She proceeded to disseminate a favorable view of black soldiers by quoting the account of his regiment that Shaw had given to his parents: "he finds so many of them more intelligent than he expected, and all of them orderly, full of pluck, and quick at acquiring military skill." The fate of the nation, Child emphasized, would depend on whether white soldiers would accept African Americans as their brothers and fight side by side with them for the freedom of all:

From the very outset of this war, I said we should never effectually put down the rebellion till we emancipated the slaves, treated them in a manner to gain their confidence, and made the fullest use of their knowledge of the rebel country, and of their natural antipathy to their masters. . . . For, say what we will, this is a war to decide whether this is to be a free country, where working-men elect their own rulers, and where free schools give all an equal chance for education, or whether we are to live under despotic institutions, which will divide society into two classes, rulers and servants, and ordain ignorance as the convenient, nay, even *necessary* condition of all who labor. . . . Our army stand before God the champions of human freedom, which includes their own. May they prove true to their trust, and may their long-deferred hopes be crowned with victory![129]

Before the Massachusetts Fifty-fourth went into action in July, Child's attention was drawn away from military affairs by personal concerns. Indeed, with the achievement of her two main war goals—an emancipation proclamation and the recruitment of black troops—her correspondence shifted its orientation. Increasingly, Child either retreated from the war into her private world or looked beyond it toward the task of reconstructing the United States as a truly egalitarian republic.

In the winter of 1862–63, partly to "divert [her] mind from the perpetual horrors of war," and partly to combat the depressing effects of her advancing age and worsening rheumatism, Child started collecting writings "peculiarly likely to be cheering, consoling, or strengthening, to an *old* person."[130] At first, she thought she would use them to "make Scrap Books for a few elderly friends." But the project quickly developed into a "Christmas Gift-Book for the *Old*."[131] It had lain at the back of her mind ever since her "father's last years," she confided to Lucy Osgood, one of the "elderly friends" for whom she intended the book and whom she enlisted in locating and writing selections for it. "I found it extremely difficult to obtain books suitable to his age, and at the same time *cheerful*," she recalled.[132]

By the end of January 1863 Child was ready to send a proposal to Ticknor & Fields. The anthology would include eight or ten articles of her own composition, as well as "Poetry, Stories, Essays, extracts from remarkable Sermons, &c," drawn from "English, American, French, German, Grecian, Roman," and other sources—all "extremely simple" and "all gems in the way of producing a *cheerful, elevating* influence on the minds of the old . . . to make them 'feel chipper'. . . ." Such a book would fill a major need, Child urged: "The great fault with all that is written or preached to the old is that it is too *solemn*. It is 'carrying coals to Newcastle'; for the old are too prone to take a solemn view of things. I have endeavored to carry out the idea first suggested to me by my father's wants, and it is a cherished wish with me to make this benefaction to the old before I die." She had already thought out almost every detail of the book. It would be 300–400 pages long, she specified:

Type *large* and *clear*. . . . Paper not so dazzling white as to try the eyes. Three pieces of music to be inserted; viz: "Auld Lang Syne," "John Anderson, my Joe," and "Old Folks at Home"; these with appropriate vignettes, or tail-pieces, if deemed desirable. A frontispiece . . . representing a happy grand mother with her grand child paddling in a bowl of water; both as "*pleased* as Punch." A tail-piece at the end of the Vol. in a line engraving, copied from Thorwaldsen's basso relievo of Old Age.

Such a book would make an eminently "saleable" gift for "old parents, or grand-parents," Child predicted. She also supplied a moral sales pitch: "As a people, we Americans are far too negligent of the *old*."[133]

In the midst of this labor of love through which Child sought to raise her spirits and resolve her lingering grief over her father's death, she was suddenly summoned to the deathbed of her brother Convers. For a month during March and April, she traveled back and forth to his home in Cambridge. "I was with him the last eight days, and with him when his soul departed on its mysterious journey to the unknown," she told Sarah Shaw. "Oh, how I suffered! It tore me all to pieces." The loss roused up "a thousand memories of childhood and youth" and intensified Child's loneliness. "In my isolated position, he was almost my only medium with the world of intellect," she mourned.[134]

Then in June another devastating blow fell. The day after a visit from Sarah Shaw, who had come to Boston to attend the farewell review and parade of Robert's Fifty-fourth Massachusetts regiment—the largest and most enthusiastic send-off the state had yet accorded to Civil War troops[135]—the ell wing of the cottage in Wayland took fire. Child was napping upstairs—something she hardly did "twice in a year"—and David by extraordinary good luck had decided to forgo his usual afternoon nap in order to finish some work in the garden—or both of them would have perished. As it was, by the time David smelled smoke and awakened Child with his "terrified screams," her chamber door was "so hot that it blistered [her] hand," and the adjacent room was so full of smoke that she nearly choked to death before finding her way out. With no fire engine in town and nothing but the neighbors' garden hose to extinguish the flames, the interior of the ell wing was "entirely consumed," leaving only the roof and clapboards. Child managed to rescue all her "precious little memorials of friendship," and "[b]y almost superhuman energy, [the neighbors] saved the body of the house." But her "cozy" sitting room was a charred wreck, "the paper in some places so scorched as to be hanging in tatters; looking-glass cracked and shivered by the heat; clock blackened, broken, & stopped; every thing looking utterly funereal." What made the destruction especially hard to bear was that Child had just finished repainting and papering her "small domain," her father's tenants having finally vacated the rooms they had been occupying all these years.[136]

In the immediate aftermath of the catastrophe, Child had borne up remarkably well. "I was even cheerful. I was *so* thankful that my dear, good David was safe! I thought, too, of the Unionists in the Border States, who instead of having such kind, sympathizing neighbors, had neighbors that *set* fire to their houses. . . ." When she discovered that her insurance policy had not expired, as she supposed, because Ellis Loring had renewed it just before his death, as if his "care . . . extended over [her], even after he was gone," she wept "like a child." But several days later, a "re-action" set in. Feeling herself on the brink of a "nervous fever," she turned desperately to Samuel Sewall, the friend best qualified to fill Loring's role, and implored him for advice.[137]

More than the shock of seeing her home go up in flames lay behind Child's emotional turmoil. Abruptly, by what appeared a providential stroke, the disaster had reopened possibilities that had long seemed foreclosed. As she explained to Sewall, she had never wanted to settle in Wayland, where she was so burdened with housework that she "found no time to write, and extremely little to read; beside being almost entirely cut off from congenial society." It was David who had opted for staying there after her father's death. His "precarious health required the comfort and regularity of a *home*; exercise in a garden was essential to his body, and his mental comfort required room for piles of pamphlets and newspapers." He was "strongly attached to his garden and fixtures" and was pressing to rebuild the house. But the insurance payment of $227 would cover only a fraction of repair costs. Most disheartening to contemplate was "the immense amount of *labor*" that would be necessary to restore "torn, scorched, or stained" objects to a semblance of their former appearance. Could she not invest her $9,000 worth of property in a more comfortable mode of life? "I should myself like to get rid of housekeeping," she confessed to Sewall. "If I could find some worthy woman of the working-class, who wanted to spare several rooms of her house, and who would cook simple meals for us, it would meet *my* wishes, and I think David could find a bit of land to amuse himself with."[138]

Before Sewall had a chance to respond, the Shaws sent a check for $200, begging Child to put aside her "prejudice" against accepting financial help and to treat them "like *real relatives*."[139] For a fleeting moment, Child dreamed wildly of locking up what remained of the cottage, renting rooms in Boston, and "going a pleasuring." She would "rest from house-work"; visit the Aquarial Gardens, which she had not yet seen; return to the Athenaeum, where she had not set foot for four years; and "stroll into Williams and Everett's" gallery to "refresh [her] eyes with landscapes and photographs, in lieu of smoked ceilings and charred walls." Or, alternatively, she and David could go to Port Royal to teach the "contrabands." They could postpone deciding what to do with the cottage until the following spring. Fortunately, they had "an excellent, responsible neighbor, who ha[d] long wanted to buy the house, and who [was] willing to buy it next week, or next year" — though it seemed best not to sell until they were sure something better would turn up.[140]

These heady fantasies of freedom vanished almost overnight. They could not leave before "cleaning, mending, and packing" the damaged articles, Child reasoned. It also seemed a shame to let the "currants and early apples," which she had been planning to make into preserves for the hospitals, go to waste. The price of boarding in Boston turned out to be higher than expected. If they went to Port Royal, David's health probably would not survive the drastic change of climate and food. Moreover, it was "necessary to practise a great deal of prudence, and some diplomacy, in all situations connected with our [military] camps; and David is always under the *necessity* of trying to right all the wrongs that come under his notice." Finally, there was the danger of theft if books, furniture, and personal effects were left in a house with "demolished doors and windows," even in a "secluded village" like Wayland and even with an "excellent, responsible neighbor" to watch over them. "The fact is, I was held prisoner by my *things*," Child admitted ruefully, to Sarah. "It is a *dreadful* thing to have property!"[141] Practical considerations thus combined with David's manifest preference for remaining in Wayland and effected a decision by default. It would be Child's last attempt to escape from her "prison."[142]

Overwhelmed by the backbreaking task of making the cottage habitable in time for winter, Child hardly took notice of the twin Union victories that changed the "deep darkness of our doubt and apprehension . . . into something like the morning of hope and the sunshine of a renewed national confidence," (as the *Tribune* put it).[143] With the capture of Vicksburg after a siege of many weeks, the Union had finally secured control of the Mississippi; and with the crushing defeat at Gettysburg of Lee's second attempt to invade the North, all recognized that the Confederacy's days were numbered. David "capered about and hurraed, when the news of the surrender of Vicksburgh came," Child reported to the Shaws in a postscript. She did not mention that on hearing of the Union triumph at Gettysburg, he rushed over to the home of his neighbors, the Cuttings, "wild with excitement" and asked to borrow their U.S. flag. As the Cuttings' five-year-old son would remember, David tied the flag over his shoulders, "climbed to the top of one of the great ash trees in front of the house — an incredible feat even for a young man — and there, sixty feet in the air, he lashed the staff to the tree, and with the flag blowing over him, and with his white hair streaming to the wind, he sang the 'Star Spangled Banner,' as loudly as his strong lungs could sing it."[144]

At the outset of the war Child had written to Sarah: "When [the United States] treats the colored people with justice and humanity, I will mount its flag in my great elm-tree. . . ."[145] For David, that moment had come when the military victory at Gettysburg had vindicated abolitionists' prophecies that the Union would only be able to win by waging an antislavery war and enlisting African Americans in the struggle for their own freedom. For Child, it had not yet come. Her revulsion was no longer being aroused by the official policy of the U.S. government, which had once made her indignantly reject the gift of a brooch in the form of a flag, exclaiming to Sarah, "I would as soon wear the rattlesnake upon my bosom as the eagle."[146] But barely two weeks after Gettysburg, anti-black violence erupted in the most vicious riots New York had ever seen.

For four days in mid-July rampaging mobs of Irish workers, encouraged by Copperhead opponents of the war, expressed their resentment of the Republican administration and its newly implemented draft law by holding the city hostage. In part, the rioters were reacting against the egregious class discrimination of a draft that exempted men rich enough to pay $300 for a substitute — "almost a year's wages for an unskilled laborer."[147] They began by burning down a conscription station and fanned out into the streets attacking "every well-dressed man" in sight, raising the cry, "Down with the rich men." The rioters vented their fury chiefly against African Americans and their abolitionist or Republican allies. "As if by preconcerted action," assaults against "colored men and boys" occurred all over the city, "crowds of from 100 to 500 persons hunting them like bloodhounds." The "infuriated howl," "Kill the d — d nigger" targeted "any unfortunate black man, woman, or child" the rioters found in their path. "Insensate" mobs looted and burned down the Colored Orphan Asylum, torched black neighborhoods, and dragged black men out of their homes and off city omnibuses, lynching them, hanging their bodies from lampposts, and setting fire to them. The rioters also went in search of *Tribune* editor Horace Greeley, whom they blamed for promoting an emancipationist war policy. Foiled in their raid on the *Tribune* offices, which the last-minute arrival of a "strong police force" saved from arsonists, the mob "completely gutted" the home of Child's former coadjutor on the *Standard*, James S. Gibbons, "because, as was [erroneously] alleged, 'Horace Greeley boarded there.'" Learning that the Gibbonses had "consecrated" one room to memorials of their dead son, Child imagined "How dreadful it must have been to have had that pillaged by a mob!"[148]

The New York draft riots accomplished what the victories at Vicksburg and Gettysburg had not: they jolted Child out of her absorption in her own troubles and refocused her attention on the war. "[C]ompared with . . . the sufferings of those poor outcasts in New York, rendered homeless by that diabolical mob, *my* misfortune becomes a mere inconvenience, to be no more regarded than the sting of a gnat," she philosophized. "I reproach myself for having *cared* so much about a home, when so *many* homes are ruthlessly broken up." Returning the Shaws' check for $200, she explained, "I can not keep it with an easy conscience," and she urged them to put it back into their "fund for the relief of poor wretches, whose need is so much greater than mine."[149]

Once again, Child was rechanneling her personal sense of oppression and her thwarted aspirations for freedom into an intense identification with African Americans. She followed reports of the New York victims' sufferings with passionate concern, noting with satisfaction how admirably their "Christ-like" conduct contrasted with the "outrages" of "their oppressors and persecutors." Her friend Mattie Griffith had undertaken relief work among them and was likewise "struck with their patient, forgiving spirit." Ultimately, the riots would be "productive of good" by creating "sympathy for the colored people" and by disgusting the public with racist violence, Child believed.[150]

In her reaction to the rioters themselves, however, Child betrayed class blinders that would later skew her perception of such events as the Paris Commune and the 1877 Railroad Strikes. The New York mob reminded her of "Paris, in the time of Robespierre," she wrote to the Shaws, shuddering with "horror" as she visualized the havoc such riffraff might wreak on her friends' elegant Staten Island mansion. Although she pronounced the "political instigators" guiltier than "the reckless and ignorant mob," the attitude she expressed toward European immigrants in a letter to the *Standard* resounded with nativist overtones: "Knowing, as we do, that the work-houses and penitentiaries of Europe are continually emptying themselves into our cities, we have no reason to wonder at any amount of depravity that may be manifested by the rabble of such a place as New York, which is a sort of common sewer for the filth of nations. . . ." It was a note she had struck as early as *The First Settlers* (1829), and it would grow increasingly strident in her old age.[151]

Coinciding by a tragic irony with the draft riots, and playing an even greater role in drawing Child back into the fray, was the baptism in blood by which the Massachusetts Fifty-fourth proved the bravery of black soldiers to a skeptical nation. Six weeks after landing at Port Royal and one night after its first trial in battle, the Fifty-fourth led a suicidal assault on Fort Wagner, one of the two forts guarding Charleston. Despite a barrage of cannon fire that mowed them down right and left, the men advanced steadily across the exposed beach and up the slope to the fort, with Shaw at their head. Shaw was shot through the heart as he stood on the ramparts "with uplifted sword, shouting, 'Forward, Fifty-fourth!'" But the men continued to fight "under a fire of grape and canister from . . . howitzers . . . hand grenades, and . . . musketry," not retreating until ordered into a trench by their last remaining officer, a junior captain. Nearly half the regiment's six hundred soldiers and seven of its ten officers were killed, wounded, or missing by the time the remnant of the Fifty-fourth returned from its desperate mission on July 19.[152] It was later reported that the black soldiers captured by the Confederates had been sold as slaves and that Shaw had been "buried . . . with his niggers" in a mass grave after his body had been stripped of its uniform and rifled of the gold watch and antique ring he had been wearing.[153]

"Intense sympathy with [her] darling friends Frank and Sarah Shaw, and anxiety about those of the 54th, who were sold into slavery" affected Child so powerfully that psychosomatic symptoms incapacitated her for two days, paralleling her reaction to the beating of Sumner.[154] Nothing since the war started had been harder for her to bear, she confided to Anna Loring.[155] While attempting to comfort Sarah with the thought that Robert had "made the most of the powers and advantages God had given him, by consecrating them to the defence of freedom and humanity," Child recognized that such words would "fall coldly upon" her friend's "bereaved heart."[156] She intended her published tributes to Robert less for the Shaws than for the readers to whom she held up the martyred colonel and his no less heroic parents as models.

"With moral courage beyond all praise," the Shaws had come forward in the earliest days of the antislavery struggle to stand "side by side with a despised band of reformers against the world of wealth and fashion to which they by position belonged," Child recalled. They had "cheerfully" supported their son's nomination as colonel of a pioneer black regiment, though "well aware of the terrible risks he would incur." And on learning of his ignominious burial, they had responded with "sublime" magnanimity by saying: "'Our darling son, our hero, has received at the hands of the rebels the most fitting burial possible. They buried him with his brave, devoted followers, who fell dead over him and around him. The poor benighted wretches thought they were heaping indignities on his dead body, but . . . we would not have him buried elsewhere, if we could.'" For his part, the "young hero" had shown that he shared his parents' abolitionist principles not only on the battlefield, but in day-to-day interactions with people of color. When "two intelligent, well-bred colored strangers" visited his regiment's camp in Massachusetts, he had invited them to dine with him "and treated them with the same unpatronizing courtesy with which he would have treated the Duke of Argyle." He had taken great pleasure in being "brought into contact" with so many "intelligent colored people" and had "seemed to rejoice over all indications of their progress, as a generous heart does over the good luck of a brother who has been kept down by misfortune."[157]

Child invoked her readers' sympathies for the men of the Fifty-fourth as well, hailing the "cheerful bravery" with which they had sacrificed their lives "to achieve the freedom of their cruelly oppressed race." If Shaw deserved a monument, "the colored soldiers who fell ought to have a monument also," she asserted. In the meantime, however, the government ought at least to take stronger measures to protect black troops against mistreatment by Confederate captors. Lincoln had ordered that for every Union soldier enslaved by the Confederates, "a rebel soldier shall be placed at hard labor on the public works." Child felt this was not enough. "Rebel prisoners of rank and influence ought to work in chains, as hostages" for enslaved black soldiers, she argued.[158]

In the midst of Child's grief for the Shaws, her anxiety about the fate of black prisoners of war, and her frenetic labor supervising the renovation of the cottage, she and David were invited to Anna Loring's wedding. It was an antislavery event, attended by Sumner, Wendell Phillips, Mattie Griffith, and many other cherished friends, but Child had no time to enjoy them. "[T]ied, hands and feet by workmen," she had to rush home "by the earliest morning train" the day after the wedding, without even a chance to visit with Louisa. The frustration she felt lay deeper than its immediate cause, for the decision to remain in Wayland was only the latest in a long series of sacrifices and disappointments since her marriage thirty-five years ago. "[S]ome how or other, a wedding never seems to me a festive occasion," she admitted to her spinster friend, Eliza Scudder. "The irrevocableness of the step is somewhat appalling, and the success of the experiment always seems to me mighty [']onsartain.'" Thinking sadly of her own blighted hopes and wondering whether Anna would fare any better, she may also have envied her surrogate daughter the fulfillment of fantasies she had once entertained for herself, since the bridegroom, Otto Dresel, was a concert pianist and composer.[159]

Child was doomed to yet another disappointment before 1863 was out. She had completed the manuscript of her anthology for old people and was looking forward to being able to present copies to her friends, when a printers' strike broke out at Ticknor & Fields's establishment. As a Christmas gift book, the anthology could not be sold after the season had passed. Hence, publication had to be delayed for a full year. Her elderly friends were falling "like autumn leaves," Child lamented. "Three have died since the book was in press. How many will survive till the close of another year, God alone knows."[160]

Until New Year's the repairs on the cottage kept Child "almost crazed with confusion and dirty work." While awaiting the plastering of her closets, her "goods and chattels" either lay "heaped up pell-mell under the bed" or "kicked about in the middle of the floor." Masons and carpenters were constantly "off and on, keeping everything in a clutter." They would turn up just when she had scheduled a visit from a friend or a trip into Boston, and then "go away to other jobs," leaving her "stumbling over piles of bricks and boards." When they appeared, she had to cook for them. For two solid weeks she spent all morning cooking, all afternoon "clearing away the cooking," and all evening mending while David read the newspapers aloud to her, edifying her with accounts of "stabbing and shooting, and burning and starving." Exhausted and disgruntled, she tried to console herself with the unexpected improvement in David's health. Usually prone to break down with the slightest exertion, he had been "remarkably well" since undertaking the work on the house, Child reported to his sister Lydia: "He has a strong appetite, and his food agrees with him, and why he don't grow fat I cannot imagine. We have made many improvements connected with the repairs, and the planning has been a pleasant occupation to his mind, which of course affects the body." During a visit to Lydia in West Boylston, he had bought a secondhand stove (although he could easily have obtained one in the vicinity of Wayland, Child noted with annoyance) and was planning to use it for apple-drying. "It is his *hobby* for the present, and if he is only careful not to spend too much in experimenting, I shall not be sorry for him to have an amusement. He is a dear, good soul, and has had hard times in the world," she commented indulgently to Lydia.[161] After all these years David was still dreaming up grand schemes for making a fortune, and she was still sacrificing her needs to his, albeit at less risk to her survival.

Perhaps because she was feeling more overwhelmed with work than usual, Child tallied up her "Employments in 1864" at the end of the year — something she had never done before. The list occupied three pages, with professional and intellectual occupations filling up less than half of the first page:

> Wrote 235 letters
> Wrote 6 articles for newspapers.
> Wrote 47 autograph articles for Fairs.
> Wrote my Will.
> Corrected Proofs for Sunset book
> Read aloud 6 pamphlets and 21 volumes.
> Read to myself 7 volumes

A line across the middle of the page divided this section from the interminable list of domestic tasks that followed, ranging from the charitable — "Made 25 needle books for Freed women," "Gathered and made peck of pickles for hospitals," and "Tended upon invalid friend two days" — to the routine: more than a page of items sewn or mended for David and herself in addition to daily chores:

> Cooked 360 dinners
> Cooked 362 breakfasts.
> Swept and dusted sitting-room & kitchen 350 times.
> Filled lamps 362 times
> Swept and dusted chamber & stairs 40 times.
> Besides innumerable jobs too small to be mentioned. . . .

It had been a year of almost unremitting drudgery, yet only one item on Child's list referred to anything beyond her normal workload: "Spent 4 days collecting and sorting papers & pamphlets scattered by the fire."[162]

In January, Child enjoyed a fleeting respite from her labors, thanks to the combined insistence of Garrison and Louisa Loring that she help preside over the annual Anti-Slavery Reception again and spend a few days visiting Boston.[163] Child heartily disliked the receptions, which Maria Chapman had substituted for the Christmas fairs in 1858. They were too noisy and chaotic to allow for either listening to speeches or renewing ties with old friends, she complained, and the task of collecting and recording contributions to the society left "no moments for conversation with anybody." Besides, she doubted whether patrons would have much money to spare when war charities made such heavy demands on them. But she let herself be persuaded to attend when she learned that Helen Garrison had just suffered a paralytic stroke. "[I]t seemed absolutely necessary that the friends should rally round Mr. G. who seemed determined to have a Reception, if he had it all alone by himself," Child confided to Sarah Shaw.[164] Contrary to her gloomy predictions, the reception was a great financial success. Best of all, Child had been excused from fund-raising in exchange for writing up the event for the *Liberator*, and thus could take pleasure in her reunions with dear antislavery comrades. Her "heart leaped up at the sight" of Whittier and Theodore Weld, both of whom "called up a host of anti-slavery memories" from the earliest days of the movement. She could always recognize such pioneer abolitionists by "their bold, straightforward utterance, indicating souls incapable of indirectness," she wrote. "With all their imperfections, they are the noblest specimens of humanity it has been my lot to meet in this earthly pilgrimage."[165]

Child was not simply expressing her nostalgia for what she had elsewhere described as the "good old *early* times of Anti Slavery, when all our hearts moved with one pulsation."[166] She was also invoking this ideal past as a talisman against another tragic schism already brewing between Garrison and Wendell Phillips.[167] The two veteran leaders were disagreeing more and more publicly about whether or not Lincoln deserved the support of abolitionists in the November 1864 elections, as well as about the future mission of abolitionists, once they had achieved their immediate goal of emancipation. Child saw merit in both leaders' positions and tried to bridge their differences. Like Garrison, she had come to feel that Lincoln, though " 'a slow coach,' " had consistently "done better than he promised" and that "he was the very best man that the moral condition of the American people admitted of being elected." Like Phillips, she was distressed by northern politicians' failure to say, " 'The black man has been wronged; give him his rights.' " Phillips's voice of "rebuke and warning" was needed, Child contended, "for the number who sincerely and heartily acknowledge the equality of races is still very small," and abolitionists must not relax their vigilance too soon. In short, abolitionists should heed both leaders' messages and refrain from pitting them against each other.[168]

Child also used her write-up of the 1864 Anti-Slavery Reception to promote the career of an aspiring sculptor she had met there — twenty-year-old Edmonia Lewis, daughter of a "full-blooded" African American father and Chippewa mother. In a long interview that Child reproduced for her readers, Lewis had attributed her artistic gifts to her Chippewa mother, who was "always inventing new patterns for moccasons, and other embroidery" and who had taught her the traditional crafts of her people. Lewis had lived among the Chippewa for three years and pronounced their life in the "free forest" the "greatest of all luxuries." In addition, she had studied at Oberlin College. A living answer to those who denied that either blacks or Indians could be educated, Lewis embodied what Child was increasingly coming to envision as the destiny of the American republic—a fusion of "nature" and "civilization," an amalgamation of African American, "Indian," and Euro-American cultures.[169] Lewis was currently learning sculpture from Edwin A. Brackett, famous for his bust of John Brown, and she invited Child to visit her studio. "Some praise me because I am a colored girl, and I don't want that kind of praise. I had rather you would point out my defects, for that will teach me something," Lewis told her, showing a "modesty and good sense" that "prepossessed [Child] greatly in her favor." Her work had "a great deal of life and expression," Child judged: "Whether she will prove to have any portion of creative genius time will show; but she seems to possess a native talent which is capable of being developed fairly by industry and perseverance."[170]

Later that year Lewis would undertake a bust of Robert Shaw, which Child would describe to Sarah as "really . . . very good, without 'making allowance for circumstances.'"[171] Child would continue to promote Lewis's work, reviewing her sculptures, helping arrange for her to pursue her studies in Rome, and protesting against racist affronts that Lewis received from American expatriates.[172] But the two women would ultimately have a falling out when Child ventured to advise Lewis to *practice in clay* until her mind and hands were "educated enough to work in *marble*," and to "devote only a *portion* of her time to perfecting herself as a sculptor," meanwhile earning "her *living* by moulding small decorations for architects, copying small statuettes, &c." Understandably, Lewis resented the advice as patronizing. She could hardly have known that Child would "rather have given $50" than write such a letter and that she had spent her life practicing the most rigid economy to avoid incurring obligations. Nor could Child have realized that in criticizing Lewis for not cultivating "habits of balancing income and outgo" and for being "in too much of a hurry to get up to a conspicuous place, without taking the necessary intermediate steps," she may have been projecting onto the young artist some of the residual anger she felt at her husband's similar propensities.[173]

By 1864 Child saw her primary tasks as ensuring the reelection of Lincoln and preparing the way for a genuine reconstruction of American society. Lincoln himself was testing one possible reconstruction policy in Louisiana, the so-called "10 Percent Plan," announced in a proclamation of December 1863. Intended as a means of shortening the war, it offered amnesty to all who took an oath of allegiance to the United States, pledging to accept the abolition of slavery, and it provided that whenever 10 percent of those registered to vote in 1860 took such an oath, this "loyal nucleus" could form a new state government.[174] Abolitionists and Radical Republicans widely deplored the plan, because they feared it would restore the South's former ruling class to power and make "the negro's freedom a mere sham," as Wendell Phillips put it.[175] Convinced that Lincoln would never endorse a thoroughgoing reconstruction guaranteeing land, education, and the ballot to blacks, Phillips began campaigning for Frémont instead. Frémont was not running as a Republican, however. The "Radical Democratic" third party that nominated him at its May 31 convention was heavily "infiltrated" by Democrats. With the aim of splitting the Republican vote and throwing the election to the Democratic candidate, former general George B. McClellan, the infiltrators "held out to the naive Frémont the prospect of a coalition with Democrats to beat Lincoln," and he promptly swallowed the "bait."[176] Alarmed, Child swung into action to prevent a Democratic victory, which she viewed as a far greater threat than Lincoln to the reconstruction policy she, like Phillips, favored. Writing to key opinion-makers in abolitionist and Republican ranks — among them Whittier, Gerrit Smith, and Sumner — she warned that Frémont was "obviously courting the copperheads" and that Phillips was "making a great mistake" in supporting him. "I have never *entirely* trusted [Frémont]," she wrote to Whittier, who would be instrumental in persuading the antislavery general to withdraw his candidacy in September.[177] She proceeded to recall Frémont's role in fomenting the Mexican War: "He *was* a fillibuster, and one of a worse stamp than common. He went *professedly* on a scientific exploring expedition. The Mexicans treated him and his company with hospitality, kindness, and confidence; but he got up a fight with them without provocation, *before* war was declared by the government; and I have no doubt he did it in obedience to *secret* instructions from the Slave Power, who contrived the so-called Exploring Expedition as a mere farce."[178] Besides contributing to an unjust war waged for the purpose of extending slavery, Frémont's pathfinders had ruthlessly slaughtered California Indians "without . . . a *pretext* of provocation," Child reminded Gerrit Smith.[179]

Child acknowledged that Frémont's emancipation proclamation had kindled her enthusiasm in 1861, but she pointed out that his conduct since his removal from command had been disappointing. Unlike General Ambrose Burnside, who had patriotically offered to serve "in some *subordinate* capacity" after his dismissal following his defeat at Fredericksburg, Frémont had aired his "personal piques" and done "nothing for the country in her hour of extreme need," though drawing a general's pay. This record, she concluded, indicated that Frémont was not "*reliable.*"[180]

Contrasting Lincoln with Frémont, Child conceded Lincoln's faults. He had a "slow mind, apparently incapable of large, comprehensive views," she judged. Inclined toward legalism and political maneuvering, he was "forever pottering about details and calculating chances." "[R]eligious-minded as he seems to be, his fear of God is unfortunately secondary to his fear of the Democratic Party." What particularly dismayed Child was that Lincoln "obviously lack[ed] sympathy for the wrongs and sufferings of the colored race. . . ." Still, she believed he "sincerely wishes to have Slavery swept completely away," and she deemed it "no small thing to be able to trust in a man's *honesty*." Perhaps most important, Lincoln had shown himself capable of growth:

"though he has learned slowly, the four years of his administration have taught him considerable. . . ." "I know of no other public man, except Charles Sumner, on whose uprightness I should rely with such perfect certainty," she wound up—an extravagant tribute from her.[181]

As the election neared, Child's fears of a Democratic victory mounted. The war had been stalemated for months, with Sherman stymied outside Atlanta and Grant bogged down in an ill-fated siege of Petersburg. The Petersburg siege culminated in one of the worst fiascos of the war—a poorly coordinated attempt to tunnel a mine shaft under the Confederate defenses and send Union troops through the breach. Because unprepared white troops were substituted at the last minute for the blacks who had been trained for the operation, it produced 4,000 Union casualties and delivered black troops up to the murderous revenge of the victorious Confederates. So whipped was the northern mood that *New York Tribune* editor Horace Greeley actually entreated Lincoln to "submit overtures for pacification to the Southern insurgents."[182] "[I]t is the darkest hour we have yet had," Child commented. "[T]he tidings of defeat at Petersburg; the horrible slaughter of the poor blacks; and the bad use that the copperheads would make of their panic, all conspired to make me so wretched, that I longed to be 'anywhere, *any*where, out of *this* world.'" Unless the tide of the war turned, she worried, McClellan would win the election and patch up "a false peace . . . by bringing the whole country under the dominion of Slavery." She swore she would seriously contemplate "quitting the country" if that happened.[183]

Sherman's capture of Atlanta on September 3 saved the day for Lincoln. As Child explained in an update of the war news for David's relatives in Australia, Atlanta was "considered even more important than Richmond, on account of its being the focus of [the Confederacy's] railroad supplies." Further enhancing Lincoln's chances of reelection, General Sheridan won "a succession of marvellous victories in the Shenandoah Valley," and Grant was "slowly, but steadily pushing on toward Richmond, taking fortification after fortification."[184] Child expressed great confidence in Grant, whom she pronounced "a real military genius." His "courage, promptness, energy, and presence of mind; . . . the brevity and good sense of his letters; . . . the simplicity of his manners, [and] his aversion to being lionized" inspired her respect and reminded her of the great Italian general, Giuseppe Garibaldi.[185]

By November, Child thought the end was near. "The Rebel army suffers greatly by desertion," she noted. "The 'poor whites' have . . . taken to the mountains in formidable numbers, refuse to fight, receive and arm all runaway slaves that go to them, and intrench themselves so strongly, that the Rebel officers think best to let them alone." Signs of Confederate desperation were multiplying. The Davis government was talking of arming 300,000 slaves and promising them freedom in exchange for their loyalty. "Another sign of desperation in the Rebels" was the rash of conspiracies they had sponsored with Copperheads "to burn cities, rob banks, murder leading men of the Republican Party, &c." Fortunately, these revelations and the zeal of the Rebels for McClellan's candidacy "opened the eyes" of the public in time for the election, Child reported to her Australian correspondents.[186]

Lincoln won resoundingly, thanks in part to the votes of Union soldiers, who had become "overwhelmingly Republican."[187] Child attributed his reelection to "the intelligence and reason of the people" — the fruit of "Free Schools" and republican institutions. Nothing else could account for his victory, she wrote privately, since Lincoln lacked the popular appeal that most other successful candidates boasted: "There is no beauty in him, that men should desire him; there is no insinuating, polished manner, to beguile the senses of the people; there is no dazzling military renown; no silver flow of rhetoric; in fact, no glittering prestige of *any* kind surrounds him; yet the people triumphantly elected him, in spite of all manner of machinations, and notwithstanding the long, long drag upon their patience and their resources, which this war has produced."[188] Child particularly hailed the democratization portended by the American electorate's choice of candidates from humble social backgrounds. "I rejoice in having a rail-splitter for President and a tailor for vice president [Andrew Johnson of Tennessee, by birth a "poor white"]. I wish a shoe-black could be found worthy to be appointed Secretary of State; and I should be all the more pleased if he were a *black* shoe-black," she confided to her old friend Parke Godwin, editor of the *New York Evening Post*.[189]

Child took hope not only from the new Vice President's class origins, but from the "spirit-stirring addresses" he had been "delivering . . . to the colored people of Nashville." " 'They who would be *free*, *themselves* must strike the blow,' " Johnson had proclaimed at a rally, to which an ardent black crowd had "responded 'Amen!' ": "He said, 'I trust the Lord will raise up a Moses for your leader;' and they cried out '*You* are our Moses.' 'I *will* be your Moses,' said he, [']until the Lord sends you a better one.' The colored people passed through the streets of Nashville in procession, to be addressed by him, and people watching them from the windows of the houses they passed, waved hats and handkerchiefs, and saluted them with hurras." Child recalled that Nashville had been the city in which "thirty years ago Amos Dresser," a classmate of Theodore Weld's at Lane Seminary in Ohio, had been "publicly flogged" for having a few abolitionist works (including her own *Oasis*) in his trunk. "Verily, 'it is the Lord's doings, and it is marvellous in our eyes,' " she exclaimed.[190]

As she contemplated the future in the light of Lincoln's record since taking office in 1861, Child felt a surge of faith in his leadership and potential for further growth. For the first time, she credited Lincoln with being "sagacious" as well as "honest." "Considering the stubborness of prejudice, the violence of old parties, the confusion produced by the Rebels, and all the immense and complicated difficulties by which he was surrounded, . . . he has done wonderfully well," she opined.[191] A comparison of Lincoln's first and second inaugural addresses measured the enormous progress he had made in four years. His first inaugural had "bowed down to the Slave power to an *unnecessary* degree" by vowing to enforce the Fugitive Slave Law and to support a constitutional amendment guaranteeing slavery against federal interference. His second had reverberated with the "wisdom and moral power" so sorely lacking at the outset: "How impressive is that portion of the President's Inaugural, where he says that every drop of blood drawn by the lash has been repaid by drops drawn by the sword." Lincoln had clearly come to understand the lesson of the war, which Child had discerned as early as the battle of Bull Run: "that the *same* measure we have meted out [to the slave] has been measured unto *us*." Nevertheless, she cautioned abolitionists, there must continue to be "sharp critics watching him; for his good-nature and love of peace may lead him into snares," and the "Pro Slavery Devil" assailing the country would surely "assume all manner of Protean shapes for mischief" in the critical period after the war: "He will squat like a toad, twist like a snake, and coo like a dove."[192]

Repeatedly during the last year of the war Child took stock of the "marvellous and constantly increasing change in public opinion on the subject of Slavery."[193] Maryland abolished slavery without compensation, and "the vote of the *soldiers* turned the scale in favor of freedom," Child exulted.[194] The British abolitionist George Thompson, whom she and David had shielded from antiabolitionist mobs in 1835, was not only lecturing to enthusiastic audiences now, but was being received in Congress as an honored guest speaker. One of Child's Wayland neighbors, Captain Wade of the U.S. Navy, literally brought the transformation of public opinion home to her. "Two years ago," Child remembered, "he was for having us mobbed because we advocated emancipating and arming the slaves." After seeing slavery at first hand and then observing black troops in action near New Orleans, he had "come home on a furlough, an outspoken abolitionist." He had "publicly announced the total change in his sentiments since he has had 'an opportunity to *know* something on the subject.'" Even more tellingly, he had demonstrated the sincerity of his convictions by protesting when a fellow passenger in the streetcar insulted a black soldier and announced, "'I'm not going to ride with niggers'": "Capt. Wade, who sat a few seats further forward, rose up, in all the gilded glory of his naval uniform, and called out, 'Come here, my good fellow! I've been fighting along side of people of your color, and glad enough I was to *have* 'em by my side. Come and sit by *me*.'"[195]

While welcoming every such indication of progress toward the racial egalitarianism she had been promulgating for more than thirty years, Child saw it as her mission to broaden and deepen the revolution wrought by the war. Thus, she greeted another notable conversion — that of former Confederate General Edward W. Gantt of Arkansas, who electrified the northern public in February 1864 with his plea to Democrats to join in extirpating the "disease" of slavery[196] — by personally cheering him on. "Above all else in this world, I respect a man who has the moral courage to say, 'I have been going wrong, but I have faced about to the right, and am going to march straight forward,'" Child wrote Gantt in a letter published in the *Standard*. "You are doing the country incalculable service." She then nudged him gently to go one step farther. "You constantly speak of the negro as the cause of the war, but you are not careful to say that he is the *innocent* cause" and the chief victim of the blight that slavery has inflicted on the South, Child remonstrated. "I longed to have you give beautiful completeness to your manly utterance by saying, . . . 'We have all wronged Cuffee. Let us agree to leave off wronging him and give him a fair chance to find his own place in creation.'" Enclosing a copy of *The Right Way the Safe Way* with her letter, Child begged Gantt to examine it and supply her with names of Arkansas citizens to whom she could send copies "post-paid." She ended by arguing against black expatriation schemes and conjuring up the alternative vision of a multiracial, egalitarian society — the only goal she considered worth the price of so much bloodshed: "In our broad territory, nowhere thoroughly cultivated, there is room and work enough for people of all nations, and all complexions. We need the labor of all classes, and can ill afford to spare any. Give them all the benefits of schools, the protection of equal laws, and the stimulus of just wages. Remove obstructions, and they will assuredly find their own natural level, as readily and safely as the waters do."[197]

Child spelled out both the socioeconomic order she envisaged and the Reconstruction policy needed to institute it in a March 1864 letter to Congressman George Washington Julian of Indiana, a leading Radical Republican. Noting with concern that "large tracts of Southern confiscated lands were being bought by Northern capitalists," Child asserted: "They ought to be mainly distributed among the emancipated slaves, and the poor whites who will consent to become loyal citizens of the U.S. . . . ." The slave system should not be replaced by capitalist "Land-Monopoly" and wage labor, but by associations of small farmers, she emphasized. For her precedent, Child drew on the West Indies, where the best feature of British emancipation had been "the cutting up of large plantations into lots." The emancipated slaves on these farms had formed cooperatives and pooled their resources to "build small sugar-mills for their mutual convenience." Their success proved that the manufacture of sugar could be "carried on without rich capitalists," Child concluded: "*Combined* capital of the laborers is far better, every way, than the monopolizing of the mills by a few men of overgrown wealth."[198] Julian fully shared Child's beliefs. In fact, he was spearheading a campaign in Congress to grant eighty-acre homesteads to all former Union soldiers, black and white, and forty-acre homesteads to European immigrants.[199] Except where soldiers were concerned, however, Child favored selling these homesteads for a "moderate price . . . with reasonable terms of credit," rather than distributing them as outright gifts, and she sought to induce Julian to modify his proposal accordingly. "[M]en are generally injured by having property *given* to them," she reasoned. The promise of free land would "attract a swarm of idlers and vagabonds to our shores," and such recipients would quickly sell their homesteads off to speculators and "land-monopolists." They would also be easily manipulated by demagogues, just as the "ignorant Irish" had been by "Southern slaveholders and Northern democrats." On the other hand, "the sort of men who would *earn* their way to the possession of farms from the public lands would be the men most likely to *cultivate* them well, to keep them in their own hands, and gradually to increase their acres by new earnings." Since labor was currently in great demand and wages were high, "a thrifty emigrant from Europe, or elsewhere, could earn enough on his way to the public lands, to buy himself a farm in a short time, by stopping to do agricultural or mechanical jobs, of which there is urgent need in all parts of the country." The revised homestead bill Child suggested would serve the combined purposes of destroying the planter aristocracy; opening opportunities for upward mobility to blacks, poor whites, and European immigrants alike; filling the country's labor shortage; and paying off the national debt.[200]

Her eyes fixed on the future, Child lobbied incessantly in 1864 for the measures she viewed as essential to consolidating emancipation and setting the country on the path toward true republican equality. Simultaneously with her campaigning for Lincoln and her promotion of a radical reconstruction policy, she began working on the project of compiling a book for the freedpeople. The idea seems to have occurred to her when she was collecting primers to send to the "contrabands" at Fort Monroe. Very few of the ones she had procured appeared "*suitable*," she noted. "*Our* literature is not, in *any* of its departments, adapted to *their* state and condition. I think I can plan some books that will help to encourage, enlighten, and entertain them, at the same time. I have a faculty at writing with *simplicity*, and my sympathies are so entirely with them, that I think I can put myself in their stead, and imagine what *I* should like in *their* place." This exercise of imagination led her to design a reader "consisting of the best *biographies* of colored people, *stories* about slaves, good *hymns*, and the best pieces of *poetry* by colored people," together with an introductory "Address written especially for them."[201] Selections "presenting honorable examples of what *has* been done by people of color" would instill a sense of racial pride in the freedpeople and inspire them to persevere in the daunting struggle to uplift themselves. The overall moral tone of the book would also "infuse kindly feelings toward their former masters."[202]

For such a book to be accessible to the freedpeople, it would have to be "sold at the lowest possible price," Child realized. Unable to afford the cost of publishing it at her own expense, and doubtful of finding a publisher to undertake it gratis, she turned to the wealthy abolitionist Gerrit Smith in April 1864. He sent $30 in response, but the minimum she would have needed to "print two thousand copies, in the cheapest manner, consistent with durability" would have been $1,000, plus another $150 for stereotyping. Thus, she decided to return Smith's advance and postpone completing the project until she found a means of financing it.[203]

The solution turned out to be reinvesting the proceeds of her Christmas gift book for the elderly, *Looking toward Sunset*. After a year's delay, Child's loving "benefaction to the old" finally appeared on the market in early November 1864. It proved even more "saleable" than she had anticipated. The first edition of 4,000 sold out before New Year's.[204] The book would go through twelve printings in her lifetime and six more after her death — an average of almost one a year until 1887 (*NUC*). Once again Child had succeeded in meshing a personal with a cultural need and pioneering a neglected domain in the process. As Thomas Wentworth Higginson put it in a review for the *Atlantic Monthly*: "Every one of her chief works has been a separate venture in some new field, always daring, always successful, always valuable. . . . And now, still longing to look in some new direction, she finds that direction in 'Sunset,' — the only region towards which her name and her nature have alike excused her from turning her gaze before."[205] Retracing Child's prior achievements from *Hobomok* through *The Progress of Religious Ideas*, Higginson nostalgically recalled the "delight" her *Juvenile Miscellany* had aroused "when childish books were few." The link he perceived between Child's latest anthology and the magazine that had first introduced her to him was not accidental, for the opening words of her preface to *Looking toward Sunset* invoke her youthful community of readers and redefine her relationship to it:

> I occasionally meet people who say to me, "I had many a pleasant hour, in my childhood, reading your Juvenile Miscellany; and now I am enjoying it over again, with my own little folks."
>
> .   .   .   .   .
>
> When I was myself near the fairy-land of childhood, I used my pen for the pleasure of children; and now that I am travelling down the hill I was then ascending, I would fain give some words of consolation and cheer to my companions on the way.[206]

Indeed, *Looking toward Sunset* strikingly resembles the *Juvenile Miscellany* in conception and spirit. The selections are similarly varied, including fiction, poetry, biographical sketches, moral essays, pithy anecdotes, practical advice, and religious counsels by a wide variety of authors, ranging from Anacreon and Cicero to Theodore Parker and Alice Cary. Nine are by Child herself: a story ("The Friends"), an allegorical sketch about the life cycle ("The Mysterious Pilgrimage), two poems (both titled "Old Folks at Home"), a pair of essays on "Unmarried Women" (incorporating a long letter by Lucy Osgood) and "Old Bachelors," another pair furnishing "Moral Hints" and "Hints about Health," and an autobiographical "Letter from an Old Woman, on Her Birthday," in which Child speaks directly to her readers as one of them. These selections "are of the best in the volume," judged Garrison in the *Liberator*, expressing his usual enthusiasm for Child's productions: "Noble woman! what a benefactor she has been to mankind!"[207]

The virtues Child preaches to the elderly are almost identical with those she had once recommended to the young: unselfishness, usefulness to others, cheerfulness, "constant employment," generosity, religious and racial tolerance, egalitarianism (164, 168–69, 179–80). Just as she had held up child prodigies as role models for young readers, she now offers her elderly readers examples of men and women who have pursued careers as artists, scientists, or reformers into old age. Just as she had shown how even a four year old could learn to perform useful tasks in a household, she now suggests a multitude of ways in which even octogenarians can serve their families and communities and thus keep the "machinery of body, mind, and heart . . . from rusting" (173–75).

While revealing the continuities in Child's values, *Looking toward Sunset* also reflects her considerable radicalization since her heyday as a cultural spokesperson. No longer does she mute unorthodox opinions for fear of alienating a conservative audience. She tells her readers point blank that "no person has a right to be entirely indifferent concerning questions involving great moral principles." She advocates active involvement in combating slavery, war, and intemperance; "righting the wrongs of the Indians"; extending the benefits of public education; reforming prisons; or otherwise contributing to the "daily comfort . . . of mankind" (175–76). She denounces epithets that instill "[p]oisonous prejudices against nations, races, sects, and classes" — " 'Nigger,' 'Paddy,' 'old Jew,' 'old maid' " (179). She protests vigorously against the double standard that makes "old maid . . . a more reproachful term than old bachelor" (226). She defends the decision to remain single and refuses to glorify marriage and the family, maintaining that contrary to popular belief, marriage and parenthood do not make people less selfish:

[F]athers and mothers are often selfish on a large scale, for the sake of advancing the worldly prosperity or social condition of their children. Not only is spiritual growth frequently sacrificed in pursuit of these objects, but principles are trampled on, which involve the welfare of the whole human race. Within the sphere of my own observation, I must confess that there is a larger proportion of unmarried than of married women whose sympathies are active and extensive (128–29).

Though respecting her elderly readers' need for spiritual consolation, Child gives no quarter to religious bigotry. "[T]he spirit of Jesus may walk and talk with good pious Hindoos and Mahometans" as well as with Christians, she contends, and "some who were called heathens might be nearer to God than many professing Christians" (34). In holding out to her readers the comforting prospect of an afterlife with cherished loved ones, she insists that they cease to restrict it to members of their own sect.

Formerly, Child had sought to close the gap between herself and her readers by masking her radicalism. In *Looking toward Sunset*, she instead chooses to invite her readers behind the veil of her private self, sharing with them the benefit of her own struggles with aging. She is most candid in her "Letter from an Old Woman, on Her Birthday," which echoes her imaginary conversations with Ellis Loring in *Letters from New York*: "You ask me, dear friend, whether it does not make me sad to grow old. I tell you frankly it did make me sad for a while; but that time has long since past" (212). Describing the "many compensations which age brings for its undeniable losses," Child writes:

I never conformed much to the world's ways, but, now that I am an old woman, I feel more free to ignore its conventional forms, and neglect its fleeting fashions. . . . [H]aving outlived expectations, I am free from disappointments. . . .

But the most valuable compensations of age are those of a spiritual character. I have committed so many faults myself, that I have become more tolerant of the faults of others than I was when I was young. . . . I now see the wisdom and goodness of our Heavenly Father, even more in what He has denied, than in what He has bestowed. . . . My restless aspirations are quieted. . . . Having arrived at this state of peacefulness and submission, I find the last few years the happiest of my life. (220–22)

True, Child reserves these confidences for a selection in the form of a letter. But the audience she addresses there — an audience of intimate aging friends like Lucy Osgood and Henrietta Sargent, to whom *Looking toward Sunset* is dedicated — is implicit throughout the book. Though Child speaks impersonally in her other essays, the reader of her "Moral Hints," for example, senses that her prescriptions for resisting the "disease" of "despondency" are distilled from personal experience:

> Perhaps you will say: ". . . I am low-spirited by temperament; and how is that to be helped?" . . . [I]f you inherit a tendency to look on the dark side of things, resolutely call in the aid of your reason to counteract it. . . .
>
> If reason will not afford sufficient help, call in the aid of conscience. . . . If you habitually try to pack your troubles away out of other people's sight, you will be in a fair way to forget them yourself; first, because evils become exaggerated to the imagination by repetition; and, secondly, because an effort made for the happiness of others lifts us above ourselves. (165–67)

The secret of the book's enormous popularity no doubt lies at least partly in the bond Child establishes with her readers. "I, too, have suffered from lifelong depression," she seems to whisper, "but I have learned to overcome it, and so can you." The book's practical psychology must also have appealed to readers. Recognizing that moral exhortations and good resolutions do not suffice to counteract depression, Child advises those "conscious of a tendency to dejection" to "increase as much as possible the circle of simple and healthy enjoyments": "They should cultivate music and flowers, take walks to look at beautiful sunsets, read entertaining books, . . . avail themselves of any agreeable social intercourse within their reach . . . [and] surround themselves with pleasant external objects" (167).

As with all of Child's pioneering ventures, what best accounts for the brisk sales of *Looking toward Sunset* is its prescient anticipation of a cultural need. In an era when the old were losing status, churches were crumbling, and ministers were declining in influence, Child provided her aging contemporaries with alternative sources of meaning and solace.[208] "You give the closing stage of human life an atmosphere of the richest lights and warmest hues, and make its clouds add to its glory," wrote the poet William Cullen Bryant, comparing Child to an artist who excelled in "sunset views." "[N]owhere indeed is old age presented under so agreeable a form," agreed Lucy Osgood. " 'The Mysterious Pilgrimage' has traits so similar to a recent personal experience to dispose me to do more than to thank you for the beautiful lesson," divulged an abolitionist correspondent. "[I]f you saw the tears and smiles, you'd rejoice you had given even one couple so much delight," echoed Wendell Phillips. Of all the aging friends to whom Child gave *Looking toward Sunset*, Louisa Loring most touchingly summed up the mission it performed: "I am sure no person has read it without being better & happier. . . . It is the best present I have had since Ellis went (always excepting the baby)" (her first grandchild).[209]

A portrait Child sketched of herself in December 1864, shortly before her sixty-third birthday, conveys the spirit that imbues her gift book for the elderly:

> My hair is white; and Time, bringing his usual allotment of afflictions and chagrins, has cut the lines deep on my forehead and mouth. Nevertheless, I generally

feel wonderfully young, for my years. A little of the old romance and enthusiasm glows under the ashes of extinguished fires; and indignation is as ready as ever to blaze forth against any form of oppression, injustice, or pride. They say the tendency is to become more conservative, as one grows older, but I become more and more radical.[210]

Such was the self whose feisty example inspired readers to defy old age and persist in fighting for a better world.

Child vowed the profits of *Looking toward Sunset* to the freedpeople. "To comfort old folks with one hand, and give . . . out the proceeds to the suffering and the wronged with the other, is what I call the highest kind of recreation," she crowed. It was the closest she had come to playing the role of Divine Providence, which she had always coveted.[211] For the time being, however, she devoted the money to relief efforts for the freedpeople. Not until the war ended would she resume work on *The Freedmen's Book*.

The last months of the war flashed by. In January 1865 Sherman completed his march from Atlanta to the sea, leaving a trail of devastation. "It seems now as if the war really *was* drawing to a close," despite the Rebels' "blustering and bragging," Child noted, hoping that her nephew Willie would "soon be able to return permanently" from the front.[212] A few weeks afterward, Child saw the consummation of more than thirty years' struggle when the House of Representatives passed the Thirteenth Amendment, abolishing slavery. "You ought to have been in Congress on the ever-to-be-remembered 31'st of January, 1865," wrote her friend William Henry Channing. "Such an outburst of the people's heart has never been seen in the Capitol since the nation was born. It was the sunrise of a new day for the Republic."[213] On February 18 a regiment of former South Carolina slaves and the Massachusetts Fifty-fourth marched in tandem into Charleston, and, three days later, Garrison's eldest son, George Thompson, led the Massachusetts Fifty-fifth into the city singing the John Brown song. "These are exciting times, are they not?" Child exulted with Radical Congressman George Washington Julian.[214] Her friend Lucy Osgood would similarly exult when black troops marched into Richmond on April 3: "To think . . . that the down-trodden race first took possession of the haughty city! What materials for history are every hour accumulating!" That day, throngs of ecstatic freedpeople shouting "Glory, Hallelujah" and "Messiah" hailed Lincoln's entry into the fallen capital of the Confederacy.[215] Coincidentally, the African American poet Frances Harper lectured in Wayland the same night, drawing an overflow crowd and "galvanizing" this conservative "Sleepy Hollow" into life, to Child's gratified surprise. With her characteristic tendency to elevate the crusade against racial prejudice above the military aspect of the war, Child commented more volubly on Harper's triumph than on the Union army's.[216]

"[T]he good news" of Lee's surrender to Grant at Appomatox Courthouse on April 9 left Child "rejoicing . . . with trembling." Thankful for the "cessation of slaughter," she nevertheless worried about the future. Already, she discerned many bad omens. The generous terms Grant made with Lee, and the incongruous tone Lee assumed in return, "more befitting a conqueror in a righteous cause, than a defeated traitor," suggested that the nation might lack the will to finish its work by destroying the slaveholding oligarchy. Sherman's political concessions to Confederate General Joseph E. Johnston reinforced Child's fears that the erstwhile belligerents would all too soon " 'hugger-mugger' it up," aborting the vital task of reconstruction. While discountenancing "anything like revenge" toward Confederate leaders and hoping "there might be no clamoring for blood," she considered it essential to "put [them] out of the way of doing further mischief," which could only be accomplished by confiscating and parceling out their estates to small farmers, black and white. "If [the large planters] have any power left, they will certainly use it to keep down the poor whites and the emancipated blacks," she predicted.[217]

In retrospect, the most sinister omen clouding the termination of the war would prove to be the assassination of Lincoln, though Child did not realize it at the time. On April 14, five days after Appomatox and three days after delivering a speech cautiously endorsing black suffrage, Lincoln succumbed to the bullet of proslavery actor John Wilkes Booth.[218] In a letter to the New York *Independent*, Child paid final homage to the president she had criticized so unsparingly until 1863:

> Year by year he gained upon my respect and confidence. I gradually came to think that I had underrated the qualities of both his head and his heart. One rarely sees such honest unselfishness of purpose combined with so much shrewdness in dealing with men for the accomplishment of purposes. . . . It is not easy to think of another man who possessed such a combination of qualities as would enable him to hold steadily in leash so many refractory forces, and to guide them at last to the desired result. . . . Assuredly, Abraham Lincoln, notwithstanding deficiencies which sorely tried the patience of radicals, was a great gift from Providence at such a crisis.[219]

As she tried to make sense of a tragedy that had deprived the nation of Lincoln's able leadership at the dawn of an era even more critical than the war, Child could only conclude that Providence may have removed him because he was "too kind-hearted" to implement the stern measures needed to reconstruct the South. Lincoln's replacement by Andrew Johnson, a southern "poor white" with a "hearty aversion to aristocracy" and a potential for exerting great influence on his own "much injured class," might turn out to be yet "another providential event in the history of this remarkable epoch," Child hazarded.[220] It would not take many months to disabuse her of her illusions.

Lydia Maria Francis, age 24, engraving after the portrait painted by Francis Alexander in 1826; courtesy Library of Congress. The original, poorly restored, hangs in the Medford Historical Society. "There is a glow and enthusiasm about it which belongs to the author of 'Hobomok,' rather than to L. M. Francis," Child wrote to her sister Mary, claiming that the portrait flattered her too much to be a good likeness.

David Lee Child in his early thirties. This is how David appeared to Child when she confided to her diary: "He is the most gallant man that has lived since the sixteenth century; and needs nothing but helmet, shield, and chain armour to make him a complete knight of chivalry." The portrait is said to be by Francis Alexander, ca. 1828. The original hangs in the Beaman Memorial Library, West Boylston, Massachusetts.

Engraving of Convers Francis and his parsonage at Watertown, where Child wrote *Hobomok*; by permission of the Boston Athenaeum.

South Boston in the distance.

A Pier for boats, at Cottage Place, in Boston,
Where we lived from 1832 to 1835, in a very small cottage,
with a very small garden filled with flowers; The
sea dashed under the windows, and was often sparkling
with moon-beams when we went to bed. We used to
call the humble little home Le Paradis des Pauvres.

A sketch Child made in 1875 of the view from her favorite home at Cottage Place (1832–35);
courtesy of the division of Rare and Manuscript Collections, Cornell University Library.

Portraits of abolitionists Ellis Gray Loring and Louisa Gilman Loring, Child's closest friends until their deaths; by permission of the Massachusetts Historical Society.

Daguerreotype of Child made in 1856, the year she wrote "The Kansas Emigrants"; she commented of it: "I was 54 years old; and that is quite old *enough* to have one's likeness taken. It is not worth while to picture the human habitation of the soul, when the tenement is in ruins; it don't look so picturesque as old Abbeys and Amphitheatres; and even *they* look better by the dimness of moonlight." By permission of The Schlesinger Library, Radcliffe College.

Photograph of John Brown by James Wallace Black, 1859; by permission
of the Boston Athenaeum.

Cabinet Photograph of Harriet Jacobs by Gilbert Studios, Washington, D.C.;
by permission of the owners, courtesy of Jean Fagan Yellin.

Carte de visite photograph of Child at age 63 by John Adams Whipple, 1865; this was Child's favorite of the three poses in which Whipple photographed her at the behest of her friend Harriet Sewall. "It has just your earnest, sincere look," commented David. "There is only one way in which a better *could* be obtained; and that is . . . when your face was all beaming with some thought or emotion." Child herself found it "positively handsome & ladylike" and was delighted that Whipple had succeeded in making her "plain old phiz present such a good appearance to posterity."

Engraving of Child at age 63, by F. T. Stuart, Boston, after the photograph by John Adams Whipple, 1865; the best known of the three poses for which Child sat, it represented her as "wearing the somewhat defiant look of 'a strong-minded woman,' and a reformer," she remarked wryly. By permission of The Schlesinger Library, Radcliffe College.

Photograph of David Lee Child at age 75, taken in 1870;
courtesy Library of Congress.

Photograph of the Childs' cottage in Wayland, Massachusetts;
by permission of the Wayland Historical Society.

19

Visions of a Reconstructed America:
The Freedmen's Book and *A Romance of the Republic*

We have passed through the Red Sea, and here we are in the Wilderness, with multitudes ready to bow down, and worship the golden calf of trade and a doubtful sort of Moses, who seems to occupy himself more earnestly with striving to save the drowning host of pharaoh than he does with leading Israel into the promised land.[1]

Dominating the front page of the *Liberator*'s valedictory issue, Child's "Through the Red Sea into the Wilderness" expresses the intermingled jubilation and anxiety with which abolitionists contemplated the evolving political scene in the closing months of 1865. The article's prominent placement in the historic number marking the culmination of Garrison's antislavery career testifies to his recognition that the writer he had long ago hailed as the *"first woman in the republic"* now occupied the rank of the "first woman" in the abolitionist movement. No other woman and few (if any) men had published more for the antislavery cause over a period of thirty-five years. Indeed, by 1865 Child had attained the status of an antislavery oracle, with the *Liberator*, the *Standard*, and the New York *Independent* (an evangelical abolitionist organ that boasted a circulation of 70,000) vying for her contributions and featuring them as lead articles.[2] A graceful tribute, Garrison's gesture of opening the last number of the *Liberator* with Child's retrospective account of the abolitionist movement linked her with the paper's history. She returned the compliment in her own tribute the following week to "The *Liberator* and Its Work," where she credited Garrison with converting her to abolitionism.[3]

Taking stock in December 1865 of the "marvellous changes" that had occurred since she had first begun "to think seriously on the destiny and dangers of this country," Child saw many reasons to rejoice. For decades none but abolitionists had noticed "the supplicating figure of the slave standing behind the minister in his pulpit, the judge upon the bench, the writer at his desk, and senators and presidents taking their oath of office." Now the "black man," no longer supplicating but erect, as behooved a brother-in-arms who had helped the Union win the Civil War, pervaded "every form of art and literature." The "best press in the country" had just published a book designed "to encourage the black men of the South, and to diminish prejudice against color at the North" (Child's *The Freedmen's Book*). Sold at "the elegant store of Ticknor & Fields," it was not "exciting . . . any distaste in the numerous clerks" (unlike Child's *Appeal*, which had met such a hostile reception in 1833).[4] Statues commemorated the invaluable assistance of slaves who had guided wounded soldiers through the swamps to Union lines. Paintings celebrated the bravery of black soldiers who had borne the U.S. flag triumphantly through battle. Even more hearteningly, "patriotism had so far conquered prejudice" that ordinary citizens in the streets were treating black men in uniform with the respect they deserved — a sight that "repaid [Child] for thirty years of conflict."

"We early Abolitionists, you know, dreamed of great miracles to be wrought by moral influence," Child reminded her readers. She added wryly: "We greeted [James G.] Birney, and [James A.] Thome, and the Grimkes" — the small cohort of repentant slaveholders who had joined forces with abolitionists in the 1830s — "as forerunners of a regenerated South. We were mistaken in that." "[D]espotism" had guarded the South so strictly that "the leaven of freedom could be worked in only by the sword." Nevertheless, Child emphasized, abolitionist "warnings, exhortations, and rebukes" *had* leavened "the whole cold mass of public sentiment" in the North, so that "when the inevitable time for the sword came," the northern public was ready "to meet the grand emergency."

After thirty-five years of agitation, slavery was finally "abolished, and cast out of the Constitution" by the newly ratified Thirteenth Amendment. This achievement would stand as a monument to the "courage, self sacrifice and liberality of the working classes" — the rank and file of the abolitionist movement, according to Child. It would preserve the spirit if not the names of anonymous heroes like the washerwoman Child remembered from the Boston Female Anti-Slavery Society, who had "wiped the suds from her arms" when notified of the next meeting after the group's October 1835 mobbing and had said "with an air that might have defied armies: 'So you expect a mob [again], do you? I'll *certainly* be there.'" Humble though they might be, Child underscored, "[s]uch agents constitute the foundation of society; and when society heaves at its foundations, strong castles are destined to fall."

As Child gauged the challenges that lay ahead, however, she discerned worrisome signs that the fruits of abolitionists' hard-won victory were being stolen from them. Andrew Johnson had not lived up to his promise to be a Moses to African Americans. Since June he had been issuing wholesale pardons to ex-Confederates, restituting their property rights in the confiscated plantations Child had hoped the U.S. government would divide into forty-acre homesteads and allocate to Union soldiers, freedmen, and poor whites. Johnson had also indicated his willingness to readmit the former Confederate states into the Union with minimal changes in their proslavery constitutions and no provisions for black suffrage. Such a procedure would result in a Congress even more dominated by the South than before the war, for unlike slaves, who each had counted as three-fifths of a person in the census determining state representation, each free black would count as one person. Disfranchised themselves, but used to increase their former masters' voting power in Congress, the freedpeople would be entirely at the mercy of a class bent on keeping them in a condition of quasislavery. Already several of the ex-Confederate states, emboldened by Johnson's leniency, had passed draconian Black Codes restoring slavery in all but name. Meanwhile anti-black violence had reached epidemic proportions. Yet Johnson was rapidly demobilizing troops, withdrawing garrisons from the South, and replacing commanders sympathetic to the freedpeople with pro-southern bigots.[5]

To elucidate the lessons of these setbacks, Child reverted to the biblical typology she had so often invoked during the war. Like the children of Israel, she observed, the American people had left the Egypt of slavery behind them and safely crossed the Red Sea of war, which had swallowed up the institution responsible for their woes. As with the Israelites, who had wandered in the wilderness for forty years before arriving in the Promised Land, Americans were finding the next phase of their progress toward freedom beset with pitfalls. In the absence of Moses, the Israelites had gathered around his brother Aaron and persuaded him to help them resurrect the Egyptian cult of the golden calf. The American people were following the same pattern. "[M]ultitudes ready to bow down, and worship the golden calf of trade" were pressing to reestablish economic ties with the South as soon as possible. Having lost their Moses, they had found a pliant tool in his successor. But the golden calf could never lead Americans to the Promised Land. They would remain in the wilderness until they returned to the worship of the true God — the creed of liberty and equality enshrined in their Declaration of Independence.

Shifting from allegory to direct political commentary, Child warned against the ominous implications of the president's December 1865 message to Congress (which had just reconvened after an eight-month recess).[6] Johnson's assurances that the freedmen would be " 'protected in their rights as *laborers*' " suggested "a distinction between the rights of *men* and the rights of *laborers*" that "would be deemed an insult to Yankee working men, or Irish laborers," she objected. His claim that the U.S. government had no right to regulate suffrage in the rebel states was equally specious. In response, Child addressed her own New Year's message to Congress: Johnson must be prevented from carrying out his Reconstruction program. "The Republican members stand in solid phalanx, facing in the right direction," she wrote encouragingly. "May Heaven preserve them from the old chronic disease of Congress — weakness of the spine!"[7]

This eloquent article sums up the political stance Child assumed during the fateful interval that historians have termed "Presidential Reconstruction" (1865–66). It also points toward the explanation for a seeming paradox of Child's career as an abolitionist spokesperson — that she chose a moment when her political authority had reached new heights to redirect herself toward less overtly political modes of discourse as her primary media for guiding America through the transition from a slave society to an egalitarian republic: a reader (*The Freedmen's Book*, 1865) and a novel (*A Romance of the Republic*, 1867). True, she published a total of nine articles commenting on various subjects connected with Reconstruction, from the shortcomings of Johnson's policies to the debates over woman suffrage.[8] Unlike her earlier political writings, however —

which had called for concrete steps toward the goals of emancipation, black empower-ment, and racial equality—most of these articles registered her consternation as she helplessly watched America's "Ship of State . . . drifting into a Niagara-current" certain to "convey it to destruction."[9] The reasons for her loss of confidence in the efficacy of lobbying and campaigning, and the factors that prompted her to opt for the cultural rather than the political arena when she sought to propound her vision of a multiracial America, lay in the tragic derailment of Reconstruction under Andrew Johnson.

Beginning with heady expectations of building a genuinely egalitarian society, the early months of Johnson's presidency had caught abolitionists off guard and thrown them into disarray. Child's trajectory was typical. The favorable view of Johnson she had shared at the outset with the Radicals who would soon lead the campaign against him— including her friends Wendell Phillips, Charles Sumner, and George Julian—left her unprepared for a defection that initially appeared to be a misguided political ploy.[10] Though dismayed by the policy of amnesty and conciliation heralded in Johnson's first Reconstruction proclamations of May 29 and June 13, which paved the way for the readmission of North Carolina and Mississippi, Child tried to reserve judgment. After all, she told herself, Lincoln, too, had adopted a policy of conciliation at the start of his presidency, and with hindsight she had come to realize that the temporizing she had criticized so harshly had served to accomplish the very ends abolitionists had been pro-moting.[11] Moreover, her nephew-in-law George Luther Stearns had worked closely with Johnson while supervising the recruitment of black troops in Tennessee, and he retained great confidence in the president's " 'honesty, sincerity and ability,' " as well as in his openness to black suffrage.[12]

Another factor inhibiting Child from publicly censuring Johnson's course was the bitter political feuding between Garrison and Phillips, which tended to confuse the question of how to assess Johnson's conduct with the dilemma of how to avoid endors-ing either of the two veteran leaders at the expense of the other. Garrison and Phillips's disagreement on whether or not to support Lincoln in the 1864 electoral campaign had mushroomed into a dispute over the role abolitionists ought to play during Recon-struction. Garrison favored disbanding the American Anti-Slavery Society after the passage of the Thirteenth Amendment and channeling efforts toward African Ameri-can uplift into freedmen's aid and education. Originally disposed to give Lincoln's Reconstruction policy the benefit of the doubt, he extended that forbearance to Lin-coln's successor. Phillips, on the contrary, viewed the mission of the AASS as incomplete without a constitutional amendment conferring full citizenship rights, including suf-frage, on African Americans. Convinced by mid-June that Johnson was " 'implacably hostile' " to this objective, he mounted a "full-scale attack" on the president with the aim of forcing the Republican party to "repudiate his policy."[13]

The factional strife between Garrison and Phillips and the developing rupture be-tween the president and Radical Republicans deflected the campaign for the two main Reconstruction measures Child had begun advocating in 1864—black suffrage and land redistribution. Neither measure could be implemented without neutralizing

Johnson, who adamantly opposed both. That task properly fell to politicians, rather than to agitators, as Child implied when she ended "Through the Red Sea into the Wilderness" with the prayer that Republicans in Congress would stand fast. The tasks of abolitionists were to help equip the freedpeople for their new lives, to mobilize public support for black suffrage, and to create the consciousness appropriate for a multiracial, egalitarian society — the aims Child sought to fulfill in *The Freedmen's Book* and *A Romance of the Republic*.

Hence, during Reconstruction's early phase Child took little part in the drama that occupied center stage — the showdown between Congress and the president that culminated in Johnson's 1868 impeachment. "I try not to be excited about public affairs, since it is not in my power to modify them," she confided to Henrietta Sargent soon after perceiving the first signs of trouble in mid-June 1865.[14] Contrary to her practice during the war, she rarely corresponded with politicians and never sought to influence the Radicals' aims or strategy.[15] Nor did she ever publish a personal appeal to Johnson, as she had to Lincoln, though she may have hoped to sway him indirectly through her letters to the *Independent*.

Constituting her chief political statements of the period, the series of opinion pieces for the *Independent* titled "Letter[s] from Mrs. L. M[aria] Child" charted the progress of her disillusionment with Johnson. Their purpose was not to indict the president, however, for they maintained a posture of waiting for "decisive proof" before pronouncing him guilty of treachery.[16] Instead, Child's letters to the *Independent* served to reiterate the egalitarian principles at the heart of abolitionism — principles she feared Johnson may not have learned.

"What ails Andy Johnson?" Child's July 23 letter admitted asking "in tones of perplexity gradually deepening into distress. . . ." Some diagnosed the president as sharing "the prejudice of the poor whites against the negroes" and therefore deeming "the civil equality of negroes an obstacle" to the elevation of his own class, Child reported. She professed to demur. "Andy Johnson has heretofore shown himself to be a man of too much intellectual ability and largeness of vision to take such a narrow view of the subject," she argued, perhaps with an eye to recalling him to his better self:

> He must be aware that the best thing for each class in the community is to improve every class to the utmost. If any class is shut out from competition for the prizes of society, and divested of the responsibilities of such competition, it not only deprives that class of salutary educational influences for themselves, but it reacts unfavorably upon the classes more privileged. Slaveholders and poor whites have been more injured by Slavery, morally and intellectually, than the negroes have been.[17]

The message was well-suited to Johnson, but Child intended it principally for the American public, whose susceptibility to racist demagoguery she was attempting to counteract. The president's actions seemed to be unleashing the forces of bigotry, North and South, and lending respectability to Democratic propagandists who contended that the enfranchisement of African Americans would threaten white workers.

In reply, Child sought to persuade her readers that racial discrimination ultimately harmed everyone, and that all would benefit from the elimination of barriers to African Americans' advancement.

By the date of her next letter to the *Independent*, October 26, 1865, Child had privately concluded that southerners had "*bought*" the president. Unless appearances were utterly deceptive, it was a pity Lincoln's assassins had "failed in their purpose of killing Andy Johnson" with him, she remarked grimly to an abolitionist friend.[18] Publicly, however, Child still couched her "alarm" tentatively. "If Andy Johnson *does* fail to be the Moses he promised to be to a long-oppressed people," she prophesied: "if by fatuity, or perversity, or mismanagement, he makes all the sacrifices and sufferings of this people a dead loss: if he goes on proceeding in a way that will deprive us of any security for the future, he will be more deeply cursed by history than is Benedict Arnold, and he will deserve it."[19] Surely as a poor white from Tennessee, Johnson of all people ought to know that the promises of slaveholders could not be trusted, Child expostulated. In case her readers felt inclined toward misplaced charity, Child set them straight with an analogy they would have found irresistible, given the *Independent*'s evangelical orientation: "To trust men brought up in habits of slaveholding with any powers to oppress the emancipated is as rash as it would be to leave the key of the wine-cellar with a drunkard who promises fairly." Through this analogy, Child also alluded covertly to the president's tippling, betrayed in the frequently "*fuddled* sound" of his speeches, especially those addressing African Americans.[20]

A barometer of her most fervent loyalties, the occasion that elicited Child's first unqualified denunciation of Johnson was the insulting interview he held with a delegation of African American leaders in early February 1866. Headed by George T. Downing and Frederick Douglass, the delegation had come to lobby for black suffrage. In reply, Johnson had openly stated his opposition to enfranchising African Americans, claiming that the freedpeople's vote would be used by their former masters against poor whites and that a "war of races" would ensue if whites and blacks were "turned loose" on each other and "thrown together at the ballot-box" with "enmity and hate existing between them." He had gone on to suggest black emigration as the solution to the problem of mutual hatred, despite the disastrous failure of Lincoln's Colonization pilot project in 1864.[21]

Contrasting Johnson's "captious" treatment of the African American delegates with his "very courteous reception" of "Virginia rebels" the same week, Child accused him of having exchanged his blue uniform for a gray one — that is, of having become a turncoat. She went on to protest against "the obvious injustice and onesidedness" Johnson had shown in blaming blacks for causing the oppression and consequent enmity of poor whites. The reverse was true, she asserted: "The poor whites were the heady tools of the rich planters, to keep the negroes in the most abject degradation. . . . By the tone assumed in the conversation, one would suppose the negroes were guilty of a great crime in not being able to love a class of men who were ever zealous to flog them and hunt them with blood-hounds." Whichever party bore the responsibility for the enmity, she added caustically, mutual hatred hardly qualified poor whites to "vote *for*" the interests of the very group they wanted to bar from the polls. Nor did it justify urging blacks to emigrate. "[W]hy is not such reasoning equally applicable to the 'poor whites?'" exploded Child: "Why should not *they* be advised to leave their country for their country's good, if they cannot consent to live peaceably in it, under equal laws of protection and restraint? Everybody knows that the colored people are not the aggressors in the numerous outrages that occur at the South. The fact is, there is no need of *any* class being driven from the country."[22]

With the president's attitude toward African Americans now "too plain to be misunderstood," the nation was facing a "solemn" crisis, Child warned. All over the South, "returned rebel soldiers" were "murdering negroes, and ordering U.S. officers to depart." In response, Johnson was removing from office the most faithful guardians of the freedpeople's rights — men like General Rufus Saxton, who had spoken out passionately against the presidential decree restoring plantations to their antebellum proprietors and evicting the freedpeople from the lands they had been cultivating as their own.[23] The South was acting like "the victorious party, dictating terms to the conquered," and in the North all too many were "ready to fall back into their old habit of yielding to the arrogant demands of those haughty oligarchs." Only one remedy could save the nation from reverting to the antebellum status quo and reenacting the history that had led to "[t]his terrible war," Child stressed:

> The future of our country, for good or ill, depends upon [the people's] standing firmly by the cause of universal freedom and impartial justice now. The test is being applied to them, to prove whether they really and truly believe in the principles they boast of before the civilized world. What a shameful farce, to talk of a republican form of government where millions of citizens are not allowed to vote for the government that taxes them and drafts them into its armies! and where they are forbidden to be jurors in courts that have over them the power of life and death!

Child sent this letter to the *Independent* on February 14, 1866, with a cover note to Theodore Tilton, giving him "permission to strike out anything" he considered "too severe."[24] Perhaps she still harbored a faint hope that by muting their criticisms of the president, abolitionists could keep him from declaring war on the Radicals, splitting the Republican party, and effecting a realignment between conservative Republicans and Democrats (who had been assiduously wooing him for months).[25] If so, Johnson would free her from such compunctions before her article appeared in print. On February 19 he threw down the gauntlet by vetoing a bill extending the life of the Freedmen's Bureau, which Congress had established in March 1865 to "exercise a benevolent guardianship" over the emancipated slaves and to protect them from abuse.[26] Passed by large majorities in both the Senate and the House, the bill embodied moderate public consensus on the responsibility that the nation owed to the freedpeople. Johnson followed up his veto with a Washington's Birthday speech in which he assumed the mantle of the nation's Founding Father; went on to associate himself with Andrew Jackson, Lincoln, and Christ; claimed the crown of a martyr dedicated to preserving the Union and the Constitution against abolitionists and secessionists alike; and all but accused Sumner, Phillips, and Thaddeus Stevens (Pennsylvania's Republican congressman and the House's leading Radical) of plotting his assassination.[27]

For Child, this outrageous tirade was the cue to abandon all niceties. "If the President was not under the bewildering influence of whiskey," she asked in a blistering article for the *Independent*, sarcastically titled "The President of the United States," how could one escape inferring that "he had planned, with malice aforethought, to stir up the passions of a mob by imaginary charges against upright and honorable men, who disagreed with him in his theory of reconstruction"? However "mortifying" the spectacle of a drunken president, it was less dire than the possibility that "the head of the nation was consciously co-operating with rebels and copperheads for the overthrow of Northern principles of civilization and progress."[28]

The threat Child conjured up was very real. A month later, Johnson vetoed the Civil Rights Bill in the teeth of a nearly unanimous Republican vote for the measure. Even more than the creation of the Freedmen's Bureau, the passage of a law defining African Americans as U.S. citizens, spelling out the rights they were to "enjoy equally without regard to race," and invalidating discriminatory state codes, represented the fruit of the war.[29] The northern public may not have been ready for black suffrage, but it was not about to leave the former slaves without any legal protection, after the country had freed them at the cost of so much bloodshed. This time Congress overrode Johnson's veto. From then on, Congress would take the initiative in formulating Reconstruction policy. Yet the president's veto power would continue to pose a serious obstacle, forcing Republicans to mobilize a two-thirds majority for every reform they championed, and drastically limiting their options. Through appointments, pardons, proclamations, and other executive prerogatives, moreover, Johnson would continue to erode the gains of the war.[30]

Bitterly assessing the situation in the South a year after Appomattox, Child wrote in her last letter about Johnson for the *Independent*:

You remember that, in by-gone years, abolitionists were constantly warned of the danger of "turning the slaves loose upon their masters." President Johnson's policy is turning the masters loose upon their defenseless slaves, just as they were before the war; and the party that were so compassionate over the imaginary dangers to which oppressors might be exposed by a simple act of justice now have no compassion to spare over the frightful wrongs and outrages which those oppressors are constantly practicing on their helpless victims.[31]

The transmutation of a moral crusade into a political struggle between Congress and the president deprived Child of the role she had played since the Kansas crisis of 1856. She could no longer presume to advise Radical Republicans on policy or urge them to take stronger stands. The intricacies of trade-offs between different factions lay beyond her purview as a reformer, and she had always detested party jockeying. She also knew she could exert little influence on seasoned legislators who faced a choice between compromising with party moderates or allowing Johnson to seize the reins.

If she could not sway the politicians who held the destiny of the freedpeople in their hands, she could perform two missions that promised greater long-range results: empowering the freedpeople to obtain their rights for themselves; and undermining the racial prejudice that prevented her white compatriots from living up to their republican creed.[32] Thus, while Johnson and Radical Republicans were battling to determine the course of Reconstruction, Child devoted herself to completing her long-projected reader for the ex-slaves and to plotting out the novel of interracial marriage through which she symbolically reconstructed her country.

"I am at present very busy on 'The Freedmen's Book,'" Child informed Henrietta Sargent in a postscript to the letter voicing her first misgivings about "public affairs."[33] The task consisted not only in choosing and arranging selections that illustrated "colored intelligence, industry, and enterprise," but in rewriting most of the biographical sketches to compress "as *much* as possible in the *smallest space*" and to "simplify" the language for newly literate readers. "I am taking more pains with it than I should if it were intended for young princes, or sprigs of what men call nobility," she announced to Garrison, knowing how much he sympathized with her increasingly "tender feeling toward what are called 'the lower classes.'" Delighted to hear that the book would feature some samples of her own composition, Garrison took advantage of the opportunity to reiterate his admiration for her: "Every thing from your pen is read with the deepest interest and the highest satisfaction by multitudes; and your position, therefore, as a writer, is one of commanding influence. . . . [T]he millions who are now rejoicing that their fetters are broken have reason to bless your name, and look upon you as among their foremost deliverers."[34]

By late August 1865 Child was ready to to approach James T. Fields, who had published *Looking toward Sunset*, with a proposition. If he would "print & stereotype an edition of 2,000," which she calculated would cost $1,200, she would contract to "buy $600 dollars worth" and distribute them to the freedpeople at cost. "If they sell, I shall expend the money in buying *more* copies; and so on; keeping the $600 as a kind of floating capital, as long as the book continues to sell; and then use it in some other way for the Freedmen." Besides sharing in financing the project, Child engaged to minimize printing expenses by setting a strict page limit and arranging "to get as much into every page as is consistent with sizable type." Wherever blank spaces occurred between selections, she would "fill them up with short extracts," as she had in her anthology for the elderly. "I want economy rather than beauty consulted in the whole getting up; but I want the materials to be *strong*," she stipulated.[35]

To bolster the financial case for the undertaking, Child enclosed a letter from Ednah Dow Cheney, head of the Freedmen's Aid Association Committee on Teachers, attesting that the book would also have "'a rapid sale at the North.'" Cheney might be overestimating the book's commercial potential in the North, Child acknowledged with her customary honesty, but she thought she could safely guarantee Fields a "sale of more than 500 copies among the white people," and those could be retailed at a competitive price. She was anxious to have it published as soon as possible, she added, because "*just at this time*, the negro is invested with paramount interest," and the book "would have an important bearing on the Suffrage Question." Though written "*solely for the Freedmen*," it was designed to counteract white prejudice as well, by showcasing examples of black literary talent and intellectual achievement. Eliminating prejudice was "essential, to the welfare of the country," Child emphasized: "The two races are here together, and together they must stay. . . . Obviously, it is the most politic course, as well as the right course, to encourage mutual friendliness of feeling. It seems to me that such a book as this will be an agent in that good work; and therefore I wish to have it published *now*."[36]

To Child's "unspeakable joy," Fields agreed to the bargain and rushed the book through the press in time for the Christmas market.[37] Appropriately, it appeared a week before Congress reconvened in December 1865, as if to second the struggle for equal rights from another quarter.

Primer, anthology, history text, and self-help manual rolled into one, *The Freedmen's Book* anticipates twentieth-century progressive educators in conceptualizing the teaching of literacy as a process that starts with the cultivation of students' pride in their own identity.[38] Accordingly, all of the selections relate to African peoples' struggle to liberate themselves from slavery and racial proscription in the New World. The book's dedication to "the loyal and brave Captain Robert Small[s], *Hero of the Steamboat Planter*," signals its recognition of African Americans as both active agents in their own liberation and vital partners in the war for their country's soul; for Smalls, a Charleston slave, had commandeered a Confederate supply ship, delivered it into Union hands, and joined the U.S. Navy as a pilot, becoming "one of the most valuable assets of the Union blockade fleet in the South Atlantic."[39] Child's preface, "To the Freedmen," explicitly defines her purpose: to provide a "true record of what colored men have accomplished, under great disadvantages," and thereby to instill "fresh strength and courage" in readers facing the monumental challenge of lifting themselves out of the ignorance enforced on them by slavery. The pedagogical method Child recommends in the preface further conduces to developing racial pride; it enlists literate freedpeople as teachers by encouraging them to read the book aloud to their less-advanced comrades.[40]

As Child indicates in her cover letter to Fields: "The book has a continuous plan. It begins with Ignatius Sancho, because he was the *first* intelligent black of whom we have a record. It passes along through the groans and aspirations of slaves, the prayers and prophecies of their friends, till Toussaint L'Ouverture makes an *opening* for them. Then Emancipation in the West Indies. Then fugitive slaves hunted in the U.S. Then Emancipation in District of Columbia. Then Lincoln's Proclamation. Then jollification and jubilee."[41] Wherever possible, Child uses "colored authors" (marked with an asterisk in her table of contents) to commemorate the historical milestones on the road to "jubilee." Poems by James Madison Bell and Frances Harper hail "Emancipation in the District of Columbia" and "President Lincoln's Proclamation of Emancipation," and an article by Charlotte Forten captures the drama of Emancipation Day on the South Carolina sea islands. "Colored authors" account for approximately half the poems in the volume and three out of twenty-two full-length prose selections (the other two being Harriet Jacobs's portrait of her grandmother and the freedman Jourdon Anderson's sarcastic letter to his former master).

A dozen biographical sketches offer a variety of role models for the freedpeople to emulate: the poets Phillis Wheatley, George Horton, and Mingo; the astronomer Benjamin Banneker, compiler of the first almanac published in the United States; the revolutionaries Toussaint L'Ouverture and Madison Washington (leader of an 1841 slave uprising on the ship *Creole*); the self-made businessman and abolitionist James Forten; the pious self-emancipated Quaker William Boen; the resourceful fugitives William and Ellen Craft; and the orator-editor Frederick Douglass. Although Child retells their stories in her own words, she mentions the narratives published by Douglass and the Crafts, characterizing the former as "ably written" (174);[42] and she quotes copiously from the letters of Ignatius Sancho and Benjamin Banneker.

Clearly aimed at counteracting the sense of inferiority drummed into African Americans by racist ideology, the biographical sketches consistently underscore the innate intelligence their subjects display. They also show that whites have deliberately kept slaves in ignorance and fostered the myth of African inferiority because they regard intelligent subalterns as a threat. The masters of Sancho and Douglass explicitly oppose letting them learn to read and write, arguing that "knowledge [is] a very improper and dangerous thing for a black servant" (2, 165–66). Mingo's "talents would have secured him an honorable position" had he been white, "but being colored, his great intelligence only served to make him an object of suspicion," and "[h]e was thrown into prison, to be sold" (84). Banneker's "ignorant white neighbors" resented him "because he was black, and yet knew so much more than they did" (16). Allowing African Americans to speak in their own defense, Child quotes Banneker's famous letter to Jefferson: "Those of my complexion have long been considered rather brutish than human, — scarcely capable of mental endowments. . . . I apprehend you will readily embrace every opportunity to eradicate the absurd and false ideas and opinions which so generally prevail with respect to us" and that "you and others . . . [will] wean yourselves from those narrow prejudices you have imbibed. . ." (18–19).

No effort to combat anti-black prejudice or inculcate racial pride can succeed without overturning the image of African savagery, Child realizes. Thus, in her biographical sketches of Wheatley and Toussaint, she presents their African heritage in a positive light. Commenting on Wheatley's sole memory of Africa — "that she used to see her mother pour out water before the rising sun" — Child elucidates the significance of the ritual: "One of the most common modes of worship was to pour out water, or wine, at the rising of the sun, and to utter a brief prayer to the Spirit of that glorious luminary. Probably this ancient custom had been handed down, age after age, in Africa, and in that fashion the untaught mother of little Phillis continued to worship the god of her ancestors" (87). Rather than endorse Wheatley's own assertion (in a poem Child does not quote) that divine "mercy" had rescued her from paganism in her native Africa,[43] Child suggests that Wheatley may have derived her celebrated piety from her African mother and from nature itself: "The sight of the great splendid orb, coming she knew not whence, rising apparently out of the hills to make the whole world glorious with light, and the devout reverence with which her mother hailed its return every morning, might naturally impress the child's imagination . . . deeply. . ." (87). Child similarly accentuates the influence that Toussaint's African father exerted on him. The son of a chief belonging to a tribe "said to be superior" to most others "in intelligence and strength of will," Toussaint's father, Gaou-Guinou, taught him "a great deal about Africa and the customs that prevailed in the tribe of his grandfather, King of the Arradas; also the medicinal qualities of many plants, which afterward proved very useful to him" (33, 36). Child attributes Toussaint's upright moral character as much to the "lessons of honor and virtue" conveyed to him by his pagan-born father as to the Catholic theology preached by his missionary-trained godfather. True, she later refers to the "barbarous" condition of Africa, but she ascribes it to the slave trade, which she blames squarely on "nations calling themselves Christians." By causing "a constant state of warfare," she points out, the slave trade has "hindered the improvement of the Africans" (200).

Not only does Child root her biographies in a cultural context that she traces back to Africa and redefines as a source of pride rather than shame; she weaves into them a detailed analysis of the historical forces behind African peoples' oppression. The most impressive instance is the fifty-page account of the Santo Domingo uprising that frames her biography of Toussaint.[44] It opens with the Spaniards' conquest of Hayti (the island's indigenous name), their decimation of its native population, and their importation of slaves from Africa; describes the conflicting interests of eighteenth-century French Santo Domingo's various classes—wealthy planters, prosperous yet disfranchised mulattoes, *petit blancs* analogous to American "poor whites" (42), and hideously oppressed black slaves; explains how the French Revolution triggered and interacted with the rebellion of the island's slaves; and traces the uprising through its complex phases up to its victorious culmination in 1803. Child devotes special attention to the setbacks of the penultimate phase, which she obviously views through the prism of presidential Reconstruction. In a letter to Sumner she would later spell out the lesson she hoped readers would draw from the attempt of the French to reimpose slavery on Santo Domingo, and from Toussaint's tragic betrayal by Napoleon: "The great mistake of Toussaint was his disposition to sacrifice everything to his favorite project of conciliating the old planters. He thought he should secure their co-operation by forbearance and magnanimity. He was in a hurry to re-construct,—to restore outward prosperity. We all know what came of *his* confidence in slaveholders."[45] This particular lesson might seem better adapted to white readers than to the freedpeople, who hardly needed to be warned against misplaced confidence in slaveholders. However, the historical information Child intercalates into her biographies (and amplifies in a separate chapter on the results of emancipation in the British West Indies) serves larger purposes: to demonstrate that white profiteers bear the primary responsibility for the poverty and backwardness of the African peoples they have enslaved; to empower the freedpeople by acquainting them with their heritage of resistance to oppression; and to enable them to learn from the experiences of other societies that have undergone the transition from slavery to freedom.

Of course, the biographical sketches in *The Freedmen's Book*, like those Child featured in the *Juvenile Miscellany* and *Looking toward Sunset*, also inculcate moral values. The bourgeois virtues of industry, sobriety, honesty, frugality, and perseverance figure prominently in the lives of Banneker, William Boen, Toussaint, James Forten, and Harriet Jacobs's grandmother. By contrast, Ignatius Sancho's lapses illustrate the consequences of failing to practice these virtues: "He accepted invitations to go to taverns, where he gambled away his earnings" (3). Yet Sancho's reformation also reassures freedpeople who share his propensities that they, too, can reform. His patrons encourage him to "persevere in his good resolutions," and when they see that he continues "sober and industrious," they reemploy him, enabling him, with "economy," to regain a comfortable living and "educate well a numerous family of children" (3). Ultimately, Sancho himself becomes a mouthpiece of bourgeois virtues, urging his fellow blacks and his white friends alike to follow the path of rectitude, avoid "heedless extravagance," and invest in knowledge and self-improvement (6–8).

Aware that members of an oppressed group can easily swing from abject self-deprecation to an exaggerated sense of their attainments, Child stresses the virtue of modesty as well. She holds up Banneker and Wheatley as exemplars. "[F]lattery and attention" do not turn their heads (17, 89). Both handle white prejudice not by entering into personal confrontations, but by endeavoring "to live in such a way that [whites] could not help respecting" them (17). Nevertheless, they use their intellectual gifts to protest against the " 'tyrannical thraldom' " and " 'absurd' " prejudices that victimize their people (18–19, 90).

Of all the values Child commends through her biographical sketches, none ranks higher than dedication to the cause of collective freedom. Every one of her black achievers speaks out against slavery, and many perform great sacrifices for their people: boycotting slave-grown sugar and cotton (Boen); supporting abolition societies with their earnings and consecrating their lives to the antislavery cause (Forten and Douglass); risking punishment to teach slaves to read, staging collective escapes and uprisings, and braving recapture to liberate others (Douglass and Madison Washington); working for the relief and uplift of the freedpeople (Jacobs).

In addition to these indirect vehicles of moral instruction, Child includes six short pieces offering direct counsels to the freedpeople. Speeches by Senator Henry Wilson of Massachusetts and Judge William D. Kelley of Pennsylvania remind the newly emancipated slaves that liberty does not mean idleness, but "the liberty to work for yourselves, to have the fruits of your labor, to better your own condition, and improve the condition of your children" (260). Four essays by Child herself distill the lessons expounded in her domestic advice books and adapt them to men and women emerging from slavery: "Kindness to Animals," "Education of Children," "The Laws of Health," and "Advice from an Old Friend." The common thread linking them is the premise that the freedpeople must learn to overcome the dehumanizing habits ingrained in them by long abuse. Abuse sets off a chain reaction, Child suggests. Its victims do violence to each other, their children, their own bodies, other living creatures, and the environment. Liberation must therefore reverse the process.

For example, in explaining the importance of cleanliness for preventing disease, Child writes: "Dirt was a necessity of Slavery; and that is one reason, among many others, why freemen should hate it, and try to put it away from their minds, their persons, and their habitations" (249–50). She uses the same argument in promoting the gentle style of childrearing she had advocated in *The Mother's Book* (1831): "It is hard for children born in Slavery to grow up spiritually straight and healthy, because they are trodden on when they are little. Being constantly treated unjustly, they cannot learn to be just." To avoid reproducing their own "stunted growth," ex-slaves must be doubly "careful not to tread upon" their children, Child cautions (222). They must totally repudiate their slave upbringing: "The system of Slavery was all penalty and no attraction; in other words, it punished men if they did *not* do, but it did not reward them for *doing*. In the management of your children you should do exactly the opposite of this. You should appeal to their manhood, not to their fears" (224).

The most remarkable of these hortatory essays is "Advice from an Old Friend," in which Child applies the lessons encoded in her biographical sketches and historical disquisitions. The accomplishments of the men and women whose lives she has related "prove that the power of *character* can overcome all external disadvantages, even that most crushing of all disadvantages, Slavery," she asserts. Though her readers may lack the talents of a Douglass, a Charlotte Forten, or a Toussaint, they can at least emulate these models in contributing to the work of global liberation: "You can do a vast amount of good to people in various parts of the world, and through successive generations, by simply being sober, industrious, and honest." Such good conduct will demonstrate that " 'negroes *can* take care of themselves' " and thus help in the "emancipation of poor weary slaves" in Brazil, Cuba, and other countries (269–70). At the same time, Child warns that the transition from "Slavery to Freedom" will be slow and painful. American slaveholders, like those of Jamaica, may try to "drive their emancipated bondmen to insurrection." If so, American freedpeople should follow their Jamaican counterparts' example: "[T]he colored people of Jamaica . . . left the plantations where they were badly treated, or poorly paid, but they worked diligently elsewhere. Their women and children raised vegetables and fowls and carried them to market; and, by their united industry and economy, they soon had comfortable little homes of their own" (273–74).

Turning from historical analogy to the actual situation in the unreconstructed South, Child writes: "I am grieved to read in the newspapers how wickedly you are still treated in some places; but I am not surprised, for I knew that Slavery was a powerful snake, that would try to do mischief with its tail after its head was crushed" (275). Although she exhorts the freedpeople not to retaliate in kind, she specifies:

I do not mean by this that you ought to submit tamely to insult or oppression. Stand up for your rights, but do it in a manly way. Quit working for a man who speaks to you contemptuously, or who tries to take a mean advantage of you, when you are doing your duty faithfully by him. If it becomes necessary, apply to magistrates to protect you and redress your wrongs. If you are so unlucky as to live where the men in authority, whether civil or military, are still disposed to treat the colored people as slaves, let the most intelligent among you draw up a statement of your grievances and send it to some of your firm friends in Congress, such as the Hon. Charles Sumner, the Hon. Henry Wilson, and the Hon. George W. Julian. (274-75)

In short, Child urges the freedpeople to act through the legal and political channels that emancipation has theoretically opened to them. Already, however, the tactics recommended by Child were proving utterly impotent to defend the freedpeople against the counterrevolution they faced. Leaving an exploitative or abusive employer would not avail them when their employers had formed a cabal to keep them in quasislavery. Nor would resorting to magistrates help when magistrates belonged to that cabal. Petitions to Congress would work only as long as their "firm friends" remained in power. Child clearly recognizes the problem, but she sees no viable short-term solution.[46]

Through *The Freedmen's Book* she offers the key to a long-term solution: education. With that key, Child hopes, the children of America's emancipated slaves will ultimately obtain justice and equality for themselves. She explicitly articulates this message in one of the three pieces of fiction she includes in the volume: "The Meeting in the Swamp," a simplified version of her 1841 story "The Black Saxons." There, a self-taught slave resolves the debate among his fellows over whether "we [could] keep our freedom without we killed the whites," when he says: " 'Many a time I'se axed myself how de white man always git he foot on de black man. . . .' He took from his old torn hat a bit of crumpled newspaper, and smoothing it out, pointed at it, while he exclaimed: '*Dat's* de way dey do it! Dey got de *knowledge*; and dey don't let poor nigger hab de knowledge. . . . I tell ye, boys, de white man can't keep he foot on de black man, ef de black man git de knowledge' " (106, 108).[47]

From our late twentieth-century perspective, some of us might wish Child had presented education not as a substitute for revolution but as one of its weapons; that she had advocated greater militancy and less reliance on the goodwill of white lawmakers. We might also wish she had included among her African American authors a voice summoning the slaves to take up arms against their oppressors — an extract from David Walker's *Appeal* or Henry Highland Garnet's 1843 "Address to the Slaves of the United States of America," for example. And we might wish she had supplemented or replaced her samples of white-authored antislavery fiction — the "Sam and Andy" episode from *Uncle Tom's Cabin*, which caricatures blacks as clowns, and Mattie Griffith's "Ratie," which portrays them as pathetic victims — with a chapter from Martin Delany's *Blake*, whose title character organizes his fellow slaves into revolutionary cells and later leads a slave uprising in Cuba.[48] If Child had oriented *The Freedmen's Book* toward preaching rebellion rather than toward fostering "mutual friendliness of feeling," however, no commercial publisher would have issued it. More to the point, *The Freedmen's Book* should be judged by the standards of its day; and by those standards, Child reveals extraordinary sensitivity to the needs of a people striving to develop political consciousness and racial pride. It would take more than a century for the American educational establishment to grasp the principle that informs her pioneering textbook of 1865: that students learn best when the curriculum nurtures their self-esteem by affirming their cultural identity.

A brief comparison of *The Freedmen's Book* with its chief rival — *The Freedman's Third Reader*, published by the American Tract Society[49] — strikingly illustrates how far Child had advanced beyond the concept of education that predominated in her time. Unlike *The Freedmen's Book*, the American Tract Society's primer aims first and foremost to inculcate evangelical piety; secondarily, it seeks to promote unquestioning patriotism. The goals of Christianization and Americanization leave no room for acknowledging either alternative values or contradictions between precept and practice. Out of 143 lessons in *The Freedman's Third Reader*, more than twenty convey sectarian religious instruction. For example, Lesson 1 on "The Creation" asserts with magisterial disregard of other religions' sacred texts: "We have no account of the creation of the world except what we find in the Bible." The same bigotry pervades the lessons on secular subjects. An article on "Europe" contrasts the high standard of civilization that the "religion of Jesus Christ" fosters there with the ignorance and degradation that reign in Asia and Africa, where the people espouse the "false religion of Mohammed" or "bow down to idols of wood, stone, or metal." Correspondingly, an article on "Africa" notes that slavery persisted there after it had come "into general disuse" in "countries where the Christian religion prevailed" — a blatant obfuscation of the role Christian nations played in perpetuating the slave trade.[50]

The treatment of American history is similarly duplicitous. An essay on "The American Indians" credits the settlers of New England with having "made efforts to Christianize" them and laments that "as a race, [the Indians] are passing away."[51] The story of Columbus does not mention his enslavement of the Indians. The articles on the Declaration of Independence and the Revolution paper over the coexistence of slavery with ideals of liberty and equality. A total of eight selections apotheosize Lincoln as the Great Emancipator and hold up his career path from a log cabin to the presidency as a pattern all Americans can realistically emulate.

No selections by African Americans appear in *The Freedman's Third Reader*, although the book does offer nine biographical sketches of blacks: Father Henson (said to be the model for Stowe's Uncle Tom), Paul Cuffee (the earliest proponent of emigration to Africa), Lott Carey (who went to Liberia as a missionary), the Reverend Dr. Pennington (a prominent African American minister), the *Amistad* captives (native Africans who had mutinied aboard a Spanish slave ship, undergone a long trial in American courts, eventually converted to Christianity, and returned to their homeland as missionaries), a hero of the Massachusetts Fifty-fourth (who was allegedly "hoping to prepare himself for the gospel ministry"), and Wheatley, Toussaint, and Douglass. Nearly all the sketches emphasize piety more than intelligence, resourcefulness, or militancy, and the choice of several figures connected with emigration to Africa betrays the American Tract Society's strong Colonizationist bias.

In contrast to those in *The Freedmen's Book*, the biographical sketches of blacks in *The Freedman's Third Reader* consistently portray even the most enterprising of their subjects as recipients of white bounty and minimize or erase their acts of rebellion. Accordingly, the account of the *Amistad* captives devotes one sentence to their uprising, dwelling instead on the "benevolent gentlemen [who] interested themselves in [the captives'] welfare" and conversion. The biography of Douglass entirely omits his famous battle with the hypocritical Methodist slavebreaker Covey (which Child faithfully rehearses), but it expatiates on his conversion experience; it then climaxes with the gifts Douglass receives from his "friends in England" — the purchase of his freedom and the donation of a printing press. Most telling is the elision of the Santo Domingo uprising from the biography of Toussaint: "War having broken out in St. Domingo between the French and Spaniards, involving both the free people of color and the slaves, Toussaint joined his brethren in arms, and stepped in a moment from slavery to freedom." The slaves' rebellion becomes a parenthesis in a war between white European nations, and their victory over their oppressors becomes once again a gift to them: "in 1794, the French Government proclaimed all the slaves in St. Domingo free. . . ." Not only does *The Freedman's Third Reader* suppress the history of European rapacity and African resistance that Child had so painstakingly reconstructed for her newly emancipated audience; its authors also praise the very aspect of Toussaint's policy that Child had privately criticized as a "great mistake": his subordination of the former slaves' welfare to the objective of restoring prosperity as soon as possible.[52]

The differences between the two readers did not escape the freedpeople themselves. According to teachers in the field, their students exhibited a clear preference for *The Freedmen's Book*. "Their appreciation of all allusions to slave life and hardships is very marked," reported one teacher. "Sometimes they say, 'Ah, Miss Alice, we could tell you bigger things than that!'" By recording rather than glossing over those hardships, Child's text performed the therapeutic function of allowing the ex-slaves to "speak bitterness" (as Chinese communists would later put it). Child's niece Abby Francis, who was teaching at a freedmen's school in Richmond, also observed that her students derived positive lessons from the sketches of fugitives who had refused to accept their lot. "If I hadn't been a fool, I should have run away years ago, as Frederick Douglass and William Crafts did," an elderly freedman told her after she had read their stories to him. Another teacher noted how enthusiastically his students responded to selections like James Madison Bell's poem "Emancipation in the District of Columbia," which they recited "with so much expression that it seems as if they were talking their own thoughts." On one occasion, he recalled, when a fourteen-year-old boy was declaiming this poem to an audience from the community, "an old woman who was present was so affected that she vented her feelings with a *heavy sigh*, from a heart that had ached oft on account of the evils of that 'accursed thing,' slavery." No doubt she was reacting to the lines:

> The slaver's pen, the auction-block,
> The gory lash of cruelty,
>   No more this nation's pride shall mock;
> No more, within those ten miles square,
>   Shall men be bought and women sold. . . .

Because *The Freedmen's Book* analyzed and historicized as well as articulated the experience of oppression, it additionally sharpened students' critical faculties. "I have a feeling that they have improved, not only in the mere point of reading, but in thought and understanding, even in the short time they have been reading the book," commented the same teacher who had mentioned her class's decision to substitute *The Freedmen's Book* for the *Third Reader*.[53]

Unfortunately, despite its greater popularity with the freedpeople and their teachers (at least those from liberal religious backgrounds), *The Freedmen's Book* could not compete financially with a text backed by the well-funded American Tract Society and adopted in schools run by the equally well-funded American Missionary Association. Most freedpeople were too poor to be able to purchase the book, even at the low price of sixty cents a copy. As a result, Child could not maintain her "floating capital" of $600. Although she expended $875 "from [her] own purse" in sending copies of *The Freedmen's Book* to the South, she could not afford to continue at that rate. In 1869 she finally decided to ask the wealthy Evangelical abolitionist Lewis Tappan, a founder of the American Missionary Association, if his organization would adopt her book for classroom use, or at least purchase and distribute five hundred copies at cost. When he replied that the AMA would do so only if permitted "to cut out several articles, and in lieu thereof insert orthodox tracts" on Christian doctrine, Child indignantly declined.[54] Rather than let *The Freedmen's Book* be turned into a duplicate of *The Freedman's Third Reader*, she elected to keep the book in circulation as best she could through her limited means. But the progressive education she tried to offer as an alternative to catechism in the dominant value system could not survive without an infrastructure to support it. By the mid-1870s Congress had cut off funding for freedpeople's education, and a severe economic depression had forced most freedmen's aid associations to retrench or dissolve. Ultimately, Evangelical churches and missionary societies would control the process of remolding ex-slaves into pious and patriotic American citizens.[55]

In enlisting James T. Fields's sponsorship of *The Freedmen's Book*, Child had confessed an ulterior motive for the project — "to soften prejudice in the minds of white people."[56] The reeducation of white Americans, she realized, was as vital to the future health of the country as the education of the former slaves. Indeed, the two had to proceed simultaneously, since African Americans could not enjoy the benefits of education as long as whites blocked the avenues of advancement. Though expecting the biographies and black-authored selections in *The Freedmen's Book* to have a "reflex" impact on white opinion, Child did not intend to rely on an indirect appeal to her white audience. As she had prepared her reader especially for the freedpeople, so she produced a companion volume especially for their white fellow citizens.

At the dawn of her public career Child had intuitively gravitated toward the theme that prefigured her lifelong crusade for an equal union of America's diverse peoples — interracial marriage. Long before embracing the antislavery cause, she had challenged racial prejudice in her fiction. It was altogether fitting that once the immediate goal of abolition had been achieved, she should return in her twilight years to the still unsolved problem of prejudice, and it was almost inevitable that she should likewise return to the medium of fiction through which she had first approached it. As she wrote to Francis Shaw, "Having fought against *slavery* till I saw it go down in the Red Sea, I wanted to do something to undermine *prejudice*; and there is such a universal passion for novels, that more can be done in that way, than by the ablest arguments, and the most serious exhortations."[57]

The desire to stretch her wings again in the realm of the imagination had been growing on Child for almost a decade, but circumstances had repeatedly thwarted the impulse. In 1858 she had written a long story for the *Atlantic* — "Loo Loo. A Few Scenes from a True History" — that provided the nucleus of the plot she would subsequently expand into *A Romance of the Republic*. Lush and sensuous, "Loo Loo" seemed to presage the renascence of the sexual energy that had animated stories like "Hilda Silfverling" and "She Waits in the Spirit Land" at the height of Child's literary creativity. But immediately after its publication, the death of Ellis Loring had plunged her back into a crippling depression. Over the next few years, political concerns had dominated her consciousness and absorbed her intellectual powers. Still, she had recurrently felt drawn to express her vision of the nation's political future in fiction. At the very beginning of the war, perhaps impelled by the same quest for an alternative to racial conflict that had led her to the metaphor of interracial marriage in *Hobomok*, she had conceived her most original story of Indian-white reconciliation and assimilation, "Willie Wharton."[58] Some time the following year, probably during one of the phases when she was "so tired of the whole dreadful business" that she could no longer bear to think or read about the war,[59] Child drafted the first few chapters of the novel that later flowered into *A Romance of the Republic*. Overcome by a sense of "discouragement," however, she laid the manuscript aside. "I probably should never have finished it, if Mr. Fields had not earnestly importuned me to write a continuous story for the Atlantic," she admitted to Francis Shaw.[60]

While testing her wings, Child was also broadening her literary horizons. She read voraciously with a heedful eye to new literary trends, concentrating on novels by women. They had outdistanced male writers in their mastery of fiction, she judged. The trend toward realism in characterization, subject matter, and plot particularly interested her. "There is as much difference between the characters in the best novels now and in those of the olden time, as there is between the prim old portraits and the life-like photographs," she commented perceptively. "In by-gone times people liked to have their portraits taken in an *attitude*, sentimental shepherdesses with a crook, &c; and it was very much the same with the spiritual portraiture given in books. Now, how it has all changed!"[61] As if to measure the change, she tried in the winter of 1865 to reread some of the best novels of her earliest literary mentor, Sir Walter Scott, "and really his historical characters seemed like pasteboard processions on the stage, compared with [the] *living* characters" of her current favorites, Harriet Beecher Stowe and George Eliot.[62] Unlike Scott's, Stowe's characters were "all real people. One sees and knows them, as they do their friends and neighbors." With mischievous gusto, Child pointed out that Stowe elevated fidelity to human nature above moral instruction, "even at the expense of making her sinners more entertaining than her saints." What she most relished in Stowe was her "close, sly, humorous observation of the details of human life."[63] Child ranked George Eliot still higher. "I consider her the greatest woman writer that ever lived; and further even than *that*, I will say that *no* writer, *man or* woman, ever made such a powerful impression on me," she asserted boldly. "It seems to me that no writer since Shakespeare has had such insight into human nature . . .; and she *uses* her insight to far better purpose, so thoroughly is her soul pervaded by loving sympathy for the *common people*." The lowly heroes created by Eliot and Stowe — "Adam Bede the carpenter, Silas Marner the weaver, Uncle Tom, and Old Tiff" (a slave character in Stowe's *Dred*) attracted Child both because they embodied the ethic of the working classes and because they portended the advent of a new era when art would be "employed . . . in the service of the *common people*," distinctions of birth and wealth would melt away, "the devil of *property*" would be "exorcise[d] . . . out of human society," and the "dignity of labor" would be universally acknowledged in practice as well as in principle. Her literary tastes reflected her egalitarian values, Child explained to Lucy Osgood (who did not share this "ingrained democracy"): "Aristocracy is *always* my aversion, whether in the form of English noble, Southern planter, or Boston respectable. . . . I honestly *believe* in the dignity of labor. I say truly, with Eppie, in Silas Marner, 'I *like* the working-people; I like their ways.' "[64]

Along with the tendencies toward realistic characters and democratic themes, Child noted a shift away from the traditional plot culminating in marriage. "How different from the *old* style of novels!" she wrote enthusiastically of two recent works Sarah Shaw had sent her — Dinah Mulock Craik's *The Woman's Kingdom* (1868) and *A Brave Lady* (1869–70) — which exemplified the new literary mode. Praising the innovation of "[b]eginning after marriage, and depending for . . . [plot] interest entirely on the bravery with which the conflicts, and disappointments of a married life are met," she exclaimed: "But what unwritten romances we have all experienced. If we only dared to write them, how they would thrill the readers!"[65] Child did not dare to write the story of her own "conflicts, and disappointments" in married life. Yet when she at last felt ready to deliver the novel that had been gestating in her consciousness for so many years, she did carry her narrative beyond marriage into the next generation and showed her characters developing and changing in realistic ways. Her subject would not be her individual "unwritten romance"; instead, as she hinted to Sarah in the same letter, it was the collective Romance of the American Republic, then being written on the stage of history: "It is a seething cauldron, this great nation. There is a great simmering together of Jew and Gentile, Catholic and Protestant, extreme Asiatics, and extreme

Westerners, Red, and White, Yellow and Black. What will be the product, God alone knows; but I have faith that it will be good, and that we shall fulfil our mission as 'vanguard of the human race.' "[66]

The stimulus that seems to have revived Child's inclination to turn her hand to fiction again was the pleasure she derived from writing the two most "romantic" biographical sketches in *The Freedmen's Book* — the stories of Madison Washington and William and Ellen Craft. Both narratives read more like fiction than like biography. The factual details of the Crafts' thousand-mile escape across the South — Ellen disguised as an ailing planter and William as her faithful bodyservant — and of Washington's unexpected discovery that his wife, Susan, was among the slaves liberated by the revolt he had led on board the *Creole* were intrinsically "romantic." In addition, the enormous risks the two slave couples undertook to preserve their marriages from desecration seem to have appealed potently to Child's imagination. The interracial appearance of their unions must also have intrigued her. Both Susan Washington and Ellen Craft were light-skinned enough to pass for white, while Madison Washington was an "unmixed black" and William Craft a "black man" (147, 179). Even before she had finished correcting the proofs of *The Freedmen's Book*, Child announced to Fields that she had "a plot formed for a story of a number of chapters," which she thought might do for the *Atlantic*. "[W]hether I can carry out my ideas is uncertain," she warned. "When one gets to be between sixty and seventy, imaginations will not always come when they are called for; and my Pegasus is somewhat stiff in the joints, from having had a heavy cart-load of stones to drag for many years" (a metaphor curiously recalling David's stint at carting stones in Northampton).[67]

For well over a year Child heatedly denied that she was actually writing a novel. "A story for the Atlantic is the utmost I should venture to try my old brain upon," she assured Louisa Loring.[68] "[T]hat distrust of my faculties, which is apt to trouble old people" would continue to dog Child during the entire composition of her new "romance." "I am somewhat nervous about it; feeling all the while as if I were too old to write imaginative things," Child confessed to Fields in September 1866, after she had "sketched 18 short chapters." "[W]hether the spinning will be fit for market, I know not."[69] Her complaints about flagging inspiration and diminished self-confidence echo the worries she had voiced in the early 1850s while wrestling with writing blocks after John Hopper's marriage and her reunion with David. The evocation of this long-buried phase of her life is suggestive, for Child was not only tapping the same imaginative sources that she had in her fiction of the 1840s, but she was contending with drains on her energy similar to those that had paralyzed her in the 1850s. "Mr. Child has been ill very frequently [with chronic diahrrea] during the past ten months; which has added to my daily cares, beside producing an anxious state of mind, unfavorable to writing," she informed Fields in February 1867, admitting that she had "several times been tempted to . . . give it up."[70] As in the 1850s, material impediments accounted for only part of the difficulty. Then, Child's fears of offending the audience she was striving to enlighten had stymied her work on *The Progress of Religious Ideas*. Now, her concerns about the direction Reconstruction was taking chilled her faith in the utopian future she was seeking to map out for her country in *A Romance of the Republic*. "I should have more heart for work, if that tipsy tailor [Andrew Johnson] were not so misguiding the Ship of State," she lamented to Fields: "To have for Captain, in a storm, a man not fit for a cabin boy! I feel very anxious and despondent about the prospects of my poor protégées, the freedmen. There was such a capital chance to place the Republic on a safe and honorable foundation, and we have lost it, by the narrow prejudices and blind self-will of that 'poor white'!"[71] The mission of her novel would be precisely to combat those "narrow prejudices" in all whites, so as to "place the Republic on a safe and honorable foundation." But the task of completing this ambitious capstone of her literary and political career would stretch over more than eighteen months.

Meanwhile, Child limbered the "stiff . . . joints" of her Pegasus by taking wing in a series of "High-Flying Letter[s]" for the *Independent* that strikingly resemble her former *Letters from New York*. Replicating the message of her novel in another medium, they scan the creation for lessons applicable to human society. The building of a robin's nest and a "flight among the stars" lead Child by free association to the deficiencies of a system of childrearing that breeds "sickly hot-house plants" instead of "hardy wild-flowers"; similarly, a balloon flight above the earth reminds her of European travel and elitist education, both of which foster "diminished faith in republican institutions and increased belief in the necessity of strong demarcation of ranks in society."[72]

Child relived the New York phase of her life in more ways than one. Renewing her friendship with the music critic John Sullivan Dwight, she asked him to send her the libretto of Bellini's opera *Norma*, together with an English translation. "I want to make a little incidental use of it in a story," she divulged. But it was so long since she had heard *Norma*, "or any other music," that she had totally forgotten the opera. Thus, she needed to have Dwight "mark with a pencil those portions which are favorite gems with the public."[73]

Music inevitably conjured up a side of Child that she had repressed along with her sexuality since resuming the role of Frugal Housewife. "I *have* tried to abjure *all* the Fine Arts, because I found that a longing for them was not favorable to content in my present position, and I could not find any way of getting *out* of my position," she confided to Anna Loring. "But the effort is useless. That craving for beauty lies too deep in my nature ever to be uprooted."[74] Inseparable from her sexual passion and emotional ardor, Child's "craving for beauty," be it art, music, or poetry, indeed lay at the core of her being. Unfortunately, she had married a man who could not satisfy it. When she "shouted" with rapture at the sight of an elm tree "encrusted" with icy "pearls and diamonds . . . David admired it greatly, and made divers superb comparisons in a quiet, philosophic way; but I could n't get him up to the *shouting* point." When she thrilled to Elizabeth Barrett Browning's *Aurora Leigh* and George Eliot's *The Spanish Gypsy*, David yawned. "As he visited Spain in his youth, and has a great liking for many Spanish things, I thought he *would* enjoy" *The Spanish Gypsy*, Child reported ruefully to her friend Harriet Sewall, but the experiment of sharing it with him had failed dismally: "I read to him that wonderful glorification of the juggler's exhibition, which made me so wild with delightful excitement, that my *soul* heard the music, saw the transfiguring light of the setting sun, and went leaping through the dance with Fedalma. . . . Mr. Child dismissed it with the remark, 'I have seen Spanish gypsies. . . and jugglers. . .; and that description seems to me very exaggerated.'" Child summed up the problem succinctly: "[H]e is a man of *facts*, and I am always alone in the *mystical* and *poetical* chambers of my soul."[75] Hence arose yet another reason for her difficulty writing *A Romance of the Republic*: her exploration of those locked chambers was awakening forbidden desires and reviving stifled frustrations.

Nevertheless, Child persisted. Having decided to stage a scene of her novel at the opera in Rome, she plied Sarah Shaw with questions about what the opera house looked like, whether peasants as well as fashionables attended, which airs the audience encored, and how "enthusiastic" the audience response generally was. She also reread her friend's "*European* letters, in hopes they would '*heave* some light'" on the layout of Rome itself.[76] In February 1867 she told Fields she had "finished the story" and was beginning to make a fair copy for the press. By April (but not on the first day of the month "lest it should prove ominous"), she hoped to be able to bring him sixteen or eighteen chapters to sample. She was counting on him, she added, for an honest opinion as to whether "the old woman's imagination needs 'the prayers of the congregation, being in a very weak and low condition'" (the formula used by ministers "in old times, 'when I was a gal,'" to invoke divine aid "for the sick and feeble").[77] In fact, the fair copy turned out to be a thorough revision, during which Child expanded the manuscript considerably. The final version, which she delivered to Fields on May 1, would come to 442 typeset pages — a far cry from the "story" she had hazarded at the outset. "For pity's sake, keep it in a Safe," Child pleaded. "I altered it so much in copying, that if it gets lost or destroyed, I shall never try to restore it." In the same breath, she hastened to assure Fields that he was "entirely at liberty not to take" the novel unless he genuinely liked it.[78] To her immense gratification, it impressed him very favorably, and they quickly signed the contract. By July it was on the market in book form (Fields having decided against serializing it).

Her publisher's seal of approval resurrected Child's old pride as a professional. Now she wanted Field's assurance that he was offering her the same terms as other well-known authors. "Of course, neither you nor I have time to discuss what ought to be the relative profits of labor and capital," she conceded. Consistently with her democratic literary tastes, Child did not distinguish between intellectual and manual labor and identified herself as a worker. Still, she wanted to be valued at her just worth. "I am not arrogant in my claims, but I thought I ought not to be put at the *foot* of the ladder," she specified. Several years earlier, Fields had infuriated her by placing her name (without permission) at the bottom of a long list of contributors to his new children's magazine, *Our Young Folks*, and referring to her not as "editor of the *Juvenile Miscellany* and author of *Flowers for Children*," but simply as "Mrs. Child and others." At the time, the humiliation of being listed "after ten or twelve of the young fry" and relegated to the "rear, with stragglers" of an "army of contributors" had shaken her self-confidence, but in retrospect, she concluded that it had roused her "spunk": "I said to myself, 'I'll show 'em that the old woman's "no deady yet." ' And so I set to work and wrote the story, which turns out to be a novel, and rather a frisky affair to come from a snowy pate."[79]

Written against the backdrop of the betrayal Johnson was engineering of all the promises the war had seemingly endorsed—genuine emancipation for African Americans; recognition of the indispensable role they had played as soldiers, spies, and auxiliaries; and their incorporation as equal citizens into a truly reconstructed Union—*A Romance of the Republic* insistently rehearses the history that its white audience was so rapidly forgetting. At a time when the ugliness of slavery was dropping out of public consciousness, the novel refocuses on one of its ugliest features—the sexual exploitation of slave women. At a time when the North was congratulating itself on its enlightened benevolence, a scene dramatizing the pursuit of fugitive slaves in Boston by a merchant who owns a mortgage on them starkly exposes the North's complicity in slavery.[80] At a time when lifelong antiabolitionists were parading as allies of those they had so fiercely persecuted, numerous vignettes recall the insults, ostracism, and mob violence that abolitionists had had to endure from "gentlemen of property and standing." At a time when the heroes of the long crusade against slavery were receding from view, the novel pays nostalgic tribute to many of them by name—Garrison, Francis Jackson, Wendell Phillips, Samuel Sewall, Father Snowden (a black clergyman active in the rescue of fugitives)—bringing some on stage for cameo appearances and introducing others in fictional guise: Wendell Phillips as Mr. Percival, Joseph Carpenter as the Quaker Underground Railroad agent Joseph Houseman; and Ellis Loring as Alfred Royal King. Finally, at a time when the nation was turning its back on the Civil War, the last section of the narrative recapitulates the episodes Child defined as crucial: the hanging of John Brown (mourned in a black church whose congregation joins in the prayer Child had heard in 1859 and reapplied to Andrew Johnson in 1867: "O Lord thou hast taken away our Moses. Raise us up a Joshua!"); the secession crisis and the flurry of northern compromise proposals that accompanied it; the galvanization of the North by the Confederate attack on Fort Sumter; the battle of Bull Run; the enlistment of women in the war effort through the Sanitary Commission; "the raising of colored regiments"; and the gradual abatement of anti-black prejudice (interestingly, the Emancipation Proclamation is never mentioned).[81]

Not only does Child weave into the novel the public history of the struggle against slavery, but she draws on her private memories of rubbing shoulders with proslavery bigots in Northampton. Like the Childs in 1838, the Northampton boardinghouse keepers Joe Bright and his wife Betsey live next door to "a great Southern nabob" who "made a heap o' money selling women and children" before moving North to spend his fortune. Modeled on the slave-auctioneer Thomas Napier, who used to pray so loudly that David had to "strike up his accordion to drown sounds so discordant to our feelings," Deacon Stillham (or "Steal'em," as Joe Bright calls him) fills the neighborhood with a "very loud and monotonous voice of prayer." "Do hear that old thief trying to come Paddy over the Lord!" exclaims Joe Bright (320–21), echoing the words that which David had expressed the "vexation of his spirit."[82] Like the Childs, the Brights determine to intervene when Stillham's South Carolina relatives arrive bringing a slave woman in tow — and this time the intervention succeeds in liberating the woman.[83] Representing the "honest mechanics" who constituted the rank and file of the abolitionist movement, the Brights also exhibit many of the character traits and values the Childs display. Betsey Bright, a former school teacher (as was Child in her youth), believes firmly that "everybody ought to help in doing the work of the world," because "it don't seem right that some backs should be broken with labor, while others have the spine complaint for want of exercise" (339). Joe Bright enjoys singing "The Star Spangled Banner" at the top of his lungs (as David did during the Civil War) and objects strenuously to Boston aristocrats who treat "mechanics as if . . . they all had the smallpox" and who are "afraid to take hold of a rough hand without a glove on" (293–94, 336–38). When told by Deacon Stillham that " 'Northern women were mere beasts of burden,' " Bright retorts in words Child herself had once used: "I told him that was better than to be beasts of prey" (366).[84] Revealingly, however, Child confers on Joe Bright the "bubbling" (295) temperament she missed so much in David (and sought during her New York years in John Hopper and Ole Bull).[85]

The novel's autobiographical resonances indicate that the healing mission *A Romance of the Republic* performs is personal as well as political. Though aimed at healing the national divisions caused by slavery, war, and racial hatred, the novel also heals Child's deep inner divisions. It brings into harmony the dissonant phases of her life (Boston, Northampton, New York), reconciles her conflicting loyalties to men who had fulfilled different needs in her (David, John Hopper, Ole Bull, Ellis Loring), and merges her disparate selves (mechanic's daughter and adopted gentlewoman, activist and artist, frugal housewife and would-be fairy godmother, inveterate New Englander and surrogate meridional). The principal agents of this fusion are the interracial marriage plot that serves as Child's metaphor for the union of ethnic groups, classes, and cultures; and the octoroon heroines onto whom she projects her abolitionist commitment, her passion for music and art, her rebellion against convention, and her unresolved guilt over illicit sexual desires.

For a country riven by racial conflict since its very origins and still undergoing the aftershocks of bitter civil warfare, interracial marriage would seem to be a perfect symbol of reconciliation. Child's need to reconcile the inner conflicts that had bedeviled her all her life made the symbol doubly attractive. At the same time, the pattern of wifely self-abnegation she had followed in her own marriage might suggest that it would prove to be a highly problematic symbol. As bitter experience had repeatedly taught Child, marriage in the nineteenth century was not an egalitarian institution; hence, it could not provide the model she sought for an equal partnership between the races. This contradiction would seriously undermine *A Romance of the Republic*.

Child based much of her plot on actual incidents that had haunted her imagination for decades. In 1835 she had learned from the New Hampshire abolitionist George Kimball that the daughters of his own cousin had been sold at auction in New Orleans. Writing to him at Ellis Loring's behest to "obtain an accurate account of the whole transaction" for the antislavery society, she had asked him to furnish "all the minute particulars" about the girls' "*very* light complexion, . . . character, dispositions, manners — &c &c" and to explain in his account "that beauty enhances price in the slave markets." She had also requested Kimball to append details of another story he had related to her, concerning three young women whom a friend of his had rescued from sale by their elder brother, and who had "afterward respectably married, without any suspicion of the 'one drop of African blood.'" Although Kimball's reply has not survived, the communication apparently left an indelible impression on Child, for she cited it thirty years later in defending the authenticity of *A Romance of the Republic*. "I have *known* of two cases, where elegant and accomplished girls were claimed as property by creditors," she insisted to skeptics who dismissed her plot as "*very* romantic": "In one case, they were sold; in the other, they escaped, and married well at the North, where their secret remains unsuspected."[86]

A similar account Child found in the *Liberator* during the same period provided not only the kernel but the entire outline of the plot she first used in her 1858 story "Loo Loo." Child even retained the setting (Mobile, Alabama) and the initial of the male protagonist (a "Mr. N******"), merely changing the name of the heroine (Martha in the original). Like Mr. N., Child's transplanted New Englander Alfred Noble becomes enmeshed in the seductions of the slave system when he buys the beautiful nine-year-old octoroon child Loo Loo after her white father dies intestate. Instead of fulfilling his intention to send her to a northern college to be educated as a teacher, he steps into her father's place and reenacts the sins of his predecessor. He, too, fails to manumit his young charge and eventually enters into concubinage with her, as Loo Loo's father had with her mother. And he, too, subjects her by his negligence to a forced sale when the Panic of 1837 bankrupts him. Like Mr. N., Noble does manage to rescue his mistress from her lascivious purchaser and to take her North, where he marries her.[87] Nevertheless, foreshadowing the central problem Child would confront in *A Romance of the Republic*, the story ends on an ambiguous note. Marriage does not free Loo Loo from the dependent status she has all too readily embraced. For the rest of her life she continues to charm her husband by repeating the words that cemented the patriarchal relationship he assumed toward her at the outset: "I thank you, Sir, for buying me."

What evidently fascinated Child most in the real-life stories of light-skinned slave women that she retold in "Loo Loo" and would embellish in *A Romance of the Republic* was the intermarriages in which they culminated. Themselves the progeny of racial amalgamation, mixed bloods embodied the dissolution of the ethnic categories to which Child attributed the antagonisms that divided humankind. Through intermarriage, she imagined, race itself could be erased, and with it racial prejudice. Sharp distinctions would blur into imperceptible gradations, and the monotony of fixed types would give way to an infinite variety no longer reducible to classification. The intermixture of races would engender an intermixture of cultures as well, resulting in enrichment for all.

Child spelled out her ideal of a racially and culturally mixed society in a pair of articles that framed the composition of *A Romance of the Republic* — the first written ten months before she claimed to have worked out the details of her plot in October 1865, the second eight months after she completed the manuscript in May 1867. Titled "A Chat with the Editor of the Standard" and "Illustrations of Human Progress," they comment on the "half Indian and half African" sculptor Edmonia Lewis. That a young woman linked with these two races should progress "from basket-weaving and moccason-embroidery, in lonely forests among the Chippewas," to sculpture in a Boston studio, writes Child, "is one among many striking signs of the times, showing how the lines of demarcation between classes and races are melting away in the powerful sunshine of this All Souls' Day." The evaporation of racial and cultural boundaries is also apparent in the work of white artists, she notes, pointing to William Wetmore Story's *African Sibyl*, Anne Whitney's *Africa Waking from Sleep*, and William Tolman Carlton's *Midnight Watch for Freedom*. "Whenever the colored people shall become a coloring people," she predicts (alluding to the absence as yet of black painters), "we shall have gorgeous pictures . . . fraught with memories of humming-birds, parrots, and flamingoes." The contributions of "colored people," she adds, will infuse new vitality into American art: "We need their idiosyncrasy to warm up our colder tastes; and when their individualism comes out, we shall recognize it fraternally." Turning from the visual arts to music, Child observes that the African genius has so far "only been manifested in Ethiopian songs, breathing the deep sadness, or the reckless merriment of human souls in bondage." She prophesies, however, that it will find "grander utterance" before long in high art: "Some future composer will give us the Prayer of a *black* Moses in tones as inspired as those of Rossini. Operas will embody the romantic adventures of beautiful fugitive slaves; and the *prima donna* will not need to represent an Octoroon, for men will come to admire the dark, glowing beauty of tropical flora, as much as the violets and lilies of the North."[88]

In all but one respect, *A Romance of the Republic* fulfills this prophecy. Based partially on Bellini's opera *Norma* — a drama of tabooed and betrayed love between Druid priestesses and Roman conquerors — it features the "romantic adventures of beautiful fugitive slaves" and sets the "dark, glowing beauty" of its "tropical" heroines, Flora and Rosabella, against the pallid charms of a northern rival named Lily and the sober tints of a perpetually violet-clad northern matron named Lila. The prima donna it brings on stage for the role of Norma, however, remains an octoroon. Because Child sought to promote the ideal of an integrated America, she could not dispense with a figure incarnating the fusion of cultures and races. The choice of a heroine whose fictional prototype derives from Italian opera and whose mixed ancestry reveals no discernible African traits points nonetheless to a flaw in Child's concept of integration. The product she envisions emerging from the blending of diverse cultural and racial strains still reflects white European dominance. An opera celebrating the struggles of African slaves for freedom would simply translate their experiences into a European art form; unlike "Ethiopian songs," and later blues, jazz, rock, and rap, it would not constitute an authentic merging of African and European cultures. Though more exotic than her Anglo-Saxon sister, the octoroon resembles her too closely to foster the valorization of African beauty; instead, she reinforces ethnocentric preferences for approximations of white beauty. Reproducing the ambiguities of the novel's interracial marriage plot, its octoroon heroine thus embodies the limitations of the egalitarian partnership to which Child summoned her compatriots.

Despite these limitations, the novel radically challenges the ideology of white supremacy that blocked the route toward a genuine reconstruction of American society. Only by dismantling all racial barriers, it insists, can America obliterate her shameful legacy of slavery and fulfill the promise of her democratic creed. *A Romance of the Republic* is also unique among nineteenth-century American novels in centering the call for an end to racial discrimination on the institution that all but the most thoroughgoing egalitarians secretly (or openly) exempted — marriage. As we shall see, even white novelists who agreed that racial integration was an "imperative duty" typically recoiled at the prospect of intermarriage.[89] Whatever the defects of the marriage plot as a vehicle for Child's egalitarian precepts, it did lead her to brilliant insights into the complex relationship between the racial slave system that victimized African Americans and the patriarchal gender system that victimized women. *A Romance of the Republic* explores that relationship more deeply than any of Child's previous works, offering a wide-ranging historical critique of slavery and patriarchy that parallels in fiction the facts and arguments offered by her 1833 *Appeal in Favor of That Class of Americans Called Africans* and her 1835 *History of the Condition of Women, in Various Ages and Nations*.

The novel's beautiful and gifted mixed-blood heroines, Rosabella and Flora Royal, simultaneously represent the legacy of the past and foreshadow the hope of the future. Their parentage recapitulates the history of American slavery. Just as the Spaniards introduced slavery into the West Indies and transplanted it to the mainland, with the French following in their wake, so the Spanish grandfather of Rosabella and Flora bought their mulatto grandmother in the French West Indies and took her to St. Augustine. Just as Anglo-Americans inherited slavery from the Spaniards, so the girls' father — a Bostonian merchant settled in New Orleans — has in turn bought his slave mistress Eulalia from her Spanish father. Royal's New England background emphasizes another historical fact — the key role Yankee slave traders played in establishing the foundations of the South's plantation economy. Royal's emigration to the South and subsequent entanglement in slavery, finally, illustrate the connection between slavery and patriarchy, between southern and northern systems of caste, class, and economic exploitation: originally engaged to the daughter of a Boston aristocrat, Royal went South to make his fortune when her father objected to her marrying a poor clerk without prospects and forced her into a match with a wealthy man she did not love.

Following her preferred literary strategy — to "attack bigotry with 'a troop of horse shod with felt'; that is . . . to *enter* the wedge of general principles, letting inferences unfold themselves very gradually"[90] — Child introduces Rosabella and Flora to the reader without disclosing their ancestry. This is the very tactic to which the girls' father resorts when he invites his Bostonian visitor and namesake, Alfred Royal King (a more principled version of Loo Loo's Alfred Noble), home for an exhibition of his daughters' talents. "I had a desire to know first how my daughters would impress you, if judged by their own merits," Mr. Royal later explains (18). Child obviously wishes the reader to react as King does: "He could not make these peculiarities [Rosa's golden complexion and wavy black hair] seem less beautiful to his imagination, now that he knew them as signs of her connection with a proscribed race. . . . Octoroons! He repeated the word to himself, but it did not disenchant him. It was merely something foreign and new to his experience, like Spanish or Italian beauty. Yet he felt painfully the false position in which they were placed by the unreasoning prejudice of society" (14).

The first chapter raises the questions: Can this "unreasoning prejudice" be overcome? If not, what are the consequences for women like Rosabella and Flora? For American society at large?

Having fallen in love with Rosa after an evening of listening to her sing, King would like to be able to marry her, but he knows his invalid mother shares society's prejudice. Every time he returns in imagination to "that enchanting room" in Royal's house, "where the whole of life seemed to be composed of beauty and gracefulness, music and flowers . . . the recollection of Boston relatives [rises] up like an iceberg between him and fairy-land" (14, 25). The imagery suggests the heavy price a society must pay in cultural impoverishment, even frigidity and sterility, when it erects barriers against other races. King suffers keenly from the sensual deprivations of his New England home and yearns for the aesthetic pleasures that Rosabella and Flora incarnate. For the moment, however, he finds the "impediments" to marriage "insurmountable."

In the slave South, as Mr. Royal knows all too well, the impediments are not merely psychological, but legal, and the consequences for all parties are more drastic. The laws of Louisiana do not recognize interracial marriages, and since Mr. Royal never manumitted the girls' mother, Rosabella and Flora, too, are legally slaves. Unless he can fulfill his intention of taking them to France, their fate will be the concubinage that was their mother's — or worse. Personifying the dangers that threaten them is the dashing Georgia slaveholder Gerald Fitzgerald, who has been assiduously courting Rosa, to her father's dismay. "If I were the Grand Bashaw, I would have them both in my harem," Fitzgerald confides to King, as they leave the Royal house together (12). In short, the racial proscriptions that make the North an iceberg make the South a harem — the trope Child had elaborated in "Slavery's Pleasant Homes."[91]

The rest of the novel shows how the sexual results affect the family lives of both races. It also examines the impact of prejudice on various classes and ethnic groups and tests the possibilities for change.

Fitzgerald's fantasy of playing Grand Bashaw and setting up a harem with the Royal sisters turns out to be prophetic. A year after the soiree at the Royal home with which the novel opens, Mr. Royal dies bankrupt, and his daughters discover that they are property, to be sold for the benefit of creditors. When Fitzgerald proposes to spirit them away, they agree on condition that he first marry Rosa (their sheltered life having left them ignorant of southern laws against intermarriage). Some weeks later, Fitzgerald installs the girls in a secluded cottage on his Georgia sea island plantation,[92] which proves to be a more sinister version of their New Orleans household; it is "evident at a glance," Child pointedly remarks, that "the master of the establishment" has done his "utmost to make the interior of the dwelling resemble their old home as much as possible" (75–76).

The parallels between the Fitzgerald and Royal households extend further than the girls realize. Both are founded on lies. Rosa's marriage is no more legitimate than her mother's was, and once again, she and Flora are slaves, while believing themselves to be free. To "obtain a legal ownership of them," without which he can "feel no security" about retaining them, Fitzgerald has arranged with Royal's creditors to pay $2,500 for the pretended fugitives, on the chance that he can track them down (67, 74). Both households consequently require concealment and isolation from society. In New Orleans, Mr. Royal had withdrawn from circles into which he could not bring his "wife" and had carefully shielded his daughters from contact with all but a few trusted friends. In Georgia, Fitzgerald keeps the sisters' very existence literally veiled in secrecy. On the plea that neither their whereabouts nor his participation in their escape must come to light, he insists that Rosa and Flora remain "entirely out of sight of houses and people" and charges them to "wear thick veils" whenever they venture out, taking care "never to raise them" in front of strangers (79, 81).

Well might Fitzgerald boast that he does not "envy the Grand Bashaw his Circassian beauties" (84), for he, too, enjoys the exclusive possession of women confined to his premises, shrouded in purdah, and reduced to the function of entertaining their master with song and dance. His emulation of a Turkish sultan whose prize harem slaves were Caucasians involves keen ironies. The reversal of cultural roles recalls that whites were once enslaved by the dark-skinned peoples they now despise, and the adoption by a Christian of Islamic practices makes a mockery out of the argument that slavery served to Christianize the African.[93] Only one of the Grand Bashaw's privileges continues to elude Fitzgerald—a plurality of wives. Before long, he takes the last steps toward translating his fantasy into reality, first by demanding sexual favors from Flora, ultimately by acquiring a legal bride.

Through the details identifying the Royal sisters as unwitting harem slaves, Child suggests still another parallel between the Royal and Fitzgerald households. In both, patriarchy and slavery are synonymous, the women being in every sense the "property" of the household's male head.

Child unmistakably equates the two institutions. In her article "Woman and Suffrage," published in the *Independent* while she was writing *A Romance of the Republic*, she had pointed out that "patriarchism" had originated as a system of "protection," giving the "husband and father" absolute power over "wives and children" in exchange for defending them against enemies.[94] It is thus no coincidence that Fitzgerald acquires his power over Rosa by offering to protect her from the creditors, auctioneers, and lascivious purchasers who menace her (among them the aptly named Mr. Bruteman): "[H]e smiled as he thought to himself that, by saving her from such degradation, he had acquired complete control of her destiny" (66–67). Come what may, he assures Rosa, "you shall never be the property of any man but myself" (61). When she recoils with indignation from a word that smacks of the slavery she is trying to escape, Fitzgerald substitutes the more acceptable language of patriarchy: "I merely meant to express the joyful feeling that you would be surely mine, wholly mine." Because Rosa has been brought up to acquiesce in the patriarchal assumption that a wife belongs surely and wholly to her husband, she has not learned the lesson Child strives to impress on her reader — that the same reality underlies both forms of discourse.

In the Royal household (as in "Loo Loo"), patriarchy had worn a benign face, and the patriarch's true relationship to his womenfolk had lain hidden. In the Fitzgerald household, the meaning of patriarchy is spelled out. The patriarch discloses the face of the slavemaster, and the protective husband steps forward as the Grand Bashaw.

Reiterating the moral of Royal's story, Child shows that the same relationship between patriarchy and slavery obtains in the North. Like the fiancée Royal has had to renounce, Fitzgerald's bride, Lily, is the daughter of a weathy Bostonian merchant, for whom her marriage constitutes a mere financial and social arrangement. As ignorant of her status as Rosa is of hers, and unaware of Rosa's existence, the new Mrs. Fitzgerald does not realize that she, too, is a victim of patriarchy and slavery — that her husband has bought her only for her father's money, and that her father, in turn, has sold her for her husband's plantation and his own business prospects in the South. In fact, Lily shares the Boston aristocracy's virulent racism and proslavery sympathies. Yet she will learn that her fate is inextricably intertwined with Rosa's. Long after Rosa's escape from slavery and Fitzgerald's death at the hands of a slave whose wife he molested, Lily discovers that their son, born within a week of Rosa's, was exchanged in the cradle with him and is now a slave, whereas the son she has brought up as hers is a member of the race she has taught him to despise.

While the first phase of the novel explores the interconnections among slavery, racism, and patriarchy, and assesses the price American society must pay for its oppression of blacks, the second phase attempts to ascertain whether the American people can arrest the cycle of wrongs they have set in motion, transcend the prejudices that poison their society, and rebuild their Republic on a foundation of freedom and equality for all. Through a cast of characters representing a broad cross section of the American public, Child suggests different answers.

At one end of the spectrum are those who show no capacity for growth, even in the face of revelations that transform their social reality. The most obdurate example is Lily Fitzgerald's father, Mr. Bell, who represents the proslavery Cotton Whig aristocracy of the North — a class as deeply implicated in the institution as slaveholders themselves. Named for the Bell-Everetts, or Constitutional Unionists, who had led the antiabolitionist riots of 1860–61, his watchword is "I stand by the Constitution" (316).[95] Bell's ship, the *King Cotton*, symbolizes his connection with "the king that rules over us all" (314), as does the mortgage he holds on the slaves of Mr. Bruteman, who epitomizes the brute force on which slavery rests. When he hears that two of these slaves have been caught trying to escape on the *King Cotton*, Bell instructs his grandson to have an agent spirit them out of Boston and dispatch them to New Orleans without due process before an "Abolition mob" can rescue them. His heartlessness extends to his own family. Bell is prepared to disinherit Gerald on being apprised of his actual parentage. And when informed that his true grandson is the fugitive he has just returned to slavery along with his mulatto wife, Bell rages: "Do you suppose, sir, that a merchant of my standing is going to leave his property to negroes? . . . A pretty dilemma you have placed me in, sir. My property, it seems, must either go to Gerald, who you say has negro blood in his veins, or to this other fellow, who is a slave with a negro wife. . . . If you expect to arrange a pack of mulatto heirs for *me*, you are mistaken, sir" (393–94).

The vignette incisively sums up the mentality of the North's proslavery aristocracy. It also prophesies that regardless of their wishes, the Mr. Bells of America will not be able to keep their property to themselves. Integration and amalgamation are inevitable, Child implies, and the Republic's black children will eventually inherit their rightful patrimony. Nevertheless, she recognizes that no arguments or pleas will reconcile the Mr. Bells to destiny — that heedless even of self-interest, they will destroy themselves rather than relent. Accordingly, Mr. Bell dies of an apoplectic fit.

Though hardly less racist, Bell's daughter, Lily, gives some indication of being able to adapt at least superficially to a new racial order. Her impulse is simply to continue pretending that Gerald is her son. "I never will give him up," she insists. "He has slept in my arms. I have sung him to sleep. I taught him all his little hymns and songs. He loves me; and I will never consent to take a second place in his affections" (362). Her loyalty would be admirable, except that she refuses to draw any inferences from the disclosure of Gerald's racial identity. She also refuses to take any interest in the fate of her biological son. "[I]t would be very disagreeable to me to have a son who had been brought up among slaves," she protests. "I have educated a son to my own liking, and everybody says he is an elegant young man. If you would cease from telling me that there is a stain in his blood, I should never be reminded of it" (386). In short, for Lily Fitzgerald, appearances and forms are paramount. As long as Gerald looks and acts like a white gentleman, and passes for such in the eyes of the world, she can go on acknowledging him as her son. Should he ever publicly identify himself as black or take a "colored wife," however, she would sever their relationship, as she baldly declares (420). Still, a vignette at the end of the novel tentatively raises the possibility that personal tragedy and historical evolution may open her to further change. After Gerald's death in the Civil War, Lily thrown together with the quadroon grandchild born to her through her biological son and his mulatto wife — now her sole remaining progeny. She will not admit that the "yellow" baby is pretty, but she stares at her unacknowledged granddaughter and daughter-in-law "with a strange mixture of feelings" and wonders, "What *would* my father say?" (421–22).

At the opposite end of the spectrum, Child places characters embodying a variety of solutions to the problem of undoing the legacy of slavery: young Gerald; Mr. Royal's former fiancée, Lila Delano; and the upright Bostonian, Alfred Royal King, who in the first chapter falls in love with Rosa.

The revelation of Gerald's origins and, soon thereafter, his encounter in the Union army with the white half-brother who was sold into slavery in his place, and whom he himself helped send back into slavery, gradually impel him to reexamine his assumptions about forced servitude, race, and inherited wealth. From his half-brother, George

Falkner, Gerald learns what it means to be a slave, laboring without reward for the benefit of idle masters. He also learns to reevaluate the relative worth of the slave and the "fine gentleman." He realizes, for example, that he, who has received so many advantages, has less to show for them and is less useful to society than his brother, who has taught himself to read and whose mechanical ingenuity puts him perpetually "in demand to make or mend something" (408).

At the same time, Child uses the ironic reversals in the two brothers' situations to undermine racist theories about innate traits fitting blacks for slavery and whites for mastery. Here it is the "black" brother who is the gentleman and the white who is the slave. In features and coloring, moreover, the two are indistinguishable — all that differentiates them is the manners and skills each has acquired as a result of his circumstances. The point, of course, is that both men are products of their environment, rather than of their racial makeup, which is so similar as to reduce racial categories to absurdity.[96]

Through Gerald, Child offers the hope that a portion, at least, of the northern and southern aristocracies founded on slavery can be taught to repudiate hierarchies of race and class ill-befitting a republic. Gerald himself does not participate in the reconstruction of American society after the Civil War, however. Killed at Bull Run, he embodies the destruction of slavery. His death in the arms of his half-brother, who carries him off the battlefield and tries to save his life, also exemplifies the lesson Child drew from the war:

> [T]he *same* measure we have meted out has been measured unto *us*. The poor slaves had *their* children shot down, whipped to-death, and torn from them to die afar off, and we heard of it with languid indifference. . . . *They* died by slow starvation, and we heeded it not. *They* were torn by blood-hounds, and we would not believe that Southern gentlemen could train ferocious brutes for such a purpose. And lo! we learn it all now, in the terrible school of experience. Slavery tears *our* children from us, to die far away from us; she starves them to skeletons; she tracks their flight with fierce blood-hounds. And, to complete the lesson, the poor abused negro, whom we have helped to abuse, hides them, and feeds them, and guides them to their friends.[97]

Of the characters who set new directions for the nation, the most interesting is Lila Delano. Widowed after an unhappy marriage with the man for whom her father forced her to break her engagement with Royal, Lila ends up playing the role of fairy godmother to Royal's daughter Flora, whom she helps escape from Fitzgerald's Georgia plantation and eventually adopts. Until her chance meeting with Flora on a visit to the South, Mrs. Delano has shared her class's racism and opposition to "anti-slavery agitation" (155). Had Flora been recognizably black, she could never have won Mrs. Delano's sympathies, but her spontaneity, exuberance, and "impulsive naturalness" charm the older woman, who has recently lost a daughter, and the attachment proves strong enough to withstand the revelation that Flora is "allied to the colored race, and herself a slave" (146, 155). In the process of befriending Flora, Mrs. Delano comes to abjure her former prejudices and ultimately joins forces with the abolitionists. "How she has changed!" sneer her fashionable acquaintances, Mrs. Ton and Mrs. Style: "She used to be the most fastidious of exclusives. . . . Think of her, with her dove-colored silks and violet gloves, crowded and jostled by Dinah and Sambo!" at antislavery meetings. "I expect the next thing we shall hear will be that she has given a negro party" (283–84).

The cultural transformation Mrs. Delano undergoes is even more significant, heralding the results Child hoped would ensue from an intermingling of races, classes, and cultures. At first, Mrs. Delano tries to "educate [Flora] after the New England pattern" (209). But when Flora objects to her "nice ideas of conventional propriety," Mrs. Delano begins to realize that her protégée, "with her strange history and unworldly ways, is educating me more than I can educate her" (151, 269). Little by little, she overcomes her upper-class notions of "propriety," learns to share Flora's predilection for "folks that bubble over," and even refurbishes her home according to Flora's "tropical" tastes (287, 295).

The most emotionally resonant section of the novel, the subplot involving Mrs. Delano and Flora reverberates with autobiographical overtones. Clearly, Child drew on her passionate attachment to Dolores, the young Spanish woman she had befriended in New York and brought with her to West Newton in 1850.[98] By projecting herself into the role of a wealthy widow who possessed the means to play fairy godmother, she vicariously fulfilled the longing for an adopted daughter that poverty had forced her to relinquish. Reflecting Child's identification with Dolores's "tropical" temperament, however, Flora rather than Mrs. Delano screens the self-portrait sketched in Child's loving re-creation of the relationship that had meant so much to her. True, Child shared Mrs. Delano's respect for a New England education. And she herself had certainly undergone Mrs. Delano's experience, after her conversion to abolition, of being "made to feel, in many small ways, that she had become a black sheep in aristocratic circles" (284). Yet there the resemblance ceases.

Unlike Mrs. Delano — but like Flora — Child was by birth an interloper in the milieu that ejected her for espousing the cause of blacks and thus transgressing racial boundaries. She did not, of course, suffer the humiliation of having a proposal of marriage withdrawn after the disclosure of her ancestry, as Flora does. All the same, courted in her youth by the supercilious dandy Nathaniel Parker Willis — the model for the aristocratic Mr. Green who so hastily turns his back on Flora — Child did find herself lampooned by him for betraying her humble origins in *The Frugal Housewife*.[99] And upon her fall from grace in 1833, she responded to the snubbing of the antiabolitionist aristocrats who had once patronized her much as Flora does to Green's abandonment of his suit. "I don't want to be introduced to any of these cold, aristocratic Bostonians," exclaims Flora indignantly (281). Such fulminations echo through Child's letters to her friends, most of whom were renegade aristocrats like Mrs. Delano. At the very time she was writing *A Romance of the Republic*, for example, Child declined an invitation to visit the Shaws at their Staten Island mansion, explaining: "[Y]ou know you are all the time surrounded by properly behaved, stylish people; and from such people I generally have to hide, or fight. . . . I have wonderfully little patience with people of aristocratic tendencies. They arouse in me a fierce antagonism, and if I am where I can't show it, I am made very miserable."[100] Child also expressed the aversion to social conformity she attributes to Flora. "I have an increasing desire to keep out of the way of *society*, which always seems to me like an enemy lying in wait to catch me and impound me, or get me into an elegant harness," Child wrote to her friend Eliza Scudder in 1870. "[When] it comes near me, . . . I snort, kick up my heels at it, and scamper away. I always was rather coltish in this respect, and I think I grow wilder, rather than tamer, with years."[101] In almost identical language, Child describes Flora as chafing against the restrictions imposed on her by New England upper-class decorum: "[I]n her desire to behave with propriety, there was an unwonted sense of constraint. When callers came, she felt like a colt making its first acquaintance with harness" (145). Reproached by Mrs. Delano for deviating from "custom" by "nodding" repeatedly to a gentleman friend in the audience at a concert, Flora sighs, "Don't you find it very tiresome, Mamita, to be always remembering what is the custom? I'm sure *I* shall never learn" (152). In similar fashion Child had once complained to Sarah Shaw: "[A]las, I can find no *simplicity*, no spontaneousness. . . . The world seems to me one great 'Circumlocution Office,' conventionally arranged to prevent people from doing anything real, or saying anything real, or feeling anything real."[102] Looking back from the vantage point of her rural hermitage on her brief sojourn among the Boston elite, she judged: "I never did know very well how to behave, and I have forgotten what little I ever knew in that line. . . . I am too indifferent to society to take the slightest pains to conform to its regulations."[103]

Besides articulating the rebellious impulses and "pent-up volcanic fires of suppressed individual freedom" that had prompted Child to align herself with social outcasts, Flora, like her sister, Rosa, personifies the arts in which Child had luxuriated in New York and which she had vainly tried to "abjure" since settling in Wayland.[104] Flora excels at embroidery, shellwork, painting, and dancing, as Rosa does at opera singing. But like Child, she finds her "enthusiasm" continually checked in the inhospitable environment of New England. When she claps her hands and shouts with pleasure at an art gallery and sways to the music at the opera, her foster mother winces with embarrassment and genteel onlookers whisper, "It's plain that this lively little *adoptée* of Mrs. Delano's has never been much in good society" (151).

Through Mrs. Delano's adoption of Flora, Child entertains one possible scenario for overcoming white prejudice and integrating blacks into American society. With the example of Dolores in mind, she poses a hypothetical case: suppose Dolores had turned out to have African antecedents; and suppose one of the aristocratic friends who had been so charmed by her — Marianne Silsbee, for instance — had learned this fact after losing her heart to the young woman; would the discovery have enabled such an inveterate "nigger"-hater to recognize the irrationality of her prejudice, and to repudiate it? (In the midst of a political storm over the remanding of a fugitive slave, Marianne had cut Child to the quick by expostulating against " 'making a ridiculous fuss about one nigger.' ")[105] If so, how would the "*adoptée*" meet the ultimate challenge of integration—the taboo against intermarriage? As Mrs. Delano puts it in worrying about Flora's future, "would it be right to conceal her antecedents" from potential "admirers" (147)? Would anyone knowingly marry a girl of African ancestry?

The mode of realism committed Child to finding realistic solutions to these problems, but the ones she proffers do not prove adequate. Flora does find a husband—her father's former clerk and protégé, the German orphan Franz Blumenthal—and their union does serve as a model for an egalitarian partnership between the races, since both are social outsiders. Yet Blumenthal is a special case. Indebted to Mr. Royal, intimate with Flora since his youth, and foreign-born—hence, free at the outset from American race prejudice (as Child believed was generally true of Europeans)—he does not represent a genuine solution to the difficulties Mrs. Delano ponders. Indeed, Child's recourse to such a figure betrays her pessimism regarding her American compatriots' ability to transcend their prejudices—and her false illusions about the European immigrants she hoped would set an enlightened example. Further undercutting the usefulness of the Blumenthals' marriage as a symbol of future relations between whites and blacks is their decision to continue concealing Flora's racial identity and to withhold it from their children "till their characters are fully formed." Mrs. Delano justifies the secrecy on the grounds of preserving the children's sexual innocence. "[T]elling them of their colored ancestry" would involve exposing them to "a knowledge of laws and customs and experiences growing out of slavery, which might . . . prove unsettling to their principles," she contends (385). But the very possibility of secrecy raises the questions: How does the passing of an occasional light-skinned mixed-blood contribute to eradicating racial prejudice? And what of the vast majority, who cannot pass?

As a metaphor for the integration process, Mrs. Delano's adoption of Flora is no less problematic. Inescapably reproducing the built-in inequality of the parent-child relationship, it defines the white godmother as the adult and her black protégée as the child.[106] Granted, the influence Flora exerts on Mrs. Delano counteracts this inequality to a certain extent; it suggests that blacks will not be merely the recipients of white bounty but the agents of American society's regeneration—that they will infuse warmth, color, and spontaneity into a culture suffering from anemia (as Child predicted in her article on Edmonia Lewis).[107] The cultural contrasts Child draws between the sober, intellectual Mrs. Delano and the mercurial, artistic Flora tend to reinforce ethnic stereotypes, however. Flora thrills to opera, ballet, and painting, but cannot be prevailed upon to tackle the heavy scholarly fare that Child no less than Mrs. Delano deemed essential to a New England education. "One might as well try to plough with a butterfly, as to teach her ancient history," concludes Mrs. Delano in frustration (209). Even more disturbingly, the ideal of assimilation Child posits through her adoption subplot erases the ethnic identity of African Americans. They are to dissolve into American society, transforming the traditional melting pot into a spicier "*olla podrida*," or Spanish stew, but ceasing to exist as a distinct people.[108]

The same defects mar Child's most radical solution to the problem of eliminating racial hierarchies, class divisions, and cultural boundaries—the solution embodied by the

Bostonian Alfred Royal King, who marries Rosa and enacts a small-scale version of the abolitionist program for Reconstruction. Representing New England abolitionism at its best, King also epitomizes its fatal flaws, which Child's intermarriage plot brings to the fore.

Initially, the marriage of King and Rosa seems to usher in a new social order, free not only of racial proscriptions, but of patriarchal restrictions on women's freedom. To marry Rosa, King must surmount more than the Boston aristocracy's racial prejudice and social exclusiveness; he must surmount patriarchal attitudes toward "tainted" women. Between the time he first meets and falls in love with Rosa and the time he finally proposes to her, she has been "the victim of a sham marriage" and, after her escape, has taken to the stage as an opera singer—a career regarded as little more respectable than prostitution (245–46). In repudiating "the merely external distinctions of this deceptive world," King repudiates external measures of sexual purity along with external badges of racial and social status. He even rises above asking his wife to sacrifice her career and the independence it gives her, though he does express the hope that she will take up concert singing in lieu of opera (252).

Paradoxically, having provided this glimpse of an alternative to patriarchal marriage, Child retreats to a pattern of conjugal relations all too familiar in her life as well as in her fiction. Rosa abdicates her hard-won freedom, degenerating into emotional dependency on her husband, and King comes to assume a quasipaternal guardianship over her. The clues to the failure of nerve—and of imagination—reflected in the novel's principal marriage plot may lie in the unresolved sexual guilt Child projects onto Rosa and in the forbidden fantasies she consummates by supplying her heroine with a husband who irresistibly recalls Ellis Loring.

"Dear Ellis remains singularly present with me always," Child wrote to Louisa several weeks after completing *A Romance of the Republic*. "Oh, how my lonely soul calls for him, and longs for some response." Expressing a desire to "peep . . . invisibly" at Louisa while she read the novel, Child hinted that she expected her friend to recognize the nostalgic portrait of Ellis she had painted in King.[109] She also inadvertently revealed one of the mental associations that had prompted her to choose the name King. Louisa's nephew John King had just remarried, and Child commented that he deserved "sunshine" after the "long, cold storm" he had endured. She was referring to the marital incompatibility that had led him and his first wife, the former Jane Tuckerman, to separate—a step Child had warmly defended.[110]

The link is suggestive, for it points toward one of Child's major preoccupations during her New York phase, which in fact reappears in *A Romance of the Republic*—the question of whether a woman has the right to seek another chance at happiness after a sexual misalliance, be it an illicit affair or an unhappy marriage. In stories like "Hilda Silfverling" and "The Prophet of Ionia" Child had defiantly answered "yes," while recurrently betraying a deep ambivalence that prevented her from depicting a "remarriage" unclouded by guilt and patriarchal dominance. She did not succeed in dispelling that ambivalence in *A Romance of the Republic*.

The malaise that haunts Child's representation of the King marriage emerges in a variety of ways: the unconvincing characterization of Rosa (whom Theodore Tilton pronounced "less impressive in the story than in the author's conception");[111] the sense Rosa conveys of being a "guilty wretch" (350) in need of "penance" (Rosa feels she would gladly walk "to Jerusalem with peas in her shoes" [414], echoing Child's description of *The Progress of Religious Ideas* as a "pilgrimage of penance, with peas in my shoes");[112] the false ring of the scenes in which Rosa reacts to Fitzgerald's treachery and confesses to King her sin of exchanging her infant son with Lily's; the "strange conduct" toward young Gerald that leads King to fear an "unworthy passion has taken possession" of Rosa (350); and, concomitantly, the threat of incest that arises when the Kings' daughter Eulalia falls in love with Gerald, not realizing he is her half-brother. Explaining the frequency of the incest motif in novels of miscegenation, Mary Dearborn writes: "Repression is never entirely successful, the return of the repressed always a threat. . . . [M]iscegenation represents the testing of the boundaries between self and other, the conscious and the unconscious, and calls up social forms of the uncanny that . . . include incest. . . ."[113] For Child, as we have seen in "Hilda Silfverling," the incest motif also had a personal significance unrelated to fears of miscegenation: it grew directly out of the illicit love for John Hopper that she had tried to deny by passing him off as her "adopted son." Thus, it is not surprising to find it surfacing as she explores through Rosa the side of herself that had once made her identify so strongly with "fallen women": her desire for a different husband, capable of satisfying the artistic and emotional, if not the sexual, needs David did not fulfill, and of providing her with nurturance, financial security, and a comfortable home.

Still, the autobiographical elements Child has woven into the marriage of King and Rosa do not fully account for its flaws as a paradigm of gender and race relations in the post-Civil War world. Like the adoption plot in which Mrs. Delano figures, the King marriage plot defines blacks as dependents and whites as parental guardians. Significantly, it is Rosa who does "penance" for the sin of slavery (to which she has contributed by consigning Lily's son to the fate her own son would otherwise have met) and who meekly follows the advice of the husband she has " 'wisely chosen . . . for [her] confessor' " (355), while it is King who unilaterally takes the responsibility for undoing the evils slavery has entailed on the Royal, King, and Fitzgerald families.

Personifying the chief wrong King sets about righting is George Falkner, the half-brother who has been enslaved in the place of Rosa's son Gerald. Although white, he faces the same problems other former slaves do after emancipation, especially since his marriage to a mulatto makes it impossible for him to "pass." Child had offered practical solutions to these problems in *The Freedmen's Book* and in letters to politicians, where she had lobbied for programs to educate the ex-slaves and to provide them with remunerative employment and opportunities for advancement. In *A Romance of the Republic* she has King set the example. Following the precedent of Ellis Loring, who had trained his black valet, William Morris, as a law clerk and prepared him for the bar,[114] King engages George as an agent in the Marseilles branch of his business, with the aim of later taking the young man into partnership. Child herself had recently helped the Morrises to arrange for educating their son in Europe, because she believed it important for a "young soul [to] grow a while in an atmosphere entirely free from the blight of prejudice."[115] The main reason for dispatching George to Europe, however, as King notes, is that in America, "his having a colored wife would put obstructions in his way entirely beyond our power to remove" (416). Once again, realistic constraints circumscribe the solutions Child can envisage as she wrestles with how to rescue blacks from racial prejudice. Yet she does demonstrate that blacks can make rapid progress in their homeland when accorded education and respect. During George's stint in the Union army, Rosa teaches his wife, Henriet, to read, embroider, and play the piano, so that she will be "educated in a degree somewhat suitable to her husband's prospects" (414). After three years "with kindly and judicious friends, who never [remind] her, directly or indirectly, that she [is] a black sheep in the social flock, [Henriet's] faculties [have] developed freely and naturally," as evidenced by a map she has "copied very neatly" and a "manuscript book of poems, of her own selection, written very correctly, in a fine flowing hand" (433). Franz Blumenthal draws the obvious inference: "If half a century of just treatment and free schools can bring them all up to this level, our battles will not be in vain, and we shall deserve to rank among the best benefactors of the country; to say nothing of a corresponding improvement in the white population" (434). In addition to training the Falkners for middle-class occupations, King intends to make full reparation to George for his enslavement by bequeathing to him a sum equal to his rightful share of the Bell-Fitzgerald inheritance, plus interest. The projected bequest is to be kept a secret, to avoid turning the Falkners' heads until their characters have been "formed by habits of exertion and self-reliance," but King stipulates that "this judicious process must not, of course, deprive the young man of a single cent that is due to him" (415–16).

In vital respects Child's fictional plan to help blacks enter into their inheritance as American citizens goes further than the Reconstruction program eventually enacted by Congress. It includes just compensation to blacks for their centuries of unrequited toil, and it promises black men full partnership in the business of running the country.

Yet it displays the same ideological limitations that hampered abolitionist efforts to uplift the freedpeople after the Civil War. Its most glaring defect is paternalism. Never, for example, does it occur to King to consult the Falkners before deciding what is best for them; nor does he credit them with having already formed strong characters and "habits of exertion and self-reliance." Intertwined with that paternalism is the patriarchal concept of woman's role implicit in the education Mrs. Falkner receives — one "suitable to her husband's prospects." A tinge of racism also infects Child's portrayal of Henriet even as she chronicles her transformation into a "lady": "[B]elonging to an imitative race, she readily adopted the language and manners of those around her. Her features were not handsome, with the exception of her dark, liquid-looking eyes; and her black hair was too crisp to make a soft shading for her brown forehead. But there was a winning expression of gentleness in her countenance, and a pleasing degree of modest ease in her demeanor" (433, 435). Most problematically, Child's fictive Reconstruction plan is predicated on the assumption, anachronistic as early as the 1850s, that American society provided "an almost perfect opportunity for social mobility."[116] As

King puts in in his parting advice to George Falkner, which echoes the refrain of Child's *Juvenile Miscellany*: "If you are industrious, temperate, and economical, there is no reason why you should not become a rich man in time" (436). In short, Child's personification of the abolitionist conscience likewise personifies its tragic contradictions. Belying the ideal of a classless society in which whites and blacks, men and women, enjoy equal opportunities, *A Romance of the Republic* reveals that racial, sexual, and class paternalism continue to dominate the thinking of abolitionists and to mar their prescriptions for reform.

Summing up the strengths and weaknesses of the vision *A Romance of the Republic* offers of America's destiny is the series of *tableaux vivants* in which the novel culminates, as the Royal sisters' reunited families celebrate the end of the Civil War. The progeny of the two families, remarks Flora proudly to her husband Franz, are "a good-looking set . . . though they *are* oddly mixed up" (432). They no longer fit any recognizable racial category but show traces of "African and French, Spanish, American, and German" ancestry. The tableaux they stage clearly prefigure the future Child dreams of for her country.

The first represents the Republic that has risen out of the ashes of slavery and civil war. Incarnating that Republic and the racial amalgamation in which its destiny lies is the Kings' daughter Eulalia, clad in "ribbons of red, white, and blue, with a circle of stars round her head" (440). In one hand, she carries "the shield of the Union"; in the other, "the scales of Justice . . . evenly poised." By her side stands Flora's daughter Rosen Blumen, flourishing a "liberty-cap" and resting her hand "protectingly" on the head of the black child the family has most recently rescued from slavery. Complete with this kneeling figure, "looking upward in thanksgiving," the tableau recalls innumerable prints and statues commemorating the emancipation. Here, the emancipators are themselves children of emancipated slaves, yet the class relations between the two groups persist. And once again, a hierarchy of color has reasserted itself.

In the second tableau, the Northampton boarding-house keeper Joe Bright (who had gone on to serve in the war, along with King, Blumenthal, Blumenthal's son, and Gerald) leads a company of black soldiers. This tableau emblematizes the solidarity of white workers and black slaves and pays tribute to the black regiments that had helped win the Civil War. Bright's role as the company's commanding officer accurately reflects historical fact in that despite vigorous agitation by black and white abolitionists, the Lincoln administration and the military had staunchly resisted commissioning blacks as officers.[117] Yet Child gives no indication that the future holds a more egalitarian alliance between white and black workers.

The last tableau, in which the freed slaves sing Whittier's "Boat Song," symbolizes the fusion of black and white cultures that an amalgamated Republic will bring about. An emancipation poem modeled on slave songs, the Whittier piece reflects the growing interest abolitionists were taking in the rich oral culture blacks had forged out of their oppression. The very year *A Romance of the Republic* was published, the first two major collections of slave songs appeared, both issued by abolitionists.[118] No doubt

Child did not have access to these collections while she was writing her novel, but she had certainly read the songs included in the slave narratives of Frederick Douglass and William Wells Brown and in the *Atlantic Monthly* articles of her friend Charlotte Forten, one of which she had reprinted in *The Freedmen's Book*.[119] That she chose to have the slaves sing not a song of their own composing, but the pale imitation a white poet had produced of one, testifies starkly to the stranglehold that the genteel canons of white middle-class culture exerted on her imagination. Once again, she was visualizing the incorporation of black elements into a white art form — or the appropriation of black culture by whites — rather than the genuine merging of black and white elements in a new art form created by African Americans themselves.

Ultimately, Child's allegiance to an ideal of assimilation that remained white-dominated prevented her from imagining satisfactory alternatives to the social order she had so trenchantly anatomized. Though able to perceive the interconnections between slavery and patriarchy, between racial and sexual proscriptions; though able to diagnose the cultural impoverishment resulting from racial exclusiveness; Child proved unable to extricate herself from conceptions rooted in the very systems she sought to discredit. As a metaphor for equal partnership, interracial marriage foundered on the manifest inequality of a patriarchal institution in which, as Child knew painfully well, the nineteenth-century wife lost her individual identity under the law and became literally her husband's appendage.[120] Writing within the patriarchal literary conventions that a marriage plot necessarily imposed — even a marriage plot that overturned the bans against interracial unions — Child found it impossible to envision a truly egalitarian, multicultural society.[121]

Twenty-five years after the publication of *A Romance of the Republic*, the African American abolitionist Frances Harper would rewrite its marriage plot in her novel *Iola Leroy* (1892). After suffering a more brutal version of Rosa's fate, Harper's heroine, Iola, meets a white suitor akin to Alfred Royal King. The son of abolitionists, Dr. Gresham implores Iola to marry him and promises her that she will be a welcome member of his parents' household. He also makes clear that the marriage will not deny her the opportunity to work for the welfare of her people, although he protests with unwitting condescension against her insistence on identifying herself as black. Gently but firmly, Iola rejects the ambiguous assimilation that Child's Rosa and Flora embrace. Pointing out that she would find herself perpetually exposed to insult, both from those who mistake her for white and hence freely express their views of blacks, and from those who bar her from their homes once her identity is known, she replies: "I am not willing to live under a shadow of concealment which I thoroughly hate as if the blood in my veins were an undetected crime of my soul." And she adds: "I don't think that I could best serve my race by forsaking them and marrying you." Instead, Iola chooses to marry a man of her own race (and color) and to go South with him to teach the freedpeople. Such would be the response of most African Americans to the solution *A Romance of the Republic* adumbrates to the problem of racial prejudice.[122]

At the same time, African Americans were the first to acknowledge that "the broad, loving humanity breathing from Mrs. Child's 'Romance of the Republic' " presented a vivid contrast to the "spirit of caste" permeating the fiction of her white peers—as Charlotte Forten commented in a perceptive review of Rebecca Harding Davis's *Waiting for the Verdict*, published the same year.[123] While interracial marriage in itself could hardly have served to abolish the economic inequality caused by two centuries of slavery and discrimination, it did serve (in Forten's words) as a "bugbear with which the enemies of the colored man are wont to terrify his timid friends." Thus, Child rightly recognized that defusing the fear of miscegenation and redefining intermarriage as a positive good were indispensable objectives; that the campaign for equal rights could not achieve its ends if it tolerated sanctuaries of white privilege. To appreciate the radicalism of this insight and the boldness of the triple intermarriage plot through which Child propagated it, one has only to compare *A Romance of the Republic* with other novels by white progressives who attempted to grapple with the same "vexed" theme.

In Davis's *Waiting for the Verdict* (1867) Margaret Conrad recoils in horror when the light-skinned mulatto surgeon with whom she has fallen in love confesses his racial identity: "[T]he gulf between us is one which God never intended to be crossed," she pontificates. "The prejudice against the black blood seems senseless to you, Doctor Broderip, but I would have to let my own out, drop by drop, before I could eradicate it. . . . It is a thing which will exist while the two races endure. I cannot fight against nature." Despite Davis's claim to have written the novel on behalf of "all the weak and wronged among God's creatures," she seems to reaffirm the notion that white antipathy for people of color is an inborn instinct, showing misgenenation to be "against nature." Even the nine-year-old Rosslyn Burley, who grows up to become the novel's most admirable female character, reacts with disgust to the sight of a mulatto child (the future Dr. Broderip): his "dirty yellow skin . . . made her sick, she was sure; it was the same as if a toad or snake had stood upright, to see his grimaces and monkey tricks of delight at being kindly spoken to. She wished he was dead, and out of the way. . . ." Broderip himself exhibits what can only be called self-hatred, or as Davis would have it, the hatred of "his fastidious white blood" for his "few drops" of black blood. Drawn to a black slum by "the mysterious instinct of race," he feels both "disgust" and "a sense of kinship and brotherhood" as he scrutinizes his people: "swarms of drunken blacks," with "bestial limbs . . . and blubber lips." After the revelation of his racial identity destroys his reputation in Philadelphia, he nobly decides to lead a black regiment in the Civil War. He ends up dying in battle, as if to eliminate the contradiction his very existence poses to theories of fixed racial categories and impassable barriers between whites and blacks.[124]

Davis's phobia of interracial marriage can be ascribed to her southern background, but northern progressives reveal a similar tendency to flinch at the prospect. The abolitionist Anna Dickinson, for example, though she traveled around the country with Frederick Douglass lecturing in favor of black suffrage, produced a novel more akin to *Waiting for the Verdict* than to *A Romance of the Republic*. Dickinson's *What Answer?* (1868) indignantly denounces racial prejudice but offers no hope that the American public can learn to tolerate interracial marriages. Both couples who break this taboo in *What Answer?* meet tragic fates. The English wife of the mulatto Mr. Ercildoune dies in childbirth after the riot of 1838 drives the couple from Philadelphia. And their daughter, Francesca, enjoys only a few weeks of happiness with her white husband, William Surrey, before the two are murdered in the New York Draft Riots of 1863. William's father initially appears capable of transcending prejudice. He has hired a mulatto as his bookkeeper and retains him until the white office staff threatens to quit en masse. When William announces his marriage to Francesca, however, his parents disown him. Prejudice "is a feeling that will never die out, and ought never to die out, so long as any of the race remain in America," they tell him. The marriage appears to have little chance of surviving under such circumstances, and it comes as no surprise that "the mad fury of the mob" targets an interracial couple with special vindictiveness. Dickinson clearly intended the novel as a call to "[f]inish the work" of the Civil War by removing the "stain" of racism from the land. Accordingly, Child pronounced the "defects" of *What Answer?* "too unimportant to dwell upon" in "comparison with its merits." Child did not specify what she meant by "defects," but Dickinson's inability to depict either a lasting interracial marriage or a character who undergoes a change of heart on the subject leaves the reader with the impression that society's ban may well be rooted in "nature."[125]

Squeamishness about interracial marriage is even more obvious in Albion Tourgée's pseudonymously published *Toinette* (1874). A product of Ohio's abolitionist-dominated Western Reserve, Tourgée played an active part in Reconstruction as a Republican judge in North Carolina and devoted the rest of his life to crusading for racial equality. Nevertheless, his novel repeatedly balks at the marriage it tries to arrange between the defeated Confederate Geoffrey Hunter and his former slave mistress Toinette. Only after a sojourn in the wilderness that purges him of his aristocratic habits of mind does Hunter finally bring himself to propose marriage to the woman he loves so passionately. Symptomatically, when he determines to do so, he is mysteriously stricken with blindness, and he never explicitly articulates his proposal. Indeed, when Tourgée reissued *Toinette* in 1881 under the title *A Royal Gentleman*, he deleted the concluding scene, ending the novel four chapters earlier with Toinette's refusal to resume her concubinage after emancipation.[126]

Two decades later, another Ohio progressive, William Dean Howells, would at last manage to stage an interracial marriage dramatizing the conviction that "sooner or later our race must absorb the colored race." Unlike Child, however, who argued that the fusion would produce a more varied and colorful population, Howells apparently shared his protagonist's belief that it would "obliterate not only [the] color, but [the] qualities" of the "colored race" because "[t]he tame man, the civilized man, is stronger than the wild man. . . ." As the title of his 1891 novel suggests, Howells treats the subject of intermarriage as *An Imperative Duty*—an unpleasant obligation. Both the hero, Dr. Olney, and the heroine, Rhoda Aldgate, find blacks "charming" until Rhoda's guardian reveals that the young woman is "of negro descent." Both react to the disclosure with "a turmoil of emotion for which there is no term but disgust." Olney's "race instinct" asserts itself in a "merciless rejection" of the beauty he had previously admired in Rhoda (in contrast to Alfred Royal King, who had not become "disenchant[ed]" on learning of Rosa's ancestry). And Rhoda "grovel[s] in self-loathing and despair," which she projects onto her newfound blood brothers: "She never knew before how hideous they were, with their flat wide-nostriled noses, their out-rolled thick lips, their mobile, bulging eyes set near together, their retreating chins and foreheads, and their smooth, shining skin. . . ." Olney dutifully stifles his "repulsion" and proposes to Rhoda, who is only too eager to be convinced that it is not "base and cowardly to desert" her people and "live happily apart from them," passing for white. Unlike the Kings and Blumenthals, the Olneys do not work for the uplift of blacks, but they emigrate to Italy. Nor is their marriage a happy one. Rhoda continues to brood over her race, leading Olney to regret that the "sunny-natured antetypes" of her mother's people have influenced her temperament less than the "hypochondria" of her Puritan forefathers. Still, he shares her "crazy" predilection for Puritan "self-sacrifice" enough to comfort himself with the thought that he has done his duty.[127]

   This sorry catalog illustrates the tenacity of the prejudices Child sought to counteract in *A Romance of the Republic* and highlights the significance of her achievement. It likewise explains the bitterly disappointing reception of the novel she called "the Benjamin of my family, the child of my old age."[128] Many of Child's closest friends responded to it with embarrassed silence, polite platitudes, or "cold" dismissal. Louisa Loring professed to have written a letter that had gone astray. Charles Sumner never acknowledged receipt of the book (perhaps because of pressures on his time). The Shaws, to whom Child had dedicated *A Romance of the Republic*, thanked Child for the "nice book" and pronounced the plot "clever." The Sewalls, among Child's earliest coadjutors in the antislavery movement, and her niece Abby Francis, a teacher for the Freedmen's Aid Society, averred that they had been "much interested." Henrietta Sargent, one of her most dedicated comrades in the Boston Female Antislavery Society, reported that she was reading a few pages a day "alternately with [Scott's] Rob Roy." Marianne Silsbee gave no sign of having recognized the plea directed at her, but she assured Child that she had read her "charming book, right off" and considered the opening chapters very poetic. Lucy Osgood frankly admitted that she did not "like the subject" and opined that Child no longer had "imagination enough to write a novel." Wendell Phillips and Joseph Carpenter, Child's Quaker host in New Rochelle, at least expressed genuine enthusiasm, but only Eliza Scudder was both "warmly sympathizing and discriminating" in her praise. The humiliation, Child confided to Louisa, had been utterly "chilling": "When I had completed the book, I felt as if I could write another and a better novel, and was full of earnestness to set about it; but the apathy of my friends took all the life out of me, and has made me feel as if I never wanted to put pen to paper again."[129] She may well have been reliving the mortifying reception of *Fact and Fiction* in 1846, for she had again tapped her deepest psychological resources and bared the most vulnerable part of her soul. Moreover, because she had had such a "good object" in seeking to "undermine *prejudice*," she could hardly have helped being deeply disturbed by the resistance her message had aroused in fellow abolitionists she had believed to be unusually free from racism.

In her bleak mood, however, Child tended to overlook the considerable attention *A Romance of the Republic* was receiving from those who shared her commitment to eradicating racism—as well as the gratifying tributes paid to it by her African American friends. The black abolitionist Robert Purvis greeted the book as a welcome antidote at a time when "[t]he Demon of Prejudice was never more cruel and relentless."[130] Theodore Tilton, identifying "the caste prejudice against the black blood" as the "*motive*" of the plot, roundly declared: "To the believing, a book like this is a strong gospel. To the doubting, it is a mighty argument. To the faithless and the narrow, it is a terrible revelation, saying, 'Now ye have no cloak for your sin.' "[131] Thomas Wentworth Higginson judged *A Romance of the Republic* to be Child's "best fictitious work." Echoing Charlotte Forten, he credited it with a "broad spirit of humanity . . . betray[ing] no trace of that subtle sentiment of caste which runs through and through some novels written ostensibly to oppose caste." Although he complained that the plot had "too many *vertebrae*" and should not have been "prolong[ed] . . . into the second generation," he predicted that the novel would "always possess value as one of the few really able delineations of slavery in fiction. . . ."[132] Higginson's praise never reached Child, because she could not "get up the courage" to look at his 1868 biographical sketch of her. "To read my own biography seems too much like being dissected before I am dead," she told him.[133] But she ought at least to have been pleased with the review in the *Standard*, which hailed *A Romance of the Republic* as both an "opportune" weapon in the battle for a genuine Reconstruction and a valuable record for the "many thousands who have never been so fortunate as to be active participants in the great conflict for freedom"—exactly the aims Child had had in mind. "What Hawthorne was unable to find, Mrs. Child has found in American life, viz.: the material for a thrilling and powerful romance," the *Standard* proclaimed, calling it "the second *great* novel based upon slavery" (the first being *Uncle Tom's Cabin*).[134]

Whether or not Child took comfort in these accolades, she did not fulfill her threat of retreating into silence. Although she never again ventured to ride her Pegasus into the sphere of fiction, she returned with a will to political journalism. She would end her long career of activism fighting to transform her country into the multiracial family she had imagined in *A Romance of the Republic*.

20

A Radical Old Age

They say people grow more conservative as they grow older; but I grow more radical.[1]

A refrain she enjoyed repeating in letters to friends as she commented on the political scene during her last decades, Child's portrayal of herself as increasingly radical with advancing age is only partially accurate. She continued to publish a large number of political articles, covering a wide range of subjects: black suffrage and Reconstruction policy, woman suffrage, Indian rights, U.S. imperialism, labor turmoil, anti-Chinese hysteria, and the Franco-Prussian War.[2] Appearing in such progressive organs as the *Standard, Independent, Woman's Advocate*, and *Woman's Journal*, and written at intervals snatched from nursing David through long bouts of incapacitating rheumatism and chronic diarrhea, Child's newspaper articles of the late 1860s and 1870s confirm that she remained faithful until her death to her abolitionist and feminist ideals. Yet they also indicate that she never succeeded in adapting those ideals to the challenges confronting the nation in an era of relentless westward expansion, massive immigration, unprecedented industrial development, and explosive labor strife.

Child's commitment to racial and sexual egalitarianism did indeed "grow more radical" with the years. Her firm antiracist principles kept her from succumbing to the backlash against Reconstruction and the resentment of black male enfranchisement that carried off some of her abolitionist and feminist comrades in the 1870s. Concomitantly, she expressed her militant feminism in the boldest arguments she had ever formulated for women's equality. Child's fidelity to the vision of a model Republic also persisted. It impelled her to denounce postwar schemes to annex the Dominican Republic and Cuba as unsparingly as she had once exposed the spuriousness of antebellum pretexts for seizing Florida and northern Mexico. And it incited her to castigate the brutal warfare against the Plains Indians with the same moral outrage she had vented on Andrew Jackson's Cherokee removal campaign four decades earlier.

But when Child turned to the cultural and economic conflicts that polarized the country in the wake of the Civil War, she revealed the limits of her radicalism. For

Native peoples, African Americans, and immigrant workers alike, she advocated the panacea of assimilation into the dominant society, with its white middle-class Protestant values. The deep suspicion of Catholicism she derived from her New England Calvinist upbringing intensified in her old age, fueled by the Catholic church's hostility to abolitionism, Irish immigrants' espousal of the Democratic party's racist demagoguery, and the fury Irish mobs had wreaked against blacks in the New York Draft Riots of 1863.[3] Skewing her comprehension of European politics, her anti-Catholic prejudices led her to glorify Protestant Germany under Bismarck as the champion of world freedom and to vilify Catholic France under the Third Republic as the beachhead of an insidious papacy. Above all, Child's twenty-year ensconcement in a rural village untouched by the forces of change left her incapable of understanding the needs of the industrial working class, which had come of age since her days in New York. Even while proclaiming, "year by year, my sympathies go more entirely with the masses, and I keep more and more jealous watch over their interests,"[4] she rejected strikes, unions, and demands for an eight-hour day as analogous to the monopolistic practices "of which [workers] so justly complain in capitalists."[5]

Particularly where class and gender were concerned, Child tended to diagnose her society's ills in the moral terms of a bygone day, which distanced her from the postwar generation. "[T]he crying sin of the times, in *every* direction," she complained, "is deficiency in a sense of *duty*; duty to each other, and duty to society. In the relations of labor and capital, it seems to be entirely wanting on *both* sides." She applied the same critique to relations between the sexes, roundly condemning women who advocated universal "Free Love" as a cure for male licentiousness and a hypocritical double standard: "[T]hose Free Love women, how recklessly they throw overboard the question of *duty* toward households, or toward society! . . . [T]hey are so wild for *freedom*, that they forget such a [word?] as *duty* exists."[6] The opposition Child set up between "freedom" and "duty" had governed her entire life. She had consistently sacrificed "freedom" to "duty," and, as she aged, she had less and less sympathy for those who opted to do otherwise.

By early 1868, having put the disappointing reception of *A Romance of the Republic* behind her, Child felt ready to resume political journalism, which would now become her sole medium for influencing public opinion. She also resumed her role as a mainstay of the *Standard*, contributing a steady stream of articles to the paper and its short-lived successor (which marked the achievement of black suffrage in April 1870 by dropping "Anti-Slavery" from its title).[7] In coming so prominently to the support of the American Anti-Slavery Society's old organ, Child was publicly endorsing Wendell Phillips's position in the dispute with Garrison's faction over whether or not to dissolve the society and discontinue its newspaper. She had no "*partisan* feeling" regarding the two veteran leaders' "unfortunate" feud, she explained to her friend Samuel Sewall, like David one of Garrison's earliest followers. "But we have always agreed with Mr. Phillips in thinking that the Anti Slavery Society ought not to be disbanded, until the rights of the freed men were much more secure than they are at present."[8] For the same reason, she pointedly refused Garrisonian loyalist Oliver Johnson's plea for more submissions to the *Independent*, to which he and Garrison had transferred their allegiance. Though promising to furnish articles for the *Independent* whenever she had time, Child stressed that she would give priority to the *Standard* because "[a] paper that is not the voice of any theological sect, or any political party, performs a mission which no other paper can. . . ."9

Accordingly, the February 15, 1868, number of the *Standard* carried a joint New Year's message from her and David, accompanied by a $50 contribution—a huge sum, considering that her annual income came to less than $700 after taxes. Emphasizing that "the vigilance of the Anti-Slavery Society was never more needed," this "Letter from Mr. and Mrs. D. L. and L. Maria Child" exhorted *Standard* readers to redouble their agitation for measures to protect the freedpeople against the "murderous" rancor of their former masters. American abolitionists must not repeat the mistake made by their British counterparts in the 1830s, who had "deserted their post too soon" to prevent the freedpeople of the West Indies from being legislated back into quasislavery, the Childs warned. "[T]o trust those who have been slaveholders, and those who habitually sympathize with slaveholders, to frame laws and regulations for liberated slaves" was as dangerous as relying on "wolves . . . to guard a sheepfold."10

Child's fears that the country was heading toward another disastrous compromise with the South had been sharpened by the results of the November 1867 elections. Not only had voters in Ohio, Minnesota, and Kansas decisively defeated black suffrage amendments to their state constitutions, but voters in the key states of New York and Pennsylvania had elected Democratic majorities in a "renewed demonstration of northern race prejudice."11 Emboldened by these developments, President Johnson had turned his annual message to Congress into an anti-black diatribe, fulminating against the evils of allowing a race that had shown "less capacity for government than any other" to "rule the white race. . . . and shape . . . the future destiny of the whole country." Worse still, he had brazenly sabotaged the Reconstruction Acts by replacing generals who sought to enforce them and by firing Secretary of War Edwin M. Stanton, the last remaining Radical in his cabinet, despite a strong Senate vote to reinstate him.12

Like most of her fellow abolitionists, Child applauded the impeachment of Johnson that swiftly followed, though she wished Congress had acted sooner and had charged Johnson not merely with violating the Tenure of Office Act in the Stanton case but with instigating the "slaughter" of black and white Republicans in the South and obstructing the laws passed to protect them.13 Aware that moderate Republicans had shrunk from the political risks of impeachment and might vote against convicting Johnson, Child saw it as her mission to prod them to do their duty "at the point of a moral bayonet." In a caustic letter to the *Standard*, she compared the U.S. government to the hero of a Spanish romance who had tried to commit suicide by "shooting, hanging, drowning, and poisoning," until his miraculous survival finally convinced him to cease resisting the will of God. The American Republic, too, had "tried persistently to destroy itself by the many-barrelled weapon called Slavery." Driven into a war for its very existence, the nation had "contemptuously refused" the "proffered aid" of fugitive slaves and black troops until constrained by " 'military necessity.' " "Still prone to suicide" even after this aid had given it "a new lease of life," it had chosen a "morally 'low white' " as vice president in the place of the "able and upright" candidate who had occupied that post for four years. The new leader, "called Moses because he could change the staff that was placed in his hand into a serpent, and bring to life again the stiffened 'Cotton Mouth' of Rebellion, and that stunned 'Copperhead,' the 'old Democratic Party,' " had all but finished off the Republic: "Loyal men, black and white, died by thousands; industrious freedmen tried in vain to obtain little homesteads, while wealthy rebels received back again the lands they had forfeited, and even obtained offices, at the expense of the United States, as a reward for treason." Child wryly predicted that a timid Congress would undertake yet another suicide attempt by allowing Johnson to continue wielding "his vast official power while he is under trial; thereby enabling him to bribe votes of acquittal by promises of honor or emolument." But she saw reason to hope that the American Republic, like the Spanish hero, would ultimately renounce its vain efforts to "counteract the decrees of Providence," and instead choose to "marry the beautiful lady Freedom." More and more people, she noted, had come to recognize that the "venom" injected into the American body politic by the "fangs" of " 'Cotton-Mouths' and 'Copperheads' " demanded an "antidote." Without the votes of the 2 million freedmen in the South, the Republican party would lose control of Congress, and a coalition of southern planters and northern Democrats would once again govern the country: "[N]egro suffrage is forced upon us, as a political necessity, by the same over-ruling hand that compelled us to resort to emancipation as a 'military necessity.' Moreover, this dilemma adds the stimulus of policy to the benevolent wish to educate the freedmen. So, you see, on whatever beam or bough we try to hang ourselves, it breaks and brings down hidden treasures."[14]

Congress had actually imposed black suffrage on the South in the spring 1867 Reconstruction Acts, which Johnson had defied. What abolitionists wanted, however, was a constitutional amendment instituting black suffrage throughout the country—the aim Johnson was endeavoring to thwart in his message to Congress. In the end, the Senate would fail by one vote to convict Johnson—a setback some historians view as marking the beginning of the end for radical Reconstruction.[15] Assessing the damage, Child mourned: "Alas, what golden opportunities have been lost for establishing our free institutions on a solid and permanent basis! Lost by the treachery of an unprincipled President, and by the cowardice of a Congress, which has not yet learned" to heed "God's impressive teaching."[16]

Chief among the lost opportunities that Child never ceased to lament was the failure to confiscate the planter aristocracy's vast estates and to divide and sell them "in small lots, on moderate terms, to the poor laborers who had, for so many years, tilled them without wages." Such a program of land redistribution, embracing poor whites as well as slaves, would have broken the power of the former slaveholding class; "stimulated the industry of the freedmen, and inspired them with a feeling of manliness"; rescued poor whites from "the blindness of their ignorance" and taught them that "honest labor is honorable above all things"; and helped pay the national debt. Child would continue to press for this goal, and to plead movingly against a policy of estate restitution that was dooming the freedpeople to remain "landless and homeless, and compelled for daily food to submit to the hard terms of grasping, unpitying masters." "[T]his great evil *can* be remedied, and the good of all classes in the country requires that it *should* be remedied, as soon as possible," she would repeatedly insist in her newspaper articles and political correspondence.[17]

In the meantime, she concentrated on promoting black suffrage, the "vital question of the hour." Beyond "justice to an oppressed class," the enfranchisement of African Americans involved a test of the nation's ideals, Child contended in another letter to the *Standard*: "whether we will be true to the principles of our free institutions; whether we will prove by our works that we really have faith in a government by the people." Black suffrage, she pointed out, was neither a radical innovation nor a violation of the Constitution, contrary to the claims of its opponents: "When we began our career as an independent nation, it was the general, unquestioned custom for free colored people to vote," except in Connecticut and South Carolina. The right to vote had been deliberately "taken away" from African Americans by amendments to state constitutions— most recently by Pennsylvania's 1838 statute. Thus, not black suffrage, but the subsequent legislation against it, represented a departure from precedent, she asserted. Quoting Madison's caveat that a "*gradual abridgment*" of the suffrage has been "*the mode in which aristocracies have been built up on the ruins of popular forms*," she concluded: "If we wish to preserve our own rights, we must conscientiously and impartially respect the rights of others."[18]

Privately, Child also worked to allay the misgivings of conservative friends like Lucy Osgood, who worried about enfranchising illiterate black voters. She herself partly shared these misgivings, she admitted. In fact, she had originally favored imposing a "moderate educational qualification" and had always "considered it a great mistake" that such a restriction had not been mandated for ignorant white voters, both native and foreign-born. Once conferred, however, the suffrage could not be withdrawn, and to require educational tests for black voters alone would be discriminatory. The sole recourse was to "educate all classes as fast as possible." Besides, Child emphasized, "Negroes are as *well* qualified to vote as the mass of Irishmen, and circumstances make it *their* interest to vote on the *right* side." Granted that slavery was "a dreadful school for the education of citizens," it had rendered the "*masters* more unfit to be citizens of a Republic" than it had the slaves. "Having survived the citizenship of slave-holders, 'poor whites' and ignorant Irish, I have faith that the Republic can survive *any*thing," she wound up.[19]

While abolitionists were crusading for black suffrage, the 1868 election campaign had got under way, and the Republicans were facing stiff competition from a Democratic party ready to fan the flames of bigotry with threats of "Negro domination." Although Ulysses S. Grant, the Republican candidate, enjoyed great popularity as a war hero, his party was reeling from the impeachment debacle and the electoral defeats that had preceded it. The Democratic candidate, Horatio Seymour, a Copperhead who had condoned the Draft Riots during his tenure as governor of New York, had proved himself a past master of racist demagoguery. His election would mean that "the loyal whites and blacks of the South" would be "bound hand and foot and delivered over to be slaughtered by their pitiless persecutors," Child prophesied. To avert that catastrophe, she took an uncharacteristic step, publishing electioneering articles in both the *Standard* and the *Independent*. Regardless of how little sympathy Grant might feel for the emancipated slaves, argued Child, "he must needs protect them, or disgrace himself." Concern for the honor of his military record, if nothing else, would motivate him to keep his pledge "not to let the country lose the vantage-ground gained by the herculean labors of the civil war."[20]

With Grant's election, Child heaved a sigh of relief. "The Republic has certainly escaped a very great danger," she judged. In recognition of the role she and David had played in the campaign, a "handsome procession of five hundred men bearing flags and gay-colored lanterns" stopped to salute them in front of their cottage in Wayland. "I . . . joined in the hurrahs of the procession like a 'strong-minded' woman as I am. The fact is, I forget half the time whether I belong to the stronger or weaker sex," Child boasted to Sarah Shaw.[21]

The Republican victory at the polls did not mean that abolitionists could rest on their oars, Child nevertheless hastened to remind *Standard* readers: "I have no sympathy with the prevailing tendency to think that our work is accomplished, and we have nothing to do now but to congratulate and glorify each other. When people ask me if I am not thankful to have lived to see justice done to the negro, I reply, 'If I do live to see justice done him, I shall be thankful.'" Only by exercising "perpetual watchfulness, and that bold impartiality of speech which results from fearing no party and seeking the favor of none" could abolitionists prevent a general backsliding to the prewar status quo and shorten the "perilous transition-time" toward a new order of racial equality, Child underscored.[22]

When Congress reconvened in December 1868, abolitionists finally began to see the results of their tireless campaign for black suffrage — a proposed constitutional amendment stipulating that "the right of citizens of the United States to vote shall not be denied or abridged by the United States or by any State on account of race, color, or previous condition of servitude." It passed the House on January 30, 1869, and the full Congress just before the March 4 adjournment deadline. Although many abolitionists recognized that the amendment's wording left black voters vulnerable to educational and property qualifications, they reluctantly accepted it, rather than risk holding out for a more purist version that Congress might defeat or the states fail to ratify. As Wendell Phillips put it, "we are living now in the easiest hour for the accomplishment of a Constitutional Amendment" guaranteeing the vote to black men. The opportunity, if allowed to slip, might not present itself again for at least another generation.[23]

On Christmas Day 1869, as the end of the countdown toward ratification neared, Child hailed the consummation of abolitionists' long crusade with her usual realism. "The passage of the Fifteenth Amendment will give a legal finish to the Anti-Slavery work; but if the soldiers of Freedom disband and lay aside their uniform, they should be careful to turn their telescopes very frequently toward the country of the old enemy," she warned, again writing jointly with David:

> The Fifteenth Amendment may be nominally ratified, as a mere stroke of policy, and yet be so evaded, by some contrivance, that the colored population will in reality have no civil rights allowed them. . . .
>
> The experience of many years shows the necessity of distrusting the professions of Southerners, and of watching their policy very closely; not because they are worse than other men would be under similar circumstances, but simply because the effects of a system so despotic and so false as Slavery cannot be wiped away by legal enactments from the souls of a generation that have grown up under its malign influence.[24]

Child provided her fullest analysis of the challenges she discerned for the future in the last of her joint letters with David, published in the valedictory issue of the old *National Anti-Slavery Standard* and addressed to the "Anti-Slavery Friends" who had assembled in New York on April 9, 1870, to commemorate the ratification ten days earlier of the Fifteenth Amendment. In this letter she clearly revealed both the extent and the limits of her radicalism. The conferral of universal manhood suffrage, she acknowledged, was a "bold" enterprise — "the most glorious experiment that Divine Providence has ever trusted to the hands of mortals" — but it was also the practical fulfillment of the "principles on which our government is founded." Whatever anxieties the "experiment" might arouse, she stressed, black voters would not be the first to demonstrate whether "ignorant masses can be safely trusted to exercise" the right to a "voice in the laws by which they are governed":

> We have granted the right of suffrage to hordes of foreigners, who can neither read nor write, who are led blindfolded by a church bitterly hostile to every form of Protestant faith, and strongly opposed to free institutions, and the dissemination of knowledge. . . . Yet even in *their* case, we would faithfully guard their rights as citizens, and trust to time and the influence of free institutions to render them more enlightened.
>
> And have we not much *more* reason to trust in the colored people? They are natives of this country, they are fervently attached to the prevailing forms of the Protestant religion, and they are under the influence of ministers and missionaries, who everywhere encourage their zeal for knowledge.[25]

On one level, by carrying democratic ideology to its logical extreme, Child was proving the sincerity of her radical creed. On another level, however, by affirming the capacity of "free institutions" to absorb and enlighten "ignorant masses," she was implying that the goal of the nation's bold "experiment" was to bring all citizens into conformity with a white, middle-class, Protestant model. While denying that racial difference need constitute a permanent barrier between native-born whites and blacks, she was simultaneously attributing greater significance to cultural and religious differences. Grateful Protestant freedmen, she was intimating, would be easier to "influence" than rebellious Catholic foreigners. In short, Child was unwittingly perpetuating the dangerous tendency to play blacks and immigrant whites against each other.[26] Her distrust of an "alien" proletariat would become increasingly evident in her later political writings. Still, it never led her to join forces with the elitists who called for restricting suffrage and immigration to prevent the proletariat from "becoming an actual majority of the voting population." In the midst of a widespread retreat from democratic principles, Child retained a faith in the ultimate benefit of universal suffrage and education that most of her contemporaries considered radical, indeed.[27]

Though unable to undertake the arduous and expensive trip to New York for the last meeting of the American Anti-Slavery Society, the Childs did manage to attend the society's final antislavery festival and the closing meeting of the Massachusetts branch, both held on January 27, 1870, in Boston's Horticultural Hall. "[P]reternaturally mild" weather allayed Child's horror of traveling in winter, when she and David were so prone to rheumatism. Yet typically, David "stopped to talk" at the station and "missed getting into the cars," leaving Child to be "whirled into the city alone" and escorted to the meeting by Wendell Phillips. She and David, who eventually caught up with her, were assigned places of honor on the platform, along with Angelina Grimké Weld and several other veterans of the cause. Reporting on the events for the *Standard*, Charlotte Forten noted that "[t]he presence of Mrs. Child gave a peculiar charm to the occasion." She went on to pay Child a poignant tribute, holding her up as both a role model and a buffer against the racism from which Forten suffered so keenly:

> Mrs. Child is truly "embodied sunshine," — as cheering and inspiring as the brightest June day. She is young and will ever be so with the heart's perpetual youth. . . . We all know what it is that keeps her so young; how noble and generous she is; how she devotes the proceeds of her delightful books to the freedmen, how she curtails her own personal expenses in every possible way that she may give freely to the needy. . . . As it is "more blessed to give than to receive" she must be greatly blest, and not alone for material gifts nor even for the consecration of her fine mental powers but for the warm and ready sympathy, which, coming straight from her large heart, gladdens and strengthens many another heart aching with the bitter sense of injustice and wrong. . . .[28]

Among the other African American celebrants Child encountered at the festival were the former fugitives William and Ellen Craft, the story of whose daring escape she had retold in *The Freedmen's Book*. They had recently returned from a long sojourn in England and were collecting funds and supplies for an industrial school and labor colony they were planning to establish for the freedpeople in Georgia. Impressed by their intelligence, judiciousness, and "uncommon business talent," Child would devote "all the time [she] could spare from household duties . . . to hunting up and repairing books" and other "odds and ends" to send to the Crafts, along with five copies of *The Freedmen's Book* and one of *A Romance of the Republic*.[29]

Despite the attention she received from old friends and young admirers, Child found the festival too crowded and rushed for "social enjoyment." The mood of the meeting itself was solemn rather than jubilant. "The colored people and the loyal white people of the South, write us too many letters describing their persecutions and their dangers" for abolitionists to indulge in " 'ovations,' " she commented to Lucy Osgood, who persisted in believing that the work of the antislavery movement was now over. The speeches and official resolutions of the society echoed Child's oft-expressed view that a major goal of Reconstruction remained unrealized as long as the freedpeople did not own their own land.[30] The ballot alone could not secure blacks political rights, abolitionist radicals agreed, for without land they would never be economically independent of their former masters. As Child formulated it in a letter to Abby Kelley Foster, who had written to praise her articles on "Homesteads" for the freedpeople: "[w]hether they shall be disheartened vagrants, or become a class of contented and useful citizens depends upon their being enabled to have homes of their own." If she had the money, she added, she would "buy millions of acres to sell again, at low prices, to those poor homeless laborers. I say to *sell* again, first, because I believe it is more salutary to all classes of people to *earn* a home than to have it *given* to them; and because a permanent fund could be thus obtained to furnish homes to an indefinite extent."[31] But the aim of breaking up the large plantations and redistributing the land to the freedpeople and poor whites would never be accomplished. The chance to effect such a policy, if it had ever existed, had long since passed.[32]

Child's excursion to Boston for the historic January 27 valedictory meeting of the Massachusetts Anti-Slavery Society ended as it had begun. David failed to meet her at the Fitchburg Depot for the return train to Wayland. "He arrived just one minute too late, and I had to 'tote' bags and budgets back into the city, till the next day," Child reported in exasperation to her niece Sarah Parsons. Symbolically, the contretemps enabled her to attend the founding meeting of the Massachusetts Woman Suffrage Association and to meet one of the leaders who would carry the torch of radical reform into the next generation, the "electrifying" Mary Livermore, whom Child described as "the product of the untramelled West."[33]

The timing of the new suffrage group's formation was not fortuitous, signaling as it did that with the Fifteenth Amendment's ratification assured, reformers could now safely devote their energies to the next item on their agenda, the extension of the vote to women. Since 1867, women's rights advocates had been engaged in a bitter internecine conflict over whether to support a suffrage amendment that did not include women.[34] Initially, Child seems to have agreed with Elizabeth Cady Stanton and other feminist leaders that abolitionists ought to campaign for a universal suffrage amendment, which would simultaneously enfranchise black men and all women. She had been championing women's right to vote ever since the 1856 Frémont campaign,[35] and she saw considerable merit in the argument that women, like blacks, had earned the gratitude of the nation for their dedicated and efficient support of the Union war effort. Stanton later claimed in her *History of Woman Suffrage* that Child had headed a petition to Charles Sumner against using the word "male" in the Fourteenth Amendment — a usage feminists protested because it introduced "an explicit sexual distinction into the Constitution for the first time."[36] Be that as it may, when Stanton subsequently asked for her active support, Child pleaded too "little energy for enlisting in a new war," but she furnished a warm letter of endorsement for "the cause you are advocating so zealously and ably," published in the *Independent* of December 6, 1866.[37] The following month she wrote a two-part article on "Woman and Suffrage" for the *Independent*, in which she eloquently refuted an antisuffrage polemic by a conservative divine named Tayler Lewis, who had contended that "one of the most precious ordinances of God and Nature" authorized the male head of the household to vote on behalf of his female dependents. In her article, however, Child implicitly distinguished her position from Stanton's by confessing "reluctance to urge the question of female suffrage upon Congress at this time, when they have so many other difficult problems to solve," and by conceding that "[t]he suffrage of woman can better afford to wait than that of the colored people," given the imperative of counteracting white supremacist terrorism in the South.[38] Unlike Stanton, who maintained that women must take advantage of an opportunity "when the constitutional door is open" to "walk in by [the] side" of the black man,[39] Child recognized that expediency, and not principle, would be the decisive factor in swinging Republican politicians and voters over to black suffrage, and that expediency currently militated against their espousing the enfranchisement of women.

The nearly two-year interval before Child returned to the subject of woman suffrage may be ascribable in part to her preoccupation with finishing *A Romance of the Republic*, which appeared in August 1867; yet it also suggests a conscious decision to avoid taking part in the increasingly ugly dispute among feminists over which deserved the higher priority—black suffrage or woman suffrage. Indeed, Child's next public statement in favor of "universal suffrage," a letter addressed to the October 1868 New England Woman's Rights Convention, pointedly advocated suffrage for black men and for women in the same breath. "[I]t has long been my conviction . . . that society can never be established on a true and solid foundation so long as any distinction whatsoever is made between men and women with regard to the full and free exercise of their faculties on all subjects, whether of art, science, literature, business or politics," Child asserted. She went on to dissociate herself both from those who demanded educational qualifications for blacks and from those who alleged that women were not ready for the vote. "[T]he same rule ought to be impartially applied to all classes," she insisted. "If Irishmen who can neither read nor write are allowed to vote, assuredly colored men who can neither read nor write ought also to be allowed to vote." For illiterate men and unsophisticated women alike, "no element of education is so powerful as a feeling of personal responsibility with regard to subjects of serious interest."[40]

Meanwhile, Stanton and her coworker Susan B. Anthony had taken the opposite path. During their 1867 campaign in Kansas in support of the black suffrage and woman suffrage state constitutional amendments on the ballot, Stanton and Anthony had reacted against local Republican leaders' hostility to woman suffrage by turning to the Democrats. Approached by a Democratic presidential aspirant named George Francis Train, whom one historian has described as "a copperhead and a flamboyant showman given to eccentric dress and self-promotion," Stanton and Anthony had snapped up his proffered assistance. Train traveled through Kansas with Anthony, appearing in "[l]avander [*sic*] kids, black pants, closely buttoned blue coat with brass buttons, and patent leather boots" and bolstering Anthony's speeches in favor of woman suffrage with crude racist jokes aimed at convincing Democratic audiences to vote for enfranchising white women rather than "barbers, bootblacks, melons and chickens." The alliance continued after the campaign, with Train financing a newspaper for Stanton and Anthony, the *Revolution*, issued from the same building as the rabidly anti-black Democratic organ, the New York *World*.[41] "I am sorry Mrs. Stanton carries such a *Train* with her," Child quipped to Samuel Sewall. "The question of Woman's Right to Suffrage requires, more than any *other* reform, great care to avoid making it ridiculous; and George Francis Train certainly *is* ridiculous. He throws off some scintillations of eloquence, but his egotism amounts to insanity, and his judgment to o." She also objected to the willingness Stanton showed to "compromise with the Democrats, and give up negro suffrage, if they would favor female suffrage."[42]

Either because she hoped Stanton and Anthony would soon come to realize their "error of judgment," or because she feared to exacerbate the schism their actions had provoked in the ranks of abolitionists and women's rights advocates, Child confined her criticism of their course to her private correspondence until August 1869. As Stanton's calls for the defeat of the Fifteenth Amendment intensified, however, acquiring "the sneering tone habitually assumed by slaveholders and their copperhead allies," Child felt obliged to break her silence. In an article titled "Women and the Freedmen," prominently displayed on the *Standard*'s editorial page and later reprinted in the *Woman's Advocate*, she expressed her dismay that "rotten timbers were getting introduced into the foundation of our cause." Noting that Stanton was courting southern white women and was accusing the freedmen of opposing woman suffrage, Child lamented that a "party of female politicians at the North" was aping the unscrupulous tactics of certain northern male politicians in "the days of slave-holding supremacy"; by showing themselves "ready to sacrifice the rights of colored men in order to secure the co-operation of Southern ladies," these "female politicians" were discrediting the notion that "the suffrage of women would tend to purify politics," she commented acidly. She could hardly moderate her censure of "a compromise so utterly wrong in principle, so shamefully mean and selfish in its spirit," Child added: "God forbid that women should ever consent to take one iota from the rights of others for the sake of advancing their own! Will human beings never learn that no good thing can ever be firmly established on a basis of violated principle?"[43]

At the same time, Child stepped up her crusading for woman suffrage. "Though tired of battling, I cannot keep my hands off 'the woman question,'" she confided to Sarah Shaw. "It is decidedly the most important question that has been before the world."[44] The July 15 and October 21, 1869, issues of the *Independent* carried another two-part article "Concerning Women," in which Child now openly favored the leaders who had parted company with Stanton and Anthony over the issue of the Fifteenth Amendment—Lucy Stone and Mary Livermore. Both earned her praise for manifesting "womanly dignity and sound common sense," as well as for resisting the impulse to hasten the liberation of women by "violating principles of freedom with regard to other human beings."[45]

The first installment of the article reiterated Child's belief that "unlimited freedom for the development of woman's faculties, and the consequent equality of the sexes in every department of life, will prove both safe and salutary." The article went on to trace the progress women had made toward that goal from ancient times to the nineteenth century. Each gain had been "hindered by conventional prejudices," Child pointed out, yet society had gradually become accustomed to women's removal of veils, their participation in mixed social gatherings, their assumption of literary careers, and their public speaking. "Quite as easily will the world become accustomed to women's voting and holding civil offices," she predicted. Through a long digression on men's evolution from aristocratic to democratic styles of clothing, she also provided women who had been calling for dress reform with a powerful new argument: "as women become invested with larger responsibilities, and become conscious of living for more extensive usefulness, will they not [like men before them] shake off the tyranny of fashion, and learn to combine gracefulness with simplicity and convenience in their costume?"[46]

The second installment of "Concerning Women" developed the thesis that sociocultural rather than biological factors accounted for most of the sexual differences so often invoked by conservatives to justify male dominance and female subordination as inherent in nature. "Even in physical strength, I doubt whether there is so much difference between men and women as has been generally assumed," Child ventured, citing the hard physical labor performed by women under slavery and in cultures as diverse as those of American Indians and European peasants.[47] Most radical was her explanation of the "difficulty at the basis of this whole subject": "The plain, undisguised truth is that women are everywhere tacitly regarded as articles of merchandise" and are "considered as *belonging* to men." Child sarcastically denied that conservative men had any ground for "alarm at the progress of 'woman's rights' ": "They, and their sons, and their sons' sons, will find plenty of clinging vines. So long as the article is in demand, the market will be abundantly supplied with women who have been trained to consider it unfeminine to think, unladylike to work, and who spend their days in decorating their persons to catch the eye of purchasers. Meanwhile, be assured, my brethren, that you, as well as we, are losers by the present unequal arrangements."[48] More trenchant than any of her earlier feminist writings, these articles for the *Independent* explicitly drew the inferences Child had left unstated in her 1835 *History of the Condition of Women*; they constituted her strongest theoretical statements on the "woman question."

With the passage of the Fifteenth Amendment, Child joined other feminists in agitating for a Sixteenth Amendment enfranchising women — the strategy that Lucy Stone and Mary Livermore had advocated during the dispute with Stanton and Anthony. Besides participating (albeit fortuitously) in the establishment of the Massachusetts Woman Suffrage, Child allowed herself to be elected as one of its honorary vice presidents. In addition, she decided that the time had come to exert her influence on Sumner, a key figure in the Senate, whom she had hesitated to pressure while the struggle for black suffrage remained unresolved. Using the vehicle of a Fourth of July letter, she urged him to rethink his opposition to according women the vote until a majority of them demanded it. "[S]ooner or later, you will see that the republican ideas you advocate so earnestly cannot be consistently carried out while women are excluded from a share in the government," Child remonstrated. She proceeded to apply to women the principles of the Declaration of Independence and the tenets of abolitionist ideology:

> I pay taxes for property of my own earning and saving; and "taxation without representation" seems to me obviously unjust. As for representation by *proxy*, that savors too much of the *plantation*-system, however kind the masters may be. I am a human being and I hold that every human being has a right to a voice in the laws, by which he may be taxed, imprisoned, or hung. The exercise of *rights* always has a more salutary effect on character, than the enjoyment of *privileges*. Any class of human beings to whom a position of perpetual subordination is assigned, however much they may be petted, must inevitably be dwarfed morally and intellectually.

Child ended with a personal plea and a candid avowal of her private frustrations, which Sumner ought to have found deeply moving, coming from a woman he admired so much: "For forty years, I have keenly felt the cramping effects of my limitations as a woman, and I have submitted to them under a perpetual and indignant protest. . . . I have walked in fetters thus far, and my pilgrimage is drawing to a close."[49]

Despite Child's eloquent lobbying, Sumner never did come round to supporting woman suffrage. In contrast, his Radical colleague, Indiana Congressman George Julian, introduced the Sixteenth Amendment in September 1869, pressing for it even after his electoral defeat the following year. To show her appreciation, Child agreed to write an introduction to his 1872 collection of *Speeches on Political Questions*.

The disposal of the black suffrage issue did not end the schism between the Stanton-Anthony and Stone factions of the women's movement, and Child continued to side with the latter. In November 1870 she addressed a letter to Stone for public delivery at the first annual meeting of the American Woman Suffrage Association — the organization Stone had formed to distinguish her group from the National Woman Suffrage Association founded by Stanton and Anthony. Child implored the group to concentrate on obtaining the suffrage and equal educational and professional advantages for women and to refrain from bringing "collateral questions into undue prominence." The "collateral" question she most deprecated raising prematurely, Child specified, was "the present state of law and custom" on marriage and divorce — a prime target of Stanton's recent speeches and editorials in the *Revolution*. "We all know that the institution of marriage has been degraded and polluted by making woman a marketable commodity," Child acknowledged, but it could only be "purified and ennobled by [woman's] equal companionship with man in all respects," and not by "any more rapid progress." Once women had won the right to "share equally with men in the making of the laws," they would have the power to effect the changes they desired, and the two sexes could "take counsel together concerning the right settlement of a question of such vital importance to us both." If they sought to agitate "this dangerous topic" now, they would "make the 'Woman Cause' unpopular, and thereby retard its progress." Even worse, they would threaten the "well-being of society." "Licentiousness is a deep-seated, festering sore in the social system," Child stressed, and it had to be cured like other sores: "Surround it with pure air, and bring pure waters to bathe it," but allow time for "a new and healthy skin" to form underneath before "pulling off the old skin."[50]

The advice was sound and sensible, but it belied Child's claim that she was consistently growing "more radical" in her old age. After all, she had once announced to Louisa Loring that she considered it "legalized prostitution" for couples who no longer loved each other to "live together in the married relation," and she had written to Francis Shaw: "Nature is so outrageously dammed up, her strongest instincts are so repressed, her plainest laws are so violated, in the present structure of society, that nature *will* revenge herself, in spite of all we can do."[51] Not that she had ever voiced such beliefs publicly, except under the veil of fiction. But she had taken a very different attitude toward an equally controversial issue in the antislavery struggle — whether or not to defer protest against antimiscegenation laws until the achievement of abolition. Throughout her career as a reformer, she had never ceased to defend interracial marriage as an essential part of her egalitarian agenda, undeterred either by the antiabolitionist riots of the 1830s or by the Democratic press's exploitation of "amalgamation" fears in the 1860s. Far from soft-pedaling her defense of interracial marriage to assure the passage of a black suffrage amendment, she had published *A Romance of the Republic* at a critical juncture of the Reconstruction debates. Similarly, as we shall see, she had gone out of her way to introduce the topic into her 1868 *Appeal for the Indians*. It is difficult to avoid concluding that Child reacted differently to challenging the sanctity of marriage and liberalizing divorce laws not because those issues were more controversial, but because they aroused deep personal conflicts in her.[52] She had long since made her peace with David and renounced her dreams of a more satisfying marriage; perhaps she could not bear to reopen the old wounds by entertaining alternatives to the course she had chosen.

Both Stanton and Stone were likewise struggling with marital difficulties, which had led them in opposite directions — Stanton toward turning her personal discontent into a political critique of the institution, Stone toward repressing her unhappiness and devoting herself to the larger cause of woman suffrage.[53] Stone had already elected the policy Child recommended in her letter. Although the rival organizations were exploring the possibility of healing the breach caused by the black suffrage imbroglio, major disagreements on strategy still divided them. Stanton wanted to address all aspects of women's oppression, including men's ownership of women's bodies; Stone wanted to confine discussion to the less scandalous topics of suffrage, education, and employment. "Better for both to work apart, without responsibility for each other's proceedings," Child advised. Relieved to learn that the two parties had reached the same conclusion, she nevertheless cautioned against succumbing to the sectarianism that had plagued the abolitionist movement. In a letter to Stone's organ, the *Woman's Journal*, she urged: "I hope women will not slide into the error to which reformers are so easily tempted—that of impugning each other's motives, or calling each other by uncourteous names, because they cannot see eye to eye on all points. Individuals may be very just and kind neighbors, without choosing to marry each other 'for better or worse'; and I see no reason why it may not be the same with societies."[54]

Founded in 1870, the *Woman's Journal* provided Child with a new forum, and she began to sustain it as vigorously as she had the *Standard*. Over the next few years, until immobilized by David's death in 1874, she contributed to it regularly, specializing in pointed responses to antisuffrage polemicists. The theme of her articles was "What is sauce for goose is sauce for gander," as she announced in the epigraph to one essay titled "Concerning Woman Suffrage." Replying to a conservative clergyman named Joseph P. Thompson, for example, who cited the atrocities committed by Catherine de Médicis, Madame de Maintenon, and the women of the 1871 Paris Commune as instances of the horrors that might be anticipated from female rule, Child asked whether the atrocities committed by males proved that "*men* are also unfit to be trusted" with the elective franchise. The New York Draft Riots, she pointed out, had been perpetrated by men. "[I]f the depraved classes of *women* in cities would be such dangerous voters," she demanded, were "the men whose vices created such classes . . . any safer depositories of civil power"? The only means of raising men or women "out of the depths of brutality and ignorance" and of rendering them "safe subjects of a Commonwealth," Child insisted, was to "educate them in political duties" and to "trust them with political responsiblities, as a vital portion of that education." This apt rejoinder earned her a special vote of thanks from Mary Livermore. "[T]he weight of your name gave additional power to the criticism," she wrote Child.[55]

Child also took on a polemicist in the *Liberal Christian* who had complained that intellectuality was "the bane of American women." "It *is* a lamentable fact that 'we are making household work a thing only for servants, and are rendering hand-labor disreputable,'" she conceded, "but it seems to me, the evil exists to as great an extent among our young men as among our young women." In both sexes, the pursuit of "intellectual ambition" to the neglect of "physical laws" was clearly injurious, but such cases were more common among men than among women (contrary to the theories propounded by Dr. Edward Hammond Clarke in his 1873 best-seller, *Sex and Education*, which warned against damage to women's sexual organs if they studied subjects better suited to male brains).[56] As for the writer's assertion that if women were admitted to Harvard, their moral safety would be "very much due to their unattractiveness," Child retorted: "The supposition is far from complimentary to young men," especially at such an elite university, but it is not surprising "from a writer who avows that he considers women unattractive in proportion to the degree of their mental cultivation."[57]

In keeping with the caveat Child had addressed to the American Woman Suffrage Association, her articles for the *Woman's Journal* steered clear of the marriage question. Privately, however, Child anxiously tracked the gathering storm over "free love," as a flamboyant editor-orator-stockbroker-spiritualist named Victoria Woodhull surged to the forefront of the rival suffrage camp in 1871 and captured press headlines by proclaiming her "inalienable, constitutional, and natural right to love whom I may, to love as long or as short a period as I can, to change that love every day if I please!"[58] Having acquired credibility by arguing persuasively before the Senate Judiciary Committee that the Fourteenth and Fifteenth Amendments could be construed as enfranchising women, Woodhull won the endorsement of Stanton and Anthony and nearly succeeded in taking over their organization. Before Anthony repudiated her in 1872, she managed to deflect attention from the campaign for woman suffrage to her free-love doctrines and sexual dalliances. Nor would Anthony's disavowal end the matter. Woodhull would retaliate by accusing Henry Ward Beecher, first president of Stone's American Woman Suffrage Association, of carrying on an affair with the wife of Theodore Tilton, editor of the *Independent* and a staunch supporter of Stanton, citing Stanton as her source—a charge that would tar the entire women's movement with the brush of free love.[59] "Mrs. Woodhull and her associates are a great blister to my spirit," Child complained to her friends. They "are doing their utmost to mix up 'Free Love,' with the movement" and are causing "immense harm" by impeding women's "real progress."[60] Victorian sexual institutions were an "Augean stable," Child agreed, and she had always foreseen that discussion of women's rights would inevitably lead to a reexamination of sexual mores, but women ought to be "patient till society is *educated* into a better state of things!"[61] Characteristically, Child refused to speculate about Woodhull's morals and even credited her, at least initially, with sincere reformist aims. Recalling her earlier analysis of Frances Wright and George Sand, she wrote of Woodhull and other "Free Love women": "I am far from thinking that *impure* motives actuate them. Most of them have in some way suffered severely under existing laws & customs, and they generously wish to save coming generations from similar experiences." She reproached them primarily with being "lamentably deficient in discretion," as well as in a sense of "*duty*."[62]

Child's sole contribution to the debates on sexual questions during this period was a fallen woman story titled "A Soul's Victory over Circumstances," which she claimed to have recorded from a woman she had met in the stage. The heroine, Eunice ("Good-Victory") Manly, allows herself to be seduced by her self-seeking fiancé Robert Shallow on the eve of his departure to undertake a long apprenticeship that her parents have imposed as a test of his character. The mean-spirited letter he writes in response to the news of her pregnancy opens Eunice's eyes, and she resolves not to marry such a despicable man, who she realizes would make a bad father as well as a bad husband. She also decides to bear her child openly and raise it under her parents' roof, instead of secreting herself in a distant village and giving the child up for adoption.

At first, she is ostracized by her neighbors, but little by little her dignity and strength of character gain their respect. Although she receives two marriage proposals from estimable men, she turns both down, the first because she fears his family will not welcome her illegitimate daughter, the second because she does not love him. Becoming a governess after her daughter's death, she ultimately marries the father of the children she has been educating, with the blessing of their dying mother. "When I met her in the stage," Child ends the story, "she had long borne his name, and did credit to it by her domestic virtues."[63]

Compared with Child's fallen women stories of the 1840s, "A Soul's Victory" registers both the gain in her psychological well-being and the subsidence of her sexual desires. Unlike the heroines of "Rosenglory" and "Elizabeth Wilson," Eunice Manly refuses the status of pathetic victim and acts energetically to restore herself. She rejects the charade of a shotgun marriage, proves that an unwed mother can survive better on her own than by marrying her seducer, and lives down her disgrace. Yet in contrast to "Hilda Silfverling," Eunice's story offers no vision of sexual fulfillment; her late marriage, undertaken more as a "duty" to another mother's children than as an outlet for her own long-buried passion, seems at best a marriage of companionship (like the Childs'). As Child's answer to the controversy over free love, "A Soul's Victory" indicates that sexual liberation had come to seem less pressing to her in old age than other aspects of the women's rights struggle.

Whether or not Child could rightly claim to have "grow[n] more radical" on women's issues remains an open question. On the problem that her generation of reformers would have most trouble solving — how to do justice to the Indians — her writings of the 1860s show a clear advance beyond her earlier views. True, Child never transcended the limitations that even the best-intentioned of the Indian's nineteenth-century sympathizers displayed. Still, she stood in the vanguard of contemporary opinion.

The Civil War and Reconstruction had vastly improved the legal position of African Americans and white women, but the exigencies of the sectional conflict and the technological development it unleashed had spelled disaster for Indians. Both sides used Indians as pawns, enlisting them in the war when convenient, but defaulting on promises of pay, arms, provisions, and protection. In Kansas and the Indian Territory of what would become Oklahoma, troop movements and shifting battle lines between Union and Confederate forces displaced thousands of Indians from their homes, often uprooting tribes that had already been "removed" in the 1830s and '40s. In Minnesota, settlers exploited wartime security concerns and the need for bipartisan unity to agitate for transporting the tribes of the Great Lakes region out to the Dakota territory. Meanwhile, the Minnesota Sioux, faced with starvation because corrupt agents had withheld the annuities owed in exchange for tribal land, went on the warpath, forcing Lincoln to divert badly needed troops from the southern theater in 1862. Analogous conditions prevailed in New Mexico, Colorado, and the Dakota territory. The accelerating pace of road and railway construction across tribal lands threatened the buffalo herds on which Plains Indians depended for food and caused frequent clashes between them and white settlers, culminating in major Indian wars in 1864.[64]

Child had repeatedly publicized the plight of the Indians during her editorship of the *Standard* and in her fiction of the 1840s. Long after other abolitionists once involved in the Cherokee struggle had become too preoccupied with the slavery crisis to agitate for Indian rights, Child had continued to intertwine the issues of slavery and Indian dispossession. As late as 1856, at the height of the civil war between pro- and antislavery settlers in Kansas, she had integrated the issue of justice toward Indians into her story "The Kansas Emigrants."[65] Not content with devoting her own literary talents to dramatizing the connection between the Indian's and the slave's wrongs, she had implored the poet John Greenleaf Whittier to do likewise. Writing to him in January 1857, she had suggested that he undertake a "tragic poem" about the Seminole chief Osceola, who had "married a beautiful runaway slave" and "instigated his tribe to resist the aggressions" of Georgia slaveholders and U.S. troops, only to be "treacherously entrapped by a flag of truce" and thrown into prison. The fate of Osceola and the defeated Seminole, expelled from Florida and torn from their black wives and children, epitomized for Child the historical intersection of the abolitionist and Indian causes. So urgently did she feel the need to address the two questions together that she renewed her plea to Whittier at the end of the war.[66]

Thus, when an Oregon reformer named John Beeson came to Boston in 1859 and 1861 to mobilize abolitionist support for his crusade to save the Indians, Child seems to have been especially receptive. She would cite him repeatedly in her 1868 and 1870 appeals for the Indians. And early in 1861, perhaps after attending a convention over which Beeson had presided that February, she set about writing her finest story of Indian-white relations, "Willie Wharton."[67]

A companion piece to *A Romance of the Republic*, conceived within eighteen months of it, "Willie Wharton" articulates the same ideal of interracial marriage and cultural fusion, but applies it to the Indian problem.[68] The story also sums up the evolution Child's concept of assimilation had undergone since she first formulated it in *Hobomok* nearly four decades before as an alternative to Indian genocide. Set in an unnamed prairie state and written in the realistic mode of "The Kansas Emigrants," "Willie Wharton" celebrates the transformation of the wilderness into a farm-land of "luxuriant" wheat fields dotted with prosperous villages, church spires, and schoolhouses.[69] Child refuses to recognize any necessary contradiction between the imperatives of western settlement and the survival of the Indians. Hence, she radically revises the myth of the frontier derived from the captivity narrative and sketches a picture of mutually beneficial interactions between enlightened white settlers and well-disposed Indians.

As the story opens, Jenny Wharton and her brother, George, are scanning the horizon for Jenny's six-year-old son Willie, Jenny apprehensively recalling stories of Indian attacks that had "made a painful impression" on her imagination in her New England childhood, George reminding her that Indians would be "as good as Christians, if they were treated justly and kindly" (324, 326). Willie's arrival with a four-year-old Indian "pappoose" in tow, whom he has found lost on the prairie, foreshadows his destiny. "I believe the adventurous little chap has been to the land of Nod to get him a wife," comments his Uncle George (324). Prophetically, the two children fall asleep in Willie's trundle bed "with their arms about each other's necks, the dark brow nestled close to the rosy cheek, and the mass of black hair mingled with the light brown locks, . . . as cozily as two kittens with different fur" (327). When the Indian girl's parents show up the following morning, they present the Whartons with a basket as a token of thanks, and Willie gives his new friend a string of scarlet guinea peas as a souvenir. The gifts, treasured through the years by both families, symbolize the bond forged between them and suggest the reciprocal relations that would naturally form if white settlers treated Indians "justly and kindly" (324).

Six months after his adventure in the "land of Nod," Willie himself is picked up on the prairie by wandering Indians and "decoyed" away with them by a "squaw, whose pappoose had died" (324, 339). The second phase of the story recounts the Whartons' sixteen-year search for their missing son, who unknown to them has ended up marrying the very "pappoose" he had brought home with him. Reinforcing the twin themes of interracial marriage and cultural fusion, Child draws on both Swedenborgian and Indian mystical traditions in a scene that subverts the conventional Victorian deathbed vision and supplants it with a vision of the nation's future. Instead of angels coming to bear her to heaven, Willie's dying mother sees her son wearing an Indian blanket and bedecking his Indian bride with guinea peas in an idyllic woodland setting where the two lovers "look happy" (334). Simultaneously, Willie has a vision of his mother, whom he no longer remembers, but whom he sees with "blue eyes and pale hair," corresponding to his foster parents' description of her. Believing that such "clairvoyant" phenomena had occurred in all cultures across time, Child offers this "magnetic transmission of intelligence" (334) between Anglo mother and Indianized son as a metaphor for the common spirituality that can put the separated families of humankind back in touch with each other and merge them into one.[70] Accordingly, Willie's vision now impels him on a quest for his long-forgotten biological family.

The last and most provocative phase of the story reconstitutes the Whartons as an interracial and bicultural family. In the process, it redefines the meaning of "brotherhood," questions the significance of race, explores the boundaries of culture, and broadens the concept of assimilation. When Willie and his brother, Charles, finally find each other in an Indian encampment, the cultural gap between them proves as formidable as if they were literally of different races: "The uncouth costume, and the shaggy hair falling over the forehead, gave Willie such a wild appearance, it was hard for Charles to realize that they were brothers. Inability to understand each other's language created a chilling barrier between them" (337). The tie of blood that links them as sons of the same parents seems as much of an abstraction to the newfound siblings as the ideal of universal human brotherhood. Their common racial identity is so irrelevant that an Indian interpreter classifies Willie as a "red man" in explaining why Willie appears "unmoved" by the reunion that brings "tears to the eyes" of Charles: "Him sorry-glad; but red man he no cry" (337). What alienates Willie and Charles from each other is their difference of hairstyle, dress, language, behavior, and values — in short, culture.

Yet Child goes on to show that culture need pose no permanent "barrier" between white and Indian "brothers," precisely because it is not innate, but acquired. If a white boy, by being brought up among Indians, can become indistinguishable from them in his habits, manners, and thoughts, then an Indian, by being educated among whites, can become "white." The parallel difficulties Willie and his Indian bride A-lee-lah face in attempting to adapt to "civilized habits" that are as alien to him as to her further develop this point (343).

Although Child defines the problem of incorporating Indians into American society as cultural rather than racial, she emphasizes that assimilation must include intermarriage. Unless white Americans are willing to embrace Indians as full members of their national family, she intimates, they cannot expect Indians to embrace "civilization." Hence, Uncle George argues that the Whartons must welcome A-lee-lah if they hope to make Willie "feel at home" and elect to stay. Themselves embodying the marriage of cultures, interracial couples can facilitate the process of assimilation by serving as "bridges," Child suggests (341, 343).[71]

She also indicates how Anglo-Americans might benefit from adopting some facets of Indian culture. For example, when Willie's cousin and sister insist on replacing A-lee-lah's short grass skirt and blanket with the constraining clothes of nineteenth-century Anglo-American ladies, Uncle George remonstrates: "it would be far more rational for you to follow *her* fashion about short skirts." After getting perpetually "entangled in the folds of her long, full skirts" and petticoats, A-lee-lah "cast[s] aside the troublesome garments and resume[s] her blanket" (342). Ultimately, she settles on "a becoming hybrid between English and Indian costumes" — a version of the Bloomers (actually East Indian in origin), which feminist dress reformers were trying to promote:[72]

Loose trousers of emerald-green merino were fastened with scarlet cord and tassels above gaiters of yellow beaver-skin thickly embroidered with beads of many colors. An upper garment of scarlet merino was ornamented with gilded buttons, on each of which was a shining star. The short, full skirt of this garment fell a little below the knee, and the border was embroidered with gold-colored braid. At the waist, it was fastened with a green morocco belt and gilded buckle.

Willie's sister admits that this exotic outfit is both attractive and comfortable: "I should like such a dress myself, if other folks wore it," she concedes (344).

Indian manners as well as dress would bear imitation, Child hints. Decrying the "Yankee" tendency to pry into the affairs of others like "a self-elected Investigating Committee, which never adjourns its sessions," Child comments that Willie and A-lee-lah's "Indian ideas of natural politeness" make them regard the intrusive visits of their nosy white neighbors "as a breach of good manners" (344).

Despite these efforts to reconceptualize assimilation not as the obliteration of Indian culture but as a mutually enriching process of cultural interchange, "Willie Wharton" betrays the same limitations *A Romance of the Republic* does. Child's goal, like the Whartons', remains " 'winning [the Indians] over to our mode of life.' " She differs from her contemporaries chiefly in the style of acculturation she advocates through her mouthpiece, Uncle George — a style of "persevering kindness and judicious non-interference" aimed at gradually effecting "such transformations as . . . desired." Uncle George raises no objection to Willie and A-lee-lah's preference for spending most of their time wandering in the woods and "making mats and baskets." Nor does he try to prevent the young couple from continuing to speak "to each other altogether in the Indian dialect," though it "greatly retarded their improvement in English." As Child recognizes, "it was thus they had talked when they first made love, and it was, moreover, the only way in which their tongues could move unfettered" (343). The family also maintains a discreet silence about A-lee-lah's "Shetland pony" hairstyle, "which she considered extremely becoming, but which they regarded as a great disfigurement to her really handsome face" (342). Not until A-lee-lah's admiration for "side-combs ornamented with colored glass" provides an opportunity to remold her taste while appearing to gratify it does anyone propose the innovation of fastening her hair away from her face. This "conquest" is achieved by praising the "pretty forehead" that the new hairstyle reveals. "Thus adroitly, day by day," A-lee-lah and Willie are "guided into increasing conformity with civilized habits" (343).

The method of acculturation Child dramatizes in "Willie Wharton" distinguishes her from most of the missionaries who worked among Indians. An 1869 article in the *Standard* by a Quaker missionary, for example, advised removing Indian children from their families, immuring them in mission boarding schools, cutting off their hair, washing off their "paint and dirt," confiscating their earrings and bracelets, dressing them in "decent" clothes, and forcing them to "drop their lingo, and acquire our language."[73]

If Child's approach is more humane, it nonetheless produces similar results. Cut off from her people and assimilated into her husband's community, A-lee-lah retains almost nothing of her culture by the end of the story. She merely adds an exotic tinge to the dominant Anglo-American culture, blending with the other foreign elements it has absorbed: "Her taste for music improved. . . . [T]he rude, monotonous Indian chants gave place to the melodies of Scotland, Ireland, and Ethiopia. Her taste in dress changed also. She ceased to delight in garments of scarlet and yellow, though she retained a liking for bits of bright, warm color . . . [that] harmonized admirably with her brown complexion and lustrous black hair. She always wore skirts shorter than others, and garments too loose to impede freedom of motion" (345).

Even as it reaches for a more sophisticated and reciprocal concept of assimilation, Child's most radical story of Indian-white intermarriage and acculturation reveals significant continuities with *Hobomok*, Unlike Hobomok, A-lee-lah has neither disappeared nor become " 'almost like an Englishman.' "[74] But she has ceased to be an Indian. And A-lee-lah and Willie's daughter, Jenny, named for her white grandmother, has lost her Indian heritage as entirely as "little Hobomok." "Willie Wharton" succeeds no better than its companion piece, *A Romance of the Republic*, in envisioning a truly multicultural society. All the same, it represents an unmatched achievement for the period.

After imagining a solution to the "Indian problem" in fictional terms, Child proceeded, as she had so often before, to translate her message into political terms. In April 1868 she addressed the plight of the beleaguered Plains Indians in a two-part article for the *Standard*.[75] Now that slavery was abolished and Reconstruction was progressing so quickly, Child urged, the time had come when abolitionists could combine their "vigilant watch over the rights of black men" with a campaign to awaken the nation to the crimes being committed against the "red men" (225).

Her "Appeal for the Indians" led the way, initiating what would become a new abolitionist crusade by 1869.[76] Its immediate impetus was the publication of a report by the Indian Peace Commission, set up by Congress in July 1867 to investigate the causes of the incessant conflicts in the West and to negotiate with hostile tribes.[77] The commission included several prominent generals, chief among them William T. Sherman of Civil War fame, but humanitarian reformers played a prominent role in shaping the report. The sympathy it manifested for Indians was so unprecedented in an official document that Child had greeted it "almost with tears of joy." "Really, this encourages a hope that the Anglo-Saxon race are capable of civilization," she remarked wryly (216). Since the report had not appeared in the *Standard*, Child quoted from it extensively.

The commissioners denounced the army's " 'indiscriminate slaughter' " of Cheyenne women and children at Sand Creek in 1864 and blamed the bloody wars of 1864–65 squarely on the provocation of white settlers, the truculence of Indian-hating local politicians, and the brutality of U.S. troops. Estimating the price of the campaign against the Plains Indians at a million dollars per warrior killed, they concluded that " 'it costs less to civilize than to kill' " (217–18). They went on to recommend confining the Indians to reservations governed by benevolent, but firm, white authorities; weaning them from hunting to "agriculture and manufactures," from collective to individual modes of life; and compelling them to abandon their cultural and tribal identity. "The object of greatest solicitude," the commissioners spelled out, "should be to break down the prejudices of tribe among the Indians; to blot out the boundary lines which divide them into distinct nations, and fuse them into one homogeneous mass. Uniformity of language will do this — nothing else will."[78] If the differences of language, customs, and manners dividing Indians from whites could be eliminated, they held, the " 'antipathy of race' " would gradually lessen and the two races could learn to live together peacefully (218).

While welcoming the spirit of the report, Child predictably criticized the methods of "civilization" it advocated. The recommendations that practices such as polygamy be " 'punished' " and that the Indians' " 'barbarous dialects . . . be blotted out' " savored "too much of our haughty Anglo-Saxon ideas of force," she objected (219). Instead, she suggested an approach much like the one she had dramatized in "Willie Wharton." Positive incentives for living with one wife, buttressed by "reasoned" exhortations, should encourage the Indians to abandon polygamy for monogamy; "the fixed habit of many generations" could not be uprooted overnight, but must be slowly weakened until the Indians were ready for "wise laws on the subject," cautioned Child. As for instruction in English, she envisaged the creation of an analogue to her reader for emancipated slaves, *The Freedmen's Book*:

[L]et their books, at first, be printed in Indian, with English translations; and let them contain selections from the best of their own traditional stories, and records of such things as have been truly honorable in the history of their "braves." Give them pleasant associations with the English language by making it constantly the medium of just principles and kindly feelings. Let proficiency in English, and the habit of speaking it, be rewarded with some peculiar privileges and honors. (219)

Once again, Child recognized the importance of orienting education toward cultivating rather than destroying minority students' pride in their own identity. Yet she apparently conceived of bicultural education merely as a temporary expedient, aimed at easing the Indians' transition toward complete assimilation into the dominant Anglo-American culture. Therein lay the fatal flaw of the multiracial ideal she held up for the nation to follow — a flaw even more obvious in her prescriptions for the Indians than in her program of uplift for African Americans.

Reflecting the impediments to formulating adequate solutions to the "Indian problem" at a time when the conviction of white European cultural superiority prevailed throughout the Western world, the bulk of Child's "Appeal" focused on refuting the "almost universal opinion that Indians are incapable of civilization" (220).[79] As usual, her refutation took a cross-cultural and historicist form. All of the "savage" traits attributed to Indians had been exhibited by Europeans, she argued, adducing a wide range of examples. The Greeks and the Romans, like the Indians, had given "no quarter in battle" and put captives to death. "The civil laws of all European countries authorized tortures" until recent times. The Spanish Inquisition had subjected hundreds of thousands to "infernal" tortures "for differences of belief concerning theological doctrines; an insanity of cruelty of which Indians were never guilty" (220–21). The record of American history had been filled with "unvaried . . . violence and fraud" toward "the red and black members of the human family." Indians, in particular, had endured massacre after massacre at Anglo-American hands, besides the shameful violation of treaty obligations (221–24). Far from proving themselves more civilized than the "savages" they claimed the right to conquer, Child pointed out, "Christian nations, in their transactions with peoples of other religions," had consistently made a mockery of their own creed:

[They] have never considered themselves bound by the same moral principles which regulate their conduct toward those of similar faith and equal power. They are more savage toward "heathens" in war, they are more fraudulent with them in trade, and in personal intercourse they treat them with less civility. Their philanthropic labors among them are nearly deprived of efficacy by an assumption of superiority, a pride of condescension, which is so ingrained in their habits that they are unconscious of it. (226)

Despite the bigotry Europeans had displayed toward peoples of color, Child denied that racial prejudice was an inborn and ineradicable instinct, contrary to the claims of those who pronounced the coexistence of Indians and whites impossible and who called for the extermination of the Indians.[80] "[I]ntermarriages" of whites with Indians "are by no means rare," she asserted, citing several well-known instances; "and they prove, as plainly as the complexions of mulattoes and quadroons, that the 'antipathy of races' is not a *natural* antipathy" (230). A digression from the main line of her argument, ostensibly in response to the peace commissioners' acknowledgment that " 'antipathy of race' " constituted a serious obstacle, Child's defense of intermarriage subtly reiterated her long-standing faith in it as the key to resolving America's race problem.

Having demonstrated that Indians were no more "savage" than whites, Child went on to contend that in some respects they were "decidedly superior." They never broke promises, or violated treaties, or returned "kindness with treachery"; nor did they ever, "even in their wildest moments of revenge, offend the modesty of female captives" — unlike white men, who routinely raped women captured in war, female slaves, and Indian women on the frontier (224, 227–29). Moreover, Indians had more "enlight-ened" views of childrearing than Europeans: "They never strike children, giving this as a reason for it: 'Before a child is old enough to understand, there is no *use* in striking him; and when he is old enough to understand, no one has a *right* to strike him.' " In contrast, Child cited the example of "an orthodox minister in New York" who had not long before "whipped to death his child of three years old, to compel it to repeat a prayer" (229). Indians were also more tolerant in matters of religion: "Their ideas of politeness prevent them from ever ridiculing or contradicting the theological opinions of other people . . ." (232).

These qualities, Child judged, clearly indicated that Indians were as capable of being "civilized" as the primitive tribes out of which Europeans had evolved. After all, ancient Britons had once "painted their bodies with various pigments," subsisted "by hunting and raising herds of cattle," clothed themselves in the "skins of beasts," and "lived in small huts of wicker-work covered with rushes" (225). If the Britons had risen out of savagery, so could Indians. Indeed, Indians had already progressed further, since many tribes practiced agriculture well before the arrival of whites (231). Thus, it would not be difficult to promote a shift from hunting to agriculture among Indians. "[P]eoples who are less advanced than ourselves" ought to be viewed not as " 'subject races,' " concluded Child, but "[s]imply as younger members of the same great human family, who need to be protected, instructed and encouraged, till they are capable of appreciat-ing and sharing all our advantages" (220).

Admirable for its humanitarian spirit, historical insight, and cross-cultural sophis-tication, Child's "Appeal for the Indians" marked a high point in nineteenth-century analysis of the "Indian problem." Few Anglo-American reformers would surpass it.[81] Yet while rejecting biological racism and proclaiming the ability of all races to "ad-vance" toward "civilization," it remained infected by the very "assumption of [cultural] superiority" Child sought so earnestly to combat. The evolutionary theory to which she subscribed (in common with virtually all progressive thinkers of her day) posited Euro-American "civilization" as the acme of development and the model for other cultures to emulate.[82] It left no room for alternative models. Nor did it provide an adequate conceptual basis for defending the right of foreign peoples to determine their own destiny free of interference by colonialist powers. Notwithstanding her sympathy for the Indians, her outrage at the genocide being perpetrated on them, and her repudiation of the doctrine that they were "'*destined* to disappear before the white man'" (231), Child never questioned the ideal of opening the West to settlement by industrious pioneers like the Whartons, nor did she ever recognize the contradiction between the goal of providing "homesteads" for white and black farmers and the principle of respecting the Indians' right to their land.

Whatever its historical limitations, Child's "Appeal for the Indians" played a vital role in sparking abolitionists' interest in the Indian question and in cementing links between them and other Indian rights advocates. Within a week of its appearance in the *Standard*, Wendell Phillips, who would soon emerge as the most militant spokesperson of the new crusade, wrote to tell Child "how much interested" he had been in her "Indian letter." "I always feel hopeless when I think of this Indian question," he admitted, implying that Child had inspired him to act. One of his first acts was to mail a copy of Child's "Appeal" to the leading Indian sympathizer in Minnesota, Bishop Henry Benjamin Whipple, whose frontier diocese ministered to the eastern Sioux and Chippewa and whose observation of British policy toward Indians in Canada seemed to bear out what Phillips inferred from Child's recommendations — that the Indians should be "citizens not alien sovereignties."[83] Praise also came from the wealthy antislavery philanthropist Gerrit Smith, who asked Child to send an extra copy to Sarah Van Vechten Brown, a reformer in his upstate New York vicinity.[84] Brown, in turn, wished Child's "Appeal" "might be scattered in all directions, so that the thousands of humane people, who are indifferent & silent, because they do not know, might be informed about the injuries & barbarities which the Indians have suffered, & are likely still to suffer at our hands." Recalling the "widely extended & powerful influence" Child's antislavery *Appeal* had exerted on "public opinion about the blacks," she predicted the new tract would have a comparable impact.[85] Still more flattering was the news that Sumner had passed Child's "Appeal" on to General Sherman himself, one of the signers of the peace commission report and the military man whose support would be most crucial to ensuring the success of President Grant's recently announced "Peace Policy." "If I can have the least little bit of influence in changing the policy toward those much-abused tribes, it will be something worth living for," Child rejoiced.[86]

Ironically, Sherman would prove to be the peace policy's main foe. In opposition to the course reformers favored of turning the management of Indian affairs over to Quakers and other missionaries, the military wanted the Indian Bureau transferred from the Interior Department to the War Department, and administered by army officers, not "sentimental" philanthropists.[87] Sherman did not believe that Indians could be "conquer[ed] by kindness," as the humanitarian members of the peace commission maintained.[88] Though willing to give them a "chance to survive," once they were safely "corral[ed]," he was convinced that the only way to prevent perpetual warfare on the frontier was to herd Indians onto isolated reservations, confine them there by force, and retaliate mercilessly against groups guilty of attacks on whites. There should be "no kid-gloves policy for those Indians who wanted war," he insisted, and Indians caught off their reservations should be deemed hostile and subject to military chastisement.[89]

Accordingly, in the winter of 1870 Sherman and his chief subordinate, General Philip Sheridan, likewise a Civil War hero, sanctioned the massacre of 173 Montana Piegan Indians, who had allegedly participated in bloody raids led by the Cheyenne chief, Black Kettle, the previous summer. Reporting the circumstances to Sherman, Sheridan accused Black Kettle's band of having "murdered, without mercy, men, women, and children; in all cases ravishing the women—sometimes as often as forty and fifty times in succession." When "insensible from exhaustion and brutality," Sheridan elaborated with perverse relish, Indian warriors had "forced sticks up [women's] persons; and in one instance, the fortieth or fiftieth savage drew his sabre, and used it on the person of the woman, in the same manner." To attempt to coax such "savages" into peaceful ways was utterly chimerical, concluded Sheridan: "The Indian is a lazy, idle vagabond; he never labors, and has no profession except that of arms, to which he is raised from a child; a scalp is constantly dangled before his eyes, and the highest honor he can aspire to is, to possess one taken by himself. . . . [I]f he does not now give up his cruel and destructive habits, I see no other way to save the lives *and property of our people, than to punish him until peace becomes a desirable object.*"[90] Sheridan's sensational rape charges (for which he provided no substantiation) served to divert public attention both from the ongoing investigation of the 1864 Sand Creek Massacre of Black Kettle's tribe and from the inconvenient facts that soon came to light about the Piegan massacre. Not only did the Piegans have no verifiable connection with the raid of Black Kettle's warriors (itself a reprisal for the Sand Creek massacre), but of the 173 Piegans killed, "all but 15 were women, children, and old men," and at least fifty were "children under twelve years of age," "many of them in their mother's arms." Moreover, at the time of the soldiers' attack on their winter camp, the Piegans were in the throes of a smallpox epidemic that had been claiming an average of six lives a day for two months.[91]

Child reacted with revulsion to Sheridan's and Sherman's defense of their genocidal warfare: "Shame on General Sheridan for perpetrating such outrages on a people because they were poor, and weak, and despised! Shame on General Sherman for sanctioning it!" she exclaimed in the lead article of the new monthly *Standard*: "[I]ndiscriminate slaughter of helpless women and innocent babies is not war—it is butchery; it is murder." She drew a telling contrast between the two Civil War generals' conduct toward white and Indian enemies: "The rebels practiced cruelties on our soldiers unsurpassed by the worst barbarities of the Indians. Would General Sheridan have slaughtered *their* women and babies? Would he have adopted such a mode of warfare with *any* white people upon earth, under *any* amount of provocation?"[92]

Child also boldly countered Sheridan's rape charge. Rape was "certainly . . . a new feature in the history of the red men," she noted, since Puritan captivity narratives invariably testified that this was one crime Indians did not commit. Indeed, Indians' "stoical training, which taught them to be ashamed of being mastered by the senses," militated strongly against their indulgence in rape. Hence, Child attributed the change in their behavior (if factual) to "the influence of white men." Citing the authority of Father

Beeson, who had told her that "white traders and soldiers violated the wives and daughters of Indians with entire impunity," she speculated that Black Kettle's warriors might have been avenging "similar outrages on Indian women" (4). She was not far off the mark in her suspicions about white provocations. As Richard Slotkin has pointed out, "[w]hite troops at Sand Creek had mutilated the living and the dead, cut off and displayed as trophies the sexual organs of Indian men, women, and children," and ripped fetuses out of pregnant women. And after the battle of Washita, where Black Kettle was killed, General George Custer had reportedly turned captured Indian women "over to the 'unbridled lust' (as Sheridan might have called it) of soldiers and officers."[93]

Privately, Child admitted having to "struggle with considerable repugnance" to champion a people who believed in wreaking vengeance on enemies and who seemed to glorify warfare. As a pacifist, she felt too much of an aversion to "all *fighters*" to have "romantic feelings about the Indians," she explained: "But though my efforts for the Indians are mere duty-work, I do it as earnestly, as I should if they were a people more suited to my taste." Publicly, in reply to Sheridan's and Sherman's depictions of the Indians as savages whose atrocities warranted extreme measures of retaliation, she maintained simply that Indians "have been, and are, outrageously wronged and there is abundant proof that they are as capable as other human beings of being developed into noble manhood by just and kindly influences."[94]

Yet Child's last protest article on "The Indians" could not escape the ideological contradictions that resulted from accepting the right of Anglo-Americans to colonize Indian land. "Do not suppose for a moment that I have no feeling for the white settlers of the frontier," she conceded:

> They are in a horrible situation, surrounded by savages, whom we have exasperated by generations of wrong, and degraded by many years of whisky-guzzling. They *must* be protected! But let Justice be blind to color, and hold her scales with an even hand. Let an Indian who murders a white be punished in the same way that a white is punished who murders an Indian; and let both have the same fair chance for a lawful trial. If their depredations and outrages make military interference necessary, let war be carried on as it is with white people who commit outrages on life or property. (2)

This concession ultimately negated the argument Child had used to vindicate Black Kettle's warriors — that they were engaging in "reprisal" (4). It also denied the fact she had recognized in all her writings on the Indian question — that leaders like Black Kettle, Osceola, and Philip were simply defending their "territories from invaders, just as white monarchs do" ("Appeal" 222).[95] Once having granted the principle that "white settlers of the frontier" could justly claim protection of "life or property," Child could not effectively refute the logic that led inevitably to Sheridan's and Sherman's brutal policies.

In the end the only hope Child could hold out for the Indians was the very remedy the peace commission had offered — the destruction of their way of life, the eradication of their tribal cultures, and their forced schooling in "civilization":

The Indians must be incited to agricultural and mechanical labor, and be rewarded with premiums for success. They must have reason to feel perfectly secure about the possession of the land they cultivate. If certain benefits were granted as a reward for substituting the English language in place of Indian dialects, it might have a good effect. . . . If some of the civilized Indians could help in such mission-work, they might do more than others to change hunters into farmers.

But I do not believe that harmony will prevail so long as they exist as independent tribes in our midst. There was never peace on the borders of England and Scotland till clans were abolished, and they all became one people, under one government. (5–6)

Having spent her life trying to dismantle the barriers of race, caste, class, gender, and religion that divided the human race, Child could see "clans" and "tribes" in no other light than as obstacles to the creation of "one people, under one government" — the fulfillment of her abolitionist ideals.[96]

Child did add one significant element to the peace commissioners' formula, however — the extension to Indians of the citizenship and suffrage rights that had just been conferred on African Americans: "If the Indian . . . could vote for the laws that govern him, and feel that he is really and truly acknowledged as an American citizen, it would make a man of him; and his vicinity would prove a blessing instead of a curse" (6). She would develop that suggestion in a letter to the *Standard* the following year, explicitly presenting it as an alternative to the widely touted notion that the Indians were " 'a race destined to pass away.' " "What need is there of their passing away?" she demanded: "There is room enough for them in our wide world, and they have abilities that can be rendered eminently useful. . . . Let us deal justly with them, bestow upon them the rights and the responsibilities of citizens, educate them, and encourage them without assuming offensive airs of superiority, and I am thinking they will be a long time in passing away, and we shall cease to wish for their disappearance."[97]

The solution Child adumbrated in her last major statements on the Indian question would soon become official U.S. policy. In March 1871, with the blessing of Indian rights advocates like Child, President Grant would sign into law a major reversal of all previous diplomatic relations with Indians: "No Indian nation or tribe within the territory of the United States shall be acknowledged or recognized as an independent nation, tribe, or power with whom the United States may contract a treaty."[98] Not long after Child's death, reformers would achieve their other principal objectives with the passage of the 1887 Dawes Act, which provided for the allotment of reservation land "in severalty" to individual Indians and the eventual granting of citizenship.[99] The triumph of white benevolence would usher in what many Indians viewed as a worse nightmare than any their people had yet endured.[100]

Meanwhile, despite Grant's peace policy, the warfare against the Plains Indians raged on almost unabated throughout Child's remaining years, and she continued to champion the Indians. She published no more appeals, perhaps because she had said everything she had to say on this "painful and wearisome" subject and saw so "little hope" of arresting "the insane and cruel disregard of Indian rights and feelings" (as she confessed at the end of her article on "The Indians" [6]). Nevertheless, she followed Indian affairs closely. When her friends the Shaws lapsed into condemning Indian savagery after Modoc chiefs murdered a team of commissioners sent to negotiate peace terms with them in 1873, Child fired back an indignant rejoinder. "[W]ould to Heaven [the Indians] had education and newspapers to tell *their* side of the story!" "According to all the laws which we set up for *ourselves*, the Modocs are perfectly justifiable." She proceeded to recall for the Shaws the chain of incidents that had led up to the Modocs' rebellion: "When we wanted to have Oregon settled, the U.S. Government, without making any treaty with the Indians, who owned the land, without *even* notifying them of what they intended to do, offered to give 640 acres of the land to every man who would settle there. When the Modocs saw thousands upon thousands of their acres taken from them in this way, they remonstrated, and the white settlers began to be afraid they would make resistance." The U.S. Army colonel sent to negotiate with them had behaved just as treacherously toward the Modocs as they had later behaved toward the commissioners, Child went on. He had "invited several of the most influential Indians," among them the brother of Captain Jack (Kintpuash), the Modoc chief responsible for the attack on the commissioners, to "dine with him, and have a peaceable conference about the adjustment of affairs. . . . [W]hen he had entrapped them, they were all shot." Following the signing of a treaty (which Congress had taken five years to ratify, after unilaterally changing its provisions without so advising the Modocs)[101] the United States had "packed [the Modocs] off, from one place to another, till finally, they were pushed into a corner where game was scarce, and the land too barren to yield them corn." Small wonder that they had resolved in "the desperation of starvation . . . to go back to their old home, and die, if die they must, by the graves of their fathers." Small wonder, too, that after discovering the commissioners "were not authorized to restore their lands," they had concluded "their smooth talk was, like all the other promises of the U.S., *sheer* humbug." Considering how their own chiefs had previously been treated by fair-speaking U.S. negotiators, Child wound up, "who can blame them, especially as *they* do not *profess* a Gospel of 'peace, and good will toward men.' " Personally she regarded the Modoc chief, Captain Jack, like the Seminole chief, Osceola, "as worthy of an historical place in the list of heroes that have died for their oppressed peoples."[102]

By the time of the Modoc affair in mid-1873, however, Child was apparently too preoccupied with David's worsening health to join the clemency campaign for Captain Jack and his accomplices, which other Indian rights advocates were conducting. With the demise of the *Standard* the previous December, she had also lost her primary outlet for articles on the Indian question. Hence, she reserved her impassioned defense of the Modocs for letters to the Shaws.[103]

Like President Grant's peace policy, which Child found "candid and just on paper" but poorly executed and erratic in practice, his Reconstruction policy was leaving a great deal to be desired.[104] As Child had predicted in December 1869, southern states had "nominally ratified" the Fifteenth Amendment for the sake of gaining readmission to

Congress but had quickly "evaded" it by a variety of "contrivance[s]" ensuring that "the colored population [would] in reality have no civil rights allowed them."[105] In many states prohibitive poll taxes, property qualifications, complicated residency and registration requirements, gerrymandering, and the reduction or elimination of polling places in black districts effectively disfranchised black voters. Simultaneously, the laws disfranchising former Confederates were ignored or repealed, thus sweeping the old guard back into power. The single most successful "contrivance" for "redeeming" the South from Republican rule and restoring white supremacy was what one historian has described as a "wave of counterrevolutionary terror" with no analogue "either in [previous] American experience or in that of the other Western Hemisphere societies that abolished slavery in the nineteenth century." By 1870 the Ku Klux Klan and kindred terrorist organizations had "entrenched" themselves "in nearly every Southern state." Masked night riders targeted local black leaders, white Republicans, black schools and churches, educators of both races serving the freedpeople, and blacks who "achieved a modicum of economic" prosperity or who owned land or animals or who availed themselves of Reconstruction laws designed to protect them against exploitation.[106] Among the many victims were William and Ellen Crafts' Southern Industrial School and Labor Enterprise, whose buildings and crops the Klan destroyed in 1871. Child was not exaggerating when she charged in an April 1871 letter to the *Standard*: "In many places, murders are of constant occurrence. . . . No colored man who dares to vote for his friends, and no white man who is known to believe in equality of civil rights, has any security for life or property. The extensive organization bearing the mysterious name of the Ku-Klux-Klan are . . . scourging, and mutilating, and murdering loyal whites and blacks, and none give heed to the agonized cries of their victims."[107] In the face of this horrific campaign of intimidation, both Grant and Congress had hitherto displayed an "apathy" that struck Child as incomprehensible.

The truth was, large sections of the northern public and the Republican party were tired of Reconstruction and anxious to turn to other concerns. Northern taxpayers did not relish subsidizing the Federal troops that would have been necessary to control the violence in the South. Many likewise shrank from setting dangerous precedents by violating states' rights and undermining local (white) civil liberties through such measures as long-term military occupation and the suspension of habeas corpus in cases involving Klan members. Labor leaders seeking to promote the cause of white workers often resented the former slaves' claims on national attention, which some leaders saw as preventing recognition of the white laboring class's needs. Party stalwarts wanted to consolidate their political power, build municipal and state machines, finance railroads and other corporate enterprises, and enrich themselves. The politicos' increasingly flagrant corruption was prompting a revolt by a new group of "liberal Republicans" comprising "intellectuals, publicists, and professionals." Though nearly all liberals had been "early advocates of emancipation and black suffrage," they had become disillusioned by the chaos in the South, alarmed by the growing labor agitation in the North, and alienated by a political spoils system that allowed demagogues and party bosses to erect petty empires by manipulating working-class voters. They wished to put Reconstruction behind them and concentrate on reforming the civil service. Replacing the spoils system with a professional bureaucracy based on "competitive examinations and permanent tenure in office for federal employees," they thought, would eliminate government corruption. A number of liberal Republicans also leaned toward restricting suffrage for all the "dangerous classes" through "educational and property qualifications," rather than enforcing black suffrage in the South.[108]

These pressures in favor of a laissez-faire southern policy accounted for the "apathy" Child complained of in Congress and the Grant administration. By the time of her April 1871 letter to the *Standard*, however, Grant had finally recommended "decisive measures for the protection of loyal citizens at the South," and Congress was debating the Ku Klux Klan Act. Marking the "outer limits of constitutional change," the new law provided for federal prosecution of "[c]onspiracies to deprive citizens of the right to vote, hold office, serve on juries, and enjoy the equal protection of the laws," and it authorized "military intervention and the suspension of the writ of habeas corpus" in extreme cases. No doubt Child timed her letter to influence the outcome of the debate, which would culminate two weeks later in passage of the act. Once more prodding Republicans to do their duty "at the point of a moral bayonet," she argued that Congress, by its failure to sponsor a land redistribution program in the South, was "largely responsible" for the emergence of the Klan. Had " 'poor whites' " been made "proprietors of the soil," Child contended, they would have been "secured . . . as allies to the United States," instead of becoming pawns in the hands of the planter aristocracy that stood behind the Klan. Hence, Congress was "all the more bound to exert itself energetically for the protection of those whose interests and safety it has so long neglected."[109]

Unfortunately, at the very moment when Republicans were apparently uniting behind measures to break the power of the Klan, an intraparty conflict that would doom Radical Reconstruction was brewing. Just before his speech endorsing vigorous prosecution of the Klan, Grant had found himself locked in combat with the dean of Radical Republicans in the Senate, Charles Sumner, who also chaired the Foreign Relations Committee. The issue was not Reconstruction, but a "disreputable scheme" to annex the Dominican Republic, which Grant enthusiastically backed and Sumner indignantly repudiated.[110] At first, Sumner stood almost alone in opposing the annexation treaty. Even the editor of the *Standard*, Aaron Macy Powell, failed to sustain him, as Child noted with dismay. In two articles aimed at awakening the public to "the great wrong . . . being perpetrated against a weaker nation," Child sarcastically granted that Santo Domingo offered "more than common to whet" the "national greed for territory": an ideal "naval station," fertile soil, "great sources of wealth open to enterprise," and lush tropical scenery. She also pointed out that American investors who had speculated in Dominican land stood to make "millions of dollars" if the United States annexed the island. The Dominican dictator Buenaventura Báez had equally sordid reasons for wanting to sell his country to the United States, observed Child: his government was facing bankruptcy. Moreover, belying the plebiscite he had held to show that two-thirds of the people supported annexation, the countryside was rife with resistance, and two U.S. warships were cruising Dominican waters in "readiness to fire" on organized protesters.[111]

It was illegal as well as "hazardous" to "purchase territory of a political adventurer, under such circumstances," Child objected. The Dominican constitution explicitly prohibited the "transfer" of the country to a "foreign Power," and a treaty with Haiti, which shared the island with the Dominican Republic, stipulated that "no part of the Island can be alienated by either of the two governments." Whatever the Dominican people's attitude toward annexation, she added, the Haitians overwhelmingly opposed it. The former slaves of Haiti had won their independence by "great sufferings," and it was manifestly "unjust to dispossess them of their hard-earned inheritance." Yet the U.S. government was issuing threats against Haitian "interference" that seemed intended to "provoke war with Hayti" and thus furnish a pretext for seizing "the whole of that much-coveted island."

Privately, Child suspected that Grant was following the "tempting precedent" of former President Andrew Jackson, who was "*glorified* for the wholesale robbery of a weak neighbor" when he "wrested territory" from Mexico.[112] Publicly, however, she steered clear of questioning Grant's personal motives and confined herself to appealing to national honor and long-term political interests.

In analyzing the campaign against annexation waged by U.S. anti-imperialists, historian Eric Foner has commented that one of the "most striking features of the whole affair was the ease with which the treaty's critics fell back upon racism to bolster their position."[113] Although Child specifically dissociated herself from those who characterized the Hispanic Dominicans and black Haitians as "degenerate races," "incapable of governing themselves," she did echo the anti-Catholic rhetoric bandied about by liberal Republican spokesmen like *Nation* editor E. L. Godkin. The Haitians, she conceded, had had the double "misfortune to inherit the Catholic church, whose policy dwarfs the souls of the people by keeping them from thinking for themselves," and the "French language," along with "a literature brilliant but flashy, and very deficient in that steady moral light which pervades the standard literature of nations of Teutonic origin." Were the United States to acquire the island of Santo Domingo, it would also acquire "an ignorant and priest-ridden population" that was "far from being a salutary addition to our body politic." The anti-Catholic, anti-French, and anti-Irish biases Child exhibited in her writings of the 1870s seriously undermined her stand against racism and imperialism, even if they never led her to make common cause with the elitists of the liberal Republican camp.

Portentously, these liberals joined Democrats in backing Sumner's crusade against the annexation treaty, while Republican stalwarts voted with Grant. Shortly after a key speech by Sumner, which Child praised in the same letter to the *Standard* urging passage of the Ku Klux Klan Act, the Senate rejected the treaty in a "humiliating defeat" for Grant and party regulars. They retaliated by divesting Sumner of his Senate Foreign Relations Committee chairmanship, precipitating a disastrous split in Republican ranks.[114]

In September 1871 the liberals defected to form a new party in coalition with the Democrats. Their presidential candidate, *Tribune* editor Horace Greeley, had long advocated a "magnanimous Reconstruction" and amnesty for Confederate leaders (his 1867 contribution to bail for Confederate President Jefferson Davis had disgusted Child with its "sickly sentimentality . . . confound[ing] all distinctions between right and wrong").[115] Like many liberal Republicans, Greeley believed that the "best men" of the Old South—gentlemen of the same class as the disaffected elitists of the North—"held the key to regional development and national reconciliation" and should be restored to power. With the presidency dangling before his eyes, he began sounding the tried-and-true Democratic campaign slogans of "local self-government" (for southern whites) and an end to coddling for blacks, whom he branded as "an easy, worthless race, taking no thought for the morrow," and whom he exhorted to "Root, Hog, or Die!"[116] "What a strange, unexpected tangle!" lamented Child. "Horace Greely [*sic*], once a loud-spoken herald of freedom, now a tool in the hands of Southern despots, and their unprincipled allies, the democrats!" "How plainly he shows he is in the market, ready to sell himself to the highest bidder!" Greeley's head was already so "turned with vanity," that "if he should be President it will make him as crazy as a coot," she judged brutally. As for his "halabuloo about the need of amnesty . . . [t]here has been nothing *but* amnesty ever since the rebels surrendered," as indicated by the thirteen "Rebel Generals" representing their states in Congress.[117]

Far more worrisome to Child than Greeley's vagaries was the gravitation toward his ticket of Radicals who had led the vanguard of Reconstruction—among them her friends George Julian and Sumner. Julian, defeated by a Democrat in the 1870 election, had convinced himself that "Liberalism promised a reaffirmation of the politics of principle," and Sumner had become so obsessed by hatred of Grant that he had lost all sense of proportion.[118] Child urged both to reconsider, concentrating her energy on Sumner, whose endorsement of Greeley would do the most damage. To his credit, Sumner hesitated for months, torn between his personal grudge against Grant and his realization "in his heart of hearts that a Greeley victory spelled the end of Reconstruction."[119] While his decision hung in the balance, Child besieged him with letters "begging, intreating, imploring him, for the sake of the freedmen, for the sake of the country, for his own sake," not to help install an administration that would "undo all the great work of his life."[120] Again and again, she reiterated her conviction that "disguise it as they may," Greeley's election would mean the return to power of "Northern Democrats and Southern Fire-eaters" and the adoption of their policies: " 'self-government for the States'; which means the 'State Sovereignty' for which the Rebels fought . . . 'and the supremacy of civil over military authority'; which means that when the Ku Klux renew their efforts to exterminate Republicans, white and black, they shall be dealt with by *Southern* civil authorities,—that is, by Judges and Jurors who are themselves members of the Ku Klux association."[121] Greeley had proved he was nothing but the Democrats' "puppet," Child insisted. "If he were President, *they*, not *he*, would govern the country; for he would be placed in such a situation that he would be *obliged* to open or shut his eyes, just as they pulled his wires." He had already agreed to pay the South millions of dollars in indemnities for their slaves and to "pension Rebel soldiers"—campaign promises for which northern taxpapers would have to foot the bill. "[W]e shall have whip and spur with a vengeance" under such a regime, Child warned, concluding with a flourish: "If the Devil himself were at the helm of the Ship of State, my conscience would not permit me to aid in removing him to make room for the Democratic Party."[122]

Despite six letters full of cogent arguments and eloquent pleas—and despite the concern for Child's regard that impelled Sumner to write as many letters in return, beseeching her with "tears [in] his eyes" to recognize that he was acting as conscientiously as he always had—the great Radical leader could not overcome his wounded pride. Ignoring all Child's caveats about the consequences of a Democratic victory, he replied only with "invectives against Grant." At the end of July 1872 he finally announced his support of Greeley. "Would to God he had died before" taking the "fatal plunge," Child mourned. Privately, she wondered whether Sumner had gone mad. Both the "violence" of his speeches against Grant and his "intellectually flimsy, and entirely reckless" letter to African Americans advising them to vote for Greeley struck Child as signs of a mental breakdown.[123]

With deep sadness, Child found herself obliged to differ publicly with her quondam idol, and implicitly to disavow him. When an article she had written for the *Boston Journal*, protesting against a vicious caricature of Sumner by the cartoonist Thomas Nast, was construed by the Greeley forces as an endorsement, Child promptly corrected the error in a follow-up article.[124] "Painful" as it was to let cruel personal attacks on Sumner go unanswered in the future, she decided, she must "endure it, rather than utter a syllable that can be twisted into an expression of toleration of the Democratic Party."[125]

Child's electioneering also took a feminist form. Her name headed a list of seventeen signatures to an "Address of the Republican Women of Massachusetts, To the Women of America" hailing the Republican party platform's recommendation that the demand for women's rights be "treated with respectful consideration."[126] In addition, she published a long article in the *Woman's Journal* on "The Present Aspect of Political Affairs." Women who had "the good of this Republic at heart" ought to exert their political influence against Greeley, Child proclaimed:

> National honor demands that we should protect the people we have emancipated, and secure to them the civil rights we have promised. . . . Moreover, we owe a debt of gratitude to the colored people of the South, for tending our sick and wounded soldiers; for hiding them when hunted by enemies, and guiding them through forests and swamps into the camps of the United States. . . .
>
> This debt is all the more binding upon us, because the freedmen have incurred the bitter resentment of their former masters by the services they rendered to the United States; and if [the masters] regain their power, they will be sure to revenge it upon them.

A vote for Greeley, Child stressed, was a vote for "unrepentant rebels" and their instrument, the Klan, which Greeley's *Tribune* was "handl[ing] . . . with exceedingly

soft mittens." Neither the smooth professions of Greeley and his Democratic allies
nor, she hinted, the flimsy arguments of self-deluded Radicals like Sumner deceived
southern freedpeople: "A negro who was urged to vote for Mr. Greeley, because he had
been such a friend to the colored race, replied, 'I don't know nothin' bout dat, sah; but I
ax myself, What for does [ex-Confederate] Gen. Ewall vote for him?'" Educated
whites ought to follow this freedman's example and ask themselves why the ex-Confederate general Wade Hampton, the "REBEL PIRATE Semmes," Boss Tweed of the Tam-
many Ring, and former Democratic Governor Horatio Seymour of New York Draft
Riot fame were "hurrahing for Greeley."[127]

To Child's infinite relief, the Republican electorate ultimately balked at Greeley's
blatant "strategy of trying to win by ingratiating himself with the South," and Grant
won by "the largest majority in any Presidential election between 1836 and 1892."[128]
David, who had been nearly paralyzed during the campaign by "very violent rheumatism," was "well enough to hurra when the election was decided, though his hands were
too lame to throw up his cap," Child reported. Once again, the country had escaped a
grave danger, and the Republican party had seemingly received a mandate to continue
with Reconstruction. "[I]t doubtless has had many imperfections. . . . But, take it all in
all, I think it is the best party we have ever had," Child commented.[129]

She did not have long to savor the victory. The defection of so many leading Radicals
to Greeley actually "demonstrated once for all the death of Radicalism as both a
political movement and a coherent ideology." The party that survived the 1872 election would be dominated by "politicos." What that meant would become clear even
before Grant's second inaugural, as the Crédit Mobilier scandal burst upon the country. "[A] dummy corporation formed by an inner ring of Union Pacific stockholders"
who "contracted with themselves, at an exorbitant profit, to build their own [railway]
line" with government assistance, and who covered up their fraudulent activities by
distributing shares to influential congressmen, the Crédit Mobilier implicated many
prominent Republicans, including some with impeccable Radical credentials. Most
shocking was the involvement of former Massachusetts Senator Henry Wilson, now
Grant's vice president, and a warm personal friend of the Childs. Dubbing the scandal
the "*Dis*credit *Im*mobilier," which she (mis)translated as "the permanent disgrace,"
Child prophesied: "It writes Icabod! Icabod! on the Republican Party." She proceeded
to diagnose the problem much as late twentieth-century historians would: "The fact is,
all the vitality there was *in* [the Republicans] was injected into their veins from the
hearts of the old abolitionists. The perils, and sacrifices of the war kept them up to a
high standard for a time, and the *necessities* of the crisis *forced* them to go ahead in a
straight line, but now they are *mere politicians*. . . ."[130]

Beyond the fate of the party, Child worried about the future of the American Republic itself. "It seems as if universal demoralization was carrying us to ruin with a
swifter impetus than has hastened the decay of preceding Republics," she wrote de-
spairingly to the Shaws. Capping the national shame, Grant's inaugural had revived the
specter of annexation, only this time the object of "greed" was Cuba. "Our talk about
humanity, and the vindication of our national honor, is all a pretense, — too flimsy to

disguise our eagerness to grab at the possessions of Cuba," Child raged. "I do believe, if we could annex the whole world, we should try to get a quarrel with Saturn, in order to snatch his ring from him."[131]

The corruption of the Republican party, the retreat into elitism of its intellectual leadership, and the disintegration of Radicalism confronted Child and her fellow abolitionists with a major challenge. To maintain the vitality and relevance of the egalitarian vision that had inspired their long crusade against slavery, they had to adapt that vision to the changing political realities of the postwar era and to forge new alliances. The most promising alliance on the horizon was one that many abolitionists had envisaged in the past—a partnership of the white and black working classes. As a group, abolitionists fervently espoused what Eric Foner has called the ideology of "free labor"—belief in the dignity of labor and in the goals of "social mobility and economic independence," which "equal opportunity" was supposed to ensure for all.[132] Child herself had frequently appealed to white workers to recognize that they shared fundamental interests with blacks; she had also credited the "working classes" with constituting the rank and file of the abolitionist movement—a claim modern historical studies have substantiated.[133] By the 1870s, however, the "working classes" Child had known in her young adulthood had undergone a crucial transformation. No longer did skilled, native-born mechanics form the majority of American workers. Unskilled Irish immigrants now occupied the "bottom rungs of labor," and a vast permanent proletariat had replaced the artisans who could once realistically aspire to rise with hard work into the ranks of proprietors and employers.[134]

In the very decades when labor was entering the age of industrial capitalism, Child was reentering the rural world of her youth. Still largely unchanged today, the Wayland to which Child had moved in 1853 was "almost exclusively a village of small farmers." Not even a "carpenter's shop, or black-smith's shop, or any kind of shop or manufactory," could be found within a mile of the village, and the nearest railway station was six miles away.[135] In an era of such amenities for middle-class city dwellers as store-bought goods, central heating, and running water, Child was once again performing the tasks she had described forty years before in *The Frugal Housewife*—growing and canning her own vegetables, perpetually fighting "mould and fermentation" of her household provisions, mending and making clothes for herself and David, heating the house with "great armfulls" of wood chopped by David, and carrying "pailfulls" of water stored in a "hogshead" for collecting rain.[136] In short, she could hardly have been more distant—in every sense—from the working classes of the 1870s. Symptomatic of how rooted she remained in the past, almost thirty years after the demise of Fourierite utopian socialism, she clung to her "faith in Association" as the ultimate solution to the conflict between capital and labor, rich and poor.[137]

Hence, the total incomprehension with which Child reacted to one of the chief demands of postwar laborers—the passage of legislation restricting the working day to eight hours.[138] Nothing could have been more revealing of the standpoint from which she viewed the question than the objection she raised in letters to Sumner and George

Julian (both of whom supported the eight-hour movement): "It is utterly impracticable; especially in agricultural communities." "*Farms* cannot be carried on upon the eight-hour system."[139]

The eight-hour movement (though destined to fail) was in fact an ideal vehicle for bringing abolitionists and workers' advocates together in a new coalition, as many leaders of both groups recognized. Not only did Radicals push for state and federal eight-hour laws, but Massachusetts labor leaders convinced their constituents that voting for black suffrage would help rather than harm the cause of white workingmen.[140] Among abolitionists, Wendell Phillips led the vanguard of the eight-hour movement, and the Reform League that rose out of the ashes of the American Anti-Slavery Society listed advancing the rights of labor among its new objectives, as did its organ, the *National Standard*. Yet instead of following the path blazed by her friends, Child openly dissented from them in her articles for the *Standard*.

Her arguments against the imposition of an eight-hour day repeatedly invoked the cluster of values that lay at the basis of early nineteenth-century Republican ideology, as she had preached it in the *Juvenile Miscellany*. "I honor labor; I believe in labor. My father was a workingman, and I am a working-woman, both theoretically and practically," Child affirmed. "Few, who have any taste for literature, have done so much of the manual labor of the world, as I have done, and still do." Her inability to grasp the difference between a wage worker and a self-employed mechanic like her father, who owned a prosperous bakery — let alone a wage worker and a rural housewife — betrayed the confusion of Republican free-labor ideology, which typically lumped manufacturers with workingmen as members of the "producing classes," distinguishing both from "the 'capitalists' (i.e., the old elite)."[141]

Child's paean to the dignity of labor likewise showed that she conceived of labor as essentially agricultural or artisanal. Protesting against the notion that labor was a hardship and that "those whose lives were devoted to it were to be commiserated," she contrasted workers favorably with parasitic aristocrats "who have nothing to do but to race horses and play at billiards" — another typical element of early bourgeois ideology.[142] "For my own part, I consider workingmen the privileged class," she went on: "Work makes them healthier, happier, braver, every way more manly. It develops the powers of mind and body and brings them into action. Honest labor strengthens the muscles far more than any gymnastic exercise; while it has the double advantage of being useful to others, as well as to one's self. Who would not rather be plain, practical, awkward, hard-working Abraham Lincoln, than the indolent, luxurious, elegant, useless Count D'Orsay?"[143] Lincoln, of course, not only personified Republican free-labor ideology and its quintessential myth of the self-made man, but he had given it classic expression in a famous speech proclaiming: "No men living are more worthy to be trusted than those who toil up from poverty. . . ."[144] As the reference to Lincoln so clearly indicates, the kind of healthy, "[h]onest labor" Child had in mind was rural, like splitting rails, and had nothing in common with the deadening conditions that the masses of late nineteenth-century workers endured in factories, sweatshops, mines, and steel mills.

Even more anachronistic than Lincoln as a model for American workers of the 1870s was Benjamin Franklin, whose "rigid economy" and diligent industry Child held up for emulation in her article "Economy and Work."[145] Unlike those who belittled the frugality that Franklin practiced (as Wendell Phillips did in a statement with which Child took issue), she still hailed his example. "[W]hen every fragment is carefully gathered up and converted to use for the sake of increasing the comforts of others, or of enlarging one's means to help on the progress of the world," Child wrote, echoing the counsels she had given in *The Frugal Housewife* so long ago, economy "is, in my estimation, one of the noblest of human virtues." Yet she admitted sadly that it was now "almost a hopeless task to try to gain a favorable hearing for such homely, old-fashioned doctrines."

What Lincoln and Franklin epitomized for Child was the early Republican ideal: a society of hardworking, upwardly mobile individuals, all perpetually advancing from humble origins to solid economic independence, but never degenerating into wealthy parasites. "If manual labor is looked upon as a burden and a degradation," she warned, "the inevitable consequence is that classes will be set apart to do it; classes that will be looked down upon as inferior, and that will systematically be kept in a state of actual inferiority." By the 1870s, however, the development Child was prophesying had long since occurred. Indeed, even while she was harking back to the days of her parents and the hoary example of Benjamin Franklin, liberal Republicans like Charles Francis Adams and E. L. Godkin were busy modifying their party's ideology so as to justify controlling the "classes . . . set apart" for manual labor and keeping them in a state of permanent "inferiority."[146]

In explaining her opposition to legislating the hours and price of labor, Child echoed many of the same premises of laissez-faire economics to which liberal Republicans subscribed. "[I]t is *useless* to attempt to regulate the value of money, or of labor, by legislation," she lectured George Julian, who had proposed an eight-hour law for federal "mechanics and laborers" as early as December 1865. "There is an eternal law of supply and demand, by which they *will* keep returning to their level, whatever may be done to prevent it." If "left to regulate themselves, without any interference of government," both money and labor would "find their own natural level, as surely as the waters do."[147] Child could not have better summed up laissez-faire theory.

Child also agreed with the liberals that "the general welfare and prosperity of the community can never be promoted by allowing any set of men to regulate, by compulsion, the prices of articles from which they derive profit." The same principle should apply to labor as to the commodities sold by capitalists, she argued: "I dislike all monopolies; and a monopoly of labor seems to me as wrong, in spirit and principle, as a monopoly of grain or fruit. For men to combine together to fix, by a forcing process, the price of the article in which they deal, is monopoly, and nothing else."[148] Predictably, Child extended this argument to strikes. Like the "Eight Hour Law" workers were demanding, strikes were "essentially coercive," and "[c]oercion . . . never changes the real basis of things," she maintained: "One devil will never cast the other devil out. The remedy for existing evils must come by co-operation, not by rivalry in monopolies." Though conceding that "[s]trikes for higher wages do indeed perform one use" by drawing "public attention" to an "unjust inequality" between the returns that laborers and capitalists each earned on their investments, Child cautioned that "they excite a fierce antagonism between labor and capital, and thus prove injurious to both parties." Significantly, she was able to recognize the fallacy of such caveats when racist demagogues invoked them against interference with race relations, but not when bourgeois ideologues invoked them against interference with labor relations.[149]

Nevertheless, Child's undying commitment to egalitarianism ultimately distinguished her from liberal Republicans. If she never went "beyond equality" (as David Montgomery puts it in analyzing the limits of Radical Republicanism), she took her egalitarian ideals as far as they could go within a bourgeois framework. Her definition of equality, she explained in one of her last articles on the labor question, was "simply . . . that every human being, man or woman, white, red, or black, American, Irishman, or Chinese, should have an equal chance to develope and use to the best advantage whatsoever faculties he or she may possess."[150]

In mentioning the Irish alongside the Chinese, Child was simultaneously responding to the nativist movement, which had pitted American-born workers against Irish immigrants ever since the 1850s, and to the recent movement led by California workers to exclude the Chinese, allegedly because they were undercutting the price of labor. Both were ugly instances of labor monopolies, founded on selfishness and bigotry, she contended. The only attitude toward immigrants "worthy of the American people" was "embodied in the noble words" that had once stood at the masthead of the *Liberator*: "My country is the world, and my countrymen are all mankind." The Chinese were no more alien than the Irish before them (and less unruly, Child implied): "John Chinaman . . . is a patient, steady, industrious brother of the human family. There is not room enough for him at home, and we have more room than we need." As for the competition between white workers and Chinese immigrants who could "live on a rat a day," that problem "would be of very transient duration." Like the Irish, who had come to expect "turkey and plum-pudding" instead of potatoes soon after settling in the United States, the Chinese would quickly adjust to the American standard of living.[151]

Child's concept of equality specifically rejected the "separation of the human race into classes, on account of sex, color, or the accident of birth"—a separation she considered purely artificial. Gender, race, and class distinctions had "no foundation in nature," she asserted. The many examples nature produced of individuals who defied expectations for their group proved "that the true policy is to remove all legal or conventional obstacles, and leave every individual free to find his or her own place."[152] In short, her egalitarianism was utterly individualistic. "The fact is, I don't believe in *classes*. I believe only in *individuals*," she told Lucy Osgood.

Paradoxically, however, as her preoccupation with interracial marriage suggests, Child also espoused what can only be called a familial ideal. In the next sentence of the same letter to Osgood she redefined "individuals" as kindred: "It is *my* mission to help in the breaking down of classes, and to make *all* men feel as if they were brethren of the same family, sharing the same rights, the same capabilities, and the same responsibilities. While my hand can hold a pen, I will use it to this end; and while my brain can earn a dollar, I will devote it to this end."[153]

Her passionate desire to unite all human beings in the same family led Child to advocate a solution to the labor problem that would seem quite incompatible with laissez-faire economics — "Association" or "co-operation." As with her throughgoing egalitarianism, it differentiated her from the liberal Republicans whose economic assumptions she partially shared. In describing the social ideal she envisioned, Child amalgamated the old "Whig-Republican doctrine of the harmony of interests" with Fourierite utopian socialism. "Our social discords can never come into harmony," she predicted, "until every man and woman performs a fair share of the labor of the world, and glories in the doing of it; a process whereby every man and woman will attain to a fair share of mental culture and healthy recreation."[154] With labor and recreation equally apportioned, "all shall become workers, and thereby all shall become capitalists." To achieve this goal, it would be necessary to devise a "system of co-operation" that could be "introduced into all branches of business, and so managed that the interests of all are equally served." Only then would it be possible to "harmonize the clashings of self interest, which is inherent in all natures."[155]

The two models of successful cooperation and association that Child cited were both entirely inadequate for accomplishing her stipulated objectives, however. The first was literally anachronistic — the Shaker settlements founded in the late eighteenth century, which were dying out because their members were practicing celibacy, although their prosperity and innovative "manufactures" provided "a very instructive business-lesson" in the "wisdom of associated labor." The second exemplified the Whig-Republican "harmony of interests" theory and depended on the noblesse oblige of progressive employers — a "partnership," in which each worker received "a share of the profits of the whole concern, proportioned to the time and the ability" he or she invested.[156]

Her eyes fixed on the utopian forms of "association" pioneered by Fourierites, Shakers, and philanthropic businessmen, Child took no public notice of the historical event that presaged what would be the most ambitious, long-lived, and pragmatic effort to resolve the conflict between labor and capital — the 1871 Paris Commune. Even privately, she dismissed it as yet "another Communist Revolution" of "poor, crazy France." Unaware that she was witnessing Europe's first serious attempt to translate socialist ideals into practice, she merely commented of its destruction, "Gott see dank that the Prussians conquered the French!"[157]

Of all the issues Child addressed in the 1870s — Reconstruction, women's rights, Indian policy, U.S. imperialism, Chinese exclusion, and labor reform — she could least convincingly claim to have grown "more radical" on the labor question. Yet despite their ideological contradictions and laissez-faire assumptions, her articles on labor remain remarkable for their ardent humanitarian sympathies and unqualified championship of every individual's right to an equal chance for self-fulfillment, regardless of sex, class, race, or ethnicity. At a time when large sections of the intelligentsia, including many of her abolitionist and feminist comrades, were lapsing into racism and elitism, Child never abandoned her youthful commitment to a just, fully integrated society. Continuing to write while overwhelmed with household chores, she could truly describe herself (by her definition) as a "working-woman" who honored labor in practice as well as in theory. To the end, Child lived out the values she preached.

21

Aspirations of the World

I long for the time to come when men will realize that all races are children of the same Father, and that all, according to the degrees of light they have, are "feeling after God, if haply they may find Him." I do not feel so much interest in any *subject as I do in melting down all the barriers that separate different portions of the human family.[1]*

No statement better sums up Child's lifelong crusade or more clearly illuminates the form it took in her last years than the letter written three years before her death to the artist Francis Alexander, who had painted her portrait half a century earlier. Feeling himself nearing his end, Alexander had just sent a "parting keepsake" from Florence to the old friend he had known as "the brilliant Miss Francis," author of *Hobomok*. The gift (a gold ring of the style found in the catacombs), had called up Child's memories of the days when she and Alexander were "just starting together in the career of life" — days that now seemed as unreal to her as the era "beyond the Flood."[2] Reciprocating in the only way she could, by sharing the principles she valued, Child commented on the looming war among European powers "hungry for a slice of turkey." "I detest all war, as the worst of all the demoralizers of humanity; but I particularly regret a war that intensifies the hatred between different religions," she wrote, referring to the "*pretext*" that Russia and other Christian nations were using for intervention — "to protect the Christian subjects of the Grand Vizier." She then gave Alexander an indirect preview of the valedictory project she had conceived as a means of ending religious and racial conflicts by "melting down all the barriers" between "different portions of the human family." An "Eclectic Bible" entitled *Aspirations of the World. A Chain of Opals* (1878),[3] it would represent her final contribution to eliminating prejudice, the problem that had preoccupied her ever since her youth.

Distant though Child felt at age seventy-five from the vivacious young "author of *Hobomok*" remembered so fondly by Alexander, an identical impulse linked her maiden novel, her mission as a radical reformer, and her twin religious works, *The Progress of Religious Ideas* and *Aspirations of the World* — the impulse to make "men . . . realize that all races are children of the same Father, and that all, according to the degrees of light they have, are 'feeling after God, if haply they may find Him.' " Indeed, her introduction to *Aspirations of the World* — echoed in her letter to Alexander — offered a more sophisticated formulation of the very idea she had tried to express in *Hobomok* through the mouths of Mrs. Conant and Mary: "This proneness of human souls to transfuse their own increasing vitality into old forms and traditions is a beautiful provision to guard freedom without destroying reverence. In this way do all the Written Oracles of the world become like the flaming cherubim, that 'turned every way to guard the tree of life.' "[4] Mrs. Conant had surmised that "flaming cherubim" kept the truths of the Bible inaccessible, so as to steer believers away from doctrinal disputes, toward the teachings of the heart, plainly discernible in the book of nature. Her rebellious daughter, Mary, had gone further, inferring from the evening star, which "smiled on distant mosques and temples" as well as on Calvinist churches, the lesson that salvation could not be reserved only for a "small . . . remnant."[5] Now, after fifty-three more years of reflecting on these questions, Child had concluded that all the world's sacred scriptures guarded the tree of life from human grasp, that all were but "Written Oracles," to be reinterpreted by each generation, though never fully understood.

As Child's interchangeable use of the words "religions" and "races" in her letter to Alexander indicates, she did not distinguish one manifestation of bigotry from another, any more than she had in *Hobomok*. At the end of her life she was merely shifting her endeavor to unify the human family from the political arena, where the abolitionist program had met severe reversals, to the religious realm, where she had turned for consolation as one intimate after another had passed away, leaving her an increasingly lonely relic of a bygone epoch.

Political and personal losses overshadowed Child's last decade, which culminated in the dismantling of Reconstruction and the demise of the generation that had dedicated itself to overthrowing slavery. Politically, the collapse of Radicalism in 1872 and the massive Republican defeat in the 1874 election, which delivered the House of Representatives back into Democratic hands, condemned Child and her few surviving comrades to impotence. Meanwhile, depriving abolitionists of their sole remaining vehicles, the *National Standard* and its parent, the Reform League, expired in December 1872, having sputtered along for two and a half years since the termination of the American Anti-Slavery Society. The concurrent failure of the eight-hour movement ended the short-lived effort to forge a new alliance with labor reformers, which might have revitalized the abolitionist movement, once its goal of racial equality had been nominally achieved. With the catastrophic Panic of 1873, itself partly responsible for the negative electoral "referendum" on Reconstruction, financial debacle completed the ideological disarray that doomed the egalitarian program Child had devoted her life to bringing into being.[6] Stymied politically, she naturally sought an alternative sphere of influence, as she had so often before. Once again her quest for a new mode of promulgating her ideal of human brother-and-sisterhood converged with a deep personal need.

Antedating the wreck of Reconstruction, Child's private ordeal had begun with her perceived rejection as a novelist. True, she had not carried out her threat to cease writing after the poor reception of *A Romance of the Republic* thwarted her dreams of a literary comeback. Instead, she had fought off chronic depression by keeping her life "brim full of usefulness"[7] — a usefulness amounting to several dozen newspaper articles between 1868 and 1873. Yet despite her brave public front — and despite the *Standard*'s faithful promotion of *A Romance of the Republic* as "one of the most thrilling . . . books ever written" about "the rights of the colored people — not excepting Uncle Tom's Cabin" — Child had never recovered from the humiliation of having the Benjamin of her old age ignored by the literary establishment and slighted by her dearest friends.[8] Since the fizzling of her ambitions, she had "expected nothing, looked forward to nothing, hoped for nothing," Child wrote bitterly to Eliza Scudder, the only friend who had expressed a "discriminating" appreciation of the novel. "I shall never dream again, not even the merest little bit of a dream," she vowed. "I have learned to estimate myself by the standard of others. . . ."[9] "All my aspirations have dwindled down to the wish to get on quietly, from day to day, doing no harm to anybody, and as much good as I can, in my small way."[10] In view of Child's enormous output during this period, it is astonishing to find her claiming that she "almost never let anything go into print, now-a-days," because the "total want of sympathy" the public had shown for her favorite novel had sapped her "power of writing, and utterly annihilated any inclination to write." However false to the facts, her wholesale discounting of her Reconstruction-era journalism unmistakably reveals what a blow her self-confidence had suffered. At the height of her involvement in the debates over Reconstruction policy, woman suffrage, and the Indian question, Child described herself as "weary of imparting my mind to others, since it is a commodity that nobody wants." "Once in a while, when an old acquaintance *asks* for an article," she wrote dismissively of her multitudinous contributions to the *Standard* and the *Woman's Journal*, "I give one to him, as I would a cold potato to a beggar, with the feeling that he will thank me for it, and throw it into the road when he gets out of sight of the house." The "very *great* change" she felt in herself had one compensation, she added grimly: "a *frozen* limb can feel no wound."[11]

Intensifying Child's sense of having outlived her reputation, a procession of deaths dogged her old age. Each awakened memories of a happier past. The first to go was Louisa Loring in May 1868, almost ten years to the day after Ellis's death. Like Ellis's, Louisa's passing coincided with Anniversary Week, when all Boston's reform societies held their annual meetings. Child had been planning a visit to Louisa ever since March. "I lot [count] upon hiding away with you in your chamber, and talking over the old, old times," she confided, as a host of reminiscences sprang up: the domestic bliss she and David had enjoyed at Cottage Place, where they had lived within easy reach of the Lorings; the many occasions when the two couples used to "talk and laugh" together around the Lorings' "late breakfast-table"; the way Ellis used to savor Maria's "little witticisms"; the enthusiasm with which they had all read Carlyle's *French Revolution* aloud together, with Margaret Fuller's protégées Jane Tuckerman and Caroline Sturgis "for auditors." Looking back from her current vantage point (and no doubt thinking of

Carlyle's subsequent diatribe *The Nigger Question*), Child could not help sighing, even as she anticipated the pleasures of reliving the old times with Louisa: "How Carlyle has changed since then! How every*body* and every*thing* has changed! . . . I myself . . . most of all."[12] Unfortunately, just before the scheduled visit with Louisa, David's "old enemy dyspepsia came back in strong force, apparently without provocation," necessitating a postponement. No sooner was he well enough to travel than Anna Loring Dresel's children came down with scarlet fever. Once they recovered, David's "difficulties" returned. By the time the Childs finally made it to Boston, Louisa was "alarmingly ill, and her life despaired of."[13] In the place of the nostalgic private retrospection for which she had hungered, Child had to supply a public tribute to the Lorings' role as pillars of the abolitionist movement. As usual, her paean to her beloved friends' "perfect union" and "steadfast consecration . . . to the Anti-Slavery cause" served an ulterior purpose. By recalling how the Lorings had rejoiced over the conversion of Wendell Phillips after his reading of her *Appeal*, Child was subtly striving to heal the breach in abolitionist ranks between Garrison's and Phillips's partisans; and by hailing the Lorings' sacrifices and linking them with Phillips's, she was prompting comrades who had dropped out before the battle was won to join Phillips in reconsecrating themselves to the struggle for black suffrage.[14]

After Louisa, the next to be "taken alarmingly ill" was Child's "aged brother" James Francis, who "hovered between life and death" for six weeks before closing his eyes in the summer of 1869. James had never reconciled himself either to his sister's antislavery politics or to her inheritance of the four-acre woodlot he believed their father should have reserved for him. The two had seen almost nothing of each other in all the years they had lived in the same town. Still, James was Child's only surviving sibling, and she did all she could to help nurse him, make the funeral arrangements, and lodge his widow and daughter until they could resettle in Worcester.[15]

Two years later, in January 1871, followed the death of Henrietta Sargent, whom Child numbered among her four closest friends, as well as among the earliest members of the abolitionist circle that had formed around Garrison soon after he had begun publishing the *Liberator*. Within a few months, Garrison's lifelong coadjutor Samuel J. May, to whom Child had dedicated her *Appeal*, likewise succumbed. In the memorials she published of them, Child upheld both as models of the courageous dedication to principle that Americans of the 1870s needed to learn anew. She also singled out May for the example he provided of a man who had paid "respectful attention" to his female coworkers' suggestions and who had regarded women neither as "charming creatures to be idolized for their personal attractions, [n]or as helpless things to be condescended to on account of their weakness; but simply as living souls, into whom God had breathed the breath of spiritual life."[16]

Henrietta had lapsed into senility by the time of her death, and Child had all but lost touch with May since his move to Syracuse, but the "sudden departure" of Lucy Osgood in June 1873 came as a cruel shock. As in the case of Louisa, the pain of bereavement was sharpened by regret at having deferred a planned visit until it was too late (again because of David's health problems). Osgood was buried on the very day

Child was to have gone to see her in Medford.[17] "With the breaking up of her establishment, I have lost the *last* place that seemed to me like *home*; except my own little nest," Child mourned. Osgood's home in fact represented Child's last link to her girlhood, when their sixty-year friendship had begun. Though far more conservative than Child, Osgood had never failed to stimulate her in the long correspondence they had kept up about theology, politics, literature, and women's rights. Child had cherished Osgood's thoughtful letters as a special "treat" and considered her "strong and cultivated intellect . . . a tonic." Now there would be no more earnest exchanges and comforting visits to Medford.[18]

In a typical gesture of delicacy toward the friend for whom giving counted so much, and who had so little of her own money to give, Osgood had willed $2,000 to "the colored people," appointing Child trustee. The bequest enabled Child to rechannel her abolitionist sympathies toward supporting institutions for community survival and uplift, now that forums for political activism no longer existed. She donated $1,000 to a Home for Old Colored Women and "with the remainder . . . founded a scholarship at Hampton College," Virginia, where freedpeople could "defray . . . the expenses of their board and tuition" through manual labor (Booker T. Washington would soon become Hampton's most famous graduate). What gave Child particular satisfaction was a chance to confer the first Osgood Scholarship on a freedman who had lost the money he had been saving for his college education when the Freedmen's Bank failed because of the white managers' dishonesty. At least in this small way she could do something to compensate African Americans for the tragic miscarriage of Reconstruction. The freedman in question, W. A. Forsyth, had impressed her favorably because he had written to his white teacher: "Don't beg for me at the North, my good friend. I will go to work and try again. I want to row my own boat." Child volunteered to pay any incidental expenses his scholarship did not cover, on condition that "he might not *know* there was any one to help him row his boat." To her gratification, Hampton's director, General Samuel C. Armstrong, reported that her protégé was "uncommonly intelligent, sensible, and every way satisfactory."[19]

Child had not even finished apportioning Osgood's legacy, when two more deaths compounded the losses of "a very sad summer." After years of isolation in Wayland, she had finally developed an intimacy with a young woman named Louisa Parmenter, who shared some of her intellectual interests and aesthetic tastes. Together they had looked forward to reading the German books Osgood had left Child, but Louisa had come for only one session; "in a fortnight she was dead."[20] On the heels of this bereavement, news arrived that Edmund Benzon, the "intelligent, cultivated, and affectionate young German, who, thirty years ago" had fallen in love with Child and squired her to concerts in New York, had died after an illness so precipitous that her farewell letter had no time to reach him. Though Benzon's acquisition of a great fortune and his entry into the world of London high society had interposed a barrier between them, he had never forgotten his old flame. Confiding to George Eliot that Child had been "one of the beneficent influences on his younger life" (as Eliot reported to her), he bequeathed her $7,800. The interest on this sum multiplied her annual income by 50 percent—

enough to hire some much-needed domestic help to perform chores for which she and David no longer had the strength. "[C]ompletely overwhelmed," Child dissolved in tender recollections of an attachment that had meant more to Benzon than to her—an attachment that inevitably conjured up memories of the two men who had occupied the place in her heart to which Benzon had vainly aspired—John Hopper and Ole Bull.[21]

Of all the deaths Child faced as she struggled to surmount her "mortifications and disappointments as a writer," her anxieties about David's failing health, her loneliness in an uncongenial community, and her despondency over the blighting of Reconstruction, "no affliction . . . oppressed [her] so heavily as the death of Charles Sumner" in March 1874. She had not felt such grief since the loss of Ellis Loring, she confessed to Sarah Shaw. Like Loring, Sumner incarnated for Child the purity of abolitionist principles—in his case miraculously preserved from the contamination of political expediency, while fortified by the power that only the political sphere afforded. Until Sumner's descent into partisanship in the 1872 election, Child had "loved and reverenced him beyond any other man in public life," constantly holding him up as her "ideal of a hero," against whom the other great men in American history should be measured. Yet contrary to Loring's passing in 1857, which had ushered in an era of renewed harmony among abolitionists, crowned by the triumph of their cause, Sumner's marked the end of Reconstruction, which he himself had inadvertently contributed to hastening. He had died leaving his mission aborted by forces of reaction he had proved unable to combat. Nor could Child see any hope of another such moral hero's arising in Sumner's wake to "stem the overwhelming tide of corruption in this country." The sting of "remorse" exacerbated her sorrow, for Sumner had wept over Child's refusal to endorse his stand, and she had ultimately stopped writing to him, since "nothing would satisfy him but the acknowledgment that he had been entirely in the right." Convinced now that he had yielded to "artful politicians" because his "nervous system" had been "shattered," and that he had been "dying by inches" of the angina that had finally killed him, Child reproached herself bitterly for having abandoned Sumner to his enemies. But she took consolation from a memorial service she and David attended with the Shaws, at which their son-in-law, George William Curtis, rendered Sumner the homage Child felt he deserved. The "spontaneous" national outpouring of tributes to the incorruptible Radical senator also comforted her, showing as it did that there was "still great respect for integrity deeply rooted in the popular mind."[22]

The 1874 elections soon confirmed the significance of Sumner's death. But by the time the defeated Republicans took advantage of their last weeks in a lame-duck Congress to honor Sumner's memory by passing a much diluted version of his Civil Rights Bill, Child no longer noticed.[23] Instead, she was reeling under a more devastating bereavement than any she had ever endured.

David's health had deteriorated badly over the past few years. His "frequent attacks of diarrhea," lasting for months at a time, kept Child forever in a "perturbed and anxious state," besides chaining her to the house.[24] After weathering a long bout of this chronic ailment in the winter of 1871–72, David had come down with a "screaming rheumatism" the following October, which had deprived him of sleep and appetite and prevented him from dressing unassisted. "[C]ombined with a severe cold," the pains that "racked" his body had "brought him so low" that Child had started fearing "the beginning of the end had come." By dint of "spending hours every day in bathing, rubbing, poulticing and swathing him in bats of cotton," she had succeeded in restoring him to a semblance of well-being; his hands remained so swollen and disabled, however, that she did not dare "leave him alone, even for an hour, lest he should burn or scald himself."[25] Not until July did David recover sufficiently to dress himself and "hold a pen." Meanwhile, Child had been performing his chores of hauling wood and water, in addition to her own of cooking, cleaning, and mending, which had left her no time to write. Small wonder that her contributions to the *Standard* and the *Woman's Journal* had slacked off by the fall of 1872 and that she had found herself turning from political commentary to such subjects as "Temperance in Eating," "The Physical Strength of Women," and "The Intermingling of Religions."[26] In October 1873 David had felt well enough to undertake a long-postponed visit to his elderly sister, Lydia, in West Boylston, likewise crippled with rheumatism, but he had predictably returned much the worse for wear. Fortunately, by then Benzon's legacy had made it possible to hire a man to do the woodcutting and other jobs David had become too weak to manage — though the extra hand around the house also meant an extra mouth for Child to feed.[27]

A more satisfactory solution to the problem of finding domestic help eventually turned up. The husband of Child's washerwoman, an alcoholic who had spent two years in prison for having "set fire to a barn and burnt up a dozen cattle, because the man who had employed him hid his rum-bottle," had emerged determined to go straight. Child had been so sickened by his wanton abuse of his wife and of helpless animals that she had never wanted to lay eyes on him again. But when he appeared at her door on the day of his release, "his eyes had such a beseeching look, as if his soul was hungry for a friend," that she relented:

> I shook hands with him, and invited him in. I had a long private talk with him, and told him that though he was 60 years old, it was not too late to make a man of himself, if he would only resolve never to taste another drop of liquor; and I assured him that if he would only try, I would be a faithful friend to him. He promised me that he *would* try. . . . He has kept his promise, and I have kept mine. . . . His attentions to us are unbounded. Whenever there is a snow-storm, he is here, prime and early, with his shovel. He runs everywhere to do errands; and on Sundays, he brings wood, and water, and splits kindlings, and does everything he can find to do. He is in fact our "man Friday". . . . I have never in my life experienced any happiness to be compared to the consciousness of lifting a human soul out of the mire.

The bargain lasted for the rest of Child's life, and she willed her reformed "inebriate" a pension of $50 a year, payable in monthly installments, as long as he continued to abstain from alcohol.[28]

Mutual convenience similarly brought Child a housekeeper at just the right moment in the summer of 1874 — Lucy Ann Pickering, a widow in straitened circumstances, who had previously worked for the Lorings. The arrangement was supposed to be temporary, because Mrs. Pickering's "diseased pride of gentility" led her to hope for employment that did not involve manual labor. But she had engaged to stay till September, taking the domestic chores off Child's hands and leaving her free to nurse David and sort through papers. (Child "destroyed over 350 letters" that summer in the name of protecting her privacy and that of her correspondents.)[29]

Having pulled David through so many physical crises, Child was caught off guard by the onset of what proved to be his final illness in July 1874, shortly after his eightieth birthday. It began much like his other bouts of "dyspepsia," with his stomach rejecting "every kind of food, even bread, or gruel," until he was "reduced almost to a skeleton" and Child "feared he could not live through the summer." His constitution seemed so strong, however, rebounding so quickly from each attack, that she allowed herself to believe his life could be "prolonged for many years, and by great care . . . made tolerably comfortable," provided she could get him on the right diet. A consultation with a homeopath reinforced her confidence. His prescriptions were soon "working admirably," and within a week or two David was able to digest meat and bread. By early August he was back in his garden and busier than Child had ever seen him with "improvements" and preparations for winter. Only a week before his death "he took a horse and cart and went 6 miles, to Waltham, to get some blocks of granite. It was a very hot day, and he was gone over ten hours, but he came back in high spirits, and said he felt better for the job." To all appearances, he fully "expected to live through the winter." Then without warning, he took to his bed again. For three days he "suffered greatly with sharp bodily pains," but as late as the day preceding his death Child was still expecting him to "rally." "Only eight hours before he passed away, he was searching the dictionary, to trace the derivation of a word." Not until the last two hours did either of them "realize that he was going." He fell asleep in Child's arms, "as gently as a tired babe, with his head leaning on [her] shoulder." "[N]o tongue can express the desolation I feel," she kept repeating to her friends in stunned misery: "We had lived together nearly half a century, and for the last twenty years had lived alone, mutually serving each other. We had such pleasant companionship intellectually, and he was always kind and lover-like, up to the last day of his life. The tearing up roots so deeply bedded, makes the heart bleed."[30] The "*one* mission" to which Child had devoted the remainder of her life — "to care for the health and comfort of my kind old mate" — was over, and there now seemed to be "nothing to live for." "I feel like a piece of a wreck, drifting out into the ocean," she wrote poignantly to Sarah Shaw.[31]

The end had come so unexpectedly that the Childs had not completed their negotiations for a burial place. Neither had wanted to be buried in Wayland, and Child had especially dreaded the idea of "a funeral from this house, so inaccessible to the few friends we have; with none but neighbors, who would attend out of mere curiosity." But there was no chance to make other arrangements, and the "weather was so very warm and damp, that it was impossible to defer the funeral" long enough for distant family members and friends to attend. Though denied the presence of the antislavery comrades who would throng her own funeral, Child did not have to go through the ordeal of burying David alone. Her capable and affectionate niece, Sarah Preston Parsons, took over the practical details for her, aided by Mrs. Pickering, who proved to be an "inexpressible treasure." Her neighbors showered her with sympathy and touching gestures of respect for David. The service, preached by Edmund Sears, whose Swedenborgian-tinged sermons had comforted Child through the mourning for her father, was "beautiful, impressive, and consoling."[32]

Among the disappointed mourners who "endeavored in vain to find out seasonably" when David's funeral was to be held was Garrison, anxious to pay public tribute to "the character and services of this stalwart champion of the cause of the enslaved," numbering among his "very earliest . . . co-laborers" in the struggle. Garrison himself had been "suffering severely" from rheumatism for the past eighteen months, he wrote Child, but no amount of physical pain could have prevented him from attending his old friend's funeral, had he been informed of it in time. He went on to recall how much he used to admire David's editorial style in the days when he was setting type for the *Massachusetts Journal*; how indebted he felt to David for "encouragement and counsel" at the time he launched the *Liberator*; and how "masterly and exhaustive" he had found David's first reported antislavery speech, *The Despotism of Freedom*, delivered in January 1833. Summing up his eulogy of David, Garrison exclaimed: "What disgust he cherished for everything that savored of hypocrisy or cant! How he loved the right and hated the wrong! How clear was his vision, how intrepid his action, how thoroughly disinterested his aspirations and aims!" He then reiterated his "exalted appreciation" of Child's own "character, genius, literary productions, and self-denying and untiring labors in the cause of universal emancipation," political and religious. "Multitudes on both sides of the Atlantic have read your writings with profit and delight, and yours has been a conspicuous part in popular education. I honor and admire you among the very first of your sex in any age or country," he assured her.[33]

Child spent the next six weeks "breaking up [her] little nest," putting together packages of keepsakes for friends and family, assembling documents to be donated to antislavery collections in public libraries and universities, and arranging to dispose of David's Greek and Latin classics, dictionaries, Spanish and Portuguese books, *Congressional Globes*, and works on "Finance, Agriculture, Commercial Relations, &c.&c.&c.," amounting to more than 200 volumes. She also took legal measures to ensure that David's invalid sister, Lydia, could continue to occupy the family homestead in West Boylston, from which the heirs of David's younger brother, John, had been trying to evict her for several years. Promising Lydia to support her financially as long as she lived, Child apologetically explained why David had left her no money. "My good, darling David was the kindest, best soul alive; but the fact is, he never had any business-faculty," she reminded Lydia:

> It was a marvel to everybody, who knew him, that a man so intelligent, so learned, so capable, so energetic, and so industrious, was *always* in pecuniary difficulty. The reason was, that he inherited his father's deficiences [*sic*]. He had no promptitude, no system in his affairs; hence everything went into confusion. . . .
>
> For the last 45 years, I have paid, from my own funds, all the expenses for both of us. . . . Also, what I have given to the Freedmen, to other charities, and to you and [David's brother] Walter.[34]

After winding up her affairs and storing her furniture with a neighbor, Child started on a series of visits with the Sewalls, Anna Loring Dresel, her brother Convers's daughter Abby, and the Shaws, at whose home in Staten Island she planned to stay until spring.[35]

Contrary to her friends' expectation that getting away from Wayland would cheer her up, Child felt more desolate than ever in unfamiliar surroundings. "The coming and going of people, talking about subjects of common interest, makes life seem like a foreign land, where I do not understand the language," she wrote from the home of the Sewalls, her dearest friends next to the Shaws: "I go back to my darling old mate, with a more desperate and clinging tenderness. And when there comes no response, but the memory of that narrow little spot, where I planted flowers the day before I left our quiet little nest, it seems to me as if *all* was gone, and as if I stood utterly alone on a solitary rock in mid-ocean; alone, in midnight darkness, hearing nothing but the surging of the cold waves."[36] The only remedy that worked was to work for others. Finding Harriet Sewall "very much out of health, nervous, and despondent about ever getting quite well again," Child forced herself to rally: "Sympathy with *her* takes me out of *myself*; and the effort to *seem* cheerful helps me to *be* more cheerful." Unconsciously, she was echoing the advice she had given to the elderly in *Looking toward Sunset.* "I want to be of some use in the world during the time that remains to me here," she added; "and in order to do that, I must not be selfishly sorrowful."[37]

Even after reaching the Shaws', however, Child did not recover from the "confused and bewildered" feeling that accompanied her everywhere. Notwithstanding her brave resolutions, she could not banish the sense that "I belong to nobody, and nobody belongs to me." Whether alone or among friends, in Massachusetts or on Staten Island, she felt "like a hungry child, lost in a dark wood." For years she had chafed against her imprisonment in Wayland and longed to be near friends like the Shaws, who shared her taste for art and literature. Now, in a mansion "adorned with every form of artistic beauty," where she enjoyed a view of "sea-gulls, sloops, and steam-boats" that reminded her of "the best old Dutch sea-pictures," her heart yearned for her "humble little nest in Wayland," and her Wayland neighbors became her chief correspondents. Sarah, Frank, and their children overwhelmed her with loving attention, and conversations with them were as intellectually stimulating as ever. Still, Child missed being able to "wait upon *myself*" in their luxurious establishment, staffed with "seven domestics, well drilled in their various departments." "If I say a word about exercise, the coachman is straightway at the door with the carriage," she complained. Whenever her hosts' backs were turned, she slipped out to "ramble," but "walking merely for the sake of exercise" did not satisfy her. "I want some active *work* to do," she confided to a Wayland neighbor. "In the Spring, I hope to be digging in my dear old garden again."[38]

Actually, Child was doing a great deal of "active *work*," for as soon as guests arrived, she fled to her room, where she set about "sewing, or knitting, for Asylums, Hospitals &c or making and mending" for herself. Her aversion to mixing with "fashionables" had become inveterate, and social "merriment" intensified her loneliness. To escape a "very large dinner-party . . . at Christmas," she went into New York for the first time in more than twenty years and renewed contact with Rosa Hopper, widowed since 1864. The two spent the day knitting and chatting "cozily about old times" and went together to a Christmas Eve gathering for poor children, organized by Rosa's pastor, the progressive Unitarian Octavius Brooks Frothingham. Apparently the visit healed the wound John had inflicted after the imbroglio over Ole Bull's ill-starred colony. Though John's name would almost never crop up in her letters, Child would remain in close touch with Rosa for the rest of her life.[39]

In mid-March, despite the Shaws' protests, Child returned to Wayland, stopping on the way for visits with Rosa, Margaret and Joseph Carpenter in New Rochelle, Marianne Silsbee in Salem, and Anna Loring Dresel in Boston.[40] Mrs. Pickering had agreed to help Child resettle in her old home and stay with her for the summer. Back in her garden, where she could conjure up the sound of David's voice "bidding a loving good morning to my flowers, as he used to do," Child hoped she would feel closer to him. "[A]ll that love and knowledge *cannot* be *lost!*" she kept telling herself. "Surely, I shall find it again *some*where!"[41] The "solemn" rite of opening her "empty little shanty" and building fires "with the wood dear David had so carefully provided" did not dispel Child's "desolate feeling," however. To her chagrin, she also discovered that her months at the Shaws' had "spoiled" her. "My small house seems smaller, voices are coarser, hands more rough, and laughs more discordant," she noticed. Much as she had learned to appreciate the kindness of her Wayland neighbors, they could not fill her need for the sympathy of intellectual soul-mates. "I long indescribably to see you all," she wrote the Shaws, recalling their "pleasant breakfast table, where discussions on the 'eternal fitness of things' were sure to arise," and picturing to herself Sarah's youthful face, crowned by "ample braids of beautiful hair" and a "jaunty" cap, and "dear Frank's pleasant smile, his soft, silky ringlets, his snow-white collar and kerchief, his prismatic diamond, and his golden cross."[42] She would always be suspended between social worlds, too much the artist to take pleasure in the company of the "plain farmers and mechanics" among whom she was born, too much the Frugal Housewife to feel comfortable in the luxurious homes of her genteel friends.[43]

Fleetingly, being "surrounded by things that dear David made and used" brought relief. The labor of "planting vegetables, weeding, destroying caterpillars and currant-worms," and supervising the tasks David used to perform — "mending fences, shingling roof, repairing water-pipes . . . &c.&c" — exhausted her enough so that she dropped into bed every night to "sleep as soundly as a dormouse."[44] But she could not sustain the illusion of David's presence. "[D]ay by day the feeling deepens that something essential to our happiness has irrevocably gone out of our life. And even if our faith is strong that the departed spirit is still near us, *that* does not satisfy the longing to touch the dear hand and hear the beloved voice," she wrote despondently to the Shaws.[45]

The job of going through David's papers resurrected not the image of the "kind and lover-like" mate Child wanted to remember, but the specter of the professional failure she wanted to forget. As she conscientiously looked over "*two barrels* full of business-papers," containing everything from "college compositions" to unfinished manuscripts, from old copies of the *Massachusetts Journal* to "certificates of hay weighed 40 years ago," Child relived the anguish of seeing David's youthful promise come to naught. "Oh, the painful, painful memories that were waked up! I thought I should have cried my eyes out before I got through," she wrote Harriet Sewall, whose husband, Samuel, had been David's college classmate at Harvard and had built a successful law career while David was floundering from one bungled project to another.[46]

By publishing fragments of David's writings that revealed him at his best, Child salvaged something positive from this sad duty. She sent the *Woman's Journal* a few extracts from a diary David had kept during his 1837 tour of Europe, which recorded his observations of the many roles women performed there and which showed "how strong an interest he took in the enfranchisement of women."[47] And she arranged to have David's classmate Stephen Salisbury publish some "remarks concerning the mode of teaching grammar," taken from an article on education David had left uncompleted. She had never ceased to regret that her "dear husband lacked facility in imparting his great store of knowledge to others," Child admitted to Salisbury. Though not a day passed without his dipping into Horace or Virgil, "[i]t was always a laborious task to him to write, or to speak to an audience; so that few knew how to appreciate him at his real value." Thus, "it would gratify [David] extremely" to know that Salisbury considered his manuscript worth publishing. "Ah!" Child added, "what would I not give to be certain that he *does* know and care about those he loved on earth!"[48]

Besides attempting to gain posthumous recognition for David, Child comforted herself by putting together a manuscript narrative of their marriage, into which she pasted entries from the diaries of their courtship years, a poem commemorating their wedding, a drawing of the view from their "Paradis des Pauvres" at Cottage Place, tender references to her in David's European journal, samples of their playful interchanges in the twilight years both considered their happiest together, and poems she had written to David on revisiting her empty home after leaving the Shaws. "In his old age, he was as affectionate and devoted as he was when he was the lover of my youth; nay, he manifested even more tenderness," Child reminisced in this private memorial to the husband she so desperately needed to restore to ideal life.

He was often singing:

> "There's nothing half so sweet in life,
> As Love's *old* dream."

. . . . .

He always insisted upon thinking that whatever *I* said was the wisest and the wittiest, and that whatever *I* did was the best; whether it was writing a book, or making his dressing-gowns, or stuffing his rocking chair.

The simplest little jeu d'esprit of mine seemed to him wonderfully witty. Once, when he said, "I wish, for *your* sake, dear, that I were as rich as Croesus,["] I answered, "You *are* Croesus; for you are King of *Lydia*." How often he used to quote that![49]

Inevitably, Child's desire for renewed communion with David drove her to the mediums she had haunted after the deaths of her father and Ellis Loring. First, she went to a "spirit-photographer" who claimed to be able to produce visual evidence that "a dear departed friend" was hovering over his clients. The sitting resulted only in an ordinary photograph of herself. "So, [spirits] don't come, unless they're *spoken* for," she sniffed. When she requested an actual "spirit-likeness," the photographer disappeared into another room, stayed "*twice as long*" as he had in developing her photograph, and returned with one showing two faces behind her own, both unfamiliar: "A fat woman with fluffy hair, and a very vulgar looking man."[50] Later, Child accompanied Garrison to the home of a celebrated medium named Mrs. Wildes, who allegedly did not know Child's identity. Garrison, a firm believer in spiritualism, found the manifestations of David's presence "very satisfactory" and thought Child did, too.[51] But her innate skepticism and solid good sense kept her from trusting in the "wishy-washy" revelations transmitted through rappings on a table. "So much falsehood and twaddle are mixed with the communications, that I don't think I could find much comfort in the conviction that they came from the spirits of departed mortals," she told the writer Epes Sargent, whom she considered one of the most rational investigators of the subject. "I have found *this* world so common-place, and so full of shams, that the prospect of going to another one like it is rather disheartening. . . . I think I would rather go to sleep and never wake up, than be transferred to a world where rogues, liars, and fools abound, as they do here" — or where "disagreeable relatives, and tiresome acquaintance[s]" could continue to pester her, Child specified to another devotee of spiritualism, her friend Mattie Griffith.[52] In retrospect, she characterized all the professional mediums she had consulted as "vulgar, repulsive persons" who may have had sufficient "clairvoyant" faculty to read minds, but who achieved most of their effects by paying close attention to the "*slightest* clue" a client dropped. "[N]o light could be gained through *such* agencies," she decided.[53] Nevertheless, she still regarded the existence of a clairvoyant faculty as a "fixed fact," authenticated by evidence "from all ages, and all countries," and scientifically explicable by "laws of the universe at present unknown to us."[54]

Despite Child's disdain for the "charlatanry and shallowness" of spiritualist practitioners and the "wholesale credulity" of their disciples, the "loneliness and longing" that had instigated her visits to mediums, as she frankly confessed, could not be assuaged by exercising her reason. Not only did she "cling to the idea that the departed still live, and remember their lives with us" (though previously she and David had both had "many doubts about conscious, individual immortality"), but she also clung to the hope of being able to communicate with David through a disinterested person with "mediumistic powers" — preferably neither an acolyte of spiritualism nor a professional who went into a trance at the drop of a dollar.[55] Her wish was fulfilled through her housekeeper, Mrs. Pickering, of all people.

Mrs. Pickering had nothing but contempt for spiritualism, which she considered "pitiful, vulgar nonsense, and dangerous withal, as a promoter of insanity." Like Child, however, she thought electricity could account for some of the mysterious phenomena connected with spiritualism, among them the automatic writing that mediums performed on planchettes. Having been "told that *she* was uncommonly electrical," Mrs. Pickering had tried a planchette and discovered that it worked, but she had refused to have anything further to do with the "uncanny thing."[56] In the summer of 1877 Child prevailed on her to take up the planchette again for the sake of obtaining a message from David. They experimented on two different evenings, sitting in the dark and going to bed without lighting the lamp. On each occasion Mrs. Pickering's arm had " 'jerked about' " and become very stiff, without her knowing whether she had actually written anything. The first evening they had sat in silence, but on the second, Child had sought to eliminate the possibility of unconscious cheating by chattering away about "trifling subjects, so that [Mrs. Pickering] could have no chance to think." Both times they had found messages on the planchette in the morning. The mysterious author of the messages called himself "Old Truepenny" (a nickname by which David had sometimes referred to himself, as Child remembered after some cogitation). Exhorting "M" to "be patient" and "[p]ray in humility" for guidance, the oracle announced:

> I am very far from you, yet very near. Be content. I will help you through the contest, if I can.
>
> .   .   .   .   .
>
> You call us dead. We are not dead. We truly live now. I cannot tell you, you cannot know, how bright you will find — — —

The second message had broken off there because Mrs. Pickering had "suddenly pushed the pencil aside, and left off." She had been extremely disturbed by the results of the enterprise, as well as "mortified" to discover that she possessed the "so-called 'mediumistic' gift," when her ostensible purpose had been to convince Child that "there *was* no such gift; that the whole thing was a humbug and a sham."[57]

Child kept her promise never to ask Mrs. Pickering for another seance or mention spiritualism to her again. She had no "inclination" to do so, she told Sarah Shaw, because her doubts were at last satisfied. "There *is* a telephone between this world and another; or rather a tele*graph*; though it does not work very perfectly." Besides, she agreed with Mrs. Pickering that "it is not *healthy* for the mind to be *seeking* such communications." In the future, she vowed, "I shall occupy myself with performing *duties here*; but I feel happier in doing so, from the assured conviction that dear departed ones are 'not dead; but truly living now.' "⁵⁸

Among the duties Child tried to perform was to continue writing for the *Woman's Journal*. During her first summer back in Wayland she sent in three contributions — "A Woman Who Made Good Use of Her Tongue," a German story she had translated for the sake of its strong feminist overtones; the extracts from David's journal; and an article addressing the question whether women ought to refuse to pay taxes as a protest against "taxation without representation" — the strategy that Abby Kelley Foster and other radicals had been advocating. Child had been struggling to define her stand on this issue since March 1874, when she had first been asked to endorse the movement to withhold taxes, but her preoccupation with David's illness and death had hitherto prevented her from formulating a public statement of her views. She now explained why she had decided to pay her taxes under protest, even though she fully concurred with those who cited the old Revolutionary slogan "Taxation without representation is tyranny." Like "other thoughtful women," wrote Child, "I feel . . . the great injustice of having taxes levied on my property by votes of ignorant foreigners, and illiberal countrymen, while I am permitted to have no voice concerning the application of funds thus raised." But the government provided many useful services from which "the people at large" benefited, such as building and repairing roads, supporting free public schools, and sustaining courts of justice. Rather than wait for all wrongs to be righted before she would help her government defray the cost of advancing the public welfare, she was willing to pay her share. At the same time, she specified in the protest against "taxation without representation" which she appended to her check, "I consider my taxes as an outright gift from my own good will, not as the payment of anything the government have a right to demand of me." The compromise would certainly not have satisfied Abby Kelley Foster, whose farm had recently been sold at auction for nonpayment of taxes, but Child still tended to "take the 'middle extreme,[']" as she had when the two had differed on tactics in the antislavery cause.⁵⁹

Child planned to write more articles for the *Woman's Journal* over the winter of 1875–76, during which she would be cooped up in the room she was renting from a Wayland neighbor; "but perhaps, because I *ought* to do it, I shall not accomplish it," she acknowledged ruefully to Sarah Shaw, who had pleaded unsuccessfully with her to spend at least her winters in Staten Island. In fact, she ended up passing her time sewing, quilting, knitting, reading, and making a scrapbook, probably because she was too depressed to write.⁶⁰ Alone in her chilly room "twenty hours out of the twenty four," she had never felt "so utterly forlorn," as she finally confessed to Sarah after a long silence. Uncertainty about whether or not to sell the house and where to live if she did so tormented her. The death in the middle of the winter of the Reverend Mr. Sears, her last real "*friend*" in Wayland, deepened Child's despondency. "It tried my feelings very much to attend his funeral; for it brought vividly to mind that other funeral, where he made such a consoling prayer, and paid such a beautiful tribute to the memory of my dear mate," she wrote Sarah. For the next two nights she had not been able to sleep. Dozing off in the morning, she had dreamed that "David was lying dead, and I was weeping over him; but all at once he moved, and voices said, 'He is *not* dead.' Then he opened his eyes and looked very lovingly at me, as he said: '*This* is worth living for. I have *you* again.'" A classic wish-fulfillment dream, it also expressed the degree to which Child had come to identify with David; she had died emotionally when David had died physically, and without him, as she had told Anna Loring Dresel, she had felt there was "nothing to live for." In her dream she was projecting onto David her sense that it would be worth coming back to life only if she could have him with her again. "Of course, it was a *dream*, caused by the scene I had been witnessing," she commented to Sarah, "but it comforted me greatly."[61]

Under the circumstances, an obituary for the Reverend Mr. Sears was the sole article Child wrote for the *Woman's Journal* that winter. She used it not only to praise him for his "quiet courage" in speaking out against slavery and in preaching the equality of the sexes, but to articulate her own sentiments. "He had no reluctance to incur obloquy in vindication of the right; but it was simply not natural to him to work in the harness of reforms," she wrote of Sears, speaking for herself as well, though she had devoted many years to working in the "harness of reforms." She went on to endorse his views on the "spiritual" differences between the sexes, bringing them into accord with hers by "making large allowance" for individual variations. "Harmony implies a difference, and harmony is a much more complete thing than unison," she argued, reverting to her favorite metaphor: "But Nature is always making innovations upon classes; she delights in individuals. Some men have clear, sweet tenor voices; some women have deep and strong contralto voices. . . . In some men, especially in artists, feminine qualities predominate. In some women, especially in reformers, strong and masculine qualities predominate. All that is wanted is perfect freedom for each and all to develop and use their natural gifts." Such freedom would "produce the highest manifestation of social harmony." Perhaps unconsciously, Child was echoing a memorable passage of her friend Margaret Fuller's *Woman in the Nineteenth Century*.[62]

Child's spirits revived after a trip to Boston in May 1876, during which she attended the Free Religious Association meeting for the first time. Founded by progressive Unitarians in 1867, the association had invited representatives of all faiths, including non-Christian religions and agnostics, to "come together as equal brothers" and learn from each other, accepting "the *true* from any quarter." Child had joined it on the spot, hailing it as the embodiment of the principle she had sought to inculcate through *The Progress of Religious Ideas* eighteen years earlier. She had hoped to go to one of its Sunday gatherings with Louisa Loring, but her plans had been frustrated by Louisa's death, and no other opportunity had presented itself until Anniversary Week of 1876. The intercourse with people who shared her radical religious views and who "made much of" her presence was very healing, especially at a time when she was searching for spiritual consolation, yet feeling more alienated than ever from orthodoxies of all stripes.[63]

Another initiative that helped cheer her up was a visit to her "Dear Friend of the

Olden Time," Abba May Alcott, in Concord. The two had known each other since before their respective marriages and had become particularly intimate in 1838, when Child had nursed Abba through the aftermath of a stillbirth, but they had lost touch during their parallel struggles with adversity. With Abba, Child burst out of the mental prison in which she had locked herself for so many months. Later apologizing for her talkativeness, she wrote enthusiastically of her visit: "There was so *much* to say about by-gone, eventful years!" The Alcott daughters, Louisa and May, were living with their parents, and Louisa, who had inherited Child's mantle as the premiere writer for girls of her generation, was at the height of the fame she had earned with *Little Women* (1868). Clearly recognizing in Louisa a younger self, Child delighted in her "Christian hatred of lionizing" and her "straightforward and sincere" manner, which some mistook for brusqueness. "Being natural is so little in fashion, that even a natural *fool* might be welcome as a novelty; and to meet with natural *geniuses*, what a rare piece of good fortune was that!" exclaimed Child. The Alcott daughters, she informed Sarah Shaw, "don't like conventional *fetters* any better than I do." As she so often did when she identified strongly with someone, Child shifted abruptly into the first person: "There have been many attempts to saddle and bridle me, and teach me to keep step in respectable processions; but they have never got the lasso over my neck *yet*; and 'old hoss' as I am now, if I see the lasso in the air, I snort and gallop off, determined to be a free horse to the last, and put up with the consequent lack of grooming and stabling." Child did not like Bronson (who resembled David in more ways than she cared to admit) any better than she had in the past, but, admiring the renovations he had made on his house in Concord, she allowed that he had "an architectural taste, more intelligible than his Orphic Sayings." Though she could not help envying Abba for having "such gifted daughters to lean upon, after all the toil and struggle of her self-sacrificing life," Child returned to her cottage in Wayland feeling "more serene" than she had since her bereavement.[64]

There she resumed her gardening and her "sorting and packing" of David's books. But her disinclination to write persisted. When Lucy Stone asked her to furnish a letter to be read at the celebration of the United States's first centennial in Philadelphia, where suffragists had set up a woman's pavilion, Child complied halfheartedly. Her brains were "stewed by the heat," she complained: "If you knew how I hate the very sight of a pen, you would appreciate my wish to oblige you. I had rather bake, brew, knit, sew, wash, scour. . . ." Her letter arrived too late for the occasion and was published in the *Woman's Journal* instead. Hailing the enormous progress women had made, both since 1776 and in her lifetime, Child called the roll of the "brilliant" writers, "distinguished" painters and sculptors, "thoroughly educated" doctors, eloquent preachers, and promising lawyers who had advanced the cause of women by furnishing "indisputable proof" of their sex's inherent equality. She ended characteristically by reminding women that "duties are always in proportion to destinies" and by urging: "as our destiny is ever growing larger and larger, let us prepare ourselves for duties of increasing magnitude."[65]

Shortly afterward, Child responded without prodding to an article by Stone's sister-in-law, Antoinette Brown Blackwell, calling on the editors of the *Woman's Journal* "to refute the theory of certain scientific men that women are, by their natural organization, physically and intellectually inferior to men." It would be a waste of women's "mental energies," Child countered, to "expend time in arguing about intellectual equality." A far more productive strategy would be to "prove it by what we do." The astronomer Mary Somerville, the political economist Harriet Martineau, the painter Rosa Bonheur, the writer George Eliot, the sculptor Anne Whitney, and the doctor Elizabeth Blackwell had done more to demonstrate the equality of the sexes by their achievements than they could have "by the ablest argumentation," Child contended: "The only argument I think it worth while to offer on the subject is this: If women have physical or intellectual strength sufficient to earn property, and consequently be taxed for it, they have intellect enough to vote concerning the use that shall be made of their taxes; and if they have sense and feeling enough to suffer from the effects of corrupt or imbecile legislation, they have sense enough to try to improve it." To enter into disputes about biological equality, Child insisted, could not help women when it was "obvious" that they were not yet "generally speaking, the physical or intellectual equals of men." As long as obstacles to the free exercise of their talents remained, there would be no means of determining whether this gap between overall male and female performance was to be ascribed to biology or to "centuries of impeded growth, and the dwarfing effects of habitual subordination." She concluded: "All I ask is perfect liberty to choose our own spheres of action, and a fair, open chance to do whatsoever we can do well. I am very willing to leave time to decide the degree of our capabilities, and I have no anxiety concerning the verdict."[66] Always more comfortable with the practice than with the theory of feminism, Child was reiterating the advice she had given the Grimké sisters nearly forty years earlier — "not to *talk* about our right, but simply [to] go forward and *do* whatsoever we deem a duty."[67]

After this spurt of her old eloquence, Child relapsed into silence, however. The truth was, her attention was focused on the world of the spirit, and neither the woman question nor any of the other causes she had so passionately advocated held her attention these days. She had stopped following the "doings in Congress," she wrote the Shaws, "not having any one to whom I can read the Speeches and Debates, as I used to, with a running commentary of mutual remarks." She took no notice of Custer's Last Stand or of the outcry against Indian savagery it generated in the press, which would once have provoked an indignant rejoinder from her. Nor did she comment on the hotly contested 1876 presidential election, except to praise Garrison privately for reminding the public of the Democrats' virulent hostility to African Americans and for pointing out that their past record of corruption was as bad as the Republicans' under the Grant administration — the same stand she had taken in 1872. Though aware that the freedpeople needed "active friends" more than ever, as she told Wendell Phillips, she herself could only watch the return to power of the plantation oligarchy and "submit, as one *must* do, to things that cannot be helped."[68] Indeed, so out of touch had she become with political affairs that she compared Grant's successor, Rutherford B. Hayes, to Lincoln as a man "especially sent to meet the *present* crisis." Even after Hayes had agreed to recognize the ex-Confederate Wade Hampton as governor of South Carolina in the place of the former abolitionist carpetbagger Daniel Chamberlain — a step Child had at first decried — she continued to laud his "honesty and impartiality" and to echo his claim that a "better feeling" was really "dawning in the South." At last, southerners like Wade Hampton were beginning to "perceive that it is for their own true interest to protect and educate all classes of their citizens," she reported to the expatriate artist Francis Alexander as late as July 1877 in giving him news of his native land. Not until the consequences of Hayes's "*excessive* spirit of conciliation" had become too patent to be denied did Child lose "patience with his miserable time-serving policy."[69] But her disillusionment never led her to challenge his use of U.S. troops to put down the Great Strike of 1877. "These rioters are terribly in the wrong; and there is nothing for it but to subdue them with a strong hand," she averred, blaming the problem of labor strife on the "increasing tendency toward a strong *demarcation of classes* in this country."[70]

If Child had withdrawn from the political arena while fighting her way out of her crippling depression, she had not abandoned her ideals. She still felt more "interest . . . in melting down all the barriers that separate different portions of the human family" than she did in "*any*" other subject, as she wrote Alexander in the same letter.[71] She had merely redirected her desire to dispel injustice and prejudice, channeling her energies into a project better suited to her psychological needs than writing for the *Woman's Journal* (or for the commercial press, as Garrison was doing).

Her new project of compiling an "Eclectic Bible" that would help liberate the masses from superstition and "expand their human sympathies" had grown out of the religious reading she had been doing in lieu of mulling over the newspapers.[72] During the "forlorn" winter of 1875–76 that she had spent boarding with the family of Wayland's retired Unitarian minister, John B. Wight, Child had begun rereading the Bible "with very close observation of its real meaning." She had drawn little solace from the perusal. Instead, she had emerged from it increasingly convinced that "it would be salutary for mankind if large portions of [the Bible] were expunged."[73] "My ideas, as you know, have been, for years, growing more and more rational; more and more sceptical, as some would say," she wrote to Thomas Wentworth Higginson. "I do not find so much that is satisfactory in the Christian religion, as I did when I wrote The Progress of Religious Ideas. I think I am more truly religious now, than I was; but not in the way that [then?] satisfied me."[74]

Thus, Child's quest for spiritual consolation had soon led her away from the Bible and back to the Greek and Oriental texts that had fascinated her when she was researching *The Progress of Religious Ideas*. Many more had been translated in the intervening decades. While Child was at the peak of her involvement in the controversies over Reconstruction, the Unitarian scholar James Freeman Clarke had published a series of *Atlantic Monthly* articles on comparative religion, which he had collected in *Ten Great Religions* (1871). They had renewed Child's interest in the subject and prompted her to write two articles of her own for the *Atlantic*, "Resemblances between the Buddhist and the Roman Catholic Religions" and "The Intermingling of Religions," in which she had implicitly taken issue with Clarke for attempting to establish the superiority of Christianity to other faiths. Besides reiterating her theory that Christianity had derived most of its doctrines from Hindu, Buddhist, Persian, and Gnostic sources, Child set Buddha and Jesus on an equal footing as religious reformers who had cast their lot with the poor and outcast, opening the "road to holiness . . . to all classes and conditions; to women as well as men, to foreign nations as well as to" their own. "[T]hose who look upon all mankind as brethren," she wrote in "The Intermingling of Religions," recognize "something beautiful in both these great tides of reform [Buddhism and Christianity], enlarging the scope of human sympathies, and sweeping away the ancient barriers that had separated classes and peoples." One of Child's aims in her article on Buddhism and Catholicism had been to counteract anti-Chinese hysteria. Contrary to the allegations of those who "sneer[ed] at the Chinese as 'Pagans'" and pronounced them unassimilable, she noted, the religions of the Chinese and of the Irish who opposed them so bitterly had a great deal in common. In fact, the parallels were "so close that it [was] difficult to perceive any differences, except in names" — an assertion Child proceeded to substantiate with a detailed comparison of the two religions' histories, doctrines, institutions, priesthoods, and popular practices. Beyond the immediate political impetus for these articles, Child had found herself tremendously drawn to Buddhism, a religion about which much more information had become available since she had explored it in the 1850s.[75]

She had greater opportunity to pursue her study of Buddhism and other non-Judaeo-Christian religions in the winter of 1876–77, when she decided to rent rooms in Boston (a decision Mrs. Pickering facilitated by offering to stay with Child if she would spend her winters in the city). By coincidence, her rooming house on Groton Street was a stone's throw away from the home she associated with the most idyllic years of her marriage. "It seems so strange to round the circle, and come back in sight of Cottage Place, where my little minikin garden bloomed, and where dear David and I lived so lovingly and cosily, looking out on the diamond-sprinkled water, that flowed between us, and South Boston," Child wrote poignantly to Sarah Shaw. "All that has happened since then, what was it *for*? What has all the toil *accomplished*? At present it seems to me a barren record; but perhaps I shall understand it better hereafter."[76] Most of the friends Child had known in Boston had died or moved away, and she felt "like a phantom flitting about among phantoms." Although she visited occasionally with Anna Loring Dresel, the Sewalls, Garrison, and a few other old-time intimates, she did not see a single familiar face in the crowded streets where acquaintances had once greeted her at every corner. What helped most to alleviate her loneliness was to attend the Sunday meetings of the Free Religious Association, held at nearby Parker Memorial Hall. "The activity of thought is altogether unfettered there, and its range is wide as the universe," she told her former hosts, the Wights, indirectly referring to her religious differences with them.[77] The stimulation of exchanging ideas with kindred spirits no doubt furthered her religious quest and introduced her to new translations of Oriental texts, as well as to the latest scholarship in the field. It also seems to have revived her old habit of turning her private needs to public account. By spring 1877 she was confiding to Sarah Shaw that she had hopes of again doing "something in a literary way," if she could only find a permanent "*home*" in which to settle with her books around her.[78]

Child's search for a home she could afford in a less isolated suburb of Boston proved fruitless, and she and Mrs. Pickering took refuge in Wayland out of desperation, "entirely wilted down and used up." It was at this juncture that they had held the seance with the planchette through which Child had received the message she found so comforting. Combined with her two-year course of reading, her regular attendance at Free Religious Association meetings, and the healing effect of time, the assurance David's spirit had given her that he was "not dead; but truly living now" liberated her from the grief that had paralyzed her since her bereavement. Now she was indeed ready to "occupy [herself] with performing *duties here*," as she had ineffectually tried to do for the past two years.[79]

Once again, as with *The Progress of Religious Ideas* more than twenty years earlier, the duty to which Child devoted herself was to distill the research that had freed her from her own "shackle[s]" into a book aimed "at the *common* people" and the "*popular* mind." She worked on the project all summer and returned to Boston in November 1877 with a completed manuscript in hand. She offered it first to James T. Fields, since he had brought out *The Freedmen's Book* and *A Romance of the Republic*. "I do not expect to get any money, or any reputation, by the publication of it," she told Fields; "but I do want, before I go hence, to do something more toward loosening the fetters with which old superstitions shackle the minds of men."[80] Fields's new partner, James R. Osgood, had published James Freeman Clarke's *Ten Great Religions*, however, and apparently reacted unfavorably to Child's refusal to emulate Clarke in weighting the scale toward Christianity. He may also have feared (correctly, as it turned out) that a "Bible" in which the sacred texts of non-Judaeo-Christian religions predominated would not sell. Fields finally put Child in touch with the firm of Roberts Brothers, and she signed the contract in March. A fellow aficionado of Asian religions, A. W. Stevens, who had read her *Progress of Religious Ideas* long ago and pronounced *Aspirations of the World* an "admirable" expression of the same "broad and beautiful spirit," shepherded the manuscript through the press for her. It appeared on the market in late May.[81]

Child's title, *Aspirations of the World. A Chain of Opals*, encapsulates the essence of the book. It conveys a double message: first, that " 'there never has been in the world but one religion; which is the aspiration of man toward the Infinite' " (one of the quotations she had included under the heading "Fraternity of Religions"); and, second, that through their sacred texts, ranging from "antique gems" to "modern pearls and crystals," "all the great human family have contributed somewhat to the family-jewels, and left their precious legacies as heir-looms to posterity."[82] She had picked the opal as her chief symbol because "different colors glanced [from it] as the light varied" (239), typifying the beauty of diversity and the ever-changing perception of truth under ever-changing circumstances.

Child's introduction spells out her purpose of uniting the human family by stressing the "[s]entiments" in which "all mankind agree" rather than the "opinions" over which they quarrel. "[M]y impelling motive is to do all I can to enlarge and strengthen the bond of human brotherhood," she explains. Hence, she seeks to show that "the primeval impulses of the human soul have been essentially the same everywhere" and that "the fundamental laws of morality, and the religious aspirations of mankind, have been strikingly similar" throughout history (1–2, 41). Unveiling the private grief that has occasioned her wide-ranging quest for religious enlightenment, she pleads movingly with her readers to follow her example and learn to identify with all fellow mortals who share the human condition: "As we travel on, beloved companions of our pilgrimage vanish from our sight, we know not whither; and our bereaved hearts utter cries of supplication for more light. . . . Being thus closely allied in our sorrows and our limitations, in our aspirations and our hopes, surely we ought not to be separated in our sympathies" (43).

In a historical overview, Child summarizes and updates the analysis she had presented in *The Progress of Religious Ideas* of how Judaism and Christianity had developed out of other ancient religions, inheriting earlier ideas of a Supreme Being, the immortality of the soul, a "Natural Law of Justice," and an imminent millennium. She also draws a brief comparison between Christianity and Buddhism. Christianity has had the advantage of building on Greco-Roman traditions of free inquiry, while Buddhism has had the disadvantage of contending with Asiatic traditions of fatalism, she points out, unconsciously lapsing into the "Orientalist" biases she is ostensibly combating. Yet "candor compels the admission that [Buddhism] has been more true to its own professions than Christianity has been": "[I]ts progress has been uniformly peaceful. It has never offered the alternative of baptism or slaughter to conquered nations, as Christianity has done; it has never persecuted its Hindu spiritual parents, as Christianity has persecuted its spiritual parents the Jews; and it has never tried to compel a uniform profession of faith by the establishment of an Inquisition, to torture and burn nonconformists, as Christianity has done" (11–12).[83]

The most remarkable feature of *Aspirations of the World* is its choice of texts representing "the *best* portions" of all the world's religions—a choice in which quotations from Greco-Roman, Buddhist, Persian, Hindu, and Chinese sacred scriptures (approximately in that order of preference) far outnumber extracts from the Old and New Testaments.[84] Unlike *The Progress of Religious Ideas*, *Aspirations of the World* makes no attempt to exhibit the "beauties and blemishes" of each religion; nor does it invite assessment of the various faiths' respective merits. Rather, it culls the most morally and intellectually satisfying words of guidance Child has encountered in her search for "light" and incorporates them into a new Bible, summing up the collective wisdom of the human race. Child explicitly criticizes the "unfairness" of Christian authors who compare the "poorest specimens" of other "Holy Writings" with the most "sublime passages from Isaiah, or the Psalms; the Sermon on the Mount, [or] . . . the benediction on Little Children." She also reminds readers that just as pious Christians "find . . . a spiritual meaning" even in passages non-initiates might consider morally objectionable, "the same thing is true with regard to the Sacred Books of other peoples" (3–4).

Her "Eclectic Bible" differs from traditional sacred texts not only in its inclusiveness, but in its organization. To help readers consult the passages suited to their needs of the moment, Child arranges them under thirty subject headings. With a few exceptions — among them "Ideas of the Supreme Being," "Prayers," and "Immortality" — most of the categories are ethical. A large proportion emphasize values central to her career as an egalitarian reformer: "Inward Light" (Conscience), "Moral Courage," "Natural Law of Justice," "Benevolence," "Brotherhood," "Fraternity of Religions." Under each subject heading, Child sets quotations in chronological order, beginning with scriptures that antedate the Old and New Testaments by many centuries; intermingling texts that date from the same period, regardless of their religious origin; and showing that all religions have kept evolving over the centuries. She also juxtaposes texts in ways that illuminate both historical influence (as in the case of late Jewish precedents for nearly all the sayings of Jesus) and spiritual affinities (as with Buddha's and Jesus' embrace of outcasts). Another of Child's strategies for promoting the spirit of brotherhood is to draw attention to the ethnicity of the authors she cites. She pointedly labels Confucius, Lao-tzu, Mencius, and a few anonymous Buddhist texts as "Chinese," for example, and she consistently identifies Jesus and Paul as "Israelite" rather than "Christian." Lastly, quotations from modern thinkers like Thomas Paine, Emerson, Carlyle, and Theodore Parker follow extracts from ancient scriptures. The inclusion of Paine, whose *Age of Reason* had been anathemized by the American public for almost a century, is particularly bold in a book destined for religious consumption. Accounting for one of the two largest groups (the other being Greco-Roman texts), these modern selections serve to indicate that divine revelation never ceases and that every generation must write its own bibles.

The Bible she has compiled, Child hopes, will prepare the way for the "Eclectic Church of the Future which shall gather forms of holy aspirations from all ages and nations, and set them on high in their immortal beauty, with the broad sunlight of heaven to glorify them all." The model for the unity in diversity she envisions is "Milan cathedral, lifting its thousand snow-white images of saints" into the sky (48). It is a model that acknowledges the contributions of Roman Catholicism, at a time when Child had been warning against the threat the church posed to republican institutions. Yet like Child's other favorite metaphor, interracial marriage, of which it is the religious equivalent, her Eclectic Church of the Future is ultimately assimilationist in nature. She would never succeed in formulating an ideal of human brotherhood that did not involve the absorption of other cultures into her own.

Child's friends responded enthusiastically to *Aspirations of the World*, in contrast to their coolness toward *The Progress of Religious Ideas* and *A Romance of the Republic*. Anna Loring Dresel judged the introduction to be in Child's "very best style, 'Full of power and gentle; liberal-minded, great, consistent,' " and she pronounced the extracts "opals of the very first water." Ellis would have been highly pleased with the book, she ventured. Garrison praised the spirit of the introduction as "world-embracing in its sympathy and catholicity." The Shaws and George Julian wrote warm letters of approbation. *The Woman's Journal* predicted that the book would be "welcomed first by the great army of readers to whom Mrs. Child has herself been for many years a source both of aspiration and inspiration, and next, by reverent people everywhere. . . ." Child took special pleasure in a "real hearty, appreciative notice" by Epes Sargent in *The Banner of Light*.[85]

Aspirations of the World did not fulfill Child's hopes of liberating the "*popular* mind" from superstition and bigotry, however. Instead, it confirmed her wry suspicion that "the clergy of all sects [would] quietly do all in their power to impede its circulation." The book sold still fewer copies than *The Progress of Religious Ideas*, received fewer reviews, and met with less generosity from the pulpit. Even a journal as liberal as *Harper's Monthly* felt obliged to deny that Christianity could properly be put on the same footing as other religions. "[T]he Christian religion is not only an echo of the world's aspirations, it also claims to be in some sense a satisfaction of those aspirations," the reviewer objected. "[W]e look in vain for any assurances of pardon or any promises of eternal life that compare with those furnished by the Scriptures of the Old and New Testaments, and equally in vain for any expressions of that 'peace of God which passeth all understanding'. . . ." If Child had "inserted these Divine promises and these expressions of Christian experience," added the reviewer, "she would have been compelled to leave the pages devoted to pagan religion wholly blank."[86] The cavil totally missed the point of a book that had intentionally omitted doctrinal statements and had sought not to furnish a point-by-point comparison of Christianity with "paganism" (a word Child deliberately eschewed), but to make available to all future heirs the "precious legacies" each member of the "great human family" had bequeathed to posterity. The defensiveness aroused by Child's last published book showed the extent to which she had remained ahead of her time.

"It is a little saddening to be out of harmony with the prevailing opinions of one's age," Child had written to Francis Shaw while she was awaiting Fields's verdict on *Aspirations of the World*.[87] Her last winters in Boston relieved her sense of isolation by putting her in contact with freethinkers who had "wandered farther into Doubt-land" than she had. Perhaps through Fields, who enjoyed forging ties among the authors he published, Child met the "Great Agnostic," Robert Ingersoll, notorious for his mordant ridicule of theological dogma. He invited her to a dinner he had organized for a dozen fellow travelers, at which Child was astonished to find herself one of two holdouts who "retained any faith in a Deity, or another world." The raillery with which Ingersoll treated religion was foreign to Child, who did not have "the heart to joke about *anything* that furnishes any poor starving soul with consolation or support." Nevertheless, she recognized Ingersoll as a kindred spirit and relished his wit. "I am so weary of respectable shams, that I cordially welcome any one who utters his thought with honest outrightness," she told Fields. She and Ingersoll were "to a certain extent, doing the same work," she acknowledged to another militant agnostic among her new friends, the sculptor Anne Whitney: "He is *knocking* off fetters, and I am *melting* them off. Good riddance to fetters! say I. I want to see human souls stride about *freely* in search of truth.

You are overturning superstition with the crow-bar of Science, *he* brings Fun in to give a heave. By *all* our help, it will be rolled into the abyss of oblivion."[88]

Anne Whitney herself probably did more than anyone else to reawaken Child's interest in life. An artist who specialized in abolitionist and feminist subjects, having "warmly sympathized with the Anti-Slavery struggle" and ardently championed the cause of women's rights, Whitney combined all of Child's passions and embodied the fusion of her warring selves. Child could hardly have found a better candidate for her last adopted daughter. Their friendship had begun in the spring of 1877, when Whitney had written to propose doing a portrait bust of Child. Child had declined on the plea that she had too much admiration for Whitney's genius and "too much reverence for the high mission of Art" to desecrate both with her "old visage." But she had leaped at the chance to visit Whitney's studio and become "better acquainted."[89] Before long, she was again performing her favorite role as a patron of artists. Hearing that a project was under way to commission a statue of John Brown, Child wrote a private letter to Brown's biographer James Redpath, recommending Whitney as a sculptor of "decided *genius*" with an "unusual faculty of putting *life* and *character* into marble." As proof, Child cited Whitney's statue of Samuel Adams, on display at the Capitol in Washington, and her model of Charles Sumner, to which a jury had voted "the highest prize." Whitney's antislavery ideals would make her especially likely to capture Brown's character, Child hinted. She suggested that Redpath hold a contest and award the commission to whichever sculptor produced the "*best* model" of Brown.[90]

Such a contest had actually been held to choose a sculptor for the statue of Sumner, and Child had been furious when Whitney was bypassed despite having won first place. The committee had explicitly rationalized its decision by arguing that "a female artist could not have a chance to become well skilled in the structure of a masculine figure." "The Jackasses!" she raged. "By that showing, what business have men to carve feminine figures?" Her indignation—and her desire to pay public homage to Whitney's achievement, in which all women might take pride—inspired the last article she would write for the *Woman's Journal*. The skillful handling of such details as "the easy position of the figure" testified to Whitney's mastery of technique, Child wrote; moreover she had succeeded brilliantly in infusing Sumner's "soul" into her model: "The refined, scholarly gentleman sits before you, and his attitude and face express the serene strength of a pure, enlightened conscience, satisfied with the performance of duty, and free from anxiety about the consequences" (a description as applicable to Child as to Sumner). She ended with a ringing condemnation of gender discrimination: "I should be sorry to have a woman favored in any department of Art of Science, merely because she is a woman, but when she fairly distances competition in her efforts, it is surely ungenerous and unjust to make her womanhood a plea for setting aside her claims."[91]

Whitney did sculpt a model of Brown's head, and Child promptly arranged to have Garrison come look at it, allegedly because he had personally known Brown and might be able to offer helpful criticism. As she hoped, the consultation resulted in Garrison's ordering a bust of himself from Whitney, which he described to his children as a perfect likeness.[92]

The friendship was far from one-sided. Whitney shared a book of her poems with Child, visited her often at her rooming house, tried to tempt her to socialize more, and implored Child to move in with her, rather than stay in cheap lodgings and shuttle back and forth between Boston and Wayland. Child good-humoredly resisted. "I am an irreclaimable Bohemian; eschewing, above all things, both the fetters and the expenses of gentility," she protested. "I am most at home among plain farmers and mechanics." The truth was of course more complicated than Child admitted, but she was not wholly misrepresenting herself. She had lived the part of the Frugal Housewife too long to change. Besides, her innate independence balked at the idea of becoming "an appendage to another person's household." Having nursed two invalids through the infirmities of old age, she dreaded the prospect of becoming a burden in her turn. "I should be very selfish to clog your young life with the care of a helpless old woman," she remonstrated.[93]

The two women also kept up a running debate about the existence of an afterlife, Whitney denying it from her thoroughgoing materialist perspective, Child stoutly maintaining her faith in the spirit world and in the possibility of communicating with its denizens, however imperfectly. "There is no use in *reasoning* with me about this," she admonished Whitney, "for I *know* it, just as certainly as I know that water, under given conditions becomes ice. But, though I have accepted what *came* to me, I shall not follow up the subject. . . . I deem frequent visits to Cloud-land as injurious to the mind, as the habitual use of opium or gas is to the body."[94]

Whitney was not the only one to try in vain to "lasso" Child and put her into social "harness," as she invariably described her friends' well-meant efforts to drag her out of her reclusiveness. Except for the Sewalls, with whom she dined every Sunday, none succeeded.[95] Frank Shaw's sister, Sarah Shaw Russell, who enjoyed escorting Child to woman suffrage meetings and taking her out to visit old friends in outlying suburbs begged to be allowed the privilege more often.[96] James T. Fields and his wife Annie, an indefatigable promoter of women writers, besieged Child with invitations to literary soirees. On one such occasion Child replied: "I must be ungracious enough to acknowledge that my aversion to *all* 'Clubs,' and all 'Readings,' is of the extremest kind. I like to read in the chimney-corner, where I can clap my hands, or laugh, or sniff, all to myself." But she did accept an invitation to a dinner for Harriet Beecher Stowe, whose biography Annie Fields would later write. To her surprise, the Stowes emphatically agreed with her that " '*No* form of theology' " had ever benefited their souls either, as she reported with zest to Francis Shaw.[97]

Since Child could so rarely be enticed out, Annie Fields decided to take one of her latest protégées, Elizabeth Stuart Phelps, to meet this distinguished literary forebear at her lodgings. The neighborhood was "so much less than fashionable, that I felt a certain awe upon me, as if I were visiting a martyr in prison," Phelps recalled long afterward in her literary reminiscences: "We climbed the steep stairs of her boarding-house thoughtfully. Each one of them meant some generous check which Mrs. Child had drawn for the benefit of something or somebody, choosing this restricted life as the price of her beneficence. She received us in a little sitting-room which seemed to me dreariness personified. . . . The room was so devoid of color as to seem like a cell. . . ." They prevailed on Child to recount some of her antislavery experiences, which moved Phelps deeply. As they talked, "the sun battled through the clouds, and then we saw that Mrs. Child had 'the afternoon side' of her boarding-house, and knew how to make the most of it. She rose quickly and, taking a little prism which she evidently treasured, hung it in the window so that it caught the southwestern ray. Instantly the colorless room leaped with rainbows." Her eyes fixed "dreamily" on the rainbows, Child continued the conversation about old antislavery times. "Her heart had gone far back." Phelps would remember the encounter for the rest of her life. "I never see a prism without thinking of her noble life," she wrote; adding that she kept one in her "study windows to this day," to remind her of the woman who had taught her what it meant to have "sacrificed the prospect of a brilliant literary future to her convictions. . . ."[98]

More and more, Child would feel like what she seemed to Phelps — a relic from an era when, as she wrote to the abolitionist Theodore Weld, "[t]he Holy spirit *did* actually descend upon men and women in tongues of flame." In the fall of 1878 she went to visit Weld's wife, the former Angelina Grimké, "after a separation of forty years." It was a painful reunion. Already senile, Angelina did not recognize her. "We had better have remained in each other's memory as we were in the days of youthful strength and courage," Child confided to another of her old comrades, the poet John Greenleaf Whittier. The visit with Angelina also raised a frightening question: "Will the dearones from whom we parted here seem so strange when we meet again in the unknown world?"[99] A year later Angelina was dead. As she reminisced in her letter of condolence to Weld about the movement in which he and Angelina had played such a conspicuous part, what Child remembered most nostalgically was the way "[p]olitical and theological prejudices, and personal ambitions, were forgotten in sympathy for the wrongs of the helpless, and in the enthusiasm to keep the fire of freedom from being extinguished on our national altar." Her mind shifting from that early crusade (and its degeneration into sectarian squabbling) to her latest effort to melt down the barriers dividing human beings, she wrote, "Ah, my friend, that is the *only* true church organization, when heads and hearts unite in working for the welfare of the human-race." From the vantage point of the post-Reconstruction period, Child found it "very hard to realize that so much . . . has passed into oblivion, and that what remains is merely the cold record of history" — and the bitter fruits of an unfinished struggle for racial equality.[100]

The death that more than any other marked the end of an era was of course Garrison's in May 1879. Fittingly, it occurred in the midst of an event that dramatized the betrayal of the nation's commitment to African Americans and the colossal failure of President Hayes's conciliatory policy toward the South — the mass exodus to Kansas of desperate freedpeople determined to escape quasi-reenslavement. No less fittingly, Garrison spent his last days writing rousing calls for a resumption of the "battle of liberty and equal rights," which were read at public indignation meetings he was too unwell to attend.[101] Shortly before he fell ill, Garrison dropped in on Child at her rooming house and the two veteran abolitionists had a "long cozy chat" together. They talked not only about their anxiety for the freedpeople, but about their outrage over the latest congressional attempt to ban Chinese immigration, which Child thanked Garrison for denouncing in a widely reprinted letter. They also shared their hopes of rejoining their loved ones in the spirit world, and Garrison showed Child "a long account of remarkable spiritual manifestations in Ohio." As usual, she "could not entirely believe" the particulars, but she held to her conviction that communication with departed spirits was possible. "She is a rare woman," Garrison commented to his daughter.[102] "It is wonderful how one mortal may affect the destiny of a multitude," Child commented in turn to Anne Whitney as she recalled how "the whole pattern of [her] life-web" had been changed when Garrison had "got hold of the strings of [her] conscience, and pulled [her] into Reforms."[103]

Though she did not return from Wayland to attend the funeral, at which Phillips, Weld, and Whittier delivered stirring tributes, she rejoiced over the unanimous praise of Garrison in the same newspapers that had vilified him forty years ago. "In the very city where he had been dragged to prison to save his life from a mob, and where his effigy had been hung on a gallows before his own door, the flags were placed at half-mast to announce his decease," she noted in her own tribute to Garrison, published in the *Atlantic Monthly*. She used it to celebrate the values of racial equality, religious freedom, and women's rights for which he stood and to draw the empowering lesson future generations should learn from his life — that a person whose entire being "revolved round a centre of fixed principle" could revolutionize the world:

> Those who hereafter seek to redress human wrongs will derive strength from the proofs he has given that all obstacles must yield to the power of self-forgetful moral earnestness. And those who long to keep their faith in the upward and onward tendencies of the human race will be cheered by the fact that such wonderful revolutions in public sentiment were produced within the memory of one generation by the exercise of clear-sighted conscience and indomitable will.[104]

An appeal for hope in a dark time and for moral courage in an age of cowardly truckling, it would be Child's last word to the public.

Child came back to Boston for one final winter in October 1879. For four years she had navigated seasonally between Wayland and Boston, increasingly tired of being afloat but unable to find a home that suited her. In Boston she grumbled perpetually about the discomforts of city life on a low budget: the view of "brick walls and chimneys, instead of the broad open meadow and the golden sunsets"; the slushy streets and icy pavements; the stuffiness of coal-heated rooms, and the difficulty of ventilating them without freezing the water pipes; the noisy, crowded streets full of unfamiliar faces. "Boston seems like a great desert; lacking the advantage of stillness," she complained.[105] But she was no happier in Wayland. Her "nest" was unbearably dreary without David, and she could no longer "put any *heart*" into her gardening.

"[T]he total want of congenial companionship" also oppressed her. "Week in and week out," she saw "no one but Mrs. Pickering, the baker, and the provision-man." She had been just as isolated in Wayland when David was alive, but "[d]ear David's mind was so full, and we sympathized so much in our opinions and pursuits, that I let every thought bubble forth as it would, sure of a hearty response." Mrs. Pickering, on the contrary, disagreed vehemently with all of her opinions. As a result, Child confided to her niece Sarah, she had to "check [her] utterance, a dozen times a day; and that is not easy for a spontaneous nature."[106] Mrs. Pickering also had another irritating defect that exacerbated Child's loneliness: "She has laid it down, as an inflexible rule, that she will not receive any company, either for herself or me. It is an extreme case of the American pride of gentility." She was willing to wait on Child, but not to be viewed by others as a servant, even for extra pay, and she could not be budged. Her answer to all of Child's pleas and cajolery was that "I could have as much company as I liked; but that *she* should always go away to her sister's; for which she has to ride 30 miles, walk a mile and a half, and then back again." This meant Child could not reciprocate the hospitality of the Sewalls and the Russells or invite Sarah Shaw to visit her in Wayland on her rare trips to New England.[107] She would never find either a niche that met her conflicting needs or a household partner who left her unfettered.

At age seventy-seven, Child was noticeably losing the bodily vigor on which she had always prided herself. Growing deafness prevented her from taking any pleasure in public lectures, and rheumatism kept her in constant pain. Hence, she stopped going to Free Religious Association meetings and reduced her outings to a weekly dinner with the Sewalls. The pastimes that always used to cheer her were to look at photographs of monuments or landscapes through the stereoscope the Sewalls had given her for her sixty-seventh birthday and to read novels. She still enjoyed the pictures friends regularly sent for her stereoscope collection, but the novels that were currently winning the plaudits of reviewers either left her cold or offended her taste.

The Sewalls had lent her William Dean Howells's *The Undiscovered Country*, thinking its treatment of spiritualism would interest her. She found it a "weak book" that merely exploited the theme of spiritualism "as grist to grind into sensational incidents. . . ." Howells was neither a "deep thinker" nor a "keen observer," Child judged: "He deals with surfaces; but that satisfies the spirit of the age."[108] The Shaws succeeded no better when they tried to introduce Child to Henry James. The characters and social settings in *Daisy Miller* and "An International Episode" were well-delineated, she conceded, "but I despise the subjects. The fact is, my contempt of fashionable people is almost ferocious. . . . The writer who sketches shoddy fashionables wastes his talents. . . ."[109]

Even the novelist who came closest to carrying on her mission as an advocate of racial equality, Albion Tourgée, ultimately alienated Child. His bitter autobiographical novel, *A Fool's Errand* (1879), presented an eyewitness account of how the Klan had overthrown Reconstruction in North Carolina, where Tourgée had served as a Republican judge until hounded from the state. At first, it impressed Child as a "remarkable book." "[H]e reveals in a startling manner the terrible perils to which the freedmen and their friends were exposed by the blundering policy of the government," she reported to Sarah Shaw. Through "a policy more crafty than open rebellion . . . he thinks [southerners] have already virtually obtained the victory." Besides reflecting Tourgée's firsthand understanding of southern psychology, the book registered the disillusionment of a man who had risked his life to bring about a genuine Reconstruction, only to be abandoned by Republican politicians too cowardly and time-serving to implement the laws they had passed. "There is a tone of bantering satire in the book; as of a mind exasperated and saddened by the popular tendency to confuse ideas of right and wrong," Child noted. By the time she finished the novel, however, Tourgée's scathing irony, deployed even more harshly against northern politicians than against southern backers of the Klan, had thoroughly depressed Child. The book's very title suggested a "slightly veiled *sneer* at those who believed in principles of justice and freedom," she objected. The implication that Reconstruction itself had been nothing but a "fool's errand" and that the novel's idealistic protagonist had been a " 'fool for meddling with what did not concern him' " left Child "sad and discouraged"; worse, it seemed to her "to undermine faith in right principles." Rather than arouse readers to action and hold out to them the vision of a better world, as she had tried to do in *A Romance of a Republic*, a book like *A Fool's Errand* could only foster a paralyzing sense of hopelessness, she felt. The verdict was unfair to Tourgée, who would devote the rest of his life to crusading for racial justice, and whose next novel, *Bricks without Straw* (1880), would feature a panorama of African American characters treated with unprecedented sensitivity for a white author. But it indicated the generational chasm between Child and Tourgée as writers of protest fiction.[110]

In the last year of her life Child discerned renewed cause for hope on several fronts. A gift sent to her by an Indian student named Bear's Heart, enrolled at the Hampton Institute, provided cheering evidence that his "intelligent and much-wronged people" were acquiring the education needed to raise their status. Reciprocating by knitting him a scarf, she urged Bear's Heart and his fellow Indians to "[s]hun the vices of the white men: their intemperance, their dishonesty, and their falsehood; but copy them in their eager pursuit of knowledge" that was "practically *useful*." If Indians put aside tribal animosities and stood "shoulder to shoulder, like brethren of one family," they "might, even now, become a great and prosperous people," Child wrote.[111]

Another auspicious omen was the emergence of a Republican presidential candidate "imbued with the honest Anti Slavery spirit" of Ohio's Western Reserve. A Civil War general, James A. Garfield did not exhibit the current "tendency to speak of both sides as equally in the right, because they both fought bravely"—a tendency Child deplored as "utterly wrong in principle and demoralizing in its influence." Instead, he had "manfully" asserted that "it is our duty to protect the slaves we have emancipated in the exercise of their civil rights." At the prospect of electing a president who might reverse Hayes's disastrous course, Child followed the 1880 campaign with more excitement than she had ever expected to feel again—though she was "somewhat troubled" when Garfield came out in favor of Chinese exclusion.[112]

Child saw further reason for optimism when she read about two successful experiments with operating businesses on "co-operative principles" — the first by the Quaker cotton miller Jacob Bright in England, the second by the French manufacturer and reformer Jean-Baptiste André Godin, a disciple of Fourier. "[M]y faith has never for a moment wavered, that co-operation is the *only* way to solve the troublesome problem between labor and capital," she wrote Francis Shaw in the same letter commending Garfield for his pledge to protect the freedpeople. The problem of labor conflict would surely be worked out some day, she concluded. "Men's highest *aspirations* are *prophecies*."[113]

Child had left Boston in the spring determined never to spend another winter there. As she explained to Anne Whitney: "The advantages of a city are not available to one who is lame and hard of hearing; and the disadvantages are many. Lodging-house life is comfortless to an old person; and genteel boarding is worse." She had hoped the summer sun in Wayland would "expel" the excruciating rheumatism from which she had suffered all winter, but the pains "attacked [her] more furiously than ever," and she spent most of the summer bedridden. "I have an increasing longing to get out of this old body," she confessed to Whitney. Despite her weariness of life, she could not resist launching into another philosophical disquisition on her favorite subject of dialogue with Whitney: "[T]he feeling grows ever stronger that [my body] is not *I*. . . . My early enthusiasm for Plato imbued me with the idea of a dual existence, to which I cling tenaciously amid all possible whirl of opinions."[114]

Child had promised to visit the Sewalls at their summer home in Melrose and to join Rosa Hopper and Marianne Silsbee for a nostalgic reunion in Milton, but she had to cancel both excursions. "[M]y left limb is so lame that it would not only be painful and hazardous, but literally impossible for me to get in and out of the cars," she wrote regretfully.[115] By coincidence, the very week that Child had meant to spend with Rosa and Marianne, the newspapers reported the death of the three friends' former idol, Ole Bull. He had recently celebrated his seventieth birthday with great pomp in Cambridge, where he had settled after marrying a midwestern heiress, and Child had felt sentimental enough to ask a young acquaintance, Maria Porter, to send her an account of the festivities. Hence, she was doubly affected by the news of his death. "I have been living in the past to-day, and recalling" how much "his marvelous playing . . . was to my soul. It filled me with inexpressible joy and the highest aspiration," she wrote Porter.[116]

As winter drew near, Child's friends worried about how she would manage. With or without Mrs. Pickering, it was out of the question for her to remain in her cottage for the winter, but Child adamantly refused to consider returning to Boston. "Moving back and forth is too troublesome and fatiguing," she complained; it was true that she was in no condition to travel or to climb the stairs of another rooming house. Perhaps sensing that the end was near, she replied to the Sewalls' anxious inquiries that she had "formed no plans, and . . . never intend to form any." All her efforts to find a permanent home had so far "come to nothing, and been very tiresome." She would simply "drift into the nearest harbour, and strive therewith to be content." The valedictory note was unmistakable, especially in Child's last letter to Anne Whitney, dated September 6. Though filled with lively comments on subjects ranging from Tourgée's *A Fool's Errand* to Whitney's latest sculpture, with only a glancing reference to her stubborn decision "never [to] try Boston again," Child's farewell ended: "My *belief* is that no atom of truth or good is ever wasted. The forms die off, but the living force remains, and goes on forever taking new forms. I would like to help on the progress of truth and good; but if I can't, somebody else will; and I am content."[117] As Whitney understood, Child meant that she did not expect to fall asleep after her "long pilgrimage" on earth, but to continue participating in the struggle for human freedom as a departed spirit. "I *think* there is more work for me to do in the universe, and that I shall enter upon it with renovated powers," she had told Whitney earlier in the summer.[118]

For one last time, Whitney implored Child to reconsider. "It must be confessed there is a little leaven of offishness in you that will not allow of the best things possible falling to you," she wrote reproachfully, no doubt alluding to the many invitations to move in with her, which Child had unfailingly turned down: "Your senses are not so impaired that they call for seclusion. Nor should that time be anticipated—Make the night as short as possible. — Instead of drawing the shades & calling for lamps—let the gracious twilight have its hour with old friends & reminiscence & prophetic hope." Enticingly describing her progress on the equestrian statue in which Child had taken such an interest, she urged her to come at least for a week's visit. "Don't go altogether & at once," she pleaded. But knowing the answer in advance, she signed her letter "Always yours for either or both worlds."[119]

Child did not live to reply. On the morning of October 20 she succumbed to a heart attack. "I was in hopes to die before I was obliged to break up my home, and stow myself away in the corner of some other household," she had written to the Sewalls a few months before.[120] Her wish had been granted.

The funeral—simple and private in accordance with Child's instructions—took place on a "beautiful October day." The assembled mourners included representatives of her various selves—abolitionist friends like Phillips, Whittier, the Sewalls, and Sarah Shaw Russell; Wayland neighbors; members of Lucy Osgood's circle in Medford; "poor people who had been recipients of her charity"; her nieces Sarah Preston Parsons and Abby Francis; and, of course, Mrs. Pickering. Wayland's Unitarian minister William Salter took the text of his funeral sermon from *Aspirations of the World*. And Wendell Phillips "stood by his old friend, with his hand on her coffin" as he sought to do justice to her many facets: her pioneering literary achievements; her heroic sacrifice of a promising career; her courage in the face of angry mobs; her daring "religious speculation"; her "pride of independence"; the "rigid economy" she practiced "with one hand . . . that the other might be full for liberal gifts"; the "ready wit, quick retort, mirthful jest," and "storehouse of fact, proverb, curious incident, fine saying, homely wisdom, touching story, [and] brave act" that made her conversation "indescribably charming." He closed with the words Child believed "spirit hands had traced" for her epitaph: "You think us dead. We are not dead. We are truly living now."[121] Then, "[j]ust after her body was consigned to the earth," the friends who knew how much Child had "always delighted" in rainbows were thrilled to see "a magnificent rainbow [span], with its arc of glory, the eastern sky."[122]

The obituaries and tributes published in the weeks after Child's death convey an eerie sense that the epoch in which she had figured so prominently had passed forever beyond recall. Again and again, those who had fought by her side in the great battle against slavery, or who had drawn the inspiration for their life work from her writings, lamented the failure of the contemporary press to appreciate the significance of her cultural and political contributions. George William Curtis noted in *Harper's Weekly* that though Child had been "one of the most justly distinguished of American women, . . . her name had become somewhat unfamiliar to readers of to-day."[123] A commentator in the *Nation* (probably Wendell Phillips Garrison) pointed out that the New York *Times*'s obituary had "absurdly . . . narrow[ed]" Child's range when it had said that "American housewives" would mourn the author of *The Frugal Housewife*. He proceeded to list Child's innumerable works and to pay homage to the "powerful influence" exerted by her abolitionist writings.[124] The Boston special correspondent of the Springfield *Republican* (possibly Franklin Sanborn of John Brown fame) cited two reasons why most of the retrospectives on Child (including the one that had previously appeared in his own newspaper) seemed to "fall short of what she deserves": "because the age in which she did her chief work has gone by," and because the current crop of newspaper editors had "little historic connection with that period" and no awareness of American journalism's "ancestral" roots. "At one time Mrs. Child was almost at the head of journalism in America, as we now understand it," he wrote. He went on to quote from Child's editorials in the *Standard* and to remind his fellow journalists that her " 'Letters from New York' were the great 'hit' in journalism at that time. . . ."[125] A pseudonymous contributor to the *Woman's Journal* mentioned having learned in a newly published biography of John Andrew, the Radical Republican governor of Massachusetts during the Civil War, that he had presented a copy of Child's *Appeal* to his younger sisters in 1833, with an inscription exhorting them to learn from a "gifted" member of "their own sex" to "uproot" from their hearts "all prejudice . . . against those immortal beings whose only crime is . . . a skin of a darker hue than their own. . . ." But she (or he) also observed that "Mrs. Child's best work was with a former generation" and that Governor Andrew had long since "passed from our sight."[126] Even Child's abolitionist disciples in the generation that had come of age in the 1840s and 1850s betrayed an awareness of living in a rapidly changing world, where they, too, might soon be forgotten. John White Chadwick, a former divinity student of her brother Convers's and an advocate of abolition, women's rights, and religious radicalism, remembered the two volumes of Child's *Letters from New York* as "the first really good books I ever read" and hailed her *Progress of Religious Ideas* as a pioneering work whose "candor . . . has never been excelled." In the same breath, he self-consciously warranted that the journalistic sketches he had loved so well "would not be found any duller now because the New York which they so vividly portray is buried under the cosmopolitan city of to-day as deeply as Pompeii under the ashes of Vesuvius"; and he granted that in their "collective mass," more recent studies in comparative religion had "gone far to supersede" Child's.[127] Thomas Wentworth Higginson credited Child with having shaped his development "at four different times during life": with her *Juvenile Miscellany*, which had taught him his early values; with her *Appeal*, which was "pre-eminently the book that awakened [his] conscience and reason to the importance of the Anti-slavery movement, and thus did more than any other book for [his] spiritual education"; with her *Letters from New York*, which "did almost as much to develop 'aesthetic feeling' as the other book had done for moral feeling"; and with her *Progress of Religious Ideas*, which had inspired him to write *The Sympathy of Religions*, his own attempt to combat bigotry. But he had ended by wondering whether Child's fame would be "permanent enough to escape the oblivion which falls, sooner or later, on all but a few leading philanthropists, and a few of the very ablest authors" — a question as applicable to himself as to her.[128]

In an effort to preserve Child's legacy for posterity, her surviving friends pooled the letters she had written to them, and Harriet Sewall edited them for publication in a one-volume compendium. The flood of reviews that greeted it — anticipating the revival of Child's reputation sparked by the publication of her complete correspondence a century later — signaled her transformation from a ghost of bygone days into a vital witness to "a stirring period of national history."[129] Over and over, reviewers referred to the *Letters of Lydia Maria Child* as a "contribution to American history"; a "representative of ideas and manners" during a key phase of "New England literary and social history"; a "record" of the antislavery struggle enabling readers to "see the scene" of each pivotal episode "as Mrs. Child saw it"; "a transcript in glowing language of a period of our national life when a woman's sympathy was a powerful lever in the great upheaval which followed"; an encapsulation of "qualities which, in women as well as in men, have helped to make America both what it is and what it promises."[130] Merely to enumerate Child's correspondents was to underscore her historical stature, reviewers recognized. "She was the steadfast friend of Garrison, Sumner, Parker, Phillips, Whittier, Lucretia Mott, and all who belonged to the circle of the foremost American reformers, and in some respects was the leader of the whole company," expounded a reviewer in the *New York Times*, which two years before in its obituary had been able to associate Child only with *The Frugal Housewife*. Reviewers also commented with delight on the vibrant personality revealed in the letters, singling out favorite passages for quotation. The *Times* even suggested that Child's editors enlarge the volume by a third, predicting that her letters would "reach a dozen" printings. "[A] generation that knows her name rather than her works and deeds" ought to be exposed to a larger selection of her correspondence, wrote this reviewer. He then delivered an encomium rivaling Garrison's salute to Child half a century earlier as "the first woman in the republic": "Here was a most remarkable woman, one who lived a great life, but lived it so simply and with such limited consideration for herself that the more you study it the more it grows to be perhaps the truest life that an American woman has yet lived."[131]

Child's posthumously published letters thus became the last best-seller of her career.

In a sense different from the one she had intended, they vindicated her belief that beyond the grave, there would be "more work for [her] to do" for human freedom and that she would "enter upon it with renovated powers."[132] As her letters went through subsequent editions, later readers seeking to "redress human wrongs" and struggling despite crushing setbacks to "keep their faith" in the ultimate triumph of justice reacted to Child's example as she had prophesied that future generations would react to Garrison's.[133]

Among them none better summed up the lessons Child had to teach than the African American writer Pauline Hopkins. In 1903, amid a tidal wave of reaction that had already swept away the civil rights laws of Reconstruction, Hopkins reprinted a large selection of Child's letters in a biographical sketch occupying three issues of the *Colored American Magazine*. The picture of Child's "life and times" offered by her letters was now more "eminently instructive . . . to all classes of people in this Republic" than at any previous "period of our history," Hopkins asserted.[134] Child's bitter outbursts during the 1850s, when her soul had "curse[d] 'law and order,' seeing them all arrayed on the wrong side," accurately described "the present position of North and South toward the Negro. . . . We of the present day [too] are *agonized by baffled efforts for human freedom*."[135] Just as Child's "caustic criticism" had exposed the hypocrisy of the northern judges and legislators who upheld slavery in her own time, "her trenchent pen would do us yeoman's service in the vexed question of disfranchisement and equality for the Afro-American" in the early twentieth century, wrote Hopkins. "If the influence of the lives of such great-hearted Anglo-Saxons as she could radiate through space, and enwrap the Negro youth round about, how different would be the lot of a dependent race!" she concluded.[136] To recover Child's vision in our own era is to experience the same empowerment.

Afterword

Readers encountering Child's writings for the first time often ask: How could a woman so influential in her own day and so perceptive about issues still relevant to ours have just disappeared from literary and historical textbooks? Pondering this question may lead us toward a more dialectical understanding of the culture Child played a major role in shaping and critiquing. It is easy to see why the generation that overturned Radical Reconstruction and repudiated the abolitionist ideal of racial equality should have consigned Child to oblivion. It is less easy to see why a generation concerned with recovering the work of "lost" foremothers has not paid more attention to her. The explanation seems to lie in the challenge Child poses to paradigms that have dominated the scholarship of the past two decades.

Although selections from her writings have appeared in a number of recent anthologies — among them Susan Koppelman's *The Other Woman* (1984) and *Women's Friendships* (1991); Lucy M. Freibert and Barbara A. White's *Hidden Hands* (1985); Judith Fetterley's *Provisions* (1985); and Paul Lauter's *Heath Anthology of American Literature* (1990) — Child has not figured in any of the studies seeking to present an overview of nineteenth-century American women's literature. She receives only passing mention in Ann Douglas's *The Feminization of American Culture* (1977), Nina Baym's *Woman's Fiction* (1978), Mary Kelley's *Public Woman, Private Stage* (1984), and Susan K. Harris's *19th-Century American Women's Novels* (1990), and no mention in Jane Tompkins's *Sensational Designs* (1985).[1] The omission points up the extent to which feminist critics have continued to accept the longstanding characterization of women writers as sentimental, genteel, and domestic, even while revaluing "sentimental" literature and disputing the grounds for its exclusion from the canon.

Child's example suggests the need to broaden our conceptions of nineteenth-century women writers and their contributions to literary history. Unlike the female "scribblers" studied by Douglas, Baym, and Kelley, Child did not claim to have entered on a literary career only out of financial exigency; instead, she frankly avowed her ambition to achieve fame and "excellence." Nor did she limit herself to sentimental and domestic fiction—from the very beginning, she wrote political fiction and soon graduated to polemical journalism, moving back and forth between the two throughout her half century of authorship. Nor did she define herself as a "private woman"—quite the contrary, Child boldly assumed a public position on the most controversial political issue of her era, articulating abolitionist ideology in tracts, editorials, newspaper articles, and letters to politicians for forty years. Nor did Child profess the evangelical faith often regarded as the norm for women writers. Her iconoclastic bent, which ultimately took her well beyond the liberalism of her Unitarian/Transcendentalist milieu and Swedenborgian denomination, aligned her more closely with skeptics like Melville than with her less heterodoxical peers of either sex. But Child's very departures from the prevailing model of female authorship might well prompt us to revise it. Clearly such a model is too narrow to encompass a writer of Child's scope and complexity; based on women who conformed to nineteenth-century gender expectations, it tends to exclude the radicals who forged an alternative tradition.

If literary scholars' neglect of Child can be ascribed to the persistent identification of women writers with sentimentalism—and to the tenacity of modernist aesthetic canons that prevent readers from discerning the subversive art veiled by decorous linguistic codes and idioms—the dearth of articles, chapters, and books on Child by feminist historians appears more puzzling. After all, students of the abolitionist movement have long recognized Child's importance and drawn on her writings for pithy quotations.[2] Yet the paradigms constructed by feminist historians have proved no more hospitable to Child than those of literary scholars.

When abolitionist women finally emerged from the eclipse they underwent during successive eras of racist historiography and male-biased scholarship, the Grimké sisters, especially Angelina, presented themselves as the prime candidates for full-length biographies.[3] Many factors no doubt influenced the choice—among them the prominence Angelina's husband, Theodore Dwight Weld, had already acquired; the consequent availability of a two-volume published selection of Weld-Grimké correspondence highlighting the couple's romantic courtship; the drama inherent in the lives of Southern slaveholders' daughters who renounced their privileges to agitate against slavery; and the sisters' pivotal role in the dispute over women's rights that split the abolitionist movement in the late 1830s. Probably the overriding factor, however, was that as pioneer women lecturers and eloquent champions of gender equality, the Grimké sisters fit the need of feminist historians to resurrect the forerunners of the modern women's movement. Along with Elizabeth Cady Stanton, who likewise inspired more than one biography,[4] Angelina and Sarah Grimké won stardom as feminist heroines.

Child's subordination of women's rights to the abolitionist cause disqualified her for that honor (as was the case for Abby Kelley Foster and to a lesser extent Lucy Stone, whose recuperation also awaited the 1990s).[5] Lacking the glamour of the Grimkés' brief public career, Child's life and writings tell a more complicated story about nineteenth-century feminists' attempts to liberate themselves from the cult of True Womanhood—a story in fact echoed by the Grimkés' retreat into domesticity following Angelina's marriage. After a quarter-century of feminist scholarship, we are perhaps better equipped to appreciate the significance of Child's marriage as a case study in the difficulties faced by the first generation of American women to strive for egalitarian partnerships allowing wives as well as husbands to pursue fulfilling professional careers.[6] Child's experience helps illuminate private recesses of the crusade for women's rights, including the inevitable contradictions between theory and practice, ideology and emotional reality. The relative priorities Child assigned to the struggles for racial and sexual equality may also enhance rather than diminish her stature as we come to terms with the racism that infected the suffragist camp, and heed the lessons of the conflicting agendas that have repeatedly undermined alliances between white women and people of color.

However uneasily Child fits the paradigm exemplified by the Grimké sisters and Elizabeth Cady Stanton, she sustains an even more vexed relationship to the group that has supplied feminist historians with their other main paradigm — the proponents of domestic ideology against whom early women's rights advocates often positioned themselves. Although Child essentially originated the American domestic advice book, she did not promote housekeeping and childrearing as sacred vocations; far from preaching the doctrine that woman's place was in the home, she openly defied it. Moreover, Child addressed *The Frugal Housewife* (1829) and *The Mother's Book* (1831) to a segment of the middle class that did not share either the wealth or the leisure we have come to associate with the nineteenth-century "lady." Historians of domestic ideology have thus given short shrift to Child, opting rather to focus on Catharine Beecher and Sarah Hale.[7] Again, the problems posed by a writer who can neither be comfortably assimilated into the paradigm of middle-class domesticity nor categorically divorced from it should induce us to develop a more finely calibrated analysis of nineteenth-century American culture.

As feminist approaches have given way to a New Historicism heavily influenced by Foucauldian theory, yet another paradigm has arisen — the concept of a hegemonic bourgeois ideology. Child's key voice in promulgating the bourgeois ethic of hard work, frugality, and self-discipline would seem to furnish decisive proof that this paradigm, at least, does apply to her. Nevertheless, the antiracist message that distinguishes the *Juvenile Miscellany* from such rival children's magazines as the *Youth's Companion* — paralleling the egalitarian values that distinguish *The Mother's Book* from Catharine Beecher's *Treatise on Domestic Economy* (1841) — admonish us against the reductiveness of treating bourgeois ideology as a monolith. Unless we differentiate among the forms the dominant cultural creed took (ranging from radical to conservative), we will not be able to understand why some of its adherents devoted their lives to extending the promise of freedom and equality to all, while others defended inequality as divinely ordained.

Precisely because Child resists pigeonholing, eludes generalizations, and stretches the bounds of theory, she offers an exceptionally rewarding subject for cultural biography — the exploration of a culture through an individual life.[8] Accommodating a woman whom even her first recent biographer has admitted to finding "paradoxical" and "maddeningly evasive" seems to require a new methodology.[9]

Accordingly, *"The First Woman in the Republic"* has set Child in dialogue with her contemporaries as she developed her ideas — with Cooper, Catharine Sedgwick, John Neal, and others on the Indian question; with Nathaniel Willis on defining the mission of children's literature; with Catharine Beecher and Sarah Hale on domestic ideology; with Frances Wright, the Grimké sisters, Margaret Fuller, and Elizabeth Cady Stanton on women's rights; with Garrison, William Ellery Channing, Maria Weston Chapman, Abby Kelley, the African American editors of the *People's Press* and *Northern Star and Freedman's Advocate*, Charles Sumner, John Brown, J. Sella Martin, and Frances Ellen Watkins Harper on the issues that divided the antislavery movement; with James Freeman Clarke and the religious conservatives and freethinkers among Child's associates. Listening to the voices of Child's contemporaries and eavesdropping on her agreements and disagreements with them allows us to ascertain more accurately where she herself belongs in the spectrum of nineteenth-century opinion and what is distinctive in her oeuvre. More broadly, it allows us to see the formation of a culture as a dynamic social process. The dialogic method also serves to strike a balance between the opposing tendencies of biography and of cultural studies — the one celebrating the heroic individual, the other reducing all historical figures to quasiuniform products of a hegemonic ideology.

Child's twin careers as woman of letters and activist reformer invite a combination of literary and historical approaches. The close reading of texts is indispensable to illuminating Child's artistry. Extensive research in nineteenth-century newspapers, manuscript collections, tracts, and ephemera is no less indispensable to situating Child's writings in historical context and establishing her significance as a cultural spokesperson. By giving equal weight to Child's fiction, antislavery tracts, journalism, domestic advice books, and writings for children, and refusing to privilege any class of texts, I have tried to emulate her own respect for all the media she used to influence readers and promote radical reforms. The intertwining of textual explication and biographical narrative may have frustrated readers expecting a conventional life story. A conventional life story, however, would not have done justice to a woman whom we must seek in her writings if we hope to experience the full power of her mind and personality. Much of Child's vast output remains inaccessible to the general public and unfamiliar to scholars. Until her works are reprinted, the only way to expose readers to them is through quotation and exegesis.

In sum, *"The First Woman in the Republic"* has aspired to treat Child holistically — as a woman contending with the same problems many face today: an unsatisfying marriage, unfulfilled sexual desires, domestic drudgery, and thwarted professional ambitions; as a reformer dedicated to building a just society that would allow people of all races and both sexes to exercise their talents and enjoy the rewards of their labor; and as a writer searching for rhetorical strategies and narrative modes capable of transforming her readers' consciousness.

Cultural biography is a form suited not only to accommodating Child's complexity, but to mining the voluminous first-hand analysis she provided of her society. An unusually astute political commentator, she criticized her government from the perspective of a radical activist. Few observers have left so incisive a record of a nation in the throes of controversy. Furthermore, Child's career encompassed almost all the intellectual and social movements of her day, opening a panoramic window onto nineteenth-century America.

In the domain of literature, Child pioneered the American historical novel, the short story, children's literature, and the journalistic sketch, turning them into vehicles for exposing the contradictions of American society and envisioning solutions to its problems. Two years before Cooper, she oriented the historical novel toward reflecting on the relations between white settlers and Indians; and unlike Cooper, she denied the inevitability of race war. The marriage of races she imagined instead—a trope for reconciliation, partnership, and mutuality, which she refined in many subsequent works and translated into political protest against antimiscegenation laws—heralded her lifelong mission as crusader for a multiracial America. Experimenting with short fiction in a variety of modes—historical, legendary, political, ethnographic, utopian, and realistic—Child adapted it to the purposes of denouncing Indian removal, slavery, and the double standard and advocating sexual mores in harmony with "nature." The body of fiction she produced—and inspired other reformers to produce—impels revision of the theory that American literature has tended toward psychological romance rather than social criticism. Similarly, Child's daring violations of genteel taboos belie caricatures of women writers as censors responsible for American literature's sexual prudery.[10]

In another department of literature, Child opened the fields of magazine publishing and journalism to women during her editorship of the *Juvenile Miscellany* (1826–34) and the *National Anti-Slavery Standard* (1841–43). The *Miscellany* inaugurated an American children's literature and molded a generation of New England youth. The "Letters from New-York" Child launched in the *Standard* and continued in the *Boston Courier* introduced one of the nineteenth century's most popular genres. While founding a school of "feminine" journalism that included Margaret Fuller, Fanny Fern, and Gail Hamilton among its practitioners, *Letters from New York* (1843, 1845) also carried Transcendentalist literary style and its aesthetic of spontaneity to new heights. Child perfected a free association that anticipated stream of consciousness. And as with her previous literary ventures, she added a new variant to the Transcendentalist repertoire. Unlike *Walden* (1854), *Letters from New York* centered not on "Life in the Woods," but on life in the city, not on the isolated individual, but on the community. To retrace Child's literary career is to reconceive American literary history.

As a writer who put her art in the service of the causes she espoused, Child personified the link between the nineteenth century's literary and social reform movements. The obvious correlation between her fiction and her political activism challenges us to question the critical dogma that pronounces a writer's intentions irrelevant to establishing the meaning of a work. Clearly, the "intentional fallacy" itself becomes a fallacy when applied to writers with avowed political aims. Like so many New Critical theories, it privileges belletristic literature and blocks appreciation of alternative forms. Of course an author's intention no more exhausts the meaning of a polemical than of a belletristic work, nor does it preclude implications contrary to the work's declared aims. But without taking intentionality seriously, we can neither understand nor value the fiction of social criticism Child honed into a fine art.

Child's consistent pattern of dramatizing social wrongs in her fiction before arguing against them in her political tracts — of working out problems first through her imagination, then through her reason — also invites us to consider "how imaginative invention and political action shape each other."[11] Her habit of moving from imaginative invention to political action, rather than the reverse, sheds new light on the creative process of the writer with a political agenda. Detractors frequently assume that such writers begin with a priori principles and mechanically devise plots and characters to illustrate them. Yet Child's practice suggests that for writers as well as readers, imaginative fiction may often provide a medium for entertaining otherwise threatening ideas before consciously deciding on a political stand. The special power exerted by fiction may operate in two directions, enabling both its creators and its consumers to imagine their way out of political impasses. If so, the stakes in battles over the literary canon are high indeed, for they involve liberating — or stymieing — our capacity to transform the world.

Child played an even more influential role in the sphere of social reform than in the literary sphere. Hers was one of the earliest voices raised against Cherokee removal. She continued to agitate for justice toward Indians throughout her life, returning to the issue again and again. Whether commenting on the Seminole War, the threatened annexation of Texas, or the civil war in Kansas, Child never lost sight of the "Indian question" and repeatedly connected it to the slavery question. She noted that the same contempt for the rights of nonwhite peoples underlay both the seizure of Indian lands and the enslavement of Africans, and that proslavery expansionists were leading the campaigns for both the acquisition of Florida and Texas and the expulsion of their Indian inhabitants to make room for plantation agriculture. At the end of the Civil War, Child's *Appeal for the Indians* (1868) directed abolitionists toward yet another crusade — preventing the genocide of the Plains tribes and formulating more humane policies of acculturation and assimilation for all Indians.

As with the struggle over Cherokee removal, Child entered the antislavery movement just as it was getting under way. She published her groundbreaking *Appeal in Favor of That Class of Americans Called Africans* (1833) only two years after Garrison started the *Liberator* and several months before the establishment of the American Anti-Slavery Society. Never surpassed in comprehensiveness and remarkable for its detailed refutation of widely accepted racist beliefs, the *Appeal* may rank as the most enduringly significant work in white antislavery archives. In its time, it not only proved instrumental in drawing women into antislavery activism — thereby contributing to a revolution in their status — but converted a formidable array of men who subsequently assumed leadership positions in the abolitionist camp and the Republican party. In ours, it claims recognition as a classic study of slavery anticipating many trends in current scholarship — among them comparative history and research into the African origins of European civilization. With unparalleled versatility, Child went on to publish a long list of antislavery writings in many different genres — the gift book, the catechism, the economic survey, the political polemic, the short story, the novel, the school reader. Of these, Child's primer for the former slaves, *The Freedmen's Book* (1865), rivaled the *Appeal* in long-term impact, prefiguring the pedagogical theories of Paulo Freire and of multicultural and Afrocentric education proponents. During the Reconstruction era the battle to secure the benefits of freedom to the emancipated slaves found Child again in the forefront, campaigning for black suffrage, land redistribution, job training, and education, and insisting on the need to eradicate white prejudice.

It has become fashionable to portray white abolitionists not as idealists who sacrificed wealth, social status, career opportunities, friendships, and private needs to fight for the liberation of African Americans, but as self-interested zealots who used African Americans for their own ends; not as women and men of goodwill, gropingly seeking to form cross-racial alliances for which their society offered no precedents, but as unwitting racists, hardly less censurable than the slaveholders and southern apologists they excoriated. Child's life and writings surely call for a reassessment of this view. She forfeited a flourishing literary career and braved mob violence, social ostracism, economic boycott, and real poverty for the sake of her abolitionist principles; centered much of her corpus on combating racial discrimination and promoting respect for people of color; condemned sanctuaries of white privilege in abolitionist social circles; maintained warm and unpatronizing relations with African American abolitionists; and sought to treat writers like Frederick Douglass, Harriet Jacobs, and Charlotte Forten as professional colleagues rather than as satellites. Granted, Child set a standard that few white abolitionists matched — though the Grimkés, Weld, Wendell Phillips, Gerrit Smith, Ellis Loring, and above all John Brown, can be counted among those who did. Granted, too, Child did not completely transcend the ethnocentrism of her culture, nor did she ever achieve the degree of intimacy with any African American that she did with her closest white friends. This said, the abolitionist movement provided the first forum in which African Americans and whites could mingle socially and work together for a common goal. It created models for future interracial solidarity movements and institutions for educating African Americans and whites in integrated settings. In short, it laid the groundwork for attaining the ideal toward which we are still striving — a society free of racism, in which women and men of all races can live in harmony as equals.

While twentieth-century scholars have frequently charged abolitionists with hypocrisy for failing to live up to the racial creed they professed, their nineteenth-century castigators more typically accused them of parading an "incredible tenderness for black folk a thousand miles off," yet turning a blind eye to the sufferings of the white poor next door (as Emerson put it in "Self-Reliance"). In keeping with this stereotype of the "angry bigot" whose "love afar is spite at home," the narrator of Hawthorne's 1843 sketch, "The Hall of Fantasy," for example, cites an "abolitionist, brandishing his one idea like an iron flail" among the "herd of real or self-styled reformers" he satirizes.[12] Child's far from isolated example counters the misrepresentation of abolitionists as monomaniacs, which their conservative peers transmitted to posterity. Not only did she publicize the plight of white slum dwellers in her "Letters from New-York," juxtaposed with her antislavery editorials in the *Standard*, but she visited prisons and almshouses, helped rehabilitate "fallen women" and alcoholics, spoke out against capital punishment, and took a keen interest in the prison reform efforts of her New York host family the Hoppers, as well as in the utopian communities through which her friends Francis Shaw and John Sullivan Dwight were endeavoring to resolve the conflict between labor and capital. Unlike some of her abolitionist colleagues, Child did not make the transition from antebellum social experiments to postwar campaigns for the eight-hour day and the right to strike; still, she did agitate for parcelling out confiscated plantation estates to both southern poor whites and ex-slaves.

If Child took a less prominent part in the women's rights movement than many of her abolitionist sisters did, they nonetheless hailed her as a forerunner. Her encyclopaedic *History of the Condition of Women, in Various Ages and Nations* (1835), covering every corner of the known world, paved the way for the feminist treatises of Sarah Grimké and Margaret Fuller; and like the *Appeal* and *The Freedmen's Book*, it anticipated recent scholarly trends, notably a multicultural approach to Women's Studies.

Child herself best articulated the logic that led abolitionists to espouse so many different "isms." "[S]ince I have been an abolitionist," she once explained, "*every* form of human suffering has become doubly interesting. *Every* shackle on *every* human soul not only arrests my attention, but excites the earnest inquiry 'What can *I* do to break the chain'?" Linking all the causes abolitionists embraced, Child specified, was "a universal idea" that encompassed "an infinity of particulars" — the principle that "every human soul had a right to full and free opportunities for the development of all their powers; and that any laws or customs, which obstructed this, were odious. . . ." Such a principle could not be restricted in its application without fatally undermining itself, she emphasized. That was why she, like other women, had begun asking: " 'How does this principle apply to *my* condition? Do laws and customs leave *me* the free exercise of all my powers?' "[13] Ultimately, the fulfillment of the abolitionist ideal, as Child envisioned and propounded it, involved the liberation of the entire human race.

Child lived to see many signs that she and her comrades had not fought in vain. The Constitution outlawed slavery and granted African Americans citizenship rights. Massachusetts, at least, eliminated antimiscegenation laws and Jim Crow transportation systems, and some northern states followed suit. White elites no longer succeeded in preventing the establishment of educational institutions for African Americans, whether segregated or integrated (as they had in the days of Prudence Crandall and the Noyes Academy). With such barriers removed, the class of African American professionals was rapidly growing by Child's last decade, and literacy was spreading among the emancipated slaves and their children. Programs for Indian education, too, despite the ethnocentrism that marred them, were gradually creating a cadre of spokespersons who could mediate between the Indian and white worlds. Women were making enormous strides in a number of different fields and slowly expanding their legal and political rights.

Child also lived to see the forces of reaction drastically erode the hard-won gains of a forty-year crusade and a bloody Civil War. Notwithstanding the reign of Ku Klux Klan terrorism, the restoration to power of the former slaveholding oligarchy, the quasi-reenslavement of the South's black masses, the de facto nullification of black suffrage in the South, the collapse of Radical Republicanism, and the abandonment of Reconstruction by the northern public, Child refused to yield to discouragement. "[E]*very* inch of the world's progress has to be gained by a tremendous struggle," she pointed out.

Through victories and setbacks alike, Child kept her faith. When confronted with difficulties, she replied: "All we can do is to follow, patiently and fearlessly, every principle which we clearly perceive to be true."[14] She responded similarly to the sectarian infighting so endemic in progressive movements. Rising above the crossfire of factional disputes among abolitionists and women's rights advocates, she persistently summoned both groups back to their true mission.

More than a century after her death, Child's long career of activism continues to resonate with meaning as new groups come forward to carry on the struggle for a just world. Her legacy embodies the best of the American heritage. It reminds us that a national history tarnished by Indian genocide, black slavery, and white supremacy has also been contested by progressive Americans of all races, committed to translating the inspiring words of the Declaration of Independence into practice. Child's heroic fidelity to the vision of a multiracial, egalitarian America and her tenacity in the face of obstacles and defeats challenge her successors to emulate her example. We who inherit Child's unfinished revolution can take courage from the watchword that encapsulates her indomitable idealism: "Men's highest *aspirations* are *prophecies*."[15]

Notes

Preface

1 [William Lloyd Garrison], "MRS. CHILD," *Genius of Universal Emancipation*, 20 Nov. 1829, p. 85; Lydia Maria Child to Charles Sumner, 7 July 1856, *Lydia Maria Child: Selected Letters, 1817–1880*, ed. Milton Meltzer, Patricia G. Holland, and Francine Krasno (Amherst: U of Massachusetts P, 1982) 286 (in subsequent citations, this work will be abbreviated as *SL*, and Child's name will be abbreviated as LMC); Samuel Jackson to LMC, "Letter from a Colored Man in Ohio to L. Maria Child," *Liberator* 23 Dec. 1859, *The Collected Correspondence of Lydia Maria Child, 1817–1880*, ed. Patricia G. Holland, Milton Meltzer, and Francine Krasno (Millwood, N.Y.: Kraus Microform, 1980), microfiche 43, letter 1158 (in future citations, this edition will be abbreviated as *CC*, with a slash mark dividing microfiche card and letter number); Elizabeth Cady Stanton, Susan B. Anthony, and Matilda Joslyn Gage, *History of Woman Suffrage*, vol. 1: *1848–1861* (1881; New York: Arno P, 1969) 38; Theodore Parker to LMC, 3 Nov. 1855, *CC* 31/888, and LMC to J. Peter Lesley, 1 Jan. 1856 (misdated 1855), *SL* 271; "L. Maria Child," *Springfield Republican*, rpt. in *Woman's Journal* 6 Nov. 1880, pp. 354–55; [Edgar Allan Poe], Review of *Philothea*, *Southern Literary Messenger* 2 (Sept. 1836): 659–62; "The Standard," *National Anti-Slavery Standard* 20 June 1868, p. 3; Thomas Wentworth Higginson, "Lydia Maria Child" (1868), *The Writings of Thomas Wentworth Higginson*, vol. 2: *Contemporaries* (Boston: Houghton Mifflin, 1900) 108, 123.

2 L. Maria Child, "The New-England Boy's Song about Thanksgiving Day," *Flowers for Children. II. For Children from Four to Six Years Old* (New York: C. S. Francis, 1845) 25–28.

3 "Letter from L. Maria Child," *National Standard* 27 Aug. 1870, *CC* 74/1956a.

4 Helene G. Baer, *The Heart Is Like Heaven: The Life of Lydia Maria Child* (Philadelphia: U of Pennsylvania P, 1964); Milton Meltzer, *Tongue of Flame: The Life of Lydia Maria Child* (New York: T. Y. Crowell, 1965).

5 See, for example, Kirk Jeffrey, "Marriage, Career, and Feminine Ideology in Nineteenth-Century America: Reconstructing the Marital Experience of Lydia Maria Child, 1828–1874," *Feminist Studies* 2 (1975): 113–30; Susan Phinney Conrad, *Perish the Thought: Intellectual Women in Romantic America, 1830–1860* (New York: Oxford UP, 1976); and Blanche Glassman Hersh, *The Slavery of Sex: Feminist Abolitionists in America* (Urbana: U of Illinois P, 1978).

6 Deborah Pickman Clifford, *Crusader for Freedom: A Life of Lydia Maria Child* (Boston: Beacon P, 1992).

7 Child's "The Quadroons," extracts from *Hobomok*, and selected *Letters from New York* appear respectively in Susan Koppelman, ed., *The Other Woman: Stories of Two Women and a Man* (Old Westbury, N.Y.: Feminist P, 1984) 1–12; Lucy M. Freibert and Barbara A. White, eds., *Hidden Hands: An*

Anthology of American Women Writers, 1790–1870 (New Brunswick, N.J.: Rutgers UP, 1985) 116–32; and Judith Fetterley, ed., *Provisions: A Reader from 19th-Century American Women* (Bloomington: Indiana UP, 1985) 159–202.

8   Lydia Maria Child, *An Appeal in Favor of That Class of Americans Called Africans* (Boston: Allen and Ticknor, 1833) 223. The chapter in question was reprinted in Louis Ruchames, ed., *The Abolitionists: A Collection of Their Writings* (New York: Capricorn Books, 1963) 60–71.

9   Lydia Maria Child, *An Appeal for the Indians*, rpt. in Carolyn L. Karcher, ed., *HOBOMOK and Other Writings on Indians* (New Brunswick, N.J.: Rutgers UP, 1986) 220–24, 231; "Letter from L. Maria Child," *National Standard* 27 May 1871, p. 4, *CC* 75/1995a.

10 "Letter from Mrs. L. Maria Child" to Caroline Severance, 16 Oct. 1868, "The New England Woman's Rights Convention," *Standard* 5 Dec. 1868, p. 3.

11 Lydia Maria Child, *Letters from New York* (1843; rpt. Freeport, N.Y.: Books for Libraries P, 1970) 204.

12 LMC to Lucy Osgood and Sarah Shaw, 1 Sept. 1861, 31 July and 15 Aug. 1877, and 20 Mar. 1879, *SL* 392, 543–44, 557.

13 See Child's comments on her friends the Lorings, equally applicable to herself: "the rough work of reform was unavoidably distasteful to their very gentle and refined natures." In "Gone," *National Anti-Slavery Standard* 6 June 1868, *CC* 69/1837.

14 This preface has benefited from the helpful criticism of Joan D. Hedrick, H. Bruce Franklin, and Jane Morgan Franklin.

Prologue

1   Lydia Maria Francis to Convers Francis, 5 June 1817, from Lydia Maria [Francis] Child, *Letters of Lydia Maria Child with a Biographical Introduction by John G. Whittier and an Appendix by Wendell Phillips*, [ed. Harriet Winslow Sewall] (1882; New York: Negro Universities P, 1969) 1 (as quoted by Child). In subsequent footnotes referring to Child's letters her name is abbreviated as LMC. This edition is abbreviated as *Letters*. All letters in this edition are included in *The Collected Correspondence of Lydia Maria Child, 1817–1880*, ed. Patricia G. Holland, Milton Meltzer, and Francine Krasno (Millwood, N.Y.: Kraus Microform, 1980), hereinafter abbreviated as *CC*, with a slash mark dividing microfiche card number from letter number.

2   Throughout this study I refer to Lydia Maria Francis Child by her married name, Child, in order to avoid the confusion of switching from her maiden to her married name. As many feminist critics and historians have found, the choice of names for married women is problematic. To refer to a woman writer by her first name, when male writers are consistently referred to by their last names, can seem demeaning and unprofessional. In Child's case, even that solution would not eliminate the problem of dual names, since she added "Maria" to her given name in 1821, and henceforth she renounced the use of Lydia, which she disliked. Some feminists have resorted to the use of a hyphenated surname. "Francis Child" seems unnecessarily unwieldy, however. Besides, it was under her married name that Child won fame. Although she had produced a considerable body of work by the time of her marriage in 1828 (including her first two novels, more than a half-dozen short stories, and four volumes of the *Juvenile Miscellany*), nearly all of it was published anonymously or under the signature "By the author of HOBO-MOK." For most of her life Child's public knew her as "Mrs. Child," "Lydia Maria Child," "L. Maria Child," or "LMC." I have chosen to respect these designations.

3   See, for example, the following reviews of *Letters of Lydia Maria Child*: [Horace E. Scudder], "Lydia Maria Child," *Atlantic Monthly* 50 (Dec. 1882): 839–44; "Mrs. Child's Letters," *Nation* 25 Jan. 1883, pp. 87–88; and "Lydia Maria Child," *New York Times* 1 Dec. 1882, p. 3.

4   LMC to Convers Francis, Sept. 1817, *Letters* 1–2, *CC* 1/2. Convers's end of the correspondence does not appear to have survived.

5   I have decided to retain the use of the term Indian because it was consistent with nineteenth-century usage. Native American, the term preferred by many today, meant in the nineteenth century a native-

born American citizen or a member of a party advocating preferential treatment for native-born Americans and restrictions against immigrants; hence, it would be anachronistic and confusing to apply it to Indians in a nineteenth-century context. Moreover, the term Indian continues to be used by many present-day Native American scholars, among them Paula Gunn Allen and A. LaVonne Brown Ruoff. These considerations do not pertain to the use of the term Negro, which I have chosen to avoid because it has now been generally discredited. Child and other nineteenth-century writers used a range of terms besides "negro" (then uncapitalized) — among them African Americans, Afric-Americans, colored people, people of color, and blacks — several of which are still current.

6   LMC to John Weiss, 15 Apr. 1863, *Lydia Maria Child: Selected Letters, 1817-1880*, ed. Milton Meltzer, Patricia G. Holland, and Francine Krasno (Amherst: U of Massachusetts P, 1982) 425, hereinafter referred to as *SL*.

7   Quoted in William Newell, "Memoir of the Rev. Convers Francis, D.D.," *Proceedings of the Massachusetts Historical Society* 8 (Mar. 1865): 235.

8   John Weiss, *Discourse Occasioned by the Death of Convers Francis, D.D. Delivered before the First Congregational Society, Watertown, April 19, 1863.* (Cambridge, Mass.: Privately printed, 1863) 13.

9   LMC to John Weiss, 15 Apr. 1863, *SL* 425–26.

10 LMC to John Weiss, 15 Apr. 1863, *SL* 425; quoted in Newell, "Memoir" 235–36, 238; quoted in Weiss, "Discourse" 62; Guy R. Woodall, ed., "*The Journals of Convers Francis*," *Studies in the American Renaissance* 1981: 265–343, 1982: 227–84 (the quotation is from the 1982 volume: 262). For biographical and historical details about the Francis family and the town of Medford, see Deborah Pickman Clifford, *Crusader for Freedom: A Life of Lydia Maria Child* (Boston: Beacon P, 1992).

11 Weiss, "Discourse" 15. Clifford has suggested that as the youngest sibling, Lydia may often have been left unsupervised rather than being drafted into constant household work, as was Convers; see *Crusader for Freedom* 14. Child's descriptions in *The Frugal Housewife* of ways in which even very young children may learn to perform domestic tasks seems to be based on her own experience, however.

12 LMC to John Weiss, 15 Apr. 1863, *SL* 425–26. As Clifford points out, Convers's own version of the story does not mention his father's opposition, but it credits him with having "consulted . . . Dr. Osgood and other friends, who probably advised him to make a scholar of me." I do not agree with Clifford, however, in assuming Convers's version to be more accurate than Child's. See Newell, "Memoir Convers Francis" 238; and Clifford, *Crusader for Freedom* 12–13. Information about Osgood and Brooks can be found in Charles Brooks, *History of the Town of Medford, Middlesex County, Massachusetts, from Its First Settlement in 1630 to 1855.* Revised, Enlarged, and Brought Down to 1885 by James M. Usher (Boston: Rand, Avery, 1886) 132–43, 237–46. Brooks is described as taking "so deep an interest in all [his fellow townspeople's] concerns, let their station in life be ever so humble, that they could always approach him with ease and confidence" (140).

13 Quoted in Newell, "Memoir" 238–39.

14 Quoted in Newell, "Memoir" 238. On Ma'am Betty, see Anna D. Hallowell, "Lydia Maria Child," *Medford Historical Register* 3 (July 1900): 96. On Child's attendance at Miss Swan's Academy, see LMC to Lucy Osgood, 1 Jan. 1859, *CC* 40/1099; and Clifford, *Crusader for Freedom* 21–22.

15 Newell, "Memoir" 241–46. For letters expressing Child's pride in her class identity and hatred of "aristocracy," see LMC to Convers Francis and Sarah Shaw, 19 Dec. 1835, 7 Sept. 1866, and 25 Aug. 1877, *SL* 41–42, 464, 543–44. On Grimké, see Gerda Lerner, *The Grimké Sisters from South Carolina: Rebels against Slavery* (Boston: Houghton Mifflin, 1967) 17–18, 21–22; and Sarah Moore Grimké, *Letters on the Equality of the Sexes, and the Condition of Woman* (1838; New York, Source Book P, 1970) 37. On Stanton, see Elizabeth Cady Stanton, *Eighty Years and More: Reminiscences 1815–1897* (1898; New York: Schocken, 1971) 20–23, 33–34. See also the tribute to Child by Elizabeth Cady Stanton, Susan B. Anthony, and Matilda Joslyn Gage, eds. *History of Woman Suffrage* (1882–1922; New York: Arno P, 1969) 1: 38 and dedication.

16 Hallowell, "Lydia Maria Child" 97.

17 See, for example, "The Cottage Girl," *Juvenile Miscellany* n.s. 1 (Sept. 1828): 3–19, esp. 9–10, 15–16;

"Elizabeth Wilson" and "Rosenglory," *Fact and Fiction: A Collection of Stories* (New York: C. S. Francis, 1846) 126–48, esp. 130–31, and 141ff., and 241–60, esp. 246–47 and 257ff.; also "The Brother and Sister," *Autumnal Leaves* (New York: Charles S. Francis, 1857) 181–99, esp. 188–90. See also Clifford, *Crusader for Freedom* 13–14.

18 Quoted in Newell, "Memoir" 235, 237. I am indebted for this interpretation to Margaret Kellow, "Must the Baby Go Out with the Bathwater? Psychohistory, Biography and Lydia Maria Child" 7–10, paper given at the 1988 American Studies Association meeting, Miami; and to Clifford, *Crusader for Freedom* 7–8.

19 "My Mother's Grave," *Juvenile Miscellany* 3 (Jan. 1828): 310–13. Quotation on 311. Subsequent page references are given parenthetically in the text.

20 As Kellow suggests, even if Child's mother did not literally die that very night, the story conveys the guilt she felt at having been an undutiful daughter. See "Must the Baby Go Out with the Bathwater" 17–18.

21 See chaps. 16 and 17, where I discuss two specific instances of martyred abolitionists whom Child had an impulse to nurse: Charles Sumner and John Brown.

22 LMC to Lucy Osgood, 26 Mar. 1847, *CC* 25/705; *SL* 1. These sentences were scratched out, probably after Child's death.

23 L. Maria Child, "Dr. Osgood and His Daughters," *Independent* 17 Jul. 1873, pp. 893–94; see also Clifford, *Crusader for Freedom* 15.

24 L. M. Child, "Concerning Women," *Independent* 15 Jul. 1869, *CC* 71/1903.

25 Thomas Wentworth Higginson, "Lydia Maria Child" (1868), *Contemporaries*, vol. 2 of *Writings of Thomas Wentworth Higginson* (Boston: Houghton Mifflin, 1900) 112. Higginson's article was originally published in James Parton et al., *Eminent Women of the Age; Being Narratives of the Lives and Deeds of the Most Prominent Women of the Present Generation* (Hartford, Conn.: S. M. Betts, 1868) 38–65; he revised it slightly after Child's death.

26 Titled "The New-England Boy's Song about Thanksgiving Day," "Over the river" first appeared in L. Maria Child, *Flowers for Children. II. For Children from Four to Six Years Old* (New York: C. S. Francis, 1845) 25–28. Some 130 years after its first appearance, the poem is still being reprinted in lavishly illustrated editions.

27 Higginson, "Lydia Maria Child" 112–13.

28 Convers's reminiscence of his father, quoted in Weiss, "Discourse" 6, 62–63.

29 The incident is described in Brooks, *History of Medford* 355–57. Milton Meltzer, *Tongue of Flame: The Life of Lydia Maria Child* (New York: Crowell, 1965), chap. 1 and in an afterword, suggests that Convers Francis, senior, may have participated in the rescue of Caesar. On the role of mechanics and working people in the antislavery movement, see L. Maria Child, "Through the Red Sea into the Wilderness," *Independent* 21 Dec. 1865, p. 1; rpt. in *Liberator* 29 Dec. 1865, p. 205 (not included in *CC*).

30 *Authentic Anecdotes of American Slavery*, 1 [1835] 6–7. The narrator of this anecdote specifically reports it as having been told to her by her mother; it is not clear whether Child or an anonymous contributor is the anecdote's author, however. "Poor Chloe," *Atlantic Monthly* 17 (Mar. 1866): 352–64, intertwines this anecdote with another titled "Phillis's Wedding," which appears on the next page of *Authentic Anecdotes*.

31 Convers's description of his father, quoted in Weiss, "Discourse" 63.

32 On James Francis, see Alfred Sereno Hudson, "The Home of Lydia Maria Child," *New England Magazine* n.s. 2 (June 1890): 407. The disagreement between Child and Convers over abolition can be followed through her letters to him. See, for example, LMC to Convers Francis, 19 Dec. 1835, *SL* 41–42.

33 Lydia Maria Child, *Emily Parker, or Impulse, Not Principle. Intended for Young Persons* (Boston: Bowles and Dearborn, 1827) 10. See also Roger Conant in *Hobomok*, discussed below and in chap. 1. And see the description of the widowed father in "Elizabeth Wilson," *Fact and Fiction* 128: "Of clothing for the mind, or food for the heart [of his orphaned children], he knew nothing; for his own had never been clothed and fed. He came home weary from daily toil, ate his supper, dozed in his chair awhile, and then sent the children to bed."

34 LMC to Lucy Osgood[?], 17 Dec. 1870, *CC* 74/1966; Clifford, *Crusader for Freedom* 17. See Harriet Beecher Stowe, *The Minister's Wooing* (1859), chap. 23, for a memorable description of such a crisis of faith, based on the experience of her sister Catharine.

35 Hallowell, "Lydia Maria Child" 97.

36 On the chronology and psychic significance of these losses, see Kellow, "Must the Baby Go Out with the Bathwater" 22, and Clifford, *Crusader for Freedom* 19.

37 Lydia Maria Child, *HOBOMOK and Other Writings on Indians*, ed. Carolyn L. Karcher (New Brunswick, N.J.: Rutgers UP, 1986) 91, 114.

38 Hallowell, "Lydia Maria Child" 97. For more information about the town, see William Allen, *The History of Norridgewock* (Norridgewock, Me.: Edward J. Peet, 1849). Allen gives the total population of the town as 880 in 1810 and 1,454 in 1820 (115). Helene G. Baer, *The Heart Is Like Heaven: The Life of Lydia Maria Child* (Philadelphia: U of Pennsylvania P, 1964) 29, cites the figure as "four hundred families." Clifford, *Crusader for Freedom* 22–23, refers to one thousand inhabitants.

39 I am indebted to Lisa K. Johnson Ponder for drawing my attention to the importance of the Maine statehood controversy in forming Child's understanding of slavery as a legal and political issue. This paragraph is based on the fine unpublished paper she generously shared with me: "Learning Law on One's Own: Sources for Legal Learning in the Early Life of L(ydia) Maria Francis Child, 1802–33," University of Oregon School of Law, 1985, pp. 20–21, 24–27. See also her M.A. thesis, "The Making of an Abolitionist: The Early Life Jurisprudential Development of L. Maria Child, 1802–1833," University of Oregon, 1987, pp. 122–23, 134–39; and Clifford, *Crusader for Freedom* 24–26. For further details on the Maine statehood controversy and its relationship to the Missouri crisis, see Ronald F. Banks, *Maine Becomes a State: The Movement to Separate Maine from Massachusetts, 1785–1820* (Middletown, Conn.: Wesleyan UP, 1970) chap. 9.

40 LMC to Mary Francis Preston, 11 June 1826, *CC* 1/18.

41 LMC to Mary Francis Preston, 6 Jan. 1827, *CC* 1/23.

42 Child, *Emily Parker* 11. See also Clifford, *Crusader for Freedom* 24.

43 "The Little Traveller," *Juvenile Miscellany* 3 (Jan. 1828): 365–69.

44 Caroline Healey Dall, "Lydia Maria Child and Mary Russell Mitford," *Unitarian Review* 19 (June 1883): 525. The continuing Abenaki presence in Maine and Vermont has been well-documented by anthropologists, as indicated by the material culture exhibit organized by Jeanne Brink, "The Spirit of the Abenaki," at the Chandler Gallery in Randolph, Vermont, 23 Apr.–16 May 1993. See also Colin G. Calloway, *The Western Abenakis of Vermont, 1600–1800: War, Migration, and the Survival of an Indian People* (Norman: U of Oklahoma P, 1990), esp. 123, 129–30, 133, and 238–51; and Dean R. Snow, "Eastern Abenaki," *Handbook of North American Indians*, Vol. 15: *Northeast*, ed. Bruce G. Trigger (Washington, D.C.: Smithsonian Institution, 1978) 137–47.

45 L. Maria Child, "Physical Strength of Women," *The Woman's Journal* 15 Mar. 1873, p. 84. Child also cites the incident in "Concerning Women," *Independent* 21 Oct. 1869, p. 1. I have assumed that the encounter took place in Winslow, from which several of her early letters are dated, because it seems unlikely that she would have been staying with another family in Norridgewock.

46 Lydia Maria Child, *The History of the Condition of Women, in Various Ages and Nations*, 2 vols. (Boston: J. Allen, 1835) 2: 234, rpt. in Karcher, ed., *HOBOMOK and Other Writings on Indians* 175.

47 L. Maria Child, "Physical Strength of Women," *The Woman's Journal* 15 Mar. 1873, p. 84; see also "Concerning Women," *Independent* 21 Oct. 1869, p. 1.

48 Lydia Maria Child, *Letters from New York [First Series]* (1843; New York: Books for Libraries P, 1970) 29. For information on Captain Neptune, see Fanny Hardy Eckstorm, *Old John Neptune and Other Maine Indian Shamans* (Portland, Me.: Southworth-Anthoensen P, 1945), to which I was led by Ponder, "The Making of an Abolitionist" 131–32. Child's sketch "Buffalo Creek" also describes what may have been an actual excursion into Iroquois territory. See the *Juvenile Miscellany*, 3rd ser. 4 (July/Aug. 1833): 255–75.

49 Lydia Maria Child, "The Indian Boy," *Juvenile Miscellany* 2 (May 1827): 31.

50   Berenice G. Lamberton, "A Biography of Lydia Maria Child" (unpublished Ph.D. diss., University of Maryland, 1952) 9–10, was the first to suggest that Etalexis may have served as the model for Hobomok.

51   Ponder, "Learning Law on One's Own" 23 and "The Making of an Abolitionist" 133; Baer, *The Heart Is Like Heaven* 29; Clifford, *Crusader for Freedom* 22–23.

52   LMC to Convers Francis, Sept. 1817 and 26 Dec. 1819, *Letters* 2, 4, *CC* 1/2, 5.

53   LMC to Convers Francis, 3 Feb. 1819, *Letters* 3, *CC* 1/3.

54   LMC to Convers Francis, 12 Mar. 1820, *Letters* 5, *CC* 1/7.

55   Lydia Maria Child, "Letter from New-York" No. 47, *National Anti-Slavery Standard* 19 Jan. 1843, *CC* 16/444, This letter was not collected in the book version of *Letters from New York*. A possible candidate for this "Magnus Apollo" is Nathaniel Deering. See chap. 5, n. 22 below.

56   LMC to Convers Francis, 12 Mar. and 10 Apr. 1820, *CC* 1/7–8. The quotation is from the 10 Apr. letter.

57   LMC to Parke Godwin, 20 Jan. 1856, *SL* 275. Ponder, "The Making of an Abolitionist" 144, points out that a small Swedenborgian church existed in Gardiner.

58   Signe Toksvig, *Emanuel Swedenborg: Scientist and Mystic* (New Haven, Conn.: Yale UP, 1948) 314–15. Toksvig details Swedenborg's doctrine of correspondences in chap. 22. The best summary of the doctrine and of its appeal to Child's generation, however, is Ralph Waldo Emerson's essay "Swedenborg; or, The Mystic," in *Representative Men* (1850). For Child's own explanations of the doctrine of correspondences, see her *Letters from New York. Second Series* (New York: C. S. Francis, 1845), Letters 12 and 22.

59   LMC to Convers Francis, 31 May 1820, *SL* 2.

60   LMC to Theodore Tilton, 27 May 1866, *SL* 460. Louise D. Woofenden has found Lydia Maria Francis listed in church records as having joined the Boston New Church (Society of the New Jerusalem) on 17 Feb. 1822 and has kindly supplied me with a copy of this document, "Creeds, Records, &c. relative to the Spiritual Affairs of the Boston Society of the New Jerusalem. Sep. 25: 1821. to 1841." Clifford has suggested that the catalyst spurring Child's decision to join the New Church was Sampson Reed's Harvard commencement lecture, "An Oration on Genius," given in late summer 1821 (*Crusader for Freedom* 37–38).

61   LMC to Theodore Tilton, 27 May 1866, *SL* 460. This rebaptism took place in the Rev. David Osgood's Congregational church in Medford, a gesture Clifford explains as a desire to please her father. According to Clifford, Child was named after her grandmother, Lydia Francis, and also had an aunt Lydia whom she disliked (*Crusader for Freedom* 6, 35).

62   LMC to Mary Francis Preston, 26 May 1822, *CC* 1/10.

63   Clifford, *Crusader for Freedom* 38–39, 44; Joel Myerson, "Convers Francis and Emerson," *American Literature* 50 (March 1978): 17–18.

64   Woodall, *Journals of Convers Francis* 1981: 282.

1   The Author of Hobomok

1   Lydia Maria Child, *Hobomok, A Tale of Early Times* (1824), rpt. *HOBOMOK and Other Writings on Indians*, ed. Carolyn L. Karcher (New Brunswick, N.J.: Rutgers UP, 1986) 3–4. All further quotations from the novel are from this edition and are given parenthetically in the text.

2   LMC to John Weiss, 15 Apr. 1863, *SL* 426.

3   For an analysis of the more typical female response to authorship in that era, see Mary Kelley, *Private Woman, Public Stage: Literary Domesticity in Nineteenth-Century America* (New York: Oxford UP, 1984). Child presents a striking contrast with Catharine Maria Sedgwick, for example, who had to be "persuaded 'with great difficulty' " by her brothers to publish her first work, and who had been " 'filled with terror and alarm' " at the idea of appearing before the public (129).

4   LMC to Convers Francis, 5 Jun. 1817, *CC* 1/1, quoted in Prologue above.

5   Charles Brockden Brown, *Edgar Huntly: or, Memoirs of a Sleep-Walker* (1799; New York: Penguin, 1988) 3.

6   Susanna Haswell Rowson, *Reuben and Rachel; or, Tales of Old Times. A Novel* (Boston: Manning and Loring, 1798) (iv). Rowson's Columbus, for example, credits his wife, Beatina, with inspiring his quest and swears to her that "no man should ever claim a right to govern" the domains he discovers, since "it is to a woman [Isabella of Spain] I owe the means of making the great attempt" (13, 16).

7   Mary E. Sargent, "Susanna Rowson," *Medford Historical Register* 7 (Apr. 1904): 26–40.

8   Lydia Maria Child, *The Mother's Book* (Boston: Carter, Hendee and Babcock, 1831) 91.

9   See Richard Slotkin, *Regeneration through Violence: The Mythology of the American Frontier, 1600–1860* (Middletown, Conn.: Wesleyan UP, 1973) 472–73; Louise K. Barnett, *The Ignoble Savage: American Literary Racism, 1790–1890* (Westport, Conn.: Greenwood P, 1975) 28, 38–39, 65–67; Michael Davitt Bell, *Hawthorne and the Historical Romance of New England* (Princeton, N.J.: Princeton UP, 1971); and George Dekker, *The American Historical Romance* (New York: Cambridge UP, 1987) 39–42.

10 Quotations are from Walter Channing, "Essay on American Language and Literature," *North American Review* 1 (Sept. 1815): 307–9, 312–14. See also in later numbers: W. Channing, "Reflections on the Literary Delinquency of America," 2 (Nov. 1815): 33–43; [E. T. Channing], "On Models in Literature," 3 (July 1816): 202–9; and [J. Knapp], "National Poetry," 8 (Dec. 1818), 169–76. The abbreviation *NAR* is used for subsequent references to this journal.

11 For historical and critical overviews of these novelists and their solutions, see Barnett, *Ignoble Savage*, esp. chaps. 4 and 5; Bell, *Hawthorne and the Historical Romance*, esp. chaps. 1, 2, and 4; Roy Harvey Pearce, *The Savages of America: A Study of the Indian and the Idea of Civilization*, rev. ed. (Baltimore: Johns Hopkins UP, 1965) chap. 7; Richard Drinnon, *Facing West: The Metaphysics of Indian-Hating and Empire-Building* (New York: Meridian, 1980), chaps. 11, 12, 13, and 15; Annette Kolodny, *The Land Before Her: Fantasy and Experience of the American Frontiers, 1630–1860* (Chapel Hill: U of North Carolina P, 1984) chap. 4; and Leland S. Person, Jr., "The American Eve: Miscegenation and a Feminist Frontier Fiction," *American Quarterly* 37 (Winter 1985): 668–85. For a general literary history that includes much information on these writers, see Alexander Cowie, *The Rise of the American Novel* (New York: American Book Co., 1948) chap. 5.

12 John Neal, *Logan, A Family History*, 2 vols. (Philadelphia: H. C. Carey and I. Lea, 1822) I: 140–41, 185, 232.

13 See James Axtell's essay "The White Indians of Colonial America," rpt. in his *The European and the Indian* (New York: Oxford UP, 1981) 171–72. The words are J. Hector St. Jean de Crèvecœur's, but Axtell also quotes Benjamin Franklin and Cadwallader Colden to the same effect.

14 James Kirke Paulding, *Koningsmarke, or Old Times in the New World*, 2 vols. (1823; rev. ed. 1834; New York: AMS P, 1971) I: 156–58. See Paulding's *Slavery in the United States* (1836). On the connections between Paulding's views on Indians and on the slavery question, see Drinnon, *Facing West* 124–30.

15 The following generalizations are based especially on Cooper's *The Pioneers* (1823) and *The Last of the Mohicans* (1826). The death of Natty Bumppo occurs in *The Prairie* (1827).

16 See Blanche Glassman Hersh, *The Slavery of Sex: Feminist-Abolitionists in America* (Urbana: U of Illinois P, 1978).

17 See Person, "The American Eve," for a detailed demonstration of this point.

18 [John Gorham Palfrey], review of *Yamoyden, NAR* 12 (Apr. 1821): 466–88. Quotations on 480, 483–85.

19 LMC to Rufus Wilmot Griswold, [Oct.? 1846?], *SL* 232.

20 Compare James Wallis Eastburn and Robert Sands, *Yamoyden, A Tale of the Wars of King Philip, in Six Cantos* (New York: James Eastburn, 1820) 124–28, with the following passages in *HOBOMOK and Other Writings on Indians*, ed. Karcher: 36, 98, 133.

21 [Palfrey], review of *Yamoyden, NAR* 12: 486.

22 Eastburn and Sands, *Yamoyden* 78–86, 131–38, 247–52.

23 [Lydia Maria Child], *The First Settlers of New-England: or, Conquest of the Pequods, Narragansets and Pokanokets: as Related by a Mother to Her Children, and Designed for the Instruction of Youth* (Boston: Munroe and Francis, [1829]) iv. See chap. 4 for a detailed discussion of this book and the problems of dating it.

24   See Barnett, *Ignoble Savage* 80–86 on the "bad Indian" stereotype.

25   L. M. Child, "Concerning Women," *Independent* 15 Jul. 1869, *CC* 71/1903.

26   Nathaniel Morton, *New England's Memorial*, 5th ed., ed. John Davis (Boston: Crocker and Brewster, 1826) 143n. Davis cites *Higginson's Journal, in Hutchinson Collection, and his New England plantation.*

27   Child, *The First Settlers of New-England* 9–12; Nathaniel Morton, *New England's Memorial*, 5th ed. (1669; Boston, 1826) 121–22; William Hubbard, *A General History of New England, from the Discovery to MDCLXXX* (1815; New York: Arno P, 1972) 93, 248–51.

28   Hubbard, *General History of New England* 108.

29   Morton, *New England's Memorial* 148.

30   Slotkin, *Regeneration through Violence* 142.

31   Morton, *New England's Memorial* 70–71. Edward Winslow, *Good News from New England* (1624) provides the fullest account of the historical Hobomok and also discusses the deity by that name. Winslow's narrative is reprinted in Edward Arber, *The Story of the Pilgrim Fathers* (Boston: Houghton Mifflin, 1897) 509–98. See esp. 521–24, 527–28, 541–42, 547–58, 567–74. For a modern historical analysis of both Hobomoks, see Frank Shuffelton, "Indian Devils and Pilgrim Fathers: Squanto, Hobomok, and the English Conception of Religion," *New England Quarterly* 49 (Mar. 1976), 108–16. For a splendid historical study of Indian-European relations in the Northeast, which includes a great deal of information about Hobomok and other Indians referred to in the novel, see Neal Salisbury, *Manitou and Providence: Indians, Europeans, and the Making of New England, 1500–1643* (New York: Oxford UP, 1982), esp. chaps. 5 and 6.

32   The inversion appears even more daring in the light of Salisbury's discussion of the emphasis the Plymouth pilgrims put on "social segregation" between them and their Indian allies (*Manitou and Providence* 118, 124).

33   Ralph Waldo Emerson's *Nature* was not published until 1836. Whether Child is anticipating Emerson, expressing ideas that are already in the air, or echoing ideas she heard Emerson voice in conversation is difficult to determine.

34   Lydia Maria Child, *The Progress of Religious Ideas, Through Successive Ages*, 3 vols. (New York: Charles S. Francis, 1855) 1:vii.

35   The quotation is from *Letters from New York [First Series]* (1843; Freeport, N.Y.: Books for Libraries P, 1970), Letter 36, reprinted in Karcher, ed., *HOBOMOK and Other Writings on Indians* 187.

36   See Slotkin, *Regeneration through Violence* 57–65 and chap. 5.

37   Shuffelton, "Indian Devils and Pilgrim Fathers" 112.

38   Slotkin, *Regeneration through Violence* 57–65.

39   On the association of women with both nature and the darker peoples whom Europeans identify with nature, see Sherry B. Ortner, "Is Female to Male as Nature Is to Culture?," *Woman, Culture, and Society*, ed. Michelle Zimbalist Rosaldo and Louise Lamphere (Stanford, Calif.: Stanford UP, 1974) 67–87; and Kristin Herzog, *Women, Ethnics, and Exotics: Images of Power in Mid-Nineteenth-Century American Fiction* (Knoxville: U of Tennessee P, 1983) xi–xxvi.

40   As Richard Slotkin points out, "From the time of Mrs. Rowlandson's captivity in King Philip's War to the captivities of the nineteenth-century Plains Indian wars, most returning captives were treated as pariahs, on the assumption that they had been sexually and spiritually 'polluted' or racially transformed by their intimate contact with Indians." See *Regeneration through Violence* chap. 5 and *Gunfighter Nation: The Myth of the Frontier in Twentieth-Century America* (New York: Atheneum, 1992) 467 (the source of the quotation). As a woman who had voluntarily eloped with an Indian, Mary would of course have been even more of a pariah than had she been a victim of captivity. Those who read the ending as a reassertion of patriarchal values overlook the historical traditions Child is violating. See, for example, Stephen Arch, "Romancing the Puritans: American Historical Fiction in the 1820s," *ESQ: Journal of the American Renaissance*, forthcoming.

41   I am indebted to Jane Tompkins for pointing out the significance of the name Mary gives her son.

42   See Barnett, *Ignoble Savage* 86–90.

43   Barnett, *Ignoble Savage* 95, 120; and William S. Osborne, *Lydia Maria Child* (Boston: Twayne, 1980) 53. Lucy M. Freibert and Barbara A. White offer a related critique in their introduction to the selections from *Hobomok* in their collection *Hidden Hands: An Anthology of American Women Writers, 1790–1870* (New Brunswick, N.J.: Rutgers UP, 1985) 118–19: "Hobomok's low status is clear in that he plays the role usually reserved for women. He is the one who must sacrifice himself" and "see his identity erased in his child." See also a study that does not discuss *Hobomok* but provides a context in which to situate the novel: Brian W. Dippie, *The Vanishing American: White Attitudes and U.S. Indian Policy* (Middletown, Conn.: Wesleyan UP, 1982), esp. chap. 2.

44   James Everett Seaver, *A Narrative of the Life of Mrs. Mary Jemison* . . . (1824; Syracuse, N.Y.: Syracuse UP, 1990). For a stimulating discussion of *Hobomok*, Jemison's *Narrative*, and Catharine Maria Sedgwick's *Hope Leslie*, see Kolodny, *The Land Before Her* chap. 4.

45   Quotations from *North American Review* 19 (July 1824): 262; and [Jared Sparks], "Recent American Novels," *North American Review* 21 (July 1825): 87, 90.

46   Review of *Hobomok*, *NAR* 19 (July 1824): 263.

47   *NAR* 19: 263; [Sparks], *NAR* 21: 87–90. To be fair, the deathbed scene is genuinely moving, and Sparks also quotes two other passages: an exchange between Hobomok and Corbitant, illustrating Child's success at capturing Indian language (21: 90–92), and the scene in which Hobomok bequeaths Mary to Charles (21: 92–94). These two passages likewise fulfill ideological purposes, however: Corbitant is a stereotypical "bad Indian," and Hobomok's sacrifice suggests the Indian's ideal role.

48   [Sparks], *NAR* 21: 95; comments on *Hobomok* by [J. C. Gray], review of *The Rebels*, *NAR* 22 (April 1826): 401. Although Child herself played a role in procuring Sparks's review (see chap. 2), the same favorable judgments are expressed by the earlier reviewer (*NAR* 19: 262–63), as well as by J. C. Gray the following year. Sparks's omnibus review discussed ten novels in all. The others were Matthew Murgatroyd's *The Refugee; a Romance* (1825); [Harriet V. Cheney's] *A Peep at the Pilgrims* (1824); *The Witch of New England; a Romance* (anon., 1824); [Eliza L. Cushing's] *Saratoga: A Tale of the Revolution* (1824); *Adsonville, or Marrying Out; a Narrative Tale* (anon., n.d.); *A Winter in Washington; or Memoirs of the Seymour Family* (anon., 1824); *Tales of an American Landlord; containing Sketches of Life South of the Potomac* (anon., 1825); *O'Halloran, or the Insurgent Chief; an Irish Historical Tale of 1798* by the Author of "The Wilderness" (1824); and Mungo Coultershoggle's *Goslington Shadow; a Romance of the Nineteenth Century* (1825). Interestingly, Cheney and Cushing were both daughters of Hannah Webster Foster, author of *The Coquette* (1797), which rivaled Susanna Rowson's *Charlotte Temple* as an early American best-seller. For a modern evaluation that ranks Cheney's *Peep at the Pilgrims* above *Hobomok*, see Arch, "Romancing the Puritans," forthcoming in *ESQ*.

49   Cushing, *Saratoga* 1: 261–63; 2: 247.

50   Review of *The Last of the Mohicans*, *NAR* 23 (July 1826): 163.

51   James Fenimore Cooper, *The Last of the Mohicans* (1826; New York: New American Library, 1962) 21, 188, 406–7. For a superb analysis of Cora as the personification of the novel's intersecting ideologies of race and gender, see Richard Slotkin, *The Fatal Environment: The Myth of the Frontier in the Age of Industrialization, 1800–1890* (1985; Middletown, Conn.: Wesleyan UP, 1986) chap. 5.

52   Barnett, *Ignoble Savage* 119.

53   Catharine Maria Sedgwick, *Hope Leslie; or, Early Times in the Massachusetts*, ed. Mary Kelley (1827; New Brunswick, N.J.: Rutgers UP, 1987) 330. As Barnett comments, Sedgwick portrays the Indianized Faith "as almost a moron" (*Ignoble Savage* 119). For an especially insightful analysis of *Hope Leslie*'s ideological strengths and limitations, see Dana D. Nelson, "Sympathy as Strategy in Sedgwick's *Hope Leslie*," *The Culture of Sentiment: Race, Gender, and Sentimentality in Nineteenth-Century America*, ed. Shirley Samuels (New York: Oxford UP, 1992) 191–202, also appearing in Nelson's *The Word in Black and White: Reading "Race" in American Literature, 1638–1867* (New York: Oxford UP, 1992) 65–78.

54   On the popularity of *Hope Leslie*, see Kolodny, *The Land Before Her* 82; and Edward Halsey Foster, *Catharine Maria Sedgwick* (New York: Twayne, 1974) 37, 95–96. Foster mentions that the site of Sacrifice Rock, where Magawisca saved Everell Fletcher from death by interposing herself between him

and her father's tomahawk, at the cost of losing her arm, had become a tourist attraction in the Berkshires by the 1850s.

55   James Fenimore Cooper, *The Wept of Wish-ton-Wish* (1829; Columbus, Ohio: Merrill, 1970) 308, 317, 388.

56   I am grateful to Richard Slotkin for helping me articulate this insight.

2   Rebels *and "Rivals": Self-Portraits of a Conflicted Young Artist*

1   LMC to Mary Francis Preston, [1825?], *CC* 1/17, as quoted in Anna D. Hallowell, "Lydia Maria Child," *Medford Historical Register* 3 (July 1900): 99.

2   See William Charvat, "The Conditions of Authorship in 1820," in *The Profession of Authorship in America, 1800–1870: The Papers of William Charvat*, ed. Matthew J. Bruccoli (Columbus: Ohio State UP, 1968) 29–48; Patricia G. Holland, "Lydia Maria Child as a Nineteenth-Century Professional Author," *Studies in the American Renaissance* 1981: 157–67; and Mary Kelley, *Private Woman, Public Stage: Literary Domesticity in Nineteenth-Century America* (New York: Oxford UP, 1984) 7–12.

3   LMC to George Ticknor, 31 Mar. 1825, *SL* 5; Deborah Pickman Clifford, *Crusader for Freedom: A Life of Lydia Maria Child* (Boston: Beacon P, 1992) 44. I am indebted to chaps. 3 and 4 of Clifford's study for many fine insights, which I have incorporated into the revised version of this chapter.

4   See chap. 3 for a discussion of *Evenings in New England.*

5   Quoted in Clifford, *Crusader for Freedom* 44; and in David B. Tyack, *George Ticknor and the Boston Brahmins* (Cambridge, Mass.: Harvard UP, 1967) 160. On Ticknor's role as a "High Priest" who used social ostracism as a means of maintaining Brahmin hegemony, see esp. Tyack 183–87.

6   LMC to George Ticknor, 29 Mar. 1825, *SL* 4.

7   LMC to George Ticknor, 29 Mar. 1825, *SL* 3–4.

8   [Jared Sparks], "Recent American Novels," *NAR* 21 (July 1825): 78–104. The section on *Hobomok* takes up ten pages: 86–95.

9   On Child's reputation as "the brilliant Miss Francis," see Hallowell, "Lydia Maria Child" 100. For descriptions of Child, see Edgar Allan Poe, *The Works of Edgar Allan Poe*, ed. Edmund Clarence Stedman and George Edward Woodberry (1895; Freeport, N.Y.: Books for Libraries P, 1971), vol. 8, *The Literati — Minor Contemporaries, Etc.* [1846] 139–41; James Russell Lowell, "A Fable for Critics," *The Poetical Works of James Russell Lowell* (Boston: Houghton Mifflin, 1895); and Clifford, *Crusader for Freedom* 49.

10   Margaret Fuller to Susan Prescott, 10 Jan. 1827, *The Letters of Margaret Fuller*, ed. Robert N. Hudspeth (Ithaca, N.Y.: Cornell UP, 1983–   ) 1: 154. Fuller first mentions Child (though not by name) in a letter of 11 July 1825, where she tells Susan Prescott of having met a new friend who has stimulated her ambition (1: 151–52).

11   Hallowell, "Lydia Maria Child" 100.

12   LMC to George Ticknor, 24 Aug. 1825, *CC* 1/13.

13   William Tudor, *The Life of James Otis, of Massachusetts: Containing Also, Notices of Some Contemporary Characters and Events from the Year 1760 to 1775* (Boston: Wells and Lilly, 1823). See 155–60, 192–94, 197, 213–36, 269–78.

14   Thomas Wentworth Higginson, "Lydia Maria Child" (1868), *Contemporaries*, vol. 2 of *The Writings of Thomas Wentworth Higginson* (Boston: Houghton Mifflin, 1900) 115–16. See also the reviews of *The Rebels* by David Lee Child in the *Massachusetts Journal* 3 Jan. 1826, p. 1; and [J. C. Gray], *NAR* 22 (April 1826): 400–401.

15   Child seems to have based her on "Aunt Sanford," known to posterity only as the unmarried sister of Hutchinson's wife. See Peter Orlando Hutchinson, *The Diary and Letters of His Excellency Thomas Hutchinson, Esq., Captain-General and Governor-in-Chief of His Late Majesty's Province of Massachusetts Bay in North America, Compiled from the Original Documents Still Remaining in the Possession of His Descendants*, 3 vols. (1884–86; New York: Burt Franklin, 1971) 1: 49n.

16 [Lydia Maria Child], *The Rebels, or Boston before the Revolution*. By the author of *Hobomok* (Boston: Cummings, Hilliard, 1825) 150–51. Further citations from this edition are given parenthetically in the text.

17 LMC to Mary Francis Preston, [1825?], *CC* 1/16; Hallowell, "Lydia Maria Child" 99. As this book was going into production, Deborah Clifford generously put me in touch with Megan Marshall, who is currently writing a biography of the Peabody sisters and has discovered references to Child in their correspondence. Marshall kindly sent me transcripts of three letters that mention Child. Most relevant to Child's attack on Byles and Calvinism in *The Rebels* is Mary T. Peabody to Miss Rawlins Pickman, 22 Mar. [1826], Massachusetts Historical Society, Horace Mann II Papers, HM3d: "You have undoubtedly read and admired the Mohicans, and I hope are one of the *understanders* of Hawkeye, the unparalleled Hawkeye. Miss Rebels will be glad, I would suppose, to hide her diminished 'head' by this time, for she has made herself no little trouble. The Misses Byles are excessively angry at her caricature of their father. It always appeared such to me — even before I heard of their indignation. They say she has picked up all the jokes that have been sported since his time and attributed them to him — they say he was a very dignified man — and it seems he had a great respect for Miss Sandford whose relations are still living in Boston — and who was a very fine woman. Dr. Willard was intended for Gen. Warren. . . . I do not wonder at the anger of the Misses Byles, for Miss Francis went there frequently before she published her book and made most particular enquiries about their father. They thought it was merely interest in his character, and they had reason to be indignant when they found what use she made of it. Mr. Graves, one of the most disagreeable characters in Hobomok, is also entirely misrepresented. He was one of the most exemplary, deserving men of the time, and his papers are in the possession of Mr. C. Lowell (one of his descendants) who speaks highly of his character. It cannot be doubted that Miss F. has genius, but it is most unfortunate that she has so little common sense to balance it. Mr. Ticknor's praise of her first book completely turned her head, and I do not think he has acted a very generous part. He read and corrected *this* before it was sent to the press — and now he says openly that he has not been able to get through it." This letter also explains Child's reference to having made enemies in Boston; see LMC to Mary Francis Preston, 11 June 1826, *SL* 7.

18 Critics who have identified Lucretia as a self-portrait of Child include Milton Meltzer, *Tongue of Flame: The Life of Lydia Maria Child* (New York: Crowell, 1965) 19; William S. Osborne, *Lydia Maria Child* (Boston: Twayne, 1980) 58; and Clifford, *Crusader for Freedom* 57.

19 See LMC to Mary Francis Preston, 11 June 1826, *SL* 7; also LMC to [Charles?] Hazeltine, 12 Mar. 1873, *CC* 80/2094: "I never, at any period of life, had any personal beauty."

20 Lowell, "A Fable for Critics," *Poetical Works* 142.

21 See, for example, Wendell Phillips in [Harriet Sewall, ed.], *Letters of Lydia Maria Child with a Biographical Introduction by John G. Whittier and an Appendix by Wendell Phillips* (1882; New York: Negro University P, 1969) 266–67.

22 LMC to Convers Francis, 3 Feb. 1819, *Letters* 3, *CC* 1/3.

23 LMC to Convers Francis, 31 May 1820, *SL* 2.

24 This scene is loosely based on historical fact. Like Lucretia, Hutchinson's daughter Sarah had refused to flee without him. Not Sarah, but the Rev. John Eliot actually salvaged Hutchinson's manuscript, however, by fishing it out of the gutter the following day. See Peter Orlando Hutchinson, *Diary and Letters of Thomas Hutchinson* 1: 67–69; Thomas Hutchinson, *The History of the Colony and Province of Massachusetts Bay*, 3 vols. (1828; Cambridge, Mass.: Harvard UP, 1936) 3: 90; Bernard Bailyn, *The Ordeal of Thomas Hutchinson* (Cambridge, Mass.: Belknap P of Harvard UP, 1974) 68–74; and John R. Galvin, *Three Men of Boston* (New York: Crowell, 1976) 102–5. Neither Hutchinson's *Diary* nor the third volume of his *History* had yet been published when Child was writing the *Rebels* in 1825, but as in the case of her sources for *Hobomok*, she may have had access through Convers to the manuscripts in Harvard's library.

25 For more details on the Boston Athenaeum episode, see chaps. 8 and 10 below.

26 For a discussion of the ideology of Republican motherhood, see Linda K. Kerber, *Women of the Republic: Intellect and Ideology in Revolutionary America* (Chapel Hill: U of North Carolina P, 1980) chap. 9.

27   *NAR* 22 (Apr. 1826) 402; *Literary World* 7 (27 July 1850) 72 (a review of the novel's 2nd ed.). See also *U.S. Literary Gazette* 3 (15 Jan. 1826): 291–95.

28   [J. C. Gray], review of *The Rebels, NAR* 22 (Apr. 1826): 400–408. Quotations are from 402–3, 408. The *U.S. Literary Gazette* also cited "passages of true pathos" as "proofs that the author has no common mind," but it chose to reprint Child's fictionalized rendering of a Whitefield sermon.

29   James Fenimore Cooper, *The Spy. A Tale of the Neutral Ground* (1821; rpt. of 1831 ed., New York: Oxford UP, 1968) 220.

30   Eliza L. Cushing, *Saratoga; A Tale of the Revolution*, 2 vols. (Boston: Cummings, Hilliard, 1824) 1: 16. Kerber, *Women of the Republic* 272–73, suggests that Cushing's mother, Hannah Webster Foster, author of *The Coquette* (1797), may have helped her daughter write this novel. According to Kerber, *Saratoga* expresses Cushing's (and Foster's) dissatisfaction with the place of women in the new Republic: "The Republic offered political roles only to men, but the talents of a Catherine would have been of far greater use to it than those of her hostile father" (273). For a larger context in which to put the theme of the rebellious daughter in Cushing's and Child's novels of the Revolution, see Michael Davitt Bell, *Hawthorne and the Historical Romance of New England* (Princeton, N.J.: Princeton UP, 1971) chap. 4. Although the novels Bell discusses are about Puritan times, his analysis of the rebellious daughter theme and the symbolic function of the romance plot also applies to these novels of the Revolution.

31   "New Historical Novel," *Massachusetts Journal* 3 Jan. 1826, p. 1.

32   Unpublished memoir of David Lee Child by LMC, 1 Jul. 1875, with pasted extracts from their diaries, manuscript "Autobiography," LMC Papers, Anti-Slavery Collection, Cornell University Library, rpt. in *SL* 5–6.

33   I have pieced together this account of David Child's career from examining his correspondence in the following collections: Milton Emerson Ross Collection, Corona Del Mar, Calif.; Boston Public Library; and Massachusetts Historical Society, Washburn and French Collections. See also his "Reminiscences of Travel," *National Anti-Slavery Standard*, beginning 16 Nov. 1843, p. 95. Lisa Johnson Ponder has provided another vital link by connecting David's diplomatic appointment with the publication of his pamphlet, *An Enquiry into the Conduct of General Putnam in Relation to the Battle of Bunker, or Breed's Hill: and Remarks upon Mr. Swett's Sketch of that Battle* (Boston: T. G Bangs, 1819); see her unpublished M.A. Thesis, "The Making of an Abolitionist: The Early Life Jurisprudential Development of L. Maria Child, 1802 to 1833," University of Oregon, 1987, 202–4. Dearborn, who later published his own reminiscences of the Battle of Bunker Hill, must have been pleased to have David demolish the claim to fame of a rival war hero. See also the *DAB* entries on Dearborn and David. The *DAB* erroneously dates David's sojourn in Portugal from 1820; however, in a letter to his mother, Mrs. Lydia Bigelow Child, 9 July 1822, Ross Collection, he announces that he sails for Lisbon that day. I am grateful to Milton Emerson Ross for his generosity in sharing these family letters, which he allowed me not only to examine in his home, but to take home with me until I had finished going through them. In future citations of David's letters, I will be referring to David as DLC.

34   For details about the circumstances of the French invasion, I am indebted to Celia Morris Eckhardt, who shared with me a deleted chapter of her fine biography of Frances Wright.

35   John James Appleton to General Lopez Baros, 16 June 1820 [1823], BPL Ms.A.4.4, p. 4; DLC to Zachariah and Lydia Bigelow Child, 26 May 1823, Milton Emerson Ross Collection; and DLC to unknown correspondent, 29 July 1823, BPL Ms. A.4.1, p. 5. Appleton's letter is in Spanish and was kindly translated for me by Dr. Laura V. Monti, Keeper of Rare Books and Manuscripts, BPL. The date, though corroborated by the BPL cataloguer, appears to be erroneous, since the invasion took place between Apr. and Aug. 1823; all of the other letters relating to David's stint in the Spanish army date from May through Sept. 1823; moreover, David did not arrive in Portugal until 1822 (see n. 33 above).

36   DLC to unknown correspondent, 29 July 1823, BPL Ms.A.4.1, p. 5. The most likely correspondent is John James Appleton, who had written two letters to him. In a letter of 19 Sept. 1823, Appleton writes to David: "Try to inspire others with your feelings and the good cause will if not triumph at least find an honorable grave and a glorious resurrection." BPL Ms.A.4.4, p. 6.

37 Diary entry of 26 Jan. [1825], LMC manuscript "Autobiography" and memoir of DLC, *SL* 5. I will continue to refer to Lydia Maria Francis as Child, and in order to avoid confusion I will refer to David Lee Child as David.

38 Diary entry of 3 May [1825], LMC manuscript "Autobiography" and memoir of DLC, *SL* 6.

39 LMC "Autobiography" with manuscript memoir of DLC, Cornell University Library, Antislavery Collection. The transcription in *SL* 6 omits the next-to-last sentence and renders "eloquent" (in my opinion a more likely reading) as "elegant." The original is very pale and difficult to decipher. The other omitted sentence does not refer to Maria.

40 David's correspondence shows him already borrowing money from prominent political sponsors as early as 1822. See DLC to John Bailey, 7 Dec. 1822, Washburn Collection, Massachusetts Historical Society, which refers to David's hopes of soon being able to repay favors of a "pecuniary kind." Also DLC to General Henry Dearborn, 13 Mar. 1824, C. E. French Collection, MHS, which complains of having had no reply to his application for another position as secretary of legation and requests "a further loan of $300."

41 DLC to Zachariah Child, 14 Nov. 1824, Ross Collection. I am grateful to Deborah Clifford for bringing this letter to my attention. See her perceptive discussion of David's financial "recklessness," *Crusader for Freedom* 66–67.

42 LMC to Mary Francis Preston, 11 June 1826, *SL* 7; Hallowell, "Lydia Maria Child" 102; Clifford, *Crusader for Freedom* 50–51.

43 LMC to Marianne Silsbee, 5 Feb. 1867 [misdated 1866], *CC* 66/1761a. Child's reminiscences were occasioned by Willis's death. The phrase "the brilliant Miss Francis" is quoted in Hallowell, "Lydia Maria Child" 100.

44 For a discussion of Willis's snobbish reaction to Child's *The Frugal Housewife*, see chap. 6.

45 LMC to Mary Francis Preston, 11 June 1826, *SL* 7.

46 LMC to Francis Alexander, undated, Alexander Family Papers, vol. 2, pp. 5–7, Schlesinger Library.

47 Catharine W. Pierce, "Francis Alexander," *Old-Time New England* 44 (Oct.–Dec. 1953): 29–46. Quotation on 33. I am grateful to Curator Jo Goeselt of the Wayland Historical Society for bringing this article to my attention and sending me a copy of it. On Child's role as a self-appointed art patron, see chaps. 13, 16, 18, and 21.

48 LMC to Mary Francis Preston, 11 June 1826, *SL* 6–8; LMC to Francis Alexander, undated, Alexander Family Papers, vol. 2, p. 7, Schlesinger Library; Pierce, "Francis Alexander" 33–34, 39; Hallowell, "Lydia Maria Child" 101, *CC* 1/21. In another transcript generously made available to me by Megan Marshall, Mary Peabody also comments on the portrait's defiant expression: "I saw . . . at Alexander's room, a portrait of Miss Francis — I can compare the expression of her face to nothing but a tiger — (you perceive the effects of bad example) I think she must have 'called up a look' that minute, for I never heard that she looked fierce." See Mary T. Peabody to Miss Rawlins Pickman, 16 Apr. 1826, Massachusetts Historical Society, Horace Mann II papers (HM3d).

49 Clifford, *Crusader for Freedom* 52–53, explores this possibility in a stimulating reading of Child's 1829 story "Harriet Bruce."

50 The quotation is from "The Rival Brothers. A Tale of the Revolution" (39), included in Lydia Maria Child, *The Coronal. A Collection of Miscellaneous Pieces, Written at Various Times* (Boston: Carter and Hendee, 1832) 32–57. Further page references to this story are given parenthetically in the text.

51 Fred Lewis Pattee, *The Development of the American Short Story: An Historical Survey* (New York: Harper, 1923) 32. For a history and bibliography of gift books, see Ralph Thompson, *American Literary Annuals & Gift Books, 1825–1865* (New York: H. W. Wilson, 1936), esp. chaps. 1, 2, and 5.

52 The quotation is from the subtitle of Nathaniel P. Willis's gift book, *The Legendary* (Boston: Samuel G. Goodrich, 1828). See also the preface to the *Atlantic Souvenir* for 1826, quoted in Pattee, *Development of American Short Story* 30.

53 On the "*Waverley*-model," see George Dekker, *The American Historical Romance* (New York: Cambridge UP, 1987) chap. 2.

54   Pattee, *Development of American Short Story* 31–32, 46–47. *North American Review*, Apr. 1829, quoted in Pattee.

55   For examples of Sedgwick's and Leslie's sketches of domestic manners, see Sedgwick's "Cacoethes Scribendi" (1830) and Leslie's "Mrs. Washington Potts" (1832), both rpt. in *Provisions: A Reader from 19th-Century American Women*, ed. Judith Fetterley (Bloomington: Indiana UP, 1985) 41–59, 70–104, which includes superb introductions to all selections. Child's three stories in this mode are collected in her volume of fiction and poetry, *The Coronal* (1832).

56   See, for example, Paulding's "The Little Dutch Sentinel of the Manhadoes" and "Cobus Yerks," in the *Atlantic Souvenir* for 1827 (154–93) and 1828 (192–206). Both are self-consciously in the vein of Irving's "The Legend of Sleepy Hollow."

57   For a discussion of Child's Indian stories and how they differ from those of her contemporaries, see chap. 5 below.

58   *The Atlantic Souvenir* for 1826, issued in the late fall of 1825, started the practice of marketing these annuals as gifts for the coming New Year. Hence, the discrepancy between the publication date and the date on the cover. The same practice was followed by *The Token*, though not by Willis's short-lived *The Legendary*. Published in *The Atlantic Souvenir* for 1827, Child's "The Rival Brothers" dates from the fall of 1826. The text I will be citing is from Child's collection *The Coronal* (1832) 32–57.

59   L. Maria Child, "The Boys of the Old Times," *A New Flower for Children* (New York: C. S. Francis, 1856) 200–215; this story seems to be a revised version of "Conversation Between a Little Boy of Olden Times, and a Boston Boy of 1827," *Juvenile Miscellany* 3 (Sept. 1827): 105–10. See also Clifford, *Crusader for Freedom* 6.

60   Review of Child's *The Coronal, American Monthly Review* 1 (Mar. 1832): 222.

61   See chap. 16 for a discussion of William Wood in "The Eglantine," published in *Autumnal Leaves* (1857).

62   LMC to Mary Francis Preston, 6 Jan. 1827, *SL* 8.

3   The Juvenile Miscellany: *The Creation of an American Children's Literature*

1   C[aroline] [Howard] G[ilman], "A Family Scene," *Juvenile Miscellany* n.s. 3: (Nov. 1829) 215–16. The abbreviation *JM* is used in subsequent references to the magazine.

2   The Library of Entertaining Knowledge was one of Child's principal sources for informational articles in the *Miscellany*. For excellent studies of nineteenth-century American children's literature and its cultural mission, see Anne Scott MacLeod, *A Moral Tale: Children's Fiction and American Culture, 1820–1860* (Hamden, Conn: Archon, 1975); and R. Gordon Kelly, *Mother Was a Lady: Self and Society in Selected American Children's Periodicals, 1865–1890* (Westport, Conn.: Greenwood P, 1974). I am indebted to Kelly for stimulating my interest in *The Juvenile Miscellany* and children's literature and to both books for teaching me to read this literature with sensitivity to its cultural implications.

3   In 1820 Caroline Howard Gilman's husband, Samuel, a clergyman, had taken a Unitarian pulpit in Charleston. An ardent southern sympathizer by the 1830s, when she and Child broke with each other, Gilman actually sided with the Confederacy during the Civil War. Child probably met the Gilmans through Samuel's sister Louisa Gilman, with whom she was already intimate by 1827 (see LMC to Louisa Gilman, 4 June [1827?], *CC* 1/24). Louisa's future husband, Ellis Loring, mentioned in the same letter, became a member of the New England Anti-Slavery Society in 1832, along with David Lee Child, and the two couples remained close friends throughout their lives.

4   See John C. Crandall, "Patriotism and Humanitarian Reform in Children's Literature, 1825–1860," *American Quarterly* 21 (Spring 1969): 3–22.

5   Caroline Healey Dall, "Lydia Maria Child and Mary Russell Mitford," *Unitarian Review* 19 (June 1883): 519–34. Quotations in this and following paragraphs on 525–26.

6   "The Orphans," *Juvenile Miscellany* 4 (July 1828): 314–26. The heroine, Lucy Mann, like Jo March, has "long, thick, and glossy" hair of "an uncommon colour" (though "golden brown," rather than chestnut,

as in Jo's case). Lucy, too, gets the idea of selling her hair from a story she reads (about an English girl). After an agonizing conflict between her desire to "make her [grandmother] comfortable" and her attachment to her "pretty hair," she performs the sacrifice. Child moralizes that Lucy's hair is not important for its own sake, since it might have had to be cut if Lucy had become ill and since it would eventually turn gray anyway; "but it was a great thing for her own character, whether she allowed vanity, to overcome her sense of duty. . . . If she had indulged her vanity in this particular, it would have grown stronger, and been harder to overcome, the next time she was tempted; and perhaps, when she became a young lady, she would be tempted to do some very wicked thing, to gratify her vanity. . ." (314–16). In *A Hunger for Home: Louisa May Alcott's Place in American Culture* [New Brunswick, N.J.; Rutgers UP, 1987) 36, Sarah Elbert has also pointed out an episode in *Little Men* where Alcott dramatizes a method of punishment Child had suggested in *The Mother's Book* (1831). Alcott's mother, Abba, an intimate friend of Child's, had applied it to Louisa when she was six years old. For Child's reminiscenes of Abba May Alcott and assessment of Louisa, see LMC to Sarah Shaw, 18 June 1876, *SL* 534–35, partially quoted in chap. 21 below; and LMC to Louisa May Alcott, 19 June 1878, *CC* 90/2398.

7   Lucy Larcom, *A New England Girlhood, Outlined from Memory* (1889; New York: Corinth, 1961) 169–75. Child was one of the first writers Larcom solicited for contributions to *Our Young Folks* on its inauguration. See "Freddy's New-Year's Dinner," "Grandfather's Chestnut-Tree," and "The Two Christmas Evenings," which Larcom featured as lead stories in the July and Oct. 1865 and Jan. 1866 issues of *Our Young Folks*.

8   Thomas Wentworth Higginson, "Lydia Maria Child" (1868), *Contemporaries*, vol. 2 of *The Writings of Thomas Wentworth Higginson* (Boston: Houghton Mifflin, 1900) 108, 116.

9   See Isaac Kramnick, "Children's Literature and Bourgeois Ideology: Observations on Culture and Industrial Capitalism in the Later Eighteenth Century," *Culture and Politics: From Puritanism to the Enlightenment*, ed. Perez Zagorin (Berkeley: U of California P, 1980) 213–14. For a statement of this point of view by a writer of Child's generation, see [Sarah Josepha Hale], review of *The Juvenile Souvenir*, for 1828, and of *The Juvenile Miscellany*, vol. 3, *Ladies' Magazine* 1 (Jan. 1828): 47. Hale comments on the "intellectual and moral" superiority of these volumes (both edited by Child) to "the absurd tales of fairy enchantment, and the foolish chimes of 'rhymes for the nursery'" hitherto offered to children: "The worthless volumes, in the perusal of which, our childhood was wasted, have now given place to a class, which, though happily adapted to the comprehension of the youngest, may both amuse and instruct the oldest."

10   The best summary of these developments is Kramnick's "Children's Literature and Bourgeois Ideology," in Zagorin, ed., *Culture and Politics* 203–40. See also Philippe Ariès's classic study, *Centuries of Childhood: A Social History of Family Life*, trans. Robert Baldick (New York: Vintage, 1962); the essays by Mary Lynn Stevens Heininger, Karin Calvert, and Harvey Green in *A Century of Childhood, 1820–1920* (Rochester, N.Y.: Margaret Woodbury Strong Museum, 1984); Jacqueline S. Reinier, "Rearing the Republican Child: Attitudes and Practices in Post-Revolutionary Philadelphia," *William and Mary Quarterly* 39 (Jan. 1982): 150–63; and the early chapters of Carl N. Degler's *At Odds: Women and the Family in America from the Revolution to the Present* (New York: Oxford UP, 1980). The following paragraphs are based on these sources, esp. Kramnick.

11   For historical analyses of these developments, see Louise A. Tilly and Joan Scott, *Women, Work and Family* (New York: Holt, 1978), esp. chaps. 4 and 6; Heidi Hartmann, "Capitalism, Patriarchy, and Job Segregation by Sex," *The SIGNS Reader: Women, Gender and Scholarship*, ed. Elizabeth Abel and Emily K. Abel (Chicago: U of Chicago P, 1983) 193–226, esp. 203–10; Mary Lynn McDougall, "Working-Class Women During the Industrial Revolution, 1780–1914," and Theresa M. McBride, "The Long Road Home: Women's Work and Industrialization," both in *Becoming Visible: Women in European History*, ed. Renate Bridenthal and Claudia Koonz (Boston: Houghton, 1977) 255–79, 280–95. For studies focusing on American women, see Gerda Lerner, "The Lady and the Mill Girl: Changes in the Status of Women in the Age of Jackson," *Midcontinent American Studies Journal* 10 (Spring 1969): 5–15; Nancy F. Cott, *The Bonds of Womanhood: "Woman's Sphere" in New England, 1780–1835* (New Haven, Conn.: Yale

UP, 1977), esp. chaps. 1–3; and Alice Kessler-Harris, *Out to Work: A History of Wage-Earning Women in the United States* (New York: Oxford UP, 1982), esp. chap. 3 on "Industrial Wage Earners and the Domestic Ideology."

12   Ariès is particularly illuminating on this point. See his chapter "From Immodesty to Innocence," *Centuries of Childhood*, 100–127.

13   See Max Weber, *The Protestant Ethic and the Spirit of Capitalism*, trans. Talcott Parsons (1905, 1920; New York: Scribner's, 1958) chap. 4, "The Religious Foundations of Worldly Asceticism" 98–128. Also extremely useful are the section on Benjamin Franklin in "The Spirit of Capitalism" and the entire chapter "Asceticism and the Spirit of Capitalism" 48–54, 155–83.

14   Kramnick, "Children's Literature and Bourgeois Ideology" 205.

15   Kramnick, "Children's Literature and Bourgeois Ideology" 205, 209, 215, 221, 227–28.

16   [Lydia Maria Child], *Evenings in New England. Intended for Juvenile Amusement and Instruction*. By an American Lady (Boston: Cummings, Hilliard, 1824) iii. Further page references are given parenthetically in the text.

17   Review of *Evenings in New England, NAR* 20 (Jan. 1825): 230–31.

18   Kramnick, "Children's Literature and Bourgeois Ideology" 228.

19   [Anna Letitia Barbauld], *Evenings at Home; or, The Juvenile Budget Opened. Consisting of a Variety of Miscellaneous Pieces, for the Instruction and Amusement of Young Persons*, 6 vols. (London: J. Johnson, 1792) 1: 51–52, 55.

20   Barbauld, *Evenings at Home* 1: 86, 94.

21   Kramnick, "Children's Literature and Bourgeois Ideology" 225. See Barbauld, "The Kidnappers," 2: 79–86, discussed below, in which Mr. B. reads a chapter from Churchill's Voyages to his son and daughter and discusses the issue it raises. Also "The Cost of a War," 5: 54–63, in which the father uses Louis XIV's conquest of the Palatinate to make the point that war is evil.

22   Barbauld, "The Kidnappers," *Evenings at Home* 2: 80–82.

23   Barbauld, *Evenings at Home* 2: 81.

24   For a more extended discussion of early antislavery ideology and the process by which radical abolitionists like Garrison and Child came to question its premises, see chap. 8 below.

25   I am grateful to Jean Fagan Yellin for pointing out the significance of Haiti, rather than Liberia, as a haven for emancipated slaves. Among the early antislavery advocates who favored Haiti were Frances Wright and the Quaker Benjamin Lundy. Child and her fellow abolitionists would agitate vociferously for U.S. recognition of Haiti.

26   LMC to Mary Francis Preston, undated, *CC* 1/15, as quoted in Anna D. Hallowell, "Lydia Maria Child, *Medford Historical Register* 3 (July 1900): 100.

27   Review of *Evenings in New England, NAR* 20 (Jan. 1825): 231.

28   LMC to Mary Francis Preston, [28 Aug. 1826], *CC* 1/19, as quoted in Hallowell, "Lydia Maria Child" 100.

29   Benjamin Rush, "Thoughts Upon Female Education," quoted in Linda K. Kerber, *Women of the Republic: Intellect and Ideology in Revolutionary America* (Chapel Hill: U of North Carolina P, 1980) 229.

30   See William Charvat, "The Conditions of Authorship in 1820," *The Profession of Authorship in America, 1800–1870: The Papers of William Charvat*, ed. Matthew J. Bruccoli (Columbus: Ohio State UP, 1968) 29–48. Irving wrote histories, including *Astoria*, financed by the millionaire John Jacob Astor. Longfellow and Hawthorne took up children's literature, and Hawthorne filled two political appointments. Emerson and Melville lectured, and Melville repeatedly attempted to procure a political appointment, finally succeeding in 1866.

31   LMC to Mary Francis Preston, 6 Jan. 1827, *SL* 8; and [1826], *CC* 1/22, as quoted in Hallowell, "Lydia Maria Child" 101.

32   For other overviews of *The Juvenile Miscellany*, see Alice M. Jordan, " 'The Juvenile Miscellany' and Its Literary Ladies," in *From Rollo to Tom Sawyer and Other Papers* (Boston: Horn Book, 1948) 46–60; and

Ruth K. MacDonald, "*The Juvenile Miscellany: For the Instruction and Amusement of Youth*," *Children's Periodicals of the United States*, ed. R. Gordon Kelly (Westport, Conn.: Greenwood P, 1984) 258–62.

33   Willis launched a "Prospectus" of the magazine, consisting of a sample number, on 16 Apr. 1827, but the *Youth's Companion* (hereinafter referred to as *YC*) did not actually begin appearing on a regular basis until 6 June. For an overview of *YC*, see David L. Greene, "*The Youth's Companion*," *Children's Periodicals of the United States*, ed. Kelly, 507–14.

34   Compare "The Elephant," *YC* 1 (31 Aug. 1827): 55 with "Wonders of the Deep," *JM* 1 (Jan. 1827): 66–80. Quotation on 73. Barbauld, a member of Priestley's circle, uses natural history in the same way as Child, who probably drew her inspiration from the natural history articles in *Evenings at Home*. See also the section "Defining the True Revelation" in Thomas Paine's *The Age of Reason*, ed. Philip S. Foner (1794; Secaucus, N.J.: Citadel P, 1974) 68–70.

35   The earliest borrowing I have found is the poem "Ellen's May Day," signed W., 1 (14 Sept. 1827): 64. Gilman's and Sigourney's selections appear in the *Companion*, 11 Jan. (1: 132) and 6 June (2: 5–6) 1828, respectively; the three biographical sketches: 18 July, 1 and 8 Aug. 1828 (2: 29–30, 39, 43). And the two stories cited appeared 19 Sept. and 31 Oct. 1828 (2: 65–66, 89–90). In the issue containing "The Cottage Girl," Willis reviewed the *Miscellany*, describing it as "well worthy of the attention of our young friends" (2: 68). All borrowings are attributed to the *Miscellany*. Initially sporadic, borrowings become regular by March 1828. They are most frequent right after the publication of each bimonthly issue of the *Miscellany* and seem to taper off as Willis runs out of material he considers worth reprinting. In his "Prospectus," Willis had pledged to avoid "every thing frivolous." He had also objected to magazines of "mere amusement, whose influence is unfavorable to religion and morals" (1: 1).

36   A typical example is "Pious Negro," *YC* 1 (27 July 1827) 34, reprinted from the Scottish *Children's Friend*. It tells of a young girl who must refuse an old Negro's pleas for charity because she has "nothing with her that could be of use to him," but who reads him an extract from the New Testament instead and prays for his conversion. The anecdote ends with his pious death. See also "Seneca Mission," *YC* 7 (22 Feb. 1834) 157, on the achievements of Indian converts and the need for greater efforts to spread the gospel among Indian tribes.

37   Paul Faler, "Cultural Aspects of the Industrial Revolution: Lynn, Massachusetts, Shoemakers and Industrial Morality, 1826–1860," *Labor History* 15 (Summer 1974): 367–94, describes the campaign of Lynn shoe manufacturers to disseminate the new industrial morality among their workers. Quotation on 367. I am grateful to Dorothy Ross for bringing this article to my attention. It is fascinating to note that the Lynn Society for the Promotion of Industry, Frugality, and Temperance was founded the same year as the *Juvenile Miscellany*, in 1826. In *A Shopkeepers' Millennium: Society and Revivals in Rochester, New York, 1815–1837*, Paul E. Johnson describes a similar campaign. On the British precedent, see Kramnick, "Children's Literature and Bourgeois Ideology."

38   Kramnick, "Children's Literature and Bourgeois Ideology" 230. The instance he cites is from Barbauld's *Evenings at Home* 6: 250.

39   Weber, *Protestant Ethic* 48–53.

40   See the opening paragraph of Franklin's *Autobiography* and the first section of Book 2.

41   "Value of Time," *JM* 1 (Jan. 1827): 103–5. See also the dialogue "Time and Money," by "Mater," *JM* n.s. 2 (July 1829): 218–26. To explain the dictum "time is money" to her daughter, Mother uses the example of bees, who "spend their time in making honey; which is sold for money" (224). She, too, goes on to say: "If time is money, time is knowledge, too; and knowledge in connexion with virtue, is the best means of happiness, as well as usefulness." The biblical metaphor she cites evaluates knowledge in monetary terms as well: "It is among the treasures 'that neither moth nor rust corrupt, nor thieves break through and steal' " (225).

42   Elizabeth Stuart Phelps, *Chapters from a Life* (Boston: Houghton Mifflin, 1896) 182–83.

43   "Benjamin Franklin," *JM* 2 (Mar. 1827): 18–23. Quotations on 20–21. Child adopted a similar strategy when she used the proceeds from *The Freedmen's Book* to buy more copies for free distribution to former

slaves. For reminiscences of Child that describe her self-sacrificing charity, see Hallowell, "Lydia Maria Child" 115; and James Russell Lowell, "A Fable for Critics," *The Poetical Works of James Russell Lowell. Household Edition* (Boston: Houghton Mifflin, 1895) 142–44.

44   Kramnick, "Children's Literature and Bourgeois Ideology" 224, 232.

45   Obviously, the biographical sketches serve patriotic purposes as well. Thus, except for foreign heroes of the American Revolution, their subjects are all Americans. In 1831, however, Child introduced a new biographical series, "Remarkable Boys," that featured a number of European child prodigies. The sketches of Isaac Newton and James Ferguson are typical in attributing their scientific achievements to the "habits of thought and attention," "industry and perseverance" that each developed at a young age (n.s. 6 [Mar./Apr. 1831] 32, 34).

46   "The American Traveller," *JM* 1 (Sept. 1826): 14–20; "Sir Benjamin West," *JM* 1 (Jan. 1827): 19–25.

47   No selections in the first issue are signed, suggesting that Child may have written all or most of them and then solicited contributors who could follow the models she provided. At the end of the second issue she apologizes in a note for not printing a contribution from an "anonymous correspondent" because it was too similar to a selection that had already been included (1 [Nov. 1826]: 108). And in the third issue, she apologizes for errors "to be attributed to the carelessness of the editor—not to the writer of the article on botany" (1 [Jan. 1827]: 108). This would seem to indicate that she initially rewrote unsigned articles contributed by others. By the third issue, the series "Mother and Eliza" is signed by "A.B.F.," and the initials of other regular contributors begin to appear. And by the fourth, a note "To Correspondents" announces that "The editor of the Juvenile Miscellany has, as usual, received a number of excellent communications. That they are so numerous, must be an excuse for deferring some which deserve immediate notice" (2 [Mar. 1827]: 108).

48   "Mother and Eliza," *JM* 1 (Sept. 1826): 45–47. Eleven years later, the women's rights advocate Sarah Grimké would translate this critique of girls' upbringing into explicit feminist terms. See her *Letters on the Equality of the Sexes, and the Condition of Woman* (1837–38), esp. Letter 8.

49   "The Industrious Family," *JM* n.s. 6 (July/Aug. 1831): 217–30; Lydia Maria Child, *The Mother's Book* (Boston: Carter, Hendee, and Babcock, 1831) 91.

50   "The Industrious Family," *JM* n.s. 6: 218–19. Child had been emphasizing the importance of manual labor in her "Hints to Persons of Moderate Fortune," appended to the 2nd ed. of *The Frugal Housewife.*

51   Kramnick points out that books like Edgeworth's *Harry and Lucy* and Barbauld's *Evenings at Home* were "important vehicle[s] in transmitting the sexual stereotypes emergent in the new notion of the family—the superiority and usefulness of men." He adds: "Things were much more exciting . . . for the young boy readers" of Edgeworth and Barbauld, since these authors were "concerned with providing new heroes for the young male reader"—inventors, manufacturers, and engineers, rather than "'kings, lords, generals, prime ministers.'" See 225, 229.

52   "The Affectionate Brother," *JM* 4 (July 1828): 276–93. Quotations in this paragraph on 276 and 289.

53   Kramnick, "Children's Literature and Bourgeois Ideology" 217.

54   "Louisa Preston," *JM* 4 (Mar. 1828): 56–81.

55   "The Brothers, or . . . The Influence of Example," *JM* 3 (Nov. 1827): 209–26. Quotation on 211.

56   See Faler, "Cultural Aspects of the Industrial Revolution" 390–91; also Johnson, *A Shopkeepers' Millennium* 120–26. Quotations in this paragraph are from Faler.

57   Faler, "Cultural Aspects of the Industrial Revolution" 391–92.

58   "The Cottage Girl," *JM* n.s. 1 (Sept. 1828) 3–19; "Rosy O'Ryan," *A New Flower for Children (For Children from Eight to Twelve Years Old)* (New York: C. S. Francis, 1856) 158–89.

59   See Weber, *Protestant Ethic* 174–75.

60   See, for example, Hartmann, "Capitalism, Patriarchy, and Job Segregation by Sex" 193–225, esp. 203–7.

61   W. B. O. Peabody, "Origin and Progress of the Useful Arts," review of *The Frugal Housewife, NAR* 33 (July 1831): 81; reviews of *Juvenile Souvenir* and *Juvenile Miscellany, Ladies' Magazine* 1 (Jan. and July 1828): 47–48, 336, and 2 (Sept. 1829): 440; reviews of *Juvenile Miscellany, American Traveller* 29 Dec.

1826, p. 2; 11 July 1828, p. 2; 5 Sept. 1828, p. 2. A dialogue on "Coral Reefs" from the *Miscellany*, Nov. 1826, is reprinted in the *Traveller*, 7 Nov. 1826, p. 4. I am grateful to Deborah Clifford for directing my attention to the *American Traveller*.

62 LMC to Mary Francis Preston, 6 Jan. 1827, *SL* 8; LMC to Lydia Bigelow Child, 14 Jan. [1829], *SL* 13.

4 A Marriage of True Minds: Espousing the Indian Cause

1 LMC to Mary Francis Preston, 28 Oct. 1827, *SL* 9.

2 George Ticknor Curtis, "Reminiscences of N. P. Willis and Lydia Maria Child," *Harper's New Monthly Magazine* 81 (October 1890): 719–20; and Deborah Pickman Clifford, *Crusader for Freedom: A Life of Lydia Maria Child* (Boston: Beacon P, 1992) 65–66. Clifford reconciles Curtis's account with Child's own assertion that David proposed by mail (*SL* 9), suggesting that he first sent a letter and then went to the Curtis's to "try persuasion in person."

3 DLC to Lydia Bigelow Child, 20 Oct. 1827, Ross Collection. On Child's "unpleasant" associations with the name Lydia, which she no longer used, see LMC to Theodore Tilton, 27 May 1866, *SL* 460.

4 LMC manuscript "Autobiography" and memoir of DLC, LMC Papers, Anti-Slavery Collection, Cornell University Library, quoted in chap. 2 above.

5 Clifford, *Crusader for Freedom* 65; Lisa Johnson Ponder, "The Making of an Abolitionist: The Early Life Jurisprudential Development of L. Maria Child, 1802 to 1833," unpublished M.A. Thesis, University of Oregon, 1987, 200–201, 208–12; Anna D. Hallowell, "Lydia Maria Child," *Medford Historical Register* (July 1900): 100. The party system was in a transition between the old Federalist and Jeffersonian Republican parties and the new Whig and Jacksonian Democratic parties. David Child was among those who favored "National Republican" as the designation for the new party that John Quincy Adams's supporters were endeavoring to form. See DLC to Henry Clay, 11 Apr. 1829, *The Papers of Henry Clay*: vol. 8: *Candidate, Compromiser, Whig, March 5, 1829–December 31, 1836*, ed. Robert Seager II and Melba Porter Hay (Lexington: UP of Kentucky, 1984) 25–26: "I hope the designation of 'National Republican' will be acceptable to friendly & patriotic persons every where. . . . It forms a good *antithesis* to Jackson Republican." According to the editors, "Party names were still in a state of flux in 1829, although the name 'National Republicans' had been adopted by the conservative, pro-administration group in Massachusetts as early as 1827. Lee Benson, *The Concept of Jacksonian Democracy: New York as a Test Case* (Princeton, N.J.: Princeton UP, 1961) 29–30n, describes it as "the title for *one faction* of the Jacksonian opposition" and asserts that it did not become generally accepted until 1830 or 1831. On the ideology and formation of the Whig party, see Daniel Walker Howe, *The Political Culture of the American Whigs* (Chicago: U of Chicago P, 1979).

6 LMC to Mary Francis Preston, 11 June 1826, *CC* 1/18, comments on Abba's invalidism: "Always on the bed, and never feeling the least excitement about any thing that concerns her family."

7 LMC to Sarah Shaw, 25 Aug. 1877, *SL* 544.

8 Clifford, *Crusader for Freedom* 66–67. See LMC to Lydia Bigelow Child, 16 Feb. 1849, *SL* 241: "David, like his poor father, you know is not remarkably prompt, and punctual to his engagements. It has been one great cause of his want of success, poor fellow." On John Childe (he added the e to his name, perhaps to distinguish himself from his poor relations), see the *DAB*.

9 LMC to Charles Sumner, 7 July 1856, *SL* 283.

10 LMC to Lydia Bigelow Child, 16 Feb. 1849, *SL* 241–42. See Vivian Gornick, "Why Women Fear Success," *The First Ms. Reader* (New York: Warner Books, 1973) 26–35. I have found this syndrome among upwardly mobile male students of working-class background, both white and African American, as well as among women of all groups. For specific instances of these behavior patterns in David's life, see chaps. 5, 9, 11, 12, and 15.

11 I am grateful to H. Bruce Franklin for stimulating this insight by pointing out, in his comments on the first draft of this manuscript, that David's business failings can be read as evidence of the same innate distaste for patriarchy that he expressed more positively in his support of women's rights. Child's

Juvenile Miscellany dialogue "Mother and Eliza" (1: 45–47), discussed in chapter 3 above, provides evidence that the bourgeois virtue of perseverance, for example, was culturally coded as masculine.

12   DLC to Lydia Bigelow Child, 20 Oct. 1827, Ross Collection.

13   LMC manuscript "Autobiography" and memoir of DLC, Cornell Anti-Slavery Collection, partial rpt. in *SL* 5–6.

14   For a fuller discussion of Child's apparent sexual disappointment in her marriage, see chaps. 13–15. For typical references to David as "kind," see LMC to Francis Shaw and Ellis Loring, 2 Aug. 1846 and 6 Feb. 1852, *SL* 229, 263, cited in chaps. 14 and 15.

15   Quoted in Helene G. Baer, *The Heart Is Like Heaven: The Life of Lydia Maria Child* (Philadelphia: U of Pennsylvania P, 1964) 49.

16   LMC to Mary Francis Preston, 28 Oct. 1827, *SL* 10; Clifford, *Crusader for Freedom* 68.

17   For a discussion of Child's Indian tales, see chap. 5 below.

18   [Lydia Maria Child], *Emily Parker, or Impulse, not Principle. Intended for Young Persons.* By the Author of *Evenings in New England*, and the Editor of the *Juvenile Miscellany* (Boston: Bowles and Dearborn, 1827) 61–63. Compare the description of Dr. Fox, "an Apollo in beauty," with "courtier-like manners" (56) to Child's reminiscences of her "Magnus Apollo" in Maine and her characterization of Willis as a man of "very fascinating manners": "Letter from New-York" No. 47, *National Anti-Slavery Standard* 19 Jan. 1843, *CC* 16/444; and LMC to Marianne Silsbee, 5 Feb. [1867], *CC* 66/1761a, quoted, respectively, in the Prologue and chap. 2. Emily meets Dr. Fox in Hallowell, near Gardiner, where Child had taught school; in a letter to her sister Mary, 11 June 1826, *SL* 7, Child mentioned her wish that a "*first rate [school]* could be established at Hallowell," since it was the town she would most readily choose "for a constant residence" if she had the option.

19   LMC to Lydia Bigelow Child, 11 and 26 July [1828], *CC* 1/28, 29. The Thanksgiving visit is recalled in LMC to Lydia Bigelow Child (mother), 14 Nov. [1828], *CC* 1/34.

20   Andrew Jackson's party did not officially adopt the designation "Democratic" until 1840; see Benson, *Concept of Jacksonian Democracy* 62. Child refers to three libel suits in LMC to Lydia Bigelow Child, 14 Jan. [1829], *SL* 13. I have not managed to find information about the third, but it may have been the attack on John B. Derby of Dedham for which David apologized in an editorial note, *Massachusetts Weekly Journal* 10 June 1829, p. 2. In that note, he admits that when he impugned Derby's character on 6 Sept. 1827, he knew nothing personally of Derby and founded his attack only on a "communication" from a third party. This admission tends to corroborate the prosecution's charge that David had wrongfully published the results of a "preliminary enquiry *ex parte*" into the stonecutter Samuel R. Johnson's conduct and treated his guilt as already proven, and that he had "distorted" the facts by interlarding his summary of the report with "his own opinions and insinuations." For details on the charges and countercharges of the Johnson and Keyes libel cases, see "Suffolk, ss. Supreme Judicial Court, Johnson vs. Child," *Massachusetts Weekly Journal* 28 Jan. 1829, pp. 2–3; *Trial of the Case of the Commonwealth versus David Lee Child, for Publishing in the Massachusetts Journal A Libel of the Honorable John Keyes, Before the Supreme Judicial Court, Holden at Cambridge, in the County of Middlesex. October Term, 1828* (Boston: Dutton and Wentworth, 1829); and Clifford, *Crusader for Freedom* 69, 73. Quotation from *Trial* 4.

21   Clifford, *Crusader for Freedom* 69. The inaugural issue of the *Massachusetts Weekly Journal* 3 Sept. 1828, p. 3, reprints a letter of 20 May from subscribers and supporters, headed by Henry Dearborn, praising the editor's "zeal" and "strenuous support of the National Administration" and urging "increased and efficient support" for the paper. In his Editor's Address, printed just above this letter, David claims that the venture of launching the new weekly, in addition to the triweekly edition, "appears to be approved, and sufficiently encouraged to justify our commencing it." He adds: "It is idle and absurd to solicit patronage. . . . If we deserve encouragement we shall obtain it. . . ." The pattern of responding to a financial crisis by expanding operations and hoping that patronage will follow seems clear in this instance. See also the *Massachusetts Journal* file at the Massachusetts Historical Society, which provides several lists of people who agreed in Nov. 1829 to take shares in the newspaper.

22   LMC to Lydia Bigelow Child, 11 and 26 July [1828] and 14 Jan. [1829], *CC* 1/28–29, *SL* 13.

23   LMC to Mary Francis Preston, undated, *CC* 1/32, as quoted in Anna D. Hallowell, "Lydia Maria Child," *Medford Historical Register* 3 (July 1900): 103–4.

24   LMC quoted in Hallowell, "Lydia Maria Child" 103; LMC to Lydia Bigelow Child (mother), 14 Nov. [1828], *CC* 1/34.

25   Curtis, "Reminiscences of N. P. Willis and Lydia Maria Child" 720.

26   LMC to Lydia Bigelow Child (mother), 14 Nov. [1828], *CC* 1/34.

27   [Lydia Maria Child], *The First Settlers of New-England: or, Conquest of the Pequods, Narragansets and Pokanokets: As Related by a Mother to Her Children, and Designed for the Instruction of Youth*. By a Lady of Massachusetts (Boston: Munroe and Francis, [1829]). Page references are given parenthetically in the text. The title page identifies the book as having been "Printed for the Author." Of the few copies that survive, some are undated and others dated 1829. Both internal and external evidence suggests that the bulk of the book was completed before the Childs' wedding and that the preface and the last section, which refer to the ongoing Cherokee removal controversy, were written late in 1828. Child probably timed the book's publication for the Christmas and New Year's market, as was her habit, perhaps following gift book publishers' practice of issuing the work before Christmas but giving it the following year's date. In the last quarter of the book Child cites a number of works published in 1828: the congressional speeches in opposition to "Indian emigration," by Ohio Reps. John Woods and Samuel Finley Vinton, delivered on 19–20 Feb., Gales and Seaton's *Register of Debates in Congress* (Washington, D.C.: Gales and Seaton, 1828), 1548–59, 1568–84; an article on "Indian Language and Condition" in *American Quarterly Review* 6 (June 1828): 391–422; Judge Joseph Story's *Discourse Pronounced at the Request of the Essex Historical Society, on the 18th of September, 1828, in Commemoration of the First Settlement of Salem, in the State of Massachusetts*; John Neal's "Otter-Bag, the Oneida Chief," a story in *The Token* for 1829, which bears a copyright date of 30 Aug., 1828, and probably went on sale in the fall (it is reviewed in the Oct. 1828 issue of Sarah Hale's *Ladies' Magazine*). Child makes no reference either to Andrew Jackson or to the electoral campaign.

28   See untitled articles from *Phoenix*, rpt. in *Massachusetts Daily Journal* 27 June and 6 Oct. 1829, p. 2. In his editorial preface to the former, "The Cherokee Phoenix," David writes: "We have long received and read a paper printed at New-Echota, in the Cherokee Nation; . . . [It] is very respectably conducted by Mr. *Elias Boudinot*, an educated Indian; and we sincerely hope it may do good in contributing to the *civilization* both of red and *white* men. — We heartily join in cheering our red editor on, and give him our hand." For further details on the Cherokee removal crisis, see Ulrich Bonnell Phillips, "The Expulsion of the Cherokees," in Louis Filler and Allen Guttmann, ed., *The Removal of the Cherokee Nation: Manifest Destiny or National Dishonor?* (Boston: D. C. Heath, 1962), 1–13; Kenneth Penn Davis, "Chaos in the Indian Country: The Cherokee Nation, 1828–35," in Duane H. King, ed., *The Cherokee Indian Nation: A Troubled History* (Knoxville: U of Tennessee P, 1979) 129–47; Thurman Wilkins, *Cherokee Tragedy: The Ridge Family and the Decimation of a People*, 2nd ed. (Norman: U of Oklahoma P, 1986) chaps. 8–9; and John Ehle, *Trail of Tears: The Rise and Fall of the Cherokee Nation* (New York: Anchor, 1988) chaps. 12–15. For analyses of the debate over removal and its ideological limitations, see Brian W. Dippie, *The Vanishing American: White Attitudes and U.S. Indian Policy* (Middletown, Conn.: Wesleyan UP, 1982) chap. 5; and Lucy Maddox, *Removals: Nineteenth-Century American Literature and the Politics of Indian Affairs* (New York: Oxford UP, 1991) chap. 1. The quotation is from Phillips, "Expulsion of the Cherokees" 5.

29   Dippie, *Vanishing American* 56–57. As Michael Paul Rogin points out, "[l]eading southern planters, speculators, and their representatives were among those pushing with greatest militance for Indian removal; the Indians were not simply victimized by democratic masses. Soil exhaustion in the southeast, for example, caused large planters to press for removal." See his *Fathers and Children: Andrew Jackson and the Subjugation of the American Indian* (New York: Knopf, 1975) 220. On the interrelationships of slavery, soil exhaustion, and expansionism, see Eugene D. Genovese, *The Political Economy of Slavery: Studies in the Economy and Society of the Slave South* (New York: Vintage, 1967) chaps. 4 and 10. On Cherokee slaveholding, see Theda Perdue, *Slavery and the Evolution of Cherokee Society, 1540–1866* (Knoxville: U of Tennessee P, 1979), esp. chap. 4.

30 Phillips, "Expulsion of the Cherokees" 5.

31 On Jackson's Indian policy, see Rogin, *Fathers and Children* passim; and Ronald N. Satz, *American Indian Policy in the Jacksonian Era* (Lincoln: U of Nebraska P, 1975). For analyses more sympathetic to Jackson, see Francis Paul Prucha, "Andrew Jackson's Indian Policy: A Reassessment," *Journal of American History* 56 (Dec. 1969): 527–39; and Robert V. Remini, *The Legacy of Andrew Jackson: Essays on Democracy, Indian Removal, and Slavery* (Baton Rouge: Louisiana State UP, 1988) 45–82.

32 "To the People of Pennsylvania," rpt. from *Penn. Intelligencer*, *Massachusetts Journal* 22 July 1828, p. 1. For a brief modern account of the First Seminole War of 1817–18, see Richard Drinnon, *Facing West: The Metaphysics of Indian-Hating and Empire-Building* (New York: New American Library, 1980) 104–8.

33 "Extract of a letter written by Major Andrew Jackson to Major Gen. Pinckney, dated on the battle ground in the bend of the Tallapoosie," *Massachusetts Journal* 8 July 1828, p. 1. For details on the battle of the Horseshoe, at which, ironically, the Cherokees helped Jackson defeat the recalcitrant faction of the Creeks, see Wilkins, *Cherokee Tragedy* chap. 3. The figure of 557 dead is confirmed on p. 79.

34 "To Gen. Jackson," *Massachusetts Journal* 26 Aug. 1828, p. 1; "Gen. Jackson's Negro Trading," rpt. from *National Journal* 16 Oct. 1828, p. 1; "To Gen. Jackson," rpt. from *Harrisburg Gazette* 7 June 1828, p. 1.

35 On the participation of many future abolitionists in the struggle against Cherokee removal, see Linda K. Kerber, "The Abolitionist Perception of the Indian," *Journal of American History* 62 (Sept. 1975): 271–95.

36 "*The Cherokee Phoenix*," *Massachusetts Journal* 15 Apr. 1828, p. 3.

37 Linda K. Kerber, *Women of the Republic: Intellect and Ideology in Revolutionary America* (Chapel Hill: U of North Carolina P, 1980) 228–29. Kerber is quoting a graduate of Mrs. Rowson's Academy.

38 Mrs. Oliver's rebellion consisted in disturbing the church service by publicly claiming the right to receive the sacrament of the Lord's Supper without having been officially inducted into church membership. Puritan practice restricted the Lord's Supper to communicants who had qualified for church membership by showing evidence of a genuine conversion experience, but Mrs. Oliver insisted that " 'all that dwell in the same town, and will profess their faith in Christ Jesus, ought to be received to the sacraments there.' " She was imprisoned by the governor for several days until she recanted. On reiterating her heretical views five years later, she was publicly whipped and exhibited in the stocks with " 'cleft stick . . . on her tongue' " (*First Settlers* 92–93). Child is quoting the account of Mrs. Oliver in Winthrop's *Journal*.

39 Child's revisionist analysis of the Pequot War is surprisingly close to the one presented by Francis Jennings in *The Invasion of America: Indians, Colonialism, and the Cant of Conquest* (1975; New York: Norton, 1976) chap. 13. See especially Jennings's account of how the Puritans used the murder of John Stone, "a West India trader-cum-pirate," as a pretext for making war on the Pequots two years after the fact, though the Massachusetts Bay colony had banished him "on pain of death if he should ever reappear" (189–90).

40 The long digression in which Child attempts to discredit the myth of the Chosen People as a means of undermining the Old Testament basis for the Puritan creed unfortunately degenerates into a diatribe against the Jews that feeds anti-Semitic prejudices. Though crude, this section of *The First Settlers* anticipates Child's historical analysis in *The Progress of Religious Ideas, Through Successive Ages* (1855) of the debts that Judaism and Christianity both owed to earlier Near Eastern religions.

41 On white supremacism and Jacksonian ideology, see Leonard L. Richards, "The Jacksonians and Slavery," in Lewis Perry and Michael Fellman, ed., *Antislavery Reconsidered: New Perspectives on the Abolitionists* (Baton Rouge: Louisiana State UP, 1979), 99–118; and Richard H. Brown, "The Missouri Crisis, Slavery, and the Politics of Jacksonianism," *South Atlantic Quarterly* 65 (Winter 1966): 55–72. Also David R. Roediger, *The Wages of Whiteness: Race and the Making of the American Working Class* (London: Verso, 1991) chaps. 4, 7. On the extension of the suffrage, see Chilton Williamson, *American Suffrage: From Property to Democracy, 1760–1860* (Princeton, N.J.: Princeton UP, 1960).

42 The *North American Review* had published a favorable notice of *Evenings in New England* and made brief mention of *The Juvenile Miscellany* and *The Frugal Housewife*, but it merely listed *The First Settlers* in its

record of new publications (29 [Oct. 1829]: 580), erroneously categorizing it as a novel and mistitling it *The First* Letters *of New England*. For Hale's reviews in the *Ladies' Magazine*, see 1 (Jan. and July 1828): 47–48, 336, on the *Juvenile Miscellany*; 1 (June 1828): 286, on "The Indian Wife"; 2 (Nov. 1829): 530, on "Chocorua's Curse"; 3 (Jan. and Apr. 1830): 42–43, 189, on *The Frugal Housewife*. For flattering references to Child in Willis's "Editor's Table" column, see *American Monthly Magazine* 1 (July and Oct. 1829): 276, 495–96; see also his praise of "Chocorua's Curse" in a review of *The Token* for 1830, 1 (Sept. 1829) 413. Willis lampoons *The Frugal Housewife* in his "Editor's Table" of 1 (Jan. 1830): 721–23 and refers satirically to it in his sketch "A Morning in the Library" and his "Editor's Table" of the same month, 1 (Feb. 1830): 792, 803. Willis had published two of Child's Indian stories, "The Church in the Wilderness" and "The Indian Wife" (discussed in chap. 5 below), in his gift book, *The Legendary*. The *American Traveller* had been reviewing almost every number of the *Juvenile Miscellany* (see chap. 3). Child's "More Hints to People of Moderate Fortune" appears in the *Cherokee Phoenix* 7 Apr. 1830, p. 4.

43 I have checked the records of books deposited for copyright at the Massachusetts and New York District Courts from 1 Aug. 1828 through 31 Dec. 1829 and have not found *The First Settlers* listed in either. During this period the Massachusetts records list Child's *Biographical Sketches of Great and Good Men*, the first volume of the *Juvenile Miscellany*'s new series, and *The Frugal Housewife* as having been deposited for copyright on 15 July and 26 Aug. 1828 and on 12 Nov. 1829, respectively. Thus, the omission seems to be deliberate.

44 LMC to George Ticknor, [1829?], *SL* 16. See also DLC to Hon. John Bailey, 20 Dec. 1828, Washburn Collection, Massachusetts Historical Society: "You will have observed that papers which have been neutral or pretended to be so or even enough in favor of Mr Adams to retain their subscribers, are now joining the Jackson forces. Some that were supposed to be committed now affect neutrality & talk as from that vantage ground. The whole tribe is perfectly contemptible & disgrace the public press. For myself I am determined to hold on till I am convinced that my *principles* are wrong. I believe I have managed the Journal consistently [?] hitherto: & altho I can boast of no extraordinary success in any way, still a great many good & discerning men have given a spontaneous & emphatic approval of my course." Benson, *Concept of Jacksonian Democracy*, confirms that "many 'friends of Adams' hastily jumped on board the Jackson bandwagon after the 1828 election returns convinced them of the error of their ways" (30n). David's farewell editorial in the daily edition acknowledges: "An experiment of almost a year has satisfied us that it is inexpedient to attempt to crowd into our dull and declining market another daily newspaper. There were special reasons which induced us to commence one, and flattered us with the idea of success. . . . The thousands of enlightened and excellent men, who approved this [newspaper's] course; and would in a period of excitement and danger make great exertions to encourage it, will not necessarily see the importance of doing much at this time. Our expectations, therefore, from the political friendship of many merchants and men of business, have in a great measure failed. . . . [W]e might have foreseen, and ought to have known, that political excitement and political friendship seldom extend to the substantials of life." See "To Friends and Subscribers, *Massachusetts Daily Journal* 29 Oct. 1829, p. 2.

45 *Trial of Commonwealth* v. *David Lee Child* 98–103; "Suffolk, ss. Supreme Judicial Court. Johnson vs. Child," *Massachusetts Weekly Journal* 28 Jan. 1829, pp. 2–3; Clifford, *Crusader for Freedom* 73–74. Clifford reports the fine as $25.

46 "State Prison Matters" and "Measurement of Stone," *Massachusetts Weekly Journal* 18 Feb. and 11 Mar. 1829, p. 3.

47 "To the Hon. John Keyes, of Concord," *Massachusetts Weekly Journal* 8 Apr. 1829, p. 1; Horace Mann to Mary Peabody Mann, 2 Sept. 1850, Horace Mann Collection, Massachusetts Historical Society. Mann attributes the origin of the sobriquet to "Derby," who must be the John B. Derby to whom David apologized in an editorial note of 10 June 1829, p. 2.

48 *New York Commercial Advertiser*, *Wicasset Citizen*, and *Boston Daily Advertiser*, rpt. in *Massachusetts Weekly Journal* 8 Apr. 1829, p. 4.

49 LMC to George Ticknor, [1829?], *SL* 15–16.

50   The quotation is from Sarah Hale's *Ladies' Magazine* 2 (November 1829): 515–16, where it prefaces a brief extract from "An Appeal to the Ladies of the United States" by a "Southern lady," which had previously appeared in Benjamin Lundy's *Genius of Universal Emancipation*. Hale's misgivings about reprinting it are obvious from her editorial comment. Her warning to women who overstep the boundaries of their sphere shows what Child was up against: "In addressing her own sex, particularly on so momentous and really appalling subject as that of *slavery*, we presume the writer had no idea of advocating female interference or usurpation of authority, in directing the affairs of state. It is only the influence of woman on public sentiment, and this, to be truly salutary, must be exerted with a womanly delicacy and in an unobtrusive manner, that is recommended. Women certainly, have, in our country, a great influence over public opinion but — *sub rosa* — let us be cautious of making too much display about the matter. . . . Let us beware of exerting our power *politically*. . . . The influence of woman, to be beneficial, must depend mainly on the respect inspired by her *moral* excellence, not on the political address or energy she may display."

51   See William G. McLoughlin, *Cherokees and Missionaries, 1789–1839* (New Haven, Conn.: Yale UP, 1984).

52   Jeremiah Evarts, *Cherokee Removal: The "William Penn" Essays and Other Writings*, ed. Francis Paul Prucha (Knoxville: U of Tennessee P, 1981). Evarts's letters succeeded in launching a full-scale petition campaign against Cherokee removal, in which several future leaders of the abolitionist movement participated. Once again, the campaign would foreshadow abolitionist tactics of the next decade and actually provoke the same response in Congress — objections that the petitions "impeached the character of certain of the Southern States" and should therefore be tabled. See "The Indian Question," an article dated New York, 25 Nov. 1829, signed by nineteen men, including the future abolitionist Arthur Tappan, and rpt. in *Massachusetts Journal* 4 Jan. 1830, p. 1; also "The Indians" in the same issue, p. 2, which announces that women in Philadelphia, New York, and Hartford "are forming associations to do something for the relief of the poor Indians." On 11 Jan. 1830, p. 2, under the column "Congress of the U.S.," an article with the subheading "Indians" reports that a petition by citizens of New York State, praying for "protection of the Indians against injustice and oppression," was tabled after Georgia's senators objected to it. For the abolitionist parallel, see Russel B. Nye, *Fettered Freedom: Civil Liberties and the Slavery Controversy, 1830–1860* (1963; Urbana: U of Illinois P, 1972) chap. 2.

53   "The Cherokees," *Massachusetts Daily Journal*, 27 June 1829, p. 2; "The Indians," *Massachusetts Journal* 6 Aug. 1829, p. 2; untitled editorial, *Massachusetts Daily Journal* 8 Sept. 1829, p. 2. For details on the New York Indian board founded by Thomas L. McKenney, see Satz, *American Indian Policy* 15–17.

54   J[oh]n Ross to DLC, 11 Feb. 1831, Lydia Maria Child Scrapbook, Schlesinger Library. For an example of David's continued militancy, see his editorial comment on the women's appeal for "relief of the poor Indians": "We do not . . . much approve of 'appealing to the *gallantry*' of the Georgians, Alabamans, &c. We would address only their *justice*. We do hope the Indians will take the best *legal advice*, and employ the ablest counsel, say HENRY CLAY, DANIEL WEBSTER and WILLIAM WIRT, and bring their case before the Supreme Court of the United States." He also suggests that supporters "subscribe money, and send to a suitable agent to defray the expenses of bringing the case" to the Supreme Court. "The Indians," *Massachusetts Journal* 4 Jan. 1830, p. 2. The *Journal* and its successor, the *Massachusetts Journal and Tribune* covered the Cherokee removal controversy very regularly throughout 1830 and until approximately July 1831.

55   See Howe, *Political Culture of the American Whigs* 40–42; Satz, *American Indian Policy* chap. 1; U.S. 21st Congress, 1st Session, *Speeches on the Passage of the Bill for the Removal of the Indians, Delivered in the Congress of the United States, April and May, 1830* [ed. Jeremiah Evarts] (Boston: Perkins and Marvin, 1830); and Dippie, *Vanishing American* 65–71. Also Remini, *Legacy of Andrew Jackson* 81; as Remini points out: "Although the Whigs pummeled the Democrats for their unconscionable theft of Indian property and inhuman disregard of Indian life and safety, nevertheless they pursued Jackson's identical policy when they themselves came into office. . . ."

56   After Jackson refused to enforce the Supreme Court's decision in favor of the Cherokees in *Worcester* v.

Georgia, most white supporters, including Worcester himself, advised the Cherokees to accept removal while they could still obtain favorable terms. A small faction of Cherokees that included *Phoenix* editor Elias Boudinot, took this advice and negotiated a treaty with the U.S. government in 1835, which the rest of the tribe rejected as fraudulent. Despite the desertion of their white allies, the vast majority of the Cherokees, led by Chief John Ross, resisted removal until they were forcibly ejected from Georgia, and succeeded in delaying it until the presidency of Jackson's Democratic successor Martin Van Buren. See McLoughlin, *Cherokees and Missionaries* chap. 12; Rogin, *Fathers and Children* chap. 7; Satz, *American Indian Policy* 99–101; Wilkins, *Cherokee Tragedy* chaps. 11–13; Ehle, *Trail of Tears* chaps. 15–20; and Perdue, *Slavery and the Evolution of Cherokee Society* 63–69.

57 Satz, *American Indian Policy*, and Kerber, "Abolitionist Perception of the Indian," both discuss the participation of abolitionists in the campaign against Cherokee removal, but a more detailed study is still needed of relations between abolitionists and other opponents of Cherokee removal, and of the ways in which the Cherokee removal controversy served as a prelude to the struggle over slavery. Kerber discusses the transition that the Childs, Birney, and Whittier made from the Cherokee campaign to abolition. Tappan's and Garrison's participation is mentioned by Satz, *American Indian Policy* 51. Robert Winston Mardock's *The Reformers and the American Indian* (Columbia: U of Missouri P, 1971) traces the roots of post-Civil War Indian reform to abolition, but it deals only briefly with the opposite movement of Indian reformers into abolition (see pp. 8–9). Prucha discusses the activities of George B. Cheever, a Presbyterian minister who collaborated with Jeremiah Evarts and eventually became a fiery spokesman for abolition, in his Introduction to Evarts's *Cherokee Removal* 19–23. Former President John Quincy Adams's belated opposition to Cherokee removal (which he had favored as a *voluntary* policy earlier in his career) is mentioned by Dippie, *Vanishing American* 65 and analyzed by Satz, *American Indian Policy* 3–6. On Adams's "central role in fostering antislavery within Whiggery," see Howe, *Political Culture of American Whigs* 60–68.

58 For examples of Child's more sympathetic attitude toward Catholic immigrants in the 1840s, see *Letters from New York [First Series]* (1843; Freeport, N.Y.: Books Libraries P, 1970), esp. Letters 14, 28, and 33; see also her story "The Irish Heart" in *Fact and Fiction: A Collection of Stories* (New York: C. S. Francis, 1846) 77–90. Child excludes discussion of religion and of women's rights from both her 1833 *An Appeal in Favor of That Class of Americans Called Africans* and her 1868 *An Appeal for the Indians*.

5 Blighted Prospects: Indian Fiction and Domestic Reality

1 Lydia Maria Child, "The First and Last Book," *The Coronal. A Collection of Miscellaneous Pieces, Written at Various Times* (Boston: Carter and Hendee, 1832) 282–85.

2 Walt Whitman, "Song of Myself," stanza 24, line 1; Herman Melville, *Moby-Dick; or, The Whale* (Evanston, Ill.: Northwestern UP, 1988) chap. 104. On attitudes more typical of women writers, see Ann Douglas Wood, "The 'Scribbling Women' and Fanny Fern: Why Women Wrote," *American Quarterly* 23 (Spring 1971): 3–24; Mary Kelley, *Private Woman, Public Stage: Literary Domesticity in Nineteenth-Century America* (New York: Oxford UP, 1984), esp. chaps. 2, 5, and 8; and Judith Fetterley, *Provisions: A Reader from 19th-Century American Women* (Bloomington: Indiana UP, 1985). In contrast to Child, for example, Catharine Maria Sedgwick wrote: "I have a *perfect horror* at appearing in print" (Kelley 130). Child does not exhibit the discomfort with fame that characterized the "literary domestics" studied by Kelley, nor does she conform to their practice of publishing anonymously or under pseudonyms — by 1829, she was already publishing under her own name. While Fetterley differs from Douglas and Kelley in contending that many nineteenth-century women writers exhibited a high degree of "self-conscious-ness and self-confidence" in their writing, she, too, finds that these women writers "did not see themselves as 'artists' and did not aspire to fill the role of the American genius who would produce a uniquely American literature" (7). Again, Child's avowed ambition for "intellectual greatness" offers a striking contrast.

3   "The Rival Brothers" appeared in *The Atlantic Souvenir* for 1827. "The Recluse of the Lake," "The Adventures of a Rain-Drop," "The Lone Indian," "Beauty," and "Caius Marius" appeared in *The Token* for 1828; "The Indian Wife" appeared in both *The Legendary* (1828) and the *Massachusetts Journal*, 28 June 1828, pp. 1–2; "Address to the Valentine" and "The Young West Indian" appeared in *The Atlantic Souvenir* (1828); "Stanzas Occasioned by hearing a Little Boy . . . mocking the Bell . . ." and "A New Year's Offering" appeared in *The Atlantic Souvenir* (1829); and "Chocorua's Curse" appeared in *The Token* for 1830. "To the Fringed Gentian" appeared in the *Miscellany* (where it had preceded Bryant's more famous stanzas by that title). "Harriet Bruce," "The Bold and Beautiful Convict," and "Stand from Under" appeared in the *Massachusetts Weekly Journal*, 27 May, p. 3, 1 Apr., p. 2, and 8 Aug. 1829, p. 4. "La Rosiere" and "The Sagacious Papa" appeared in the *Massachusetts Journal and Tribune*, 17 Apr., p. 3, and 4 Sept. 1830, p. 1. "Romance" appeared in the *Massachusetts Journal*, 20 Nov. 1828, p. 1.

4   *The Legendary*, like *The Token*, published by Samuel Goodrich, was not marketed as a Christmas and New Year's gift book. Only two volumes of it appeared. "The Church in the Wilderness" led off vol. 1. For a brief account of its history and contributors, see Ralph Thompson, *American Literary Annuals & Gift Books, 1825–1865* (New York: H. W. Wilson, 1936) 93–94.

5   For literary and historical studies focusing on these debates, see Roy Harvey Pearce, *The Savages of America: A Study of the Indian and the Idea of Civilization*, rev. ed. (Baltimore: Johns Hopkins UP, 1965) chaps. 6–7; Louise K. Barnett, *The Ignoble Savage: American Literary Racism, 1790–1890* (Westport, Conn.: Greenwood P, 1975) chaps. 1 and 3; Brian Dippie, *The Vanishing American: White Attitudes and U.S. Indian Policy* (Middletown, Conn.: Wesleyan UP, 1982) chaps. 2–5; Sherry Sullivan, "The Literary Debate over 'the Indian' in the Nineteenth Century," *American Indian Culture and Research Journal* 9 (1985): 13–31; and Lucy Maddox, *Removals: Nineteenth-Century American Literature and the Politics of Indian Affairs* (New York: Oxford UP, 1991), esp. chap. 1.

6   William Leete Stone, "A Romance of the Border," *Atlantic Souvenir* for 1830: 187–229. Quotation on 228.

7   [William J. Snelling], "Te Zahpahtah. A Sketch from Indian History," *The Token* for 1831: 143–51. For further discussion of this theme, see Barnett, *The Ignoble Savage* 87–89; and Dippie, *Vanishing American* chaps. 2–3.

8   "The Lone Indian" (1827) was first published in the inaugural issue of Samuel Goodrich's gift book, *The Token*, for 1828. Like its predecessor *The Atlantic Souvenir*, *The Token* was advertised as a New Year's gift book for the year following its actual publication date. Thus, *The Token* for 1828 was actually published in Oct. 1827, according to its copyright. Subsequent numbers were published as early as Aug., reviewed by Sept. or Oct., and generally available for sale by Oct. of the year preceding the date given for each volume. This confusing discrepancy should be kept in mind wherever the publication date seems to conflict with the volume date.

9   James Fenimore Cooper, *The Last of the Mohicans* (1826; New York: Signet, 1962) 58, 146. The earlier passage specifically cites Mohawks and Oneidas.

10 The text of "The Lone Indian" will be drawn from Lydia Maria Child, *HOBOMOK and Other Writings on Indians*, ed. Carolyn L. Karcher (New Brunswick, N.J.: Rutgers UP, 1986) 154–60. Quotation on 158. Further page references to this story are given parenthetically in the text.

11 I am borrowing the concept of the "language zone" from Mikhail Bakhtin, *The Dialogic Imagination: Four Essays*, ed. Michael Holquist, trans. Caryl Emerson and Michael Holquist (Austin: U of Texas P, 1981). Ian Marshall's article "Heteroglossia in Lydia Maria Child's *Hobomok*," *Legacy* 10 (1993): 1–16, which I saw in manuscript, first suggested to me the idea of applying Bakhtinian theory to Child's fiction. Child's technique invites comparison with Cooper's. Although Cooper lets his evil Huron chief Magua eloquently arraign whites for their greed and hypocrisy, for example, he neutralizes Magua's voice both through Hawk-eye and through the narrator, who present alternative points of view.

12 [Lydia Maria Child], *The First Settlers of New-England: or, Conquest of the Pequods, Narragansets and Pokanokets: As Related by a Mother to Her Children, and Designed for the Instruction of Youth*. By a Lady of Massachusetts (Boston: Munroe and Francis, [1829]) 64.

13 Tecumseh's speech is partially reprinted in Paul Lauter, ed., *The Heath Anthology of American Literature*, 2 vols. (Lexington, Mass.: D. C. Heath, 1990) 1: 469.

14 I. M'Lellan, "The Hymn of the Cherokee Indian," *Atlantic Souvenir* for 1831: 265.

15 In her fine study of the fur trade in English Canada, Sylvia Van Kirk points out that this trade was unique in being "based on a commodity exchange" between Indians and whites that created "mutual dependency," "significant cultural exchange," and "widespread intermarriage between the traders and Indian women" (3–4). She shows that when English fur trading companies took over the French empire, their London owners initially tried to impose a different pattern of race relations, more consistent with the English model elsewhere, condemning intermarriage and fraternization with Indians. These French patterns persisted among the traders themselves, however (whose ranks included many French Canadians), eventually forcing the companies to accept such Indian- and French-influenced customs as intermarriage *à la façon du pays*. See *"Many Tender Ties": Women in Fur-Trade Society, 1670–1870* (1980; Norman: U of Oklahoma P, 1983).

16 "The Church in the Wilderness," by the Author of Hobomok, *The Legendary*, ed. Nathaniel P. Willis, 2 vols. (Boston, 1828) 1: 2. Further page references to the story are given parenthetically in the text.

17 The "Biographical Memoir of Father Rasles," *Collections of the Massachusetts Historical Society*, 2nd ser. 8 (1819): 250–67, reprints letters by the French, Indian, and British parties to the hostilities, as well as extracts from Rale's papers. Rale's papers had been captured in a British raid on Norridgewock in 1721 and later deposited in the Harvard College Library, along with the dictionary of the Abenaki language that Rale had been compiling for some thirty years. See also Convers Francis, "Life of Sebastian Rale, Missionary to the Indians," in *The Library of American Biography*, ed. Jared Sparks, vol. 17, *Lives of John Ribault, Sebastian Rale, and William Palfrey* (Boston: Little, Brown, 1845) 159–333; J. W. Hanson, *History of the Old Towns Norridgewock and Canaan, Comprising Norridgewock, Canaan, Starks, Skowhegan, and Bloomfield, from Their Early Settlement to the Year 1849; Including a Sketch of the Abnakis Indians* (Boston: J. W. Hanson, 1849); and William Allen, *The History of Norridgewock* (Norridgewock, Me.: Edward J. Peet, 1849). For an excellent modern analysis that weighs the merits of the French and English versions and of Indian oral tradition, see Fannie Hardy Eckstorm, "The Attack on Norridgewock, 1724" *New England Quarterly* 7 (Sept. 1934): 541–78. Child cites "the old inhabitants of Norridgewock" in "The Adventures of a Bell," *Juvenile Miscellany* 2 (March 1827): 30.

18 I am grateful to Richard Slotkin for pointing out to me that the Norridgewock massacre was being "heavily mythologized" at this moment as "part of the literary movement that displaced current race and Indian issues into the distant past, and resolved them through the workings of romance."

19 See Paula Gunn Allen, *The Sacred Hoop: Recovering the Feminine in American Indian Traditions* (Boston: Beacon P, 1986) 196–200, 202; and Sarah M. Evans, *Born for Liberty: A History of Women in America* (New York: Free P, 1989) 17. Evans points out that the fluidity of Indian gender roles "allowed a few women quite literally to live the lives of men. In some societies manly hearted women were noticed very young and raised with extreme favoritism and license" (17). The Sioux writer Zitkala-Sa describes such a woman in her story "The Warrior's Daughter" (1902), *American Indian Stories* (1921; Lincoln: U of Nebraska P, 1985) 137–53. Like Saupoolah, the heroine of Zitkala-Sa's story is heterosexual. Child's description of Saupoolah suggests that she may have observed transsexual or "manly hearted" women among the Abenaki, though probably without perceiving them as "lesbian." In her *History of the Condition of Women*, she presents a conventional European misinterpretation of transsexual men among the Hohay (probably drawn from a travel account): "men who dress in a female garb, and perform all manner of female avocations . . . are called *Winktahs*, and treated with the utmost contempt." See the excerpt reprinted in *HOBOMOK and Other Writings on Indians* 173.

20 Child cites oral tradition in "The Adventures of a Bell," where she reports: "Some said the priest killed himself and the boy, when he found it was impossible to escape from the English; but obscurity rests on this part of the story," *JM* 2 (Mar. 1827): 28. Convers Francis also refers to a "tradition . . . sometimes mentioned in that neighborhood [Norridgewock], that when the English troops reached Rale's village, the Indians and their priest were all in their church, engaged in some religious service"; but he claims

that he has never found "the slightest historical evidence for such a story." See his "Life of Sebastian Rale" 321–22. The same tradition is invoked by the anonymous author of "Narantsauk" in the *Atlantic Souvenir* for 1829, discussed below. According to Eckstorm, "Attack on Norridgewock" 543–45, a variant of this tradition was widespread among the Abenakis and Penobscots.

21   Eckstorm, "The Attack on Norridgewock" 576.

22   *The Legendary* was deposited for copyright on 15 May 1828 and was reviewed in the *Ladies' Magazine* in June (1: 285–87). On *Carabasset*, see Leola Bowie Chaplin, *The Life and Works of Nathaniel Deering (1791–1881). With the Text of Deering's Plays "Carabasset" and "The Clairvoyants"* (Orono: UP of Maine, 1934); chap. 3 provides biographical details. Forrest issued his call in New York *Critic*, 22 Nov. 1828 (Chaplin 79). The contest was won by John A. Stone's *Metamora* (1829). *Carabasset* was not published until 1830. Child had addressed a witty poem to Deering: "Whoever weds the young lawyer at C—— / Will surely have prospects most cheering; / For what must his person and intellect be / When even his name is N. Deering" (Chaplin 64). The message she sent to "N. Deering" in a letter to her sister Mary no doubt alludes to the same play on his name; see LMC to Mary Francis Preston, 6 Jan. 1827, *SL* 8. According to biographers, Child met Deering shortly after he arrived in Canaan, Maine, near Norridgewock, in 1822. By then, however, Child was already living with Convers in Watertown. He may be another candidate for the "Magnus Apollo" who courted her during her stint of schoolteaching in Gardiner the previous year. The *Atlantic Souvenir* for 1829 appeared on the market in time to be reviewed by Nov. 1828.

23   John Greenleaf Whittier, "Mogg Megone," *Whittier's Poetical Works*, 7 vols. (Boston: Houghton Mifflin, 1888), vol. 4, *Personal Poems: Occasional Poems: The Tent on the Beach* 325–52. A year after writing the poem Whittier admitted ruefully: "It is not, I fear, calculated to do good." For the rest of his life he tried to suppress it. Only at his publisher's insistence did he agree to include "Mogg Megone" in his collected writings, where he relegated it to an appendix. See John B. Pickard, ed., *The Letters of John Greenleaf Whittier*, 3 vols. (Cambridge, Mass.: Belknap P of Harvard UP, 1975) 1: 198, 258; 2: 325–28.

24   "Narantsauk," *Atlantic Souvenir* for 1829: 32–60. According to Thompson, *American Literary Annuals* 55, the records of Carey and Lea, publishers of the *Atlantic Souvenir*, assign "Narantsauk" to "an author designated only as 'Sedgwick's friend.'" Whether the Sedgwick in question is Catharine Maria or her brother Theodore, who also wrote fiction, is unclear. The story seems more characteristic of women's Indian fiction than of men's.

25   [Sarah Josepha Hale], review of *The Atlantic Souvenir* for 1829, *Ladies' Magazine* 1 (Nov. 1828): 521.

26   "Narantsauk" 43–44, 59–60.

27   "The Indian Wife," *Coronal* 165. I shall be citing *The Coronal*, rather than *The Legendary*, as the text of "The Indian Wife," since it is more accessible.

28   Evans, *Born for Liberty* 14–15. Evans is summarizing the conclusions of Van Kirk's *"Many Tender Ties,"* cited in n. 15 above. Van Kirk's chapters on mixed-blood wives are also relevant to "The Indian Wife."

29   "A Legend of the Falls of St. Anthony," *HOBOMOK and Other Writings on Indians*, ed. Karcher, 207, 212. Further page references are to this edition and are given parenthetically in the text.

30   See James Everett Seaver, *A Narrative of the Life of Mary Jemison* (1824; New York: Garland, 1977). See also James Axtell, *The European and the Indian: Essays in the Ethnohistory of Colonial North America* (New York: Oxford UP, 1981), esp. the essay "The White Indians of Colonial America," 168–206. On the popularity of Jemison's narrative, see Annette Kolodny, *The Land Before Her: Fantasy and Experience of the American Frontiers, 1630–1860* (Chapel Hill: U of North Carolina P, 1984) chap. 4; and her "Among the Indians: The Uses of Captivity," *New York Times Book Review* 31 Jan. 1993, pp. 1, 26–29.

31   [Sarah Josepha Hale], review of *The Legendary*, *Ladies' Magazine* 1 (June 1828): 286.

32   "The Indian Bride," *Atlantic Souvenir* for 1832: 117–39. Quotations on 131–32.

33   Child, "An Appeal for the Indians," *HOBOMOK and Other Writings*, ed. Karcher, 227.

34   Unsigned review of Cooper's *The Wept of Wish-ton-Wish*, *Massachusetts Weekly Journal* 21 Nov. 1829, p. 4. The only direct acknowledgment of Child's participation in editing the paper is David's announcement in "Prospectus of a New Plan of the Massachusetts Journal" that the author of "Hints to People of

Moderate Fortune" will furnish "a series of original tales" illustrating those hints, "besides the constant assistance upon which the Editor can depend, from the same source" (30 Jan. 1830, p. 2). Several of the unsigned pieces in the column "For the *Massachusetts Journal*" reappear in *The Coronal*, however, and the "Hints to People of Moderate Fortune" were later included as an appendix to *The Frugal Housewife*. Since selections borrowed from other sources are acknowledged as such, it seems safe to assume that unsigned literary pieces are by Child.

35 See Garrison's comments on "Comparative Strength" and "Hints," quoted in chap. 8 below.

36 [Lydia Maria Child], "Comparative Strength of Male and Female Intellect," *Massachusetts Weekly Journal* 4 Mar. 1829, p. 2. Garrison reprinted this article in the *Genius of Universal Emancipation* 30 Oct. 1829, pp. 60–61. In his editorial preface to it he identified the author as "unquestionably Mrs. Child," and he mentioned that he had cut it out "for insertion in the Journal of the Times" (the newspaper he was then editing), but not finding space for it at the time, he had "hoarded it up ever since." See chap. 8 for further details on Garrison's early recognition of Child's talents.

37 See LMC to Parke Godwin, 20 Jan. 1856, *SL* 275, in which Child refers to the hold that Swedenborg's doctrine of correspondences exerted on her youthful imagination: "I then '*experienced religion*'; and for a long time lived in a mansion of glories."

38 "Letter from a Lady, concerning Miss Wright," *Massachusetts Weekly Journal* 14 Aug. 1829, p. 3. For an account of Wright's lecture tour and a brief summary of her ideas, see Celia Morris Eckhardt's superb biography, *Fanny Wright: Rebel in America* (Cambridge, Mass.: Harvard UP, 1984) chap. 7. For an indication of what Child may have heard Wright say in her Boston lecture, see Frances Wright D'Arusmont, *Life, Letters and Lectures, 1834/1844* (New York: Arno P, 1972). From these published lectures it is difficult to see why Wright was accused of preaching free love. In fact, Child would end up presenting very similar ideas, often unconsciously echoing Wright's language, in her later writings about women's rights and even about religion.

39 LMC to Ellis Loring, 16 June 1843, *CC* 17/499.

40 Eckhardt, *Fanny Wright* chaps. 8–9, provides a moving account of Wright's forced retreat and its psychological costs.

41 [Lydia Maria Child], "Annals of a Village. Marian Russell," and "Annals of the Village. The Sudden Match," *Massachusetts Weekly Journal* 7 Jan. 1829, p. 4, and 15 Apr. 1829, p. 2; the other three selections, all under the heading "For the Massachusetts Journal," are pasted into a scrapbook preserved in the Schlesinger Library. On the "narrative of community," see Sandra A. Zagarell, "The Narrative of Community: The Identification of a Genre," *Signs: Journal of Women in Culture and Society* 13 (1988): 498–527.

42 See Lawrence Shaw Mayo, "The History of the Legend of Chocorua," *New England Quarterly* 19 (Mar. 1946): 302–14. I am grateful to Robert McGrath for bringing this article to my attention.

43 "Chocorua's Curse" (1829), *HOBOMOK and Other Writings*, ed. Karcher, 165–67. Further page references to this edition are given parenthetically in the text.

44 [Timothy Flint], "The Indian Fighter," by the Author of 'Francis Berrian,' *Token* for 1830: 37–58. Quotation on 57–58.

45 LMC to Lydia Bigelow Child, 14 Jan. 1829, *SL* 12–14.

46 LMC to Carey and Lea, [before 25 July 1829?], *SL* 14–15.

47 In 1831 Carter and Hendee had also just bought the *Juvenile Miscellany* from Putnam and Hunt.

6 The Frugal Housewife: *Financial Worries and Domestic Advice*

1 LMC to Lydia Bigelow Child, [Feb.? 1830], *SL* 16–17.

2 Meltzer and Holland, editorial headnote, *SL* 17; Deborah Pickman Clifford, *Crusader for Freedom: A Life of Lydia Maria Child* (Boston: Beacon P, 1992) 81. The exact duration of his stay in prison is not known, but David was back home by Aug. 1830. On the continuing crisis of the *Massachusetts Journal*, see LMC to Henry A. S. Dearborn [May 1829], *CC* 1/37; also the *Massachusetts Journal* file at the

Massachusetts Historical Society, which indicates another round of borrowing and a retrenchment of operations in Nov. 1829.

3   LMC to Lydia Bigelow Child, 14 Jan. [1829] and [Feb.? 1830], *SL* 12–14, 16–17. Lydia Maria Child, *The Frugal Housewife* (Boston: Marsh and Capen, and Carter and Hendee, 1829). As noted on the back of the title page, the first edition was deposited for copyright on 12 Nov. 1829. Page references in the text will be to the more accessible 16th ed. (Boston: Carter and Hendee, 1835). The phrase "glass beads" is from Child's sketch "The First and Last Book," *The Coronal. A Collection of Miscellaneous Pieces, Written at Various Times* (Boston: Carter and Hendee, 1832) 284. For estimates of Child's profits on the book, see Patricia G. Holland, "Lydia Maria Child as a Nineteenth-Century Professional Author," *Studies in the American Renaissance* (1981): 159; and Clifford, *Crusader for Freedom* 81.

4   For studies of the impact that the industrial revolution had on European women's work, see Louise A. Tilly and Joan W. Scott, *Women, Work, and Family* (New York: Holt, 1978), esp. chaps. 4 and 6; Heidi Hartmann, "Capitalism, Patriarchy, and Job Segregation by Sex," *The SIGNS Reader: Women, Gender & Scholarship*, ed. Elizabeth Abel and Emily K. Abel (Chicago: U of Chicago P, 1983) 193–226, esp. 203–10; Mary Lynn McDougall, "Working-Class Women During the Industrial Revolution, 1780–1914," and Theresa M. McBride, "The Long Road Home: Women's Work and Industrialization," both in *Becoming Visible: Women in European History*, ed. Renate Bridenthal and Claudia Koonz (Boston: Houghton Mifflin, 1977) 255–79, 280–95. For a detailed study of American working women, see Alice Kessler-Harris, *Out to Work: A History of Wage-Earning Women in the United States* (New York: Oxford UP, 1982). Chap. 3 on "Industrial Wage Earners and the Domestic Ideology" is particularly relevant. Kessler-Harris specifies that by the mid-nineteenth century "probably less than 5 percent of the total of married [American] women worked outside their own homes for wages" and that only about "2.25 percent of all females over ten years old worked in industry" (46–47).

5   For Child's own analysis of her place in the American class structure, see LMC to Sarah Shaw, 31 July and 25 Aug. 1877, *SL* 542–44. The phrase "respectable mechanics" is from Kessler-Harris, *Out to Work* 46, though Child often uses it. Historians have been engaged in a lively debate over whether the ideology of domesticity and the redefinition of middle-class women's roles represented a gain or a loss in status and power. For different viewpoints on this question, see Gerda Lerner, "The Lady and the Mill Girl: Changes in the Status of Women in the Age of Jackson," *Midcontinent American Studies Journal* 10 (Spring 1969): 5–15; Ann Douglas, *The Feminization of American Culture* (New York: Knopf, 1977); Kathryn Kish Sklar, *Catharine Beecher: A Study in American Domesticity* (New Haven, Conn.: Yale UP, 1973); and Nancy Cott, *The Bonds of Womanhood: "Woman's Sphere" in New England, 1780–1835* (New Haven, Conn.: Yale UP, 1977).

6   Lydia Maria Child, *The Mother's Book* (Boston: Carter, Hendee and Babcock, 1831) vii.

7   [Lydia Maria Child], "Domestic Duties," *Massachusetts Weekly Journal* 17 Dec. 1828, p. 3.

8   Mrs. William [Frances] Parkes, *Domestic Duties; or, Instructions to Young Married Ladies, on the Management of Their Households and the Regulation of Their Conduct in the Various Relations and Duties of Married Life* (1825; New York: Harper, 1846) 201–9. For a complete list of the cookbooks available in the United States in the 1820s, see Eleanor Lowenstein, *Bibliography of American Cookery Books, 1742–1860* (Worcester, Mass.: American Antiquarian Society, 1972).

9   [Eliza Leslie], *Miss Leslie's Seventy-Five Receipts for Pastry, Cakes and Sweetmeats* (Boston: Munroe and Francis, 1827). The quotation is from the preface. Although the title page lists it as the 20th ed., the National Union Catalogue does not cite any earlier edition. Munroe and Francis published Child's *The First Settlers of New England* in early 1829.

10 From the 8th ed., 1832, Child retitled her book *The American Frugal Housewife* to avoid confusing it with its English competitor: Susannah Carter's *The Frugal Housewife, or, Complete Woman Cook; wherein the Art of Dressing All Sorts of Viands is explained in upwards of Five Hundred Approved Receipts . . . To which is added an Appendix containing Several New Receipts Adapted to the American Mode of Cooking* (1772; New York: G. and R. Waite, 1803). These examples come from the Alphabetical Index that serves as a table of contents. For another example of a book that belies its title, see *A New System of Practical Domestic*

Economy; Founded on Modern Discoveries, and the Private Communications of Persons of Experience . . . To Which Are Now First Added, Estimates of Household Expenses, Founded on Economical Principles, and Adapted to Families of Every Description, 3rd ed. (London: Henry Colbern, 1823). The chapter on "Principal Apartments" covers such matters as "Diamonds, &c. — Trinkets — Pearls . . . Fine Arts — Sculpture — . . .Gems — Antiques," and an entire chapter is devoted to the "Servants'-Hall."

11   Catharine E. Beecher, *Treatise on Domestic Economy, for the Use of Young Ladies at Home, and at School* (1841; rev. ed., New York: Harper and Brothers, 1845) devotes a whole chapter to "Difficulties Peculiar to American Women," heading the list (40) with the dwindling number of those "willing to go to domestic service." "The anxieties, vexations, perplexities, and even hard labor, which come upon American women, from this state of domestic service, are endless," she claims (41). Evidently the term "American women" did not apply to domestics themselves. William A. Alcott, *The Young House-keeper or Thoughts on Food and Cookery* (Boston: George W. Light, 1838), anticipates Beecher in recommending that housekeeping should be treated as a "science" (18). He advocates that a mother "at least direct" housework, even "if she does not perform all the labor with her own hands," and he expresses the wish that "every mother could perform all the duties of her family, without that aid which in fashionable life is now quite common, and which seems to involve the idea of a superior and an inferior class of citizens" (27–28). Mostly a treatise on the advantages of a vegetarian diet, the book includes only one chapter of "Recipes for Plain Cooking," two of which are lifted unacknowledged from *The Frugal Housewife* (Alcott 394–95; Child 76–78). See also William A. Alcott, *The Young Wife, or Duties of Woman in the Marriage Relation* (Boston: George W. Light, 1837), which cites *The Frugal Housewife* as a "valuable" aid to brides "whose education has been so defective, as to leave [them] ignorant on the subject of house-keeping" (190).

12   LMC to Lydia Bigelow Child, 14 Jan. [1829], *SL* 13.

13   See Beecher, *Treatise on Domestic Economy* 6, 157; and Alcott, *The Young House-keeper* chap. 1.

14   The original title used the word "People" rather than "Persons." William Lloyd Garrison was among those who may have suggested the idea of appending the "Hints" to *The Frugal Housewife* when he urged Child to reissue her "Hints" in book form. See his article "Mrs. Child," *Genius of Universal Emancipation*, 20 Nov. 1829, p. 85, quoted in chap. 8.

15   Clifford, *Crusader for Freedom* 24.

16   *National Union Catalogue.* The *NUC* lists the 1855 edition as the 33rd and does not count the two subsequent printings as increasing the number of editions to 35.

17   Caroline Healey Dall, "Lydia Maria Child and Mary Russell Mitford," *Unitarian Review* 19 (June 1883): 525.

18   Quotations are from the first edition of *The Frugal Housewife* 38, 58. Child deleted the word "cheap" from the headings of subsequent editions.

19   See, for example, Parkes, *Domestic Duties* (1846): 203–4: "Rice, or indeed any kind of seed, should not be bought in large quantities, because an insect is apt to breed in it. . . ."

20   See, for example, LMC to Louisa and Anna Loring, Sarah Maria Preston Parsons, and Marianne Silsbee, 24 Sept., 6 Nov., 29 Dec., and undated, 1850, and 8 Aug. 1852, *CC* 28/792, 795, 798, 800, and 29/827, quoted in chap. 15 below. These letters refer, for example, to baking bread, churning butter, making straw beds, patching and darning carpets, "seeing that nothing moulds, ferments, or freezes." Similar complaints can be found in Child's letters of the 1860s and 1870s. See LMC to Harriet Sewall, 19 June 1871, *CC* 75/1998.

21   [Sarah Josepha Hale], review of "*The Frugal Housewife. By the Author of Hobomok*," *Ladies' Magazine* 3 (Jan. 1830): 42–43. Quotations that follow are from this review.

22   For a brief biographical sketch of Hale, see Nancy Woloch, "Sarah Hale and the *Ladies Magazine*," *Women and the American Experience* (New York: Knopf, 1984) 97–112. Hale's reviews of Child's writings had hitherto been warmly supportive in every respect.

23   Nathaniel Parker Willis, review of *The Frugal Housewife*, "Editor's Table," *American Monthly Magazine* 1 (Jan. 1830): 721–22. Quotations that follow are from this review.

24 Willis's quotations (slightly inaccurate, though not in ways that distort the text) come from pp. 3, 46, 58, 70, and 72 of the 1829 ed.

25 *The Frugal Housewife* 21; Hale, review appears in *Ladies' Magazine* 3: 43.

26 [Sarah Josepha Hale], review of *The Frugal Housewife*, 2nd ed., *Ladies' Magazine* 3 (Apr. 1830): 189.

27 Nathaniel Parker Willis, "A Morning in the Library," *American Monthly Magazine* 1 (Feb. 1830): 792.

28 Nathaniel Parker Willis, "Editor's Table," *American Monthly Magazine* 1 (Feb. 1830): 803.

29 LMC to DLC, 8 Aug. 1830, *SL* 18.

30 Catharine Maria Sedgwick to LMC, 12 June 1830, *CC* 2/43.

31 LMC to Lydia Bigelow Child and DLC, [Feb.? 1830] and 8 Aug. [1830], *SL* 17, 18.

32 Clifford, *Crusader for Freedom* 81; Samuel Eliot Morison, *Harrison Gray Otis: The Urbane Federalist* (Boston: Houghton Mifflin, 1969) 492–96; Caroline Healey Dall, *Alongside* (Boston: Thomas Todd, 1900) 7. Child is quoted as having described her house on Harvard Street as a "proper little martin box" in Anna D. Hallowell, "Lydia Maria Child," *Medford Historical Register* 3 (July 1900): 103.

33 LMC to DLC, 8 Aug. [1830], *SL* 18–19; Clifford, *Crusader for Freedom* 82.

34 DLC to LMC, 29 Sept. and 3 Oct. 1830, *CC* 2/45.

35 LMC to Lydia Bigelow Child, 2 Aug. 1831, *SL* 19.

36 LMC to Lydia Bigelow Child (mother), 23 June 1831, *CC* 2/48.

37 LMC to Lydia Bigelow Child (mother), 23 June 1831, *CC* 2/48. Clifford finds the "candor" of Child's letter to David's mother "suspicious" and suggests the possibility that David may have been impotent (*Crusader for Freedom* 84). My own impression is that Child would not have written so openly to her mother-in-law about wanting children if David had been impotent at this stage. As Clifford points out, however, many indications do point to his failure to satisfy Child sexually, whether or not this failure was related to the couple's infertility.

38 Lydia Maria Child, *The Mother's Book* (1831; New York: C. S. Francis, 1844) v. All further page references, given parenthetically in the text, are to this edition. I have collated it with the 1831 edition and found it almost identical, with several significant exceptions noted below.

39 Quotations are from the table of contents of *The Mother's Book*. *The Mother's Book* is the first book I have found by an American author to cover all aspects of childrearing. The anonymous *Thoughts on Domestic Education, the Result of Experience. By a Mother* (Boston: Carter and Hendee, 1829) is a reprint edition of an English book concerned with the formal education at home of older children; the course of study it recommends is clearly designed for upper-class English children. The American works on education that preceded *The Mother's Book* include Bronson Alcott's anonymously published "Maternal Instruction — Hints to Parents," *American Journal of Education* 4 (Jan. 1829): 53–58, actually a review of an English book "[i]n the spirit of Pestalozzi's method," and his pamphlet on infant schools, *Observations on the Principles and Methods of Infant Instruction*, 1830, rpt. Walter Harding, ed., *Essays on Education* (Gainesville, Fla.: Scholars Facsimiles, 1960); also Jacob Abbott's *The Little Philosopher, or the Infant School at Home* (Boston: Carter and Hendee, 1830). In many respects the educational dialogues in Child's *Evenings in New England* and the *Juvenile Miscellany* anticipate these writers' approaches. Sarah Elbert, *A Hunger for Home: Louisa May Alcott's Place in American Culture* (New Brunswick, N.J.: Rutgers UP, 1987) chap. 2, credits *The Mother's Book* with having influenced the Alcotts' childrearing methods. She also points out that Bronson Alcott and Child both derived their ideas from Pestalozzi.

40 John S. C. Abbott's *The Mother at Home; or, The Principles of Maternal Duty Familiarly Illustrated* and *The Child at Home; or the Principles of Filial Duty Familiarly Illustrated* were both published by the American Tract Society (New York, 1833). The latter quotes in full Child's autobiographical story in the *Juvenile Miscellany*, "My Mother's Grave," though without mentioning her name (*JM* 3 [Jan. 1828] 310–13; *The Child at Home* 22–25). Many passages in Lydia Huntley Sigourney's *Letters to Mothers* (New York: Harper and Brothers, 1839) also suggest that she took hints from *The Mother's Book* even while defining a somewhat different position on certain issues; see, for example, pp. 35, 58–59, and 151ff. on kindness to animals, courtesy toward domestics, and religious education. *The Mother's Book* also predates such periodicals as *Mother's Magazine*, founded in 1833; *Mother's Monthly Journal*, 1836; and *The Mother's*

Assistant and Young Lady's Friend, 1841. For secondary studies of nineteenth-century American child-rearing literature, see Anne L. Kuhn, *The Mother's Role in Childhood Education: New England Concepts, 1830–1860* (New Haven, Conn.: Yale UP, 1947); Mary Ryan, *Cradle of the Middle Class: The Family in Oneida County, New York, 1790–1865* (New York: Cambridge UP, 1981), chap. 2, and *The Empire of the Mother: American Writing about Domesticity, 1830–1860* (New York: Haworth P, 1982). On earlier childrearing practices, see Philip J. Greven, *The Protestant Temperament: Patterns of Child-Rearing, Religious Experience, and the Self in Early America* (New York: Knopf, 1977). Greven's collection, *Child-Rearing Concepts, 1628–1861: Historical Sources* (Itasca, Ill.: F. E. Peacock, 1973), includes selections from Abbott but neglects women writers. Also relevant are Kathryn Kish Sklar, *Catharine Beecher: A Study in American Domesticity* (New Haven, Conn.: Yale UP, 1973) chap. 11; and Elbert, *A Hunger for Home* chap. 2.

41   Quotations in this paragraph are from the "Concluding Chapter" Child added to the 1844 ed. (New York: C. S. Francis, 1844) 170.

42   Deposited for copyright on 25 Dec. 1830, *The Little Girl's Own Book* (Carter, Hendee and Babcock, 1831) was briefly mentioned among the "Literary Notices" in the Jan. 1831 issue of the *Ladies' Magazine.* The National Union Catalogue lists a total of sixteen editions, about half published under the title *The Girl's Own Book.* Five are published in London and adapted by other editors for English audiences. The last of these is dated 1875.

43   Eliza Leslie, *The Girl's Book of Diversions; or, Occupation for Play Hours,* 3rd ed. (London: T. Tegg, 1837). I was unable to procure a copy of the original edition. Instead of a preface enunciating its philosophy, Leslie's book opens with a dialogue between a mother and her daughters about what kinds of games the book contains. Like Child, Leslie included stories as well as games, sports, and riddles. Leslie's stories, borrowed from other authors, are much more conventional than Child's, however. For example, Child's "Mary Howard" (257–70) concerns an orphan captured and brought up by savages in New Zealand; like so many of Child's stories in the *Juvenile Miscellany,* discussed in chap. 7 below, it inculcates tolerance toward other peoples.

44   "To the Public," *Massachusetts Journal & Tribune* 14 Jan. 1832, p. 3. Child also specifies that she did not see Leslie's book in print until she herself was preparing the third edition of *The Little Girl's Own Book.*

45   The *American Journal of Education* reviewed the first and third numbers of the *Juvenile Miscellany* in Oct. 1826 (1: 640) and Mar. 1827 (2: 191), respectively, noticed it briefly along with Child's *Juvenile Souvenir* in Dec. 1827 (2: 750), and reviewed her *Emily Parker; or Impulse, not Principle. Intended for Young Persons* in Sept. 1827 (2: 576). Its successor the *American Annals of Education* reviewed *The Mother's Book* in Sept. 1831 (3rd ser. 1: 440–41). "Pestalozzi's Principles and Methods of Instruction," *American Journal of Education* 4 (Mar.–Apr. 1829): 97–107, mentions a text called *The Mother's Book,* used in Pestalozzian schools and intended as "the companion of the nursery, and the agent by which maternal affection should regulate the development of the faculties of her child" (100, 102). The National Union Catalogue does not list any book by Pestalozzi under that title, however. Possibly this was the author's rendition of *Letters of Pestalozzi: on the Education of Infancy. Addressed to Mothers* (Boston: Carter and Hendee, 1830), which in turn was an abridged version of Pestalozzi's *Letters on Early Education. Addressed to J. P. Greaves, Esq.* (London: Sherwood, Gilbert and Piper, 1827). For secondary studies of Pestalozzi's influence on American educators, see Will S. Monroe, *History of the Pestalozzian Movement in the United States* (1907; New York: Arno, 1969); and Thomas A. Barlow, *Pestalozzi and American Education* (Boulder: U of Colorado P, 1977).

46   Compare Pestalozzi, *Letters on Early Education* (Syracuse, N.Y.: C. W. Bardeen, 1898) on how "the attention of the child is . . . excited and fixed by a great variety of external impressions" including the "brilliant colors of a flower, or the pleasing sounds of music" (17–18). Further quotations are from this edition.

47   Sigourney's preface is typical: "You are sitting with your child in your arms. So am I. And I have never been as happy before. Have you? How this new affection seems to spread a soft, fresh green over the soul. Does not the whole heart blossom thick with plants of hope, sparkling with perpetual dew-drops?

What a loss, had we passed through the world without tasting this purest, most exquisite fount of love" (*Letters to Mothers* vii).

48   Sigourney, *Letters to Mothers* 86, 88.

49   Note Child's adaptation of Pestalozzi's Letter 30: "When I recommend to a mother to avoid *wearying* a child by her instructions, I do not wish to encourage the notion that instruction should always take the character of an amusement or even of play. . . . A child must very early in life be taught . . . that exertion is indispensable for the attainment of knowledge. But a child should not be taught to look upon exertion as an unavoidable *evil*," *Letters on Early Education* (1898: 130). Compare also the following passages: "[S]hould you, while tossing a ball, stop and say, 'This ball is *round*; this little tea-table is *square*. Now George knows what *round* and *square* mean. . . . When he has a new toy, he will think to himself whether it is round or square" (Child 11–12); "Show him a certain quality in one thing, and let him find out the same in others. Tell him that the shape of a ball is called round; and if, accordingly, you bring him to point out other objects to which the same character belongs you have employed him more usefully than by the most perfect discourse on rotundity" (Pestalozzi 1898: 149–50).

50   Sigourney, *Letters to Mothers* 33; Abbott devotes two whole chapters of *The Mother at Home* to "Maternal Authority" and the inculcation of obedience (chaps. 2–3).

51   Compare Abbott, *Mother at Home* 62–65, 73; Sigourney, *Letters to Mothers* 56, 62–63. For a perceptive Foucauldian critique of this nineteenth-century style of childrearing, see Richard H. Brodhead, "Sparing the Rod: Discipline and Fiction in Antebellum America," *Representations* 21 (Winter 1988): 67–96. Brodhead does not note the differences of emphasis between *The Mother's Book* and the other childrearing and educational manuals he analyzes, however.

52   On Child's meeting with Garrison, see chap. 8 below. On the increasing antislavery content of the *Juvenile Miscellany* from Sept. 1830 on, see chap. 7 below.

53   Quotations from Beecher, *Treatise on Domestic Economy* 27, 48–49, and 138–41. Notwithstanding such statements, Catharine Beecher was a pioneer in the education of women, and the Hartford Female Seminary she founded taught rhetoric, logic, natural and moral philosophy, chemistry, history, Latin, and algebra. See Sklar, *Catharine Beecher* 59–63. Beecher argued against abolitionism, and especially women's involvement in it, in *An Essay on Slavery and Abolitionism, with Reference to the Duty of American Females* (Philadelphia: Henry Perkins, 1837).

54   Except for an appended "Concluding Chapter" in which she announced her new opinion that parents should never resort to whipping, this chapter is the only one Child revised for the 1844 edition. Besides amplifying her defense of "imagination," she updated her "List of Good Books for Various Ages" to incorporate recent works, especially those by American authors. Child's views should be contrasted with the attitudes toward fiction that Mary Kelley has found characteristic of the "literary domestics," *Private Woman, Public Stage: Literary Domesticity in Nineteenth-Century America* (New York: Oxford UP, 1984) 117–23.

55   Reviews of *The Mother's Book*, *American Annals of Education*, 3rd ser. 1 (Sept. 1831): 440–41 (this was a continuation of the *American Journal of Education*); and *American Monthly Review* 1 (Jan. 1832): 75–76.

56   [Sarah Josepha Hale], review of *The Mother's Book*, *Ladies' Magazine* 4 (July 1831): 333–34.

57   LMC to Lydia Bigelow Child, 2 Aug. 1831, *SL* 20. Confirming the extent to which *The Mother's Book* reflects Child's evolution toward abolitionism, the same letter asks Lydia to return "Abbott's Letters from Cuba," which Child had lent her sister-in-law but now wanted to use for an antislavery article in the *Juvenile Miscellany*.

58   LMC to Lydia Bigelow Child, 2 Aug. 1831, *SL* 19–20.

59   LMC to DLC, [2 Oct. 1831], *SL* 20.

60   LMC to DLC, [2 Oct. 1831], *SL* 20.

61   For a discussion of Child's *History of the Condition of Women*, see chap. 10 below.

62   Lydia Maria Child, *The Biographies of Madame de Staël, and Madame Roland*, vol. 1 of *The Ladies' Family Library* (Boston: Carter and Hendee, 1832).

63   See Ellen Moers, *Literary Women* (New York: Anchor, 1977) 268–69.

64 Lydia Maria Child, *The Biographies of Lady Russell, and Madame Guyon*, vol. 2 of *The Ladies' Family Library* (Boston: Carter and Hendee, 1832) 45–46, 62–63; LMC to DLC, 22 May 1835, *CC* 3/72.

65 Lydia Maria Child, *Good Wives*, vol. 3 of *The Ladies' Family Library* (Boston: Carter and Hendee, 1833). For passages that credit the virtues of wives to their husbands, see the biographies of Mrs. Hutchinson, Mrs. Fletcher, and Lady Fanshawe, *Good Wives* 37–38, 59, 89.

66 Margaret Fuller refers to both de Staël and Roland in *Woman in the Nineteenth Century* (1845), rpt. Jeffrey Steele, ed., *The Essential Margaret Fuller* (New Brunswick, N.J.: Rutgers UP, 1992) 283, 296–97; she also cites several other women mentioned in Child's series: Mrs. Hutchinson (279, 341), Panthea (291–95), and Lady Russell (324, 327–28, 341). Elizabeth Cady Stanton took "Mrs. Child's sketches of Mmes. De Staël and Roland" on one of her lecture tours and consoled herself for the discomforts she was experiencing on her travels by recalling the much more severe "persecutions" de Staël and Roland had suffered. See her *Eighty Years & More: Reminiscences 1815–1897* (1898; New York: Schocken, 1971) 277.

67 Reviews of *The Biographies of Madame de Staël, and Madame Roland* and *The Biographies of Lady Russell, and Madame Guyon*, *American Monthly Review* 2 (Sept. and Dec. 1832): 230–35, 452–57; [Sarah Josepha Hale], review of *The Biographies of Madame de Staël, and Madame Roland*, *Ladies' Magazine; and Literary Gazette* 5 (July 1832): 329–35; U.U., review of *Good Wives*, *Ladies' Magazine; and Literary Gazette* 6 (May 1833): 237–39; review of *Good Wives*, 1846 ed., *Southern Quarterly Review* 9 (Apr. 1846): 539. The praise of the *Southern Quarterly Review* is especially remarkable because Child had forfeited her southern readership in 1833.

68 *The Family Nurse; or, Companion of the Frugal Housewife* (Boston: Charles J. Hendee, 1837). Page references are given parenthetically in the text.

69 The publication history of *The Mother's Book* suggests a direct correlation between this eleven-year gap and Child's ostracism after issuing her abolitionist manifesto, *An Appeal in Favor of That Class of Americans Called Africans*. *The Mother's Book* was reprinted twice in 1831, twice in 1832, and once in 1833 before suddenly going out of print. In 1844 when Child had it "republished at the request of a few friends" (*MB* 1844: 170), she had just resigned from the American Anti-Slavery Society and was trying to rebuild her literary reputation.

70 Significantly, Child returned to the genre only after the Civil War, in *Looking toward Sunset* (1865), her anthology of writings for the elderly. The bulk of the volume consists not of domestic advice but of fiction, sketches, essays, and poetry, however. See chap. 18 below.

7 *Children's Literature and Antislavery: Conservative Medium, Radical Message*

1 "Note," *Juvenile Miscellany* 3rd ser. 6 (July/Aug., 1834): 323. The abbreviation *JM* is used in further references to the magazine.

2 See chap. 4 on *The First Settlers*. Quotation from [Lydia Maria Child], *The First Settlers of New-England: or, Conquest of the Pequods, Narragansets and Pokanokets: As Related by a Mother to Her Children, and Designed for the Instruction of Youth*. By a Lady of Massachusetts (Boston: Munroe and Francis, 1829) iv.

3 For details on that meeting, see chap. 8.

4 See Richard Slotkin, *The Fatal Environment: The Myth of the Frontier in the Age of Industrialization, 1800–1890* (Middletown, Conn.: Wesleyan UP, 1985), esp. chaps. 6 and 15.

5 Compare the Declaration of Independence with the racial theories Jefferson advances in *Notes on the State of Virginia* (1785; New York: Harper and Row, 1964), esp. Query 14. Jefferson cites Africans' color, "strong and disagreeable odor," and "difference of structure in the pulmonary apparatus" as evidence of physical inferiority. He goes on to argue that "in reason [they are] much inferior [to whites] . . .; and that in imagination they are dull, tasteless, and anomalous. . . . [N]ever yet could I find that a black had uttered a thought above the level of plain narration; never saw even an elementary trait of painting or sculpture." He ends by dismissing or ignoring the examples of black achievement cited by others: the poetry of Phillis Wheatley ("below the dignity of criticism"), the essays of Ignatius Sancho ("do more

honor to the heart than the head"), and the mathematical genius of Benjamin Banneker (*Notes* 133–38). Jefferson did not apply these theories of biological inferiority to Indians, whom he defended as symbols of America itself, but others did.

6   Donald L. Noel, "Slavery and the Rise of Racism," *The Origins of American Slavery and Racism* (Columbus, Ohio: Merrill, 1972) 153–74. Quotation on 164.

7   "Adventure in the Woods," *JM* 1 (Sept. 1826): 5–13. Subsequent page references are given parenthetically in the text.

8   "William Penn," *JM* 2 (July 1827): 40–49; "Rev. John Eliot," *JM* 3 (Nov. 1827): 140–44. The biography of Penn is accompanied by an illustration showing Penn signing a treaty with the Indians. The caption reads: "The red men then solemnly pledged themselves."

9   See the historical dialogues between Aunt Maria and James in the series "American History," *JM* n.s. 1 (Sept. 1828): 99–108; and n.s. 2 (May 1829): 199–205. The *Miscellany* dialogues, however, are considerably less radical than those between Mother and her daughters in *The First Settlers*, written during roughly the same period. Evidently, Child decided to publish *The First Settlers* anonymously because she wanted to express herself more freely than she could in the *Miscellany*, where she had to beware of alienating her subscribers. See also "The Adventures of a Bell," *JM* 2 (Mar. 1827): 24–30, on the Norridgewock massacre.

10 In addition to "The Indian Boy" and the anecdote included in "Pol Sosef," both discussed in this chapter at 154–56 below, see "Buffalo Creek," *JM* 3rd ser. 4 (July/Aug. 1833): 255–75, an apparently autobiographical account of a visit to the Mohawk settlement by that name. Since the visit is offered as a reward to a young white boy, as a means of inciting him to discipline himself and study for four hours a day, the contradiction between bourgeois ideology and Indian culture (whose attraction for whites lies precisely in its freedom from bourgeois constraints) is particularly obvious. For evidence linking the boy in "Buffalo Creek" to Child's nephew Francis Preston, see LMC to Mary Francis Preston, *CC* 1/18, in which Child advises Mary to send Francis to "some good school, where his native restlessness will be a little curbed, and his *emulation* excited."

11 "The Indian Boy," *JM* 2 (May 1827): 28–31.

12 "Pol Sosef. The Indian Artist," *JM* n.s. 5 (Jan./Feb. 1831): 278–84.

13 Child identifies the proprietor as a "Mr. Paine, of Winslow." She had stayed with friends in Winslow in March and April 1820. Compare the similar incident in "The Lone Indian," probably based on the same memory, *HOBOMOK and Other Writings* 157.

14 Child may be referring to Chief John Ross, whose letter to David of 11 Feb. 1831 she preserved in her scrapbook; although the story was published in Jan. 1831, David may have been in correspondence with Ross earlier; his handwriting was indeed ornate. Other possibilities are Elias Boudinot, editor of the *Cherokee Phoenix*; David reprinted many articles from the *Phoenix* in the *Massachusetts Journal*, some of which Boudinot may have sent to him with cover letters; also David Brown, whom Child quoted in *The First Settlers*.

15 "Sir Benjamin West," *JM* 1 (Jan. 1827): 19–25; quotation on 1: 20.

16 See, in order, "Chinese Children," *JM* n.s. 3 (Sept. 1829): 3–6; "A Few Words about Turkey," *JM* 3rd ser. 5 (Jan./Feb. 1833): 310–11; "New Zealanders," *JM* n.s. 5 (Nov./Dec. 1830): 189; "Polar Regions," *JM* n.s. 6 (Mar./Apr. 1831): 89–101; "Letter from a Native of Tongataboo," *JM* n.s. 5 (Jan./Feb. 1831): 307–10. Also relevant are "William Burton; or, the Boy Who Would Be a Sailor," 3rd ser. 1 (Sept./Oct. 1831): 1–46, about two youths captured and adopted by Mulgrave islanders; and "Life in the Desert," n.s. 6 (May/June 1831): 160–89, about a Tibboo African woman saved by a panther (discussed at the end of this chapter). Child acknowledges travel accounts as her sources in "William Burton" and "A Few Words about Turkey." Not all of Child's exotic sketches succeed in combating ethnocentrism, however. At least two perpetuate ethnocentric stereotypes of South Sea islanders. See "Lealea Hoku," *JM* 4 (May 1828): 206–17; also "The Young Adventurers" in the gift book Child edited for children, *The Juvenile Souvenir* (Boston: Marsh and Capen, and John Putnam, 1828) 86–123.

17 As an index of how much "safer" the Cherokee cause was to espouse than abolitionism, some of the very

New England politicians and clergymen who spoke out most eloquently against Cherokee removal — Edward Everett and Jeremiah Evarts, for example — either became bitter foes of abolitionism or remained indifferent to it.

18   The thirty-year lull in antislavery activity after the adoption of the federal Constitution is discussed by Betty Fladeland, *Men and Brothers: Anglo-American Antislavery Cooperation* (Urbana: U of Illinois P, 1972) chaps. 3–4. On the debates over Colonization vs. abolition and the beginnings of the Garrisonian abolitionist movement, see chap. 8 below.

19   See Lydia Maria Child, *An Appeal in Favor of That Class of Americans Called Africans* (Boston: Allen and Ticknor, 1833) 150: "The Anti-Slavery Society is loudly accused of being seditious, fanatical, and likely to promote insurrections. . . . I once had a very strong prejudice against anti-slavery; — (I am ashamed to think *how* strong . . .) but a candid examination has convinced me, that I was in an error." For further details on Child's reasons for initially opposing agitation of the slavery question, see chap. 8 below.

20   "Extracts from a Journal," *JM* 3 (Nov. 1827): 227–36; quotation on 232. I am indebted to Margaret Kellow for drawing my attention to Convers's description in his journal of his trip to Baltimore. See Guy R. Woodall, ed., "*The Journals of Convers Francis* (Part 2)," *Studies in the American Renaissance* 1982: 237–38.

21   In the chapter of *An Appeal* titled "Moral Character of Negroes," for example, Child reproduces the same long quotation from the Rev. Robert Walsh's *Notices of Brazil* that she had used in her *Miscellany* article "Some Talk about Brazil," *JM* 3rd ser. 3 (Sept./Oct. 1832): 31–50; that chapter also reproduces a famous passage from Mungo Park's *Travels in the Interior Districts of Africa* (1799), which she had cited in her *Miscellany* article "Kindness of the Africans," *JM* 3rd ser. 5 (Nov./Dec. 1833): 111–18. See *Appeal* 189–92, 198–99.

22   LMC to Caroline Weston, 7 Mar. 1839, *SL* 109.

23   "New Books," *JM* 3rd ser. 2 (July/Aug. 1832): 320–21.

24   "All about Brazil," *JM* 3rd ser. 3 (Sept./Oct. 1832): 31–50; the quotation is from 47–48. See also "Some Talk about Cuba," *JM* 3rd ser. 2 (May/June 1832): 198–215.

25   "William Peterson, the Brave and Good Boy," *JM* 3rd ser. 6 (Mar./Apr. 1834): 66–67.

26   "The St. Domingo Orphans," *JM* n.s. 5 (Sept. 1830): 81–94.

27   Jefferson, *Notes on the State of Virginia* 132–33 (Query 14).

28   "Jumbo and Zairee," *JM* n.s. 5 (Jan./Feb. 1831): 285–99. See "The Unfortunate Moor," *African Repository* 3 (Feb. 1828): 364–67; and "Unfortunate Moorish Prince," *Youth's Companion* 2 (11 July 1828): 25–26.

29   See "The Unfortunate Moor," *African Repository* 3 (Feb. 1828): 364–67; "Abduhl Rahahman, the Unfortunate Moorish Prince," *African Repository* 4 (May 1828): 77–81; "Abduhl Rahahman, the Unfortunate Moor," *African Repository* 4 (Oct. 1828): 243–50; and "Unfortunate Moorish Prince," *Youth's Companion* 2 (11 July 1828): 25–26.

30   The quotation is from "Abduhl Rahahman, the Unfortunate Moor," *African Repository* 4 (Oct. 1828): 246, but the summary is based on all of the articles mentioned in n. 29.

31   "Slavery," *Youth's Companion* 2 (18 July 1828): 32.

32   "Slavery," *Youth's Companion* 2 (18 July 1828): 32.

33   See "The Little Master and His Little Slave," *Evenings in New England* 138–47, discussed in chap. 3 above. Unlike Child, Willis did not evolve away from the position he took in 1828.

34   Anne Scott MacLeod, *A Moral Tale: Children's Fiction and American Culture, 1820–1860* (Hamden, Conn.: Archon, 1975), 115; John C. Crandall, "Patriotism and Humanitarian Reform in Children's Literature, 1825–1860," *American Quarterly* 21 (Spring 1969): 13–16.

35   For quotations from Park, see *Appeal* 161–62, 188–96; for a brief summary of Equiano's narrative, see *Appeal* 168–69. The latter may have suggested to Child the creation of her child protagonists, since Equiano was captured at the age of twelve along with his younger sister. In other respects, however, Equiano's narrative would not have served Child's purpose, since his captors were African, not white. See chaps. 1–2 of *The Interesting Narrative of the Life of Olaudah Equiano, or Gustavus Vassa, the African* (1789), reprinted in Arna Bontemps, ed. *Great Slave Narratives* (Boston: Beacon P, 1969).

36   Garrison strongly criticized Colonization in editorial comments appended to a pro-Colonization article he reprinted in the *Liberator* from the *Massachusetts Journal* on 15 Jan. 1831 ("Liberia Colony," p. 10), but he did not fully repudiate it until an editorial of 22 Jan. 1831: "Removal to Texas," p. 13. His full-length exposé of the Colonizationist movement's racism, *Thoughts on African Colonization*, did not appear until 1832. In that work he reprinted anti-Colonization statements by many African American leaders. The most famous African American attack on Colonization is David Walker's *Appeal, in Four Articles; Together with a Preamble, to the Coloured Citizens of the World, but in Particular, and Very Expressly, to Those of the United States of America*, ed. Charles M. Wiltse (1829; New York: Hill and Wang, 1965). For further details, see chap. 8 below.

37   Lydia Maria Child, "The *Liberator* and Its Work," *Independent* 28 Dec. 1865, p. 1, *CC* 64/1698.

38   "Mary French and Susan Easton," *JM* 3rd ser. 6 (May/June 1834): 186–202. Another antislavery story that followed "Jumbo and Zairee" is "The Little White Lamb and the Little Black Lamb," *JM* 3rd ser. 4 (March/April 1833): 53–56, discussed briefly at the end of this chapter. The articles "Some Talk about Cuba," "New Books," and "Some Talk about Brazil," discussed above, all date from 1832. The *Appeal* is listed in copyright records of the District Court of Massachusetts (available on microfilm) as having been deposited for copyright on 5 Aug. 1833.

39   See Vincent Harding, *There Is a River: The Black Struggle for Freedom in America* (1981; New York: Vintage, 1983), chap. 6. The most famous case of a free black kidnapped into slavery was Solomon Northup. See his *Twelve Years a Slave. Narrative of Solomon Northup, a Citizen of New-York, Kidnapped in Washington City in 1841, and Rescued in 1853, from a Cotton Plantation Near the Red River, in Louisiana* (1854; New York: Dover, 1970).

40   "New Books," *JM* 3rd ser. 2 (Mar./Apr. 1832): 108. I have not been able to locate the original edition of "The Travelling Tin-Man," which is collected in Eliza Leslie's *Pencil Sketches; or, Outlines of Character and Manners* (Philadelphia: Carey, Lea and Blanchard, 1833) 1: 145–61. As the title of her collection indicates, Leslie focuses on regional character types and manners, rather than on slavery. The Quakers' intervention in the slave kidnapping occurs late in the story, and the black child ends up being bound out to her rescuers with the consent of her parents. Leslie apparently does not see that her protagonist remains in a status much like a slave's. A drastically abbreviated version of the story, omitting racially offensive language in the original, can be found in the antislavery children's magazine *The Slave's Friend* 2 (1837): 132–44, published by the American Anti-Slavery Society and funded by the wealthy New York abolitionists Arthur and Lewis Tappan. For an overview, see John R. Edson, "*Slave's Friend*," *Children's Periodicals of the United States*, ed. R. Gordon Kelly (Westport, Conn.: Greenwood P, 1984), 408–11. I am grateful to Karen Sánchez-Eppler for drawing my attention to both Leslie's story and the magazine.

41   "Mary French and Susan Easton," *The Slave's Friend* 1 (1836): 125–39. I have not been able to track down the case to which Child refers.

42   Karen Sánchez-Eppler also notes the significance of this emblem in her article "Bodily Bonds: The Intersecting Rhetorics of Feminism and Abolitionism," *Representations* 24 (Fall 1988), rpt. in Shirley Samuels, ed. *The Culture of Sentiment: Race, Gender, and Sentimentality in Nineteenth-Century America* (New York: Oxford UP, 1992) 92–114; see 102.

43   "Mary French and Susan Easton," *The Slave's Friend* 1 (1836): 137.

44   "Descriptive Catalogue of Anti-Slavery Works," *Liberator* 27 Oct. 1837, p. 176. This advertisement was reprinted in many subsequent issues.

45   "Note," *JM* 3rd ser. 6 (May and July 1834): 216, 323.

46   See esp. John Greenleaf Whittier, "Biographical Introduction," *Letters of Lydia Maria Child* (1882; New York: Negro Universities P, 1969) ix; subsequent biographers have generally relied on Whittier's testimony: e.g., Anna D. Hallowell, "Lydia Maria Child," *Medford Historical Register* 3 (July 1900): 106–7; Helene G. Baer, *The Heart Is Like Heaven: The Life of Lydia Maria Child* (Philadelphia: U of Pennsylvania P, 1964) 67; Milton Meltzer, *Tongue of Flame: The Life of Lydia Maria Child* (New York: Crowell, 1965) 42; and Clifford, *Crusader for Freedom* 106.

47   Compare the impact of "The Little Master and His Little Slave" in *Evenings in New England*, which had

taught children to channel their antislavery sympathies toward Colonization, with that of "Jumbo and Zairee" and "Mary French and Susan Easton." Willis's article on "Slavery" (*Youth's Companion* 2 [18 July 1828]: 32) provides a good example of the standard view northern parents wanted to inculcate in their children. I am grateful to H. Bruce Franklin for helping me reconceptualize my analysis of parents' reactions and distinguish more clearly between the reactions of the *Miscellany*'s parental subscribers and juvenile readers.

48   The *Traveller* reviewed the Nov. 1830 issue of the *Miscellany* and Child's *Girl's Own Book* on 5 Nov. and 24 Dec. 1830, p. 3. The next and last review of the *Miscellany* is on 13 May 1831, p. 2. Meanwhile, in subsequent months the *Traveller* continued to review other juvenile works and ladies' periodicals along with magazines and books for the general public. I found no reviews of *The Mother's Book*, the *Biographies of Madame de Staël, and Madame Roland*, or the *Appeal*. The issue of 6 Nov. 1832, p. 2, did carry a highly favorable review of the *Biographies of Lady Russell, and Madame Guyon*, however. Child quotes the *Traveller* as having reported that she had tried to steal the idea of the *Little Girl's Own Book* from Eliza Leslie (*Massachusetts Journal* 14 Jan. 1832). On 8 July 1834, p. 4, the *Traveller* reprinted Child's story "Tahmiroo: The Indian Wife" without attribution. On 4 Jan. 1831 the *Traveller* reported neutrally that Garrison had just published the first number of the *Liberator* ("The Newspaper Press," p. 2). On 30 Aug. and 6 Sept., it provided extensive coverage of the Nat Turner rebellion. On 16 Sept. it sympathetically reported that citizens of New Haven were trying to prevent the founding of a college for blacks there ("College for Blacks," p. 2). In 1833 the paper gave extensive coverage to Colonization. Although it printed one letter from an abolitionist correspondent replying to Colonizationist attacks, the *Traveller* generally tilted toward the Colonizationists.

49   "Note," *JM* 3rd ser. 3 (Jan./Feb. 1833): 323.

50   MacLeod, *Moral Tale* 111–17, confirms that antislavery protest was rare and muted in children's literature: "Publishers and authors who hoped to see their products widely sold walked carefully around those places where angels feared to tread" (116). Crandall, "Patriotism and Humanitarian Reform in Children's Literature" 13–16, finds more examples of antislavery children's literature, but he does not distinguish clearly between abolitionist and mainstream children's writers; he also agrees that the " 'giants of the juveniles,' Samuel Goodrich (Peter Parley) and Jacob Abbott, approached the subject [of slavery] with great caution" and that "The American Sunday School Union, The American Tract Society and the other Sabbath School agencies did not see fit to make a concentrated attack on slavery" in their publications for children (13). The two magazines of the 1840s that Crandall cites as forthrightly addressing the issue of slavery were singled out in the abolitionist press as exceptions. The *Liberator* reprints an advertisement in the *Oberlin Evangelist* that gives "special notice" to the *Youth's Cabinet* because "It is the only youth's publication that heartily espouses the cause of the slave. All the rest seem to preserve a studied silence over his wrongs" (26 July 1839, p. 118). The *National Anti-Slavery Standard* announced the launching of a new periodical, *The Child's Friend*, ed. by the abolitionist Eliza Lee Cabot Follen, with these words: "When Mrs. Follen was asked to take charge of this periodical, she declined doing it, unless free to say whatever she liked on the subject of slavery; and the publisher replied that this was no objection. . . . This marks progress" (12 Oct. 1843, p. 75).

51   *Flowers for Children, 1 (For Children Eight or Nine Years Old)* (New York: C. S. Francis, 1844); *Flowers for Children, 2 (For Children from Four to Six Years Old)* (New York: C. S. Francis, 1845); *Flowers for Children, 3 (For Children of Eleven and Twelve Years of Age)* (New York: C. S. Francis, 1847). "The Little White Lamb and the Little Black Lamb" is in *Flowers* 2: 132–34, and "Lariboo" in *Flowers* 3: 154–84; they originally appeared in *JM* 3rd ser. 4 (Mar. 1833): 53–56 and in n.s. 6 (May 1831): 160–89, respectively. Child revised Lariboo considerably for *Flowers*, eliminating ethnocentric details that had marred the earlier version, introducing more information about African culture, and strengthening the story line. The revisions reflect the growth of her consciousness and indicate that she did hope to use the story as a "troop of horse shod with felt."

52   "Jamie and Jeannie," *A New Flower for Children (For Children from Eight to Twelve Years Old)* (New York: C. S. Francis, 1856) 9–102.

53 Caroline Healey Dall, "Lydia Maria Child and Mary Russell Mitford," *Unitarian Review* 19 (June 1883): 528. Both Dall and Higginson came from conservative aristocratic families that opposed antislavery agitation.

54 Samuel Johnson to LMC, [1–3] Feb. 1860, *CC* 44/1196.

55 See Lydia Maria Child, *The Mother's Book* (1831; New York: C. S. Francis, 1844) 38–44, cited in chap. 6 above. Johnson was responding to the recent publication of *Correspondence between Lydia Maria Child and Gov. Wise and Mrs. Mason, of Virginia* (Boston: American Anti-Slavery Society, 1860), discussed in chap. 17 below.

56 Sarah Van Vechten Brown to LMC, 2 Mar. 1869, *CC* 71/1887.

57 Melissa E. Dawes to LMC, 12 Feb. 1868, *CC* 68/1813.

8 "The First Woman in the Republic": An Antislavery Baptism

1 "MRS. CHILD," *Genius of Universal Emancipation*, 20 Nov. 1829, p. 85. Garrison joined the paper on 2 Sept., as indicated by his salutatory address "To the Public" of that date. For the details of Garrison's acquaintance with David Lee Child, see *The Letters of William Lloyd Garrison*, ed. Walter M. Merrill and Louis Ruchames (Cambridge, Mass.: Belknap P of Harvard UP, 1971–81) 1: 38 and 6: 352, hereinafter cited as *GL*; and Wendell Phillips Garrison and Francis Jackson Garrison, *William Lloyd Garrison, 1805–1879: The Story of His Life Told by His Children* (1885–1889; New York: Arno P, 1969) 1: 73, hereinafter cited as *Life*.

2 "Comparative Strength of Male and Female Intellect," from the *Massachusetts Journal, Genius of Universal Emancipation* 30 Oct. 1829, pp. 60–61. The article is reprinted in the "Literary" column. Garrison writes that he had "cut [it] out, in February last, for insertion in the Journal of the Times; but, as the press of other matter prevented its publication at that time, I have hoarded it up ever since for that purpose, and to praise a very meritorious woman."

3 Garrison's efforts to recruit Whittier for the cause provide indirect evidence of the high priority he assigned to enlisting the best writers of the day as propagandists for antislavery. In a letter to Harriott Plummer dated 4 Mar. 1833, he writes: "You excite my curiosity and interest still more, by informing me that my dearly beloved Whittier is a *friend* and townsman of yours. Can we not induce him to devote his brilliant genius more to the advancement of our cause . . .?" (*GL* 1: 209).

4 The ostensible purposes of Garrison's June 1830 trip to Boston and Newburyport, as he explains in a letter to Ebenezer Dole of 14 July 1830 (*GL* 1: 104–6), written on his return to Baltimore, were to collect "some essential evidence to be used in the civil action" pending against him and to explore the possibility of obtaining funds to reestablish the *Genius*, which had suspended publication after his imprisonment. *Life* 1: 192 reports Garrison as "passing through Boston on the 10th of June, and paying his respects to friendly Mr. Buckingham of the *Courier*," before proceeding to Newburyport. Garrison's letter to Dole implies that he returned to Boston on his way back from Newburyport to Baltimore, however, and suggests that his stay in Boston may have been somewhat longer.

5 LMC to Samuel J. May, 29 Sept. 1867, *SL* 474–75.

6 LMC to May, 29 Sept. 1867, *SL* 474–75; "W. L. Garrison," *Massachusetts Journal and Tribune* 13 Nov. 1830, p. 1.

7 Lydia Maria Child, "The *Liberator* and Its Work," *Independent* 28 Dec. 1865, p. 1, *CC* 64/1698.

8 WLG to Editor of Newburyport *Herald* 21 Apr. 1827, *GL* 1: 38; WLG to LMC, 25 Oct. 1874, *GL* 6: 352. On the chronology of Garrison's involvement with Lundy and antislavery work, see *Life* 1: 92–98; *GL* 1: xxvii, 63–65.

9 LMC to Anne Whitney, 25 May 1879, *SL* 558. Unfortunately, Child's reminiscences to Whitney and to Samuel J. May (*SL* 473–75) about her first meeting with Garrison supply no dates. The appearance of her first antislavery story in the Sept. 1830 issue of the *Miscellany*, however, and the succession of antislavery pieces that follow on its heels provide strong evidence that the meeting took place before

that date. Hence, I am assuming that it took place during Garrison's brief visit in June, rather than after his permanent return to Boston in Sept.-Oct., the other possible date.

10 Garrison's seven-week imprisonment in a jail that served as a depot for apprehended runaways and slaves waiting to be transported south intensified his identification with the slaves. See his letter to Ebenezer Dole, 14 July 1830, *GL* 1: 105–6, in which he contrasts his own situation in prison with that of "the poor slave."

11 See *Life* 1: 142–48 on the development of Garrison's thinking during this period. Garrison had proclaimed his commitment to immediate rather than gradual abolition in his inaugural editorial for the *Genius* (2 Sept. 1829, rpt. in *Life*), but he had not fully spelled out what that entailed. Nor had he repudiated the Colonization Society or questioned the desirability of reducing the black population through a voluntary emigration program. He began to do so after a black correspondent of the *Genius*, who styled himself "A Colored Baltimorean," pointed out the racist implications of the repatriation scheme in an article of 27 Nov. 1829, reprinted in Garrison's *Thoughts on African Colonization: or an Impartial Exhibition of the Doctrines, Principles and Purposes of the American Colonization Society. Together with the Resolutions, Addresses and Remonstrances of the Free People of Color* (1832; New York: Arno P, 1968), pt. 2: 52–54. Two historians have identified this "Colored Baltimorean" as William Watkins (presumably the uncle of Frances Ellen Watkins Harper); see Floyd J. Miller, *The Search for a Black Nationality: Black Emigration and Colonization, 1787–1863* (Urbana: U of Illinois P, 1975) 84; and R. J. M. Blackett, *Building an Antislavery Wall: Black Americans in the Atlantic Abolitionist Movement, 1830–1860* (Baton Rouge: Louisiana State UP, 1983) 50–51. As late as 8 Jan. 1831, Garrison was not yet ready to take a public stand against the Colonization Society. Though he had criticized it in a private letter to Lundy, he was disconcerted when Lundy published the letter in the *Genius* without his authorization. In response, however, Garrison promised on 8 Jan. to "thoroughly sift . . . [the society's] pretensions," and by 22 Jan. he was announcing that "it is time to repudiate all colonization schemes, as visionary and unprofitable" and advocating that blacks be educated and "made useful in society." See "Another Libel," *Liberator* 8 Jan. 1831, p. 7; and "Removal to Texas," 22 Jan. 1831, p. 13.

12 For an excellent history of antislavery protest in England and the United States, from the colonial period through the Civil War, see Betty Fladeland, *Men and Brothers: Anglo-American Antislavery Cooperation* (Urbana: U of Illinois P, 1972). For a brilliant analysis of early antislavery ideology and the international socioeconomic context in which it developed, see David Brion Davis, *The Problem of Slavery in the Age of Revolution, 1770–1823* (Ithaca, N.Y.: Cornell UP, 1975).

13 For a fascinating account of how early African American leaders who had been receptive to selective voluntary repatriation were induced by the militant opposition of the black masses to change their stand and present a united front against Colonization schemes, see William Loren Katz's introduction to the Arno rpt. edition of Garrison's *Thoughts on Colonization*. Katz also details the influence that African Americans exerted on Garrison, prompting him to investigate the subject and change his stand. It should be noted that even those African American leaders who had favored repatriation never supported a program of forced mass emigration; also, many of the early supporters of repatriation — Prince Hall and Paul Cuffee, for example — were influenced by African parents. African American interest in repatriation declined in direct correlation with the Colonization Society's ascendancy.

14 Garrison reprinted the anti-Colonization statements he had collected from black correspondents in "Sentiments of the People of Color," Part II of *Thoughts on African Colonization*. Surprisingly, he did not include extracts from Walker's *Appeal*, though he had commented on it in both the *Genius* and the *Liberator*; see *Life* 1: 159–62. For a modern edition, see *David Walker's Appeal, in Four Articles; Together with a Preamble, to the Coloured Citizens of the World, but in Particular, and Very Expressly, to Those of the United States of America*, ed. Charles M. Wiltse (New York: Hill and Wang, 1965). The comments by Garrison and review by "V" are reprinted in Truman Nelson, ed., *Documents of Upheaval: Selections from William Lloyd Garrison's THE LIBERATOR, 1831–1865* (New York: Hill and Wang, 1966) 4–6, 12–26. "V" may be Garrison's black friend from Pittsburgh, John B. Vashon. Among those who suggest a

relationship between Walker's and Child's titles are Thomas Wentworth Higginson, "Lydia Maria Child," *Contemporaries*, vol. 2 of *Writings of Thomas Wentworth Higginson* 121; and Jean Fagan Yellin, *Women and Sisters: The Antislavery Feminists in American Culture* (New Haven, Conn.: Yale UP, 1989) 54. It is possible that David Child, rather than the *Liberator*, first brought Walker's *Appeal* to Child's attention. In an editorial note of 11 Dec. 1830 (p. 3), titled "Walker's Appeal," David comments on Walker's death, refers to having made inquiries about its cause, and invites "our colored friends" to send the *Massachusetts Journal* any evidence they can find of Walker's having been assassinated.

15 See "Liberia Colony," reprinted under the heading "Colonization," *Liberator* 15 Jan. 1831, p. 11. The original article appeared in the *Massachusetts Journal and Tribune* on 1 Jan. 1831, p. 1.

16 "A Noble Commentary," *Liberator* 13 Aug. 1831, pp. 129–30. The original appeared in the editorial column of the *Massachusetts Journal and Tribune*, 6 Aug. 1831, p. 3, under the title "Novel Incident."

17 I have compared this editorial to both David Lee Child's *The Despotism of Freedom; or the Tyranny and Cruelty of American Republican Slave-Masters, Shown to be the Worst in the World; in a Speech, Delivered at the First Anniversary of the New England Anti-Slavery Society, 1833* (Boston: Young Men's Anti-Slavery Association, 1833) and Lydia Maria Child's *An Appeal in Favor of That Class of Americans Called Africans* (Boston: Allen and Ticknor, 1833) and found it much closer in style and content to the latter. For example, although both Childs cite the Prince Saunders anecdote, Lydia Maria Child's version of it in the *Appeal* is stylistically more similar to the version in the *Massachusetts Journal* (see *Appeal* 142; *Despotism* 11). The *Appeal* also cites a second anecdote that appears in the *Massachusetts Journal* article, but not in *The Despotism of Freedom*: the reference to a man who defended his refusal to hire blacks by saying: " 'I am too great a democrat . . . to have any body in my house, who don't sit at my table; and I'll be hanged, if I ever eat with the son of an Ethiopian' " (*Appeal* 217–18; *Liberator* 13 Aug. 1831, p. 130). Other close verbal parallels between the *Massachusetts Journal* article and the *Appeal* are discussed in the paragraphs below.

18 See the *North American Review* 19 (1824): 262–63; [Jared Sparks], "Recent American Novels," *NAR* 21 (1825): 87; and *The First Settlers of New-England: or, Conquest of the Pequods, Narragansets and Pokanokets: As Related by a Mother to Her Children, and Designed for the Instruction of Youth*. By a Lady of Massachusetts (Boston: Munroe and Francis, [1829]) 66. The context makes clear that she intended the argument to apply to intermarriage with blacks as well as with Indians.

19 See *Appeal* 209–10, quoted and discussed in this chapter below.

20 Garrison, *Thoughts on African Colonization* 145–46n.

21 For Garrison's reaction, see the editorial on "The Insurrection" in the *Liberator* 3 Sept. 1831, rpt. in Nelson, ed., *Documents of Upheaval* 28–31; for David's see "*Insurrection in Virginia*," rpt. under the heading "Remarks of Editors," *Liberator* 10 Sept. 1831, pp. 146–47. The issue containing the original is missing from the *Massachusetts Journal and Tribune* file at the American Antiquarian Society. David provided extensive and sympathetic coverage of the Turner rebellion in other issues, however. For example, in an article on "The Virginia Slave Insurrection," he comments that "nearly twice as many [blacks] have been put to death as were concerned in it." And in one titled "Gen. Nat," he disputes a Virginia newspaper's claim that Turner had "sold his body for Gingercakes which he ate before his Execution." David retorts: "We think this improbable. In the first place he was a slave and by the laws of Virginia a slave cannot make a bargain nor own anything. In the next place it is the policy of the Southern press to make the black race appear despicable. In the third place the fact is totally in consistent [*sic*] with the heroism with which he met death, which is described by a witness as follows. . . ." See the *Massachusetts Journal and Tribune* 15 Oct. 1831, p. 1; and 26 Nov. 1831, p. 3. For Turner's own account of the rebellion, though filtered through the judgments of his Virginian interrogator, see Thomas R. Gray, *The Confession, Trial and Execution of Nat Turner, the Negro Insurrectionist; also, a list of persons murdered in the insurrection in Southampton County, Virginia, on the 21st and 22nd of August, 1831, with Introductory Remarks* (1831; New York: AMS P, 1975); for a modern historical account, see Vincent Harding, *There Is a River: The Black Struggle for Freedom in America* (New York: Vintage, 1981) 94–100.

22 "The Insurrection" in Nelson, ed., *Documents of Upheaval* 30; Garrison had already spelled out his posi-

tion on slave revolt in a comment of 8 Jan. 1831 on David Walker's *Appeal*, rpt. in Nelson 5–6: "Believing, as we do that men should never do evil that good may come; that a good end does not justify wicked means . . . and that we ought to suffer, as did our Lord and his apostles, unresistingly — knowing that vengeance belongs to God . . . *[w]e* do not preach rebellion — no, but submission and peace. . . . We say, that the possibility of a bloody insurrection at the South fills us with dismay; and we avow, too, as plainly, that if any people were ever justified in throwing off the yoke of their tyrants, the slaves are that people."

23 See the *Liberator* 21 May 1831, p. 84; 21 Jan. 1832, p. 12; 28 Jan. 1832, p. 16. The aphorism titled "Marriage," excerpted from *The Mother's Book*, appears 10 Dec. 1831, p. 200; Child included "Stand from Under!" in *The Coronal. A Collection of Miscellaneous Pieces, Written at Various Times* (Boston: Carter and Hendee, 1832) 184–89. Quotation on 184.

24 Garrison's fellow abolitionist and first biographer, Oliver Johnson, vividly re-creates the setting and recalls the antislavery pioneers who gathered there, *W. L. Garrison and His Times* (1881; Miami, Fla.: Mnemosyne, 1969) 51–53. He does not mention any visits by Maria Child, though he speaks of her elsewhere.

25 LMC to Anne Whitney, 25 May 1879, *SL* 558.

26 Garrison and Garrison, *Life* 1: 213n; Nina Moore Tiffany, *Samuel E. Sewall: A Memoir* (Boston: Houghton Mifflin, 1898) 12–13, 36–42.

27 LMC to Louisa May Alcott, 19 June 1878, *CC* 90/2398. Child specifies that her acquaintance with Abba (and probably with her brother Samuel) "began at her father's house, before either of us was married."

28 See the *DAB* articles on David Lee Child and Ellis Gray Loring. David Child taught at the Boston Latin School from 1817 to 1820, the year of Loring's graduation. On Child's earlier relationship with Louisa Gilman, see LMC to Louisa Gilman, 4 June [1827?], *CC* 1/24.

29 "Gone," *National Anti-Slavery Standard* 6 June 1868, in *CC* 69/1837. For examples of letters confessing to a similar distaste for "the rough work of reform," see LMC to Ellis Gray Loring, Augusta G. King, and Mary Ann Brown, 6 Mar. and 19 and 26 Sept. 1843 and 2 Dec. 1860, *SL* 192–97, 202–4, and *CC* 47/1271.

30 Johnson, *Garrison and His Times* 83–84, takes issue with the statement by Samuel J. May, in *Some Recollections of Our Antislavery Conflict* (Boston: Fields, Osgood, 1869) 31, that the naysayers disagreed with the principle of immediate emancipation. The details in the following paragraphs are from Johnson 83–85.

31 Johnson, *Garrison and His Times* 83–85; *Life* 1: 279. The earliest notices in the *Liberator* of the society's monthly meetings read: "All persons interested in the subject of slavery are invited to attend." On 23 June 1832 "Ladies are particularly invited to be present" at a debate over the merits of Colonization. Beginning in July 1832, notices of meetings read: "Ladies and gentlemen are respectfully invited to attend." See the *Liberator* 28 Jan. 1832, p. 15; 23 June, p. 99; 28 July, p. 119; 25 Aug., p. 135; 22 Sept., p. 151; 27 Oct. 1832, p. 171. In her preface to *The Oasis*, ed. Lydia Maria Child (Boston: Allen and Ticknor, 1834) xv–xvi, Child affirms: "I have, for the last two years, attended almost every Anti-Slavery meeting in this neighborhood. . . ."

32 Oliver Johnson's explanation of why blacks were "not conspicuous among the formers of the new society" underscores how paternalistically abolitionists conceived of the two races' roles in the movement: "It was because they instinctively knew that their presence and co-operation would serve only to increase and intensify the prejudices which the society must encounter. Their very anxiety for its success kept them aloof at first. They were careful not to embarrass in its infancy a movement on which were staked their dearest hopes" (*Garrison and His Times* 99). See also "New-England Anti-Slavery Society," *Liberator* 10 Mar. 1832, p. 39, which invites "friends of the people of color, *and the people of color themselves,*" in other New England towns to "form auxiliaries to this Society." For accounts of black antislavery activity during this period, see Harding, *There Is a River*, esp. chaps. 4 and 6; Benjamin Quarles, *Black Abolitionists* (New York: Oxford UP, 1969); Blackett, *Building an Antislavery Wall*, esp. chaps. 1–2; and Sterling Stuckey, *Slave Culture: Nationalist Theory and the Foundations of Black America* (New York: Oxford UP, 1987), esp. chaps. 2–3.

33   Quoted in Child's *Appeal*, chap. 5, p. 146; also in *Life* 1: 281.

34   *Life* 1: 279–80; "Annual Meeting of the New-England Anti-Slavery Society," *Liberator* 2 Feb. 1833, p. 17; "Proceedings of the New-England Anti-Slavery Society, at its First Annual Meeting," in *First Annual Report of the Board of Managers of the New-England Anti-Slavery Society* (Boston: Garrison and Knapp, 1833) 8.

35   May, *Some Recollections* 97–98. Quotation continues in next paragraph.

36   "Works of Mrs. Child," *NAR* 38 (July 1833): 138–64. The quotations are from 138–39.

37   [Harriet Winslow Sewall, ed.], *Letters of Lydia Maria Child with a Biographical Introduction by John G. Whittier and an Appendix by Wendell Phillips* (1882; New York: Negro Universities P, 1969) 264.

38   See, for example, Amos A. Phelps, *Lectures on Slavery and Its Remedy* (1834; St. Clair Shores, Mich.: Scholarly P, 1970), which concentrates on showing that slavery is sinful and on answering objections to "immediate emancipation" (frequently quoting Child on emancipation); William Jay, *Inquiry into the Character and Tendency of the American Colonization, and American Anti-Slavery Societies* (1835; rpt. in *Miscellaneous Writings on Slavery* (Freeport, N.Y.: Books for Libraries P, 1970), which borrows heavily, without acknowledgment, from Child's discussion of slave law; [Theodore Dwight Weld, Angelina Grimké Weld, and Sarah Grimké], *American Slavery As It Is: Testimony of a Thousand Witnesses* (1839; New York: Arno P, 1968), which concentrates on demonstrating the brutality of slavery; and [Richard Hildreth], *Despotism in America; or an Inquiry into the Nature and Results of the Slave-holding System in the United States* (Boston: Whipple and Damrell, 1840), which amplifies the economic analysis offered in chap. 3 of the *Appeal*, as well as aspects of Child's first two chapters.

39   May, *Some Recollections* 98.

40   See, for example, Frank Tannenbaum, *Slave and Citizen: The Negro in the Americas* (1946; New York: Vintage, n.d.); David Brion Davis, *The Problem of Slavery in Western Culture* (Ithaca, N.Y.: Cornell UP, 1966); Carl N. Degler, *Neither Black Nor White: Slavery and Race Relations in Brazil and the United States* (New York: Macmillan, 1971); and Donald Noel, "Slavery and the Rise of Racism," in Noel, ed., *The Origins of American Slavery and Racism* (Columbus, Ohio: Charles E. Merrill, 1972) 153–74, quoted in chap. 7 above. Child's main source on slave law, George Stroud's, *A Sketch of the Laws Relating to Slavery in the Several States of the United States of America* (Philadelphia, 1827), also compares American slave law with biblical, classical, and European colonial slave law, but Stroud's analysis is more narrowly focused. The theoretical insights Child derives from these comparisons seem to be original.

41   For studies of women's antislavery discourse, see Blanche Glassman Hersh, *The Slavery of Sex: Feminist-Abolitionists in America* (Urbana: U of Illinois P, 1978); Nancy A. Hewitt, *Women's Activism and Social Change: Rochester, New York, 1822–1872* (Ithaca, N.Y.: Cornell UP, 1984); and Yellin, *Women and Sisters*. For examples of women's antislavery discourse in the *Liberator*, see [Elizabeth Margaret Chandler], "Our Own Sex," 7 Jan. 1832, p. 2; L.H., "Duty of Females," 5 May 1832, p. 70; "A Dialogue on Slavery" ("Altered from a British Anti-Slavery Tract"), 2 June 1832, p. 86; "The Abuse of Liberty" signed "Magawisca" after the Indian heroine of Catharine Maria Sedgwick's *Hope Leslie*, 26 Mar. 1831, p. 50 (the author was Sarah Louise Forten, identified by Dorothy Sterling, *We Are Your Sisters: Black Women in the Nineteenth Century* [New York: Norton, 1984] 121); Sarah Douglass is identified on 21 July 1832, p. 114, as an "accomplished young colored lady" and the author of "several original and truly beautiful articles which have appeared in the Ladies' Department of the Liberator"; a number of speeches by Maria Steward [*sic*] were reprinted in the *Liberator* and later published in books, which, in turn, were advertised in the *Liberator*. Stewart's speeches have been reprinted in Stewart, *Maria W. Stewart: America's First Black Woman Political Writer*, ed. Marilyn Richardson (Bloomington: Indiana UP, 1987).

42   Thomas Clarkson, *The History of the Rise, Progress, and Accomplishment of the Abolition of the African Slave-Trade by the British Parliament*, 2 vols. (1808). Child also drew most of her information on the Santo Domingo uprising and some of her economic arguments from Clarkson's pamphlet, *Thoughts on the Necessity of Improving the Condition of the Slaves in the British Colonies, with a View to Their Ultimate Emancipation; and on the Practicability, the Safety, and the Advantages of the Latter Measure* (New York, 1823). See n. 40, above, for a full citation of Stroud. Henri Grégoire, *An Enquiry Concerning the*

Intellectual and Moral Faculties and Literature of Negroes Followed with an Account of the Life and Works of Fifteen Negroes and Mulattoes Distinguished in Science, Literature and the Arts (1808), trans. D. B. Warden (1810; College Park, Md.: McGrath, 1967). Alexander Everett, *America, or a General Survey of the Political Situation of the Several Powers of the Western Continent,* ed. Michael Hudson (1827; New York: Garland, 1974) 212–25. Child also drew on American antislavery tracts, but these provided her mostly with instances of cruelty and descriptions of the domestic slave trade rather than with analysis of the workings of the slave system. See, for example, John Rankin, *Letters on American Slavery, Addressed to Mr. Thomas Rankin* (1826; New York: Arno P, 1969), which had been reprinted in the *Liberator* beginning in Aug. 1832; and Jesse Torrey, *A Portraiture of Domestic Slavery, in the United States: with Reflections on the Practicability of Restoring the Moral Rights of the Slave, without Impairing the Legal Privileges of the Possessor; and a Project of a Colonial Asylum for Free Persons of Colour: Including Memoirs of Facts on the Interior Traffic in Slaves, and on Kidnapping* (1817; St. Clair, Mich.: Scholarly P, 1970).

43   "Annual Meeting of the New-England Anti-Slavery Society," *Liberator* 26 Jan. 1833, p. 14; John Greenleaf Whittier and William Lloyd Garrison to LMC, 23 Sept. and 25 Oct. 1874, *CC* 83/2180, 2191.

44   See n. 17 above for a full reference to *The Despotism of Freedom.* Verbal parallels between *Despotism* and the *Appeal* include the following: (1) Both works refer to the "quarantine" provision of the Colored Seamen Laws and comment: "as if freedom were as bad as the cholera!" (*Appeal* 69), "as if they had the *cholera*" (*Despotism* 58); (2) both works sum up their analysis of American slave laws by saying: "Our republic is a perfect Pandora's box to the negro, only there is no *hope* at the bottom" (*Appeal* 75), "Our Republic is a complete Pandora's box to the slave, except that *there is no hope at the bottom*" (*Despotism* 21); (3) both works, pointing out that the slaves are ruled by laws they cannot read, comment: "This is worthy of Nero, who caused his edicts to be placed so high that they could not be read, and then beheaded his subjects for disobeying them" (*Appeal* 62), "The standing illustration of Nero's tyranny was, that he issued and executed edicts which he caused to be fixed so high that the subjects could not read them" (*Despotism* 48).

45   Eric Foner, *Free Soil, Free Labor, Free Men: The Ideology of the Republican Party before the Civil War* (New York: Oxford UP, 1970). See esp. intro. and chap. 1.

46   Edward P. Crapol, "Lydia Maria Child: Abolitionist Critic of American Foreign Policy," in Crapol, ed., *Women and American Foreign Policy: Lobbyists, Critics, and Insiders* (Westport, Conn.: Greenwood P, 1987) 1–18.

47   It is perhaps significant that a French Enlightment philosophe, the Abbé Grégoire, was Child's only precursor and that later abolitionists do not follow Child's lead in devoting comparable space to refuting racist ideology.

48   "Report on the Domestic Slave Trade," *Proceedings of the New-England Anti-Slavery Convention, Held in Boston on the 27th, 28th and 29th of May, 1834* (Boston: Garrison and Knapp, 1834) 25–36.

49   See, for example, Basil Davidson, *Africa in History: Themes and Outlines,* rev. ed. (New York: Collier, 1968), 192–94; Walter Rodney, *How Europe Underdeveloped Africa* (Washington, D.C.: Howard UP, 1982), esp. chap. 4.

50   Mungo Park, *Travels in the Interior Districts of Africa* (1799; New York: Arno P, 1971); Major Denham, Captain Clapperton, and the late Doctor Oudney, *Narrative of Travels and Discoveries in Northern and Central Africa, in the Years 1822, 1823, and 1824. . . .* 2 vols., 3rd ed. (London: John Murray, 1828); Olaudah Equiano, *The Interesting Narrative of Olaudah Equiano, or Gustavus Vassa, the African* (1789), rpt. in Arna Bontemps, *Great Slave Narratives* (Boston: Beacon P, 1969) 1–192; Michaud, *Biographie Universelle, Ancienne et Moderne. . . .* (Paris, 1828). I have not been able to locate the *English Family Library.* The two sources Child quotes and paraphrases most extensively are Park and the Abbé Grégoire (see n. 42 above for a full citation), but she drew her account of Zhinga from the *Biographie Universelle* 52: 314–22.

51   See *The First Settlers of New-England* 131–74, esp. 168–69.

52   See Karen Sánchez-Eppler, "Bodily Bonds: The Intersecting Rhetorics of Feminism and Abolition," *Representations* 24 (Fall 1988), rpt. in Shirley Samuels, ed., *The Culture of Sentiment: Race, Gender, and Sentimentality in Nineteenth-Century America* (New York: Oxford UP, 1992) 106–7.

53   May, *Some Recollections* 40–72 offers an eyewitness account.

54   "Comment Is Needless!," *Liberator* 6 April 1833, p. 54.

55   "Mrs. Child's Appeal in Favor of the Africans," *Quarterly Christian Spectator* 6 (Sept. 1834): 445–56. Quotation on 448.

56   Convers's attitude can be inferred from Child's replies to his (no longer extant) letters. See LMC to Convers Francis, 22 Nov. 1833 and 25 Sept. and 19 Dec. 1835, *SL* 27, 38–39, 41–42. James Francis is described by a Wayland neighbor as "quite unlike his sister in politics, being an 'old line Democrat' of the Jefferson-Jacksonian stripe, and perhaps more pro- than antislavery in sentiment. It is said, he used to declare that 'his sister's attitude on the slavery question had caused him much grief' "; see Alfred Sereno Hudson, "The Home of Lydia Maria Child," *New England Magazine* n.s. 2 (June 1890): 407. Gravestones in the cemetery at Wayland bear the names of James's daughters Lydia Maria and Mary Conant Francis. Child mentions her namesake in LMC to Mary Francis Preston, 26 May 1822, *CC* 1/10. Convers, Sr.'s attitude can be inferred from letters of the 1840s, cited in chapter 11 below, and from Convers, Jr.'s reminiscences of his father, quoted in the prologue and quoted in John Weiss, *Discourse Occasioned by the Death of Convers Francis, D.D. . . .* (Cambridge, Mass.: Privately printed, 1863) 62. On the names of Lucretia Child Haskins's children, see Meltzer and Holland, *SL* 67n.

57   George Ticknor Curtis, "Reminiscences of N. P. Willis and Lydia Maria Child," *Harper's New Monthly Magazine* 81 (Oct. 1890): 720; presumably what Curtis says of himself applies to his mother: "I very seldom met her after the first year or two of her married life. . . . [M]y associations, sympathies, and opinions were with those conservative forces of society which were . . . antagonistic to those in which Mrs. Child's life became absorbed." Lucy Osgood to LMC, 8 May 1843, *CC* 17/493; renewing acquaintance with the "Apostle of Freedom" who "might have lost sight, in her passage down the stream of time, of the scenes & associates of other days," Osgood's letter hints at a long estrangement, probably caused by their disagreement over abolition. Also, LMC to Marian Marshall, 28 Aug. 1836, *CC* 4/105.

58   See Catharine Maria Sedgwick to LMC, 27 May 1834, Sedgwick Collection, Historical Room, Stockbridge Library (courtesy of Patricia G. Holland and Laurie Robertson-Lorant); and LMC to Sarah Shaw, 20 May 1872, *SL* 506.

59   On Ticknor's tactics of enforcing ostracism against abolitionists and other "heretics," see David B. Tyack, *George Ticknor and the Boston Brahmins* (Cambridge, Mass.: Harvard UP, 1967) 185–86. For accounts by Child's friends of the reaction to the *Appeal*, see May, *Some Recollections* 100, and the introduction by Whittier and the appendix by Phillips in the 1882 ed. of Child's *Letters* ix, 264. See also LMC to Samuel J. May, 29 Sept. 1867, *SL* 473–75, written in response to his reminiscences about her ordeal. It was Phillips who supplied the anecdote about Austin, which acquires added significance when we remember that Austin's diatribe at the public meeting called to protest the murder of the abolitionist editor Elijah Lovejoy brought Phillips to his feet with a fiery speech that launched his career as an abolitionist orator. See James Brewer Stewart, *Wendell Phillips: Liberty's Hero* (Baton Rouge: Louisiana State UP, 1986) 59–63. Austin also prosecuted the Johnson libel case against David. See "Suffolk, ss. Supreme Judicial Court," *Massachusetts Weekly Journal* 28 Jan. 1829, pp. 2–3.

60   "Mrs. Child's 'Appeal,' " rpt. in *Liberator* 14 Dec. 1833, p. 200.

61   "New publication," *Liberator* 10 Aug. 1833, p. 127 (this was by Oliver Johnson, who was editing the *Liberator* in Garrison's absence); "Mrs. Child's New Work," rpt. from the *Christian Watchman*, *Liberator* 7 Sept. 1833, p. 141; "Mrs. Child's Appeal," *Liberator* 7 Sept. 1833, pp. 142–43; "An Appeal in favor of the Africans," rpt. from *Newburyport Advocate*, *Liberator* 2 Nov. 1833, p. 175.

62   "Facts," *Liberator* 15 Feb. 1834, p. 25; "A Noble Young Lady," *Liberator* 26 July 1834, p. 117.

63   "Mrs. Child's New Work" (rpt. from *Christian Watchman*) and "Mrs. Child's Appeal," *Liberator* 7 Sept. 1833, pp. 141, 142–43.

64   See LMC to Charles Sumner, 7 July 1856, *SL* 286, in which she thanks him for telling her that "your public course had been influenced by the effect my anti-slavery writings had on your mind, when you were a younger man"; in this letter Child also mentions similar acknowledgments she has received from Wilson, Channing, and Palfrey. For her influence on Wendell Phillips, see "Gone," *CC* 69/1837,

quoted in chap. 9 below. See Higginson, "Lydia Maria Child" 123–24, on the "formative influence" the *Appeal* exerted on him.

9   An Antislavery Marriage: Careers at Cross-Purposes

1   "Annual Meeting of the State Society," rpt. from the *Friend of Man, Liberator* 5 Nov. 1836, p. 178. Child may have been present on this occasion. In a letter of 19 Oct. 1836 to her mother-in-law Lydia Bigelow Child, written immediately after her return from New York, she mentions having "heard the Revd Mr. Ludlow, a Presbyterian minister, who is the heartiest abolition preacher I ever heard" (*SL* 55). The Rev. Henry Ludlow also gave the opening prayer at the Grimké sisters' first public lecture in New York in Dec. 1836. See Gerda Lerner, *The Grimké Sisters from South Carolina: Rebels Against Slavery* (Boston: Houghton Mifflin, 1967) 153–54. Ludlow's tribute to Child occurs in his speech on "Female Influence," where he defends the participation of women in the abolitionist movement as vital to its success. Ironically, he would shortly turn into one of the most vociferous critics of abolitionist women who addressed "promiscuous" audiences or occupied public offices in gender-mixed antislavery societies. Note the echo of Gen. 1.2–3: "And the earth was without form, and void; and the darkness was upon the face of the deep. And the Spirit of God moved upon the face of the waters. And God said, Let there be light. . . ." The reference to the "voice of mercy from Calvary" also suggests Acts 1–2, where the apostles are "baptized with the Holy Ghost" in accordance with the promise. Chaps. 9 and 10 have benefited greatly from the incisive criticisms of Milton Meltzer, Joyce Adler, Andrea Kerr, Jane Tompkins, Deborah Clifford, and H. Bruce Franklin (in chronological order).

2   "A.W.," untitled letter to Garrison, dated 23 Feb., *Liberator* 7 Mar. 1835, p. 38. Child was probably on her way to Washington (see this chapter below).

3   "*Extracts from an Address*," *Liberator* 30 June 1837, p. 105.

4   Articles on slavery or related topics in the *Massachusetts Journal and Tribune* include the following: "Walker's Appeal," 11 Dec. 1830, p. 3; "Liberia Colony," 1 Jan. 1831, p. 1; "The Slave Trade in the Capital," 8 Jan. 1831, p. 1; "A Fact," 30 Apr. 1831, p. 1 (rpt. from *Liberator*); "The Slave Trader" (a serialized story by LMC) and "Destruction of a Slave Trader," 7 May 1831, pp. 1–2; "The Marriage Law," 7 May 1831, p. 1 (rpt. from *Boston Courier*); "Negro Slavery," 16 July 1831, p. 2; "Novel Incident," 6 Aug. 1831, p. 3; "The Slave Question, No. 1," 13 Aug. 1831, p. 1; "Gabriel's Defeat" (rpt. from *Albany Argus*) and "College for Colored People," 17 Sept. 1831, pp. 1 and 3; "Inside of a Slave Ship" and "New Slave Insurrection," 24 Sept. 1831, pp. 2–3; "The Slave Insurrection," 1 Oct. 1831, p. 2; "College for Colored People," 1 Oct. 1831, p. 2; "College for Colored People" and "The Virginia Slave Insurrection," 15 Oct. 1831, pp. 1–2; untitled article on Garrison, 29 Oct. 1831, p. 1 (rpt. from *Portsmouth Journal*); "The Slave Question, No. 2," 12 Nov. 1831, p. 1; "The Slave Question, No. 3," "Incendiary Publications," and "Gen. Nat," 26 Nov. 1831, pp. 1, 3; "Vermont Colonization Society," 3 Dec. 1831, p. 1; "The Moral of an Alarm Watch" (LMC story) and "Slaves," 17 Dec. 1831, pp. 1, 3; "Colony of Liberia," 24 Dec. 1831, p. 1; "The Slave Question, No. 4" and untitled editorial note praising the *Liberator*, 7 Jan. 1832, p. 3; "Some of the Evils of Slave Labor," 21 Jan. 1832, p. 1; "Free Negroes and Slaves," 28 Jan. 1832, p. 1; "The American Colonization Society," 4 Feb. 1832, p. 1; "Liberia," 11 Feb. 1832, p. 3. David's articles on Colonization indicate that he had not yet come to see support for the Colonization Society as incompatible with abolitionism. The issue of 18 Feb. 1832 appears to be the last, though it contains no editorial farewell.

5   "Speech of David Lee Child, Esq.," rpt from *New-England Telegraph, Liberator* 4 Jan. 1834, p. 1.

6   LMC to Stephen Salisbury, 13 June 1875, *CC* 85/2238a.

7   See LMC to Louisa Loring, 28 Feb. and 14 Aug. 1843, *CC* 16/459, 17/505, quoted in chaps. 11 and 12 below.

8   [Wendell Phillips Garrison?], "Mrs. Child's Letters," review of *Letters of Lydia Maria Child* (1882), *Nation* 25 Jan. 1883: 87–88.

9   LMC "Autobiography," Cornell University Anti-Slavery Collection, Child Papers. Child wrote this

description of her domestic paradise at the bottom of a sketch she drew of "A Pier for boats, at Cottage Place." See the photograph reproduced in this book. See also Deborah Pickman Clifford, *Crusader for Freedom: A Life of Lydia Maria Child* (Boston: Beacon P, 1992) 89–90.

10 "Gone," *CC* 69/1837; for a description of abolitionists' social lives, see Lawrence J. Friedman, *Gregarious Saints: Self and Community in American Abolitionism, 1830–1870* (Cambridge: Cambridge UP, 1982), esp. chap. 2 on the Boston Clique.

11 LMC to Henrietta Sargent, 17 Aug. 1870, *CC* 74/1956; "Another Friend Gone," *National Standard* 28 Jan. 1871, p. 1.

12 LMC to Charles Sumner and Lucy Osgood, 4 and 6 Apr. 1860, *CC* 45/1211, *SL* 349. Child cites other witticisms of Chapman's in letters to Louisa Loring, 24 June 1849, *CC* 27/753, and to Henrietta Sargent, 24 July 1870, *CC* 74/1953. For a brief (and hostile) biographical sketch of Chapman, see Jane H. Pease and William H. Pease, "The Boston Bluestocking: Maria Weston Chapman," *Bound with Them in Chains: A Biographical History of the Antislavery Movement* (Westport, Conn.: Greenwood P, 1972) 28–59; the quotations describing her are from p. 29. On Ann Terry Greene and the Weston sisters, see James Brewer Stewart, *Wendell Phillips: Liberty's Hero* (Baton Rouge: Louisiana State UP, 1986) 44–45. On the gatherings of the Boston Clique in the Chapmans' home, see Friedman, *Gregarious Saints* 55–57.

13 LMC to Gerrit Smith, 4 Apr. 1864, *SL* 441. See also LMC to Louisa Gilman Loring, 19 July 1836, *CC* 4/100: "I do not know of a single member in my own church, who has the least sympathy with me" on the issue of slavery.

14 For excellent histories of antiabolitionist mob violence, see Russell B. Nye, *Fettered Freedom: Civil Liberties and the Slavery Controversy, 1830–1860* (1963; Urbana: U of Illinois P, 1972), esp. chap. 5; and Leonard L. Richards, *"Gentlemen of Property and Standing": Anti-Abolition Mobs in Jacksonian America* (New York: Oxford UP, 1971).

15 Richards, *"Gentlemen of Property and Standing"* chap. 2.

16 Richards, *"Gentlemen of Property and Standing"* 25; James Brewer Stewart, *Holy Warriors: The Abolitionists and American Slavery* (New York: Hill and Wang, 1976) 65.

17 "Declaration of Sentiments of the American Anti-Slavery Society," *Selections from the Writings and Speeches of William Lloyd Garrison* (1852; New York: Negro Universities P, 1968) 66–71.

18 David Lee Child, *Oration in Honor of Universal Emancipation in the British Empire, Delivered at South Reading, August First, 1834* (Boston: Garrison and Knapp, 1834).

19 *Proceedings of the New-England Anti-Slavery Convention, Held in Boston on the 27th, 28th, and 29th of May, 1834* (Boston: Garrison and Knapp, 1834) 17–18; rpt. of "Report on the Domestic Slave Trade" on 25–36.

20 See Vincent Harding, *There Is a River: The Black Struggle for Freedom in America* (1981; New York: Vintage, 1983), 120–23.

21 See the appendix to David Lee Child, *The Despotism of Freedom* (Boston: Boston Young Men's Anti-Slavery Association, 1833) 69–71. The libel accusation occurs in the letter by Isaac Stone (the alleged kidnapper), rpt. from *Newburyport Herald*, *Liberator* 11 Jan. 1834, p. 6. On 8 Mar. 1834, David's correspondence with Stone and the affidavits of the three people whose testimony contradicted Stone's were published in the *Liberator* at David's request (p. 38). Although evidently nothing came of Stone's accusation, the successful libel suit against Garrison by the Newburyport captain he had charged with slave trading, Francis Todd (not to mention David's own conviction for libel), shows that being accused of libel could have serious consequences.

22 On David's appointment as paramount instructor, see George Kimball to DLC, 28 Oct. 1834, BPL Ms.A.1.2.V4, p. 70. A letter "To the American Public," signed by the academy's ten trustees, including David and Sewall, announced the "unanimous vote" to integrate the school; see the *Liberator* 25 Oct. 1834, p. 169. For eyewitness accounts of the school's destruction, see "Colored School at Canaan," rpt. from *Concord Patriot*, *Liberator* 5 Sept. 1835, p. 141; and the letter by John H. Harris, one of the academy's trustees, *Liberator* 3 Oct. 1835, p. 159. According to Harris, the vast majority of the towns-

people supported the school. A British abolitionist who visited Canaan, New Hampshire, with David Child while the trustees were voting on the school's charter makes the same assertion; see Edward S. Abdy, *Journal of a Residence and Tour in the United States of North America, from April, 1833, to October, 1834* (1835; New York: Negro Universities P, 1969) 3: 265–69. Of the fourteen black youths forced to flee the town at gunpoint for the crime of trying to obtain an education, two would win fame as leaders and leave major intellectual legacies: Henry Highland Garnet and Alexander Crummell. Their experience at the school is described in Sterling Stuckey, *Slave Culture: Nationalist Theory and the Foundations of Black America* (New York: Oxford UP, 1987) 148–49.

23   The letter nominating David as a candidate for U.S. senator is signed "P.H.," *Liberator* 24 Jan. 1835, p. 13. Garrison endorsed the nomination in a short note on p. 16. In 1835 "Massachusetts" replaced "New-England" in the Anti-Slavery Society's name, reflecting the large number of regional and state societies that had since been formed.

24   Wendell Phillips Garrison and Francis Jackson Garrison, *William Lloyd Garrison, 1805–1879* (1885–1889; New York: Arno P, 1969) 2: 49n, hereinafter cited as *Life*; also Jack Mendelsohn, *Channing: The Reluctant Radical* (Boston: Little, Brown, 1971) 236–37.

25   Child describes the encounter and reminisces about her relationship with Channing in a tribute to him published in his *Memoirs* after his death; rpt. in 1882 ed. of *Letters of Lydia Maria Child* [ed. Harriet Winslow Sewall] (New York: Negro Universities P, 1969) 48–50. By then, Channing had come to support abolitionists, and she had modified her original impression of him as "time-serving."

26   William Ellery Channing, *Slavery* (1835; New York: Arno P, 1969) 154–57; "Letter to Dr. Channing," *Liberator* 2 Apr. 1836, *CC* 4/91. For another interesting assessment of Channing's book and character by an abolitionist who shared Child's reservations but still revered Channing, see Samuel J. May, *Some Recollections of Our Antislavery Conflict* (Boston: Fields, Osgood, 1869) 177–85.

27   LMC to Henrietta Sargent, 13 Nov. 1836, *SL* 57.

28   LMC to Louisa Gilman Loring, 19 July 1836, *CC* 4/100.

29   LMC to Henrietta Sargent, 13 Nov. 1836, *SL* 56–57.

30   For studies of Channing's career that discuss his evolution on the slavery question, see Mendelsohn, *Channing: The Reluctant Radical*, chap. 6; Andrew Delbanco, *William Ellery Channing: An Essay on the Liberal Spirit in America* (Cambridge, Mass.: Harvard UP, 1981), chap. 4; and David P. Edgell, *William Ellery Channing: An Intellectual Portrait* (1955; Westport, Conn.: Greenwood P, 1983) 42–51, 179–83.

31   *Letters of Lydia Maria Child* 44–47.

32   Lydia Maria Child, ed., *The Oasis* (Boston: Allen and Ticknor, 1834). I am grateful to Peter Van Wingen, former Head of the Reference Section of the Rare Book Room at the Library of Congress, for directing me to a copy of *The Oasis* in the original binding. Evidently the book also came with an "ornamental cover" that no longer survives. The other titles I have cited are listed in the catalog appended to Ralph Thompson's *American Literary Annuals & Gift Books, 1825–1865* (New York: H. W. Wilson, 1936) 102–63.

33   Of nine full-page engravings, six present sympathetic and attractive images of Africa, Africans, or mulattoes: the ruins of Thebes; the illustrations of African children and their mother accompanying "Malem-boo," discussed in this chapter below; and the portraits of the beautiful mulatto Joanna, of the black military hero of France, Scipio Africanus, and of a Hottentot herdsman. Completing the set are portraits of two white abolitionist heroes, one male the other female (William Wilberforce and Prudence Crandall), and a scene showing a "Negro Hunt."

34   For a discussion of "Jumbo and Zairee," see chap. 7 above. So far I have found only one example of antislavery fiction that antedates Child's "The St. Domingo Orphans" and "Jumbo and Zairee" in the *Juvenile Miscellany* (Sept. 1830 and Jan./Feb. 1831): "The Harmans" in the *Genius of Universal Emancipation*, 13 Nov. 1829, pp. 76–77. I have found a handful of antislavery stories in the *Liberator*, all dating from 1831 to 1832: see "A Dream" and "Another Dream" by "T.T." (2 Apr. 1831, p. 53; 30 Apr. 1831, p. 70); "Uncle's Story" by T.E. in the Juvenile Department (31 Mar. 1832, pp. 50–51); and "Story of 1793" (29 Sept. 1832, p. 156). None bears the slightest resemblance to "Malem-Boo." Nor do the two

earliest antislavery novels of which I am aware: Gustave de Beaumont's *Marie ou l'Esclavage aux États-Unis* (1835) and Richard Hildreth's *The Slave, or Memoirs of Archy Moore* (1836), both published after "Malem-Boo."

35 "'The Oasis — Edited by Mrs. Child,'" *Liberator* 11 Oct. 1834, p. 163; "The Oasis — By Mrs. Child," *Liberator* 18 June 1836, p. 99.

36 "The Oasis," rpt. from *Boston Daily Advocate, Liberator* 22 Nov. 1834, p.187.

37 "The Oasis, by Mrs. CHILD," *Liberator* 29 Nov. 1834, p. 189. Garrison printed this review under the column "Refuge of Oppression," reserved for proslavery and antiabolitionist cullings from the mainstream press, and followed it with a defense of *The Oasis* by someone who signed himself "Howard" after the English philanthropist and prison reformer. The review had originally appeared in a "monthly miscellany" run by Harvard students.

38 Untitled note, *Liberator* 9 May 1835, p. 74.

39 "Amos Dresser's Own Narrative," *Liberator* 26 Sept. 1835, p. 156.

40 "The Election — Mr. Lawrence's Letter," *Liberator* 8 Nov. 1834, p. 179.

41 J. H. Le Roy, "READ IT. *Written in Mrs. Child's 'Oasis,' presented to a friend," Liberator* 8 Nov. 1834, p. 179.

42 Allen and Ticknor also published the *Appeal*. For a discussion of the curious exception Ticknor seems to represent among commercial publishers, who generally refused to have anything to do with abolitionists, see my article "Censorship, American Style: The Case of Lydia Maria Child," *Studies in the American Renaissance* 1986: 283–303, esp. 285–87.

43 See LMC to Ellis and Louisa Loring, 5 Dec. 1838, *SL* 95, and Ellis Loring to LMC, 22 Feb. 1839, *CC* 7/170.

44 Quoted in Thompson, *American Literary Annuals* 84. See his chap., 82–90, on *The Liberty Bell*. For an illuminating discussion of *The Liberty Bell* and the fair as intertwined forums of women's antislavery activism, see Karen Sánchez-Eppler, "Bodily Bonds: The Intersecting Rhetorics of Feminism and Abolition," *Representations* 24 (Fall 1988), rpt. in Shirley Samuels, ed., *The Culture of Sentiment: Race, Gender, and Sentimentality in Nineteenth-Century America* (New York: Oxford UP, 1992) 92–114, esp. 97–99 and 300–301, nn. 17–21. The first of *The Liberty Bell's* fifteen volumes was published in 1839. Except for a few missing years, it appeared annually until 1858.

45 For details on the *Panda* case, see Anna D. Hallowell, "Lydia Maria Child," *Medford Historical Register* 3 (July 1900): 104; Helene G. Baer, *The Heart Is Like Heaven: The Life of Lydia Maria Child* (Philadelphia: U of Pennsylvania P, 1964) 77–82; Deborah Pickman Clifford, *Crusader for Freedom: A Life of Lydia Maria Child* (Boston: Beacon P, 1992) 114–15; Edward C. Battis, "The Brig Mexican of Salem, Captured by Pirates, and Her Escape," *Essex Institute Historical Collections* 34 (June 1898): 41–63; the "Biography of Lydia Maria Child" by Holland and Meltzer in the guide and index to the microfiche edition of Child's *Collected Correspondence* 36, n. 16; "Trial of the Pirates," *Liberator* 15 Nov. 1834, p. 183; "The Pirates: Verdict of the Jury," *Liberator* 29 Nov. 1834, p. 191; and Child's letters of 25 and 28 Feb. 1835 to Attorney General Benjamin F. Butler and of 22 May 1835 to David, *CC* 3/70–72. Quotations in this and the next paragraph are from the *Liberator* articles, Hallowell, and Child's letters.

46 LMC to DLC, 22 May 1835, *CC* 3/72.

47 Battis, "The Brig Mexican of Salem" 63.

48 LMC to DLC, 22 May, 1835, *CC* 3/72.

49 See LMC to DLC, 22 May 1835, *CC* 3/72; LMC to Lydia Bigelow Child, 19 Oct. 1836, *SL* 55; LMC to Louisa Loring, 19 July 1836, *CC* 4/100; LMC to DLC, 31 July 1836, *CC* 4/103. On David's prior interest in going West, see DLC to General Henry Dearborn, 13 Mar. 1824, C. E. French Collection, MHS.

50 See C. Duncan Rice, "The Anti-Slavery Mission of George Thompson to the United States, 1834–1835," *Journal of American Studies* 2 (Apr. 1968): 13–31. Though hostile to Thompson and the Garrisonians, this article is useful for its detailed reconstruction of the tour.

51 Rice, "Anti-Slavery Mission of Thompson" 22, mentions Thompson's trip to New York and Philadelphia. "A.W.," untitled letter to Garrison, dated 23 Feb., *Liberator* 7 Mar. 1835, p. 38 describes Child in the company of Thompson.

52   Caroline Weston to Mrs. L. R. G. Hamatt, 1 Aug. 1835, BPL Ms.A.9.2.V7, p. 62.

53   Caroline Weston to Anne Warren Weston and Deborah Weston?, 13 Aug. 1835, BPL Ms.A.9.2.V7, p. 63; "House Furniture, To be sold at public vendue, at No. 3, *Cottage Place*, on Thursday, Aug. 6th, at 9 o'clock, A.M.," *Liberator* 1 Aug. 1835, p. 123; Caroline Weston to Mrs. L. R. G. Hamatt, 1 Aug. 1835, BPL Ms.A.9.2.V7, p. 62.

54   LMC to Louisa Loring, 15 Aug. [1835], *SL* 31.

55   I am indebted to Deborah Clifford for suggesting to me that Child may have developed a crush on Thompson (a suggestion she did not incorporate into her biography). See also the much reprinted poem Child wrote to Thompson while she was hiding from the mobs. And see chaps. 13–14 below on Child's platonic love relationships with other men. She later confessed to her friend Francis Shaw that " 'The strong necessity of loving' has been the great temptation and conflict of my life' " (2 Aug. 1846, *SL* 229). Rice, "Anti-Slavery Mission of Thompson" 24 cites Deborah Weston's diary of 8 Nov. 1835 for evidence of Weston's "school-girl crush" on Thompson. Another young abolitionist who seems to have developed a "school-girl crush" on Thompson is Sarah H. Southwick. See her *Reminiscences of Early Anti-Slavery Days* (1893; Macon, Ga.: Kingsley P, 1971) 12–13.

56   LMC to Louisa Loring, 15 Aug. [1835], *SL* 32; Harriet Martineau, *The Martyr Age of the United States* (1839; New York: Arno P, 1969) 15.

10   The Condition of Women: *Double Binds, Unresolved Conflicts*

1   The inscription was reproduced in the accompanying letter by Anna Purinton for the Ladies of Lynn, 8 Aug. 1835, *CC* 3/78, rpt. in the *Liberator* 29 Aug. 1835. The same issue contains a similar letter by the ladies of Salem and Child's reply (*CC* 3/77, 79). The watch, chosen by Maria Chapman and George Thompson, was presented to Child at the Lorings' farewell party. See Caroline Weston to Anne Warren Weston and Deborah Weston?, 13 Aug. 1835, BPL Ms.A.9.2.V7, p. 63.

2   Anna Purinton [for the Ladies of Lynn and Salem], 8 Aug. 1835, *CC* 3/78.

3   Samuel J. May, *Some Recollections of Our Antislavery Conflict* (Boston: Fields, Osgood, 1869) 101. In her preface to *The Oasis* (Boston: Allen and Ticknor, 1834) Child writes: "I have, for the last two years, attended almost every Anti-Slavery meeting in this neighborhood" (xv–xvi).

4   See Jane H. Pease and William H. Pease, "The Boston Bluestocking: Maria Weston Chapman," *Bound with Them in Chains: A Biographical History of the Antislavery Movement* (Westport, Conn.: Greenwood P, 1972) 34.

5   May, *Some Recollections* 101.

6   For an eyewitness account, see May, *Some Recollections* 79–87, esp. 91–93 on the participation of Mott and two other Quaker women, Esther Moore and Lydia White. For a modern account, see Blanche Glassman Hersh, *The Slavery of Sex: Feminist-Abolitionists in America* (Urbana: U of Illinois P, 1978) 13–14.

7   LMC to the Editor of the *Liberator* 6 Mar. 1840, *SL* 128. The meeting Child refers to in this letter took place in 1836.

8   See the reminiscences by John Greenleaf Whittier and Wendell Phillips in the introduction and appendix to [Harriet Winslow Sewall], ed. *The Letters of Lydia Maria Child* (1882; New York: Negro Universities P, 1969) xvii, 266–67. Also Margaret Fuller to Susan Prescott, 10 Jan. 1827, *The Letters of Margaret Fuller*, ed. Robert N. Hudspeth (Ithaca, N.Y.: Cornell UP, 1983–) 1: 154, quoted in chap. 2.

9   LMC to Louisa Loring [Mar.? 1837], *SL* 64.

10   See "Letter from a Lady, concerning Miss Wright," *Massachusetts Weekly Journal* 14 Aug. 1829, p. 3, quoted in chap. 5 above.

11   See the criticisms of David's style in "Speech of David Lee Child, Esq.," rpt. from the *New-England Telegraph*, *Liberator* 4 Jan. 1834, p. 1, quoted in chap. 9 above.

12   See LMC to Stephen Salisbury, 13 June 1875, *CC* 85/2238a, quoted in chap. 9. See also LMC to Ellis

Loring, 22 Mar. [1842], *SL* 167: "My peculiar situation is sufficiently disagreeable to me, without adding anything which seems like giving me the superiority over my gifted and beloved husband."

13   WLG to Editor of the *Newburyport Herald*, 21 Apr. 1827, Walter M. Merrill, ed. *The Letters of William Lloyd Garrison*, vol. 1: *I Will Be Heard! 1822–1835* (Cambridge, Mass.: Belknap P of Harvard UP, 1971) 38, hereinafter cited as *GL*. Garrison was commenting on a speech David made in favor of John Quincy Adams at a Faneuil Hall meeting.

14   DLC to Angelina Grimké, 12 Feb. 1838, *Letters of Theodore Dwight Weld, Angelina Grimké Weld and Sarah Grimké, 1822–1844*, ed. Gilbert H. Barnes and Dwight L. Dumond (1934; Gloucester, Mass.: Peter Smith, 1965) 2: 544, hereinafter referred to as *Weld-Grimké Letters*.

15   "Anti-Slavery Convention," rpt. from the *Emancipator*, *Liberator* 28 Dec. 1833, p. 206. The *Liberator* 14 July 1832, p. 110, announced with fanfare "the formation of the first 'Female Anti-Slavery Society' in New-England," the Providence Female Anti-Slavery Society, and expressed the hope that it would be "the forerunner of a multitude of similar associations. . . ." According to Keith E. Melder, however, credit for forming the first female antislavery society (in Feb. 1832) belongs to the African American women of Salem, Massachusetts; see his *Beginnings of Sisterhood: The American Woman's Rights Movement, 1800–1850* (New York: Schocken, 1977) 59. For an excellent study of women's activism, see Nancy A. Hewitt, *Women's Activism and Social Change: Rochester, New York, 1822–1872* (Ithaca, N.Y.: Cornell UP, 1984), esp. chap. 2 for this formative period; see also Hersh, *Slavery of Sex*.

16   LMC to Charlotte Phelps [2 Jan. 1834], *SL* 28.

17   Wendell Phillips Garrison and Francis Jackson Garrison, *William Lloyd Garrison, 1805–1879* (1885–1889; New York: Arno P, 1969) 2: 49n., hereinafter referred to as *Life*.

18   LMC to Lucretia Mott, 5 Mar. 1839, *SL* 107.

19   This can be inferred from one of the resolutions she proposed at the 1837 Anti-Slavery Convention of American Women, discussed at the end of this chapter. The importance Child ascribed to sitting beside blacks can also be inferred from a letter of 10 July 1862 to William P. Cutler, in which she criticizes the "vulgar, shallow fools . . . who consider it a degradation to be seated by [the] side" of one of her African American acquaintances, probably Charlotte Forten (*SL* 414).

20   LMC to Jonathan Phillips, 23 Jan. 1838, *SL* 69–71. Jonathan Phillips was a relative of Wendell Phillips.

21   LMC to Jonathan Phillips, 26 Feb. 1838, *CC* 96/2533. This was a letter of thanks for the $30 Phillips sent Paul. In it Child frankly avowed her desire to convert him to abolition.

22   On 22 Nov. 1834 a brief notice in the *Liberator*, p. 187, titled "Anti-Slavery Ladies—Attention!" invites members of other female antislavery societies in New England to contribute articles combining "utility with ornament" to the antislavery fair being organized by "MRS. CHILD and other ladies" and to send them to the *Liberator* office. The fair is advertised in a notice of 13 Dec. 1834, p. 199. It took place on 16 Dec. beginning at 9 A.M. and continuing throughout the day. The article "Anti-Slavery Fair," 20 Dec. 1834, p. 203, describes the event and the items sold.

23   Deborah Pickman Clifford, *Crusader for Freedom: A Life of Lydia Maria Child* (Boston: Beacon P, 1992) 109; Sarah H. Southwick, *Reminiscences of Early Anti-Slavery Days* (1893; Macon, Ga.: Kingsley P, 1971) 7–8.

24   Lydia Maria Child, "The Ladies' Fair," *Liberator* 2 Jan. 1837, p. 3.

25   Child, "The Ladies' Fair," *Liberator* 2 Jan. 1837, p. 3. See also LMC to Lydia Bigelow Child, 17 Jan. 1837, *SL* 60, which reports: "My cradle-quilt sold for $5." For a fine analysis of the female discourse of antislavery fairs, see Karen Sánchez-Eppler, "Bodily Bonds: The Intersecting Rhetorics of Feminism and Abolition," Shirley Samuels, ed., *The Culture of Sentiment: Race, Gender, and Sentimentality in Nineteenth-Century America* (New York: Oxford UP, 1992) 98–99.

26   LMC to Lucretia Mott, 5 Mar. 1839, *SL* 106.

27   Deborah Weston to Mrs. Anne B. Weston, 8 May 1835, BPL Ms.A.9.2.V7, p. 45, quoted in *SL* 28–29; see also Deborah Weston Diary, BPL Ms.A.9.2.V7, pp. 43–44, 8 May 1835: "Maria called having succeeded in getting 75 dolls since yesterday morning for Mrs Child to have a right in the Athaneum library."

28   LMC to Maria Weston Chapman and Other Ladies, 1 June 1834 [1835], *SL* 29. In her letter, Child goes on to say that she may have to appropriate the money to different, though comparable, uses if David decides to leave Boston. According to the Athenaeum's list of books borrowed, however, Child returned her most crucial sources for her *History of Women* (discussed in this chapter below) on 14 May 1835. No further records of borrowings appear after that date. (The Athenaeum's register includes date borrowed and date returned. Child's first borrowing is on 14 Jan. 1832, the last on 2 Feb. 1835.) This would seem to indicate that Child never purchased a paying membership in the Athenaeum. Since it was a private library, it would no doubt have had the right to exclude an undesired member on other than financial grounds. Clifford reaches the same conclusion, *Crusader for Freedom* 106.

29   According to a notation on the title page, the book was deposited for copyright on 7 Sept. 1835. Child apparently left the Lorings in charge of final arrangements for the book. See LMC to Louisa Loring, 15 Aug. [1835], *SL* 33. The book appeared in time to be reviewed in the Oct. 1835 issue of Hale's *American Ladies' Magazine*.

30   Lydia Maria Child, *The History of the Condition of Women, in Various Ages and Nations*, vols. 4 and 5 of the *Ladies' Family Library* (Boston: John Allen, 1835). I will be quoting from the 5th edition, retitled *Brief History of the Condition of Women, in Various Ages and Nations* (New York: C. S. Francis, 1845), reissued with identical pagination in 1854 (still described as the 5th edition). Page references will be given parenthetically in the text. I have compared the 1835 and 1854 editions and found a few significant revisions, including the addition of a preface, the deletion of a negative reference to Frances Wright, and a more radical formulation of Child's views on the woman question (2: 210–11). Child's *History of Women* anticipates Gerda Lerner's *The Creation of Patriarchy* (New York: Oxford UP, 1986). Child's emphasis on women's cultural diversity and class differences is also very much in line with the recent trend away from monolithic theories about women based largely on white middle-class experience.

31   I am grateful to Deborah Clifford for expediting my research on Child's sources by sharing with me her list of the books Child borrowed from the Boston Athenaeum.

32   In a lecture at the University of Maryland in 1977, Hilda Smith described this as a problem facing the scholars who reinvented women's history in the 1970s.

33   William Alexander, M.D., *The History of Women, from the Earliest Antiquity, to the Present Time; Giving an Account of Almost Every Interesting Particular Concerning That Sex, among All Nations, Ancient and Modern. With a Complete Index*, 2 vols. (1779; New York: AMS P, 1976). This book seems to have enjoyed great popularity. It went through several editions, both in England and in the United States, and it seems also to have been widely read in France. The first American edition was published in Philadelphia in 1796. I have been unable to find any information about the author in biographical dictionaries. It would appear, however, that his book was part of a late eighteenth-century trend toward encouraging the education of women. Child checked the book out of the Boston Athenaeum on 18 Jan. 1834, along with a French work titled *Les Femmes*, renewing both several times. The latter, Vicomte J. A. de Ségur's *Les Femmes, leur condition et leur influence dans l'ordre social, chez différens peuples anciens et modernes; Augmentés de l'influence des Femmes sous l'Empire, et de notes historiques, par M. Ch. N****, 3 vols. (Paris, 1803), also went through many editions and was translated into English in 1803. The author acknowledged his debt to an unnamed English work, obviously Alexander's *History*. Child seems to have relied mostly on Alexander.

34   See Martin Bernal, *Black Athena: The Afroasiatic Roots of Classical Civilization*, vol. 1: *The Fabrication of Ancient Greece, 1785–1985* (New Brunswick, N.J.: Rutgers UP, 1987; and Cheikh Anta Diop, *The African Origin of Civilization: Myth or Reality?*, trans. M. Cook (Westport, Conn.: Lawrence Hill, 1974). As Bernal shows, the facts Child cites (along with other abolitionists) were widely accepted until the late eighteenth century, when a campaign began to redefine Egypt as part of Europe and to minimize the debt of the Greeks, and of European civilization generally, to Egypt. Archaeological and linguistic research has confirmed the theory of Ethiopian origin.

35   Alexander 1: 279–84. The best he can say of Africa is that the "gloomy scene is here and there chequered with a few of the virtues" (281).

36   [Sarah Josepha Hale], "The History of the Condition of Women, in Various Ages and Nations. By Mrs. D. L. Child," *American Ladies' Magazine* 8 (Oct. 1835): 588.

37   Jean Fagan Yellin, *Women and Sisters: The Antislavery Feminists in American Culture* (New Haven, Conn.: Yale UP, 1989) 55–56.

38   Sarah M. Grimké, *Letters on the Equality of the Sexes, and the Condition of Woman. Addressed to Mary S. Parker, President of the Boston Female Anti-Slavery Society* (1838; New York: Source Book P, 1970) 10, 27, 29, 60.

39   Margaret Fuller, *Woman in the Nineteenth Century* (1845), in Jeffrey Steele, ed. *The Essential Margaret Fuller* (New Brunswick, N.J.: Rutgers UP, 1992) 346–47.

40   Steele, ed. *Essential Margaret Fuller* 281. Also echoed in this passage is Child's assertion that in the United States "mothers are not wanting who will consent to sell their daughters to the highest bidder, though the bargain is accompanied with formalities, supposed to render it much more respectable than the sale of Circassian girls in the Turkish markets" (2: 269).

41   Steele, ed., *Essential Margaret Fuller* 319–33. The quotations are from 322, 329. Fuller goes on to cite Child as a model, praising her for having publicly befriended a "fallen woman" who had tried to murder her seducer (330). For a discussion of this incident, see chap. 14 below. Fuller's discussion of prostitution is part of a long section analyzing the "transition state" (324) of marriage in the Western world, from its roots in the Asian customs described by Child toward an equal partnership of the sexes that includes intellectual and spiritual companionship (see also 281–95). In tracing this evolution, which Fuller viewed as still in progress, she drew for examples on Child's *Good Wives* and her biographies of Madame Roland and Lady Russell. See 283 on the marriage of the Rolands; also the examples of Colonel and Mrs. Hutchinson (279, 341), Panthea and Abradatus (291–95) and Lady Russell (324, 327–28). Though Fuller clearly went directly to Child's sources, her reading of Child must have suggested these examples to her.

42   LMC to Louisa Loring, 8 Feb. 1845, *SL* 219.

43   [Margaret Fuller], "History of Women. By L. M. Child," *New York Tribune* 20 Nov. 1845, p. 1, col. 1. Yellin, *Women and Sisters* 193, n. 8, credits the discovery of this review to Bell Gale Chevigny.

44   Elizabeth Cady Stanton, Susan B. Anthony, and Matilda Joslyn Gage, *History of Woman Suffrage*, vol. 1: *1848–1861* (1881; New York: Arno P, 1969) 38. This statement is actually an unacknowledged quotation from Thomas Wentworth Higginson, "Lydia Maria Child" (1868), *Contemporaries, The Writings of Thomas Wentworth Higginson*, vol. 2 (Boston: Houghton Mifflin, 1900) 120.

45   "What Have Ladies to Do with the Subject of Anti-Slavery?," *Liberator* 29 Mar. 1834, p. 50. For a similar statement reflecting a transition toward a more radical position, see "The Mandate!," *Liberator* 19 Dec. 1835, p. 203. Quotations in this paragraph are drawn from both articles.

46   "The Mob at Concord [New Hampshire]," *Liberator* 13 Dec. 1834, p. 198.

47   "Letter from New-York" No. 33, *National Anti-Slavery Standard* 18 Aug. 1842, *CC* 15/399; "A Reminiscence of George Thompson's First Visit to the United States. Letter from Mrs. Child," *National Anti-Slavery Standard* 27 Feb. 1864, *CC* 58/1544.

48   For contemporary accounts of this event, which came to be known as the "Boston mob," see [Maria Weston Chapman], *Right and Wrong in Boston*, No. 1: *Report of the Boston Female Anti-Slavery Society; with a Concise Statement of Events, Previous and Subsequent to the Annual Meeting of 1835*, 2nd ed. (Boston: Boston Female Anti-Slavery Society, 1836); and *"Triumph of Mobocracy in Boston . . . ," Liberator* 7 Nov. 1835, pp. 178–79, rpt. in Nelson, ed., *Documents of Upheaval* 85–95. Chapman's report reprints the major newspaper accounts of the event. Quotations are from pp. 32–34.

49   LMC to the Boston Female Anti-Slavery Society, [undated, before 19 Nov. 1835], *SL* 41; Lydia Maria Child, *The Biographies of Madame de Staël, and Madame Roland*, vol. 1 of *The Ladies' Family Library* (Boston: Carter and Hendee, 1832) 74n.

50   "Annual Meeting of the Boston Female Anti-Slavery Society," *Liberator*, 21 Nov. 1835, p. 187; *Right and Wrong in Boston* 90–94.

51 Parker actually suggested the topic "The Province of Woman" and helped arrange for the serial publication of Sarah Grimké's letters in the New England *Spectator*, beginning in July 1837. The letters were concurrently reprinted in the *Liberator* before being reissued the following year in book form. See Gerda Lerner, *The Grimké Sisters from South Carolina: Rebels against Slavery* (Boston: Houghton Mifflin, 1967) 187–88; and Angelina Grimké to Theodore Weld and John Greenleaf Whittier, *Weld-Grimké Letters*, 1: 427–28.

52 Lydia Maria Child, "Letter from New-York" No. 50, *National Anti-Slavery Standard* 16 Feb. 1843, *CC* 16/452. Child is quoting her friends' letters.

53 See LMC to George Thompson, 18 Sept. 1835, *SL* 35.

54 The comparison that springs to mind is Frances Wright's pilot project in Nashoba, Tennessee, which had proved a costly failure. See Celia Morris Eckhardt, *Fanny Wright: Rebel in America* (Cambridge, Mass.: Harvard UP, 1984) chaps. 5–6.

55 "Mexican Colonization," *Liberator* 13 June 1835, p. 95.

56 DLC to Señor Castillo, chargé d'affaires of Mexico, 26 Dec. 1835, BPL Ms.A.4.1, p. 45. This appears to be a rough draft. David sent the original to Castillo care of Lundy. See Benjamin Lundy to DLC, 25 Jan. 183[6?], *CC* 4/89. David's radicalism can best be appreciated against the backdrop of the debates over annexation, as summarized by Reginald Horsman, *Race and Manifest Destiny: The Origins of American Racial Anglo-Saxonism* (Cambridge, Mass.: Harvard UP, 1981) chaps. 11–13. None of David's fellow Whigs shared his passionate sense of solidarity with the Mexicans, and his fellow abolitionists tended to express their solidarity through pacifist agitation.

57 Benjamin Lundy to DLC, 25 Jan. 183[6?], *CC* 4/89 (italics in original); Meltzer and Holland headnote, *SL* 42; Merton L. Dillon, *Benjamin Lundy and the Struggle for Negro Freedom* (Urbana: U of Illinois P, 1966) 217–18.

58 LMC to Ellis and Louisa Loring, 30 Jan. 1836, *SL* 43–46.

59 LMC to Ellis and Louisa Loring, *SL* 45. The publication of *The Evils of Slavery, and the Cure of Slavery* was announced in the *Liberator* on 16 Jan. 1836, p. 11; see "Much in Little." Child's *Anti-Slavery Catechism* was advertised in the *Liberator* on 30 Jan. 1836, p. 19. None of the three tracts was reviewed.

60 Lydia Maria Child, *Anti-Slavery Catechism* (Newburyport: Charles Whipple, 1836) 17–18, 29–33. Further page references are given parenthetically in the text.

61 Though Child's formulation of the abolitionist creed may seem surprisingly conservative, it is in fact consistent with Garrison's. See his statement in the *American Anti-Slavery Almanac for 1836*, ed. Nathaniel Southard (Boston: Webster & Southard, 1835) 29:

> By immediate emancipation we do not mean —
> That the slaves shall be turned loose upon the nation, to roam as vagabonds or aliens — nor
> That they shall be instantly invested with all political rights and privileges. . . . But we mean —
> That, instead of being under the unlimited control of a few irresponsible masters, they shall really receive the protection of law. . . .
> That the slaves shall be employed as free laborers, fairly compensated, and fully protected in their earnings:
> That they shall be placed under a benevolent and disinterested supervision, which shall secure to them the right to obtain secular and religious knowledge, to worship God according to the dictates of their own consciences, to accumulate wealth, and to seek an intellectual and moral equality with their white competitors.

In the context of the 1830s, moreover, merely to suggest that the avenues of upward mobility should be opened to Northern free blacks, let alone to Southern slaves, was radical enough to provoke a race riot, as the examples of Prudence Crandall's school and the Noyes Academy testify.

62 LMC to Lydia Bigelow Child, 10 Mar. 1836, *SL* 47.

63 LMC to Ellis Loring, 30 Jan. 1836, *SL* 45.

64 Lydia Maria Child, *Philothea. A Romance* (Boston: Otis, Broaders, 1836) vi–vii. All further page references to this edition will be given parenthetically in the text.

65 See Robert E. Streeter, "Mrs. Child's 'Philothea' — A Transcendentalist Novel?," *New England Quarterly* 16 (Dec. 1943): 648–54; Kenneth Cameron, *Philothea, or Plato Against Epicurus: A Novel of the Transcendental Movement in New England, by Lydia Maria Child. With an Analysis of Background and Meaning for the Community of Emerson and Thoreau* (Hartford, Conn.: Transcendental Books, 1975) 2–3, 41–49, 135–36; Joel Myerson, "A Calendar of Transcendental Club Meetings," *American Literature* 44 (May 1972): 197–207; and his "Convers Francis and Emerson," *American Literature* 50 (Mar. 1978): 17–36.

66 On Greek civilization's Afroasiatic roots, see Bernal, *Black Athena*, cited in n. 34 above.

67 For an interesting topical interpretation of the novel's political allegory, see William Osborne, *Lydia Maria Child* (Boston: Twayne, 1980) 74–81. Osborne not only identifies Pericles with Andrew Jackson, but Aspasia with Margaret Eaton, "installed by Jackson as mistress of the White House" (79). In another topical interpretation, Cameron more convincingly identifies Aspasia with Frances Wright. He argues that Child is responding to Wright's Greek novel, *A Few Days in Athens* (1822, rev. ed. 1835) by countering an Epicurean with a Transcendentalist intepretation of Hellenism. See his edition of *Philothea* (1), which includes a reprint of *A Few Days in Athens*.

68 LMC to Francis Shaw, 2 Aug. 1846, *SL* 228. Osborne, *Lydia Maria Child*, also suggests that "the ideal love of Philothea and Paralus" can be read "as a thinly veiled allusion to what may have been the innocent love of Maria and David Child." He interprets Child's statement "We always continued child-like in our love-making" to mean that the couple lacked a "sexual life" (89, 180n); see her unpublished "Autobiography" (8) LMC Papers, Anti-Slavery Collection, Cornell University Library.

69 Clifford, *Crusader for Freedom*, wonders whether "Philothea's creator is not expressing an unconscious desire for her own husband's death" (123).

70 DLC to Lydia Bigelow Child, 20 Oct. 1827, Ross Collection, quoted in Chapter 4; "Letter from a Lady, concerning Miss Wright," *Massachusetts Weekly Journal* 14 Aug. 1829, p. 3, discussed in chap. 5.

71 Reviews of *Philothea* by [Sarah Josepha Hale], *American Ladies' Magazine* 9 (Aug. 1836): 480–81; [Cornelius Conway Felton], *North American Review* 44 (Jan. 1837): 77–85; [Edgar Allan Poe], *Southern Literary Messenger* 2 (Sept. 1836): 659–62. The Felton and Poe reviews are reprinted in Cameron's edition of *Philothea*. See also the *Knickerbocker* 8 (Sept. 1836): 370: "We can but counsel all lovers of a pure, classical style, and of a narrative imbued with more than common power and interest, to possess themselves of a volume which reflects honor upon the taste and genius of the author."

72 Cameron, ed., *Philothea* 3, 135–36; Higginson, "Lydia Maria Child" 124–25; Anne Warren Weston to M. Weston, 15 Apr. 1836, BPL Ms.A.9.2.8, p. 19. The one exception was Margaret Fuller, who expressed a low opinion of *Philothea* in a letter of 16 Aug. 1837 to her and Child's friend Caroline Sturgis; see *The Letters of Margaret Fuller*, ed. Robert N. Hudspeth (Ithaca, N.Y.: Cornell UP, 1983) 1: 297.

73 Meltzer and Holland, headnote, *SL* 50; Dillon, *Benjamin Lundy*, chap. 13; May, *Some Recollections* 316–21; Harriet Martineau, *The Martyr Age of the United States* (1839; New York: Arno P, 1969) 48–49.

74 LMC to Louisa Loring, 3 May [1836], *SL* 49; for a partial list of English editions, see Jacob Blanck, *Bibliography of American Literature* (New Haven, Conn.: Yale UP, 1957).

75 LMC to Louisa Loring, 3 May and 19 July 1836, *SL* 49, *CC* 4/100.

76 *The Oasis* might be considered an exception, but it was not a purely commercial venture. The hostility to abolition that prevented its commercial success in the U.S. did not exist in England.

77 LMC to Louisa Loring, 23 or 24 Apr. 30 May, and 19 July 1836, *CC* 4/94, 98, 100.

78 LMC to Louisa Loring, 19 July 1836, *CC* 4/100.

79 LMC to DLC, 24 July 1836, *CC* 4/101.

80 LMC to DLC, 28 July 1836, *SL* 51.

81 LMC to DLC, 31 July [1836], *CC* 4/103.

82 WLG to DLC, 6 Aug. 1836, Louis Ruchames, ed., *The Letters of William Lloyd Garrison*, vol. 2: *A House*

Dividing Against Itself, 1836–1840 (Cambridge, Mass.: Belnap P of Harvard UP, 1971) 152–54, hereinafter referred to as *GL*.

83   *GL* 2: 215n.

84   LMC to Esther Carpenter, 4 Sept. 1836, *SL* 52–53. Loring's argument and Massachusetts Supreme
Court Chief Justice Lemuel Shaw's opinion in the Med case are reproduced in the *Liberator* of 3 and 24
Sept. and 8, 15, and 22 Oct. 1836; see also Leonard W. Levy, *The Law of the Commonwealth and Chief
Justice Shaw* (Cambridge, Mass.: Harvard UP, 1957) 62–68. The quoted portion of Loring's argument
is from "Case of the Slave Child, Med," *Liberator* 22 Oct. 1836, p. 169. On the renaming of Med, see
[Maria Weston Chapman], *Right and Wrong in Boston, in 1836: Annual Report of the Boston Female Anti-
Slavery Society; Being a Concise History of the Slave Child, Med, and of the Women demanded as Slaves of the
Supreme Judicial Court of Mass. With All the Other Proceedings of the Society* (Boston: Boston Female Anti-
Slavery Society, 1836) 67. For an analysis of the Somerset case, see David Brion Davis, *The Problem of
Slavery in the Age of Revolution, 1770–1823* (Ithaca, N.Y.: Cornell UP, 1975) 480–82.

85   Clifford, *Crusader for Freedom* 127, suggests that the Childs went to New York to await "confirmation
of their sailing date for England." Child's letters do not specify the reason for the trip.

86   LMC to Lydia Bigelow Child, 19 Oct. 1836, *SL* 54–55.

87   LMC to Gerrit Smith, 17 Sept. 1836, *CC* 4/107. Child was writing to Smith on behalf of David and his
sponsors in Alton to request a $50,000 loan for the purchase of a large tract of land and the "settlement
of a sober and industrious Colony."

88   Clifford, *Crusader for Freedom* 127.

89   LMC to Lydia Bigelow Child, 19 Oct. 1836, *SL* 55.

90   LMC to the Boston Female Anti-Slavery Society [Oct.? – before 19 Nov. 1835], *SL* 40. See also
Lerner, *Grimké Sisters* 130, on the encounter between Angelina and Child.

91   "From a highly respectable Southern Lady," *Liberator* 16 May 1835, p. 78. This letter is not mentioned
either in Lerner's *Grimké Sisters* or in Katharine DuPre Lumpkin's *The Emancipation of Angelina
Grimké* (Chapel Hill: U of North Carolina P, 1974). Lumpkin's biography indirectly supplies proof of
Angelina Grimké's authorship, however, by citing a letter to Angelina by a Charleston, South Carolina,
Quaker, replying to her inquiries about the punishments inflicted on slaves in the Charleston Work-
House. According to Lumpkin, "No evidence can be found that Angelina mentioned this letter [from
her Quaker correspondent] in her writings" (76). Contrary to this claim, Angelina identifies herself in
her letter to the *Liberator* as a native of Charleston currently residing in Philadelphia and explains that
having been "led to query, 'Lord, what wilt thou have me to do?',," she has solicited information about
the Charleston Work-House, which she is sending to the *Liberator* as her contribution to the antislavery cause. "I lived in this city [Charleston] from childhood, and have so often mourned over the
cruelties practised there that I am willing to bear the obloquy, reproach or penalty that may be attached
to . . . exposure" of her identity, she avows. The document she attached on the Work-House was
published in the *Liberator* along with her letter.

92   Angelina Grimké to Jane Smith, 10 Aug. 1837, quoted in Lumpkin *Emancipation of AEG* 106.

93   LMC to Lydia Bigelow Child, 2 Apr. 1837, *SL* 67. See also LMC to DLC, 24 July 1836, *CC* 4/101,
which cites several humorous examples of her father's "tendency to look on the dark side."

94   LMC to Louisa Loring, [Mar.? 1837], *SL* 63–64; LMC to Lydia Bigelow Child, 17 Jan. and 2 Apr.
1837, *SL* 59–60, 65.

95   LMC to Louisa Loring, [Mar.? 1837], *SL* 63.

96   LMC to Louisa Loring, [Mar.? 1837], *SL* 63 (*CC* 5/121 conjectures 8 or 15 Apr.), and 30 Apr. 1837, *CC*
5/123. It is not clear whether Child had received a third letter in the meantime (only two have
survived), or was simply revising her reaction to the letter she had received in late March.

97   DLC to LMC, 12 Feb. and 7 June 1837, *CC* 5/117, 124; quotations from 5/124. In contrast, when
Garrison traveled to England, he wrote innumerable letters to his wife, even during the voyage across
the Atlantic, and filled them with loving words and anxious questions about her wellbeing and the
children's health. The same is true of Ellis Loring's letters to Louisa.

98   LMC to Lydia Bigelow Child, 2 Apr. 1837, *SL* 65.

99   LMC to Lydia Bigelow Child and Henrietta Sargent, 2 and 17 Apr. 1837, *SL* 66–68.

100 See Dorothy Sterling, *Turning the World Upside Down: The Anti-Slavery Convention of American Women Held in New York City, May 9–12, 1837* (New York: Feminist P of CUNY, 1987) 3; further page references given in the text. Sterling notes that "Black men had participated in the founding of the American Anti-Slavery Society" in 1833, and that "a token few had been elected officers." Although the number of black women attending the Convention was larger, the minutes do not show much participation by them. None proposed any resolutions, and only one, the Grimkés' friend Grace Douglass, was elected to an office or served on a committee. Black women testified to their experience of prejudice, but their remarks were not recorded. The women's convention did go further than the men's in addressing the problem of racial prejudice in abolitionist ranks.

101 See also Lerner, *Grimké Sisters* 161: "Angelina seemed to take particular pleasure in giving Weld [the above-mentioned] message from one of the convention secretaries . . . [t]o which she added her own comment: 'The Boston and Philadelphia women were so well versed in business that they were quite mortified to have Mr. Weld quoted as authority for doing or not doing so and so.'"

102 "Billingsgate Abuse," rpt. from the *New York Commercial Advertiser*, *Liberator* 2 June 1837, p. 90.

103 Child presented sixteen, not counting amendments and reconsiderations, and Angelina eleven, compared to four by Sarah Grimké and one or two each by other delegates.

104 Because the constitution gave the states control over their own internal affairs, slavery could not be abolished by the federal government without the consent of the states. Abolitionist petitions therefore concentrated on those areas over which Congress had legal jurisdiction: slavery in the District of Columbia, a federal territory; the interstate slave trade; and the admission to the Union of territories in which slavery existed, such as Florida and Texas.

105 LMC to Caroline Weston and Lucretia Mott, 13 Aug. 1838 and 5 Mar. 1839, *SL* 83–84, 106–7.

106 LMC to the Editor of the *Liberator*, 6 Mar. 1840, *SL* 128–29.

107 "Letter from Mrs. Child on the Present State of the Anti-Slavery Cause," *Liberator* 6 Sept. 1839, *CC* 8/186. Lerner, *Grimké Sisters*, discusses a similar debate between Angelina Grimké and Theodore Weld during the same period and comments of Angelina's position: "[S]he had caught hold of a fundamental organizational principle. . . . To mobilize activists in an embattled cause, they must be mobilized as equal participants, not as tolerantly suffered inferiors" (199).

108 Lerner, *Grimké Sisters* chaps. 16–17; Lumpkin, *Emancipation of AEG* chap. 4.

109 LMC to Angelina Grimké Weld, 2 Oct. 1838, *SL* 91.

11   Schisms, Personal and Political

1   LMC to Henrietta Sargent, 18 Nov. 1838, *SL* 93.

2   LMC to Lemuel Shaw, 18 Aug. 1839, *CC* 7/185.

3   LMC to Ellis and Louisa Loring, 16 Aug. and 5 Dec. 1838, *SL* 95, *CC* 6/145.

4   LMC to Gerrit Smith, 28 Sept. 1841, *CC* 11/266; see also *CC* 7/185 (n. 2 above); and LMC to Lydia Bigelow Child, 6 Apr. 1838, *SL* 73. Meltzer and Holland explain that the cultivation of mulberry trees and silkworms was "the rage when the Childs lived" in Northampton, and that the Northampton Silk Company "suddenly went bankrupt in 1840" (*SL* 101 n. 17). David was renting his land from the silk company (*SL* 136).

5   LMC to Ellis Loring, 24 Mar. 1839, *CC* 7/176; DLC to LMC, 25 June 1839, *CC* 7/182.

6   See Ellis Loring to LMC, 22 Feb. 1839, *CC* 7/170: "I feel a strong desire to know whether Mr. Child has a right to require any *certain* salary of his employers at Northampton, *independently* of the success of the manufacture — and whether you consider his employment there as likely to be permanent. Not one of your personal friends here seems to have the slightest information on these points, which of all others interests us most —"

7   LMC to Ellis and Louisa Loring, 10 July 1838, *SL* 76–77. Ellis Loring describes these "loitering

breakfasts, . . . full of animated argument, wild fun & raillery" in a letter of 22 Feb. 1839, *CC* 7/170. On the "exhausted" soil of David's rented farm, see LMC to Ellis Loring, 9 Feb. 1841, *SL* 136–37.

8   LMC to Ellis and Louisa Loring, 10 July 1838, *SL* 77.

9   LMC to Louisa Loring, 16 Aug. 1838, *CC* 6/145.

10   LMC to Caroline Weston, 13 Aug. 1838, *SL* 83.

11   LMC to Henrietta Sargent, 18 Nov. 1838, *SL* 93.

12   See the following articles in the *Liberator*: "The Marriage Law," 15 Feb. 1839, p. 27; "Doings in the Legislature, Satirical Petition on the fair Ladies who admire 'Gentlemen of Color,'" "Scurrilous Petition from Lynn," and "Equal Laws — The Lynn Petition," 22 Feb. 1839, p. 30; "Report Respecting Distinctions of Color," 15 Mar. 1839, p. 41; "The Law of Caste," 22 Mar. 1839, p. 47.

13   "The Marriage Law," *Liberator* 15 Feb. 1839, p. 27; LMC "To the Legislature of Massacusetts," 20 Mar. 1839, *SL* 111, printed in *Liberator* 26 Apr., p. 67.

14   LMC to Ellis and Louisa Loring and Caroline Weston, 10 July and 13 Aug. 1838, *SL* 76, 83.

15   See Susan I. Lesley, *Memoir of the Life of Mrs. Anne Jean Lyman* (Cambridge, Mass.: Privately printed, 1876) 57, 408–9. Lesley recalls an incident in which her mother read "a fine passage" of *Philothea* aloud to "a knot of young girls" she overheard making fun of Child's "unfashionable bonnet": "'Girls,' she said, when she had finished, 'never again speak of what that woman wears on the *outside* of her head; think only of what she carries in the *inside*.'"

16   LMC to Ellis and Louisa Loring, 10 July 1838, *SL* 77–78.

17   LMC to Susan I. Lesley, 3 Aug. 1874, *CC* 83/2167, rpt. in Lesley, *Memoir* 528–29.

18   LMC to Louisa Loring, 9 June 1838, *CC* 5/136.

19   LMC to Ellis Loring, 9 Feb. 1841, *SL* 136.

20   LMC to Caroline Weston, 27 July 1838, *SL* 80.

21   LMC to Louisa and Ellis Loring, respectively, 12 Jan. and 15 Jan. 1839, *CC* 7/162, 164.

22   LMC to Theodore Weld, 18 Dec. 1838, *SL* 98–99. Child was writing in response to a circular letter from Weld asking a series of questions about the residents of the recipient's town in order to show "what the free states have to do with Slavery." For a copy of this circular, see Weld to Gerrit Smith, *Letters of Theodore Dwight Weld, Angelina Grimké Weld, and Sarah Grimké, 1822–1844*, ed. Gilbert H. Barnes and Dwight L. Dumond (1934; Gloucester, Mass.: Peter Smith, 1965) 2: 718–19, hereinafter abbreviated as *Weld-Grimké Letters*.

23   LMC to Caroline Weston and Abigail Kelley, 27 July and 1 Oct. 1838, *SL* 80, 81, 90.

24   For a complete version of the story, see LMC to Angelina Grimké Weld, 26 Aug. and 2 Oct. 1838, *CC* 6/147, 150, *SL* 87–89, 91–93; also LMC to Caroline Weston, 27 July and 13 Aug. 1838, *SL* 81–84.

25   LMC to Abby Kelley, 1 Oct. 1838, *SL* 90.

26   Garrison expressed this view in a letter of 6 Nov. 1837 to the British abolitionist Elizabeth Pease. Noting that "Upon the slaveholding States, we make no perceptible impression," he acknowledged: "I have relinquished the expectation, that they will ever, by mere moral suasion, consent to emancipate their victims. I believe that nothing but the exterminating judgments of heaven can shatter the chain of the slave, and destroy the power of his oppressor." See Louis Ruchames, ed., *The Letters of William Lloyd Garrison*. vol. 2: *A House Dividing Against Itself, 1836–1840* (Cambridge, Mass.: Belknap P of Harvard UP, 1971) 324, hereinafter abbreviated as *GL*. Weld's similar opinion can be inferred from his comments on congressional debates of 1842, written to Angelina from Washington. See *Weld-Grimké Letters*, 6 and 17 Feb. 1842, 2: 911–12, 923–24. In the latter he writes: "Satan never retreats without a death struggle. . . . That slavery has *begun* to fall is plain, but . . . its fall will be resisted by those who cling to it, with energy and desperation and fury such as only fiends can summon when they know their hour has come. . . ."

27   LMC to Henrietta Sargent, 18 Nov. 1838, *SL* 93–94.

28   LMC to Lydia Bigelow Child, 7 Aug. 1838, *CC* 6/142.

29   LMC to Abby Kelley, 1 Oct. 1838, *SL* 89–90.

30   I shall be using the terms "orthodox" and "evangelical" interchangeably to refer to abolitionists who espoused some form of Calvinist theology.

31   The author of the pastoral letter was the Rev. Nehemiah Adams, who became known derisively as "Southside Adams" after the publication of his apologia, *A Southside View of Slavery* (1854). Garrison reprinted the pastoral letter in his Refuge of Oppression column, *Liberator* 11 Aug. 1837, p. 129, as did Maria Weston Chapman in her *Right and Wrong in Boston: Annual Report of the Boston Female Anti-Slavery Society, with a Sketch of the Obstacles thrown in the way of Emancipation by certain Clerical Abolitionists and Advocates for the subjection of Woman, in 1837* (Boston: Isaac Knapp, 1837) 45–48. Quotations are from Chapman.

32   "Divide and Conquer!," signed "Z.," reprinted from the *Concord Freeman, Liberator* 8 Sept. 1837, p. 146.

33   Wendell Phillips Garrison and Francis Jackson Garrison, *William Lloyd Garrison, 1805–1879. The Story of His Life Told by His Children* (1885–1889; New York: Arno P, 1969) 2: 137–38, hereinafter cited as *Life.*

34   I have borrowed (and put in the plural) the apt phrase of an African American correspondent of the *Colored American* who signed himself "A.," rpt. in the *National Anti-Slavery Standard*, 9 July 1840, p. 18.

35   Although the explanation that follows is my own, I have benefited greatly from the work of the many scholars who have analyzed the schisms in the antislavery movement. The best book on the subject is still Aileen S. Kraditor's *Means and Ends in American Abolitionism: Garrison and His Critics on Strategy and Tactics, 1834–1850* (1969; New York: Vintage, 1970); nevertheless, my study of Child's experience leads me to feel that Kraditor underplays the extent of factional feuding among the Garrisonians themselves. Also useful is Merton L. Dillon, *The Abolitionists: The Growth of a Dissenting Minority* (De Kalb: Northern Illinois UP, 1974), chap. 6. Ronald G. Walters, *The Antislavery Appeal: American Abolitionism After 1830* (Baltimore: Johns Hopkins UP, 1976), chap. 1, provides a counterweight to Kraditor's argument by emphasizing the cultural commonalities that united abolitionists, as well as the personal and sectarian aspects of the quarrel. Lawrence J. Friedman, *Gregarious Saints: Self and Community in American Abolitionism, 1830–1870* (New York: Cambridge UP, 1982), claiming that historians have exaggerated both the ideological and the personal aspects of the quarrel, contends that abolitionists simply belonged to several different cliques. Recent scholarship has generally repudiated the long dominant anti-Garrisonian interpretation of the schism propounded by Gilbert H. Barnes, *The Antislavery Impulse, 1830–1844* (1933; New York: Harcourt, 1964). Biographies of leading figures in the orthodox camp furnish a better introduction to the anti-Garrisonian viewpoint. Particularly helpful for its nonpartisan analysis is Gerda Lerner's *The Grimké Sisters from South Carolina: Rebels Against Slavery* (Boston: Houghton Mifflin, 1967), chap. 16, because the Grimké sisters and Weld initially belonged to opposite factions. For accounts of the schism from the viewpoint of Child's associates, see Chapman, *Right and Wrong in Boston* (1837) and *Right and Wrong in Massachusetts* (1839; New York: Negro Universities P, 1969); also Oliver Johnson, *W. L. Garrison and His Times* (1881; Miami, Fla.: Mnemosyne, 1969), chaps. 16–17; and *Life* 2: chaps 3, 5, and 6.

36   Lydia Maria Child, *Anti-Slavery Catechism* (Newburyport, Mass.: Charles Whipple, 1836) 35.

37   These events are best summarized by Russel B. Nye, *Fettered Freedom: Civil Liberties and the Slavery Controversy, 1830–1860* (1963; Urbana: U of Illinois P, 1972), chaps. 2, 4, and 5. The Pinckney gag rule is quoted in Nye 45.

38   LMC to Abby Kelley and Angelina Grimké Weld, 1 and 2 Oct. 1838, *SL* 90, 92.

39   LMC to Theodore Weld, 29 Dec. 1838, *SL* 104–5.

40   "Speech of a Colored Brother, Delivered at the late meeting of the N.Y. State Anti-Slavery Society at Utica," rpt. from *Friend of Man, Liberator* 13 Oct. 1837, p. 165.

41   "Prospectus of THE LIBERATOR," 15 Dec. 1837, *Documents of Upheaval: Selections from William Lloyd Garrison's THE LIBERATOR, 1831–1865*, ed. Truman Nelson (New York: Hill and Wang, 1966) 141. The best analysis of the Non-Resistance movement is Lewis Perry's *Radical Abolitionism: Anarchy and the Government of God in Antislavery Thought* (Ithaca, N.Y.: Cornell UP, 1973).

42   Kraditor, *Means and Ends* 78–79. Lerner, *Grimké Sisters* 284, argues that such factional splits are "necessary in order to break out of sectarian isolation. Typically, in the American setting, factionalism is the symptom of a weak minority movement trying to find new organizational forms. The most radical leadership, unable to admit that its methods are no longer valid, turns utopian and retreats into isolation

in order to maintain its purity of purpose, while the majority compromises its program in order to win alliances." For discussions of African American responses to the schism in abolitionist ranks, see Benjamin Quarles, *Black Abolitionists* (New York: Oxford UP, 1969), chaps. 3 and 8; Jane H. Pease and William H. Pease, *They Who Would Be Free: Blacks' Search for Freedom, 1830–1861* (New York: Atheneum, 1974), chap. 5; Vincent Harding, *There Is a River: The Black Struggle for Freedom in America* (1981; New York: Vintage, 1983), chap. 6, esp. 133–39; and Sterling Stuckey, *Slave Culture: Nationalist Theory and the Foundations of Black America* (New York: Oxford UP, 1987), chaps. 3 and 4, passim.

43 LMC to Lucretia Mott, 5 Mar. 1839, *SL* 107.

44 LMC to Ellis Loring, 30 Apr. 1839, *SL* 114.

45 LMC to Caroline Weston, 7 Mar. 1839, *SL* 108–9.

46 LMC and DLC, "To the Massachusetts Anti-Slavery Society," 15 Jan. 1839, *CC* 7/165; published in the *Liberator*, 8 Feb. 1839.

47 LMC to Caroline Weston, 7 Mar. 1839, *SL* 108.

48 LMC to Lydia Bigelow Child, 9 June 1839, *CC* 7/181; LMC to Lemuel Shaw, 18 Aug. 1839, *CC* 7/185; *SL* 96, n. 4; LMC to Louisa Loring, 30 Apr. 1839, *CC* 7/179.

49 "Beet Sugar," *Liberator* 3 Apr. 1840, p. 55; LMC to Louisa Loring, 30 Apr. 1839, *SL* 113.

50 LMC to Louisa Loring, 30 Apr. 1839, *SL* 113.

51 LMC to DLC, 18 Aug. 1839, *SL* 116–18.

52 LMC to Lydia Bigelow Child, 12 Dec. 1839, *SL* 125.

53 "Beet Sugar," reprinted in the *Liberator* 28 Feb. 1840, p. 36. David's book is advertised in the *Liberator* of 17 Jan. 1840, p. 11.

54 "Beet Sugar," rpt. in *Liberator* 13 Mar. 1840, p. 44.

55 "Adelphic Union Lecture," *Liberator* 22 Nov. 1839, p. 187; "Beet Sugar," *Liberator* 3 Apr. 1840, p. 55.

56 LMC to Lydia Bigelow Child, 12 Dec. 1839, *SL* 125.

57 LMC to Lydia Bigelow Child, 18 Nov. 1839, *SL* 125.

58 LMC to Ellis Loring, 21 Feb. 1843, *SL* 189 (Child is reminiscing about 1839).

59 Margaret Fuller to [Sophia Ripley?], 27 Aug. 1839, Robert N. Hudspeth, ed., *The Letters of Margaret Fuller*, 5 vols. (Ithaca, N.Y.: Cornell UP, 1983) 2: 86–89. See also Fuller's answer to Chapman's request that she devote one of her Conversations to abolition, 26 Dec. 1840, 2: 197–98; and Francis E. Kearns, "Margaret Fuller and the Abolition Movement," *Critical Essays on Margaret Fuller*, ed. Joel Myerson (Boston: G. K. Hall, 1980), 247–54. Emerson furnishes a list of women who attended Fuller's Conversations in his contribution to *Memoirs of Margaret Fuller Ossoli*, [ed. William Henry Channing, James Freeman Clarke, and Ralph Waldo Emerson], 2 vols. (Boston: Phillips, Sampson, 1852) 1: 338. Among the Boston Female Anti-Slavery Society members it includes are Child, Louisa Loring, Maria White, Sarah Shaw, Caroline Sturgis, and Ann Greene Phillips.

60 "New England Anti-Slavery Convention" and "Proceedings," *Liberator* 31 May and 7 June 1839, pp. 87, 90–91; "Meeting of Friends to the Liberator," *Liberator* 7 June 1839, p. 91; Samuel J. May to William Lloyd Garrison, 15 June 1839, BPL Ms.A.1.2.V8, p. 36; "First Annual Meeting of the New-England Non-Resistance Society," and "Eighth Annual Meeting of the Massachusetts Anti-Slavery Society," *Liberator* 11 Oct. 1839, p. 164, and 31 Jan. 1840, p. 18. At the Non-Resistance Society meeting, Child identified herself as one taking a "friendly interest" in the subject rather than necessarily agreeing with the society's objectives.

61 Chapman, *Right and Wrong in Massachusetts* 124–28; "Fairs," *Liberator* 14 June 1839, p. 95.

62 LMC to Lydia Bigelow Child, 12 Dec. 1839, *SL* 125.

63 "Proceedings of the Boston Female Anti-Slavery Society at Its Annual Meeting," *Liberator* 1 Nov. 1839, p. 174. Unless otherwise noted, the account that follows is based on these proceedings, supplied by Anne Warren Weston. According to Dorothy Sterling, "there was an ugly aspect to the fight that was never mentioned in Maria Chapman's acount, 'Right and Wrong in the Boston Female Anti-Slavery Society,' or in numerous private letters of the participants. Except for Mary Parker and Catharine Sullivan, the conservative leaders and many of their followers were black." Sterling identifies Lucy and

Martha Ball as African Americans who spent their last years living as whites. See her splendidly researched biography *Ahead of Her Time: Abby Kelley and the Politics of Antislavery* (New York: Norton, 1991) 100–102.

64   "The Split in the Female Anti-Slavery Society," rpt. from *Boston Transcript, Liberator* 18 Oct. 1839, p. 167. Seventy-eight women who had voted against Parker (among them the leading African American members, Susan Paul, L. Hilton, Louisa Nell, and Nancy Prince) signed a certificate disputing the official count, which had omitted seventeen negative votes. And the *Liberator* exulted when the fair organized by Chapman brought in twice as much as the Parker faction's. See "Important Certificate," *Liberator* 15 Nov. 1839, p. 183; "The Massachusetts Anti-Slavery Fair," 8 Nov. 1839, p. 179; "Fairs," 27 Dec. 1839, p. 207; "Fairs," 10 Jan. 1840, p. 7. See also the refutations by the Parker faction in "Contradiction," 8 Nov. 1839, p. 179; "Proceedings of the Boston Female Anti-Slavery Society, at Its Annual Meeting," 15 Nov. 1839, p. 182; "Correction" and "Miss Ball's Correction," 22 Nov. 1839, p. 187; "Boston Female Anti-Slavery Society," 17 Apr. 1840, p. 63; and "Miss Ball's Explanation," 1 May 1840, p. 75.

65   "To the Members of the Boston Female Anti-Slavery Society," 3 Apr. 1840, p. 54, *CC* 8/201. In an editorial note Garrison comments that this letter is characteristic of Child's "excellent mind."

66   "Boston Female Anti-Slavery Society" and "Statement of the Boston Female A.S. Society," *Liberator* 17 Apr. 1840, p. 63, give Parker's and Child's rival versions of the quarterly meeting. "Special Meeting of the Boston Female Anti-Slavery Society . . . April 11, 1840" describes the meeting over which Child presided, *Liberator* 24 Apr. 1840, p. 67. See also [Maria Weston Chapman], *Seventh Annual Report of the Boston Female Anti-Slavery Society. Presented October 14, 1840* (Boston: Boston Female Anti-Slavery Society, 1840) 5–13.

67   LMC to Ellis Loring, 6 Mar. 1843, *SL* 193.

68   LMC to William Lloyd Garrison, 2 Sept. 1839, *SL* 119–24, *Liberator* 6 Sept. 1839, p. 142. Quotations on 120, 124.

69   LMC to WLG, 2 Sept. 1839, *SL* 122–24. In another interesting instance of the different views Child expressed in public and in private, she went on to say, in answer to a question from Garrison, "I am *not* discouraged by these dissensions. . . . [U]nder God's Providence, they will mightily promote the cause of general freedom." It is true that she also took this position in a letter to Louisa of 28 June 1840, *CC* 8/208, but in the overwhelming majority of her private letters, she admits to discouragement.

70   William Comstock, "Mrs. Child," *Liberator* 13 Sept. 1839, p. 147.

71   LMC to William Lloyd Garrison, 6 Mar. 1840, *SL* 127–29.

72   Caroline Weston to Anne Warren Weston, 14 Mar. 1840, BPL Ms.A.9.2.V13. pp. 39–40.

73   "Letter from Lewis Tappan," *Liberator* 20 Mar. 1840, pp. 45–46.

74   LMC to Lydia Bigelow Child, 7 June 1840, *CC* 8/205.

75   As at the New-England Anti-Slavery conventions of 1838 and 1839, the right of women to register and vote as members was put to the test at the May 1840 anniversary. Ironically, both sides allowed their women supporters to vote on this point. The Garrisonians won by a large majority and proceeded to appoint Abby Kelley to serve on the business committee. Thereupon all but one member of the orthodox-dominated executive committee resigned. They immediately founded a rival national organization, the American and Foreign Anti-Slavery Society. Child, Chapman, and Lucretia Mott were appointed to fill the vacancies on the executive committee. Child declined to serve because of her immobilization in Northampton, but David accepted his election to the board of managers. According to Meltzer and Holland, neither of the Childs attended the anniversary meeting. Child's letter to Loring of 7 May does gives this impression, since she mentions sending "a copy of a letter, which Mr. Child intended to have sent to the Anniversary" (*SL* 130–31). Yet her letter of 7 June to her mother-in-law says that "My dear husband worked quite effectually at N. York" (*CC* 8/205). David is also listed in the convention's "Roll of Members and Delegates" as a delegate from Northampton, quoted in the proceedings, and mentioned in a letter by Anne Warren Weston as having "spoke[n] capitally" in favor of allowing women full participation. See "American Anti-Slavery Society" and "Annual Meeting of the

National Society," *Liberator* 29 May 1840, p. 86; *National Anti-Slavery Standard* 11 June 1840, p. 1; and Anne Warren Weston to Maria Weston Chapman, 13 May 1840, BPL Ms. A.9.2.V13, p. 74.

76   LMC to Maria Weston Chapman, 10 Apr. 1839, *CC* 7/178.

77   See LMC to Francis Shaw and Louisa Loring, 27 May 1841, *SL* 141–42, 30 Apr. 1839, *CC* 7/179.

78   The *Liberator* reported the first signs of the Panic in an article reprinted from the *Journal of Commerce* "The Pressure in New York," 12 May 1837, p. 79. See also on the same page "Arthur Tappan & Co.," rpt. from *New York Evangelist*, which announced with "deep regret" that "the house of Arthur Tappan & Co. have been obliged to suspend payment." Tappan, who had been the antislavery movement's largest financial contributor, filed for bankruptcy in 1843. David left for Europe in the fall of 1836, but by the time he returned the following fall, the Panic was in full swing.

79   LMC to Francis Shaw, 27 May 1841, *SL* 140; LMC to Louisa Loring, 19 July 1840, *CC* 8/209.

80   LMC to Francis Shaw, 27 May 1841, *SL* 141.

81   LMC to Lydia Bigelow Child, 7 June 1840, *CC* 8/205, partial rpt. in *SL* 131–32.

82   LMC to Louisa Loring, Ellis Loring, and Francis Shaw, 19 July 1840, 9 Feb. and 27 May 1841, *CC* 8/209, *SL* 136, 140–43.

83   LMC to Louisa Loring and Convers Francis, 17 Feb. 1841, *CC* 9/226, and 20 Oct. 1840, *CC* 9/215, partial rpt. in *SL* 132–34.

84   LMC to Louisa Loring, 19 July 1840, *CC* 8/209. She was alluding specifically to the "pecuniary connection" that obliged her to share the household with her father, but the context invites a more general interpretation of her "position."

85   LMC to Francis Shaw, 27 May 1841, *SL* 140–41. Garrison regarded the *Liberator* as his personal mouthpiece, not as the society's organ.

86   LMC to Louisa Loring, 16 May 1841, *CC* 9/228; Mr. Francis's departure is mentioned in Anne Warren Weston to Deborah Weston, 29 Mar. 1841, BPL Ms.A9.2.V15, p. 32.

87   The beet sugar industry is now flourishing both in the United States and in Europe, but efforts to establish it did not begin to pay off until the turn of the century.

88   LMC to the Board of the Massachusetts Anti-Slavery Society, 21 Feb. 1843, *SL* 190.

89   LMC to Ellis Loring, 12 June 1843, *CC* 17/498; LMC to Lydia Bigelow Child, 16 Feb. 1849, *SL* 241.

90   LMC to Louisa Loring, 14 Aug. 1843, *CC* 17/505, and 28 Feb. 1843, *CC* 16/459.

91   LMC to Francis Shaw, 18 July 1844, *SL* 210.

92   LMC to Louisa Loring, 29 Apr. 1847, *SL* 237.

12   The National Anti-Slavery Standard: *Family Newspaper or Factional Organ?*

1   "To Abolitionists," *National Anti-Slavery Standard* 20 May 1841, p. 198, hereinafter abbreviated as *Standard*.

2   The dispute over what the Garrisonians considered the theft or "embezzlement" of the *Emancipator* can be followed in the columns of the *Standard* and the *Liberator*. See "The Transfer of the Emancipator," *Standard*, 12 Nov. 1840, p. 90, and the editorials by David Child, Maria Weston Chapman, and Edmund Quincy cited in nn. 74 and 90 below. In contrast to the *Liberator*, which Garrison had always considered his personal mouthpiece, the *Standard* was meant to represent the official viewpoint of the American Anti-Slavery Society.

3   "National Anti-Slavery Standard," *Standard* 11 June 1840, p. 2. Oliver Johnson, *W. L. Garrison and His Times* (1881; Miami, Fla.: Mnemosyne, 1969) 296–97, describes the editorial arrangements for the paper prior to Child's accession in 1841. N. P. Rogers was already editing the *Herald of Freedom* in New Hampshire and did not want to move to New York. He agreed to supply editorials for the *Standard* if Oliver Johnson would manage the paper in New York.

4   I counted twenty-two among the articles on which I took notes. They appear most frequently in July 1840; in Oct. and Dec. 1840 and Jan. and Mar. 1841 they average two a month.

5   "New Organization," *Standard* 31 Dec. 1840, p. 118. See also "The Standard," 18 Feb. 1841, p. 146: "Is

it *wild* to rank our friends of the Emancipator and the Reporter [antislavery papers edited by "New Organization" partisans Joshua Leavitt and Lewis Tappan] above the Herald [a rabidly racist and antiabolitionist Democratic paper] in the pro-slavery class? Which of the two is most dangerously at war with the only policy that can achieve our enterprise? Which of them could have detached a body from the anti-slavery phalanx, and made them fire into the camp they had deserted?"

6   "John G. Whittier," *Standard* 7 Jan. 1841, p. 123 (as the title indicates, the Quaker poet Whittier, who had also gone over to the opposing faction, is the main target of this editorial).

7   "Colored Convention," *Standard* 18 June 1840, p. 6.

8   See the eloquent letters to the *Standard* and the *Colored American* by Samuel Ringgold Ward, Charles B. Ray, and Samuel Cornish, as well as Jackson's responses to them: [S. R. Ward], "For the National Anti-Slavery Standard," "S. R. Ward's Letter," and "Colored American," *Standard* 2 July 1840, p. 14; "The National Anti-Slavery Standard *vs.* the Convention," 16 July 1840, p. 23; "National Anti-Slavery Standard and New-York Convention," 30 July 1840, p. 31; and "Aristocracy of the Skin," 20 Aug. 1840, p. 43. Quotations are from Cornish's letter in the issue of 30 July 1840, p. 31. Ray points out that "no people ever succeeded in establishing their principles, or regaining their rights without 'exclusive action'" and explains that "If we act [only] with our white friends, . . . the words we utter will be considered theirs, or their echo" (16 July). On the significance of this exchange and the choices faced by African American abolitionists in the wake of the schisms, see Benjamin Quarles, *Black Abolitionists* (New York: Oxford UP, 1969), chap. 3, esp. pp. 55–56.

9   "The National Anti-Slavery Standard," *Standard* 6 May 1841, p. 191.

10   Loring to LMC, 29 Apr. 1841, *CC* 9/227.

11   Edmund Quincy to Maria Weston Chapman and Henry G. Chapman, 18 May 1841 [misdated 1840], BPL Ms.A.9.2.V13, pp. 71–72; Anne Warren Weston to Deborah Weston, 29 Mar. 1841, BPL Ms.A.9.2.V16, p. 32; Anne Warren Weston to Maria Weston Chapman, 15 Apr. 1841, BPL Ms.A.9.2.V15, p. 42. The Chapmans had gone to Haiti in hopes that the warm climate would cure or arrest Henry's T.B.

12   "Prospectus of the Anti-Slavery Standard for 1841–42," *Standard* 20 May 1841, p. 199.

13   "To Abolitionists," *Standard* 20 May 1841, p. 198.

14   Ellis Loring to LMC, 22 May 1841, *CC* 9/230. I have deciphered as "dividing" the word for which the transcript of Loring's letter suggests a conjectural reading of "deciding[?]." For another letter praising Child's opening editorial, see Jacob Ferris to LMC, published in the *Standard* of 22 July 1841, *CC* 10/242.

15   LMC to Ellis Loring, 17 May [1841], *CC* 9/229; in her letter of 21 Feb. 1843, *CC* 16/456, to the Board of the Massachusetts Anti-Slavery Society, Child writes: "An addition of $300 (making our salary $1,500 per annum) was voted to Mr. Child and myself; but we declined to accept it; and when I see Mr. Child, I presume that he will agree not to take more than $1,000." Van Rensalaer and Powell are identified in Walter M. Merrill, ed., *The Letters of William Lloyd Garrison*, vol. 3: *No Union with Slave-holders, 1841–1849* (Cambridge, Mass.: Belknap P of Harvard UP, 1973) 72, hereinafter abbreviated as *GL*.

16   LMC to Ellis Loring, 28 Sept. [1841], *SL* 146.

17   "To the Readers of the Standard," *Standard* 20 May 1841, p. 198. This salutation precedes the editorial "To Abolitionists."

18   Untitled editorial note, *Morning Courier and New-York Enquirer*, 4 Jan. 1842, p. 2. Surprisingly, this seems to have been editor James Watson Webb's introduction to the *Standard*, which someone had sent him because it contained strong criticism of a proannexation editorial he had published, rpt. in the *Standard*. He did not respond to the Childs' criticism, deeming it "ungallant" toward a lady and "unmanly" toward a "male child."

19   Garrison and Benjamin Lundy had followed the same practice during their joint editorship of the *Genius of Universal Emancipation*. Oliver Johsnson, Edmund Quincy, and Maria Weston Chapman also initialed their editorials when they stood in for Garrison during his absences or illnesses. Otherwise, it was not customary for editors to sign their pieces, and David ceased to do so when he assumed sole editorship of the *Standard* in Aug. 1844.

20 LMC to James Miller McKim and Philadelphia Friends, 24 [and 25] Nov. 1841, *SL* 154.

21 LMC to Maria Weston Chapman, 26 Apr. 1842, *CC* 14/365: "I suppose you are aware that, from the beginning, I have had the *entire* charge of the paper, unassisted by any individual. . . ." This statement confirms that unsigned editorials are also by Child.

22 LMC to Ellis Loring, 17 June and 27 May, 1841, *SL* 143, *CC* 9/231.

23 LMC to Ellis Loring, [21 Sept. 1841], *CC* 11/262.

24 "Letter from the Editor," 2 Nov., *CC* 11/279, *Standard* 11 Nov. 1841.

25 LMC to Ellis Loring, 24 Nov. and 13 Dec. 1841, *SL* 151–53, *CC* 12/299.

26 LMC to Ellis Loring and to James Miller McKim and Philadelphia Friends, 14 and 24 [and 25] Nov. 1841, *SL* 151–55.

27 LMC to Louisa Loring, 27 Apr. 1842, *CC* 14/366.

28 See Garrison's letters to Elizabeth Pease and Henry C. Wright, in which he complains that the *Liberator*'s "list of subscribers is very much reduced," 1 and 16 Dec. 1843, *GL* 3: 227, 239.

29 "Farewell," *Standard* 4 May 1843, pp. 190–91.

30 Headnote to the first installment of Frances Trolloppe's *Jonathan Jefferson Whitlaw*, 10 June 1841, p. 4. This was also the first issue of the *Standard*'s second year.

31 The serialization of "Forest Life" begins on 30 June 1842, p. 16; it is attributed to "Mrs. Mary Clavers [Kirkland's pseudonym], author of the very lively and pleasant volume, called 'A New Home; Who'll Follow?'" Extracts from Emerson's "Man, the Reformer" and "Extract from De Tocqueville's Travels" (*Democracy in America*) appear on 20 May 1841, p. 200. Extracts from Dickens's *American Notes*, which Child praises for its "hard hits at the peculiar institution" ("Charles Dickens," p. 95), begin on 17 Nov. 1842, p. 93 (the front page). "A Rill from the Town Pump" appears on 7 July 1842, p. 20, and extracts from "Miss Beecher's Domestic Economy" in the column "For Housekeepers and Farmers" of 24 Mar. 1842, p. 168. Child reviewed Martineau's *The Hour and the Man* in her editorial column, 10 June 1841, p. 2.

32 "Annette Gray," 22 July 1841, pp. 26–27; "They have not wit enough to take care of themselves," 5 Aug. 1841, p. 35; "Follow the North Star," 21 July 1842, pp. 26–27; "Lewis Clark," 20 and 27 Oct. 1842, pp. 78–79, 83; "The Slaveholder Seeking Light," 26 Jan. 1843, pp. 134–35. See also "The Conscientious Slave," 7 Apr. 1842, pp. 174–75.

33 "The Deserted Church," *Standard* 27 May 1841, p. 203.

34 "The Iron Shroud," *Standard* 3 Mar. 1842, pp. 154–55. Child reprinted the story from which she borrowed this trope — "The Iron Shroud. A Tale of Italy" — on 8 and 15 Dec., p. 108 and p. 112.

35 "Great Race between the North and the South," *Standard* 9 June 1842, p. 2. I am grateful to Donald Dingledine for drawing my attention to the "slave" donkey's blinders and the contrasting head positions of the two donkeys.

36 The column "A, B, C, of ABOLITION" opens with the serialization of Child's *Anti-Slavery Catechism* on 5 Aug. 1841, p. 34. Samuel J. May's "Anti-Slavery Reminiscences," written in the form of letters to Child, begin on 16 Dec. 1841, p. 110. Child refers to the "brave old days" of "holy zeal" in her inaugural editorial, cited in n. 1 above.

37 "The Press," 24 Mar. 1842, pp. 166–67. In this editorial Child theorizes that "What the priesthood once were to the world, the press now is" and compares its power and coruption to the medieval church's: "'a sale of indulgencies' for sin is carried on, as actively as it was in the fifteenth century." She also castigates the press for fomenting war and riots and then hypocritically churning out "eloquent elegies for the fallen."

38 "The Press," *Standard* 23 Dec. 1841, p. 115; "Independence of the American Press," 30 Dec. 1841, p. 119; the statistics are reproduced in David's editorial "Texas and the New-York Courier and Enquirer," pp. 118–19. That leading Whig newspaper had just called for annexing Texas, and the Childs were responding to its sophistic and misleading arguments. Two and a half years later, John Gorham Palfrey decided to free the slaves he had inherited from his father's estate and sought Child's help in finding jobs for them. He credited her with his conversion to abolition (*SL* 208, 286).

39   Child describes her practice of rewriting news articles and abolitionist communications in letters to Ellis Loring, 27 July and 11 Aug. 1841, *CC* 10/244, 246, and to Francis Shaw, 7 Dec. 1841, *CC* 12/297 (the quotation is from her letter to Shaw and refers to her rewriting of J. C. Fuller's "Gerrit Smith's Slaves," *Standard* 30 Sept. 1841, p. 65). On Douglass, see Henrietta Sargent to LMC, "Anti-Slavery in New Bedford and Nantucket," *Standard* 26 Aug. 1841, p. 46, reproduced in *CC* 10/247.

40   Lucretia Mott to Anne Warren Weston, 8 July 1841, BPL Ms.A.9.2.V8, p. 20; William Ellery Channing to LMC, 21 Dec. 1841, *CC* 12/308; LMC to Ellis Loring, 31 Aug. 1841, *CC* 10/253, and LMC to Gerrit Smith, 28 Sept. [1841], *CC* 11/266; Oliver Johnson to Maria Weston Chapman, 3 Sept. 1841, BPL Ms.A.9.2.V15, p. 61; "The Emancipator," *Standard* 3 June 1841, p. 207; Wendell Phillips to LMC, 21 Feb. 1842, *CC* 13/339.

41   Oliver Johnson to Maria Weston Chapman, 3 Sept. 1841, BPL Ms. A.9.2.V15, p. 61.

42   "Rev. Jonathan Davis," *Standard*, 26 Aug. 1841, p. 46 (Davis was a proslavery minister who was currently touring the North); "Colonization," 28 July 1842, p. 31.

43   "Unwritten Wrongs," *Standard* 29 Dec. 1842, p. 119. See also "My Friend Jane," a moving personal reminiscence Child commissioned from a white abolitionist. The writer reflected on her youthful friendship with an African servant girl, now dead, and commented: "[P]rejudice is so early imbibed, and so constantly cherished, by circumstances, that we are scarcely conscious of it; yet, I suspect a strict self-examination will detect it within our own breasts to a far greater extent than we are now aware of. . . . The fact, that we feel a warm interest in some persons of color, deceives us . . .; while a more critical inspection of the springs of action within us, might detect a deep-rooted prejudice, which will allow none of the race equal rights with ourselves." *Standard* 15 Dec. 1842, p. 112.

44   "Our Anglo-Saxon Ancestry," *Standard* 28 Apr. 1842, pp. 186–87. This analysis represents a major revision of current Anglo-Saxonist ideology, which insisted on the uniqueness and racial superiority of the Anglo-Saxons whom Americans liked to claim as ancestors. See Reginald Horsman, *Race and Manifest Destiny: The Origins of American Racial Anglo-Saxonism* (Cambridge, Mass.: Harvard UP, 1981), esp. chap. 9.

45   "A Word to Abolitionists," rpt. from *Northern Star and Freeman's Advocate*, *Standard* 7 Apr. 1842, p. 173.

46   Garrison reprinted twelve major editorials by Child and five by David over a two-year period. He also reprinted many short pieces and minor editorial statements. Those concerning moral versus political action include "The Third Political Party," "Union of Old and New Organization," "Moral Influence – The Third Party," and "Talk about Political Party," *Liberator* 9 July 1841, p. 109; 1 Oct. 1841, p. 157; 10 Dec. 1841, p. 197; 5 Aug. 1842, p. 122. See also David's "The Third Party" and "Political Action," *Liberator* 27 Aug. and 3 Sept. 1841, p. 138 and p. 141.

47   "The Third Political Party," *Standard* 24 June 1841, pp. 10–11; "Moral Influence," 2 Dec. 1841, p. 102.

48   "Talk about Political Party," *Standard* 7 July 1842, pp. 18–19.

49   "Moral Suasion – Political Action," *Liberator* 2 Sept. 1842, p. 139; Green's letter appeared in the 16 Aug. number of the *Cazenovia Abolitionist*.

50   "The Williamsburg Resolutions" and "Address To their Fellow-Citizens, by the Executive Committee of the American Anti-Slavery Society," *Standard* 27 Jan. 1842, pp. 134, 135; "Peterboro Convention," 10 Feb. 1842, p. 142; "Address To the Slaves of the United States, by the Convention of the 'Liberty Party' Abolitionists, held in Peterboro, N.Y. January 19th, 1842" and "Gerrit Smith's Address to the Slaves" 24 Feb. 1842, pp. 149–51.

51   "Letters from New-York," No. 12, *Standard* 2 Dec. 1841, p. 103, *CC* 12/293; see also Child's *Appeal in Favor of That Class of Americans Called Africans* (Boston: Allen and Ticknor, 1833) 161–65, 175–78.

52   "Address to their Fellow-Citizens, by the Executive Committee of the AASS," *Standard* 27 Jan. 1842, p. 135; "Peterboro Convention," 10 Feb. 1842, p. 142.

53   "Gerrit Smith's Address to the Slaves," 24 Feb. 1842, pp. 150–51; "Case of Nelson Hackett," *American and Foreign Anti-Slavery Reporter*, rpt. in *Standard* 1 Sept. 1842, p. 49.

54   "Meeting of Colored Citizens of Boston" and "The Decision of the Supreme Court," *Standard* 7 July 1842, pp. 18–19. The *People's Press* editorial is quoted by Child in the latter article.

55   "The Union," *Standard* 24 Feb. 1842, p. 151.

56   That campaign, in turn, had grown out of a petition by citizens of Haverhill, Massachusetts, calling for a dissolution of the Union in protest against the gag rule. When John Quincy Adams presented the Haverhill petition to the U.S. House of Representatives on 24 Jan. 1842, it provoked an uproar in Congress, leading to an attempt to have him censured or expelled.

57   See the three articles titled "The Union" in the *Standard* 17 Mar. 1842, pp. 161–62. The first two are reprinted from the *Philanthropist* and the *New-York American*; the third is extracted from a letter of Loring's. All three take the position: "we love the Union, but we love liberty more." They differ on whether or not the time has come to dissolve the Union. See also a second article from the *Philanthropist* on "The Union," in which that newspaper criticizes Child's earlier editorial, *Standard* 31 Mar. 1842, p. 169.

58   "The Union," *Standard* 31 Mar. 1842, pp. 170–71.

59   "The Annual Meeting at New-York," *Liberator* 22 Apr. 1842, p. 63.

60   LMC to Maria Weston Chapman, 11 May [1842], *SL* 174–76.; see also LMC to Wendell Phillips, 3 May 1842, *CC* 96/2535: "Garrison's unguarded editorial seemed to hand us all over to a line of policy, which we had had no time to examine."

61   "*Abolitionism. Treason to the Union*," *Morning Courier and New-York Enquirer* 27 Apr. 1842, p. 2; "Legal Diabolism," *Liberator* 6 May 1842, p. 71; in *Liberator* 20 May 1842, p. 77, Garrison reprinted Noah's charge under the headlines "Daring Judicial Attempt to excite a Mob, and to suppress Freedom of Speech!!" "Extract from a Charge delivered by Judge Mordecai Manasseh Noah, (a Jewish unbeliever, the enemy of Christ and of Liberty,) to the Grand Jury of the Court of Sessions of New-York, May 3d, 1842." In an editorial note of 18 Aug. 1842, p. 43, titled "Colorphobia," Child decried "remarks" that "evince some degree of that spirit which has so wickedly oppressed and persecuted the Jews." The target of those "remarks" was again Judge Noah.

62   "Correction," *Morning Courier and Enquirer* 3 May 1842. This circular is prefaced by an editorial headnote identifying it as an official communication from the AASS and commenting: "[W]e are gratified to perceive by it that Garrison's authority to bring the subject of a dissolution of the Union before the approaching session of the Abolition Society in this city, is distinctly disclaimed. . . . The chairman of the 'Executive Committee,' and Mrs. Child its Secretary, certify to us·that the meeting 'stands entirely uncommitted' as to the subjects which occupy the deliberations of the meeting. We trust the Executive Committee will see the necessity very soon of 'committing' the society *against* anything in the nature of such a discussion . . .; for we have no idea that it would be consistent with the peace of the city."

63   "Extraordinary Disclaimer," *Liberator* 6 May 1842, p. 71. What particularly mortified Garrison was that Child's and Gibbons's disclaimer reached him via the *Courier and Enquirer*.

64   "Repeal of the Union," *Liberator* 6 May 1842, p. 71.

65   LMC to Maria Weston Chapman, 11 May [1842], *SL* 174–76; LMC to Wendell Phillips, 3 May 1842, *CC* 96/2535; LMC to Ellis Loring, 6 Mar. 1843, *SL* 193.

66   LMC to Maria Weston Chapman, 11 May [1842], *SL* 174–76. Even Loring wrote to rebuke Child for the circular. See LMC to Ellis Loring, 6 May 1842, *CC* 14/372.

67   "The Anniversary," *Standard* 19 May 1842, p. 198; Garrison to Elizabeth Pease, 2 July 1842, *GL* 3: 89; LMC to Maria Weston Chapman, 11 May [1842], *SL* 175.

68   "The National Anti-Slavery Standard," *Liberator* 17 June 1842, pp. 94–95.

69   "Diversity of Gifts with Unity of Purpose," *Standard* 30 June 1842, p. 13 (Child does not identify the author as Garrison); LMC to Ellis Loring, [July? 1842], *CC* 14/396.

70   Wendell Phillips to LMC, 21 Feb. 1842, *CC* 13/339.

71   Maria Weston Chapman to Caroline Weston, n.d. BPL Ms.A.9.2.V4, p. 88. Internal evidence dates this letter around July 1844, since it refers to David's departure and his replacement by Sidney Howard Gay as local editor.

72   James S. Gibbons to "My dear friend" [probably Chapman], 21 Feb. 1843, BPL Ms.A.9.2.V18, p. 10; Abby Kelley to Maria Weston Chapman, 8 Mar. 1843, BPL Ms. A.9.2.V18, p. 19. Frederick Douglass

and Charles L. Remond later broke with Collins over precisely this issue. See Jane H. Pease and William H. Pease, *They Who Would Be Free: Blacks' Search for Freedom, 1830–1861* (New York: Atheneum, 1974) 75–76; and Dorothy Sterling, *Ahead of Her Time: Abby Kelley and the Politics of Antislavery* (New York: Norton, 1991) 177–79.

73 Abby Kelley to Maria Weston Chapman, 8 Mar. 1843, BPL Ms.A.9.2.V18, p. 19. For the classic come-outer denunciation of the church, see Stephen S. Foster, *The Brotherhood of Thieves: or, A True Picture of the American Church and Clergy: A Letter to Nathaniel Barney, of Nantucket* (Boston: Anti-Slavery Office, 1844). For a sympathetic and insightful analysis of the come-outer strategy Kelley favored, see Sterling, *Ahead of Her Time* 167–69.

74 LMC to Ellis Loring, 16 May 1844, *SL* 207. See also LMC to Ellis Loring, 6 Mar. 1843, *SL* 193, where Child complains of Chapman's efforts to make her "say *editorially* that *I* considered Joshua Leavitt a knave." Chapman's attacks on Leavitt in the *Liberator* begin with her letter "Mr. Leavitt and Mr. Colver," 25 Nov. 1842, p. 187, in response to an attempt by Leavitt to join forces with the Garrisonians during the demonstrations occasioned by the Latimer case. The attacks continue in editorials by Chapman and Quincy on 16, 23, and 30 Dec. 1842, pp. 198, 202, 207: "Emancipator and Massachusetts Abolition Society," "The Present Crisis, and its Dangers," and "Divisions of Abolitionists." Explicit attacks on the Liberty party follow in "The Origin of Liberty Party," "Third Party Statistics," and "Freedom in the Choice of Measures," *Liberator* 13 Jan. 1843, p. 6. Another motive for the attacks seems to have been the hope of completing the destruction of the *Emancipator*, whose vulnerable financial state was revealed in an *Emancipator* extra that the Garrisonians got hold of in early Dec. 1842. See the gleeful letter citing the details of the *Emancipator*'s debts, Caroline Weston to Anne Warren Weston, 9 Dec. 1842, BPL Ms. A.9.2.V17, p. 134. For an indication that the opposing party interpreted these attacks as part of a campaign to defeat the Liberty party, see Lewis Tappan, "Transfer of the Emancipator," *Standard* 7 Dec. 1843, p. 106.

75 LMC to Wendell Phillips, 3 May 1842, *CC* 96/2535.

76 LMC to Maria Weston Chapman, 11 May [1842], *CC* 14/374, *SL* 174–76; LMC to Ellis Loring, 6 Mar. 1843, *SL* 192–96.

77 LMC to the Board of the Massachusetts Anti-Slavery Society, 21 Feb. 1843, *SL* 190–91.

78 LMC to Ellis Loring, [29? Oct. 1842], *SL* 178–79; James S. Gibbons to "My dear friend" [Caroline Weston], 6 Mar. 1843, BPL Ms.A.9.2.V18, p. 15.

79 James S. Gibbons to "My dear friend" [Caroline Weston], 6 Mar. 1843, BPL Ms.A.9.2.V18, p. 15; LMC to Ellis Loring and Francis Shaw, [29? Oct. 1842] and 15 Jan. 1843, *SL* 179, 185; Deborah Pickman Clifford, *Crusader for Freedom: A Life of Lydia Maria Child* (Boston: Beacon P, 1992) 178–79.

80 "Arthur Tappan," *Standard* 15 Dec. 1842, p. 111; "Arthur Tappan," *Liberator* 23 Dec. 1842, pp. 202–3.

81 LMC to Ellis Loring, 6 Mar. 1843, *SL* 193.

82 "Sects and Sectarianism," *Standard* 16 Feb. 1843, p. 146.

83 James S. Gibbons to "My dear friend" [Caroline Weston], 6 Mar. 1843, BPL Ms.A.9.2.V18, p. 15.

84 LMC to Ellis Loring, 6 Mar. and 26 Sept. 1843 and 16 May 1844, *SL* 193, 196; 204, 207–8.

85 "Farewell," *Standard* 4 May 1843, pp. 190–91; untitled editorial note, *Standard* 25 May 1843, p. 203; "The Anti-Slavery Standard," *Liberator* 19 May 1843, p. 79; LMC to Ellis Loring, 26 June [1843], *CC* 17/500. Garrison must have felt all the more uncomfortable about Child's implication that editing an official organ had interfered with her freedom, since he himself had always refused to let the *Liberator* become the official organ of the Massachusetts or American Anti-Slavery Societies for that very reason. See Child's letter of 2 Sept. 1839 to the *Liberator*: "The Liberator is not and never, was the organ of the Mass. Anti-Slavery Society. . . . I was present at the meeting where it was decided to appropriate funds to assist the Liberator, then considerably involved in debt; and I well remember how earnestly Mr. Garrison protested against being considered the organ of any Society. He said he could not be the organ of other men's opinions, nor could he be impeded in the free utterance of his own" (*SL* 122).

86 Caroline Weston to Anne Warren Weston, 9 Dec. 1842, and Amos Farnsworth to Maria Weston Chapman, 13 Dec. 1842, BPL Ms.A.9.2.V17, pp. 134, 142; Maria Weston Chapman, "Our Cause — Its

Present Position. DEPARTURE OF MR. CHILD FOR WASHINGTON," *Liberator* 16 Dec. 1842, p. 198. David's "Letters from Washington" began appearing in the *Liberator* on 30 Dec. 1842 and in the *Standard* on 5 Jan. 1843.

87   The objections of Mott and her fellow Philadelphian, the Democrat Thomas Earle, are quoted in James S. Gibbons to "My dear friend" [probably Chapman], 21 Feb. 1843, BPL Ms.A.9.2.V18, p. 10. See also David's exchange of correspondence with the board on the editorial policy he would follow, rpt. as "Our Position," *Standard* 9 Nov. 1843, pp. 90–91.

88   LMC to Ellis Loring, 28 Sept. [1841] and 6 Mar. 1843, *SL* 147, 193. On Garrison's hope of retaining Child as a contributor, see "The Anti-Slavery Standard," *Liberator* 19 May 1843, p. 79; on his respect for David's talents, see his letter of 6 Aug. 1836, *GL* 2: 153–54; Chapman praises David in "Our Cause — Its Present Position," *Liberator* 16 Dec. 1842, p. 198; also Maria Weston Chapman to Abby Kelley, 26 July 1843, quoted in Sterling, *Ahead of Her Time* 177: "I rely with the most unhesitating confidence on his honesty, uprightness, noble mindedness & devoted love of the cause." On the sobriquet David Libel Child, see Horace Mann to Mary Peabody Mann, 2 Sept. 1850, Horace Mann Collection, Massachusetts Historical Society, quoted in chap. 4. For private comments on the relative merits of the two Childs, see Maria Weston Chapman to Anne Warren Weston, [12 Feb. 1843], BPL Ms.A.9.2.V4, p. 14; and Abby Kelley to Maria Weston Chapman, 3 May 1843, BPL Ms.A.9.2.V18, p. 32. Garrison's letter of 9 Sept. 1843 imploring Chapman to edit the *Standard* was omitted from his published correspondence; see BPL Ms.A.9.2.V19, p. 33.

89   See LMC to Maria Weston Chapman, [11 May? 1842?], *CC* 14/374: "With regard to Mr. Child's coming here, in the employ of *any* society, I should feel the strongest opposition to it. I am not his ruler, and [*sic*] more than he is mine; but if he felt it to be his duty to take such a step, I should feel under the *necessity* of withdrawing from the Standard, and taking up some other employment, for support." Quotations are from LMC to Ellis Loring and Francis Shaw, 26 Sept. 1843 and 18 July 1844, *SL* 204, 210.

90   Occupied with winding up his personal affairs in Northampton, David did not formally assume his responsibilities until August. He stopped in Boston on the way to consult with the board and clarify his ideological position on matters that worried several board members (for the inside story of David's appointment, see Memoranda of Business Committee of 25, Annual Meeting 10 May 1843, and Anne Warren Weston to Caroline and Deborah Weston, 22 May 1843, BPL Ms. A.9.2.V18, pp. 34, 40). David's first editorial, "Where We Are," which horrified Abby Kelley with its disparagement of come-outism, appeared on 24 Aug. 1843, pp. 46–47. See Abby Kelley to Maria Weston Chapman, 4 Sept. 1843, BPL Ms.A.9.2.V.19, p. 29. Edmund Quincy's article on "Liberty Party," appears on 5 Oct., p. 69, and David's "The Embezzlement of the Emancipator" on 12 Oct., pp. 74–75. Mention of the libel threats by Charles T. Torrey and a Mr. Willey can be found in the article by the same title of 19 Oct., p. 79. Thereafter editorials on the "Embezzlement" appear every week until 16 Nov., with one last article on 7 Dec.

91   See chap. 9 above; LMC to DLC, 31 July [1836], *CC* 4/103; and William Lloyd Garrison to DLC, 6 Aug. 1836, *GL* 2: 153–54.

92   For example, David never reports on the Colored Convention in Buffalo of Aug. 1843, at which Henry Highland Garnet gave his pivotal "Address to the Slaves of the United States," exhorting them, "Let your motto be resistance!" Besides engaging in personal attacks, David departed from Child's editorial policy in reprinting and responding to praise or criticism of his own editorial style. See, for example, his responses to qualified praise by Chapman and Garrison and criticism by Abby Kelley and Stephen Foster: [Chapman], "Where We Are," *Standard* 28 Sept. 1843, p. 65; [Garrison], "The Anti-Slavery Standard," *Liberator* 17 Nov. 1843, p. 183 (David reprints this editorial in full and adds in response to Garrison's hint that he is not fully satisfied: "Mr. Garrison will oblige us by specifying our shortcomings. He cannot do us a greater favor"; see "Something New," *Standard* 23 Nov. 1843, p. 99); "Letter from Abby Kelley," *Standard* 18 Jan. 1844, p. 130 (see also 28 Dec. 1843, p. 118); "Letter from Stephen S. Foster," *Standard* 25 Jan. 1844, p. 136. Compare Child's statement about her own editorial

policy: "While I was editor, I always drew my pen heavily through all compliments to myself, and all criticisms upon my own, or other people's style of editing" (*SL* 201).

93   LMC to Ellis Loring, 6 Mar. 1843, *SL* 194.

94   For criticisms of David's editorials and the political opinions they expressed, see "Letter from S. S. Foster," 25 Jan. and 15 Feb. 1844, pp. 136, 146; Thomas Earle, "The Whiggery of the Standard," 7 Mar. 1844, p. 158 (this is the first of a series of such articles by Earle, a Democrat); Abby Kelley to Maria Weston Chapman, 4 Sept., 10 Oct., and 2 Nov. 1843, BPL Ms.A.9.2.V19, pp. 29, 59, 69; and J. Miller McKim to Maria Weston Chapman, 6 Nov. 1843, BPL Ms.A.9.2.V19, p. 71. David endorses Clay's position on the annexation of Texas in his "Washington Correspondence" of 2 May 1844, p. 191. See also his editorials of 2 May and 9 May, respectively, "Tenth Annual Meeting of the American Anti-Slavery Society" (p. 191) and "The Issue" (p. 195), in which he strongly implies that abolitionists ought to vote for Clay and the Whigs in order to prevent the annexation of Texas — a stand he would openly take by July 1844. See Garrison's comments in the *Liberator* of 5 July (p. 107) and 8 Nov. 1844 (p. 174); see also Child's response to a letter from her friend Francis Shaw, 18 July 1844, *SL* 210. Child had repeatedly condemned Henry Clay during her editorship of the *Standard* (as had David then). On Child's rejection of "temporary expediency," see "The Third Political Party," *Standard* 24 June 1841, pp. 10–11; and "Moral Influence," 2 Dec. 1841, p. 102.

95   Anne Warren Weston describes a business meeting called by Ellis Loring, at which this matter was taken up. "Saying that 'between friends, Mr Child was very careless about money matters,'" Loring asked the board to pay him David's salary, and let him take care of David's financial obligations. The others indignantly refused, and Loring did not feel at liberty to explain that he was trying to protect Child's earnings in his capacity as her lawyer. See Anne Warren Weston to unidentified correspondent, 8 Jan. 1845, BPL Ms.A.9.2.V21, p. 3.

96   LMC to Louisa and Ellis Loring, 28 Feb. and 12 June [1843], *CC* 16/459, 17/498.

97   LMC to Ellis and Louisa Loring, 16 June and 14 Aug. 1843, *CC* 17/499, 505; Clifford, *Crusader for Freedom* 179.

98   LMC to Francis Shaw, 18 July 1844, *SL* 209.

99   LMC to Ellis Loring, 21 Mar. [1843], *CC* 17/470.

13   Letters from New York: *The Invention of a New Literary Genre*

1   "Phrenological Character of Mrs. L. M. Child," *American Phrenological Journal*, rpt. in *Liberator* 24 Sept. 1841, p. 156.

2   "Lydia Maria Child," *Liberator* 17 Sept. 1841, p. 151.

3   It was Garrison who made this claim, *Liberator* 17 Sept. 1841, p. 151; LMC to Ellis Loring, 27 July 1841, *CC* 10/244.

4   See chap. 7 for a brief discussion of *Flowers for Children* (New York: C. S. Francis, 1844, 1846), a three-volume series of children's stories reprinted from the *Juvenile Miscellany* along with some new selections; chap. 12 for an analysis of Child's editorials; and chap. 14 for an analysis of her short stories of the 1840s, partially collected in *Fact and Fiction* (New York: C. S. Francis, 1846). It has often been erroneously asserted that the "Letters from New-York" were published from the beginning in the *Boston Courier*. Although occasionally reprinted in other newspapers, they were written for the *Standard* as a means of increasing its circulation — a purpose they could not have served had Child simultaneously published them in a commercial newspaper. It was not until after leaving the *Standard* that Child contracted to publish her "Letters from New-York" in the *Courier*. See LMC to Ellis Loring, 26 Dec. 1843 [misdated 1844], *CC* 21/595.

5   I am grateful to Richard Slotkin for helping me to formulate this insight.

6   LMC to John Sullivan Dwight, 23 Oct. 1844, *SL* 214.

7   LMC to Francis Shaw, 27 May 1841, *SL* 142.

8   LMC to DLC, 11 July 1841, *CC* 10/241.

9   LMC to Ellis Loring, 27 July 1841, *CC* 10/244. Loring's letter has not survived.

10 LMC to Ellis Loring, 6 Mar. 1843, *SL* 195.

11 LMC to Ellis Loring [21 Sept. 1841], *CC* 11/262.

12 LMC to Ellis Loring, 11 Aug. 1841, *CC* 10/246.

13 LMC to Maria White Lowell and Francis Shaw, 18 Feb. 1845, *CC* 21/606; 29 May 1843, *CC* 17/497.

14 LMC "Autobiography," Anti-Slavery Collection, Cornell University Library.

15 LMC to Louisa and Ellis Loring, 29 Apr. [1847] and 6 June 1850, *SL* 237, *CC* 28/782; LMC to Susan Lyman, 9 Apr. 1847, *CC* 25/707; Frank Preston Stearns, *The Life and Public Services of George Luther Stearns* (1907; New York: Arno P, 1969) 76–77, 120; Anna D. Hallowell, "Lydia Maria Child," *Medford Historical Register* 3 (July 1900): 100.

16 LMC to Francis Shaw and Ellis Loring, 27 May, 17 June, and 31 Aug. 1841, *SL* 142, 145, *CC* 10/253. See also the sensitive discussion of Child's relationship with John in Deborah Pickman Clifford, *Crusader for Freedom: A Life of Lydia Maria Child* (Boston: Beacon P, 1992) chap. 12.

17 LMC to Ellis Loring and Augusta King, 26 Sept. and [13? Nov.] 1843, *CC* 18/515, 521.

18 LMC to Ellis Loring, 11 Apr. 1843, *CC* 17/481.

19 L. Maria Child, *Letters from New York* (1843; Freeport, N.Y.: Books for Libraries P, 1970) 13. Subsequent page references, given in parentheses in the text, are to this comparatively accessible reprint of the third edition. New-York was hyphenated in the first edition, but not in the third.

20 LMC to Ellis Loring, before 25 Jan. 1842, *CC* 13/326.

21 Lucy Osgood to LMC, 8 May 1843, *CC* 17/493.

22 [Charles F. Briggs], review of *Letters from New York. Second Series, Broadway Journal* 1 (10 May 1845): 295–96. Since this review is not listed among Poe's collected works, I am assuming it must be by Briggs.

23 LMC to Ellis Loring, before 25 Jan. 1842, *CC* 13/326.

24 See the Literary Notices in the *New York Tribune* of 22 Mar. 1843, p. 1, and 23 Aug. 1843, p. 4 (the quotation is from the 23 Aug. review of the first edition); also the "Editor's Table," *Graham's Magazine* 22 (Apr. 1843): 264. Child mentions her negotiations with the Langleys, publishers of the *Democratic Review*, in her letters to Loring of 21 Feb. 1843, *SL* 188, and 18 Apr. 1843, *CC* 17/484. For a fuller discussion of the compromises Child had to make to get the book published, see Carolyn L. Karcher, "Censorship, American Style: The Case of Lydia Maria Child," *Studies in the American Renaissance* (1986): 283–303.

25 LMC to Ellis Loring, 18 Apr. 1843, *CC* 17/484.

26 LMC to Ellis Loring, 21 Mar. [1843], *CC* 17/470. Loring's marginal comments have been preserved in the Loring family papers at the Schlesinger Library.

27 LMC to Ellis Loring, 21 Feb., 6 Mar., and 11 Apr. 1843, *CC* 16/455, *SL* 195, and *CC* 17/481. The three antislavery letters Child cut were no. 12, which championed the *Amistad* captives and defended the slave's right to fight in self-defense; no. 14, an interview with a fugitive, which graphically exposed the cruel treatment to which slaves were subjected; and no. 33, which reminisced about the mob violence targeting George Thompson.

28 LMC to Francis Shaw, 18 July 1844 and [Oct. 1846], *SL* 209–10, 230.

29 "Farewell," *National Anti-Slavery Standard* 4 May 1843, pp. 190–91.

30 See Letters 1, 8, 11, 20, 21, 22, 23, 25, and 36. For an analysis of Child's strategy of sapping and mining proslavery assumptions and racist attitudes in Letters 11, 20, and 23, see Karcher, "Censorship, American Style," 290–93.

31 This critique of asylums and institutions for the segregation of the poor actually distinguishes Child from most of the reformers cited by David J. Rothman in his pathbreaking study, *The Discovery of the Asylum: Social Order and Disorder in the New Republic* (1971; rev. ed., Boston: Little, Brown, 1990).

32 See Letter 29 in *Letters from New York. Second Series* (New York: C. S. Francis, 1845) 258–72; see also the uncollected "Letters" to the *Courier* of 12 Mar. 1846 and 23 Feb. 1847, reproduced in *CC* 23/654 and 25/697.

33 Rothman, *Discovery of the Asylum* 229, quotes this passage as an endorsement of "precision and regularity" in the management of asylums.

34   Garrison's voyage to Liverpool in June 1840 awakened him to the plight of sailors, whom he described in a letter to his brother (a sailor) as "awfully oppressed, degraded and contemned as a class"; in England he found himself unable to "enjoy the beautiful landscapes . . . because of the suffering and want staring me in the face, on the one hand, and the opulence and splendor dazzling my vision, on the other"; see WLG to James Garrison, 4 June 1840, and WLG to Samuel J. May, 6 Sept. 1840, *Letters of William Lloyd Garrison*, vol. 2: *A House Dividing Against Itself, 1836–1840*, ed. Louis Ruchames (Cambridge, Mass.: Belknap of Harvard UP, 1971) 636, 696–97. For a similar reaction by N. P. Rogers, who accompanied Garrison on this trip, see his editorials "The British Steerage" and "Treatment of Sailors," *National Anti-Slavery Standard* 26 Nov. 1840, p. 98, and 28 Jan. 1841, p. 135. On Wendell Phillips's sensitization to issues of poverty and class during his trip to Europe in 1839–41, see James Brewer Stewart, *Wendell Phillips: Liberty's Hero* (Baton Rouge: Louisiana State UP, 1986) 79–80, 113–16. In contrast, Edmund Quincy, Arthur and Lewis Tappan, Maria Weston Chapman and her sisters, and many other prominent leaders remained much less sensitive to the plight of the white working class than Child became during her stay in New York. On Child's belief that "the re-construction of society on a new basis is the *only* thing that can arrest the frightful increase of pauperism and crime" and her consequent interest in the ideas of the French socialist Charles Fourier and the utopian socialist experiment of Brook Farm, see LMC to Ellis Loring and Robert Cassie Waterston, 9 Mar. 1842 and 27 Aug. 1844, *SL* 165–66, 212–13. Child is mentioned among the visitors to Brook Farm in John Thomas Codman, *Brook Farm: Historic and Personal Memoirs* (1894; New York: AMS P, 1971) 80. I am grateful to Lucy M. Freibert for this reference. One visit probably took place in June 1841 during Child's vacation with the Lorings (also listed among the visitors). She may have returned for another visit during her Dec. 1847 trip to Massachusetts. The Shaws' sojourn at Brook Farm is discussed in Russell Duncan, ed., *Blue-Eyed Child of Fortune: The Civil War Letters of Colonel Robert Gould Shaw* (Athens: U of Georgia P, 1992) 3–4.

35   For a fine discussion of Child's attitude toward the city, see Patricia G. Holland, "Lydia Maria Child and New York City in the 1840s," unpublished Henry Whitney Bellows Lecture, Unitarian Church of All Souls, New York, 10 May 1990. I am grateful to Holland for sharing this paper and the list of accompanying illustrations.

36   Thomas Wentworth Higginson, "Lydia Maria Child," *The Writings of Thomas Wentworth Higginson*, vol. 2: *Contemporaries* (Boston: Houghton Mifflin, 1900) 127–28.

37   "Letter from the Editor," 2 Nov. 1841, written from Northampton and published in the *Standard* 11 Nov., *CC* 11/279. Child incorporated this paragraph into Letter 28 of *Letters from New York. Second Series* 257.

38   LMC to Louisa Loring, 29 May 1843, *CC* 17/496; see also LMC to Ellis Loring, 11 and 18 Apr. 1843, *CC* 17/481, 484.

39   For a more detailed exposition of this argument, see Karcher, "Censorship, American Style," 293–97. Strikingly exemplifying the northern press's subserviency to southern pressure, the Harpers publicly apologized on two separate occasions for having unwittingly printed books containing antislavery commentary to which southern reviewers objected. See the article by William Jay, "Renwick's Life of John Jay," *New-York American*, rpt. in *Liberator* 19 Feb. 1841, p. 30. In the letter quoted by Jay from the *Charleston Mercury*, the Harpers assure their southern critic that they were "entirely ignorant of the fact" that an English novel they had published, titled *Woods and Fields*, contained "the objectionable matter" the southern newspaper had cited. "[W]e uniformly decline publishing works calculated to interfere, *in any way*, with Southern rights and Southern institutions," they assert, adding: "Our INTERESTS, not less than our opinions, would dictate this course, if there were no other less selfish considerations." They end by saying that in deference to southern objections, they have printed a new edition of the novel, "in which the offensive matter has been *omitted*." For analyses of the Democratic party's political orientation, see Leonard L. Richards, "The Jacksonians and Slavery," *Antislavery Reconsidered: New Perspectives on the Abolitionists*, ed. Lewis Perry and Michael Fellman (Baton Rouge: Louisiana State UP, 1979) 99–118; Richard H. Brown, "The Missouri Crisis, Slavery, and the Politics of Jacksonianism," *South Atlantic Quarterly* 65 (Winter 1966): 55–72; and John M. McFaul, "Expediency vs. Morality: Jacksonian

Politics and Slavery," *Journal of American History* 62 (June 1975): 24–39. On the political orientation of the *Democratic Review*, see Frank Luther Mott, *A History of American Magazines 1741–1850* (1930; rpt. Cambridge, Mass.: Belknap P of Harvard UP, 1957) 681; see also the 1841 editorial statement reproduced on the inside wrapper of many numbers.

40   LMC to Ellis Loring, 11 Apr. 1843, *CC* 17/481.

41   LMC to Louisa Loring and Francis Shaw, 29 May 1843, *CC* 17/496, and 15 Jan. 1843, *SL* 185. Munroe and Francis had previously printed *The First Settlers of New-England* at Child's expense. According to Caroline Healey Dall, the senior Convers Francis and the publishers Francis descended from two different sons of John Francis (born 1650), "the ancestor of all the branches in New England." See Dall, "Lydia Maria Child and Mary Russell Mitford," *Unitarian Review* 19 (June 1883): 522.

42   *Letters from New York* came on the market at the end of August and was sold out by the end of December. See LMC to Louisa Loring, 14 Aug. 1843, *CC* 17/505, announcing that the book would be "out in a week," and LMC to James Munroe, 20 Dec. 1843, *SL* 205, reporting that not enough copies remain on hand to meet the orders pouring in. The book was first advertised in the *Standard* on 31 Aug., p. 51. The *Standard* 8 Feb. 1844, p. 143, advertises the second edition, to be available "in a few days," and specifies: "The first edition of 1,500 sold, and orders for several hundred more were received, in four months."

43   LMC to Francis Shaw, 18 July 1844, *SL* 209.

44   "H" [Thomas Wentworth Higginson], "Mrs. Child's Letters from New York," *The Present* 1 (15 Nov. 1843): 133–36.

45   [Higginson], "Mrs. Child's Letters from New York," *The Present* 1: 135; [John O'Sullivan], review of *Letters from New York*, *United States Magazine and Democratic Review* 13 (Oct. 1843): 443–45; *Knickerbocker* 22 (Oct. 1843): 372–74; [Margaret Fuller], *The Dial* 4 (Jan. 1844): 407.

46   [Donald G. Mitchell], "Notes upon Letters," *The American Review: A Whig Journal of Politics, Literature, Art and Science* 1 (Jan. 1845): 60–74. Quotations on 62, 63, 68, 73, and 74; I have also paraphrased from 61, 63, and 73. *Letters from New York* was also reviewed in two British journals: *The Athenaeum* no. 831 (30 Sept. 1843): 880–81; and *Chambers's Edinburgh Journal* 12 (25 Nov. 1843): 358–59. *The Athenaeum* was more critical than *Chambers's* or Child's American reviewers, but it conceded that "after all due and large allowances are made for endless digressions and sentimental small talk, there are many clever papers in the volume — good magazine articles. . . ." Garrison reprinted two glowing reviews of the book in the *Liberator* 10 Nov. 1843, p. 180: one from the *Cincinnati Philanthropist*, which quoted from the *Boston Courier*; the other from the *Baltimore Saturday Visitor*. The *Courier* praised the book in the flowery language typically applied to women writers, but the *Saturday Visitor* judged the *Letters* "enough to put to rout, utterly, the notion, so prevalent, of an inferiority of mental capacity in the opposite sex. No one can read them as here congregated, without being surprised not only at the vigor of thought and felicity of utterance, but the variety of the topics treated with such striking equality and effort."

47   Edgar Allan Poe, *The Works of Edgar Allan Poe*, vol. 8: *The Literati — Minor Contemporaries, Etc.* (1846), ed. Edmund Clarence Stedman and George Edward Woodberry (1895; New York: Books for Libraries P, 1971) 139–41.

48   James Russell Lowell, "A Fable for Critics," *The Poetical Works of James Russell Lowell*, household ed. (Boston: Houghton Mifflin, 1895) 142–44; partially quoted in Higginson, "Lydia Maria Child" 129.

49   LMC to Ellis Loring, 26 Dec. 1843 [misdated 1844], *CC* 21/595.

50   Dall, "Lydia Maria Child," *Unitarian Review* 19: 526.

51   See LMC to Francis Shaw, 12 Oct. 1841, *SL* 149–50; William H. Furness, 28 Apr. 1845, *CC* 22/612; John Jay, 24 May 1845, *SL* 221–22; Parke Godwin, 30 May 1845, *CC* 22/618, and 7–9 Nov. 1845, *CC* 23/638; Antony Philip Heinrich, 29 Apr., 5 Sept., and 19 Nov. 1845, *SL* 219–20, *CC* 22/630, 23/639; "Letter from New-York," *Boston Courier* 7 Nov. 1845, rpt. *Evening Post* 11 Nov. 1845; and LMC to William Wetmore Story and Charles Sumner, 3 Mar. 1846, *CC* 23/652, 653. Fuller to James Nathan, 5 June 1845, *Letters of Margaret Fuller*, ed. Robert N. Hudspeth, 5 vols. (Ithaca, N.Y.: Cornell UP, 1987), vol. 4 (1845–47): 113–15.

52   LMC to Anna Loring, 23 Mar. 1846, *SL* 224–25.

53   LMC to John Sullivan Dwight, 23 Oct. 1844, *SL* 214.

54   Mortimer Smith, *The Life of Ole Bull* (1943; Westport, Conn.: Greenwood, 1973) 64–67, 88–89, 92–96.

55   "Letter from New-York," *Boston Courier* 23 Dec. 1843, reproduced in *CC* 18/525 and partial rpt. in altered form in *Letters from New York. Second Series* 22–27.

56   LMC to Ellis Loring, 22 May 1844, *CC* 19/557.

57   LMC to Marianne Silsbee, 5 Feb. 1847, *CC* 24/693; Louisa Loring, 2 Aug. 1846, *CC* 23/663; Maria White, 25 Dec. 1844, *CC* 21/594; Anna Loring, 28 Dec. 1844, *CC* 21/597. Child's letter to Maria White, which apologizes for not having written sooner to congratulate her on her forthcoming marriage to James Russell Lowell, explains that she has been "unusually depressed" for several months and later mentions in passing that David is not with her and that John is "recently betrothed."

58   LMC to Louisa Loring, 31 May 1846, *CC* 23/659.

59   LMC to Anna Loring, 13–14 Oct. 1844, *CC* 20/578.

60   LMC to John Sullivan Dwight, 23 Oct. 1844, *SL* 214.

61   See the discussion of "Thot and Freia," below, and *Letters from New York. Second Series* 177. Child used Freia, the Norse goddess of Love and Feeling, as a symbol of "inspiration, because genius resigns itself wholly to a *feeling* of the beautiful. . ." (177).

62   LMC to Anna Loring, 28 Dec. 1844, *CC* 21/597.

63   LMC to Marianne Silsbee, 5 Feb. 1847, *CC* 24/693; see also LMC to John Sullivan Dwight, 23 Oct. 1844, *SL* 214–15.

64   LMC to Anna Loring, 8 Dec. 1845, *CC* 23/641. Ole Bull numbered the poet Anne Charlotte Lynch among his other feminine admirers; see Smith, *Life of Ole Bull* 66–68.

65   LMC to Marianne Silsbee, 5 Feb. 1847, *CC* 24/693.

66   Child reports that it is "going through the press" in LMC to Louisa Loring, 8 Feb. 1845, *CC* 21/605.

67   See Letters no. 2, "Ole Bul heard for the first time. The vast significance of Music"; no. 12, "Spiritual Correspondences, illustrated largely by Music. . . ."; no. 19, ". . . The Alhamra. Philharmonic Concerts. Italian Opera. Castle Garden. Niblo's Garden. Vauxhall. . . ."; no. 25, "The Violin. Effects of Scenery on Music. The Northmen. Expression of Scotch and Irish Music. Lizst's Piano-playing. Lines to Ole Bul"; no. 28, " . . . The perfect chord of Music and of Colours. Fourier's perfect Social Chord. The Major and Minor Mode"; and no. 30, "Ole Bul's Niagara and Solitude of the Prairie. Genius and Criticism. Anecdote of Haydn and of Beethoven. The tone of an Instrument. changed by the manner of playing upon it." Music also crops up incidentally in Letters no. 3 on New Year's festivities in New York; no. 24 on church bells; and even no. 29 on prison reform, where Child describes the effects of music and flowers on prisoners' attitudes.

68   See LMC to Louisa Loring, 31 May 1846, *CC* 23/659: "I am grateful to Edmund Benzon for his lavish kindness, and I sympathize with the loneliness of his position in the world." She is assuring Louisa that none of her new friends have replaced the Lorings.

69   "Charity Bowery" was originally published in the *Liberty Bell* of 1839: 26–43. "The Deserted Church" (Letter 16) first appeared as an editorial in the *Standard*, 27 May 1841, p. 203. The paragraphs on emancipation in the British West Indies incorporated into Letter 10 also derive from earlier statements.

70   J[ohn] S[ullivan] D[wight], review of *Letters from New York. Second Series*, *The Harbinger* 28 June 1845, pp. 41–43. Quotation on 41. I am grateful to Deborah Clifford for drawing this review to my attention.

71   [Margaret Fuller], "Mrs. Child's Letters," *New York Tribune* 10 May 1845, p. 1.

72   In addition to the reviews by John Sullivan Dwight and Margaret Fuller, see "Mrs. Child's Letters from New York. — Second Series," *United States Magazine, and Democratic Review* 16 (June 1845): 569–76; the *Knickerbocker* 25 (June 1845): 547–48; and the review by Briggs in the *Broadway Journal* 1 (10 May 1845): 295–96.

73   See Child's response to such criticisms of Ole Bull in her letter to John Sullivan Dwight, *SL* 214–15.

74   Nathaniel Hawthorne's "The Birthmark" was first published in the March 1843 issue of *The Pioneer*, approximately two years before "Thot and Freia."

75   LMC to Sarah Shaw, 12 Nov. 1844, *CC* 20/585. Among these periodicals was Poe's *Broadway Journal*, in whose opening number Child published "Ole Bul's Niagara" (1 [4 Jan. 1845]: 9–10).

76   LMC to Israel Post, [1844? Nov.–Dec.?] *CC* 21/598 (Post was the publisher of the *Columbian*, whose editors were John Inman and Robert A. West); "Thot and Freia. A Romance of the Spirit Land," *Columbian Lady's and Gentleman's Magazine*, 3 (Jan. 1845): 1–7. Child omitted the preface to the story that she supplied for *Letters from New York*.

14   Sexuality and Marriage in Fact and Fiction

1   LMC to Francis Shaw, 2 Aug. 1846, *SL* 229.

2   LMC to Francis Shaw, 2 Aug. 1846, *SL* 228. Child's letters to Shaw often refer to Swedenborgianism and reminisce about the days when they used to sit side by side in church; see, for example, those of 17 Aug. 1838 and 27 May 1841, *SL* 87, 142; 24 Oct. 1840, *CC* 9/217; and esp. 11 Feb. 1869, *CC* 70/1881. On Shaw's translation of Sand's *Consuelo*, see LMC to Lucy Osgood, 28 Jun 1846, *SL* 226–27.

3   LMC to Francis Shaw, 2 Aug. 1846, *SL* 229. Margaret Fuller, *Woman in the Nineteenth Century* (1845), rpt. in Jeffrey Steele, ed., *The Essential Margaret Fuller* (New Brunswick, N.J.: Rutgers UP, 1992) 321–22, 331–33. Child mentions Fuller's departure for Europe later in the same letter, again apparently in reply to a comment by Shaw.

4   For a brilliant analysis of Owen's ideas and of the socialist feminist movement to which Owen and Frances Wright belonged, see Barbara Taylor, *Eve and the New Jerusalem: Socialism and Feminism in the Nineteenth Century* (New York: Pantheon, 1983). Taylor summarizes Owen's sexual philosophy as follows: "Natural/unnatural, instinctual/artificial, spontaneous/constrained: these polarities dominate all of Owen's writings on human relations. . . . Above all, sexual love is a spontaneous expression of the most joyous and pleasurable of our instincts; its repression within conventional marriage is a desecration of the natural order, a violation of 'the most sacred laws of our nature.'" She adds that Owen's "favourite metaphors" for natural sexual relations "tended to be watery ones: sexual love was a flood, current, tide, which could not be dammed, channeled, bottled up. . ." (41–42). Fourier's ideas were very similar; see the extensive summary provided by Jonathan Beecher, *Charles Fourier: The Visionary and His World* (Berkeley: U of California P, 1986) 195–352. According to Beecher, a "recurrent theme" in Fourier's writings was that "civilization was an edifice built on the repression of man's instinctual drives, and its cornerstone was the institution of monogamous marriage," whose chief victims were women. Fourier saw human behavior as "dictated by fundamental instinctual drives that could not be permanently altered or suppressed. . . . In his view the real task confronting the social theorist was to find a way to liberate and utilize the repressed passions" (204, 206, 220). For allusions to Fourier in *Letters from New York*, see Letter #37 on Swedenborg and Fourier, *Letters from New York [First Series]* (1843; Freeport, N.Y.: Books for Libraries P, 1970) 273–74; and Letter #28 on "Fourier's perfect Social Chord" in *Letters from New York. Second Series* (New York: C. S. Francis, 1845) 256–57; Letter #10 of the Second Series also refers in passing to Fourier's investigation of "the causes of social evils and their remedy" (107). Child cites Fourier frequently in her personal letters as well; see esp. LMC to Ellis Loring, 9 Mar. 1842, *SL* 165: "I have never intended to endorse Fourier's system. But is he unphilosophical in saying that *every* passion and emotion of the human heart was made to be exercised in a healthy sphere, and no one made to be stifled?" For Child's early association of Frances Wright with "infidel" attacks on religion, see "Letter from a Lady, concerning Miss Wright," *Massachusetts Weekly Journal* 14 Aug. 1829, p. 3, quoted in chap. 5.

5   Child's two "Letters from New-York" on women's rights, #50 and #51, appeared in the *Standard* of 16 and 23 Feb. 1843. They are reproduced in *CC* 16/452 and 457. Child announced her decision "not to follow David's movements any more" in a letter to Louisa Loring of 28 Feb. [1843], *CC* 16/459, where she concludes, "If I had done this six years ago, it would have been better for us both. . . ."

6   "Speaking in the Church," *Standard* 15 July 1841, p. 22. See also LMC to William Lloyd Garrison, 2 Sept. 1839, *SL* 122–23, *Liberator* 6 Sept., p. 142.

7 "Speaking in the Church," *Standard* 15 July 1841, p. 22.

8 Child refers to her friends' demands that she "come out" on the issue in the opening paragraph of "Letters from New-York" #50, 16 Feb. 1843. She deleted this paragraph and the one that follows from the book version of *Letters from New York* [*First Series*] 245–52, which amalgamates Letters #50 and #51 in the *Standard* into one (#34) and reorganizes the argument. Subsequent quotations from the book version will be given parenthetically in the text. Since the excised passages concern the debate among abolitionists over whether or not women's rights "is a legitimate branch of the anti-slavery enterprise," removing them has the effect of redefining women's rights as an issue important in its own right, relevant not only to abolitionists, but to a broad audience outside of reformist circles. Her other minor deletions also have the effect of strengthening her argument by eliminating qualifications. The first is a brief passage near the end of #50, in which Child offers her answer to those who claim (as Frances Wright did) that "there is no sex in souls": "I believe that the natures of men and women are spiritually different, yet the same," like flutes in "different keys" playing the same tune. The second is the next-to-the-last paragraph of #51, referring to the common association of women's rights with "infidelity" of the sort imputed to Wright and Mary Wollstonecraft.

9 These sentences were added to the book version. See her correspondence with Ellis Loring over whether or not to include the letters on women's rights in the book, 21 Feb. and 11 Apr. 1843, *CC* 16/455 and 17/481.

10 Lucy Osgood to LMC, 8 May 1843, *CC* 17/493.

11 LMC to Lucy and Mary Osgood, 12 June 1858, *SL* 315–16.

12 LMC to Marianne Devereux Silsbee, 12 Feb. 1847, *CC* 25/694. Deborah Pickman Clifford describes Silsbee as "an old acquaintance but a new friend"; see *Crusader for Freedom: A Life of Lydia Maria Child* (Boston: Beacon P, 1992) 202. Child may have met Silsbee through Louisa Loring's relatives in Salem, the Kings.

13 LMC to Marianne Silsbee, 17 Apr. 1848, *SL* 238. See the fine analysis of this passage by Susan K. Harris, *19th Century American Women's Novels: Interpretive Strategies* (Cambridge: Cambridge UP, 1990) 18–19.

14 LMC to Louisa Loring, 15 Jan. 1847, *SL* 235. See also Child's frequent expressions of sympathy for the artist William Page in his chronic marital troubles. One of the best examples is LMC to Sarah Shaw, 16 Jan. 1859, *CC* 40/1096: Child refuses to condemn Page and his second wife, Sarah, for their marital infidelities and denies that the Shaws' daughters are " 'naturally depraved,' because they don't seem to mind Sarah [Page]'s having left her husband."

15 See LMC to Francis Shaw, *SL* 228–29: "my husband's deficiences [*sic*] in business matters are *incurable*; . . . he inherits the causes in his organization, and can no more help having them than he can help the color of his eyes, or the inches of his stature."

16 See also LMC to Marianne Silsbee, 24 Jan. 1850, *CC* 27/775, written after reuniting with David: "I sometimes wish that he was more mercurial, or I was less so. . ."; also LMC to Harriet Sewall, 30 July 1868, *CC* 69/1843: "he is a man of *facts*, and I am always alone in the *mystical* and *poetical* chambers of my soul" (quoted in chaps. 15 and 19, respectively).

17 Margaret Fuller to LMC, 13 Mar. 1844, *The Letters of Margaret Fuller*, vol. 3, *1842–44*, ed. Robert N. Hudspeth (Ithaca, N.Y.: Cornell UP, 1984) 183, hereinafter cited as *Fuller Letters*. The summary of Fuller's career is based on this five-volume edition of her complete correspondence.

18 Compare Child's and Fuller's articles on their visits to Blackwell's Island in *Letters from New York* [*First Series*], Letter #29, 199–212, and in "Our City Charities. Visit to Bellevue Alms House, to the Farm School, the Asylum for the Insane, and Penitentiary on Blackwell's Island," *New-York Daily Tribune* 19 Mar. 1845, reprinted in Jeffrey Steele, ed. *The Essential Margaret Fuller* 385–91. See chaps. 10 and 13 for Fuller's reviews of the 1845 edition of *History of the Condition of Women* and the First and Second Series of *Letters from New York*. Child's review of Fuller's *Woman in the Nineteenth Century* is discussed below. Although Child told Louisa Loring that she did not see Fuller "*very* often," because of the

three-mile distance between their residences (22 June 1845, *SL* 223), Fuller wrote to Anna Loring that she saw Child "often" (2 Apr. 1845, *Fuller Letters* 4: 66).

19   Fuller to Anna Loring, 2 Apr. 1845, *Fuller Letters* 4: 66; LMC to Anna Loring, 28 Dec. 1844, *CC* 21/597; LMC to Louisa Loring, 8 Feb. 1845, *SL* 219. Fuller reviewed the performance of Niagara in "Ole Bull" *New-York Daily Tribune* 20 Dec. 1844, expressing her indignation at the public's "cold and dull reception" of a concert she had found as soul-stirring as Child had.

20   LMC, "Woman in the Nineteenth Century," *Boston Courier*, 8 Feb. 1845, p. 2; *New-York Daily Tribune* 12 Feb. 1845, p. 1; *Broadway Journal* 1 (15 Feb. 1845): 97. Quotations in the following paragraphs are from the *Broadway Journal* review, which differs from the version Child wrote for the *Courier*.

21   See Fuller to James Nathan, 5 June 1845, *Fuller Letters* 4: 113–14, for a description of an occasion when Fuller accompanied Child and Benzon to the theater immediately after Nathan's departure.

22   LMC to Margaret Fuller, undated [Jan.? 1846?], *CC* 23/649.

23   Fuller to James Nathan, 5 June and 22 [July]. 1845, *Fuller Letters* 4: 114, 138. In the 5 June letter, Fuller draws a parallel between Child's marriage and her befriending of the actress Jeannie Barrett. In the 22 July letter, Fuller is responding to a letter of 5 June from Nathan, written immediately after his departure. On Nathan's sexual proposition to Fuller, see Hudspeth's preface, 4: 7–8, and Fuller to Nathan, 14 Apr. and [15 Apr.] [1845], 73–79.

24   Steele, ed., *Essential Margaret Fuller* 329. For details of Fuller's Oct. 1844 visit to Sing Sing and her conversations with the prostitutes imprisoned there, see *Fuller Letters* 3: 236–38. For another example of Fuller's interest in the rehabilitation of women prisoners and prostitutes, see her article in support of a new "Asylum for Discharged Female Convicts," *New-York Daily Tribune* 19 June 1845, p. 1.

25   On the Moral Reform movement of the 1830s, see Carroll Smith-Rosenberg, "Beauty, the Beast, and the Militant Woman: A Case Study in Sex Roles and Social Stress in Jacksonian America" (1971), rpt. in her *Disorderly Conduct: Visions of Gender in Victorian America* (New York: Oxford UP, 1985) 109–28; and Mary P. Ryan, "The Power of Women's Networks: A Case Study of Female Moral Reform in Antebellum America," *Feminist Studies* 5 (Spring 1979): 66–85. On Abby Hopper Gibbons and other women prison reformers, see Estelle B. Freedman, *Their Sisters' Keepers: Women's Prison Reform in America, 1830–1930* (Ann Arbor: U of Michigan P, 1981) chap. 2. See also Lydia Maria Child, *Isaac T. Hopper: A True Life* (Boston: J. P. Jewett, 1853) 408ff., on her host's prison reform activities. For a brilliantly original perspective on prostitution as a realistic choice among unattractive alternatives, by which working-class women earned better wages than they could at legitimate trades and exacted some reciprocity for sexual relations, see Christine Stansell, *City of Women: Sex and Class in New York, 1789–1860* (Urbana: U of Illinois P, 1987) chap. 9.

26   Steele, ed., *Essential Margaret Fuller* 283–86.

27   "Letter from New-York," *Boston Courier* 6 Feb. 1844, rpt. in the *Standard* 22 Feb. and reproduced in *CC* 19/536. Quotations in the next paragraph will be drawn from this text. Child did not collect it in the Second Series of her *Letters from New York* (1845).

28   Steele, ed., *Essential Margaret Fuller* 330.

29   LMC to Maria White Lowell, 22 Dec. 1845, *CC* 23/643.

30   LMC to ? 23 Apr. 1844, *CC* 19/550.

31   Margaret Fuller to James Nathan, 5 June 1845, *Fuller Letters* 4: 113–14.

32   Yet years later Child admitted to Sarah Shaw that her efforts had all failed in the end: "In three cases, I tried the experiment of taking a cast-a-way into my own room for several months. While they were with me, all went well; but every case proved a failure after they went out into the world to earn their living; one after a probation of a few months, the other two after a term of years. I confess that if I had known human nature as well as I now know it, I never should have had courage to try such experiments. But is it not strange that some way cannot be discovered by which the elements of human society can be so harmonized as to prevent such frightful discords?" LMC to Sarah Shaw, 9 July 1878, *SL* 552.

33   LMC to the Rev. John Pierpont, 19 Nov. 1844, *CC* 20/586.

34   LMC to Eliza F. Merriam, 13 July 1846, *CC* 23/661.

35   LMC to Lucy and Mary Osgood, 12 June 1858, *SL* 316. She was referring here to George Sand, but the point is the same. For an intriguing snippet of evidence that Child may have viewed herself as a "fallen woman," see LMC to Parke Godwin, 17 Feb. 1846, *CC* 23/651. Thanking him for having sent her a copy of his latest book, she writes that she "cut out" his complimentary inscription to her because "I sincerely feel that I am *not* an 'excellent woman.' Again and again I have lost my way in the mazes of life."

36   I am using the phrase in the double sense suggested by Nancy Cott and Sarah Grimké: "that woman-hood bound women together even as it bound them down." See Cott's fine study, *The Bonds of Womanhood: "Woman's Sphere" in New England, 1780–1835* (New Haven, Conn.: Yale UP, 1977) 1. On Child's distaste for "distinct female societies," see LMC to Charlotte Phelps and Lucretia Mott, [2 Jan. 1834], and 5 Mar. 1839, *SL* 28, 106–7, quoted in chap. 10.

37   "The Quadroons" and "The Black Saxons" were subsequently reprinted in Lydia Maria Child, *Fact and Fiction: A Collection of Stories* (New York: C. S. Francis, 1846) 61–76, 190–204. All subsequent quotations from the stories in this collection will be from this edition and will be given parenthetically in the text. "Slavery's Pleasant Homes," *Liberty Bell*, 4 (1843): 147–60. The latter was never collected.

38   "Speaking in the Church," *Standard* 15 July 1841, p. 22.

39   LMC to Maria Weston Chapman, [21 Nov. 1840, misdated 1841], *CC* 11/285. This letter, accompany-ing the manuscript of "The Black Saxons," is undated, but postmarked Northampton, 21 Nov. After the first volume in 1839, *The Liberty Bell*, like other Christmas gift books, was always dated "for" the following year. The 1841 volume was issued in Dec. 1840 "for" 1841. Thus, Child's story could not have been written in Nov. 1841 "for" the 1841 volume. Moreover, Child's letter refers to her desire to escape from Northampton "in any way not involving separation from my dearest and best friend"; yet by Nov. 1841 she was living in New York.

40   LMC to Francis Shaw, 2 Aug. 1846, *SL* 229.

41   My count of twenty-seven stories includes all those published in the *Liberty Bell*, the *Columbian Lady's and Gentleman's Magazine*, and the *Union Magazine of Literature and Art* between 1840 and 1849, with the exception of a few prose selections that cannot properly be considered fiction. Of the works mentioned in this paragraph, all but the following are collected in *Fact and Fiction*. "Home and Politics," "The Rival Mechanicians," and "The Prophet of Ionia," were collected much later in Lydia Maria Child, *Autumnal Leaves: Tales and Sketches in Prose and Rhyme* (New York: C. S. Francis, 1857) 96–118, 143–64, 269–90, where the third was retitled "The Ancient Clairvoyant." "The Hindoo Anchorite" (never collected) appeared in the *Union Magazine* 2 (Apr. 1848): 151–53. "Home and Politics" and "The Prophet of Ionia" first appeared in the same journal (Aug. 1848 and Feb. 1849), and "The Rival Mechanicians in the *Columbian Magazine* (Jan. 1847).

42   On David's propensity for gambling on schemes of quick enrichment, see the letters quoted in chap. 15: LMC to Louisa Loring, 22 June 1845, and [Dec.? 1849?], *SL* 223–24, *CC* 27/770; to Convers Francis, [23 May? 1846?], *CC* 23/658; to DLC, 31 Aug. 1849, *SL* 248. On his political ambitions, see LMC to DLC, 31 Aug. 1849, *SL* 248: "Oh if we only *could* have ever so small a home, where you could be contented, and have no dreams about Congress!" See also LMC to Francis Shaw, 2 Aug. 1846, *SL* 228–30.

43   See LMC to Francis Shaw, 18 July 1844, *SL* 210: "You ask whether Mr. Child has inoculated me *again* with politics. Your memory is better than mine if you can recollect any period of my life when I regarded politics otherwise than with extreme aversion. . . . As for Henry Clay, I have no confidence whatever in him." Also LMC to Ellis Loring, 26 Dec. 1843 [misdated 1844], *CC* 21/595: "David talks of going to Washington next week. I am sorry. We were just getting comfortably and cozily settled. I hate politics worse and worse." On the prior relationship between David Child and Henry Clay, see "Henry Clay and Texas," *Standard* 15 Feb. 1844, pp. 146–47. In this editorial, David complains that Clay has not answered a letter he sent three months before, asking for the Kentuckian's views on the annexation of Texas. He adds: "we were his early, constant, and ardent friend, and supporter, having by

the steadiness and singleness of our attachment, carried among those most devoted to him, the cognomen of 'Old Kent,' at the time his star, like the flickering life of Lear, seemed ready to go out forever. Moreover, we had often communicated with Mr. Clay on public affairs; and we expected the courtesy of a reply." See also *An Appeal from David L. Childs. [sic] Editor of the Anti-Slavery Standard, to the Abolitionists*, a pamphlet enumerating the reasons why abolitionists ought to vote for Clay (published and distributed by the *Albany Evening Journal*, 1844). Given the story's Aug. 1848 publication date, Child may have been aware that David even wrote to Clay in July 1848, urging him to run as the Free Soil candidate for president. See DLC to Henry Clay, 26 July 1848, BPL Ms.A.4.2, p. 23.

44 *Autumnal Leaves* 110. For a more detailed analysis of the autobiographical resonances in "Home and Politics," see Deborah P. Clifford, "Creating a Biography of Lydia Maria Child," unpublished paper given at American Studies Association convention, Miami, Fla., 1988; also her *Crusader for Freedom* 190–91.

45 See, for example, LMC to Francis Shaw, 2 Aug. 1846, *SL* 230.

46 LMC to DLC and Francis Shaw, 18 Aug. 1839, 27 May 1841, *SL* 118, 142.

47 *Autumnal Leaves* 104, 108.

48 In many ways "The Children of Mount Ida" invites comparison with *Philothea*, also set in Greece and featuring examples of clairvoyance. In *Philothea*, Child attributes the withdrawal of Paralus to a mysterious malady and idealizes Philothea's self-sacrifice. In "The Children of Mount Ida" she blames the withdrawal of Corythus on his ambition. Clearly, she is now willing to blame the breakup of the marriage on the husband.

49 [Charles F. Briggs], "The Children of Mount Ida. By MRS. CHILD," *Broadway Journal* 1 (29 Mar. 1845): 193. Although he published Child's warm review of Fuller's *Woman in the Nineteenth Century*, he himself excoriated the book and impugned Fuller's character in several "squibs" that Child called "very ungentlemanly." Child pronounced Briggs's "ideas of women . . . at least a century behind the age." See LMC to Francis Shaw, undated [Oct. 1846], *SL* 231; and [Charles F. Briggs], "WOMAN IN THE NINE-TEENTH CENTURY," *Broadway Journal* 1 (1 Mar. 1845): 130–31; continued on 8 and 22 Mar., pp. 145–46, 182–83.

50 LMC to Francis Shaw, 29 May 1843, *CC* 17/497.

51 JSD, review of *Fact and Fiction*, *Harbinger* 4 (2 Jan. 1847): 57–58. This is the only review I have been able to locate of the book, except for a brief notice in the *New-York Daily Tribune*, 24 Dec. 1846, p. 2.

52 I am using the term "documentary" tale in the sense suggested by Barbara Foley's fine study, *Telling the Truth: The Theory and Practice of Documentary Fiction* (Ithaca, N.Y.: Cornell UP, 1986).

53 See chaps. 7 and 9 for analyses of "The St. Domingo Orphans," "Jumbo and Zairee," and "Mary French and Susan Easton" in the *Juvenile Miscellany* and of "Malem-Boo" in *The Oasis*.

54 "ARCHY MOORE," LMC to William Lloyd Garrison, *Liberator* 18 Mar. 1837, p 47, rpt. in *CC* 5/118.

55 LMC to Lydia Bigelow Child, 17 Jan. 1837, *SL* 60.

56 LMC to Lydia Bigelow Child, 2 Apr. 1837, *CC* 5/120.

57 Caroline Weston to Anne Warren Weston, n.d., BPL Ms.A.9.2.4, p. 55. This letter reports that "Mrs. Child's novel [*Philothea*] is coming out immediately," which would seem to date it before fall 1836. If so, Child must have begun her antislavery novel before the publication of Hildreth's, which Weston reports having heard is "in *press*."

58 See, for example, E. J. Hobsbawm, *Primitive Rebels: Studies in Archaic Forms of Social Movement in the 19th and 20th Centuries* (1959; New York: W. W. Norton, 1965); and "Our Anglo-Saxon Ancestry," *Standard* 28 Apr. 1842, pp. 186–87, discussed in chap. 12. This is another example of the way Child's fictional imagination dramatizes political insights before her polemical essays formulate them analytically.

59 Lydia Maria Child, *An Appeal in Favor of That Class of Americans Called Africans* (Boston: Allen and Ticknor, 1833) 180.

60 See her editorial, "The African Race," *Standard* 27 Apr. 1843, p. 187, which develops this idea in detail.

61 See Frederick Douglass, *Narrative of Frederick Douglass, An American Slave. Written by Himself* (1845;

New York: Doubleday, 1963) chap. 6. "The Black Saxons" was published about nine months before Douglass's memorable debut as an antislavery orator in Aug. 1841.

62   Child, *Appeal in Favor of Americans Called Africans* 19.

63   "Slavery as it is," *Pennsylvania Freeman*, rpt. in *Liberator* 12 June 1840, p. 93.

64   For analyses of the "tragic mulatto" theme and the problems it raises, see Jules Zanger, " 'The Tragic Octoroon' in Pre-Civil War Fiction," *American Quarterly* 18 (Spring 1966): 63–70; Sterling A. Brown, *The Negro in American Fiction* (1937; Port Washington, N.Y.: Kennikat P, 1968) 45–46; Barbara Christian, *Black Women Novelists: The Development of a Tradition, 1892–1976* (Westport, Conn.: Greenwood P, 1980) 22–23; Alice Walker, *In Search of Our Mothers' Gardens: Womanist Prose* (New York: Harcourt Brace Jovanovich, 1983) 290–312; and Jean Fagan Yellin, *Women and Sisters: The Antislavery Feminists in American Culture* (New Haven, Conn.: Yale UP, 1989) 71–74.

65   The story of Cassie in *Uncle Tom's Cabin* combines elements of Rosalie's and Xarifa's stories. Brown acknowledged his debt to the story and lifted whole passages from "The Quadroons" in chaps. 4 and 8 of *Clotel*. His plagiarism (which he eliminated from subsequent editions of the novel) betrays both his discomfort with the white-invented "tragic mulatto" theme and his understanding of its strategic value in appealing to white readers. See William Edward Farrison, *William Wells Brown, Author and Reformer* (Chicago: U of Chicago P, 1969), 224, 228, 325; Jean Fagan Yellin, *The Intricate Knot: Black Figures in American Literature, 1776–1863* (New York: New York UP, 1972) 172; and Carolyn L. Karcher, "Lydia Maria Child's *A Romance of the Republic*: An Abolitionist Vision of America's Racial Destiny," in *Slavery and the Literary Imagination: Selected Papers from the English Institute, 1987*, ed. Deborah E. McDowell and Arnold Rampersad (Baltimore: Johns Hopkins UP, 1989), 101 n.6.

66   LMC to Maria Weston Chapman, 1 Dec. [1841], *CC* 12/292. Deborah Clifford suggests that the romantic strain of "The Quadroons" reflects Child's developing romance with John Hopper; see *Crusader for Freedom* 174.

67   These features, in my view, clearly distinguish "Slavery's Pleasant Homes" from the typical "tragic mulatto" narrative. Hence, I cannot agree with Yellin in classifying it as such (*Women and Sisters*, 71–74).

68   *Appeal* 205; "The Slave Murders," *Standard* 23 June 1842. This editorial refers to the earlier incident while commenting on a similar case that has just been reported.

69   Quotations are from Child's paraphrases of the *Liberator* story in the *Appeal* (206) and the *Standard* (see n. 68 above); for the original, see "Diabolical Wickedness, to which a citizen of Boston was a party," *Liberator* 11 Aug. 1832, p. 127. A comparison of the three accounts once again reveals Child's evolution toward greater freedom of expression in sexual matters. Garrison's article in the *Liberator* is much more explicit than Child's version of the story in the *Appeal*, where she merely says that the overseer "compelled" the women to "remain as long as he thought proper" (206). In the *Standard*, Child supplies the details she had earlier censored from Garrison's account.

70   "The Slave Murders" and "Horrible Events, " *Standard* 23 June 1842, pp. 10–11.

71   See "Annette Gray" and "Follow the North Star," *Standard* 22 July 1841, pp. 26–27, and 21 July 1842, pp. 26–27. I have put the names in quotation marks because they are fictitious.

72   "Peculiar Traits of Southern Life — Condition of Woman — Her Strange Seclusion — True and False Civilization — Southern Chivalry," *Portsmouth Journal*, reprinted in *Standard*, 8 Dec. 1842, p. 108. Child generally sent in her contributions to the *Liberty Bell* by 1 Dec., since the volume had to be published in time for the pre-Christmas fair. The *Portsmouth Journal* article had probably arrived at the *Standard* office well before Child reprinted it. She often held articles for several weeks when space constraints prevented her from inserting them. Late twentieth-century readers will of course note the relevance of Edward W. Said's *Orientalism* (New York: Pantheon, 1978) to analyzing these tropes.

73   Lydia Maria Child, *The History of the Condition of Women* . . . (Boston: John Allen, 1835) 1: 2, 24, 45.

74   "Slavery's Pleasant Homes," *The Liberty Bell* 4 (1843): 147–60. Page references to the story are given parenthetically in the text. I am using the term "romance" in the sense that Child uses it, not in the sense established by Hawthorne. I do not mean to claim that "Slavery's Pleasant Homes" is an example

of literary realism, as defined by Howells. Nevertheless, I would like to suggest that antislavery fiction may be profitably examined as one of the sources or precursors of literary realism, which recent critics have traced back to mid-nineteenth century women writers. See, for example, *Provisions: A Reader from 19th-Century American Women*, ed. Judith Fetterley (Bloomington: Indiana UP, 1985), 10–11.

75 I am indebted to Lucy Freibert for this analysis of Child's imagery. It should be noted that the image of the "dark carnation" represents a departure from the model of the near-white heroine. Rosa's skin color is described as "transparent brown," resembling "claret [shining] through a bottle in the sunshine" when she blushes (148).

76 "Annette Gray" and "Follow the North Star," *Standard* 22 July 1841, pp. 26–27, and 21 July 1842, pp. 26–27.

77 Child leaves ambiguous whether Frederic or George is the father of Rosa's child. In either case, the pregnancy would still be the result of illicit sex, since Child make clear that George and Rosa's marriage is informal (slave marriages were not legally recognized).

78 In "Benito Cereno" (1855), Melville appends the legal deposition of the master, which the Spanish court has used to convict the slave rebels; in *Billy Budd*, he appends a newspaper account in "a naval chronicle of the time, an authorized weekly publication," whose version represents a complete distortion of the story he has narrated (chap. 29).

79 Caroline Healey Dall, "The Inalienable Love," *The Liberty Bell* 15 (1858): 87.

80 "Speaking in the Church," *Standard* 15 July 1841, p. 22. See also LMC to William Lloyd Garrison, 2 Sept. 1839, *SL* 122–23, published in the *Liberator* of 6 Sept., p. 142.

81 For letters referring to Child's activities on behalf of fugitive slaves, see *SL* 208, 244.

82 On the ideology of passionlessness constructed by eighteenth-century Evangelicals, see Nancy Cott, "Passionlessness: An Interpretation of Victorian Sexual Ideology, 1790–1850," *Signs* 4 (Winter 1978): 219–36. The *Columbian Lady's and Gentleman's Magazine* and *Godey's Lady's Book* both featured a number of fallen women stories during the 1840s, but I have found none that take as liberal an attitude toward sexuality as Child's do. Other authors occasionally allow the heroine to repent, but do not defend her sexual impulses as "natural" and often lash out against men's licentiousness. See Catharine Maria Sedgwick, "Fanny McDermot," *Godey's Magazine and Lady's Book* 30 (Jan. and Feb. 1845): 13–20, 75–83; Emma C. Embury, "The Convict's Daughter," *Godey's* 30 (Jan. 1845): 21–26; Walter Whitman, "Dumb Kate. An Early Death," *Columbian Lady's and Gentleman's Magazine* 1 (May 1844): 230–31; Mrs. C. H. Butler, "The Minister's Family," *Columbian* 7 (Feb. 1847): 71–76; Miss Martha Russell, "Melinda Dutton and Her Old Relations," *Columbian* 7 (Apr. 1847): 161–68; and Miss C. M. Sisson, "The Reclaimed," *Columbian* 8 (Oct. 1847): 159–61. For surveys of the fallen woman theme in British literature, see Françoise Basch, *Relative Creatures: Victorian Women in Society and the Novel*, trans. Anthony Rudolf (New York: Shocken, 1974) pt. 3; and Sally Mitchell, *The Fallen Angel: Chastity, Class and Women's Reading, 1835–1880* (Bowling Green, Ohio: Bowling Green U Popular P, 1981). David S. Reynolds has described the 1840s as flooded with erotic fiction. The fiction he discusses, however, was written exclusively by men and articulates male fantasies about female sexuality (often extremely misogynist). See Reynolds, *Beneath the American Renaissance: The Subversive Imagination in the Age of Emerson and Melville* (Cambridge, Mass.: Harvard UP, 1989) chaps. 6–7. The image of voracious female sexuality conveyed by this body of writing is actually a holdover from an earlier era and dates back to ancient times, but it was displaced from mainstream culture in the nineteenth century, as Cott has shown in "Passionlessness."

83 On the moral reform movement, see the articles by Carroll Smith-Rosenberg and Mary Ryan cited in n. 25 above.

84 LMC to Francis Shaw, 2 Aug. 1846, *SL* 229.

85 "Rosenglory" was published in the *Columbian* of Oct. 1846. Child had called the women's rights question "distasteful" to her in "Speaking in the Church," *Standard* 15 July 1841, p. 22.

86 See LMC to ? 23 Apr. 1844, *CC* 19/550; and Child's indictment of the criminal justice system in #29 of *Letters from New York* [*First Series*].

87 Miss Martha Russell, "Melinda Dutton and Her Old Relations," and Miss C. M. Sisson, "The Reclaimed," *Columbian Lady's and Gentleman's Magazine* 7 (Apr. 1847): 161–68, and 8 (Oct. 1847): 159–61. "Rosenglory" had appeared in Oct. 1846.

88 Child had registered her protest against capital punishment in *Letters from New York* [*First Series*] #31, 220–30.

89 LMC to Louisa Loring, 15 Jan. 1847, *SL* 235 (Child is projecting her own feeling onto Mrs. Jameson); LMC to Louisa Loring, 28 Feb. [1843], *CC* 16/459.

90 See Carolyn L. Karcher, "Patriarchal Society and Matriarchal Family in Irving's 'Rip Van Winkle' and Child's 'Hilda Silfverling,'" *Legacy* 2 (Fall 1985): 31–44. I am indebted to Margaret Kellow for pointing out the autobiographical implications of Hilda's freedom from aging.

91 Frank Preston Stearns, *The Life and Public Services of George Luther Stearns* (1907; New York: Arno P, 1969) 76–77. The author was the son of Child's niece, Mary Preston Stearns.

92 See Child's descriptions of Ole Bull in "Letter from New-York," 23 Dec. 1843, *CC* 18/525; and LMC to Anna Loring, 13–14 Oct. 1844, *CC* 20/578, quoted in chap. 13. To a certain extent, Child also transformed her relationship with Bull into a mother-son bond, at least in retrospect. See LMC to Ole Bull, 22 Oct. 1853, *CC* 30/853, where she explicitly defined their relationship in those terms; also LMC to Marianne Silsbee, 5 Feb. 1847, *CC* 24/693 (quoted in chap. 13).

93 See the examples collected in Carol Farley Kessler, *Daring to Dream: Utopian Stories by United States Women: 1836–1919* (Boston: Pandora P, 1984); Charlotte Perkins Gilman's feminist utopia *Herland* (1915); Ursula Le Guin's *The Left Hand of Darkness* (1969); and Marge Piercy's *Woman on the Edge of Time* (1976).

94 See Carroll Smith-Rosenberg's brilliant analysis of the Trickster characters created by Virginia Woolf in *Orlando* and by Djuna Barnes in *Nightwood* (1936), "The New Woman as Androgyne," *Disorderly Conduct: Visions of Gender in Victorian America* (New York: Oxford UP, 1985) 290–95; also her essay "Davy Crockett as Trickster: Pornography, Liminality, and Symbolic Inversion in Victorian America," in the same volume, 90–108. By providing a model for feminist analysis of the Trickster and by pointing me toward Barbara Babcock-Abrahams' indispensable article, "'A Tolerated Margin of Mess': The Trickster and His Tales Reconsidered," *Journal of the Folklore Institute* 11 (Dec. 1974): 147–86, Smith-Rosenberg's essays helped me to reformulate the interpretation of Alerik as Trickster that I presented in "Patriarchal Society and Matriarchal Family," 37–40.

95 Quotations are from Karl Kerenyi, "The Trickster in Relation to Greek Mythology," appended to Paul Radin's classic book, *The Trickster: A Study in American Indian Mythology* (London: Routledge and Kegan Paul, 1956) 182; Smith-Rosenberg, *Disorderly Conduct* 291; and Babcock-Abrahams, "Tolerated Margin of Mess" 159–60. Of the sixteen attributes Babcock-Abrahams lists, thirteen apply to Alerik.

96 See H. R. Ellis Davidson, *Gods and Myths of the Viking Age* (New York: Bell, 1981) 66–68; and G. Dumézil, *Mythes et dieux des Germains* (Paris: Librairie Ernest Leroux, 1939) 81–85, cited in Davidson 67. Dumézil's analysis deserves to be quoted verbatim: "Les berserkir, en effet, sont les 'jeunes'; ils assument dans la vie des sociétés germaniques cette fonction de fantaisie, de tumulte et de violence qui n'est pas moins nécessaire à l'équilibre collectif que la fonction conservatrice (ordre, tradition, respect des tabous) qu'assument les ... vieux." Child's reference to the Berserkers is only one indication of how extensive her knowledge of Norse mythology was. She seems to have derived her information on the Berserkers from Samuel Laing's translation of the Ynglinga Saga, in *The Heimskringla; or, Chronicle of the Kings of Norway. Translated from the Icelandic of Snorro Sturleson, with a Preliminary Dissertation* (London: Longman, Brown, Green, and Longmans, 1844). The other main source to which she would have had access is Paul Henri Mallet, *Northern Antiquities: or A Description of the Manners, Customs, Religion and Laws of the Ancient Danes, including those of Our Own Saxon Ancestors. With a Translation of the Edda, or System of Runic Mythology, and Other Ancient Pieces, from the Ancient Icelandic Tongue,* trans. Thomas Percy, 2 vols. (Edinburgh: C. Stewart, 1809). Both sources were very well known and formed part of a vogue for Norse mythology that Reginald Horsman has attributed to "racial Anglo-

Saxonism"; see his *Race and Manifest Destiny: The Origins of American Racial Anglo-Saxonism* (Cambridge, Mass.: Harvard UP, 1981) 67.

97   Mallet, *Northern Antiquities* 2:61; Davidson, *Gods and Myths* 178.

98   Child's description of Orpheus in *The Progress of Religious Ideas, Through Successive Ages* (New York: C. S. Francis, 1855) 1: 333–34, suggests that she views him as a Trickster figure: "he travelled into Egypt, where he obtained some knowledge of their religious mysteries, and became skilful in music, poetry, philosophy, astrology, and medicine. Thus accomplished, he returned to the Greeks, who were at that time in such a rude condition, that any man of moderate attainments would have seemed a prodigy. Accordingly, he became as famous among them as was Hermes among the Egyptians." This account of Orpheus also explains why she has Alerik refer to the Egyptian belief that "the soul was obliged to live three thousand years, in a succession of different animals, before it could attain to the regions of the blest" (235).

99   Kerenyi in Radin, *The Trickster* 185.

100   Babcock-Abrahams, "A Tolerated Margin of Mess" 184. Carroll Smith-Rosenberg has also indicated some of the device's limitations for the feminist modernists she has examined; see *Disorderly Conduct* 292.

101   LMC to Francis Shaw, 29 May 1843, *CC* 17/497.

102   "She Waits in the Spirit Land" was collected in *Fact and Fiction* along with Child's other stories for the *Columbian Lady's and Gentleman's Magazine*. For convenience, however, I will be citing the reprint edition included in *HOBOMOK and Other Writings on Indians*, ed. Carolyn L. Karcher (New Brunswick, N.J.: Rutgers UP, 1986) 192–201. Page references to this edition will be given parenthetically in the text.

103   Ellis Loring to LMC, 6 Jan. 1847, *CC* 24/689.

104   LMC to Anna Loring, 13 Jan. 1847, *CC* 24/690.

105   Ellis Loring to LMC, 6 Jan. 1847, *CC* 24/689.

106   JSD, review of *Fact and Fiction*, *Harbinger* 2 Jan. 1847, pp. 57–58.

107   LMC to Francis Shaw, 18 Feb. [1847], *CC* 25/696.

108   LMC to Francis Shaw, 11 July 1847, *CC* 25/711.

109   LMC to Francis Shaw, 18 July 1844, *SL* 209.

110   LMC to Susan Lyman, 28 Mar. 1847, *CC* 25/706, and 9 Apr. [1847], *CC* 25/707.

111   LMC to Ellis Loring, 27 Oct. 1851, *SL* 261.

15   The Progress of Religious Ideas: *A "Pilgrimage of Penance"*

1   LMC to Ellis Loring, 6 June 1850, *CC* 28/782.

2   LMC to Lucy Osgood, [11?–19? Feb. 1856], *SL* 276.

3   LMC to Ellis Loring, 1 Feb. 1850, *SL* 252.

4   See chap. 10; Child had also used their home as a refuge from unwelcome visitors during the New Year's holidays and the May anniversary meetings of the American Anti-Slavery Society. See *SL* 38, 226.

5   LMC to Convers Francis, 20 Jan. 1848; Marianne Silsbee, 6 Feb. 1848; and Relief Loring, 12 Feb. 1848, *CC* 26/725, 726, 727.

6   LMC to Louisa Loring, 29 Apr. 1847, *SL* 236–37.

7   Child shared her worries about David with Susan Lyman, 8 Aug. and 10 Oct. 1847, *CC* 25/712, 715.

8   LMC to Relief Loring, 12 Feb. 1848, *CC* 26/727.

9   "The Hindoo Anchorite," *Union Magazine of Literature and Art* 2 (Apr. 1848): 151–53.

10   LMC to Lucy Osgood, 28 June 1846, *SL* 226. See also *Letters from New York* 1: Letters 6, 11, 26, 33, 36, and 2: Letters 12, 13, 23. For a fine account of the spiritual pilgrimage Child began in New York and consummated in *The Progress of Religious Ideas*, see Patricia Holland, "Lydia Maria Child and New York

City in the 1840s," Henry Whitney Bellows Lecture, Unitarian Church of All Souls, New York City, 10 May 1990.

11   LMC to Louisa Loring, 8 Mar. 1849, *SL* 242.

12   LMC to Susan Lyman, 8 Aug. 1847, *CC* 25/712.

13   LMC to Marianne Silsbee, 9 Nov. 1848, *SL* 240.

14   LMC to Susan Lyman, 28 Jan. 1849, *CC* 26/745.

15   LMC to Louisa Loring, 8 Mar. 1849, *SL* 242–45. Child also refers to this recurrent dream in letters to the Lorings of 7 and 24 Mar. 1850, *CC* 28/777, *SL* 253–54.

16   I am indebted for this suggestion to Margaret M. R. Kellow, "Must the Baby Go Out with the Bathwater? Psychohistory, Biography and Lydia Maria Child," unpublished paper presented at the American Studies Association convention, Miami, Fla., 1988. Child recorded her mother's age under a lock of hair clipped at her death and carefully preserved; see Hair Clippings, Lydia Maria Child Papers, Cornell University Library Anti-Slavery Collection.

17   LMC to Sarah Maria Preston Parsons, 27 Sept. 1847, *CC* 25/714. Child acknowledges apologetically that "during the last twenty years . . . I have seen [Mary] but twice." Even more suggestively, she omits any reference to the eight years she spent in Norridgewock, during which Mary had played the role of a surrogate mother to her.

18   LMC to Louisa and Ellis Loring, 8 Mar. 1849 and 7 Mar. 1850, *SL* 242–43 and *CC* 28/777.

19   LMC to Convers Francis, 27 Feb. 1856, *CC* 32/909.

20   LMC to Marianne Silsbee, 17 Apr. 1848, *CC* 26/729.

21   LMC to Susan Lyman, 7 Aug. 1848, *CC* 26/735.

22   LMC to Parke Godwin, 22 Aug. 1848, *CC* 26/737.

23   LMC to Marianne Silsbee, 9 Nov. 1848, *SL* 240–41.

24   LMC to Susan Lyman, 28 Jan. 1849, *CC* 26/745.

25   LMC to Convers Francis, 14 July [1849], *CC* 27/755a.

26   LMC to Mary Preston Stearns, 13 May 1850, *CC* 28/781.

27   LMC to Louisa Loring, 22 June 1845, *SL* 224. See also LMC to Convers Francis, 23 May? 1846?, *CC* 23/658: "[A]s usual [David] lost money by his last year's speculation. Yet he is for curing the difficulty by another bite of the same dog. I *cannot* persuade him out of these things." Susan I. [Lyman] Lesley, *Memoir of the Life of Mrs. Anne Jean Lyman* (Cambridge, Mass.: Privately printed, 1876); quoted in Anna D. Hallowell, "Lydia Maria Child," *Medford Historical Register* 3 (July 1900): 110–11.

28   Lesley, *Memoir*, quoted in Hallowell, "Lydia Maria Child": 110–11.

29   LMC to Susan Lyman, 24 Jan. 1848, *CC* 26/724.

30   LMC to DLC, 31 Aug. 1849, *SL* 248.

31   LMC to Susan Lyman and Louisa Loring, 28 Jan. and [Dec.?] 1849, *CC* 26/745 and 27/770.

32   LMC to Louisa and Ellis Loring, 21 Oct. 1849, *SL* 249–50, and 6 June 1850, *CC* 28/782. For a brief sketch of John Childe's lucrative career as a civil engineer and surveyor for the railroads, see the *DAB*. (He added the *e* to the family name, perhaps to distinguish himself from his abolitionist relatives.)

33   LMC to DLC, 2 Nov. 1846, *SL* 234; Lydia Bigelow Child, 16 Feb. 1849, *SL* 242; Ellis Loring, 24 Mar. 1850, *SL* 253.

34   LMC to Louisa Loring, 21 Oct. 1849, *SL* 250.

35   LMC to Louisa Loring, 12 Nov. 1849, *CC* 27/764.

36   LMC to Louisa Loring, 21 Oct. 1849, *SL* 250. See also LMC to Ellis Loring, 26 Dec. 1843, *CC* 21/595.

37   LMC to DLC, 31 Aug. 1849, *SL* 248.

38   LMC to DLC, 31 Aug. 1849, *SL* 248–49.

39   LMC to Louisa Loring, 21 Oct. 1849, *SL* 250. See also LMC to Ellis Loring, 1 Feb. 1849, *SL* 252–53, which once again juxtaposes comments on the Childs' reconciliation with references to Fuller's marriage.

40   LMC to Marianne Silsbee, 29 Oct. 1849, *CC* 27/762.

41   LMC to Louisa and Ellis Loring, 21 Oct. 1849 and 1 Feb. 1850, *SL* 250, 252.

42   LMC to DLC, 31 Aug. 1849, *CC* 27/758. See also LMC to Francis Shaw, 18 July 1844, *SL* 210.

43   LMC to Ellis Loring, 7 Nov. and 14 Dec. 1849, *CC* 27/763, 768; see also LMC to Lucy Osgood, 28 June 1846, *SL* 226.

44   LMC to Marianne Silsbee, 24 Jan. 1850, *CC* 27/775.

45   LMC to Lydia Bigelow Child and Ellis Loring, 16 Feb. 1849 and 24 Mar. 1850, *SL* 241–42, 253–54.

46   LMC to Louisa Loring, 12 Nov. 1849, *CC* 27/764.

47   LMC to Ellis Loring, 24 Mar. and 6 June 1850, *SL* 254, *CC* 28/782.

48   LMC to Ellis Loring, 1 Feb. 1850, *SL* 252–53.

49   LMC to Ellis Loring, 6 Jun 1850, *CC* 28/782.

50   LMC to Ellis Loring, 6 Jun 1850, *CC* 28/782.

51   LMC to Ellis Loring, 13 Apr. 1851, *SL* 258–59.

52   LMC to Louisa and Ellis Loring, 12 Nov. 1849 and 13 Apr. 1851, *CC* 27/764 and *SL* 258–59.

53   LMC to Ellis Loring, 6 June 1850, *CC* 28/782. Quotations in the next paragraph are also from this letter.

54   Ellis Loring to LMC, 26 Mar. 1850, *CC* 28/779.

55   LMC to Louisa and Ellis Loring, 12 Nov. and 14 Dec. 1849, *CC* 27/764, 768.

56   LMC to Ellis Loring, 30 Dec. 1851, *CC* 29/819; Anna Loring, 7 Aug. 1856, *CC* 33/934; and Henry Wadsworth Longfellow, [after 10 June 1850], *CC* 28/784.

57   LMC to Marianne Silsbee, Susan Lyman, and Ellis Loring, 17 Apr. and 7 Aug. 1848 and 3 Dec. 1849, *CC* 26/729 and 735 and 27/766.

58   LMC to Marianne Silsbee, 10 July 1848, *CC* 26/732.

59   LMC to Ellis Loring, 7 Nov. 1849, *CC* 27/763.

60   LMC to Sarah Shaw, 9 Nov. 1856, *SL* 298–99.

61   LMC to Susan Lyman, 7 Aug. 1848, *CC* 26/735.

62   LMC to Lucy Osgood, 26 Mar. 1847, *CC* 25/705. This fantasy may explain why Child keeps resorting to the plot device of babies exchanged in the cradle, which recurs in both *The Rebels* (1825) and *A Romance of the Republic* (1867).

63   LMC to Susan Lyman, 7 Aug. 1848, *CC* 26/735.

64   LMC to Marianne Silsbee, 3 Mar. and 6 Dec. 1849, *CC* 26/749, 27/767.

65   LMC to Marianne Silsbee, 6 Feb. and 3 Mar. 1849, *CC* 26/746, 749.

66   LMC to Ellis Loring, 14 Dec. 1849, *CC* 27/768.

67   LMC to Marianne Silsbee and Susan Lyman, 3 Mar. and 28 Jan. 1849, *CC* 26/749 and 745.

68   LMC to Ellis and Anna Loring, 30 Dec. 1851, *CC* 29/819, and 7 Aug. 1856, *CC* 33/934.

69   LMC to Ellis Loring, 14 Dec. 1849, *CC* 27/768.

70   LMC to Ellis Loring, 7 Nov. and 14 Dec. 1849, *CC* 27/763, 768.

71   See LMC to Louisa and Anna Loring, Sarah Maria Preston Parsons, and Marianne Silsbee, 24 Sept., 6 Nov., 29 Dec., and undated, 1850, and 8 Aug. 1852, *CC* 28/792, 795, 798, 800, and 29/827.

72   LMC to Ellis Loring, 13 Apr. and 27 Oct. 1851, *SL* 258, 260–61.

73   LMC to Ellis Loring, 6 Feb. 1852, *SL* 262.

74   LMC to Ellis Loring, 27 Oct. 1851, *SL* 260.

75   For an account of the North American Phalanx and its many rivals, see John Humphrey Noyes, *History of American Socialisms* (1870), rpt. as *Strange Cults and Utopias of 19th-Century America* (New York: Dover, 1966), esp. chaps. 36–38.

76   LMC to Francis Shaw, 11 Feb. 1869, *CC* 70/1881. See also LMC to Ellis Loring and Robert Cassie Waterston, 9 Mar. 1842 and 27 Aug. 1844, *SL* 165–66, 212–13.

77   LMC to Ellis Loring, 6 Feb. 1852, *SL* 263; also 1 Feb. 1850, *SL* 252. The allusion is to *David Copperfield*.

78   LMC to Ellis Loring, 6 Feb. 1852, *SL* 263.

79   On the Oleana episode and John Hopper's role in it, see Mortimer Smith, *The Life of Ole Bull* (1943; Westport, Conn.: Greenwood P, 1973) 101–23. Child's surviving correspondence contains no references to Oleana. In a letter to Ole Bull of 22 Oct. 1853, *CC* 30/853, however, she implores him to "avoid politicians, and speculators, like evil spirits; for they *are* evil spirits, whose mission it is to blight all the flowers in a poet's soul." For cryptic references to her painful associations with New York and her rupture with John, see LMC to Sarah Shaw, 8 and 20 Dec. 1856 and 29 May 1858, *CC* 34/964, 35/969, and 38/1058.

80   LMC to Ellis Loring, [1852?], *CC* 29/836.

81   LMC to Louisa Loring, 8 Aug. 1852, *CC* 29/827.

82   LMC to Francis Shaw, 5 Sept. 1852, *CC* 29/828.

83   LMC to John Hopper, undated [before 30 Apr. 1853?], *CC* 30/842.

84   Lydia Maria Child, *Isaac T. Hopper: A True Life* (Boston: John P. Jewett, 1853), 248–49, 492. Subsequent page references to this edition are given parenthetically in the text.

85   See LMC to Convers Francis, 20 Oct. 1840, *SL* 133, where Child complains about the "Lilliputian cords" entangling her in housework.

86   An obvious example is her willingness to forgo her own salary as *Standard* editor until the printers were paid. See also Wendell Phillips's anecdotes in his funeral tribute to Child: "It was like her to refuse a gift of several thousand dollars, and, again when I suggested that the large-hearted friend who offered it had more than she could do to wisely distribute her income, . . . it was like her also to . . . accept the trust, portion out every dollar of income while she lived, and devise it, at her death, to the ideas and movements she loved"; [Harriet Sewall, ed.], *Letters of Lydia Maria Child* with a Biographical Introduction by John Greenleaf Whittier and an Appendix by Wendell Phillips (1882; New York: Negro Universities P, 1969) 266.

87   LMC to Sarah Shaw, 31 July and 25 Aug. 1877, *SL* 543–44.

88   See her letters to Maria White Lowell, Francis Shaw, Louisa Loring, and Marianne Silsbee, 18 Feb. 1845, *CC* 21/606; 29 May 1843, *CC* 17/497; 15 Jan. 1847, *SL* 235; 8 Mar. 1849, *SL* 243; 5 Feb. 1847, *CC* 24/693.

89   LMC to Ellis Loring, [1852?], *CC* 29/836.

90   LMC to Francis Shaw, 22 Jan. 1854, *CC* 30/858.

91   LMC to Ellis and Louisa Loring and Francis Shaw, 2 Sept. 1850, 8 Aug. 1852, 26 Dec. 1852, *CC* 28/789 and 29/827, 835.

92   LMC to Francis Shaw, 26 Dec. 1852, *CC* 29/835.

93   LMC to Ellis Loring, 5 Mar. 1854, *CC* 30/862.

94   LMC to Ellis and Louisa Loring, 1 and 12 Sept. 1853, *CC* 30/849, 851. Dolores remained in New York until Aug. 1856, when she returned to Spain after her uncle had arranged a legal separation for her from her "brutal husband." See LMC to Anna Loring and Marianne Silsbee, 7 and 21 Aug. 1856, *CC* 33/934, 936. Child's subsequent letters indicate that Dolores suffered from culture shock on her return to Spain: "The men seem to her so narrow and bigotted, the women such fools and slaves"; Dolores also chafed against not being allowed to earn her own living or to go out "without a servant to attend upon her" (LMC to Marianne Silsbee, 9 Dec. 1856, *CC* 34/965). By Sept. 1857 Dolores had returned to New York with an "affectionate attentive husband," by whom she had several children in quick succession (LMC to Marianne Silsbee, 6 Jan. 1860, *CC* 43/1176). Child's references to her in letters are too numerous to cite. The correspondence with Dolores herself seems to have been lost, however.

95   LMC to Marianne Silsbee, 1 Jan. 1854, *CC* 30/857a.

96   LMC to Francis Shaw, 22 Jan. 1854, *CC* 30/858.

97   LMC to Francis Shaw, 22 Jan. 1854, *CC* 30/858.

98   LMC to Ellis Loring, 5 Mar. 1854, *CC* 30/862.

99   Charles S. Francis to LMC, 3 and 19 Oct. 1854, *CC* 31/870, 871. See, for example, the reviews in the *New-York Evangelist* 6 Dec. 1855, p. 194; and in the *Christian Examiner* 4th ser. 73 (Jan. 1856): 150. Child's original title was "A Glance at Religious Ideas. . . ."

100 A letter Child misdated 1 Jan. 1855 instead of 1856 gives the mistaken impression that the book was already being reviewed in late 1854 (*SL* 271). All the reviews Child refers to in that letter date from late 1855, however. They are in weekly newspapers and refer to the book as having been just published.

101 Lydia Maria Child, *The Progress of Religious Ideas, Through Successive Ages* (New York: C. S. Francis, 1855) 1: viii–ix. Subsequent page references to this edition are given parenthetically in the text.

102 See, for example, *New-York Evangelist* 6 Dec. 1855, p. 194; *Christian Register* 15 Dec. 1855, p. 198; *Christian Inquirer* 5 Jan. 1856, p. 2.

103 See Frederic Ives Carpenter, *Emerson and Asia* (1930; New York: Haskell House, 1968); and Arthur Christy, *The Orient in American Transcendentalism: A Study of Emerson, Thoreau, and Alcott* (1932; New York: Octagon, 1963).

104 LMC to Lucy Osgood, [11?–19? Feb. 1856], *SL* 277–78.

105 LMC to Louisa Loring, 30 July [1849], *CC* 27/757.

106 To some extent Child's idealization of the Greeks also reflects larger cultural tendencies. See Martin Bernal, *Black Athena: The Afroasiatic Roots of Classical Civilization*, vol. 1: *The Fabrication of Ancient Greece, 1785–1985* (New Brunswick, N.J.: Rutgers UP, 1987), on the advance in tandem with Western imperialism of an ideology valorizing the ancient Greeks as standard bearers of a progressive "European" civilization destined to triumph over the decadent "Orient." Child disputed many of the racist claims made by the proponents of this ideology, notably their efforts to obscure the Greeks' debt to the Egyptians and to characterize the Egyptians as "Caucasians" rather than "Negroes," but she could not entirely escape its insidious influence.

107 Review of *The Progress of Religious Ideas*, *Knickerbocker* 46 (Dec. 1855): 629.

108 James Freeman Clarke, *Ten Great Religions: An Essay in Comparative Theology* (Boston: James R. Osgood, 1871) 3–4. Subsequent page references to this edition are given parenthetically in the text.

109 Review of *The Progress of Religious Ideas*, *New-York Evangelist* 6 Dec. 1855, p. 194.

110 Review of *The Progress of Religious Ideas*, *New-York Observer* 15 Nov. 1855, p. 366.

111 Review of *The Progress of Religious Ideas*, *The New Englander* 54 (May 1856): 319, 321.

112 Review of *The Progress of Religious Ideas*, *Christian Inquirer* 5 Jan. 1856, p. 2.

113 LMC to the Editors of *Life Illustrated*, 30 Dec. 1855, *CC* 32/895. Child was especially pleased with this journal's review, but I have not succeeded in tracking it down. The balance between negative and positive reviews shifted in 1856.

114 LMC to [Lucy and Mary Osgood?], 12 Jan. 1856, *CC* 32/898.

115 LMC to Convers Francis and Lucy Osgood, 21 Nov. 1855, *CC* 32/892, and [11?–19? Feb. 1856], *SL* 278.

116 LMC to Lucy Osgood, 9 July 1856, *CC* 33/928.

117 Lucy Osgood to LMC, 11 Feb. and 5 May 1856, *CC* 32/901, 914.

118 LMC to Peter Lesley, 1 Jan. 1856 [misdated 1855], *SL* 271.

119 LMC to Peter Lesley and Lucy Osgood, 1 Jan. and [11?–19? Feb. 1856], *SL* 272, 277.

120 Parker's "Discourse" is reprinted in Perry Miller, *The Transcendentalists: An Anthology* (Cambridge, Mass.: Harvard UP, 1950) 259–83. Like Child, Parker considered Christianity's theological doctrines "transient" and the example of Jesus "permanent." On Convers Francis's "defection" from Parker, see Joel Myerson, "Convers Francis and Emerson," *American Literature* 50 (Mar. 1978): 21–22.

121 Theodore Parker to LMC, 3 Nov. 1855, *CC* 31/888; Samuel May to LMC, undated [Jan.? 1856?], *CC* 32/900; LMC to Peter Lesley, 1 Jan. 1856, *SL* 271.

122 LMC to Lucy and Mary Osgood, 11 May 1856, *CC* 33/915.

123 Lucy Osgood to LMC, 6 July 1856, *CC* 33/924.

124 George T. Angell to LMC, 16 Dec. 1874, Cornell University Library Anti-Slavery Collection, LMC Papers, "Aspirations of the World" Mss. Fragment (Child wrote her manuscripts on the reverse side of old letters).

125 "Woman's Kingdom: Elizabeth Cady Stanton on the Work of Lydia Maria Child," *Inter-Ocean* (Chicago) 6 Nov. 1880, courtesy of Patricia G. Holland; Elizabeth Cady Stanton, *Eighty Years and More:*

Reminiscences 1815–1897 (1898; New York: Shocken, 1971) 467. See also the tributes of the Orientalist Samuel Johnson to LMC, [1–3] Feb. 1860, *CC* 44/1196, quoted in chap. 7; and of the ex-Unitarian minister A. W. Stevens to LMC, 27 Apr. and 19 June 1878, *CC* 90/2384, 2399.

16 Autumnal Leaves: *Reconsecrated Partnerships, Personal and Political*

1   LMC to Charles Sumner, 7 July 1856, *SL* 283.

2   The most complete account, including reprints of many newspaper articles and congressional documents, is Edward L. Pierce, *Memoir and Letters of Charles Sumner* (1893; Miami, Fla.: Mnemosyne, 1969) 3: 461–524. Quotations on 442, 446, and 470–71. See also *Liberator* 30 May 1856, p. 87; and David Donald, *Charles Sumner and the Coming of the Civil War* (New York: Ballantine-Fawcett Columbine, 1960) chap. 11.

3   LMC to Francis Shaw, 5 Sept. 1852, *SL* 265. Shaw must have passed on Child's praise to Sumner.

4   Charles Sumner to LMC, 14 Jan. 1853, *CC* 29/837. He was referring not only to his political position but to his physical position in the Senate, where he was seated between Butler of South Carolina and James M. Mason of Virginia, author of the Fugitive Slave Law. Ironically (as Child would point out [*SL* 285–86]), both of the proslavery senators with whom Sumner prided himself on having maintained cordial relations would heartily endorse Brooks's deed.

5   LMC to Charles Sumner, 7 July 1856, *SL* 286.

6   LMC to Anna Loring and Charles Sumner, 8 June and 7 July 1856, *CC* 33/918, *SL* 283. Quotations that follow are also from these letters.

7   LMC to Anna Loring, 8 June 1856, *CC* 33/918.

8   LMC to Anna Loring, 8 June 1856, *CC* 33/918.

9   LMC to Marianne Silsbee, 1 Jan. 1854, *CC* 30/857a.

10   LMC to Francis Shaw, 3 June 1854, *CC* 30/866.

11   LMC to Henrietta Sargent, Lucy Osgood and Anna Loring, 29 Jan. and 5 June 1855 and [11?–19? Feb. 1856], *CC* 31/878, 884, *SL* 277.

12   LMC to Lucy Osgood and Sarah Shaw, [11?–19? Feb.] and 27 Oct. 1856, *SL* 277 and *CC* 34/952.

13   LMC to Ellis Loring, [27 Nov. 1856], *CC* 34/961.

14   LMC to Henrietta Sargent and Anna Loring, 29 Jan. and 5 June 1855, *CC* 31/878, 884.

15   LMC to Sarah Shaw, 23 Mar. 1856, *CC* 32/911.

16   LMC to Marianne Silsbee, 27 Aug. 1855, *CC* 31/886.

17   LMC to Sarah Shaw, 3 Aug. 1856, *CC* 33/933.

18   David Lee Child, *The Taking of Naboth's Vineyard, or History of the Texas Conspiracy, and an Examination of the Reasons Given by the Hon. J. C. Calhoun, Hon. R. J. Walker, and Others, for the Dismemberment and Robbery of the Republic of Mexico* (New York: S. W. Benedict, 1845). See also David's 1844 campaign plea for Henry Clay, *An Appeal from David L. Childs,* [sic] *Editor of the Anti-Slavery Standard, to the Abolitionists.* (Albany, N.Y.: *Albany Evening Journal,* [1844]); it urged abolitionists to support Clay on the strength of his statement opposing annexation (Clay's statement was in fact extremely equivocal). On David's role in the anti-annexation struggle, see Samuel J. May, *Some Recollections of Our Antislavery Conflict* (Boston: Fields, Osgood, 1869) 316–21.

19   For a detailed account of the 1850 Compromise and how it was engineered, see James M. McPherson, *Battle Cry of Freedom: The Civil War Era* (1988; New York: Ballantine, 1989) 68–77.

20   LMC to Francis Shaw, 3 June 1854, *SL* 269. On public opinion of the Kansas-Nebraska Act as a betrayal of the 1820 and 1850 compromises, see Stanley W. Campbell, *The Slave Catchers: Enforcement of the Fugitive Slave Law, 1850–1860* (1968; New York: Norton, 1972) chap. 4.

21   LMC to Marianne Silsbee, 6 Feb. 1849, *CC* 26/746; also LMC to Ellis and Louisa Loring, 28 Jan. and 8 Mar. 1849, *CC* 26/744, *SL* 244–45.

22   LMC to Marianne Silsbee, 27 Mar. 1851, *SL* 257–58. For a summary of the Fugitive Slave Law's provisions, see Campbell, *Slave Catchers* 23–25.

23 LMC to Francis Shaw, 3 June 1854, *SL* 269–70; also LMC to Charles Sumner, 12 Feb. 1855, *CC* 31/879. The model Child probably had in mind was Boston blacks' dazzlingly successful rescue of the slave Shadrach, whom they had whisked out of the courtroom and sped on his way to Canada under the astonished noses of the officers in charge. Meltzer and Holland conjecture that Shadrach was the fugitive whom Nathaniel Silsbee had been involved in apprehending (*SL* 257n). Shadrach was rescued on 15 Feb. 1851, and Child's letter to Marianne Silsbee is dated 27 Mar. 1851. Accounts of the Shadrach case do not mention Silsbee, however. See Campbell, *Slave Catchers* 148–51.

24 For details of the rescue plan, see the reminiscences of Thomas Wentworth Higginson, *Cheerful Yesterdays* (1898; New York: Arno P, 1968) 147–60.

25 LMC to Marianne Silsbee and Francis Shaw, 27 Mar. 1851 and 3 June 1854, *SL* 257, 269.

26 LMC to Susan Lyman Lesley and Francis Shaw, 29 Mar. and 5 Sept. 1852, *SL* 264–65.

27 Child wrote *A New Flower for Children* in late 1855 and published it in time for Christmas. It was already being reviewed in Dec. 1855 (*New York Tribune*, 25 Dec., p. 7). "The Adventures of Jamie and Jeannie" is an expanded version of "The Bewildered Savage," originally published in the *Union Magazine of Literature and Art* 2 (Jan. 1848): 23–26. *The Liberty Bell* "for 1856" came off the press in Dec. 1855, in time to be sold at the Anti-Slavery Fair.

28 LMC to Marianne Silsbee and Henrietta Sargent, 1 Jan. 1854, *CC* 30/857a and 29 Jan. 1855, *CC* 31/878; see also LMC to DLC, 20 Dec. [1857], *CC* 38/1041: "I am having the same sort of time that I usually have at the Fair. A great deal of hurry and discomfort, with snatches of pleasant intercourse with old friends. . . . I am at [Mrs. Greene's] house. . . . She almost kills me with kindness, but the arrangements are so elegant, and the ways so different from *my* ways, that I don't like it so well as I do 'my nest and my mate.'"

29 LMC to Sarah Shaw, 20 Mar. 1857, *SL* 307.

30 LMC to Anna Loring, 7 Aug. 1856, *CC* 33/934.

31 LMC to Charles Sumner, 7 July 1856, *SL* 285. See also LMC to Sarah Shaw, 9 Nov. 1856 and 20 Mar. 1857, *SL* 299–300, 307–8.

32 LMC to Sarah Shaw, 20 Mar. 1857, *SL* 308.

33 The Liberty party had siphoned enough votes away from the Whigs in 1844 to throw the election to the expansionist Democrat James K. Polk. In 1848, disaffected Whigs and Democrats had joined with former Liberty party members in a broader antislavery coalition, the Free Soil party, whose platform called for containing rather than abolishing slavery. David, who had opposed the Liberty party for tactical reasons, had enthusiastically supported the new coalition and even tried to enlist his old idol Henry Clay as its presidential candidate (a colossal misjudgment of the politician who would sponsor the Compromise of 1850 and its Fugitive Slave Law). See DLC to Henry Clay, 26 July 1848, BPL Ms. A.4.2, p. 23. In this letter, David blames the defeat of the Whigs in 1844 on their failure to take an "unambiguous" stand against annexation. Had Clay won the election, he would have been "the best President that has administered the government since the great Washington," David asserts. Like its predecessor, the Free Soil party had failed at the polls, but it furthered the process of realignment, which culminated in the founding of the Republican party in 1854. For a more detailed account of these realignments, see McPherson, *Battle Cry of Freedom* 60–64, chap. 4 passim, and 153–62.

34 LMC to Sarah Shaw, 3 Aug. 1856, *SL* 291.

35 "The Kansas Emigrants" was serialized in the 23, 24, 25, 28 Oct. and 4 Nov. numbers of the daily *New York Tribune* and in the 25 Oct. and 1 Nov. numbers of the weekly *Tribune*. The first two pages of the daily are taken up with advertisements; Child's story fills from one and a half to three colums of p. 3, the equivalent of the front page, where it is the lead item. "The Crime Against Kansas" was the title of Sumner's speech. Child included the story in her last collection of fiction, *Autumnal Leaves: Tales and Sketches in Prose and Rhyme* (New York: C. S. Francis, 1857) 302–63.

36 For an excellent article on the struggle in Kansas, which led me to many of the primary sources cited below, see Michael Fellman, "Rehearsal for the Civil War: Antislavery and Proslavery at the Fighting Point in Kansas, 1854–1856," *Antislavery Reconsidered: New Perspectives on the Abolitionists*, ed. Lewis

Perry and Michael Fellman (Baton Rouge: Louisiana State UP, 1979) 287–307. Also extremely useful are Allan Nevins, *Ordeal of the Union*, vol. 2, *A House Dividing, 1852–1857* (1947; New York: Harper and Row, 1960); and McPherson, *Battle Cry of Freedom* chap. 5. Child uses the phrase "wiped out" in quotation marks in "The Kansas Emigrants" 358.

37   LMC to Sarah Shaw, 3 Aug. 1856, *SL* 290.

38   Besides articles in the *Tribune*, the *Liberator*, and the *National Anti-Slavery Standard*, Child's main sources for "The Kansas Emigrants" were William Phillips's *The Conquest of Kansas, by Missouri and Her Allies. A History of the Troubles in Kansas, from the Passage of the Organic Act Until the Close of July, 1856* (Boston: Phillips, Sampson, 1856); and the anonymous *Six Months in Kansas. By a Lady* (Boston: John P. Jewett, 1856). Phillips was the *Tribune's* special correspondent in Kansas. Child refers to some incidents mentioned in his book, but not in his *Tribune* dispatches. The anonymous lady's narrative of her sojourn in Kansas, extracts of which appeared in the *Liberator* 27 June 1856, pp. 101–2, under the title "Scenes in Kansas," provided Child with many of the details that make "The Kansas Emigrants" such a surprisingly vivid and realistic rendering of life in a western frontier town.

39   "The Kansas Emigrants," *Autumnal Leaves* 303. Subsequent citations are to this edition and are given parenthetically in the text.

40   Phillips, *Conquest of Kansas* 90–91. For a fuller discussion of the role Child accords this proslavery settler in the story, see Carolyn L. Karcher, "From Pacifism to Armed Struggle: Lydia Maria Child's 'The Kansas Emigrants' and Antislavery Ideology in the 1850's," *ESQ: A Journal of the American Renaissance* 34 (3rd quarter, 1988): 141–58.

41   "The Civil War in Kansas," *Liberator* 4 Jan. 1856, p. 2. Child's niece, Mary Preston, had married George Luther Stearns, one of the "Secret Six" who later helped finance John Brown's raid on the Federal arsenal at Harpers Ferry. The distant relationship between Charles and George Luther Stearns can be traced in Willard E. Stearns, *Memoranda of the Stearns Family, Including Records of Many of the Descendants* (Fitchburg, Mass.: Sentinel, 1901). For an extensive discussion of Charles Stearns and the debate among Garrisonians over whether or not to adhere to their peace principles, see Lewis Perry, *Radical Abolitionism: Anarchy and the Government of God in Antislavery Thought* (Ithaca, N.Y.: Cornell UP, 1973) chap. 8, "Accommodation to Violence."

42   "Remarks," appended to "The Civil War in Kansas," *Liberator* 4 Jan. 1856, p. 2.

43   WLG to James Miller McKim, 14 Oct. 1856, rpt. in the *Standard* 25 Oct. 1856 and included in *The Letters of William Lloyd Garrison*, vol. 4: *From Disunionism to the Brink of War, 1850–1860*, ed. Louis Ruchames (Cambridge, Mass: Belknap P of Harvard UP, 1975) 404–10, hereinafter abbreviated as *GL*.

44   LMC to Charles Sumner, 7 July 1856, *SL* 285; the quotations that follow are also from this letter; for another expression of the conflict Child was undergoing at the prospect of relinquishing her peace principles, see LMC to Lucy Osgood, 9 July 1856, *CC* 33/928.

45   For the incident Child used as her source, see "The Civil War in Kansas," *Liberator* 4 Jan. 1856, p. 2; *Six Months in Kansas* 134–37; and the extracts from the latter published in the *Liberator* under the title "Scenes in Kansas," 27 June 1856, pp. 101–2. For a fuller discussion of the parallels between this incident and Bruce's murder, see Karcher, "From Pacifism to Armed Struggle" 149. The words "stern adherence" are Garrison's, *GL* 4: 409.

46   The Frémont campaign slogan is quoted in McPherson, *Battle Cry of Freedom* 161. The best and most comprehensive analysis of Republican ideology is Eric Foner's *Free Soil, Free Labor, Free Men: The Ideology of the Republican Party before the Civil War* (New York: Oxford UP, 1970).

47   Phillips, *Conquest of Kansas* 12–19.

48   Stearns, "Letter from Kansas," *Liberator* 12 Jan. 1855, p. 10.

49   *Liberator* 26: 42, as quoted in Wendell Phillips Garrison and Francis Jackson Garrison, *William Lloyd Garrison, 1805–1879: The Story of His Life Told by His Children* (1885–1889; New York: Arno P, 1969), hereinafter abbreviated as *Life* 3: 438–39.

50   LMC "To the Women of Kansas," 28 Oct. 1856, *CC* 34/954; rpt. from the *Herald of Freedom* in the *Standard*, 3 Jan. 1857.

51   LMC to DLC, 27 Oct. 1856, *SL* 295.

52   See LMC to Marianne Silsbee, 27 Aug. 1855, *CC* 31/886: "The strong affections, which have made me expend all my resources so unreservedly for those I love . . . [have] been the source of my greatest virtues, and my worst mistakes."

53   Child apparently changed her heroine's name to Alice at a late stage of composition. She sometimes calls Alice "Ellen" or "Mary" in the manuscript draft of "The Kansas Emigrants," Child Papers, New York Public Library.

54   See DLC to LMC, 18 Oct. 1856, *CC* 34/948; and LMC to Lucy and Mary Osgood, 28 Oct. 1856, *CC* 34/953. For historical background, see Ralph Volney Harlow, "The Rise and Fall of the Kansas Aid Movement," *American Historical Review* 41 (Oct. 1935): 1–25. David's services were no doubt engaged by George Luther Stearns (husband of Child's niece Mary Preston), the head of the Massachusetts Kansas Aid Committee.

55   LMC to Charles Sumner and Sarah Shaw, 7 July and 3 Aug. 1856, *SL* 283, 289.

56   Phillips, *Conquest of Kansas* 209.

57   Phillips, *Conquest of Kansas* 208–9.

58   I am indebted to Roger Stein for pointing out the sexual connotations of this passage. On the sexual connotations of "luggage" or "baggage," see Eric Partridge, *Shakespeare's Bawdy: A Literary & Psychological Essay and a Comprehensive Glossary*, rev. ed. (New York: Dutton, 1969) 134.

59   LMC to Charles Sumner and Sarah Shaw, 7 July and 3 Aug. 1856, *SL* 285, 291. Child also wrote a number of openly political articles on the Kansas question, which she sent to newspapers "far and wide" (see LMC to Louisa Loring and Sarah Shaw, 26 and 27 Oct. 1857, *CC* 34/949, 952. These articles have not been located. By its own account, the *Weekly Tribune* boasted a circulation of 175,000 in 1856.

60   On Henry B. Stanton's role in launching the Liberty party, see Aileen S. Kraditor, *Means and Ends in American Abolitionism: Garrison and His Critics on Strategy and Tactics, 1834–1850* (New York: Vintage, 1969) chaps. 5–6. On the radical significance of the demand for woman suffrage, see Ellen Carol DuBois, *Feminism and Suffrage: The Emergence of an Independent Women's Movement in America, 1848–1869* (Ithaca, N.Y.: Cornell UP, 1978).

61   LMC to Sarah Shaw, 12 Jan. 1859, *CC* 40/1092. Child expresses this opinion repeatedly; see, for example, her editorials in the *Standard* warning against forming an abolitionist political party (cited in chapter 12 above).

62   LMC to Sarah Shaw, 3 Aug. 1856, *SL* 291.

63   In her punning reference to the table-rappings through which departed spirits supposedly manifested their presence to the living, Child was associating the women's rights movement with the woman-dominated spiritualist cult, coincidentally inaugurated in the same vicinity the very year of the Seneca Falls Convention. On the spiritualist cult and its connection with women's rights, see Howard Kerr, *Mediums, and Spirit-Rappers, and Roaring Radicals: Spiritualism in American Literature, 1850–1900* (Urbana: U of Illinois P, 1972); Cindy S. Aron, "Levitation and Liberation: Women Mediums in Nineteenth-Century America," M.A. thesis, University of Maryland, 1975; R. Laurence Moore, *In Search of White Crows: Spiritualism, Parapsychology, and American Culture* (New York: Oxford UP, 1977); and Ann Braude, *Radical Spirits: Spiritualism and Women's Rights in Nineteenth-Century America* (Boston: Beacon P, 1989).

64   LMC to Sarah Shaw, 3 Aug. 1856, *SL* 290–91.

65   LMC to Sarah Shaw, 14 Sept. and 9 Nov. 1856, *SL* 293 and *CC* 34/956.

66   LMC to Lucy and Mary Osgood, 20 July 1856, *SL* 289.

67   LMC to Sarah Shaw, 3 Aug. 1856, *SL* 291.

68   DLC to LMC, 18 Oct. 1856, *CC* 34/948.

69   LMC to DLC, 27 Oct. 1856, *SL* 294–96.

70   LMC to John Sullivan Dwight, 18 Oct. 1856, *CC* 34/947; LMC to DLC, 27 Oct. 1856, *SL* 295; DLC to LMC, 18 Oct. 1856, *CC* 34/948. A copy of the song has been preserved in the Child Papers, New York Public Library.

71   LMC to Ellis Loring, 3 July 1856, *SL* 282. On the sale of the Northampton farm, see LMC to Ellis Loring, 17 Feb. 1856, *CC* 32/905.

72   LMC to Ellis Loring, 24 Feb. 1856, *SL* 279.

73   LMC to Ellis Loring, 6 Feb. 1852, *SL* 263, and 5 Mar. 1854, *CC* 30/862. Rent from the Northampton farm also tided them over until its sale in Feb. 1856.

74   DLC to Lydia Bigelow Child, 29 May 1858, Ross Collection.

75   LMC to DLC, 27 Oct. 1856, *SL* 296. See also LMC to Parke Godwin, DLC, and Louisa Loring, 18, 19, and 23 Nov. 1856, *CC* 34/958–60.

76   LMC to Sarah Shaw and Parke Godwin, 9 and 18 Nov. 1856, *CC* 34/956, 958.

77   McPherson, *Battle Cry of Freedom* 162. A third candidate, Millard Fillmore, the vice president who had succeeded Whig president, Zachary Taylor, on Taylor's death in the second year of his term, also ran in 1856 on the ticket of the nativist "Know-Nothing" or "American" party, winning 44 percent of the southern vote and 13 percent of the northern.

78   LMC to Louisa Loring, 23 [and 24] Nov. 1856, *CC* 34/960.

79   LMC to DLC, 19 Nov. 1856, *CC* 34/959.

80   LMC to Louisa Loring, 23 [and 24] Nov. 1856, *CC* 34/960.

81   LMC to Ellis Loring and DLC, 16 and 19 Nov. 1856, *CC* 34/957, 959.

82   LMC to Louisa Loring, 23 [and 24] Nov. 1856, *CC* 34/960.

83   LMC to Sarah Shaw, 8 Dec. 1856, *SL* 300–301. See also LMC to Ellis Loring and Marianne Silsbee, [27 Nov.] and 9 Dec. 1856, *CC* 34/961, 965.

84   LMC to Lucy and Mary Osgood, 12 Mar. 1857, *CC* 36/997.

85   LMC to Susan Lyman Lesley and Lucy Osgood, 7 Aug. 1857, *CC* 36/1017, 37/1018.

86   LMC to Charles Follen, 3 Jan. 1857, *CC* 35/976.

87   LMC to Lucy Osgood, 7 Aug. 1857, *CC* 37/1018.

88   For histories of the spiritualist movement, see Frank W. Podmore, *Modern Spiritualism: A History and Criticism*, 2 vols. (London: Methuen, 1902); Moore, *In Search of White Crows*; and Braude, *Radical Spirits*. Garrison's letters frequently reiterate his belief in the authenticity of spirit manifestations and refer to many of the séances he attended. See, for example, WLG to LMC, 6 Feb. 1857, *GL* 4: 421–22, and WLG to Helen E. Garrison, 16 Feb. 1854, 17 Feb. 1857, and 18 May 1857, *GL* 4: 293, 431, 442. Higginson described his séance experiences in *The Rationale of Spiritualism* (New York, 1859), a pamphlet Child specifically requested him to send her. See LMC to Thomas Wentworth Higginson, 4 July 1859, *CC* 41/1113.

89   LMC to Charles Follen, 3 Jan. 1857, *CC* 35/976.

90   LMC to William Lloyd Garrison, 1 Feb. 1857, *CC* 35/986.

91   LMC to Marianne Silsbee and Sarah Shaw, 4 and 12 Jan. 1859, *CC* 40/1091–92. The spirits who allegedly manifested themselves at this séance were those of Jeannie Barrett and Ellis Loring.

92   Alfred Sereno Hudson, "The Home of Lydia Maria Child," *New England Magazine* n.s. 2 (June 1890): 407. James is said to have belonged to the pro-southern Copperhead faction during the Civil War.

93   LMC to Ellis Loring, 12 Feb. and 14 Dec. 1856, and 22 Jan. 1857, *CC* 32/902 and 35/967, 983. Child quotes the sum of $4,000 in LMC to Sarah Shaw, 3 May 1857, *CC* 36/1001. For records of the settlement, see Loring Papers, Schlesinger Library, A-160, Box 1, Folder 25 and Box 2, Folder 42.

94   LMC to Sarah Shaw, 3 May 1857, *CC* 36/1001.

95   LMC to Sarah Shaw, 20 Feb. and 3 May 1857, *CC* 36/992, 1001.

96   LMC to Sarah Preston Parsons and Thomas Wentworth Higginson, 29 Dec. 1850 and 4 July 1859, *CC* 28/798 and 41/1113.

97   LMC to Sarah Shaw and Lucy Osgood, 20 Feb. 1857, *CC* 36/992, and 7 Aug. 1857, *CC* 37/1018.

98   LMC to Sarah Shaw, 20 Feb. 1857, *CC* 36/992.

99   LMC to Marianne Silsbee and Sarah Shaw, 27 Aug. 1855 and 8 Dec. 1856, *CC* 31/886, *SL* 300–301.

100   LMC to Sarah Shaw, 9 Nov. 1856, *SL* 298, and [18 June to 22 July? 1859], *CC* 41/1114.

101   DLC to LMC, 27 June 1858, *CC* 39/1066.

102   LMC to DLC, 20 June 1858, *CC* 38/1063. The particular love letter referred to here does not seem to have survived.

103   DLC to LMC, 17 Mar. 1859, *CC* 40/1104. See also DLC to LMC, 17 Sept. 1857, *CC* 37/1024, where he urges Child (then on a visit to Marianne Silsbee in Salem) to "stay as long as you find it enter-tai[ni]ng" and assures her that "My bones are really better, tho far from being good ones."

104   LMC to Sarah Shaw, 20 Mar. 1857, *SL* 306–307.

105   LMC to Sarah Shaw, 20 Feb. 1857, *CC* 36/992. This is the only mention Child makes of Fuller after her drowning in 1850. It seems to reflect the image of Fuller projected in the bowdlerized *Memoirs of Margaret Fuller Ossoli*, ed. Ralph Waldo Emerson, William Henry Channing, and James Freeman Clarke (2 vols., 1852).

106   LMC to DLC, [15 July 1857], *CC* 36/1011a.

107   LMC to Anna Loring and Marianne Silsbee, 4 Jan. 1859, *CC* 40/1090–91; cf LMC to Ellis Loring and Sarah Shaw, [27 Nov.] and 8 Dec. 1856, *CC* 34/961, 964.

108   "The Rival Mechanicians" was first published in the *Columbian Lady's and Gentleman's Magazine* 7 (Jan. 1847): 13–18.

109   "The Catholic and the Quaker," "The Man That Killed His Neighbors," and "The Juryman" all have real merit. "The Juryman" is especially remarkable for its insights into the violent impulses that the partisans of capital punishment share with the criminals they would chastise.

110   I am indebted to H. Bruce Franklin's brilliant interpretations of these stories, and of the driven inventor figure in nineteenth-century science fiction. See his *Future Perfect: American Science Fiction of the Nineteenth Century*, rev. ed. (New York: Oxford UP, 1978) 15–18, 141–50.

111   See chap. 15 above for a brief discussion of "The Hindoo Anchorite," *Union Magazine of Literature and Art* 2 (Apr. 1848): 151–53. Its omission is doubly suggestive because all but one of the other stories Child published after *Fact and Fiction* found their way into *Autumnal Leaves*; the other exception, "The Bewildered Savage" (*Union Magazine of Literature and Art* 2 [Jan. 1848]: 23–26), reappears in *A New Flower for Children*, where Child incorporated it into "The Adventures of Jamie and Jeannie."

112   "Home and Politics" and "The Ancient Clairvoyant" (originally titled "The Prophet of Ionia") appeared in *Sartain's Union Magazine of Literature and Art* 3 (Aug. 1848): 63–68 and 4 (Feb. 1849): 94–97.

113   "The Prophet of Ionia," *Sartain's Union Magazine of Literature and Art* 4 (Feb. 1849): 94–97. Comparison between the magazine and book texts indicates that Child made only minor revisions in the other stories she collected in *Autumnal Leaves*.

114   LMC to Ellis Loring, 16 June 1843, *CC* 17/499. See also LMC to Louisa Loring, 21 Oct. 1849, *SL* 250.

115   See LMC to Louisa Loring, 15 Jan. 1847, *SL* 235.

116   See, for example, LMC to Susan Lyman, 7 Aug. 1848, *CC* 26/735, where Child says of Dolores's "tropical exuberance": "I am guilty of being rather partial to the excessive warmth of foreigners. . . . I *ought* to have been a foreigner, myself." Also LMC to Sarah Shaw, 9 Nov. 1856, *SL* 299: "my last letter . . . *seemed* cool to you because I have accustomed you to such tropical heat. . . ." Dolores may well have been the model for Praxinoe, since the story dates from the period of Child's most intense identification with her young Spanish friend as an unappreciated wife.

117   Asked about how she has spent her time since completing *The Progress of Religious Ideas*, Child mentions having written *A New Flower for Children* and "Jan and Zaida," both published late in 1855, and having been tied up with her father's "severe illness" in Jan.–Feb. 1856. By late May, her preoccupation with the beating of Sumner and the events in Kansas were turning her toward the composition of "The Kansas Emigrants." That would leave the intervening months as the most likely period of composition for the four other prose selections in *Autumnal Leaves*, which Child describes in a prefatory note as having been "recently written, during the hours that could be spared from daily duties." See LMC to Lucy Osgood and Sarah Shaw, [11?–19? Feb.] and 3 Aug. 1856, *SL* 276–77, *CC* 33/933.

118   Child uses this phrase in her discussion of "Woman's Rights," Letter 34 of *Letters from New York* (1843; Freeport, N.Y.: Books for Libraries P, 1970) 250.

119   Reviews of *Autumnal Leaves* appear in the "New Publications" column of the *Liberator*, the *Standard*, and the *Tribune* on 12 Dec. 1856, p. 198; 13 Dec. 1856, p. 3; and 17 Dec. 1856, p. 7, respectively; and in the *Knickerbocker* 49 (Feb. 1857): 199.

120   LMC to Convers Francis, 8 Aug. 1858, *CC* 39/1073, *SL* 317. The original of this letter has been lost, and two different printed versions have been preserved of it.

121   LMC to Francis Shaw, 5 Sept. 1852, *SL* 265. This letter refers to Stowe and to the young sculptor Harriet Hosmer.

122   LMC to Susan Lyman Lesley and Peter Lesley, 29 Mar. [1852], *SL* 264, and 2 May 1859, *CC* 40/1107.

123   LMC to Louisa Loring, [26? Oct.? 1856], *SL* 294.

124   LMC to Marianne Silsbee, Peter and Susan Lesley, and Sarah Shaw, 9, 12, and 20 Dec. 1856, *CC* 34/965, 35/966, 969; and LMC to Marianne Silsbee and Peter and Susan Lesley, 1 Feb. and 10 Mar. 1857, *CC* 35/987, *CC* 36/996.

125   LMC to Lucy and Mary Osgood, 12 June 1858, *SL* 315, and 30 Jan. 1859, *CC* 40/1099.

126   LMC to Francis Shaw, 5 Sept. 1852, *SL* 265.

127   LMC to Sarah Shaw and Marianne Silsbee, 25 Oct. 1857, *CC* 37/1026, 1027.

128   LMC to Harriet Hosmer, 21 Aug. 1858, *CC* 39/1074.

129   LMC to John Gorham Palfrey? and Louisa Loring, 28 Jan. and 8 Feb. 1857, *CC* 35/985, 990.

130   LMC to Charles Sumner, 17 June 1860, *SL* 354.

131   LMC to Sarah Shaw, 20 Mar. 1857, *SL* 307.

132   Lydia Maria Child, "The Stars and Stripes. A Melo-Drama," *Liberty Bell* 15 (1858): 122–85.

133   "Loo Loo. A Few Scenes from a True History," *Atlantic Monthly* 1 (May 1858): 801–12 and 2 (June 1858): 32–42. For a brief discussion of the story and its relationship to *A Romance of the Republic* (1867), see chap. 19 below.

134   LMC to Lucy and Mary Osgood, 12 June 1858, *SL* 314–15. See also LMC to Sarah Shaw and Louisa Loring, 29 May 1858 and 4 May 1859, *CC* 38/1058, 41/1109.

135   LMC to Thomas Wentworth Higginson, 4 July 1859, *CC* 41/1113.

136   LMC to Louisa Loring, 19 Sept. 1852, *CC* 29/829. See also Loring Papers, Schlesinger Library A-160, Box 1, for letters that Ellis, Louisa, and Anna wrote to each other.

137   LMC to Sarah Shaw, 11 Oct. 1858, *CC* 39/1083. After trying in vain to cheer Louisa, Child eventually stopped writing to her and corresponded with Anna instead.

138   LMC to Sarah Shaw and Henrietta Sargent, 3 May 1857, *CC* 36/1001, and 2 Aug. 1858, *CC* 39/1072. See also LMC to John Greenleaf Whittier, 2 Dec. 1856 and 20 June 1858, *CC* 34/962, 39/1065.

139   LMC to John Greenleaf Whittier, Henrietta Sargent, and Sarah Shaw, 20 June and 2 Aug. 1858, 16 Sept. 1860, *CC* 39/1065, 1072, and 46/1252.

17   The Example of John Brown

1   LMC to Maria Weston Chapman, 11 Jan. 1860, *CC* 43/1181.

2   LMC to Charles Sumner, 7 July 1856, *SL* 283.

3   LMC to Mary Ann Brown, 2 Dec. 1860, *CC* 47/1271.

4   LMC to Sarah Shaw, 17 June 1859, *CC* 41/1112. By 1859 Garrison had moved much closer to the position Child had held in 1856. He, too, now acknowledged that the Republican party had played an important role in preventing the extension of slavery and that it was helping to lead the country in the right direction. See Wendell Phillips Garrison and Francis Jackson Garrison, *William Lloyd Garrison, 1805–1879: The Story of His Life Told by His Children* (1885–1889; New York: Arno P, 1969) 3: 483–85, hereinafter referred to as *Life*; and Garrison's comments at the convention, as reported in "New England Anti-Slavery Convention," *Liberator* 3 June 1859, pp. 85–87. Most of the speakers noted the changed temper of public opinion and the great advances in the antislavery cause. Child served on the business committee.

5   Brown's words have been rendered differently by different sources. See Franklin B. Sanborn, ed., *The*

Life and Letters of John Brown, Liberator of Kansas, and Martyr of Virginia (Boston: Roberts Brothers, 1891) 131, 421; Garrison and Garrison, *Life* 3: 488; and Stephen B. Oates, *To Purge This Land with Blood: A Biography of John Brown*, 2nd ed. (Amherst: U of Massachusetts P, 1984) 271–72.

6   The other two members of the "Secret Six" who backed Brown were Samuel Gridley Howe, also personally known to Child, and Franklin B. Sanborn. By May 1859 Parker was dying of tuberculosis in Rome, but he had helped fund Brown until his departure and "wished to see [Brown's plan] tried, believing that it must do good even if it failed" (Sanborn, *Life and Letters of John Brown* 440). In addition to Sanborn, see Thomas Wentworth Higginson, *Cheerful Yesterdays* (1898; New York: Arno P, 1968) 216–34; and Frank Preston Stearns, *The Life and Public Services of George Luther Stearns* (1907; New York: Arno P, 1969) chaps. 10, 12, 13.

7   LMC to John Brown, 16 Nov. 1859, *SL* 328.

8   LMC to Charles Sumner, 7 July 1856, *SL* 285.

9   See Frederick Douglass, *Life and Times of Frederick Douglass* (1892; New York: Collier, 1962) 314–15, 319; and Sanborn, *Life and Letters of John Brown* 425, 434–36, 438–40, 450, 466, 541–42. Quotation from Sanborn 542. A letter to Sanborn of 24 Feb. 1858 suggests that Brown may even then have been conceiving of a suicide mission like "the last victory of Samson" (Sanborn 444).

10 Sanborn, *Life and Letters of John Brown* 552, 554; Osborne P[erry] Anderson, *A Voice from Harper's Ferry* (1861; New York: World View, 1980) 68.

11 Brown's letter of 7 Mar. 1858 to Theodore Parker indicates that he was already planning to use hostage-taking as a means of educating slaveholders, first by making them "virtually slaves themselves," and then by trying to appeal to their consciences through "abolition lectures" and "kindness and plain dealing, instead of barbarous and cruel treatment, such as they might give. . . ." (quoted in Sanborn, *Life and Letters of John Brown* 449). Some historians have suggested that Brown may have been waiting for slaves to join him; see Oates, *To Purge This Land with Blood* 294, and James M. McPherson, *Battle Cry of Freedom: The Civil War Era* (1988; New York: Ballantine, 1989) 206. The first to "infer" this was James Redpath in *The Public Life of Capt. John Brown*, by James Redpath, *with an Auto-Biography of His Childhood and Youth* (1860; Sandusky, Ohio: Kinney Brothers, 1872) 251. Anderson's *Voice from Harper's Ferry* indicates that "many colored men" did in fact join the raiders and that several anonymous slaves were killed in the battle (71–73, 96–98). See also Redpath 254, 267–68.

12 Sanborn, *Life and Letters of John Brown* 562.

13 This is the conclusion I have drawn from comparing the reminiscences of Brown's acquaintances and the surviving participants in the raid, and from reading the letters Brown addressed to them (cited throughout this chapter). My interpretation differs from most other historians'.

14 Sanborn, *Life and Letters of John Brown* 559, 568; Anderson, *Voice from Harper's Ferry* 79; Oates, *To Purge This Land with Blood* 300.

15 For biographical sketches of Francis Jackson Merriam and the other raiders, based partly on interviews with the survivors, see Richard J. Hinton, *John Brown and His Men: With Some Account of the Roads They Traveled to Reach Harper's Ferry* (1894; New York: Arno P, 1968). Child refers to Merriam's role in the raid in letters to Francis Jackson and Anna Loring, 4 Nov. and 13 Dec. 1859, *CC* 41/1130, 42/1146.

16 Sanborn, *Life and Letters of John Brown* 565–68, 584. Originally published in the *New York Herald*, this interview was reprinted in newspapers across the country, including the *Liberator*, and in most early biographies of Brown. Oates flatly asserts that Brown lied about his purposes (*To Purge This Land with Blood* 278–81, 306, 326–27, 345). I have decided to take Brown's denial seriously, since it accords with the testimony of Douglass, Higginson, and others to the effect that Brown may have envisaged a series of guerrilla raids, rather than a massive slave insurrection on the model of Nat Turner's or the Santo Domingo revolutionaries'. After drafting the original version of this chapter, I came across Herbert Aptheker's *Abolitionism: A Revolutionary Movement* (Boston: Twayne, 1989), which similarly gives credence to Brown's denial and holds that he was still planning to "set up . . . maroon bases, throughout the Alleghenies and thus shake the slaveholding edifice to its foundations" (132–33).

17 LMC to William Lloyd Garrison, 28 Oct. 1859, *SL* 326.

18   Whittier refused because his pacifist convictions did not allow him to "lend *any* countenance" to violence; see John Greenleaf Whittier to LMC, 21 Oct. 1859, *CC* 41/1122. Child's letter to Whittier has not been preserved, but its contents can be inferred from his reply and from her 28 Oct. 1859 letter to Garrison. The quotation is from Emerson's "Concord Hymn."

19   LMC to John Brown, 26 Oct. 1859, *SL* 324–25.

20   LMC to Lucretia Mott, 26 Feb. 1861, *SL* 377.

21   LMC to Mary Ann Brown, 2 Dec. 1860, *CC* 47/1271.

22   "Letters of L. Maria Child to Gov. Wise and Capt. Brown," *Liberator* 11 Nov. 1859, p. 179, ed. headnote; LMC to Henry Wise, [1859, after 29 Oct.], *CC* 41/1128.

23   LMC to Governor Henry Alexander Wise, 26 Oct. 1859, *SL* 325–26.

24   Henry Wise to LMC, 29 Oct. 1859, *CC* 41/1127. I am quoting the manuscript letter, which differs slightly from the printed version.

25   John Brown to LMC and LMC to the Editor of the *New York [Daily] Tribune*, 4 and 10 Nov. 1859, *CC* 42/1132–33. Child's letters to Brown and Wise, with Wise's reply, appear in the *New York Weekly Tribune* of 12 Nov. 1859, p. 7, under the title "MRS. CHILD, GOV. WISE, AND JOHN BROWN." Her own letter to the *Tribune*, with Brown's reply, appears in the *New York Weekly Tribune* of 19 Nov. 1859, p. 6. The entire body of correspondence was published in the tract *Correspondence between Lydia Maria Child and Gov. Wise and Mrs. Mason, of Virginia* (Boston: American Anti-Slavery Society, 1860). Page references to the letters in this tract are given parenthetically in the text.

26   Child is no doubt referring to Mary Stearns, who had come to love the old man intensely over the course of his many visits with her family. See the reminiscence by Mary Stearns, rpt. in Sanborn 509–11. Child's reference to her niece seems surprisingly indiscreet, considering that George Luther Stearns and several of Brown's other supporters had fled to Canada after the discovery of letters implicating them in the Harpers Ferry attack.

27   John Brown to LMC, 4 Nov. 1859, *CC* 42/1132; the page numbers cited are to *Correspondence between LMC and Gov. Wise*.

28   LMC to Edward Fitch Bullard, Aaron Stevens and Oliver Johnson, 19 and 20 Dec. 1859, *CC* 42/1151–53 and *SL* 335.

29   "LYDIA MARIA CHILD'S REPLY TO GOV. WISE," *New York Weekly Tribune* 26 Nov. 1859, p. 4.

30   LMC to Parke Godwin, 27 Nov. 1859, *SL* 330.

31   LMC to Horace Greeley, 18 Dec. 1859, *SL* 333.

32   Review of *Correspondence between Lydia Maria Child and Gov. Wise and Mrs. Mason, of Virginia*, *Liberator* 27 Jan. 1860, p. 14.

33   LMC to Parke Godwin, Maria Weston Chapman, and Daniel Ricketson, 27 Nov. 1859, *SL* 330; 28 Nov. and 22 Dec. 1859, *CC* 42/1141, 43/1156.

34   "Mrs. Child's Humanity," rpt. in *Liberator* 30 Mar. 1860, p. 49.

35   Rpt. from *Worcester Bay State*, *Liberator* 27 Jan. 1860, p. 13. "Fragrant" is misprinted as "fragment."

36   LMC to Peter and Susan Lesley and Parke Godwin, 20 and 27 Nov. 1859, *SL* 329–30. Child preserved only a small fraction of the letters she received, which averaged fifteen to twenty a week for several weeks. She refers to answering as many as twenty-three letters in a single week. See LMC to Sarah Shaw, 22 Dec. 1859, *CC* 43/1157.

37   William H. Armstrong to LMC, 25 Dec. 1859, *CC* 43/1166.

38   Samuel Johnson to LMC, [1–3] Feb. 1860, *CC* 44/1196.

39   Eliza Lee Cabot Follen to LMC, [7 Dec. 1859], *CC* 42/1144.

40   Watkins [Harper]'s letter is quoted in LMC to Mary Ann Brown, 23 Dec. 1859, *SL* 337–38. Child told Mrs. Brown that she had received letters "from colored people in various parts of the country."

41   Samuel Jackson to LMC, "Letter from a Colored Man in Ohio to L. Maria Child," *Liberator* 23 Dec. 1859, *CC* 43/1158.

42   Review of *Correspondence between Lydia Maria Child and Gov. Wise and Mrs. Mason, of Virginia*, *Liberator* 27 Jan. 1860, p. 14; *SL* 333.

43 LMC to Maria Weston Chapman, 7 and 11 Jan. 1860, *CC* 43/1177, 1181.

44 LMC to Sarah Shaw, 28 Dec. 1859, *CC* 43/1169. This letter comments directly on the letter to Mrs. Mason.

45 A number of historians have commented on the many violations of due process committed during the hasty trial—among others the anomaly of trying Brown for treason against a state of which he was neither a citizen nor a resident. See, for example, Richard Morris, *Fair Trial* (1953), quoted in Louis Ruchames, *A John Brown Reader: The Story of John Brown in His Own Words, in the Words of Those Who Knew Him, and in the Poetry and Prose of the Literary Heritage* (New York: Abelard-Schuman, 1959) 29.

46 LMC to Peter and Susan Lesley, 20 Nov. 1859, *SL* 329.

47 Quoted in Hinton, *John Brown and His Men* 362–63. Like Brown's interview with Wise, Mason, and Vallandigham, this statement to the court was widely reprinted in the newspapers. Garrison read it to the audience at the Tremont Temple commemoration on 2 Dec.. See "Great Meeting in Boston on the Day of the Execution of Captain John Brown," *Liberator* 9 Dec. 1859, p. 194.

48 LMC to [Maria Weston Chapman?], 28 Nov. 1859, *CC* 42/1141.

49 LMC to Peter and Susan Lesley, 20 Nov. 1859, *SL* 329.

50 On Child's role in organizing the meeting, see LMC to [Maria Weston Chapman?], 28 Nov. 1859, *CC* 42/1141. "Speech of Wm. Lloyd Garrison, At the Meeting in Tremont Temple, Dec. 2d, relating to the Execution of John Brown," *Liberator* 16 Dec. 1859, p. 198; partial rpt. in Truman Nelson, ed., *Documents of Upheaval: Selections from William Lloyd Garrison's* THE LIBERATOR, *1831–1865* (New York: Hill and Wang, 1966) 263–67.

51 LMC to Sarah Shaw, 22 Dec. 1859, *CC* 43/1157. See also LMC to Sarah Preston Parsons, 25 Dec. 1859, *CC* 43/1165.

52 "Great Meeting in Boston on the Day of the Execution of Captain John Brown. Speech of Rev. J. S. Martin," *Liberator* 9 Dec. 1859, p. 194, rpt. in Benjamin Quarles, ed. *Blacks on John Brown* (Urbana: U of Illinois P, 1972) 25–31. The quotation is on p. 28. Anderson implies a similar critique in his comments on the confusion Brown seemed to be showing on the morning of the attack (*Voice from Harper's Ferry* 73, 75).

53 LMC to Sarah Preston Parsons, 25 Dec. 1859, *CC* 43/1165. Sarah Parsons and Mary Stearns were the daughters of Child's sister Mary Francis Preston.

54 Comments appended to "Letter from a Colored Man in Ohio, to L. Maria Child," *Liberator* 23 Dec. 1859, *CC* 43/1158.

55 LMC to [Maria Weston Chapman?], 22 Dec. 1859, *CC* 42/1155.

56 LMC to Mary Ann Brown, 2 Dec. 1860, *CC* 47/1271; also 23 Dec. 1859, *SL* 337–38.

57 LMC to Edward Fitch Bullard and Sarah Shaw, 19 and 22 Dec. 1859, *CC* 42/1151, 43/1157.

58 LMC to Edward Fitch Bullard, 19 Dec. 1859, *CC* 42/1151.

59 LMC to Sarah Shaw, 22 Dec. 1859, *CC* 43/1157.

60 LMC to Aaron D. Stevens, 19 Dec. 1859 and 11 Jan. 1860, *CC* 42/1152, 43/1183.

61 Aaron D. Stevens to LMC, 15 Jan. 1860, *CC* 44/1190.

62 LMC to Rebecca Spring, 19 Mar. 1860, *CC* 45/1210.

63 Eliza Lee Cabot Follen to LMC, [7 Dec. 1859], *CC* 42/1144.

64 LMC to Richard Webb, 30 Apr. 1861, *CC* 48/1303. Apparently the Irish abolitionist Webb had added his voice to the chorus.

65 LMC to Mary Ann Brown, 2 Dec. 1860, *CC* 47/1271.

66 See Eugene D. Genovese, *The Political Economy of Slavery: Studies in the Economy and Society of the Slave South* (1965; New York: Vintage, 1967), esp. chaps. 4 and 10.

67 For a splendid historical analysis of the terms "wage slavery" and "white slavery," see David R. Roediger, *The Wages of Whiteness: Race and the Making of the American Working Class* (London: Verso, 1991) chap. 4. I will be citing the second ed. of L. Maria Child, *The Right Way the Safe Way, Proved by Emancipation in the British West Indies, and Elsewhere* (New York: 5 Beekman Street, 1862). Page numbers are given parenthetically in the text. Quotation from LMC to Samual May, Jr., 26 Feb. 1860, *SL* 342.

68 LMC to Samuel May, Jr., 26 Feb. 1860, *SL* 342.

69 LMC to John Curtis Underwood, 26 Oct. 1860, *SL* 362.

70 Of all the Caribbean islands, Jamaica turned out to be the one most relevant to the American South. Like their Jamaican counterparts, American slaveholders revealed a "violent and unyielding" spirit and a "stubborn determination to make [abolition] operate badly" (55). But learning a lesson from the Jamaican experience, they made it virtually impossible for their ex-slaves to purchase land and thereby rise into the "middling class" (81). American freedpeople had to accept the very conditions of peonage against which their Jamaican analogues had rebelled: "If the tenant expressed dissatisfaction, or gave offence in any way, or if his capricious landlord merely wanted to make him feel that he was still in his power, he was ejected at once, and obliged to take for his crops whatever the despotic employer saw fit to value them at" (70). A recent historian has also pointed out that the islands on which sugar production remained the most profitable were those on which the ratio of population to land was too high to make landownership an option for significant numbers of former slaves. On the other islands, landowners ended up replacing slave labor with indentured immigrant labor. See William A. Green, *British Slave Emancipation: The Sugar Colonies and the Great Experiment, 1830–1865* (Oxford: Clarendon P, 1976), esp. the chaps. "Free Labour and Plantation Economy," "Immigration," and "Free Society: Progress and Pitfalls."

71 James M. McPherson, "Was West Indian Emancipation a Success? The Abolitionist Argument during the American Civil War," *Caribbean Studies* 4 (July 1964): 28–34; quotation on 29. Of the other tracts McPherson lists, two are extremely rare, and the others are scattered through newspapers and periodicals. None comes anywhere near the length of Child's: 96 pages, with a 12-page appendix added in the second edition of 1862.

72 LMC to Wendell Phillips, [Oct.? 1860], *SL* 364. In letters to Robert Folger Walcutt of the Anti-Slavery office, Child mentions having received two hundred names from Underwood by 15 Nov. and two hundred more by 5 Dec. (*CC* 47/1267, 1272). The Hovey Fund underwrote Child's mailing expenses.

73 LMC to Sidney Edgerton, 6 July 1860, *CC* 45/1232. I am grateful to Donald Dingledine for this conjectural reading.

74 Underwood's letters have not survived, but Child quotes portions in her letters to Robert F. Wallcut, 15 Nov. and 5 Dec. 1860, *CC* 47/1267, 1272.

75 For an analysis of the many factors that led to emancipation in Maryland, see Barbara Jeanne Fields, *Slavery and Freedom on the Middle Ground: Maryland during the Nineteenth Century* (New Haven, Conn.: Yale UP, 1985) chap. 5. Fields makes no mention of Child's tract, but as in West Virginia it was presumably cited in debates by some of the pro-emancipation legislators who received copies of it.

76 LMC to Robert F. Wallcut, 20 Apr. 1862, *CC* 52/1405. The same letter mentions that Child has been trying in vain to obtain names and addresses of Missouri and Kentucky legislators.

77 L. Maria Child, *The Patriarchal Institution, As Described by Members of Its Own Family*. Compiled by L. Maria Child (New York: American Anti-Slavery Society, 1860). Page references to this edition are given parenthetically in the text.

78 LMC to Wendell Phillips, 22 July 1860, *SL* 356.

79 See Child's *The Evils of Slavery, and the Cure of Slavery* . . . (1836) and Theodore Dwight Weld, *American Slavery As It Is: Testimony of a Thousand Witnesses* (1839). Child draws heavily on Weld's tract for quotations from southern newspapers, though she also supplements it with many new quotations from newspapers of the 1840s and 1850s. Child was not the first to exploit such quotations. On the capital that Republican newspapers made of them, see McPherson, *Battle Cry of Freedom* 196–98.

80 LMC to Charles Sumner and Wendell Phillips, 17 June and 22 July 1860, *SL* 355–56.

81 For David Child's correspondence relating to these pamphlets, see DLC to Henry Wilson, 13 Mar. 1860, BPL Ms.A.4.2.pp. 45–46; and a series of letters addressed to George Luther Stearns, who was underwriting publication of the tracts, Stearns Collection, MHS. The first pamphlet was supposed to be ready in time for the May nominating convention in Chicago, but David appears to have attempted

a pamphlet too ambitious to meet the deadline; the last letters to Stearns find David apologizing for having taken until the end of September to finish the job.

82 LMC to Henry Wilson, 10 Mar. 1861, *CC* 47/1293. Child compliments Wilson on showing himself to be an exception to that generalization. See also LMC to Lucy Osgood, 8 Jan. 1862, *CC* 50/1365. The last quotation is from LMC to Wendell Phillips, 10 Oct. 1860, *CC* 96/2547.

83 LMC to Wendell Phillips, 10 Oct. 1860, *CC* 96/2547.

84 L. Maria Child, *The Duty of Disobedience to the Fugitive Slave Act: An Appeal to the Legislators of Massachusetts* (Boston: American Anti-Slavery Society, 1860). Page references to this tract are given parenthetically in the text. The quotation is from LMC to Sarah Shaw, 28 Dec. 1859, *CC* 43/1169.

85 Harriet A. Jacobs, *Incidents in the Life of a Slave Girl*, ed. Lydia Maria Child (1861), rpt. ed. Jean Fagan Yellin (Cambridge, Mass.: Harvard UP, 1987) 1–2. Further page references to this work are given parenthetically in the text.

86 Harriet Beecher Stowe, *Uncle Tom's Cabin or Life Among the Lowly* (1852; New York: New American Library, 1966) 102.

87 Notice of *The Duty of Disobedience to the Fugitive Slave Act*, *Liberator* 16 Nov. 1860, p. 182, listed under "New Tracts."

88 LMC to Wendell Phillips, 22 July 1860, *SL* 355.

89 LMC to Robert F. Wallcut, 13 Oct. 1860, *CC* 46/1259.

90 LMC to Samuel Sewall, 20 Sept. 1860, *CC* 46/1253.

91 LMC to Lucy Searle, 4 Feb. 1861, *CC* 47/1282.

92 LMC to Lucy Osgood, 8 Aug. 1860, *CC* 46/1241.

93 Harriet Jacobs to Amy Post, 8 Oct. [1860], *Incidents* 246–47.

94 LMC to John Greenleaf Whittier, 4 Apr. 1861, *SL* 378.

95 LMC to Harriet Jacobs and Lucy Searle, 13 Aug. 1860, *SL* 357, and 4 Feb. 1861, *CC* 47/1282. From Child's comment to Jacobs — "the remarks are also good, and to the purpose" — it is clear that passages of antislavery moralizing were already in the text, contrary to what many readers have assumed.

96 LMC to Daniel Ricketson and Lucy Searle, 14 Mar. and 4 Feb. 1861, *CC* 47/1295, 1282.

97 LMC to Lucy Searle, 4 Feb. 1861, *CC* 47/1282.

98 See chaps. 12 and 13 for examples of the way Child edited both her own writing and that of others. For a more extensive discussion of Child's revision of *Letters from New York* for commercial publication, see Carolyn L. Karcher, "Censorship, American Style: The Case of Lydia Maria Child," *Studies in the American Renaissance* 1986: 283–303. For another illuminating example of Child's editorial practice, see her letter to her friend Caroline Sturgis (10 July 1847, Sophia Smith Collection, Smith College, courtesy of Patricia G. Holland, Amherst) explaining the modifications she was making in the manuscript of Sturgis's *Rainbows for Children*: "If you find a sentence of mine inserted now and then, you must not attribute it to the vanity of authorship. . . . The truth is, half a page *must* be left blank at the end of every story, or they cannot insert the tail-piece. The printer's types are inexorable. . . . Therefore, I add a sentence, when it is necessary to stretch over on a new page." Child also patronizes Sturgis, who was seventeen years her junior and a novice in the literary profession: "Please attend to this matter *soon*, that's a good girl; otherwise, you will not merely make me wait, but the printer and engraver likewise."

99 LMC to Harriet Jacobs, 13 Aug. 1860, *SL* 357. Unfortunately, just before Jacobs's scheduled meeting with Child to go over the manuscript, her employer, Cornelia Willis, went into premature childbirth on 31 Oct. Already committed by then to a November publication date, Child delivered the manuscript to Thayer and Eldridge without waiting until Jacobs could find time for a later meeting. This, too, was consistent with her usual practice. For example, when James T. Fields agreed to publish her own *The Freedmen's Book*, after Child had sought in vain for a publisher, Child dropped everything else to rush the book through the press in time for the Christmas market. See LMC to Sarah Shaw and Eliza Scudder, 3 Sept. and 15 Oct. 1865, *CC* 63/1680, 1688. In the latter Child writes: "I engaged to do something for Ticknor & Fields, and, being death on engagements, I *must* keep my word, or per-

ish. . . ." For other opinions of Child's editing, see Karen Sánchez-Eppler, *Touching Liberty: Abolition, Feminism and the Politics of the Body* (Berkeley: U of California P, 1993) chap. 3; Bruce Mills, "Lydia Maria Child and the Endings to Harriet Jacobs's *Incidents in the Life of a Slave Girl*," *American Literature* 64 (June 1992): 255–72; Yellin, *Incidents* xxii; Alice Deck, "Whose Book Is This?: Authorial Versus Editorial Control of Harriet Brent Jacobs' *Incidents in the Life of a Slave Girl: Written by Herself*," *Women's Studies International Forum* 10 (no. 1, 1987): 33–40; and F. Elaine De Lancey, "Harriet Jacobs's Narrative, Lydia Maria Child's Bump of Mental Order on It, and Critical Response to This Collaboration," unpublished paper, Temple University.

100   LMC to Wendell Phillips, 2 and 9 Dec. 1860, *CC* 96/2549–50.

101   LMC to Daniel Ricketson and John Greenleaf Whittier, 14 Mar. and 4 Apr. 1861, *CC* 47/1295, *SL* 378.

102   See LMC to Robert F. Wallcut, William Lloyd Garrison, and Stephen Salisbury, 15 Dec. 1861, 10 Apr. 1863, and 14 Dec. 1864, *CC* 50/1358, 55/1475, and 60/1605a; and Harriet Jacobs to LMC, 18 Mar. 1863 and 26 Mar. 1864, *CC* 55/1474 and 58/1552, *Liberator* 10 Apr. 1863, *Standard* 16 Apr. 1864.

103   LMC to Lucy Osgood, [Nov.? 1866]?, *CC* 66/1748.

104   LMC to Lucy Osgood, 1 Apr. 1866, *CC* 64/1715; Harriet Jacobs to Ednah Dow Cheney, 25 Apr. [1867], *Incidents* 250.

105   LMC to John Fraser, 20 Nov. 1866, *CC* 66/1746. John Fraser was the husband of David's niece Ruth Child, daughter of his brother Levi (*SL* 447).

106   The extant correspondence indicates that Child and Jacobs regularly exchanged letters, at least during the Civil War. For example, Child quotes a letter she had received from Jacobs about Robert Gould Shaw in LMC to [Francis Shaw], 18 Oct. 1863, *CC* 56/1508, and Jacobs thanks Child for a letter and refers to earlier correspondence in Harriet Jacobs to LMC, 18 Mar. [1863] and 26 Mar. 1864, *CC* 55/1474 and 58/1552, *Liberator* 10 Apr. 1863, *Standard* 16 Apr. 1864. See also Jacobs's letter to Child about the Emancipation Proclamation, which Child quotes in *Looking toward Sunset. From Sources Old and New, Original and Selected* (Boston: Ticknor and Fields, 1865) 361 and in *The Freedmen's Book* (Boston: Ticknor and Fields, 1865) 218. Jacobs's only surviving letters to Child are the ones cited above, from which private portions, if any, were deleted before publication. Of Child's letters to Jacobs, only the ones relating to the editing of *Incidents* have been preserved.

107   LMC to Samuel Sewall and Sarah Shaw, 27 Sept. and [after 20 Nov.] 1860, *CC* 46/1256, 47/1270. Child had received a long and detailed letter of 9 Sept. 1860 from Francis Jackson, answering her request for information about the rendition of Sims (*CC* 46/1249). Jackson knew Sims's sister and included an extract of Sims's letter to his sister in his reply to Child.

108   "A Letter from Mrs. L. Maria Child," *Independent* 26 Oct. 1865, *CC* 63/1689.

109   Brown added: "I had, as I now think vainly, flattered myself that without very much bloodshed it might be done." As quoted in Sanborn, *Life and Letters of John Brown* 620. See Oates, *To Purge This Land with Blood* 351 for an accurate reproduction of Brown's idiosyncratic punctuation and italics.

110   For an analysis of the election, see McPherson, *Battle Cry of Freedom* chap. 7.

111   LMC to Henrietta Sargent, 27 May 1860, *SL* 352.

112   LMC to Rebecca Spring and Lucy Osgood, 19 Mar. and 10 Apr. 1860, *CC* 45/1210, 1213.

113   "Senator Seward on the Crisis," *Liberator* 18 Jan. 1861, p. 10; McPherson, *Battle Cry* 256.

114   For an excellent account of "The Counterrevolution of 1861," see McPherson, *Battle Cry* chap. 8. The phrase "triggered a chain reaction" appears on p. 235.

115   "Hon.(!) Lucius Slade on the Crisis. An Infamous Letter," *Liberator* 8 Feb. 1861, p. 21. Slade was "a prominent member of the Massachusetts Legislature," and his letter to a confrere in Georgia had been published in the *Literary and Temperance Crusader* (Georgia), of 3 Jan. and widely reprinted.

116   "Mayor Wightman and the Abolitionists," *Boston Pilot*, rpt. in *Liberator* 8 Feb. 1861, p. 21.

117   "To the Citizens of Massachusetts," *Liberator* 28 Dec. 1860, p. 205.

118   LMC to Lemuel Shaw, 3 Jan. 1861, *SL* 367–68. Among the signers whom the Childs had once known as literary or political patrons were Benjamin Curtis, George Ticknor, Jared Sparks, Levi Lincoln, and Emory Washburn. Also on the list is Edward Dickinson of Amherst, father of Emily Dickinson.

119 LMC to Lemuel Shaw, 3 Jan. 1861, *SL* 367–68.

120 "Hon. (!) Lucius Slade on the Crisis," rpt. in *Liberator* 8 Feb. 1861, p. 21. See also "Freedom of Speech Violated in Boston. A John Brown Meeting Broken Up," *New York Weekly Tribune* 8 Dec. 1860, p. 1: "A determination to prevent this proposed public expression of anti-Southern feeling in Boston had been very noisily avowed by the merchants and bankers of this city. . . ."

121 "Freedom of Speech Violated . . .," p. 1, cited in n. 120 above. Except where otherwise noted, quotations in this paragraph are drawn from the above article.

122 E. Heywood to Samuel May, Jr., 19 Dec. 1860, BPL Ms.B.1.6.Vol. 13, p. 81; LMC to Henrietta Sargent and Charles Sumner, 9 Feb. and 28 Jan. 1861, *SL* 375, 373.

123 "Another Bell-Everett Mob," *Liberator* 21 Dec. 1860, p. 203; E. Heywood to Samuel May, Jr., 19 Dec. 1860, BPL Ms.B.1.6.Vol. 13, p. 81.

124 LMC to Sarah Shaw, 25 Jan. 1861, *SL* 370–72. The description that follows is taken from this letter, except where otherwise noted. Maria and David Child are listed among the seventeen members of the business committee in "Annual Meeting of the Massachusetts Anti-Slavery Society," *Liberator* 1 Feb. 1861, p. 17.

125 Quoted in Hinton, *John Brown and His Men* 345; see also Sanborn, *Life and Letters of John Brown* 500.

126 "Annual Meeting of the Massachusetts Anti-Slavery Society. Speech of Wendell Philips," *Liberator* 1 Feb. 1861, p. 18.

127 LMC to Charles Sumner, 28 Jan. 1861, *CC* 47/1281. McPherson presents a more charitable interpretation of Adams's "maneuver": "to divide the upper and lower South and cement the former to the Union by the appearance of concession on the territorial question" (*Battle Cry* 256).

128 LMC to Sarah Shaw, 25 Jan. 1861, *SL* 371.

129 "Boston Under Mob Law—Mayor Wightman Enforcing It," *Liberator* 1 Feb. 1861, p. 19. See also pp. 18–19 for an account of "Proceedings of the Evening," based on extracts from the Boston *Journal*.

130 LMC to Sarah Shaw, 28 Jan. 1861, *SL* 371.

131 LMC to Henrietta Sargent, Charles Sumner, and Maria Weston Chapman, 9 Feb. 1861, *SL* 374–76, and 11 Jan. 1860, *CC* 43/1181.

132 LMC to Charles Sumner, 9 Feb. 1861, *SL* 375–76.

133 LMC to Henrietta Sargent, 9 Feb. 1861, *SL* 374.

134 McPherson, *Battle Cry* 256.

135 LMC to Lucretia Mott, 26 Feb. 1861, *SL* 377.

136 LMC to Francis Shaw, 8 Jan. 1861, *SL* 369.

137 LMC to Henrietta Sargent, 9 Feb. 1861, *SL* 374.

138 LMC to Maria Weston Chapman, 11 Jan. 1860, *CC* 43/1181; John Brown's valedictory as quoted in Sanborn, *Life and Letters of John Brown* 620.

18 Child's Civil War

1 "Letter from Mrs. L. M. Child, 23 July 1865, *Independent* 3 Aug. 1865, *CC* 63/1672.

2 LMC to Parke Godwin, [Maria Weston Chapman?], and Sarah Shaw, 27 and 28 Nov. and 22 Dec. 1859, *SL* 330, *CC* 42/1141, 43/1157.

3 LMC to Lucy Osgood, 7 May 1861, *SL* 381. Child is quoting an editorial in the *Boston Advertiser*.

4 LMC to Lydia Bigelow Child, 11 Feb. 1864, *CC* 57/1535.

5 LMC to Sarah Shaw, 12 Jan. 1859, *CC* 40/1092.

6 LMC to Eliza Scudder, 8 July 1869, *CC* 71/1901: "Wayland has always been a prison to me."

7 LMC to Lucy Searle and Henrietta Sargent, 9 June and 26 July 1861, *SL* 384, *CC* 49/1321.

8 See "Letter from L. Maria Child to Gen. Gantt," 7 Feb. 1864, *Standard* 22 Apr. 1865, p. 4, *CC* 57/1531.

9 Child refers to these articles in her correspondence. See, for example, LMC to Mary Stearns, 22 Dec. 1862, *CC* 54/1444: "I write emancipation articles, and find them readily accepted by the Wheeling,

Virginia, Intelligencer, and the St. Louis *Democrat*." Also LMC to Sarah Shaw, [after 18 Jan. 1862], *CC* 50/1368. I have succeeded in tracking down two of Child's anonymous and pseudonymous articles in the *New York Weekly Tribune*: one signed "Straight Line," discussed in this chapter below, and "Can Emancipated Slaves Take Care of Themselves?" 25 Jan. 1862, p. 2, an account of a McDonough's slaves. A systematic search through contemporary newspapers would surely uncover many more.

10   On the political activism and lecturing of Stanton, Dickinson, and others, see Wendy Hamand Venet, *Neither Ballots nor Bullets: Women Abolitionists and the Civil War* (Charlottesville: UP of Virginia, 1991), esp. chaps. 3, 5, and 6.

11   LMC to James Freeman Clarke, 16 Feb. 1863, *CC* 55/1471.

12   LMC to Peter and Susan Lesley, 8 Feb. 1861, *CC* 47/1284.

13   LMC to Lucy Osgood, 8 Aug. 1860, *CC* 46/1241.

14   LMC to: Anna Loring, 26 Aug. 1858, *CC* 39/1076; Lucy Osgood, 8 Aug. 1860, *CC* 46/1241; Sarah Shaw, 16 Sept. 1860, *CC* 46/1252; Convers Francis, 28 July 1862, *CC* 53/1421; and Samuel Sewall, 21 June 1863, *CC* 55/1484. Lucy Osgood to LMC, 4 Sept. 1860, *CC* 46/1248.

15   LMC to Peter and Susan Lesley and to Lucy Searle, 8 Feb. and 4 Feb. 1861, *CC* 47/1284, 1282.

16   LMC to Lucy Osgood, 8 Aug. 1860, *CC* 46/1241.

17   LMC to Lucy Osgood, 14 July 1861, *CC* 48/1317.

18   LMC to Lydia Bigelow Child, 3 Oct. 1862, *CC* 53/1432.

19   For an excellent summary of the crisis over Fort Sumter and the choices Lincoln and Confederate President Jefferson Davis faced, see James M. McPherson, *Battle Cry of Freedom: The Civil War Era* (1988; New York: Ballantine, 1989) 264–75; see also Kenneth M. Stampp, "Lincoln and the Secession Crisis," in his *The Imperiled Union: Essays on the Background of the Civil War* (New York: Oxford UP, 1980) 163–88.

20   "The Result," *New York Weekly Tribune*, 20 Apr. 1861, p. 2.

21   LMC to Lucy Osgood, 26 Apr. 1861, *SL* 380.

22   LMC to Lucy Osgood, 26 Apr. and 7 May 1861, *SL* 380–81.

23   LMC to Lucy Osgood, 7 May 1861, *SL* 381–82.

24   LMC to Lucy Osgood, 26 Apr. 1861, *SL* 380. I have not succeeded in finding any mention of the Fort Pickens incident in the *Liberator*, the *Standard*, or the *New York Weekly Tribune*. However, Ira Berlin has generously located for me a letter of 18 Mar. 1861 from Lt. A. J. Slemmer to Lt. Col. Lorenzo Thomas announcing that eight fugitive slaves had come to the fort on 12 Mar. "entertaining the idea that we were placed here to protect them and grant them their freedom" and that he had done what he could "to teach them the contrary" by delivering them to the Pensacola "city marshal to be returned to their owners." See *The War of the Rebellion: A Compilation of the Official Records of the Union and Confederate Armies*, 128 vols. (Washington, D.C.: U.S. Government Printing Office, 1880–1901), ser. 2, vol. 1, p. 750.

25   LMC to Lucy Searle and Henrietta Sargent, 28 and 26 July 1861, *CC* 49/1322, 1321.

26   James M. McPherson, *The Struggle for Equality: Abolitionists and the Negro in the Civil War and Reconstruction* (Princeton, N.J.: Princeton UP, 1964) 69–70, 72; [Edward L. Pierce], "The Contrabands at Fortress Monroe," *Atlantic Monthly* 8 (Nov. 1861): 626–40; "General Butler on the Contraband Question," *New York Weekly Tribune* 10 Aug. 1861, p. 2.

27   McPherson, *Battle Cry* 222, 506.

28   Meltzer and Holland, *SL* 393; McPherson, *Struggle for Equality* 75–79. The campaign was initiated by Samuel Gridley Howe and included two other members of John Brown's "Secret Six," George Luther Stearns and Frank Sanborn. Also participating were Garrison, Wendell Phillips, Edmund Quincy, the Childs, the reformist Unitarian minister William Henry Channing, and Republican Frank Bird.

29   LMC to John Greenleaf Whittier, 10 Sept. 1861, *SL* 394. I am inferring Child's influence on the group's strategy from two facts: (1) the resemblance of this strategy to the one Child had recommended for distributing *The Right Way the Safe Way*; (2) her independent initiative of sending an anonymous letter to the *Tribune* several weeks before the group's first meeting.

30   LMC to John Greenleaf Whittier, 10 Sept. 1861, *SL* 394.

31   David Lee Child, *Rights and Duties of the United States Relative to Slavery under the Laws of War. No Military Power to Return Any Slave. "Contraband of War" Inapplicable between the United States and Their Insurgent Enemies* (Boston: R. F. Wallcut, 1861) 6. The pamphlet is an expanded version of the articles David published in the *Liberator* under the title "Gen. Butler's Contraband of War," 26 July, 16 and 23 Aug., and 6 Sept. 1861. David considered Butler's "contraband of war" doctrine legally "unfounded" as well as "narrow and impracticable . . . because it applies to property only, and does not recognize men and women as persons" (28). His aim was to supply a sounder legal basis for emancipation and, in the long run, for amending the Constitution. His pamphlet was one of three studies produced by abolitionists to prove that a presidential emancipation decree would be constitutional under the war power. It was ultimately superseded by William Whiting's more thorough and influential *The War Powers of the President, and the Legislative Powers of Congress in Relation to Rebellion, Treason, and Slavery* (1862). See McPherson, *Struggle for Equality* 67–69.

32   LMC to Sarah Shaw, 24 Nov. 1861, *CC* 50/1350, and 11 Aug. 1861, *SL* 390–91.

33   LMC to Sarah Shaw, 11 Aug. 1861, *SL* 391.

34   "Straight Line," "What is to be done with the Contrabands?" *New York Weekly Tribune* 17 Aug. 1861, p. 5. This letter to the *Tribune* can be identified as Child's because it is almost identical with her letter to Sarah Shaw of 11 Aug. (*SL* 390–91), in which she says that she has just sent the *Tribune* a brief statement "to that effect."

35   LMC to Oliver Johnson, 3 June 1861, *CC* 48/1310.

36   LMC to Samuel and Harriet Sewall, 16 June 1861, *CC* 48/1314. See also LMC to Sarah Shaw, 14 June 1861, *SL* 386.

37   LMC to Samuel and Harriet Sewall, 16 June 1861, *CC* 48/1314. On Scott's opposition to a "war of conquest" against the South and on the criticism his strategy generated in the *Tribune* and other northern newspapers, see McPherson, *Battle Cry* 333–35.

38   LMC to Oliver Johnson and Samuel and Harriet Sewall, 3 and 16 June 1861, *CC* 48/1310, 1314.

39   LMC to Henrietta Sargent, 26 July 1861, *CC* 49/1321.

40   For these alternative explanations, see "The Battle of Bull's Run," *New York Weekly Tribune* 27 July 1861, p. 8; and McPherson, *Battle Cry* 344. For a full account of the battle and an analysis of its impact on northern and southern public opinion, see *Battle Cry* 334–50.

41   "Brutalities of the Rebels," *New York Weekly Tribune*, 3 Aug. 1861, p. 3.

42   LMC to Lucy Searle and Henrietta Sargent, 28 and 26 July 1861, *CC* 49/1322, 1321.

43   Meltzer and Holland, *SL* 385, n. 1; LMC to Sarah Shaw, 11 Aug. 1861, *CC* 49/1324; Russell Duncan, ed., *Blue-Eyed Child of Fortune: The Civil War Letters of Colonel Robert Gould Shaw* (Athens: U of Georgia P, 1992).

44   LMC to Lucy Searle, 28 July 1861, *CC* 49/1322.

45   LMC to Henrietta Sargent, 26 July 1861, *CC* 49/1321. For a fine historical summary of intellectuals' reactions to the war in 1861, see George M. Fredrickson, *The Inner Civil War: Northern Intellectuals and the Crisis of the Union* (1965; New York: Harper and Row, 1968) chap. 5.

46   "Straight Line," "What is to be done with the Contrabands?," *New York Weekly Tribune* 17 Aug. 1861, p. 5.

47   LMC to Lucy Searle, 28 July 1861, *CC* 49/1322.

48   LMC to Sarah Shaw and to Theodore Tilton, 21 July 1861, *SL* 388–89.

49   LMC to Sarah Shaw and Henrietta Sargent, 11 and 24 Aug. 1861, *SL* 391–92, *CC* 49/1328. In the latter, Child writes of telling the anecdote at a gathering of abolitionists.

50   LMC to George William Curtis, 1 Sept. 1861, *CC* 49/1329.

51   "General Frémont's Proclamation," *New York Weekly Tribune* 7 Sept. 1861, pp. 4, 5, 7. Child would first have seen the news announced in a daily paper, however, since she mentions it in letters dated 1 Sept.

52   Caption to "Gen. Frémont's Proclamation," *Liberator* 6 Sept. 1861, p. 143.

53   LMC to Lucy Osgood, 1 Sept. 1861, *CC* 49/1330.

54   For an analysis of Frémont's and Lincoln's motives, see McPherson, *Battle Cry* 352–54.

55   LMC to John Greenleaf Whittier, 22 Sept. 1861, *CC* 49/1337.

56   LMC to William Cullen Bryant, 19 Sept. 1861, *CC* 49/1336.

57   "A Letter from Mrs. Child. To 'Our Jessie,' " *New York Evening Post* 1 Oct. 1861, rpt. in the *Liberator* 11 Oct. and the *Standard* 19 Oct., *CC* 49/1335.

58   "*Fre*mont might be thanked for his energy and bravery, without saying anything against the President," Child wrote to Whittier, 22 Sept. 1861, *CC* 49/1337.

59   LMC to Sarah Shaw, 24 Nov. 1861, *CC* 50/1350.

60   LMC to John Greenleaf Whittier and Sarah Shaw, 22 Sept. and 24 Nov. 1861, *CC* 49/1337, 50/1350.

61   LMC to John Greenleaf Whittier, 22 Sept. 1861, *CC* 49/1337.

62   For an excellent analysis of the economic and political factors governing British policy toward the two sides in the Civil War, see McPherson, *Battle Cry* 382–91.

63   Quoted in "England and America. A Letter from Mrs. L. Maria Child," *Standard* 18 Jan. 1862, p. 2, *CC* 50/1363.

64   Quoted in LMC to Sarah Shaw, 24 Nov. 1861, *CC* 50/1350, and in William Lloyd Garrison to George Thompson, *Liberator* [21 Feb. 1862], rpt. in *The Letters of William Lloyd Garrison*, vol. 5; *Let the Oppressed Go Free, 1861–67*, ed. Walter M. Merrill (Cambridge, Mass.: Belknap P of Harvard UP, 1979) 66, hereinafter abbreviated as *GL*. This was the first of a series of letters to Thompson in which Garrison defended the Lincoln government against criticism by British abolitionists.

65   McPherson, *Battle Cry* 390; LMC to Lucy Searle and Lucy Osgood, 3 and 8 Jan. 1862, *CC* 50/1362, 1365. Child was responding to "Letters from Harriet Martineau. LIX," *Standard* 28 Dec. 1861, p. 2. Martineau begins by acknowledging "the great fact that the free states were in antagonism with the slave States, and that slavery must go down when the people of the North had gained strength and wisdom by suffering." The bulk of her letter is devoted to presenting the British point of view on the *Trent* incident. Her tone is indeed chauvinistic: she finds it "inconceivable" that the seizure of the *Trent* was not authorized beforehand by the Lincoln administration; she calls it an act of "piratical audacity"; she asserts that "there is no hope of peace but in immediate retraction and apology from Washington"; and she says that "[t]he temper and manners of the Northern people towards England" have destroyed "the *confidence* of your European well-wishers" at least for the present generation. Martineau's biographer defends her against her American abolitionist critics and asserts that during the *Trent* affair "she sought to placate ruffled British pride rather than to further inflame it." See Valerie Kossew Pichanick, *Harriet Martineau: The Woman and Her Work, 1802–76* (Ann Arbor: U of Michigan P, 1980) 216.

66   "England and America. A Letter from Mrs. L. Maria Child," *Standard* 18 Jan. 1862, p. 2, *CC* 50/1363.

67   W. L. Garrison to George Thompson, [21 Feb. 1862], *GL* 5:64.

68   See Betty Fladeland, *Men and Brothers: Anglo-American Antislavery Cooperation* (Urbana: U of Illinois P, 1972) chap. 16.

69   LMC to Fanny Garrison, 5 Nov. 1861, *SL* 397–98.

70   See Paulo Freire, *Pedagogy of the Oppressed* (New York: Herder, 1970).

71   LMC to Lucy Searle, 19 Nov. 1861, *CC* 50/1349.

72   LMC to Col. James Montgomery, 26 Dec. 1861, *CC* 50/1360.

73   LMC to Mary Stearns, Robert F. Wallcut, and Col. James Montgomery, 15 and 26 Dec. 1861, *CC* 50/1357, 1358, 1360.

74   LMC to Sarah Shaw, 15 Dec. 1861 and [after 18 Jan.? 1862], *CC* 50/1356, 1368.

75   LMC to John Greenleaf Whittier, 21 Jan. 1862, *CC* 51/1370. Tubman was then in Boston, where she had been summoned by Governor Andrew, who wished to send her to South Carolina as a spy and scout for Union troops—a commission she accepted and discharged without ever receiving pay or pension from the U.S. government. See Sarah Bradford, *Harriet Tubman, The Moses of Her People* (1886; Secaucus, N.Y.: Citadel P, 1974) 94–95.

76   LMC to Lucy Osgood, 24 Feb. 1862, *CC* 51/1390.

77   See Willie Lee Rose, *Rehearsal for Reconstruction: The Port Royal Experiment* (Indianapolis, Ind.: Bobbs-

Merrill, 1964). For contemporary accounts, see [Edward Pierce], "The Freedmen at Port Royal," *Atlantic Monthly* 12 (Sept. 1863): 291–315; Charlotte L. Forten [Grimké], *The Journals of Charlotte Forten Grimké*, ed. Brenda Stevenson (New York: Oxford UP, 1988) 382–511; and [Charlotte L. Forten (Grimké)], "Life on the Sea Islands," *Atlantic Monthly* 13 (May–June 1864): 587–96, 666–76.

78   LMC to John Greenleaf Whittier, 17 June 1864, *CC* 59/1569; Charlotte L. Forten, "New-Year's Day on the Islands of South Carolina, 1863," in L. Maria Child, *The Freedmen's Book* (1865; New York: Arno P, 1968) 251–56. Child refers to Forten and the "intelligent productions of her pen" in LMC to William P. Cutler, 10 July 1862, *SL* 414.

79   LMC to Sarah Shaw, [Mar.?] 1862, *CC* 51/1398, and 18 May 1862, *SL* 411, *CC* 52/1410 (the earlier letter is a transcript in another hand dated only "Wayland 1862"; the second half is identical with the letter of 18 May, but the first half seems to date from the second week of March, since it refers to Lincoln's speech of 6 Mar.). Also LMC to Lucy Osgood, 29 Jan. 1865, *CC* 61/1630.

80   LMC to Lucy Osgood, [10–17 Aug. 1861], *CC* 49/1326.

81   In joining the educational commission, Child pointedly took "the liberty to suggest that no person even suspected of a pro-slavery bias ought to be employed." LMC to William Endicott, 2 Mar. 1862, Atkinson MSS, Massachusetts Historical Society, quoted in Rose, *Rehearsal for Reconstruction* 39.

82   LMC to Sarah Shaw, [Mar.?] 1862, *CC* 51/1398.

83   LMC to Gerrit Smith, 7 Jan. 1862, *CC* 50/1364. Child attributes the desire to play the role of Divine Providence to Madame Roland; see *Letters from New York* (1843; Freeport, N.Y.: Books for Libraries P, 1970), Letter 12, p. 87.

84   See Frederick Law Olmsted, *A Journey in the Seaboard Slave States, with Remarks on Their Economy* (1856; New York: Negro Universities P, 1968); *A Journey through Texas; or, a Saddle-Trip on the South-western Frontier* (New York: Dix, Edwards, 1857); and *A Journey in the Back Country, 1853–54* (1860; New York: Schocken, 1970); see also *The Cotton Kingdom: A Traveller's Observations on Cotton and Slavery in the American Slave States*, a one-volume abridgment of these three studies (1861; New York: Modern Library, 1984). Olmsted's *Seaboard Slave States* was one of the few books Child allowed herself to purchase "[i]n the low state of [her] finances," and she was "much pleased with its candid good-natured tone toward the masters, and its obvious sympathy with the slave"; see LMC to Lucy and Mary Osgood, 11 May 1856, *SL* 280–81.

85   LMC to Francis Shaw, 28 Jan. 1862, *SL* 401–2.

86   LMC to Anna Loring, 7 Dec. 1862, *CC* 53/1440. Child's friend, the wealthy abolitionist Francis Jackson, had died in Nov. 1861, leaving her a legacy of $100, which she devoted in its entirety to the "contrabands." See *SL* 401.

87   LMC to Sarah Shaw, [after 18 Jan.? 1862], *CC* 50/1368.

88   McPherson, *Battle Cry* 498. Lincoln's message was dated 6 Mar. The full text was reprinted in the *New York Weekly Tribune*, 15 Mar. 1862, p. 6, under the headlines: "Message from the President. Highly Important Proposition. The Gradual Abolition of Slavery. A Vigorous Blow at the Hopes of the Rebels." See also the editorial "The Message of Freedom," p. 4. For an accessible modern text (slightly different in wording) see Roy P. Basler, ed., *The Collected Works of Abraham Lincoln* (hereinafter abbreviated as *CWL*), 8 vols. (New Brunswick, N.J.: Rutgers UP, 1953) 5: 144–46.

89   *CWL* 5: 145–46.

90   LMC to Horace Greeley, 9 Mar. 1862, *SL* 407; also LMC to Sarah Shaw, [Mar.?] 1862, *CC* 51/1398. The *Weekly Tribune* editorial of 15 Mar. 1862, p. 4, "The Message of Freedom," may have been a response to Child's letter, since it offers an interpretation of Lincoln's message quite similar to hers. Although the weekly *Liberator* reprinted it on 14 Mar. ("Message from the President. Proposal to Aid the States in the abolishment of Slavery," p. 43), Garrison was among the editors who evidently did not grasp the "*full* import" of Lincoln's message. Instead of recognizing that it indicated Lincoln was already seriously considering emancipation as a war measure, Garrison roundly excoriated Lincoln for "perversely" recommending gradual rather than immediate emancipation ("The President's Message," p. 42). Child was not alone in her hopeful interpretation of the 6 Mar. message, however. See

also the editorial in the *Anglo-African*, rpt. in James M. McPherson, *The Negro's Civil War: How American Negroes Felt and Acted during the War for the Union*, 2nd ed. (Urbana: U of Illinois P, 1982) 45–46.

91   LMC to Horace Greeley, 9 Mar. 1862, *SL* 406–7.

92   LMC to Sarah Shaw, [Mar.?] 1862, *CC* 51/1398.

93   McPherson, *Struggle for Equality* 97; *Battle Cry* 498.

94   LMC to Anna Loring, 20 Apr. 1862, *CC* 52/1402.

95   McPherson, *Battle Cry* 499; Ira Berlin, Joseph P. Reidy, and Leslie S. Rowland, *Freedom: A Documentary History of Emancipation, 1861–1867*: Series 2, *The Black Military Experience* (New York: Cambridge UP, 1982) 38.

96   LMC to Charles Sumner, 22 June 1862, *SL* 412.

97   "Faithful Champions of Freedom in Congress," *Standard* 5 July 1862, *CC* 52/1416.

98   LMC to William P. Cutler, 10 July 1862, *SL* 413, *CC* 52/1417. Child also wrote to Congressman George Washington Julian of Indiana, who had made a key speech on "Confiscation and Liberation," and, of course, to Sumner. See her letters of 16 and 22 June 1862, *CC* 52/1414, 1415, and *SL* 411–12.

99   "Address on Colonization to a Deputation of Negroes," *CWL* 5: 370–75; "The President on African Colonization," *Liberator* 22 Aug. 1862, p. 134; Lincoln's address is reprinted in full under the *Liberator*'s Refuge of Oppression column, p. 133. See also the excellent chapter on "The Colonization Issue" in McPherson, *The Negro's Civil War* 77–97. Historians disagree as to whether Lincoln himself believed in Colonization or was merely using the proposal to deflect criticism of emancipation. For the former view, see David M. Potter, *Division and the Stresses of Reunion, 1845–1876* (Glenview, Ill.: Scott, Foresman, 1973) 159–61; George M. Fredrickson, *The Black Image in the White Mind: The Debate on Afro-American Character and Destiny, 1817–1914* (New York: Harper and Row, 1971) 149–51; Benjamin Quarles, *Lincoln and the Negro* (New York: Oxford UP, 1962) 108–16; and the testimony of Lincoln's navy secretary, Gideon Welles, *Civil War and Reconstruction: Selected Essays by Gideon Welles*, ed. Albert Mordell (New York: Twayne, 1959) 234, 250–51. For the latter, see McPherson, *Battle Cry* 509; LaWanda Cox, *Lincoln and Black Freedom: A Study in Presidential Leadership* (Columbia: U of South Carolina P, 1981) 22–24; and Don E. Fehrenbacher, "Only His Stepchildren" (1974), rpt. *Lincoln in Text and Context: Collected Essays* (Stanford, Calif.: Stanford UP, 1987) 110–11.

100   McPherson, *Battle Cry* 509, quotes a Republican politician who admitted that Colonization "is a damn humbug. But it will take with the people."

101   "A Letter from L. Maria Child. Emancipation and Amalgamation," *New York Daily Tribune* 3 Sept. 1862, p. 9; rpt. in the *Standard* 13 Sept. 1862, p. 1, *CC* 53/1423. In a letter of 15 Sept. to Oliver Johnson, editor of the *Standard*, Child complained that she had sent the article to the *Tribune* "[a]bout four weeks ago" and that she had neither seen the article in the *Tribune* nor heard from editor Horace Greeley that he could not use it (*CC* 53/1428). Child subscribed to the much more widely circulated *Weekly Tribune* and probably expected Greeley to publish her article there, rather than in the *Daily*, where she evidently did not catch it, if indeed she regularly read the *Daily*.

102   LMC to William P. Cutler, 10 July 1862, *SL* 414.

103   "A Letter from L. Maria Child. Emancipation and Amalgamation," *New York Daily Tribune* 3 Sept. 1862, p. 9, rpt. in the *Standard* 13 Sept. 1862, p. 1, *CC* 53/1423.

104   "Mrs. L. Maria Child to the President of the United States," *National Republican* 22 Aug. 1862, p. 1; rpt. in the *Liberator* 29 Aug. 1862, p. 139, and in the *Standard* 6 Sept. 1862, p. 4, *CC* 53/1426. The *National Republican* featured Child's letter in the most prominent position on the front page, and Garrison printed it in the column adjacent to Lincoln's famous statement of 22 Aug. that his "paramount object is to save the Union, and is not either to save or destroy slavery" (a statement Lincoln made in reply to a pro-emancipation letter of 19 Aug. by Horace Greeley, "The Prayer of Twenty Millions," *New York Daily Tribune*, 20 Aug. 1862, p. 4).

105   See the useful distinction made by George M. Fredrickson, *The Black Image in the White Mind: The Debate on Afro-American Character and Destiny, 1817–1914* (New York: Harper and Row, 1971) chaps. 3–4.

106   "Mrs. L. Maria Child to the President of the United States," *CC* 53/1426.

107 The following paragraph is based on McPherson, *Battle Cry* 504–5, which led me to the reminiscences of Secretary of the Navy Gideon Welles, "The History of Emancipation," originally published in *Galaxy* 14 (Dec. 1872), rpt. *Civil War and Reconstruction* 228–55; see esp. 235–40. See also Cox, *Lincoln and Black Freedom* 14–15; and *CWL* 5: 337n.

108 LMC to Sarah Shaw, 9 June 1862, *CC* 52/1413. Child quotes Sarah's letter in *CC* 52/1412 to Lucy Searle, written the same day. For Robert Shaw's accounts of the incident, see Robert G. Shaw to Francis and Sarah Shaw, 27 May and 13 June 1862, Duncan, ed., *Blue-Eyed Child of Fortune* 203–6, 209–11. For press accounts quoted in this paragraph, see "From Gen. Banks's Department" and "Gen. Banks's Retreat," *New York Weekly Tribune* 31 May 1862, p. 5, and 7 June, p. 3.

109 For accounts of these battles, see McPherson, *Battle Cry* chaps. 15, 17. Quotation on 511.

110 LMC to Sarah Shaw, 18 May 1862, *CC* 52/1410. I was unable to find any account of this incident in the *New York Weekly Tribune*, the *New York Daily Tribune*, the *Liberator*, or the *Standard*.

111 LMC to Lucy Searle, 10 Aug. 1862, *CC* 53/1422.

112 McPherson, *Battle Cry* 544.

113 "The Pursuit of the Enemy — Illness of Gen. McClellan — the Rest on Thursday — the Casualties on Both Sides — The Gallant Conduct of Our Army," *New York Weekly Tribune* 27 Sept. 1862, p. 3.

114 Quoted in McPherson, *Battle Cry* 545.

115 LMC to Charles Sumner, 3 Oct. 1862, *SL* 416–17.

116 LMC to Sarah Shaw, 30 Oct. 1862, *SL* 418. Both the *Tribune* and the antislavery press were full of anti-McClellan articles during this period. See also McPherson, *Battle Cry* 504–6, 524–25, 559–60. McPherson's rendition of the admission Child quotes is even more damning: "Lee's army had not been 'bagged' at Sharpsburg because 'that is not the game. The object is that neither army shall get much advantage of the other; that both shall be kept in the field till they are exhausted, when we will make a compromise and save slavery' " (559).

117 McPherson, *Battle Cry* 557. For the complete text of the 22 Sept. Emancipation Proclamation, see *CWL* 5: 433–36.

118 LMC to Eliza Scudder, 30 Sept. 1862, *CC* 53/1430.

119 LMC to Eliza Scudder, 30 Sept. 1862, *CC* 53/1430. See also the "Remarks" Garrison appended to the text of the proclamation in the *Liberator*, 26 Sept. 1862, p. 154.

120 LMC to Charles Sumner, 3 Oct. 1862, *SL* 417. Most abolitionists agreed that the Union would have been better off without the border states, but historians generally maintain that the border states were militarily essential to the Union's survival. See, for example, McPherson, *Battle Cry* 284: "Maryland, Kentucky, and Missouri . . . would have added 45 percent to the white population and military manpower of the Confederacy, 80 percent to its manufacturing capacity, and nearly 40 percent to its supply of horses and mules." Also Potter, *Division* 157.

121 LMC to Sarah Shaw, 30 Oct. 1862, *SL* 419. For an interesting explanation of Lincoln's refusal to put the Emancipation Proclamation on "*high moral grounds*," see Cox, *Lincoln and Black Freedom* 13–14.

122 Quoted in McPherson, *Battle Cry* 559–62.

123 LMC to Sarah Shaw, 11 Nov. 1860, *SL* 420.

124 *CWL* 6: 28–30. The complete text of the 1 Jan. Emancipation Proclamation was reprinted in the *Liberator* 2 Jan. 1863, p. 3, under the headline "The Proclamation. Three Million of Slaves set Free! 'Glory, Hallelujah!' " In an untitled editorial note Garrison called the Proclamation "a great historic event, sublime in its magnitude, momentous and beneficent in its far-reaching consequences, and eminently just and right alike to the oppressor and oppressed. . . ."

125 See LMC to Lydia Bigelow Child, 14 Dec. 1862, *CC* 54/1442, in which Child mentions having written to George and worries about having received no reply. I am indebted to Milton Emerson Ross, grandson of Lydia Maria Child Haskins, for information about George's death. On the diseases that decimated Civil War soldiers, see McPherson, *Battle Cry*, 485–88: "twice as many Civil War soldiers died of disease as were killed and mortally wounded in combat." Black soldiers suffered even higher rates of death from disease. See Berlin et al., *Black Military Experience* chap. 15.

126   LMC to William Lloyd Garrison Haskins, 28 Dec. 1862, *SL* 423.

127   "L. Maria Child to the President of the United States," *CC* 53/1426; LMC to William Lloyd Garrison Haskins, 28 Dec. 1862, *SL* 424.

128   For the inside story of Robert Shaw's reluctant acceptance, see Duncan's introduction and Robert G. Shaw to Annie Kneeland Haggerty, 4 and 8 Feb. 1863, Duncan, ed., *Blue-Eyed Child of Fortune* 21–27, 283–86. From these and other letters, it seems clear that fear of his fiancée's objections and his racist acquaintances' mockery were his main motives for initially refusing this assignment.

129   LMC to Willie Haskins, 30 Apr. 1863, *SL* 427–28.

130   LMC to Lucy Osgood and Mary Stearns, 11 Jan. 1863, *CC* 54/1452, and 22 Dec. 1862, *CC* 54/1444.

131   LMC to Ticknor and Fields, 22 Jan. 1863, *CC* 54/1458.

132   LMC to Lucy Osgood, 11 Jan. 1863, *CC* 54/1452.

133   LMC to Ticknor and Fields, 22 Jan. 1863, *CC* 54/1458. In LMC to James T. Fields, 22 Feb. 1863, *CC* 55/1472, Child further explains how she has grouped the selections and discusses possible illustrations (none of which ultimately appeared in the book, perhaps due to financial constraints).

134   LMC to Sarah Shaw, [Apr?] 1863, *CC* 55/1478.

135   See "Departure of Fifty-Fourth Regiment of Massachusetts Volunteers," *Traveller*, rpt. in *Liberator* 5 June 1863, p. 91; and "The Fifty-Fourth Massachusetts, *New York Weekly Tribune*, 6 June 1863, p. 2; also Duncan, *Blue-Eyed Child of Fortune* 39–40, 331, 335, 336.

136   LMC to Sarah Shaw and Samuel Sewall, 16 and 21 June 1863, *CC* 55/1483, 1484. LMC to Anna Loring, 24 May 1862, *CC* 52/1411, explains the circumstances under which Child became "monarch of all I survey" and describes the redecorating she and David have been doing with their own hands.

137   LMC to Samuel Sewall and Francis Shaw, 21 and 25 June 1863, *CC* 55/1484, 1486.

138   LMC to Samuel Sewall, 21 June 1863, *CC* 55/1484.

139   Sarah Shaw to LMC, [21 June? 1863], *CC* 55/1485; LMC to Francis Shaw, 25 June 1863, *CC* 55/1486. Francis's letter has not been preserved, but its contents can be inferred from Sarah's and from Child's response.

140   LMC to Francis Shaw and Samuel Sewall, 25 and 29 June 1863, *CC* 55/1486, 1487.

141   LMC to Sarah and Francis Shaw, 14 and 17 July 1863, *CC* 56/1489–90; also LMC to Samuel Sewall, 29 June 1863, *CC* 55/1487.

142   LMC to Eliza Scudder, 8 July 1869, *CC* 71/1901.

143   "The Fourth Last Past," *New York Weekly Tribune* 11 July 1863, p. 4.

144   Alfred Wayland Cutting, *Old-Time Wayland* (privately printed, 1926) 46. I am grateful to Deborah Clifford for generously drawing my attention to this anecdote and to Jo Goeselt of the Wayland Historical Society for sending me a photocopy of *Old-Time Wayland*.

145   LMC to Sarah Shaw, 5 May 1861, *CC* 48/1305.

146   LMC to Sarah Shaw, 5 May 1861, *CC* 48/1305. In the wake of the Emancipation Proclamation and the recruitment of African American soldiers, Child was naturally less critical of official policy than when army officers were following orders to surrender fugitive slaves to their masters. But on learning that the government had reneged on its promise of equal pay to African American troops and was paying them $3 a month less than white troops, deducting an additional $3 for their uniforms, she wrote: "the mean conduct of the government toward the negroes fills me with shame." See LMC to Eliza Scudder, 22 Apr. 1864, *SL* 443.

147   McPherson, *Battle Cry* 602. See also the interesting analysis that follows, showing that in fact, cities, counties, Democratic ward committees, factories, businesses, and railroads all contributed to funds to buy exemptions for drafted workers, tending to equalize opportunities to buy substitutes.

148   LMC to Francis Shaw, [25? July 1863], *CC* 56/1492. Quotations describing the depredations of the mob and the attack on Gibbons's home are drawn from "The Draft. Riot in the City of New-York...," and "The Riot," *New York Weekly Tribune* 18 July 1863, pp. 3–5. For full-scale accounts of the New York Draft Riot and historical analyses of its causes, see Adrian Cook, *The Armies of the Streets: The New York City Draft Riots of 1863* (Lexington: UP of Kentucky, 1974); and especially Iver Bernstein, *The New*

York City Draft Riots: Their Significance for American Society and Politics in the Age of the Civil War (New York: Oxford UP, 1990).

149   LMC to Anna Loring and Francis Shaw, 9 Aug. and [25? July] 1863, *CC* 56/1494, 1492.

150   LMC to Henrietta Sargent, 14 Aug. 1863, *CC* 56/1497.

151   LMC to Francis and Sarah Shaw, 17 July 1863, *CC* 56/1490; and to Oliver Johnson, printed as "Parts of Two Private Letters," in the *Standard* 22 Aug. 1863, *SL* 435–36. On the anti-immigrant views Child expresses in *The First Settlers*, see chap. 4.

152   "Fort Wagner" (editorial) and "The Attack on Fort Wagner—A Bloody Night-Assault and Repulse" (news dispatch), *New York Weekly Tribune* 1 Aug. 1863, pp. 2–3; Luis F. Emilio, *A Brave Black Regiment: History of the Fifty-Fourth Regiment of Massachusetts Volunteer Infantry, 1863–1865*, rev. ed. (1894; New York: Arno P, 1969), chap. 5, esp. pp. 79, 82, 84, 90–91; Duncan, ed., *Blue-Eyed Child of Fortune* 48–56; Lawrence Lader, *The Bold Brahmins: New England's War Against Slavery: 1831–1863* (New York: Dutton, 1961) 289; Fredrickson, *Inner Civil War* 151–56. See also "Testimony by a Special Correspondent of the *New York Tribune* before the American Freedmen's Inquiry Commission," *Black Military Experience* 534–36, which quotes General Truman Seymour as having suggested putting "those d——d niggers from Massachusetts in the advance," since "we may as well get rid of them, one time as another."

153   "Later from Charleston," *New York Weekly Tribune*, 8 Aug. 1863, p. 3; Lader, *Bold Brahmins* 290; Emilio, *Brave Black Regiment* 95–103. Actually, the fate of the black soldiers did not become known until much later, "the enemy absolutely refusing information" (Emilio 97). The question of what to do with the black soldiers was hotly debated among Governor M.L. Bonham of South Carolina, Confederate Secretary of War J. A. Seddon, and President Jefferson Davis. Bonham wanted the black soldiers turned over to the state of South Carolina to be tried and executed for supporting slave insurrection. Seddon and Davis feared retaliation by the Union and decided instead to return former slaves to their masters but to hold the free black soldiers without formally recognizing them as prisoners of war. See *Black Military Experience* 567–68, 579–81.

154   LMC to Henrietta Sargent, 14 Aug. 1863, *CC* 56/1497.

155   LMC to Anna Loring, 9 Aug. 1863, *CC* 56/1494.

156   LMC to Sarah Shaw, 25 July 1863, *CC* 56/1491.

157   "A Tribute to Col. Robert G. Shaw," *New York Evening Post*, rpt. in the *Standard* 15 Aug. 1863, *CC* 56/1498; "Parts of Two Private Letters," *Standard*, 22 Aug. 1863, *CC* 56/1499. Actually, as Duncan shows, Robert Shaw fell far short of his parents' abolitionist ideals, and often expressed racist views in his letters, even using the word "nigger." See Duncan's introduction and Robert G. Shaw to Sarah Shaw, Mimi (Elizabeth Russell Lowell), Effie (Josephine Shaw), Francis Shaw, and Charles Fessenden Morse, *Blue-Eyed Child of Fortune* 7, 10, 12–13, 35, 42–43, 289–90, 292, 299–301, 304–5. Child could not have known this, however, and Sarah Shaw indicated her own disappobation by editing out offensive statements in the selection of her son's letters that she published after his death.

158   "A Tribute," cited in n. 157 above; "Parts of Two Private Letters," *Standard* 22 Aug. 1863, *CC* 56/1499; McPherson, *Battle Cry* 794. No such policy was ever adopted, of course. Indeed Lincoln never implemented his order. Though the U.S. government ended all prisoner exchanges rather than acquiesce in the Confederacy's exclusion of black prisoners from exchanges, the net result was to leave soldiers of both races in enemy hands for the duration of the war.

159   LMC to Anna Loring, Eliza Scudder, and Louisa Loring, 9 Aug., 6 Nov., and 9 Nov. 1863, *CC* 56/1494, 1510, 1511. Child had to forgo attending another antislavery wedding, that of Garrison's son William. See LMC to Fanny Garrison, 26 Oct. 1863, *CC* 56/1509.

160   LMC to Lucy Osgood and James T. Fields, 18 and 10 Dec. 1863, *CC* 57/1521, 1519.

161   LMC to Eliza Scudder and Lydia Bigelow Child, 6 Nov., 23 Nov. and 13 Dec. 1863, *CC* 56/1510, 57/1517, 1520. Also to [Louisa Loring?, 1–27 Jan.? 1864], *CC* 57/1528. Compare LMC to Lydia Bigelow Child, 3 Oct. 1862, *CC* 53/1432.

162   "Employments in 1864," Child papers, Slavery Collection, Cornell University Library.

163   LMC to William Lloyd Garrison and [Louisa Loring?] 27 Dec. 1863 and [1–27 Jan.? 1864], *CC* 57/1525, 1528.

164   LMC to Sarah Shaw, [Feb. 1864], *CC* 58/1548.

165   "Letter from L. Maria Child," *Liberator* 19 Feb. 1864, *Standard* 27 Feb. 1864, *CC* 58/1538.

166   LMC to Henrietta Sargent, 2 Aug. 1858, *CC* 39/1072.

167   See McPherson, *Struggle for Equality* chap. 13; James Brewer Stewart, *Wendell Phillips: Liberty's Hero* (Baton Rouge: Louisiana State UP, 1986) 243–55. The developing schism can also be followed through vol. 5 of Garrison's letters.

168   "Letter from L. Maria Child," *Liberator* 19 Feb. 1864, *Standard* 27 Feb. 1864, *CC* 58/1538.

169   Child makes this explicit in "A Chat with the Editor of the *Standard*," 14 Jan. 1865, *CC* 61/1616, rpt. in *Liberator* 20 Jan. 1865, quoted in chap. 19 below.

170   "Letter from L. Maria Child," *Liberator* 19 Feb. 1864, *Standard* 27 Feb. 1864, *CC* 58/1538.

171   LMC to Sarah Shaw, 3 Nov. 1864, *SL* 446.

172   On Child's efforts to assist Lewis, see LMC to Robert Wallcut and James T. and Annie Fields, 26 Aug. 1864, 13 Oct. and 25 Nov. 1865, *CC* 59/1582, 63/1685, 1695; for her promotion of Lewis's work in newspapers, see "A Chat with the Editor of the *Standard*," 14 Jan. 1865, *CC* 61/1616, and "Letter from L. Maria Child. To the Editor of the *Independent*," 5 Apr. 1866, *Independent*, *CC* 64/1716.

173   LMC to Sarah Shaw, 8 Apr. 1866, *CC* 64/1717, and [Aug.? 1870], *CC* 74/1958; LMC to Harriet Sewall, 10 July 1868, *SL* 480–81. Child's letter to Sarah of 8 Apr., which reveals her sensitivity to the twin dangers of unreasonable expectations and condescension in judging the work of black artists at this transitional stage, deserves extensive quotation. Sarah had not liked the bust of Robert and objected to what she called Lewis's "self-conceit." Child replies: "I do not think she has any genius, but I think she has a good deal of imitative talent, which, combined with her indomitable perseverance, I have hoped might make her something above mediocrity, if she took *time* enough. But she . . . is in too much of a hurry to get up to a conspicuous place, without taking the necessary intermediate steps. I do not think this is so much 'self-conceit,' as it is an uneasy feeling of the necessity of making things to sell, in order to pay for her daily bread. Then you must remember that *youth*, in its fresh strength and inexperience, naturally thinks itself capable of doing *anything*. How contemptuously I smile now to read things which seemed to me very beautiful when I wrote them, years ago!. . . . I agree with you that, looked at in the light of *Art*, nothing she has produced is worth a second glance; but I am more disposed than *you* seem to be to give her time for a fair trial. . . . I doubt whether we *can* treat our colored brethren *exactly* as we would if they were white, though it is desirable to do so. But we have kept their minds in a state of infancy, and children *must* be treated with more patience and forbearance than grown people. How can they learn to swim, if they don't dive into the water? They will sprawl about, at first, doubtless, but they will find the use of their limbs by dint of trying." Child drew the line, however, at praising work she considered inferior. She refused to review Lewis's statue of the Freedman and his Wife, saying: "*Art* is sacred, as well as *Philanthropy*; and I do not think it either wise or kind to encourage a girl, merely because she is colored, to spoil good marble by making it into poor statues" (*CC* 74/1958). Unfortunately, Child's correspondence with Lewis herself has been lost. Lewis went on to make a very successful career for herself. "Her works have gained several gold medals and diplomas," reported the *Woman's Journal* in an article of 22 Nov. 1873 ("Edmonia Lewis," p. 375). She exhibited a statue in the 1876 Centennial Exposition and produced a statue of Lincoln for New York's Central Park, one of John Brown for the Union League Club, and one of Longfellow for Yale College (*Woman's Journal*, untitled note, 7 Dec. 1872, p. 387). She remained in Italy for the rest of her life, returning to the United States for periodic visits. See LMC to Lydia Bigelow Child, 12 Feb. 1866, *CC* 64/1708 for an example of similar advice Child gives her nephew Willie (to tend store while studying bookkeeping, so as to be "earning something"). Revealingly, Child proceeds to contrast her own attitude with David's: "David is very prone to look ahead to *prospective* advantages; but *my* way has always been to earn money by *any* honest means that came to hand, and be prepared to do something better, as soon as anything better presented itself."

174 McPherson, *Battle Cry* 698–713; Eric Foner, *Reconstruction: America's Unfinished Revolution, 1863–1877* (New York: Harper and Row, 1988) chap. 2.

175 Quoted in McPherson, *Battle Cry* 700, 716. See also David Child's vehement criticism of the "Louisiana scheme" in a letter of 20 Apr. 1865, apparently to Sumner, BPL Ms.A.4.2.p.53. Cox, *Lincoln and Black Freedom* 36–43, 75–81, 93–100, 103–4, 112, offers a convincing refutation and argues persuasively that the alternative Wade-Davis bill, which Lincoln angered radicals by pocket-vetoing in July, did not embody a more thoroughgoing approach to reconstruction.

176 McPherson, *Battle Cry* 716.

177 McPherson, *Struggle for Equality* 284–85.

178 LMC to John Greenleaf Whittier, 19 June 1864, *CC* 59/1569.

179 LMC to Gerrit Smith, 23 July 1864, *SL* 446.

180 LMC to John Greenleaf Whittier, 19 June 1864, *CC* 59/1569.

181 LMC to Gerrit Smith and Charles Sumner, 23 and 31 July 1864, *SL* 445, *CC* 59/1577; also to Sarah Shaw, [May–June? 1864], *CC* 59/1570.

182 Private letter quoted in McPherson, *Battle Cry* 762; see *Battle Cry*, 758–60 for a description of the fiasco at Petersburg.

183 LMC to Eliza Scudder, Lucy Osgood, Lydia Bigelow Child, and Anna Loring, 3 and 21 Aug., 18 Sept., and 11 Oct. 1864, *CC* 59/1578, 1580, 1583, 1584.

184 LMC to John Fraser, 10 Nov. 1864, *SL* 448. Fraser had married David's niece Ruth Child, and the couple had recently moved to Australia.

185 LMC to Eliza Scudder and Gerrit Smith, 22 Apr. 1864, *SL* 444, *CC* 58/1562.

186 LMC to John Fraser, 10 Nov. 1864, *SL* 448–50. For details on these conspiracies, see McPherson, *Battle Cry* 762–65.

187 McPherson, *Battle Cry* 804–5.

188 LMC to Eliza Scudder, 14 Nov. 1864, *CC* 60/1593.

189 LMC to Parke Godwin, 13 Dec. 1864, *CC* 60/1605.

190 LMC to John Fraser, 10 Nov. 1864, *SL* 449.

191 LMC to Sarah Parsons, 27 Nov. 1864, *CC* 60/1598.

192 LMC to Theodore Tilton, editor of the *Independent*, 7 Mar. 1865, *Independent* 16 Mar., *CC* 61/1640; partially published in *Liberator* 24 Mar. 1865. For her criticism of the First Inaugural, see LMC to John Greenleaf Whittier, 22 Sept. 1861, *CC* 49/1337. For complete texts of the First and Second Inaugurals, see *CWL* 4: 262–71, and 8: 332–33.

193 LMC to Eliza Scudder, 22 Apr. 1864, *SL* 444.

194 LMC to John Fraser, 10 Nov. 1864, *SL* 449.

195 LMC to Eliza Scudder, 22 Apr. 1864, *SL* 444.

196 See "Gen. Gantt at Cooper Institute. Slavery the Cause of the Rebellion, and a Nuisance—Necessity of Its Destruction," and "Gen. Gantt's Converts" (editorial), *New York Weekly Tribune* 6 Feb. 1864, pp. 6 and 4.

197 "Letter from L. Maria Child to Gen. Gantt," 7 Feb. 1864, published in the *Standard* 22 Apr. 1865, p. 4, *CC* 57/1531.

198 LMC to George W. Julian, 27 Mar. 1864, *SL* 439.

199 See Julian's speech, "Homesteads for Soldiers on the Lands of Rebels," U.S. House of Representatives, 18 Mar. 1864, rpt. in George Washington Julian, *Speeches on Political Questions* (1872; Westport, Conn.: Negro Universities P, 1970) 212–28. Child wrote an introduction to the volume.

200 LMC to George W. Julian, 27 Mar. 1864, *SL* 439–40, and 8 Apr. 1865, *CC* 62/1651.

201 LMC to Gerrit Smith, 4 and 22 Apr. 1864, *SL* 441, *CC* 58/1562.

202 LMC to John Greenleaf Whittier, 19 June 1864, *CC* 59/1569.

203 LMC to Gerrit Smith, 4 Apr. and 23 July 1864, *SL* 441, 445.

204 LMC to Henrietta Sargent, 8 Jan. 1865, *CC* 61/1614. Quotations are from LMC to Ticknor and Fields, 22 Jan. 1863, *CC* 54/1458.

205 [Thomas Wentworth Higginson], review of *Looking toward Sunset*, *Atlantic Monthly* 15 (Feb. 1865): 255. David Hackett Fischer, in *Growing Old in America*, rev. ed. (New York: Oxford UP, 1978), cites Child's *Looking toward Sunset* as "representative of a genre of 'gathered gems for the aged' which appeared in the mid-nineteenth century" (121). All but two of the nine works he mentions appeared after Child's. The two exceptions, John Stanford's *The Aged Christian's Cabinet* (1829) and Joseph Lathrop's *The Infirmities and Comforts of Old Age* (1802), typified the earlier literature for the old against which Child was reacting in attempting to compile a "cheerful" and undoctrinal work. In *The Journey of Life: A Cultural History of Aging in America* (Cambridge: Cambridge UP, 1992), Thomas R. Cole describes Stanford's *Aged Christian's Companion* (1829) as having "initiat[ed] the genre of American advice literature for older people" (67). According to Cole, the late Calvinist view of aging and death articulated in Stanford's book gave way in the mid-nineteenth century to an ideal of " 'civilized' old age," which he finds typified by Lydia Huntley Sigourney's *Past Meridian* (1854), Child's *Looking toward Sunset*, Cora S. Nourse's *Sunset Hours of Life* (1875) and S. G. Lathrop's *Fifty Years and Beyond; or, Gathered Gems for the Aged* (1881). He takes a highly critical view of the "sentimental" advice literature of the mid- to late-nineteenth century and its advocacy of an active, cheerful, and useful old age, arguing that it tended to promote unrealistic expectations of being able to control aging and escape bodily decrepitude by forming good moral and physical habits. Of these works, none approached Child's in popularity. Sigourney's went through eight printings, Nourse's one printing, and Lathrop's four printings (*NUC*). Sigourney's resembles Child's in spirit but not in form (it is an advice book, rather than an anthology). The latter two differ strikingly from Child's in promulgating doctrinal religious views (Nourse's was published by the American Tract Society). Child's thoroughgoing religious tolerance and advocacy of radical causes are unique among these works addressed to the aged. I am grateful to Rodney Olsen for bringing Cole's and Fischer's books to my attention.

206 L. Maria Child, *Looking toward Sunset. From Sources Old and New, Original and Selected* (Boston: Ticknor and Fields, 1865) v. Further page references are given parenthetically in the text.

207 Review of *Looking toward Sunset*, *Liberator* 16 Dec. 1864, p. 202.

208 For historical analyses of these trends and their consequences, see Cole, *Journey of Life* chaps. 4–7; and Fischer, *Growing Old* chap. 2.

209 William Cullen Bryant, Lucy Osgood, Stephen Salisbury, Wendell Phillips, and Louisa Loring to LMC, 26 Dec. 20 Nov., and 21 Nov. 1864, and 10 Feb. [1865], *CC* 60/1608, 1595, 1596, and 61/1632.

210 LMC to Parke Godwin, 13 Dec. 1864, *CC* 60/1605.

211 LMC to Anna Loring, 18 Jan. 1865, *CC* 61/1619.

212 LMC to Lydia Bigelow Child and Henrietta Sargent, 8 Jan. 1865, *CC* 61/1613, 1614.

213 Quoted in LMC to Lucy Osgood, 12 Feb. 1865, *CC* 61/1634.

214 Benjamin Quarles, *The Negro in the Civil War* (1953; Boston: Little, Brown, 1969) 326–27; LMC to George W. Julian, 8 Apr. 1865, *CC* 62/1651.

215 Lucy Osgood to LMC, 9 Apr. 1865, *CC* 62/1652; McPherson, *Battle Cry* 846–47.

216 LMC to Harriet Sewall, 4 Apr. 1865, *CC* 62/1649.

217 LMC to George Julian, Lucy Osgood, and Sarah Shaw, 8, 13, and [after 15 Apr.], 1865, *CC* 62/1651, *SL* 451–54.

218 *CWL* 8: 399–405. On the implications of the speech, see McPherson, *Battle Cry* 851–52; Foner, *Reconstruction* 74; Cox, *Lincoln and Black Freedom* 150–52.

219 "Letter from Mrs. L. M. Child," to Theodore Tilton, editor of the *Independent*, 6 May 1865, *Independent* 11 May, reprinted in *Liberator* 26 May 1865, *CC* 62/1659.

220 "Letter from Mrs. L. M. Child," to Tilton, cited in n. 219 above. See also LMC to Sarah Shaw, [after 15 Apr.] 1865, *SL* 453–54. Child's erroneous appraisal of Johnson was shared by most abolitionists and Radical Republicans; see Foner, *Reconstruction* 177–82. One of the few exceptions was Frederick Douglass, who "caught a glimpse of the real nature of this man" from the "bitter contempt and aversion" Johnson inadvertently revealed toward him on Inauguration Day; see Douglass, *Life and Times of Frederick Douglass* (1892; New York: Collier, 1962) 364.

19   Visions of a Reconstructed America: The Freedmen's Book and A Romance of the Republic

1   "Through the Red Sea into the Wilderness," *Independent* 21 Dec. 1865, p. 1; rpt. *Liberator* 29 Dec. 1865, p. 205 (not included in *CC*). Except where otherwise indicated, all quotations from Child in the next few paragraphs are taken from this article.

2   On the history and circulation of the *Independent*, see James M. McPherson, *The Struggle for Equality: Abolitionists and the Negro in the Civil War and Reconstruction* (Princeton, N.J.: Princeton UP, 1964) 87–88. Founded as a Congregational antislavery journal of conservative cast, the *Independent* became "for all practical purposes . . . an abolitionist organ" in 1863, when Theodore Tilton took over the editorship from Henry Ward Beecher. Child was invited to contribute to the *Independent* as early as 1859, when it was controlled by orthodox clergymen, but she refused on three grounds: (1) "I never write for a periodical that restricts my liberty"; (2) "the thing I detest most, next to Slavery, is Calvinism"; and (3) she objected to the *Independent's* supercilious treatment of Garrison and Theodore Parker; see LMC to Sydney Howard Gay, 21 Dec. 1859, *SL* 335. She began writing regularly for the *Independent* in 1865.

3   "The *Liberator* and Its Work," *Independent* 28 Dec. 1865, p. 1, *CC* 64/1698. Tilton printed both this article and "Through the Red Sea into the Wilderness" in the lead column generally reserved for the pronouncements of Congregationalist clergymen.

4   For contemporary reminiscences of the hostile public reception of the *Appeal*, see "Remarks of Wendell Phillips at the Funeral of Lydia Maria Child, October 23, 1880," published as an appendix to *Letters of Lydia Maria Child* [ed. Harriet Winslow Sewall] (1882; New York: Negro Universities P, 1969) 263–68; and Edward Everett Hale, *Memories of a Hundred Years*, 2 vols. (New York: Macmillan, 1902) 2: 118. See also chap. 8 above.

5   See McPherson, *Struggle for Equality* chap. 14; Eric Foner, *Reconstruction: America's Unfinished Revolution, 1863–1877* (New York: Harper and Row, 1988) chap. 5; and Ira Berlin, Joseph P. Reidy, and Leslie S. Rowland, *Freedom: A Documentary History of Emancipation, 1861–1867*, Series 2: *The Black Military Experience* (New York: Cambridge UP, 1982) chap. 17. On Johnson's promise to be a Moses to African Americans, see the famous speech quoted in LMC to John Fraser, 10 Nov. 1864, *SL* 449.

6   It is important to realize that Congress was not in session during the entire period when Johnson was defining Reconstruction policy through presidential proclamations. As Eric Foner explains: "It was a peculiarity of nineteenth-century politics that more than a year elapsed between the election of a Congress and its initial meeting. The Thirty-Ninth Congress, elected in the midst of war, assembled in December 1865 to confront the crucial issues of Reconstruction. . . ." See *Reconstruction* 228.

7   "Through the Red Sea into the Wilderness," *Independent* 21 Dec. 1865, rpt. *Liberator* 29 Dec. 1865, p. 205. Johnson's Annual Message of 4 Dec. 1865 is reprinted in Edward McPherson, *The Political History of the United States of America during the Period of Reconstruction. . . .*, 2nd ed. (1875; New York: Negro Universities P, 1969) 64–66.

8   Besides "Through the Red Sea into the Wilderness," these include "Letter from Mrs. Child," 5 July 1865, *Boston Transcript*, rpt. *Liberator* 21 July, *CC* 63/1669; "Letter from Mrs. L. M. Child," 23 July, *Independent* 3 Aug., *CC* 63/1672; "A Letter from Mrs. L. Maria Child," *Independent* 26 Oct. 1865, *CC* 63/1689; "Letter from L. Maria Child," *Independent* 29 Feb. 1866, *CC* 64/1710; "The President of the United States," *Independent* 8 Mar. 1866 (not included in *CC*); "Letter from L. Maria Child," *Independent* 5 Apr. 1866, *CC* 64/1716; and "Woman and Suffrage," *Independent* 10 and 17 Jan. 1867, *CC* 66/1759, 1760, *SL* 468–72. I am omitting Child's tributes to "The *Liberator* and Its Work" and "Friend Joseph," *CC* 64/1698, 66/1751, since neither deals explicitly with Reconstruction. Her articles on woman suffrage are discussed in chap. 20 below.

9   "A Letter from Mrs. L. Maria Child," *Independent* 26 Oct. 1865, *CC* 63/1689.

10   Interestingly, many African American leaders appear to have followed the same trajectory. See the views quoted in Leon F. Litwack, *Been in the Storm So Long: The Aftermath of Slavery* (1979; New York: Vintage, 1980) 528–30.

11   LMC to Eliza Scudder, 15 and 22 Oct. 1865, *CC* 63/1688; "Letter from Mrs. L. M. Child," *Independent* 11 May 1865, p. 4; rpt. *Liberator* 26 May 1865, *CC* 62/1659: "How completely [Lincoln] transferred the laboring oar into the hands of those refractory Border States, when he gave them a chance to make a good bargain out of Emancipation, if they would but accept the generous terms! Perhaps he took it for granted that they would reject them; but, doubtless, he also foresaw that, if they did so, circumstances would eventually compel them to give up slavery without pecuniary recompense, while at the same time they would have silenced, by their own act, the sympathy of Democrats at home and aristocrats abroad."

12   McPherson, *Struggle for Equality* 336–37; Frank Preston Stearns, *The Life and Public Services of George Luther Stearns* (1907; New York: Arno P, 1969) 360–61.

13   McPherson, *Struggle for Equality* 329–30. See Phillips's editorials "The Fatal Step," "The Administration," and "The President Tylerizes," on p. 2 of *Standard* 3 and 24 June and 1 July 1865, which reflect his own progression from reserving judgment to bitterly denouncing Johnson.

14   LMC to Henrietta Sargent, 18 June 1865, *CC* 62/1667.

15   For example, Child wrote only one letter to Sumner (27 Nov. 1865) and one to Julian (22 Jan. 1866) during this period; see *CC* 64/1697, 1704. In neither letter did she urge any particular course of action or express any difference of opinion on policy.

16   "Letter from Mrs. L. M. Child," 23 July 1865, *Independent* 3 Aug., rpt. in *Liberator* 11 Aug., *CC* 63/1672.

17   "Letter from Mrs. L. M. Child," 23 July 1867, *Independent* 3 Aug., rpt. in *Liberator* 11 Aug., *CC* 63/1672.

18   LMC to Sarah Shaw and Eliza Scudder, 29 Oct. and 15 and 22 Oct. 1865, *CC* 63/1690, 1688.

19   "A Letter from Mrs. L. Maria Child," *Independent* 26 Oct. 1865, *CC* 63/1689.

20   "A Letter from Mrs. L. Maria Child," *Independent* 26 Oct. 1865, *CC* 63/1689. See LMC to Eliza Scudder, 15 and 22 Oct. 1865, *CC* 63/1688 for comments on the "*fuddled* sound" of the "prosy repetitions" in Johnson's "Address to the Colored Soldiers." The speech, which is indeed rambling and repetitious, is reprinted in McPherson, *Political History of Reconstruction* 49–51.

21   "Interview with a Colored Delegation respecting Suffrage," rpt. in McPherson, *Political History of Reconstruction* 52–55.

22   "Letter from L. Maria Child," *Independent* 29 Feb. 1866, p. 1, *CC* 64/1710. Quotations in the next paragraph are also from this letter.

23   Child also mentions General John A. Palmer, who had defended black soldiers and their families against abuse by their Kentucky masters; and General Charles Devens, whom she had elsewhere praised for volunteering to pay $1,800 for the freedom of Thomas Sims. On Saxton's vigorous protest against the expulsion of the freedpeople from the lands they had been cultivating, see Foner, *Reconstruction* 159. On Palmer, see Berlin et al. *Black Military Experience* 278.

24   LMC to Theodore Tilton, 14 Feb. 1866, *CC* 64/1711. She need not have worried that he would object to her severity; his own editorial in the *Independent* 15 Feb., p. 4, "The President's Re-statement of His Views," took a similar position: "In its political significance, the President's speech [to the Black delegation] is a turning-point in affairs. It draws a definite line between the President's Policy and the Negro's Rights — putting the President and his partisans on one side, and the Negro and his friends on the other. Good men are called to take sides."

25   Both Phillips and Tilton pointed out early signs that Johnson was contemplating such a move. See their respective editorials, "The Administration" and "The President Tylerizes," *Standard* 24 June and 1 July 1865, p. 2; and "The Present Political Aspect," *Independent* 24 Aug. 1865, p. 4. In his editorial "Courage in Politics," *Standard* 20 Jan. 1866, p. 2, Phillips complained that Republican politicians were still paralyzed by this fear. He argued that if the president were capable of being driven into the hands of Democrats, "he ought to be. If he means to betray his party, the sooner the better." For modern historical analyses of Johnson's motives, see Foner, *Reconstruction* 184, 191, 248–51; LaWanda Cox and John H. Cox, *Politics, Principle, and Prejudice, 1865–1866* (New York: Glencoe P, 1963), esp.

chaps. 5 and 8; and W. R. Brock, *An American Crisis: Congress and Reconstruction, 1865–1867* (London: St. Martin's, 1963), esp. chap. 2 and 172–75. Cox and Cox also provide an extremely illuminating and detailed account of the struggle between conservative Republicans and Democrats for control over the new party each group hoped to build around Johnson.

26 Foner, *Reconstruction* 68–69 and chap. 4; McPherson, *Struggle for Equality* 347–48.

27 "Speech of 22d February 1866," rpt. in McPherson, *Political History of Reconstruction* 58–63.

28 "The President of the United States," Mrs. L. Maria Child, to the Editor of the *Independent*, 8 Mar. 1866, p. 1.

29 Foner, *Reconstruction* 243–44.

30 Johnson vetoed ten bills between Feb. 1866 and Mar. 1867. See McPherson, *Political History of Reconstruction* 68–82, 147–81. Brock's *American Crisis* provides a fascinating blow-by-blow account of the jockeying between Johnson, moderate Republicans, and Radicals for control of Reconstruction policy. Brock also argues throughout that the success of the Radicals in mobilizing support for their aims cannot be understood without taking into account the northern public's strong desire to secure the fruits of the war.

31 "Letter from L. Maria Child," *Independent* 5 Apr. 1866, p. 1, *CC* 64/1716.

32 I am grateful to H. Bruce Franklin for helping me to arrive at and formulate this perception.

33 LMC to Henrietta Sargent, 18 June 1865, *CC* 62/1667.

34 LMC to Ednah Dow Cheney and William Lloyd Garrison, 22 Oct. 1865, *CC* 63/1687, and 7 July 1865, *SL* 456–57; WLG to LMC, 10 July 1865, *CC* 63/1671.

35 LMC to James T. Fields, 27 Aug. 1865, *SL* 458–59.

36 LMC to James T. Fields and Ticknor and Fields, 27 Aug. and 3 Sept. 1865, *SL* 459, *CC* 63/1681. See also LMC to Sarah Shaw and Ednah Dow Cheney, 3 Sept. and 22 Oct. 1865, *CC* 63/1680, 1687. Cheney's letter, quoted by Child, has not been preserved.

37 LMC to Sarah Shaw, 3 Sept. 1865, *CC* 63/1680.

38 See, for example, Paulo Freire, *Pedagogy of the Oppressed* (New York: Herder, 1970); James Lynch, *Multicultural Education in a Global Society* (London: Falmer, 1989); and Paul Lauter, ed., *The Heath Anthology of American Literature*, 2 vols. (Lexington, Mass.: D. C. Heath, 1990).

39 James M. McPherson, *The Negro's Civil War: How American Negroes Felt and Acted during the War for the Union* (1965; Urbana: U of Illinois P, 1982) 157.

40 Page references to *The Freedmen's Book* (1865; New York: Arno P, 1968) are given parenthetically in the text.

41 LMC to James T. Fields, 27 Aug. 1865, *SL* 459. At one point Child apparently planned to include Gustavus Vassa (Olaudah Equiano) as well as Ignatius Sancho. See LMC to Robert Morris, 19 June 1864, *CC* 59/1567, in which she asks to borrow *The Life of Olaudah Equiano, or Gustavus Vassa, The African*, which she had presented to Morris many years earlier. It is not clear whether she omitted it because she could not find a copy of the work or because she decided that space limits precluded using it.

42 Child requested Douglass's permission to write an abridged version of his narrative and asked if he would now supply the details of his escape from slavery, which he had hitherto refused to divulge. Her letter has been lost, but it can be reconstructed from his reply: "Use the story of my life in any way you see fit. I am sure it will not, in your hand, be employed to the injury of myself or the cause of my people. . . . I have always read with grateful pleasure what you have from time to time written on the question of slavery." Douglass felt "[n]o good end could be served" by revealing the manner of his escape, however. See Frederick Douglass to LMC, 30 July 1865, *CC* 63/1673. Child follows Douglass's 1845 *Narrative* and 1855 *My Bondage and My Freedom* very closely, faithfully reflecting his political viewpoint, but neglecting to preserve his voice — a defect irritating to a modern reader. Her dramatic account of the Crafts is drawn from many sources, including "verbal information," as she told Fields. Garrison supplied her with their 1860 narrative, *Running a Thousand Miles for Freedom*. See LMC to William Lloyd Garrison and James T. Fields, 7 July and 27 Aug. 1865, *SL* 456–60; and William Lloyd Garrison to LMC, 10 July 1865, *CC* 63/1671.

43 See the often anthologized poem "On Being Brought from Africa to America":

> 'Twas mercy brought me from my *Pagan* land,
> Taught my benighted soul to understand
> That there's a God, that there's a *Saviour* too:
> Once I redemption neither sought nor knew.
> Some view our sable race with scornful eye,
> "Their colour is a diabolic die."
> Remember, *Christians*, *Negros*, black as *Cain*,
> May be refin'd, and join th'angelic train.

Instead, Child reprints Wheatley's poem to the Earl of Dartmouth, which explains that her "love of Freedom sprung" from her experience of being kidnapped, which led her to "pray / Others may never feel tyrannic sway." Elsewhere in the anthology she also reprints Wheatley's "The Works of Providence" (90, 94–96).

44 Theodore Tilton singled it out for praise in his review of *The Freedmen's Book*, *Independent* 1 Feb. 1866, p. 3.

45 LMC to Charles Sumner, 27 Nov. 1865, *CC* 64/1697. This letter accompanied the copy she presented to Sumner of *The Freedmen's Book*.

46 For a vivid account of the obstacles the freedpeople faced when they tried to assert their rights in the ways Child suggests here, see Litwack, *Been in the Storm So Long* 274–91 and chap. 7. Child's "Advice from an Old Friend" invites comparison with Clinton B. Fisk's *Plain Counsels for Freedmen: In Sixteen Brief Lectures* (Boston: American Tract Society, 1866). Despite his evangelical abolitionist background, Fisk betrays more sympathy for the former master than for his slave. He admonishes the freedpeople: "Now it is natural that he [the former master] should feel sore; that he should grieve over his loss; that he should be slow to adapt himself to the new state of things. . . . It is natural, too, that he should feel severe toward you. . . . [W]henever he sees you he can not but think of the great change, and can not avoid blaming you for it, although his better judgment tells him he ought to praise, rather than blame you" (10–11). Fisk follows up his plea to "think kindly of your old master," with a similar appeal to "avoid every thing you can which will inflame" white people's "strong prejudices": "You know how easy it is to hurt a sore toe. Prejudices are like tender toes. Do not step on them when it is possible to avoid it" (13).

47 Child's revisions of the story for *The Freedmen's Book* shed much light on her ideological purposes, racial sensibilities, and perceptions of different audiences. Consonantly with her aim of promoting "mutual friendliness of feeling" between blacks and whites, she abridged and toned down the speeches of slaves advocating "[b]lood for blood" (*FB* 107). Yet she also eliminated the racial comments she had made in the earlier version, which had credited mulattoes with greater militancy and ascribed it to their Anglo-Saxon blood. Finally, to reorient the story from a white to a black audience and to make it more accessible to uneducated freedpeople, she shifted the focus from the slaveholder Mr. Duncan to the slaves themselves and dropped the entire analogy with Saxon history. For comparison, see "The Black Saxons," *Fact and Fiction: A Collection of Stories* (New York: C. S. Francis, 1846) 190–204.

48 Martin Delany's *Blake; or the Huts of America* was not published in book form until 1970 (ed. Floyd J. Miller; Boston: Beacon P), but it was serialized in the *Anglo-African Magazine* (Jan. to July 1859) and the *Weekly Anglo-African* (26 Nov. 1861 to late May 1862). Child subscribed to the latter. See LMC to Oliver Johnson, [after 16 Apr. 1861], *CC* 48/1301, in which she asks to have it sent to Wayland again.

49 *The Freedman's Third Reader* (Boston: American Tract Society, 1866); For an excellent discussion of this and other texts used in the freedmen's schools, see Robert C. Morris, *Reading, 'Riting, and Reconstruction: The Education of Freedmen in the South, 1861–1870* (Chicago: U of Chicago P, 1981), esp. chap. 6. I do not agree with Morris's judgment that Child's book was "almost as moderate as those published by the American Tract Society," however (206).

50 *Freedman's Third Reader* 11, 227, 235.

51 *Freedman's Third Reader* 237–38.

52 *Freedman's Third Reader* 83–86; LMC to Charles Sumner, 27 Nov. 1865, *CC* 64/1697.

53 "The Freedmen's Book," *Freedmen's Record* 2 (Apr. 1866): 69; Sarah E. Chase, "From Columbus," *Freedmen's Record* 2 (June 1866): 119; Joshua E. Wilson to Ednah D. Cheney "From a Native Teacher," *Freedmen's Record* 5 (Feb. 1870): 61–62. I am indebted to Morris, *Reading, 'Riting, and Reconstruction* chap. 5, for guiding me to these sources. Child quotes at length from Abby Francis's letter in "Letter from L. Maria Child," *Independent* 5 Apr. 1866, *CC* 64/1716.

54 LMC to James T. Fields, 27 Aug. 1865, *SL* 459; LMC to Lewis Tappan and Lucy Osgood, 30 Jan. and 28 Mar. 1869, *CC* 70/1875, 71/1893; Lewis Tappan to LMC, [after 30 Jan. 1869], *CC* 70/1876. Revealingly, Tappan pleaded "lack of funds" as a reason for being unable to purchase five hundred copies at cost, but he claimed that had Child "seen fit to make the alterations . . . the AMA would have circu[lat]ed thousands of copies."

55 Morris, *Reading, 'Riting, and Reconstruction* 243–49.

56 LMC to James T. Fields, and Ticknor and Fields, 27 Aug. and 3 Sept. 1865, *SL* 459, *CC* 63/1681.

57 LMC to Francis Shaw, 28 July 1867, *CC* 67/1789.

58 LMC to Oliver Johnson, 3 June 1861, *CC* 48/1310, requests him to take back from the *Knickerbocker* a story then titled "Willie and Wikamee," which they had not published as promised. The story seems to have been written during Child's stay with Lucy Osgood in the winter of 1860–61. She would eventually submit it to the *Atlantic Monthly*, adding a prefatory note at Fields's request, and it would appear in the Mar. 1863 number. See LMC to James T. Fields, 26 Feb. 1862, *CC* 51/1391. See chap. 20 below for an analysis of this story.

59 LMC to Lucy Osgood, 24 Feb. 1862, *CC* 51/1390.

60 LMC to Francis Shaw, 28 July 1867, *CC* 67/1789. Child dates this early draft back "four of [*sic*] five years ago," that is, in midsummer of 1862 or 1863. The former seems the more likely date, since in the spring of 1863 Child was preoccupied by the death of Convers, and in June the burning of her house drove everything else from her mind. She may have turned to her other project of 1862–63, *Looking toward Sunset*, as a means of counteracting the "discouragement" produced by her inability to continue with the novel.

61 LMC to Lucy Searle, 9 June 1862, *CC* 52/1412.

62 LMC to Lucy Osgood, 5 Sept. 1866, *CC* 65/1737.

63 LMC to Lucy Searle and Sarah Shaw, 9 June and 18 May 1862, *CC* 52/1412, 1410. In these two letters Child was referring in particular to *The Pearl of Orr's Island*. Though she pronounced it inferior to *The Minister's Wooing*, she found much to admire in it.

64 LMC to Lucy Osgood and Sarah Shaw, 1 Sept. 1861, 5 Sept. 1866, and 16 Oct. 1866, *SL* 392, *CC* 65/1737, 1742. The 1866 letters refer to Eliot's latest novel, *Felix Holt*.

65 LMC to Sarah Shaw, undated, *CC* 66/1757. The attractions of these novels are deducible from the plot summaries furnished by Sally Mitchell, *Dinah Mulock Craik* (Boston: Twayne, 1983). *The Woman's Kingdom* depicts a marriage of equals that "fills both physical and emotional needs" while leaving "the balance of power . . . in the woman's hands" (69). *A Brave Lady*, written in support of a Married Women's Property Act giving women "legal right to their own property and earnings," provides a "realistic picture of a confined, hopeless, emotionally unsatisfying married life" (69, 71).

66 LMC to Sarah Shaw, undated, *CC* 66/1757.

67 LMC to James T. Fields, 19 Oct. 1865, *CC* 63/1686. In a letter written three days later, Child confirms that she is still correcting proof sheets of *The Freedmen's Book*, which Ticknor and Fields was mailing in small batches several times a week. See LMC to Ednah Dow Cheney, 22 Oct. 1865, *CC* 63/1687; LMC to Harriet Sewall and Sarah Shaw, 9 and 29 Oct. 1865, *CC* 63/1683, 1690.

68 LMC to Louisa Loring, 10 Dec. 1866, *CC* 66/1752.

69 LMC to James T. Fields, 9 Sept. 1866, *CC* 65/1739.

70 LMC to James T. Fields, 18 Feb. 1867, *CC* 66/1764.

71 LMC to James T. Fields, 9 Sept. 1866, *CC* 65/1739.

72 "Letter from L. M. Child" and "A High-Flying Letter" by Mrs. L. M. Childs [*sic*], *Independent* 21 and 28 June 1866, *CC* 65/1726, 1727. See also "Illustrations of Human Progress," *Independent* 31 Jan. 1867, *CC* 68/1809, which salutes the invention of "chromo-lithography" as a sign of the democratization of art and proceeds to comment on Edmonia Lewis, "half Indian and half African" as the embodiment of the coming new era when artists of color will "warm up our colder tastes." In addition to these letters for the *Independent*, Child wrote another story for the *Atlantic* in Oct. 1865 — "Poor Chloe" (published in Mar. 1866) — and three stories for Fields's children's magazine, *Our Young Folks*: "Freddy's New-Year's Dinner" (July 1865), "Grandfather's Chestnut-Tree" (Oct. 1865), and "The Two Christmas Evenings" (Jan. 1866).

73 LMC to John Sullivan Dwight, 13 Oct. 1866, *CC* 65/1741.

74 LMC to Anna Loring, 13 Feb. 1866, *CC* 64/1709.

75 LMC to Anna Loring and Harriet Sewall, 13 Feb. 1866, 30 July 1868, *CC* 64/1709, 69/1843.

76 LMC to Sarah Shaw, 7 and 25 Sept. 1866, *CC* 65/1738 and *SL* 466.

77 LMC to James T. Fields, 18 Feb. and 1 Mar. 1867, *CC* 66/1764, 1766.

78 LMC to James T. Fields, 30 Mar. 1867, *CC* 66/1768.

79 LMC to James T. Fields, 14 and 17 May 1867, *SL* 473, *CC* 67/1775.

80 This is also the theme of Child's last story for the *Atlantic*, "Poor Chloe" (Mar. 1866), which depicts the harshness of slavery in New England.

81 Lydia Maria Child, *A Romance of the Republic* (1867; Miami, Fla.: Mnemosyne, 1969) 401, 403, 409, 412, 428–29, 433. Further page references to this edition are given parenthetically in the text.

82 LMC to Caroline Weston, 27 July 1838, *SL* 80.

83 See chap. 11 above for an account of Child's unsuccessful attempt to enable the slave woman Rosa to claim her freedom.

84 For one of Child's tributes to the role of "mechanics" and working people in the abolitionist movement, see "Through the Red Sea into the Wilderness," cited and discussed at the beginning of this chapter. For an allusion to David's singing of "The Star Spangled Banner," see Alfred Wayland Cutting, *Old-Time Wayland* (privately printed, 1926) 47, quoted in chap. 18 above; Child also refers frequently in her Civil War correspondence to David's singing of the anthem. For Child's retort that she had "rather be a beast of *burden*, than a beast of *prey*," see LMC to William Cutler, 10 July 1862, *SL* 413. Thanks to Donald Dingledine for tracking down this quotation for me.

85 See LMC to Louisa Loring, 22 June 1845, *CC* 22/623: "Don't grudge me my enthusiasm about Ole Bul. . . . Such a gushing bubbling nature always had great charms for me. . . ." Also LMC to Anna Loring, 13–14 Oct. 1844, *CC* 20/578: "[Y]our father . . . does not admire free, gushing, spontaneous characters so much as I do."

86 LMC to George Kimball, 10 Apr. 1835, Cornell University Library Anti-Slavery Collection (not included in *CC*); LMC to Francis Shaw, 28 July 1867, *CC* 67/1789.

87 Compare "Romantic Story: The Beautiful Slave," *Liberator* 7 July 1837, p. 112, with "Loo Loo. A Few Scenes from a True History," *Atlantic Monthly* 1–2 (May–June 1858): 801–12, 32–42.

88 "A Chat with the Editor of the Standard," *Standard* 14 Jan. 1865, *Liberator* 20 Jan. 1865, *CC* 61/1616; "Illustrations of Human Progress," *Independent* 31 Jan. 1867, *CC* 68/1809.

89 See Rebecca Harding Davis's *Waiting for the Verdict* (1867), Albion Tourgée's *Toinette* (1874), and William Dean Howells's *An Imperative Duty* (1891), discussed at the end of this chapter.

90 LMC to Caroline Weston, 7 Mar. 1839, *SL* 109.

91 See chap. 14 above for an analysis of the harem trope in "Slavery's Pleasant Homes."

92 Child based her description of the island scenery on Fanny Kemble's *Journal of a Residence on a Georgian Plantation in 1838–1839* (1863; New York: Knopf, 1961). Praising it as "one of the most powerful of the agencies . . . at work for the overthrow of slavery" during the war, she wrote of Kemble: "For a woman of her transcendent powers, accustomed to ease, elegance, and the excitement of perpetual adulation, to sympathize with those poor loathsome slaves as she did, and persist in rendering them such personal services as were in her power, indicates great nobility of soul. Then she saw through all

the apologies for slavery with such clear, practical good sense!" See LMC to Oliver Johnson, published in the *Standard* 22 Aug. 1863, *SL* 435. Kemble's husband, Pierce Butler, may have been one of Child's models for Gerald Fitzgerald.

93 See Child's account of the Circassians and her comments on the practices of the Turkish sultans in *The History of the Condition of Women, in Various Ages and Nations* (Boston: John Allen, 1835) 1: 43–47.

94 "Woman and Suffrage," *Independent* 10 Jan. 1867, *CC* 66/1759. See chap. 20 below for a discussion of these articles and of the part Child took in the campaign for woman suffrage.

95 John Bell, a Tennessee slaveholder, was the Constitutional Union candidate for president in 1860, and Edward Everett of Massachusetts was his vice presidential running mate. By naming her Massachusetts merchant Bell, Child is identifying him as a northern man with southern principles and underscoring the North's complicity in slavery.

96 Child's use of this device should be compared with Twain's in *Pudd'nhead Wilson* (1894). She is careful to avoid the "blood will tell" interpretation of the two men's characters, not only by stressing the influence of environment more heavily than Twain does, but by portraying Gerald as an essentially good-hearted young man capable of outgrowing the defects of his slaveholder's upbringing. In contrast, Twain's Tom is an irredeemable villain. The device nevertheless remains double-edged, since the mechanical ingenuity, intelligence, and drive exhibited by Gerald's half brother could still be attributed by racist readers to his white identity. The body of criticism on *Pudd'nhead Wilson* is vast, and critics are divided as to whether Twain is exposing or succumbing to racist theories, or simply reflecting his own and his culture's confusion about race. See, for example, the essays collected in Susan Gillman and Forrest G. Robinson, eds., *Mark Twain's* Pudd'nhead Wilson: *Race, Conflict, and Culture* (Durham, N.C.: Duke UP, 1990).

97 LMC to Theodore Tilton, 7 Mar. 1865, *CC* 61/1640.

98 For an extended discussion of Child's relationship with Dolores, see chap. 15 above. Child was still corresponding with Dolores in the 1860s. Indeed, what may have helped suggest the idea of using her as a model for a fugitive slave was the fact that Dolores because of health problems requiring a warmer climate had moved to Charleston, South Carolina, with her husband and children just before the outbreak of the war.

99 Willis's death occurred while Child was writing *A Romance of the Republic*, reawakening her memories of their courtship; see LMC to Marianne Silsbee, 5 Feb. [1867], *CC* 66/1761a, quoted in chap. 2 above; on Willis's reviews of *The Frugal Housewife*, see chap. 6 above.

100 LMC to Sarah Shaw, 7 Sept. 1866, *SL* 464.

101 LMC to Eliza Scudder, 6 Feb. 1870, *SL* 488–89. See also LMC to Sarah Shaw, 18 June 1876, *SL* 535: "There have been many attempts to saddle and bridle me, and teach me to keep step in respectable processions; but they have never got the lasso over my neck *yet*; and 'old hoss' as I am now, if I see the lasso in the air, I snort and gallop off, determined to be a free horse to the last, and put up with the consequent lack of grooming and stabling."

102 LMC to Sarah Shaw, 20 Feb. 1857, *CC* 36/992.

103 LMC to Sarah Shaw, 7 Sept. 1866, *SL* 464.

104 See LMC to Louisa and Anna Loring, 24 June 1849, *CC* 27/753, and 13 Feb. 1866, *CC* 64/1709.

105 LMC to Marianne Silsbee, 1 Feb. 1857, *SL* 303–4. Responding to a peace overture from Marianne, Child is recalling the circumstances of their estrangement.

106 I am indebted to Jean Fagan Yellin for pointing this out in her commentary on a paper that provided the basis for the present chapter.

107 "Illustrations of Human Progress," *Independent* 31 Jan. 1868, *CC* 68/1809.

108 I am indebted for this insight to H. Bruce Franklin's critique of an early draft of this chapter. "*Olla podrida*" is the phrase Child uses to describe the mixture of English, Spanish, and French that Flora and Rosa speak between themselves (32, 149).

109 LMC to Louisa Loring, 24 May 1867, *CC* 67/1776. The occasion for the letter was the ninth anniversary of Loring's death.

110   See LMC to Louisa Loring, 15 Jan. 1847, *SL* 235; quotations are from LMC to Louisa Loring, 24 May, 1867, *CC* 67/1776.

111   [Theodore Tilton], review of *A Romance of the Republic, Independent* 10 Oct. 1867, p. 2.

112   LMC to Lucy Osgood, [11?–19? Feb. 1856], *SL* 276. See chap. 15 above on the feelings of guilt for illicit sexual desires that lie behind this "pilgrimage of penance."

113   Mary V. Dearborn, *Pocahontas's Daughters: Gender and Ethnicity in American Culture* (New York: Oxford UP, 1986) 151.

114   For a brief account of Loring's relationship with Morris, see James Oliver Horton and Lois E. Horton, *Black Bostonians: Family Life and Community Struggle in the Antebellum North* (New York: Holmes and Meier, 1979) 56. I have also drawn on notes compiled by the research assistants who worked on Meltzer and Holland's edition of Child's letters. I am grateful to Milton Meltzer for passing them on to me. Morris met the Lorings while working as a "table boy" for the King family, and they subsequently hired him from the Kings. Loring first promoted Morris to the status of law copyist in his office, then of law clerk, and finally trained him for the bar. In 1849 Morris helped Charles Sumner argue the desegregaton case of *Sarah C. Roberts* vs. *The City of Boston* before the Massachusetts Supreme Court — a case decided against them by Chief Justice Lemuel Shaw. Child knew Morris well and presented him with a copy of Olaudah Equiano's narrative while he was clerking for Loring. See LMC to Robert Morris, 19 June 1864, *CC* 59/1567.

115   LMC to John Greenleaf Whittier and Henrietta Sargent, 22 Sept. 1861 and 3 Mar. 1865, *CC* 49/1337 and 61/1639. The "intelligent colored friend" mentioned in the letter to Sargent may be another person Child helped, but she was certainly involved in the abolitionist community's efforts on Morris's behalf.

116   Eric Foner, *Free Soil, Free Labor, Free Men: The Ideology of the Republican Party before the Civil War* (New York: Oxford UP, 1970) 25.

117   See Berlin et al., *Black Military Experience*, chaps. 6 and 8.

118   [Thomas Wentworth Higginson], "Negro Spirituals," *Atlantic Monthly* 19 (June 1867): 685–94; William Francis Allen, Charles Pickard Ware, and Lucy McKim Garrison, *Slave Songs of the United States* (New York: A. Simpson, 1867). For a superb discussion of those songs and their reception by nineteenth-century white audiences, see H. Bruce Franklin, *The Victim as Criminal and Artist: Literature from the American Prison* (New York: Oxford UP, 1978) 73–98.

119   See the *Narrative of the Life of Frederick Douglass, An American Slave. Written by Himself* (1845; New York: Doubleday, 1963), chap. 2; Frederick Douglass, *My Bondage and My Freedom* (1855; New York: Dover, 1969) 252–53, 278–79; *Narrative of William W. Brown, A Fugitive Slave. Written by Himself* (Boston: Anti-Slavery Office, 1847) 51–52; and [Charlotte L. Forten], "Life on the Sea Islands," *Atlantic Monthly* 13 (May/June 1864): 587–96, 666–76.

120   See Child's letter to Ellis Loring of 24 Feb. 1856, expressing her "towering indignation" at the legal necessity of having her will signed by David: "[I]f you had been by, you would have made the matter worse by repeating your old manly 'fling and twit' about married women being dead in the law. . . . I was indignant for womankind made chattels personal from the beginning of time, perpetually insulted by literature, law, and custom. The very phrases used with regard to us are abominable. 'Dead in the law,' 'Femme couverte.' How I detest such language!" (*SL* 279).

121   Three recent interpretations of *A Romance of the Republic* arrive at similar conclusions by different routes. See Dana D. Nelson, *The Word in Black and White: Reading "Race" in American Literature, 1638–1867* (New York: Oxford UP, 1992) 78–89; Shirley Samuels, "The Identity of Slavery," *The Culture of Sentiment: Race, Gender, and Sentimentality in Nineteenth-Century America*, ed. Shirley Samuels (New York: Oxford UP, 1992) 157–71; and Mark R. Patterson, "Redefining Motherhood: Surrogacy and Race in American Reconstruction," paper presented at the American Studies Association convention, Baltimore, fall 1991.

122   See Frances E. W. Harper, *Iola Leroy; or, Shadows Uplifted* (1892; Boston: Beacon P, 1987) chaps. 8, 13, and 25. Quotations on 233, 235.

123   C[harlotte] L. F[orten], "Waiting for the Verdict," *Standard* 22 Feb. 1868, p. 3.

124   Rebecca Harding Davis, *Waiting for the Verdict* (1867; Upper Saddle River, N.J.: Gregg P, 1968). Quotations from prefatory note and on 10, 295, and 310. In her review Forten points out these and other passages implying that "prejudice against color is instinctive in and natural to the whites." She also criticizes Davis's portrayal of Broderip as unrealistic: a man of Broderip's attainments "is not 'cowed' before a white skin, even if his own be black. Imagine Frederick Douglass (and he was a slave until manhood) cringing before a man because his skin is white!" Writing to Charlotte Forten to thank her for her "beautiful allusion to 'The Romance of The Republic,'" Child commented of Davis: "I have not read 'Waiting for the Verdict.' . . . [*A*]*ll* her writings excite more or less antagonism in my mind. In her views of things she seems to me to drift about, without any rudder or compass of moral principles. It is a pity, for she has a powerful intellect. I have thought several times that she was confused in her ideas as to which was the *right* side, the U.S. or the Rebellion; a thing not to be wondered at, considering she is a Virginian." See LMC to Charlotte Forten, 6 Mar. 1868, rpt. in Anna J[ulia] Cooper, ed., *The Life and Writings of the Grimké Family* (privately printed, 1951) 14–15; not included in *CC*. Child was probably referring particularly to Davis's stories "John Lamar" and "Blind Tom," *Atlantic Monthly* 9 (Apr. 1862): 411–23 and 10 (Nov. 1862): 580–85. For a similar reading of *Waiting for the Verdict*, which concludes that the novel offers "no hope for mulattoes," short of "avoiding the miscegenation which produces them," see James Kinney, *Amalgamation! Race, Sex, and Rhetoric in the Nineteenth-Century American Novel* (Westport, Conn.: Greenwood P, 1985) 106–9. For a reading that presents Davis as critiquing rather than endorsing her heroine's prejudice, see Sharon M. Harris, *Rebecca Harding Davis and American Realism* (Philadelphia: U of Pennsylvania P, 1991) 133–36. Judith R. Berzon, *Neither White Nor Black: The Mulatto Character in American Fiction* (New York: New York UP, 1978), also finds Broderip sympathetically treated (146–48, 195–96). The most nuanced and sensitive reading of *Verdict* to date is Donald Dingledine's introduction to the forthcoming NCUP edition.

125   Anna E. Dickinson, *What Answer?* (1868; Freeport, N.Y.: Books for Libraries P, 1972) 9–11, 174–75, 185, 237–38, 264–65, 297–98; LMC to the Editor of the *Independent*, *Independent* 8 Oct. 1868, *CC* 70/1856. Chief among the "merits" Child found in *What Answer?* was that Dickinson's "terribly graphic account" of the Draft Riots would deter voters in the upcoming election from supporting the Democratic candidate, Horatio Seymour, an "accomplice" of the mob. The anonymous review of *What Answer?* in the *Nation* by young Henry James provides yet another telling instance of the ideological forces (here masquerading as aesthetic principles) arrayed against Child's efforts to use fiction as a means of transforming her readers' political consciousness. See "Injurious Works and Injurious Criticism," *Nation* 29 Oct. 1868, pp. 346–47. James begins by deriding "Mrs. Stowe and Mrs. Lydia Maria Child" for having "praised [*What Answer?*] lavishly on the ground that, whatever it may be as a novel, it is, as 'a deed,' a noble deed and a brave one." I am grateful to Joan Hedrick for bringing this review to my attention and identifying its author as James.

126   *Toinette*, by Henry Churton (New York: J. B. Ford, 1874), chap. 50; Albion W. Tourgée, *A Royal Gentleman* (1881). Tourgée's squeamishness is all the more disconcerting in view of the extraordinary insights he displays in his powerful novels about Reconstruction, *A Fool's Errand* (1879) and *Bricks without Straw* (1880). For Child's reaction to *A Fool's Errand*, see chap. 21 below.

127   William Dean Howells, *An Imperative Duty* (1891; New York: Harper and Brothers, 1893) 25–26, 38, 44, 85, 87, 142, 148–49. Howells's title refers ostensibly to the duty Rhoda's guardian feels to disclose her racial identity, but it seems to have broader implications. Harper may well have intended *Iola Leroy* as an answer to Howells's misplaced condescension. Other critics have interpreted *An Imperative Duty* more charitably. Kinney, for example, argues that "Howells debunks the romantic emotionalism surrounding miscegenation" and "ridicules the stereotypic characters and situations found in" earlier novels on the subject (*Amalgamation* 137). Berzon claims that "Howells manages to transcend . . . formula . . . and produce a genuine satire which exposes the racist assumptions and ideology of the tragic mulatto novel" (*Neither White Nor Black* 114). Edwin H. Cady, *The Realist at War: The Mature*

Years, 1885–1920, of William Dean Howells (Syracuse, N.Y.: Syracuse UP, 1958), concedes that Howells "was devoted to ideas about race which now seem outmoded," but he argues that "Howells' views were not limited to those of Dr. Olney. Howells does not hope that the Negro will disappear into the general nation via miscegenation or any other route" (160, 162). See also Anne Ward Amacher, "The Genteel Primitivist and the Semi-Tragic Octoroon," *New England Quarterly* 29 (June 1956): 216–27; and Thomas W. Ford, "Howells and the American Negro," *Texas Studies in Literature and Language* 5 (Winter 1964): 530–37. Scenes in which characters react with physical revulsion to blacks after discovering their hidden ancestry abound in white-authored fiction, however, and are rare or nonexistent in black-authored fiction. For another example, see Sarah Barnwell Elliott, "The Heart of It," *The Signet Classic Book of Southern Stories*, ed. Dorothy Abbott and Susan Koppelman (New York: New American Library, 1991) 116–31.

128 LMC to Francis Shaw, 28 July 1867, *CC* 67/1789.

129 LMC to Eliza Scudder and Louisa Loring, 11 Aug. 1867 and 1 Jan. 1868, *CC* 67/1791, 68/1806. The views of Child's friends, quoted above, are all drawn from these two letters, since Child unfortunately did not preserve the originals.

130 LMC to Robert Purvis, 14 Aug. 1868, *SL* 482–83. Again, Child is quoting from Purvis's letter, which she did not preserve.

131 [Theodore Tilton], review of *A Romance of the Republic, Independent* 10 Oct. 1867, p. 2. In her letter thanking Tilton for "so complimentary" a review, Child nevertheless expressed some annoyance that he had confessed to preferring the "agreeable" Fitzgerald to the high-minded King, on whom he complained that "his broadcloth sits a trifle stiffly." Child replied that she had deliberately accentuated King's "Bostonian" primness and "conscientiousness" as a "contrast to the impulsive and slippery S. Carolinian." She added: "That you *prefer* the latter is a proof of your total depravity" (a joking reference to his Calvinistic belief in Original Sin). See LMC to Theodore Tilton, 27 Oct. 1867, *CC* 67/1797.

132 Thomas Wentworth Higginson, "Lydia Maria Child" (1868), in *Contemporaries*, vol. 2 of *The Writings of Thomas Wentworth Higginson* (Boston: Houghton Mifflin, 1900) 137–38.

133 Higginson had written to the Shaws and Louisa Loring to ask whether he might have access to Child's letters for the purposes of preparing his biographical sketch of her. Although Child liked and admired Higginson, she reacted with outrage to "[t]his mousing round after my private sentiments" and complained: "I don't think anybody has a *right* to make a biography of a person who does not *wish* to have it done." She later offered mollifyingly to leave her papers to him as a legacy (a pledge she did not keep). See LMC to Sarah Shaw and T. W. Higginson, 18 Feb. 1868, 21 Feb. 1871, *SL* 477, 499.

134 Review of *A Romance of the Republic, Standard* 10 Aug. 1867, p. 3. The novel also received a favorable review in the *Nation*, a moderate abolitionist journal. See "Two Books by Mrs. Child," *Nation* 15 Aug. 1867, pp. 127–28 (the second book was, appropriately, a new edition of *Fact and Fiction*). However, the reviewer judged that neither book was fit for young readers.

20   *A Radical Old Age*

1 LMC to Sarah Shaw, 7 Sept. 1866, *SL* 464. For similar statements, see LMC to Sarah Shaw, 18 May 1862, *CC* 52/1410; LMC to Parke Godwin, 13 Dec. 1864, *CC* 60/1605; and LMC to [Lucy Osgood?], 14 Aug. 1865, *CC* 63/1677, and 9 July 1869, *CC* 71/1902. This chapter has benefited from the helpful criticisms of Deborah Clifford and members of the 1993 Dartmouth Spring Institute on the U.S. and Its Others, especially Amy Kaplan, Donald Pease, Nancy Bentley, Shalom Goldman, and Keith Walker.

2 In addition to the many included in Meltzer and Holland's microfiche edition of Child's *Collected Correspondence*, I have found the following important articles on Reconstruction, Indian policy, woman suffrage, the annexation controversy, economic issues, and the Franco-Prussian War in the *Standard*, the *Independent*, the *Woman's Advocate*, and the *Woman's Journal*: "Indian Civilization," *Independent* 11

Feb. 1869, p. 1; "Hon. Geo. W. Julian vs. Land Monopoly," *Standard* 13 Mar. 1869, p. 2; "Home-steads," *Standard* 20 Mar. 1869, p. 2; "The Radicals," *Independent* 19 Aug. 1869, p. 1, rpt. in *Standard* 28 Aug. 1869, p. 1; "Women and the Freedmen," *Standard* 28 Aug. 1869, p. 2, rpt. in *Woman's Advocate* 1 (Oct. 1869): 190–92; "Concerning Women," *Independent* 21 Oct. 1869, p. 1, rpt. in *Standard* 30 Oct. 1869, p. 1; "Women and Minors," *Standard* 23 Oct. 1869, p. 2; "The Indians," *Standard* n.s. 1 (May 1870): 1–6; "Letter from Lydia Maria Child, 15 Dec. 1870, *Woman's Journal* 24 Dec. 1870, p. 405; "Dominica and Hayti," *National Standard* 28 Jan. 1871, pp. 4–5; "The Franco-Prussia War," *Independent* 9 Feb. 1871, p. 1; "Rejection of the Hon. Charles Sumner," *National Standard* 18 Mar. 1871, pp. 4–5; "Economy and Work," *National Standard* 5 Aug. 1871, pp. 4–5; "Two Significant Sculptures," *Woman's Journal* 9 Mar. 1872, p. 76; "Diamonds in the Dirt," *Woman's Journal* 30 Mar. 1872, p. 99; "A Glance at the State of Things," *Boston Journal* 16 July 1872, p. 3; "The Present Aspect of Political Affairs," *Woman's Journal* 10 Aug. 1872, p. 252; "Physical Strength of Women," *Woman's Journal* 15 Mar. 1873, p. 84; "A Mistake Corrected — Letter from Mrs. Child," *Woman's Journal* 22 Mar. 1873, p. 92; "Is Intellectuality the Bane of American Women?," *Woman's Journal* 19 July 1873, p. 228; "Samuel J. May," *Woman's Journal* 30 Aug. 1873, p. 276. This list does not include articles on miscellaneous nonpolitical subjects, nor does it include the letters and articles Patricia G. Holland has kindly made available to me from her file of those found since the microfilming of *CC*.

3   Child showed great sympathy for Irish immigrants in the 1840s; see, for example, her story "The Irish Heart," in *Fact and Fiction: A Collection of Stories* (New York: C. S. Francis, 1846) 77–90; also Letter 33 of *Letters from New York* (1843; Freeport, N.Y.: Books for Libraries P, 1970), in which she proclaimed: "I love the Irish. Blessings on their warm hearts, and their leaping fancies!" (243). Like many abolitionists, she turned against them only after Irish Americans embraced the Democratic party's implacable hostility to abolition and blacks. The increasing power they acquired as a voting bloc may also account for her change of attitude.

4   LMC to Lucy Osgood, 9 July 1869, *CC* 71/1902.

5   "Letter from L. Maria Child," *National Standard* 17 Sept. 1870, *CC* 74/1959a.

6   LMC to Harriet Sewall and Sarah Shaw, 27 Nov. and 12 Dec. 1871, *CC* 76/2017, 2018.

7   The *National Anti-Slavery Standard* ceased publication on 16 Apr. 1870, to be replaced on 30 Apr. 1870 by the monthly *Standard* (May–July 1870), subsequently retitled the *National Standard* and reissued as a weekly through Dec. 1871, then as a monthly throughout 1872, after which it merged with the *National Temperance Advocate*. Child's last article for the monthly *National Standard* dates from Aug. 1872. By then, however, she had shifted to such concerns as the "intermingling of religions," temperance, and the ill effects of tobacco smoking, in addition to woman suffrage (though she reserved articles on suffrage for the *Woman's Journal*). I will continue to refer to the *National Anti-Slavery Standard* simply as the *Standard*, but I will use the title *National Standard* in footnotes referring to the latter.

8   LMC to Samuel Sewall, 21 Mar. 1868, *SL* 478. See chaps. 18 and 19 above for more discussion of the factional dispute between Garrison's and Phillips's adherents; for a full-length study, see James M. McPherson, *The Struggle for Equality: Abolitionists and the Negro in the Civil War and Reconstruction* (Princeton, N.J.: Princeton UP, 1964) chap. 13.

9   LMC to Oliver Johnson, 22 Sept. 1868, Medford Public Library. I am grateful to Patricia Holland for making available to me the file of newly discovered Child letters that contains this one.

10   "Letter from Mr. and Mrs. D. L. and L. Maria Child," 1 Jan. 1868, *Standard* 15 Feb. 1868, p. 2, *CC* 68/1807. Child details her income in LMC to Sarah Shaw, 2 Feb. 1868, *SL* 475. On the lessons that abolitionists drew from the West Indian experience during Reconstruction, see Eric Foner, *Nothing But Freedom: Emancipation and Its Legacy* (Baton Rouge: Louisiana State UP, 1983).

11   McPherson, *Struggle for Equality* 382; William Gillette, *Retreat from Reconstruction, 1869–1879* (Baton Rouge: Louisiana State UP, 1979) 7–10.

12   McPherson, *Struggle for Equality* 383–84; "The President's Message," *Standard* 14 Dec. 1867, pp. 1–2.

13   LMC to Samuel E. Sewall, 21 Mar. 1868, *SL* 478; also LMC to Louisa Loring, 6 Mar. 1868, *CC* 68/1816.

14   "Letter from Mrs. Lydia Maria Child," *Standard* 28 Mar. 1868, p. 2, *CC* 68/1822.

15   See, for example, Gillette, *Retreat from Reconstruction* 11–12; and Hans L. Trefousse, *The Radical Republicans: Lincoln's Vanguard for Racial Justice* (New York: Knopf, 1969) chap. 11. For less negative interpretations of the impeachment attempt, see Eric Foner, *Reconstruction: America's Unfinished Revolution, 1863–1877* (New York: Harper and Row, 1988) 333–38; and McPherson, *Struggle for Equality* 384–85.

16   "Letter from L. Maria Child," [before 13 May 1868], *Standard* 23 May 1868, p. 1, *CC* 69/1831.

17   "Hon. Geo. W. Julian vs. Land Monopoly," *Standard* 13 Mar. 1869, p. 2; "Homesteads," *Standard* 20 Mar. 1869, p. 2; LMC to George W. Julian, 27 Mar. 1864, *SL* 439–40, quoted in chap. 18. "Homesteads" is especially effective, using as a vehicle the story of a freedman named Moses Fisher, who "after wearing out his muscles with incessant toil for three years, will not own one rood of the land he has cleared." See also "Letter from L. Maria Child," *National Standard* 8 Apr. 1871, pp. 4–5 *CC* 75/1989a, discussed at the end of this chapter.

18   "Letter from L. Maria Child," *Standard* 23 May 1868, p. 1, *CC* 69/1831.

19   LMC to Lucy Osgood, 4 and 28 Feb. 1869, *SL* 484, *CC* 70/1886; LMC to Theodore Tilton, 7 Mar. 1865, *CC* 61/1640.

20   "The Importance of One Vote," *Independent* 8 Oct. 1868, *CC* 70/1857; "A Word to Voters," *Standard* 26 Sept. 1868, p. 2, *CC* 69/1853.

21   LMC to Anna Loring and Sarah Shaw, 10 Nov. 1868 and [before 17 Jan. 1869], *CC* 70/1860, 1872.

22   "Letter from L. Maria Child," *Standard* 12 Dec. 1868, p. 2, *CC* 70/1862.

23   McPherson, *Struggle for Equality* 424–27; Theodore Tilton, "The New Architecture of Reconstruction," *Independent* 11 Feb. 1869, p. 4; Wendell Phillips, "Congress," *Standard* 20 Feb. 1869, p. 2. Phillips was instrumental in encouraging abolitionists and Radicals to settle for pragmatism; he astutely predicted that under Grant, whose tendency was toward moderation and reconciliation, Radicals would not succeed in mobilizing as much support for their programs as they had under Johnson, whose bitter hostility had polarized Congress and driven moderates into the Radical camp.

24   D. L. Child and L. Maria Child, "A Few Words about the Standard," *Standard* 25 Dec. 1869, *CC* 97/2562.

25   "Letter from D. L. and L. Maria Child," *Standard* 16 Apr. 1870, p. 1, *CC* 73/1942.

26   Note the continuities with *The First Settlers of New-England* (1829), where Child had argued that incorporating Indians into the American body politic would serve as a buffer against hordes of ignorant white immigrants (see chap. 4 above).

27   On the views of elitists like Charles Francis Adams and E. L. Godkin, see Richard Slotkin, *The Fatal Environment: The Myth of the Frontier in the Age of Industrialization, 1800–1890* (Middletown, Conn.: Wesleyan UP, 1985) 298–99; and Foner, *Reconstruction* 492–93. For a succinct expression of Godkin's views, see his article "Legislation and Social Science," *Journal of Social Science* 3 (1871): 115–32.

28   "Annual Meeting of the Massachusetts Anti-Slavery Society," *Standard* 5 Feb. 1870, pp. 1–2; C[harlotte] L. F[orten], "The Festival," *Standard* 12 Feb. 1870, p. 2.

29   LMC to Sarah Parsons, Eliza Scudder, and Lucy Osgood, 5, 6, and 14 Feb. 1870, *CC* 72/1924 and 1926, *SL* 489–90; Lucy Osgood to LMC, 9 Feb. 1870, *CC* 72/1927.

30   "Annual Meeting of the Massachusetts Anti-Slavery Society," *Standard* 5 Feb. 1870, pp. 1–2. Wendell Phillips and Aaron M. Powell, editor of the *Standard*, both stressed the importance of securing land to the freedpeople, as did the business committee's resolutions. On Osgood see n. 20 above.

31   LMC to Abby Kelley Foster 28 Mar. 1869 *SL* 485–86; also LMC to Harriet Winslow Sewall, 5 Dec. 1869, *CC* 72/1917; see also Child's articles "Hon. Geo. W. Julian vs. Land Monopoly," *Standard* 13 Mar. 1869, p. 2; and "Homesteads," *Standard* 20 Mar. 1869, p. 2. Abby and her husband Stephen Foster were members of the business committee that drafted the society's resolutions on land, which went even further than Child was prepared to by specifying that the freedpeople needed "pecuniary aid" to purchase land. See also Wendell Phillips's editorial, "The Negro's Claim," *Standard* 29 Jan. 1870, p. 2, which argues (against *Tribune* editor Horace Greeley's dictum that "Root, hog, or die" was

the best advice to give blacks): "The Nation *owes* [blacks] one-seventh of all the wealth we hold. Freedom is only an instalment of the debt we owe the Negro. Every Negro family can justly claim forty acres of land, one year's support, a furnished cottage, a mule and farm tools, and free schools for life."

32   On the reasons for the failure to achieve the goal of land redistribution, see Foner, *Reconstruction* 153–70.

33   LMC to Sarah Parsons and Eliza Scudder, 5 and 6 Feb. 1870, *SL* 488–89, *CC* 72/1924.

34   For different versions of this internecine conflict, see Elizabeth Cady Stanton et al., *History of Woman Suffrage* (New York: Fowler and Wells, 1882) 2: chaps. 17–19, 21; Ellen Carol DuBois, *Feminism and Suffrage: The Emergence of an Independent Women's Movement in America, 1848–1869* (Ithaca, N.Y.: Cornell UP, 1978); Elisabeth Griffith, *In Her Own Right: The Life of Elizabeth Cady Stanton* (New York: Oxford UP, 1984) chap. 8; and Andrea Moore Kerr, *Lucy Stone: Speaking Out for Equality* (New Brunswick, N.J.: Rutgers UP, 1992) chaps. 8–9. I am grateful to Kerr for making her manuscript available to me before its publication.

35   See LMC to Sarah Shaw and DLC, 3 Aug. and 27 Oct. 1856, *SL* 289–91, 294–96, and other letters cited in chap. 16 above; see also "The Kansas Emigrants."

36   DuBois, *Feminism and Suffrage* 60, 62; Stanton et al., *History of Woman Suffrage* 2: 96–97. Meltzer and Holland report that "[n]othing in Child's papers or the National Archives collection of such petitions either supports or refutes the claim," *SL* 467.

37   "Mrs. L. M. Child, in a letter to Mrs. E. C. Stanton, thus expresses her sentiments. . . ," *Independent* 6 Dec. 1866, *SL* 467–68.

38   "Woman and Suffrage," *Independent* 10 Jan. 1867, p. 1, and 17 Jan. 1867, p. 1, *CC* 66/1759–1760, *SL* 468–72. The article Child was refuting was by Tayler Lewis, "Household Suffrage," *Independent* 6 Dec. 1866, p. 1, and 20 Dec. 1866, p. 1. Lewis favored black suffrage, but not woman suffrage, which, he warned, would endanger the unity of the family and the authority of the husband and father.

39   Quoted in DuBois, *Feminism and Suffrage* 63; *History of Woman Suffrage* 2: 94n.

40   "Letter from Mrs. L. Maria Child" to Caroline Severance, 16 Oct. 1868, "The New England Woman's Rights Convention," *Standard* 5 Dec. 1868, p. 3. Interestingly, the version of this letter reprinted in the Jan. 1869 *Woman's Advocate* deleted the references to black suffrage (1: 58–59). Child's letter was also quoted by Theodore Tilton in his Editorial Notes, *Independent* 3 Dec. 1868, p. 4.

41   Kerr, *Lucy Stone*, 127–29, 131 (my quotations are taken partially from the original manuscript; the published version omits a description of Train's clothing). For accounts of the Train alliance from Stanton's and Anthony's point of view, see DuBois, *Feminism and Suffrage* chap. 3, and Griffith, *In Her Own Right* chap. 8.

42   LMC to Samuel Sewall and Sarah Shaw, 21 Mar. 1868, *SL* 478; [Sept.? 1869], *CC* 72/1909.

43   LMC to Samuel Sewall, 21 Mar. 1868, *SL* 478; "Women and the Freedmen," *Standard* 28 Aug., 1869, p. 2; rpt. in *Woman's Advocate* 1 (Oct. 1869): 190–92. For a similar viewpoint, see the response of Abby Kelley Foster to Lucy Stone, quoted in Dorothy Sterling's splendid biography *Ahead of Her Time: Abby Kelley and the Politics of Antislavery* (New York: Norton, 1991) 347. Stone eventually abandoned her own opposition to a Fifteenth Amendment that did not include women. For corroboration of Child's assertions regarding the "sneering" racist tone of Stanton's attacks on the Fifteenth Amendment, her opportunistic appeal to southern white women, and her characterization of the freedmen as antifeminist, see Stanton et al., *History of Woman Suffrage* 2: 316, 318, 333–35, 353–55.

44   LMC to Sarah Shaw, [Sept.? 1869], *SL* 486–87.

45   "Concerning Women," *Independent* 15 July 1869, p. 1, *CC* 71/1903, and 21 Oct. 1869, p. 1 (not in *CC*). The latter is the lead article.

46   "Concerning Women," *Independent* 15 July 1869, p. 1, *CC* 71/1903.

47   "Concerning Women," *Independent* 21 Oct. 1869, p. 1. See also "Physical Strength of Women," *Woman's Journal* 15 Mar. 1873, p. 84, in which Child develops this theme in greater detail.

48   "Concerning Women," *Independent* 21 Oct. 1869, p. 1 (not in *CC*).

49   LMC to Charles Sumner, 4 July 1870, *SL* 495. Child expressed herself even more strongly in a letter of

9 July 1872, Sumner Papers, Houghton Library, bMS Am 1 (not in *CC*): "If I were to give free vent to all my pent-up wrath concerning the subordination of women, I might frighten *you*. . . . Either the theory of our government is *false*, or women have a right to vote."

50   LMC to Lucy Stone, 11 Nov. 1870, published in *Cleveland Daily Leader* 24 Nov. 1870, p. 1, under "Woman Suffrage, Second Day's Proceedings," not in *CC*, courtesy of Patricia Holland.

51   LMC to Francis Shaw, 2 Aug. 1846, *SL* 229; LMC to Louisa Loring, 15 Jan. 1847, *SL* 235.

52   For evidence that other feminists did not view the issue of interracial marriage as less controversial than divorce, see Anthony's caution to Stanton against publicly approving of Frederick Douglass's marriage to a white woman: "I do hope you won't put your foot into the question of intermarriage of the races. You know very well that if you plunge in . . . your endorsement will be charged upon me and the whole association." Quoted in Griffith, *In Her Own Right* 184.

53   On the two suffragists' marriages, see Griffith, *In Her Own Right* chap. 6, and Kerr, *Lucy Stone* chaps. 9–10.

54   "Letter from Lydia Maria Child," 15 Dec. 1870, *Woman's Journal* 24 Dec. 1870, p. 405 (not in *CC*).

55   "Concerning Woman Suffrage," *Woman's Journal* 1 July 1871, p. 204 (not in *CC*); Mary Livermore to LMC, 1 Aug. 1871, *CC* 76/2007. Child was replying to Joseph P. Thompson, "Lessons from the Fate of Paris," *Independent* 8 June 1871, p. 1. As its title indicates, Thompson's article was aimed primarily at drawing lessons from the Paris Commune; in fact, his analysis of the Franco-Prussian War was very similar to Child's, except that one of the lessons he drew from the French troubles was that government would be further degraded, rather than purified, by the conferral of political power on women. Besides praising Child's refutation of Thompson, Livermore asked Child to "furnish four articles" she could use as editorials for four successive weeks beginning 12 Aug. Child apparently tried to comply — she furnished two.

56   Here, Child was simultaneously replying to the author of the *Liberal Christian* article and to Clarke, whose theories the former was invoking. Child does not seem to have undertaken a direct refutation of Clarke, though she praised Elizabeth Stuart Phelps for cutting him up "with a sharp knife" in an article in the *Independent*. "With regard to Dr. Clarke, I do not believe his theory," she wrote to her niece. She added in language echoing her reply to the *Liberal Christian* polemicist: "Doubtless, women who are so much engrossed with study as to neglect physical exercise, will lose their health; and so will men. I have known many more cases of young men who have injured their health in that way, than I have of young women." See LMC to Sarah Parsons, 31 Jan. 1874, *CC* 81/2132. On Clarke, see Kerr, *Lucy Stone* 181.

57   "Is Intellectuality the Bane of American Women?," *Woman's Journal* 19 July 1873, p. 228 (not in *CC*).

58   Quoted in Kerr, *Lucy Stone* 168–69.

59   On the long-term impact of Victoria Woodhull and the Beecher-Tilton scandal, see Kerr, *Lucy Stone* 175–77, 188–89; Griffith, *In Her Own Right* 147–53, 156–58; and Nancy Woloch, *Women and the American Experience* (New York: Knopf, 1984) chap. 13. For a fascinating inside view of the scandal from the different perspectives of Harriet Beecher Stowe and Isabella Beecher Hooker, see Jeanne Boydston, Mary Kelley, and Anne Margolis, eds., *The Limits of Sisterhood: The Beecher Sisters on Women's Rights and Woman's Sphere* (Chapel Hill: U of North Carolina P, 1988). The scandal dragged on until 1875, when a hung jury in effect exonerated Beecher. Child eventually became convinced of Beecher's innocence, though she found his behavior "very deficient in *common* sense." She especially deprecated the effect of the scandal on "public morals." See LMC to Sarah Shaw, Sarah Parsons, and Sarah and Francis Shaw, 7 Aug. 1874, *SL* 525–26; 3 Sept. 1874, *CC* 83/2174; and 11 and 18 Apr. 1875, *CC* 85/2227, 2229.

60   LMC to Lucy Osgood and Anna Loring Dresel, 12 Feb. and 1 Mar. 1872, *SL* 504, *CC* 78/2041.

61   LMC to Harriet Sewall, 27 Nov. 1871, *CC* 76/2017.

62   LMC to Sarah Shaw, 12 Dec. 1871, *CC* 76/2018; also LMC to Harriet Sewall, 27 Nov. 1871, *CC* 76/2017.

63   "A Soul's Victory over Circumstances," *Woman's Journal* 16 Sept. 1871, pp. 294–95.

64   See David A. Nichols, *Lincoln and the Indians: Civil War Policy and Politics* (Columbia: U of Missouri P, 1978), esp. chaps. 3–7, 9, and 12.

65   See the discussion of "The Kansas Emigrants" in chap. 16 above.

66   LMC to John Greenleaf Whittier, 2 Jan. 1857 and [May ? 1865], *SL* 301, *CC* 62/1666. Child also tried to persuade Wendell Phillips to do a lecture on Osceola: 5 July 1868, *CC* 96/2561.

67   On Beeson's Indian advocacy work, see Robert Winston Mardock, *The Reformers and the American Indian* (Columbia: U of Missouri P, 1971). According to Mardock, "Beeson's pre-Civil War crusade reached its climax on October 9, 1859, at a public meeting in Boston's Faneuil Hall," at which Wendell Phillips likewise spoke (11). The *Liberator* of 8 Mar. 1861, p. 40, also reports that Beeson presided over a "Convention for the Indians" on 26 Feb. 1861 (not mentioned by Mardock). Child refers in her "Appeal for the Indians" to hearing Beeson's "public testimony concerning the outrages committed within his own knowledge" (in Carolyn L. Karcher, ed. *HOBOMOK and Other Writings on Indians* [New Brunswick, N.J.: Rutgers UP, 1986] 224). She also reports a conversation with Beeson in "The Indians," *Standard* n.s. 1 (May 1870): 4. Whether Child attended the 1859 or the 1861 meeting or both is not clear, but by mid-October 1859 she would have been too preoccupied by John Brown to turn her attention to the Indian question. The composition of "Willie Wharton" in early 1861 suggests that it may have been inspired by the Feb. 1861 convention, or possibly by a personal encounter with Beeson during his visit to Boston at that time. Child was unusually active in attending meetings during the winter of 1860–61, when she was staying in Medford with Lucy Osgood. Although "Willie Wharton" was not published until 1863, Child reports having submitted a story titled "Willie and Wikanee" to the *Knickerbocker*, which she expected to appear in the Mar. or Apr. 1861 number, and which she asked to have returned to her when it did not. See LMC to Oliver Johnson, 3 Jun. 1861, *CC* 48/1310. She resubmitted the story, now titled "Willie Wharton," to James T. Fields, publisher of the *Atlantic*, by Feb. 1862 and added an introductory paragraph at his request. See LMC to James T. Fields, 26 Feb. 1862, *CC* 51/1391.

68   On the composition of *A Romance of the Republic*, see LMC to Francis Shaw, 28 July 1867, *CC* 67/1789, cited and discussed in chap. 19 above.

69   "Willie Wharton," *Atlantic Monthly* 11 (March 1863): 324–45. Quotation on 335. Further page references to the story are given parenthetically in the text.

70   Child airs her theories about clairvoyance in many works, among them *Philothea*; *Letters from New York. Second Series*, Letters 4, 22; "The Ancient Clairvoyant" and "Spirit and Matter" in *Autumnal Leaves* 269–301; and *The Progress of Religious Ideas*. She submitted another article about clairvoyant phenomena to the *Atlantic* at the same time as "Willie Wharton." See LMC to James T. Fields, 26 Feb. 1862, *CC* 51/1391, and "Spirits," *Atlantic Monthly* 9 (May 1862): 578–84. See also her article "Things Unaccountable," *Independent* 25 Mar. 1869, *CC* 71/1891. Child's leaning toward mysticism gave her an intuitive sympathy for the visionary aspect of American Indian culture. For an American Indian analogue to the simultaneous visions of Jenny Wharton and her son, see *Black Elk Speaks: Being the Life Story of a Holy Man of the Oglala Sioux, as Told Through John G. Neihardt (Flaming Rainbow)* (1932; Lincoln, U of Nebraska P, 1988) 226–29.

71   Child's views on assimilation and intermarriage should be compared with those of the writers cited by Brian W. Dippie, *The Vanishing American: White Attitudes and U.S. Indian Policy* (Middletown, Conn.: Wesleyan UP, 1982) chap. 15. According to Dippie, a few writers of the late nineteenth century maintained that " 'the harmonious blending of the two races' was 'the great solution of the Indian question,' " and this opinion became quite "widely accepted" at the turn of the century (248). Dippie points out, however, that "red-white amalgamation was being proposed in a context of racial segregation in the South, imperialism abroad, and nativism at home" and that it was never extended to other racial groups; nor was it ever "generally condoned," even in the case of Indians: "Acceptance was almost always conditional on circumstances and the pairings involved" (250, 257).

72   For a description of the "bloomer costume" and a brief account of mid-nineteenth-century dress reform efforts, see Griffith, *In Her Own Right* 71–72. A very similar costume, minus the belt, is still worn today in Turkey, Pakistan, and India. The only American Indian features of A-lee-lah's costume are the gaiters.

73   " 'Friends' among the Indians. Letter from Mary B. Lightfoot," *Standard* 4 Sept. 1869, p. 1. The turn-of-the-century Sioux writer Zitkala-Sa describes the traumatic effects of such forced "civilization" in "The School Days of an Indian Girl," *Atlantic Monthly* 85 (Feb. 1900): 185–94, rpt. in her *American Indian Stories* (1921; Lincoln: U of Nebraska P, 1985) 47–80. For a splendid analysis and critique of this forced schooling in "civilization," see Laura Wexler, "Tender Violence: Literary Eavesdropping, Domestic Fiction, and Educational Reform," *The Culture of Sentiment: Race, Gender, and Sentimentality in Nineteenth-Century America*, ed. Shirley Samuels (New York: Oxford UP, 1992) 9–38.

74   Karcher, ed., *HOBOMOK and Other Writings on Indians* 137.

75   "A Plea for the Indian," *Standard* 11 Apr. 1868, p. 3, and 18 Apr. 1868, pp. 2–3, rpt. as a pamphlet retitled *An Appeal for the Indians* (New York: William P. Tomlinson, 1868). Page references are to Karcher, ed., *HOBOMOK and Other Writings on Indians* 216–32.

76   A thorough canvassing of the *Standard* reveals no articles on the Indian question before Child's 11 Apr. "Plea." Instead, the impeachment question dominated the paper. The next article after Child's is an exchange of "Correspondence on the Enslavement of the Indians" between John Beeson and George M. Hanson, *Standard* 27 June 1868, p. 3. On 18 July 1868 a communication "From the West," signed L.B.C., quotes some corroborating statements about Indian honesty, which "might be worthy to place beside some of Mrs. Child's testimonies regarding the Indians" (*Standard*, p. 3). Thereafter, articles begin to appear at regular intervals, though they do not become numerous until the following year. In *Reformers and the American Indian* Mardock indirectly confirms Child's role in initating the new abolitionist crusade by beginning his discussion of it with her 1865 letter to Whittier and citing her "Appeal for the Indians" as the earliest response to the peace commission's report (15, 31–32).

77   Mardock, *Reformers and the American Indian* 25, 30–32; U.S. Cong., House of Representatives, *Annual Report of the Commissioner on Indian Affairs*, 40th Cong., 3rd Sess.; 1868, "Report to the President by the Indian Peace Commission, January 7, 1868," House Executive Document 1: 486–510, hereinafter cited as *Annual Report* (1868).

78   *Annual Report* (1868): 504. This passage is not quoted in Child's "Appeal." Page numbers given in the text refer to Child's quotations from the report in her "Appeal," marked by double quotation marks.

79   Child also devoted another article to this theme: "Indian Civilization," *Independent* 11 Feb. 1869, p. 1. In that article she cited as evidence of the Indian's capacity for civilization the progress made by Indian students at the Quaker-run Asylum at Cattaraugus for Orphan and Destitute Indian Children, as well as the specimens of Indian achievement at an Iroquois agricultural exhibition.

80   See the western newspapers quoted by Mardock, *Reformers and the American Indian* 22, 94–100, 144–45. See also A. J. Grover, "The Indians. A Plea for the Sheridan Policy," *Standard* 19 Mar. 1870, p. 1 (Grover was a consistent critic of the "sentimental" policy advocated by the *Standard*).

81   According to Mardock, in June 1869 Wendell Phillips "demanded that the government abandon the railroad and give the Great Plains back to the Indians" (62), but there is no evidence that Phillips seriously pursued this demand. Nor does Phillips explicitly exhort the U.S. government to give the Great Plains back to the Indians in any of the newspaper articles Mardock cites as sources. In his editorial "The Pacific Railroad" (*Standard* 12 June 1869, p. 2), Phillips urges the Indians to continue disrupting railroad traffic until their rights are respected: "We would tell [every Indian chief], lay down your gun, but allow no rail to lie between Omaha and the mountains. . . . The Pacific Railway is the Indians [*sic*] Alabama. Every blow struck on those rails is heard round the globe. Haunt that road with such dangers that none will dare use it." Phillips goes on to say that Indians should continue to use their "right to make war . . . and never yield it till 'Citizenship' means more than it does now." In 1864 John Beeson also offered a "radical citizenship proposal" suggesting the "formation of four Indian states to be governed by laws made and administered by their own authority . . . to be subject to the United States only as 'dependent friendly allies' [and] . . . to be represented in Congress by delegates of their own choice." He abandoned this plan by the mid-1870s, however, replacing it "with the more realistic one of citizenship for the Indians" (Mardock 57). These are the only proposals I have encountered that go further than Child's.

82 Marx and Engels are no exceptions. Although Marxist theory recognizes the virtues of "primitive communism," it still posits the necessity of historical evolution toward higher stages of socioeconomic development. See, for example, Frederick Engels, *The Origin of the Family, Private Property and the State*, ed. Eleanor Burke Leacock (1884; New York: International Publishers, 1972). Edward Said has similarly pointed out the extent to which Marx shared the Orientalist assumptions of his day: "In article after article [Marx] returned with increasing conviction to the idea that even in destroying Asia, Britain was making possible there a real social revolution"; see *Orientalism* (New York: Vintage, 1979) 153–55. For a broader context in which to place Child's evolutionary assumptions about the relationship between Indian cultures and "civilization," see Robert F. Berkhofer, Jr., *The White Man's Indian: Images of the American Indian from Columbus to the Present* (1978; New York: Vintage, 1979) 49–55. Throughout the book Berkhofer argues that the assumption of Indian deficiency and European cultural superiority has persisted from Columbus to the present, creating more similarities than differences among "friends" and "enemies" of the Indian.

83 Wendell Phillips to LMC, 24 Apr. 1868, *CC* 68/1826. On Whipple's activities in Minnesota, where he had tried to prevent the 1862 Sioux war, see Mardock, *Reformers and the American Indian* 9–14.

84 LMC to Gerrit Smith, 18 Feb. 1869, *CC* 70/1885.

85 Sarah Van Vechten Brown to LMC, 2 Mar. 1869, *CC* 71/1887. Another portion of this long and moving tribute to Child has been quoted in chap. 7 above.

86 LMC to Charles Sumner and Harriet Sewall, 8 and 10 May 1868, *SL* 479–80, *CC* 69/1829.

87 Mardock, *Reformers and the American Indian* 21–22, 26.

88 *Annual Report* (1868): 489.

89 Mardock, *Reformers and the American Indian* 37–38, 62, 147; "Sheridan and the Indians," *New York Evening Post*, rpt. in *Standard* 19 Mar. 1870, p. 1.

90 Sheridan's report to Sherman, as quoted in A. J. Grover, "The Indians. A Plea for the Sheridan Policy," *Standard* 19 Mar. 1870, p. 1. For a brilliant analysis of this incident and of the rape charges "Sheridan deploys as his most powerful argument against the supporters of the Peace Policy," see Slotkin, *Fatal Environment* 391–92, 398–404.

91 Mardock, *Reformers and the American Indian* 67; "The Indian Massacre. Sheridan's Reports, and a Letter from Mr. Colyer," *Standard* 19 Mar. 1870, p. 1.

92 "The Indians," *Standard* n.s. 1 (May 1870): 2. Subsequent page references to this article are given parenthetically in the text.

93 Slotkin, *Fatal Environment* 401–2; see also Dee Brown, *Bury My Heart at Wounded Knee: An Indian History of the American West* (New York: Holt, 1970) 87–92. Brown portrays Black Kettle as doing all in his power to maintain peaceful relations with whites and as being the victim, rather than the perpetrator, of atrocities such as those with which Sheridan charged Black Kettle's band.

94 LMC to Charles Sumner, 4 July 1870, *SL* 496–97.

95 See also Child's *First Settlers of New-England* 168–69, quoted in chap. 3 above.

96 Linda K. Kerber also makes this point in her splendid article, "The Abolitionist Perception of the Indian," *Journal of American History* 62 (Sept. 1975): 271–95, esp. 288–89.

97 "Letter from L. Maria Child," *National Standard* 27 May 1871, p. 4, *CC* 75/1995a.

98 Quoted in Dippie, *Vanishing American* 144.

99 Dippie, *Vanishing American* 174–75, 189–96; Berkhofer, *White Man's Indian* 166–75.

100 See, for example, Zitkala-Sa's "The School Days of an Indian Girl," cited in n. 73 above; also Luther Standing Bear, *Land of the Spotted Eagle* chap. 9, rpt. in *The Portable North American Indian Reader*, ed. Frederick W. Turner III (New York: Penguin, 1974) 567–77. For a historical overview of post-Civil War Indian educational programs and of the erosion of Indian land holdings under the allotment in severalty policy, see Dippie, *Vanishing American* 113–21, 273–81.

101 Mardock, *Reformers and the American Indian* 115–28. Four Modoc chiefs including "Captain Jack" (Kintpuash) were ultimately executed.

102 LMC to Sarah Shaw, 22 June and [July?] 1873, *SL* 514–17.

103 Since so many new articles by Child have turned up, it is not inconceivable that one on the Modoc case may yet be found. I have checked the *Independent* from Apr. through Aug. 1873 and found nothing by Child (except an obituary for Lucy Osgood), though there were several sympathetic articles by others about the Modocs. Child seems to have stopped publishing regularly in the *Independent* after 1869. I found only two articles in Feb. and Mar. 1870, both about kindness to animals, and one article on the Franco-Prussian War in Feb. 1871 (see n. 2 above). I checked systematically from Jan. through June 1871 and from June through early Nov. 1872 without turning up anything at all by Child. After Theodore Tilton was forced to resign from the editorship of the *Independent* in Dec. 1870, it reverted to its original character as an evangelical weekly. Although Garrison continued to write for the *Independent*, Child, who had objected strenuously to contributing to the *Independent* when it was under evangelical domination, may have felt that it no longer provided a hospitable vehicle for her (see LMC to Sydney Howard Gay, 21 Dec. 1859, *SL* 335). I also checked the *Boston Journal* for all of June 1873 without turning up any articles by Child on the Modocs.

104 LMC to Sarah Shaw, 22 June 1873, *SL* 515.

105 D. L. Child and L. Maria Child, "A Few Words about the Standard," *Standard* 25 Dec. 1869, *CC* 97/2562.

106 Foner, *Reconstruction* 412–14, 422–23, 425–30.

107 "Letter from L. Maria Child," *National Standard* 8 Apr. 1871, pp. 4–5, *CC* 75/1989a. The attack on the Crafts' industrial school is mentioned in a note by Meltzer and Holland, *SL* 490. At the time the Crafts established the school, Child wrote to Lucy Osgood: "I think they will do a great and good work, provided the devilish Ku Klux Klan does not murder them" (14 Feb. 1870, *SL* 490.) The Crafts rebuilt the institution and ran it until 1878, when they sold the land in small tracts to the freedpeople.

108 Foner, *Reconstruction* chaps. 9–10. Quotations on 488, 492–93. See also Slotkin, *Fatal Environment* 298–99, 310–11.

109 "Letter from L. Maria Child," *National Standard* 8 Apr. 1871, *CC* 75/1989a; Foner, *Reconstruction* 454–55; Gillette, *Retreat from Reconstruction* 26.

110 Foner, *Reconstruction* 494.

111 "Dominica and Hayti," *National Standard* 28 Jan. 1871, pp. 4–5 (not in *CC*) and "Annexation of Dominica," *National Standard* 4 Mar. 1871, *CC* 75/1985a. Quotations in the following paragraphs are drawn from these two articles.

112 LMC to George William Curtis, 22 July 1872, *CC* 78/2056.

113 Foner, *Reconstruction* 496.

114 Foner, *Reconstruction* 495–96; "Letter from L. Maria Child," *National Standard* 8 Apr. 1871, *CC* 75/1989a.

115 LMC to Charles Sumner, 8 May 1868, *SL* 480.

116 Quoted in Foner, *Reconstruction* 503.

117 LMC to Sarah Shaw and Sarah Parsons, 23 June, 13 July and 26 Sept. 1872, *CC* 78/2051, *SL* 508, *CC* 79/2064. See also LMC to Charles Sumner, 21 June 1872, Sumner Papers, Houghton Library, bMS Am 1. I am grateful to Jennie Rathbun and the reference librarians at the Houghton for locating these letters, inexplicably omitted from *CC*, and mailing me copies of them. My search for the missing letters, to which Child refers in her correspondence with other friends, was initiated by a quotation from one of these letters in Foner, *Reconstruction* 507.

118 Foner, *Reconstruction* 500, 506–7.

119 Foner, *Reconstruction* 506–7.

120 LMC to Eliza Scudder, 5 Aug. 1872, *CC* 78/2058. See also LMC to George Julian, 31 Jan. 1872, *CC* 77/2034. To Sumner, Child writes: "If you are persuaded to [endorse Greeley], I believe you will regret it the longest day you have to live; for the consequences will be the undoing of all your life's great work" (9 July 1872, Sumner Papers, Houghton Library bMS Am 1; not in *CC*).

121 LMC to Sarah Shaw, 13 July 1872, *SL* 507–8. See also LMC to Charles Sumner, 28 June 1872, Sumner

Papers, Houghton Library, bMS Am 1 (not in *CC*): "There is no mistaking the fact that Greely [*sic*] manifests [an?] unprincipled readiness to make *any* concessions to Rebels and Democrats, for the sake of obtaining their votes."

122   LMC to Sarah Shaw and Eliza Scudder, 13 and 24 July and 5 Aug. 1872, *SL* 507–8, *CC* 78/2057, 2058; LMC to Charles Sumner, 9 and 24 July 1872, Sumner Papers, Houghton Library, bMS Am 1 (not in *CC*). In her letters to friends, Child reports what she has said to Sumner, often repeating the same sentences or phrases verbatim.

123   LMC to Eliza Scudder and Sarah Shaw, 5 Aug. 1872 and [after 11 Mar.] 1874, *CC* 78/2058, *SL* 519–20. Only four of the six letters Child claimed to have written to Sumner have survived in the Sumner papers; none of Sumner's six replies is extant. Child lovingly preserved all of Sumner's earlier letters to her, but she seems to have destroyed these.

124   "A Glance at the State of Things," *Boston Journal* 16 July 1872, p. 3. This article reiterates all the points made in Child's letters to friends.

125   LMC to George William Curtis, 22 July 1872, *CC* 78/2056.

126   "Address of the Republican Women of Massachusetts, to the Women of America," *Woman's Journal* 28 Sept. 1872, p. 308. This "friendly, but vague and . . . noncommittal" gesture toward the American Woman Suffrage Association was so minimal that "some suffragists called it a 'splinter' rather than a plank" of the party's platform. See DuBois, *Feminism and Suffrage* 199.

127   "The Present Aspect of Political Affairs," *Woman's Journal* 10 Aug. 1872, p. 252; Child also heads a list of forty notable women who supported Grant, in contrast to four who supported Greeley. See "A Contrast," *Woman's Journal* 2 Nov. 1872, p. 349. A comparison of Child's rhetoric and arguments in her electioneering articles for the *Boston Journal* and the *Woman's Journal* once again reveals her fine-tuned sense of audience. The *Boston Journal* article says nothing about a debt of gratitude toward blacks but concentrates on the sectional arguments that had helped mobilize northerners unsympathetic to blacks to go to war against the South.

128   Gillette, *Retreat from Reconstruction* 69; Foner, *Reconstruction* 510.

129   LMC to Lydia Bigelow Child and Sarah Parsons, 13 Nov. and 1 Dec. 1872, *CC* 79/2070, 2071.

130   LMC to Sarah Shaw and Sarah Parsons, 17 and 24 Mar. 1873, *CC* 80/2096, 2098–99, *SL* 512–13; compare Foner, *Reconstruction* 468, 484–88, 510.

131   LMC to Sarah Shaw, 24 Mar. 1873, *SL* 512–13, *CC* 80/2099.

132   See Eric Foner, *Free Soil, Free Labor, Free Men: The Ideology of the Republican Party before the Civil War* (New York: Oxford UP, 1970), esp. chap. 1. Quotations on 11 and 29.

133   See, for example, *The Patriarchal Institution. . .*, discussed in chap. 17 above, and "Through the Red Sea into the Wilderness," *Independent* 21 Dec. 1865, discussed in chap. 19 above. For a contemporary corroboration of Child's claim, see Thomas Wentworth Higginson, *Cheerful Yesterdays* (1898; New York: Arno P, 1968) 114–15. For more recent historical studies substantiating it, see David Montgomery, *Beyond Equality: Labor and the Radical Republicans, 1862–1872* (1967; Urbana: U of Illinois P, 1981) 118; and Edward Magdol, *The Antislavery Rank and File: A Social Profile of the Abolitionists' Constituency* (Westport, Conn.: Greenwood P, 1986).

134   Montgomery, *Beyond Equality* 25–44, 119.

135   LMC to Ellis Loring, 22 Jan. 1857, *CC* 35/983.

136   LMC to Harriet Sewall, 19 June 1871, *CC* 75/1998, and 3 Jan. 1873, *SL* 510–11.

137   "Letter from L. Maria Child, *National Standard* 27 May 1871, p. 4, *CC* 75/1995a; LMC to Lucy Osgood, 13 Apr. 1870, *CC* 73/1939.

138   For a detailed account of the eight-hour movement, see Montgomery, *Beyond Equality* chaps. 5–8.

139   LMC to Charles Sumner and George Julian, 4 July 1870, *CC* 73/1951, 12 July 1871, *SL* 500–501. On Sumner's and Julian's support for the eight-hour movement, see Montgomery, *Beyond Equality* 240–41, 313, 318. Julian pioneered eight-hour legislation in Congress, but Sumner did not convert to the cause until 1872.

140   Montgomery, *Beyond Equality* 273, 275–76.

141 "Letter from L. Maria Child," *National Standard* 17 Sept. 1870, p. 5, *CC* 74/1959a. On free-labor ideology, see Montgomery, *Beyond Equality* 14; also Foner, *Free Soil, Free Labor* 18–23.

142 See the discussion of early bourgeois ideology in chap. 3 above on the *Juvenile Miscellany*.

143 "Letter from L. Maria Child," *National Standard* 17 Sept. 1870, p. 5, *CC* 74/1959a.

144 Quoted in Montgomery, *Beyond Equality* 15; see also Foner, *Free Soil, Free Labor* 12, 16, 23, 29–30.

145 "Economy and Work," *National Standard* 5 Aug. 1871, pp. 4–5 (not in *CC*).

146 See Slotkin, *Fatal Environment* chaps. 13–15, 19. Quotation from "Economy and Work."

147 LMC to George Julian, 12 July 1871, *SL* 500; "Letter from L. Maria Child," *National Standard* 17 Sept. 1870, p. 5, *CC* 74/1959a; Montgomery, *Beyond Equality* 313. George William Curtis similarly argued in *Harper's Weekly* that "[n]o law of a Legislature can outwit the law of nature and society," i.e., the law of supply and demand (11 [25 May 1867]: 323; quoted in Montgomery, 304).

148 "Letter from L. Maria Child," *National Standard* 17 Sept. 1870, *CC* 74/1959a. Compare the report of the 1865 Griffin Committee on the hours of labor, which "condemned any state action designed to interfere in 'the bargain between [the worker] and the capitalist, and give him a larger share of the value that is or may be produced, than the capitalist is willing to agree to' as 'subverting the right of individual property, and establishing communism'" (Montgomery, *Beyond Equality* 267).

149 "Letter from L. Maria Child," *National Standard* 31 Dec. 1870, p. 4, *CC* 74/1966a, and 27 May 1871, p. 4, *CC* 75/1995a.

150 "Letter from L. Maria Child," *National Standard* 1 July 1871, p. 4, *CC* 76/2000a.

151 "Letter from L. Maria Child," *National Standard* 17 Sept. 1870, p. 5, *CC* 74/1959a.

152 "Letter from L. Maria Child, *National Standard* 1 July 1871, p. 4, *CC* 76/2000a.

153 LMC to Lucy Osgood, 4 Feb. 1869, *SL* 484.

154 "Economy and Work," *National Standard* 5 Aug. 1871, pp. 4–5 (not in *CC*). On Whig-Republican doctrine, see Foner, *Free Soil, Free Labor* 20.

155 "Letter from L. Maria Child," *National Standard* 27 May 1871, p. 4, *CC* 75/1995a.

156 Foner, *Free Soil, Free Labor* 20; "Letter from L. Maria Child," *National Standard* 31 Dec. 1870, p. 4, and 1 July 1871, p. 4, *CC* 74/1966a, 76/2000a. The particular model of a cooperative business Child had in mind was the dry-goods store of the abolitionist Charles Hovey, who willed the proceeds of his business to abolition, women's rights, and other progressive causes. Similar cooperative enterprises were currently being tried in England, France, and Germany. Economic "partnerships" or "profit-sharing" relationships between employers and workers were the form of "cooperation" favored by some Liberals, notably E. L. Godkin. See Godkin's articles, "The Labor Crisis," *North American Review* 105 (July 1867): 177–213; and "Co-operation," *North American Review* 106 (Jan. 1868): 150–75. As Montgomery shows, however, "Sentimental" labor reformers and working-class labor leaders were also attracted to "cooperative" and "profit-sharing" schemes, and "no clear line of distinction was drawn" between these approaches to solving the conflict between capital and labor. Liberals, "Sentimentalists," and labor reformers, he argues, were all "committed to the illusion of harmonious society." See *Beyond Equality* 383–84, 437–46. Montgomery's analysis of the differences between Liberals and "Sentimentalists" tends to confirm that Child's antielitist beliefs and class origins aligned her much more closely with the "Sentimentalists"; see esp. *Beyond Equality* 410–14.

157 LMC to Anna Loring Dresel, 25 Jan. 1871, *SL* 498–99, and 5 Apr. 1872, *CC* 78/2044. Child also wrote three articles championing Prussia: "Letter from L. Maria Child," *National Standard* 10 Sept. 1870, p. 4, and 24 Sept. 1870, p. 5, and "The Franco-Prussia [*sic*] War," *Independent* 9 Feb. 1871, p. 1.

21 Aspirations of the World

1 LMC to Francis Alexander, 1 July 1877, *CC* 88/2329.

2 LMC to Francis Alexander, Sarah Shaw and Sarah Parsons, 1, 7, and 8 July 1877, *CC* 88/2329, 2331, 2332.

3 Child uses the phrase "Eclectic Bible" in a letter to James T. Fields, 28 Oct. 1877, *SL* 545.

4   See Child's assertion in the preface to *Aspirations of the World* (Boston: Roberts Brothers, 1878): "All the people on earth, from the beginning of time, have been 'feeling after God, if haply they might find him'. . ." (13). Quoted passage on 5.

5   Lydia Maria Child, *HOBOMOK and Other Writings on Indians*, ed. Carolyn L. Karcher (New Brunswick, N.J.: Rutgers UP, 1986) 48, 76.

6   For analyses of the various factors behind the dismantling of Reconstruction, see Eric Foner, *Reconstruction: America's Unfinished Revolution, 1863–1877* (New York: Harper and Row, 1988), esp. chaps. 10–11; William Gillette, *Retreat from Reconstruction, 1869–1879* (Baton Rouge: Louisiana State UP, 1979), esp. chap. 10; and David Montgomery, *Beyond Equality: Labor and the Radical Republicans, 1862–1872* (1967; Urbana: U of Illinois P, 1981), esp. chaps. 7–11.

7   LMC to Susan Lyman Lesley, 18 Feb. 1869, *CC* 70/1884.

8   LMC to Francis Shaw, 28 July 1867, *CC* 67/1789; "The Standard," *Standard* 20 June 1868, p. 2. This advertisement was regularly carried in the *Standard* and its successor. Until the demise of the successor, those who renewed their subscriptions and brought in at least one new subscriber received free copies of either *A Romance of the Republic*, Wendell Phillips's *Speeches*, or Caroline Healey Dall's *College, Market and Court*.

9   LMC to Eliza Scudder, 8 July 1869, *CC* 71/1901.

10 LMC to Susan Lyman Lesley, 18 Feb. 1869, *CC* 70/1884.

11 LMC to Eliza Scudder, 8 July, 1869 and 10 July 1870, *CC* 71/1901, 73/1952.

12 LMC to Louisa Loring, 6 Mar. 1868, *CC* 68/1816.

13 LMC to Henrietta Sargent and Eliza Scudder, 16 Mar., 12 and 14 Apr., and 10 May 1868, *CC* 68/1818, 1824, 69/1828.

14 "Gone," *Standard* 6 June 1868, *CC* 69/1837.

15 LMC to Harriet Sewall, 30 Sept. 1869, *CC* 72/1908.

16 "Another Friend Gone," *National Standard* 28 Jan. 1871, p. 1 (not in *CC*); LMC to Anna Loring Dresel, 25 Jan. 1871, *CC* 74/1972; LMC to Eliza Scudder and John Greenleaf Whittier, 17 and 24 July 1871, *CC* 76/2005, 2006; "Samuel J. May," *Woman's Journal* 30 Aug. 1873, p. 276. The latter is not an obituary, but an article occasioned by George B. Emerson's *Life of Samuel J. May*.

17 LMC to Anna Loring Dresel, 26 Sept. 1873, *CC* 81/2113.

18 LMC to Anna Loring Dresel, 26 Sept. 1873, *CC* 81/2113; L. Maria Child, "Dr. Osgood and His Daughters," *Independent* 17 July 1873, pp. 1–2. See also LMC to Sarah Shaw and Sarah Parsons, 22 June and 8 July 1873, *CC* 80/2106, 2107.

19 LMC to Stephen Salisbury and Sarah Shaw, 12 June 1874, *CC* 82/2154a, and 27 Jan. 1876, *SL* 532.

20 LMC to Anna Loring Dresel, 26 Sept. 1873, *CC* 81/2113.

21 LMC to Harriet Sewall, 16 Dec. 1873, *SL* 517; George Eliot to LMC, 30 Mar. 1879, *CC* 92/2440a.

22 LMC to Eliza Scudder, 10 July 1870, *CC* 1873/1952; and LMC to Sarah Shaw, Samuel and Harriet Sewall, and John Greenleaf Whittier, [after 11 Mar.], 2 Apr., 6, 12, and 18 June 1874, *SL* 519–20, *CC* 82/2146, 2155, 2156.

23 See Gillette, *Retreat from Reconstruction* chaps. 10–11; and Foner, *Reconstruction* chap. 11.

24 LMC to Lucy Osgood, 21 Dec. 1871, 12 Jan. 1872, *CC* 77/2021, 2031; LMC to Eliza Scudder, 29 Jan. 1872, *CC* 77/2033.

25 LMC to Anna Loring Dresel, Sarah Shaw, Sarah Parsons, Lucy Osgood, and Susan Lesley, 16, 24, and 31 Oct., 6 Nov., and 1 Dec. 1872, 8 Jan., 14 Feb., and 15 June 1873, *CC* 79/2065, 2066, 2067, 2069, 2071, 2082; 80/2087, 2105.

26 DLC and LMC to Lydia Bigelow Child, 30 July 1873, *CC* 81/2109; LMC to Harriet Sewall, 3 Jan. 1873, *SL* 510; "The Intermingling of Religions," *Atlantic Monthly* 28 (Oct. 1871): 385–95, extracted in the *National Standard* 30 Sept. 1871, p. 3, 7 Oct., pp. 2–3, and 14 Oct., pp. 3, 6. "Temperance in Eating," *National Standard* June 1872, p. 5; "Physical Strength of Women," *Woman's Journal* 15 Mar. 1873, p. 84; also concerned with religious and health-related subjects are "Resemblances between the

Buddhist and the Roman Catholic Religions," *Atlantic Monthly* 26 (Dec. 1870): 660–65; "A Memory" and "Tobacco," *National Standard* Feb. and Mar. 1872, pp. 1, 4–5.

27 LMC to Harriet Sewall, 16 Dec. 1873, *CC* 81/2123.

28 LMC to Sarah Shaw, 2 Apr. 1874, *SL* 521–22 and 25 Apr. 1875, *CC* 85/2230; Meltzer and Holland, *SL* 522 n. 1. Child's will is reprinted in Helene G. Baer, *The Heart Is Like Heaven: The Life of Lydia Maria Child* (Philadelphia: U of Pennsylvania P, 1964) 311–16.

29 LMC to Anna Loring Dresel, 5 Aug. 1874, *CC* 83/2168. It is not clear in what capacity Mrs. Pickering worked for the Lorings.

30 LMC to Lydia Bigelow Child, Anna Loring Dresel, Sarah Shaw, John Greenleaf Whittier, and Susan Lesley, 22 July, 5 and 7 Aug., 16, 18, and 24 Sept., and 7 Oct. 1874, *CC* 82/2164, 83/2168, 2170, 2175, 2176, 2177, 2181, 2187.

31 LMC to Sarah Shaw and Anna Loring Dresel, [Aug.?] 1870, and 18 Sept., and 7 Oct. 1874, *CC* 74/1957, 83/2177, 2188.

32 LMC to Sarah Shaw, Anna Loring Dresel, and Lydia B. Child, 18 Aug. and 18 and 24 Sept. 1874, *CC* 83/2172, 2177, 2181.

33 WLG to Anne Weston, 22 Sept. 1874, BPL Ms.A.1.1.Vol.8, p. 63(a-b); WLG to LMC, 25 Oct. 1874, *CC* 83/2191.

34 LMC to Lydia Bigelow Child and James T. Fields, 29 and 30 Sept. 1874 and 11 Feb. 1875, *CC* 83/2182, 2184, *SL* 530.

35 LMC to John Greenleaf Whittier, 30 Oct. 1874, *CC* 84/2195.

36 LMC to Sarah Shaw, 29 Oct. 1874, *CC* 84/2192.

37 LMC to Sarah Shaw, 4 Nov. 1874, *CC* 84/2197; compare *Looking toward Sunset* (Boston: Ticknor and Fields, 1865) 166–67: "In this world of sorrow and disappointment, every human being has trouble enough of his own. It is unkind to add the weight of your despondency to the burdens of another, who, if you knew all his secrets, you might find had a heavier load than yours to carry.... If you habitually try to pack your troubles away out of other people's sight, you will be in a fair way to forget them yourself ... because an effort made for the happiness of others lifts us above ourselves."

38 LMC to Sarah Shaw, 11 Apr. 1875, *CC* 85/2227; LMC to Hannah Baldwin, John B. Wight, and Emily F. Damon, 6, 12 and 22 Dec. 1874, *CC* 84/2202, 2204, 2206.

39 LMC to Martha Wight, 24 Feb. 1875, *CC* 85/2223; LMC to Sarah Parsons and Harriet and Samuel Sewall, 1 and 10 Jan. 1875, *CC* 84/2211, 2212. See chap. 15 on the breach between Child and John Hopper.

40 LMC to Marianne Silsbee, 7 Mar. 1875, *CC* 85/2224.

41 LMC to John B. Wight, 12 Dec. 1874 *CC* 84/2204.

42 LMC to Sarah and Francis Shaw, 4, 11, and 18 Apr. and 13 May 1875, *CC* 85/2226, 2227, 2229, 2232.

43 LMC to Anne Whitney, 14 Aug. 1878, *CC* 90/2406.

44 LMC to Sarah Shaw, 13 May and 8 June 1875, *CC* 85/2232, 2236.

45 LMC to Sarah Shaw, 31 May 1875, *CC* 85/2234. This letter ostensibly refers to the recent death in a shipwreck of the Shaws' niece, Bessie Green, but Child is clearly expressing her own feelings.

46 LMC to Harriet Sewall, 1 July 1875, *CC* 85/2241.

47 "Extracts from a Journal by David Lee Child," *Woman's Journal* 11 Sept. 1875, p. 289.

48 LMC to Stephen Salisbury, 13 June and 12 Oct. 1875, *CC* 85/2238a, 86/2251a.

49 Manuscript "Autobiography," Lydia Maria Child papers, Anti-Slavery Collection, Cornell University Library. Quotations on 13–14.

50 LMC to Sarah Shaw, 31 May 1875, *CC* 85/2234.

51 WLG to Fanny Garrison Villard, 9 Feb. 1877, BPL Ms.A.1.1.Vol.9, p. 19, a-b.

52 LMC to Mattie Griffith and Epes Sargent, 12 Jan. 1875 and 14 Mar. 1879, *CC* 84/2213, 92/2439.

53 LMC to Thomas Wentworth Higginson and Lucy Ann Brooks, 9 Sept. 1877 and 1 and 11 Apr. 1879, *CC* 88/2340, 92/2441, 2442. By 1879 Child had stopped frequenting mediums, but she agreed to accompany Brooks at Brooks's insistence.

54   LMC to Harriet Sewall and Francis Shaw, 11 June 1875 and 1 Apr. 1877, *CC* 85/2237, 87/2311.

55   LMC to Francis Shaw, Thomas Wentworth Higginson, and Epes Sargent, 17 June 1875, 1 Apr., 20 June and 9 Sept. 1877, 19 Dec. 1878, and 15 Jan. 1879, *CC* 85/2240, 87/2311, 88/2325, 2340, 91/2418, 2426.

56   LMC to Francis Shaw, 17 June 1875, *CC* 85/2240.

57   LMC to Sarah Shaw, 13 July 1877, *CC* 88/2333.

58   LMC to Sarah Shaw, 7 and 13 July 1877, *CC* 88/2331, 2333.

59   "Mrs. L. Maria Child on Taxation," *Woman's Journal* 28 Aug. 1875, p. 276; LMC to Abigail May and Sarah Shaw, 15 Mar. 1874 and 4 Oct. 1875, *SL* 521, 531. On the courageous crusade waged by Abby and Stephen Foster, see Dorothy Sterling, *Ahead of Her Time: Abby Kelley and the Politics of Antislavery* (New York: Norton, 1991) 367–72.

60   This scrapbook, one of several Child put together over her lifetime, is also preserved among her papers in the Anti-Slavery Collection, Cornell University Library.

61   LMC to Sarah Shaw, 6 Dec. 1875 and 27 Jan. and [14] Mar. 1876, *CC* 86/2256, 2261, 2267; LMC to Anna Loring Dresel, 18 Sept. 1874, *CC* 83/2177.

62   "One of Our Benefactors," *Woman's Journal* 25 Mar. 1876, p. 100. Compare Margaret Fuller, *Woman in the Nineteenth Century* (1845), in Jeffrey Steele, ed., *The Essential Margaret Fuller* (New Brunswick, N.J.: Rutgers UP, 1992): "Male and female represent the two sides of the great radical dualism. But, in fact, they are perpetually passing into one another. . . . There is no wholly masculine man, no purely feminine woman. History jeers at the attempts of physiologists to bind great original laws by the forms which flow from them. . . . Nature provides exceptions to every rule. She sends women to battle, and sets Hercules spinning. . . . Let us be wise, and not impede the soul" (310–11). Fuller had also argued that "[h]armony exists in difference, no less than in likeness, if only the same key-note govern both parts"; and she had predicted that if "every arbitrary barrier" against women's free development were "thrown down . . . a ravishing harmony of the spheres would ensue" (260, 288).

63   Quoted in "Letter from L. Maria Child," 20 July 1868, *Standard* 25 July 1868, *CC* 69/1842; LMC to Louisa Loring and Abigail May Alcott, 12 Feb. 1868 and 7 June 1876, *CC* 68/1812, 87/2274a.

64   LMC to Abigail May Alcott, Sarah Shaw, Susan Lyman Lesley, and Louisa May Alcott, 3, 7, and 18 June 1876 and 19 June 1878, *CC* 86/2273, 87/2274a, *SL* 534–35, and *CC* 90/2398; Sarah Elbert, *A Hunger for Home: Louisa May Alcott's Place in American Culture* (New Brunswick, N.J.: Rutgers UP, 1987) 41.

65   LMC to Lucy Stone, 1 July 1876, *SL* 536; "Letter from Mrs. Child," *Woman's Journal* 15 July 1876, p. 225.

66   L. Maria Child, "Equality of the Sexes," *Woman's Journal* 5 Aug. 1876, p. 252.

67   "Letter from Mrs. Child, on the Present State of the Anti-Slavery Cause," *Liberator* 6 Sept. 1839, *CC* 8/186. See chap. 10 above for a fuller discussion of Child's differences with the Grimkés on this issue.

68   LMC to Sarah Shaw, Wendell Phillips, and Sarah Parsons, 8 Apr., 4 June, and 28 Dec. 1876, *SL* 533, *CC* 87/2274, 2293; Child refers to Garrison's letter to James Freeman Clarke, 2 Dec. 1876, published in the *Boston Journal* 4 Dec. and rpt. in *The Letters of William Lloyd Garrison*, vol. 6: *To Rouse the Slumbering Land, 1868–1879*, hereinafter abbreviated as *GL*, ed. Walter M. Merrill and Louis Ruchames (Cambridge, Mass.: Belknap P of Harvard UP, 1981) 428–37.

69   LMC to Francis Alexander, Sarah Shaw, and Sarah Parsons, 1 and 7 July 1877 and 12 Feb. and 20 Nov. 1878, *CC* 88/2329, 2331, *SL* 549, and *CC* 91/2415. Because Child referred so rarely to public events in her letters of this period, it is difficult to pinpoint the date of her disillusionment with Hayes. Her vehement assertion that Wade Hampton was "totally *incapable* of doing justice to the colored citizens of South Carolina," unless he had "gone through some wonderful process of regeneration," is also difficult to reconcile with her "delighted" acceptance of Hampton's claim that he had indeed changed his sentiments. The first occurs in an undated fragment (*CC* 89/2356), the second in a letter written in July (*CC* 88/2331). In contrast, from the moment of Hayes's inauguration, Garrison expressed "the gravest apprehensions as to what is to be the 'policy' of the new administration," and by mid-April he was already publicly attacking it as a "policy of compromise, of credulity, of weakness, of subserviency, of surrender," though he credited Hayes with "the best intentions." See WLG to Neal Dow, 16 Mar.

1877, and WLG to Editors of the *Boston Daily Advertiser*, 20 Apr. 1877, *GL* 6: 460–62, 469–75. For historical analyses of the "Compromise of 1877" and its aftermath, see Foner, *Reconstruction* 575–87; Gillette, *Retreat from Reconstruction* chap. 14; and Rayford W. Logan, *The Betrayal of the Negro from Rutherford B. Hayes to Woodrow Wilson* (rev. ed.; New York: Collier, 1965) chap. 2.

70 LMC to Sarah Shaw, 31 July 1877, *SL* 542–43.

71 LMC to Francis Alexander, 1 July 1877, *CC* 88/2329.

72 LMC to James T. Fields, Sarah Parsons, and Francis Shaw, 28 Oct. 1877, *SL* 545, and 21 May and 7 June 1878, *CC* 90/2386, *SL* 551–52.

73 LMC to Francis Shaw, 16 Dec. 1877, *CC* 89/2350. Child identifies the Rev. Mr. Wight and discusses her boarding arrangements with his son and daughter-in-law in LMC to Sarah Shaw, 19 Nov. 1875, *CC* 86/2253.

74 LMC to Thomas Wentworth Higginson, 9 Sept. 1877, *CC* 88/2340. The letter is mutilated at its middle fold, and one or two words may be missing.

75 James Freeman Clarke, *Ten Great Religions: An Essay in Comparative Theology* (Boston: James R. Osgood, 1871). For a brief comparison of this work with Child's *Progress of Religious Ideas*, see chap. 15 above. L. Maria Child, "Resemblances between the Buddhist and the Roman Catholic Religions" and "The Intermingling of Religions," *Atlantic Monthly* 26 (Dec. 1870): 661–65, and 28 (Oct. 1871): 385–95. Quotations are from "Resemblances" 660 and "Intermingling" 387.

76 LMC to Sarah Shaw, [Nov.?] 1876, *SL* 537–38.

77 LMC to Susan Damon, [Sarah] Wight, Marianne Silsbee, and Sarah Parsons, 12 Nov. and 10 Dec. 1876, 6 Feb. 1877, and 20 Nov. 1878, *CC* 87/2287, 2289, 2303, and 91/2415.

78 LMC to Sarah Shaw, undated, 1877, *CC* 89/2356. A reference in the letter to President Hayes's promise to "sustain Wade Hampton's government of South Carolina" would date this letter around Apr. 1877.

79 LMC to Sarah Shaw, 20 June and 7 and 13 July 1877, *CC* 88/2326, 2331, and 2333.

80 LMC to James T. Fields, 28 Oct. 1877, *SL* 545.

81 LMC to James T. Fields, 3 Feb. and 11 Mar. 1878, *CC* 89/2364, 90/2377; A. W. Stevens to LMC, 27 Apr. and 19 June 1878, *CC* 90/2384, 2399. Stevens describes himself as a former Unitarian minister who had outgrown his profession and been led "out of conservative, partisan Christianity into the 'large place' of universal appreciation and charity." It is not clear whether he was an editor at Roberts Brothers or simply an acquaintance Child met at Free Religious Association meetings.

82 L. Maria Child, *Aspirations of the World. A Chain of Opals* (Boston: Roberts Brothers, 1878) 2, 257. Subsequent page references are given parenthetically in the text.

83 See Edward Said, *Orientalism* (New York: Vintage, 1978). Actually Child's assertions about Buddhism need to be qualified. Religious wars and persecution have occurred under Buddhism, though not to anything like the same extent as under Christianity.

84 Child also includes a significant number of extracts from the Koran, and the Muslim Sufis are well represented among her Persian texts. In addition, she cites a handful of inscriptions from Egyptian tombs and verses from the Egyptian Book of the Dead. Surprisingly, in view of the anti-Judaic biases Child showed in *The Progress of Religious Ideas*, Jewish texts outnumber Christian, though many of them are from the Talmud and Apocryphal books, rather than from the Old Testament.

85 Anna Loring Dresel and WLG to LMC, 21 May and 25 Aug. 1878, *CC* 90/2387, 2407; LMC to Francis Shaw, George Julian, and Epes Sargent, 7 June, 28 Sept., and 19 Dec. 1878, *SL* 551, *CC* 91/2411, 2418 (their letters to her have not been preserved); review of *Aspirations of the World*, *Woman's Journal* 29 June 1878, p. 205.

86 Review of *Aspirations of the World* under "Editor's Literary Record," *Harper's New Monthly Magazine* 57 (Oct. 1878): 786–87.

87 LMC to Francis Shaw, 16 Dec. 1877, *CC* 89/2350.

88 LMC to James T. Fields and Anne Whitney, 11 Mar., 22 May, and 28 Sept. 1878, *CC* 90/2377 *SL* 550–51, *CC* 91/2412, Ingersoll is identified as the "Great Agnostic" by Meltzer and Holland, *SL* 550 n. 3.

89 LMC to Anne Whitney and WLG, 8 Apr. 1877 and 28 Feb. [1878], *SL* 540–41, *CC* 89/2371.

90 LMC to James Redpath, 10 Jan. 1878, *SL* 547–48.

91 L. Maria Child, "Anne Whitney's Model of Charles Sumner's Statue," *Woman's Journal* 5 May 1877, p. 137. Child makes the same point in her letter to Redpath.

92 LMC to WLG, 28 Feb. [1878], *CC* 89/2371; WLG to Wendell Phillips Garrison and Fanny Garrison Villard, 29 Mar. 1878, 28 Mar. 1879, *GL* 6: 515, 572.

93 LMC to Anne Whitney, 18 Apr., 14 Aug. and 28 Sept. 1878, *CC* 90/2383, 2406, 91/2412.

94 LMC to Anne Whitney, 28 Sept. 1878, *CC* 91/2412.

95 LMC to Anne Whitney and Sarah Parsons, 25 Nov. 1878, *SL* 555, and 19 Jan. 1879, *CC* 91/2427.

96 Sarah S. Russell to LMC, 21 May [1878], *CC* 90/2388; LMC to Sarah Shaw and Sarah Shaw Russell, 14 June 1878, 28 May 1879, *CC* 90/2397, 92/2453.

97 LMC to Annie Fields, 22 Jan. 1877, *CC* 87/2300; LMC to Francis Shaw, 16 Dec. 1877, *CC* 90/2350.

98 Elizabeth Stuart Phelps, *Chapters from a Life* (Boston: Houghton Mifflin, 1896) 182–85.

99 LMC to Theodore Dwight Weld, 10 July 1880, *SL* 563; LMC to John Greenleaf Whittier, 25 Oct. 1878, *CC* 91/2413.

100 LMC to Weld, 10 July 1880, *SL* 562–64. This letter was written in response to the memorial that Weld had just published of Angelina. Child had also written a letter of condolence on 16 Nov. 1879, immediately after Angelina's death, enclosing a check for $100, which she had accepted as a gift from a friend "only on condition that I might transfer it to Theodore Weld, who had lost his earnings [in the aftermath of the Panic of 1873], while mine were yielding a good per cent." An extract from this letter, reprinted in Paul Richards, Catalog 184, item 43, was graciously made available to me by Patricia Holland from her file of material accumulated since the publication of *CC*.

101 See Garrison's letters to Robert Morris and George T. Downing, 22 Apr. 1879, *GL* 6: 578–81.

102 WLG to Fanny Garrison Villard, 19 Mar. 1879, *GL* 6: 569. In a letter to John A. Collins the following day, he also quotes extensively from a letter of Child's that seems to have been lost, in which she thanked him for his "strong and earnest words about the wrongs done to the Chinese"; 20 Mar. 1879, BPL Ms.A.1.1.Vol.9, p. 71 (a-b). Child briefly described their visit in letters to Sarah Russell and Sarah Shaw, 28 May and 30 June 1879, *CC* 92/2453, 2462.

103 LMC to Anne Whitney, 25 May 1879, *SL* 558.

104 L. Maria Child, "William Lloyd Garrison," *Atlantic Monthly* 44 (Aug. 1879): 237–38.

105 LMC to Susan Damon, Sarah Parsons, and Lydia Bigelow Child, 12 Nov. and 28 Dec. 1876, 8 Dec. [1877], 20 Nov. 1878, *CC* 87/2287, 2293, 89/2349, 91/2415.

106 LMC to Sarah Parsons and Sarah Shaw, 8 and 22 July 1877, and 29 Apr. and 21 May 1878, *CC* 88/2332, 2334, 90/2385, 2386.

107 LMC to Sarah Shaw, 20 July 1879, *CC* 92/2464.

108 LMC to Harriet Sewall, 11 July 1880, *CC* 94/2510.

109 LMC to Sarah Shaw, 20 Mar. 1879, *SL* 557.

110 LMC to Sarah Shaw, 28 Dec. 1879, *CC* 93/2486, and 6 Sept. 1880, *SL* 567.

111 "Letter to Bear's Heart from Mrs. Lydia Maria Child," Sept. 1879, *Southern Workman* (Dec. 1879): 123–24, *CC* 93/2472.

112 LMC to Theodore Weld and Francis and Sarah Shaw, 10 July and 10 and 23 Aug. 1880, *SL* 564, 565–66, *CC* 94/2517.

113 LMC to Francis Shaw, 10 Aug. 1880, *SL* 566.

114 LMC to Anne Whitney, 22 June and 6 Sept. 1880, *CC* 94/2506, 95/2520.

115 LMC to Marianne Silsbee, Sarah Shaw, and Harriet Sewall, 27 July and 23 and 24 Aug. 1880, *CC* 94/2513, 2517, 2518.

116 LMC to Maria S. Porter and Sarah Shaw, circa Feb. and mid-Aug. 1880 and 23 Aug. 1880, *CC* 97/2566, 94/2517, 97/2569; Maria S. Porter, "Lydia Maria Child," *National Magazine: An Illustrated American Monthly* 14 (May 1901): 161–70; Mortimer Smith, *The Life of Ole Bull* (1943; Westport, Conn.: Greenwood P, 1973), pp. 156–61, 199–203, 209; Sara C. Bull, *Ole Bull: A Memoir* (1882; New York: Da Capo P, 1981) 256–57, 299–305.

117　LMC to Harriet Sewall and Anne Whitney, 24 Aug. and 6 Sept. 1880, *CC* 95/2518, 2520.

118　LMC to Anne Whitney, 16 July 1880, *CC* 94/2511.

119　Anne Whitney to LMC, 22 Sept. 1880, *CC* 95/2521.

120　Deborah Pickman Clifford, *Crusader for Freedom: A Life of Lydia Maria Child* (Boston: Beacon P, 1992) 297; *Letters of Lydia Maria Child with a Biographical Introduction by John G. Whittier and an Appendix by Wendell Phillips*, [ed. Harriet Winslow Sewall] (1882; New York: Negro Universities P, 1969) xxiii; LMC to Samuel and Harriet Sewall, 15 June 1880, *CC* 94/2505.

121　Phillips slightly misquotes Child's epitaph; see "Remarks of Wendell Phillips at the Funeral of Lydia Maria Child, October 23, 1880," Appendix, [Sewall, ed.], *Letters of Lydia Maria Child* 263–68; "In Memoriam. L. Maria Child," *Woman's Journal* 30 Oct. 1880, p. 345; Anna D. Hallowell, "Lydia Maria Child," *Medford Historical Register* 3 (July 1900): 117. Child's will strikingly illustrates the connection between her "rigid economy" and the charity she liked to practice. She left an estate valued at over $36,000, which she willed to "needy friends and relatives and a variety of worthy causes." Mrs. Pickering received one of the largest bequests: $8,000. As Clifford notes, the size of Child's estate testifies to "her ability to prosper on her own" and "raises the tempting, if speculative, question of what her life would have been like if she had never married David" (*Crusader for Freedom* 298); also Baer, *Heart Is Like Heaven* 311–16.

122　Whittier Introduction, *Letters of Lydia Maria Child* xxiii.

123　Curtis's obituary is reprinted as part of a longer retrospective incorporating other tributes in "Lydia Maria Child," *Woman's Journal* 13 Nov. 1880, p. 366.

124　Untitled article, *Nation* 31 (28 Oct. 1880): 309.

125　"L. Maria Child," rpt. in *Woman's Journal* 6 Nov. 1880, pp. 354–55.

126　"Lydia Maria Child and Gov. Andrew," *Woman's Journal* 20 Nov. 1880, p. 374.

127　"Lucretia Mott and Lydia Maria Child," *Woman's Journal* 18 Dec. 1880, pp. 409–10.

128　T[homas] W[entworth] H[igginson], "Lydia Maria Child," *Woman's Journal* 27 Nov. 1880, p. 377.

129　"Maria Edgeworth and Lydia Maria Child," *The Critic* 2 (2 Dec. 1882): 325.

130　[Wendell Phillips Garrison], "Mrs. Child's Letters," *Nation* 36 (25 Jan. 1883): 87–88; "Maria Edgeworth and Lydia Maria Child" 325; [Horace Scudder], "Lydia Maria Child," *Atlantic Monthly* 50 (Dec. 1882): 839–44; [George William Curtis], "Editor's Easy Chair," *Harper's New Monthly Magazine* 66 (Feb. 1883): 471–72.

131　"Lydia Maria Child," review of *Letters of Lydia Maria Child*, *New York Times* 1 Dec. 1882, p. 3; actually the *Letters* went through five editions, the last dated 1888. The reviews in the *Atlantic Monthly* and the *Nation* also comment on Child's personality as revealed in her letters, illustrating it by quoting extensively. George William Curtis's review in *Harper's* regrets that "much of the 'spice' must be omitted from purely personal and intimate letters when they are published, or these would be still more piquant and graphic." For full citations, see n. 130 above.

132　LMC to Anne Whitney, 16 July 1880, *CC* 94/2511.

133　Child, "William Lloyd Garrison," *Atlantic Monthly* 44 (Aug. 1879): 237–38.

134　Pauline R. Hopkins, "Reminiscences of the Life and Times of Lydia Maria Child," *Colored American Magazine* 6 (Feb. 1903): 279. As Carla Peterson pointed out to me, this article, part of a series of biographical sketches of notable women, is the only one in the series devoted to a white woman, as well as the only one to occupy more than one issue.

135　Hopkins, "Reminiscences of Lydia Maria Child," *Colored American Magazine* 6 (Mar. 1903): 354.

136　Hopkins, "Reminiscences of Lydia Maria Child," *Colored American Magazine* 6 (May and June 1903): 454; 6 (Feb. 1903): 280.

Afterword

1　For a reprint of Child's "The Quadroons," see Susan Koppelman, ed., *The Other Woman: Stories of Two Women and a Man* (Old Westbury, N.Y.: Feminist P, 1984) 1–12; for a reprint of "The Neighbour-in-

Law," see Koppelman, ed., *Women's Friendships: A Collection of Short Stories* (Norman: U of Oklahoma P, 1991) 3–15; for selections from *Hobomok*, see Lucy M. Freibert and Barbara A. White, eds., *Hidden Hands: An Anthology of American Women Writers, 1790–1870* (New Brunswick, N.J.: Rutgers UP, 1985) 116–32; for selections from *Letters from New York*, see Judith Fetterley, ed., *Provisions: A Reader from 19th-Century American Women* (Bloomington: Indiana UP, 1985) 159–202; for a reprint of "Slavery's Pleasant Homes" and selections from *An Appeal in Favor of That Class of Americans Called Africans* and "Letters from New-York" (the column rather than the book), see Paul Lauter, ed., *The Heath Anthology of American Literature* (Lexington, Mass.: D. C. Heath, 1990) 1: 1795–1812. For passing references to Child, see Ann Douglas, *The Feminization of American Culture* (1977; New York: Avon Books, 1978) 65–66, 72, 81, 101, 113, 114, 184, 185, 404–5; Nina Baym, *Woman's Fiction: A Guide to Novels by and about Women in America, 1820–1870* (Ithaca, N.Y.: Cornell UP, 1978) 52–53; Mary Kelley, *Private Woman, Public Stage: Literary Domesticity in Nineteenth-Century America* (New York: Oxford UP, 1984) 15, 204, 319–20; and Susan K. Harris, *19th-Century American Women's Novels: Interpretative Strategies* (Cambridge: Cambridge UP, 1990) 18–19. The one exception to this pattern, significantly, is a study that focuses on women intellectuals, among whom Child figures prominently: Susan Phinney Conrad's *Perish the Thought: Intellectual Women in Romantic America, 1830–1860* (New York: Oxford UP, 1976).

2   For studies of abolitionism that frequently cite Child's opinions, see Louis Filler, *The Crusade Against Slavery, 1830–1860* (New York: Harper and Row, 1960); James M. McPherson, *The Struggle for Equality: Abolitionists and the Negro in the Civil War and Reconstruction* (Princeton, N.J.: Princeton UP, 1964); Aileen S. Kraditor, *Means and Ends in American Abolitionism: Garrison and His Critics on Strategy and Tactics, 1834–1850* (New York: Vintage, 1969); Carleton Mabee, *Black Freedom: The Nonviolent Abolitionists from 1830 Through the Civil War* (New York: Macmillan, 1970); Jane H. Pease and William H. Pease, *Bound with Them in Chains: A Biographical History of the Antislavery Movement* (Westport, Conn.: Greenwood P, 1972); Merton L. Dillon, *The Abolitionists: The Growth of a Dissenting Minority* (DeKalb: Northern Illinois UP, 1974); Ronald G. Walters, *The Antislavery Appeal: American Abolitionism After 1830* (Baltimore: Johns Hopkins UP, 1976); James Brewer Stewart, *Holy Warriors: The Abolitionists and American Slavery* (New York: Hill and Wang, 1976); and Herbert Aptheker, *Abolitionism: A Revolutionary Movement* (Boston: Twayne, 1989). For discussions of Child in studies that focus on the connections between abolitionism and women's rights, see Blanche Glassman Hersh, *The Slavery of Sex: Feminist-Abolitionists in America* (Urbana: U of Illinois P, 1978); and Jean Fagan Yellin, *Women and Sisters: The Antislavery Feminists in American Culture* (New Haven, Conn.: Yale UP, 1989) chap. 3 and passim.

3   For a pioneering exposé of the racist historiography that took over the universities in the post-Reconstruction era, see the chapter "The Propaganda of History" in W. E. B. Du Bois, *Black Reconstruction in America: 1860–1880* (1935; New York: Atheneum, 1977) 711–29. Until the 1960s the scholarship on abolitionists remained largely hostile, caricaturing the movement as "extremist" and "fanatic." Although Gilbert Hobbs Barnes's *The Antislavery Impulse, 1830–1844* (1933) partially rehabilitated Evangelical abolitionists, it did so by shifting the onus of "extremism" and "fanaticism" to the Garrisonians. Louis Filler's *The Crusade Against Slavery, 1830–1860* (1960) marked the beginning of a more balanced approach to the movement as a whole. Not until Kraditor's *Means and Ends in American Abolitionism* (1969) did Garrisonians receive genuinely sympathetic treatment, however. Meanwhile, most studies of abolitionism paid little attention to the role of women in the movement, except to blame them for precipitating the schism between Evangelicals and Garrisonians. The pioneering feminist scholarship of Gerda Lerner and the emergence of women's history in the 1970s helped turn the tide. As indices of the Grimkés' status as feminist heroines, see Gerda Lerner, *The Grimké Sisters from South Carolina: Rebels against Slavery* (Boston: Houghton Mifflin, 1967); and Katharine DuPre Lumpkin, *The Emancipation of Angelina Grimké* (Chapel Hill: U of North Carolina P, 1974); also Larry Ceplair, ed., *The Public Years of Sarah and Angelina Grimké: Selected Writings, 1835–1839* (New York: Columbia UP, 1987).

4   Lois W. Banner, *Elizabeth Cady Stanton: A Radical for Woman's Rights* (Boston: Little, Brown, 1980); and Elisabeth Griffith, *In Her Own Right: The Life of Elizabeth Cady Stanton* (New York: Oxford UP, 1984).

5   Dorothy Sterling, *Ahead of Her Time: Abby Kelley and the Politics of Antislavery* (New York: Norton, 1991);

Andrea Moore Kerr, *Lucy Stone: Speaking Out for Equality* (New Brunswick, N.J.: Rutgers UP, 1992); and Deborah Pickman Clifford, *Crusader for Freedom: A Life of Lydia Maria Child* (Boston: Beacon P, 1992).

6   Both Hersh, *Slavery of Sex*, and Kirk Jeffrey, "Marriage, Career, and Feminine Ideology in Nineteenth-Century America: Reconstructing the Marital Experience of Lydia Maria Child, 1828–1874," *Feminist Studies* 2 (2/3, 1975) 113–30, treat the Childs' marriage as a case study, but Hersh tends to underplay its problematic aspects, and Jeffrey underestimates the degree to which Child did in fact criticize marriage as an institution.

7   See, for example, Kathryn Kish Sklar, *Catharine Beecher: A Study in American Domesticity* (New Haven, Conn.: Yale UP, 1973); Mary P. Ryan, *The Empire of the Mother: American Writing about Domesticity, 1830–1860* (New York: Haworth P, 1982); and the chapter "Sarah Hale and the *Ladies Magazine*," in Nancy Woloch, *Women and the American Experience* (New York: Knopf, 1984) 97–112.

8   I have borrowed the term "cultural biography" from Sacvan Bercovitch, who originated it to describe his work in progress on Melville.

9   Clifford, *Crusader for Freedom* 4.

10 For influential articulations of these theories, see Richard Chase, *The American Novel and Its Tradition* (New York: Doubleday, 1957); and Leslie Fiedler, *Love and Death in the American Novel* (New York: Criterion Books, 1960).

11 I owe this formulation and inquiry to Richard Slotkin.

12 Quotations are from "Self-Reliance," Stephen E. Whicher, ed., *Selections from Ralph Waldo Emerson* (Boston: Houghton Mifflin, 1957) 150; and from Nathaniel Hawthorne, "The Hall of Fantasy," *The Pioneer* 1 (Feb. 1843): 53. In a letter to Jonathan Phillips, Child refers to the common "assertion that we abolitionists live 'but for one idea' " (26 Feb. 1838, *CC* 96/2533).

13 LMC to Jonathan Phillips, 26 Feb. 1838, *CC* 96/2533; "To Abolitionists," *Standard* 20 May 1841, p. 198.

14 Both quotations are from LMC to Sarah Shaw, 2 Mar. 1880, *SL* 561.

15 LMC to Francis Shaw, 10 Aug. 1880, *SL* 566. I would like to thank Richard Slotkin and Milton Sernett for suggesting this Afterword and H. Bruce Franklin, Jane Morgan Franklin, Martin Karcher, and Reynolds Smith for their incisive criticisms of earlier drafts.

Works of Lydia Maria Child

No bibliography of Child's writings can yet claim to be definitive. New articles of hers keep turning up, not only in hitherto unexamined journals but in those already searched by other scholars. Child also published a large number of articles anonymously or pseudonymously, both in her husband's newspaper, the *Massachusetts Journal* (ca. 1828 until 1832), and during the Civil War, in mainstream political newspapers. Many of those articles remain to be located. In addition, newspapers, magazines, and gift books often reprinted her stories, articles, and extracts from her longer works under different titles. Space limitations preclude listing these reprints, but they can be found in the following publications: *The Lady's Cabinet Album; The Boston Book; The Rover; The Slave's Friend; The Anti-Slavery Record; Rural Repository; The New World; The Gem of the Season; The Casket; Gems by the Wayside; The Dew-Drop; The Gem Annual; The Marriage Offering;* and *Merry's Museum.*

A complete listing of all Child's publications in *The Juvenile Miscellany,* the *Liberator,* the *National Anti-Slavery Standard,* the *Boston Courier,* and the *Independent,* including her weekly editorials and "Letters from New-York," would require a volume in itself. Hence, I have adopted the following principles of selectivity: (1) of the stories and sketches Child published in the *Juvenile Miscellany,* I have listed only the ones cited in this biography; (2) of the innumerable newspaper articles Child published in the form of letters, I have listed only those omitted from the microfiche edition of her *Complete Correspondence;* (3) of her "Letters from New-York," I have listed only those omitted from the book versions of the First and Second Series; (4) of her weekly editorials, I have listed only those mentioned in chapter 12. With these exceptions, I have listed both the periodical and the book publication of Child's stories and essays. In the case of her uncollected fiction and journalism and her unpublished manuscripts and letters, I have tried to provide a complete bibliography of all items found to date.

This bibliography is arranged chronologically to allow readers to follow the development of Child's career. Annuals and gift books have been listed in the order of their actual publication date (or date of deposition for copyright), rather than by the year announced in their title (e.g., *The Token* "for" 1828 was actually published in October 1827 and is listed accordingly). For easier reference, the bibliography is also subdivided into the categories of books and pamphlets; stories, sketches, and anecdotes; journalism and miscellaneous nonfiction; poems; unpublished manuscripts; collected letters; and uncollected letters.

Books and Pamphlets

Hobomok, A Tale of Early Times, By An American. Boston: Cummings, Hilliard, 1824.
Evenings in New England. Intended for Juvenile Amusement and Instruction. By An American Lady. Boston: Cummings, Hilliard, 1824.

"Preface"; "Personification"; "History"; "General Lee. A Drama"; "Trees"; "Riddling Forest"; "The Uneasy Oak. A Fable"; "The Rainbow"; "The Adventures of a Dandelion"; "Gobelins Tapestry"; "The Man with One Bad Habit"; "Oracles"; "The Hospitable Dog of St. Bernard"; "Conversation on Wealth"; "The Triumphal Arch. A Drama"; "Process of Making Sugar"; "The Indians Outwitted"; "Indian Tribes"; "Botanical Hints"; "Flax and Dodder. A Fable"; "Association of Ideas. Anecdote of a Horse"; "Origin of Names, Phrases, Customs"; "The Sailor and His Babe"; "Trees" (cont.); "Aurora Borealis"; "Flora's Timekeepers. —A Fable"; "The Morning Adventures of a Stupid Schoolboy"; "Gems, Fossils, &c."; "The Little Master and His Little Slave"; "Astronomical Hints"; "The Young Bookseller"; "Anecdote of a Parrot"; "Heraldry"; "The Young Hero"; "Key to the Riddling Forest"; "Farewell."

The Rebels, or Boston before the Revolution. By the author of *Hobomok.* Boston: Cummings, Hilliard, 1825; rpt. Boston: Phillips, Sampson, 1850.

Emily Parker, or Impulse, Not Principle. Intended for Young Persons. By the Author of *Evenings in New England,* and Editor of the *Juvenile Miscellany.* Boston: Bowles and Dearborn, 1827.

The Juvenile Souvenir (edited, with the following anonymous contributions by Child). By the Editor of "The Juvenile Miscellany." Boston: Marsh & Capen, and John Putnam, 1827.

"Emma Forsyth"; "Anna and Her Dog"; "The Little Irish Girl"; "The Young Adventurers"; "The Happy Family"; "George and Georgiana"; "The New Year."

Biographical Sketches of Great and Good Men. Designed for the Amusement and Instruction of Young Persons. Boston: Putnam & Hunt/Philadelphia: Thomas T. Ash, 1828.

"Benjamin Franklin"; "Captain John Smith"; "General Israel Putnam"; "Christopher Columbus"; "John Ledyard"; "Sir Benjamin West"; "William Penn"; "Rev. John Elliot"; "Baron De Kalb."

Moral Lessons in Verse (ed.). Cambridge: Hilliard and Brown, 1828.

The First Settlers of New-England: or, Conquest of the Pequods, Narragansets and Pokanokets: As Related by a Mother to Her Children, and Designed for the Instruction of Youth. By a Lady of Massachusetts. Boston: Munroe & Francis/New York: Charles S. Francis, [1829].

The Frugal Housewife. Boston: Marsh & Capen, and Carter & Hendee, 1829; revised and enlarged, 1830; retitled, from the 8th ed. on, *The American Frugal Housewife.* Boston: Carter & Hendee, 1832.

Editions from 1830 on include "Hints to Persons of Moderate Fortune," rpt. from *Massachusetts Journal.*

The Little Girl's Own Book (rpt. eds. occasionally titled *The Girl's Own Book*). Boston: Carter, Hendee and Babcock, 1831; London: Tegg, 1832; enlarged ed. Boston: Carter, Hendee, 1834.

Includes two children's stories: "Mary Howard" and "The Palace of Beauty."

The Mother's Book. Boston: Carter, Hendee & Babcock/Baltimore: Charles Carter, 1831; Glasgow: Griffin/London: Tegg, 1832; revised and enlarged ed., New York: C. S. Francis/Boston: Joseph H. Francis, 1844.

The Coronal. A Collection of Miscellaneous Pieces, Written at Various Times. Boston: Carter and Hendee, 1832; slightly enlarged as *The Mother's Story Book; or, Western Coronal. A Collection of Miscellaneous Pieces. By Mrs. Child . . . To which are added, a few tales, by Mary Howitt, and Caroline Fry.* London, Edinburgh, Dublin, and Glasgow: T. T. & J. Tegg, 1833.

"Caius Marius. Lines, Suggested by Vanderlyn's Fine Picture of Caius Marius among the Ruins of Carthage"; "The Lone Indian"; "The Sagacious Papa"; "To a Lady celebrated for Music"; "The Rival Brothers"; "You've been Captain long enough"; "On hearing a Boy mock the Bell"; "Thoughts"; "La Rosiere"; "Address to the Valentine"; "Blessed Influence of the Studies of Nature"; "Recluse of the Lake"; "Spring"; "Lines to Beauty"; "Harriet Bruce"; "Miseries of Wealth"; "To the fringed Gentian"; "The Bold and Beautiful Convict"; "Romance"; "Lines to a Wealthy Lady"; "The Indian Wife"; "Fable of the Caterpillar and Silk-Worm"; "Lines occasioned by a beautiful Thought"; "Stand from Under"; "Adventures of a Rain-Drop"; "The Young West-Indian"; "A New-Year's Offering to a Friend"; "Nature and Simplicity"; "Chocorua's Curse"; "Lines to a Husband"; "The First and Last Book."

The Biographies of Madame de Staël, and Madame Roland. Vol. 1 of **Ladies' Family Library.** Boston: Carter and Hendee, 1832; rpt. in part as *The Biography of Madame de Staël.* Edinburgh: Thomas Clark, 1836; 1832 ed. rpt. as *Memoirs of Madame de Staël, and of Madame Roland.* New York: C. S. Francis/Boston, J. H. Francis, 1847.

The Biographies of Lady Russell, and Madame Guyon. Vol. 2 of **Ladies' Family Library.** Boston: Carter, Hendee, 1832; rpt. in part as *The Biography of Lady Russell.* Edinburgh: Thomas Clark, 1836.

Good Wives. Vol. 3 of **Ladies' Family Library.** Boston: Carter, Hendee, 1833; rpt. as *Biographies of Good Wives.* New York: C. S. Francis/Boston: J. H. Francis, 1846; London: Griffin, 1849; rpt. as *Celebrated Women: Or, Biographies of Good Wives.* New York: Charles S. Francis, 1861; rpt. as *Married Women: Biographies of Good Wives.* New York: Charles S. Francis, 1871.

An Appeal in Favor of That Class of Americans Called Africans. Boston: Allen and Ticknor, 1833; rpt. New York: John S. Taylor, 1836.

The Oasis (edited, with the following contributions by Child). Boston: Allen and Ticknor, 1834.
"To the Public"; "Preface"; "William Wilberforce"; "How to effect Emancipation"; "Malem-Boo"; "Illustration of the Strength of Prejudice"; "I thank my God for my humility"; "Safe Mode of Operation"; "The Hottentots"; "Conversation between the Editor and a Colonizationist"; "Contrast"; "Voices from the South"; "Scale of Complexions"; "Dangers of Emancipation"; "Knowledge in the United States"; "Old Scip"; "Arguments and Men"; "Derivation of Negro"; "Mobs in Jamaica."

The History of the Condition of Women, in Various Ages and Nations. Vols. 4 and 5 of **Ladies' Family Library.** Boston: John Allen, 1835; London, 1835; rev. ed. retitled *Brief History of the Condition of Women, in Various Ages and Nations.* New York: C. S. Francis/Boston: J. H. Francis, 1845.

Authentic Anecdotes of American Slavery (edited anonymously, with unspecified contributions by Child). Nos. 1–2. Newburyport, Mass.: Charles Whipple, 1835.

Anti-Slavery Catechism. Newburyport, Mass.: Charles Whipple, 1836.

The Evils of Slavery, and the Cure of Slavery. The First Proved by the Opinions of Southerners Themselves, the Last Shown by Historical Evidence. Newburyport, Mass.: Charles Whipple, 1836.

Philothea. A Romance. Boston: Otis, Broaders/New York: George Dearborn, 1836; rpt. as *Philothea: A Grecian Romance.* New York: C. S. Francis, 1845.

The Family Nurse; or Companion of The Frugal Housewife. Boston: Charles J. Hendee, 1837.

Authentic Anecdotes of American Slavery (edited anonymously with unspecified contributions by Child). No. 3. Newburyport, Mass.: Charles Whipple, 1838.

Memoir of Benjamin Lay: Compiled from Various Sources (ed.). New York: American Anti-Slavery Society, 1842.

American Anti-Slavery Almanac [for 1843] (ed.). New York: American Anti-Slavery Society, 1843.

Letters from New-York [First Series]. New York: C. S. Francis/Boston: James Munroe, 1843; London, Bentley, 1843.

Flowers for Children. I. (For Children Eight or Nine Years Old). New York: C. S. Francis/Boston: J. H. Francis, 1844; rpt. as *The Christ Child, and Other Stories.* Boston: D. Lothrop/Dover, N.H.: G. T. Day, 1869.
"The Christ-Child and the Poor Children"; "The New-York Boy's Song"; "Mannikins, or Little Men"; "George and His Dog"; "The Squirrel and Her Little Ones"; "The Young Artist"; "How the Birds Make Their Nests"; "The Present. A Drama"; "The Indolent Fairy"; "Little Bird! Little Bird!"; "Deaf and Dumb"; "Louisa Preston"; "Life in the Ocean"; "The Sister's Hymn."

Flowers for Children. II. (For Children from Four to Six Year Old). New York: C. S. Francis, 1844; rpt. as *Good Little Mitty, and Other Stories.* Boston: D. Lothrop/Dover, N.H.: G. T. Day, 1869.
"Good Little Mitty"; "The Saucy Little Squirrel"; "The Visit"; "The New-England Boy's Song"; "The Impatient Little Girl"; "Little Runaways"; "Robins"; "The Spring Birds"; "Little Mary Is Cross To-Day"; "Little Lucy and Her Lamb"; "Little Francis"; "The Autumn Bird"; "Happy Little George"; "The Donkey"; "The Sailor's Dog"; "Father Is Coming"; "Anna and Her Kitten"; "The House of Little Tom Thumb"; "The Unlucky Day"; "The Hen and Her Ducks"; "The Little Glutton"; "The Twins"; "The Parrot"; "Who Stole the Bird's Nest?"; "The Little White Lamb and the Little Black Lamb"; "May-Day"; "Little Jane"; "My Sister Mary"; "Discontented Dora"; "Little Emma"; "The Young Traveller"; "Gertrude and Her Birds"; "Our Playthings."

Letters From New York. Second Series. New York: C. S. Francis/Boston: J. H. Francis, 1845.

Fact and Fiction: A Collection of Stories. New York: C. S. Francis/Boston: J. H. Francis, 1846; London: William
   Smith, 1847; rpt. as *The Children of Mt. Ida, and Other Stories.* New York: C. S. Francis, 1871.
   "The Children of Mount Ida"; "The Youthful Emigrant. A True Story of the Early Settlement of New
   Jersey"; "The Quadroons"; "The Irish Heart. A True Story"; "A Legend of the Apostle John"; "The
   Beloved Tune"; "Elizabeth Wilson"; "The Neighbour-in-Law"; "She Waits in the Spirit Land"; "A
   Poet's Dream of the Soul"; "The Black Saxons"; "Hilda Silfverling. A Fantasy"; "Rosenglory"; "A
   Legend of the Falls of St. Anthony"; "The Brothers."

With M. Kendrick. *The Gift Book of Biography for Young Ladies.* London: Thomas Nelson; and Edinburgh,
   1847.

Flowers for Children. III (For Children of Eleven and Twelve Years of Age). New York: C. S. Francis/Boston: J. H.
   Francis, 1847; rpt. as *Making Something, and Other Stories.* Boston: D. Lothrop/Dover, N.H.: G. T. Day,
   1869.
   "Making Something"; "The Tulip and the Ladies' Delight"; "Lines to Annette"; "Musical Children";
   "A Dream"; "William Burton, the Boy who would be a Sailor"; "Aunt Maria's Swallows"; "Lariboo.
   Sketches of Life in the Desert."

Sturgis, Caroline. *Rainbows for Children.* Ed. Lydia Maria Child. New York: C. S. Francis, 1848.

Rose Marian and the Flower Fairies. New York: C. S. Francis/Boston: J. H. Francis, 1850.

Sketches from Real Life. I. The Power of Kindness. II. Home and Politics. Philadelphia: Hazard & Mitchell, 1850;
   London: Collins, 1850; rpt. as *The Power of Kindness; and Other Stories.* Philadelphia: Willis P. Hazard,
   1853.

The Childrens' [sic] Gems. The Brother and Sister: And Other Stories. Philadelphia: New Church Book Store,
   1852.

Isaac T. Hopper: A True Life. Boston: John P. Jewett/Cleveland: Jewett, Proctor & Worthington/London:
   Sampson Low, 1853.

The Progress of Religious Ideas, Through Successive Ages. 3 vols. New York: C. S. Francis/London: S. Low, 1855.

A New Flower for Children. New York: C. S. Francis, 1856.
   "Jamie and Jeannie"; "The Sagacious Cat. A True Story"; "Willie Wild Thing"; "The New England
   Boy's Answer to a May-Day Invitation"; "Rosy O'Ryan"; "A Welcome to June"; "The Boy's Heaven";
   "The Boys of the Old Times"; "Secrets of Nature"; "The Real Giants"; "The Royal Rose Bud";
   "Farewell to the Birds."

Sturgis, Caroline. *The Magician's Showbox.* Ed. Lydia Maria Child. Boston: Ticknor & Fields, 1856.

Autumnal Leaves: Tales and Sketches in Prose and Rhyme. New York: C. S. Francis, 1857.
   "The Eglantine"; "A Serenade"; "The Juryman"; "The Fairy Friend"; "Wergeland, the Poet"; "The
   Emigrant Boy"; "Home and Politics"; "To the Trailing Arbutus"; "The Catholic and the Quaker"
   (earlier titled "The Power of Love" and "The Power of Kindness"); "The Rival Mechanicians"; "A
   Song"; "Utouch and Touchu"; "The Brother and Sister"; "The Stream of Life"; "The Man that Killed
   His Neighbours"; "Intelligence of Animals"; "The World that I am Passing Through"; "Jan and Zaida";
   "To the Nasturtiums"; "The Ancient Clairvoyant" (earlier titled "The Prophet of Ionia"); "Spirit and
   Matter"; "The Kansas Emigrants"; "I Want to go Home."

Correspondence between Lydia Maria Child and Gov. Wise and Mrs. Mason, of Virginia. Boston: American Anti-
   Slavery Society, 1860.

The Right Way the Safe Way, Proved by Emancipation in the British West Indies, and Elsewhere. New York: 5
   Beekman Street, 1860; rpt. and enlarged, 1862.

The Patriarchal Institution, As Described by Members of Its Own Family (ed.). New York: American Anti-Slavery
   Society, 1860.

The Duty of Disobedience to the Fugitive Slave Act: An Appeal to the Legislators of Massachusetts. Boston: American
   Anti-Slavery Society, 1860.

Jacobs, Harriet A. *Incidents in the Life of a Slave Girl.* Ed. Lydia Maria Child. Boston: Privately published,
   1861.

Looking toward Sunset. From Sources Old and New, Original and Selected (edited, with the following contributions by Child). Boston: Ticknor and Fields, 1865.

"Preface"; "The Friends"; "Old Folks at Home"; "The Mysterious Pilgrimage"; "Unmarried Women"; "Moral Hints"; "Letter from an Old Woman, on Her Birthday"; "Old Bachelors"; "Old Folks at Home" (another poem by the same title); "Hints about Health."

The Freedmen's Book (edited, with the following contributions by Child). Boston: Ticknor and Fields, 1865.

"Ignatius Sancho"; "Benjamin Banneker"; "William Boen"; "Toussaint L'Ouverture"; "Phillis Wheatley"; "Kindness to Animals"; "James Forten"; "The Meeting in the Swamp" (abbreviated and simplified version of "The Black Saxons"); "Progress of Emancipation in the British West Indies"; "Madison Washington"; "Frederick Douglass"; "William and Ellen Crafts" [sic]; "Education of Children"; "John Brown"; "The Laws of Health"; "Advice from an Old Friend."

A Romance of the Republic. Boston: Ticknor and Fields, 1867.

An Appeal for the Indians. New York: Wm. P. Tomlinson, 1868.

Aspirations of the World. A Chain of Opals (edited, with introduction by Child). Boston: Roberts Brothers, 1878.

Periodical Stories and Sketches (Uncollected Items Marked with Asterisk)

"The Rival Brothers. A Tale of the Revolution." *The Atlantic Souvenir* for 1827. Philadelphia: H. C. Carey & I. Lea: 1826. 208–26; rpt. *American Traveller* 28 Nov. 1826: 4; rpt. *The Coronal* 32–57.

*"Adventure in the Woods." *Juvenile Miscellany* 1 (Sept. 1826): 5–13.

*"Adventures of a Bell." *Juvenile Miscellany* 2 (Mar. 1827): 24–30; rpt. *Massachusetts Journal* 8 Mar. 1827: 4.

*"The Indian Boy." *Juvenile Miscellany* 2 (May 1827): 28–31.

"The Recluse of the Lake." *The Token* for 1828. Boston: S. G. Goodrich, 1827. 59–76; rpt. *The Coronal* 87–119.

"The Adventures of a Rain Drop." *The Token* for 1828. Boston: S. G. Goodrich, 1827. 78–83; rpt. *Massachusetts Journal* 29 Jan. 1828: 1; rpt. *The Coronal* 190–200.

"The Lone Indian." *The Token* for 1828. Boston: S. G. Goodrich, 1827. 101–10; rpt. *The Coronal* 3–19.

"The Young West Indian." By the Author of Hobomok. *The Atlantic Souvenir* for 1828. Philadelphia: Carey, Lea, & Carey, 1827. 230–69; rpt. *The Coronal* 201–62.

"Conversation Between a Little Boy of Olden Times, and a Boston Boy of 1827." *Juvenile Miscellany* 3 (Sept. 1827): 105–10; revised and rpt. as "The Boys of the Old Times" in *A New Flower for Children* 200–215.

*"The Brothers, or . . . The Influence of Example." *Juvenile Miscellany* 3 (Nov. 1827): 209–26.

*"My Mother's Grave." *Juvenile Miscellany* 3 (Jan. 1828): 310–13.

*"The Little Traveller." *Juvenile Miscellany* 3 (Jan. 1828): 365–69.

"Louisa Preston." *Juvenile Miscellany* 4 (Mar. 1828): 56–81.

*"Lealea Hoku." *Juvenile Miscellany* 4 (May 1828): 206–17.

*"The Church in the Wilderness." *The Legendary.* Ed. Nathaniel P. Willis. Boston: Samuel G. Goodrich, 1828. 1–23.

"The Indian Wife." *The Legendary.* Ed. Nathaniel P. Willis. Boston: Samuel G. Goodrich, 1828. 197–208; rpt. *Massachusetts Journal* 28 June 1828: 1–2; rpt. *The Coronal* 162–80.

*"The Orphans." *Juvenile Miscellany* 4 (July 1828): 314–26.

"The Cottage Girl." *Juvenile Miscellany* n.s. 1 (Sept. 1828): 3–19.

*"Annals of a Village. Marian Russell." *Massachusetts Weekly Journal* 7 Jan. 1829: 4.

*"Kirby Simpson." *Massachusetts Journal* 29 Nov. 1828: 1 [authorship uncertain].

"You've been Captain long enough!" *Massachusetts Weekly Journal* 18 Feb. 1829: 4; rpt. *The Coronal* 58–60.

"Harriet Bruce." *Massachusetts Journal* 23 May 1829: 2; *Massachusetts Weekly Journal* 27 May 1829: 2; rpt. *The Coronal* 125–42.

"The Bold and Beautiful Convict." *Massachusetts Weekly Journal* 1 Apr. 1829: 2; rpt. *The Coronal* 148–55.

*"Annals of the Village. The Sudden Match." *Massachusetts Weekly Journal* 15 Apr. 1829: 2.

"Stand from Under!" *Massachusetts Weekly Journal* 8 Aug. 1829: 4; rpt. *Liberator* 28 Jan. 1832: 16; rpt. *The Coronal* 184–89.

*"Captain Gregg and His Dog." *Massachusetts Daily Journal* 24 Aug. 1829; *Massachusetts Weekly Journal* 29 Aug. and 10 Oct. 1829: 1.

"Chocorua's Curse." *The Token* for 1830. Ed. Samuel Goodrich. Boston: Carter and Hendee, 1829. 257–65; rpt. *The Coronal* 270–80.

*"Black Dennis." *Massachusetts Weekly Journal* 27 Feb. 1830: 1.

*"The Rivals." *Massachusetts Weekly Journal* 20 Feb. 1830: 1.

*"The Favorite Guest." *Massachusetts Weekly Journal* 27 Feb. 1830: 2.

*"Aunt Betty." *Massachusetts Weekly Journal* 14 Mar. 1830: 2.

*"The School Mistress." *Massachusetts Weekly Journal* 10 Apr. 1830: 3.

"La Rosiere." *Massachusetts Journal* 17 Apr. 1830: 3; *Massachusetts Weekly Journal* 17 Apr. 1830: 1; rpt. *The Coronal* 67–77.

*"Caroline Swan." *Massachusetts Weekly Journal* 1 May 1830: 2.

*"The St. Domingo Orphans." *Juvenile Miscellany* n.s. 5 (Sept. 1830): 81–94.

"The Sagacious Papa." *Massachusetts Journal and Tribune* 4 Sept. 1830: 1; rpt. *The Coronal* 20–29.

"The Indolent Fairy" (1830). *Youth's Keepsake; a Christmas and New Year's Gift for Young People.* Boston: Carter and Hendee, 1831. 199–206; rpt. *Flowers for Children. I* 130–38.

"The Spider, Caterpillar and Silk Worm." *Massachusetts Journal and Tribune* 27 Nov. 1830: 2; rpt. and retitled "Fable of the Caterpillar and Silk-Worm." *The Coronal* 181–82.

*"First and Last Thanksgiving." *Massachusetts Journal and Tribune* 4 Dec. 1830: 2.

"The Palace of Beauty. A Fairy Tale." *Massachusetts Journal and Tribune* 25 Dec. 1830: 3; rpt. *The Little Girl's Own Book* 271–80.

*"Pol Sosef. The Indian Artist." *Juvenile Miscellany* n.s. 5 (Jan. 1831): 278–84.

*"Jumbo and Zairee." *Juvenile Miscellany* n.s. 5 (Jan. 1831): 285–99.

*"Letter from a Native of Tongataboo." *Juvenile Miscellany* n.s. 5 (Jan. 1831): 307–10.

*"Darby and Joan." *Massachusetts Journal and Tribune* 26 Feb. 1831: 2.

*"The Gipsey Wife. Founded on Facts Stated in an English Law Book." *Massachusetts Journal and Tribune* 16 Apr. 1831: 1.

*"The Sultana of the Desert. Translated for the *Massachusetts Journal* from *Le Courier des Etats Unis*." *Massachusetts Journal and Tribune* 23 Apr. 1831: 1 (possible source for LMC's "Life in the Desert").

"Life in the Desert." n.s. 6 (May 1831): 160–89; retitled "Lariboo" and revised for *Flowers for Children. III* 154–84.

*"The Slave Trader." *Massachusetts Journal and Tribune* 7 and 14 May 1831: 1.

*"The Industrious Family." *Juvenile Miscellany* n.s. 6 (July 1831): 217–30.

"William Burton; or the Boy Who Would be a Sailor." *Juvenile Miscellany* 3rd ser. 1 (Sept. 1831): 1–45; rpt. *Flowers for Children. III.* 97–143.

*"The Despot's Favorite." *Massachusetts Journal and Tribune* 29 Oct. 1831: 2.

*"The Stage Coach." *Massachusetts Journal.* [Pasted into a scrapbook, LMC Papers, Schlesinger Library, date unknown].

*"Annals of a Village. Founded on Fact." *Massachusetts Journal.* [Pasted into a scrapbook, LMC Papers, Schlesinger Library, date unknown.]

*"Annals of a Village. The Blacksmith's Daughter." *Massachusetts Journal.* [Pasted into a scrapbook, LMC Papers, Schlesinger Library, date unknown.]

*"Annals of a Village. The Runaway Marriage." *Massachusetts Journal.* [Pasted into a scrapbook, LMC Papers, Schlesinger Library, date unknown.]

*"Buffalo Creek." *Juvenile Miscellany* 3rd ser. 4 (July 1833): 255–75.

*"William Peterson, the Brave and Good Boy." *Juvenile Miscellany* 3rd ser. 5 (Mar. 1834): 66–67.

*"Mary French and Susan Easton." *Juvenile Miscellany* 3rd ser. 6 (May 1834): 186–202.

"The Black Saxons" (1840). *The Liberty Bell*. Boston: Massachusetts Anti-Slavery Fair, 1841. 19–44; rpt. *Liberator* 8 Jan. 1841: 5–6; rpt. *Fact and Fiction* 190–204; rpt., revised and retitled "The Meeting in the Swamp." *The Freedmen's Book* 104–10.

"The Quadroons" (1841). *The Liberty Bell*. Boston: Massachusetts Anti-Slavery Fair, 1842; rpt. *Fact and Fiction* 61–76.

*"Slavery's Pleasant Homes. A Faithful Sketch" (1842). *The Liberty Bell*. Boston: Massachusetts Anti-Slavery Fair, 1843. 147–60.

"The Remembered Home." *The Present* 1 (Sept. 1843): 11–18; rpt. *Letters from New York. Second Series* 32–47.

"Thot and Frela." *Columbian Lady's and Gentleman's Magazine* 3 (Jan. 1845): 1–7; included in *Letters from New York. Second Series* 176–95.

"Elizabeth Wilson." *Columbian Lady's and Gentleman's Magazine* 3 (Feb. 1845): 79–85; rpt. as "Lizzy. A Thrilling Story." Philadelphia *Saturday Courier* 1 Feb. 1845: 1, 4; rpt. *Fact and Fiction* 128–48.

"The Children of Mt. Ida." *Columbian Lady's and Gentleman's Magazine* 3 (Apr. 1845): 145–54; rpt. *Fact and Fiction* 9–39.

"The Youthful Emigrant." *Columbian Lady's and Gentleman's Magazine* 3 (June 1845): 241–47; rpt. *Fact and Fiction* 40–60.

"The Irish Heart. A True Story." *Columbian Lady's and Gentleman's Magazine* 4 (July 1845): 17–21; rpt. *Fact and Fiction* 77–90.

"A Legend of the Apostle John." *Columbian Lady's and Gentleman's Magazine* 4 (Sept. 1845): 123–30; rpt. *Fact and Fiction* 91–115.

"Hilda Silfverling. A Fantasy." *Columbian Lady's and Gentleman's Magazine* 4 (Oct. 1845): 169–78; rpt. *Fact and Fiction* 205–40.

"The Beloved Tune." *Columbian Lady's and Gentleman's Magazine* 4 (Nov. 1845): 193–96; rpt. *Fact and Fiction* 116–25.

"She Waits in the Spirit Land." *Columbian Lady's and Gentleman's Magazine* 5 (Mar. 1846): 97–101; rpt. *Fact and Fiction* 163–76.

"The Neighbour-in-Law." *Columbian Lady's and Gentleman's Magazine* 5 (June 1846): 241–45; rpt. *Fact and Fiction* 149–62.

"A Poet's Dream of the Soul." *Columbian Lady's and Gentleman's Magazine* 6 (Sept. 1846): 117–20; rpt. *Fact and Fiction* 177–89.

"Rosenglory." *Columbian Lady's and Gentleman's Magazine* 6 (Oct. 1846): 181–86; rpt. *Fact and Fiction* 241–60.

"The Rival Mechanicians." *Columbian Lady's and Gentleman's Magazine* 7 (Jan. 1847): 13–18; rpt. *Autumnal Leaves* 143–64.

"The Fairy Friend." *Columbian Lady's and Gentleman's Magazine* 7 (Mar. 1847): 97–98; rpt. *Autumnal Leaves* 65–71.

"The Man That Killed His Neighbours." *Columbian Lady's and Gentleman's Magazine* 7 (May 1847): 193–97; rpt. *Autumnal Leaves* 203–20.

"The Emigrant Boy." *Union Magazine of Literature and Art* 1 (July 1847): 4–8; rpt. *Autumnal Leaves* 79–95.

"The Brother and Sister." *Union Magazine of Literature and Art* 1 (Oct. 1847): 155–59; rpt. *Autumnal Leaves* 181–99.

"Utouch and Touchu." *Union Magazine of Literature and Art* 1 (Dec. 1847): 241–44; rpt. *Autumnal Leaves* 166–80.

"The Bewildered Savage." *Union Magazine of Literature and Art* 2 (Jan. 1848): 23–26. Incorporated into "The Adventures of Jamie and Jeannie." *A New Flower for Children*. New York: C. S. Francis, 1856. 9–102.

*"The Hindoo Anchorite." *Union Magazine of Literature and Art* 2 (Apr. 1848): 151–53.

"The Power of Love." *Union Magazine of Literature and Art* 2 (May 1848): 213–18; rpt. and retitled "The Power of Kindness." *Sketches from Real Life. I. The Power of Kindness. II. Home and Politics*. Philadelphia:

Hazard & Mitchell, 1850; rpt. as *The Power of Kindness; and Other Stories*. Philadelphia: Willis P. Hazard, 1853; rpt. and retitled "The Catholic and the Quaker," *Autumnal Leaves* 121–42.

"Home and Politics." *Sartain's Union Magazine of Literature and Art* 3 (Aug. 1848): 63–68; rpt. *Sketches from Real Life. I. The Power of Kindness. II. Home and Politics*. Philadelphia: Hazard & Mitchell, 1850; rpt. as *The Power of Kindness; and Other Stories*. Philadelphia: Willis P. Hazard, 1853; rpt. *Autumnal Leaves* 96–118.

"The Prophet of Ionia." *Sartain's Union Magazine of Literature and Art* 4 (Feb. 1849): 94–97; revised and retitled "The Ancient Clairvoyant." *Autumnal Leaves* 269–90.

*"The Stars and Stripes. A Melo-Drama" (1857). *The Liberty Bell*. Boston: Massachusetts Anti-Slavery Fair, 1858. 122–85.

*"Loo Loo. A Few Scenes from a True History." *Atlantic Monthly* 1 (May 1858): 801–12; (June 1858): 32–42.

*"Willie Wharton." *Atlantic Monthly* 11 (Mar. 1863): 324–45.

*"Freddy's New-Year's Dinner. A Story for Small Young Folks." *Our Young Folks* 1 (July 1865): 421–29.

*"Grandfather's Chestnut-Tree." *Our Young Folks* 1 (Oct. 1865): 613–27.

*"The Two Christmas Evenings." *Our Young Folks* 2 (Jan. 1866): 2–13.

*"Poor Chloe. A True Story of Massachusetts in the Olden Time." *Atlantic Monthly* 17 (Mar. 1866): 352–64.

*"A Soul's Victory over Circumstances." *Woman's Journal* 16 Sept. 1871: 294–95.

*"A Woman Who Made Good Use of Her Tongue." Trans. from the German. *Woman's Journal* 31 July 1875: 246–47; 7 Aug. 1875: 254–55.

Journalism and Miscellaneous Nonfiction (Uncollected Items Marked with Asterisk)

"The American Traveller." *Juvenile Miscellany* 1 (Sept. 1826): 14–20; rpt. *Biographical Sketches of Great and Good Men* 49–55.

*"Mother and Eliza." *Juvenile Miscellany* 1 (Sept. 1826): 45–47.

"Sir Benjamin West." *Juvenile Miscellany* 1 (Jan. 1827): 19–25; rpt. *Biographical Sketches of Great and Good Men* 56–63.

*"Wonders of the Deep." *Juvenile Miscellany* 1 (Jan. 1827): 66–80.

*"Value of Time." *Juvenile Miscellany* 1 (Jan. 1827): 103–5.

"Benjamin Franklin." *Juvenile Miscellany* 2 (Mar. 1827): 18–23; rpt. *Biographical Sketches of Great and Good Men* 9–14.

"William Penn." *Juvenile Miscellany* 2 (July 1827): 40–49; rpt. *Biographical Sketches of Great and Good Men* 64–75.

"Rev. John Eliot." *Juvenile Miscellany* 3 (Nov. 1827): 140–44; rpt. *Biographical Sketches of Great and Good Men* 76–80.

*"On the Importance of Mental Resources." *Massachusetts Journal*. Pasted into a scrapbook, LMC Papers, Schlesinger Library; may date from ca. 1827–28; rpt. as "The Importance of Resources among Ourselves. *Written fourteen years ago, by L. M. Child.*" *National Anti-Slavery Standard* 20 May 1841: 198.

*"American History." *Juvenile Miscellany* n.s. 1 (Sept. 1828): 99–108.

"Romance." *Massachusetts Journal* 20 Nov. 1828: 1; rpt. *The Coronal* 156–60.

*"Review of Frances Parkes, *Domestic Duties. Massachusetts Weekly Journal* 17 Dec. 1828: 3.

"Philosophy and Consistency." *Massachusetts Weekly Journal* 7 Jan. 1829: 2; rpt. *Frugal Housewife* from 1830 ed. on.

*"Politeness." *Massachusetts Weekly Journal* 18 Feb. 1829: 4.

*"Comparative Strength of Male and Female Intellect." *Massachusetts Journal* 3 Mar. 1829; *Massachusetts Weekly Journal* 4 Mar. 1829: 2.

*"Fish." *Massachusetts Weekly Journal* 25 Mar. 1829: 1.

*"Rambling Thoughts." *Massachusetts Weekly Journal* 8 Apr. 1829: 2.

*"American History." *Juvenile Miscellany* n.s. 2 (May 1829): 199–205.

"Hints to People of Moderate Fortune." *Massachusetts Weekly Journal* 27 May 1829: 2; rpt. *Frugal Housewife* from 1830 ed. on.

*"Criticisms on the Gallery." *Massachusetts Weekly Journal* 3 June 1829: 1.

"Hints to People of Moderate Fortune." *Massachusetts Weekly Journal* 17 June 1829: 4; rpt. *Frugal Housewife* from 1830 ed. on.

*"Hints." *Massachusetts Weekly Journal* 1 July 1829: 2.

"More Hints to People of Moderate Fortune." *Massachusetts Weekly Journal* 15 July 1829: 1; rpt. *Frugal Housewife* from 1830 ed. on.

*"Filial Piety." *Massachusetts Weekly Journal* 22 July 1829: 4 (authorship uncertain).

*"Satire." *Massachusetts Weekly Journal* 22 July 1829: 4 (authorship uncertain).

*"Letter from a Lady, concerning Miss Wright." *Massachusetts Weekly Journal* 14 Aug. 1829: 3.

*"Chinese Children." *Juvenile Miscellany* n.s. 3 (Sept. 1829): 3–6.

"More Hints to People of Moderate Fortune." *Massachusetts Weekly Journal* 12 Sept. 1829: 2; rpt. *Frugal Housewife* from 1830 ed. on.

*"Letter from a Lady in Boston to her Friend in the Country." *Massachusetts Weekly Journal* 19 Sept. 1829: 2.

*Review of *The Token* [for 1830]. *Massachusetts Weekly Journal* 24 Oct. 1829: 2.

"More Hints to People of Moderate Fortune." *Massachusetts Weekly Journal* 24 Oct. 1829: 2; rpt. *Frugal Housewife* from 1830 ed. on.

*Review of *The Wept of Wish-ton-Wish*. *Massachusetts Weekly Journal* 21 Nov. 1829: 4.

"More Hints to People of Moderate Fortune." *Massachusetts Weekly Journal* 30 Jan. 1830: 2; rpt. *Frugal Housewife* from 1830 ed. on.

*"Wealth." *Massachusetts Weekly Journal* 14 Mar. 1830: 3.

*"Rules for a Young Lady." *Massachusetts Weekly Journal* 1 May 1830: 4.

*"Hints on Education." *Massachusetts Weekly Journal* 15 May 1830: 3.

*"Straw Bonnets." *Massachusetts Weekly Journal* 22 May 1830: 3.

*"Popular Manners." *Massachusetts Weekly Journal* 3 July 1830: 2.

*"Prudential Matches." *Massachusetts Weekly Journal* 21 Aug. 1830: 2.

*"Domestic Happiness — Its Influence, &c." *Massachusetts Journal and Tribune* 18 Sept. 1830: 1–2.

*"Hiding in the Sand." *Massachusetts Journal and Tribune* 2 Oct. 1830: 1–2.

*"Female Labor." *Massachusetts Journal and Tribune* 9 Oct. 1830: 1 (authorship uncertain).

*"News and Newspapers." *Massachusetts Journal and Tribune* 9 Oct. 1830: 2.

*"Comfort." *Massachusetts Journal and Tribune* 30 Oct. 1830: 2.

*"New Zealanders." *Juvenile Miscellany* n.s. 5 (Nov. 1830): 189–95.

"The First and Last Book." *Massachusetts Journal and Tribune* 13 Nov. 1830: 1; rpt. *The Coronal*. 282–85.

*"Literature below Stairs." *Massachusetts Journal and Tribune* 1 Jan. 1831: 1.

*"The Mismanagement of Children." *Massachusetts Journal and Tribune* 22 Jan. 1831: 2.

*"Polar Regions." *Juvenile Miscellany* n.s. 6 (Mar. 1831): 89–101.

"Thoughts." *Massachusetts Journal and Tribune* 11 June 1831: 2; rpt. *The Coronal*. 63–66.

*"Man-Traps." *Massachusetts Journal and Tribune* 16 July 1831: 1.

*"Novel Incident." *Massachusetts Journal and Tribune* 6 Aug. 1831: 3.

*"Woman's Love Strong in Death." *Massachusetts Journal and Tribune* 24 Sept. 1831: 2.

*"The Moral of an Alarm Watch." *Massachusetts Journal and Tribune* 17 Dec. 1831: 1; rpt. *Liberator* 21 Jan. 1832: 12; rpt. and retitled "The Alarm-Watch." *Juvenile Miscellany* 3rd ser. 6 (May 1834): 210–11.

*"To the Public" (letter in response to accusation of having copied idea for *Little Girl's Own Book* from Eliza Leslie). *Massachusetts Journal and Tribune* 14 Jan. 1832: 3.

*"The Miseries of Knowledge." *Massachusetts Journal* [pasted into scrapbook in LMC Papers, Schlesinger Library; date unknown].

*"The Winds." *Massachusetts Journal* [pasted into scrapbook in LMC Papers, Schlesinger Library; date unknown].

*"Leaf from a Reviewer's Journal." *Massachusetts Journal* [pasted into a scrapbook, LMC Papers, Schlesinger Library, date unknown].

*"New Books." *Juvenile Miscellany* 3rd ser. 2 (March 1832): 108.

*"All about Cuba." *Juvenile Miscellany* 3rd ser. 2 (May 1832): 198–215.

*"New Books." *Juvenile Miscellany* 3rd ser. 2 (July 1832): 320–21.

"Some Talk about Brazil." *Juvenile Miscellany* 3rd ser. 3 (Sept. 1832): 47–50; partially incorporated into *An Appeal* 189–92.

*"A Few Words about Turkey." *Juvenile Miscellany* 3rd ser. 5 (Jan. 1833): 310–11.

"Kindness of the Africans." *Juvenile Miscellany* 3rd ser. 5 (Nov. 1833): 114–18; partially incorporated into *An Appeal* 198–99.

"Charity Bowery." *The Liberty Bell*. Boston: Massachusetts Anti-Slavery Fair, 1839. 26–43; rpt. *Letters from New York. Second Series* 43–56.

"Anecdote of Elias Hicks." *The Liberty Bell*. Boston: Massachusetts Anti-Slavery Fair, 1839. 65–68. Incorporated into *Isaac T. Hopper* 274–82.

*"The Emancipated Slaveholders." *The Liberty Bell*. Boston: Massachusetts Anti-Slavery Fair, 1839. 71–74.

*"To the Readers of the Standard." *National Anti-Slavery Standard* 20 May 1841: 198.

*"To Abolitionists" [inaugural editorial]. *National Anti-Slavery Standard* 20 May 1841: 198.

*"Prospectus of the Anti-Slavery Standard for 1841–42." *National Anti-Slavery Standard* 20 May 1841: 199.

"The Deserted Church." *National Anti-Slavery Standard* 27 May 1841: 203; partially incorporated into *Letters from New York. Second Series* 144–50.

*"The Third Political Party." *National Anti-Slavery Standard* 24 June 1841: 10–11.

*"Speaking in the Church." *National Anti-Slavery Standard* 15 July 1841: 22.

*"Annette Gray." *National Anti-Slavery Standard* 22 July 1841: 203.

*"They have not wit enough to take care of themselves." *National Anti-Slavery Standard* 5 Aug. 1841: 41.

*"Rev. Jonathan Davis." *National Anti-Slavery Standard* 26 Aug. 1841: 46.

*"Moral Influence." *National Anti-Slavery Standard* 2 Dec. 1841: 102.

*"Letters from New-York." No. 12 [on the *Amistad* captives]. *National Anti-Slavery Standard* 2 Dec. 1841: 103.

*"Letters from New-York." No. 14 [interview with an ex-slave woman]. *National Anti-Slavery Standard* 16 Dec. 1841: 111.

*"The Press." *National Anti-Slavery Standard* 23 Dec. 1841: 114.

*"Independence of the Press." *National Anti-Slavery Standard* 30 Dec. 1841: 119.

*"Address to their Fellow-Citizens, by the Executive Committee of the American Anti-Slavery Society." *National Anti-Slavery Standard* 27 Jan. 1842: 135.

*"Peterboro Convention." *National Anti-Slavery Standard* 10 Feb. 1842: 142.

*"Gerrit Smith's Address to the Slaves." *National Anti-Slavery Standard* 24 Feb. 1842: 150–51.

*"The Union." *National Anti-Slavery Standard* 24 Feb. 1842: 151.

*"The Iron Shroud." *National Anti-Slavery Standard* 3 Mar. 1842: 154–55.

*"Letters from New-York." No. 18 [description of Delevan Temperance Institute]. *National Anti-Slavery Standard* 3 Mar. 1842: 155.

*"The Press." *National Anti-Slavery Standard* 24 Mar. 1842: 166–67.

*"The Conscientious Slave," *National Anti-Slavery Standard* 7 Apr. 1842: 174–75.

*"Our Anglo-Saxon Ancestry." *National Anti-Slavery Standard* 28 Apr. 1842: 186–87.

*"The Anniversary." *National Anti-Slavery Standard* 19 May 1842: 198.

*"Great Race between the North and the South." *National Anti-Slavery Standard* 9 June 1842: 2.

*"Talk about Political Party." *National Anti-Slavery Standard* 7 July 1842: 18–19.

*"The Decision of the Supreme Court." *National Anti-Slavery Standard* 7 July 1842: 18–19.

*"Follow the North Star." *National Anti-Slavery Standard* 21 July 1842: 25.

*"Colonization." *National Anti-Slavery Standard* 28 July 1842: 31.

*"Letters from New-York." No. 33 [on antiabolitionist mob at George Thompson's lecture of 1 Aug. 1835]. *National Anti-Slavery Standard* 18 Aug. 1842: 43.

*"Colorphobia." *National Anti-Slavery Standard* 18 Aug. 1842: 43.

*"Letters from New-York." No. 36. *National Anti-Slavery Standard* 22 Sept. 1842: 63.

*"Lewis Clark." *National Anti-Slavery Standard* 20 and 27 Oct. 1842: 78, 83.

*"Arthur Tappan." *National Anti-Slavery Standard* 15 Dec. 1842: 111.

*"Unwritten Wrongs." *National Anti-Slavery Standard* 29 Dec. 1842: 119.

*"The Slaveholder Seeking Light." *National Anti-Slavery Standard* 26 Jan. 1843: 134–35.

*"Sects and Sectarianism." *National Anti-Slavery Standard* 16 Feb. 1843: 146.

*"Farewell." *National Anti-Slavery Standard* 4 May 1843: 190–91.

*"The Missionary of Prisons." *The Present* 1 (Dec. 1843): 210–12.

*"Progress and Hope." *The Present* 1 (Jan. 1844): 230–34.

*"Letter from New-York." [on Amelia Norman]. *Boston Courier* 6 Feb. 1844; rpt. *National Anti-Slavery Standard* 22 Feb. 1844.

"Letter from New-York." No. 8 [denunciation of Nativism]. *Boston Courier* 19 Apr. 1844.

"Ole Bul's Niagara." *Broadway Journal* 1 (4 Jan. 1845): 9–10; rpt. *Letters from New York. Second Series* 272–79.

*Review of *Woman in the Nineteenth Century* by Margaret Fuller. *Boston Courier* 8 Feb. 1845: 2.

*Review of *Woman in the Nineteenth Century* by Margaret Fuller. *New York Daily Tribune* 12 Feb. 1845: 1.

*Review of *Woman in the Nineteenth Century* by Margaret Fuller. *Broadway Journal* 1 (15 Feb. 1845): 97.

*"Monsieur Edouart's Silhouette Rooms." *Broadway Journal* 1 (15 Feb. 1845): 101–2.

*"Letter from New-York." [on Julia Northall and New York church architecture]. *Boston Courier* 2 Oct. 1845.

*"Letter from New-York." [on Antony Philip Heinrich]. *Boston Courier* 7 Nov. 1845; *New York Evening Post* 11 Nov. 1845.

*"The Beauty of Peace." *Columbian Lady's and Gentleman's Magazine* 4 (Dec. 1845): 251–53.

*"The Self-Conscious and the Unconscious." *Columbian Lady's and Gentleman's Magazine* 5 (Jan. 1846): 43.

"Letter from New-York." No. 3 [on the Prison Association]. *Boston Courier* 30 Jan. 1846.

*"Recollections of Ole Bull." *Columbian Lady's and Gentleman's Magazine* 5 (Feb. 1846): 72–76.

*"Letter from New-York." [on prison reform]. *Boston Courier* 12 Mar. 1846.

*"Letter from New York." [on John Sullivan Dwight's lectures, Christopher Cranch's paintings, Dickens's letters against capital punishment, and the achievements of women]. *Boston Courier* 2 Apr. 1846; partial rpt. *National Anti-Slavery Standard* 30 Apr. 1846.

*"Letter from New-York." [on concerts in New York]. *Boston Courier* 27 Oct. 1846.

*"Letter from New York." [on a fugitive slave case]. *Boston Courier* 31 Oct. 1846.

*"Letter from New York." [another installment on the same case]. *Boston Courier* 3 Nov. 1846.

*"Letter from New-York." [on Art Union, Horace Kneeland, and Edward L. Walker]. *Boston Courier* 11 Nov. 1846.

*"The Northmen." *Columbian Lady's and Gentleman's Magazine* 6 (Dec. 1846): 241–47.

*"Letter from New-York." [on Viennese dancers]. *Boston Courier* 14 Dec. 1846.

*"Letter from New-York." [on prison reform]. *Boston Courier* 23 Feb. 1847.

"Correspondence between Mrs. M. J. C. Mason, of Virginia, and Mrs. L. Maria Child, of Massachusetts. *Echoes of Harper's Ferry.* Ed. James Redpath. Boston: Thayer and Eldridge, 1860. 333–47.

*"Spirits." *Atlantic Monthly* 9 (May 1862): 578–84.

*"Through the Red Sea into the Wilderness." *Independent* 21 Dec. 1865: 1; rpt. *Liberator* 29 Dec. 1865: 205.

*"The President of the United States." *Independent* 8 Mar. 1866: 1.

*"All Soul's Day." *National Anti-Slavery Standard* 9 May 1868: 3.

*"Letter from Mrs. L. Maria Child" [included in article on "The Woman's Rights Convention"]. *National Anti-Slavery Standard* 5 Dec. 1868: 3; partially rpt. *Woman's Advocate* 1 (January 1869): 58–59.

*"About Santo [sic] Claus." *Independent* 24 Dec. 1868: 1.

*"Indian Civilization." *Independent* 11 Feb. 1869: 1.

*"Hon. Geo. W. Julian vs. Land Monopoly." *National Anti-Slavery Standard* 13 Mar. 1869: 2.

*"Homesteads." *National Anti-Slavery Standard* 20 Mar. 1869: 2.

*"The Radicals." *Independent* 19 Aug. 1869: 1; rpt. *National Anti-Slavery Standard* 28 Aug. 1869: 1.

*"Women and the Freedmen." *National Anti-Slavery Standard* 28 Aug. 1869: 2; rpt. *Woman's Advocate* 1 (Oct. 1869): 190–92.

*"The Byron Controversy." *Independent* 14 Oct. 1869: 1; rpt. *National Anti-Slavery Standard* 23 Oct. 1869: 4.

*"Concerning Women." *Independent* 21 Oct. 1869: 1; rpt. *National Anti-Slavery Standard* 30 Oct. 1869: 1.

*"Women and Minors." *National Anti-Slavery Standard* 23 Oct. 1869: 2.

*"Little Dog Pink." *National Anti-Slavery Standard* 12 Feb. 1870: 4.

*"The Relations of Man to Animals." *Independent* 3 Mar. 1870: 3; rpt. *National Anti-Slavery Standard* 12 Mar. 1870: 1.

*"The Indians." *The Standard* n.s. 1 (May 1870): 1.

*"Resemblances between the Buddhist and the Roman Catholic Religions." *Atlantic Monthly* 26 (Dec. 1870): 660–65.

*"Letter from Lydia Maria Child" (15 Dec. 1870). *Woman's Journal* 24 Dec. 1870: 405.

*"Another Friend Gone." *National Standard* 28 Jan. 1871: 1.

*"Dominica and Hayti." *National Standard* 28 Jan. 1871: 4–5.

*"The Franco-Prussia War." *Independent* 9 Feb. 1871: 1.

*"Rejection of the Hon. Charles Sumner." *National Standard* 18 Mar. 1871: 4–5.

*"Concerning Woman Suffrage." *Woman's Journal* 1 July 1871: 204.

*"Chromos." *Woman's Journal* 15 July 1871: 221.

*"Economy and Work." *National Standard* 5 Aug. 1871: 4–5.

*"The Intermingling of Religions." *Atlantic Monthly* 28 (Oct. 1871): 385–95.

*"A Memory." *National Standard* Feb. 1872: 1.

*"Tobacco." *National Standard* Feb. 1872: 1; Mar. 1872: 4–5.

*"Two Significant Sculptures." *Woman's Journal* 9 Mar. 1872: 76.

*"Diamonds in the Dirt." *Woman's Journal* 30 Mar. 1872: 99.

*"Temperance in Eating." *National Standard* June 1872: 5.

*"A Glance at the State of Things." *Boston Journal* 16 July 1872: 3.

*"The Present Aspect of Political Affairs." *Woman's Journal* 10 Aug. 1872: 252.

*"Physical Strength of Women." *Woman's Journal* 15 Mar. 1873: 84.

*"A Mistake Corrected — Letter from Mrs. Child." *Woman's Journal* 22 Mar. 1873: 92.

*"Dr. Osgood and His Daughters." *Independent* 17 July 1873: 893–94.

*"Is Intellectuality the Bane of American Women?" *Woman's Journal* 19 July 1873: 228.

*"Samuel J. May." *Woman's Journal* 30 Aug. 1873: 276.

*"Mrs. L. Maria Child on Taxation." *Woman's Journal* 28 Aug. 1875: 276.

*"One of Our Benefactors." *Woman's Journal* 25 Mar. 1876: 100.

*"Letter from Mrs. Child." *Woman's Journal* 15 July 1876: 225.

*"Equality of the Sexes." *Woman's Journal* 5 Aug. 1876: 252.

*"Anne Whitney's Model of Charles Sumner's Statue." *Woman's Journal* 5 May 1877: 137.

*"William Lloyd Garrison." *Atlantic Monthly* 44 (Aug. 1879): 237–38.

*"The Underground Railroad." Pasted into a scrapbook in LMC Papers, Anti-Slavery Collection, Rare and Manuscript Collections, Cornell University Library; journal and date unknown.

Poems (Uncollected Items Marked with an Asterisk)

"The Valentine." By the Author of Hobomok. *The Atlantic Souvenir* for 1828. Philadelphia: Carey, Lea, & Carey, [Aug.] 1827. 3–4; rpt. and retitled "Address to the Valentine." *The Coronal* 78–79.

"Beauty." *The Token* for 1828. Boston: S. G. Goodrich [Oct.] 1827. 282–83; rpt. and retitled "Lines to Beauty." *The Coronal* 123–24.

*"Introduction." George W[ashington] Julian. *Speeches on Political Questions by George W. Julian. With an Introduction by L. Maria Child.* New York: Hurd and Houghton, 1872. v–xvii.

"Stanzas occasioned by hearing a Little Boy, just let loose from School, mocking the Bell, as it struck the hour of Twelve." *Atlantic Souvenir* for 1829. Philadelphia: Carey, Lea, [August] 1828. 159–60. [signed L. M. Francis]; rpt. and retitled "Lines To a little boy mocking the Old South Bell, as it rung the hour of twelve," By the Author of Hobomok." *Massachusetts Weekly Journal* 8 Oct. 1828: 4; rpt. and retitled "Lines, Occasioned by Hearing a Little Boy Mock the Old South Bell Ringing the Hour of Twelve." *The Coronal* 61–62.

"A New Year's Offering." *Atlantic Souvenir* for 1829. Philadelphia: Carey, Lea, [Aug.] 1828. 246–47 [signed L. M. Francis]; rpt. as "A New-Year's Offering to a Friend" *The Coronal* 263–64.

"To the Beautiful Flower, Called the Fringed Gentian." *Juvenile Miscellany* n.s. 1 (Sept. 1828): 49–50; rpt. *Massachusetts Journal* 20 Sept. 1828: 4; rpt. and retitled "The Fringed Gentian." *The Coronal* 143–46.

*"Lines Suggested by a very pretty picture of Cupid filling his quiver with dollars." *Massachusetts Weekly Journal* 20 Dec. 1828: 4.

*"The Snow—The Snow!" *Massachusetts Weekly Journal* 25 Feb. 1829: 3.

*"Suggested by the Play called 'The Bottle Imp.'" *Massachusetts Weekly Journal* 25 Feb. 1829: 4.

*"Auld Lang Syne." *Massachusetts Weekly Journal* 25 Mar. 1829: 4.

*"Turn Out." *Massachusetts Weekly Journal* 8 Apr. 1829: 2.

*"May Day." *Juvenile Miscellany* n.s. 2 (May 1829): 211–15; rpt. *Massachusetts Weekly Journal* 6 May 1829: 4.

*"The Dandy Poet's Appeal." *Massachusetts Weekly Journal* 22 July 1829: 4.

*"The Caravan of Animals." *Massachusetts Weekly Journal* 10 Oct. 1829: 3.

"Lines, Occasioned by seeing an Indian employed as a Sawyer in Boston." *Massachusetts Journal*. [Pasted into a scrapbook, LMC Papers, Schlesinger Library, date unknown.]

"Lines, Suggested by Vanderlyn's Fine Picture of Caius Marius among the Ruins of Carthage." rpt. *The Coronal* 1–2. *The Token* for 1828. Boston: S. G. Goodrich [Oct.] 1827. 255–56.

*"To George Thompson." *Liberator* 14 Nov. 1835: 183; rpt. "Letters from New-York.—No. 33." *National Anti-Slavery Standard* 18 Aug. 1842: 43.

*"Lines to Those Men and Women, Who Were Avowed Abolitionists in 1831, '32, '33, '34, and '35." *The Liberty Bell*. Boston: Massachusetts Anti-Slavery Fair, 1839. 5–9.

"A Welcome to Ole Bull, on his return from Canada." *U.S. Magazine and Democratic Review* 15 (Sept. 1844): 285; rpt. *Letters from New York. Second Series*, Letter No. 25, 232–35.

*"Lines. Suggested by a Lock of Hair from Our Departed Friend, Catherine Sargent." *The Liberty Bell* for 1856. Boston: National Anti-Slavery Bazaar, 1856. 159–60.

*"The Hero's Heart." *Echoes of Harper's Ferry*. Ed. James Redpath. Boston: Thayer and Eldridge, 1860. 348.

*"God Bless Our Soldier Boy." *The Prairie Chicken* 1 (Nov. 1864): 1.

*"The Woodland Poet's Alchemy." *The Prairie Chicken* 1 (May 1865): 4.

*"Our Legion of Honor." *The Prairie Chicken* 1 (June 1865): 1.

*"A Voice from Memory. Written on the 24th of May, the Anniversary of the Day on which Ellis Gray Loring Departed from This Life." *The Standard* 1 (June 1870): 1–2.

Unpublished manuscripts in LMC Papers, Anti-Slavery Collection, Rare and Manuscript Collections, Cornell University.

"How a very small Mouse helped to gnaw open a net that held a great Lion." 1860.

"Employments in 1864."

"Autobiography" (1875).

"To the Spirit of my Beloved Old Mate. Copied in the Summer of 1875."

"Duplicity. A tale from real life" (date unknown).

"A Song in Gold" (date unknown).

"Simplicity of the Olden Time" (date unknown; seems to be part of a longer mss.).

"Short pieces to be put in to fill up pages, if needed" (date unknown; seems to be part of a longer mss.).

"From her lone path she never turns aside" (poem fragment, date unknown; seems to be part of a longer mss.)

"The child counted 1, 2, 3 . . ." (mss. fragment, date unknown).

"Mr. Graeter told a story . . ." (mss. fragment, date unknown).

"Aspirations of the World" (draft).

Unpublished manuscripts in Other Collections.

"Bring flowers for the artist's brow." Unpublished poem, [Francis] Alexander Family Papers, Vol. 2, p. 6. Schlesinger Library.

"The Kansas Emigrants" (draft). Lydia Maria Child Papers, New York Public Library.

"Song for the Free Soil Men," Lydia Maria Child Papers, New York Public Library.

"The Colored Mammy and her White Foster-Child. A True Story." Lydia Maria Child Papers, New York Historical Society.

"Negro Song, During the War of The Rebellion." Unpublished manuscript, provenance unknown, Patricia G. Holland File, Amherst, Mass.

Collected Letters

[Harriet Winslow Sewall, ed.]. *Letters of Lydia Maria Child with a Biographical Introduction by John G. Whittier and an Appendix by Wendell Phillips.* Boston: Houghton Mifflin, 1882.

The Collected Correspondence of Lydia Maria Child, 1817–1880. Ed. Patricia G. Holland, Milton Meltzer, and Francine Krasno. Millwood, N.Y.: Kraus Microform, 1980.

Lydia Maria Child: Selected Letters, 1817–1880. Ed. Milton Meltzer, Patricia G. Holland, and Francine Krasno. Amherst: U of Massachusetts P, 1982.

Uncollected Letters (Copies of Most on File with Patricia G. Holland, Amherst, Mass.; Items Listed in Dealers' Catalogs Can Be Traced through the American Antiquarian Society, Worcester, Mass.)

LMC to Catharine Maria Sedgwick. 21 Aug. 1826. Catharine Sedgwick Papers, Section 3, Folder 3, item 5, Massachusetts Historical Society.

LMC to Catharine Maria Sedgwick. [1826?]. Catharine Sedgwick Papers, Section 3, Folder 1, item 15, Massachusetts Historical Society.

LMC to Francis Alexander. [1826?]. Francis Alexander Papers. Vol. 2, p. 5. Schlesinger Library, Radcliffe College.

LMC to Francis Alexander. [1826?]. Francis Alexander Papers. Vol. 2, p. 7. Schlesinger Library, Radcliffe College.

LMC to Catharine Maria Sedgwick. 5 June 1828. Catharine Sedgwick Papers, Section 3, Folder 3, item 8, Massachusetts Historical Society.

LMC to Messrs. Carey & Lea. 2 Jun 1830. Paul Richards, Inc. Catalog 175, item 108.

LMC to Catharine Maria Sedgwick. 16 July 1831. Catharine Sedgwick Papers, Section 3, Folder 3, item 12, Massachusetts Historical Society.

LMC to William D. Ticknor. 1 Apr. 1835. Benjamin Holt Ticknor Papers, Vol. 3, Manuscript Division, Library of Congress.

LMC to [George] Kimball. 10 Apr. 1835. Lydia Maria Child Papers, Anti-Slavery Collection, Rare and Manuscript Collections, Cornell University Library.

LMC to William D. Ticknor. 18 Apr. 1835. Benjamin Holt Ticknor Papers, Vol. 3, Manuscript Division, Library of Congress.

LMC to Benjamin Lundy. 14 Mar. [1836]. William Clinton Armstrong. *The Lundy Family and Their Descendants of Whatsoever Surname, with a Biographical Sketch of Benjamin Lundy.* New Brunswick, N.J.: J. Heidingsfeld, 1902. 391–92.

LMC to [Ellis Loring]. 25 Mar. 1844. Rare Books and Special Collections, Pennsylvania State University.

LMC to William D. Ticknor, 28 Dec. 1844, Benjamin Holt Ticknor Papers, Vol. 3, Manuscript Division, Library of Congress.

LMC to Caroline Sturgis. 10 July 1847. Sophia Smith Collection, Smith College.

LMC to [Convers Francis]. 18 Sept. 1847. Olive Kettering Library, Antiochana, Antioch College.

LMC to Isaac T. Hopper. [after 15 Aug. 1848]. L. Maria Child. *Isaac T. Hopper: A True Life.* Boston: John P. Jewett, 1853. 462–64.

LMC to Susan Hopper. 19 July [1854?]. David Schulson Autographs. Catalog n.d., item 21.

LMC to ?. 30 Mar. 1856. J. W. Johnson Collection, Beinecke Library, Yale University.

LMC to Progressive Friends?. 14 Apr. 1856. *Proceedings of the Pennsylvania Yearly Meeting of Progressive Friends, 1853–94.* Meeting of May 1856, p. 69. Haverford College.

LMC to ?. 7 July [1856]. Schlesinger Library A/C 536b, Radcliffe College.

LMC to Rudolph Lehman. 24 Oct. 1856. Diana J. Rendell, Inc. List No. 6, item 22.

LMC to [Edmund H. Sears]. 21 Apr. 1859. Wayland Historical Society.

LMC to Progressive Friends?. 2 May 1859. *Proceedings of the Pennsylvania Yearly Meeting of Progressive Friends, 1853–94.* Meeting of May 1859. Haverford College.

LMC to [Edmund H. Sears]. 11 May [1859]. Wayland Historical Society.

LMC to James Manning Yerrinton. 25 Jan. 1860. Anti-Slavery Collection. Boston Public Library.

LMC to A. F. Green. 7 Feb. 1861. Essex Institute[?].

LMC to Henry Wilson. 10 Mar. 1861. Schlesinger Library, Radcliffe College.

LMC to Mrs. Sears. 16 Feb. 1862. Wayland Historical Society.

LMC to William Endicott. 2 Mar. 1862. Atkinson MSS, Massachusetts Historical Society.

LMC to Mr. Lasar. 4 Sept. 1862. Walter R. Benjamin Autographs. *The Collector* 1987: 5.

LMC to ?. 5 July 1863. David Schulson Autographs, Catalog 4, item 31.

LMC to ?. 5 Aug. 1863. Sotheby's *Fine Printed and Manuscript Americana . . . Auction Wednesday, May 13, 1987. . . .* New York, 1987, in lot 154.

LMC to Theodore Tilton. 1 Oct. 1865. *New York Herald* 11 Aug. 1874. From Beecher-Tilton Scrapbook 7: 13. New York Public Library.

LMC to Edmund H. Sears. undated, after publication of *The Freedmen's Book* in Dec. 1865. Wayland Historical Society.

LMC to Elizabeth Cady Stanton. 28 Apr. 1866. Elizabeth Cady Stanton, Susan B. Anthony, and Matilda Joslyn Gage, *History of Woman Suffrage* 1882; New York: Arno P and New York Times, 1969. 2: 910.

LMC to Charlotte Forten. 6 Mar. 1868 (extract). *The Life and Writings of the Grimké Family.* Ed. Anna Julia Cooper. 2 vols. in 1. Privately printed, 1951. 1: 14–15.

LMC to American Anti-Slavery Society Annual Meeting [paraphrase]. *New York World.* 14 May 1868.

LMC to Oliver Johnson. 22 Sept. 1868. Medford (Mass.) Public Library.

LMC to Caroline Healey Dall. 30 Aug. 1870. Caroline Healey Dall, review of *Letters of Lydia Maria Child,* source unidentified, clipping in Scrapbook 5, n.p., Caroline Healey Dall Papers, Massachusetts Historical Society.

LMC to Lucy Stone. 22 Nov. 1870. *Cleveland Daily Leader* 24 Nov. 1870: 1.

LMC to Mary ?. 19 Feb. 1872. Paul Richards, Catalog 239, item 132.

LMC to Charles Sumner. 21 June 1872. Sumner Papers, Houghton Library, bMS Am 1, Harvard University.

LMC to Charles Sumner. 28 June 1872. Sumner Papers, Houghton Library, bMS Am 1, Harvard University.

LMC to Charles Sumner. 9 July 1872. Sumner Papers, Houghton Library, bMS Am 1, Harvard University.

LMC to Charles Sumner. 24 July 1872. Sumner Papers, Houghton Library, bMS Am 1, Harvard University.

LMC to Charles Alfred Cutting. 1 Jan. 1873. Wayland Historical Society.

LMC to Mrs. Cole. 12 Feb. 1873. *Index* 1 Mar. 1873: 108.

LMC to Progressive Friends?. *Proceedings of the Pennsylvania Yearly Meeting of Progressive Friends, 1853–94.* Meeting of May 1873, p. 6. Haverford College.

LMC to Thomas Wentworth Higginson. 10 Nov. 1873. Inscription in James Smith. *The Divine Drama of History and Civilization.* London, 1854. Harvard University Library.

LMC to Lucinda Hinsdale Stone. 20 Apr. 1874. *Proceedings of the Michigan State Woman-Suffrage Association, at its Fifth Annual Meeting, Held at Lansing, May 6 and 7, 1874.* [Kalamazoo]: State Woman Suffrage Association, 1874. 23–25. Galatea Collection, Boston Public Library.

LMC to [Charles Alfred Cutting]. 16 Dec. 1874. Society for the Preservation of New England Antiquities.

LMC to Mrs. Sears. 3 Jan. 1875. Wayland Historical Society.

LMC to Middlesex County Woman Suffrage Association. Clipping, source unidentified, Robinson-Shattuck Papers, Scrapbook 48, following p. 82, reel 6. Schlesinger Library, Radcliffe College.

LMC to Agnes W. Lincoln. 20 Oct. 1877. Medford (Mass.) Public Library.

LMC to Charlotte Forten. 16 Dec. 1878. *The Life and Writings of the Grimké Family*. Ed. Anna Julia Cooper. 2 vols. in 1. Privately printed, 1951. 1: 14.

LMC to Gov. Talbot of Massachusetts. 19 Mar. 1879. Paul Richards, Catalog 204, item 234.

LMC to Theodore Dwight Weld. 16 Nov. 1879. Paul Richards, Catalog 184, item 43.

LMC to [Oliver Wendell Holmes, Sr.] 17 Dec. 1879. Oliver Wendell Holmes Papers, Container 1, Letterbooks alphabetically arranged. Manuscript Division, Library of Congress.

LMC to? [draft fragment]. Anti-Slavery Collection, Rare and Manuscript Collections, Cornell University Library.

The Society for the Preservation of New England Antiquities also holds a large collection of letters, too numerous to list individually, addressed to young "Allie" (Afred Wayland Cutting), dating from ca. 1865 to ca. 1875.

Index

In lieu of a bibliography, the index includes citations in the notes of important secondary sources and of full references to frequently used primary works and biographical sources.

Carolyn L. Karcher is Associate Professor of English,
American Studies, and Women's Studies at Temple
University. She is author of *Shadow over the Promised Land:
Slavery, Race, and Violence in Melville's America* and the editor
of *HOBOMOK and Other Writings on Indians* by Lydia Maria
Child.

Karcher, Carolyn L., 1945–
The first woman in the republic : a cultural biography of
Lydia Maria Child / by Carolyn L. Karcher.
Includes bibliographical references and index.
ISBN 0-8223-1485-1 (cl)
1. Child, Lydia Maria Francis, 1802–1880. 2. Women social
reformers — United States — Biography 3. Authors,
American — 19th century — Biography. I. Title.
HQ1413.C45K37   1994
303.48'4'092 — dc20
[B]   94-9151 CIP